# China

## a travel survival kit

**China – a travel survival kit**

**Published by**
Lonely Planet Publications
PO Box 88, South Yarra, Victoria, 3141, Australia
Also at: PO Box 2001A, Berkeley, California, USA 94702

**Printed by**
Colorcraft, Hong Kong

**Photographs by**
Alan Samagalski & Michael Buckley

**Maps & Design by**
Graham Imeson

**First published**
October 1984

National Library of Australia
Cataloguing-in-publication entry

Samagalski, Alan.
China, a travel survival kit.

Includes index.
ISBN 0 908086 58 X.

1. China – Description and travel – 1976-
– Guide-books. I. Buckley, Michael.
II. Title.

915.1'0458

**Alan Samagalski** came to Lonely Planet after a lengthy stay on the Indian subcontinent, where he'd fled from a life of genetics at Melbourne University and a stumbling career as the world's first 'Atomic Folk Musician' – putting spontaneity back into music at Melbourne's legendary 'Comedy Cafe' and 'Last Laugh'. After an initial research trip to Ballarat, Bendigo and Geelong, better things awaited with an update of Lonely Planet's Hong Kong book, before he was packed off for five months in China. At the time this book went to press Alan was paddling down a tropical river in the jungles of South-East Asia.

**Michael Buckley** was raised in Australia and has been on the loose since graduating from class 7C. Now resident in Vancouver, Canada, he makes a living out of freelance journalism and (so it is rumoured) teaching English to immigrants. Michael first fell into the Middle Kingdom through the Hong Kong trapdoor back in 1981 when solo travel became possible. Lonely Planet sent him back to China to help research this guide, and though his plans to roller-skate the Great Wall backwards failed miserably, he did burn up a bicycle or two on the highways and backstreets.

## CREDITS

Michael Buckley covered much of the north-eastern and south-western provinces and cities: Jiangsu, Shanghai, Shandong, Hebei, Beijing, Tianjin, Liaoning, Jilin, Heilongjiang, Guizhou, Guangxi, Sichuan and Yunnan. Alan did the slab in the middle from the south-east coast out as far as Kashgar in Xinjiang, with a few odd places like Nanjing, Chongqing and the Guilin/Yangshuo area thrown in for good measure. Where personal comments are included in the text you'll just have to guess whose they are.

The authors were helped by a host of other people and thanks must go to all those who wrote notes and letters, and gave advice and moral support. Among them: Geoff Bonsall, Lonely Planet's Hong Kong distributor, who comforted our weary souls when we trudged back from China, whose flat became a storeroom for copious quatities of notes, and whose taste in restaurants was much appreciated; Richard Strauss (UK), gentleman and scholar, who provided background info and the section on the Trans-Siberian railway; Graham Harrop, a troglodyte from Vancouver and perpetrator of cartoons about weather reports and ordering beers (bears); Carol Ryffel (USA) for her notes on Tibet and living and working in China; Hari Huberman

(USA) for a notepad full of general notes; Joe Greenholtz for notes on Guilin, Yangshuo and Xishagubanna; Fabian Pedrazzini (Switzerland); Geoffry Martin (USA); Linda Rogers (Canada); Nan Rudy (USA); Klaus Jahn (West Germany); Rocky Dang (Hong Kong); Ian Taylor (Australia); Lorelei Cotovsky (USA); John Spowart (UK); Jill Stanley (Canada); Helgard Ziegler (West Germany); Mark Brazier (UK); Patrick Whitehouse (UK); Andrew Scrimgeour (Australia); Martyn Patterson and Lucie Lolicato (Australia) for thrilling pictures of Tibet, their ideas and anything else I might have stolen from them.

Thanks also to various other people along the way who may not wish to be or who have asked not to be named, and to anyone we have forgotten to mention . . .

## A NOTE FROM THE PUBLISHER

This book is the largest we've done at Lonely Planet, both for its physical size, and in terms of the effort that went in from many people.

After many months on the road in China, Alan and Michael spent many more at their desks in Melbourne and Vancouver. In the back room of Lonely Planet's Melbourne office, surrounded by inspirational posters of China's leaders, Alan typed away on his Kaypro word processor; periodically the mail brought large envelopes with Vancouver postmarks. Michael's text was transcribed and edited by Ginny Bruce onto another Kaypro, and incorporated by Alan into the growing opus. Just when we were wondering if Alan would ever stop writing, he boarded a plane to Kalimantan, leaving us with the inspirational posters, plus a heap of carefully labelled folders and boxes, several km of computer print-out, 30 floppy diskettes, about 150 sketch maps, hundreds of Kodachrome transparencies, and a cardboard cutout of himself.

The posters and the cardboard replica are still there but somehow the rest has all been transformed into a finished book, with the help of many people, many cups of tea and coffee, many floppy diskettes and the RS-232 interface. Graham drew more maps than he ever wanted to know about; Ann masterminded the typesetting; proofreading, correcting, and indexing were handled by Mary, Margit, Lindy, Michael and Todd; the Chinese calligraphy was done by Rita; in the art department Fiona laid out page after page after page; and through all this Andy and Marianne kept the office functioning, Jim exhorted, Tony and Maureen waited, Pooh Bear slept.

## AND A REQUEST . . .

All travel guides rely on new information to stay up-to-date. At Lonely Planet we get a steady stream mail from travellers, and it all helps, whether it's a few lines on a postcard or a stack of closely-written pages. Everywhere prices go up, new hotels open, old ones close, bus routes change – this happens in China just as much as in any other country, probably even more. So if you find that something isn't quite the way it's described in this book, don't blame the authors; instead, write to Lonely Planet and help make the next edition even better. As usual, the most useful letters will get a free copy of the next edition, or another Lonely Planet book if you prefer.

## LONELY PLANET NEWSLETTER

To make the most use out of all the information that comes in to Lonely Planet, we publish a quarterly newsletter with extracts from many of the letters we get from travellers 'on the road', plus other facts on air fares, visas, etc. It comes out quarterly, usually in January, April, July and November. To subscribe, write to Lonely Planet in either Australia or California; a year's sub costs $5 (A$ in Australia, US$ in the US). Some back issues are available.

# Contents

# Introduction

After being closed for repairs for almost 30 years the Middle Kingdom suddenly swung open its big red doors – but not quite all the way. Comrades! We must raise the production of tourists! China desperately needs the foreign exchange that tourism so conveniently provides – and they have done very well out of the deal so far. Today the tallest buildings in China are, appropriately, hotels. Come back in five years time and there will be Marco Polo pizza bars dotted along the Great Wall and revolving pagoda-topped restaurants everywhere.

China's policy on tourism is 'promote it'. Since 1949, the number of tourists has increased by seven million per cent; the vast majority of these are Overseas Chinese but amongst the 7.76 million tourists who came to the country in 1981 there were 675,000 Westerners. The combined rake-in from both groups was US$780 million – a tidy little sum.

In the late 1970s the tour groups started rolling in but the prospects for individual travel looked extremely dim. It has always been possible for individuals to travel to the PRC, but invitation only, and until the late 1970s few managed an invite. The first regulars were from Sweden and France (nations favoured by China) who stepped off the Trans-Siberian in 1979 when it re-opened after 30 years. Then, in 1981, the Chinese suddenly started issuing visas to solo, uninvited, all and sundry travellers through a couple of their embassies overseas, but mainly through various agencies in Hong Kong. Just about anyone who wanted a visa could get one but, since there was no fanfare, news spread slowly by word of mouth. By 1982, and certainly by 1983, it seemed that just about *everyone* who landed in Hong Kong was going to China. After all, we'd been waiting for over 30 years for the chance to travel in the country unfettered by tour guides. As it turned out, for most people China was *not* what they expected.

Although many guide books speak of the country in glowing terms, a lot of people quickly discovered that China is not the easiest of countries to travel through – at least not on your own. At some stage you're almost certain to find yourself at the end of your tether with both the place and the people. A lot depends, of course, on where you go, how long you stay in the country and how you travel.

Many of the hassles stem from the same problems that afflict other Asian countries: too few resources and too many people. Yet the outstanding feature of China is that, after what seems like several hundred years of utter stagnation, it is now making a *determined* effort to modernise itself and catch up with the west. The size of the task is staggering, and now is a unique opportunity to get some whiff of what the Communists have been doing for the last 35 years. The sleeping giant stood up in 1949 and, however you feel about the place, China is a country that cannot be ignored.

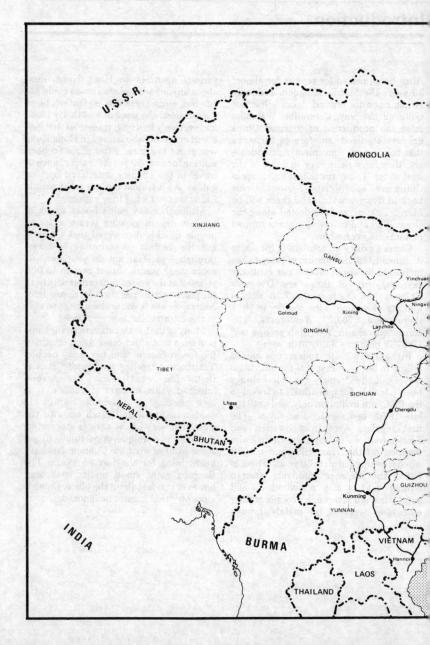

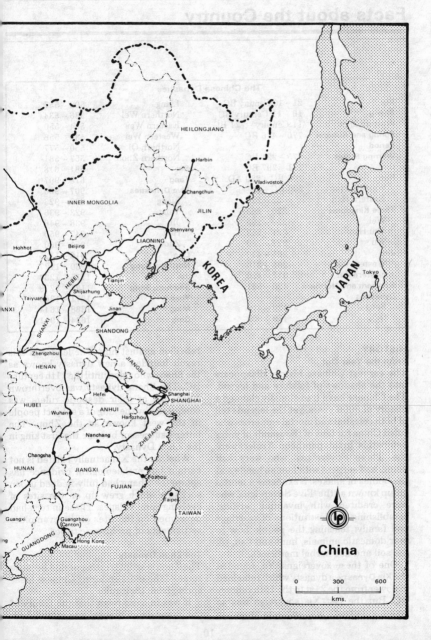

# Facts about the Country

## HISTORY

### From the Year Dot

The earliest Chinese history disappears into the shadows of folklore and legend. The Chinese have traditionally claimed a history of 5000 years, yet the legends tell of both celestial and mortal emperors who ruled China for tens of thousands of years before this. In this pantheon of rulers were the 'Three Sovereigns' who were half being, half serpent with human heads and the bodies of snakes. Next came a mortal group known as the 'Five Sovereigns' who were credited with inventing writing; establishing the institutions of marriage and family; teaching the people how to rear domestic animals, hunt and fish, till the soil and use herbal medicines.

One of these sovereigns, Yu, founded the **Xia Dynasty**, a dynasty which remained in power from the 21st to the 16th century BC. But the last Xia sovereign was so tyrannical that his subjects rose in rebellion against him. The leader of this revolt founded a new dynasty known as the **Shang** who ruled until the 11th century BC. The Shang dynasty was overthrown when one of their despotic rulers was conquered by the king of a subject people in the west known as the Zhou. The latter's successor became the first king in the Zhou Dynasty.

Whether the Xia actually existed is not certain but archaeological evidence has shown the Shang had fully-fledged urban societies which grew up on the sites of evolving rural villages. These in turn had developed on the sites of the even older settlements of prehistoric tribes.

### The Zhou Dynasty

The Zhou is an interesting period because some of the most enduring Chinese ideas spring from their rule.

It was in their reign that the theory of the 'mandate of heaven' was established.

10

It was supposedly adopted by early Zhou rulers who used it as a justification for overthrowing the tyrannical Shang king, and embodies the idea that heaven gives wise and virtuous leaders a mandate to rule and removes it from those who aren't. It has since become a fundamental tenet in Chinese political thinking. Very probably, the concept of the emperor being the 'Son of Heaven' also originated at this time. Whatever the case, the Zhou are shown in history as model rulers and paragons of virtue. Later, the theory of the 'mandate of heaven' was extended to incorporate the Taoist theory that heaven expresses disapproval of bad rulers through natural disasters – such as earthquakes, floods and plagues of locusts.

Another refinement of the 'mandate of heaven' theory is the 'right of rebellion', which says that the will of heaven is expressed through the people in their continuing support of the ruler or the withdrawal of that support. This doctrine therefore justified rebellions against tyrannical rulers and allowed successful rebel leaders to claim a mandate of heaven to rule. From this comes the third important concept called the 'dynastic cycle', which maintains that as the moral quality of the ruling family declines, heaven passes power on to another dynasty. Thus there is an endless cycle in which governments rise, pass through a period of prosperous and just rule but gradually grow weak and corrupt until heaven has no alternative but to hand the power over to a new, strong, just ruler.

It was also during the Zhou period that the Chinese developed a concept of themselves as a separate identity. Though they were split into separate kingdoms, the Chinese were united by a common belief in the superiority of the Shang-Zhou culture. These states came to be known as the 'Chung-kuo' or 'Central States' whilst outsiders were considered barbarians.

### The decline of the Zhou & the growth of the Warring States

The Zhou dominated the area north and south of the Yellow River. Theirs was a feudal society; over 1700 feudal states are said to have existed within the Zhou realm. Their lords swore allegiance to the emperor and gave military aid when required. But by 771 BC the power of the Zhou royal family had declined while the power of the feudal states increased. Big states swallowed little ones, until by 700 BC only 200 independent states existed. Continuing annexations over the following centuries reduced the number to a handful. It was a period of perpetual war known as the 'Warring States Period'.

One of China's most influential philosophers, Confucius, lived during the Warring States Period – around 500 BC – in the turmoil of incessant wars, unbridled power of rulers and great extremes of wealth and poverty. His attempts at finding a solution to the excesses of the Warring States Period and restoring peace to the people led him to uphold the Zhou period as the golden age of good government. Confucius' solution ultimately resulted in the custom of venerating the alleged good government of a distant past and the people and literature of that past. Though Confucianism was not the only school of thought – there were several major schools around in this period of upheaval – it was the one which eventually took hold of China.

The perpetual wars were also having their effect on the structure of society, and the period from 500 BC onwards is notable for the development of the landlord class. It was a class distinct from the long-established aristocracy of the former states. One explanation for its development is that feudal rulers rewarded their ranking soldiers with grants of land. Another explanation is that the defeat of various feudal lords freed large numbers of peasants from their feudal bonds, and their new masters allowed them to start farming on their own. As poorer farmers foundered under the burden of increased taxes, they sold out to wealthier farmers who then rented the land to the highest bidder. The poor peasants thus slipped into the role of tenant farmers to these wealthy families. The trend continued throughout the succeeding Qin period during which heavy taxes ruined the peasants, while the landlord class, based on private ownership of land rather than on aristocratic inheritance coupled with a serf population, continued to grow.

### The Empire of Qin Shihuang

The Warring States Period came to an end in the 3rd century BC when the state of Qin conquered all the other states, and for the first time united the Chinese into a single empire. The Qin ruler took the title of Shihuangdi, First Exalted Emperor (he is usually referred to as Qin Shihuang). His was a brief rule which lasted only from 221 to 207 BC. It is remembered more for the tyranny and cruelty of the emperor than for anything else.

But it was also a time of dramatically increased centralised control; the power of the aristocracy was broken by depriving them of land and apportioning it to private farmers. Books written before the Qin period were destroyed to wipe out ideas which conflicted with the emperor's. Prisoners of war and peasants who had lost their land were drafted into gangs to build public works, which included imperial palaces and the emperor's mausoleum as well as the Great Wall, snaking all the way across northern China for 3200 km and designed to keep the northern nomads at bay.

Centralisation also enabled the destruction of fortifications built by the independent feudal states, the building of a network of roads from the capital, and the standardisation of weights and measures, of coinage and the writing system. The foundations for a large and unified Chinese empire were laid.

With the death of Qin Shihuang, it seemed that heaven had once again taken care of the downtrodden. A rebellion broke out. The Qin capital near modern-day Xian was captured by a commoner, Liu Pang, who by 202 BC had taken the title of emperor and established the Han Dynasty.

### The Han Dynasty

The Han Dynasty lasted for 400 years, from 206 BC to 220 AD. It was during this period that the pattern of the modern Chinese state was established and the empire reached its zenith.

Theoretically the Han emperor had unlimited power, but in practice he had to contend with conflicting power groups. These included regional governors and princes who maintained a strong grasp of authority, wealthy merchant families who commanded influence because of their wealth, the landed gentry, the emperor's own immediate family, relatives, palace servants and eunuchs – all had access to the emperor and could exercise influence over him. After the cruelty of the Qin period the power of the emperor had to be tempered, and since the Han emperors were never able to rule with the same degree of absolute power as Qin Shihuang,

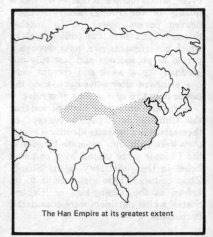

The Han Empire at its greatest extent

they had no choice but to accept the power-sharing structure. Lower in the echelons, but equally important, was the remarkably well-developed government bureaucracy, ranked in 20 (later 16) grades, each with its own carefully defined privileges.

Under the fifth Han Emperor, Wu, who came to power in 147 BC, the empire reached its furthest boundaries with far-flung military campaigns. Wu was an intensely autocratic monarch, but it was he who decreed Confucian texts and teachings to be the yardstick for everyone who aspired to the position of government official. A university was set up in the capital specifically to teach Confucianism, and examinations in the Confucian classics were instituted for those hoping to take up positions as government officials. Confucianism thus became the basis of education and admission to the civil service for the next 2000 years.

### The Problem of Dealing With Foreigners

Until the 19th century the Pacific Ocean shut China off from the rest of the world. China looked inward and was a land power, not a maritime nation (during the Southern Song Dynasty China developed a substantial navy and merchant fleet, and during the reign of the second Ming emperor vast sea-going expeditions were undertaken, but these were very much exceptions to the general trend). Mountains and deserts isolated China from continental neighbours. Contacts with the outside world existed, but they made little impact on the civilisation that grew up along the Yellow River.

The Shang and Zhou had their own customs for dealing with all those outside the 'Central States'. By the 2nd century BC a vocabulary had developed for dealing with foreigners. The 'barbarians' were expected to 'come and be transformed' by contact with the higher Chinese civilisation; they were expected to 'observe the rites' of the Chinese court, to 'offer tribute' and in return they would be

treated courteously and be presented with gifts. The expansion of the empire into Central Asia brought the Han Chinese into contact with numerous peoples. Diplomatic missions and envoys from foreign countries had even brought the Han into contact with the Roman Empire and the last Greek settlements in the mountains of north-west India that had been left over from Alexander's invasion, but again, with little or no impact on the Chinese world.

The Chinese view of themselves as a superior race continued to develop through the later Han period, but the awkward fact remained that the Han armies could never quite defeat the barbarians that plagued the empire's boundaries. Often they were forced to receive the barbarian ambassadors as guests or equals, but they still recorded them as the visits of vassals who brought tribute – a thinking which entrenched itself deeper and deeper in the Chinese mentality.

### Invasions & Migrations: 300 years of Disunity

300 years of disunity followed the collapse of the Han Dynasty in 220 AD. Strains on the empire's economy and a succession of weak rulers led to power struggles between powerful regional rulers and their armies, and the empire finally split into three separate kingdoms. The rivalry between them invited invasion by China's northern neighbours and caused great migrations of Chinese people. Despite the disunity, the concept of a unified empire remained and there were always rulers who aspired to be, or claimed to be, the legitimate sovereign of all China. It was also a period in which the north of China came under the control of the Turkish-speaking people known as the Tobas, while the south split into separate Chinese kingdoms.

The conquest of northern China by the foreigners brought to light two interesting developments. The first was the growing power of Buddhism, which was probably first introduced to China by Indian merchants who were accompanied by Buddhist priests. It entered a boom period between the 3rd and 6th centuries when most of the northern invaders, many of whom had been acquainted with the religion before they came to China, patronised the Buddhist monks, partly to generate a group of educated officials who were not Confucians.

The second development was the absorption of the northern barbarians into Chinese culture. The Toba eventually disappeared as a race – either rejoining the Turkish tribes in the north, or successfully assimilating the Chinese way of life. The seduction of the northern invaders by the civilised style of Chinese life was repeated later on; both the Manchus and even the warrior Mongols succumbed to it.

### The Sui & Tang Dynasties

The country was finally united again in the 6th century under the Sui Dynasty, founded by a general of mixed Chinese-Toba descent who had usurped the northern throne and went on to conquer southern China.

However the Sui dynasty was short lived and in 618 AD the throne was again usurped, by a noble family of Chinese-Toba descent who founded the Tang Dynasty. Like Confucius who turned to the Zhous as a source of inspiration, the Chinese now look on the Tang as a golden age of Chinese power and prosperity, and a brilliant period in Chinese culture and creativity.

At the height of Tang power, their capital at Changan (on the site of modern-day Xian) was one of the greatest cities in Asia, if not the world. It held a million people within its walls and there were perhaps another million outside: a cosmopolitan city of courtiers, merchants, foreign traders, soldiers, artists, entertainers, priests and bureaucrats. It was a thriving imperial metropolis of commerce, administration, religion and culture, and the political hub of the empire. During this time the Chinese empire covered the greatest area since the Han dynasty. Unlike the Han dynasty, government became highly centralised; power radiated from the capital and increasingly from the emperor.

With the conquest of the last of the Chinese rulers in the south in 589 AD, the first Sui emperor had been able to embark on an administrative reorganisation of the empire. A nation-wide examination system enabled more people from the eastern plains and the increasingly populous southern regions to serve in the government bureaucracy in Changan, thus ensuring that the elite were drawn from all over the country. The examination system was continued and developed by the Tang. Communications had also been developed by the Sui emperors through the construction or reconstruction of canals strategically linking important parts of the empire. Canal links were further improved and developed during the Tang dynasty, and roads were made and inns were built for officials, travellers, merchants and pilgrims.

These communication systems radiated

The Tang Emperor Li Shih – Min

out to the sea ports and to the caravan routes which connected China to the rest of the world, allowing it to import the world's ideas and products. The capital became a centre for international trade and a large foreign community established itself here. Numerous foreign religions established themselves, including Islam, the Zoroastrian sect of Persia, and the Nestorian Christian sect of Syria, and temples and mosques were built as the outward manifestation of these faiths. During this period China was in contact with a greater variety of foreign peoples and was more exposed to foreign ideas and culture than at any time until the present. The success of the Sui and the Tang in creating a centralised bureaucratic government impressed surrounding countries, and embassies were sent to the Tang court by Tibet, Japan and Korea to learn the techniques of government. So the barbarians came to learn from the Chinese (just as the Chinese expected them to) and, though others – the Javanese, the Malays, and the Indians – came only to trade, they too had to comply with the tribute system because the Chinese demanded it. As in the Han period, the Tang continued to record all meetings with foreigners in terms of vassals giving tribute.

The Tang system of government was to have a profound influence on future dynasties, particularly the Ming who modelled themselves on the Tang, and the Ming in turn were scrupulously copied by the Manchus of the Qing Dynasty. At the apex of the social order was the emperor and his entourage whose lives were shaped by the triple responsibilities of ceremonial duties, political administration and the pursuit of pleasure. The Tang emperors had inherited the traditional ideology of kingship and the rituals and roles attached to it. The emperor was not only the Son of Heaven who maintained the balance between the world of mankind and the forces of nature, he was also the *first farmer* of a peasant empire, the

ceremonial head of a ruling class, and the guardian of the state ideology of Confucianism, and the patron and devotee of the popular religions of Buddhism and Taoism. He presided over government policy and state affairs with his ministers and other high officials, honoured officials and foreign dignitaries with audiences and banquets, and in wartime took part in devising strategy and issued orders and commissions to his officers. He was also the stud of the harem. The day-to-day task of government was handled by the emperor's personal staff, the palace eunuchs and the huge government bureaucracy.

### Tang to Song: China's Economic Revolution

Towards the end of the 8th century the Tang Dynasty was starting to decline. From 775 AD onwards the armies of central government were suffering defeats at the hands of provincial warlords and Tibetan and Turkish invaders. The setbacks exposed weaknesses in the empire and, though the Tang still maintained overall supremacy, they gradually began to lose control of the transport networks and the tax collection

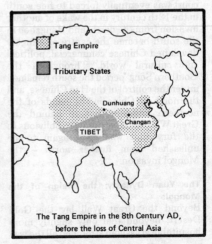

The Tang Empire in the 8th Century AD, before the loss of Central Asia

system on which their power and prosperity depended. Between 841 and 845 AD the government went on a campaign of wholesale destruction of Buddhist temples and temples belonging to other non-Chinese religions; an indication, perhaps, of the dismal state of the dynasty. The Tang dynasty finally fell in 907 AD and China once again split into a number of independent states.

Nevertheless it was during this period of disunity that the Chinese embarked on a period of rapid economic development. When Marco Polo got to China in the 13th century he found huge and prosperous cities on a scale quite unlike anything in Europe, an orderly society and large-scale inter-regional trade. The establishment of trade was partly spurred on by the fall of the Tang empire; the south split into separate kingdoms which remained peaceful, and trade and commerce developed rapidly in the absence of central government controls.

The empire was reintegrated in 960 AD by a southern general who founded the Song Dynasty. He used political skill rather than military means to achieve this and peace helped to maintain the prosperous economic structure. The Song court was eventually forced to flee south in the 12th century in the wake of another invasion from the north, and Hangzhou in the south became the centre of a highly developed Chinese commercial, political and cultural world. Throughout the 'Southern Song' period the south remained under the control of the Han Chinese, and the north of China in the hands of the northern invaders. Secure behind the Great Wall, both parties were oblivious to the fury that was once again to be unleashed from further north – the Mongol invasion.

### The Yuan Dynasty; the Reign of the Mongols

Beyond the Great Wall lay the Gobi Desert; beyond that only slightly more hospitable grassland stretched all the way

from Manchuria to Hungary, inhabited by nomadic Turk and Mongol tribes who endured a harsh life as shepherds and horse-breeders. The Mongols occasionally went to war with the Chinese but in the past had always been defeated, and they were despised for their ignorance and poverty.

By the year 1206, after 20 years of internal war, the roaming Mongol tribes had united under Genghis Khan. He gathered the tribes together and proclaimed a new nation, the 'Blue Mongols', under the protection of the heavenly sky. Genghis Khan began the invasion of China in 1211, penetrated the Great Wall two years later and in 1215 took Beijing. Stubborn resistance from the Chinese rulers, conflict within the Mongolian camp, and campaigns in Russia delayed the conquest of Song China for many years, but by 1279 the grandson of Genghis, Kublai Khan, had brought southern China under his sway.

The Mongols made Beijing their capital, and Kublai Khan became the first emperor of the Yuan dynasty. Kublai established a government in China with power concentrated in the cities and towns. The Mongols improved the road system linking China with Russia and promoted trade throughout the empire and with Europe. They instituted a famine relief scheme, and expanded the canal system which brought food from the countryside to the cities.

Overall the Mongols had little effect on China itself, but their rule is interesting for two reasons. Firstly, an ideological schism emerged in the Mongolian party. Kublai Khan realised that an empire won on horseback could not be governed by the same means, but there were those who wanted to preserve their own way of life – they wanted to extract wealth from their new subjects without integrating. They alienated the Chinese by staffing the government bureaucracy with Mongols, Moslems and other foreigners; the Chinese were excluded from government and relegated to the lowest levels. Landowners and wealthy traders were favoured, taxation was high and the prosperity of the empire did little to improve the lot of the peasant. However, the Mongols, like the Toba before them, were seduced by the Chinese civilisation; the warriors who had conquered almost all the known world grew soft.

Secondly, the Mongol rule generated a growing European interest in the Far East. The Mongol armies had swept into Eastern Europe and the whole continent had been on the verge of an invasion; the invasion was called off at the last minute, but it forced the Europeans to take notice of the Orient. Trade and contacts across Asia were made easier by Mongol supremacy which cut the boundaries between separate nations. It was to the China of the Mongols that Europeans like Marco Polo came, and their books revealed the secrets of Asia to an amazed Europe.

Kublai Khan died in 1294, the last Khan to rule over a united Mongol empire. With the collapse of the Mongol empire, China isolated itself from the rest of the world at a time when interest in China had just been stimulated. In the years to come the Chinese were to be confronted by a different type of foreigner; unlike the northern barbarians who had little culture of their own and succumbed to Chinese civilisation, the Europeans came armed with a sense of their own superiority and relatively advanced technology against which the Middle Kingdom was unprepared.

## The Ming Dynasty

The Mongol reign over China was rapidly disintegrating by the 1350s and several rebel armies vied for power, the chief contender being the army led by Zhu Yuanzhang.

Zhu was born of a poor peasant family in Anhui Province. His parents died of starvation when he was a boy and he entered a Buddhist monastery, but eventually left to become a beggar. In 1352, at the age of 25, he joined a rebel group which rapidly grew into a huge band of insurgents, so powerful that it was able to capture Nanjing in 1356. By 1367 Zhu had secured most of southern China and was able to move north to attack Beijing and drive out the Mongols.

Zhu Yuanzhang proclaimed himself the first emperor of the Ming dynasty and took the name Hong Wu. He established Nanjing as the capital, far from the north and safe from enemy attacks.

Under General Xu Da, who had led the attack on Beijing, the war against the Mongols was carried successfully into the Mongol homeland; their capital of Karakorum was sacked and the threat to China was curbed for some time. Meanwhile Hong Wu set about organising a new government structure. Buddhism and Taoism were made state religions, the competitive examination system to select government officials was revived, and a civil government apparatus modelled on that of the Tang Dynasty was set up.

The reign of Hong Wu is, however, noted for two developments which ultimately weakened China. The first was a dramatic increase in the power of the emperor versus the bureaucracy. China had always lived under authoritarian rulers and administrations, but the rule of Hong Wu approached the totalitarian, and bureaucrats came to rely more on orders from above than on their own initiative. Intellectual life, original thought and imagination came to a standstill. The second development was the isolation of China from the rest of the world; the Ming emperors saw China as culturally superior and economically self-sufficient with nothing to learn from other countries. At a time when Europe was entering its most dynamic phase since the Roman Empire, China was becoming stagnant.

There was one great exception to this trend, and it came from the third Ming emperor, Yong Le. It was during Yong's reign that the Chinese embarked on spectacular maritime adventures, and great Chinese fleets sailed to South-East Asia, India, Persia and Arabia and even to

the east coast of Africa. The purpose of these voyages is not exactly clear; Yong Le may have been interested in founding a commercial or even colonial empire and, at this period in history, half a century earlier than the voyages of Columbus and Vasco de Gama, he had every possibility of doing both. Seven voyages were led by the palace eunuch, Zheng He, over 28 years from 1405 onwards, but the voyages came to an end when Yong Le died in 1424, and neither commercial bases nor colonies had been established.

The Ming Dynasty collapsed in the early 17th century, ending a line of young, weak and incompetent rulers, and a government whose power lay largely in the hands of the palace eunuchs, the emperor's personal servants. A severe famine in Shaanxi in 1628 precipitated the inevitable uprising, and a rebel army led by Li Zicheng captured Beijing in 1644.

### The Qing Dynasty

Meanwhile the Manchus to the north of China took advantage of the turmoil in China and launched an invasion. Initially held back by the Great Wall, the Manchus were let in by a Ming general and expelled the rebel army from Beijing. They set up their own dynasty, the Qing.

The north succumbed to the Manchus without resistance but the south held out for 20 years, led by various claimants to the throne. The wars left a bitterness between the Chinese and the Manchus which has lasted to this day. Today 'triads' are the descendants of the secret societies that were set up to resist the northern barbarians, the Manchus in turn continue to be suspicious and mistrustful of the south.

The Manchus were the second foreigners to rule over all of China and, like the Mongols, they set themselves apart and above their subjects, concentrating power in their own hands and alienating the Han Chinese. Nevertheless, the reign of the Qing emperors from 1663 to 1796 was a period of great prosperity and the throne

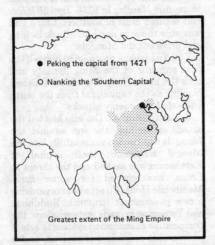

● Peking the capital from 1421

○ Nanking the 'Southern Capital'

Greatest extent of the Ming Empire

was occupied by three of the most able rulers China has known: Kangxi, Yong-cheng and Qianlong. The blood flowed like an old friend as the Qing carried the expansion of the empire to its greatest limits, and Mongolia and Tibet came under Qing suzerainty. On the domestic front, reduced taxation and massive flood control and irrigation projects benefited the peasants.

The competence of the emperors also led to a further concentration of power in their hands and the responsibilities of the throne became too great for the successors of Qianlong to cope with; their successes became their undoing. Like the Mongols, the Manchu rulers succumbed to the civilisation of the Chinese and soon became culturally indistinguishable from their conquered peoples. They painstakingly modelled their government on that of the Ming, having no political traditions of their own capable of governing a huge state. Thus the moribund isolationism and intellectual conservatism which came to characterise the Ming government was passed on to the Qing. China continued as an inward-looking nation, oblivious to the tech-nological and scientific revolutions that were taking place in Europe. The Europeans had made massive advances and were about to expand their power on a scale undreamt of by the Chinese. European power was one which the Qing were simply not equipped to meet, and the coming of the west was to hasten the fall of the Qing and help mould the China that we know today.

### The coming of the west

The Europeans couldn't be held out by the Great Wall – they came by sea. The first European ships to make it to China were those of the Portuguese who arrived in 1516; in 1557 they were permitted to set up a trading base in Macau, possibly as a reward for clearing nearby waters of pirates. In the following century the British, Dutch, and Spanish all landed in China. The trade overtures of the foreign merchants were initially rebuffed by the Qing government, but they eventually opened the distant port of Canton in 1685. The foreigners were thus kept at arm's length, far from the centre of the nation in the north. Trade flourished, mainly in China's favour, but the Chinese soon proved to be no match for the commercial ambitions and the firepower of the westerners.

In 1773 the British started unloading chests of Indian opium in Canton with the intention of evening up the balance of trade. With Chinese silver fast disappearing from the country in payment for the opium and an increasing number of opium addicts, the Emperor thundered an edict in 1800 banning the trade, which the foreigners, Chinese merchants and corrupt Cantonese officials duly ignored.

More drastic measures were taken in 1839 when the Chinese seized 20,000 chests of opium in Canton, but when the subsequent negotiations broke down, the British attacked Canton in the first of what became known as the 'Opium Wars'. There were three more 'Opium Wars'. The second was in August 1842 when British

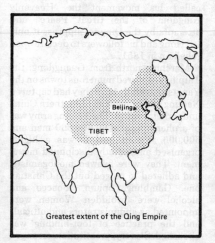

Greatest extent of the Qing Empire

Beijing

TIBET

warships sailed up the Yangtse River to threaten Nanjing. The third, the 'Arrow War', broke out over the interpretation of earlier treaties and the boarding of the British-owned merchant ship, the *Arrow*, by Chinese soldiers searching for pirates. French troops joined the British in this war and the Russians and Americans lent naval support. The Fourth Opium War was in 1859-1860 after the first British envoy to Beijing was fired on as he made his way to the city.

Each war was ended by an 'Unequal Treaty' which, amongst other things, opened more Chinese ports to foreign ships, gave foreigners the right to settle in certain areas and later to travel freely in China. The Chinese were forced to pay large war indemnities, customs tariffs on imported western goods were severely reduced, western diplomats were permitted to take up residence in Beijing, and freedom of movement was eventually accorded to missionaries. By 1860 the opening of China was virtually complete.

Another treaty introduced two provisions which had a profound effect on China's subsequent history. The first was the 'most favoured nation' principle in which China agreed to give privileges won by any foreign country to all other foreign countries with whom it had treaties containing 'most favoured nation' clauses. ·This meant that no one nation could receive special privileges from the Chinese; the western powers would be able to deal with the Chinese with a united front since concessions granted to one country would also be granted to the others. The second provision was 'Extra-territoriality'; foreigners who committed crimes or offences in China could only be tried by their own consuls. This meant that foreigners were immune to Chinese laws and the Chinese government had little control over their actions.

There were further encroachments on Chinese territory. The Russians seized the area of Siberia east of the Amur River in 1860. The French annexed Cochin-China from Annam, part of Vietnam today, over which the Chinese claimed suzerainty. The Chinese were utterly powerless to prevent these annexations and proved themselves at the mercy of the western armies in battle. The Emperor's attempts to reform the navy after the defeat of 1842 were blocked by conservative mandarins; the army was inefficient and, divided to prevent rebellion, it couldn't unite against the foreigners. The government was corrupt: official posts could now be obtained by purchase, foreign trade was expanded by bribery, and the power of the emperor was weakened.

## The Taiping Rebellion
In the second half of the 19th century there were two dramatic events which could have halted this process of decay. The first was the Taiping Rebellion, founded and led by Hong Xiuquan, a native of Guangdong. Convinced he was on a mission from God and professing to be the younger brother of Jesus Christ, he gathered around him a group of followers who went from strength to strength preaching Christianity whilst smashing Buddhist, Taoist and Confucian idols and razing their temples to the ground. Hong called his movement the 'Heavenly Kingdom of the Great Peace' and attempts by the Qing to suppress it only led Hong and his followers to declare open rebellion in 1851.

Marching north from Guangdong, the Taipings captured numerous towns on the Yangtse River; by 1853 they had captured Nanjing and brought all of southern China under their control. The Taiping army was of a phenomenal size, 600,000 men and 500,000 women, and it was a highly organised and strictly disciplined movement. They were avowed monogamists, and adhered to no god but the Christian one. Gambling, opium, tobacco and alcohol were forbidden. Women were appointed as administrators and officials and the practice of foot-binding was abolished. Slavery, prostitution, arranged

A Taiping Coin

marriages and polygamy were also abolished. What particularly attracted the peasants was their policy of agrarian reform and lighter and more equitable taxation in those areas they controlled, plus the idea of public rather than private ownership. In many ways the movement was a forerunner of the Communist movement of the following century.

The Taipings failed to gain the support of the western powers, however, who until then had remained neutral. In fact, it was probably the success of the Taipings which worried the westerners. It was more expedient for them to deal with a corrupt and weak Qing government than with the united and strong Taipings. So after 1860 the western powers allied with the Qing and a counter-offensive began. By 1864 the Taipings had retreated to their capital city of Nanjing. A Qing army aided by British army regulars and mixed European and American mercenaries besieged and captured the city, slaughtering the defenders. Hong Xiuquan committed suicide and the rebellion was ended.

## Interlude before a storm: the decline of the Qing

The years after the Taiping Rebellion were a time of further intrusion by the foreign powers into China. The Qing government grew progressively weaker and the lot of the peasants became increasingly miserable.

In 1861, at a time when China needed a strong government more than ever, it found itself with the six-year-old Emperor Guangxu who had just ascended the throne. Real power remained in the hands of his aunt the Empress Dowager, Wu Cixi a former concubine. Wu Cixi saw reform and modernisation as a threat to the conservative power base of the Qing Dynasty and, in clinging to this belief, spent the next 48 years presiding over the disintegration of China.

At this time, China's own colonial empire began to break up; a war with the French between 1883-85 ended Chinese suzerainty in Indo-China and allowed the French to maintain control of Vietnam and eventually gain control of Laos and Cambodia (Kampuchea). At the same time Chinese suzerainty in Burma was ended by the British who occupied the region. In 1894 a rebellion broke out in Korea against the Korean king and the Chinese sent 2000 troops to assist him; Japan sent 10,000 troops to attack the Chinese who were defeated by March 1895. The Chinese were forced to sign the Treaty of Shimonoseki which ceded Taiwan, the Pescadores and the Liaoning Peninsula to Japan. Four new ports were opened to foreign trade, an indemnity was paid to Japan, and the Japanese were given the right to set up factories in China.

Japan's power alarmed the Russians, French and Germans who forced Japan to return the Liaoning Peninsula to China. As a 'reward' for this intervention, the Russians were allowed to build a railway through Manchuria to their treaty port of Port Arthur (Lushun); by moving troops in with the railway, the Russians effectively gained control of Manchuria for the next 10 years. Soon Germany, Russia, Britain and France rushed in to lease various chunks of territory in a spree of land-grabbing.

The powers mapped out their own 'spheres of influence': Russia claimed Manchuria, Germany Shandong and the north of China, Britain the Yangtse Valley, Japan Fujian, and France the southern borders of Yunnan and Guangxi. By June 1898 they seemed to be on the verge of carving China up. But the partition was delayed by an American proposal, an 'open-door' policy which would leave all of China open to trade with any foreign power.

Economically the Chinese government fared disastrously; China was indebted to the western powers, Japan, and, short of money, it began to borrow from other countries and raised the taxes on its own people which added to the general misery of the peasants. Coastal trade by foreign ships developed at the expense of the Chinese junk trade. Foreigners built railways and telegraph lines and opened coalmines and ironworks, but these were used by them to exploit the country. Missionaries arrived in large numbers, threatening traditional Chinese society with foreign religion, science, education and morals. Chinese students, returning from studying abroad, brought back anti-Manchu sentiment and European-influenced political ideologies.

The Chinese government embarked on a 'self-strengthening' programme in 1881 which built naval yards and arsenals, and laid some railways; it made a start towards industrialisation with the opening of coal mines, iron works and textile mills, while seeking to maintain the conservative ideology on which the Qing regime was based. However the defeat of the supposedly modern Chinese army in the Sino-Japanese War of the mid-1890s showed the self-strengthening programme to be a dismal failure. What China needed was radical reform.

In 1898 there was a dramatic attempt by the imperial court to halt the disintegration of China. The Emperor Guangxu had come under the influence of the reformer Kang Youwei and his Beijing supporters who advocated the modernisation and liberalisation of China if it were to survive intact. But the 'Hundred Days Reform' of June to September 1898 was opposed by Cixi. The Emperor tried to have her arrested but his military officials changed sides, imprisoned him, returned Cixi to power, and executed the emperor's supporters. Kang escaped to Japan.

For almost 40 years the foreigners in China had been doing very much as they pleased. Then quite unexpectedly there came strange and bizarre retribution – the Boxer Rebellion. This was the second event which could have changed the course of Chinese and world history.

## The Boxer Rebellion and the Fall of the Qing

The rebels' Chinese name cumbersomely translates as 'Righteous and Harmonious Fists'. They began as an anti-Manchu organisation supported by the peasantry. Its members developed a form of 'boxing', which was a kind of calisthenic exercise aimed at harmonising the mind and the body in preparation for combat, and they added rituals so that spirits would possess their bodies and make them invincible in battle.

The Boxer rebellion was encouraged by the economic misery of Shandong in the last few years of the 19th century; there was an influx of demobilised troops after the Chinese defeat in the war with Japan in 1894. Famines in the south, floods and drought, drove refugees north. The imperial government was either incapable or unwilling to help the local people, and foreigners were blamed for disregarding the gods and angering the spirits. The slogan of the Boxers, 'Overthrow the Qing; destroy the foreigner' had immediate appeal. The Boxers suffered a heavy defeat by government troops in October 1899, but the Qing court saw the strength and popularity of the Boxers as an instrument to throw the foreigners out of China. Towards the end of 1899 the Boxers and the government had united in an anti-foreigner alliance. In the winter of that year the Boxers began the massacre of Chinese Christians, missionaries and other foreigners, and destroyed churches and ripped up railroads. They converged on Beijing in June 1900 and laid siege to the foreign legations' compound; the day after the Boxers attacked, the imperial government declared war on the foreign powers. The legations, however, held out until a relief force of foreign troops arrived to end the siege and put down the rebellion.

By late 1900 there were 45,000 foreign troops in China, the imperial court had fled to Xian and the Boxers were dispersed. But although the foreign powers punished China with executions of government officials and Boxer leaders and forced the Chinese to pay a huge indemnity, they did not break up the Chinese empire. Instead they preserved the dynasty with Cixi as ruler, holding the empire together and thus maintaining their own supremacy. The Chinese had once again been defeated and foreign privileges preserved. With the defeat of the Boxers even the Empress realised that China was too weak to survive without reform. The civil service examinations based on the irrelevant 1000-year-old Confucian doctrines were abolished. A draft constitution was devised but this only allowed the throne to retain absolute power; the court-sponsored reform was a sham. By now there were secret societies being set up all over the country and by Chinese abroad aimed at bringing down the Qing Dynasty. In 1905 several of these merged to form the Alliance for Chinese Revolution, headed by the Cantonese Dr Sun Yat-sen.

The Empress Dowager died in 1908 and the throne was ascended by the two-year-old Emperor Puyi. The power of the central government rapidly fell apart. When the court announced the nationalisation of the railways in 1911, the move was viewed by provincial governors and wealthy merchants as an attempt to restrict their autonomy. An army coup in Wuhan siezed control of the city and the heads of many other provinces declared their loyalty to the revolutionaries. By the year's end, most of southern China had repudiated Qing rule and given its support to the Alliance. On 1 January, 1912 Sun Yat-sen was proclaimed President of the Chinese Republic.

### The Early Days of the Republic

When China became a republic in 1912 it was in name only. In that year Sun was declared the President of the Republic and head of a provisional government which had been set up in Nanjing. But the new government needed a substantial armed force to reinforce its authority. In the north, the former chief of the imperial armies and the foremost military leader, Yuan Shikai, held power. To prevent civil war Sun Yat-sen relinquished the presidency and handed it over to Yuan. The short-lived revolutionary army which had been formed by the Nanjing government was now disbanded, along with the Nanjing government itself. Yuan began concentrating power in his own hands hoping to found an imperial dynasty with himself as emperor. But it seemed that he was not blessed by the 'mandate of heaven' for his grandiose plans were cut short – with devastating finality – by his sudden death in June 1916.

The combination of internal upheaval and the self-interest and imperialism of other countries was beginning to make China's survival as an autonomous nation seem no more than an illusion. Externally the gravest threat came from Japan. During the first World War Japan had joined the Allies and taken over Germany's port of Qingdao and German ships, railways and industries in the Shandong

Peninsula along with it. In 1915 Japan presented China with the 'Twenty-One Demands' which would have reduced China to the level of a Japanese colony. Under the threat of a Japanese military advance out of Shandong, Yuan Shikai was forced to accept the economic concessions, but some of the more extreme political demands (like attaching Japanese 'political advisers' and 'police' to the provincial governments in China) were resisted.

Internally, China was exposed to nationwide warlordism, made worse because there was no real political centre after the death of Yuan. Civilian authorities in the towns and cities were forced to work hand-in-glove with the most powerful local military leaders who were backed by their own armies. Supplies and requisitions for the armies were taken from those who were the least able to resist – the peasants. As they became increasingly destitute, the peasants were forced to join the warlord armies in order to survive by looting others. These waves of militarism and the consequent decline in productivity led to an ascending spiral of poverty – not a new situation in China.

At this time Sun Yat-sen initiated moves to set up a government in the south to challenge the northern warlords. In 1917 he went to Canton and called on all the surviving members of the Kuomintang Party – the party which had emerged as the dominant political force after the abdication of the Manchus – to join him and form a government. But it was more an empty gesture than a significant challenge, for with no public recognition and no military backing, the southern warlords were able to put an end to Sun's scheme – and very nearly to his life – before it had even got started. He and his wife just managed to escape to the International Settlement in Shanghai.

## The Intellectual Revolution
Meanwhile, the intelligentsia in China were continuing to search for solutions to China's crisis. Following Yuan's death, his opponents returned from abroad; the conservative Confucian order came under attack once again; and the struggle for a new ideology began. The mainstream of the intellectual revolution came from Beijing University, but in nearly all the major cities and towns discussion societies, with their own journals, emerged. One of the leaders of the movement, Li Dazhao, worked as a librarian at Beijing University. Later a founder of the Chinese Communist Party and and still regarded as one of the best Chinese interpreters of Marxism, Li was instrumental in getting Mao Zedong a job in the library.

In 1918 Li started a society for the study of Marxism which was joined by Mao and Zhang Guodao, a student leader at the university and later a founder of the Communist Party. Another Beijing intellectual who organised Marxist study groups throughout China and became a founder of the Chinese Communist Party, was Chen Duxiu, dean at the university until 1919.

In Tianjin a Marxist study group was started by a young scholar, Zhou Enlai, who went to France in 1920 and, with other Chinese in that country, formed a Socialist Youth League and later a Communist Party which became a branch of the Chinese Communist Party. When Mao returned from Beijing to Changsha he started his own Marxist study group, whose members included Liu Shaoqi and Xiao Chen (later a founder of the Communist Party). He also made contact with Li Lisan. Another society was formed at the same time in Hebei called the 'Social Welfare Society' of which Lin Biao was a member.

## The May 4th Movement
In May 1919, the intellectual revolution was given impetus when the news reached China that the Allies at the Versailles Peace Conference had agreed to support Japan's claims to German concessions on Chinese territory. Student protests against

the Japanese and the warlord regime in Beijing – the city which had supported the treaty – were broken up by the police. But still the protests did not end. A wave of nationalist, anti-Japanese, anti-foreign, anti-warlord feeling swept through the country's intellectuals. The aims of the movement were clear: to unite China, to bring the warlords under control, establish a central government, throw off the shackles of the unequal treaties which had been forced on China in the 19th century, and modernise the country sufficiently for it to cope with the foreign powers. But the question of how this was to be done remained unanswered.

## The Formation of the Chinese Communist Party (CCP)

From 1920 a few Russians who had taken part in the Bolshevik Revolution in Russia began to appear in China as representatives of the Soviet Foreign Office or of the Communist International (Comintern), the international body dedicated to world revolution with its headquarters in Moscow. But it was noticeable to all interested parties that they were not merely representatives but were being used as an important part of the Soviet foreign policy machinery. Talks with Li Dazhao in Beijing and Chen Duxiu in Shanghai eventually resulted in several Chinese Marxist groups banding together to form a Chinese Communist Party (CCP) at a meeting in Shanghai in 1921.

In 1922 the CCP members were urged by the Moscow representatives to join the Kuomintang. Much of Soviet policy was governed by fear of the Japanese threat to their Far Eastern flank. They supported the Kuomintang as being the party most likely to strengthen China against foreign intervention, particularly from the Japanese. There was a great deal of uneasiness within the CCP about adopting this line since the CCP feared the Kuomintang was interested only in a national revolution which would unify the country and eliminate foreign interference, and not in the wider social revolution so important to the CCP. The Moscow representatives insisted that a social revolution could not occur without a national revolution, and under threat of having their support from the Comintern withdrawn, the CCP members joined the Kuomintang.

Russian military, economic and political advisers were sent to China between 1923 and 1927 to help the Kuomintang unify China internally and strengthen it against further foreign intrusions, which explains – in part – Russia's insistence on the Chinese Communist Party working with, rather than against the Kuomintang. But it was a tenuous alliance.

## The Struggle for Unification & Leadership

With a secure political base established in Canton, the Kuomintang began training its National Revolutionary Army, brought southern China under its control and set about subduing the northern warlords. In the hope of coming to some agreement with the warlord regime in Beijing, Sun Yat-sen went there at the end of 1924. But he had cancer and in March of the following year he died.

Sun's death removed the unifying influence in the faction-ridden party. The power struggle was between Wang Jingwei on the political wing and Chiang Kai-shek on the military wing. Wang Jingwei was sympathetic to the social reform policies of the Communists; Chiang Kai-shek's policies were basically antipathetic to the CCP, being founded on a capitalist state dominated by a privileged elite and ruled over by a military dictatorship.

The son of a middle-class merchant and landlord, Chiang Kai-shek was born in 1887 and grew up near Ningbo in the small village of Chikou in Zhejiang Province. At the age of 20 he entered a Chinese military school but stayed only a month before going to another in Japan, which he graduated from in 1909. In Japan he met Sun Yat-sen, joined the Kuomintang, returned to China and worked with Sun, until he became frustrated with attempts to play the warlords off against each other and found a government. He left the political scene in 1917 but returned to Sun's entourage when the Kuomintang allied itself with the Soviet Union. He was eventually made commander of the Whampoa Military Academy in Canton – a sort of Chinese West Point, where both Kuomintang and Communist youths were trained as officers for the National Revolutionary Army. In 1927 he married the sister of Madame Sun Yat-sen, strengthening his claims as legitimate successor to the late president.

In 1924 Zhou Enlai went to Canton to work as deputy director of the Whampoa Academy under Chiang Kai-shek. Under the direction of the Communist Party member, Peng Bai, the Kuomintang set up a Peasant Training Institute in Canton to train leaders for the peasant organisations. Hundreds of potential peasant leaders from Guangdong and Hunan and other provinces trained there for six months before returning to their own areas to organise the peasants. The peasant organisations grew much faster than their urban industrial counterparts, and began pressing for radical changes. They demanded that rent be reduced to only 25% of the crop, high taxes be removed, taking land as payment for debts be prohibited, higher payment for farm labourers, and the abolition of the landlord's private armies and gangs. Impressed by the strength of the peasant movement Mao, who taught at the Institute around 1925-26, tried to persuade the Kuomintang leadership that the greatest potential strength for revolution lay in the countryside. But he was ignored as attention was focused at the time on the impending 'Northern Expedition'.

## The Northern Expedition

In an effort to unify China, the Kuomintang decided to tackle the problem full-on. In 1926 they embarked on the Northern Expedition to wrest power away from the warlords who were still operating individually. Chiang Kai-shek was appointed commander-in-chief by the Kuomintang and the Communists. One force of the NRA moved up through Hunan, under the command of Tang Shengzhi, and eventually took the city of Wuhan, which became the seat of the Kuomintang government. Meanwhile Chiang Kai-shek's force had captured Nanchang. Following this victory Chiang tried to persuade the political and military leaders of the Kuomintang and the Russian advisers to join him. It became obvious that there was now a struggle for power within the Kuomintang. With the NRA about to move on Shanghai – the largest industrial city in China – Chiang took the opportunity to put down his opponents in the Party and the Communists along with them.

## The Shanghai Coup: the Betrayal of the Revolution

Shanghai was under the control of a local warlord, but his strength was being undermined by a powerful industrial movement organised in the city by Liu Shaoqi and Zhou Enlai for the Communist Party.

The Kuomintang strategy of the 1927 Northern Expedition called for the Shanghai workers to take over key installations in the Chinese city (but not in the foreign concessions) while the Kuomintang armies advanced on the city. On March 21 a general strike was called and Shanghai industry shut down. The police stations and the military arsenals were seized and 5000 workers were armed; the Kuomintang Army entered the city not long after. It seemed that the strategy had worked perfectly, but it was a short-lived victory.

Supported by the Shanghai industrialists who were worried about the trade union movement, and foreigners who feared the loss of trade and privileges, Chiang let loose a reign of terror against the Communists, Communist sympathisers and anyone who advocated revolutionary change in China. With the help of Shanghai's underworld leaders, money from Shanghai bankers and the blessings of the International Settlement, 'Chiang armed hundreds of gangsters, dressed them in Nationalist uniforms, and launched an overnight surprise-attack on the workers' militia which wiped out the Communists in the city. This was quickly followed by the massacre of Communists and other anti-Chiang factions in Canton, Changsha and Nanchang. Zhou Enlai, who later estimated the massacre in Shanghai alone at something like 5000, managed to escape by a hair's breadth. Li Dazhao, a founder of the Communist Party, was not so fortunate; he was executed by slow strangulation.

The political leadership of the Kuomintang was thrown into turmoil once again, and the military arm of the party attempted to sieze control. Chiang was officially dismissed and discreetly went off to Japan. But there were now two Nationalist governments in China; Chiang's creation in Nanjing, and the one based in Wuhan which had organised the Northern Expedition. With the military supporting Chiang Kai-shek and the massacre of most of its supporters, by September 1927 the Wuhan government was forced to bow to Chiang's Nanjing regime. By the middle of 1928 the Northern Expedition had reached Beijing and a national government was established with Chiang holding the highest political and military positions.

## The Kuomintang and the Futility of Reform

When Chiang set up the Kuomintang regime in Nanjing in 1927 it not only did not represent the majority of China, it did not even represent the majority of the party. Rivalry for the leadership of the party and struggles between local warlords for control of territory (even at the end of the Northern Expedition perhaps only 50% of the country was under direct

Kuomintang control) continued. Chiang was obsessed with his campaigns against the Communists, and blamed them for the Kuomintang's failure to achieve any social reform or unity during the 1930s.

Although there were genuine reformers in the Kuomintang, they did not have any influence. The party was more interested in maintaining a small and privileged elite than the rest of the people. Any prospects of social and rural reform were forgotten. In 1934 Chiang started the 'New Life Movement' to encourage the population to adopt martial discipline and unquestioning obedience to his leadership. The movement was a failure but it did indicate the future direction of the Kuomintang in a public way.

A kind of moral rearmament, the New Life Movement reverted to appealing to the traditional Confucian virtues of frugality and obedience. But this was neither the time nor the place to be preaching frugality to the great mass of Chinese. Not when labourers were treated little better than beasts of burden; when children were used as slave labor in factories, standing at machines for 12 or 13 hours a day and sleeping under them at night; and when women and children were sold as concubines, prostitutes or domestic slaves. The American journalist, Edgar Snow, recorded that in 1935 in Shanghai alone, more than 29,000 bodies were picked up from the streets, rivers and canals – bodies of the destitute, the starved, of babies and children that could not be fed.

Strikes were suppressed ruthlessly by foreign and Chinese factory owners. The situation was made even worse by a famine in 1929 which swept across Inner Mongolia and took five million lives. The military stopped food from being shipped to the famine-stricken regions because it wanted to protect its rolling stock, being afraid this vital machinery would be seized by enemies if sent eastwards to pick up supplies. For the same reason Kuomintang generals wouldn't send rolling stock westwards. In the towns of the famine-stricken areas there were rich men, rice hoarders, money-lenders and landlords, with armed guards to defend them, who profited enormously from the misfortune of others. As the famine set in, the opportunists descended on rural areas like vultures, buying up parcels of land from the starving farmers for a pittance.

In the countryside the Kuomintang 'government' consisted of a Kuomintang-appointed county magistrate who ruled in collusion with the landlords and money lenders of the district and their private armed guards – 10 to 20% of the rural population. Any attempts at reform were blocked by these 'unholy triumvirates' because it was not in their interests to see rents reduced or rural banks set up which would lend money to peasants at low interest rates. They themselves used money made available by the government at low interest and lent it at higher interest to the farmers. If rural reformers (and there were some operating in China in the first half of this century) managed to persuade farmers to use fertiliser to produce a better crop, the farmers had to borrow money at high interests to buy fertiliser – and if a better crop resulted, the local merchants who bought the crop simply lowered the buying price. Peasant protests were dealt with by the magistrates, landowners, money-lenders and merchants, often one and the same person. Repeated protests were dealt with by the private armies and gangs that many landlords retained, whilst the peasants' wives and children were taken into the landlords' households as domestic slaves in lieu of debts.

Between 80 and 90% of the rural population was illiterate. Tax collectors had police powers and could imprison peasants for failing to pay taxes and rent; peasants who did not want to go to jail were forced to borrow money from the money-lenders – more often than not the same person as the landlord and tax collector – at interest rates which meant paying the loan back at 400% over six months, 700% a year. In some instances land taxes were collected 60 years in advance.

Not only were most peasants destitute, but they were terrified of taking any step which would bring them into conflict with armed authority. The Communists quickly realised that the only way to win a social revolution was with guns.

## The Civil War: Communist versus Kuomintang

After Chiang Kai-shek staged his massacre of Communists and other opponents in March 1927, what was left of the Communist Party went underground. At this time the Chinese Communist Party had a policy of urban revolution, believing that victory could only be won by organising insurrections in the cities. Units of the Kuomintang Army led by Communist officers happened to be concentrated around Nanchang at the time, and there appeared to be an opportunity for a successful insurrection.

On 1 August, a combined army of 30,000 under the leadership of Zhou Enlai and Zhu De (who held a high-ranking post in the Kuomintang Army but was sympathetic to the Communists and helped organise the insurrection) seized the city and held it for several days until they were driven out by troops loyal to the Nanjing regime. The revolt was basically a fiasco, but it is marked in Chinese history as the beginning of the Red Army. The Communist forces retreated south from Nanchang to Guangdong.

In the autumn of 1927, Mao was sent to Changsha to organise what became known as the 'Autumn Harvest Uprising'. By September the first units of a peasant-worker army were formed with troops drawn from the peasantry, miners from the town of Hengyang further south, and rebel Kuomintang soldiers. Mao's army moved south through Hunan, fighting Kuomintang troops, and climbed into the Jinggang Mountains.

Despite opposition from the Central Committee of the Party which considered the rural movement doomed to failure, the rebel army held out until May 1928, reinforced by Zhu De's troops who had backtracked from Guangdong. A strategy was mapped out to consolidate control over the Communist-held areas and slowly expand.

But the Party hierarchy, led by Li Lisan, ordered the Communist army to attack Nanchang and Changsha. After two costly defeats at Changsha in 1930 Mao and Zhu refused to obey Li's orders to attack Changsha again, and they were supported by Lin Biao and Peng Dehuai. There ensued a brief Party war in which a number of anti-Maoists were killed or imprisoned. But from then on the 'Li Lisan line' was completely repudiated. The power base of the revolution was moved permanently to the country and the peasants and away from the cities where the Communists had always been defeated.

Communist-led uprisings in other parts of the country had also brought various parts of the country under their control: in Hubei, Fujian, Hunan, Sichuan and across northern China in Shaanxi, Ningxia and Gansu. But the Red Armies were still small, with limited resources and weapons. The Communists adopted a strategy of guerilla warfare with emphasis on mobility and rapid concentration and deployment of forces for short attacks on the enemy, followed by swift separation once the attack was over. Pitched battles were avoided except where their force was overwhelmingly superior. It was summed up in a four-line slogan;

*The enemy advances, we retreat;*
*The enemy camps, we harass;*
*The enemy tires, we attack;*
*The enemy retreats, we pursue.*

By 1930, the few hundred ragged and half-starved revolutionaries had been turned into an army of perhaps 40,000 –

such serious challengers to the power of the Kuomintang government that Chiang Kai-shek had to hurl a number of full-scale 'extermination campaigns' against them. But each time he was defeated and the Reds killed many Kuomintang troops, captured supplies and ammunition, enlisted new soldiers and expanded their territory.

The fifth campaign began in October 1933. For some reason the Communists changed their strategy. It seems that Mao and Zhu's authority was undermined by other members of the Party (notably Bo Gu, the Party General Secretary) who advocated meeting Chiang's troops in pitched battles. By October 1934 the Communists were hemmed into a small area in Jiangxi and had suffered heavy losses through a year of constant fighting. With the Communists tottering on the brink of defeat, Mao was able to win back the support of army officers, the Party Politburo and Central Committee, and supreme military and political command was given to him by a conference of army and political leaders. At this conference the decision was also made to retreat from Jiangxi and march north to Shaanxi.

### The Long March
In the mountains to the north of China the Communists controlled an area which spread across Shaanxi, Gansu and Ningxia. The troops in the north were led by Liu Zhitan (later killed in battle, March 1936), a graduate of the Kuomintang's Whampoa Military Academy in Canton who had sided with the Communists when the Kuomintang and Communists split in 1927.

On 16 October 1934 the main force of the Red Army in Jiangxi, about 90,000 troops, began the march west to Sichuan, to link up with the Red Army led by Xu Xiangqian in July 1935. Later that year 40,000 Red troops marched from their base in Hunan – only 15,000 or so reached Sichuan. The march from Sichuan to Shaanxi began in August 1935; they broke through the Kuomintang troops that had been mobilised in southern Gansu and joined the Red Army in Shaanxi in late October.

The Long March took a year and covered 5000 miles over some of the world's most inhospitable terrain. It was forced on the Communists by their defeats in the south, but it quickly became a legendary retreat. They passed through areas where the peasants had never heard of or knew little of the Red Army, and as they marched they confiscated the property of officials, landlords and tax-collectors, redistributed the land to the poor peasants, armed thousands of these peasants with weapons captured from the Kuomintang and left soldiers behind to organise guerilla groups which could harass the enemy. Of the 90,000 who started in Jiangxi only 20,000 made it to Shaanxi. Fatigue, sickness, exposure, and enemy attacks took their toll. Some deserted, but there were always more to fill their ranks. The Long March proved that peasants all over China would fight if they were given a method, an organisation, leadership, hope and weapons.

## Jinggangshan & the Communist Leadership

It's worth noting that Jinggangshan brought together many of the Communist leaders who rose to prominence in the following few years and held key positions in the People's Republic after 1949.

Of those who survived, **Zhu De**, regarded as the father of the Red Army, was the most prominent apart from **Mao Zedong** and **Zhou Enlai** who was political commissar to Zhu's army. **Peng Dehuai** was an officer in the Kuomintang Army commanded by the Hunanese warlord He Jian. The warlord began a purge of leftists amongst his troops in the winter of 1927 and then launched a massacre of thousands of radical 'Communist' Hunanese farmers and workers – but he hesitated to act against Peng because of his widespread popularity amongst the troops. In July 1928 Peng led his troops in

revolt, and joined the peasant uprising. **Ye Jianying** was also here; he was born in Canton in 1898 into a merchant family, graduated from the Yunnan Military Academy and joined the Communist Party in 1922. He was an instructor at Whampoa and commanded a division during the Northern Expedition until Chiang Kai-shek's coup. He went to Moscow in 1927 for two years and returned to China to join the Communist forces in Jiangxi. **He Long**, born in 1896 in Hunan, was organising peasant rebellions a decade before Mao. He joined the Kuomintang in 1920 and the Communist Party in 1926, helped lead the Nanchang uprising of August 1927 after which he escaped to Shanghai and Jiangxi where he became an army leader. **Lin Biao** was born in 1908, the son of a factory owner in Hebei Province ruined by extortionate taxation. Lin became a cadet at the Whampoa Military Academy in Canton and by 1927 was a colonel in the Kuomintang Army. After the coup he led his troops to join the Communist Army in the Nanchang Uprising and then retreated to Jiangxi. **Deng Xiaoping** joined the Communist Party in France and spent five years working there in the early 1920s. Returning to China via Moscow he transferred to the Chinese Communist Party and in 1927 helped set up a peasant army in Jiangxi. After the coup he worked underground in Shanghai and then went to Guangxi in 1929 to set up another Communist army. The army was defeated by Kuomintang troops but the survivors made their way to Jiangxi. In Jinggangshan Deng backed Mao's 'peasant line' and also supported him against Zhang Guodao during the Long March. Deng was closely associated with **Liu Bo-cheng** throughout the revolutionary war. Liu Bo-cheng joined the Communist Party in 1926, took part in the Nanchang Uprising and went to the Soviet Union before returning to China and Jinggangshan. He commanded the vanguard forces during the Long March. **Liu Shaoqi** worked closely with Zhou Enlai in Shanghai to organise the labour unions before their suppression in 1927. In 1932 Liu went to Jiangxi and made the Long March as far as Zunyi where he backed Mao in the struggle against Bo Gu; Liu was then sent to make contact with the guerilla forces north of the Yangtse and to head the party underground in Northern China until going to Yanan in 1937.

Among those who stayed behind in Jiangxi to fight the rearguard action when the Long March got under way was **Ye Ding** who had trained at Whampoa. He led a division during the Northern Expedition and was one of the principals in the Nanchang Uprising.

The split in the Communist Party between the 'peasant line' and the 'Li Lisan line' widened at Jinggangshan after repeated failures of attacks on the cities. Much of the struggle was between two factions in the Party and the relative importance they placed on the cities and the countryside to gain victory; between those like Mao who had been trained by bitter experience in China itself, and those who had been trained in Moscow and became known as 'Stalin's China Section' and later the 'Twenty-eight Bolsheviks'. In 1930 their leader was **Wang Ming**(aged 24), supported by his close comrade **Bo Gu**(age 23). Wang was the leader of the faction which opposed Mao's 'peasant line'. Li Lisan also opposed the 'peasant line' and dominated the Party from 1929 until 1930 when he too came into conflict with Wang and Po and was sent back to Moscow, allowing the two to assume leadership. From 1932 to 1935 Bo Gu was Mao's chief antagonist and responsible for policies which Mao, in 1945, asserted 'cost more Communist lives than enemies'. In 1935, during the Long March, a meeting of the Party hierarchy at Zunyi in Guizhou Province recognised Mao's leadership and he assumed supreme responsibility for strategy; Bo Gu and his supporters were forced to step down.

The last great challenge to Mao's supremacy came from **Zhang Guodao** who commanded the Red Army which marched from north of the Yangtse River to link up with Mao's forces in Sichuan in June 1935; Zhang and his supporters refused to recognise Mao's supreme command. The deadlock was broken by the sudden advance of the Kuomintang troops which threatened to drive a wedge between the two armies, and by a sudden rise in water level of one of Sichuan's rapid rivers which physically cut them off from each other. Zhang's army was left on the southern bank and Mao's pushed on to Shaanxi. When Zhang's army crossed the Yellow River a year later, it was nearly annihilated; the remnants of his army were left under the commmand of the **Li Xiannian**. In 1938 Zhang went over to the Kuomintang.

## The Japanese invasion & the United Front

In September 1931 the Japanese invaded and occupied the potentially wealthy but underdeveloped area of Manchuria, setting up a puppet state with the last Chinese Emperor, Puyi, as the symbolic head. The invasion provoked a crisis in the Kuomintang which saw Wang Jingwei temporarily become President, but Chiang still presided over the army. By skilful handling of the groups who supported him and the destruction of those who opposed him he was able to keep himself on top.

Despite the Japanese invasion Chiang seemed obsessed with putting down the Communists; 'Pacification first, resistance afterwards' was his slogan. Meanwhile the Communists held the view that unless the Japanese were defeated there would be no China for either Communists or Kuomintang to control, and advocated an anti-Japanese alliance with the Kuomintang. Even a surprise air-raid by Japanese bombers on Shanghai in 1932 and massacres of Shanghai Chinese by Japanese troops left Chiang unmoved. He launched into his series of 'extermination' campaigns against the Communists in the south, the last of which drove them out on their long march to Shaanxi.

In December 1936, Chiang flew to Xian to oversee yet another extermination campaign against the Communists. The deadlock between the Communists and the Kuomintang was about to be broken, but not by Chiang. In what became known as the 'Xian Incident' Chiang was taken prisoner by his own generals, led by Marshal Zhang Xueliang who commanded an army of Manchurian troops whose homeland was occupied by the Japanese and who were sympathetic to the Communists. Chiang was forced to call off his extermination campaign and to form an alliance with the Communists to resist the Japanese. In 1937 the Japanese launched an all-out invasion of China and by 1939 had all of eastern China under control. The Kuomintang government retreated west to Chongqing.

When war broke out in Europe in 1939 the immediate effect on China was to cut off the Kuomintang's most important source of supplies – Germany. Despite their anti-Soviet pact with Japan, the Nazis supplied the Kuomintang with over 60% of its munitions until July 1939. On the other hand, Japan got more than half its imported war materials from the USA. Most of the Russian arms arrived in China via Burma or Indochina. But in June 1940 Japan compelled the French to close the railway into Yunnan. Then the British complied with Japanese demands and closed the Burma highway. China was left with only one route of supply – the desert road from Xinjiang into the Soviet Union.

The situation changed dramatically after the Japanese bombing of Pearl Harbour in December 1941 and the entry of the Americans into the war. The Americans now hoped to use the Chinese to tie up as many Japanese troops as possible, and planned to use China as a base for attacking Japanese shipping, and Japanese troops in South-East Asia – and ultimately Japan itself. At the same time, Chiang Kai-shek hoped the Americans would win the war against the Japanese,

and provide him with the munitions he required to finally destroy the Communists.

The Kuomintang armies relied on conscription for their soldiers, but those with money and privilege could buy their way out so the burden fell on the poor. Areas under Kuomintang control each had a quota of recruits and, where numbers were short, men were press-ganged and roped together to prevent them escaping before reaching recruitment centres. Treated badly, underfed, underpaid, beaten by officers, and provided with hopeless medical attention, to be conscripted into the Kuomintang Army was to be doomed to death by injury, disease or starvation. From 1938 until the end of the war the Japanese were never seriously harassed by the Kuomintang troops as Chiang attempted to save his troops for renewed attacks on the Communists once the Americans had defeated the Japanese. General Joseph Stiwell, who was sent by President Roosevelt to China in 1942 to improve the combat effectiveness of the Chinese army, concluded that 'the Chinese government is a structure based on fear and favour in the hands of an ignorant, arbitrary and stubborn man ... ' and that its military effort since 1938 was 'practically zero'.

### The collapse of the United Front

Since the American commitment to defeating Japan was in their own interests, Chiang Kai-shek saw no need to maintain the alliance with the Communists – reasoning that the Americans would support him regardless. He had been putting pressure on the Communists before the American entry into the war, blockading the Communist areas in the north with 500,000 troops and moving away the sympathetic Manchurian troops.

The collapse of the United Front came in 1941 when Kuomintang troops ambushed the rear detachment of the Communists New Fourth Army while it was in an area which Chiang had assigned it, behind Japanese lines. This non-combat detachment was annihilated and its commander, Ye Ding, was imprisoned in Chongqing. Chiang ruled that the massacre was caused by the New Fourth's 'insubordination' and henceforth all aid was withdrawn from that army and also from the Communists' Eighth Route Army. From then on the Communists received neither pay nor ammunition, and a blockade was thrown up around their areas to prevent access to supplies. Although the Communists did not retaliate against the Kuomintang – which would have made Japan's task much simpler – clashes between Kuomintang and Communist were frequent, often on the scale of all-out civil war.

Nevertheless the Communist armies moved into and expanded in areas that were occupied by the Japanese. The Japanese burned villages and killed Chinese in their scorched earth policies that were meant to wipe out Chinese resistance, but the survivors joined the Communist armies. Communist armies led by He Long and Liu Bocheng moved into Shanxi and others now operated in parts of Hebei and Shandong. Another important base was in northern Jiangsu where the New Fourth Army had moved after its rear detachment was massacred in 1941. Other pockets of Communist guerrilla resistance also existed in southern China, in Hainan Island, near canton, in Hunan, Hubei, and Anhui. When the war against Japan was over in 1945 the Communist Army numbered 900,000 and were backed by militia and active supporters in the millions – and although widely scattered geographically they were held together by a common policy and leadership – a state within a state.

### The defeat of the Kuomintang

In 1945 the Soviet Union betrayed the Chinese Communists. It was Chiang's fear that once the Nazis were defeated in Europe the Russians would invade China and install the Communists as rulers.

Instead the Russians concluded a treaty with Chiang Kai-shek in 1945 and promised to aid his troops exclusively, and recognise his authority in Manchuria. Both the Americans and the Russians were committed to supporting the Kuomintang. The treaty came as a complete surprise to the Communists leaving them with no alternative but to compromise in the first round of a postwar struggle.

Peace negotiations between the Kuomintang and the Communists were opened in 1945 after the defeat of Japan. They came up against two fundamental problems. Chiang knew that if the Communists were admitted to government their dynamism and popular support would ultimately win them political control. Chiang refused to reorganise the Kuomintang government and admit the Communists unless their armies were placed under his control. The Communists knew that if their armies were disbanded, their movement would be finished. The talks carried on to the inevitable stalemate amidst clashes between Kuomintang and Communist troops.

It was probable that in 1945 Stalin believed – as did most observers – that once the war with Japan was over the Kuomintang's well-equipped army of 2½ million troops would quickly disperse the poorly-armed and outnumbered Communists, and that if necessary the USA would intervene to save the Kuomintang from destruction. Stalin's advice to the Communists was to dissolve their armies and enter into an alliance with the Kuomintang as a minority in Chiang's government. But the Chinese Communists had fought for too long and were too formidable a power to be vanquished by a scrap of paper signed in Moscow.

With the surrender of Japan in August 1945, Soviet troops moved into Manchuria (as agreed by the Allied Powers at the Yalta conference of February that year), and occupied the main cities and took over the railroads. The Communist armies were in areas behind Japanese lines and the Kuomintang armies were concentrated in south-west China where they had been countering Japanese pressure on US air bases there. There was a dramatic struggle for position. The Americans transported Kuomintang troops to northern China to accept the surrender of the Japanese, and American-trained and equipped Kuomintang armies were moved to the cities along the Yangtse and then to Beijing and Tianjin. The American Navy moved into Qingdao and landed 53,000 marines to protect the railways leading to Tianjin and Beijing and the coal mines which supplied these railways. The Communists moved into Manchuria by foot and by sea from Shandong, and set themselves up in the countryside. In three months the 100,000 Communist troops were joined by 200,000 Manchurian troops who had been forcibly incorporated into the Japanese army, and within the next two years the Communist army and its support units grew to several million.

In November 1945 Chiang launched the first attacks against the Communists in Manchuria. The general strategy of the Communists, under the command of Lin Biao, was to surround the Manchurian cities where Chiang's armies were based and pinch off their flanking units one by one. This time it was the Kuomintang who found themselves surrounded by the enemy. The Kuomintang troops had no reason to fight and they were commanded by incompetent and corrupt generals. By 1948 the Communists were gaining the initiative in Manchuria and Shandong. Having captured American-supplied Kuomintang equipment and recruited Kuomintang soldiers to their side, by the middle of the year they equalled the Kuomintang in both numbers and supplies. The turning point was a campaign in the middle of the year in which the Kuomintang lost 500,000 men, most of whom, along with their equipment, were incorporated

into the Communist Army. The second great battle was fought between November 1948 and January 1949 with 500,000 troops on either side. In the end whole divisions went over to the Communists who captured 375,000 troops. The Kuomintang lost seven generals, dead or captured, and seven divisional commanders crossed sides. The third decisive campaign was fought around Beijing and Tianjin at the same time; Tianjin fell on 15 January and Beijing on 23 January. The victories brought another 500,000 troops over to the Communists.

The Communists moved south and were deployed along the north bank of the Yangtse River, Kuomintang peace overtures were rejected, and in April the Communists crossed the river in small boats along a 480 km front. Nanjing fell on April 23 and the Kuomintang government fled to Canton and then to Chongqing. By October all the major cities south of the Yangtse had fallen to the Communists and on 1 October Mao Zedong proclaimed the formation of the People's Republic of China in Beijing.

Chiang Kai-shek fled to Taiwan, taking with him the entire gold reserves of the country and what was left of his air force and navy. By December, the hierarchy of the Kuomintang had joined him, and alltold some 2,000,000 refugees and soldiers from the mainland crowded onto the island and have been there ever since – the last remnant of 20 years of civil war.

### The Communist Era: Revolution to Cultural Revolution

It was inevitable that the Chinese would embrace Communism. When Marx's books were being read by young Chinese intellectuals and would-be revolutionaries in the early part of this century, they recognised a description of China as they knew it: child and female slave labour, starvation wages, exploitation of workers by capitalists, no protection against sickness, injury, unemployment and old age, and no bargaining power for better working conditions. This was not only an academic description of life in industrial Europe in the 1800s, it fitted China to a T. Famine, war, invasion by foreign powers and massive indemnities, heavy taxation and the plundering and squandering of public money by bureaucrats and militarists had brought about massive unemployment and poverty.

Chinese communism was also Chinese nationalism; foreign armies defended western and Japanese rights and interests which had been gained by force. Immunity to Chinese laws gave foreigners a free hand to do what they wanted, and the country lay at the mercy of Japan and a host of western powers. Marxism advocated the eradication of imperialism, which appealed to many nationalists. The Communists wanted to form a united front of workers, peasants and 'progressive bourgeoisie' which would end imperialist rule and win complete independence.

The Chinese Communists overturned the orthodox Marxist view that a Communist revolution could not succeed without the organisation of the urban workers as the main fighting force. After the initial disasters of the urban insurrections of 1927-30, the Communists had to fall back on the countryside where Mao and Zhu De set up the first Communist armies drawn largely from the peasants. The Communists came to represent the poor peasants, the greater mass of the Chinese population. They promised them land and relief from ruinous taxes, usury, starvation. In the areas they controlled they eliminated the landlord-gentry class and distributed the land equally amongst the poor peasants – in fact the Chinese name for Communist Party literally translates as the 'Share-Property-Party'. Chiang Kai-shek and his Kuomintang supported the landlords and saw the peasants only as a source of soldiers and supplies for its armies.

The vast spaces, the lack of roads, railways and bridges made it possible for the Communists to set up power bases in the countryside. They supplied themselves with weapons and ammunition captured from the enemy and gained more troops as the Japanese and Kuomintang killed more villagers. The heavily-policed cities could always be held down by their enemies, but in the countryside the Communists were virtually invincible because they carried with them the decisive political factor which the Japanese and the Kuomintang lacked – the support of the people.

## The 1950s – the Early Years of the People's Republic

The People's Republic started its official life as a bankrupt nation. The economy was in chaos following Chiang Kai-shek's flight to Taiwan with China's only gold reserves. The country had a mere 12,000 miles of railways and 48,000 miles of usable roads, all in chaotic condition and need of repair. Irrigation works had broken down, livestock and animal populations were greatly reduced. Industrial production fell to 50% of the pre-war days and agricultural output plummeted. Since the mid-19th century the Chinese harvest had been unable to feed the population even if the food had been distributed equitably. Famine was endemic and millions died of malnutrition and disease.

With the Communist takeover China seemed to become a different country; its obsessive haste to catch up with history and become one of the world's great nations, or the world's greatest nation, was positively awesome.

Unified by the elation of victory and the immensity of the task before them, and further bonded by the Korean War and the necessity to defend the new regime from possible American invasion, the 1950s were a dynamic period for the Communists. By 1953 inflation had been halted, industrial production restored to pre-war levels and the land had been confiscated from the landlords and redistributed to the poor peasants. In the mid-1950s industry was nationalised and the farmers were encouraged to pool land and equipment in mutual-aid teams and co-operatives with a view to using resources more efficiently and increasing production.

## The Great Leap Forward

Despite the rapid advances which China was making in both agricultural and industrial output, Mao and his supporters embarked on the ill-fated 'Great Leap Forward', an ambitious plan designed to transform the country at one stroke into a developed nation. The seasonally under-employed peasantry were to work on local small-scale industrial projects like small steel furnaces and fertiliser plants, as well as on labour-intensive dams and irrigation networks. Ironically, while industry was being decentralised, the programme was combined with the establishment of gigantic rural communes which would supposedly allow a more efficient use of land and resources. Having won their land, the peasants now found it being taken away from them again; inefficient management combined with little incentive to work on the common field, and large numbers of the rural work-force now engaged on industrial projects, resulted in a massive slump in agricultural output.

With industry in confusion and agriculture at an all-time low, China was struck by two disasters: the floods and droughts which ruined the harvests of 1959 and 1960, and the withdrawal in 1960 of all Soviet Union aid from China.

## 1960-1964: Prelude to the Cultural Revolution

The Soviet withdrawal, the failure of the Great Leap Forward and the communes, unprecedented bad weather and poor harvests, all contributed to the severe food shortages and famine of 1959, 1960 and 1961. By 1964-65 the economy had recovered some of its equilibrium and the hardship years of 1959-62 were past; industry and agriculture started to pick up and there was a general sense of optimism,

clouded only by a growing fear of war with the United States spreading from Vietnam. However, the disasters of the late 1950s and early 1960s opened a rift between Mao and the rest of the Communist Party.

One of the first clashes occurred in 1959 when Mao came under attack from Marshal Peng Dehuai at the Lushan conference of the Party Central Committee. Peng attacked the Party's failures and inferentially blamed Mao for the heavy losses of the Great Leap Forward, the people's communes and the split with the Soviet Union. Peng was defeated at the conference, dropped from the Politburo and lost his job as Minister of Defence, though he still remained on the Central Committee. In 1960-61, allegedly encouraged by Liu Shaoqi to persevere, Peng travelled through China on field studies and produced a long report which he presented to the Central Committee meeting in 1962. The report made further criticisms of Mao's leadership and was preceded by several shorter reports circulated to the members of the Central Committee. Although Peng had lost two important positions, Mao also found himself in a political recession with much of the responsibility for the Great Leap Forward and the commune failures laid on him.

Thus began a period in which Liu Shaoqi and Deng Xiaoping and their supporters were in the ascendancy. In contrast to Mao, they took a pragmatic view of economics; they encouraged effort by material incentives first and ideological zeal second, pushed production without class struggle, boosted technology through experts and intellectuals. Ownership of land was turned over to the individual villages, family ownership of land and small private plots was guaranteed, limited free markets were permitted and a bonus system and material incentives introduced into industry. In 1960 and 1961 agriculture took priority over heavy industry; Liu and Deng continued their policies of free markets, private plots and small enterprises with sole responsibility for their own losses and profits. To put their policies into effect they built up an enormous government and Party bureaucracy, labour unions, Party schools and Communist Youth Leagues over which Mao had little or no influence. For Mao these policies reeked of 'revisionism' – a return to the capitalist past which would breed a new herd of capitalist opportunists who would lead China back into the misery and oppression which the revolution had sought to destroy.

Mao still had one power base – the army – but even army leadership was polarised. On the one hand, there were officers who backed Peng Dehuai's policies; Peng felt that China was not ready to stand alone and favoured a temporary compromise with the USSR. This group wanted Russian help to complete the technological modernisation of the army, including the development of the nuclear bomb. They wanted to break Mao's grip on the army, which he had had since 1935 as Chairman of the Military Affairs Commission, so that the army could determine military policy, and they wanted to free the army of non-military production tasks. On the other hand, Mao and Lin Biao felt that another alliance with the USSR would make China a junior partner in an unequal alliance and subservient to Russian interests. Lin was Mao's faithful Army disciple and Vice-Chairman of the Military Affairs Commission; Liu controlled the civilian government apparatus, but Mao and Lin controlled the Army – *the* trump card in any showdown.

Both the Maoist and Liuist factions aimed to create a strong and independent China, and the conflict arose mainly from differing views about where that strength lay and how to go about using it to best advantage. Liu and Mao came from rich peasant stock and had similar backgrounds, but their philosophies differed markedly. Mao disliked city life and was contemptuous of experts and intellectuals who had never fired a gun or dug a field. Mao learned about revolution by recruiting peasant guerilla fighters; he respected the peasants who had been his best soldiers. Liu did not care for peasant life, preferred to organise urban-based conspiracies and was a skilled organiser of workers and intellectuals. Liu tended to see results emerging less from zeal and exhortation than from the efforts of a professional human machine with co-ordinated staff.

By 1964, the pragmatic economic policies of Liu and Deng were under attack by Mao in a campaign known as the 'Socialist Education Movement'. Through the party section of the army, Lin Biao had built up a corps of about a million Maoist activists whose job was to put down the 'spontaneous desire to become capitalists' amongst the peasants. The first point of the SEM was to denounce and demand the removal of 'those in the Party in authority who are taking the capitalist road' and this was to form the basis of a new drive, the 'Cultural Revolution'.

### 1966-1970: the Cultural Revolution

With the rise of the bureaucratic elite, Mao believed that China was slipping away from the spirit of the revolution; it needed recharging. A 'Cultural Revolution' would put it back on the revolutionary path. Mao advocated policies of self-reliance, initiative, decentralisation, priority for the needs of the peasants (70% to 80% of the population), and a campaign to destroy bourgeois influences. He believed that Liu Shaoqi's bureaucracy was divorced from the people, a new elitist class that was reverting to capitalism. He opposed Liu's desire to reactivate the USSR-China alliance as a defence against possible US aggression after that country started bombing Vietnam in 1965; Mao wanted China to stand alone and not be in a position of dependence.

In August 1966 the Party Central Committee adopted a programme for the Cultural Revolution. The resolution stated that the bourgeoisie was attempting to stage a comeback using 'old ideas, culture, customs and habits of the exploiting class to corrupt the masses, capture their minds'. The aim of the Cultural Revolution was 'to struggle against and crush those persons in authority who are taking the capitalist road, to criticise and repudiate the reactionary bourgeois academic "authorities" and the ideology of the bourgeoisie and all other exploiting classes and to transform education, literature, and art and all other parts of the superstructure that do not correspond to the socialist economic base, so as to facilitate the consolidation and development of the socialist system'.

There was no doubt as to the ideological basis of the campaign; the resolution declared that 'In the Great Proletarian Cultural Revolution, it is imperative to hold aloft the great red banner of Mao Zedong's thought and put proletarian politics in command. The movement for the creative study and application of Chairman Mao Zedong's works should be carried forward among the masses of the workers, peasants, and soldiers, the cadres and the intellectuals, and Mao Zedong's thought should be taken as the guide for action in the Cultural Revolution'.

The 'Revolution' rapidly turned into political mayhem personally directed by Mao. Backed by his supporters in the Army and by the Socialist Education Movement he was able to purge anti-Mao officials in the Party and government institutions. The effects on Liu's bureaucracy were devastating. Thousands of administrative personnel in the central government lost their jobs; about 80% of these cadres were sent to 'May 7th Schools' (the name deriving from a Mao directive of that day in 1968) where re-education in socialism and the Thought of Mao Zedong was combined with labour on commune farms. The training organisations of Liu Shaoqi's bureaucracy, the Young Communist League, and the Party

Training Schools were all disbanded; the army was going to be the source of new cadres.

The battle was effectively over for Liu – though it was not until 1967 that he was actually named as China's Krushchev, and not until early 1968 that he was expelled from the Communist Party, dismissed from all offices and declared a scab, renegade and traitor. Deng Xiaoping was also purged as the second-ranking 'Capitalist Roader'; many senior army officers were retired and replaced by younger officers.

Liu Shaoqi died in prison in 1969; Deng was sent off to work as a waiter. They were not the only two high-ranking Communist leaders to be purged. Peng Dehuai was accused of being a counter-revolutionary who conspired with Liu Shaoqi as early as 1959 and was held guilty of collusion with reactionary and revisionist elements who sought to overthrow Mao; he disappeared and it was not until 1980 that it was announced that he had died in 1974. Peng Zhen, the mayor of Beijing, also disappeared. Even Zhou Enlai and Zhu De were attacked in the occasional Red Guard wall-poster.

### The Red Guards

The Red Guards changed the face of the Cultural Revolution. They appeared at Beijing University in May 1966. Exactly how they got started is unknown, but it seems that neither side planned nor foresaw them. The group at the university was initially suppressed but Mao was quick to recognise their potential. Encouraged by his support they rose again in Beijing University and then spread elsewhere. In June Mao gave his support to the movement and the nation saw a Red Guard explosion. With the unleashing of the Red Guards in August 1966, Mao set loose on the country a madness that may have surprised even him. The people who had been bottled up for 4000 years suddenly found the corkscrew removed; millions of teenagers were suddenly given an opportunity to attack and humiliate people in authority, their teachers, professors, and cadres.

In some places new leaders arose, but in others the Red Guards failed to agree on a choice of leaders and fell into factions. Arms – even mortars – were seized from local militia and Red Guard factions fought each other until civil war was close. With the country fast self-destructing, Mao was forced to call in the army in 1967 to end the chaos, using weapons when necessary to disarm the Guards and end the factional fighting.

### The Cultural Dissolution

The name of the revolution did, after all, include the word 'Culture'. But it was really a time of cultural dissolution, reminiscent of the book-burning of Qin Shihuang 2000 years ago.

This time round it was Mao's wife, Jiang Qing, the former B-grade Shanghai film actress who became the cultural supremo. Theatres, movies, radio and television, loudspeakers in train carriages were dominated by a handful of her 'Revolutionary Model Operas', with titles like *Taking Tiger Mountain by Strategy* or *Red Lantern* portraying themes from the Chinese revolution or the post-1949 period, with performers dressed as PLA troops strutting around on stage toting wooden rifles. Western instruments were introduced into the orchestra and the music had elements of Western classical music in it – ironic developments for this time of xenophobia. Connoisseurs of music could enjoy brilliant compositions like *The Chuang Minority Loves Chairman Mao with a Burning Love* or *The Production Brigade Celebrates the Arrival in the Hills of the Manure Collectors*.

The dissolution of art and culture and the subjugation of what was left originated at least as far back as 1942 in Yanan when Mao delivered his 'Talk on Arts and Letters'. In this lecture he laid down the principles that have governed the Party approach to culture ever since; Mao said there was no such thing as art for art's sake, no art which transcended class or party, no art which was independent of politics; all art and literature serves political ends, and under the Communist Party it must serve the interests of the Party.

The reform of the Chinese opera began soon after to put these ideas into practice; new scenarios were written with themes related to actual events and old operas were revised so as not to continue propagating outdated ideas. The Communists recognised the opera as a moving force among the Chinese masses and in a country which had suffered oppression for so long it made sense to eradicate the tools of oppression.

The Cultural Revolution was the ultimate product of Mao's lecture in 1942 and led to a cultural sterility which could only have been matched by the Nazis or the Khmer Rouge. Universities and secondary schools were closed; intellectuals were dismissed, persecuted and sent to labour in the countryside, some were killed or they committed suicide. Publication of scientific, artistic, literary and cultural magazines and periodicals ceased. Movies, plays and operas from before the Cultural Revolution disappeared and movie studios closed. Library collections were destroyed.

All books published prior to the Cultural Revolution were banned; bookstores sold works by Mao Zedong and little else. The 1966 Central Committee resolution had listed some of the works of Mao which must be studied: *On the New Democracy, Talks at the Yenan Forum on Literature and Art, On the Correct Handling of Contradictions Among the People, Speech at the Chinese Communist Party's National Conference on Propaganda Work, Some Questions Concerning Methods of Leadership, and Methods of Work of Party Committees*. Lin Biao summarised the teacher's teachings by publishing a book of Mao quotations, the 'little red book'; it was first published in 1964 for the use of the army and the peasants, and in 1966 copies flooded the cities. Literally hundreds of millions of 'little red books' rolled off the presses in every significant language of the world.

The Red Guards attacked writers, artists and intellectuals; their works were destroyed and they were sent to labour in the countryside. Temples were ransacked, monasteries disbanded and the monks, too, were sent to the countryside. Anything that was a physical reminder of China's past – temples, monuments, works of art – was considered inextricably bound up with exploitation, capitalism and feudalism, and it was destroyed.

## The Communist View of History

Contemporary Communist historians see history as developing in a 'linear' manner rather than the 'cyclical' manner observed by their predecessors. The Communist view of history also shifts attention from the rulers to the common people, judging a historical period by the conditions under which the ordinary people lived rather than that of the ruling group with which most historians have been concerned. In the mid-19th century, Marx interpreted European history as having progressed through a series of stages, each growing out of the last; from primitive village communalism, through slavery to feudalism and to capitalism. In the 1920s and 1930s, Chinese historians sympathetic to Marxism tried to fit their own history into this theory of stages. Neolithic villages fitted the first stage, the evidence of human sacrifice and slavery in the Shang and part of the Zhou period seemed to fit the second. The growth of a landlord class, which reduced free peasants to a serf-like status through the control of rents, interest and market rates, provided enough reason to call the period from 500 BC onwards a 'feudal society'. The next stage of Chinese history was to emerge out of the 'class struggle' between slaves and aristocrats, peasants and landlords.

## Maoist China: 1969-1976

Three years after Mao began his revolution the Red Guards had risen and been suppressed, Liu Shaoqi had been locked away and millions of cadres had been sent to the fields to labour. Mao's victory was so complete that at the Ninth National Party Congress in April 1969 Lin Biao stated that 'whoever opposes Chairman Mao Zedong's Thought, at any time or under any circumstances, will be condemned and punished by the whole Party and the whole country'.

Mao Zedong and the Thought of Mao Zedong was the unifying force behind the Party-government-military and the man was raised almost to the level of a god, at least an emperor. It was no accident that Mao hailed his people from the Gate of Heavenly Peace which the Son of Heaven had presided over for ages past. Curiously, in 1970 Mao told Edgar Snow that the cult of personality which prevailed in China during the Cultural Revolution had been overdone. Mao called the 'Four Greats' – Great Teacher, Great Leader, Great Supreme Commander and Great Helmsman – a nuisance, and promised they would all be dispensed with sooner or later. He said only the word 'teacher' would be retained; that is, schoolteacher. He had always been a schoolteacher and still was one. It is possible that Mao didn't mean what he said, but he certainly wasn't oblivious to the cult that had grown up around him.

The ideals of the Cultural Revolution were high: to erase the difference between city and country, subordinate selfishness to service, create a superior 'socialist man' from the poor peasants and workers, and prevent the rise of a fat and bloated bureaucratic elite which would lead China back into the bog. China was to become a self-sufficient nation and was to enter an age of self-sustaining growth. But it didn't work out that way.

## The Rise and Fall of Lin Biao

In 1969 the National Congress of the Communist Party had adopted a new constitution, reportedly drafted by Mao himself. It designated Lin Biao, Defence Minister and Vice-Chairman of the Party, referred to as Mao's 'closest comrade in arms', as Mao's successor. Of the 279 members in the new Central Committee, a hundred of them were of military rank. The army had emerged more powerful than ever from the Cultural Revolution.

The army was always an integral part of the Communist movement, having begun as an army drawn mainly from the peasants and poor workers. Political leaders often held military positions as well; Mao was both Chairman of the Party and effective commander-in-chief of the army by virtue of his chairmanship of the Military Affairs Commission. Zhou Enlai was a general in command of the Eastern Front Army in Shanxi in the 1930s.

In China, unlike other countries, the army was involved in non-military activities, mainly construction programmes: afforestation, housing projects, and the building of strategic dams, power plants, bridges, tunnels and roads. It built the Chengdu-Kunming railway during the Cultural Revolution. It built the Beijing subway and supervised the communications network and the building of air-raid shelters all over China. Naval officers were in charge of the Shanghai shipbuilding yards. All military and nuclear industries were, of course, run by the army. The army dominated ideological indoctrination in almost every organisation, industry and institution in China after the Cultural Revolution. Today it may exist as a separate entity as it does in other countries, but the army then was the lynchpin of society.

Mao was not oblivious to the trend towards separatism in the army – its desire to set itself up as an autonomous force. In the 'Red Book' he points out that 'Political power grows out of the barrel of a gun' and 'Without a People's Army the people have nothing and neither has the Party'. They are as inseparable as 'the lips and the teeth' as the Chinese say. But Mao also maintained that the 'Party commands the gun and the gun must never be allowed to command the Party'.

In 1972 it was suddenly announced that Lin Biao, the 'closest comrade in arms', had been killed in a plane crash in September 1971, fleeing to the Soviet Union after an assassination attempt and coup against Mao had failed. Unless there was some unknown schism in the leadership, with the army firmly in power and Lin designated as Mao's successor, there seems to be no reason for Lin to try and wrest command from a man in the last few years of his life. It's possible Lin may have been planning a coup or Mao may have feared he was and had him executed. Whatever the truth, the story of the plane crash is effective on two counts. It suggests that Lin was actually planning a coup and was therefore a traitor, and also that in Mao's China political foes were not disposed of in a manner offensive to the western world. The truth will never be known.

### The Rise of Zhou Enlai

In 1972 Mao Zedong was 79 years old. *The* paramount force in China and probably the most inspiring revolutionary force in the world, China now had to face the imminent prospect of a time without him. With Lin dead and Mao's health steadily declining, it was the 73-year-old Premier Zhou Enlai who commanded the most substantial influence in the day-to-day governing of China, exercised the most influence and commanded the most loyalty and respect.

Zhou was a remarkable survivor of the Cultural Revolution. Not really allied to Liu Shaoqi, but very much an adherent to the same pragmatic economic policies, Zhou was always third in line to Mao and Lin. In the late 1920s he was definitely a candidate for the supreme leadership of the Party but never seemed to go for it. During the Kuomintang-Communist alliance he was the Communist political

chief at Canton's Whampoa Military Academy and won the confidence of people like Lin Biao and Ye Jianying. His years spent in Moscow and France enabled him to make connections with and win the respect of many factions in the Party. And in the Jiggang Mountains of Jiangxi he was the political commissar to Zhu De's army. But when Mao attained supreme leadership of the Party, Zhou never wavered in his loyalty to him. As Premier, his main preoccupation during the Cultural Revolution was to hold the administrative machinery of the government together, and after the 1969 Congress he set about reorganising the government structure and restoring and expanding China's diplomatic and trade contacts with the outside world – particularly with the United States.

### The 1970s – the Parting of the Bamboo Curtain

Despite the finality of the Communist victory in 1949, Chiang Kai-shek's regime on Taiwan continued to receive the support of the Americans who feared that a Communist victory had established a giant Communist monolith bent on world conquest dominated by the Soviet Union. American foreign policy seemed to ignore the fact that the Communists had fought for 20 years to throw off imperialist aggression and had no intention of submitting to the Soviet Union or anyone else.

During those early years the United States saw the People's Republic as a pliant puppet of Moscow and believed that Soviet expansion would continue indefinitely. But such universal world domination by one power was a technical impossibility; the power of the Kremlin could only extend to those countries which were occupied by their armed forces, and China was not one of them.

During the 1950s and 1960s the United States followed a policy of armed encirclement or containment of China which aimed to isolate and eventually bring about its collapse. The fallacy of the 'Communist monolith' theory was demonstrated in 1960 when the alliance split – by 1959 the fissures between China and Russia had widened so much that Khrushchev reneged on his promise to give China a 'sample atom bomb'. The following year Khrushchev withdrew all Soviet technical advisers and cancelled hundreds of contracts vital to China's industrialisation. The Marxist myth that class solidarity was stronger than nationalism was shattered. China and the Soviet Union now vied with each other for the ideological leadership of the Communist movements around the world.

In reality the Soviet Union and China were containing each other. It was a confrontation which the USA could exploit by favouring China, the weaker of the two powers, but refused to do so. In the 1950s the Chinese made an attempt at reconciliation with the USA. They offered visas to many Americans but until 1957 the Secretary of State, John Foster Dulles, had banned *all* Americans from visiting China, threatening any violators with the loss of passport, fines or imprisonment. America's paranoid fear of Red China continued through the 1960s and China fell into a period of isolationism aggravated by the Cultural Revolution.

Around 1970, with the major campaigns of the Cultural Revolution finished, the Chinese leadership turned its attention to what it considered the greatest threat to its security – the Soviet Union. The Soviets also looked on China as an immediate threat, and by 1969 the borders of the two countries bristled with arms and border skirmishes were frequent. Meanwhile in a propaganda war they tried to destroy each other's credibility in world opinion. With the Chinese growing more apprehensive about the Soviets, a possible reconciliation with the USA looked more attractive.

Indeed, reconciliation with China must have seemed more urgent after 1964; in October of that year the country exploded

its first atom bomb and in 1968 it exploded its first hydrogen Bomb, permitting the Chinese to take an active role in Armageddon. Although the country could hardly bear the burden of building missiles and bombs, the potential to do so certainly put a new perspective on China's position in the world. On the Chinese side, growing fear of the Soviet Union was high among the reasons why rapprochement with the Americans interested the Chinese. They also saw a possibility for negotiating the recovery of Taiwan and for China to be accepted as a power in world affairs.

In 1969 the Nixon administration cancelled most of the restrictions against trade with China, as well as travel, cultural and newspaper contacts. Early in 1970, in Warsaw, Chinese and American diplomats resumed discussions concerning terms of peaceful co-existence and the dissolution of the American armed protectorate of Taiwan. China also moved towards greater contact with the outside world: it vilified the USSR for the invasion of Czechoslovakia in 1968; moved towards closer relations with Rumania; opened trade with the arch-revisionist Yugoslavia, and attempted to establish diplomatic relations with Canada. The invasion of Cambodia by the Americans in 1970 and the overthrow of Prince Sihanouk (whom the Chinese supported) by General Lon Nol's coup may have suggested to the Chinese that Nixon could not be taken seriously, but the President persisted and the possibility of a presidential visit preceded by an envoy (Henry Kissinger) was put to the Chinese. The bamboo curtain finally parted when Nixon stepped off the plane at Beijing Airport in 1972, to be greeted by Zhou Enlai. Whatever the Chinese may have thought of Nixon's motives, he earned some appreciation by the courtesy of coming to see them.

### The Second Coming of Deng Xiaoping
Zhou's pragmatic approach to politics, economics and government was so

successful that in 1973 he was able to return to power none other than Deng Xiaoping, vilified as China's Number Two Capitalist Roader during the Cultural Revolution.

Just as before the Cultural Revolution, there were now two factions vying for power in the Chinese leadership: one being the 'moderates' or 'pragmatists' led by Zhou Enlai and Deng Xiaoping; the other the 'radicals', 'leftists' or 'Maoists'. Yet there was no open conflict between Zhou and Mao, and certainly Deng must have been brought back with Mao's approval, however begrudging.

The 'Maoist' faction was led by Mao's wife Jiang Qing, who rode to power during the Cultural Revolution on Mao's name and her marriage certificate. With their power threatened by the resurgence of Zhou and the return to power of Deng, the radicals mounted the oddly-named 'Criticise Lin Biao and Confucius' campaign, in reality an attack on their contemporary adversaries, particularly Deng.

### The death of Zhou Enlai

Whilst Zhou lived the inevitable power struggle was kept at bay. But his health was rapidly deteriorating and in the midst of the radical resurgence he died in early January 1976. A memorial service was held in the Great Hall of the People in Beijing. Mao was inexplicably absent, though he had met 10 foreign ministers in the previous four months, all of whom found him very much alive, and was due to meet ex-President Nixon a few weeks later.

After the memorial service the period of mourning was unexpectedly declared over. Deng Xiaoping, who had read the eulogy at the service, suddenly disappeared from public view and the newspapers (which were all controlled by 'leftists' in the Party opposed to Zhou and Deng's policies) started propagating the line that China was now threatened by people in authority who were taking the 'capitalist road'. The post of Acting Premier went to

the fifth-ranking Vice-Premier Hua Guofeng, little known in the west. Deng had been passed over for what appeared to be a compromise candidate for the job.

### The Tiananmen Incident & the End of an Era

Late March was the Qing Ming Festival, the time when Chinese traditionally honour their dead. On 30 March the first wreath dedicated to Zhou was placed on the Heroes Monument in Tiananmen Square, and from then on more and more people came to honour Zhou with wreaths and eulogies until the square was filled with thousands of people. Other wreaths were sent by ministries of the central government, departments of the central command of the PLA, and from other military units as well as factories, schools, stores and communes in the Beijing area. For the Chinese, Zhou represented the antithesis of the madness and fanaticism of the Cultural Revolution and its instigators, and though there were bits and pieces of official support for the demonstration, on the whole it was a rare spontaneous display of how the Chinese *felt* about what was happening. Indirectly it was an attack on Mao himself, as well as being open defiance of the leftists who had commanded that there would be no more mourning for Zhou.

One could go on endlessly discussing the relative merits of Zhou Enlai and the ambivalent role he played in the Cultural Revolution, when he survived while his lifetime colleagues fell by the wayside. Whatever he really was he remained a revered figure in China, and at least his image transcended the worst Communist politics. Zhou Enlai seemed to be the last vestige of goodness and justice in the government; with him alive there still seemed some hope for China, and without him everything seemed lost.

In the early hours of April 5, the wreaths and poems in Tiananmen were torn down from the square and carted away. Those who tried to prevent the removal of the tributes were arrested, and guards surrounded the monument. The same day tens of thousands of people swarmed into the square demanding the return of the wreaths and the release of those arrested, only to be attacked and dispersed by thousands of men wearing the armbands of the Workers Militia and armed with staves. The demonstrations and riots became known as the 'Tiananmen Incident'. On 7 April a meeting of the Politburo stripped Deng of all his offices and Hua Guofeng was made Vice-Chairman of the Party and continued in the post of Premier. The Tiananmen demonstrations were declared counter-revolutionary; the blame was laid on Deng.

As for Mao, he was still in public view, receiving the Prime Ministers of three foreign countries in April and May. But after that, it was announced that he would receive no more foreigners and he was not seen publicly again. Who had access to him, what he was being told, whether he still had the capacity to grasp or influence any of the events that were taking place, is unknown. The Chinese were now going through another struggle – Mao had led them in the struggle against the Kuomintang, the Japanese, the Americans in Korea, and then into the depths of a cultural revolution. Finally at Tiananmen his own people had turned against him – just a few blocks from his home behind the walls of the Zongnanhai compound.

The ominous sign came in late July, when the massive Tangshan earthquake struck northern China claiming half a million lives. For the Chinese great natural disasters foreshadow the end of dynasties and once again it seemed like the cycle of Chinese history had come full swing. With the portentious sign from heaven that he had lost the mandate to rule, Mao died in the early hours of the morning on 9 September.

## The Gang of Four

With Mao gone the two factions had to stand on their own feet. There was no 'ultimate power' to help or hinder them. But without Mao the leftists found themselves in a weaker position: lacking political competence, closely identified with the system of repression that was spawned by the Cultural Revolution, lacking mass support and too young to command the respect engendered by having taken part in the revolution. On their side they had the military commanders of the Beijing and Shenyang regions, both of whom had benefited from the Cultural Revolution. They had a powerful civilian militia in Shanghai and a strong political base in Shanghai and Liaoning Province.

Their foremost opponent was Deng Xiaoping, who commanded widespread support and influence from powerful people like Defence Minister Marshal Ye Jianying, Li Xiannian the economic and financial expert and former Minister of Finance, and the military commanders in Guangdong Province.

The meat in the sandwich was Hua Guofeng. His authority rested largely on his status as the chosen successor to Mao Zedong. Mao had supposedly said to him 'With you in charge, I am at ease'. A native of Shanxi, Hua rose to become a Party leader in Hunan Province before coming to the attention of Mao. Hua's career in Beijing was largely developed with Mao's support and in the 1970s he was appointed head of the Public Security Ministry.

## The Arrest

The change came swiftly and dramatically. Less than a month after the death of Mao, Jiang Qing and a number of other leftist leaders and their supporters were arrested.

Out of this was born the 'Gang of Four'. Jiang Qing and three other principal allies of Mao were selected as scapegoats for this latest ideological change and became known as the 'Gang of Four'.

**Jiang Qing** was Mao's third wife (discounting an unconsummated childhood-arranged marriage). During the 1930s she worked as a B-grade Shanghai movie actress and then joined a patriotic drama troupe which took her to Wuhan and Chongqing. She moved to Xian and later to Yanan in 1938. Jiang attended Mao's lectures, became one of his most assiduous students, and married him late in 1938 or early in 1939. She had little or no *official* involvement in politics until the Cultural Revolution when she became the supreme overlord of Chinese culture and the No 1 authority on acceptable proletarian art. Arrested with her were **Yao Wenyuan, Zhang Chunqiao** and **Wang Honqwen**, the other members of the 'gang'.

Yao Wenyuan, a relatively young writer in the late 1950s, won praise from Mao in 1957 after writing an article against the bourgeois influence in the arts and journalism. At Mao's request he fired the opening propaganda shot of the Cultural Revolution – a critique of the play *Hai Jui Dismissed from Office* which, by innuendo, had criticised Mao for having secured the removal of Marshal Peng Dehuai. The critique was published in a pamphlet in Shanghai in October 1965, Mao being unable to get it published in any of the newspapers in Beijing which were then all controlled by supporters of Liu Shaoqi. During the Cultural Revolution Yao became a Politburo member, responsible for party propaganda and mass media.

For most of his career Zhang Chunqiao was involved in literary propaganda work, as a political commissar, overseer and writer. During the Cultural Revolution he became Vice-Premier.

At the beginning of the Cultural Revolution Wang Hongwen was a political activist at factory floor level in Shanghai. By 1973 he was Vice-Chairman of the Communist Party – and not yet 40 years of age! It was a truly meteoric rise to power. When former Australian Prime Minister Gough Whitlam asked Mao where he had

discovered Wang, Mao replied with an offhand 'I don't know'. One of Wang's responsibilities was to oversee the civilian militia – which the leftists hoped would be a counterforce to the rather better-trained PLA – to defend their cause in a confrontation with the rightists.

## The Third Coming of Deng Xiaoping

In the middle of 1977 Deng Xiaoping returned to power for the third time – two more than Christ had managed – and was appointed to the positions of Vice-Premier, Vice-Chairman of the Party and Chief of Staff of the PLA. His return indicated yet another battle royal in the leadership – this time between Deng and Hua whose appointment to the post of Premier had in part been responsible for Deng's downfall in 1976. But Hua didn't have the unequivocal support of the Party; he was a compromise leader for both left and right factions.

It was not until September 1980 that Hua finally relinquished the post of Premier to **Zhao Ziyang**. In June the following year **Hu Yaobang** was named as Party Chairman in place of Hua. Hu had first met Deng in 1941 when as a 26-year-old political commissar he was assigned to work under Deng in the Red Army operating in north-west China. They served together for eight years, and in 1949 went to Sichuan where they set up the Communist administration there. When Deng was purged in the Cultural Revolution, Hu toppled with him and the same pattern was repeated when Deng was purged a second time in 1976. Zhao Ziyang was the former Party leader of Sichuan after 1975; his economic policies and reforms had overcome the province's bankrupt economy and food shortages and had won him Deng's favour.

## The Future

With the Gang of Four imprisoned and Hua Guofeng demoted, final power now resided in the collective leadership of the six-man Standing Committee of the

Communist Party; Deng Xiaoping, Ye Jianying, Li Xiannian, Chen Yun, Hu Yaobang and Zhao Ziyang. (Ye Jianying, a frail 86-year-old, was finally retired in the middle of 1983). All six men have impeccable Communist pedigrees: all are veterans of the revolution, all fought against the Kuomintang and Japanese, all served in Yanan, all but one made the Long March. More importantly perhaps, all suffered or had family who suffered during the Cultural Revolution.

The China that these men took over was racked with problems. They still had to face the problem of modernising a backward country and improving the material standard of living of its people. They had to find ways to rejuvenate and replace an aged leadership (themselves); overcome the problem of a possible leftist backlash; reconcile the need for order with the popular desire for more freedom; reward those in responsibility but guard against the misuse of privilege; overcome the crisis in faith in the Communist ideology and try to legitimise a regime dependent on the power of the police and military to maintain its authority.

## The Leadership Problem

Power struggles within the leadership had plagued the Party even before Mao led his little band up into the Jiggang Mountains. There was the struggle against Li Lisan, then others against Bo Gu and Wang Ming, and Zhang Guodao. After the Communist victory came the purge of Liu Shaoqi and Deng Xiaoping, of Lin Biao and then the chain of events which saw Deng's return and fall from power, the purging of Jiang Qing, the return of Deng and the demotion of Hua.

The long period between 1935 and 1958 was one of stable and collective leadership, but conditions have changed since then. At that time the Party leaders were united by the civil war, the war with Japan, then the elation of victory followed by the Korean War, and the immense task ahead of them. There was no room for

disunity and, when there was, it was settled quickly. But while the old guard were united by common experience and a desire to implement the promise of their revolution, the problem remained of passing the leadership on to a younger generation who had no experience of those tumultuous years. It was a problem which Mao faced – and tried to solve – but the Cultural Revolution which was intended to instil the revolutionary spirit into every Chinese for time immemorial simply didn't work out.

## The Trial of the Gang of Four

The present leadership also has to guard against a possible leftist backlash. The first dramatic step was taken with the trial of the Gang of Four and their supporters.

The Gang of Four and a number of their supporters in the armed forces were placed on trial from November 1980 to January 1981. Jiang Qing was accused of framing and persecuting to death Liu Shaoqi and other high-ranking Party members as well as making false charges against others. She was labelled a 'ringleader of the Lin Biao and Jiang Qing counter-revolutionary cliques' and was accused of working to overthrow the government and 'tyrannizing the people'. Zhang Chunqiao was accused of working 'hand in glove' with Jiang Qing to sieze power; of making false charges against Party members; and of plotting an armed rebellion in Shanghai. Yao Wenyuan was accused of actively participating in Jiang Qing's plot to sieze power by conducting propaganda campaigns; of agitating for a counter-revolution and being instrumental in creating violent disturbances across China in 1976; of smearing the people who mourned Zhou Enlai's death as 'counter-revolutionaries'; of falsely charging Deng Xiaoping as being the party behind the 'Tiananmen Incident'; and of persecuting numerous party members. Wang Hongwen was accused of taking an active part in Jiang Qing's plot to sieze power, and of collaborating with the gang to create disturbances throughout the country in 1976. He was held responsible, along with Yao Wenyuan, of engineering several incidents during the Cultural Revolution which led to the death, wounding or maiming of many innocent people. He was also accused of building up a militia force in Shanghai with the intention of staging an armed rebellion.

Also standing trial were Chen Boda, boss of the Ministry of Culture and Mao's ghost-writer during the Cultural Revolution, plus five high-ranking military leaders who were variously accused of being instrumental in the framing and imprisonment of Peng Dehuai; of framing Ye Jianying as the plotter of a coup; of framing and slandering leading cadres in the PLA, Navy and Air Force; of persecuting to death high-ranking Party and military leaders; of extorting confessions through torture and of conspiring with Lin Biao to seize power and to assassinate Mao.

For China, the demise of the radicals came as more than a relief. Jiang Qing and Zhang Chunqiao were sentenced to death but were given a two-year reprieve in which to repent their sins (an innovation of Chinese justice) and their sentences were commuted to life imprisonment. The others were all sentenced to long prison terms.

But the trial was reminiscent of Stalin's show-trials of the 1930s. 'Guilty' was a foregone verdict, and what could have been used as an example of justice by the new regime was a public display of one faction reeking revenge on another.

### The Resolution of a Theological Crisis

The new regime was able to ward off immediate threats from the radicals by locking them up. But it still had to deal with the theological crisis which gripped the country – what to do with Mao Zedong. One step taken towards resolving this crisis was the resolution on the historical roles of Mao Zedong and Liu Shaoqi issued in the middle of 1981 by the Central Committee of the Communist Party.

The moderates had every intention of pulling Mao off his pedestal and making a man out of the God. But they couldn't denounce him as Krushchev had denounced Stalin; Mao had too many supporters in the party and too much respect amongst the common people. An all-out attack might only provoke those who might otherwise, if only begrudgingly, fall in line with Deng and his supporters, so a compromise stand was taken.

The resolution cited Mao as 'a great Marxist and a great proletarian revolutionary, strategist and theorist. It is true that he made gross mistakes during the Cultural Revolution, but, if we judge his activities as a whole, his contributions to the Chinese revolution far outweigh his mistakes'. The resolution went on to blame Mao for initiating and leading the Cultural Revolution which 'was responsible for the most severe setback and the heaviest losses suffered by the Party, the state and the people since the founding of the People's Republic'. Liu Shaoqi and his pragmatic economic policies were given an unequivocal rehabilitation.

### The Purge of the Party

The trial of the 'Gang of Four' and the military leaders was a major step towards breaking the power of Deng's opponents. But there were still thousands and thousands of supporters of Mao in lesser official positions. In the vast bureaucracy of China such people could effectively obstruct or slow down the new pragmatic economic policies. A way had to be found to get rid of them without calling it a purge. In October 1983 the Central Committee of the Communist Party launched a three-year campaign which was referred to as an 'overall rectification of party style and consolidation of party organisations' – a purge by any other name. Between two to four million people are expected to lose their Party membership and the main objective is to remove those who still support the 'Gang of Four' and those not committed to Deng's policies. It is also Deng's campaign to ensure the survival of his policies beyond the grave – something which Mao couldn't manage to do.

### China & the Future World

Chinese foreign policy has taken a turn away from the xenophobia that characterised the Cultural Revolution. At the time, though, the xenophobia of the Chinese was understandable as foreign imperialism had encroached to such an extent that the country was in danger of losing its identity altogether.

Today, the Chinese are still dealing with the aftermath of both the civil war and foreign imperialism. Two increasingly pressing problems relate the position of Hong Kong after 1997 and the future of Taiwan. To the Chinese, Hong Kong and Macau are the last bastions of foreign imperialism on Chinese soil and Taiwan is the last outpost of the Kuomintang.

Taiwan was seized from China by Japan in 1895; the Cairo Conference in 1943 and the Potsdam Conference in 1945 promised to return it to China, but the Kuomintang fled to the island from the Communists in 1949 and set up an independent government under Chiang Kai-shek. In 1950 President Truman placed a naval blockade around the island to prevent any possibility of a mainland attack and in 1955 Eisenhower formalised this de facto American protectorate in an alliance with Chiang. The USA continued to recognise and finance Chiang's delusions as the legitimate sovereign of all China. For the Communists on the mainland, the Taiwan problem is not ancient history; the scars of the bitter civil war run deep in the Communist leadership. Today the Beijing government no longer talks of 'liberating' Taiwan but of a peaceful solution which would allow Taiwan to become part of the PRC.

Britain's lease on Hong Kong is up in 1997, and common sense dictates that Hong Kong should be left alone by the People's Republic since it is of immense economic benefit to that country. But common sense does not always prevail in Bejing – or in any other country for that matter – and no one knows who will be ruling China in 1997. Theoretically, when the lease expires the Chinese border moves south as far as Boundary Rd in the Kowloon peninsula, taking in the whole colony except for Hong Kong Island, Stonecutters Island and Kowloon. China could force a takeover of the colony at any time, by cutting off the colony's water supply from the Shenzhen reservoir for example, or by ripping down the fence on the border and sending the masses over to peacefully settle on Hong Kong territory (in 1962 China actually staged what looked like a 'trial run' and sent 70,000 people across the border in 25 days). Others have suggested turning it into an independent state like Singapore, or setting it up as an 'autonomous region' (Hong Kong minority people?) with either a Hong Kong or PRC governor and letting it carry on very much as it does now.

The position of Macau is simpler. In 1974 the new left-wing government in Portugal tried to give Macau back to China as part of their efforts to pack up the rag-tag empire, but the Chinese wouldn't take it. The Portuguese constitution now regards Macau as Chinese territory under Portuguese administration.

On its southern borders the 'Communist monolith' theory of the 1950s and 1960s took another beating with the Chinese invasion of Vietnam and the continuing border fighting. In their desperation to drum up support against the Vietnamese the Chinese allied themselves with the Khmer Rouge regime of Pol Pot, who brutally exterminated two million of his own people – making the Chinese accomplices to one of the greatest mass murders of modern history. Fearful of the Soviet domination of Vietnam, the Chinese have continued their support and seem willing to fight to the last Kampuchean.

Relations with western countries and Japan are largely governed by the present pragmatic economic policies of the Chinese government, their desire to rapidly modernise the country by importing technology and teachers, though relations with the USA are complicated by the the continuing support that country gives to Taiwan. In the past few years the Chinese have emphasised the historic links between the Middle Kingdom and the outside world; whether that be the foreign traders stationed in the imperial city of Changan, the exploratory voyages of the Ming fleets or the Silk Road that connected China to Central Asia and ultimately to Europe. Primarily, it is technology and scientific expertise that China wants from the west; western ideas and culture are another thing altogther.

### The Suppression of Dissidence & the Pursuit of Privilege

There has been one unifying facet of the characters of all the Communist leaders, Mao, Zhou, Deng and Hua. They have all been authoritarians; they are not liberals and they do not accept challenges to their power and authority. For a band of revolutionaries who sought to overthrow the old order of China they all became dictatorial and the record of the Communists on human rights has been a miserable one. The right to set up a political party in opposition to the Communist Party, the right to publish independent newspapers, the right to voice ideas or philosophies in opposition to the official line of the Party (whatever it happens to be at any particular time) have all been suppressed by the Communist regime.

The first example resulted from the 'Hundred Flowers' campaign of 1956. In that year the Communist leadership encouraged the Chinese to speak out and voice their opinion on the new regime. To their horror the leadership found that many intellectuals challenged the right of the Party to be the sole political force in the country, and the following year saw a wave of repression in which untold numbers of people who had voiced opposition to the Communists were arrested and imprisoned.

The second great repression was, of course, the Cultural Revolution, which raised the Thought of Mao Zedong to a state religion and smashed those who opposed or questioned it.

Then there was the event known as the 'Democracy Wall Movement' of 1978, in which a wave of political wall-posters were glued from November onwards on a wall in the middle of Beijing by anyone with an opinion or a grievance to air. The movement was initially supported by Deng Xiaoping, possibly to drum up some mass support for his campaign against Hua Guofeng, or even to make a good impression in the United States which Deng was going to visit the following month, and with which full diplomatic relations would be established in January 1979. Later that year the government decided to close down Democracy Wall; plain-clothes police were sent in to disrupt the crowds that gathered at the wall each day, and the leading activists were arrested and imprisoned. On 16 January 1980 Deng gave an important speech in which he insisted that the right to put up wall-posters be stripped from China's constitution, and that that right had been used by a 'handful of reactionaries with ulterior motives' to undermine China's 'stability and unity' and threaten plans for economic development.

Some observers likened the Democracy Wall Movement to the May 4th Movement of 1919. Back in the early years following the overthrow of the Manchu Dynasty, the intellectual ferment in China had given birth to numerous societies dedicated to the overthrow of the old order, to Marxist study groups which included people like Mao, Zhou, Lin Biao and Liu Shaoqi. Yet once these people came to power they exercised the same degree of repression which characterised the society they fought to overthrow.

Able to suppress all political opposition, the Party has been able to establish itself as a privileged elite. High-ranking cadres are provided with higher standard housing, they are provided with cars befitting their rank (like the *Red Flag* limousines), they can shop at special stores stocked with goods of better quality or in short supply to the ordinary people, they receive higher pay for their work, their children are sent to better schools and have a greater chance of entering university or even studying abroad. The higher up the scale, the greater the number of privileges and the better the standard of living.

In fact, there are 24 separate rankings for the country's Party and government workers, from the lowest clerk upwards. It was a system which was established in the 1950s and has remained largely unchanged since then, although the system of ranking is deeply rooted in the Chinese mentality and probably derives from the careful ordering of society prescribed by Confucianism.

Mao realised that there was a growing elite of fat bureaucrats in control of China, and he tried to wipe them out with the Cultural Revolution. But those who got thrown out of their apartments and mansions were soon replaced by others. Mao himself and his entourage continued to live their own similarly privileged existence. Again, his policies just didn't work.

The Communist leadership rapidly fell into the way of life which they had originally attempted to overthrow; like the Kuomintang that preceded them the Communists have established a system which maintains a small and privileged elite, supported by the police and military and requiring unquestioning obedience from those lower on the social ladder. Privilege remains a dilemma for a government which espouses egalitarianism and whose leaders fought for 20 years to overthrow the miserable poverty of old

China. It remains to be seen whether the gap between the haves and the have-nots will be closed, though certainly the pragmatic economic policies of the present government are aimed at significantly raising the material standard of living of the ordinary people.

It seems unlikely that China, in the near future, will approach anything like the democratic system of government known in the west. Totalitarianism has been a feature of the Chinese government since the first Ming Emperor Hong Wu came to the throne, and authoritarianism for 1500 years before. These political traditions can't be wiped out in a decade and the present government is no exception. It should also be remembered that the problems that faced the Communists were immense and are still immense, and for China to have come even as far as it has today is extraordinary. So far the Communists have not delivered all that they promised, yet it seems unlikely that anyone else could have done a better job.

## GOVERNMENT

Precious little is known about the inner workings of the Chinese government and, from a distance, westerners can only make educated guesses as to the outlines.

The highest authority rests with the Standing Committee of the Politburo. The Politburo is composed of 25 members. Below that is the 210-member Central Committee which is composed of younger party members and provincial party leaders. At grass-roots level the Party forms a parallel system to the administrations in the army, the universities, the government, and industries; the real authority is exercised by the Party representatives at each level in these organisations. They, in turn, are responsible to the Party officials in the hierarchy above them, thus ensuring strict central control.

Between 1921 and 1935 the Chinese

Communist Party followed the Soviet model; the General Secretary of the Central Committee and the Politburo held chief responsibility for the leadership of the Party. But a change in the significance of this title took place at the Zunyi conference in 1935 during the Long March. At Zunyi, Mao Zedong, who had been Chairman of the Communist government in Jinggangshan, won over the support of the Politburo from General Secretary Bo Gu; the conference transferred top authority to the Chairman, the post of General Secretary was subordinated to him and eventually abolished in 1945. Provision was then made for a Chairman and four Vice-Chairmen to constitute a Standing Committee of the Politburo.

The Standing Committee of the Politburo still retains supreme power but today its members are accorded a hodgepodge of titles. Foremost on the Standing Committee is diminutive Deng Xiaoping, Chairman of the Military Affairs Commission of the Central Committee which gives him overall command of the army (a position which Mao held since the Zunyi conference and of which Lin Biao eventually became Vice-Chairman, thus allowing them to wield enormous power). Deng is also Chairman of the Central Advisory Commission whose function is to deal with elderly leaders standing down from their posts. Other members include General Secretary of the Central Committee, Hu Yaobang, and Premier, Zhao Ziyang. The post of General Secretary was restored in 1956 as a top job of administration, though today it seems to be regaining its original mantle as the foremost leadership position in the Party. However, in the Chinese political sphere titles and appearances are slippery things and often the name belies the real power and influence its holder may (or may not) have.

The day-to-day running of the country lies with the State Council which is directly under the control of the Communist Party. The State Council is headed by the Premier, and is composed of himself and four Vice-Premiers, 10 State Councillors, a Secretary-General, and 45 ministers and sundry other agencies. The function of the State Council is to implement the decisions made by the Politburo: it draws up quotas, assesses planning, establishes priorities, organises finances. The ministries include Public Security, Education, Defence, Culture, Forestry, Railways, Tourism, Minority Affairs, Radio and Television, the Bank of China, Family Planning . . .

Rubber-stamping the decisions of the Communist Party leadership is the National People's Congress (NPC). The NPC is usually referred to as a legislative body but its job is to approve everything which comes down from above. In theory it is empowered to amend the constitution, and choose the Premier and members of the State Council. The catch is that all these must first be recommended by the Central Committee, and thus the NPC is only an approving body. The composition of delegates to the NPC is surprising: it has a sizeable number of women, non-Communist Party members, intellectuals, technical people and industrial managers; the Army is not well represented and the rural areas supply only a fraction of the total. Just why so much effort is spent to maintain the NPC and why so much publicity is given to its sessions (via the national television and newspapers) is anyone's guess, but it seems important for the Communist leadership to maintain the illusion of democracy. Whether the NPC will ever be transformed into a truly representative parliament with real power is also anyone's guess.

If the NPC is a white elephant then the great stumbling block of the Chinese political system/government is the bureaucracy. There are 24 ranks on the ladder, each accorded its own particular privileges; the term 'cadre' is usually applied to all workers in the bureaucracy – but that term includes the lowliest clerks and political leaders with real power (such as the work unit leaders and, at the other end of the scale on the No 2 or No 3 level, Deng Xiaoping himself), Party and non-Party members. Despite attacks on the bureaucratic system by the Red Guards the system survived intact, if many of its former members did not. Today it is once more being weeded out, this time by Deng's three-year purge (headed by Hu Yaobang) aimed at ridding it of Maoist officials who could slow down the implementation of the new economic policies. Other offenders, according to the 'Selected Works of Deng Xiaoping' published in 1983, include the despotic, the lazy, the megalomaniac, the corrupt, the stubborn and the unreliable.

Problems with the Chinese bureaucracy really began with the Communist takeover in 1949. When the Communist armies entered the cities the peasant soldiers were installed in positions of authority as Party representatives in every office, factory, school and hospital. Former revolutionaries who had rebelled against the despotism of the Kuomintang, once in power reverted to the inward-looking, conservative values of their rural homes – respectful of authority, suspicious of change, interested in their families' comfort, sceptical of the importance of technology and education, suspicious of intellectuals. Their only real training had been in the Red Army which had taught them how to fight, not how to run a modern state. During the 1950s Liu Shaoqi and Deng Xiaoping instituted programmes aimed at producing a competent bureaucracy, but their training organisations were decimated by Mao's Cultural Revolution. The bureaucratic system survived but the Revolution left the new officials with neither competence nor the ideological zeal and idealism which was supposed to push China on to greater glories. The slothfulness, self-interest, incompetence and preoccupation with the pursuit of privilege continued.

At grass-roots level, amongst the 'masses' (the 'proletariat'), the basic unit of social organisation, outside the family, is the *danwei* or work unit. Every Chinese, whether he works in a hospital, school, office, factory, or village, is a member of one. While westerners may admire the co-operative spirit this system seems to engender they would cringe if their own lives were so intricately controlled. Nothing can proceed without the work unit: it issues ration coupons for grain, oil, cotton and coal, it decides if a couple may marry and when they can have a child or if they can divorce, it assigns housing, sets salaries, handles mail, recruits party members, decides who will get to buy a TV set or a bicycle this year or next, keeps files on each unit member, arranges transfers to other jobs or other parts of the country, gives permission to travel. The list goes on into every part of the individual's life.

White elephants, stumbling blocks, work units – and there's a bogey-man to be added to the Chinese political spectre, the Army. The People's Liberation Army covers the land forces, the navy and the air force, and grew out of the Chinese Workers and Peasants Red Army of the 1920s and 1930s. The total force numbers 4.2 million, and an additional 12 million workers and peasants of the local militias would be mobilised in time of war. In 1949 and also during the Cultural Revolution the army took control of every institution in China; there still is a considerable overlap between the Party, Army and State. Mao wanted the people and the army to be closely integrated, and for the army to be integrated with the Party and State yet somehow subordinate to the Party.

However, the army appears to have drawn away as a separate elitist force. Back in the 1950s Marshal Peng Dehaui wanted to build an army of professionals, released from non-military duties like flood control, harvesting and land reclamation, which would decide its own military policies. But 'Purging' Peng and his supporters during the Cultural

Revolution didn't solve the problem of keeping the army under control, and the next to go was Lin Biao in 1971 (either killed in a plane crash after his assassination attempt on Mao, or knocked off by Mao who perceived him as a threat). Deng Xiaoping dealt the army another blow by putting on trial (along with the Gang of Four) a number of high-ranking military leaders opposed to him; in 1978 he persuaded the elderly Generals to clear out of the Central Committee's offices and return to their barracks. In a delicate transfer of power the army is being weaned away from participation in the the political scene and more into target practice and the modernisation of its equipment and fighting techniques. Mao said that political power grows out of the barrel of a gun; the gun has remained a bogey-man in Chinese politics because whoever had control of it could do away with their opponents. Mao may have lost almost all influence in the civilian government during the early 1960s but he held sway over the army and that was the deciding factor in the show-down with Liu Shaoqi. Likewise Deng Xiaoping probably couldn't have made a comeback after the death of Zhou Enlai had the military been in support of a B-grade movie actress; as to the other manipulations involved, if you can work out how Deng could come back twice from the dead then you have probably unlocked the secrets of political power in China today.

## POPULATION & PEOPLE

The national census of 1982 revealed that the population of mainland China (excluding Taiwan, Hong Kong and Macau) had reached a staggering 1,008,175,288 people. Of that figure, Han Chinese number about 93.3% – the rest is composed of China's 55 or so minority nationalities.

These billion people have to be fed with the produce of just 15% of the land they live on, the total of China's arable land. The rest is barren wasteland or can be only lightly grazed. To make things worse much of the productive land is vulnerable to flood and drought caused by the vagaries of China's summer monsoons or her unruly rivers. Since the revolution, irrigation and flood control schemes have improved the situation but the afflictions of the weather cannot be completely overcome. In 1981, for instance, there were devastating floods in Sichuan province, and simultaneously a drought in the Beijing area. Despite these problems and the limited supply of land the Communists have managed to double food production since 1952, but this has almost been equalled by the increase in the population – which leaves the amount of food available per person pretty much what it was 30 years ago. Even as late as 1982 China had to import 15 million tons of grain to feed the extra mouths.

Of these one billion people, just under 236 million are rated by the census as illiterates (people 12 years of age and older who cannot read or who can only read a few words). Those with school education number a respectable 600 million, but more than half that figure have been to primary school only. University graduates number 4.4 million and there are a paltry 1.6 million undergraduates. The task of educating so many people is a formidable one; certainly a greater percentage of Chinese are better educated than 20 years ago, but statistics indicate that this staggering population still has very little technical and scientific expertise to draw upon. So, even if the population can be adequately fed, the prospects of substantially improving their lot, let alone modernising the country without foreign help, doesn't look such a hot proposition (as the government appears to have realised).

Food supplies, access to higher education, transport, housing and medical services are all under pressure from a huge population which continues to grow. Cessation of the civil war in 1949, and improved medical services and a larger

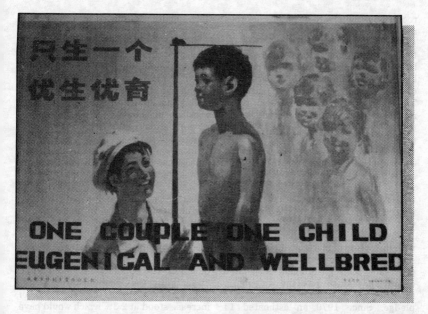

and more stable food supply since then, has raised the average life span of the Chinese from 40 years to close on 70 years (a United Nations estimate), as well as allowing the population to double since the Communists took power. Birth-control programmes were instituted by the Communist government in the 1950s with some heartening success, but with the Cultural Revolution these programmes were abandoned. The responsibility lies with Mao Zedong, and was probably his greatest mistake. He believed that birth control was some sort of capitalist plot to make China weak and that the country would find strength in a large population. His ideas very much reflected his background – that of the peasant farmer who wants many hands to make light work on the fields. It was not until 1973 that population growth targets were again included in China's economic planning, and campaigns like 'Longer, Later, Fewer' were launched. Planning for the future is a nightmare; Chinese estimates of how many people the country can support range up to 1.4 billion. The current plan is to limit growth to 1.2 billion by the year 2000 and then hold steady somehow – and presumably allow birth control and natural mortality to reduce that figure.

**Birth control** Huge billboards in Chinese cities spell out the goals for the year 2000 – modernisation and population control. The posters look like ads for a Buck Rogers sci-fi movie re-run: planes, UFOs and helicopters fill the skies; strange vehicles glide down LA-type freeways, and skyscrapers poke out of metropolises of the future – and often the only people visible are a smiling couple with their one child, usually a girl. The figure on the poster is 1.2 billion, the quota set for the year 2000. So what will life be like then? A Western teacher put this question to his university students in China and got back the following predictions in writing. Most of them envisaged a quiet family-orientated life; husband, wife and one child, living in a roomy apartment with no granny or other relatives (they'll be retired and kept busy elsewhere). People will have private telephones, travel abroad will be easy, large meals will be prepared in modern kitchens equipped with labour-saving devices like fridges and washing machines. The bicycle will be a museum piece replaced by private cars, cities will be full of skyscrapers, and colour TVs and picnics will occupy leisure time. The CCP will still be in charge but politics is expected to play a minor role in their lives and there will be a free press. Progress will, of course, bring about pollution and traffic congestion, but generally the place will be quiet and orderly. Few envisage war.

The one-child campaign is bound up with this vision of materialistic splendour – but how do you get a billion people to procreate at a government-designated quota? The main thrust of the campaign in the cities is for couples to sign a one-child pledge. Since 1979 an estimated 14 million couples have done so, encouraged by the extra month's salary per year they receive until the child is 14, and their entitlement to housing normally reserved for a family of four (a promise often not kept because of the housing shortage). If the couple have a second child then the privileges are rescinded and penalties, such as demotion at work or even loss of job, are imposed. Other material incentives are offered to encourage birth control: if a woman has an abortion it entitles her to a vacation with pay; the legal age for marriage is 22 for men and 20 for women, but if the woman delays marriage until after the age of 25 then she is entitled to longer maternity leave. All methods of birth control are free. The most common methods are the IUD, female sterilisation and abortion; other methods of contraception and male sterilisation rate low on the scale. Forcing women to have abortions and falsifying figures are two methods taken by local officials in their enthusiasm to meet the 'quotas' of new-

born children permitted for a particular area.

Population pressure is more particularly a rural problem; of China's 1008 million people, only 206 million live in cities or towns, and 80 per cent of the population live in rural areas (which means that something like –1/5th of the world's population are Chinese peasants!). So population control is going to be most acutely felt in the villages – with much of Chinese agriculture still reliant on human muscle, the peasant requires many hands to make light the work on his private plots. In Anhui Province this is countered by giving the peasant double-sized plots if he has only one child and no plot at all if a Number 2 child appears.

Certainly the birth control measures are working, but whether the target of zero growth can ever be reached is another question. The population doubled in the 30 years after the Communists took power and, as late as 1971, the yearly rate of increase stood at 2.3% which would have doubled the population again in another 30 years. By 1979 the rate was down to 1.2% and at that rate the population would double in 59 years, but at least it was close to the 1% target which former Chairman Hua Guofeng had set for 1980. In comparison to other third world countries (such as Bangladesh which continues to expand at a rate of 3% each year) China's birth-rate hardly seems catastrophic – but even at the relatively modest rate of 1.2% reported for 1979 that still meant an additional 12 million people to feed, not far below the total population of Australia.

If the Chinese can be convinced or cajoled or persuaded or pressured into accepting birth control, the one thing they cannot agree to accept is the sex of their only child. The desire for male children is deeply ingrained in the Chinese mentality, and the ancient custom of female infanticide continues to this day – as the Chinese government and press will freely admit. In 1982 a young man in Liaoning was sentenced to 13 years imprisonment for smothering his two-month old daughter and throwing her body down a well. According to one Chinese news source 195 female infants in a county in Anhui Province were drowned between 1978 and 1979. The *People's Daily* has called the imbalance of the sexes a 'grave problem' and reported that in one rural area of Hebei Province the ratio of male to female children (under the age of five) was 5:1. The paper also reported a case in Zhengzhou (Henan Province) where two applications for divorce were rejected, having been made by husbands on the grounds that their wives had given birth only to female children. In one attempt to counter this age-old prejudice against female offspring the family-planning billboards depict, almost without fail, a rosy-cheeked little girl in the ideal family.

**The National Minorities** The Chinese government officially recognises 55 national minorities. They account for a bit less than 7% of the population but are distributed over some 50% of Chinese-controlled territory, mostly in the sensitive border regions. Some minority groups, like the Zhuang and the Manchu, have become so assimilated over the centuries that to the western eye they look indistinguishable from their Han counterparts; only language and religion separates them. Other minority groups no longer wear their traditional clothing except for market or festival days. Some have little or nothing in common with the Han Chinese, like the Turkish-descended Uygurs of Xinjiang who are instantly recognisable by their swarthy Caucasian appearance, their Turkish-related language, Arabic script and Islam religion.

Han migrations and invasions over the centuries have pushed many of the minorities into the more isolated, rugged areas of China. Traditionally the Han have regarded them as barbarians – in fact, it was only with the formation of the People's Republic that the symbol for 'dog', which was incorporated in the characters for minority names, was replaced with the symbol for 'man'.

Separatism amongst the minorities has always posed a threat to the stability of the Chinese state, particularly from the Uygurs and Tibetans whose homelands form the border regions of the People's Republic and whose relations with the Han continue to be poor or volatile. Nevertheless it is the minority regions that provide China with the greater part of its livestock, hold vast deposits of untapped mineral resources, and whose military importance – particularly around the borders with the Soviet Union and Vietnam – are paramount.

Keeping the minorities under control has been a continuous problem for the Han Chinese. Tibet and Xinjiang are heavily garrisoned by Chinese troops, partly to protect China's borders and partly to prevent rebellion amongst the local population (as happened in Tibet in 1959). Chinese migration to minority areas has been encouraged as a means of controlling these areas by sheer weight of numbers. The Chinese government has also set up special training centres, like the National Minorities Institute in Beijing, to train loyal minority cadres for these regions. Since 1976 the government has also relaxed its grasp on the day-to-day life of the minority people, allowing temples and mosques to reopen (having closed them down during the Cultural Revolution).

Up until now the minorities have been exempt from the birth-control regulations applied to the Han Chinese, but it now seems that this policy has or is about to change. It was probably an inevitable step since the Chinese certainly don't want the minorities turning into majorities. Since 1982 the Li and Miao peoples on Hainan Island have been limited to four children per family, and the birth of a fifth child incurred a penalty fee of 100 kg of unhusked rice and 50 yuan (about 25 American dollars) per year, payable until the child was 14. It now appears that they have been further limited to two or three children. However, there is very little information and it's not known if the same policy applies to other minority groups.

Your chances of seeing many of the minority peoples in their 'natural habitat' are fairly small. A few places in Xinjiang are open, Tibet is only accessible on expensive tours, and most of the other minority areas are closed to western tourists. On the other hand, Nepal, Thailand and the area of Ladakh in India offer a smattering of the same groups that can be found along those borders with China and are far more accessible to the traveller. If it's minorities you're interested in then it might be worth venturing to these countries rather than hassling through China.

## ECONOMY

When the Communists came to power in 1949 some change in the economic conditions of the people and the country was inevitable, for the old China could not have been worse off. The cessation of war, the setting up of a stable government and a redistribution of the fat of the past regimes could only improve China for the better. The official Chinese press readily describes China as a developing nation – it still has enormous difficulties to overcome before it catches up with countries like Japan, the United States or West Germany.

China's economic policies have undergone a radical change since the death of Mao Zedong and the fall of the so-called 'Gang of Four'. Under Mao, China had largely isolated itself from the economy of the rest of the world, apprehensive that economic links with other countries would make China dependent on them. Although the country was opening up in the later years of Mao's life this was only on a limited basis.

The usual label applied to present economic policies is the 'Four Modernisations' – the modernisation of industry,

agriculture, defence, and science and technology. It is the government's intention to turn China into a modern state by the year 2000, to quadruple production and boost the average annual income to something like 2000 yuan (the present average is about 700 yuan). To achieve these goals the national economy has been increasingly decentralised and the country has also turned away from the narrow path of self-reliance which characterised the Maoist era.

The PRC's centrally-planned economy is now moving towards a three-tiered system; on the first rung is the state which rigidly controls consumer staples (such as grains and edible oils) and industrial and raw materials; on the second rung come services and commodities which can be purchased or sold privately within a price range set by the state; at the lower end is the rural and urban 'free marketing' where prices are established between buyer and seller, except that the state can step in if there are unfair practices. Modernisation is to be achieved mainly by two means; increasing production in both industry and agriculture by turning over responsibility for production to the workers and peasants themselves, and by importing sorely needed foreign technology and expertise.

China has committed itself to an open-door policy on foreign trade, foreign investment and joint-venture enterprises with foreign companies. There are hundreds of joint-venture enterprises on the go, including oil and gas drilling in the South China Sea, construction of commercial nuclear power plants in Guangdong and Zhejiang, lychee production in Fujian and modernisation of the Beijing Auto Works. In an attempt to attract foreign investment to China, the government has also set up 'Special Economic Zones' such as Shenzhen county which borders Hong Kong. Foreign companies are encouraged to set up businesses in these areas with reduced taxation, low wages, abundant labour supply and low operating costs as encouragement. Not all goes smoothly – foreign businessmen are driven mad by the Kafkaesque paperwork needed for contracts, inefficient use of equipment, closure of factories once quotas are filled(!), and even unwillingness on the part of the Chinese to accept advice on how to increase production.

Incentives for workers and peasants are one of the main thrusts of the new economic policies. Early in 1983 the central government began testing a system where workers are hired on contract – they can be fired for causing economic losses or breaking rules. Bonus systems are increasingly used to spur on urban workers who are used to doing little or nothing and getting the same pay for it. In the countryside the government has introduced an agricultural responsibility system. This varies from province to province – in the north-east state-owned farms and mechanised agriculture prevail, whilst in the south-west 'market gardening' controlled by individual villages or families is more appropriate, given the difficult terrain. Under the system a work team or family is contracted to work a plot of state land – they decide what to grow and when, provide the government with its quota, and are then allowed to sell any surplus at rural free markets. They can keep any profit from free market sales. In 1983 the total number of urban and rural free markets was placed at 46,000.

Along with the peasants who bring their produce to the rural and urban free markets has arisen a new breed of entrepreneur – the private businessman, and the related subspecies the pedlar. Faced with a return of rusticated youth from the countryside and with swelling unemployment amongst those born in the 1960s, the government has tended to encourage this form of private enterprise. Pedlars now sell just about anything; shoes, clothing, produce from distant provinces, tickets to sporting events and shows, and sometimes goods from state stores. Licences issued to small-time retailers, restaurateurs, repairmen and small shops reached 15,000 in Beijing alone by early 1983.

How well the economic policies work could be anyone's guess. Chinese government figures state that the average annual rural income doubled from 1978 to 1982 (to 270 yuan), and that over this period agricultural output increased by a robust 7.5% as compared to only 3.2% over the 26 years from 1953 to 1978. On the industrial side, for example, figures released in 1983 put rolled steel production up by 5.7% on 1982, coal by 5%, cement by 11%, machine-tools by 18%, power-generating equipment by 65% and walking tractors by up to 60% (these tractors can be used to draw loads or to plough fields).

The money to finance the economic programmes comes from the burgeoning tourist industry, as well as from a favourable surplus of exports over imports. Large loans have been made from foreign governments and from international financial organisations. China also has vast untapped oil and mineral deposits, particularly in the outlying regions of Qinghai, Tibet and Xinjiang, and these could very well become the forte of an expanding economy.

**Cost of Living** Urban incomes average around Y50 to Y80 a month. The figure is deceptively low; housing rental is fixed at between three and six per cent of income (but that could mean a tiny house or flat inhabited by several people per room), and there are various perks that go with some jobs, such as bus travel passes, free child day-care services, non-staple food allowances, haircut and public bath allowances, bonuses and so on. Education and medical care are free and personal income tax is non-existent or negligible. Up to 50% of a person's income can be spent on food – food in short supply or staple foods are rationed, and these include rice, grains and cooking oil. While prices for things like clothing and cooking utensils are low, other items depend on which shortage is operating – it could be light bulbs or bicycle tyres or women's high-heel shoes.

It's when you look at the cost of luxury or high-quality goods that you notice the huge gap in the buying power between the Chinese and most westerners. In China, a Xingfu motorcycle costs Y1000 (say, a year to 20 months' wages for the average urban worker), a motor scooter is Y700, a bicycle starts from Y150, and a Chinese would pay Y28 or half a month's wages for a hard-seat ticket on the train from Beijing to Shanghai. Luxury appliances are also expensive; a small sewing machine is Y150, a multi-speed desk fan is Y150 to Y200, a wristwatch is Y50 to Y100, a calculator is Y50 to Y70, leather shoes may be Y25 plus, canvas shoes are Y7.50, men's running shoes are Y11, a down jacket is Y45. Food prices per kg: rice for Y0.30 to Y0.80 depending on quality, cooking oil Y1.80, pears Y0.92, potatoes Y0.24, cabbage Y0.12, pork Y2.60, chicken Y2.90, eggs Y2.20. Smaller bills include bicycle parking at Y0.02, newspapers Y0.05, movies Y0.30, comic books Y0.20, bus maps Y0.10, cigarettes Y0.30, inter-city letter postage Y0.08.

Over the last few years there has been a substantial increase in the availability of consumer goods. The four modernisations may not be industry, agriculture, defence and science at all, but cassette players, washing machines, TV sets and electric fans, all of which are being produced in greater quantities for the home market. At least for the moment, the government is giving the people what they want. However, production cannot meet the demand for such goods; certain commodities, such as TV sets and bicycles, are rationed, and the work unit decides which of its members will able to buy them. Though money will buy goods, access to those goods is restricted so many Chinese are still very much reliant on their connections (*guanxi*) – such as Hong Kong

relatives – to supply them with luxury items. The system of privilege is another means by which a minority of Chinese are able to accumulate a disproportionate share of available luxuries; while no private individual could possibly afford to buy a car, for example, a high-ranking cadre will have a car placed at his disposal by the state – which amounts to the same thing as owning one. Likewise, better housing, even hot running water, is the domain of the Chinese elite.

## GEOGRAPHY

The insularity of the Chinese is very much a product of geography; the country is bounded to the north by deserts, and to the west by the inhospitable Tibetan plateau. The Han Chinese, who first built their civilisation around the Yellow River, moved south and east towards the sea. The Han did not develop as a maritime nation so expansion was halted at the coast; they found themselves in control of a vast plain cut off from the rest of the world by oceans, mountains and deserts.

China is the third largest country in the world, after the Soviet Union and Canada. But only half of China is occupied by Han Chinese; the rest is inhabited by Mongols, Tibetans, Uygurs and a host of other 'national minorities' whom the Chinese have long regarded as barbarians. These minorities occupy the periphery of Han China, on the strategic border areas. Distance, isolation and inhospitable terrain have made the Han control of these people a tenuous affair and the boundaries of the empire have often changed during the Han expansion.

Beyond this periphery of 'barbarians' lay a multitude of other powers with whom China has shared borders for centuries – not always happily. Today, China is bordered by North Korea in the east; Mongolia in the north; the Soviet Union in the north-east and north-west; Afghanistan, Pakistan, India, Nepal, Sikkim and Bhutan in the west and south-west; Burma, Laos and Vietnam in the south.

The capital is Beijing, and from here the government rules over 21 provinces and the five 'autonomous regions' of Inner Mongolia, Ningxia, Xinjiang, Guangxi and Tibet. Beijing, Tianjin and Shanghai are administered directly by the central government. China also controls about 5000 islands and lumps of rock which occasionally appear above water level; the largest of these is Hainan off the southern coast.

Taiwan, Hong Kong and Macau are all firmly regarded by the People's Republic as Chinese territory. There is a constant conflict with Vietnam concerning sovereignty over the Nansha and Xisha island groups in the South China Sea; Vietnam claims both and has occupied some of the Nansha Islands.

Two-thirds of China is mountainous, desert, or otherwise unfit for cultivation. Even if you exclude the largely barren regions of Inner Mongolia, Xinjiang and the Tibet-Qinghai Plateau from consideration of what's left, only 15 to 20% can be cultivated. All this to feed a billion people!

China's topography varies from mountainous regions with towering peaks to flat, featureless plains. The land surface is a bit like a staircase descending from west to east.

At the top of the staircase are the plateaux of Tibet and Qinghai in the south-west of the country. These areas average 4500 metres above sea level and for this reason, Tibet is referred to as the 'Roof of the World'. At the southern rim of the plateau is the Himalayan mountain range with peaks averaging 6000 metres high, and with 40 peaks 7000 metres or more. Mount Everest, known to the Chinese as *Qomolangma Feng*, lies on the China-Nepal border.

The melting snow from the mountains of western China and the Tibet-Qinghai plateau provides the water for the headstreams of many of the country's largest rivers; the Yangtse (Chang), the Yellow (Huang), the Mekong (Lancang)

and the Salween (the Nu, which runs from eastern Tibet into Yunnan province and on into Burma).

Across the Kunlun and Qilian mountains on the northern rim of the Qinghai-Tibet plateau and the Hengduan mountains on the eastern rim, the terrain drops abruptly to between 1000 and 2000 metres above sea-level. The second step of the staircase is formed by the Inner Mongolia, Loess and Yunnan-Guizhou plateaux, and the Tarim, Sichuan and Junggar basins.

The Inner Mongolia plateau has open terrain and expansive grasslands. Further south, the Loess plateau is formed of loose earth 50 to 80 metres in depth – in the past the soil erosion which accompanied a torrential rainfall often choked the Yellow River. The Yunnan-Guizhou plateau in the south-west of China has a lacerated terrain with numerous gorges, rapids and waterfalls, and is noted for its limestone pinnacles and large underground caverns such as those at Guilin and Yangshuo.

The Tarim Basin is the largest inland basin in the world and is the site of the Xinjiang Autonomous Region. Here you'll find the Taklamakan Desert (the largest in China) as well as China's largest shifting salt lake, Lop Nur, where they test their nuclear bombs. The Tarim Basin is bordered to the north by the Tian mountains, and to the east of this range is the low-lying Turfan Depression. The Turfan Depression is the hottest place in China and is known as the 'oasis of fire'. The Junggar Basin lies in the far north of Xinjiang Province, beyond the Tian mountains.

Crossing the mountains on the eastern edge of the second step of the staircase, the altitude drops to less than a thousand metres above sea level. Here, forming the third step, are the plains of the Yangtse River valley and northern and eastern China. These plains are the homeland of the Han Chinese, their 'Middle Kingdom'. They're the most important agricultural areas of the country and the most heavily populated.

In such a vast country, the waterways quickly took on a central role as communication and trading links. Most of China's rivers flow eastwards. At 6300 km the Yangtse is the longest in China and the third longest in the world after the Nile and the Amazon. It originates in the snow-covered Tanggula mountains of south-western Qinghai, and passes through Tibet and several Chinese provinces before emptying into the East China Sea. The Yellow River is about 5460 km long, second only to the Yangtse. It originates in the Bayan Har mountains of Qinghai, and winds its way through the north of China to the Bo Sea east of Beijing. The Yellow River is the birthplace of Chinese civilisation and the cradle of the Chinese nation. The third great waterway of China is man-made; the 1800 km Grand Canal, the oldest and longest man-made canal in the world, stretches all the way from Hangzhou in the south of China to Beijing in the north.

## CLIMATE

Spread over such a vast area, China is subject to the worst extremes in weather, from the bitterly cold to the unbearably hot. There doesn't really seem to be an 'ideal' time in which to visit the country, so use the following information as a rough guide to avoid the extremes of temperature.

**North** Winters in the north fall between December and March and are incredibly cold. Beijing's temperature doesn't rise above 0°C (32°F) although it will generally be dry and sunny. North of the Great Wall, into Inner Mongolia or Heilongjiang, it's much colder – the temperatures can drop to –44°C (–40°F). In Inner Mongolia you'll see the curious phenomenon of sand dunes covered in snow.

Summer in the north is around May to August. Beijing temperatures can rise to 38°C (100°F) or more. July and August are also the rainy months in the city. In both

the north and south of the country, most of the rainfall comes in the summer.

Spring and autumn are the best times for visiting the north. Daytime temperatures are in the 20°C to 30°C (70°F to 80°F) range and there is *less* rain.

**Central** In the Yangtse River Valley area (and this includes Shanghai), summers are long, hot and humid. Wuhan, Congqing and Nanjing have been dubbed 'the three furnaces' by the Chinese.

You can expect very high temperatures any time between April and October. Winters are short and cold, with temperatures dipping well below freezing, almost as cold as Beijing. It can also be wet and miserable at any time apart from summer. So it is impossible to pinpoint an ideal time, but spring and autumn are probably the best times to visit the area.

**South** In the far south, around Canton, the hot, humid period lasts from around April through to September, and temperatures can rise to 38°C (100°F) as in the north. This is also the rainy season. *Typhoons* are liable to hit the south-east coast between July and August.

There is a short winter from January to March, nowhere near as cold as the north, but temperature statistics don't really indicate just how cold it can get in the south; bring warm clothes. If you flop into China around this time, wearing thongs, shorts and a T-shirt, you'll see what I mean!

Autumn and spring can be a good time to visit, with day-time temperatures in the mid-20°C. But it can be miserably wet and cold, with perpetual rain or drizzle, so be prepared.

**Xinjiang** Try to avoid the Xinjiang region (in the north-west of China) at the height of summer. Industrial Urumqi is dismal at this time (although it's a good time to visit the Lake of Heaven in the mountains to the east of the city), and Turpan (which is worse off for being situated in a depression) deserves the title of the 'hottest place in China' with maximums of around 47°C.

In winter, though, this region is as formidably cold as the rest of northern China. In Urumqi the average temperature in January is around −10°C, with minimums down to almost −30°C. Temperatures in Turpan are only slightly more favourable to human existence.

**Tibet** Tibet deserves a special mention since the high altitude creates its own problems. Winter at high altitudes can be endless days and nights of incredibly piercing, dry cold. Summers are warm and dry but, because of the thin air, a cloud across the sun will make the temperature drop suddenly and dramatically and you'll always need to carry a jacket with you. For more details, see the section on Tibet.

**Other regions** The warmest regions in winter are Xishuangbanna near the Laotian border, the south coast of China and Hainan Island. In summer, high spots like Emei Shan would be a welcome relief from the heat.

## RELIGION

Chinese religion has been a bizarre mixture of philosophy and superstition. It has been influenced by three great trends in human thinking: Taoism, Confucianism and Buddhism. In their pure forms all of these are more philosophies than they are religions, but they have all been inextricably entwined in the religious consciousness of the Chinese and the popular religion of China is a fusion of ancient superstition with the three philosophies. The founders of these philosophies have all been deified and the Chinese have worshipped both them and their disciples as fervently as they've worshipped their own ancestors and a multiplicity of gods and spirits, and the whole lot is permeated with sorcery and magic.

The most important word in the Chinese popular religious vocabulary is *joss*. It means luck, and the Chinese being so astute did not leave something as important as luck to chance. Gods had to be appeased, bad spirits blown away and sleeping dragons soothed to keep joss on your side. No house, wall or shrine was built until an auspicious date for the start of construction had been chosen and the most propitious location selected. Incense had to be burned, gifts presented and prayers said to appease the spirits who might inhabit the future construction site; it all stemmed from a combination of traditional superstition with Taoism which taught man to maintain harmony with the universe, not to disturb it. Confucianism, on the other hand, took care of the political and moral aspects of life, and buddhism took care of the after-life. At one time or other, in various places around the country, Islam, Christianity and even Judaism have taken root.

### Taoism

According to tradition, the founder of Taoism is a man known as Lao Tzu. He is said to have been born around the year 604 BC, but some say he was born three centuries earlier, and some doubt if he ever lived at all. If he did live, then almost nothing is known about him – we don't even know his name. 'Lao Tzu' simply translates as 'the old boy' or the 'Grand Old Master'.

The legends depict Lao Tzu as having been conceived by a shooting star, carried in his unfortunate mother's womb for 82 years, and born as a wise old man with white hair. But the story also goes that he was the keeper of the government archives in a western state of China, and that Confucius was supposed to have visited him. At the end of his life, Lao Tzu is supposed to have climbed on a water buffalo and ridden west towards what is now Tibet, in search of solitude for his last few years. On the way, he was asked to leave behind a record of his beliefs, and the product was a slim volume of only

5000 characters, the *Tao Te Ching*, or *The Way and its Power*. He then rode off on his buffalo, and that, as far as he was concerned, was the end of the matter.

The concept of *Tao* itself is the centre of Taoism. Tao is the way of ultimate reality, the basic mystery of life – it cannot be perceived, because it exceeds the senses, all thoughts and all imagination. It can be known only through mystical insight which cannot be expressed with words. Tao is also the way of the universe, the driving power in nature, the order behind all life, the spirit which cannot be exhausted. And Tao also refers to the way man should order his life to keep it in line with the natural order of the universe.

Just as there have been three interpretations of the 'way', there have also been three interpretations of *Te* – the power. And this led to three distinct forms of Taoism taking hold in China.

*Popular Taoism* was the Taoism of the masses; the power of the universe is the power of gods, magic and sorcery. It was probably inevitable since the lofty concepts of Taoism couldn't be interpreted in any other way by the average villager. But it was basically Taoism reduced to the level of a funeral racket.

*Esoteric Taoism* was the Taoism of a small, enlightened minority and as such left very little mark on Chinese culture. Its followers advocated that the power of the universe was basically psychic in nature. By practising yogic exercises and meditation – the same as that practised in India, if not actually imported from there – a number of individuals could become receptacles for *Tao*. Thereafter, these persons could radiate a kind of healing, calming, psychic influence over those around them, a power over people and things. Esoteric Taoists made little or no attempt to propagate their beliefs, but they did have an appreciable core of devotees in the five centuries before the birth of Christ. This form of Taoism has now vanished.

*Philosophical Taoism* held that the power of Tao is not magical (as in Popular Taoism), nor mystical (as in Esoteroc Taoism), but philosophical. The philosophical Taoist, by reflection and intuition, orders his life in harmony with the way of the universe and achieves the understanding or experience of Tao.

The Taoists rejected self-assertiveness, competition and ambition. They revered humility and selflessness, and were disinterested in the things the world prizes like rank and material goods. Nature was also to be made friends with, rather than conquered, dominated or controlled – the idea was to blend in harmony with *Tao*, which flows through everything. Civilisation tended to be condemned, simplicity encouraged, and travel discouraged as pointless and conducive to idle curiosity.

Both the Philosophical Taoists and the Confucians had similar values, but what set them apart was their approach. The Taoists rejected all formalities, show, ceremony – to them it was pointless, artificial, repressive. The Confucians sought to arrange life within the framework of a meticulous code of moral conduct. And to the Taoists, there was no absolute distinction between good and bad – instead good and bad are just aspects of the all-embracing Tao. Confucianism stresses social responsibility, but Taoism reveres spontaneity and naturalness. Confucianism focuses on man, but Taoism focuses on *Tao* and Tao runs through everything:

*There is a being, wonderful, perfect;*
*It existed before heaven and earth.*
*How quiet it is!*
*How spiritual it is!*
*It stands alone and it does not change.*
*It moves around and around, but does not on this account suffer.*
*All life comes from it.*
*It wraps everything with its love as in a garment, and yet claims no honour, it does not demand to be Lord.*
*I do not know its name, and so I call it*

Top: Painting in Mao Museum, Shaoshan [AS]
Left: Street sign, Hangzhou [AS]
Right: No translation required [AS]

*Tao, the Way, and I rejoice in its power.*

The society which the Taoists envisaged was a democratic and class-free one, compared to the precisely ordered and rank-conscious structure of the Confucians. One consequence of this was that Taoists tended to be associated with political dissent. The Taoists were also associated with alchemy and the search for immortality; and partly because of this the Taoists often attracted the patronage of various rulers – though it was the Confucians who eventually gained the upper hand in China.

## Confucianism

With the exception of Mao, the one name which has become synonymous with China is Confucius. He was born of a poor family around the year 551 BC in what is now Shandong Province. His ambition was to hold a high government office and to re-order society through the administrative apparatus. At best, he seems to have held several insignificant government posts and, though he had his followers, his career was permanently blocked. At the age of 50 he perceived his 'divine mission', and for the next 13 years tramped from state to state offering unsolicited advice to rulers on how to improve their governing, looking for an opportunity to put his own ideas into practice which never came. In a time of perpetual conflict and war in China, state after state disregarded his philosophy of peace and concern for the people. He returned to his own state on invitation from a new government, but realising that he was too old for public office anyway, he spent the last five years of his life quietly teaching and editing classical literature. In 479 BC, at the age of about 72, he died.

The glorification of Confucius began only after his death, but within several generations his ideas had permeated every level of Chinese society: government offices presupposed a knowledge of the Confucian classics, and spoken proverbs trickled down to the illiterate masses.

It is not difficult to see why Confucianism became so popular in China. What characterised the China of his time was the multiplicity of states in perpetual conflict. The long reign of the Zhou dynasty had come to an end around 770 BC as the emperor's power declined and the vassal states asserted their independence. The following centuries were a period of war between these states; the larger ones annexed the smaller ones and by 400 BC only seven remained, locked in a perpetual state of conflict, the 'Warring States Period'.

Against this background of disorder, Confucius sought to find a way which would allow people to live together peacefully. For Confucius, the answer was tradition. Like others of his time, he believed that there had once been a period of great peace and prosperity in China. This period, he said, had been brought about because people lived by certain traditions which maintained order, and he advocated a return to the traditon of this period. Traditions had to be passed on from generation to generation; if the continuity is ruptured then the society breaks down, people form separate groups and conflict between the groups leads to war. He did not simply recount the traditions of the past; he devised what he thought were the values necessary for collective well-being. The study of 'correct attitudes' then became the primary task; moral ideas had to be driven into the people by every possible means, in the temples, theatres, homes, schools, at festivals and in proverbs and folk stories.

Confucius aimed to instil a feeling of humanity towards others and a respect for oneself, a sense of the dignity of human life. Courtesy, selflessness, magnanimity, diligence, empathy would all follow automatically, the ideal relationships between human beings. His ideal person was free of violence and vulgarity; competent, fearless, even-tempered ...

Confucius had another concept, *Li*, which has two meanings. The first meaning is propriety – how things should be done, a knowledge of how to behave in a given situation, a set of manners. Behind the concept of Li stands the presumption that the various roles and relationships of life have been clearly defined. In the Confucian scheme of things there are five main relationships; father-son, elder brother-younger brother, husband-wife, elder friend-junior friend, and ruler-subject. What you do affects others, you are never alone when you act; your actions must not damage or create conflict with other individuals. The family retains its central place as the basic unit of society (Confucianism reinforced this idea, but did not invent it). The key to family order is children's respect for and duty towards their parents, *filial piety*. Also embedded in the concept of Li is respect for age; age gives everything – people, objects, institutions – their value, dignity and worth. The old may be at their weakest physically, but they are at the peak of their wisdom, knowledge and experience. Respect flows upwards, from young to old.

The second meaning of Li is *ritual*. When life is detailed to Confucian lengths, the individual's entire life becomes stylised into a vast, intricate, ceremonial rite. Life becomes completely ordered. There is a pattern to every act, no room for improvisation, since everyone knows exactly how to act in any given situation.

Out of *Li* stem two other ideas. First is the *rectification of names* – that words are clearly defined and that the language with which ideas are expressed is a perfect instrument for communication. Secondly, the *doctrine of the mean* – moderation in all things, nothing to excess, to be equally removed from enthusiasm as from indifference, to reject fanaticism, to prevent the growth of pride, to seek pleasure but never to excess.

After Li, the next bulwark of Confucianism is *Te*, the power by which people are ruled. Confucius rejected the use of force; he advocated that there must be spontaneous consent from the people if they are to accept a government, and this can only happen if the people perceive the government as competent, capable, sincere and devoted to the common good. Goodness is spread through society by the personal example of the ruler, whose sanction to rule lies in his inherent righteousness.

The final bulwark of Confucianism is *Wen*, the arts of peace; music, painting, poetry – not just for the sake of art itself, but as an instrument of moral education, to arouse the mind and induce self-contemplation. And furthermore, to have the greatest art, the noblest philosophy, the grandest poetry is to show the world that you have the greatest civilisation, and thereby to gain their respect and admiration.

Although Confucius shifted the emphasis of Chinese thought away from heaven and the supernatural and set it firmly down on earth, its people and the relationships between people, he did not deny the existence of the supernatural or of a spiritual power behind the material world. Confucianism thus becomes something of a social order set against the cosmic order; like Taoism it seeks a way of living in harmony with the world, but Confucianism tends to narrow the horizons to the material world, whereas Taoism sees the world as part of an all-encompassing whole which has to be befriended.

Confucius' impact on China has been immense. Under the Han dynasty (206 BC – 220 AD) Confucianism effectively became the state religion. In 130 BC it was made the basic discipline for training government officials, and remained so until the establishment of the Republic of China in 1912. In 59 AD, sacrifices were ordered for Confucius in all urban schools, and in the 7th and 8th centuries, during the Tang dynasty, temples and shrines were built to him and his original disciples. Under the Song dynasty the Confucian bible *The Analects* became *the* book, the basis of all education. But the greatest testament to the impact of Confucian thought can be seen in traditional Chinese life itself.

The tightly-bound Confucian society, with strict codes of conduct and clearly defined patterns of obedience became seemingly inextricably bound up in the Chinese mentality. Women obeyed and deferred to men, younger brothers to elder brothers, sons to fathers; age was venerated. Teamed up with traditional superstition Confucianism also led to the practice of ancestor-worship. These strict codes of obedience were further held together by concepts of filial piety, ancestor worship, and concepts of 'face' – to let down the family or group, to fall short of their expectations is one of the greatest shames a Chinese can endure. All people rendered homage to the emperor, who was regarded as the embodiment of Confucian wisdom and virtue, the head of the great family-nation. Dynasties rose or fell, but the Confucian pattern never changed. Administration under the emperor lay in the hands of a small Confucian scholar class; in theory anyone who could pass the examinations could qualify, but in practise the monopoly of power was held by the educated upper classes enmeshed in an extraordinarily stable bureaucratic system. There has never been a rigid code of law, because Confucianism rejected the idea that conduct could be enforced by some organisation set up for the purpose, and taking legal action also implied an incapacity to work things out by sensible compromise and negotiation; but the result was arbitrary justice and oppression by those who held power.

## Buddhism

Buddhism was founded in India around the 6th century BC. The founder was Siddhartha Guatama of the Sakyas; Siddhartha was his given name, Guatama his surname and Sakya the name of the clan to which his family belonged. He was a prince and was brought up in luxury, but in his 20s he became discontented with the world when, so the story goes, he was confronted with the sights of old age, sickness, and death. He despaired of ever finding fulfilment on the physical level, since the body was inescapably involved with disease, decrepitude and death. Around the age of 30 he made his break from the material world, and plunged off in search of 'enlightenment'.

He began by studying Hindu philosophy and yoga. Then he joined a band of ascetics, and tried to break the power of his body by inflicting severe austerities on himself. But holding his breath until his head burst and starving his body until his ribs jutted out failed to enlighten him, and he gave it up as futile. From this experience he established the principle of the *Middle Way*, to live somewhere between the extremes of asceticism on the one hand and indulgence on the other. Having turned his back on mortifying the body, he devoted the final phase of his search for enlightenment to meditation and mystic concentration, and one evening, so the story goes, he sat beneath a fig tree, slipped into a deep meditation and emerged from it having achieved enlightenment.

Buddha founded an order of monks and for the next 45 years or so preached his ideas until his death around 480 BC. To his followers he was known as *Sakyamuni*, the 'silent sage of the Sakya clan' to express the unfathomable mystery that surrounded him. Guatama Buddha is not the only Buddha, but the fourth, and he is not expected to be the last one either.

Strictly speaking, Buddhism is more of a philosophy and a code of morality than a religion, since it is not centred on a god. Buddha rejected the supernatural and the traditions and rituals which clogged religion. But with his death, all these things stampeded back with a vengeance.

Buddha taught that all life is suffering, that everyone is subjected to the trauma of birth, to sickness, decrepitude, death, and that one is always tied to what one abhors (an incurable disease or an ineradicable personal weakness), and separation from what one loves. Real happiness cannot be achieved until suffering is overcome. The cause of unhappiness is *tanha* which is usually translated as 'desire', specifically the desires of the body and the desire for personal fulfilment. Happiness can only be achieved if these desires are overcome, and this requires following the eight-fold path.

*Right knowledge* is the first step in the path – to believe that all life is suffering, that suffering is caused by desire for personal gratification, that suffering can be overcome, and that the way to overcome it is to follow the eight-fold path.

*Right aspiration* is the second step – to become passionately involved with the knowledge of what life's problems basically are.

*Right speech* is the third step – to avoid lies, idle talk, abuse, slander, and deceit, since all these things remove a person from the prospect of attaining happiness.

*Right behaviour* is to show kindness and to avoid self-seeking and personal fulfilment in all actions. It also includes five rules, a Buddhist variation on the second half of the Ten Commandments; 'Do not kill', 'Do not steal', 'Do not lie', 'Do not be unchaste', and 'Do not drink intoxicants'.

*Right livelihood* – Buddha considered spiritual progress impossible if one's occupation, such as slave-dealing or prostitution, pulled in the opposite direction.

*Right effort* is the will to develop virtues and to curb passions.

*Right mindfulness* is to practise self-examination and to cultivate knowledge of oneself, to overcome the state of semi-alertness and to become aware of what is happening to onself.

*Right absorption* involves the techniques of Hinduism's *raja yoga* and leads to the same goal. There are several branches of yoga. *Hatha yoga* is a discipline designed to teach control over all the functions of the body, and was originally taught as a preliminary to spiritual yoga, but has largely lost its connection. There are four branches of spiritual yoga, and each is designed to unite man with the universal, all-pervading 'God'. They differ in their approach: *jnana yoga* is the way to God through knowledge, *bhakti yoga* is the way to God through love, *karma yoga* is the way to God through work, and lastly *raja yoga* is the way to God through psychological exercises. Raja yoga was the yoga that Buddha studied under his Hindu teachers at the outset of his search for enlightenment. Raja yoga involves practising mental exercises and observing the effects on one's spiritual condition, to penetrate deep into the psyche where the real problems and answers lie, to achieve a personal experience of what lies hidden away within.

By following the eightfold path the Buddhist aims to attain *nirvana*, a condition beyond the limits of the mind, thoughts, feelings, desire, the will; a state of bliss, ecstasy.

Buddha's total outlook on life is hard to grasp; he wrote nothing and the writings that have come down to us date from about 150 years after his death. By the time these texts appeared, divisions had already appeared in Buddhism.

Some writers tried to emphasise his break with Hinduism, others to minimise it. It appears that Buddha accepted the Hindu concept of reincarnation, the cycle of rebirths. And he seems to have accepted the concept of *karma*, the law of cause and effect; your actions in one life determine the role you will play and what you will have to go through in the next. Karma is a doctrine essential to the maintenance of the Hindu caste system, which was probably anathema to Buddha. The Buddhism that Guatama taught is probably dead; there is no way of knowing precisely what it was, or how drastically it had split from traditional Hinduism.

Later, Buddhism split into two major schools. The *Hinayana* or 'little raft' school holds that the path to nirvana is an individual pursuit. It centres on the monks, on individuals who make the search for nirvana a full-time profession; man is alone in the world and he must tread the path to nirvana on his own; Buddhas can only show the way. The *Mahayana* or 'big raft' is the second school and this holds that since all life, all existence, is one, thien the fate of the individual is linked to the fate of all others; the Buddha did not just point the way and float off into his own Nirvana, he also continues to exude spiritual help to those also seeking Nirvana.

The Hinayana school is the Buddhism of Sri Lanka, Burma and Thailand and Kampuchea. The Mahayana School is the Buddhism of Vietnam, Japan, Tibet, Korea, Mongolia and China.

The outward manifestation of the difference between the two schools is the cosmology that was either spawned or taken up by the Mahayana school, as the Hinayana was too heady a doctrine to appeal to the Chinese masses. Mahayana Buddhism is replete with innumerable heavens, hells and descriptions of nirvana; prayers of thanks and prayers for guidance are addressed to the Buddha, mixed up with elaborate ritual. Buddhist deities were created; the worship of *bodhisattvas*, a rank of supernatural beings in their last incarnation before nirvana, became important. Temples were filled, and are filled today, with images of Maitreya, the future Buddha, portrayed as fat and happy over his coming promotion; Amitabha, a saviour who rewards the faithful with admission to

a sort of Christian paradise. The ritual, tradition and superstition that Buddha rejected came tumbling back in with a vengeance. Today, the lines of demarcation between Mahayana Buddhism, Taoism and Confucianism are irrevocably blurred in China. The great mass of Chinese worship Buddha, the bodhisattvas, the Taoist immortals, Confucius and their own ancestors with equal vigour.

Buddhism developed in China during the 3rd to 6th centuries. It was probably introduced by Indian merchants who took Buddhist priests with them on their land and sea journeys to China. Later, an active effort was made to import Buddhism into China; in the middle of the 1st century the religion had gained the interest of the Han Emperor Ming, who sent a mission to the west in search of Buddhism; they returned in 67 AD with two Indian monks, scriptures and images of the Buddha. Centuries later, other Chinese monks like Xuan Zang journeyed to India and returned with Buddhist scriptures which were then translated from the original Sanskrit to Chinese – a massive job involving Chinese as well as foreign scholars from Central Asia, India and Sri Lanka.

Buddhism spread rapidly in the north of China where it was patronised by most of the invading rulers, who in some cases had been acquainted with the religion before they came to China. Others deliberately patronised the Buddhist monks because they wanted educated officials who were not Confucians. In the south Buddhism spread more slowly, carried down during the times of the Chinese migrations from the north. To a people who were constantly faced with starvation, war and poverty its appeal probably lay with the doctrines of reincarnation and nirvana. Monasteries and temples sprang up everywhere, in great numbers, and these played a role similar to the churches and monasteries of medieval Europe; they were guest houses for travellers, hospitals, orphanages and refuges. With gifts obtained from the faithful, the monasteries were able to build up considerable wealth which enabled them to set up money-lending enterprises and pawn-shops; the monastery pawnshops were the poor man's bank right up until the middle of the 20th century.

An interesting form of Buddhism is the Tantric (Lamaist) Buddhism of Tibet. It's a form of Buddhism heavily influenced by the preBuddhist Bon religion of Tibet. At the pinnacle of the Lamaist pantheon is the divine trinity of Avalokitesvara, (a male bodhisattva who was transformed by the Chinese into the female Goddess of Mercy, Guanyin) Manyushri and Vayrapani, but there are an extraordinary number of gods and demons. To make matters even more complicated, there are unique incarnations only recognised in certain monasteries. Lamaism is the monastic side of the religion, and revolves around the concerted meditation of monks. This essential basis of the religion contrasts with the visible rituals observed by the Tibetans, such as pilgrimages to temples or holy tombs, the turning of prayer wheels or the chanting of prayers and the flying of prayer flags. Lamaism has been the religion of Tibet since the early 7th century AD.

## Islam

The founder of Islam was the Arab prophet, Mohammed. Strictly speaking, it was not Mohammed who shaped the religion but God, and Mohammed merely transmitted it from God to his people. To call the religion 'Mohammedanism' is also wrong, since it implies that the religion centres around Mohammed and not around God. The proper name of the religion is *Islam*, derived from the word *salam* which means primarily 'peace', but in a secondary sense 'surrender'. The full connotation is something like 'the peace which comes by surrendering to God', and the corresponding adjective is *Moslem*.

The prophet was born around 570 AD. He came to be called Mohammed, which means 'highly praised'. His descent is traditionally traced back to Abraham who had two wives, Hagar and Sarah. Hagar gave birth to Ismael, and Sarah had a son named Isaac. But Sarah demanded that Hagar and Ismael be banished from the tribe. According to the *Koran*, the Moslem's holy book, Ismael went to Mecca. His line of descendants is then traced down to Mohammed. There have been other true prophets before Mohammed, but he is regarded as the culmination of them and there will be no more. There is only one God, *the* God, Allah – the name derives from joining *al* which means 'the' with *Illah* which means 'God'.

The initial reaction to Mohammed's message was one of hostility; the uncompromising monotheism conflicted with the pantheism and idolatry of the Arabs – instead, Allah is the God, all-powerful, all-pervading. Mohammed's moral teachings conflicted with what he believed was a corrupt and decadent social order, and in a society which was afflicted with class divisions Mohammed was preaching a universal brotherhood in which all men are equal in the eyes of God. Mohammed and his followers were forced to flee from Mecca to Medina in 622 AD, and there Mohammed built up a political base and an army which eventually defeated Mecca and brought all of Arabia under his control. Mohammed died in 632 AD, two years after taking Mecca. By the time a century had passed the Arab Moslems had built a huge empire which stretched all the way from Persia to Spain, and though the power of the Arabs was eventually superseded by the Turks, the power of Islam has continued to the present day.

Islam was brought to China by two routes; by sea by the Arab traders who landed on the southern coast of China and established their mosques in great maritime cities like Canton and Quanzhou, secondly by Moslem merchants who travelled the 'Silk Road' through Asia to

China, established mosques and won converts among the Han Chinese in the north of the country.

## Christianity

The earliest record of Christianity in China dates back to the Nestorians, a Syrian Christian sect. They first appeared in China in the 7th century when a Syrian named Raban presented Christian scriptures to the Chinese imperial court at Xian (now Chang'an). This, and the construction of a Nestorian monastery in Chang'an, is recorded on a large stone stele made in 781 AD, and now on display in the Shaanxi Provincial Museum in Xian.

Then came Father John Montecorvino of Rome in the 13th century. The Jesuits were the next Christian sect to propagate the faith in China. The first of them were the priests Matteo Ricci and Michael Ruggieri who, in the 1580s, were permitted to set up base at Zhaoqing in Guangdong Province, and eventually made it to the imperial court in Beijing.

Parallel with the expansion of the western powers, Protestant and Roman Catholic missionaries came in large numbers during the 19th and early 20th centuries. By the end of the 19th century there were thousands of Catholic and Protestant missionaries in China. Their presence was no more welcome to the imperial government than were the foreign armies. The western governments used the missionaries as an excuse to expand the areas under their control, claiming the need to protect the missions. Besides winning converts, the missions posed a threat to traditional Chinese society since they introduced an alien religion, science, education and morals.

## Judaism

One of the curiosities of the country are the Chinese Jews, and Kaifeng in Henan Province was the home of their largest community. The religious beliefs and almost all the customs associated with it

have died out, yet the descendants of the original Jews still consider themselves Jewish. Just how the Jews got to China is unknown; they may have come there as traders and merchants along the Silk Road when Kaifeng was the capital, or they may have emigrated from the Jewish populations in India. For more details, see the section on Kaifeng in this book.

## Religion, Culture & Communism

Today, the Chinese Communist government professes atheism, and considers religion a superstition, a tool of the ruling class to keep power and privilege and an archaic remnant of old China.

The Cultural Revolution of the 1960s had a massive impact on organised religion in China. Temples and monasteries were ransacked, the monks and priests disbanded and sent out to the countryside to till the fields. Many temples and monasteries are now derelict or are used as schools, libraries, restaurants, offices, museums or parks.

Over the last few years there has been a resurgence in active, organised religion in China. At some places the monks and priests have been allowed to return, and some of the renovated temples seem to be attracting many worshippers, but they are invariably the elderly. The situation in the villages may be quite different though, particularly in isolated areas were old beliefs and customs are likely to have remained intact.

The individual religions all came under attack during the Cultural Revolution. Confucius seems to have been singled out, as his teachings permeate so deeply the mentality of the Chinese. Confucius has often been used as a political symbol, his role 'redefined' to suit the needs of the time. At the end of the 19th century he was upheld as a symbol of reform because he had worked for reform in his own day; after the fall of the Qing Dynasty, Chinese intellectuals vehemently opposed him as a symbol of a conservative and backward China; in the 1930s he was used by Chiang

Kai-shek and the Kuomintang as a symbol of proper, traditional values. During the Cultural Revolution Confucius was attacked as a symbol of the decadence and oppression of old China; the Red Guards descended on the philosopher's birthplace of Qufu and destroyed many of the statues and relics in the Confucius temple, and other edifices around the country were also wrecked. It hit another low point in the early 1970s with the 'Criticise Lin Biao and Confucius' campaign, which was actually a veiled attack on Deng Xiaoping and his pragmatic economic policies. With the downfall of the 'Gang of Four' that campaign has also been buried, but just what line to take with the Confucian teachings remains a problem for the Chinese government. Today it's making something of a comeback as the government emphasises stability and respect for order and authority, co-opting some of the traditional values to its own service.

As for the Christian churches, they take on a different meaning to the Chinese government, because they are a reminder of foreign intrusion and imperialism on Chinese soil. A common criticism of Christianity in China is that many of its Chinese adherents would only have been 'rice Christians' – those attracted to the power and wealth of the church rather than to the faith itself. True or not, the church has survived since the Communists took over in 1949 and the country was largely cut off from foreign contact.

Since 1957 the affairs of the Christian Churches, which include an estimated three million Catholics and an equal number of Protestants (although the Chinese delegation to a religious conference in the USA in 1979 reported the number of Protestants as only 700,000), have been controlled by the Bureau of Religious Affairs. This Bureau is a department of the government, answerable to the State Council and the Premier.

Freedom of religion is guaranteed under the Chinese constitution, but it carries a crucial rider 'Relgious bodies and religious affairs are not subject to any foreign domination'. In the late 1950s the Chinese government moved to sever the loyalties of the churches from their foreign masters and to place the churches under the control of the government. For the Chinese leadership, Christianity has simply been another facet of western imperialism. The 'Three-Self Patriotic Movement' was set up as an umbrella organisation for the Protestant churches, and the 'Catholic Patriotic Association' was set up to replace Rome as the leader of the Catholic churches.

The government's relations with the Catholic church has probably caused the most friction since the church refuses to disown the Pope as its leader and because the Vatican maintains diplomatic relations with Taiwan. In March 1983, four elderly priests who had already spent long terms in prison were again sentenced to long terms of imprisonment on charges which included subversion and collusion with foreign countries, though it is thought that their main offence was maintaining illicit contacts with the Vatican. The former Roman Catholic Bishop of Shanghai, Kong Pingmai, has been in prison since 1955. Exactly what will become of the churches in China is unknown. Like the monasteries and temples many of them are being restored, since they too were sacked during the Cultural Revolution; many are once again active places of worship.

The Cultural Revolution also caused the closure of the Moslem mosques, even in far off Xinjiang – again, many of these have been re-opened. Perhaps it was in Tibet that a minority people were subjected to the full brunt of Mao's mayhem. The Dalai Lama and his entourage had fled to India in 1959 when the Tibetan rebellion against Chinese rule was put down by Chinese troops. In that year there were 1600 monasteries operating in the region; by 1979 there were only 10 (these are statistics supplied by the Chinese; another writer puts the original number of monasteries as over 2400). Whatever the figure, the revolution was certainly devastating. Most of the monasteries were closed during the Cultural Revolution and the monks were sent to work in the fields, to labour camps and some were, no doubt, executed. Of the more than 100,000 monks in Tibet in 1959, perhaps only 2000 remain – the feudal theocracy which had ruled Tibet for centuries was wiped out overnight. A few Tibetan temples and monasteries have been reopened on a very limited basis to worshippers, and by all accounts the strength of the Tibetan religion is still powerful amongst the ordinary people.

For whatever reason, the government has finally permitted open, if rather controlled, religious worship. More cynical observers say it's to curry favour with the oil-rich Moslem Arab states and the predominantly Buddhist countries of South-East Asia. It might be because so much of the Chinese land mass is occupied by Moslem, Buddhist or Lamaist minority groups, and allowing them to worship makes for better relations with their Chinese rulers. But I would like to think it was just another aspect of a more sensible approach that the Chinese government is taking to running the country. Westerners tend to project their own desires onto China, hoping that the resurgence of religion indicates the Chinese are 'thirsting' for something more spiritual than Communism is, does or could offer them – well, there may be such a 'thirst', but I really wouldn't know one way or another.

## THE ARTS OF CHINA

Chinese art is like its religion – it has developed over a period of more than 2000 years and absorbed many influences. Two of China's most revered arts, calligraphy and painting, have been inspired by the Taoist respect for nature and deeply influenced by Confucian morality.

## Calligraphy

Calligraphy has traditionally been regarded in China as the highest form of visual art. A fine piece of calligraphy was often valued more highly by a collector of art than a good painting. Children were trained at a very early age to write beautifully and good calligraphy was a social asset. A scholar, for example, could not pass his examination to become an official if he was a poor calligrapher. A person's character was judged by his handwriting, and elegant handwriting was believed to reveal a person of great refinement.

The basic tools of calligraphy are paper, ink, ink-stone (on which the ink is mixed) and brush. These are commonly referred to as the 'four treasures of the scholar's study'. A brushstroke must be infused with the creative or vital energy which, according to the Taoists, permeates and animates all phenomena of the universe: the mountains, rivers, rocks, trees, insects, animals. Expressive images are drawn from nature to describe the different types of brush strokes; for example, 'rolling waves', 'leaping dragon', 'a startled snake slithering off into the grass', 'a dewdrop about to fall' or a 'playing butterfly'. A beautiful piece of calligraphy would therefore conjure up the majestic movements of a landscape. The quality of the brushstrokes are referred in the organic terms of 'bone', 'flesh', 'muscle' and 'blood'; blood, for example, refers to the quality of the ink and the varied ink tones created by the degree of moisture of the brush.

Calligraphy itself is regarded as a form of self-cultivation as well as self-expression. It is believed that calligraphy should be able to express and communicate the most ineffable of thoughts and feelings which cannot be conveyed by words. It is often said that looking at calligraphy 'one understands the writer fully, as if meeting him face to face'.

All over China, examples of calligraphy can be found in temples, adorning the walls of caves, on the sides of mountains, monuments and anything else with a flat or roughly flat surface.

## Painting

Looking at Chinese paintings for the first time, the Italian Jesuit priest Matteo Ricci (who reached China in 1582), criticised Chinese painters for their lack of knowledge of the illusionistic techniques of shading, with the result that their paintings 'look dead and have no life at all'. The Chinese were in turn astonished by and admired the oil paintings brought to China by the Jesuits, which to them resembled images reflected in a mirror, but at the same time they rejected them as paintings because they were devoid of brushwork.

Chinese painting is the art of brush and ink; the basic tools are those of calligraphy, which influenced painting in both technique and theory. The brush line, which varies in thickness and tone, is the important feature of a Chinese painting. Shading is regarded as a foreign technique (introduced to China via Buddhist art from Central Asia during from the 3rd to 6th centuries), and colour plays only a minor symbolic and decorative role. As early as the 9th century, ink was recognised as being able to provide all the qualities of colour.

Although you will see artists in China painting or sketching in front of their subject, traditionally the painter works from memory. The painter is not so much interested in imitating the outward appearance of his subject, but of capturing its life-like qualities, to imbue his painting with the energy that permeates all nature.

From the Han Dynasty until the end of the Tang Dynasty, the human figure occupied the dominant position in Chinese painting, as it did in pre-modern European art. Figure painting flourished against a Confucian background, illustrating moralistic themes. Landscape painting for its own sake started in the 4th and 5th

centuries. The practise of seeking out places of natural beauty and communing with nature first became popular among Taoist poets and painters, stimulated by Taoist attitudes and ideas. By the 9th century the interests of artists began to shift from figures to landscapes, and from the 11th century onwards landscape has been the most important aspect of Chinese painting.

The function of the landscape painting was to serve as a substitute for nature, allowing the viewer to wander in imagination within the landscape. The painting is meant to surround the viewer, and there is no 'viewing point' as such as there is in western painting. The painter, Guo Xi, of the 11th century wrote, 'Contemplation of such pictures arouses corresponding feelings in the breast; it is as if one has really come to these places ... without leaving the room, at once, he finds himself among the streams and ravines'. Guo also spoke of landscape elements in organic terms, the watercourses as the arteries of mountains, the grass and trees as its hair, the mist and haze its complexion.

In the 11th century a new attitude to painting was formulated by a group of scholar-painters led by Su Dongpo (1036-1101). They came to recognise that painting could go beyond mere representation; it could also serve as a means of expression and communication in much the same way as calligraphy.

Painting became accepted as one of the activities of a cultured man, along with poetry, music and calligraphy. The scholar-amateur painters, who were either officials or living in retirement, did not depend on painting for income. They became their own patrons and critics, and painted for pleasure. They were also collectors and connoisseurs of art, the arbiters of taste. Their ideas on art were voiced in voluminous writings and in inscriptions on paintings.

Moralistic qualities appreciated in a virtuous man (in the Confucian frame of things) became the very qualities appreciated in paintings. One of the most important of these qualities was the 'concealment of brilliance' under an unassuming exterior; any deliberate display of technical skill was considered vulgar. Creativity and individuality were highly valued – but within the framework of tradition. The artist created his own style of painting by transforming the styles of the ancient masters, and the scholar-artist saw himself as part of the great continuity of painting tradition. This art-historical approach to painting became a conscious pursuit in the late Ming and early Qing Dynasties.

## Funeral Objects

As early as neolithic times (around 2500 BC and earlier) offerings of pottery vessels and stone tools or weapons were placed in graves to accompany the departed. During the Shang Dynasty, precious objects such as bronze ritual vessels, weapons, and jade were buried with the dead. For the tombs of great rulers, dogs, horses and even human beings were sacrificed for burial. When this practice was abandoned, replicas (usually in pottery) were made of human beings, animals and precious objects. A whole repertoire of objects for the dead were produced especially for burial. By making substitutes for the real objects you make provision for the dead in a symbolic way, without waste of wealth or human sacrifice.

Burial objects made of earthenware were very popular from the first to the eighth centuries AD. In the Han Dynasty, pottery figures were produced, cast in moulds and painted in bright colours after firing. Statues of attendants, entertainers, musicians, acrobats, and jugglers were all made, along with models of granaries, watchtowers, pig-pens, stoves . . .

Close trade links with the west are illustrated by the appearance of the two-humped Bactrian camel which carried merchandise along the Silk Road; warriors with Western Asian faces and heavy beards appear as funerary objects during the Northern Wei Dynasty, a foreign dynasty founded by the Turkish-speaking Tobas of Central Asia. The cosmopolitan life of Tang China is further illustrated by its funerary wares – western and central Asians flocked to the capital at Changan, and were portrayed in figurines of merchants, attendants, warriors, grooms, musicians and dancers. Tall western horses with long legs, introduced to China from Central Asia at the beginning of the first century BC, were also popular subjects for tomb figurines.

Other funeral objects that are commonly seen in Chinese museums are what appear to be military figures dressed in full armour, often trampling oxen underfoot. These figures may have served as tomb guardians and may represent the *Fangxiangshi*, the four heavenly kings. The Fangxiangshi seem to have been assimilated by or developed by Buddhism; the four kings are supposed to guard four quarters of heaven and protect the state. Large statues of the guardians can be seen in numerous Buddhist temples – notably the Lingyin Temple at Hangzhou – and the tomb figures tend to resemble the figures of the Fengxiansi Cave at the Longmen Grottoes near Luoyang.

Guardian spirits are some of the strangest of funerary objects; common ones are those with bird's wings, elephant ears, human face, the body of a lion, the legs and hoofs of a deer or horse all rolled into one. There are some variations, but you get the general idea. One suggestion is that the figures represent *Tubo*, the earth-spirit or lord of the underworld, who is endowed with the power to ward off demons and evil spirits and is therefore entrusted with guarding the tomb of the deceased. Those figures with human faces may represent the legendary Emperor Yu, said to be the founder of the Xia Dynasty, who was transformed into *Tubo* after his death.

For several thousand years looking after the dead played the most important role in the religious life of China. Concepts of after-life and rituals for the dead may have originated from popular superstitions as well as Buddhism and Taoism, but it was probably because of Confucianism that the rituals and customs surrounding the deceased were carried on. Serving the dead was stated by Confucius as part of the duties of 'filial piety' – that is *xiao*, devotion to one's parents. The notion of filial piety was seen as the starting point for all virtue and the basis of the family – and the family was the social, political and religious unit of traditional China. The ancient customs and rituals regarding burial were fostered by Confucianism to serve the moral purpose of filial piety, to perpetuate the family system, and to contribute to the harmony and political stability of Chinese society. The Confucian *Liji*, the Book of Rites, says 'Funeral and sacrificial rites serve to inculcate benevolence and love ... when the mourning and sacrificial rites are clearly understood, the people are filial'.

## Ceramics

Earthenware production has a long history in China, beginning with the primitive pottery of prehistoric times. As many as 8000 years ago primitive Chinese tribes were making earthenware artefacts with clay. The primitive 'Yangshao' culture (so-named because the first excavation of an agricultural village was made in the region of the village of Yangshao, near the confluence of the Yellow, Fen and Wei Rivers) is noted for its distinctive painted pottery, with flowers, fish, animals, sometimes human faces, and geometric designs painted on by brush. Around 3500 BC the 'Lungshanoid' culture (so-named because the first evidence of this ancient culture was excavated near the village of Lungshan in Shandong Province) was making eggshell-thin black pottery, as well as a type of white pottery.

Pottery-making was well advanced by the Shang period; the most important development occurred around the middle of the dynasty with the manufacture of a high-fired greenish glaze applied to stoneware artefacts. It was during the Han Dynasty that the custom of glazing pottery became fairly common. A yellowish -grey glaze applied to a reddish surface, for example, resulted after firing in a pale shade of green. The production of terracotta pottery – made of a mixture of sand and clay, fired to produce a reddish-brown colour and left unglazed – continued to survive however.

During the Southern and Northern Dynasty periods, a type of proto-porcelain was developed. This is a type of pottery halfway between Han glazed pottery and true porcelain. The proto-porcelain was made by mixing clay with quartz and the mineral feldspar to make a hard smooth-surfaced vessel. Feldspar was mixed with traces of iron and produced an olive-green glaze. Few examples survive but the technique was perfected under the Tang. By the 8th century, Tang proto-porcelain and other types of pottery had found an international market, and were exported as far afield as Japan and the east coast of Africa. Chinese porcelain did not find its way into Europe until the Ming period and it was not until the 17th century that porcelain was manufactured in Europe. The Tang period also saw the introduction of tri-colour glazed vessels.

Chinese pottery reached its artistic peak under the Song. During this time true porcelain was developed, made of fine gaolin clay, white, thin, transparent or translucent. The art of the Song is generally regarded as the finest China has ever produced. The production of porcelain continued under the Yuan but gradually lost the delicacy and near-perfection of the Song period. However, it was probably during this time that the 'blue and white' porcelain – as it became known under the Ming – made its first appearance.

The blue and white type (blue decoration on a white background) was obtained from the gaolin clay quarried near Jingdezhen coupled with a type of cobalt imported from Persia. Also produced during this period were the three-colour and five-colour porcelain (the former usually green, yellow and violet, the latter with light blue and red as well) with floral decorations on a white background. Another notable invention was mono-coloured porcelain, in ferrous red, black or dark blue.

A range of new mono-coloured vessels was developed under the Qing. The tradition of coloured porcelain also continued with the addition of new colours and glazes and more complex decorations. This was the age of true painted porcelain, decorated with delicate landscapes, birds and flowers; elaborate and ornate designs and brilliant colouring became the fashion, along with the imitation, in porcelain, of all sorts of other materials such as gold and silver, mother of pearl, jade, bronze alloy, wood and bamboo.

### Ancient Bronze Vessels

Bronze is an alloy, the chief elements being copper, tin and lead. Tradition ascribes the casting of bronze to the Xia Dynasty of 4000 years ago (the dynasty may or may not have existed). Emperor Yu, the founder of the dynasty, is said to have divided his empire into nine provinces and then cast nine bronze tripods to symbolise his dynasty. But it was the discovery of the last Shang Dynasty capital at Anyang in Henan Province in 1928, which provided the first evidence that the ancient Chinese had developed a bronze technology.

It is believed that a large number of bronze vessels were used for ceremonial purposes, for preparing or holding offerings of food and wine in sacrificial ceremonies performed by the ruler and the aristocracy. Through ritual sacrifices the spirits of the ancestors were persuaded to look after their descendants. The vessels were often buried with the deceased, along with other earthly provisions. Most of the late Shang funeral

vessels have inscriptions which are usually short and pictographic, recording the names of the clan, the ancestor, the maker of the vessel, or recording events, wars. Zhou Dynasty bronze vessels tend to have longer messages and the characters are ideographic, relating wars, rewards, ceremonial events, the appointment of officials.

The early bronzes were cast in sectional clay moulds, an offspring of the advanced pottery technology with high temperature kilns and clay-mould casting. Each section of the mould was covered with the required designs which were either impressed, incised or carved. During the Eastern Zhou period (771-256 BC), by the 5th century BC geometric designs and scenes of hunting and feasting formed using inlays of precious metals and stones were introduced.

Bronze mirrors were used as early as the Shang Dynasty and had already developed into an artistic form by the Warring States Period. Ceramics gradually replaced bronze utensils by the Han Dynasty, but bronze mirrors were not displaced by glass mirrors until the Qing Dynasty. In China, the mirror is a metaphor for self inspection in philosophical discussion. The wise man has three mirrors: a mirror of bronze in which he sees his own physical appearance, a mirror of the people by which he examines his own inner character and conduct, and a mirror of the past by which he learns to emulate successes and to avoid the mistakes of earlier recorded history. The backs of bronze mirrors are decorated and inscribed; the inscriptions express wishes for good fortune and for protection from evil influence. Post-Han writings are full of fantastic stories of the supernatural powers of mirrors. One of them relates the tale of Yin Zhongwen who held a mirror to look at himself but found that his face was not reflected; soon after he was executed.

### Jade

The jade stone has been revered in China

since Neolithic times. The pure white form is the most highly valued, but the stone varies in translucency and colour to include many shades of green, brown and black. To the Chinese, jade has symbolised nobility, beauty and purity; its physical properties have become metaphors for the Confucian ideal of the *junzi*, the noble or superior man. A Chinese dictionary of the second century AD defines the character of *yu* (jade) in these terms:

*Yu is the fairest of stones.*
*It is endowed with five virtues.*
*Charity is its lustre, bright yet warm;*
*Rectitude is its translucency, revealing the colour and markings within;*
*Wisdom is its pure and penetrating note when struck.*
*It is courage, for it can be broken but does not bend;*
*Equity is its sharp edges which injure none.*

Jade was also empowered with magical and life-giving properties; Taoist alchemists, hoping to become immortal, ate an elixir of powdered jade. Jade was a guardian against disease and evil spirits; plugs of jade were placed over the orifices of a corpse to prevent the life force from escaping. Opulent jade suits, clothing meant to prevent decomposition, have been found in Han tombs – examples can be seen in the Nanjing Museum and in the Anhui Provincial Museum in Hefei.

### The Chinese Temple
Architecturally, the roof is the dominant feature of a Chinese temple. It is usually green or yellow and is decorated with figures of divinities and lucky symbols such as dragons and carp. Stone lions often guard the entrance to the temple. Inside is a small courtyard with a large bowl where incense and paper offerings are burnt. Beyond it is the main hall with an altar table, often with an intricately carved front. Here you'll find offerings of fruit and drinks. Behind is an altar with its

images framed by red brocade, embroidered with gold characters. Depending on the size and wealth of the temple, there are gongs, drums, side altars and adjoining rooms with shrines to different gods, chapels for prayers for the dead and displays of funerary plaques. There are also living quarters for the temple keepers. There is no set time for prayer and no communal service except for funerals. Worshippers enter the temple whenever they want to make offerings, pray for help or give thanks.

The most striking feature of the Buddhist temples are the pagodas. These were probably introduced from India along with Buddhism in the 1st century AD. The early pagodas were constructed of wood, they were easily destroyed by fire and subject to corrosion, so materials such as brick, stone, brass and iron were substituted. They were often built to house religious artefacts and documents, to commemorate important events or built simply as monuments. During the Northern Wei Period (4th to 6th centuries) the construction of cave temples began, and cave temples continued to be built during later dynasties. The caves at Longmen near Luoyang, at Magao near Dunhuang, and Yugang near Datong, are some of the finest examples.

In Buddhist art the Buddha is frequently displayed in a basic triad, with a bodhisattva on either side. The latter are Buddhist saints who have arrived at the gateway to nirvana but have chosen to return to earth to guide lesser mortals along righteous paths. Their faces tend to express joy, serenity or compassion. Sometimes the bodhisattvas are replaced by the figures of Buddha's first two disciples, the youthful Ananda and the older Kasyapa.

### FLORA & FAUNA
The following description of China's flora and fauna, and its wildlife reserves was contributed by Murray D Bruce and Constance S Leap Bruce.

Unknown to the West, China created its first natural reserve in 1956. Since that time, the work of preserving China's rich wildlife has grown steadily in strength and complexity and today encompasses over 100 nature reserves, with plans to establish some 500 by the end of the century.

However, coordinated efforts to study and appreciate China's natural history began many centuries ago and were influenced by Taoist beliefs as well as a vast pharmacopeia of medicines of plant and animal origin. The first encyclopaedia of natural history was the *Erh Ya* (Literary Expositor), which was written between the 4th and 2nd Century BC.

China possesses a vast selection of plants and animals, including many so called 'relict' species that survived in protected niches of China during glaciation (Ice Age) periods, most notably the Giant Panda and the Dawn Redwood, the only living relative of the famous California Redwoods.

China's abundant botanical residents include some 30,000 species of higher plants (10% of the world's total). Included in these are many wild prototypes of commonly cultivated plants such as oranges, chestnut, rice and walnut. Cultivation has been practiced intensively for many centuries and a vast array of ornamental plants such as chrysanthemum, peony and rose originated here.

A variety of animals have also been raised and bred in China, including many insects, such as the silkworm and the fighting cricket. Among the 4,400 species of vertebrates (mammals, birds, reptiles, etc.) many are found nowhere else. There are some 200 species of amphibians (frogs, toads etc.) including a giant salamander. There are over 300 reptile species, including the Chinese Alligator, the focal point of serious conservation efforts. The diversity of China's bird life, with about 1200 species, includes spectacular pheasants and peacocks and the largest number of the world's crane species (featuring several that are endangered and supported by conservation projects).

The 450 or so species of mammals still found in China include some of the world's rarest deer, wild horses, mountain sheep and wild cats (notably more forms of the tiger than any other country, with the Manchurian, or Siberian tiger the world's largest). China has its Yeti too, here called *Yen ren* (wild man) and major scientific expeditions have recently been launched to investigate its existence. By far, China's most famous mammal is the Giant Panda, the chosen

symbol for the World Wildlife Fund and the Subject of considerable conservation efforts by the Chinese, including the establishment of 12 sanctuaries or panda reserves.

The Giant Panda (to distinguish it from the smaller, reddish Lesser Panda of the Himalayas) is a bamboo specialist (in fact one of the most specialised large animals in the world). It is only found where there is sufficient vegetation to support its limited diet (eating habits perhaps only matched by the Australian specialist, the koala). In recent times their natural range has been much reduced and many pandas are restricted to small areas. Unfortunately, this has meant that many can no longer move elsewhere when their local food supply diminishes. Bamboo follows a natural dying and regeneration process with cycles ranging from a few years to 100 years, depending on the species. After bamboo flowers, it quickly dies and then reseeds itself. Until the new plants are established, pandas living in an affected area must either move or starve. Some 140 pandas died of starvation in a reserve in 1975 where the bamboo flowered. Another important panda reserve began its bamboo flowering in late 1983. When this was discovered, the Chinese and international advisers took drastic steps to save the local pandas, including bringing in emergency substitute food supplies such as sugar cane, and moving pandas to new sites from which the resident Chinese were evacuated.

In spite of the real progress made in the last few years with establishing protected areas, the sheer size of the country is still a daunting prospect to overcome. So far, most protected areas are concentrated in the east and south, especially the southeastern regions. Here can be found the most diverse and most vulnerable areas. In broad terms, China is divided into three regions: – the steppe and desert regions in the north-west and north-east: – the forest regions in the east: – and the high mountains and plateaus in the west and south-west. The steppes (vast plains) range from forested to arid desert. The forested east ranges through a variety of types from conifers and pines to tropical rain forest. The complex, mountainous region extends from high, isolated ranges through the massive hills and gorges of east Tibet to the Tibetan plateau ('the roof of the world').

Under the term 'natural protected area', China currently recognises three main types. First are the areas protected for the whole natural landscape, particularly large areas with a diverse range of forest and other habitat types, including many important watershed areas for some of China's larger rivers. The main priority now in this category concerns the mountains and plateaus in the south, and the deserts of the north (it may already be too late for the last known herds of pure wild horses). The second category is for special types of habitats (or ecosystems) which contain rare and unique plants and animals and which are of immense importance for scientific research. There are many such areas protecting fragments of tropical and subtropical habitat in the southeast. Many more such areas are proposed. The third category is for the special protection of rare animals and plants. The panda reserves are a good example of this group, as are the alligator sanctuaries, bird, and snake islands. Amongst plants, the efforts to protect the last 3000 Dawn Redwoods is notable.

Although many areas of scenic as well as natural beauty have been designated for tourism and recreation, the emphasis is still more towards the scenic. Fortunately, the concept of multiple use protected areas is being developed now and many natural protected areas should be far more accessible in the near future.

Current internationally aided conservation projects are focussing on the areas where pandas live. The research priority is to develop a better understanding of the intricate and varied life cycles of the bamboo species eaten by pandas. At three of the panda reserves under study, there are now research and visitor centres being developed (in some cases taking over settlements used for logging and clearing the forests – an everpresent problem in China, as elsewhere). These reserves are:

### Wangland Panda Reserve

This reserve is a steep sided basin of 27,700 ha protecting the headwaters of major tributaries of the Chang Jiang (Yangtze) River, in northern Sichuan. Although initially established for the pandas in 1965, it is also being used to study other endangered species. It is located 430 km north of Chengdu; the last 90 km from Pingwu, with good roads if taken before the summer rains. The new reserve headquarters (2450 m) is 9 km from the border station.

### Tangjiahe Panda Reserve

This 40,000 ha reserve is southeast of Wangland and part of the same ridge system. It was established in 1978 to conserve the panda, takin (a bizarre antelope) and golden monkey – 'the rare and precious animals of China'. The reserve headquarters is 370 km by road from Chengdu (170 km from Pingwu). About 200 pandas live here, restricted to a narrow bamboo belt at 2100 to 2800 metres. This reserve strikingly illustrates the problem of survival for pandas. The dominance in areas of certain types of bamboos increases the risks of sudden flowering – above the bamboo are open rock and meadows, below are logged areas.

### Fengtongzhai Panda Reserve

This 40,000 ha area was established in 1979 in the watershed of the upper Qingyi Jiang in the Qionglai (Chunglai) Shan. Reserve headquarters is 271 km by road from Chengdu (30 km north of Baoxing). It was here that Pere Armand David, the famous French missionary explorer, obtained the first panda specimen in 1869, and also from here that the pandas presented to the USA, UK, France, Japan and Mexico were taken. There is no logging here and pandas can move about, even to feed beyond commune farms along the reserve's boundary.

Murray D Bruce &
Constance S Leap Bruce

" ... IT SAYS HEAVY SPITTLE, EASING TO LIGHT DRIVEL, WITH A CHANCE OF CULTURAL FALL-OUT OVERNIGHT ..."

# Facts for the Visitor

## VISAS

Visas for individual travel in China are easy to get. The only people who are automatically excluded from entering China are holders of South Korean, South African, Israeli and Rhodesian passports. Don't worry if you have a Taiwanese visa in your passport.

**Where to get Them** China visas are readily available in Hong Kong. Several agents issue the visa and most do it in as little as 24 hours, and one place issues it same day. If you're prepared to wait a few days, the cost of the visa is reduced.

Outside Hong Kong the situation is variable to say the least! Going by the experience of other travellers the embassy in Moscow was readily giving visas to anyone who asked; the embassy in Stockholm was readily giving visas to Swedish citizens; and the embassy in one of the African countries gave one girl a visa with unlimited time in China! Some embassies in Europe will give transit visas for people travelling by train across the Soviet Union and China to Hong Kong, and you may be able to extend the visa in China. The embassy in the USA was only giving visas to individuals who wanted to visit relatives in China, and the one in Australia was simply referring people to travel agents and their tours.

Remember, this was the situation in 1983; it's extremely variable. If you've got the time, then it's worth trying the embassy in your own country or one that you're passing through since the regulations seem to be changing all the time.

**Visas in Hong Kong** There are a number of agents in Hong Kong who are responsible for issuing China visas. Generally they offer a choice of visa by itself, or a package deal including visa fee and the cost of transport to China.

Visa applications require two passport-size photos, your application must be written in English, and you're advised to have one entire blank page in your passport for the visa. You'll generally be issued either a two-week or a one-month visa but even that varies; on one occasion three of us applied for a visa at the same agent on the same day and paid the same price; one of us was given a 35-day visa, I got 33 days and the other got 31 days!

The cost of visas and the type of package-deals you get in Hong Kong change quite frequently, so use this information as a guide only. For instance, during one Canton Trade Fair, tours to the city were off because of lack of accommodation.

There appear to be only three agencies which issue visas directly; these are *Trinity Express*, *Wah Nam Travel* and *China Travel Service*. Others such as *Phoenix Services* and *Travellers Hostel* take passports and applications to Trinity Express which is staffed by People's Republic Chinese.

*Travellers Hostel*, 16th floor, Block A, Chungking Mansions, Nathan Rd, Tsimshatsui, Kowloon (tel 3-687710 or 3-682505).
– Visa only for HK$130; takes three working days to issue. The visa is valid for one month although in reality the actual number of days varies from person to person.
– Visa only for HK$180 if issued Monday to Friday; takes 24 hours and is valid for two weeks.
– Visa only for HK$200 if issued Saturday, Sunday, or public holidays; takes 24 hours and is valid for two weeks.
– Visa plus train ticket to Canton for HK$330; takes 24 hours and includes visa fee, transport by bus and train to the

81

border, lunch at the border and train ticket from the border to Canton. The visa is valid for two weeks.

*Wah Nam Travel*, Rm 1003, Eastern Commercial Centre, 397 Hennessey Rd, Wanchai, Hong Kong Island (tel 5-8911161). There is a second office at Rm 602, Sino Centre, 582-592 Nathan Rd, Kowloon (tel 3-320367). This is probably the best place to get your visa. They issue one-month visas and the fee varies depending on how long you're prepared to wait for it.
– Visa only for HK$70; takes one week to issue (though may be issued in as little as four days).
– Visa only for HK$120; takes two working days.
– Visa only for HK$180; issued on the same day – drop your passport in early in the morning and get it back in the afternoon.

*Phoenix Services*, Rm 11, 1st floor, Bowring Centre, corner of Bowring and Woosung Sts, Tsimshatsui, Kowloon (tel 3-7227378). Lots of people have spoken highly of this place; friendly and exceptionally helpful staff. Their visas are valid for two weeks, but they say they'll try and get you three weeks (how this works I've no idea).
– Visa only for HK$130; takes two working days.
– Visa only for HK$200; takes 24 hours.

*Hong Kong Student Travel Bureau*, Rm 1024, 10th floor, Star House, Salisbury Rd, Tsimshatsui, Kowloon.
– Visa plus ferry to Canton, plus one night's accommodation in Canton for HK$510; takes three to four working days. They don't supply visas by themselves.

*Trinity Express*, Rm 614, 6th floor, New World Centre, Salisbury Rd, Tsimshatsui, Kowloon.
– Visa plus train ticket to Canton for HK$350; takes 24 hours. They pick you up in Kowloon, bus and train you to the border where you have lunch, and provide you with a soft-seat train ticket from the border to Canton. The visa is valid for 14 days. You may get three weeks, but don't count on it.

*China Travel Service*, Head Office; China Travel Building, 77 Queens Rd, Central, Hong Kong Island (tel 5-259121). There is a branch office conveniently located on 1st floor, 27-33 Nathan Rd, Kowloon (tel 3-667201), across the road from Chungking Mansions and the entrance is on the Beijing Rd side.
– Visas for individual travel are issued by CTS, but they charge a fortune and are only valid for 10 days, and take two to three days to issue.

The Visa Office of the Ministry of Foreign Affairs of the People's Republic (tel 5-744163) is at 287 Queen's Road East. Inquiries can be made on the ground floor and the 7th floor – but they will deny that you can get into China by yourself, or without a proper invitation!

**Visa Application Form** Apart from personal details, the visa application form also asks you to specify your religion and political party, occupation and previous occupation, whether you have been in China before and the names of relatives and friends in China. It asks you to specify what languages you know and the purpose of your journey to China. For religion and political party, say 'none'. For occupation the safest job is 'student' – *don't* tell them you're a journalist, priest, government worker or something similarly naughty. *Don't* list relatives and friends in China. If you speak Chinese *don't* say so. Tell them you're going to China for 'sightseeing'.

It also asks you to specify your itinerary of travel and your means of transport, but you can deviate from this as much as you want; just list a few major places that are officially open to foreigners. You *don't* have to leave from the place you specify on your visa application form. List your means of transport as train and plane.

**Visas for Foreign Students** Quite a few Chinese universities are taking foreign students, usually for Chinese language courses. Most students stay a year or two, but there are also six-week summer courses available. Once you're accepted by a Chinese university you're automatically given a visa. You can then go to China to study and after that you're free to travel – *and* you'll get student discounts on trains and in hotels. If you're a foreign student in Taiwan you'll also get student discounts, since Taiwan is considered to be part of China.

**Visa Extensions** Extending visas in China is also very variable They might have the situation sorted out by the time this book is out, so again use this information as a rough guide only.

From the middle of 1983 it was generally possible to get a one-month extension on your visa and that was all. Before then it was possible to get two one-month extensions, but the rules suddenly changed.

Visa extensions are handled by the Foreign Affairs Section of the local Public Security Offices. China International Travel Service has *nothing* to do with extensions. Extensions cost Y5 (about US$2.50).

The problem in the past has been that some Public Security Offices wouldn't or were highly unwilling to give visa extensions. Others were more than happy to. Some wouldn't give extensions if you'd already had two extensions, and some wouldn't give you another if you'd had just one. So if you only got a two-week visa in Hong Kong you'd find your total time in China severely limited – despite the reassurances from the Hong Kong agents that the visa could be easily extended.

Then there were the oddities to contend with; if you made it to Lhasa in the middle of 1982 there was a friendly police officer who was letting people stay for as long as they liked, so long as they had valid permits. Beijing Public Security, on the other hand, was handing out just a few extra days – enough time to allow you to leave the country. Guilin in late 1982 was under the impression that visas could be extended only once, though I did manage to wangle two more weeks out of them on top of my first extension. Various places were reported as no-goers for extensions, but there was rarely any consistency; it all seemed to depend on who was sitting behind the desk at the time and the relative position of the sun and the moon. One place was actually giving two-month extensions, but by the time this book is out they will probably have been told not to.

You should at least be able to get one extension of one month's duration – that seems to be the rule now. You could always try bargaining; in Jinan they only wanted to give me a two week extension, so I refused to hand over my passport until they guaranteed a month. If you're planning on a lengthy stay in China, you should be sure to get a one-month visa in Hong Kong. Otherwise, try the embassy in your home country or elsewhere – you may be able to get a longer visa than you'll get in Hong Kong.

## CUSTOMS

Immigration procedures are so streamlined they're almost a formality these days. The third-degree at Customs seems to be reserved for Seiko-smuggling Hong Kongers, much more of a problem than the odd stray backpacker.

Customs require that you declare on the 'Baggage Declaration for Incoming Passengers' the number of cameras, wristwatches, recorders (including multi-purpose combination sets), radios, calculators, electric fans, bicycles, sewing machines, TV sets and cine-cameras you're taking into China; this is to prevent you from selling them in the country or giving them away as presents. They also ask you to declare the quantity of foreign currency and travellers' cheques you're carrying, and any gold, silver, jewellery, antiques, calligraphy and other works of art. When you leave China, you'll be asked to show that you still have all the items listed. Don't lose the declaration form!

You're allowed to import 600 cigarettes or the equivalent in tobacco products, two litres of alcholic drink and one pint of perfume. You're allowed to import only 3000 feet of movie film, and a maximum of 72 rolls of still film. Importation of fresh fruit is prohibited.

It's illegal to import any printed material, film, tapes, etc 'detrimental to China's politics, economy, culture and ethics'. But don't get too paranoid about what you take to read. Leaving China, any tapes, manuscripts, books, etc, 'which contain state secrets or are otherwise prohibited for export' can be seized – as in any other country. Cultural relics, handicrafts, gold and silver ornaments, and jewellery purchased in China has to be shown to Customs on leaving. You'll also have to show your receipts otherwise the stuff may be confiscated. Again, don't get paranoid – they usually check only that you've still got your Walkmans and your camera with you and that you're not departing with large doses of Chinese currency.

Lastly, an item for the travelling herbalist: export of musk, toad-cake, cinnabar, euconmia, gastrodia-elata, pianzihuang, caterpillar fungus, Liu-Shen pills and Angongniuhuang pills is prohibited.

## MONEY

The basic unit of Chinese currency is the *yuan*, which is divided into *jiao* and *fen*. 10 fen make up one jiao, and 10 jiao make up one yuan. Most Chinese use the term 'mao' instead of 'jiao'. There are, in fact, two types of currency in use in China: Renmibi and Foreign Exchange Certificates.

**Renmibi**, RMB or 'People's Money' is issued by the Bank of China. Paper notes are issued in denominations of 1, 2, 5 and 10 yuan; 1, 2 and 5 jiao; and 1, 2 and 5 fen. Coins are in denominations of 1, 2 and 5 fen. The one fen note is a small yellow note, the two fen is blue and the five fen is a small green note.

**Foreign Exchange Certificates**, FECs or 'Tourist Money' have been issued in China for use by foreign tourists, diplomats, Overseas Chinese and Chinese from Hong Kong and Macau. FECs come in six denominations: 50 yuan, 10 yuan, 5 yuan, 1 yuan, 5 jiao and 1 jiao. There are no coins. Apparently there's a 100 yuan note but I've never seen it. You're meant to use FECs in places which serve foreigners only, such as Friendship Stores, hotels and foreign trade centres. They're supposed to be used for payment of through-train fares to Hong Kong or ship fares to Hong Kong or Macau, international and domestic airfares, international telecommunications charges and parcel post and for the payment of imported goods.

In practice, if you buy your train ticket at a railway station you can pay with either RMB or FEC, or a mixture of both. If you buy through CITS they may insist you pay in FECs. Some hotels insist you pay with FECs but I've met people who always paid with RMB. Friendship Stores are a bit variable; for some goods they'll accept either currency, and much depends on what city you're in. Some people have even paid for air tickets partly in RMB and partly in FECs; or paid taxis with RMB despite the signs in the cab saying to pay in FECs. Basically it's a rather confused situation out there.

As for those places which do insist on FECs, there's really no sense in arguing as some people do; life will be easier for both sides if you just pay up in FECs.

## Changing Money

Foreign currency and travellers' cheques can be changed at the main centres of the Bank of China or at its branch offices in the tourist hotels, some shops such as the Friendship Stores, and some of the big department stores. You'll be issued FECs and small change will be made up of the RMB 1, 2 and 5 fen notes and coins.

Foreign currency which is acceptable in China includes the Australian dollar (A$); Austrian schilling (Sch); Belgian franc (FB) Canadian dollar (Can$); Danish krone (DKr); West German Mark (DM); French franc (FF); Japanese yen (Y); Malaysian dollar (M$); Dutch gilder (FL); Norwegian krone (NKr); Singapore dollar (S$); Swedish krona (SKr); Swiss franc (SF); Pound sterling (£); US dollar (US$); and Hong Kong dollar (HK$).

Travellers cheques from most of the world's leading banks and issuing agencies are now acceptable in China – stick to the major companies such as Thomas Cook, American Express, Bank of America, and you'll be OK.

The exchange rate varies but is usually about two yuan to the US dollar. The rates listed below are approximate and were current at the time of publication (when the US dollar was particularly strong). Check the latest rates when you go.

| USA | US$1 | = Y2.3 |
| UK | £1 | = Y3.0 |
| Australia | A$1 | = Y1.9 |
| Canada | C$1 | = Y1.7 |
| Germany | DM1 | = Y0.81 |
| Hong Kong | HK$1 | = Y0.29 |
| Japan | 1000 yen | = Y9.5 |

## Changing FECs for RMB

Getting hold of RMB (which you'll need if you want to buy things at the little street-stalls, restaurants or in the markets) is no trouble. Many Chinese will swap them on a one-to-one basis so they can buy imported goods in the Friendship Stores (some Friendship Stores only serve foreigners and others will sell to anyone with the foreign cash). A number of hotel staff will insist you pay with FECs so they can get them for themselves. You may get approached outside the hotels to change

money – if not, just try paying for anything with FECs and you'll soon meet someone who wants a fresh supply. Or ask the reception desk at the hotel to swap some for you. Banks may also give you RMB if you ask for it. In more remote areas, where tourists don't go, you'll find that the locals have no idea what tourist money is, so you'll *have* to use RMB. Some people seem to think it's illegal for foreigners to have RMB – it's *not*.

## Reconverting Chinese currency

You can change Chinese currency, both RMB and FEC, back to hard currency when you leave China. But you *must* have your exchange receipts with you.

Foreign Exchange Certificates can be taken in and out of the country as you please, but RMB is not supposed to be taken out. Unless you're definitely going back to China, change the whole lot to hard currency since Chinese yuan are useless outside the country. If for some reason you do get stuck with a heap of yuan, ask around at the travellers' hang-outs in Hong Kong as someone who's going to China will probably buy it. If you're returning to Hong Kong, the bank in Shenzhen Railway Station changes yuan to Hong Kong dollars.

## Credit Cards

In general, credit cards are gaining more acceptance in China for use by foreign visitors. Federal Card is accepted at several places in Beijing, Tianjin, Nanjing, Canton, Hangzhou, Shanghai, Fuzhou, Hankou and Kunming; Visa in Canton, Beijing, Shanghai, Tianjin and Hangzhou; Mastercard in Shanghai, Canton, Hangzhou Beijing and Nanjing; American Express in Canton and Shanghai and Diners Club in Shanghai and Canton. It wouldn't be worth getting a credit card especially for your trip to China, but if you already have one there are a few places you might find it handy – but remember that their acceptance is still very limited.

## Foriegn Exchange Certificates

**10 Fen**

**50 Fen**

**1 Yuan**

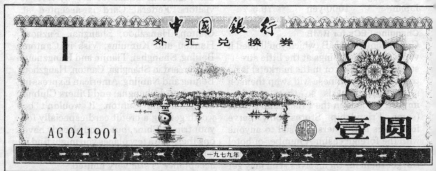

Renmibi

1 Fen

2 Fen

5 Fen

1 Yuan

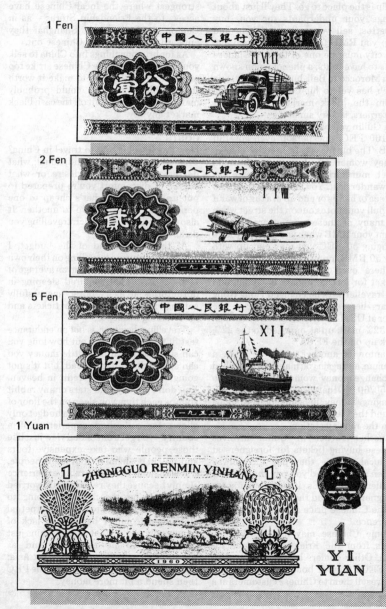

### Black Market

Guilin is the place to go. They'll just about change your underpants for you, buy cassettes, sell you railway tickets and swap you RMB for FECs at a premium. The city must be one of the few Chinese cities to have touts, a phenomenon known from Morocco to Bali, but (mercifully) one which has yet to hit China. Apart from Guilin the black market, at least for westerners, is very small.

In Guilin you can readily get 120 RMB for 100 FEC; one person even got 130 RMB. The business is fronted by 'change money' women, who hang out in the main street murmuring 'fifatee/sicksatee' as you wander past. You may get surrounded by a sea of hands or end up in a tug of war if you pull your notes out on the street when too many of these women are around. Count your RMB when you get it; if you're changing 50 FEC you may end up with only 50 RMB, no premium.

There even appears to be a black market for foreign dollars in Guilin, and one traveller says he changed Hong Kong dollars here as well as US dollars, the latter at US$110 cash for RMB 220 which is a 32% mark up as opposed to the 22% mark up on the FECs.

Canton is another place to make a premium, and again you may get approached by 'change money' women who offer up to at 50/60. Otherwise, you could try changing money in some of the shops around the Liu Hua Hotel across the road from the railway station.

Another racket in Guilin involves Chinese buying tickets for foreigners at the local price – they pay the railway station in RMB and you pay the Chinese middleman in FECs. It seems that some foreigners have had their tickets checked for the Chinese price and had to pay the difference.

Some Chinese may ask you to buy goods from the Friendship Stores for them. Other dealers buy the goods with the FECs they've bought from you and then resell them to Chinese customers at a mark-up. The black markets may be strongest where the local Chinese have access to the Friendship Stores – as in Canton. In Beijing and Shanghai they appear to keep the local Chinese out.

As for bringing things into China to sell, you'll probably find the Chinese strike too much of a hard bargain to make it worth the trouble – and you could probably make just as much profit off the cash black market anyway.

### COSTS

How much will it cost to travel in China? That's largely up to the individual; what degree of comfort you desire or what degree of discomfort you're prepared to put up with – and what's cheap to one person may be expensive to another. It also depends on how much travelling you do and where you go.

At the bottom end of the budget, I didn't meet anyone travelling on their own in China doing it on less than an average of US$7 a day. That required sleeping in dormitories at every hotel, successfully getting local price on all train tickets and *never* taking a sleeper.

Travelling, however, is *not* an endurance test; if you want to find out how long you can stay away and how little money you can spend doing it go ahead, but it's not going to earn you any credit in heaven. You don't get any gold stars or any rabbit stamps each time you sleep on the floor of a train. Travelling on too low a budget only allows for a limited experience of a country – you get a one-sided view just like those people who take expensive tours and stay in posh hotels. For many people, travelling can be a miserable experience simply because they're constantly worried about how far the money is going to stretch; being forced to live in a perpetual state of discomfort because of lack of money only adds to that misery. China just *isn't* going to be as cheap and as comfortable as India or South-East Asia; if you want to have a good time in the PRC then spend a bit more money.

If you care about your sanity take a sleeper. Train trips in China are almost always *long*; sitting for 30 hours in a hot, crowded hard-seat carriage, the lights on all night, people staring at you and constantly spitting on the floor is no fun at all – if that's your bag, you can have it.

Similarly, hotel dormitories can be incredibly aggravating; most people who go to China take the well-trodden tourist route which means they end up in dormitories where a degree of western sanity prevails – though we can be noisy and impolite enough. Once you're off that route, you're pretty much on your own. If you're sharing with Chinese you'd had better be able to cope with a language that's spoken late into the night at 140 decibels and spitting from five paces – China and its people are friendly enough, but if you're there for any length of time you'll soon appreciate being able to come back to a hotel room at night and shutting the door on it all.

China can be cheap, but it's hard to do it cheaply and comfortably. Most people do the place on US$10 a day – staying in dormitories and getting local price on the trains. But that is with some difficulty, and you'd be better off going up to US$15 a day. Most of your money gets spent on transport and accommodation. If you take dorm beds accommodation costs are fairly low by Chinese standards. If you're travelling alone but want your own room, the cost of living will probably soar to US$20 or US$25 a day – this is mainly because hotels generally only supply double rooms. If you're on your own they may give you the room for half price, but quite often they won't – so you end up paying for two people and that really gets expensive. Even food costs decrease if you're with somebody else; 'eating Chinese' with a few other people not only gives you greater variety of food to choose from, but also brings the price down.

Costs also vary from place to place. Beijing has an extreme shortage of cheap accommodation, but in the obscure town of Zhanjiang in Guangdong you can get a decent little room for Y3.50 – but where would you rather go? In heavily-touristed places like Guilin, it's *almost* impossible to get local price on the trains, but in other places it's easy. It's hard to say how much you're going to spend on the trains, since you don't know how lucky you'll be getting local price – but it's likely to get harder in the future. Taking buses and boats is a good idea; you pay the same as the locals and you get to see more of the countryside as well. Travelling at night on the trains will also save on hotel bills.

At the other end of the scale, if money is no object, you'll get plenty of opportunity in China to use it up.

## OFFICIALDOM, DOCUMENTS AND PAPERWORK

Of all the striking Chinese sayings a particularly applicable one is 'With one monkey in the way, not even 10,000 men can pass'. Three of the major monkeys in China today are CITS (China International Travel Service), the PSB (Public Security Bureau) and the mass of little bits of paper collectively referred to as 'red tape'.

**CITS (China International Travel Service)** deals with China's foreign tourist hordes, and mainly concerns itself with organising and making travel arrangements for group tours. It is known in Chinese as *Luxingshe*. CITS existed as far back as 1954 when there were few customers; now they're inundated with a couple of hundred thousand big-noses a year and it will take a while for them to get their act together.

CITS will buy train and plane tickets for you (and some boat tickets), reserve hotel rooms, organise city tours, and even get tickets for the cinema, opera, acrobatics and other entertainment as well as organise trips to communes and factories, and provide vehicles (taxis, minibuses) for sightseeing or transport. Remember that all rail tickets bought through CITS will be tourist-priced (an extra 75% on top of the Chinese price) and that there will usually be a two or three yuan service charge added on to the price of rail, boat or plane tickets. Also remember that CITS has nothing to do with issuing travel permits or visa extensions – for that you must go direct to the Public Security offices (in Beijing and possibly in Fujian Province CITS acts as an intermediary).

CITS offices and desks are usually located in the major tourist hotels in each town or city open to foreigners; sometimes they are located elsewhere but if you need their services either go and see them or get the hotel reception desk to phone them.

Service varies and some offices are more helpful than others. Some CITS people are friendly and full of useful information about the places they're stationed in; others can be downright rude. In some cases you'll even find CITS offices manned by people who speak sparse or even zero English (a situation which should improve with time). It tends to be pot-luck with what you get; Beijing CITS is housed in a tiny room manned by three to five people at any one time – all this to deal with the full onslaught of the western hordes; Shanghai CITS, on the other hand, has more people to do the work so the Basil Fawlty blood pressures that characterise the Beijing office are held at bay; Canton has got it all worked out – they've erected screens around their front desk that they can hide behind – you'd think they were hibernating. On the other hand, the offices at Nanchang, Lu Shan, Guiyang, Yeuyang, Turpan and Fuzhou (to give a few examples) were exceptionally friendly, helpful and efficient.

Getting information out of CITS is also pot luck; again, it depends who you're dealing with. I already knew the answer to a question I asked of Beijing CITS:

'How do I get to Zunhua?'

'You can't go, it's closed'.

I showed the lady my permit for Zunhua. 'Oh, well, I suppose you can go'.

'How do I get to Zunhua?'

'I don't know.'

It's almost comical; the tour bus for Zunhua could be booked a few blocks west of Beijing CITS and it departed in the morning right opposite CITS.

I had a similar experience with Datong CITS; I asked them how I could get to the 'Mass Graves Class Education Exhibition Hall'. I was told the hall was closed – which it was not – another westerner has bussed out there that morning. At Canton CITS I asked how I could get to Zhanjiang and was told I'd have to fly – I took the long-distance bus the next day.

The point is, that if CITS tells you that something cannot be done, that you cannot go somewhere or you can only go by such-and-such a means of transport – then check it out for yourself. Go to the bus station and see if you can buy a ticket, or go to Public Security and see if they will give you a permit for a given destination. A good example of this is Haikou on Hainan Island – if you go to CITS they'll tell you that the rest of Hainan is off-limits to westerners except if you go on one of their organised tours – so you trundle off to the bus station and after they've refused three times to sell you a ticket to anywhere else on the island you can be assured that it really is off-limits to westerners.

One of the more maddening aspects of travel in China – and one which seems to infect certain CITS offices – are the tales the Chinese make up hide inefficiency, or to avoid doing anything for you. Usually it's something aggravating like being told that a hotel is full and 15 minutes later being told that a room has become available because someone just checked out even if it is 11 o'clock at night! The standard excuse used by China Airlines to explain a delayed or cancelled flight is bad weather. Sometimes though, the stories get quite out of hand and reach utterly comic proportions. One couple who walked into Lonely Planet's office in Melbourne told us that CITS had refused to sell them tickets on the boat from Chongqing to Wuhan because a large rock had fallen into the river and blocked it! But that wasn't the best – a western tour group had their bookings on the boat cancelled by CITS because their were no boats plying the river that day. And why weren't there any boats? Because the Yangtse River was being cleaned!

**CTS & OCTS (China Travel Service & Overseas Chinese Travel Service)** are two branches concerned with tourists from Hong Kong, Macau, possibly Taiwan, and those foreign nationals of Chinese descent (that is, Overseas Chinese) who visit China in groups or individually – perhaps for sightseeing or for visiting relatives. CTS doesn't tend to deal with western tourists but in Hong Kong, where they speak English, you can use their services to book trains, planes, hovercraft etc. to China and they also issue China visas (the last service is not recommended as they charge more than other agencies and the visa is usually only 10 days' duration). In China CTS is sometimes mixed in with the CITS offices and desks in the tourist hotels, particularly in towns with only one major tourist hotel where both westerners and Overseas Chinese stay. CTS seem to have a wider range of services than CITS; one advantage is that they will book transport that CITS won't, such as boats plying routes not normally open to western tourists. You're also more likely to get cheap tickets out of them.

**CYTS (China Youth Travel Service)** is the travel department of the All-China Youth Federation and was established in 1979. Its purpose is to establish ties with youth the world over, including foreign and overseas Chinese youth as well as those from Hong Kong, Macau and Taiwan. It stresses more active pursuits like camping and cycling and provides some concessions to the lower budgets of students in other countries. They only deal with groups – such as academic and cultural exchanges and also with professional groups (doctors, teachers, etc). Like CITS and CTS, CYTS has offices in Hong Kong and Beijing but their network in Chinese cities is not yet large, though offices may be attached to local youth organisations.

Exactly what the relationships are between CITS, CYTS, OCTS and CYTS is anyone's guess. For a while some independent operators out of Hong Kong managed to bypass both CITS and CTS to make their own cheaper arrangements by dealing direct with hotels and transport booking offices – Beijing quickly put an end to that, though some of it probably continues. Beijing has made it clear that tourism is part of the national economy – no bypassing the money channels.

**PSB (Public Security Bureau)** The Public Security Bureau is the name given to China's police, both uniformed and plain-clothes. It's responsible for the whole range of activities, including suppression of political dissidence, crime detection, mediating family quarrels and directing traffic. The Foreign Affairs Branch of the Public Security Bureau deals with foreigners. This branch is responsible for issuing visa extensions and Alien Travel Permits – for details, see below.

What sets the Chinese police aside from their counterparts in, say, Mexico and South America, is their amiability towards foreigners (what they're like with their own people may be a different story). They'll sometimes sit you down, give you a cup of tea and practice their English – and the frequency of competent English speakers is surprisingly good. The only run in you may have with the PSB is when you end up in a closed place and it's the job of the PSB to put you on your way. For misdemeanours such as being in a town without a permit, or being off-course without a good alibi, there could be a fine – figures mentioned are around Y30, but one violator was fined Y200.

One traveller covered up an expulsion order issued to him by Guiyang PSB. The Wuhan PSB caught up with him, kept him for six days, fined him US$100 and slung him out via Canton. The expulsion was not so much for visiting closed places but for overstaying his visa. He also used an unusual device to get into Chinese hotels on the way – telling them he was from Xinjiang, where a different language is spoken and a Caucasian face is the norm. Chinese, however, carry all sorts of odd ID like swimming licences, work unit cards, bicycle licences, and probably travel authorisation. This was a bit of an extreme case – the worst you can really expect to happen is to be ejected from the country at your own expense. We haven't heard of anyone languishing in a Chinese prison – yet.

## Documents & Paperwork

There is a plethora of useless jobs in China involving the issuing and organising of small bits of paper. Failing computers and trust this is the way they keep track of everything – or do they? Well, whether or not the system works is besides the point – the Chinese are crazy about chops, seals, signatures and official looking letterheads – so carry as many of these as you can muster. Apart from your invaluable passport and its visa stamp, there are a couple of bits of paper which actually are important amidst the red-tap:

**Baggage Declaration for Incoming Passengers** is a slip of paper you'll be given at Customs when you enter China. On it you have to list the number of cameras, wristwatches, recorders (including multi-purpose combination sets), radios, calculators, electric fans, bicycles, sewing machines, TV sets and cinecameras you're taking into China; the number is checked when you leave the country to ensure that you haven't sold the stuff or given it away as presents. They also ask you to declare the quantity of foreign currency and travellers' cheques you're carrying, and any gold, silver, jewellery and calligraphy and other works of art in your possession. When you leave China you'll be asked to show that you still have all the objects in your possession. Don't

lose the declaration form! If you leave without the form but have all the goodies a foreigner is expected to be carrying then you probably won't be hassled, but if you have no form and no goodies then there could be problems.

**Money-exchange vouchers** Whenever you change foreign currency into Chinese currency you'll be given a money exchange voucher recording the transaction. If you've got any leftover Chinese currency when you leave the country and want to reconvert it to hard currency you will require those vouchers – not all them, but at least equal to the amount of RMB you want to change.

**Health Certificate** is required if you're arriving in China from an infected area – see the section on 'Health' for details.

**Passport Photos** Although obtainable in China, it's more convenient if you bring them along. Particularly useful if you're going to Europe on the Trans-Siberian, as that may require three visas (Mongolian, Soviet and Polish).

**Alien Travel Permit** There are about 130 or so places in China which are officially open to foreign tourists – the number keeps on slowly increasing. Of these, there are 29 places in China which you may go to *without* a permit. These are:

| | |
|---|---|
| Beijing | Nanjing |
| Canton | Nanning |
| Changchun | Qingdao |
| Changsha | Qinghuangdao |
| Chengdu | Shanghai |
| Chongqing | Shenyang |
| Foshan | Suzhou |
| Gullin | Taiyuan |
| Hangzhou | Tianjin |
| Harbin | Wuhan |
| Jinan | Wuxi |
| Kaifeng | Xian |
| Kunming | Zhaoqing |
| Luoyang | Zhengzhou |
| Lunan Country | |
| (Stone Forest) | |

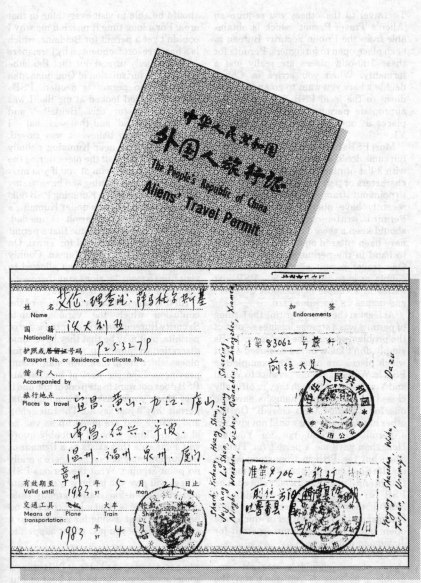

To travel to the others you require an 'Alien's Travel Permit' which is obtainable from the Public Security Bureau in each place open to foreigners. Permits for these 100-odd places are really just a formality. When you arrive in China, decide where you want to go and then go down to the local PSB and ask for the appropiate permits; you're allowed ten places at one go and the permit costs Y1.

Most PSBs have an English interpreter, but some don't, so you should go equipped with a list of places you want in Chinese characters or perhaps a map (in Chinese) to point out strange new places which may recently have opened up. The Travel Permit is written out in Chinese, so you should keep a record of the places which have been entered on it. You do not have to hand in the permit after it's expired. One travel permit can be issued to a couple or even three people – PSB just writes in a couple of passport numbers and names on the same card.

At least at the time of writing the issuing of permits was a strange business – part of the problem seems to be that many PSBs simply don't know or are confused about which places are open. For example the PSB in Wuhan gave me permits to Wuhu and Yingtan even though they're officially closed to foreigners. Changsha gave me one for Zhuzhou (also closed). On the other hand, Chongqing would not give me a permit for Wuhu, nor for Yingtan. Hangzhou gave me a permit for Tiantai Shan but the PSB in Chongqing would not. Lu Shan gave me permits for Yingtan, Guichi and Tunxi, all officially closed. The PSB in Luoyang was exceptionally helpful; they gave me permits for both Kashgar and Xining, neither of which were open, but wouldn't give me a permit for Jiayuguan which was.

Places which are within day trip range of open places shouldn't present any problem, so long as you don't stay the night there. The jurisdiction of some open cities is enormous and theoretically you

should be able to visit everything in that area. For a long time it puzzled me why I couldn't get a permit for Beidaihe, which is a beach resort frequented by foreigners – it eventually turned out that Beidaihe fell into the jurisdiction of Qinghuangdao for which no permit is needed. PSBs where I applied looked at me like I was crazy asking for this 'Beidaihe' and mumbled 'closed' and that was that – I really started to believe it was closed. Down at Anning near Kunming nobody will object if you visit the place during the day, but they'll scream at you if you miss the bus back to Kunming and have to stay the night – meanwhile Kunming PSB tells you that Anning comes under Kunming's jurisdiction and no permit is needed. Hangzhou PSB also told me that a permit for Huang Shan was good for Tunxi. On the other hand there's Lunan County which is open but you're not allowed to visit Lunan town, let alone stay there – it's the Stone Forest which is open.

All this may just be an indication of the confusion which the various Public Security Bureaux were in over the issue of permits, or it may be that they have some discretionary power to give permits for places which are in their own or adjaceant provinces. Like the best of bureaucrats PSB does not want to step out of line and if they think you're asking for an unusual permit they'll just say no. The rules chop and change and are made up as you go along in China – they'll probably quote you some rule that exists as a figment of the current imagination and there's really no point arguing. What the various PSB offices will give you in the way of permits and visa extensions varies greatly from office to office – remember, there is no harm in at least asking for a permit to a strange place – you just might happen to get it.

Alien Travel Permits can be demanded when registering at a hotel, at PSB offices, sometimes when purchasing boat or bus tickets, spot checks by police in unusual areas. If you're off the track but heading towards a destination for which you have a permit PSB will either stop you and cancel the destination, or they will let you continue on your way. The permit also lists the modes of transportation you're allowed to take; plane, train, ship or car – and if a particular mode is crossed out then you can't use it. If a mode is cancelled it can be reinstated at the next PSB, but that may only be for a single trip from Point A to Point B – or you could try and carry on regardless – or you could lose the permit in the next one of the 29 open cities and start again.

Some unscrupulous people have even tried altering the contents of the travel permit. In the days of Lhasa travel one guy did this, got to Lhasa, and was last heard of being chased around the mountains of upper Sichuan by a posse of angry PSB men. The way *not* to do things is to alter the permit – PSB is not stupid and they can easily spot mistakes and alterations particularly since the document is in their own language. Remember also that as things stand now the Public Security police are quite amiable towards foreigners and the best thing to do is *keep them this way*. If you cheat your way through, or insist on hassling endlessly for permits and visa extensions, you'll stuff things up for future travellers and maybe even for individual travel in China!

If you manage to get a permit for an unusual destination then the best strategy is to get to that destination as fast as possible (by plane if possible). Remember, other PSBs do not have to honour the permit and can cancel it and send you back. Take your time getting back from that strange destination – you're hardly likely to be hassled if you're on your way back to civilisation.

Transit points to destinations usually don't require a permit, and you can stay the night, so long as you have the destination on the permit – though if a trip is going to take three days PSB may refuse you permission. Railway stations seem to be open just about anywhere – so long as you don't venture out into the closed town (people travelling by rail from Guilin to Chongqing used to get incarcerated in Guiyang railway station while they waited for their connecting train – Guiyang is now open though).

**Visa Extensions** are an additional stamp in your passport and the local Public Security Offices are responsible for issuing them. Visa extensions cost Y5 and the standard rule now is that you're entitled to one extension of one month's duration – for more details, see the section on Visas.

**Other Bits of Paper** Given the Chinese preoccupation with impressive bits of paper it's worth carrying around a few business cards, student cards and anything else that's printed and wrapped in a plastic envelope. These sort of additional ID are useful for leaving with bicycle-renters who often want a deposit or some sort of security for their bikes – sometimes they ask you to leave your passport but you should insist on leaving another piece of ID or perhaps a deposit. Most hotels also require you to hand in your passport but will sometimes accept the Alien's Travel Permit as security – or if you prefer, offer to pay in advance.

It's also worth hanging onto cheap room or dormitory hotel receipts – the fact that you've been allowed to stay cheaply at some other hotel will weigh in your favour at the next place you're trying to get cheap accommodation. Likewise, hang on to any Chinese-price tickets you happen to buy.

Officially, the only foreigners who qualify for student discounts in China are those studying in China or in Taiwan. They have their own ID cards. Some travellers have got student discount using driver's licences, youth hostel cards, international student cards, forgeries, made-in-Hong Kong imitations, and the like – but be warned that more and more places in China are catching on.

## HEALTH
### Vaccinations

Vaccinations against cholera are required if you arrive within five days of leaving an infected area. Yellow Fever vaccinations are required if you're arriving within six days of leaving an infected area. If you're coming from a 'clean' area then inoculations against cholera, yellow fever, typhoid and smallpox are not necessary.

### Malaria

Malaria is spread by mosquitos which transmit the parasite that causes the disease when the mosquito bites you. The disease has a nasty habit of recurring in later years, even if you're cured at the time – and it can be fatal.

Malaria is a risk in the southern and south-eastern provinces of China, almost as far north as Beijing. Beijing itself and the provinces of Heilongjiang, Jilin, Inner Mongolia, Gansu, Xingjiang, Shanxi, Ningxia, and Qinghai are considered to be free of malaria. Tibet is also considered free of malaria, except along the Zangbo River Valley in the extreme south-east. North of the 33°N latitude malarial transmission occurs from July to November. Between 33°N and 25°N it's between May and December, and south of 25°N transmission occurs the year round.

You can't be inoculated against malaria but protection is simple; either a daily or weekly tablet depending on which your doctor recommends. The tablets kill the parasites if they get into your bloodstream. You usually have to start taking the tablets about two weeks before entering the malarial zone and continue taking them for several weeks after you've left it. Resistance to two types of anti-malarial tablets, chloroquine and fansidar, has been reported in China. There is little information on the extent of the resistance, but Guangdong (including Hainan Island), Guangxi and Yunnan Provinces have been reported as chloroquine-resistant areas.

Another precaution is to avoid being bitten in the first place; a lot of Chinese

hotels have mosquito-nets. Mosquito repellent is available but you may have trouble finding it, so bring your own. Mosquito coils are readily available.

### Hepatitis

If any serious disease is likely to become an affliction of travellers to China, then it will probably be infectious hepatitis (there are several varieties of hepatitis, of differing severity, but infectious hepatitis is the one you're most likely to pick up).

Hepatitis is a disease of the liver, which occurs in countries with poor sanitation – of which China is definitely one. It's spread from person to person via infected food or water, or contaminated cooking and eating utensils. Salads which have been washed in infected water or fruit which has been handled by an infected person might carry the disease.

Symptoms appear 15 to 50 days after infection (generally around 25 days) and consist of fever, loss of appetite, nausea, depression, complete lack of energy, and pains around the bottom of your rib cage (the location of the liver). Your skin turns progressively yellow and the whites of your eyes yellow to orange. The best way to detect it is to keep watch on your eyes and also on your urine, which will turn a deep orange no matter how much liquid you drink – but if you haven't drunk much liquid and/or you're sweating a lot, don't jump to conclusions!

The severity of the disease varies; it may last less than two weeks and give you only a few bad days. Or it may last for several months and give you a few bad weeks. You could feel depleted of energy for several months after.

The usual protection against hepatitis is a gamma-globulin injection but the effectiveness is debatable – improved shots may provide protection for as much as six months, but some say it's not worth it at all.

The only way to guard against hepatitis is to avoid eating contaminated food or drinking contaminated water. It's easy to

Top: Typical market scene [AS]
Left: Cricket cages, Lanzhou [AS]
Right: Chestnut roaster, outside Beijing [MB]

Top: Healthy body, healthy mind [MB]
Left: China succumbs to western influences [AS]
Right: Beijing acrobats putting their heads together [MB]

get paranoid about where to eat – most Chinese restaurants are incredibly scungy places though the food itself usually looks OK – it's probably more a problem of who's been handling it. Using eating utensils that other people have been using can be a source of infection – particularly wooden chopsticks with their cracked ends and accumulated dirt. There are lots of water-coolers on the streets selling glasses of cold drink – but then you don't know who was drinking out of the glass immediately before you.

If you get hepatitis, then rest and good food are the only cures; don't use alcohol or tobacco since that only gives your liver more work to do. In China, that's easier said than done; unlike India and South-East Asia there are very few places you can go which are cheap enough to hole up in for a long convalescence. You could sit it out in hotel dormitories but you're only going to risk infecting the people around you – and if you're constantly surrounded by people, you probably won't get any rest anyway. On top of that, good food is hard to come by in China.

## Tetanus

Due to a bacillus which usually enters the blood system through a cut, or as the result of a skin puncture by a rusty nail, wire, etc. It is marked by sever and painful muscle cramps. It is worth being vaccinated against since there is more risk in warm climates as cuts take longer to heal. You have to have two shots, several weeks apart. Protection is variable, but it usually lasts about two years.

## Diarrhoea

Diarrhoea (the 'Hong Kong dog') is often due simply to a change of diet or because your digestive system is unused to spicey or oily food (both a feature of Chinese cooking). A lot depends on what you're used to eating and whether or not you've got an iron-gut. If you do get diarrhoea, then the first thing to do is nothing – it rarely lasts more than a few days. If it

persists then the usual treatment is Lomotil tablets – in the west it's a prescription drug, so ask your doctor for a supply. If the condition persists for a week or more, it's probably not simple travellers' diarrhoea and you should see a doctor.

If you get a severe bout of diarrhoea, you'll get dehydrated – keep up your fluid intake as well as your salt intake.

## Drinking Water

Getting sick from drinking the water is less of a problem in China than it is in other Asian countries. Even the cheap hotels have thermoses of boiled water in their rooms and dormitories. It's worth carrying a water-bottle with you and refilling it in the hotels. The trains also have boilers on them for the passenger's use.

If you don't have any boiled water with you then you could use water purification tablets. If you don't have either, you have to consider the risks of drinking unboiled water against the risks of dehydrating – the first is possible, the second is definite. In China you shouldn't really have any problems, unless you get to isolated areas or if you manage to stay in villages. You could use water-purifying tablets, but remember that many of these are not safe for prolonged use.

## Other

The climate of China is going to be one of the biggest strains on your health. Winter in the south is not only cold, it is *miserably wet.* Everyone is coughing and spluttering and you'll inevitably come down with the same. If you're travelling in winter than it's wise to bring something to relieve the symptoms of flu and colds – respiratory ailments are prevalent in China and shouldn't be taken lightly.

Summer is another problem. The north and north-west are incredibly dry and hot. It's easy to dehydrate if you don't keep up your fluid intake – which is why it's a good idea to carry a water-bottle with you. You are dehydrating if you find you are urinating infrequently or if your urine turns a deep yellow or orange; you may also find yourself getting headaches. The sun is bright and good sunglasses are a must. Sunburn is also a problem. Bring something to cover your head – cheap, wide-brimmed straw hats are readily available in China.

You sweat just as much in hot, dry climates as you do in hot, humid climates. In dry climates your sweat evaporates. In humid climates your sweat can't evaporate because the air itself is already moist, so you become bathed in sweat.

Summer in the south is hot and humid and the sweat stays on you. Prickly heat becomes a common problem with people from temperate climates. Small red blisters appear on the skin where the sweat glands have been blocked. Sogginess of the skin is the prime factor at the start of this condition, and this is caused by the inability of the sweat to evaporate because the atmosphere is already saturated, or because you're wearing clothes which prevent the sweat either evaporating or being absorbed. To prevent (or cure it), wear clothes which are light and leave an air space between the material and the skin; stop wearing synthetic clothing like nylon since it can't absorb the sweat; dry well after bathing and use calamine lotion or a zinc-oxide based talcum powder. Anything that makes you sweat more – exercise, tea, coffee, alcohol – only makes the condition worse.

If you're sweating profusely, you're going to lose a lot of salt – that leads to fatigue and muscle cramps – make it up by putting extra salt in your food (a teaspoon a day is enough), but don't increase your salt intake unless you also increase your water intake.

Tibet deserves special mention; you probably won't get there, but if you do you had best be prepared for a couple of problems stemming from the high altitudes and thin air. Winter at high altitudes can be endless days and nights of incredibly piercing, dry cold that seems impossible to keep out. Summers are warm and dry, but because of the thin air the rays of the sun are much more penetrating and it's easy to get sunburnt. By the same token, a cloud across the sun will cause the temperature to drop suddenly and dramatically and you'll always have to carry a jacket with you. Altitude sickness is the other problem. Rapid ascent from low altitudes, overexertion, obesity, lack of physical fitness, dehydration, fatigue, advanced age or sickness, can bring on symptoms which include headache, dizziness, lack of appetite, nausea and vomiting. (Breathlessness and a pounding heart are normal at these altitudes and are *not* part of altitude sickness; your body will eventually start making more blood cells to carry extra oxygen). If you get altitude sickness, the best cure is to go to a lower altitude. A pain-killer for headache and an anti-emetic for vomiting will also help.

Milk, yoghurt and cheese are rarely available in China, which means you get no calcium. Canned and bottled fruit is readily available all over China but fresh fruit is of extremely poor quality except along the south-east coast. Vitamin C tablets are worth considering if you're going to be in the country for any length of time. Multi-vitamin tablets are also worth taking.

Some travellers have reported getting sick on the boxed meals served on the trains. One westerner contracted encephalitis in Dalian and was in hospital for a month.

## Medical Clinics and Hospitals

Don't get too concerned about your health in China; by taking tablets you can generally avoid malaria (remember that some resistance has been reported) and by eating sensibly you can greatly reduce your chances of contracting hepatitis and diarrhoea. Tour groups probably have a higher frequency of sickness as their members are invariably elderly and find it difficult to cope with the long days and jam-packed schedules.

If you get seriously sick in China then you have a certain advantage doing it here than in other Asian countries; a sick and dying foreigner is *not* something the Chinese want to have on their hands. You'll get medical attention – the quality of which may be dubious, but you won't be left to rot. If you've got something that looks like it's going to get worse they'll probably pack you off to Hong Kong just so it doesn't get worse in China.

In Beijing, Canton and Shanghai there are medical clinics set aside to treat foreigners, and in some of the provincial towns there are clinics in the tourist hotels. In the three main cities, these clinics are at: Capital Hospital Clinic for Foreigners, Dongdan Beilu, Beijing (tel 55-3731); Shanghai No 1 Hospital, 190 Suzhou Beilu, Shanghai (tel 24-0100); Canton No 1 Hospital, Renmin Beilu, Canton (tel 33-090).

An unusual medical problem occurred when a fellow-traveller had piping hot tea spilled over him, burning the skin off the top of his foot. Back in town a doctor pierced the blisters with the locals crowding into the room to watch. The hospital looked pretty dirty. Doctors fees were Y6, including penicillan (penicillan is the mainstay of Chinese antibiotics) and the foot healed up eventually.

### Medical Supplies
If you really need something, take it with you. There are lots of well-stocked pharmacies in China, supplying both western and Chinese medicines. *But you shouldn't count on getting what you want; if you really need something then bring it with you.* The other problem with buying medicines in China is that the labels are in Chinese and you may have trouble figuring out the appropriate dose.

### Blood Supplies
If you're RH-negative, try not to bleed in China. The Chinese do not have RH-

negative blood and their blood banks don't store it. Type O blood is also rare. If you're a Type O RH-negative, then you're in worse luck since you can only accept a transfusion of the same and nothing else – and there aren't very many of us around.

### WHAT TO TAKE AND HOW TO TAKE IT
The usual travellers' rule applies; bring as little as possible. It is much better to have to get something you've left behind than to have to throw things away because you've got too much to carry. If you have to get something, go to the department stores – there are large, well-stocked stores in almost every town in China. Some people have all sorts of strange and wise ideas about what to take to China – perhaps a collapsible chair for when you're stuck for a seat on a crowded train?

**Carrying bags** For budget travellers the backpack is still the best carrying container. Adding some thief-deterrent (and there are thieves in China as anywhere else) by sewing on a few tabs so you can shut your pack with a padlock is a good idea. On the other hand, packs can be cumbersome and difficult to get on crowded buses and trains. You should also remember that the opportunities for camping and hiking in China are limited in the extreme, so unless you're absolutely determined a large pack with a frame is unnecessary. A soft pack, with no frame or with a semi-rigid frame, is much better all round.

A large soft zip-bag with a wide shoulder strap is less prone to damage and a bit more thief-proof. Shoulder bags are easier to wield on crowded buses and trains, but they're hard to carry for any distance – so if you've got any walking to do you're better off with a pack. Whatever you bring, try and make it small; long distance buses have very little space to stow baggage and city buses are so crowded that a large bag or pack will be unpleasant to lug around.

A small day-pack is useful; you can

dump your main luggage in a hotel or the left-luggage room at the train station and head off for a few days. It's good for hiking and for carrying extra food on long train rides.

**Clothes** If you're travelling in the north of China at the height of winter, prepare yourself for the most incredible cold. Good down jackets, woollens, fur-lined boots, gloves and cap are what you need in this sort of weather. You can buy down jackets in a few of the big cities, but not in large sizes and the supply is limited; they cost around Y35 to Y40. Alternatively, you can buy one of the huge padded jackets which the Chinese wear – very functional. Warm fur-lined hats with ear-covers that make you look like Snoopy are sold in many department stores, but fur-lined gloves and boots seem to be unavailable. You shouldn't need a sleeping bag since sheets and blankets are provided in even the hard-sleeper carriages of the trains, and the hotels always provide warm bedding. Taking a collapsible umbrella with you is a *good* idea; plastic raincoats can be bought in China.

Jackets with silk wadding will be more than sufficient to guard against the cold, but *not* the wind or rain. A silk T shirt or other silkwear will also give good insulation. Silk is light and will pack small, and absorbs 30% of its weight in moisture and still feels dry.

In summer, the lightest of clothes will do for daytime wear; T-shirts, sandals and shorts. But remember, if you go up into the hills it can still get very cold, and it can get cold travelling on the trains at night. Wandering out of the summer heat into an air-con hotel room is a good way to catch a chill if you don't have some trousers and a jacket to put on. Remember also that there is wide variation in weather conditions across the country and that the weather can be very fickle.

Generally speaking the usual standards of Asian decorum apply, and while shorts are less acceptable for women plenty of Chinese girls wear them and you shouldn't get any unpleasant reactions. Skirts and dresses are frequently worn in places like Beijing, Shanghai and Canton where the Chinese women are more fashion conscious, but wearing any dress of a revealing nature is considered risque. Chinese women as a rule don't wear makeup, but mild use of makeup and jewellery is acceptable for foreigners. If you want to blend in then conservative dress and darker colours, blues, greens and khakis, are advised. The Chinese place little importance on what foreigners wear, as long as they remain within an acceptable level of modesty; casual clothes are always acceptable.

Functional, though baggy clothes are readily available from the department stores, small shops and street markets. Apart from the usual blue garb, there are lots of surplus Army uniforms. The main problem with buying clothes in China, particularly shoes, is that big sizes are hard to come by. Shirts are the usual Asian long-short sleeves and extended body so that they hang out over your baggy trousers. There's a great variety of shoes available; gym boots, sneakers, lace-ups, high-heels, sandals and plastic boots. In Hong Kong you can buy large size running shoes from 'Marathon Sports', at Shop 6, Ambassador Hotel, Kowloon (tel 3-674666).

Absolutely essential is a good pair of sunglasses, particularly in the Xinjiang desert or the high altitudes of Tibet where the sunlight can be extraordinarily bright. In summer the Chinese sun can be fierce. Good, wide rimmed straw hats are very cheap and are sold everywhere in China, so there is no problem getting one if you haven't brought one with you.

Sewing a map pocket to the inside of your jacket is useful – you collect a lot of maps in China and it's an idea to have something handy to hold them in. If it's hot, then perhaps a pocket sewn inside a vest.

**Medicines and toiletries** There are lots of well-stocked pharmacies in China, selling both western and Chinese medicines, but if you really need something you'd be better off bringing it with you. One of the problems of buying medicines in China is that the labels on the bottles are in Chinese and you may have trouble figuring out what the right dose is.

Aspirin, medicine for diarrhoea and medicine for relief of cold symptoms are recommended, and you should definitely take with you any prescription medicines you may need. Given the lack of fresh fruit in the country you would be wise to take some Vitamin C tablets if you're going to be there for any length of time. Multi-vitamin tablets are also worth considering.

It seems that tampons (Tampex) are available in China but the supply could be limited, so you would be wise to stock up in Hong Kong. Sanitary napkins are available but they're somewhat similar to the medieval concept of the chastity belt. The large tissues used to line this contraption, however, are useful since they're softer than local brands of toilet paper and cheaper; they can be found, after a search, in local dry-goods stores. Any medicines you use for menstrual cramp should be brought with you.

Shampoo, razor blades and make-up are available in China but are inferior to western brands. Suntan lotion is not available and you should bring sunburn cream with you. Toilet paper is sold at the department stores and some of the smaller shops.

Mosquito coils are readily available and it seems the Chinese use a rub-on mosquito repellent, a camphor or menthol-based lotion that goes under the name *Shui Cho Yeow* – but it will save you time hunting around if you bring your own.

**Food** Chinese tea is sold everywhere. Indian tea is unavailable and coffee can only be bought in a few large cities, so if you cannot do without, bring your own. If you're into endless cups of Chinese tea, a mug and a teaspoon is useful for those long train trips where there's a continuous supply of hot water.

**Cigarettes and Alcohol** Locally-made cigarettes, beer and spirits are sold everywhere. Cigarettes have the gentle eastern aroma of old socks, but Chinese beer is consistently excellent – with only a few exceptions to the rule.

Foreign-made cigarettes and alcohol are available from the shops in the big tourist hotels and from the Friendship Stores. To give you some idea of what you'll be paying, the Friendship Store in Hangzhou sells Johnny Walker Black Label for Y35 and Red Label for Y21, Boodles British Gin for Y18, Chivas Regal Y46, Captain Morgan Rum Y18, and Napoleon Augier Cognac Y46. The Beijing Hotel even sells bottles of Manischewitz for just Y12 for when that Jewish holiday sneaks up on you . . . For packs of 100 cigarettes, the Hangzhou Friendship Store sells Marlboro for Y18, State Express 555's for Y18, Camel Y17, Kent Deluxe Y18 and Dunhill Y18.

**Books** If you want to read, bring your own books. American and British paperbacks are available from the bookshops in the tourist hotels in the big Chinese cities, but the supply and range is extremely limited. Foreign Language Bookshops cater for Chinese learning foreign languages, not for western reading interests. For info about foreign newspapers and journals available in China, see the section on Media.

**Films, Camera and Electronics** Agfa, Kodak, Fuji and Polaroid film is available in China from the Friendship Stores and tourist hotels, but it's usually about 50% more expensive than in Hong Kong. And you can't rely on being able to get what you want when you want it – some places are better stocked than others and offer a wider range of film types. For details of film and camera equipment available in

China, see the section on Photography. Some people bring a Walkman with them, though keeping the power supply up is a problem since Chinese alkaline batteries are not too reliable. Alternatively you could just bring a stock of cassette tapes; quite a few hotel dining rooms and hotel bars have three-in-one cassette players, and I'm sure if you asked you could play your tapes as you ate. Transistor radios will pick up music from local stations. A compact shortwave reciever is easy to carry and will let you get news from the outside world – again, the problem of batteries.

**Gifts** If you must give the Chinese something then give them an English book; if you have to teach them something then teach them English. It's the one element of western culture that's universally desired. Other than that stick to simple things; stamps make good gifts. Chinese are avid stamp-collectors, congregating outside the philatelic sections of the post offices and dealing on the footpath. A few stamps to give away will help you make friends. They seem to go for readily recognisable subject matter like people and scenery rather than abstract designs. Pictures of you and your family are very popular gifts with the Chinese. Don't – as some people have done – insult them by trying to give away your old jacket; don't turn every kid on the block into a scrounger and a beggar by indiscriminately giving away stamps, pens and coins; don't give away Walkmans, radios and the like unless you really have made a close friend – apart from the fact that these are listed on your Customs Declaration form and you'll have to show them to Customs when you leave, you'll only help advance the cargo cult to China.

**PHOTOGRAPHY**

**Film** Film can be bought at the major tourist hotels and Friendship Stores in the major tourist cities. The range is rarely complete and depending on where you are you may not be able to get the film type or speed you need. As an example of prices and what's available, the Hangzhou Friendship Store was selling the following varieties:

| | |
|---|---|
| Kodacolor II, C135-36 (prints) | Y6.40 |
| Kodacolor II, 110-24 (prints) | Y4.70 |
| Kodacolor II, C120 (prints) | Y3.90 |
| Kodak Ektachrome 64, ER135-36 | Y9.70 |
| Fujicolor F-II, CN110-24 (prints) | Y4.00 |

One of the most commonly used films which is not widely sold in China is Kodachrome 64 KR135-36P film for colour slides. It *is* sold at the Beijing Hotel for Y18.80 (includes processing) and also at the Friendship Store in Xian and you should be able to get it in Shanghai, Canton and Chengdu – but it's surprisingly uncommon. In Hong Kong, you can pick up rolls of 36 exposures for around HK$45 (including processing) which is about 40% less than the price in China. Film will inevitably be cheaper in Hong Kong than in China and you should stock up there. Prices vary slightly from place to place in China, presumably due to transportation expenses. Black & white film is not well stocked as tourists are expected to need colour film. Officially, you're allowed to bring in 72 rolls of film – which is a lot – but it's amazing how fast you can whip through the stuff.

**Polaroid Film** We all know the amazing effects of polaroid photography on the natives – so you can easily set yourself up in the magic business in China. At the Hangzhou Friendship Store, the following Polaroid film was available:

| | |
|---|---|
| Polaroid 600 High-speed Colour Land Film (10 photos) | Y16.00 |
| Polaroid Type 88 (8 photos) | Y12.40 |
| Polaroid Polacolor 2 Land Pak Film Type 668 (8 photos) | Y15.80 |

**Movie Film** 8 mm cameras are permitted into China; 16 mm or professional equipment is not permitted without the

Kafkaesque red tape. The Beijing Hotel in Beijing has the following types of 8 mm movie film:

Ektachrome 40, Super 8 colour – Y11.20 15 m ELA 464.
Ektachrome 160 Type A colour – Y12.90 15 m ELA 464.
Kodachrome 40 sound colour, Y21.30 Type A Super 8 – 15 m KMA 594P

**Video Cameras** There don't seem to be any firm regulations on video cameras at the moment. One traveller got his equipment held for two weeks by Shanghai customs before he could reclaim it. Another foreigner working in northern China was permitted to bring in video equipment with no problems. The biggest problem of course is the power source and recharging your batteries off the strange mutations of plugs and voltages in China!

**Film Processing** You can get your film processed in 24 hours in some of the major tourist cities, like Beijing, Shanghai, Canton, Guilin – usually through the major tourist hotels. Colour prints (around 9 cm by 12 cm) cost around Y0.55 to Y1.10 each – they make ideal gifts for Chinese friends. Kodachrome film cannot be processed in China nor in Hong Kong – the closest countries which process them are Japan and Australia. Undeveloped film can be sent out of China – but there are always those dreadful airport X-ray machines lurking in the background to worry about – if you're going to post film you might consider stocking up on valium as well. If you're getting film processed in China you should also remember that pictures of 'controversial' subjects may get 'lost'.

**Technical Problems** Dim interiors, lit by 40-watt bulbs or low-voltage fluorescent. Camera batteries are unavailable except in places like Shanghai, and even then they can be unreliable. You should also be wary of X-rays at airports, which may fog your film. Dust is a major hazard, take your own cleaning devices along. Polarising filters are useful, and in places like Xinjiang a UV filter is good for reducing the haze. Photography from moving trains doesn't work unless you have high-speed film; if you have low-speed film then train-window shots tend to get blurred.

**Prohibited Subjects** Photography from planes, photographs of airports, of military installations, harbour facilities and railroad terminals are prohibited – bridges may also be a touchy subject. These rules do get enforced if the people to enforce them happen to be around; one traveller, bored at the airport, started photographing the X-ray procedure in clearance. PLA men promptly pounced on her and ripped the film out. A foreign journalist had all his film and camera equipment confiscated – he wasn't sure why, but perhaps he was close to a military installation without knowing it. In an age where satellites can zoom down on a number plate it all seems a bit ridiculous, but there you have it – most countries have these sorts of restrictions on photography.

Taking photos is not permitted in many temples and museums and archaeological sites – this is mainly to protect the postcard and slide industry. It also prevents westerners publishing their own books about these sites and taking business away from the Chinese-published books. It also prevents valuable works of art being damaged by countless flash-photos – but in most cases you're not even allowed to take harmless time-exposures. Beware that these rules *are* generally enforced – if you want to snap a few photos of these places then start with a new roll of film – if that's ripped out of your camera at least you don't lose 20 other photos as well. A few places where photos are forbidden are the terracotta soldiers at Xian, the Dunhuang Cave Temples, the Bilingisi caves near Lanzhou, and the Lama Temple in Beijing (In the Lama

Temple in Beijing I couldn't resist one quick shot – I quickly aimed the camera, but faster than me was an agile monk who bounded across the courtyard and snapped a hand right over the lens – scared the daylights out of me. He must have had some special camera martial arts training).

**People Photos** In China you'll get a fantastic run for your money; for starters there are one billion portraits to work your way through. Religious reasons for avoiding photographs are absent amongst the Han Chinese – for instance, some guy isn't going to stick a spear through you for taking a picture of his wife and stealing part of her soul – though the taboo may apply to some of the minority groups, and you probably won't be allowed to take photos of idols in Buddhist temples. Some Chinese shy away from having their photo taken, even duck for cover; others are proud to and will ham it up for the camera – and they're especially proud if you're taking a shot of their kid. Nobody expects any payment for photos – so don't give any or you'll set a precedent. What the Chinese would go for though is a copy of a colour photo, which you could mail to them – black and white photography is a big thing in China but colour photos are a rarity. The Chinese also have the idea that the negative belongs to the subject as well, and they'll ask for both the negative and the print – but through the post there's no arguments.

There are three basic approaches to photographing people; one is the polite ask for permission and pose it shot (which is often rejected); another is the no-holds-barred and upset everyone approach; the other is surreptitious, standing half a kilometre away with a metre long telephoto lens. Many Chinese will disagree with you on what constitutes good subject matter; they don't really see why anyone would want to take a street-scene, a picture of a beggar or an old man's bald head. Another barrier often brought up is

that the subject is not 'dignified' – be it a laborer straining down the street with a massive load on his hand-cart, or a barrel of excrement on wheels – it seems a bit absurd in an age where the poor peasant and worker is glorified on huge billboards, but you'd have a tough time informing your subject of this. During the Beijing winter I spotted a bicycle-hauler with a load of charcoal bricks headed my way – grimy face looking like something out of the Industrial Revolution – when I went click the man shielded his face. My companion spoke Chinese and the coal-hauler said 'come back when I've got my suit on'. Taking this as an invitation to try again (hmmh?) I raised the camera – and the coal hauler reached for a brick. End of photo session!

**Chinese Photography** Shutterbugs abound in the PRC these days, although a good-quality camera is still the mark of a cadre. The common Chinese camera harks back to the age of the Box Brownie, or bellows-type twin-lens Rolleiflex with a top speed of 1/300th of a second using 120-size film. Top of the line is the Seagull Goeland DF, an SLR which sells for around Y500 – it's a chunky looking camera that does what most Japanese cameras can do. There is Seagull brand black and white film to go with it. Japanese cameras are sold in some photographic stores in China, but they're prohibitively expensive which explains why you have to record your own camera on your customs declaration form – ensures you don't sell it.

A lot of Chinese cannot afford a camera in the first place and they resort to photographers who have set themselves up in business at key tourist places. The photo-men also supply dress-up clothing for that extra touch – Chinese change from street clothing into spiffy gear for the shot. Others have cardboard cut-outs as props, an opera star or a boat perhaps. In Beijing one prop is a *real* car (after all, your average Chinese has about as much hope of riding in a car as you've got of hitching on the space shuttle). Some of the photo merchants hand-tint the black and white results; one of the stranger sights is the customer riding home on his bicycle with a roll of negatives flapping from the handle-bars – a unique method of drying the results. (The tourist areas abound with places which develop black & white film in a few hours).

Heroic statues or important vintages of calligraphy are considered suitable back-grounds for a shot – in fact the Chinese will pose in front of just about anything that can vaguely rate as a 'sight' – and the pose is usually stiff. If you hang around these places you can clip off some portrait shots for yourself – people expect photos to be taken and are more at ease with the cameras. The important thing for them is not the composition but what's in the photo – a photo is a precious thing and not to be wasted on a street-scene – so Chinese photography is an endless succession of people shots in front of identifiable sights, such as the Mao portrait on the Gate of Heavenly Peace in Beijing. They'll sometimes even drag you into the photo as an exotic backdrop.

Use of colour film is a rarity in China – simply too expensive (in some cities Japanese Sakura colour film is available to the locals – with developing it costs about Y15 which is a massive slice of the wages. The same film in a Friendship Store costs Y9 with developing, payable in FECs). There are numerous colour portrait studios in China – those along Nanjing Road in Shanghai seem to do a job comparable to the west.

## THEFT AND OTHER CRIMES

Like anywhere else in the world, there is crime in China. At best, it is unlikely that it will affect you – it's certainly safer travelling through China than it is through other countries, and you're also less likely to have stuff stolen. Don't worry too much about personal obliteration at the hands of a marauding gang – but don't be oblivious to the possibility of theft.

Hotels are usually safe places to leave your stuff; each floor has an attendant whose job it is to keep watch over who goes in and out of the hotel; if anything does go missing from your room then they're going to be obvious suspects since they've got keys to the rooms. But don't expect them to watch over your room like a hawk – they don't. Dormitories could be a problem; some hotels have large storage rooms where you check your bags in (they insist that you do). Some have left-luggage rooms where you can leave your bag if you want to. In other hotels you may have to leave your stuff in the dorm which is sometimes locked so that all and sundry don't go wandering in and out. The dormitory at the Pujiang Hotel in Shanghai even has little lockers you can keep your valuables in. Unfortunately, your fellow travellers can be a problem – there are a few around who make the money go further by helping themselves to other people's. So far only a few creeps seem to have made it to China.

If you get your passport stolen it's a long trip to Beijing to get a replacement (if you're American there are consulates in Canton and Shanghai which should help you, and if you're French there is a consulate in Shanghai). Stolen traveller's cheques can be replaced, but again the company will probably have its office in Beijing. Don't leave your valuables (passport, traveller's cheques, money, health certificates, air tickets) lying around in dormitories. A money-belt is the safest way to carry those things, particularly when travelling on the buses and trains. If you lose your money-belt, then one precaution would be to leave a small stash of money (say US$50) in your hotel room, with a record of the traveller's cheque serial numbers and your passport number, you'll need the money if you've got a long trip to a replacement office. And remember, something may be of little or no value to the thief, but to lose it would be a real heartbreak to you – like film. Another thing worth making a copy of before you leave home is your address book.

Again, don't get paranoid in China – but also remember that people *have* been ripped off there. If you wander off from your pack in a crowded railway station (as one person seems to have done in Canton), don't expect to find it when you come back. The Chinese don't trust each other and there's no reason you should trust them; the Chinese run around with rings full of keys as if they were in a gaol – *everything* is scrupulously locked; the walls of buildings have jagged glass concreted to the top and iron bars are fitted on first floor windows. It seems to be safe enough to leave your bags on the racks of the trains (at least in hard-sleeper class) and go to sleep or wander off – but it's been noted in trains that the Chinese secure their own bags to the racks with bicycle chains . . .

A couple of theft stories: one traveller in Beijing had the whole kaboodle (passport, money, documents) ripped off him in a crowded bus – he was asking for it, wearing his money belt on the outside! He lost US$2000 and it took two weeks to get the rest back. One couple in Xian had the entire works stolen overnight from their locked hotel room – apparently the thief came through the window and ran off with two cameras, a wad of lenses, cheques, watches and luggage. Rip-offs have also occurred in Guilin and Leshan, but these are probably related to the Chinese hotels. Another traveller had two attempts made on his pockets on the one bus – the first by a child judging from the size of the hand intercepted, and the second from a 'friendly drunk'. I was almost pick-pocketed on a Shanghai bus on my first trip to China in 1981 – I reached down and found a hand in my pocket, ripped the hand out and flung it away. There's no way you'll get your message across to the other passengers on the bus though.

To date I haven't heard of any assaults on foreigners. While I was in China there was mention of western girls being harassed by Chinese men in Beijing's parks, and there are stories of lone western female cyclists being harassed while riding at night. A level of prudence is worth keeping, but the paranoia that may be justified in other countries is inappropriate in China.

As to more serious crime in China – that is anyone's guess. The Chinese don't release statistics on how many rapists, murderers and muggers roam the streets committing their heinous offences. There is nothing on official corruption or white-collar crime, although the Chinese newspapers constantly report arrests and even the occasional execution of frauds and embezzlers.

Justice in China seems to be dispensed entirely by the police who also decide the penalty. The standard manner of execution is to be shot in the back of the head, often at a mass gathering in some sports stadium – a punishment usually reserved for deserving rapists and murderers. Afterwards your mugshot and maybe even a photo of your extinguished body gets plugged up on a public notice-board; a common sight in southern China, although less so in the north. A couple of years ago a tour group arriving in Xian were 'lucky' enough to witness one such event as they stepped out of the railway station. A protracted and embarrassed silence ensued! A public execution had just taken place and the dead bodies, with bullet holes in the backs of their necks, were lying on the pavement outside the station, surrounded by a large crowd. The police quickly dragged the corpses out of sight.

On the other hand, an executed body has little chance of performing any useful work. If your crime is a little less serious, you may be given a chance to visit the prison camps in Qinghai Province and be 'reformed through labour' for the next few years – and perhaps even have the opportunity to die here.

The Chinese don't want tourists running amok in Qinghai since the province is the centre of the labour camp system, a sort of Chinese Siberia. Over the years, the inmates have included Kuomintang police and army officers rounded up after the Communists came to power in 1949, common criminals, 'rightists' who were arrested in 1957-58 when the Hundred Flowers got their blooms amputated, Overseas Chinese who patriotically returned to China and were then arrested as spies, and now 'leftists' who have been convicted of 'counter-revolutionary crimes' because of their activities 'during the Cultural Revolution. Other travelling possibilities include being sent to join landscape gardeners in China's frontier regions, building roads and railways, clearing forests, filling in swamps, and planting virgin fields.

There is definitely no shortage of bullets in China; the executions continue unabated, and more people are being sent to the labour camps. The most recent crime purge began in the middle of 1983 with two waves of arrests, one beginning on 8 August and another on 17 September. In a single day 61 men were shot after a mass rally beside the Yangtse River in the city of Chongqing, and there were reports of more than 300 people being shot in the space of one month in more than 25 cities in southern and eastern China. The government seemed to be intent on rounding up about 100,000 suspected criminals and executing as many as 5000 of them. Thirty people were shot after a big rally in the Beijing Worker's stadium on 23 August, bringing the total of executions in Beijing up to 80. Another 94 were shot in Guiyang.

## PLACES TO STAY

One of the reasons tourism has suddenly expanded in China is because the Chinese need the foreign exchange, and tourists are a convenient source. Hotel prices are steadily rising towards what you'd pay for a similar standard of accommodation in the west; there aren't too many bargains around, but at present the room prices in

many of the middle range hotels still compare very favourably against prices in the west. By the same token you may find that too often you pay too much for too little.

The hotels themselves deserve a separate chapter; they're tourist attractions in themselves and a visit to China is memorable for the places you stayed in, would have liked to stay in or would have preferred not have stayed in. The enormous, rambling hotels in the major cities are like mini-states; they have post offices, banks, restaurants, art and craft shops, beauty parlours, taxi services, travel agents . . . the Dong Fang Hotel in Canton is so big that the top floor suites have their own gardens. The Jianguo Hotel in Beijing is the height of western decadence with ultra-suede walls, computerised cash registers, glass ceilings and staff that have been trained not to bite tourists. There are plans afoot to dispense bits of the west out of this bizarre landmark of opulence via a kiosk which will sell hotdogs, hamburgers and doughnuts. The Jingling in Nanjing is spectacular; a gleaming white, 36-storey tower with a revolving restaurant on top, and, so I'm told, its own helipad!

These hotels are still the exception in China, but their number is steadily increasing. And they are an indication that the Chinese are learning that they must provide value for money if they are to attract more tourists to the country.

You'll often find yourself staying in gigantic Soviet-built mammoths, constructed to house the Russian technicians and experts who came to China in the 1950s. Then there are a number of European and British-built hotels, mainly in the coastal cities and a few of the inland river cities which were once foreign concessions. These often have that 'run down' look about them; as you get further and further off the main tourist track the quality of the accommodation steadily decreases, but then so do the prices.

**Segregation** Hotels in China are split basically into three categories. First there are the tourist hotels where westerners are expected and generally do end up staying. These hotels also accommodate Hong Kong and Macau and Overseas Chinese. Secondly, there are hotels which only accommodate Hong Kong and Macau and Overseas Chinese and exclude the westerners. Thirdly, there are the innumerable hotels and guest houses which cater solely for citizens of the People's Republic.

Segregation is not strictly applied, and depends on where you are. In a small more obscure town, such as Quanzhou in Fujian Province, there may only be one or two good standard hotels, so westerners, Hong Kongers and high-ranking Chinese all get thrown into the same bag.

At the other end of the price scale, it *is* possible for westerners to stay in Chinese hotels. Again, it depends where you are. If you're out in the sticks there might be nowhere else to stay; if you land in Canton during the trade fare you'll probably find that the major hotels really are full and they'll *have* to find a place for you in one of the small hotels.

If you front up at the door of a Chinese-only hotel it's more a question of luck if you get a room or a bed; they're not supposed to take you and may be worried about breaking the rules; it's unfair to them to argue the point – most likely they'll just point you off in the direction of the nearest tourist-hotel. If you do get into a Chinese-only hotel, you may get a visit from the Public Security Police who may just look at your passport and travel

## 外 国 人 临 时 住 宿 登 记 表
### REGISTRATION FORM OF TEMPORARY RESIDENCE FOR FOREIGNER

| 姓　　名<br>Name in full | 中　　文<br>In Chinese | | 性　　别<br>Sex | |
| --- | --- | --- | --- | --- |
| | 原　　文<br>In original language | | 生　　年<br>Date of birth | |
| 国　　籍<br>Nationality | 来华身份或职业<br>Identity or occupation | | | |
| 签证或旅行证号码及期限<br>Visa or travel document number and date of validity | | | | |
| 停留事由<br>Object of stay | | | 抵达日期<br>Date of arrival | |
| 何处来何处去<br>Where from and to | | | 拟住日期<br>Duration of stay | |
| 房号或住址<br>Room number or address | | | | |

旅　馆　或　户　主　签　章
Stamp of the hotel or signature of the householder

日 期
Date

permit and go away, or they may take you down to the tourist hotel. There are no really hard and fast rules; places like Canton, Beijing and Shanghai are more restrictive as to where you stay; Guilin, on the other hand, seems to be fairly liberal.

**Prices** The cost of hotel rooms depends on *what* you are. If you have a white face and a big nose then you pay the most. The Chinese also attempt to plug you into the most expensive of the tourist hotels, and to give you the most expensive rooms. They do this for two reasons; they want the money, but also they think you're spectacularly wealthy, and that you'll want to do things in spectacular style. They may offer you a room for Y23 because it has a colour TV rather than the Y20 room which doesn't; they're not trying to rip you off, they're just trying to please you. Unfortunately for low-budget travellers, a lot of the problem stems from the Asian illusion that every westerner just stepped out of John Paul Getty's bank account. You're considered to be rolling in cash and the natives are going to charge accordingly.

The category of 'Overseas Chinese' is a curious invention; these are people of Chinese descent who are now resident in foreign countries; even if you've got an American passport and West coast accent and your ancestors came to join in the California goldrush of the 1840's, a yellow face and slant eyes will still get you cheaper prices in Chinese hotels. The People's Republic has been trying to instil a sense of patriotism in the descendants of people who left the motherland decades ago; that Chinese have a responsibility to their 'motherland' no matter where they are or how long ago their ancestors left. The fact that their ancestors left for the simple reason that they had nothing to eat is quite beside the point.

Hong Kong and Macau Chinese pay less than the Overseas Chinese. People's Republic Chinese stay in the cheapest

hotels; those who stay in the top hotels can do so because their rank entitles them that privilege. The 'masses' are not even permitted to tread the grounds of these hotels let alone stay there.

**Rooms & Dormitories** The price of rooms in the tourist hotels depends on where you are. For westerners, prices in Canton start around Y30 a double; in Beijing the starting price is about Y35 a double, but such accommodation is scarce and you should expect to pay more. In a more mid-range town such as Xiamen or Xian, you would be looking at around Y20 on average for a double. On the other hand, if you go to an obscure southern town like Zhanjiang you can get a room for Y3.50, since there is no tourist hotel and you have to stay in lower standard accommodation. So there is quite a bit of variation in room prices across the country.

Value for money is the sore point of Chinese hotels; in too many places you pay a high price for very basic accommodation – there is not actually anything wrong with the rooms, or with the hotel, but too often they're just not worth the money. Since there may only be one or two hotels in town where foreigners are allowed to stay, you don't get much choice of accommodation. For example, a double room at Datong's run-down Guest House will cost you Y32 – about the same as you'd pay for an excellent double in the Liu Hua Hotel in Canton. On the other hand, in Shantou in Guangdong I must have been the first foreigner to front up at one particular hotel – and was given an enormous room to myself for just Y8.

Another problem with Chinese hotels is that rooms are inevitably doubles; hardly any have single rooms. Some hotels will give you a double for half-price if you're travelling alone, but generally they won't. (That problem is by no means unique to China – in many countries you pay by the room, not by the number of people in it).

Dormitory accommodation is generally easy to get; most towns now have at least one tourist hotel which offers it. Most dormitories have lots of space, sheets, blankets, often mosquito nets and sometimes air-conditioning; not your usual batch of bunk-beds and everyone falling over each other. In most touristy places a bed usually costs between Y3 and Y10. By Chinese standards, that's the cheapest you can really hope for except in the most obscure towns.

There are a few places where getting a dorm bed involves a battle, although they're notable exceptions to the rule now. In such a case you'll be told that there is no dormitory, or that the dormitory is full. After a few hours of waiting it out at the reception desk they may finally condescend to give you a bed. The Liu Hua Hotel in Canton has the worst reputation for playing games with foreigners; on one occasion when I ventured through Canton they kept people waiting six hours and still didn't give them beds, although there were several available.

Dormitories are always sexually segregated (there have been one or two exceptions made where foreigners are concerned). Many have an attached bathroom; if not, there'll be a shower-room down the hallway. You may find in the odd place that only communal showers are available.

If there are no dormitories, there are usually three-bed rooms and you should be able to pay for just one bed. Anyone else who comes along will get thrown in with you. Some hotels have the most incredible variations on rooms and beds; the one I stayed in at Jingdezhen had single rooms with two double-beds each ... hmmmh. If you get a bed in a triple room then it's probably going to cost you about Y10 or Y12.

**Getting Cheaper Prices** If you keep your receipts for cheap rooms and dormitories you can show these at other hotels – the fact that other hotels have given you cheap accommodation will weigh in your favour. On one occasion, three of us were charged Y12 each for a three-bed room in Taiyuan

– a few days later when two of the beds were vacant, a couple were charged only Y8 each for the same beds because they'd showed their receipts for cheap rooms from previous hotels.

A bit of vocabulary also helps in the search for cheaper accommodation; a 'fandian'(hotel) is likely to have cheap rooms, but a 'binguan' (guest house) almost certainly won't. There's no point, however, going into hotels with a siege mentality determined to get the ultra-cheapest regardless; it's only going to aggravate the hotel staff and make it harder for people who come after you. By the same token, if you pay whatever ridiculous price the Chinese ask you to they'll treat the next person with the same degree of contempt.

Always ask for *all* the room prices if the first quote is too high for you. You'll quite often find that some of the staff simply don't know all the prices. Always bargain– we even heard of one person who bargained with such determination that he was given a free room!

**Student and 'Student' Discount** If you're a foreign student in the People's Republic or in Taiwan (the PRC considers Taiwan to be part of China) then you'll be able to get a discount on room prices. Students usually have to show their student card, which is a little card bound in bright red plastic. As for other travellers, the receptionist will sometimes accept your word that you're a student and will give you a cheaper price – other people have used false student cards, or made in Hong Kong student cards or whatever – but be warned that it's getting harder and will get harder still to get away with these sort of lies and tricks.

**Registering** Once you've negotiated the room price you fill out a short registration form in English, and give them your passport and travel permit. The hotel may keep one or both of these until you leave, or it may give them both back to you.

They'll give them back to you if you have to change money or go to Public Security. You're usually given a room card, and you take this to the service desk on the appropriate floor where the attendant will show you to your room.

The Chinese method of designating floors is the same as used in the USA, but different from, say, Australia. In China there is no 'ground floor' as there is in Australia. The 'ground floor' in China is referred to as the '1st floor', the 1st floor in Australia is the Chinese 2nd floor, and so on . . .

**Room Service** Not good, but gradually getting better. Of course, you can't expect much in the cheap Chinese hotels, but in the tourist hotels the price warrants some attention. A lot of hotels don't provide very good service; there's no need to get angry, but you'll often have to *tell* the attendants that you want the bedsheets and bath towels changed, the water mopped off the bathroom floor, the bathtub cleaned, and the tea-cups washed. A lot of people don't complain because they're afraid of offending the Chinese, but unless you do the Chinese won't learn how to treat western visitors.

Each floor of just about every hotel in China has a service desk usually located near the elevators. An attendant sits here and his job is to clean the rooms, make the beds, and collect and deliver laundry (just about all the tourist hotels have a laundry service, and if you hand in clothes one day you should get them back a day or two later).

The attendant also keeps an eye on the people staying in the hotel, both the Chinese and the westerners. This is partly to prevent theft, partly to stop you bringing any of the locals back for the night. Some hotels will turn away a local Chinese at the gate; others require that the Chinese registers his name, address, work unit and purpose of visit at the reception desk. Since many Chinese are reluctant to draw attention to themselves

like this you'll find they may be reluctant to visit you at the hotel – even if they are allowed in.

Something else you'll have to be prepared for is a lack of privacy. Some visitors to China are adamant that the Chinese lack the very concept of privacy, others say that privacy is one of the most valued things amongst the Chinese. Anyway, what happens is that you're sitting starkers in your hotel room, the key suddenly turns in the door and the roomboy or girl casually wanders in . . . it's becoming less of a problem as the Chinese gradually learn how to handle foreign visitors but it's still a frequent occurence. Don't expect anyone to knock first before entering – you could try teaching them if you like – but don't get angry; remember that in this country people live in crowded rooms – consequently the custom of knocking-before-entering hasn't developed. One suggestion worth trying is to tape a sign over the keyhole – it doesn't matter if it's in English, apparently they get the idea.

And one last note on privacy in China, it was pointed out to me that privacy is another privilege of rank; the high-ranking cadres live in large houses surrounded by high walls and are driven around in cars with drawn curtains. They stay in hotel rooms (not dormitories) and if they're sufficiently high then they stay in government guest houses far from the milling proletariat.

**THE PROBLEMS OF INDIVIDUAL TRAVEL**
Just how long independent travel will last in China is a good question. It may go on for as long as the Chinese feel they're making enough money out of it to justify the effort. They may stop it if they feel they are losing control over where individuals go, or if they feel that individuals are coming away with unfavourable impressions of the country. Other people have suggested that individuals create too many problems with the Chinese; we argue for cheaper

prices at the hotels, and get angry when things don't go right, unlike the better behaved tour groups who don't make trouble and are much easier to control. One Chinese even suggested to a foreign traveller that the People's Republic is letting individuals in because they *do* get angry and therefore give an unfavourable impression of the west to the Chinese proletariat . . . worth considering.

One thing that solo travellers were quick to find out about China is that it's not plain sailing. A lot of travellers seem to come away with the impression that China is well worth the trip – but ask them if they *liked* it and the responses are too often negative; it's highly educational, it's different from other parts of the world, it has its moments, it's interesting . . . but it can also be immensely frustrating.

## Coping With China

Whether or not you have to cope with China very much depends on how long you stay there, where you want to go, what you want to do and how much you want to learn, how tolerant and even-tempered you are, and how much money you're prepared to spend. The problems of travelling in China are usually the same as those in other Asian countries; generally they're all petty irritations, but they tend to get worse the longer you hang around. In China a couple of those irritations stand out.

**Staring Squads** The programme is the 'Alien' and you are the TV set – and cinema-sized audiences will gather to watch the box. You can get stared at in any Asian country, particularly when you get off the beaten track where the locals have seen few or no tourists at all. But China is certainly phenomenal for the size and enthusiasm of its staring squads. With the exception of Beijing and Shanghai, I'd be hard pressed to think of one place in China where I didn't get even a small audience and it's not uncommon to get a little horde of 50 or more.

Sometimes you don't even have to be doing anything to get a crowd; stop for a minute or two on the street to look at something, or to look at nothing at all, and several Chinese will also stop. Before long the number of onlookers swells until you're encircled by a solid wall of people.

My initial reaction was one of amusement, but gradually the novelty wore off and I began to wave people away; then it became tedious, and after a while just outrightly aggravating not being able to do anything without an audience. Even using a communal toilet involves a few starers – and after a while that gets to be a real drag.

Some people get used to being stared at and some don't. There are a few things you can do to reduce the frequency of audiences; don't wear fancy watches (particularly digitals) and keep the camera-case on when you're not taking a photo – western cargo tends to attract a lot of attention. If a Chinese comes up to talk to you on the street, then talk to him as you walk since a conversation with a foreigner automatically attracts a crowd and makes a decent conversation fairly difficult anyway. If you stand on the street scribbling in a note book someone is sure to come right up to you and poke their head right over the book to see what you're writing, and sometimes they'll lift the book straight out of your hands for a closer inspection.

The other way to cope with staring squads is to limit your time in obscure places which have seen few foreigners; or break them up by going to places which have been well-trampled by tourists (yet even in the lesser-trampled environs of a place like Beijing you can still attract a crowd). Travelling with someone else also helps; if you've got someone to talk to it's easier to ignore the crowd. Staring back never seems to help. Getting out your camera and taking a photo sometimes parts the waves but doesn't send people scurrying for cover. Hiring a bicycle is a good idea – you're zooming along so fast the crowds can't accumulate.

There are times when you've just had the lamington; I got on a train after being stared at for fully an hour by a massive crowd in the waiting room, and was in no mood to deal with another crowd on the train. When the umpteenth Chinese came up and started the old English-lesson syndrome I retreated to a book. 'Where do you come from?' he asked. 'Moldavia' I said. 'Where's that?' he asked. 'Russia' I replied. I rather got the idea that Russia wasn't the most favoured nation at the time – the man was up like a rocket and back the other end of the car, and I was left in peace and quiet for the rest of the trip. The solution to the waiting room dilemma, by the way, is to find the first-class waiting room, which is where the cadres hide from the masses.

One of the reasons the Chinese crowd around and look at you is because you've got things that they don't have; big eyes, beards, blonde hair, hairy arms and legs and big breasts have an enduring fascination for the Chinese. The Chinese men can't grow anything resembling a beard until after 40 or 50 years of age. The only 'blondes' I saw in the whole country were two albino Chinese and a light-haired Uygur girl. Chinese skin is smooth and almost hairless or grows only very fine hair. The women are among the most flat-chested on earth (admittedly, difficult to determine under the baggy clothes they wear). So don't be surprised if you begin to feel like a circus freak. You may even get curious people rubbing their fingers up and down or pulling at the hairs on your arms.

**Noise** is the second great affliction. Chinese is spoken at about 140 decibels and 120 km/h. It is said to be the only language in the world that can't be whispered – I've been told by a speaker of Cantonese that this is *not* true, but when you get to China you'll find that it's a distinct possibility. Cheap Chinese hotels can be an utterly miserable experience since the vast, empty concrete corridors and rooms amplify the sound. The Chinese enjoy conversing with their friends at the other end of the corridor and often sit up until late at night amiably shouting at their acquaintances. There are a couple of ways to avoid all this; pack a good set of earplugs, go to China with the of tolerance of a saint, or else spend more money and stay at the tourist hotels. A noisy hotel is *not* what you want to fall into after long, tiring train or bus rides.

**Spitting** is the third affliction; if you thought the Indians were bad for spitting, then go to China! The Chinese don't just clear their throats and spit – they'll come to a halt on the street, lean over and let it slowly dribble from the mouth. Everyone does it, on the streets, and even on the floors of train carriages and buses – try not to get caught in the crossfire.

**Queues** for tickets, particularly at the larger railway stations can be *long*. Sometimes it may be worth that extra money to have CITS get your tickets – otherwise be patient and just accept that this is China and there ain't nothing you can do about one billion people.

One way to cope with China is to limit your time there; leave before the people and the place get irritating and go away with happy memories. Spend more time in the places you visit and less time actually travelling on buses and trains tiring yourself out. China doesn't deserve glowing reviews, but the irritations of travel there can also make you oblivious to the good in the country.

If you're in the country for any length of time then at some point you're going to explode. On some occasions it worked; I finally got that train ticket or a cheaper room in the hotel. Other people have found that Chinese who are familiar with the eccentricities of foreigners simply turn off if we get angry – the wall comes down and nothing is achieved. Whatever happens, try not to strip-mine somebody's face – this is not good for international relations.

## Making Contact

A Chinese travel guide had this to say about encountering foreign guests: 'In trains, boats, planes or tourist areas one frequently comes across foreign guests. Do not follow, encircle and stare at them when you meet. Refrain from pointing at their clothing in front of their face or making frivolous remarks; do not vie with foreign guests, competing for a seat and do not make requests at will. If foreign guests take the initiative to make contact, be courteous and poised. Do not be flustered into ignoring them by walking off immediately, neither should you be reserved or arrogant. Do your best to answer relying on translation. When chatting with foreign guests be practical and realistic – remember there are differences between foreign and home life. Don't provide random answers if you yourself don't know or understand the subject matter. Refrain from asking foreign guests questions about age, salary, income, clothing costs and similar private matters. Do not do things discreditable to your country. Do not accept gifts at will from foreign guests. When parting you should peel off your gloves and then proffer your hand. If you are parting from a female foreign guest and she does not proffer her hand first, it is also adequate to nod your head as a farewell greeting.'

Educating a billion Chinese to be courteous to foreigners is a formidable task. For thirty years few foreigners set foot in the country, let alone were seen in the flesh by the common people. Tourism was a dirty word and unauthorised contact with a foreigner was tantamount to asking for a prison sentence; come the Cultural Revolution and the xenophobia reached its greatest heights. Even before the Communist takeover foreigners could hardly expect to be viewed in a sympathetic light; contact with westerners came largely in the form of policemen and soldiers who protected foreign settlements and business interests, established via gunboat diplomacy and a couple of Opium Wars – then add to that another 600 years of xenophobia from the time Emperor Hong Wu founded the Ming Dynasty and you'd wonder whether it really was safe to walk down a Chinese street at night. Whether or not the Chinese actually *like* foreigners is a matter of opinion – but they *are* curious about us.

Making contact with the Chinese can be a frustrating affair. Inevitably it begins with someone striking up a conversation with you on the street, in your hotel or on a train. Unfortunately many of these conversations have a frustrating habit of deteriorating into 'You speak English very well... Oh no, my English is very poor...' You can hardly expect anyone to start revealing the intimate details of their private life; think of how you'd feel if a stranger from another country suddenly started asking you lots of personal questions!

Conversations with Chinese usually begin with 'What country are you from?' followed quite often by 'How long have you been here?' or 'Is this your first time to China?' which may be followed by 'What is your name?' and 'Are you married?' and 'How old are you?' If you're lucky the person will have advanced beyond the first few phrases that everyone learns in foreign-language classes; but conversations too often deteriorate into English lessons that become more and more tedious the longer you stay in China or the less patient a person you are. Even worse and far more boring, you end up talking about talking English.

Before long you may find yourself an unwilling teacher overwhelmed by a horde of willing students. It's not uncommon for someone to knock on your hotel room at 10 pm, shyly asking to come in and practice their English with you – and then front up the following night with a couple of enthusiastic friends in tow. You end up spending the first six weeks in China trying to make contact with the people and the last six weeks trying to avoid them.

If a Chinese doesn't want to answer one of your questions he'll suddenly become evasive; he may 'forget' how to speak English, fail to understand the question or how to translate the answer from Chinese to English, or he may tell you that the subject is complex and that he has forgotten the answer. On one occasion I was with a Chinese who didn't want to translate something another had just said; he used the excuse that this second person spoke a different dialect which he *suddenly* didn't understand anymore.

You should also remember that the Chinese are highly sensitive to talking about political issues; just about everyone you meet will criticise the Cultural Revolution – but that's official policy nowadays. You simply can't expect the Chinese to express their real views on the present government, though many will. At the same time, don't necessarily expect these 'real views' to be negative just because *you* think they should be. Many Chinese simply won't broach any political subject at all and may say that they have no interest in politics. Don't expect anyone to be too liberal with their views if they're in earshot of others; it's even more difficult in China since a conversation with a foreigner on the street automatically attracts a crowd of onlookers.

The official policy on Chinese talking to foreigners tends to vary. During the Maoist era, it was absolutely forbidden. Presently it's probably even encouraged; modernisation of the country requires foreign technology – if a foreign technical journal is going to be of any use you have to be able to read the thing. Fluency in English is a path to a better job, even a chance to travel overseas to work or study in a foreign country, and that explains the enthusiasm with which the Chinese are learning the language and seeking spontaneous tuition from stray foreigners. Although the Chinese are curious about foreigners don't think they come up and speak to you purely out of curiosity or a desire to make friends – the majority simply want to practice their English and unlike other Asian countries, 'Can I practice my English with you?' is not simply a line they start with before dragging you off to their 'uncle's' souvenir shop – 99% of the time anyway.

Interesting people to talk to are the elderly Chinese who learnt English back in the 1920s and 1930s when there were large foreign communities in China. Then there are the middle-aged who were learning English just before the Cultural Revolution but were then forced to stop and are only now starting to pick it up again. Next comes the younger generation of Chinese, those who went to school or university after the Cultural Revolution and have been able to take foreign-language courses. Even the level of proficiency that self-taught Chinese have attained by listening to English-language programmes on the radio or on the television is quite impressive. You will probably never meet another group of people who are trying so hard to learn English!

If you do make a Chinese friend and you want to stay in contact through letters, then it's suggested that before you leave China you buy several stamps sufficient for letters from China to your home country. The first time you write to your Chinese friend enclose the stamps – say that you had them left over when you left China, and that you're sending them to him because you have no use for them. One of these stamps could be half a day's wage to some people in China – so for them to write to you really does involve a sacrifice. While you're in China you can keep in contact by arranged meetings, by having the Chinese person phone your hotel or post a letter. If you get him to write down his address on several envelopes you can post them to him with messages;

in the towns and cities a letter posted before 9 am should reach him that same afternoon. It *is* possible to visit people's homes – many Chinese feel greatly honoured by your visit.

## And a warning

A lot of people go to China expecting a profound cultural experience – and this has led to a lot of disappointment. Whilst the Forbidden City and the caves of Dunhuang still stand intact, it's worth remembering that many of China's other ancient monuments were ransacked during the Cultural Revolution, vandalised or even razed to the ground.

In the early 1970s, with the new turn in China's foreign policy towards rapprochement with the West, the Chinese government began a superficial revival of their ancient culture aimed at presenting a more acceptable 'human face' towards the outside world. A very *few* of the ransacked temples and monasteries were restored as showpieces. Exhibitions were set up to display 'archaeological objects found during the Cultural Revolution' in some attempt to cover up the vandalism of that period – but these exhibits were open only to foreigners and Overseas Chinese. Even some antique shops and art-reproduction shops reopened – but again only for the benefit of foreigners and Overseas Chinese. A few Chinese classics were reprinted in a few hundred copies each, but these were mainly for export anyway.

While the government may still be trying to eradicate 'feudal' ideas from the Chinese mentality it's generally accepted that wanton vandalism is no way to go about it. In the past few years there's been a determined effort to restore many of these ruined sites, but many of the temples remain abandoned and derelict or are used as schools, libraries, restaurants, offices, museums, parks, factories or warehouses. The amount of damage done both by deliberate vandalism on the part of the Red Guards and by the years of neglect is evident in so many ancient buildings in China. A few of the restored temples are attracting worshippers once again, mainly old people. But on the whole the temples are just mummified remains of their former selves – lifeless museum pieces. There are some marvellous cultural attractions; the Beijing Opera, the Provincial Dance Ensemble of Gansu Province, the acrobatics of Beijing and Shanghai, and some stunning performances of Chinese music are often organised for the tour groups – but culture in China is very much like the availability of good food – don't expect to find it on every street corner. The Cultural Revolution almost put an end to the old culture and the country is only now starting to recover.

## Itineraries

There's an awful lot of China, but planning a route around it isn't really very difficult if you only want to stick to the major towns and cities. The only problem is travelling time; on the whole, transport isn't bad, but distances are immense and if you can afford it, you might find the odd plane trip well worth the money.

There is a fairly definite 'tourist route' in China now. Most people take the train or the overnight ferry from Hong Kong to Canton, then the boat up the Pearl and Xi (West) rivers to Wuzhou. They bus to Yangshuo or Guilin and in Guilin take the train to Kunming and then to Chengdu. From Chengdu it's one of two things – either north to Xian or south to Chongqing. Those who go to Xian head off along the railway line to Turpan and Urumqi, or north to Beijing. Those who go to Chongqing take the boat down the Yangtse River – some go all the way to Wuhan but many people are getting off at Yichang and taking the train to Luoyang. From Luoyang they either head to Urumqi or to Beijing. After Beijing many people go straight down to Shanghai and take the boat to Hong Kong.

Other places are becoming increasingly popular (and some are quickly losing popularity as people find they're not all they were made out to be). The main tourist cities are Beijing, Shanghai, Canton, Guilin, Hangzhou, Suzhou, Kunming and Xian. Beijing and Shanghai will always maintain their fascinating character. Most people flit through Canton not giving it the time it really deserves. Guilin is being replaced by the superior scenery of Yangshuo. In the north-west, Urumqi but *particularly* Turpan remain the favourites of many travellers. Kunming invariably gets rave reviews from everyone who goes there. Other places like Datong and Luoyang with their Buddhist caves attract much attention, and it's likely that the towns of the south-east coast will become increasingly popular.

Of course, it very much depends what you're interested in seeing or doing. If you want to get off the tourist track there are a host of small towns and places where few people ever go – and of course, there are thousands and thousands of villages to explore ... One important thing to remember about planning a trip through China is timing. The weather ranges from furiously hot to bitterly cold – see the Climate section of this book for details.

## TOURS & TOUR GROUPS

Even if China *is* letting individuals travel around, tour groups are still considered the darlings of Chinese who have to deal with foreigners. It is much easier for the Chinese if you arrive in a tour group, if all your accommodation is pre-booked; Everyone sits down at a table at the same time to eat, if there's a CITS interpreter on hand so that someone doesn't have to struggle with a phrasebook or pidgeon-English. Groups don't make a nuisance of themselves by trying to go to 'closed' places, they usually keep their complaints to themselves or channel them through the tour leader rather than shouting at the desk clerk. Tour groups spend more money than individuals and they probably go away with a more positive attitude

towards the country.

So are tours worth it? Unless you simply can't get around on your own, probably not. Apart from the expense, they tend to screen you even more from the realities of China. Most people who come back with glowing reports of the People's Republic are those who have been looked after by their Chinese hosts, and who never had to battle their way on board a bus in the whole three weeks of their stay. On the other hand, if your time is limited and you just want to see the Forbidden City and the hills of Guilin, the brief tours from Hong Kong are definitely worth considering – expensive, but if you have to whip around the country then a tour is the best way to do it.

One thing you will never be able to complain about on a tour is not being shown enough. Itineraries are invariably jam-packed with as much as can possibly be fitted into a day and the Chinese expect stamina from their guests. The day may start early in the morning with breakfast, a visit to a market, a morning's sightseeing, an afternoon visit to a school, a shopping session and not finish until 10 pm after a visit to the local opera. Stays in cities are short and in your few weeks in the country you're whisked from place to place at a furious rate. The other thing you won't be complaining about is the quantity of food – you may complain about the quality or the degree of imagination involved in the cooking – but there is no way the Chinese will let you starve.

On tours or at official functions you may find yourself being applauded – this is a Chinese custom and is used as a form of greeting or approval. The correct response is to applaud back! For official functions and banquets the Chinese are exceedingly punctual – to be late is considered very rude.

### Short tours from Hong Kong and Macau

There are innumerable tours you can make from Hong Kong or Macau. The best people to go to if you want to find out what's available are the Hong Kong travel agents, the Hong Kong Student Travel Bureau (10th floor, Star House, Tsimshatsui, Kowloon) or China Travel Service. You usually have to book one or two days in advance.

Tours to **Shenzhen** just across the border are probably the most popular. These are usually daily except on Sundays and public holidays, and the price hovers around HK$250 for visa, transport and lunch. The tour usually includes a trip to the Shenzhen Reservoir from which Hong Kong gets most of its water, a visit to the Shenzhen art gallery, a kindergarten and the local arts and crafts shop. Most people seem to find the trip fairly enjoyable. There are also two-day tours which take you to Shenzhen, Humen, the Shajioo Fortress at the mouth of the Pearl River Estuary and the town of Shekou.

There are day-trips from Hong Kong to **Zhongshan**, the Special Economic Zone north of Macau. Cost is around HK$370 and you're taken by hydrofoil to Macau and then by bus to Zhongshan, to visit either Shaqi or Zhuhai town, and to Cui Heng village the birthplace and former residence of Sun Yat-sen. There are also 1½ day tours which include both Zhongshan and Macau.

There's a four-day **Pearl River Delta** tour, including Macau, Zhongshan, Shiqi, Zhaoqing, Foshan and Canton costing around HK$1480. There are also three-day tours to Canton costing around HK$1200 to 1300, which includes Foshan.

Essentially the same tours can be booked in Macau, and if you're in that city and want to book a tour it's probably best to do so at the China Travel Service Office (Metropole Hotel, Rua de Praia Grande) or the travel agents in the large tourist hotels – they'll have someone around who speaks English. An enthusiastic one-day visitor described her tour as follows:

The tour starts in Macau at 9.30 am at the Mondial Hotel. Chinese customs are no problem ... Our whole bus group (about 20 people) crossed the border in just 15 minutes.

The programme then was a 20-minute visit to the Dr Sun Yat-sen Memorial Middle School followed by a half-hour visit (with a tea break) to the late founder of the Republic of China's residence. We then had an excellent 1½ hour lunch in Shaqi with prawns, fish soup, chicken, pork, duck, and real beer .... We then had a half-hour walk around Shaqi, a short visit to a farmer's house in a small village and tea back at the border before we crossed into Macau.

The guide would stop the bus while we were driving through the country if we wanted to take pictures. The Chinese guide was very well-informed, and to me he seemed very open. It was a well-organised, friendly and helpful tour– money well spent.

**Other tours** Tours further afield can be bought in Hong Kong and there's an infinite variety available – combinations, permutations and prices change all the time, so use this info as a rough guide only. For example you can get a six-day tour from Hong Kong to Beijing and Shanghai for HK$5340, an eight-day tour to Beijing, Guilin and Canton for HK$5880, or a 12-day tour to Shanghai, Xian, Beijing, Guilin and Canton for HK$8480. China Travel Service has four-day tours to Guilin; you fly from Hong Kong to Guilin and back again for an all-inclusive HK$2550.

China Travel Service in Hong Kong organises what are known as 'individual tours', one to Shanghai, Hangzhou, Nanjing and Wuxi combined, and others to Beijing, to Canton and to Shanghai. They put together a package deal which includes visa fee, transportation to and within China, one or two nights' hotel accommodation, sightseeing tour, and transport from the airport or railway station to your hotel. If you've got little time and only want to zoom off to one or two places then these individual tours may be worth considering. You have to submit your passport with a visa application form in triplicate and three passport photos at least five days before departure. The tours are expensive; *excluding* airfare, for a person travelling alone, the tour to Beijing is HK$1205 (includes only one night's accommodation) to Shanghai HK$1050 (with one night's accommodation), and the eight-day combined tour of Shanghai, Nanjing, Wuxi, and Hangzhou HK$5676. Prices decrease if there are two people travelling together.

Longer tours of two or three weeks are also available from Hong Kong. For example, a 16-day tour of eastern China would carry you round Beijing, Xian, Nanjing, Suzhou, Shanghai, Guilin and Canton. A 21-day 'Silk Road' tour would also include Urumqi, Turpan, Dunhuang, Jiuquan and Lanzhou. Again, there are all sorts of combinations, durations and prices available, so see the travel agents. Tours to Tibet are also available from Hong Kong, but tend to be booked up several months in advance.

**Tours from Western countries** are handled by innumerable travel agents and any of them worth their commission will tell you that you can't go to China except on a tour. There are the standard couple of week tours that whip you round Beijing, Shanghai, Guilin, Xian etc, but in an attempt to spice up the offerings the Chinese have come up with some new formulas; honeymoon tours (how many in the group?), acupuncture courses, special interest tours for botanists, railway enthusiasts, lawyers and potters, trekking tours to Tibet and Qinghai, women's tours, bicycle tours, Chinese language courses . . .

It is unlikely that tour operators are going to lose much money because individual travel has opened up in China; tour groups are invariably the affluent elderly, and these people would go on a tour regardless. As for the slightly more adventurous tours, the Chinese worked out years ago that westerners would fork out great sums of money for the opportunity to tear into little-visited holes over the most uncomfortable roads possible, in order to be the first white man

on the scene. Young people are going to make up the majority of individual travellers and these have been precluded from travelling to China in the past because of the high cost of tours.

**Mountaineering & Trekking Tours** to China are organised by various agents in the west, but the prices are too high for low-budget travellers. Trekking is administered and arranged by the Chinese Mountaineering Association under the same rules as apply for mountaineering in China. The CMA makes all arrangements for a trek with the assistance of provincial mountaineering associations and local authorities. The first few trekkers were allowed into China only in 1980 and the first groups were arranged in 1981. Because trekking is under the mountaineering rules, all treks must be near one of the peaks open for mountaineering – these regions span the country and include spectacular mountain scenery that varies from the plains of Tibet to the lush bamboo forests of Sichuan Province and the open plains of Xinjiang. If you can afford it, a few mountaineering, trekking (and cycling) tour operators are:

**USA** Mountain Travel, 1398 Solano Avenue, Albany, CA 94706; Wilderness Travel, 1760 Solano Avenue, Berkeley, CA 94707; Ocean Voyages, 1709 Bridgeway, Sausalito, CA 94965; China Passage, 302 Fifth Avenue, New York 100001.

**Australia** Australian Himalayan Expeditions, 159 Cathedral Street, Woolloomooloo, Sydney, 2011.

**England** Voyages Jules Verne (tel 01-486 8080) 10 Glentworth Street, London NW1. Society for Anglo-Chinese Understanding (tel 01-267 9841) 152 Camden High Street, London NW1. Both of these will provide individual travel arrangements (including visa) as well as tours. Voyages Jules Verne also has an office in

Hong Kong at Rm 214, 2nd Floor, Lees Garden Hotel, Hysan Avenue, Hong Kong Island.

Various travel agents will book you through to these operators. Scan their literature carefully – sometimes the tours can be done just as easily on your own. What you want are places that individuals would have trouble getting into to.

In Hong Kong there are several operators who organise some interesting trips, cycling and living on communes; try the Hong Kong Student Travel Bureau, Rm 1024, 10th floor, Star House, Salisbury Road, Tsimshatsui, Kowloon; and the China Youth Travel Service, Rm 904, Nanyang Commercial Bank Bldg, 151 des Voeux Rd, Hong Kong Island – CYTS is the younger arm of CITS and they liase with many foreign student organisations and groups. The Hong Kong Cycling Tour Association on 1st floor, 17 Mei king Street, Tokwawan, Kowloon, promotes bike touring to China.

**Non-profit Touring** Some organisations require paying helpers to assist on projects. This is a contribution to the cost of the project and you have to pay your own airfares and living expenses to and on site. Two organisations which have made such trips to China are Earthwatch, 10 Juniper Road, Box 127, Belmont, Mass. 02178, USA; and the University Research Expeditions Programme, University of California, Berkeley, California, 94720, USA. You can send for a catalogue – they expect you to work hard when joining an expedition. Costs are tax-deductible for US citizens.

## LANGUAGE
**The Spoken Language** The official language of the People's Republic is the Beijing dialect, usually referred to in the West as 'Mandarin'. It's spoken mainly in the north-east and south-west of the country. In China it's referred to as *putonghua* or 'common speech' and the Chinese

government set about popularising it in the 1950s.

China has eight major dialects, though about 70% of the population speaks Mandarin. The other major dialect is Cantonese, spoken in the south and basically the same as that spoken in Hong Kong. But Cantonese is almost unintelligible to the northerners and vice-versa.

To further confuse the issue, Chinese is a 'tonal' language. The difference in intonation is the deciding factor in the meaning of the word. For example, *gaai* can mean chicken, street or prostitute depending on the way you say it. There is another phrase in Chinese which means 'grass for your horse' unless you get the tones wrong in which case it's something quite unspeakable.

For all its thousands of characters, Chinese has only a bit more than 400 syllables to pronounce them, so the tones are used to increase the number of word sounds available. There are few phonetic similarities between any of the Chinese dialects and any of the European languages – which makes it difficult for both sides to learn the other's language. The Chinese have come up with the saying 'nothing is more terrible above or below than a foreigner speaking Chinese'.

**The Written Language** Written Chinese has something like 50,000 'pictographs' – characters which symbolise objects or actions. About 5000 are in common use and you need about 1500 to read a newspaper easily.

The origin of the written script dissolves into myth; the story goes that Chinese characters were invented by the official historian of China's mythical 'Yellow Emperor', who is supposed to have ruled over the country 4000 years ago. The earliest known characters are the *Jiaguwen*, simple inscriptions carved on bones and tortoise shells by primitive Chinese tribes; about 4500 such characters have been discovered. Some of these are

Jiaguwen

Jinwen

Xiaozhuan

Lishu

Caoshu

Kaishu

still in use, like *mouth* –

and a picture of a tree for *wood* –

A system of pictographs known as *Dazhuan* continued under the Emperor Qin Shihuang, but under the succeeding Han Dynasties, these gave way to a system known as *Lishu* which used constructions of dashes and dots and horizontal and vertical strokes. The succeeding *Caoshu* script was written with swift brush stokes and many of these strokes were joined together to make handwriting easier. The *Kaishu* script shaped during the Wei and Jin Dynasties was further simplified for ease of handwriting.

In the early stages of developing the script, each character stood for a single word. Later, two or more characters were combined to form new characters. Today, 90% of characters in common use are made up of two or more original characters; that is, each character has two

or more *components*.

Each character has a phonetic component which gives some clue to the pronunciation, and an idea component which gives a clue to the meaning. The idea component is called a *radical* and is often written on the left-hand side of the character. Characters with related meanings will all contain the same radical; for example, the characters for mud, lake, river and oil all contain the radical which represents the character for water. There are somewhat more than 200 radicals and Chinese dictionaries are often arranged according to them.

The phonetic component, like the idea component, is often a character in itself. If you know the pronunciation of the character which the phonetic component is based on, then you can know or approximate the pronunciation of many characters in which that component is used.

Chinese characters are all the same size when written, although some have more strokes than others. All the characters can be constructed using about 13 basic stokes, and these individual strokes are always written in a certain order. Often the difference of one stroke produces an entirely different character with a different meaning. For example, this character means *large* –

If a dot is added at the top right corner, it becomes *dog* –

Take out the dot, add another horizontal line, and you get *sky* –

And if both horizontal lines are removed it becomes *person* –

The Communist government has also simplified many characters in an effort to make the written script easier to learn and increase the literacy rate in the country. Many of the characters you'll see in Hong Kong are written quite differently from the same ones in China. In China itself there are regional variations, with some characters written in abbreviated forms in certain locales but nowhere else.

**The Pinyin System** In 1958 the Chinese officially adopted a system known as 'pinyin' as a method of writing their language using the Roman alphabet. Since the official language of China is the Beijing dialect, it is this pronunciation which is used. The popularisation of this spelling is still at an early stage, and though literate Chinese read and write the same language of course, don't expect them to be able to use pinyin. Off in the countryside and the smaller towns you may not see a single pinyin sign anywhere, so unless you speak Chinese you'll need a phrase book with Chinese characters if you're travelling in these areas. And though pinyin is helpful, it's not an instant key to communication since westerners usually don't get the pronunciation and intonation of the romanised word correct.

Pinyin is noticeably used on shop fronts, street signs and advertising billboards. It is of help to have a passing knowledge of the system. Basically the sounds are read as they're pronounced in English. There are a few oddities though:

c is pronounced 'ts' as in *its*
q is pronounced 'ch' as in *choose*
x is pronounced as 'sh' as in *short*
z is pronounced as 'ds' as in *bids*
zh is pronounced as the initial *j*

For example, the second syllable of *Guangzhou* is pronounced so that it rhymes with 'joe'. *Xian* is pronounced 'Shi-arn'. *Chongqing* is pronounced 'Chong ching'.

Since 1979 all translated texts of Chinese diplomatic documents and Chinese magazines published in foreign languages have used the pinyin system of spelling names and places. The system replaces the old Wade-Giles and Lessing systems which were previously used to romanise the Chinese script. Under pinyin, 'Mao Tse-tung' becomes *Mao Zedong*, 'Chou En-lai' becomes *Zhou En-lai* and 'Peking' becomes *Beijing*. The name of the country remains as it has been generally written; 'China' in English and German, and 'Chine' in French.

**Tones** The four basic tones used in pinyin are usually indicated by the following marks:

‾ high level
´ rising
∨ falling-rising
` falling

An unmarked syllable is unstressed and is pronounced lightly and quickly with no particular tone.

**Communication Difficulties** With so many people learning English, communicating in China is not as difficult as it appears. There always seems to be someone around who speaks even a little bit of the language who will emerge from the crowd to help you. And there are lots of Chinese who speak the language extremely well. In the tourist hotels and at the CITS offices there is nearly always someone around who speaks at least communicable English. Hong Kongers are usually very friendly and helpful despite their reputation in Hong Kong itself.

Phrasebooks are invaluable – but it's better to copy out the appropriate sentences in Chinese rather than show someone the book otherwise they'll take the book and read every page! Reading place names or street signs is not difficult; often the Chinese name is accompanied by the pinyin form, and, if not, you'll soon learn lots of characters just by repeated exposure. A small dictionary in English, Pinyin and Chinese characters is also useful for learning a few words.

Watch out for Lonely Planet's *China Phrasebook* in our series of 'Language Survival Kits'.

## PHRASES

yes
*shì*
是

no
*bù*
不

I want to go to
*wǒ yào dào*
我要到

I want to see
*wǒ yào kàn*
我要看

I want to buy
*wǒ yào mǎi*
我要买

I want to go at . . . . . . . .
*wǒ yào zài . . . . . . . . diǎn dào*
我要在.....点到

Could you buy a ticket for me?
*kě yǐ tì wǒ mǎi yì zhāng piào ma?*
可以替我一张票吗?

I am a student
*wǒ shì yí ge xué shēng*
我是一个学生

I cannot read or write Chinese
*wǒ bú huì kàn huò xiě zhōng wén*
我不会看或写中文

## Toilets
*cè suǒ*
厕所

men
*nán rén*
男人

women
*nǚ rén*
女人

## Places

Public Security Bureau
*gōng ān jú*
公安局

China International Travel Service
*zhōng guó guó jì lǚ xíng she*
中国国际旅行社

CAAC
*zhōng guó mín yòng háng kōng zǒng jú*
中国民用航空总局

Main Train Station
*huǒ chē zǒng zhàn*
火车总局

Post Office
*yóu jú*
邮局

Long Distance Bus Station
*cháng tú qì chē zhàn*
长途汽车站

Airport
*fēi jī chǎng*
飞机场

## Public Security

I want to extend my visa
*wǒ yào yán cháng wǒ de qiān zhèng*
我要延长我的签证...

by two weeks
*dào liǎng xīng qī*
到两星期

by one month
*dào yì ge yuè*
到一个月

by two months
*dào èr ge yuè*
到二个月

I need an Alien's Permit for the following places
*wǒ xū yào yí fèn yǔn xǔ wài guó rén lǚ yóu de zūn zhèng dào yí xià de dì fāng qù*

我须要一份允许外国人旅游的尊证到以下的地方去.

## Street Names and Nomenclature

street
*dà jiē*

大街

road
*lù*

路

north
*běi fāng*

北方

south
*nán fāng*

南方

east
*dōng fāng*

东方

west
*xī fāng*

西方

Streets and roads are usually split up into sectors. Each sector is given a number or (more usually) labelled according to its relative position to the other sectors according to compass points. For example *Zhongshan Lu* (Zhongshan Road) might be split into an east and a west sector. The east sector will be designated *Zhongshan Donglu* and the west will be *Zhongshan Xilu*.

## Hotels

a single hotel which rarely admits foreigners
*lǚshè*

旅社

a reception lodge usually reserved for officials
*zhāodàisuǒ*

招待所

guest house
*bīnguǎn*

宾馆

tourist hotel
*lǚguǎn*

旅馆

tourist hotel
*fàndiàn*

饭店

I want a single room
*wǒ yào yì jiān dān rén fáng*

我要一间单人房

I want a double room
*wǒ yào yì jiān shuāng rén fáng*

我要一间双人房

I want a dormitory bed
*wǒ yào yì zhāng chuáng wèi*

我要一张床位

How much is it per night?
*měi wǎn zhè jiān yào duō shǎo qián?*

每晚这间多少钱?

That's too expensive
*Zhè tài guì le*

这太贵了

Is there anything cheaper?
*Yǒu pián yi de yì diǎn ma?*

有便宜一点的吗?

## Transport

How long does the trip take?
*zhè cì lǚ xíng yào duō jiǔ?*

这次旅行要多久?

How much is a hard seat?
*yìng xí duō shǎo qián?*

硬席多少钱?

How much is a hard sleeper?
*yìng wò duō shǎo qián*
硬卧多少钱?

How much is a soft sleeper?
*ruǎn wò duō shǎo qián?*
软卧多少钱?

Could I have a middle berth?
*wǒ kě yǐ yào yí ge zhōng pù ma?*
我可以要一个中铺吗?

Train number
*chē hào*
车号

Where is the first class waiting room?
*tóu děng hǔo chē shì zài nǎr?*
头等候车室在哪儿?

Where is the left luggage room?
*xíng lǐ shì zài nǎr?*
行李室在哪儿?

I want to refund this ticket
*wǒ yào tuì diào zhè zhāng piào*
我要退掉这张票

When does the train leave?
*hǔo chē shén me shí hòu kāi?*
火车什么时候开?

When does the bus leave?
*qì chē shén me shí hòu kāi?*
汽车什么时候开?

When is the first bus?
*tóu bān qì chē jǐ diǎn zhōng kāi?*
头班汽车几点钟开?

When is the last bus?
*mò bān qì chē jǐ diǎn zhōng kāi?*
末班汽车几点钟开?

When is the next bus?
*xià yì bān qì chē jǐ diǎn zhōng kāi?*
下一班汽车几点钟开?

When does the boat leave?
*lún chuán shén me shí hòu kāi?*
轮船什么时候开?

When does the plane leave?
*fēi jī shén me shí hòu kāi?*
飞机什么时候开?

**Bicycles**

I want to hire a bicycle
*wǒ yào zū yí liàng zǐ xíng chē*
我要租一辆自行车

How much is it per day?
*duō shǎo qián yì tiān*
多少钱一天?

How much is it per hour?
*duō shǎo qián měi xiǎo shí?*
多少钱每小时?

**Post Office**

I want to send this letter by airmail to........
*wǒ yào háng yóu zhè fēng xìn dào........*
我要航邮这封信到....

package
*bāo gǔo*
包果

surface mail
*lù lù yóu zhèng*
陆路邮政

**Time**

tonight
*jīn wǎn*
今晚

today
*jīn tiān*
今天

tomorrow
  *míng tiān*　明天
the day after tomorrow
  *hòu tiān*　后天
in the morning
  *zài shàng wǔ*　在上午

in the afternoon
  *zài xià wǔ*　在下午
in the evening
  *zai wǎn shang*　在晚上
at night
  *zai wǎn shàng*　在晚上

## Countries

Australia
  *aò dà lì yà*　澳大利业
USA
  *měi guó*　美国
Germany
  *dé guó*　德国

New Zealand
  *xīn xī lán*　新西兰
Britain
  *yīng guó*　英国
Canada
  *jiā ná dà*　加拿大

## Food

chicken
  *jī*　鸡
pork
  *zhū ròu*　猪肉
beef
  *niú ròu*　牛肉
duck
  *yà*　鸭
frogs
  *qīng wā*　青蛙
snake
  *shé*　蛇
rice
  *mí fàn*　米饭
dumplings
  *jiǎo zi*　饺子
prawns
  *xiā*　虾
squid
  *yóu yú*　鱿鱼
octopus
  *zhāng yú*　章鱼

crab
  *xiè*　蟹
fish
  *yú*　鱼
eel
  *shàn yú*　鳝
tea
  *chá*　茶
water
  *shuǐ*　水
beer
  *pí jiǔ*　啤酒
soup
  *tāng*　汤

beancurd
  *dòu fù*　豆腐
vegetables
  *shū cài*　蔬菜
pepper
  *hú jiāo*　胡椒
mushrooms
  *mó gu*　蘑菇

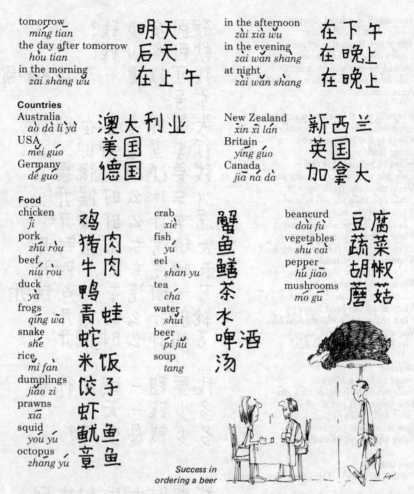

*Success in ordering a beer*

## FOOD

Many people who go to China expect a marvellous banquet to be available on every street corner. There is indeed some excellent food available in China, and some fascinating culinary exotica – but it's in limited supply, restricted to places like Canton, Shanghai, Beijing and Guilin.

Be warned that what's been dreamt up by Chinese chefs is not what's readily available for you to eat. Most of the time you're going to find yourself living on rice (steamed or fried), a few varieties of fried meat and vegetables, dumplings, beancurd, noodles and soup. And too often the food seems to be amazingly oily, as if they fry it up in a wok, scoop it out and douse it with a ladleful of grease. Food in the south is generally better than in the north of China, and during the winter northern

Chinese food can be perfectly dreadful.

Every so often though an extraordinary meal does crop up in the most unlikely place; in the small railway-junction town of Hengyang four of us were served an enormous meal of fish, egg, vegetables, meat, soup and rice – more than we could eat – and the bill came to a *total* of only Y8.90!

**Traditional Fare** Chinese cooking is famine cooking. The Chinese will eat anything and everything that moves, and no part of an animal or plant is wasted. What we now regard as Chinese culinary exotica is really a product of the need to make the most of everything available, salvaging the least appetising ingredients which wealthy nations reject as waste, and making them into appetising food. This has led to some interesting dishes; fish heads, ducks feet, dog and cat meat, bird saliva, fish lips and eyeballs to name a few. Even the method of cooking is a consequence of the shortage of fuel; cutting the food into small pieces and stir-frying it in a wok is more fuel-efficient than baking or spit-roasting. Pigs and chicken have always been a feature of the cuisine, because they have unchoosy eating habits and can be raised on very small areas of land.

Traditional Chinese food can be divided into four major categories; Beijing (sometimes called Mandarin) and Shandong, Cantonese, Shanghainese and Jiangzhenese, and Sichuan.

**Beijing and Shandong** food comes from one of the coldest parts of China and uses heaps of spices and chilli to warm the body up. Bread and noodles are often used instead of rice.

The chief speciality is Beijing Duck, eaten with pancake and plum sauce. Another chicken speciality is Beggar's Chicken, supposedly created by a beggar who stole the emperor's chicken and then had to bury it in the ground to cook it – the dish is wrapped in lotus leaves and baked all day in hot ashes.

Some good Beijing dishes: chicken or pork with soya-bean sauce; bean curd with pepper sauce; fried shredded beef with chilli sauce; stewed mixed vegetables; barbecued chicken; fried shrimp eggs and pork pancakes. Another speciality is Mongolian barbecue – assorted barbecued meats and vegetables mixed in a hotpot. Birds' nest soup is a speciality of Shandong cooking, as is sweet and sour Yellow River carp. The latter is served singed on the outside but tender inside.

**Shanghainese and Jiangzhenese** food is noted for its use of seafoods. It's heavier and oilier than either Beijing or Cantonese, and uses lots of chilli and spices. Eels are also popular and so is drunken chicken – the bird cooked in *shaoshing* a potent Chinese wine which tastes a bit like warm sherry. Other things to try are Tientsin cabbage, some of the cold meat and sauce dishes, ham and melon soup, bean curd and brown sauce, braised meat balls, deep-fried chicken, and pork rib with salt and pepper.

Jiangzhe cooking specialises in poultry and seafood, and the dishes are cooked in their own juices to preserve their original flavour.

**Sichuan** is the hottest of the four categories and is characterised by heavy use of spices and peppers. Specialities include frogs' legs and smoked duck; the duck is cooked in peppercorns, marinated in wine for 24 hours, covered in tea leaves and cooked over a charcoal fire. Other dishes to try are shrimps with salt and garlic; dried chilli beef; vegetables and beancurd; bears' paws braised in brown sauce; fish in spicy bean sauce and aubergines in garlic.

**Cantonese** is southern Chinese cooking – lots of steaming, boiling and stir-frying. It's the best of the bunch if you're worried about cholesterol and coronaries, as it uses the least amount of oil. It's lightly cooked and not as highly spiced as the other three. Lots of seafood, vegetables, roast pork, chicken, steamed fish and fried rice. Specialities are abalone, thousand-year-old-eggs (which are actually only a few months old), shark's fin soup, roast pig and a snake dish known as 'dragon's duel tiger', which combines wild cat and snake meat.

**Culinary exotica** Guilin is the place to go for strange animals; anteaters, pangolins (a sort of Chinese armadillo), cats, owls, monkeys and snakes can be found in cages outside several restaurants on the main street. Headless skinned and roasted dogs are quite a common sight in many of the markets in China. Turtles, tortoises, toads and frogs can be found in abundance in Canton. If you like seafood then the coastal towns of Shantou, Xiamen and Quanzhou will stuff you full of prawns, squid and octopus.

One of the stranger Chinese delicacies is pig faces; having removed the meat from the head, pour hot tar over the pig's face and wait until dry. Then peel the tar off, removing the hair and leaving the skin intact. The skin is then used as an ingredient in soup.

Live rat embryos are a southern delicacy from Guizhou Province, I believe – and really I don't know whether this one is true or whether someone just made it up. The dish is nicknamed the 'three squeals' since the embryo squeals when you pick it up with your chopsticks, once again when you dip it in soya sauce, and finally when you put it in your mouth . . .

**Drinks** Tea is probably the most commonly served brew in China; it didn't originate in China but in South-East Asia. Coffee and Indian tea is not generally available – you might get it in the Friendship Store in Beijing or Shanghai and there may be some locally-produced coffee around in the major cities. If you can't live without the stuff then you'd better bring it with you. One of the interesting brands of tea in China is the 'Silver Needle Tea' which is grown on the island of Junshan in Dongting Lake in Hunan Province. The tea is supposed to stand upright in the water like tiny needles and emit a delicate fragrance, though the stuff I had wallowed around on its back or sank to the bottom.

Beer is probably the next most popular drink, and by any standards it's great stuff. The best-known is *Tsingtao* made with a mineral water which gives it its sparkling flavour. It's really a German beer since Tsingtao was once a German concession. Local brews are found in all the major cities of China and are of varying quality but almost always very good. (Chinese women, by the way, don't drink or smoke, but it's considered permissable for western women).

*Mao tai* is a favourite of the Chinese. It's a spirit made from sorghum (a type of millet) and is used for toasts at banquets. You can get drunk very quickly on this stuff – personally I like it, though it's probably what methylated spirits taste like.

China is plagued by innumerable local wines and spirits; the sort of thing they run tanks on. The *Dynasty* white-wine is produced near Tianjin in conjunction with the French company Remy Martin. *Hejie Jiu* is 'lizard wine' and is produced in the southern province of Guangxi; each bottle

contains one dead lizard floating perpendicularly in the clear liquid.

Coca Cola is produced in Beijing and is sold in the tourist hotels. It's also sold in the streets in Canton and along the southeast coast. Fanta and Sprite are also available in the tourist hotels.

Western liquor is available at the Friendship Stores and the large tourist hotels in the major cities. For details of what's available and how much it costs (a lot!) see the section on 'What to Take and How to Take it'.

Fizzy soft drinks are available everywhere; they're also locally brewed, manufactured in backyards by entrepreneurs who mix together a bit of artificial colouring and flavouring with bicarbonate-of-soda. To be avoided like the plague!

Milk is almost unavailable; I've seen a few restaurants selling hot milk by the cupful, and you can also buy bottles of milk in the Friendship Store in Beijing – but other than that it's a great rarity.

The Tibetans have an interesting brew called *qingke* – a beer or spirit made from barley, and the Mongolians serve the sour-tasting *koumiss* made of fermented mare's milk.

**Fruit** Getting fresh fruit is a problem in China. Canned and bottled fruit is readily available everywhere, in the department stores and food stores and is also sold in the dining cars on the trains. Poor quality oranges, mandarins and bananas are commonly sold in the street markets, but good fresh fruit is very rare. Good watermelons are sold in the north of China, and there is good fruit (oranges, pineapples, bananas and lychees) along the south-east coast, but other than that

there is little available. Lychees come into season around April to August. The lychee is an evergreen tree grown mainly in Guangdong, Fujian and Guangxi; the fruit of the tree is called the lychee nut which has a reddish coloured skin enclosing a jelly-like pulp filled with sweet, milky juice.

**Western food** You can usually get western breakfasts (eggs, and toast with jam and butter) in the tourist hotels, and a few of them serve western dishes. Again, outside of Beijing and Shanghai, it's only the odd place – such as the Seamen's Club in Shanghai or the *Jinghang Hotel* in Nanjing – which has a large Western menu. When in Rome . . .

**Vegetarianism** Difficult to cater for, though possible. Get someone to write down for you in Chinese a note saying that you're a vegetarian and that you don't eat *any* sort of meat. Remember that most food in the dining-cars of the trains has meat in it.

**Chopsticks** in China are blunt at the end, unlike those in Japan which are pointed. Most public restaurants and privately-run restaurants use wooden chopsticks. Some people think that the wooden chopsticks are unhealthy, harbouring dirt in the cracks that may be a source of hepatitis and they buy their own chopsticks rather than using the restaurant's. Plastic chopsticks are commonly sold in China.

The best way to master chopsticks is to be hungry in a place where there are no knives and forks; hopefully the following diagrams will help;

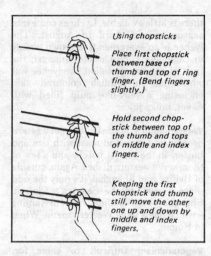

Using chopsticks

Place first chopstick between base of thumb and top of ring finger. (Bend fingers slightly.)

Hold second chopstick between top of the thumb and tops of middle and index fingers.

Keeping the first chopstick and thumb still, move the other one up and down by middle and index fingers.

Don't worry about making a mess on the table – everyone does. If you want to, raise the bowl right up to your lips and shovel in the rice – this is how the Chinese eat so don't be embarrassed, though it will probably take a lot of practice to master the shovelling process.

**Ration coupons** The Chinese have to pay for rice and food grains with ration coupons. They're not issued to foreigners. Sometimes you get asked for them, but if you don't have any it usually doesn't matter. You may be charged a bit extra for the food instead, but not much.

**RESTAURANTS** Chinese restaurants are another thing altogether. In the towns the government-run establishments are like great canteens that might seat several hundred people at any one time. In Beijing, Shanghai and Canton, the older establishments have private rooms where small groups of people can eat away from the crowd. Nor do the Chinese go in for the western fashion of eating in dimly-lit, intimate surroundings. In fact, the Chinese have a word *renao* which is the flip-side of privacy and intimacy; literally it means 'hot and noisy' suggesting the

pleasure that Chinese find in having a large group of friends and relatives who get together for a meal in a noisy brightly lit room, the chopsticks clicking, and everyone talking.

There's a multitude of privately-run restaurants in China, part of the boom in free enterprise since Mao died. Like everywhere else, foreigners often end up paying more than the locals. On some occasions the rip-off gets a bit too much to tolerate, like being charged a yuan for a bowl of soupy noodles when the Chinses might pay as little as 20 or 30 fen. Sometimes polite insistence will bring the price down, but at other times the Chinese can be frustratingly stubborn. On the positive side, you'll often find these small privately-run restaurants much more pleasant to eat in than the large crowded and noisy canteens, and the speed of the service and sometimes the quality of the food can be substantially better.

One of the peculiarities of the larger restaurants in China, (more in the north of the country, very rarely in the south) is the foul smell that characterised so many of them. Some people thought it was caused by an over abundance of garlic; to me it smells more like an accumulation of decomposing grease. Whatever it is it hits you full in the face as soon as you walk through the door and, for this reason alone, there are a lot of restaurants I simply wouldn't recommend.

The restaurants in the tourist hotels are usually good places to eat and the food is generally better than at the public restaurants. One advantage is that you don't get stared at like you do in the big public restaurants. The small street stalls can sometimes be good places to eat, particularly for snacks.

In places like Beijing and Shanghai there are several restaurants with rooms reserved for foreigners; but generally speaking you can't expect just to wander in and be served. Generally you have to phone ahead, a day in advance if possible, and specify the number of people in the party, the price per head you're willing to pay and your nationality – then the restaurant will make a booking for you.

**Getting Served** Tourist hotels almost always have their menus in Chinese and English. If not, there's usually someone around who speaks some English. Sometimes they dispense with menus, you pay a flat rate and you're served a bowl of steamed rice together with several small plates of fish and different types of vegetables and meat – which is not a bad way to eat.

Most public restaurants have counters where you buy tickes for the individual plates of food; then you go to a window facing into the kitchen, hand in your tickets and get your food. Menus and prices are usually chalked up on a blackboard and scrubbed out as the restaurant runs out.

Unless you can speak Chinese, the best way to order a meal in a Chinese restaurant is to point at something that somebody else already has – easy enough in the small privately-run restaurants, but more difficult in the large canteens where there are usually lines of people waiting to be served. Sometimes somebody takes you in hand, leads you into the kitchen where you can point out what you want, and then goes and buys the tickets for you.

**Banquets** Visiting delegations, cultural groups, etc, are usually given a welcoming banquet by their host organisation. At the very highest levels there'll be formal invitations and a detailed seating plan based on rank and higher algebra. At lower levels it's a more simple affair, though the ritual and etiquette is much the same.

A formal dinner usually lasts about 1½ hours, and is preceded by 10 or 15 minutes of tea and polite conversation. The party is then seated with the host presiding at the head of the table and the high-ranking guests (that is, the leaders of the delegation) seated to his left or right. Dishes are served in sequence, beginning with cold appetisers and continuing to 10 or more courses, with soup usually served after the main course, and used to wash the food down.

Sometimes the host will serve the guest, as is the Chinese custom. If not, use the small china spoon to take food from the large serving plates to your own bowl. The

**Food Ration Coupons**

other small bowl is for tea, which will probably be constantly refilled. Small dishes in the middle of the table are soya sauce and chilli.

The usual rule is to serve everyone too much. Empty bowls imply that the host hasn't served a sufficient quantity of food, so if you see a bit left in a bowl then leave it there. Similarly, though rice may be the staple, at banquets it is used only as a filler and to consume great quantities, implying you are still hungry, is considered an insult to your host.

In a formal setting it is impolite to drink alcohol alone; toasts are usually offered to neighbours or to the whole table. It is appropiate for the leader of the guests to offer a toast to everyone at the table, and the Chinese host usually begins the toasts after the first course. Avoid excessive toasting since inebriation is frowned upon. There are usually three glasses per person on the table; one for soft drinks, one for beer and another for toasts. Toasts are often made using the fiery mao-tai with the expression 'Gan bei!' which literally implies 'empty the cup'. In the course of a banquet there may be several 'gan bei' toasts, but custom dictates that you need only drain your glass on the first one. Subsequent toasts require only a small sip – the Chinese are *not* great drinkers. The Han Chinese don't clink their classes when toasting.

Don't be late for a formal banquet; it's considered extremely rude. The banquet ends when the food and toasts end – the Chinese don't linger after the meal.

You may find yourself being applauded when you enter an official function, such as a large banquet. This is a Chinese custom which is used as a greeting or indicates approval; the correct response is to applaud back!

## READING

There is enough literature on China to keep you reading for another 5000 years of their history. The problem with China is the amount of nonsense written about the

place. At the risk of either boring or misleading you a few suggestions are listed below.

The classic on the Chinese revolution is *Red Star Over China* by Edgar Snow. Snow managed to break through the Kuomintang blockade of the Communists and spend four months with them in Yan'an in 1936; his was the first personal account by a western journalist of the Red Army and its leaders. Since the book was written before the Communists came to power its information about the top Chinese leaders is undistorted by the power-struggles and propaganda of the post-Liberation period. It's been criticized as naive, glossing over some of the worst aspects of the Communist movement, but I think it conveys the hope and idealism of the time.

Snow's later books *The Other Side of the River*, *Red China Today* and *The Long Revolution* recount his visits to China in the 1960s, before and just after the Cultural Revolution. *Edgar Snow's China* is a compilation of his writings with photos taken by him, his friends or from Chinese archives – graphic reminders of why the Communists carried on 22 years of war with the Kuomintang and the Japanese.

*Chinese Shadows* by Simon Leys is one of the most critical books on Mao and the Cultural Revolution. It was published in 1974, based on Ley's visits to China in 1972 and 1973. It's interesting to draw comparisons between the China of the post-Mao era with the one that Leys visited.

Roger Garside's *Coming Alive – China After Mao*, describes the events which led to the downfall of the 'Gang of Four' and the rise of Deng Xiao-ping to power. Garside served at the British embassy in Beijing for two years at the end of the Cultural Revolution in 1968-1970, and was First Secretary from 1976-1979.

George Orwell's *1984* was ahead of its time predicting the political trends in Communist China. *Animal Farm* is perhaps a closer approximation to post-

1949 China and its bloated cadres more equal than others. And equally interesting is *Political Imprisonment in the People's Republic of China*, a report published by Amnesty International in 1978.

Over the last few years, since foreign journalists were permitted to take up residence in China, there has been a spate of books delving into Chinese life, the universe and everything. Fox Butterfield's *China – Alive in the Bitter Sea* is one of the biggest sellers, and tells you everything from the location of the Chinese labour-camps to what the women use as substitutes for tampons. Canadian, John Fraser lived in China at the time of the 'Democracy Wall Movement' of 1978, and much of his book *The Chinese – Portrait of a People* centres on this event and its aftermath. Another worthy account is *The Chinese* by David Bonavia.

Then there's the sort of stuff that fits more into the 'Mad Dogs & Englishmen' genre; probably long out of print, but if you can find a copy you won't fail to be amused by two books written by a young Englishmen, Peter Fleming, in the mid 1930s. *One's Company* describes his travels across Siberia and eastern China meeting such notables as Pu Yi, the puppet-emperor of the Japanese-occupied Manchuria. *News from Tartary* describes his epic six-month trek on the backs of camels and donkeys across southern Xinjiang and into the north of Pakistan. More recent is Vikram Seth's *From Heaven Lake*, another rather amusing account by a young Indian student who hitched from northern China to his home in Delhi via Lhasa and Nepal in 1981 – battles with bureaucracy and the agonising discomfort of long-distance trucking in graphic detail.

### Other Guidebooks

Graham Earnshwaw's *On Your Own in China* is rather scanty on practical information but he's got some fascinating background info. Highly recommended for additional reading.

Brian Schwartz's *China – Off the Beaten Track* is also rather scant on information but it was one of the first China guidebooks orientated to low-budget independent travellers. Just about *everybody* who went to China in 1983 had this in hand like the yellow bibles of South-East Asia. Future editions could be worth watching out for since Schwartz spent seven weeks in Tibet in the middle of 1982.

Frederic Kaplan and Arne Keijzer's *The China Guidebook* lists the major cities, sights and hotels and includes some other useful info. It's really a book designed for people on tours who want some background reading, not for low-budget solo travellers. Kaplan is a member of the National Board of directors of the US-China People's Friendship Association and is also president of of China Passage Inc., which organises specialised tours to China. Keijzer is the founder of a consulting firm which specialises in the development of trade between the US and China – which all goes to explain the style of the book.

There have been a number of do-it-yourself guidebooks orientated to low-budget, independent travel. These were usually written by people who travelled a month or two in the country in the early days of independent travel. Amidst the dearth of information and the lack of any comprehensive guidebooks they all seem to have been quite profitable ventures.

**Living in China** If you're about to condemn a large portion of your existence to residence or extensive travelling in the People's Republic, then there are a couple of books worth picking up:

*The Administrative Divisions of the People's Republic of China* is a little booklet with extensive lists of Chinese cities and towns in both Pinyin and Chinese characters – useful if you're going to travel to obscure places. It's sold in Hong Kong and in China.

*The China Phone Book and Address*

*Directory* is published annually by the China Phone Book Company, GPO Box 11581, Hong Kong and is also available from some of the major bookshops in Hong Kong. If you're living in China or visiting the country frequently it may be invaluable. It's in English and Chinese and contains the addresses and phone numbers of industrial firms, hospitals, government departments and the like in the major cities and towns.

Excellent background information can be had from *China Bound: A Handbook for American Students, Researchers and Teachers* published by the US-China Education Clearing House. It's available from the National Association for Foreign Student Affairs, 1860 19th Street, NW Washington, DC 20009, USA. There's also *Living in Hong Kong* which contains a *brief* but very good section on living in Beijing. The book is published by the American Chamber of Commerce in Hong Kong, and is available on order from the Book Society at GPO Box 7804, Hong Kong; costs HK$90 plus a mailing charge of US$6.10 to the USA and Europe.

**Phrase Books** are an essential for China. There probably isn't a single one which will match all your needs but you'll need something. The well-known Berlitz series has a Chinese phrase book which is particularly useful if you find yourself in a rape-type situation in the middle kingdom, with useful phrases like 'Go Away', 'Leave me alone' and 'Stop or I'll scream'.

### Bookstores in Hong Kong

There are a couple of bookstores in Hong Kong which are good for books from or about China. The best is probably *Swindon Books* on Lock Rd, Tsimshatsui, Kowloon. Other shops to try are the *Chueng Wah Bookstore* at 740A Nathan Rd, Kowloon or their other shop at 450-452 Nathan Rd, Kowloon. The *Commercial Press* has a shop at 35 Queens Rd, Central, Hong Kong Island. *Kelly and Walsh* on Ice House St, Central, Hong Kong Island, are also worth trying but they don't have a big selection. For glossy magazines and the like, try *Hong Kong China Tourism Press*, 1C Tsing Wan Building, 334-336 Kings Rd, North Point, Hong Kong Island.

### General Thoughts

If you think it's hard deciding what to read on China, then spare a thought for the Chinese who don't have the right to choose. Books come and go in China – as the political winds change so does the availability of certain books. In a bookshop in Wuhan I came across a copy of a book printed in 1974 called 'Criticise Lin Biao and Confucius' – it should have been removed long ago since that campaign was actually an attack on 'rightists' like Deng Xiao-ping. The employees in the shop tried to take it off me when I picked it off the shelves and despite a furious argument they refused to sell it to me. They claimed it was a damaged book (the front cover had been torn off) and they couldn't sell a damaged book. One bystander said it was an 'old' book and I couldn't learn anything from an old book. In utter frustration I left the shop. I returned the next day and all copies of the book had been taken off the shelves. So if you see something that looks interesting you'd better get it now, because in ten years time when the Chinese leadership is aiming in a different direction it just won't be available.

The other problem with Chinese bookshops is that some books are *neibu* – restricted or forbidden except to those who have been granted access. Of course they won't tell you the book is neibu but will make up some excuse like the book has no price on it. Books are neibu for various reasons; sometimes it's because they're illegally printed copies of Western books and the Chinese are sensitive about infringing international copyright. A more common reason – and this one afflicts university libraries throughout China – is that only certain people have permission to use certain books – a law student can only use the law books, an economics student can only use the economics books and so on. To use books outside your field requires permission from the unit in charge of the library which houses those books. Foreign students and foreign teachers right up to professorial level are not immune to the system – even they are restricted in their access to books, and this has become one of the most serious complaints made against the Chinese by foreigners who are either teaching or studying in the country.

## MAPS

The most useful map of China is the one published by the **Cartographic Publishing House** in Beijing. It's detailed and is available in both pinyin and Chinese script. It's called simply the *Map of the People's Republic of China (Zhonghua Renmin Gonghegua Ditu)* You should be able to get it in your home country, otherwise it's readily available in Hong Kong and in the large cities in China. It does have a few peculiarities; like referring to North and South Korea simply as 'Korea' with the capital in Pyongyang, and showing Taiwan as part of China. Hong Kong and Macau are referred to as 'occupied' territories.

*Bartholomew's* maps are usually excellent, but not for China. Their China map is extremely detailed but uses the old Wade-Giles system for naming towns, which is a distinct nuisance. The map also leaves out Tibet and Xinjiang.

The *Rand McNally* map is not very detailed, but it covers the whole country and uses pinyin names. It's useful for plotting a route at a glance, and probably has most places marked.

City maps are often sold by hawkers outside the railway and long-distance bus stations. These are in Chinese and show the bus routes, and in most cases are very good and definitely worth buying. They only cost around 10 to 30 fen. Maps in English are sometimes sold at the larger tourist hotels, but their usefulness varies depending on where you are.

Large maps of 20 major cities in China have been made by the **Cartographic Publishing House** in Beijing, and are usually available from most tourist hotels. There are versions both in Chinese and in English, and they usually come complete with sub-maps of the area around the city, and of parks and sights within the city. The cities mapped so far are Beijing, Shanghai, Guangzhou, Chengdu, Dalian, Xian, Kunming, Guilin, Suzhou, Wuxi, Wuhan, Qingdao, Hangzhou, Nanjing, Jinan, Tianjin, Nanning, Changsha, Chongqing and Shenyang. They also carry a lot of background info on the reverse side, and only cost around 25 fen each. They're excellent maps, although sometimes the sights are carelessly marked and it's hard to tell whether a building is on a main street or off down some side alley. It can be a bit of nuisance getting these maps when you need them – if you see a map of a city you'll be going to buy it, because it may not be available in that city, and that even applies to maps of Beijing!

If you're after detail, then you can sometimes get booklets of maps (in Chinese) of the counties in the individual provinces, and these usually include maps of the main towns. There are little booklets of detailed maps of the individual Chinese provinces (in Chinese) sold on the trains and at the railway stations.

Generally, there are pretty good maps available of most of the touristy places in China; the problem is mainly one of supply; so as I said, if you see a map you're going to need, then get it!

If you arrive in a place where there is no map available, take a look in the waiting room of the railway or long-distance bus-station; there are often large maps of the town hung up on the wall. They're always in Chinese, but you may be able to orientate yourself from them, and they sometimes show the bus routes.

Chinese cities built or rebuilt under the Communists are laid out on neat grid patterns; curvy streets or wandering streets on a map may indicate an old area, where the houses have traditional architecture and courtyards, and are separated by narrow alleys and walkways; these small streets are often the location of free markets.

## MEDIA
### News Agencies

China has two news agencies, the Xinhua News Agency and the China News Service. The Xinhua (New China) Agency is a national agency with its headquarters in Beijing and branches in each province and autonomous region, as well as branches in the PLA and about 85 foreign countries. It provides news for the national, provincial and local papers and radio stations, transmits radio broadcasts abroad in foreign languages, and is responsible for making contact with and exchanging news with foreign news agencies. The main function of the China News Service is to supply news to overseas Chinese newspapers and journals, including those in Hong Kong and Macau. It also distributes Chinese documentary films abroad.

Newspapers and periodicals are distributed through the post office and the major distributor of books is the Xinhua Bookstore, which has around 5000 stores throughout China. There are also Foreign Language Bookstores in the major cities. The Guoji Shudian (China Publications Centre) is the chief distributor of books and periodicals abroad.

### Chinese language publications

In 1980 there were 188 national and provincial newspapers. The main one is *Renmin Ribao (People's Daily)* which was founded in 1946 as the official publication of the Central Committee of the Communist Party which is circulated nationally. There are also around 39 newspapers specifically for the minority nationalities.

There were almost 2200 periodicals published in 1980, of which about half were technical or scientific – the rest were concerned with social sciences, literature,

culture and education, or were general periodicals, pictorials or children's publications. One of the better-known periodicals is the monthly *Hongqi (Red Flag)* which is the main Communist philosophical and theoretical journal.

In China the last place news appears is in the papers, or on the radio or television. Westerners tend to be numbed by endless accounts of heroic factory workers and stalwart peasants, and dismiss China's media as a huge propaganda machine. Flipping through journals like *China Reconstructs*, *Women of China* and *China Pictorial* only serves to confirm this view. But information is also a privilege of rank in China, and the official information system allows some Chinese to be better informed about what is happening both inside and outside China than many foreigners might expect.

Apart from the classified documents which move through the Party, government and army, and which only high-ranking cadres have access to, there is also a hierarchy of *neibu* or 'restricted' publications. At the bottom of the hierarchy is *Reference News*, a four-page paper which reprints articles from the foreign press about international affairs and which also carries copies of reports by foreign journalists about events in China. It has a circulation of about 10 million, nearly double that of *People's Daily* and any Chinese can subscribe to it for only 50 fen per month. At the next level is *Reference Material*, a thick digest of foreign news articles distributed only to Party members and cadres. And above that there are information bulletins for distribution to even higher-ranking cadres. Ordinary Chinese who have connections with ranking cadres will be able to tap into the government's official information network, rather than rely on the public media.

Nevertheless, the Chinese press does warrant serious attention since they it provides clue to what is happening in China. When Deng Xiaoping returned to public view after being disposed of in the Cultural Revolution, the first mention was simply the inclusion of his name in a guest list at a reception for Prince Sihanouk of Kampuchea, printed in the *People's Daily* without elaboration or comment. Political struggles are expressed in articles in the Chinese newspapers as a means of warning off supporters of the opposing side and undermining its position rather than resorting to an all-out and dangerous conflict. 'Letters to the editor' of *People's Daily* provides something of a measure of public opinion, and complaints are sometimes followed up by reporters.

Newspapers and journals are useful for following the 'official line' of the Chinese government – though in times of political struggle they tend to follow the line of whoever has control over the media. For example in the immediate post-Mao days when the 'rightists' were making a comeback, the 'leftists' controlled the media.

## Foreign language publications

China publishes various newspapers, books and magazines in a number of European and Asian languages.

The papers you're most likely to come across are *China Daily*, the only English-language daily newspaper which was first published in June 1981, *Beijing Review*, a weekly magazine on political and current affairs, and *China Reconstructs* which is a monthly magazine. They all suffer from an over-supply of political rhetoric, but there are usually some interesting articles on archaeological discoveries or travel. China Daily is notable for reporting crime and the executions of criminals and even stories about corrupt officials (a very popular theme in the papers at the moment).

## Radio and Television

Domestic radio broadcasting is controlled by the Central People's Broadcasting Station (CPBS). Broadcasts are made in *putonghua*, the standard Chinese speech, as well as in the local Chinese dialects and the minority languages. There are also broadcasts to Taiwan in *putonghua* and Fukianese. Radio Beijing is China's overseas radio service and broadcasts in about 40 foreign languages, as well as in *putonghua* and several local dialects. It also exchanges programmes with radio stations in a number of countries and has correspondents in some. The other station, Chinese Central Television (CCTV) began broadcasting in 1958, and ·colour transmission began in 1973.

There are only something like eight million TV sets in the country, distributed among a billion people. Yet the Chinese seem to be addicted to TV, at least in the urban areas where sets are more common. Television has also bred a desire for more television sets and God knows how many get carried across the border every day by Hong Kong relations! The most watched shows are probably the English-language programmes; if you need a laugh watch the afternoon English-language show 'Follow Me'. Private ownership of TVs is limited, but just about everyone has access to one: communes, factories and hotels usually buy a TV and put it in their recreation rooms or dining halls for collective viewing, or there may even be one set serving a whole apartment block.

## Foreign papers and journals on sale in China

Some western journals and newspapers are sold in a few of the major tourist hotels. The *Herald Tribune* and the Asian edition of the *Wall Street Journal* are sold in Beijing, Shanghai and Canton. *Time*, *Newsweek* and *Reader's Digest* have wide distribution; *Newsweek* is even sold in some Foreign Language Bookshops. Time and Newsweek sell for around Y3 or Y3.50 each. If you want to keep up with the news, a short-wave radio receiver would be worth bringing with you. There are various compact and easy-to-carry units on the western (and South-East Asian) market.

**Public notice-boards and big-wall posters**

Apart from the media – television, radio and the press – the public notice-board retains its place as a means of educating the people or influencing public opinion. Other people who want to get a message across glue up 'big wall-posters' in public places – it's a traditional form of communicating ideas in China and if the subject matter catches the attention of even a few beholders, the word can spread very quickly.

Public notice-boards abound in China. Two of the most common subjects are crime and road accidents. In China it's no holds barred. Before-and-after photos of executed criminals are plugged up on these boards along with a description of their heinous offences. Photos of people squashed by trucks are even more frequent. Industrial safety is another common theme, and displays may include photos of a severed and mangled foot.

Model workers are another common theme; the 'face of China' for 1983 was Zhang Haidi. Zhang was paralysed at the age of five from the chest down by a spinal tumour, but she . . .

. . . has valiantly fought her disease and persisted in her studies, thus acquiring various skills. She has tutored other young people so that they could pass the college entrance exam. She studied acupuncture enabling her to treat thousands of patients suffering from paralysis, and she also learnt to repair radios and TV sets .

Her photos, artists' sketchings of episodes in her life, descriptions of her work, could be seen all over China – in magazines, on notice-boards, posters and huge billboards.

Stories of 'model workers' abound in the Chinese press. One recent article in *China Pictorial* told the heart-warming story of Wei Yu, a Chinese student who completed a PhD in Germany:

Refusing to take a home leave, Wei Yu extended her stay in Germany, and worked intensively, sleeping only four or five hours a night. She lost weight and suffered from fatigue. The doctor wanted to hospitalize her, but she took some traditional Chinese medicine and continued her rigorous schedule. In eight months she finished writing her doctoral dissertation'.

In another story, Yang Xun, a cotton-mill worker from Nantong . . .

. . . arrives early at the factory and gets everything ready before the shift starts. When she was still in her apprenticeship, she trained two other apprentices. Although Yang is highly skilled she is not conceited and has many friends . . . she was so excited when she got her first months wage that she bought fruit and bottles of tonic water for her grandmothers, parents and aunt and uncle. What's more, she gave her younger sister a satchel and some stationery.

## SHOPPING

Some people buy nothing in China while others come back loaded with souvenirs; it largely depends on what you're interested in. There's a variety of goods available and a variety of places to buy them. Some items, like cloth, require ration coupons (except in the Friendship Stores), so you may find occasionally that the shop can't sell you what you want to buy.

**Chinese department stores in Hong Kong**

It's worth remembering that the Chinese government runs large department stores in Hong Kong which sell almost everything that China exports. Everything from antiques to chopsticks is available and you'll get a greater variety and often cheaper prices than you can in China itself! There are two types of stores; the 'China Products' and 'China Arts and Crafts'. The first sells the ordinary, domestic, down-market end of merchandise like cloth, garments, household goods and furniture, but it also stocks silk kimonos, short 'happi' coats and negligees you wouldn't believe came out of staid China. The second stocks the arty/crafty, curio/antiquity stuff. There are several of these stores in Hong Kong; the best is the one opposite Central Market in Queens Road, on the Hong Kong Island side. Another good store is at the corner of Percival St and Hennessy Rd in Causeway Bay.

If you are going to buy stuff in China, it's a good idea to get a few guidelines by checking out the prices in the Hong Kong stores first.

**Friendship Stores** stock goods which are either imported from the west and/or are in short supply in the ordinary stores. You usually have to pay for goods in these stores with Foreign Exchange Certificates, which have become the subject of a black market since they enable ordinary Chinese to buy goods which are otherwise obtainable or would require a long wait – like televisions or cassette-players. You don't need ration coupons or approval from your work unit to buy stuff in the Friendship Stores, all you need is the right type of money and that's why the Chinese are so anxious to get FECs.

Some of these stores are reserved for foreigners and high-ranking Chinese, while others serve anyone with the cash. Some stores are just small shops in the tourist hotels while others are large-scale affairs like the stores in Canton, Beijing and Shanghai. The Beijing store has a supermarket selling imported western food – so if you can't stand one more noodle, this is a chance to stock up.

At some Friendship Stores you can get things crated up and sent home for you.

**Department Stores** If you need something, the big department stores are the places to go. With the rebirth of consumerism these stores are stocked with all types of goods, both daily needs and sometimes luxuries. If you need toilet paper and haven't 'borrowed' any from your last hotel, the department stores are where you'll get it. Most of the goods are very expensive in comparison with Chinese wages, but cheap for westerners. Before you buy something in the Friendship Store, it's worth checking to see if it's available in the local department store as it may be cheaper there.

**Hotel Shops** sell things which foreigners either need or like, such as western and Japanese film, western cigarettes and alcohol, Coca-Cola, biscuits, souvenirs, toothpaste, postcards, maps and books.

**Free Markets** started up around 1979-1980. These are street markets where people can sell their produce and goods for their own profit. They usually sell clothes and foodstuffs, and you'll also see a lot of people selling secondhand books and magazines on the side-walks.

## THINGS TO BUY

You won't fail to notice China's efforts to expand its arts and crafts industries with a view to profiteering from the tourist trade. If you're on a tour, visits to arts and craft 'factories' and handicrafts shops figure heavily on the itinerary. There is a mass of stuff to buy – perhaps the only rule is that if you see something you like then get it there and then – you may not see it again anywhere else! **Books and Posters** Chinese propaganda books and magazines are interesting souvenirs, as are wall-posters. These are readily available in the bookshops and are very cheap. One delightful poster I bought showed Mao Zedong, Zhou Enlai, Zhu De and Liu Shaoqi amiably chatting in what looks like a communist heaven, surrounded by trees and flowers with a most beautiful waterfall behind them! One of the most interesting posters showed Zhu, Mao and Liu welcoming Zhou at the airport on his return from the USSR in the 1950s; older versions of this poster (which you'll still see in China) have Liu scrubbed out. Another version of the updated poster even includes Deng Xiaoping!

All over China you'll see people on the footpath presiding over shelves full of little books. These are the Chinese equivalent of comic books and are about the size of your hand. Popular with both children and adults, the Chinese rent them from the stall-keeper and sit down on benches to read them. The stories range from fantasies about animals to tales from classical China and episodes from the Communist revolution. They're all in Chinese but they make nice little souvenirs – you can buy them in the shops for around 20 fen each.

The fashion magazines printed in Beijing and Shanghai are interesting mementoes, with their western and Chinese beauties whose looks, hairstyles and dress are eons away from the blue-garbed socialist women of the Maoist era. Some of them include dress patterns.

**Arts and Crafts** Chinese musical instruments are sold in the department stores and there are quite a few private shops which manufacture and sell instruments. Some shops are devoted entirely to the sale of traditional Chinese opera costumes, so if you want something unique for the next masquerade party ... and if you take a liking to the music itself, then it's available on record and cassette in some of the music stores.

Brushes, paints and other art materials may be worth checking out – a lot of this stuff is being imported by western countries and you should be able to pick it up cheaper at the source. Scroll paintings are sold everywhere and are invariably very expensive, partly because the material on which the painting is done is expensive. There are many street artists in China, who often sit out on the sidewalk making on-the-spot drawings and paintings and selling them to passers-by.

Beautiful kites are sold in China and are worth getting, even just to hang on your wall. Paper rubbings of stone inscriptions are cheap and make nice wall hangings when framed. Paper-cuts are sold everywhere and some of them are exquisite.

**Clothes and Jewellery** China is a hat-collector's paradise. The woven straw coolie hats vary from province to province. The women from the villages near Xiamen lacquer their hats a bright yellow; in Hunan the peasants wear hats which are a distinctive squat conical shape. In Xinjiang the Moslems wear attractive little embroidered caps. Discarded PLA caps (or imitations) are available everywhere, as are the blue so-called 'Mao caps'.

In Xinjiang and in Hohhot in Inner Mongolia you can buy, or have made for you, decorative leather riding boots. Kashgar is the hat and knife-making centre of Xinjiang and both are available in an extraordinary variety of designs.

Check out the cashmere jumpers, cardigans and skirts in the Beijing Friendship Store and its branch in the Beijing Hotel.

Jade and ivory jewellery is commonly sold in China – but remember that some countries like Australia and the USA prohibit the import of ivory.

**Antiques** Many of the Friendship Stores have antique sections, and some cities have separate antique shops, but prices are high so don't expect to find a bargain. Only antiques which have been cleared for sale to foreigners may be taken out of the country. When you buy an item over 100 years old it will come with an official red wax seal attached – this seal does *not* necessarily indicate that the item is an antique though! You'll also get a receipt of sale and you must show this to Customs when you leave the country, otherwise the antique will invariable be confiscated.

Imitation antiques are sold everywhere. Some museums have shops which sell replicas of some of their exhibits.

**Stamps and Coins** China issues quite an array of beautiful stamps – generally sold at post offices in the hotels. Outside many of the post offices you'll find amateur philatelists with books full of stamps for sale and these are worth checking out. It's extraordinarily hard bargaining with these guys though. Old coins make good souvenirs, and these are sold by individuals in places that have had a few tourists come through – like Yangshuo or the Bilingisi Caves near Lanzhou.

**Oddities** If plaster statues take your liking, the opportunities to stock up in China present themselves in abundance! Fat Buddhas everywhere, and 60 cm high Venus de Milos and multi-armed gods are not uncommon. They're all incredibly crass, but the Chinese haven't had these things for 30 years and so the market for them has really taken off.

Fireworks are sold all over China. One problem is that you're not allowed to bring them into Hong Kong and Customs may ask you for them or inspect your bags. It's also prohibited and dangerous to carry fireworks on aircraft. Some countries, like Australia, do not permit the import of fireworks.

There are lots of shops selling numerous medicinal herbs and spices which could be worth checking out. Your home country may not allow the import of these drugs though, and they may be taken off you at Customs when you you return.

In Kashgar you can buy wooden horse saddles, and Hotan is the carpet-making centre of Xinjiang.

### Advertising

It'd be fun to handle the advertising campaigns for some of China's charming brand names. There's Double-Bull Underwear, as well as Pansy Underwear (for men); Fang-Fang Lipstick, and another anagrammatic brand called Maxam which sounds vaguely familiar. For your trusty Walkman it may be best to stay away from White Elephant Batteries, but you might try the space-age Moon Rabbit variety. Flying Eagle Safety Razors don't sound too safe either. Then there's the Golden Cock Alarm Clocks – but they've gone and changed the name on that one to Golden Rooster. Out of the psychedelic 60s come White Rabbit Candy; the rarer brand to look for is the Flying Baby series which appears to have been discontinued – there used to be some Flying Baby Toilet Paper around. As for Coca-Cola, the ideographs sound something like 'Kokuh-Koluh' and translate as 'tastes good, tastes happy'.

## POST & COMMUNICATIONS

As well as the local post offices there are branch post offices in just about all the major tourist hotels where you can send letters, packets and parcels (the contents of packets and parcels is checked by the post office staff before mailing). In some places, you may only be able to post printed matter from these branch offices. Other parcels may have to have a Customs form attached at the central post office, where its contents will be checked.

The international postal service seems to be efficient and airmailed letters and postcards will probably take around five to ten days to reach their destinations. There is also an International Express Mail Service now operating in many Chinese cities. If possible, write the country of destination in Chinese as this should help speed up the delivery.

Large envelopes are a bit hard to come by; try the stationary stores and the department stores; if you expect to be sending quite a few packets, stock up when you come across such envelopes. String, glue, and sometimes cloth bags are supplied at the post offices. The Friendship Stores will sometimes package and mail purchases for you.

### International Post

Listed below are ordinary postal rates for international mail (other than to Hong Kong or Macau)

**Letters** Surface mail Y0.50 up to 20 g, Y1.00 up to 50 g. Airmail letters are an additional Y0.30 for every 10 g or fraction thereof.

**Postcards** Y0.40 surface mail or Y0.70 air mail anywhere in the world.

**Aerogrammes** Y0.70 anywhere in the world.

**Printed Matter** Surface mail is Y0.30 up to 20 g, Y0.55 up to 50 g, Y0.90 up to 100 g, Y1.80 up to 250 g, Y3.40 up to 500 g, Y5.40 up to 1 kg, Y9.00 up to 2 kg; Y3.80 for each additional kg.

Air mail is an additional Y0.15 for every 10 g.

航空
PAR AVION

LONELY PLANET
P.O. BOX 88
SOUTH YARRA, 3141.
MELBOURNE
AUSTRALIA

澳大利亚

漓江饭店

地址：桂林市杉湖北路

BY AIR MAIL
PAR AVION

Lonely Planet
P.O. Box 88
South Yarra, 3141,
Melbourne,
AUSTRALIA.

中国人民邮政

澳大利亚

T 30/50

Par Avion

LONELY PLANET,
P.O. BOX 88
SOUTH YARRA, 3141,
MELBOURNE,
AUSTRALIA

澳大利亚

人民大厦
REN MIN HOTEL

**Small packets** Surfcae mail charges are Y1.20 up to 100 g, Y2.40 above 100 g and upto 250 g, Y4.30 above 250 g and up to 500 g, Y7.20 above 500 g and up to 1kg. Air mail for small packets is an additional Y0.15 for every 10 g.

**Parcels** Rates vary depending on the country of destination. Surface mail for a 1 kg parcel to England is Y18.40, to Australia Y13.40, to Hong Kong Y9.60.

Post offices are very picky about how you pack things; don't finalise your packing until the thing has got its last Customs clearance. If you have a receipt for the goods, then put it in the box when you're mailing it, since it may be opened again by Customs.

**Registered mail** The registration fee for letters, printed matter and packets is Y0.50. Acknowledgment of receipt is Y0.40 and enquiry fee is Y0.50.

**Film** You *can* post undeveloped film out of China. But it's likely to be a nerve-racking experience with the prospect of the dreaded X-ray machines always lurking in the background ... at the moment your peace of mind is better off if you keep your film with you.

Some of the restrictions on what you can post out of the country almost reach the point of comical absurdity. In Wuhan I picked up a copy of a volume of the *Acta Academiae Medicinae Wuhan* a journal of medical research published (in English) by the Wuhan Medical College, freely available from the pamphlet shelf of the dining room of the Jianghan Hotel. I scurried off to the post office to send it back to Hong Kong but the staff there looked at it dubiously and telephoned someone who obviously told them that it wasn't to be posted. No doubt it was some sort of secret research which wasn't supposed to leave the confines of hotel dining rooms. In the next town I posted it, no questions asked.

**Poste Restante**

There is a poste restante in just about every city and town and these seem to work OK. Apart from these you can receive mail at some of the major tourist hotels – which may be easier all round. Some of these hotels have a mail box or a desk where incoming mail, both for residents of the hotel and others, is kept. Other hotels have notice boards where letters are displayed (one letter I saw in Canton was for Mr Wolf-doctor Kunler... hmmmh, strange people roaming these parts).

You should be able to rely on getting mail if it's posted to any one of the following hotels: the Dong Fang (Canton), the Beijing Hotel (Beijing), the Renmin Daxia (Xian) and the Peace Hotel (Shanghai). You should also be able to receive mail at the Kunming Hotel (Kunming), the Renmin Hotel (Chongqing), the Friendship Hotel (Tianjin) and the Jinjiang Hotel (Chengdu). They will hold mail for several months if you write such an instruction on the outside of the letter.

Other than these, your chances of receiving mail at a given hotel are rather haphazard. It's worth noting that some foreigners living in China have had their mail opened before they receive it – and some have evidently had their outgoing mail opened and read. Whether that applies to tourists also we don't know. Your mail is less likely to be opened if it's sent to cities that handle high volumes of mail, like Beijing. There are several items which the People's Revolution prohibits from being mailed to it. This includes matter such as books, magazines, notes, manuscripts, etc ...

**International Telephone, Telex and Telegram**
The tourist hotels have long-distance telephone facilities, and again the service is quite efficient. Lines are a bit faint but OK and depending on where you are you probably won't have to wait more than half an hour before you're connected (on the other hand a call to the USA I made from Harbin took 1½ hrs to get through).

The usual procedure is to fill out a form

with the relevant information concerning who you want to call and hand it to the attendant at the telephone desk. Calls to Western countries are charged around Y9.60 per minute with a minimum charge of three minutes; there is no call cancellation fee. Collect calls are cheaper than calls paid for in China. Time the call yourself; the operator will not break in to tell you that your minimum period of three minutes is approaching. After you have completed the call and hung up the operator will ring back to tell you how much the call cost.

If you are expecting an international call, if possible advise the caller beforehand of your hotel room number; the operators frequently have difficulty understanding western names and the hotel receptionist may not be able to locate you.

Telexes and telegrams can also be sent from some of the major tourist hotels and from the central telegraph offices in some of the bigger cities. International telexes (other than those to Hong Kong or Macau) cost Y8.40 per minute with a three minute minimum charge. International telegram rates vary considerably, but are usually around Y1.20 to Y1.50 per word, and more for the express service. For example, telegrams to the USA cost Y1.30 per word – the rate is double for a four hour urgent delivery.

### Services to Hong Kong & Macau

If you have some person or place of contact in Hong Kong then it's worth sending parcels there and picking them up when you get back from China – it greatly reduces the cost of postage and you can send everything by train.

Postcards cost Y0.04 to send. Letters up to 20g are Y0.08 for every extra 20g or fraction thereof. Letters up to 20g are Y0.10 air mail. Printed matter is considerably cheaper to send to Hong Kong and Macau, but rates for small packets are the same as the international rates. To send a 1kg parcel to Hong Kong by surface mail will cost you Y9.60.

Registeration fee is Y0.12 and there is a Customs fee of Y0.80 on packets and parcels.

Phone calls to Hong Kong are charged between Y6 and Y12 for the first three minutes, and Y4 for each additional minute; the call cancellation fee is Y1.20. the Liu Hua Hotel in Canton, across the road from the railway station, has a direct-dial service to Hong Kong which is quite cheap.

### Domestic Services

Postcards cost Y0.02; letters up to 20g are Y0.04. By all accounts the internal post seems to be very fast – say one or two days from Canton to Beijing. I sent one letter in Shanghai to another address in the city, and it arrived on the same day. Many hotel rooms are equiped with phones and local phone-calls from these are free. Local calls made from public phones (they are said to exist) cost four fen. There are also internal telex, telegram and long distance phone services.

## GENERAL INFORMATION

### Time

Time throughout China is set to Beijing time and does not vary throughout the year. When it's noon in Beijing it's also noon in far off Lhasa, Urumqi and all other parts of the country.

And when it's noon in Beijing the time in cities around the world is:

| | |
|---|---|
| Bangkok | 11 am |
| Chicago | 10 pm |
| Frankfurt | 5 am |
| Hong Kong | 12 noon |
| London | 4 am |
| Los Angeles | 8 pm |
| Melbourne | 2 pm |
| Montreal | 11 pm |
| New York | 11 pm |
| New Delhi | 9.30 am |
| Paris | 5 am |
| Rome | 5 am |
| Singapore | 11.30 am |
| Stockholm | 5 am |

| Tokyo | 1 pm |
| Vancouver | 8 pm |
| Wellington | 4 pm |
| Zurich | 5 am |

## Beggars

Yes, beggars do exist in China – but at least in the cities, towns and places you're likely to go to there are not as many as there are in countries like India. You may see as many beggars in a week in China as you would in an hour in India. There seem to be more in the north of China, standing out in Xian, Kashgar and Kaifeng, though there are quite a few hanging around Canton. As specimens of humanity some of them look no less wrecked than their counterparts in other Asian countries. More common than beggars are the people who hang around in the public restaurants waiting to move in on the food scraps. The beggars tend not to pounce on foreigners – the exception are the kids – in Yantai I couldn't get rid of kids in a restaurant who tugged at my trousers.

## Dope

There's not much information on this at the moment. One traveller found grass growing around the town of Dunhuang in Gansu province ' ... but sad to say, I picked some, dried it in a plastic bag, smoked it and never got stoned. Some people in Beijing say Chinese dope is quite poor quality. Have seen it from the train near the Great Wall in Peking ... '

Another traveller writes of the Kunming area in Yunnan Province ' ... if you walk around and explore the stone forest you might come across some marijuana. I had some from a Kiwi and we smoked it in the long bamboo bong which one sees all over Kunming. You could say we were stoned in the stone forest!'

We have no idea what the attitude of the Chinese police is to foreigners using dope – it's simply too early to tell. And if they do take an unfavourable view of it, we've no idea what the penalties would be if you get caught. Discretion is strongly advised!

## Tipping

China is one of those wonderful countries where tipping is not done and almost no one asks for it. In five months in China I came across only one exception, and that was in one of the new ultra-luxury hotels.

## Toilets

Chinese toilets are the usual Asian style holes in the ground which you crouch over. Public toilets can often be found in the side streets of the cities and towns. They have very low or no partitions at all between the individual holes, and if there are partitions there are usually no doors. The Chinese seem to crouch over these for ages reading books and newspapers; toilet paper is not provided. The toilets themselves vary between quite clean to absolutely filthy – some look like they haven't been cleaned since the Han dynasty. Often the problem is not the filth but the smell from the ground several feet below the floor of the toilet. Nothing is wasted; it's eventually shovelled up and sent to the countryside for use as fertiliser.

Toilet paper is readily available in China from the big department stores, although it's a good idea to hang on to whatever's left in your hotel room. Dormitory rooms are *not* provided with toilet paper, probably because if they were people would steal it. The tourist hotels have western-style 'sit-down' toilets.

Remember:

men 男

women 女

## Electricity

Electricity is 220 volts, 50 cycles AC. Plugs are usually two pin American type, so take conversion plugs if you're bringing any electrical equipment with you. Chinese cities are thankfully free of the frequent power black-outs which afflict countries like India and the Philippines.

### Holidays

The People's Republic has nine national holidays during the year:

**New Year's Day** 1 January.
**Spring Festival,** usually in February. This is otherwise known as Chinese New Year and starts on the first day of the old lunar calendar. This is China's only three-day holiday.
**International Working Women's Day** 8 March.
**International Labour Day** 1 May.
**Youth Day** 4 May, commemorates the student demonstrations which took place in Beijing on 4 May 1919, when the Versailles Conference decided to give Germany's 'rights' in the city of Tianjin to Japan.
**Children's Day** 1 June.
**Anniversary of the founding of the Communist Party of China** 1 July.
**Aniversary of the founding of the Chinese People's Liberation Army** 1 August.
**National Day** 1 October, which celebrates the founding of the People's Republic of China on 1 October, 1949.

### Weights & Measures

The metric system is widely used in China and most information you come across will have weights and measures recorded using this system. However the traditional Chinese measures are often used for domestic transactions and you may come across them:

| | | |
|---|---|---|
| 1 metre | = 3 shichi | = 3.28 feet |
| 1 kilometre | = 2 shili | = 0.62 miles |
| 1 hectare | = 15 mu | = 2.47 acres |
| 1 litre | = 1 sheng | = 0.22 gallons |
| 1 kilogram | = 2 jin | = 2.20 pounds |

### Business Hours

Banks, offices, government departments, Public Security Bureaux, etc, are open Monday to Saturday. *As a rough guide only* they tend to open around 8 am to 9 am, close for two hours in the middle of the day, and then re-open until 5 pm or 6 pm.

Sunday is a public holiday. CITS offices, Friendship Stores and the foreign exchange counters in the tourist hotels and some of the local branches of the Bank of China have similar opening hours, and will generally be open on Sundays as well.

Many parks, zoos and monuments have similar opening hours, but they are also open on Sundays and are often open at night. Restaurants are open for early morning breakfast (sometimes as early as 5.30 to 7.30 am), then for lunch and again in the evening from around 5 pm to 8 pm or 9 pm. Chinese eat early and go home early – by 9 pm you'll probably find the chairs stacked and the cooks gone home, though some places stay open quite late depending on where you are. Cinemas and theatres finish by 9.30 or 10 pm as well.

Railway station and long-distance bus stations open their ticket offices quite early in the morning – often around 5 am or 5.30 am before the first trains or buses pull out – and apart from the one or two-hour break in the middle of the day, usually stay open until late at night, say 11 or 11.30 pm.

### Admission Fees

Gardens, parks and tourist sights usually have an admission fee; usually around five fen. In some cases, fees for foreigners can be much higher, such as Y3 at the Longmen Caves outside Luoyang.

### Chinese Embassies Abroad

**Australia** 247 Federal Highway, Watson, Canberra, 2602 ACT.
**Canada** 411-415 Andrews St., Ottawa, Ontario KIN 5H3.
**England** 31 Portland Place, London WIN 3AG.
**France** 11 George V Avenue, 75008, Paris.
**West Germany** 5307 Wachtbergniederbachen, Konrad-Adenauer Str, 104, Bonn.
**Italy** Via Giovanne, Paiseillo 39, Roma 00198.
**Japan** 15-30 Minami– Azabu, 4-Chome, Minato-ku, Tokyo.

**Netherlands** Adriaan Goehooplaan 7, Den Haag.

**Sweden** Bragevagen 4, Stockholm.

**Switzerland** Kalcheggweg 10, Berne.

**United States** The Chinese Embassy is at 2300 Connecticut Ave., NW Washington, DC 20008. there are also consulates at Guest Quarters, Suite 1509, 2929 South Post Oak Rd, Houston, TX 77056; San Francisco Hotel, Rm 1040, Union Square, San Francisco, CA 94119; 520 12th Avenue, New York, NY 10036.

### China International Travel Service (CITS)

The head office is located at 6 East Changan Avenue, Beijing (tel 551031; cable Luxingshe, Beijing; telex 22350 CITSH CN). The international offices are at :

**Britain** 4 Glenworth Street, London NW 1, (tel 01-9359427).

**France** 7 Rue Jean Goujon, 75008, Paris (tel 359-74-85).

**Hong Kong** Unit 601/605/606, 6th Floor, Tower II, South Sea Centre, Tsimshatsui East, Kowloon, (tel 3-7215317, cable 2320 Hong Kong, telex 38449 CITC HX)

**Japan** 1st Floor, A K Building, 6-1, 5 Bancho, Chiyoda-ku, Tokyo, (tel 03-234-5366).

**USA** 60E, 42nd Street, Suite 465, New York, NY 10165 (tel 212-867-0271).

### China Travel Youth Service (CYTS)

The head office is at 23 Dongjiaomin Xiang, Beijing (tel 551531; cable CHINAYS) The office in Hong Kong is at Room 904, Nanyang Commercial Bank Building, 151 des Voeux Road, Hong Kong Island (tel 5-410975-8; cable HON-SHANG; telex 61679 YOUTH HX)

### China Travel Youth Service (CYTS)

The head office is at 23 Dongjiaominxiang, Beijing (tel 551531; cable CHINAYS). The office in Hong Kong is at Room 904, Nanyang Commercial Bank Building, 151 des Voeux Road, Hong Kong Island (tel 5-410975-8; cable HONSHANC; telex 61679 YOUTH HX).

### CAAC

The overseas offices of the China National Aviation Corporation, the domestic and international carrier of the People's Republic are listed below (there are also offices in Addis Ababa, Baghdad, Belgrade, Bucharest, Sharjah, Teheran, and, for academic interest, in Pyongyang).

**Burma** 67 Prome Rd, Rangoon (tel 75714, Airport 40113).

**England** 5A Whitehorse St, London W1 (tel 4497601). The Gatwick Airport office is in Rm 601, North Roof Office Block (tel 02 93502021).

**Japan** Minato Ku Motoazabu 3-4-38 Tokyo (tel 4043700, Narita Airport *0476* 323941); 4F Matsufuji Bldg, 3-25 Gotomachi, Nagasaki (tel 281510).

**Pakistan** 25/C, 24th Street, Block 6, PECHS Karachi-29 (tel 435570).

**Philippines** 4816 Velanzuela St. Sta, Mesa, Metro Manila (tel 608111, Airport 8316351).

**Switzerland** CH-8058 Zurich Airport, terminal B 1-101, Zurich (tel 8163090 or 8163091).

**Thailand** 286/3-4 Surawong Rd, Bangkok (tel 2344122, 2332899, 2351880-2).

**United States** 2500 Wilshire Boulevard, Los Angeles, California 90057 (tel 3842703, Airport 6468104); 51 Grant Avenue, San Francisco, California 94108 (tel 3922156, Airport 8770750); 477 Madison Avenue, Suite 707, New York, NY 10022 and at 4230E Pan Am Terminal Building, J F Kennedy International Airport (tel 37 19898, Airport 6564722).

**USSR** Leninskye Gory UL, Druzhby 6 (tel 143-15-60, Airport 578-27-25).

**West Germany** Limburger Str, 37, 6246 Glashutten Airport, Frankfurt/main Room 201 2342 (tel 06174/63188, Airport 0611/690 5214).

# Getting There

## FROM HONG KONG

For most travellers, Hong Kong is going to be the jumping-off point for China. Most people head to Canton but there are a couple of other alternatives available. If you are going to Canton, the one rule to remember is to try to avoid going on weekends and even more so, holiday times like Easter and Chinese New Year. At these times everything is booked out and the crowds pour across the border from Hong Kong, trampling back-packers in their wake. Also avoid taking the local train from Kowloon to the border on weekends; queues of Hong Kongers are miles long – one person who went on the weekend had to line up for 90 minutes just to buy a ticket for the train and then had to queue for two hours to get to the emigration desks! You can get to Canton by express or ordinary train, ferry, hydrofoil or plane. There are also boats to towns on the south-east coast of China, Shanghai, and even direct to some towns in Guangdong province.

You can also enter or leave China via Macau. There is a bus from Canton to the border and a ferry between Canton and Macau; for details see the Canton section.

**Overnight Ferry to Canton** The Pearl River Shipping Company runs two ships between Hong Kong and Canton. They are the *Tianhu* and the *Xinghu*. One ship departs Hong Kong daily from the Tai Kok Tsui Wharf in Kowloon at 9 pm and arrives in Canton the following morning at 7 am. You can book tickets at the China Travel Service offices at 77 Queens Rd, Central, Hong Kong Island (tel 5-259121) or at the office on 1st floor, 27-33 Nathan Rd, Kowloon (tel 3-667201) – the entrance to the office is around the corner from Nathan Road on the Beijing Rd side. Some of the agencies that issue China

visas will also make bookings on this boat for you. There are no ferries on the 31st of each month. In Canton, the other ship leaves at 9 pm from Zhoutouzi Wharf; see the Canton section for details.

The ferry is one of the best and increasingly one of the most popular ways of getting to Canton. The boats are large, clean and very comfortable – but bring a light jacket because the air-conditioning is fierce! The fares per person are:

|  | Xinghu | Tianhu |
|---|---|---|
| 2-person cabin | HK$160 | HK$140 |
| 4-person cabin | HK$130 | HK$110 |
| Dormitory | HK$90 | HK$90 |
| Seat only | HK$70 | not available |

The *Xinghu* departs from Hong Kong on even number dates. The *Tianhu* departs on odd number dates.

An adult can bring one child under five free of charge. Once you have paid for a ticket, there is no refund available if you cancel.

**Express Train** The express train between Hong Kong and Canton is a comfortable and convenient way of entering China. Apart from tourists, the train is mainly used by businessmen.

There are two express trains daily from Hong Kong to Canton; Train No 92 departs Kowloon (Hunghom) Station at 12.55 pm and arrives in Canton at 3.35 pm. Train No 94 departs Kowloon (Hunghom) Station at 2.57 pm and arrives in Canton at 5.35 pm. The Adult fare is HK$80 and the Child fare is HK$40.

Returning to Hong Kong, Train No 91 departs Canton at 8.30 am and arrives at Kowloon (Hunghom) Station at 11.18 am; Train No 93 departs Canton at 10.10 am and arrives at Kowloon at 1.08 pm.

In Hong Kong, tickets can be booked up to seven days before departure at the CTS office at 24-34 Hennessey Rd, Wanchai, and at 62-72 Sai Yee St, Tak Po Building, Mong Kok, Kowloon. Tickets for the day of departure can be bought from Kowloon Railway Station. CTS charges a service fee of HK$5 on a one-way adult ticket, and HK$2.50 on a one-way child ticket. One child under five years of age may be brought free of charge so long as the child does not occupy a seat – each additional child must buy a ticket. Children over 10 years of age require adult tickets. Return tickets are also sold, but only seven to 30 days before departure.

If you cancel your trip you can get a 50% refund but you must apply at least 22 hours before departure time. On return tickets you can get a 50% refund on the first journey (Kowloon to Canton) and a 100% refund on the second journey (Canton to Kowloon), but you must apply at least seven days before the departure time of the train. If the Kowloon to Canton journey has already been made, you can get a 50% refund on the return journey, but you must apply in Canton at least 22 hours before departure.

For the travelling nature-lover, please be aware that you're not permitted to carry vegetables, plants, fish, poultry, livestock, roast pigs, birds and animals on the train.

You are allowed to take bicycles on the express train, and the freight rate is HK$0.11 per km with an unloading charge of HK$2.

**Local Trains between Hong Kong and Shenzhen and between Shenzhen and Canton** Rather than take the express train, a cheaper alternative is to take the electric train from Kowloon (Hunghom) Station to the Hong Kong/China border (Lo Wu station), walk across the border to the town of Shenzhen on the Chinese side and take the local train to Canton. This is the way most Hong Kongers enter China, so don't be surprised if you're sharing a train carriage with a couple of dozen colour TV sets and Sony three-in-ones.

The electric train from Kowloon (Hunghom) Station to Lo Wu is HK$5 ordinary class and HK$10 first class – both classes are air-conditioned and it's only a 35 minute trip to Lo Wu. The first electric train departs Kowloon at 7.05 am. The border closes at 4 pm so the last train you could get which would allow you to cross to China on that day would be the one at 3 pm. The first train from Lo Wu to Kowloon departs Lo Wu at 6 am.

The train from Shenzhen to Canton costs Y5.50 hard-seat, and Y11.50 soft-seat. Timetables on this route change frequently and during holiday periods you'll probably find several extra trains running. Departure times are shown below, but use them as a rough guide only.

| Train | dep. Shenzhen | arr. Canton |
|---|---|---|
| 98 | 9.33 am | 12.54 am |
| 100 | 11.33 am | 2.29 pm |
| 96 | 1.00 pm | 3.00 pm |
| 102 | 3.02 pm | 5.50 pm |
| 502 | 4.30 pm | 9.42 pm |

| Train | dep. Canton | arr. Shenzhen |
|---|---|---|
| 97 | 6.25 am | 8.44 am |
| 99 | 7.32 am | 10.00 am |
| 95 | 9.15 am | 11.20 am |
| 101 | 10.02 am | 1.35 pm |
| 501 | 9.40 am | 3.30 pm |

Once you've been through Customs at Shenzhen station, you usually have to wait for the Canton-bound train; the waiting hall in Shenzhen station is always packed, but there are two large restaurants upstairs if you want to eat and it's also worth taking the opportunity to wander around in the town (see the Shenzhen section for details).

**Hovercraft to Canton** The route taken by the hovercraft is the same as that used by the earliest navigators in these waters. At the mouth of the Pearl River (Zhu Jiang) is Lintin Island, where just over a century ago British merchant ships offloaded their cargoes of opium. The real gateway to

Canton is Tiger Gate (Hu Men), popularly known to earlier generations of Europeans as The Bogue, only five km wide at its greatest point. From here the traffic on the river becomes noticeably busier.

In Hong Kong the hovercraft depart from Tai Kok Tsui Wharf in Kowloon and dock at Canton's Zhoutouzui Wharf in the south-west of the city (see the Canton section for details). Hovercraft depart Tai Kok Tsui daily at 8.45 am, 9.45 am and 10.00 am and the fare is HK$140. They depart Zhoutouzui daily at 12.45 pm, 1.45 pm and 2 pm.

There are also hovercraft on the route between Tai Kok Tsui and the Whampoa Passenger Terminus in Canton. These depart Hong Kong at 9.30 am and 10.15 am and the fare is HK$100. They depart Whampoa at 2.15 pm and 2.45 pm and the fare is Y30.

Tickets for the hovercraft can be bought at the China Travel Service Offices in Hong Kong, or at the offices of the Hong Kong and Yaumati Ferry Company at the Jordan Rd Ferry Pier (tel 3-305257) in Kowloon or the Central Harbour Services Pier (tel 5-423428) on Hong Kong Island. In Canton, tickets can be bought from the China Travel Service office at 40 Kiu Kwong Rd, Haizhu Square (tel 61112) and at the Liuhua Hotel Service Desk.

**Hovercraft between Hong Kong and Shekou** Shekou is a port in the Shenzhen Municipality Special Economic Zone, situated on a peninsula of Chinese territory which juts out into Hou Bay on the north-west of Hong Kong's New Territories. There are hovercraft running between Tai Kok Tsui in Hong Kong and Shekou.

Mondays to Saturdays, the hovercraft leave Tai Kok Tsui at 9 am and 3.30 pm. They depart from Shekou at 10 am and 4.30 pm. Tickets for the hovercraft can be bought from the offices of the China Travel Service in Hong Kong, and from the offices of the Hong Kong & Yaumati

Ferry Company.

On Sundays, the hovercraft depart Tai Kok Tsui at 9 am and 3.30 pm. They depart Shekou at 2.40 pm and 4.30 pm. Tickets can be bought from the Passenger Terminus, Shekou Industrial Zone Pier.

**Jetcat to Zhuhai** There is a Jetcat service between Hong Kong to Jiuzhou Port in Zhuhai, the Special Economic Zone north of Macau. These high-speed catamarans take just an hour to do the trip. Departures from Hong Kong are at 7.45 am, 11 am and 2.30 pm. Departures from Jiuzhou Port are at 9.30 am, 1 pm and 4.30 pm. In Hong Kong tickets can be bought from the offices of China Travel Service and from the offices of the Hong Kong Hydrofoil Company (Ground Floor, Nathan Centre, 580 Nathan Rd, Mongkok, Kowloon; Tai Kok Tsui Ferry Pier, Kowloon (tel 3-954795); Hong Kong Macau Terminal, Hong Kong Island (tel 5-444441). In China tickets can be bought at the office of the Hong Kong China Hydrofoil Company at the Zhuhai Ferry Terminal at Jiuzhou Port, and at some of the major bus stations in Guangdong Province: Shiqi, Daliang, Canton, Jiangmen, Xihui, Taicheng, Jingan.

**Boat to Shanghai** There are two boats, the *Shanghai* and the *Haihing* which ply the south-east coast between Hong Kong and Shanghai. Most people take a boat when they leave China to return to Hong Kong and the trip gets rave reviews. Details of tickets and fares for the trip from Shanghai to Hong Kong are given in the Shanghai section. The fares for the trip from Hong Kong to Shanghai per person are:

| Class | The *Shanghai* | The *Haihing* |
| --- | --- | --- |
| Special A | 2 people, HK$800 each | 2 people, HK$800 each |
| Special B | Not available | 2 people, HK$740 each |

| 1st class A | Single person cabin, HK$680 | Single person cabin, HK$680 |
|---|---|---|
| 1st class B | 3-person cabin, HK$620 | 3-person cabin, HK$620 |
| 2nd class A | 2 or 3 people, HK$590 each | 3 people, HK$590 |
| 2nd class B | 3 people, HK$540 each | 2 people, HK$540 each |
| 3rd class A | 2 people, HK$500 | 2,3 or 4 people, HK$500 |
| 3rd class B | 4 people, HK$450 | 2 people, HK$450 |
| Economy | HK$380 (20 person dorm) | HK$380 (20 person dorm) |

In Hong Kong tickets for the boat can be bought from the offices of China Travel Service and from the China Merchants Steam Navigation Company on the 18th floor, 152-155 Connaught Rd, Central District, Hong Kong Island (tel 5-440558 and 5-430945). In Shanghai, tickets can be bought from the office of the China Ocean Shipping Agency at 255 Jiangxi Rd (tel 216327 extension 79) – for details see the Shanghai section.

**Ferries along the Chinese Coast** There are a couple of boats which go to Chinese ports on the south-east coast. These are worth investigating since the coast is one of the most attractive parts of China and some of the most interesting towns are located here. The *Dinghu* plies the water between Hong Kong and Shantou and the *Jimei* and *Gulangyu* run between Hong Kong and Xiamen.

There is also a direct boat to Zhanjiang departing Hong Kong once a week at 4 pm and arriving in Zhanjiang at 8.30 am the next day.

**Hovercraft to Wuzhou** There is a direct hovercraft from Hong Kong to Wuzhou. It departs Hong Kong on even-number dates from the Tai Kok Tsui Wharf at 7.20 am. The adult fare is HK$270 and child (under four years of age) fare is HK$150. Round trip tickets can also be booked, but you must return within a month. From Wuzhou you can get a bus to Guilin which takes nine hours, though you will *have* to overnight in Wuzhou. Coming back to Hong Kong, the hovercraft departs Wuzhou on odd number dates at 7.30 am. The journey takes 11 hours upstream (Hong Kong to Wuzhou) and nine hours downstream (Wuzhou to Hong Kong).

Tickets in Hong Kong can be bought at the offices of the China Travel Service and from some of the other agencies that issue China visas. The big advantage of the hovercraft is that it's probably the easiest way of getting to Guilin from Hong Kong. It may also be possible to take a boat further down the river from Wuzhou to Nanning.

**Ferry to Jiangmen** There are two ferries, the *Mingjuhu* and the *Yinzhouhu*, which travel from Hong Kong to the town of Jiangmen in Guangdong Province.

**Air to China** The Civil Aviation Administration of China (CAAC) operates flights between Hong Kong and six Chinese cities. In Hong Kong flights can be booked at the CAAC office on the ground floor of Gloucestor Tower, des Voeux Rd, Central, Hong Kong Island (tel 5 216416). The office is open Monday to Friday 9 am to 1 pm and 2 to 5 pm, Saturday 9 am to 1 pm, and is closed on Sundays and public holidays. The free baggage allowance on the flights is 15 kg and excess baggage is charged 1% of the fare per extra kg. There are flights to the following cities:

Canton – five flights a day; the fare is HK$260 (Y74) economy class or HK$340 (Y97) first-class. The 35-minute flight probably rates as one of the most expensive civilian flights in the world!

Beijing – five flights a week; HK$1158 (Y330) economy class or HK$1506 (Y429) first class.

Hangzhou – five flights a week; HK$832 (Y237).

Kunming – two flights a week; HK$860 (Y245).

Tianjin – two flights a week and the fares are the same as those for Beijing.

Shanghai – five flights a week; HK$832 (Y237) economy class and HK$1162 (Y331) first class. Cathay Pacific also fly Hong Kong – Shanghai for HK$799.

There may be direct flights from Hong Kong to Xiamen.

## FROM THE WEST

Apart from the Trans-Siberian from Europe, most westerners will probably enter China via Hong Kong. CAAC, the carrier of the People's Republic, also has flights between China and several European and US cities and Pan Am and Japan Airlines also fly between the USA and China (for a listing of flights between Europe and China, see the 'Getting Away' section).

Getting from the West to Hong Kong almost inevitably ends up gouging an enormous slice out of anyone's budget but there are a couple of ways of reducing the cost – usually by buying some sort of discounted fare which may (or may not) involve restrictions on route, advance purchase requirements cancellation charges, laborious route, non-refundable or non-reroutable clauses, etc. Some of the tickets available are listed below;

APEX (Advance Purchase Excursion) tickets usually have to be purchased two or three weeks ahead of departure, have a cancellation fee, do not permit stopovers and may have minimum and maximum stays as well as fixed departure and return dates.

Excursion fares are priced mid-way between APEX and full-fare economy class tickets. There are no advance booking requirements, but often a minimum stay overseas is required. Unlike APEX fares you can change your bookings and can also stopover in places en route.

Point-to-point tickets offer discounts on the full fare in return for loss of stopovers.

A back-to-front ticket is when a ticket is bought in, say Hong Kong, to fly to Sydney – but is actually used to fly from Sydney to Hong Kong. More about this later.

Another useful ticket is the round-the-world ticket. They're good value if you're going to China from Hong Kong and if Hong Kong is just going to be one stop on an across Asia or world tour. Booking restrictions, maximum and minimum stays, and penalties for changes of itinerary vary from airline to airline.

Combined ticketing is where a couple of tickets are issued at the same time to cover several projected trips. This method guards against fare increases, and since the tickets are sold at the normal price they can be altered if your plans change.

As well as these there are a host of legal, semi-legal and mostly illegal contortions that some travel agents go through to sell you a cheaper ticket.

## FROM AUSTRALIA

Direct flights to China began in 1984, with Qantas flying Melbourne/Sydney–Beijing and CAAC flying Sydney–Canton; both services operate weekly.

APEX fares are available with 21 days advance booking. There's a short high season in December-January; the rest of the year is low-season. Low-season return fares are A$908 to Canton, A$1102 to Beijing; in high-season it's A$1100 and A$1334 respectively.

Regular one-way economy fares are A$1258 to Canton, A$1374 to Beijing.

**Melbourne/Sydney to Hong Kong** Low-season APEX from Qantas or Cathay Pacific is A$591 one-way, A$908 return. In the high season (December-January) it's A$714 one-way, A$1100 return.

**Perth to Hong Kong** Low-season APEX fare is A$498 one-way, A$768 return;

high-season costs A$602 one-way, A$928 return.

It *is* possible to get discounts on APEX fares if you go to a travel agent. This may only be 5% but I know of one case where it was 15% off the low-season fare including a stopover in Manila with a night at the Hilton Hotel paid for by the airline. So it's worth shopping around. In Melbourne one of the best and most helpful discount-agents is The Flight Shop, 386 Little Bourke St (tel 67 6921).

If you've got the time then it is possible to arrange your visa and transport to China before you leave Australia. The company handling this is Access Travel, 5th floor, 58 Pitt St, Sydney (tel 241 1128). They organise a package deal which costs A$995 and includes a return airfare Sydney-Hong Kong (flying in the off-peak season on Cathay Pacific), return hovercraft Hong Kong-Canton, two nights accommodation in Canton, and a China visa valid for one month. You collect your visa when you arrive in Hong Kong. Access Travel can also book you on to the Trans-Siberian from Beijing to Europe and will arrange your Soviet, Mongolian and Polish visas – but this takes between six to eight weeks. They may also be able to book international flights out of China.

## FROM NEW ZEALAND

APEX fares between New Zealand and Hong Kong can only be bought in New Zealand. The low-season fare is NZ$1326 return and the high-season fare is NZ$1563 return. Tickets have to be paid for at least 30 days ahead of your departure date and there are no one-way APEX fares. The cheapest one-way ticket is the Standard Economy fare which is NZ$1129. There is also a 90 day excursion fare for NZ$1780 return – on this ticket you have to stay overseas for at least seven days and no longer than 90 days. Flights from New Zealand to Hong Kong depart from Auckland and Air New Zealand and Air Niugini take it in turns to carry passengers.

## FROM BRITAIN

British Airways, British Caledonian and Cathay Pacific (the Hong Kong based carrier part-owned by British Airways) fly London-Hong Kong. All offer the same APEX fares. One-way fares are: off-peak £225, shoulder £240, peak £290. Return fares are double the one-way fares.

Ticket discounting is a long running business in the UK and it's wide open – the various agents advertise their fares and there's nothing under-the-counter about it at all. To find out what's going and where to get it pick up a copy of the giveaway newspaper *Australasian Express* or the weekly 'what's on' guide *Time Out*. The magazine *Business Traveller* also produces a regular survey listing and analysing what's available on air-fares throughout the world.

Discount tickets are almost exclusively available in London – you won't find your friendly travel agent out in the country offering exciting deals. The danger with discounted tickets in the UK is that some of the 'bucket shops' (as ticket-discounters are known) are more than a little shonky, and sometimes the backstairs over-the-shop travel agents fold up and disappear after you've handed over the money and before you've got the tickets – get the tickets before you hand over the folding stuff.

A couple of excellent places to try for tickets are Trail Finders at 46 Earls Court Rd, London W8 and the Student Travel Association at 74 Old Brompton Rd, London W7. Also try Budget Holidays at 40 New Oxford St, London WC1 (tel 01 637 1414), Reho Travel at Commonwealth House, 15 New Oxford St, London WC1A 1BH, Flightdeck at 181 Earls Court Rd, London SW5 (tel 01 370 6437) and All Points Travel at Michelle House, 45/46 Berners St, London W1 (tel 580 0984). You can expect a London-Hong Kong return ticket to cost £400 to £500.

## FROM USA AND CANADA

There are direct flights from the USA to China; the limiting factors for flying direct are the expense and visas – weighed against this is the inconvenience of flying to Hong Kong if you're aiming for the north of China. Some American and Canadian travellers have managed to squeeze two-month visas out of home base – which takes care of one problem. It's also worth considering buying a return ticket from the USA or Canada rather than a one-way, as cheap tickets bought in Hong Kong may be less than spectacular value on this route, or the saving may be minimal.

**Discount flights to Hong Kong from the USA** Flights from the US West coast to Hong Kong are available from around US$300 to US$400 with a number of airlines, usually with no stopovers. But by shopping around you may be able to add a few stopovers for the same price. However if you stopover on a cheap ticket you may find yourself at the back of the queue getting a seat on the next leg and end up spending more time in the mid-Pacific than you bargained for. Again the best deals are from the travel agents, not from the airline itself.

A recent (maybe current?) price war started in Seattle when United Airlines considerably stepped up flights between that city and Hong Kong (via Tokyo), including one direct flight daily. United Airlines and North-West Orient quote US$820 return from the west coast to Hong Kong if you fly mid-week (Monday to Thursday) with no advance purchase and only a 15% cancellation fee.

**Discount flights to Hong Kong from Canada** Rock-bottom fares (low season, special deal, several restrictions) for the Vancouver -Hong Kong route seem to be around C$900 return – but you'll have to hunt around for it. Cathay Pacific and CP Air have an interchangeable deal for Vancouver -Hong Kong at C$1090 return (flying mid-

week, 25% non-refundable, 21-day advance booking, travelling in the Sept-May low-season – high season is June-August and the fare rises to C$1230); no stopover is allowed in Tokyo and there is a minimum stay overseas of 14 days and a maximum of six months. Cathay Pacific also has some direct flights to Hong Kong, thus appealing to Canadians who hate being frisked by US Customs men. China Airlines charges C$1090 return in the low season, but for some reason high season jumps to C$1400 return.

Undercutting these three carriers is Korean Airlines whose bookings only go through agents – and apparently the reduced deals are only available to Canadian residents (though some naughty US travellers have found their way around this). Return fare is C$980 low season and C$1020 return high season. The ticket is valid for a year, advance purchase is not necessary and few stops are allowed. Agents in Vancouver that book Korean Airlines flights are Kowloon Travel, 425 Abbott Street (Chinatown); Westcan Treks, 3415 West Broadway; Travel Cuts, 1516 Duranleau St, Granville Markets. Travel Cuts is Canada's national student bureau and has offices in Vancouver, Victoria, Edmonton, Saskatoon, Toronto, Ottawa, Montreal and Halifax – you don't necessarily have to be a student.

Getting discount tickets in Canada is much the same as in the USA – go to the travel agents and shop around until you find a good deal. A good agent for cheap tickets in Vancouver is Ed Polanin, No 7, 2065 W, 4th Avenue, Vancouver, BC, V6J-IN3.

**Direct flights to China** The general route for direct plane flights from the USA to China is from San Francisco (with connections from New York, Los Angeles and Vancouver) to Tokyo, Shanghai and up to Beijing. So you could go through to Beijing and pick up the return flight in Shanghai.

A plane change is generally made in

Tokyo, usually requiring a one-night stop. CAAC, Pan Am and Japan Airlines (JAL) fly the route and flights are dreadfully expensive. Pan Am and JAL, one-way from San Francisco to Shanghai costs US$790, and one-way from New York to Shanghai costs US$976. Return flights are a slightly better deal; Pan Am APEX (30-45 day advance booking) is US$1310 San Francisco-Beijing return; CAAC San Francisco-Shanghai return is US$1130 return. (JAL has recently been given rights to Canton airport and it also has Hangzhou on the list. CAAC flies the routes between China and Tokyo as well as Osaka and Nagasaki).

From Vancouver you can take a JAL flight direct to Tokyo and then on to China. An APEX flight (21-day advance booking) Vancouver-Tokyo-Shanghai is around C$1550.

Another possibility worth investigating is to hop over the Atlantic and pick up a plane to China from the European end where there are a lot more direct carriers – but again it's a problem of getting a Chinese visa. One traveller flew Paris-Karachi-Beijing-Tokyo on Pakistan International for just US$900 return.

## ROUND-THE-WORLD TICKETS

If you intend to go to China via Hong Kong and this is just one stop on a round-the-world trip then there are special fares worth considering. The best known of thse is Pan Am's 'Round the World in 180 Days' ticket which is just what it says – you've got a limit of 180 days to circumnavigate the globe and you can go anywhere that Pan Am goes, as long as you don't backtrack. Other airlines have similiar tickets, some of which last for a year; sometimes two or more airlines team up to provide a round-the-world service. You are free to stopover wherever the airline flies so long as you don't backtrack. Often the RTW tickets have to be bought at least a few weeks in advance of your intended departure date.

The Pan Am ticket is US$1999 if you buy the ticket and start in the USA. There's an additional charge of around US$500 if you want to go to Australia and New Zealand using this ticket. The ticket can be bought in Australia for A$2537 and that includes flights in and out of Australia and New Zealand.

Singapore Airlines teams up with Trans World Airlines to offer a round the world ticket for S$4198 (Singapore dollars) and you can start and finish in places other than in Singapore, with the exception of Australia which is not covered by the ticket. The ticket is valid for 180 days. If you buy the ticket in Australia and use it to fly in and out of there it will cost you A$2499.

Qantas has a RTW ticket for A$2519 economy class – valid for one year – and of course that includes routes in and out of Australia.

There are a number of round the world tickets available in England. Singapore Airlines' ticket costs £998 there. US Airline Northwest teams up with 10(!) other airlines and their ticket is £999.

Other options to consider are the agencies who can put together a collection of cheaper fares to create one continuous ticket – try Columbus Travel (tel 01 638 1101) in London. Such tickets may knock £100 or £150 off the cost of a normal round-the-world ticket.

Outside the UK sales of round the world tickets tend to be limited, notably in West Germany. The Swiss agents, SOF Travel in Zurich (tel 01 301 3333) and Stohl Travel in Geneva (tel 022 316560) offer lots of round the world tickets starting from several European countries, at similar prices.

Worth considering is a ticket which will take you from point A to point B with multiple stopovers. For example, such a ticket could fly you Sydney to London with stopovers in Manila, Hong Kong, Bangkok, Calcutta, Delhi and Istanbul. Airlines don't encourage this sort of imaginative ticketing because it's a lot of trouble and the airline issuing the ticket might only carry you on the first leg with a dozen other carriers sharing the rest of the trip.

## BACK-TO-FRONT TICKETS

Back-to-front tickets are an interesting consideration if you're not in a hurry and have a Hong Kong connection. Usually this means buying, for example, a Hong Kong-Sydney-Hong Kong ticket but using it to fly Sydney-Hong Kong-Sydney. In other words you use the return coupons before the outward coupon. Such a ticket can be bought in Hong Kong by a friend or by mail or telex if you know a reliable travel agent. It may even be possible to do this with just a one-way ticket. Check prices first as they're not always such a bargain as to be worth the trouble–they're often only a little bit less expensive than discount tickets available in your own country.

For back-to-front tickets try the following Hong Kong travel agents: Hong Kong Student Travel Bureau, Asian Express, and Overseas Travel (their addresses are given in the 'Getting Away' section) Remember though, a mention does not necessarily entail a recommendation!

## THE TRANS-SIBERIAN RAILWAY

For the purpose of travelling east the Trans-Siberian can best be divided into three alternatives.

**Trans-Siberian (Moscow-Khabarovsk -Nakhodka)** This is the route for those heading for Japan; from the Soviet port of Nakhodka near Vladivostok there is a boat to Yokohama and there is also one to Hong Kong. You should probably allow about seven days for the Nakhodka-Hong Kong boat journey. Your Intourist rail ticket will be timed to connect with the specific sailing. The 'Rossia' express departs Moscow's Yaroslav Station daily in the morning and the trip to Nakhodka takes about 8½ days. It is also possible to travel part of the route by air, stopping at

Irkutsk, Bratsk or at Khabarovsk where you'll have to stay overnight to pick up the train connection to Nakhodka and Japan. Prices for the complete rail/ship journey from Moscow to Yokohama start from 264.50 roubles (about US$320) for a 2nd class sleeper on the train and a four-berth cabin on the ship. Intourist recommends a minimum of four weeks notice to take care of visas, hotel bookings and train reservations. Further details are available in a special Intourist folder 'Independent Travel to the USSR – the Trans-Siberian Railway').

**Trans-Manchurian (Moscow-Manzhouli-Beijing)** This is a Russian service which skirts Mongolia. The train departs Moscow on Fridays late at night, and arrives in Beijing the Friday after early in the morning.

**Trans-Mongolian (Moscow-Ulan Bator-Beijing)** This is the Chinese service which passes through Mongolia. Trains depart Moscow every Tuesday in the afternoon and arrive in Beijing the following Monday in the afternoon.

A traveller sent the following suggestion to Lonely Planet:

It might be helpful to readers of your guides to let them know about the very real and reasonable possibility of transitting Asia through the USSR on the Trans Siberian Railroad. The Peking-Irkutsk section of the Trans Siberian is also becoming popular.

As you probably know individual independent travel in the USSR ir rather expensive therefore a budget traveller will have to hook up with a tour group. I made the Yokohama-Helsinki trip in July '82 with a student tour arranged by Scandinavian Student Travel Service which was absolutely outstanding (and you don't have to be a student). All transport, meals, tours, transfers, everything for 22 days was US$825. Since it is a 'student' tour they arranged opportunities to meet Soviet students which was fun. This tour was a small group of only 10 people. I understand that it is limited to 20. Free time is allowed at all the stops along the way and you may occasionally miss a scheduled city tour and go off on your own. The Russians always seem very eager to talk even about politics. I went for a motorcycle ride outside of Moscow with a friendly Muscovite I met on the street.

SSTS has its head office in Copenhagen and offers a wide range of Budget tours to Russia and Eastern Europe. These trips can be booked through Student Travel agencies, but I recommend dealing directly with SSTS. Mail service is very fast to/from Denmark. Copenhagen/Seattle mail was taking 4 to 6 days, express only 3. They kept me up to date on all aspects of the trip and answered all my questions promptly and fully. They can get Soviet visas quickly and cheaply too, US$3.00. AUS and student organisations to other countries should have the address.

**Visas** The average time required to complete the visa and ticket hurdles would be about two months. It would probably be less for a simple route on a trip during winter and more for a complex routing on a trip taken in the summer peak period. Visas should be obtained in reverse order; so if you decide to do the Trans-Mongolian trip you should get a Chinese, Mongolian, Soviet, Polish and East German visa in that order. A Mongolian visa is unecessary if you take the Trans-Manchurian. East German transit visas are available at the border on the train.

**China visa** There are several ways to obtain a visa for individual travel to China. The first thing to do is try the embassy in whatever country you happen to be in; the embassy in Sweden for example was readily handing out visas to Swedish citizens. Failing a full tourist visa, between 1 December and 31 March the Chinese embassies will give transit visas of seven days duration (sometimes three-day extensions are possible) – this will allow you to cross China to Hong Kong where you can pick up a tourist visa and re-enter the country. The Chinese embassy in Moscow has also been issuing visas to travellers on their way through to China, but don't rely on it.

You can also get a visa if you have an invitation from a diplomat or a foreign expert working in China (the invitation should include all the relevant details such as passport particulars, places to be visited, etc). Take the invitation to the Chinese embassy in your home country, who will then probably seek authorisation from China International Travel Service in Beijing. This usually gets you a tourist visa of 30 to 35 days duration with extensions possible.

Another, more complicated possibility is to send a letter or telex the Comprehensive Service Department, China International Travel Service Head Office, Beijing (telex 22350 CITSH CN). State your full name, sex, occupation, nationality, passport number, intended entry date to China, places you want to visit and how long you intend to stay in China. At the same time send 40 yuan (about US$20) by telegraphic transfer to the Bank of China, Head Office, Banking Department, Beijing. (This is best done through the Bank of China in your own country; there is a branch at 8/10 Mansion House Place, London EC4N, tel 01-026 8301). The 40 yuan is a handling fee, payable to CITS. To expediate a receipt you should state your own name and 'For Comprehensive Service Department' on the remittance advice. If your trip is accepted a confirmation letter will be sent to you while the Chinese embassy in your home country is authorised to issue the visa. On receipt of the confirmation letter you should go to the embassy with your passport, and the visa will be issued in a few days. The whole process should take about a month – advised for patient people only.

**Soviet Visa** If you apply for a visa through a Soviet embassy you must supply a confirmed Intourist itinerary and timetable. If you're applying through Intourist you must have an appropiate visa for your country of destination. Intourist will process visa and ticket applications together and they require four to five weeks. During summer ticket reservations are essential as trains – especially the Trans-Mongolian which runs only once a week – are quickly booked out. For your Soviet visa you must supply three photos.

**Other visas** Mongolian transit visas, Polish transit or tourist visas, and East German transit or tourist visas are readily obtainable from the appropiate embassies. East German transit visas can also be obtained on the train at the border – no need to get one beforehand.

**Tickets** Tickets from London to Beijing via Berlin, Moscow and Ulan Bator, including one nights accommodation in Moscow, start from about £270. Intourist provides an excellent timetable of the international passenger routes with rail prices. You could also book an itinerary starting from Berlin or Helsinki, or you

could fly to Moscow and continue by rail on from there.

Other routes also exist; prices from Budapest are astoundingly low. You have to reserve a Moscow-Beijing ticket at least two months in advance at the Central Office of the Hungarian State Travel Company (IBUSZ), Tanacs Korut 3/c, Budapest V (office closes at 5 pm on weekdays and 12 noon on Saturdays) or at MAV-IRODA, Nekoztarsasag Utca, Budapest. Obtain your Chinese and Soviet visas as usual. The Mongolian embassy is on the outskirts of Budapest and issues visas within the hour for US$3 cash. There are daily train services from Budapest to Moscow departing Budapest at night – it's about a 33 to 35 hour trip to Moscow. There are two trains each night, and the earlier one is usually certain to catch the connection to Beijing – reservations for this train should also be made well in advance.

# Getting Around

## TRAINS

Trains are the best way to get around in reasonable speed and comfort. The network covers every province except Tibet, and that's next. There are an estimated 52,000 km of rail in China, most built since 1949 when the system had either been blown to bits or was non-existent in certain regions.

### Classes

In socialist China there are no classes; instead you have hard-seat, hard-sleeper, soft-seat and soft-sleeper.

**Hard-seat** Except on the trains which serve some of the branch or more obscure lines, hard-seat is not in fact hard but is actually padded. But it's hard on the brains and you'll get little sleep on the upright seats; since it's really the only thing the locals can afford it's packed out to the gills, the lights stay on all night, passengers spit on the floor, and the carriage speakers drone on endlessly broadcasting news, weather, information and music. Hard-seat is OK for a day-trip; some people don't take more than five hours of it, whilst others have a threshold of 12 hours or even longer; a few brave, determined, mad, penniless souls have even been known to travel *long-distance* this way – some even roll out a mat on the floor under the seats and go to sleep on top of the gob . . . well don't look at me for a rabbit stamp.

**Hard-Sleeper** Very comfortable and only a fixed number of people are allowed in the sleeper carriage. The car is made up of doorless compartments with a half dozen bunks in three tiers, and sheets, pillows and blankets are provided. It does very nicely as an overnight hotel. The best bunk to get is a middle one since the lower one is invaded by all and sundry who use it

as a seat during the day, while the top one has little head-room. The worst possible bunks are the top ones at either end of the car or right in the middle; they're right up against the speakers and you'll get a rude shock in the morning at about 6 am. Lights and speakers in hard-sleeper go out at around 9.30 to 10 pm. Few ordinary Chinese can afford hard-sleeper; those that use it are either the new class of got-rich-recently or they're city folk on their way to one conference or other and whose travel is being paid for by the state.

**Soft-Seat** On shorter journeys (such as Shenzhen to Canton) some trains have soft-seat carriages – the seats are a bit like reclining aeroplane seats and are used by higher-ranking cadres. They cost about the same as hard-sleeper and you may consider them if there are no hard-sleepers available or if you just want a break from everyone.

**Soft-Sleeper** Luxury; softies get the works with four comfortable bunks in a closed compartment – complete with straps to stop the top fatso from falling off in the middle of the night – wood panelling, pot plant, lace curtains, teacup set, clean washrooms, carpets (so no spitting), and many have air-conditioning. And as for those speakers, not only do you have a volume control but you can also turn the bloody things off! The carriages appear to be of East German origin. Soft-sleeper costs twice as much as hard-sleeper and is worth trying once to experience the heights of bourgeois decadence in egalitarian China.

Train composition varies from line to line and also from day to night, and largely depends on the demand for sleepers on that line. A typical pattern on a high-frequency train line is about 12 carriages;

six hard-seat, one soft-seat, three hard-sleeper, one soft-sleeper, one dining car, one guard and baggage car. Half a car, or even an entire car may be devoted to crew quarters on the longer trips. If the journey time is more than 12 hours then the train qualifies for a dining car. The dining car often separates the hard-seat cars from the hard sleeper and soft sleeper carriages. The conductor is to be found at a little booth in a hard-seat car around the middle of the train – usually car 7, 8 or 9. Wood-fired samovars are found in the ends of the hard class sections, and from these you can draw a supply of hot water; the disc-jockey has a little booth at the end of one of the cars with a door marked 'Boyinshi' which, apart from the reel-to-reel tape, radio and record-player, also contains her bed. On some of the small branch lines there are various types of passenger carriages – some have long bench seats along the walls, others are just cattle cars without seats or windows.

## Classes of Trains

Not all trains come complete with all of the aforementioned fare classes – there are also classes of trains, usually recognised by the train number.

**1 to 90** Special express and usually diesel-hauled. They have all classes and there is a surcharge for the speed and superior facilities. The international trains are included in this group.

**100 to 350 (approximately)** These make more stops than special expresses. They have soft and hard sleepers but fewer of them. The speed surcharge is half that of the special expresses but the difference in overall price is minimal.

**400 and 500 series** They are slow, and stop at everything they can find. They may have hard wooden seats and no sleepers. They should have soft-seats, but these will be equivalent to the hard-seats on the fast

The following is a Chinese price rail ticket; the ticket is for a hard seat on train No. 304 from Shanghai to Nanjing. Total price is Y6.50. The sticker attached to the rear of the ticket shows the train number, departure time, date of travel, and the reserved seat number.

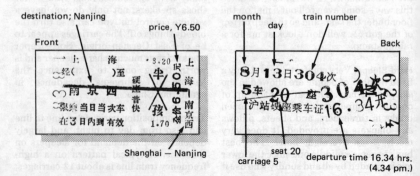

destination; Nanjing

price, Y6.50

Front

month

day

train number

Back

Shanghai — Nanjing

carriage 5

seat 20

departure time 16.34 hrs.
(4.34 pm.)

trains. Antique fittings, lamps, wood panelling and usually steam-pulled. There is no speed surcharge as there is no speed.

**700 series** Suburban routes.

Apart from the speed breakdown, the train numbers don't really tell you much else about the train. As a general rule the outbound and inbound trains have matching numbers; thus trains 79/80 divide into train 79 leaving Shanghai and going to Kunming, and train 80 leaving Kunming and going to Shanghai. However, there are for example at least six different trains listed in the Chinese train timetable under 301/302, and the sequence-number match is not always the case. Trains also appear to shift numbers from one timetable to the following year's time-table, so train 175 becomes train 275.

### Prices

Calculation of train prices is a complex affair based on the length of the journey, speed of the train and the relative position of the sun and the moon.

There is a double-pricing system on Chinese trains: most foreigners are required to pay 75% more than People's Republic Chinese for their rail tickets. Other fares apply to Overseas Chinese, Chinese students, foreign students in China ...

**Chinese Price** The table gives some typical Chinese prices. The hard-sleeper sup-plement is that for a middle berth. The special express supplement applies to trains 1-90. The last column shows the total price of a hard-sleeper ticket, got by adding the first three columns.

There are a few variables such as air-con charges, whether a child occupies a berth or not – but nothing worth worrying about. The express surcharge is the same regardless of what class you use on the train.

| Dist-ance | Hard-seat fare | Hard-sleeper suppl. | Special express charge | Hard-sleeper total |
|---|---|---|---|---|
| km | Y | Y | Y | Y |
| 110 | 1.90 | 5.40 | 0.80 | 8.10 |
| 320 | 5.40 | 5.40 | 2.10 | 12.90 |
| 580 | 9.30 | 7.30 | 3.60 | 20.20 |
| 1020 | 14.70 | 11.50 | 5.80 | 32.00 |
| 1660 | 21.20 | 16.70 | 8.30 | 46.20 |
| 2020 | 24.50 | 19.20 | 9.60 | 53.30 |
| 3060 | 35.50 | 27.90 | 13.90 | 77.30 |
| 5100 | 57.30 | 103.19 | 22.50 | 125.60 |
| 6000 | 67.00 | 121.60 | 26.30 | 147.00 |

**Tourist price** – the fare paid by foreign travellers – is an additional 75% of the total Chinese price.

An example of a fare calculation:
Route: Beijing to Nanchang
Train: No 146
Distance: 2005 rail km

Train No 146 is ordinary express, so halve the special express charge; the ordinary express charge is now Y4.80.

The Chinese hard-sleeper (middle berth) fare is:

Y24.50 + Y19.20 + Y4.80 = Y48.50.
For the tourist price add 75% to this:
= Y84 approximately.

Trains are definitely cheaper than either long-distance buses or planes, but if you get a tourist-price soft-sleeper then the gap between train and air travel narrows considerably. For example it costs Y244 for a foreigner to fly from Beijing to Canton; a tourist-price soft-sleeper on a train will cost about Y190. So, given the saving in time and trouble, it's worth considering flying when the price gap is so narrow.

Tourist price is the real crunch – it will clean your wallet out. Higher prices for foreign tourists in the hotels can be justified to some extent – the facilities and the quality of the accommodation are far better than in Chinese hotels. But on the trains and planes conditions are identical

– so the tourist pricing is purely a profit-making venture. In hard-seat there is absolutely no reason why you should pay more to ride in the same agony.

## Calculating Rail Distances

The distances, in km travelled by rail are shown in the tables below for some of China's major cities. To calculate the *approximate* cost of your rail ticket, all you have to do is look up the appropriate distance table, and then read off the Chinese-priced fare for hard-seat and hard-sleeper in the table above. From this you can calculate the approximate tourist price.

### Distances by rail (km) – main cities

|  | Bei | Shan | Can | Chan | Wuha | Nanj | Qin | Xian | Kunm | Chen | Chon |
|---|---|---|---|---|---|---|---|---|---|---|---|
| Beijing | Bei | | | | | | | | | | |
| Shanghai | 1462 | Shan | | | | | | | | | |
| Canton | 2313 | 1811 | Can | | | | | | | | |
| Changsha | 1587 | 1187 | 726 | Chan | | | | | | | |
| Wuhan | 1229 | 1534 | 1084 | 358 | Wuha | | | | | | |
| Nanjing | 1157 | 305 | 2116 | 1492 | 1229 | Nanj | | | | | |
| Qingdao | 887 | 1361 | 2677 | 1951 | 1593 | 1056 | Qin | | | | |
| Xian | 1165 | 1511 | 2129 | 1403 | 1045 | 1206 | 1570 | Xian | | | |
| Kunming | 3179 | 2677 | 2216 | 1592 | 1950 | 2982 | 3512 | 1942 | Kunm | | |
| Chengdu | 2048 | 2353 | 2544 | 1920 | 1887 | 2048 | 2412 | 842 | 1100 | Chen | |
| Chongqing | 2552 | 2501 | 2040 | 1416 | 1774 | 2552 | 2916 | 1346 | 1102 | 504 | Chon |
| Zhengzhou | 695 | 1000 | 1618 | 892 | 534 | 695 | 1059 | 511 | 2453 | 1353 | 1857 |

### Distances by rail (km) – South-East Provinces

|  | Han | Shan | Suz | Wux | Nanj | Shao | Nanc | Fuz | Xia | Cant |
|---|---|---|---|---|---|---|---|---|---|---|
| Hangzhou | Han | | | | | | | | | |
| Shanghai | 189 | Shan | | | | | | | | |
| Suzhou | 275 | 86 | Suz | | | | | | | |
| Wuxi | 317 | 128 | 42 | Wux | | | | | | |
| Nanjing | 494 | 305 | 219 | 177 | Nanj | | | | | |
| Shaoxing | 60 | 249 | 335 | 377 | 554 | Shao | | | | |
| Nanchang | 636 | 825 | 911 | 953 | 1130 | 592 | Nanc | | | |
| Fuzhou | 972 | 1161 | 1247 | 1289 | 1466 | 990 | 622 | Fuz | | |
| Xiamen | 1187 | 1376 | 1462 | 1504 | 1681 | 1247 | 838 | 603 | Xia | |
| Canton | 1633 | 1811 | 1897 | 1936 | 2116 | 1640 | 1042 | 1608 | 1834 | Cant |
| Beijing | 1651 | 1462 | 1376 | 1334 | 1157 | 1711 | 2005 | 2623 | 2838 | 2313 |

### Distances by rail (km) – South-West Provinces

|  | Bei | Sha | Nan | Wuh | Zhu | Can | Liu | Nann | Che | Cho | Guiy |
|---|---|---|---|---|---|---|---|---|---|---|---|
| Beijing | Bei | | | | | | | | | | |
| Shanghai | 1462 | Sha | | | | | | | | | |
| Nanchang | 2005 | 825 | Nan | | | | | | | | |
| Wuhan | 1229 | 1545 | 776 | Wuh | | | | | | | |
| Zhuzhou | 1638 | 1136 | 367 | 409 | Zhu | | | | | | |
| Canton | 2313 | 1811 | 1042 | 1084 | 675 | Can | | | | | |
| Liuzhou | 2310 | 1808 | 1039 | 1081 | 672 | 1079 | Liu | | | | |
| Nanning | 2565 | 2063 | 1294 | 1336 | 927 | 1334 | 255 | Nann | | | |
| Chengdu | 2048 | 2353 | 2236 | 1887 | 1869 | 2544 | 1574 | 1829 | Che | | |
| Chongqing | 2552 | 2501 | 1732 | 1774 | 1365 | 2040 | 1070 | 1325 | 504 | Cho | |
| Guiyang | 2540 | 2038 | 1269 | 1311 | 902 | 1577 | 607 | 862 | 967 | 463 | Guiy |
| Kunming | 3179 | 2677 | 1908 | 1950 | 1541 | 2216 | 1246 | 1501 | 1100 | 1102 | 639 |
| Guilin | 2134 | – | | | | 903 | 176 | – | – | – | – |

**Distances by rail (km) – North-Eastern Provinces**

| | Bei | Tia | Jinz | Shen | Chan | Har | Qiq | Jil | Dan | Dal | Jin |
|---|---|---|---|---|---|---|---|---|---|---|---|
| Beijing | Bei | | | | | | | | | | |
| Tianjin | 137 | Tia | | | | | | | | | |
| Jinzhou | 599 | 462 | Jinz | | | | | | | | |
| Shenyang | 841 | 704 | 242 | Shen | | | | | | | |
| Changchun | 1146 | 1009 | 547 | 305 | Chan | | | | | | |
| Harbin | 1388 | 1251 | 789 | 547 | 242 | Har | | | | | |
| Qiqihar | 1448 | 1311 | 849 | 760 | 530 | 288 | Qiq | | | | |
| Jilin | 1287 | 1150 | 688 | 446 | 128 | 275 | 563 | Jil | | | |
| Dandong | 1118 | 981 | 519 | 277 | 582 | 824 | 1037 | 723 | Dan | | |
| Dalian | 1238 | 1101 | 639 | 397 | 702 | 944 | 1157 | 843 | 674 | Dal | |
| Jinan | 494 | 357 | 819 | 1061 | 1366 | 1608 | 1668 | 1507 | 1338 | 1458 | Jin |
| Jiamusi | 1894 | – | – | – | – | 506 | – | – | – | – | – |
| Mudanjiang | – | – | – | – | – | 357 | – | – | – | – | – |

**Distances by rail (km) – North-West Regions**

| | Bei | Zhen | Xian | Lan | Xini | Urum | Hoh |
|---|---|---|---|---|---|---|---|
| Beijing | Bei | | | | | | |
| Zhengzhou | 695 | Zhen | | | | | |
| Xian | 1165 | 511 | Xian | | | | |
| Lanzhou | 1813 | 1187 | 676 | Lan | | | |
| Xining | 2098 | 1403 | 892 | 216 | Xini | | |
| Urumqi | 3774 | 3079 | 2568 | 1892 | 2108 | Urum | |
| Hohhot | 668 | 1363 | 1292 | 1145 | 1361 | 3037 | Hoh |
| Yinchuan | 1346 | 1654 | 1143 | 467 | 683 | 2359 | 678 |

## Getting Cheaper Tickets

Getting a Chinese-priced ticket is possible but getting more difficult. Officially the only foreigners entitled to local-Chinese-priced tickets are foreign students studying in the People's Republic or in Taiwan (which is considered part of China) and probably foreign experts working in China. In the past travellers have been using all sorts of impressive looking 'student cards' or made in Hong Kong imitations to pass themselves off as students, but more railway stations are catching on to these lies and tricks – still, it's worth trying.

Some railway workers don't care if you get a Chinese-priced ticket; but if you do get such a ticket the conductor on the train can still charge you the full fare, or you could be stopped at the exit gate of the railway station at your destination and your tickets checked – again, if you don't have the right tickets you can be charged the full fare. When you do get Chinese-priced tickets, hang on to them as they'll count in your favour when you have to wrangle for another one at the next station. Other people have asked Overseas Chinese, Hong Kongers or local Chinese to buy tickets for them, since these people also get the lower prices – but that method could get a local Chinese into trouble. Sometimes one railway station in a town will refuse to sell a Chinese-price ticket, but another one will. Sometimes when CITS and CTS are located in the same place they get their wires crossed and issue Chinese-priced tickets. Another thing – before you argue at the railway station, ask yourself if it's really worth it – for short hauls it's hardly worth the hassle.

## Tickets & Reservations

Tourist-price tickets are slips of paper with various details scribbled out all over them; Chinese-price tickets are little stubs of cardboard. Getting either can be

The following is a tourist price rail ticket; the ticket is for a hard seat on train No. 143 from Wuhan to Yeuyang. The train travels a total distance of 238 railway kilometres and the ticket is valid for two days. Total price is Y8.60, of which Y1.40 is the express train supplement. The triangular-bottomed stamp in the bottom right-hand corner of the ticket shows the train number and the time of departure.

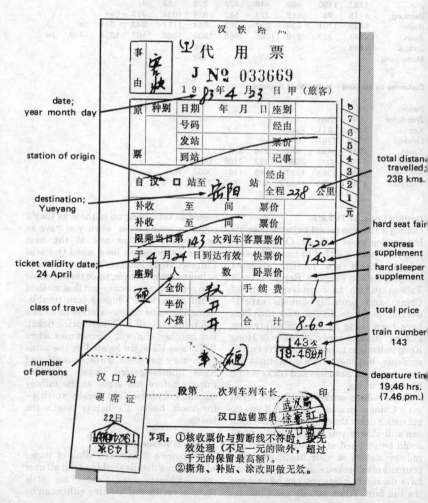

date; year month day

station of origin

destination; Yueyang

ticket validity date; 24 April

class of travel

number of persons

total distance travelled; 238 kms.

hard seat fair

express supplement

hard sleeper supplement

total price

train number 143

departure time 19.46 hrs. (7.46 pm.)

If a sleeper had been reserved at the time of booking, an additional sticker would have been attached to the ticket, showing date of travel, train number, carriage number and position of the sleeper:

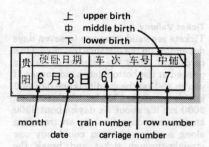

上 upper birth
中 middle birth
下 lower birth

| 贵阳 | 硬卧日期 | | 车次 | 车号 | 中铺 |
|---|---|---|---|---|---|
| | 6 月 | 8 日 | 61 | 4 | 7 |

month — date

train number — carriage number

row number

one of the most frustrating exercises you'll undertake in China.

Tickets can be bought in advance from CITS and CTS offices (usually attached to the major tourist hotels), and from advance booking offices of which there may be several in a large city. Both of these will issue tickets one to four days in advance.

You can buy tickets the night before departure or on the day of departure from the railway station. This involves queues – long queues – towards the tail they follow a traditional queue-type configuration, but at the front they can be bulbous with queue jumpers, people buying tickets for people 10 metres back, others unable to extricate themselves from the jumble – some stations are better than others. Some of the larger stations have separate foreigners' ticketing offices – they'll charge tourist price but you'll get the ticket faster than with CITS and you'll avoid the queues. Tickets bought on the same day will usually be unreserved – you get on board and try and find a place for your bum.

If you get on the train with an unreserved seating ticket, you can seek out the conductor and upgrade yourself to a hard-sleeper if there are any available. The conductor sits in a little booth, usually in carriage 7, 8 or 9 (all carriages are numbered on the outside). On many trains you should be able to get a sleeper – sometimes it's easy, particularly on the uncrowded runs like Lanzhou to Urumqi (except during the holiday season), but other trains are notoriously crowded (like

the Shanghai-Kunming express). A lot of intermediary stations along the rail lines aren't empowered to issue sleepers, so you just have to buy a hard-seat ticket, hop on the train and hope ... along with whatever number of Chinese are also trying to get a sleeper. If the sleeper carriages are full then you may have to wait until it's vacated when someone gets off. That sleeper may only be available to you until the next major station which is empowered to issue sleepers, but you may be able to get several hours sleep out of it, and the sleeper price will be calculated for the distance that you used it for.

Another possibility is not bothering with a ticket at all and just trying to walk on to the train; it's difficult, to say the least – railway stations in China are pretty well controlled, and you're not too likely to get on board without a ticket. Still, if the worst comes to worst it could be worth a try ... then go and see the conductor and get a ticket. One way of getting onto the platform would be to buy a zhantaipiao, a platform ticket, which is available from the station's information kiosk for 5 fen.

If you're buying a ticket from the railway station, or an advance booking office, then you should write down clearly on a piece of card or paper what you want; train number, time, date, class of travel – the appropriate characters and phrases can be copied out from a phrasebook. Learn a few key phrases like 'tomorrow' and 'hard-sleeper'. English-speaking Chinese are always willing to translate if necessary – there always seem to be one or two around in the larger places.

## Ticket Validity

Tickets are valid from one to seven days depending on the distance travelled. On a cardboard ticket the number of days is printed at the bottom left hand corner. If you go 250 km the validity is one day; 500 km it's two days; 1000 km it's three days; 2000 km it's about six days; about 2200 km it's seven days. So if you are travelling along a major line you could buy one straight-through ticket and break the journey where you feel like it. This will only work for unreserved seating though (hard-seat). When you leave the train the station may be able to sell you a hard-sleeper ticket – if not you'll have to try and get one from the conductor when you re-board. The advantage of this method is that you can keep away from railway ticket windows for a while. When you buy a ticket get one for special express so that you can take both special and ordinary express trains after that – they may quibble if you use an ordinary express ticket to ride a special express train (though that would only be a case of paying a couple of yuan as a supplement).

An ideal route for trying such a ticket is the Shanghai-Nanjing line, a 305 km route, where you could get off at Wuxi, Suzhou and Changzhou, and continue on to Nanjing all on the one ticket. Because these places are very close together you needn't worry about sleepers – it takes only one or two hours to travel between each point.

Another possibility is the Shanghai-Kunming express which is around 2500 km. Starting from Shanghai you could get a sleeper as far as Guilin, hang around there for a few days, get back on (not much hope of a sleeper on this line anyway) and off again at Anshun to visit the Huangguoshu Falls, then carry on to Kunming before this seven-day ticket expires.

A few things which follow from this system; if you miss a train you do not need to get a refund and book a new ticket (unless your ticket is only valid for one day and there is no other train within that period). If you're unable to get a sleeper and are sick of sitting hard-seat you can get off, trundle off to a refreshing hotel, and get back on board the next day on the same ticket. It also allows you to pass through cities or towns where it's difficult to get Chinese-price tickets. If you get sick and can prove it, the ticket validity period is extendable.

## Food

Trains on longer journeys have dining cars and depending on the train these are quite adequate. Cheapest meals are the 'rice boxes' that are brought down the carriages on trolleys and distributed to those who previously bought meal tickets (one of the train staff walks down the train shortly before hand selling them ). These are cardboard boxes of rice, meat and vegetables and cost about 50 fen – fairly filling, though some travellers have got the runs off them. Meals in the dining car cost about Y1 to Y3, depending on what you have (usually you've got a choice of soup and maybe two plates of meat and/or vegetables; noodles for breakfast cost about 30 fen). There is also a separate sitting for passengers in the soft-class carriages – as a foreigner you can join in even if you're in hard-class, and you can even get a western breakfast sometimes.

The order of meal servings at breakfast is hard-seat, hard-sleeper and soft class; dinner is done in reverse. That makes sense since soft class passengers get up later, and for dinner the staff don't want the dining car in a mess by the time the soft class passengers get there. After about 8 pm when meals are over you can probably wander back into the dining car– though the staff may want to get rid of you – but if you just sit down and have a beer it may be OK. One traveller (who speaks Chinese) recalled getting drunk in the dining car with the train crew, one of whom stood up and loudly cursed the powers that be saying they were all rotten to the core. This particular crew member was threatened with ejection from the train at the next stop if he didn't sit down and shut up!

It's worth stocking up with your own supplies for long train trips – particularly if you're an obsessive nibbler; jam, biscuits and fruit juice, can be bought at department stores beforehand. If you like coffee or tea then bring your own – the trains have boilers at the end of the hard class carriages from which you can draw a constant supply of boiled water. Sometimes the dining car will have stocks of canned fruit for sale, even whole chickens in plastic bags. At station stops you can buy food from the vendors.

### Timetables

A paperback rail timetable comes out every October but it's almost impossible to lay your hands on it – in any case, unless you read Chinese it's a drag working your way through it. Thinner versions listing the major trains can sometimes be bought from hawkers outside the railway stations. Hotel reception desks and CITS offices have copies of the timetable for trains out of their city or town; they'll be able to fill you in. The railway booking office of CITS in Beijing puts out a little booklet in English listing major trains out of Beijing. Thomas Cook publishes an overseas railway timetable, which includes China – single copies are expensive but you might be able to get a xerox of the relevant pages from your friendly neighbourhood travel agent.

### Railway Stations

Once you have your ticket, you hang around in the railway station's waiting room – or in the smaller stations outside in a designated area. There's always a sign put up with the train number and destination telling passengers where to wait. If you can't find the right line or the right waiting room then show your ticket to one of the railway staff who will lead the way. If the horde of starers in the waiting room is annoying you can usually head to the soft class waiting rooms, which

you'll generally be able to use even if you've got a hard class ticket. These soft class waiting rooms can also serve as overnight hotels if you arrive somewhere at some disgusting hour of the morning – the staff may let you sleep there until 5 am or 6 am when you can get a bus to the hotel – worth a try. You might also be able to shack up here if you arrive in or are in transit through a place closed to foreigners. Just about all railway stations have left-luggage rooms where you can safely dump your bags.

If you have a sleeper ticket the carriage attendant will take it from you and give you a metal or plastic chit – when your destination is close she will swap it back and give you the original ticket. Keep your ticket until you get through the barriers at the other end, as you'll need to show it there.

### Smile – it helps

It's worth remembering that many of the railway staff in China are exceedingly polite and can be very helpful – particularly if you look like a lost orphan. Sometimes they'll give you their own train seats – on one occasion I was allowed to use the special car reserved for the rail staff sleepers until they found another place for me. So it helps to be nice. In Jinan, two of us boarded a train with hard-seats to Qingdao – it was about 10 pm and the lights had gone out in the hard-sleeper section so the conductor took us into the soft compartment to write out an upgraded ticket for the hard-sleeper. Well, those soft bunks looked real nice at that hour. My friend stretched out on a bunk and indicated that it would do just fine – the conductor looked in amazement, motioning that the hard-sleepers were a few cars off – finally he gave up and let us have the soft class for Y5 each. Quite a bargain! It's China all over – one moment you're down in the dumps, the next you're up in the soft department clouds ...

## BUSES

Long-distance buses are one of the best means of getting around the country. Services are extensive, though roads tend to be poor and you'll be in for a lot of rough rides. Nevertheless, since the buses stop every so often in small towns and villages you get to see bits of the countryside you wouldn't otherwise see if you only travelled on the trains.

Bus travel is not especially cheap when compared to hard seats on trains; it will probably cost slightly more than trains, but you have to take into account that there is *no* double-pricing system on buses. So if it's a choice between a tourist-price hard seat ticket on the train and a bus ticket then the bus might come out slightly cheaper. As a rule of thumb buses work out to around Y1 for every hour of travelling time.

As with the trains it's a good idea to book a seat in advance – all seats are numbered. Buses depart from separate bus stations which are often large affairs with numerous ticket windows and waiting halls. The symbol for a bus station is

汽车站

One disadvantage are the Chinese roads; those that run along the railway lines are in better condition, but away from the rails a lot of them are just wide dirt tracks (one exception is Shandong Province which has an extensive surfaced road network) and in some places (like Canton to Shantou) you'll be in for some long *rough* rides. Try to avoid sitting at the rear of the bus since it's painful for the shock-absorbers in your back – and try to avoid the front since the noise from the engine and the multiple horns will drive you mad/deaf (Chinese law requires a driver to announce his presence to cyclists, and for this he uses a tweeter for preliminaries, a bugle or bullhorn if he

gets annoyed and an ear-wrenching air-horn if he really gets stirred up – the horns always seem to sound like they're located *inside* the bus).

Astronaut-type backpacks will be a nuisance to stow on buses – there's little space under the seats, there are no overhead racks, and sparse space in the aisles. If you intend doing a lot of bus travelling then travel light. In China, unlike other Asian countries, people do not ride on the roof – though luggage is sometimes stowed there.

Buses do not travel at night – eight to about 14 hours a day appears to be the maximum driving time. This includes a short lunch-break and assumes that there are no breakdowns; some of the older geriatric models are prone to suffer some relapse somewhere on a longer trip, but you'll be amazed how they keep these old crates going. If the trip is a long one you'll overnight at a hotel en route and the bus will carry on the next morning.

## PLANES

CAAC – Civil Aviation Administration of China – is China's domestic and international carrier. There are flights covering about 80 cities and towns right throughout the country. For details of international flights, see the sections on 'Getting There' and 'Getting Away'.

**Timetables** CAAC publishes a combined international and domestic timetable in both English and Chinese in April and November each year. It's almost impossible to get a copy in China but they're readily available from the CAAC office in Hong Kong (Ground Floor, Gloucester Tower, des Voeux Rd, Central District, Hong Kong Island (tel 5-216416). It also comes in useful as a sort of phrasebook catalogue of Chinese place-names.

**Fares** CAAC charges foreigners a surcharge of 100 to 160% of the fare charged local Chinese. Unlike the trains, there is no way past this regulation, except

perhaps for foreign experts. If you do somehow happen to get Chinese price and it's discovered you'll probably have your ticket confiscated and no refund will be given.

Children under 12 must travel with an adult passenger. Children over 12 are charged the adult fare. Children between 2 and 12 years of age are charged 50% of the adult fare. Children under two who do not occupy a seat are charged 10% of the adult fare.

On domestic flights, a cancellation fee of Y4 is charged if you cancel more than two hours before the flight is due to depart. If you cancel within two hours of departure time the cancellation fee is 20% of the fare. If you don't show up for a domestic flight your ticket is cancelled and there is no refund.

**Baggage** On domestic and international flights the free baggage allowance for an adult passenger is 20 kg in economy class and 30 kg in first class. You are also allowed 5 kg of hand luggage, though this is rarely weighed.

**Stand-by** does exist on CAAC flights. Some seats are always reserved in case some high-ranking cadre turns up at the last moment. If no one shows up it should be possible to get on board.

**Airport Transport** Your ticket includes the cost of transport from the CAAC office on the CAAC bus to the airport, and from the airport to the office at your destination.

The time of departure of the bus will be noted on your ticket. You can also take a taxi to the airport.

**Airport Tax** There is no airport tax on domestic flights. On international flights there is an airport tax of Y10.

**Service** Basically there is none. On international flights there is a concerted attempt to keep up appearances though, and the hostesses have spiffy uniforms and make-up and get their training in Japan – which makes for a pleasanter flight. On domestic flights you'll probably be given a little bag or two of sweets, or a key-ring as a souvenir – almost makes up for the 100% tourist surcharge doesn't it?

CAAC also stands for China Airlines Always Cancels (the usual excuse is bad weather) but more importantly China Airlines Almost Crashes. The airline's safety record appears to be a poor one – but no information on crashes or incidents is released unless there are foreigners on board. Probably one of the worst accidents was a crash in April 1982 near Guilin which killed 112 people. CAAC profits in 1982 were estimated at about US$120 million but it seems little is spent on maintenance, equipment or upgrading the vintage planes or purchase of new aircraft. New airports are sprouting up everywhere though to accommodate the tourist influx – like those at Dunhuang and Xiamen, and there is one planned for Qufu ... but you still get the same crappy old planes. Things are improving on some runs – there are Boeing 737s on some runs out of Canton, 707s and 747s out of Beijing and Shanghai, and Yun-5, Yun-7 and Yun-10 jets, (made-in-Xian copies of Western aircraft) are coming into service.

Riding through the clouds I picked up CAAC's marvellous in-flight magazine, a glossy magazine produced in Japan. It's full of heroic folk tales about air crews and their flawless safety records, doctored folk tales, how the attendant at a CAAC hostel in Beijing found a million yen and rushed after the passenger to whom it belonged ... there were even some safety tips – if you put enough magazines together you could figure out where the exits were, since the stewardess did not dwell upon the ceremony. My attention was drawn by an unusual piece of airline photography–a passenger evacuating a meal into a paper bag held by a hostess. On the facing page was a picture of a passenger being served a cake; in the middle was a bunch of testimonials in Chinese, Japanese and English. One of the passenger's comments (September 1982) read 'Having travelled around the world twice, we have never heard of asking passengers to move from the front to the back because the plane was too heavy! If it is truly that risky the plane should not be flown!'

The basic problem with CAAC is old technology. For the international runs they use nice, relatively new Boeings – but on the domestic runs its sometimes old Russian turbo-props (like the Antonovs) designed and built back in the 1950s. The worst models are relegated to the lesser-known runs and may have no seat-belts, oxygen masks, life jackets, fire extinguishers, and the freight sometimes blocks the emergency exits. We don't want to scare you off flying CAAC – but these stories persist.

The classic story is this one: amused passengers watched the pilot (returning from the toilet) locked out of the cockpit by a jammed door. The co-pilot opened the door from within, then both men fiddled with the catch and succeeded in locking themselves out of the cockpit. As passengers stared in disbelief the pilot and co-pilot attacked the door with a fire-axe, pausing for a moment to draw a curtain between themselves and the audience.

Skyjackings have added a new dimension to the fire-axe routine. In January 1983 a hijacker fatally shot a pilot after ordering a diversion to Taiwan; the hijacker was then axed by the navigator. Heroics in the air is the Chinese way of dealing with the menace of pirates aloft – the motherland does not like to lose planes, especially to Taiwan. In July 1982 a Shanghai-bound plane was hijacked by five Chinese youths armed with sticks of dynamite, who ordered the plane to go to Taiwan. The pilot's response was to fly around in circles until the fuel was almost exhausted, whereapon the crew led passengers in an attack on the pirates with umbrellas and mop handles. The CAAC version of this near-calamity reads 'The heroic deeds of the crew... showed the firm standpoint of their love for the Party and our socialist motherland... they feared no sacrifice... 'The captain of the flight was awarded a special title created by the State Council 'Anti-Hijacking Hero'. Similar honours were bestowed on the crew of a plane hijacked to South Korea on May 5, 1983.

## BICYCLES

What the car is to the west, the bicycle is to China. The bicycle is the main mode of private transport. There are collective trucks, chauffeured cadre limos and private motorcycles but the bicycle is still the king of the road. There are 120 million bikes in China and they're produced at a rate of 17 million a year, with some exported to Burma and India. Production can never keep up with demand because the Chinese will do anything to lay their hands on one rather than be at the mercy of the bus system. Much more than this the bicycle is a workhorse, carrying anything up to a 100 kg slaughtered pig or a whole couch ... you name it. Bikes are also rationed commodities and permission to purchase goes through the individual's work-unit; five years would be the minimum turn-over period for getting a new bike but in a lot of cases it may be one bike for life – so a brand new one is a status symbol, a sign of wealth.

A bike licence is obligatory and costs 90 fen for life (the licence is *not* necessary for foreigners). Some cities have bicycle licence plates, and in Beijing bikes owned by foreigners have special licence plates so that they can't be sold to a Chinese. If a person has an accident or is drunk whilst riding a bike a fine can be imposed – up to Y10 – and the bike is impounded for the first two weeks for the first drunk-riding offence (there are posters to this effect in Chinese cities). Police also occasionally stop cyclists to do spot checks on the brakes and other equipment. Bike repair shops are everywhere and repairs are dirt cheap (say 50 fen per shot).

**Accidents** As for accidents, there are plenty of picture displays around Chinese cities showing what happened to cyclists who didn't look where they were going and got creamed – and I mean creamed! These displays also give tips on how to avoid accidents and show 're-education classes' for offenders who have had several accidents. If you keep your eyes peeled and your head alert you shouldn't have an accident; after you get over the shock of seeing the old lady up front balancing a boxed TV set over her rear wheel and a couple of chickens dangling off the front handlebars it shouldn't be too difficult. Many of the larger towns and cities have separate bicycle lanes on each side of their main streets. Night riding is particularly hazardous though – the only time buses and cars use their headlights is to flash them on and off to warn cyclists up ahead to get out of the way – so if you do ride at night watch out for the motorised monsters. One advantage is that there are no cars parked on the roadside to open their doors on you. One traffic hazard is that cyclists who spot you may glide by staring gape-mouthed sideways, crash into something in front and cause the traffic behind to topple like ten-pins.

**Bicycle Rental** Bicycles are definitely the best way of getting around Chinese cities, even to get some distance out of them. Chinese cities are built for bikes – long,

wide avenues, and flat as pancakes (one exception is hilly Chongqing where there's hardly a bike in sight) so even those heavy gearless monsters ride OK. There are now established bicycle rentals dealing with foreigners in Beijing, Guilin, Nanning, Yangshuo and Hangzhou – no doubt the list will increase with time. Other renters, intended mainly for Chinese, can be found in Shanhaiguan, Chengde, Beidaihe, Shenyang and Hohhot. Some bicycle rentals are attached to Chinese hotels or operate out of an independent rental shop of which there are many. Some places will only rent to Chinese.

Day rental, 24 hour rental or rental by the hour is the norm. It's also possible to rent for a stetch of several days so touring becomes a possibility if the bike is in good condition. Rates for westerners average around Y2.20 for 24 hours, or about Y0.20 per hour – though places like Guilin and Yangshuo are much more expensive. If you rent over a long period you should be able to reduce the rate. Most rental places will ask you to leave some sort of ID. Sometimes they ask for your passport which is asking a lot. Give them some other sort of ID instead like a student card or a drivers licence and they should be happy. Some rentals may require a deposit; in Yangshuo one renter wanted Y50 in lieu of a passport. At Beijing's high-class Bamboo Garden Hotel the stipulation was Y200 deposit, which is more than the value of the bike. Before taking a bike, check the brakes (are there any?) and get the tyres pumped up hard – and make sure that none of the moving parts is about to fall off. Get the saddle raised to maximum leg-power. It's also worth tying something on – a handkerchief for example – to identify your bicycle amidst the zillions at the bicycle parks.

**Bicycle Parks** There are designated places in the cities where you can park your bicycle. Bicycle parks are womanned by attendants (usually old ladies) who give you a token when you park; the charge is usually two or three fen. In China bicycles can be 'towed' just as mis-parked cars can be in the west; one traveller who didn't use the parking lots finally found his bike after a lengthy search down at the police station – and was fined 30 fen! Bicycle theft does exist; the bicycle parks with their attendants help prevent this; for the same reason keep your bike off the streets at night, at least within the hotel gates. If the hotel has no grounds then take it up the elevator to your room. Most rented bicycles will have a lock around the rear wheel.

**Bicycle Touring** Organised bicycle tours for groups have operated in China since the beginning of 1981. The style is for a bus up front to clear traffic hazards and break the wind, followed by a mob of westerners on 10-speeds and a luggage van bringing up the rear in case anyone gets tired. It's a bit like climbing a mountain and having a helicopter hovering overhead in case you get tired or chicken out.

Probably the very first bike the Chinese saw was when a pair of globe trotting Americans bumbled into Beijing around 1891 after a three-year journey from Istanbul. They wrote a book about it – *Across Asia on a Bicycle* by Allen and Sachtlaken. The novelty was well-received by the Qing court and the last bum on the dragon throne, the boy-emperor Puyi was given to tearing around the Forbidden City on a cycle. Modern Chinese are great bicycle tourists – one farmer notched up 40,000 km over a couple of years covering everwhere except Tibet and Taiwan; a retired Chinese couple did 10,000 km from Gansu to Guangdong in two years; a 69 year-old retired worker set off on a self-made tricycle the back of which could be converted into a bed and kitchen.

On a 22 kg standard Chinese bike, loaded with 10 kg of gear, no gears, on a flat sealed road you could do about 10 km per hr. On an unweighted 10-speed you could do twice that. With amiable weather conditions on a flat sealed road you could cover 50 to 80 km a day on a Chinese bike – but 100 km would be possible. On the other hand you could stick your bike on a train or boat (buses may or may not let you take it) and travel from town to town that way.

The legalities of the Chinese cycling on the roads from town to town are open to conjecture; but until someone official (like the Public Security Police) tells you not to then you should assume you can. Other problems include road-blocks and where to stay overnight (camping?). There is an unconfirmed report of a German cycling from Guilin to Canton in seven days; some foreigners have cycled from Beijing to Tianjin but that's boring. A Hong Konger did Beijing to Canton with official sanction.

Officialdom does have the potential to get nasty if you get off the track. A female German traveller set off on her 10-speed from Wuhu, heading for Maanshan which is 60 km away. She got caught in the rain and took shelter in a local factory where the workers played guitar for her, gave her lunch and generally treated her like a princess. A princess however is not supposed to be cycling and Public Security descended on the factory with a CITS translator. 'Uncomfortable for a tourist, dangerous too' said the translator examining the dropped handle-bars on the bike. They took her off in a taxi to the hotel five km away (the interpreter rode the bike through the rain!) and the crowds gathered – must have been the first western customer there. She decided to get out when the rain let up and was allowed to cycle to the station but the CITS man insisted the panniers were too heavy and they'd have to go in a taxi (this lady had been half-way around the world with those panniers). Two minutes before the train was due to leave the CITS man presented her with a whopping great taxi-bill and she had no choice but to fork out the ransom to get herself out of there – that's the way they do things in China. No one, however, stopped her proceeding altogether on this set of wheels.

**Western Bicycles** You *can* bring a bicycle into China; there is no tariff and the bicycle is simply marked on your customs declaration form to ensure that you leave with it. If a foreigner is to be resident in China then there's a 100% tax on the cost of the bicycle which is believed to be non-refundable.

One problem with a western bike is that they attract a lot of attention. Another problem is the unavailability of spare parts. One westerner brought a fold-up bicycle with him – but in most places it attracted so much attention that he had to give it to the locals to play with until the novelty wore off. One advantage of that latter type of bike is that you can stick it in a bag and stow it on the luggage racks of the trains; unfold it when you arrive at your destination and trundle off, no hassles. They are, however, quite useless for long-distance travel and can be very expensive to buy in the west – still, they're definitely worth considering.

It's essential to have a kick-stand for parking, a bell, and a headlight and reflector would be a good idea. Make sure it's all bolted down, otherwise you'll be inviting theft. I added a cageless water bottle to my Chinese bike, but had to take it off in the cities because it attracted too much attention. Adhesive reflector strips also got ripped off.

**Chinese Bicycles** Only a few basic tyes of bikes are available in China – small wheel, light roadster (14 kg), black hulk (22 kg) and farmer's models (25 to 30 kg). Then there are arrays of tricycles with spokes thicker than a motor-cycle's, reinforced forks and double tubing – a sort of poor man's truck, and the loads are stupendous. Other bikes have little side-cars tacked on to carry children, or for use as makeshift rickshaws or by invalids. An average bicycle costs around Y120 to Y275, but on average is around Y150 –

that's three months wages for a city worker. Prestigious brands are the Phoenix, the Shanghai-built Black Rooster, Forever, and the Tianjin-built Flying Pigeon. An interesting variation is the motorised bicycle; the better ones cost almost as much as a moped at Y300 to Y800.

The standard Chinese bicycle is a copy of ye olde English Raleigh Roadster, complete to the last detail – even mimicking the crest. The Phoenix is a heavy-duty bike, built to last with thick spokes, chaincase, upright bars, rear rack, heavy-duty tubing, wide wheelbase for heavy loads, rod-type brakes and no gears, headlights or reflectors. Dynamo sets haven't appeared on the market; a few of the lighter Chinese bikes are starting to appear with three-speed gears, as are a few expensive Phoenix models.

**Buying a Chinese Bike** The greatest problem is buying a Chinese bike in China. As of 1982 those in the Friendship Store in Beijing were stashed in the basement and only foreign experts had access to them. In other places they may not be aware or may not follow this regulation, so once you've bought the thing and got a receipt you shouldn't have any problems. The odd Friendship Store around China (such as Taiyuan) sells bicycles. Bikes can also be bought from second hand stores but their resale value is not high; Chinese acquaintances may be able to help you buy one somewhere. In terms of resale value, the best thing is one of the prestigious makes – if you get one you can generally resell it for 10 to 30% less than what you paid. So if the bike costs Y150 you could resell for Y130. Second-hand bikes are in demand because it allows the Chinese to jump the queue on the ration-system – he has to explain how he got it to register it, but that's his problem. Some bike shops will also accept foreigners' bikes for resale – but that mostly applies to foreign residents.

Bikes in Hong Kong are cheaper than they are across the border and better made. There's a Raleigh agent, British Bicycle Company, and bike shops in the Mongkok area of Kowloon as well as over on Hong Kong Island. Hong Kong bikes are related to the Chinese versions so parts between Raleighs and Chinese brands should be roughly compatible – or at least your Chinese bicycle repairman should know what he's looking at. You can also buy three-speed bikes in Hong Kong.

**Train transport** Bikes are not cheap to transport on trains. On a train it can cost as much as a hard-seat fare (Chinese price). Boats are the cheapest means of transport – around a third of the 3rd class passenger fare, which is not much. Trains have quotas for the number of bikes they may transport. As a foreigner you will get preferential treatment in the luggage compartment and the bike will go on the first available train. But your bike won't arrive at the same time as you unless you send it on a couple of days in advance. At the other end it is held in storage for three days free, and is then charged a small fee. The procedure for getting a bike on a train and getting it at the other end is as follows:

1 They would like to see a train ticket for yourself (not entirely essential).
2 Go to the baggage transport section of the station. Get a white slip and fill it out to get the two or three tags which are for registration. Then fill out a form (it's only in Chinese, so just fill it out in

English) which reads – Number/to station x/send goods person/recieve goods person/total number of goods/ from station y.
3 Take the white slip to another counter, where you pay and are given a blue slip.
4 At the other end (delays of up to three days for transporting a bike) you present the blue slip, and get a white lip in return. This means your bike has arrived. The procedure could take 20 minutes to an hour depending on who's around. If you lose that blue slip you'll have real trouble reclaiming your bike at the other end.

Chinese cyclists spend ages at the stations mummifying their bicycles, wrapping everything up in cloth in preparation for transport. For the one scratch the bike will get it's hardly worth going through this elaborate procedure. Again, you can avoid all of this by taking a fold-up bicycle.

## DRIVING

At the moment, taking a car or motor cycle into China is not possible. There are plans to introduce a bus service from Hong Kong to Shenzhen and perhaps to Canton, and to open up parts of Shenzhen as tourist resorts for Hong Kongers. That suggests that at some time it may become possible to drive across the border, at least into the Shenzhen region.

Even if you did manage to bring a vehicle across the border, you'd probably have a hard time finding somewhere to refuel; apart from the roadside service stations for the buses and trucks, I only saw *one* gas station in the whole of China and that was in Wuhan. At the moment, it's probably just completely impractical to try bringing in your own vehicle – you wouldn't want to ship it all the way to Hong Kong only to be refused entry for it!

So far the only westerner we've heard of who has motor-cycled through China is the multi-millionaire Malcolm Forbes, editor-in-chief of Forbes business magazine. Back in October 1982 he did an 11-day trip from Xian, through Henan and Hebei provinces up to Beijing – after getting permission from Deng Xiao-ping himself!

## HITCHING

Many people have hitchhiked in China; some have been amazingly successful. It's not officially sanctioned, so don't bother trying to get permission to hitch a lift. Like anywhere else, the best way to get a lift is to get out onto the outskirts of town. There are usually lots of trucks on the roads, and even army convoys are worth trying.

Hainan Island used to be a good place to hitch, or so it seems. But then the Chinese stopped people travelling around there on their own and even hitching may now be difficult. Back in the good old days when a few people made it on their own to Tibet, hitching was fairly easy and often was the only way of getting from one spot to another apart from walking.

As a means of getting into closed or isolated areas, hitching is probably going to become increasingly popular – though you'll probably find that the truck drivers will be told to stop picking up westerners. In places where there is poor, or infrequent, public transport you may have to hitch: such as between Turpan and the railway station at Daheyon, or between Dunhuang and the station at Liuyuan. Both these routes are served by only two buses a day.

As far as we know, there is no Chinese signal for hitching, so just try waving down the trucks. Unless you speak Chinese, you'll need to have where you want to go written down in Chinese – otherwise there's not much hope of being understood. Again, a phrasebook would be useful.

To some extent the success of hitch-hiking depends on the novelty value of picking someone up. If truck drivers are constantly confronted by little herds of foreigners hitchhiking they're less likely to pick anyone up. Like everywhere else in Asia, people are friendlier and more curious where few foreigners have gone. If you can take a bus, take it! Leave hitching

to someone who really is stuck for transport.

## BOATS

Apart from the ships which ply the coast of China (see the 'Getting There' section for details), there are several inland shipping routes which are worth considering. For details of each trip see the appropiate city sections.

The best known is the three-day boat ride along the Yangtse River from Chongqing to Wuhan (see the sections on these cities for details). A number of people find the trip a bore, the Yangtse simply not being as amazing as it's cut out to be, but it's a good way to get from Chongqing to Wuhan, and it's also a relief from the trains. You can also carry on down the Yangtse River from Wuhan the whole way to Shanghai (which lies on the Huangpu River, which branches off the Yangtse).

Hangzhou to Suzhou along the Grand Canal is another popular ride. The situation with this trip in early 1983 was an odd one. You could readily buy a ticket to go from Hangzhou to Suzhou, but people were always refused tickets for the Suzhou to Hangzhou direction.

Canton to Wuzhou along the West(Xi) River is popular with budget travellers as it is the cheapest way to get from Canton to Guilin and Yangshuo, disembarking at Wuzhou and then taking a bus to Guilin the next morning. It is possible to travel by water the whole way to Guilin – see the Yangshuo section for details.

The Li River boat trip from Guilin to Yangshuo is a popular tourist ride taking around six hours – see the Guilin section for details.

## LOCAL TRANSPORT

Long-distance transport in China is not really a problem – it just takes a long time to get from point A to point B. The real problem is when you finally make it to point B. Like American and Australian cities where the automobile is the key to movement, the bicycle is the key in China – and if you don't have one, life is rather more difficult. Walking is not usually recommended since Chinese cities tend to be very spread out.

**Buses** are the most common means (apart from bicycles) of getting around in the cities. Services are fairly extensive and the buses usually go to most places you will want to go. The problem is that they are almost always packed. If an empty bus pulls in at a stop then the battle for seats ensues, and a passive crowd of Chinese suddenly turns into a stampeding herd. Even more aggravating is the speed at which a mobile pile of humanity moves, accentuated by a peculiar habit which Chinese drivers have of turning off their motors and letting the bus roll to the next stop. There is no solution to this. You just have to be patient, never expect anything to move rapidly and allow lots of time to get down to the railway station to catch your train. One consolation is that buses are cheap; you'll rarely pay more than 15 fen per trip, and more usually only five or 10 fen.

Good maps of Chinese cities together with the bus routes are readily available; often sold by hawkers outside the railway stations. When you get on a bus, point to where you want to go on the map, and the conductor (who is seated near the door) will be able to sell you the right ticket. They usually tell you where you have to get off.

You may be offered a seat in a crowded bus, although this is becoming less common in the big cities. It's that peculiar Chinese politeness which occasionally manifests itself, and if you're offered a seat it's best to accept as refusal may offend unnecessarily.

**Tour Buses** Most major cities have companies operating short-range tour buses which carry both Chinese and foreigners to the local sites. Places where tour companies regularly carry westerners include Beijing (trips out to the Ming Tombs and Great Wall), Kunming (trips to the Stone Forest) and Xian (trips to the terracotta soldiers and several other sights). Prices are low but sometimes the buses will whizz through interesting spots and make long stops at dull places – depends where you are. Sometimes you might have difficulty getting a ticket because the destination is closed to foreigners, or the bus is booked out or they think you're too much trouble. In some places CITS organises tour buses for foreigners, and these are usually good value (Turpan for example). You can sometimes hitch up with a western tour group for which you will be charged a fee – and sometimes that's the only way of getting a look at certain places (such as the steam locomotive factory in Datong). Oh yes, some of these buses go a long way, like Beijing to Nanning – a 10 day trip with hotels and food included in the price – but I think I'd prefer the train.

**Taxis** These do not cruise the streets in China, except in Canton. They're available from the tourist hotels which have separate desks for booking them. You can hire them for a single trip or on a daily basis – the latter is definitely worth considering if you've got the money or if there's a group of people who can split the cost. The fare usually works out to around Y0.60 to Y0.80 per km. Some of the tourist hotels also have mini-vans and even minibuses on hand.

**Cycle-rickshaws** have not disappeared from China. In most places they are the usual three-wheeler bicycle-rickshaws that you see in India, with the driver at the front and a seat for two behind him. In some places along the south-east coast they're improvised from ordinary bicycles with a little wooden side-cart in which two people can sit. Rickshaws congregate outside railway and bus stations and sometimes outside the tourist hotels. Unlike other countries the drivers aren't predatory, though some of them are becoming more so in Hangzhou and Quanzhou. Beijing and Shanghai and hilly Chongqing seem to be the only places completely devoid of rickshaws. Bargaining with the drivers is usually a hassle, as they seem to have the attitude that if they can't rip you off, they don't want your money. Agree on a price beforehand otherwise you'll be in for a furious argument when you reach your destination. If there is more than one of you make sure the agreed fare covers both people.

**Auto-rickshaws** are neat little three-wheel vehicles with a driver at the front, a small motor-bike engine below and seats for two passengers behind. Again, they congregate outside the train and bus stations, but generally only in larger towns and cities. Some of these vehicles have trays at the rear with bench seats along the sides so that several people can be carried at once.

**Tempos** are rather large, ugly versions of the auto rickshaws and seat five or six passengers. They're not very common and the only place I've seen them is Fuzhou.

**Airport Transport** Your air ticket entitles you to free transport on the CAAC bus from the CAAC office on the airport, and from the airport to the CAAC office when you arrive at the other end. Alternatively, you can take a taxi to the airport, but you will have to pay for that yourself.

# Getting Away

## FROM HONG KONG

Most travellers will probably also leave China via Hong Kong – though the Trans-Siberian to Europe is an increasingly popular trip and CAAC does fly from Beijing and Shanghai to various destinations around the world – for details see the section below on 'Getting Away – from China'.

Hong Kong is a good place to pick up a cheap air ticket to somewhere else. You'll have to go to the travel agents as airlines tend to be too respectable to do anything naughty like fare discounting. Cheap tickets come and go, change price rapidly, have between zero to a whole range of restrictions attached to them and are offered by both reliable and unreliable travel agents. Travel agents advertise cheap air tickets in the classified sections of the 'South China Morning Post' and the 'Hong Kong Standard'.

### Hong Kong Student Travel Bureau

This is one of the more popular places for buying tickets. The office is in Room 1020, 10th floor, Star House, Tsimshatsui, Kowloon. A few examples of their tickets are listed below; the only restrictions applied to stopovers and tickets should be bought a couple of days before the intended departure date. All fares shown are one-way. Remember that tickets come and go with great rapidity and you should use this information as a rough guide only to what's available.

**Britain & Europe** One-way fares to Frankfurt, Zurich, Paris for HK$1900. To Rome for HK$1900 with stopovers permitted in Bangkok or Colombo. To Frankfurt, Athens, London or Rome for HK$2150 with a stopover in Manila. To London or Paris for HK$1825 with a stopover in Kuala Lumpur. It's worth remembering that June and early July is a

holiday season in Hong Kong when lots of expatriates fly back to Britain – consequently the planes are heavily booked and it's difficult to get a seat.

**USA** To Los Angeles or San Francisco for HK$1900 with stopovers permitted in Manila or Honolulu. To New York for HK$2730, no stopovers. To Seattle for HK$1900 with stopovers permitted in Taipei or in Tokyo.

**Canada** To Vancouver for HK$2500. Toronto, HK$3100.

**India** To Bombay for HK$1416 with stopovers permitted in Bangkok and Colombo. To Calcutta for HK$1488 and Delhi for HK$1920 with a stopover allowed in Bangkok. To Madras for HK$1500 with stopovers allowed in Bangkok, Colombo or Kuala Lumpur.

**South-East Asia** To Bangkok HK$630, Brunei HK$1086, Denpasar (Bali) HK$2202, Jakarta HK$1734, Kuala Lumpur HK$1260, Manila HK$650, Seoul HK$1050, Taipei HK$564, Singapore HK$1272 – all with various stopovers and restrictions on stopovers.

**Other** To Tokyo HK$900, Rangoon HK$1266, Kathmandu HK$2030, Karachi HK$1500, Colombo HK$1300, Dacca HK$1711 – all with various stopovers and restrictions on stopovers.

### Other Travel Agents

Some of the other travel agents in Hong Kong who offer cheap tickets are listed below. Also listed are some examples of the air fares they offer. Advance Purchase tickets usually have to be bought two to three weeks ahead of departure; other tickets need only be bought a few days ahead. Remember that prices of cheap tickets change and bargains come and go rapidly. Some travel agents are more reliable than others – and a mention here does *not* entail a recommendation.

Travellers Hostel, 16th floor, Chungking Mansions, Nathan Rd, Kowloon.

Overseas Travel, Rm 603, Commercial House, 35 Queen's Rd, Central (tel 5-246196).

A & J Travel, Rm 906, United Overseas Bank Building, 48-54 des Voeux Rd, Central (tel 5-222153).

Asian Express, Rm M4, General Commercial Bldg, 158-162 des Voeux Rd, Central (tel 5-440263).

Viking Travel, Rm 1006, Mohan's Bldg, 14 Hankow Rd, Kowloon (tel 3-699568).

Prestige Travel, 4th Floor, Houston Centre, Mody Rd, Kowloon.

Travel World, Rm 1403, Sam Cheong Bldg, 216 des Voeux Rd, Central (tel 5-438876).

Edwynn Travel, Suite 1, 13th floor, Imperial Building, 58-66A Canton Rd, Kowloon (tel 3-688231).

**Europe** The following fares apply to London but similar prices and conditions apply to destinations on the Continent. Asian Express and Prestige Travel have APEX tickets for HK$1600 and HK$1500 respectively. Non-APEX tickets from A & J HK$1790, Viking HK$1750, Overseas Travel HK$1900, Travellers Hostel HK$1900.

**USA** Viking and Asian Express have tickets to Los Angeles and San Francisco for HK$1400 and Travellers for HK$1820. APEX tickets to Seattle for HK$1550 from Asian express and HK$1850 from A & J.

**Canada** APEX tickets are available from Asian Express and Prestige Travel for HK$1690 and HK$1550 respectively. Overseas Travel has ordinary tickets for HK$1850.

**Australia** Overseas Travel and Travel World have tickets for around HK$2700 to HK$2850 to Melbourne and Sydney. It's unlikely you'll find anything very much cheaper.

**Burma** Edwynn Travel has tickets to Rangoon for HK$1390, Travel World for HK$1450.

**India** APEX tickets to Bombay from Prestige Travel for HK$1400; tickets to Calcutta from Viking for HK$1100.

**Indonesia** APEX tickets to Jakarta for HK$1050 from Asian Express and ordinary tickets for HK$1750 from Travel World.

**Japan** APEX tickets for HK$700 from Prestige and HK$800 from Asian Express. Ordinary tickets from Viking for HK$850.

**Nepal** To Kathmandu for HK$1350 from Viking; also try Edwynn Travel and see what they have available.

**Philippines** APEX tickets for HK$350 from Prestige, HK$400 from Asian Express. Ordinary tickets for HK$685 from the Travellers Hostel and HK$600 from Viking.

**Singapore** APEX for HK$850 from Asian Express.

**Taiwan** APEX tickets for HK$390 from Prestige, HK$450 from Asian Express. Also try the Travellers Hostel.

**Thailand** APEX tickets to Bangkok for HK$580 from Prestige, HK$650 from Asian Express. Ordinary tickets from the Travellers Hostel for HK$630 and from Viking for HK$600.

## FROM CHINA

Most travellers will probably leave China via Canton and go back to Hong Kong. But there are several interesting and sometimes more convenient options worth considering, notably the Trans-Siberian from Beijing to Moscow and then on to West Berlin – see below for details.

### South-East Asia

The most interesting possibility is the direct flight from Kunming to Rangoon on the once-weekly CAAC plane. You have to have a Burmese visa, and that's available in Beijing but not in Kunming. Your stay in Burma is limited to one week and you usually have to have an air ticket out of the country before they'll give you a visa. The flight costs Y390 plus Y10 airport tax, and it would be much more expensive to go back to Hong Kong and then fly Hong Kong-Bangkok and Bangkok-Rangoon. One Swiss couple who flew the route had problems with CAAC in Kunming who wanted to refer their reservation back to Beijing – but the flight turned out to have only them and three businessmen on it!

CAAC has a once-weekly flight from Beijing to Manila via Canton. There may be direct flights from Xiamen in Fujian Province to Manila, and a once-weekly flight from Beijing to Bangkok, also via Canton. Back in the days when Vietnam and China were fraternal Communist allies there was a once-weekly express train from Beijing to Hanoi via Nanning – today, if you can get a visa and if the two of them aren't at war . . .

### Japan and Korea

CAAC has several flights a week from Beijing to Tokyo and Osaka, via Shanghai. Japan Airlines flies from Beijing and Shanghai to Tokyo, Osaka and Nagasaki. Economy-class fares from Beijing are Y581, Y508 and Y442 respectively. Economy-class fares from Shanghai are Y408, Y318 and Y284 respectively. JAL also has rights to land at Canton and Hangzhou, so it's worth watching out for services opening on these routes.

China and South Korea have no direct links since the two have no diplomatic relations with each other. As for North Korea, *if* you can get a visa there are twice-weekly trains between Beijing and Pyongyang. There is also a once-weekly flight from Beijing. I haven't met *anyone* who has gone to North Korea as an ordinary tourist and I'd give you absolutely no hope whatsoever of getting a visa.

### Pakistan

At present the only way of going directly to Pakistan from China is by air. CAAC has direct flights from Beijing to Karachi and from Beijing to Karachi via Islamabad.

The land route is currently open only to Chinese and Pakistani nationals. When the Chinese clamped down on individual travel to Tibet in 1982, many travellers turned their attention to Kashgar, a town in the far west of the Xinjiang Autonomous Region which is connected by the Karakoram Highway to the north of Pakistan. Although the town is officially closed to foreign tourists, in 1983 several Public Security Offices were dispensing permits; a few people managed to get out to the oasis but were not allowed to exit to Pakistan.

If you do make it to Kashgar and can avoid the police, or if the regulations change, then going to Pakistan will allow you to experience some of the most dramatic scenery in the world –the huge snow-covered Karakoram mountain ranges which stretch across the north of Pakistan are stunningly beautiful. A couple of people got out to Kashgar around the end of 1983 and were told by Public Security that if they had visas to Pakistan they would have been allowed to cross the border.

From Kashgar there is *apparently* a bus which will take you to the town of Taxkorgan on the Karakoram Highway. From here you would probably have to try to hitch on one of the trading convoys which travel between the two countries, though there may be a bus, or there might be a direct bus to Pakistan from Kashgar.

### Nepal

Back in the good old days of the early '80s, a few people managed to travel from Lhasa to Kathmandu by road, but since the Chinese clamped down on individuals roaming around Tibet, it's virtually impossible to do this any more. For details of the route, see the Tibet section.

### USA

CAAC has several flights a week from Beijing and Shanghai to San Francisco, Los Angeles and New York. Sample fares: Shanghai to San Francisco Y1300 one-way, Shanghai to New York Y1857 one-way.

### Europe and the Middle East

CAAC has flights from Beijing to Belgrade (via Dubai), Bucharest, Frankfurt, London, Moscow, Paris (via Karachi and Athens) and Zurich (sometimes via Athens).

There are also flights from Beijing to Addis Ababa (via Bombay), Baghdad, and Sharjah (in the United Arab Emirates).

Other international airlines operate flights out of Beijing but there are very few, if any, cut-rate fares from the Chinese end. Aeroflot, for example, costs Y1150 Beijing to Moscow one-way, which is the same price as CAAC. Tarrom, the Rumanian airline, has some cheaper flights from Beijing to Europe – shop around.

### Australia

Qantas and CAAC now have flights from Beijing to Melbourne and Sydney, direct or via Canton.

### The Trans-Siberian Railway

Travelling from China to Europe on the Trans-Siberian is easy to organise. All arrangements can be made in Beijing. (It is possible to do it in Hong Kong but the travel agency which handles tickets and visas charges a hefty fee and has to get visas via the Soviet Embassy in Japan. However, Hong Kong is a good place to replenish some US dollars and visa photos). In Beijing, between seven to 10 days should be allowed for completing all visa and ticket arrangements.

There are two train routes out of China into the Soviet Union. The Trans-Mongolian train is the Chinese service which goes through Mongolia; it goes from Beijing, through Datong, crosses the China/Mongolia border at Erlan and carries on to the Soviet Union via Ulan Bator. In terms of overall comfort it is generally rated as preferable to the Russian train. The Trans-Manchurian train is the Russian service and this train skirts around Mongolia; it goes from Beijing and crosses the China/Soviet border at Manzhouli. The Trans-Mongolian train takes about six days to reach Moscow from Beijing and the Trans-Manchurian takes about seven days.

**Tickets** These can be obtained from the China International Travel Service (CITS) Office in Beijing, which is located in the Chongwenmen Hotel (see the section on Beijing for details). Book your seat and sleeper on the train before you start getting your visas. Once you have got your visas, return to CITS and pay for your ticket.

December to May is the quiet end of the season, but if you intend travelling in the peak periods of June to September (summer) then you should reserve as soon as possible. Provided your visas are in order a ticket can be made out to virtually any destination served by the USSR railways. The information here concentrates on the Beijing-Moscow-Berlin routes, but there are other options worth considering such as connections from the USSR to Japan, Finland, Hungary, Turkey, etc.

Fares from Beijing to Moscow:

| Route | deluxe | soft-sleeper | hard-sleeper |
|---|---|---|---|
| Trans-Mongolian | Y440.70 | Y386.00 | Y275.50 |
| Trans-Manchurian | Y457.60 | Y401.10 | Y286.02 |

**Visas for the Trans-Siberian** The basic rule when getting visas is to start with the final destination and work backwards. For details of locations of the foreign embassies, see the section on Beijing.

Most travellers will probably need a Mongolian, Soviet and Polish visa. If you are taking the Trans-Manchurian train (which skirts around Mongolia) then you do not need a Mongolian visa. If you intend going to Finland from Moscow then you do not need a Polish visa – but the Soviet Embassy may not issue you a visa unless you have first obtained a Polish visa. If you are taking the Trans-Mongolian train then your Soviet visa can, if you wish, be issued for the day *after* departure from Beijing, thus giving you an extra day in the USSR since the train takes a day to go through Mongolia.

**Mongolia** The Mongolian Embassy is located at 2 Xiushui Beijie, Jianguomenwai Compound. Opening hours: Monday 2 to 3 pm; Tuesday and Friday 9 am to 12 noon. Transit visas take between 10 minutes and 24 hours to issue, require two photos, and must be paid for in US dollars (cash). It is possible to break your journey in Ulan Bator for one or two days – enquire at the embassy.

**USSR** The USSR Embassy is located just off Dongzhimen, Baizhongjie 4, just west of the Sanlitum Embassy Compound. Opening hours; Mon, Wed, Fri 9 am to 1 pm (the embassy is closed on 7 and 8 November, New Years Day, 8 March, 1, 2 and 9 May, and 7 October). Transit visas are valid for a maximum of 10 days and tourist visas are required if the journey is broken. Resumption of the journey will require purchase of a costlier Russian ticket. Transit visas take five days to issue but a cogent reason could speed things up. Three photos are required. The embassy does not keep your passport, so you are free to travel while your application is being processed.

All travel arrangements including overnight stays *have* to be arranged at the embassy and paid for in US dollars. Do not be deterred – theoretically the train should arrive in Moscow in time to catch the connection to Berlin, so it is not imperative to book a horribly expensive hotel room in Moscow – in fact you can sleep in transit in the waiting hall of Belaruski Station (not Yaroslav Station when you arrive) but lock up your bags in the luggage lockers near the hall.

**Poland** The embassy is at 1 Ritan Lu, Jianguomenwei Compound. Opening Monday to Friday; in winter 8 am to 3 pm, and in summer 8 am to 12 noon, and 2 pm to 5 pm. Transit visas are available in two hours and are valid for two days, require two photos and cost Y15. Apparently the visa can also be obtained, more expensively, on the train at the Polish-Soviet border.

**Finland** The embassy is at 30 Guanghua Lu, Jianguomenwai Compound. Many western nationalities do not require Finnish visas – if in doubt, check.

**East Germany** The embassy is located at 3 Sanlitun Dongsijie, Sanlitun Compound. Open; Tuesday and Thursday 9 am to 12 noon. Transit visas are immediately available and cost Y4.50. It is not necessary to get an East German transit-visa in Beijing as they are issued free of charge on the train when you cross the Polish-East German border.

**Food en route** Provisioning on the train is better in summer than in winter. Once the restaurant car has been uncoupled at the Chinese border lean times are in store.

Stock up in the Chinese restaurant car with whatever fuels your system. Better still the Friendship Store in Beijing is an excellent source of all sorts of goodies like coffee, tea, bread, sausage, cakes, sweets and fruit. Apparently the Russians are uneasy about Californian fruit-fly and have been known to dissect incoming fruit at the border. Trundling through the Soviet Union you'll find the Russian dining car has an impressive menu but 90% of it is bluff. Station kiosks en route sell buns, stuffed rolls, etc.

**Customs** At the Chinese border the train's bogies are changed from narrow gauge to broad gauge while passengers wander around the terminus building. A film theatre here offers some distraction. You can change renminbi back into foreign currency here, but you'll have to be content with whatever foreign currency happens to be in the sack. Photography is prohibited.

Mongolian Customs have a reputation for unpredictable reactions. Various stories include slight molesting of females alone in a compartment, films ripped out of the cameras of foreigners who tried taking photos and requests for 'fees'.

At the Soviet border your baggage will be searched. Suspicious literature is usually confiscated. One Dutch guy brought a five day hoard of reading bliss — obviously inability to read Dutch was the root of the problem and after a furious argument his newspapers were confiscated — two soldiers duly trundled off with them leaving their owner pining for news. You should also be able to buy Russian roubles here. When you enter the Soviet Union you'll be required to produce your foreign currency and fill in a currency-declaration form. Make sure you retain all your bank receipts as unused roubles can be exchanged for foreign currency at the border on leaving the USSR only on production of the bank receipts. Check your finances are in order as body and baggage searches are rigorous.

**Arrival in Moscow** The train usually gets into Moscow's Yaroslav Station late, if you have encountered blizzards then very late. For those who have booked a hotel room the Intourist man will be waiting with a transfer taxi usually included in the hotel price. If you haven't booked you could try sharing with someone who has. If you want to hire a taxi they are notoriously scarce (although foreign currency helps) and drivers are renowned for stinging the unwary with extravagant prices. The metro (underground) is another choice and providing you obtain some 20 kopeck coins and some reluctant advice from Intourist you can find your way to Belaruski Station (for all trains to the West). There is an Intourist office at Belaruski Station (open 9 am to 8 pm) where you can buy tickets to the west. You can sleep on the seats in the huge waiting hall but do not forget to use the luggage lockers as cameras, etc, often disappear. Stock up on food for the rest of the journey — the restaurant car sometimes disappears at the Polish border where the bogies are changed again. At the Polish border you will have your visas, currency forms, etc, scrutinised and your baggage searched (there's a special interest in Russian correspondence intended for the outside world). For those staying a few days in Moscow you'll find students from developing countries very friendly and a mine of information regarding accommodation, food, currency, etc, for those on a low budget.

**Arrival in East Berlin** When you reach Berlin you will, in fact, be in East Berlin. Take the underground to Friedrichstrasse to cross to the west. This border crossing shuts late in the evening and if it is closed then you can trudge off to Checkpoint Charlie. In case you feel like waiting until early morning, just down the road from Friedrichstrasse there is a palatial, exorbitantly-priced hotel with an all-night bar above a gleaming foyer serving, amongst other things, frankfurters and coffee. You may also witness the bouncer of unbelievable stature in action against an irritating, midget Glaswegian.

**Arrival in West Berlin** Whether you feel a sense of elation or deflation, West Berlin is definitely the west. Amble down the Kuhdam (*the* shopping street) and observe the shops bulging with wares while stout ladies spoon double portions of cream into their coffee.

The *Mitfahrerzentrale* at Willibald-Alexis Strasse 11 (tel 6939101) offers a cheap service for lifts all over Europe. From the *Busbahnhof* at Masurenallee (almost opposite the *Kongresszentrum ICC*) excellent buses run to most major German cities and have reductions for student-card holders. Onward train connections are available from *Bahnhof Zoo*. For those under 26 the *Transalpino* tickets are recommended. And don't forget things like *Eurail* and *Interail* Passes.

Unless you travel in a group then the selection of travelling companions for the journey is delightfully or excrutiatingly random – a judgement upon which you have five or six days to ponder. A couple of years ago the combined complement of first and second class carriages included a Dutch bargee returning from a stint as an au pair in Beijing; an all-American college boy who nonplussed all he met with his staggering naivety; a know-all American college girl, a Chinese with long brown hair, innocent looks and a bull-dozing intellect, a gracious Polish diplomatic couple, two Chinese students returning to Sweden to study Swedish and a Chinese diplomat returning to Moscow.

The Dutchman indulged in chain smoking and a pungent style of clothing which was too much for the Chinese family in his compartment – they beat a hasty retreat before the train had even pulled out of Beijing station. On the other hand

you could also get stuck in the cross-fire of American Ivy League debates on baseball, or a bunch of earnest Germans solemnly cataloguing, photographing and testing everything for seminars in Frankfurt. The discussions rage or drag on past Naushki, Krasnojarsk – some retreat to chess games, epic novels, epic paralytic drinking bouts, or teach English to the train attendant – or they might just stare for mile after mile of melancholic birch trees as twilight descends.

At sub-zero temperatures you can exercise along the platform, start snowball fights or wonder about the destination of teenage recruits milling around a troop train; one recruit had a guitar with a Beatles sticker over one shoulder and a gun over the other. A chess set soon makes friends. The Russians produce not only talented players but also courteous ones– perhaps as a gesture of friendship they'll quickly cede the first game but the rest are won with monotonous regularity. Prodigious amounts of alcohol disappear down Russian throats so expect a delighted interest in consuming your hoard of Chinese alcohol – for which there is plenty of time. On the other hand, if you want to repulse freeloaders you might try injecting a bottle of some of those ghastly Chinese liqueurs – the recipient is either going to stagger out in absolute revulsion or he'll be vaccinated and your stocks are doomed. Crimean champagne is a best buy and an excellent contribution to hilarious parties generating chaotic Soviet friendship in transit.

For those interested in the barter trade or fund-raising; tea, watches, jeans, Walkman cassette recorders are all sources of inspiration to passengers. Various sombre figures parade down the corridors so use your discretion as to the extent and type of transaction. Import of roubles is forbidden and changing money on the black market (at rates of up to five times the official rate) is also forbidden.

# Eastern
# &
# Southern
# China

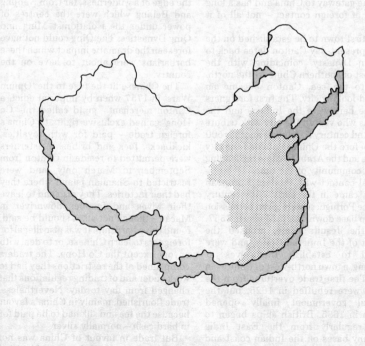

# Canton

The Chinese have a saying to the effect that 'everything new begins in Canton'. Certainly as far as tourism is concerned this seems to be the case, since it's the most accessible city in China for the ordinary tourist. Most people make the mistake of not spending enough time in Canton, tending to skip through on their way to or from Hong Kong. The city is much more than the biannual Trade Fair or an overnight stop on the way to the north. It's one of the most ancient cities in China and today is the political, economic and cultural centre of Guangdong Province. For over a thousand years Canton has been the gateway to China and has a long history of foreign contact – not all of it happy.

The first town to be established on the site of present-day Canton dates back to the Qin Dynasty, coinciding with the conquest of southern China by the north. Close to the sea, Canton became an outward-looking city. The first foreigners to come here were the Indians and the Romans who visited the city with tribute in the 2nd century AD. It was another 500 years before the Chinese opened the city to trade and the Arabs became the leading foreign community of the time.

Initial contact with modern European nations came in the early 16th century when the Portuguese were given permission to set up base downriver in Macau in 1557. Then the Jesuits came, aroused the interest of the Imperial Court, and were allowed to establish themselves at Zhaoqing, a town north-west of Canton, in 1582. The first trade overtures from the British were rebuffed in 1625, but the Imperial government finally opened Canton in 1685. British ships began to arrive regularly from the East India Company bases on the Indian coast and the traders were allowed to establish a warehouse (or 'factory') near Canton as a base to ship out tea and silk. But the opening of Canton alone was an indication of how little importance was placed on trading with the western barbarians: Canton was always considered to exist on the edge of a wilderness, far from Nanjing and Beijing which were the centres of power under the isolationist Ming and Qing Dynasties. The Qing could not have foreseen the dramatic impact which these barbarians were about to have on the country.

The Chinese lit the fuse to the 'Opium Wars' in 1757 when by imperial edict, a Canton merchants' guild called the 'Co Hong' gained exclusive rights to China's foreign trade – paid for with royalties, kickbacks, fees and bribes. Westerners were permitted to reside in Canton from September to March only, and were restricted to Shamian Island where they had their factories. They also had to leave their wives and families downriver in Macau – though not all, it should be said, found this a hardship. It was also illegal for foreigners to learn Chinese, or to deal with anyone except the Co Hong. The traders complained of the restrictions they had to work under and of trading regulations that changed from day to day. Nevertheless, trade flourished, mainly in China's favour because the tea and silk had to be paid for in hard cash – normally silver.

But trade in favour of China was not what the western merchants had in mind and in 1773 the British unloaded a thousand chests at Canton, each chest containing 150 pounds of Bengal opium. The intention was to balance, and eventually more than balance, their purchases of Chinese goods. The Chinese taste for opium, or 'foreign mud' amounted to 2000 chests a year by about 1800. The Emperor, Tao Kung, alarmed at the drain of silver from the country, issued an edict totally banning the drug trade. But the foreigners had different ideas, and with the help of the Co Hong and corrupt Cantonese officials the trade continued. By 1816 yearly imports were 5000 chests.

In 1839 opium was still the key to British trade in China. The Emperor appointed Lin Tse-hsu Commissioner of Canton with orders to stamp out the opium trade once and for all. It took Lin just a week to surround the British in Canton, cut off their food supplies and demand all the opium in their possession. In stiff-upper-lip tradition the British stuck it out for six weeks until they were ordered by their own Superintendent of Trade, Captain Elliot, to surrender 20,000 chests of opium. Elliot had been under instructions from Lord Palmerston, the British Foreign Secretary, to solve the trade problems with China. He tried negotiating with Kishen, Lin's representative, but when this failed he attacked Canton in the first 'Opium War'. The attack was ended by the Convention of Chuen Pi which ceded Hong Kong to the British. (The convention was due to be signed on 20 January 1841 but never was. Nevertheless the British ran the flag up on Hong Kong Island – a later treaty ceded the island and a piece of Kowloon 'in perpetuity'.)

The first Opium War signalled the coming fall of the Qing Dynasty and it was also from the south that internal opposition to the Qing was to arise. This Cantonese reputation for thinking for themselves has long been a problem for the rulers in the north – rebellions and uprisings were a feature of the town right from its foundation, and in the 10th century it

became independent along with the rest of Guangdong Province. The assimilation of southern China was a slow process, reflected in the fact that the southerners refer to themselves as men of Tang (of the Tang dynasty of 618 to 907 AD), while the northerners refer to themselves as men of Han (of the Han Dynasty of 206 BC to 220 AD).

In the 19th century the Guangdong region became a cradle of revolt aginst the north; the leader of the anti-dynastic Taiping Rebellion, Hong Xiu-quan (1814-1864), was born at Huaxian, north-west of Canton, and the early activities of the Taipings centred around this area. Canton was a stronghold of the republican revolutionaries who overthrew the Manchus in 1911. Sun Yat-sen, the first provisional president of the newly established Republic of China, was born at Cuiheng Village south-west of Canton. Sun founded the Kuomintang (Nationalist) Party in Canton in 1923, so having been a base to fight the Qing, Canton became a base to fight the northern warlords.

During the 1920s, Canton was the centre of activities of the fledgeling Communist Party, and the scene of the tumultuous Canton -Hong Kong strike in 1925. In December 1927, the Communists staged an uprising in the city in an attempt to oust the Republican government, now under the control of Chiang Kai-shek. The revolt was quelled by Chiang's troops in just three days and thousands of Communists were slaughtered. With the exception of the Japanese occupation from 1938-45 the city remained in Kuomintang hands until their final defeat in 1949.

Today, five million people live in Canton and its surrounding suburbs. Although there are no signs of armed revolt, the traditional sense of independence and resistance against the north is maintained. Part of it stems simply from Cantons geographical position – the Cantonese live a mere 111 km from Hong Kong and 2313 km from their

1 流花宾馆
2 东方饭店
3 广东迎宾馆
4 白云宾馆
5 人民大厦
6 广州饭店
7 华侨饭店
8 人民路旅社
9 白天鹅饭店
10 旅社
11 沙面饭店
12 胜利饭店
13 农民运动讲习所
14 黄花岗烈士陵园
15 七十二烈士之墓
16 六榕花塔
17 光孝寺
18 罗马天主牧会
19 怀圣寺
20 中山纪念碑
21 镇海楼
22 五羊塑象
23 中山纪念堂
24 满真先贤古墓

25 友谊商店
26 广东古董商店
27 广州古董商店
28 大同饭店
29 莫莫饭店
30 海味饭店
31 蛇饭馆
32 广州酒家
33 西园饭店
34 菜根香食馆
35 回民饭店
36 北园茶馆
37 洋溪酒家
38 西园茶馆
39 长途汽车站
40 白云山路汽车站
41 汽车(从化)
42 汽车(佛山,西樵)
43 大沙头
44 洲头咀港澳客运站
45 中国民用航空总局
46 公安局
47 中国国际旅行社

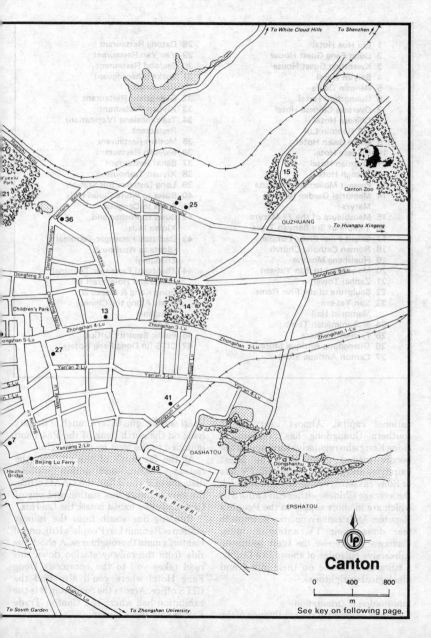

# Canton

```
0        400       800
         m
```

See key on following page.

| | |
|---|---|
| 1 Liu Hua Hotel | 28 Datong Restaurant |
| 2 Dong Fang Guest House | 29 Yan Yan Restaurant |
| 3 Kwantung Guest House | 30 Seafood Restaurant |
| 4 Baiyun Hotel | 31 Snake (Shecanguan) |
| 5 Renmin Daxia | Restaurant |
| 6 Guangzhou Hotel | 32 Guangzhou Restaurant |
| 7 Overseas Chinese Hotel | 33 Xiyuan Restaurant |
| 8 Chinese Hotel | 34 Tsaikenhsiang (Vegetarian) |
| (22 Renmin Lu) | Restaurant |
| 9 White Swan Hotel | 35 Moslem Restaurant |
| 10 Chinese Hotel | 36 Beiyuan Restaurant |
| 11 Shamian Hotel | 37 Banxi Restaurant |
| 12 Shengli Hotel | 38 Xiyuan Teahouse |
| 13 Peasant Movement Institute | 39 Long Distance Bus Station |
| 14 Memorial Garden to the | 40 Buses to White Cloud Hills |
| Matyrs | 41 Buses to Conghua |
| 15 Mausoleum of the 72 Matyrs | 42 Buses to Foshan and |
| 16 Temple of Six Banyan Trees | Xiqiao Hills |
| 17 Bright Filial Piety Temple | 43 Dashatou Passenger Terminal |
| 18 Roman Catholic Church | (Boats to Wuzhou & |
| 19 Huaisheng Mosque | Zhaoqing) |
| 20 Monument to Sun Yat-sen | 44 Zhaotouzi Passenger Terminal |
| 21 Zenhai Tower | (Boats and Hovercraft to |
| 22 Sculpture of the Five Rams | Hong Kong & Macau & |
| 23 Sun Yat-sen | Boats Along the Chinese |
| Memorial Hall | Coastline) |
| 24 Mohammedan Tomb | 45 CAAC |
| 25 Friendship Store | 46 Public Security Office |
| 26 Guangdong Antique Store | 47 CITS (in Dong Fang Hotel) |
| 27 Canton Antique Store | |

national capital. Almost everyone in southern Guangdong has relatives in Hong Kong who regularly storm across the border loaded down with the latest hairstyles and gifts of cooking oil, TV sets or Sony cassette recorders – goods which the average Chinese either can't afford or which are in short supply in the People's Republic. And despite numerous attempts to tear down their TV antennas, many Cantonese can receive the latest bourgeois/ subversive episodes of shows like *Dallas*, a ruinous influence on their moral and ideological uprightness.

### Information & Orientation

Canton is situated at the confluence of the Pearl and Zengbu Rivers, much of the city lying on the north bank of the Pearl and bounded to the west by the Zengbu.

At the far north of the city lies the railway station, and within walking distance of it you'll find the CAAC office, the long-distance bus station and one of Canton's largest tourist hotels, the Lui Hua.

Running due south from the railway station is Renmin Lu (People's Rd), one of Canton's main thoroughfares. A short bus ride from the railway station down this road takes you to the enormous Dong Fang Hotel where you'll also find the CITS office. Across the road from it is the exhibition hall where the Canton Trade Fair is held twice a year.

Renmin Lu leads to the Pearl River. A bit more than half-way down from the railway station it passes through Zhongshan Lu, the main east-west street. From here on the buildings are older and more interesting than the modern northern section of the city. Hugging the northern bank of the Pearl River is Yanjiang Lu and to the west of the intersection of Renmin and Yanjiang Lu lies Shamian Island, the old foreign enclave notable for its colonial buildings and also for the city's newest tourist hotel, the massive White Swan. Heading east from the intersection you come to another large, older hotel, the Renmin Daxia (People's Mansions). Further up is Haizhu Square, site of the Guangzhou Hotel, and beyond that are the Dashatou wharves where you catch the boats to Wuzhou. The waterfront area, particularly around the Renmin Lu and Yanjiang Lu intersection is a hive of activity with numerous shops, restaurants and street stalls.

Running approximately parallel to Renmin Lu, to the east is Jiefang Lu (Liberation Rd), which cuts across the entire width of the city. East of Jiefang Lu and running parallel to it is Beijing Lu. The area bounded by Zhongshan Lu in the north, Renmin Lu in the west, Beijing Lu in the east and the river to the south, is a fairly good area for restaurants.

Across the Pearl River, approximately opposite Shamian Island, is Zhoutouzui Wharf where you get boats and hovercraft to Hong Kong and boats to Hainan Island.

**CITS** has two offices. The main one is in room 2366 in the old wing of the Dong Fang Hotel. The office is open daily from 8.30 to 11.30 am and 2.30 to 5.30 pm. For the most part they seem to be either unwilling or unable to answer enquiries from tourists who are not part of a group. They're terribly unfriendly and seem to spend most of their time hiding behind the screens they've put up around the front desk. You may have to stick your fingers

down their throats to get anything out of them. There's a friendlier CITS office at 179 Huanshi Lu, right next to the CAAC building – you'll see it on your left as you come out of the railway station. Opening hours are the same as for the Dong Fang Hotel office. Unfortunately, they speak next to no English here. The White Swan Hotel has a ticket booking office on the ground floor, but they probably only handle people who are staying at the hotel. The hotel office is open from 7 am to 11 pm.

**Public Security** is on Jiefang Lu opposite the road that leads up to the Zenhai Tower. It's about a 15 minute walk from the Dong Fang Hotel and is open daily 8 am to 12 noon and 2.30 to 5.30 pm. It's closed on public holidays. They're quite friendly here and one of the women who sits at the front desk speaks fluent English.

**CAAC** is at 181 Huanshi Lu, to your left as you come out of the railway station.

**Post and Communications** There's a post office in the Dong Fang Hotel open daily from 7.30 am to 9 pm and another on the ground floor of the Liu Hua Hotel. The Liu Hua also has a separate telephone office where you can dial direct to Hong Kong. There is a post office in the White Swan Hotel, open from 7.30 to 10.30 am and 6 to 9 pm and a telegram/telex office open from 1.30 to 8.30 pm.

**Bank** Change cash and travellers cheques at the bank in the White Swan Hotel (open 8 am to 8.30 pm), at the Dong Fang Hotel, or the Liu Hua Hotel. There is also a black market operating in Canton and you can get Y120 RMB for Y100 FEC; the change-money women hang around the Liu Hua Hotel and around the Overseas Chinese Hotel at Haizu Square – although they don't seem to be as numerous nor as easy to come across as the ones in Guilin.

**Friendship Store** is right next to the Baiyun Hotel

**Maps** of Canton are readily available; hawkers outside the railway station sell excellent bus maps in Chinese. Across the road in the Liu Hua Hotel you can get a good tourist map (in English) at the shop on the ground floor of the south building; a similar map is available free from the CITS office in the Dong Fang Hotel.

**Consulates** The *USA Consulate* (tel 1100) is in the Dong Fang Hotel, on the 11th floor of the old wing. It's open Monday to Friday 8.30 am to 12.30 pm and 1.30 to 5.30 pm. For American citizens only, there's an after-hours emergency service you can reach by telephoning 69900 and asking for extension 1000.

The *Japanese Consulate* (tel 69900 and ask for extension 2785) is in the Dong Fang Hotel on the 7th floor of the old wing. It's open Monday to Friday 9 am to 12 noon and 2 to 5.30 pm, and on Saturday 9 am to 12 noon (closed on the first and third Saturday of each month).

**Getting Away**
Canton is a transport bottleneck; from here you can bus, train, fly or sail to numerous other places in China. There are even a few international flights which pass through here (see the 'Getting Away' section in the introductory part of this book for details).

**Bus** The Long Distance Bus Station is on Huanshi Xilu, a 10-minute walk west of the Railway Station. From here you can get buses to a large number of places both in and beyond Guangdong Province.

One possibility is to head from Canton up the south-east coast of China. The first major town on the route is Shantou. Buses for Shantou leave Canton at 5.30 am and 5.45 am; the fare is Y11.70. The ride has got to be one of the roughest in China; there are a few sections of surfaced road, otherwise it's a solid, miserable bone-shake the whole way. The trip takes about 15 hours, including a few stops. It's green, rolling countryside the whole way, mainly rice and sugar-cane fields. About mid-way you pass briefly by a beautiful section of coastline with turquoise water and small islands close to the shore. You arrive at Shantou around 9.30 pm and a ferry takes the bus across the river to the main part of town; you should be in the city centre around 10 pm.

The bus to Zhanjiang departs at 5.30 am and the trip takes about 13½ hours. The fare is Y12.30. From Zhanjiang you can get a bus/boat combination to Haikou on Hainan Island. It's a fascinating bus-ride from Canton to Zhanjiang, mainly because it's a route very much untravelled by Westerners. You pass through a lot of grott-looking villages and small towns; after the first nine hours the countryside seems to spread out, it's neater and seemingly less heavily populated. And don't be suprised if at one or two places you get *surrounded* by people, many of whom have obviously never seen a foreigner before! Everyone is curious, but reluctant to be photographed, and the little children just don't know what to make of you at all!

There is a direct bus to *Guilin* which takes two days though it seems some travellers have been refused tickets. Alternatively you can bus or boat to the town of Wuzhou and then take another bus from there to Guilin or Yangshuo.

The bus to Wuzhou departs at 6.15 am; the fare is Y8.40. Wuzhou is open to westerners but only if you want to stay overnight don't worry about getting a permit – though you'll probably need one if you want to stay longer.

Buses to Jiangmen depart at 7.30 am, 11.30 am, 1.30 pm and 2.30 pm; the fare is Y2.55.

Buses to Zhaoqing depart at 7 am, 8 am 12 noon, 1 pm and 2 pm; the fare is Y2.80.

Buses to Macau depart at 7.15 am, 8 am and 2 pm; the fare is Y7.60. There are also buses to Macau leaving from the Overseas Chinese Hotel in Haizhu Square, though the fare is Y13.50. (For this second bus, buy your ticket from the booking office next to the hotel – it's open from 8.30 to 11.30 am and 2 to 5.30 pm. The bus leaves at 6.30 am.)

**Trains** Canton railway station is notable for its crowds; you seem to end up waiting forever in long queues of people. It's difficult but not impossible to get local price.

**To Hong Kong** There are two ways of getting to Hong Kong by train; you can take the express train straight through to Kowloon, or else you can take the local train from Canton to the border town of Shenzhen, walk across the border and pick up the electric train on the other side. For details of these trains see the section on 'Getting There' in the introductory section of this book.

**To Beijing** The fastest express to Beijing takes about 33½ hours and the main line passes through Changsha, Wuhan, Zhengzhou and Shijiazhuang. To get to Taiyuan and Datong from Canton you must change trains at Zhengzhou. The fare from Canton to Beijing is around Y39 hard seat, Y60.5 hard seat Chinese price; and around Y68 hard seat and Y109 hard sleeper tourist price.

**To Shanghai** Express to Shanghai takes about 33 hours, and the line passes through Zhuzhou, Nanchang and Hangzhou. Canton to Shanghai is around Y32 hard seat, Y50 hard sleeper Chinese price; and around Y56 and Y87.5 tourist price.

**To Nanjing** There is no direct train from Canton to Nanjing. You must first go to Shanghai and switch trains. An alternative would be to take the train as far as Hangzhou and then bus to Nanjing.

**To Guilin** The train connection from Canton to Guilin is poor. The entire trip takes 24 hours, including a couple of hours stopover in Hengyang where you have to change trains; there is no direct train. If you take a hard sleeper and are charged tourist price (which you most likely will be in Canton), then the ticket will cost you Y40. At that price you may as well fly (Y60) and save all that time.

**To Fuzhou & Xiamen** The Canton-Shanghai railway line branches off at Yingtan in Jiangxi Province. From Yingtan a line runs southwards, and splits again with one branch leading to Xiamen and the other to Fuzhou. There may be direct trains from Canton to Xiamen and Fuzhou, but more likely you'll have to change at Yingtan. However, you'll probably find it much more interesting to take a bus up the south-east coast from Canton; you'll have to overnight in Shantou and then carry on the next day to Xiamen, where you can get another bus to Fuzhou.

**Plane** Canton's Baiyun Airport is located in the northern suburbs, 12 km away from the city centre. For details of international flights, see the 'Getting Away' section in the introductory part of this book.

There are domestic flights to:

| | |
|---|---|
| Beijing (Y244 2nd class) | Nanchang (Y81) |
| | Nanjing (Y153) |
| Changsha (Y68) | Nanning (Y75) |
| Chengdu (Y201) | Quanzhou (Y96) |
| Chongqing (Y164) | Shanghai (Y155) |
| Fuzhou (Y106) | Shantou (Y56) |
| Guilin (Y60) | Shengyang (Y324) |
| Guiyang (Y117) | Tianjin (Y265) |
| Haikou (Y74) | Wuhan (Y106) |
| Hangzhou (Y135) | Xian (Y221) |
| Harbin (Y335) | Xingning (Y48) |
| Kunming (Y163) | Zhanjiang (Y55) |
| Lanzhou (Y284) | Zhengzhou (Y166). |

**Boats** Canton has two main wharves, Zhoutouzi and Dashatou. There is another harbour, Whampoa (also known as 'Huangpu') 25 km east of Canton. The

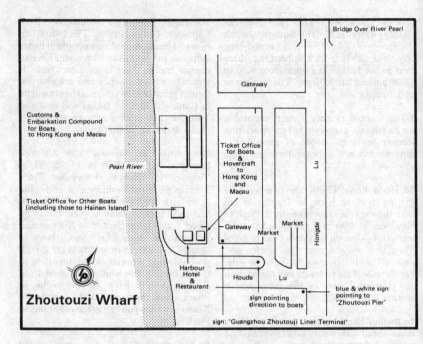

Chinese intend to build a 206 km highway from Huangpu Highway to Hong Kong.

**Zhoutouzi Wharf** is in the Honan area on the south side of the Pearl River. To get to it you have to cross Renmin Bridge and continue straight ahead down Hongde Lu until you come to Houde Lu – look for a blue and white sign which says 'Zhoutouzi Pier'. The sign is in both English and Chinese and hangs on the side of a building on the corner of Hongde and Houde Lu. Turn down Houde Lu, past the first street-market on the right to the second and larger street-market also on the right. Houde Lu splits in two here, and to get to the wharf you follow the road on the right – you'll also see a faded sign here pointing the way.

After a few minutes' walk you'll come to a road and gateway on the right, and the sign 'Guangzhou Zoutouji Liner Terminal'.

The ticket office for ferries and hovercraft to Hong Kong and Macau is at the gateway and these depart from the wharf about 10 minutes' walk down the road on the right. You may find that this ticket office only sells tickets for same-day departure. Bookings can be made at the booking-office next to the Overseas Chinese Hotel in Haizhu Square.

Further down Houde Lu, behind this ticket office, is the *Harbour Hotel and Restaurant* and around the corner from that, to the right, you'll find the ticket office for boats to Haikou.

Getting to Zhoutouzi Wharf is a bit of a problem; bus No 10, bus No 9 and trolley-bus No 25 stop fairly close by, but you'd probably be better off getting a taxi as it takes about 15 minutes to walk from Hongde Lu down Houde Lu to the wharf. If you come in from Hong Kong on the ferry, there's a bus which goes directly from the wharf to the railway station via the Renmin Daxia Hotel and the Dong Fang Hotel; it costs Y1, but is well worth it. Otherwise there are taxis, but the drivers are starting to pounce on people as they emerge from the Customs office.

From Zhoutouzi you can get boats to Hong Kong, Macau and Haikou, and hovercraft to Hong Kong.

The 'Red Star' to Macau departs at 5.30 am and arrives about 20 hours later.

There are two ferries to Hong Kong, the 'Xinghu' and the 'Tianhu' ply the Pearl River between Canton and Hong Kong. One ship departs Canton daily at 9 pm with a simultaneous departure of the other from Hong Kong. The trip takes about 10 hours. There are no boats on the 31st of the month. For more details, see the 'Getting There' section in the introductory part of this book. The hovercraft to Hong Kong depart Canton at 12.45 pm, 1.45 pm and 2.00 pm daily. The fare is Y30 and the trip takes about three hours.

There are daily departures for Haikou; fares are Y14, Y15.80 and Y18 and the trip takes about 26 hours.

**Dashatou** Dashatou is on the north side of the Pearl River in eastern Canton, on Yanjiang 3-Lu. From here you can get boats to Zhaoqing, Wuzhou and Jiangmen.

There is a daily departure for Wuzhou at 12 to 12.30 pm; the fare is Y4.80 and you should get into Wuzhou around 6 the next morning. (Apparently it's possible to buy a combined boat/bus ticket in Canton which will take you the whole way to Guilin). There are no seats as such, only two tiers of sleeping spaces – which one person described as 'uncomfortably reminiscent of pictures of concentration camp bunks'.

There is a daily departure for Zhaoqing at 7 am; the fare is Y2.45.

**Places to Stay**

Canton has quite a number of hotels to choose from, but only a few provide relatively cheap accommodation and there is not much in the way of cheap dormitory accommodation.

The *Liu Hua Hotel* (tel 68800 or 34304) is a large tourist hotel directly across the road from the railway station; it's easily recognisable by the big 'Seagull Watch' sign on the roof. It's also one of the most aggravating hotels in China and one of the few places where the Chinese have gone out of their way to be nasty to foreigners. Dormitory accommodation here costs Y8 in the men's dormitory (a seven-bed room) and Y10 in the women's (three bed) . . . if you can get in. Whether or not you get in depends on who's behind the desk that day; sometimes they'll readily give you the beds, other times they have kept people waiting for as much as *six hours* and still refused to let them into the dormitory. Sometimes they say the dormitory is full, or that there is no dormitory, or that the only accommodation left in the whole hotel is just one last double room for Y45. In any case, when they do condescend to give you a bed they usually put the men in Room 1595 (5th floor, south building) and women next door in Room 1572. How long this situation will go on is anyone's guess . . . it's a great introduction to China, but be assured that the rest of the country is *not* like this. If you want a room, there are no singles, but there are double rooms ranging in price from Y29 to Y45.

There used to be a sign up in the men's dormitory which said that guests should . . .

*conscientiously observe the rules and regulations of the hotel . . . small arms carried by the guests shall be registered and kept safely or trusted to the public security departments . . . prostitution, drug-taking, gambling, speculation or any illegal activities are strictly prohibited in the hotel.*

The *Bai Yun Hotel* (tel 67700) on Huanshi Donglu is a large tourist hotel east of the railway station. A lot of foreign tour groups get put up here. Singles from Y28 and doubles from Y38 (there may be cheaper double rooms – the hotel staff have an aggravating habit of quoting different prices every time you ask) The hotel is in an exceptionally dull part of town, and you'd be better off staying somewhere else – it's convenient for the Friendship Store but that's about all. 'Bai' is pronounced 'bye' and the vowel in 'Yun' is a short 'o' as in 'book'. The hotel is named after the White Cloud Hills (Bai Yun Shan) to the immediate north. Bus No 30 from the railway station goes straight past the hotel.

The *Dong Fang Hotel* (tel 69900, 32644 or 32810) is directly across from the Trade Fair building and is regarded as Canton's No 1 hotel though that honour will no doubt be taken by the White Swan Hotel. The Dong Fang mainly caters to business people and foreign tour groups. Single rooms for Y50 and doubles for Y60 and Y70. 'Fang' is pronounced 'fung' to rhyme with 'hung'. It's about a 15 minute walk from the railway station, or else take bus No 31. When all else fails you can come here and commit intergalactic mayhem on the video games on the 2nd floor of the old wing; there are more games to massacre aliens in a separate room at the rear of the Liu Hua Hotel. There are concerts every evening at the Dong Fang Hotel from 9.30 pm to midnight. There is also a disco on the second floor of the old building, open 8.30 to midnight.

The *Kwantung Guest House* is at 655 Jiefang Lu, in between Dongfeng Lu and Zhongshan Lu. It's a pleasant hotel, friendly staff but it's a bit out of the way. Rooms from Y40.

There are a couple of hotels down near the waterfront that are worth trying:

The *Renmin Daxia (People's Mansions)* (tel 61445) was formerly known as the 'Love of the Masses'. It's an older hotel, finished in 1937. If you can afford something upmarket then this is probably the best place to stay in Canton; it's cleaner than the Bai Yun and cheaper than the Dong Fang and unlike both of them is in a fascinating part of town on Yanjiang Lu next to the river. Singles for Y22 and doubles for Y33. Take bus No 31 from the railway station, get off as soon as you come to the river, turn left and walk up Yanjiang Lu for about 10 minutes; you can't miss the hotel which is a big white tower. Great views across the city or across the Pearl River from the upper storeys.

The *Guangzhou Hotel* (tel 61556) is at Haizhu Square, east of the Renmin Daxia. Double rooms for Y29, although they may have some cheaper ones. One couple got a triple room here for Y34 and student cards brought the price down to Y23 for three people. Bus No 29 from the front of the railway station goes straight past the hotel. Haizhu Square is a big roundabout with a giant statue in the middle; you can't miss it.

The *Overseas Chinese Hotel* (tel 61112) is just near the Guangzhou Hotel. A few people have managed to get into the dormitory here which costs Y4 each, but you'll probably be wasting your time.

Another place that may be worth trying is at *17 Renmin Nanlu*, not far from the Renmin Daxia. The hotel sign is in Chinese, but there is an pinyin sign above the shop next door which says 'Kunlun'. The people at the hotel are amazingly friendly and they may take you. Give it a try. Singles are Y8 and doubles are Y24. The hotel is just a few minutes' walk up Renmin Nanlu from the intersection with Yanjiang Lu.

Shamian Island is almost a happy hunting ground for hotels and it's here you'll find some of the cheaper accommodation. To get to the hotels on Shamian Island, take bus No 5 from Huanshi Xilu out front of the railway station. The bus runs along Liuersan Lu on the northern boundary of the canal which separates Shamian Island from the rest of Canton. Two footbridges connect Shamian Island to the rest of Canton.

The *White Swan Hotel* (tel 86968) is a good place to orientate yourself. It's on the south-eastern shoreline of the island and is the huge white tower which looks like a direct transplant from Hong Kong. It's also got a first for China – a waterfall in the lobby! There are no single rooms but doubles range from Y65 to Y80; the more expensive rooms face the river. The White Swan also has the 'Palm Disco' on the ground floor – which comes complete with illuminated dance floor. It's open every night from 8.30 pm to 1 am. Admission is Y12 on Fridays and Saturdays and Y8 other days (the price includes one drink). And, says the sign at the front door, you're not allowed to take in fireworks.

Near the White Swan is a small hotel which has been letting foreigners stay for Y6 each in a triple. The hotel is a grey concrete building on the corner of the T-intersection immediately to the east of the entrance to the White Swan.

The *Shamian Island Hotel* is a minute's walk from the front entrance of the White Swan Hotel, on the opposite side of the road heading east. The hotel has a new and old section; the new section is an uninspiring concrete block, but the old section is a red brick building with ornate colonnaded front and iron railing, typical of the European colonial buildings which cover the island. No singles but double rooms are Y22. The reception desk is in the new building.

The *Shengli (Victory) Hotel* (tel 61223) is on the northern side of the island at 55 Shamian Beijie. To get to it, you cross the bridge opposite Qingping Market and turn left – the hotel is a two minute walk down the road. Double rooms are Y42 and they say there's no dormitory – they're not worth arguing with. If you turn right from the bridge, a minute's walk up the road on the corner of the first T-intersection is a Chinese hotel which may take you, but they quote room prices as Y30 for a double.

There are numerous Chinese-only hotels around Yanjiang Lu down on the waterfront and also down the laneway on the western side of the Liu Hua Hotel. But it's highly unlikely you'll be allowed to stay in any of these places, and you'd be wasting your time to try.

The Chinese have built another luxury tourist hotel on the banks of a lake, a half-hour drive from central Canton; the *Nanlu Hotel* (tel 77930 or 78053) has 300 rooms, swimming pool, European and Chinese restaurants, convention facilities(!) and a free pick-up service from the airport, railway station and the ferry and hovercraft terminuses. No single rooms, but doubles for US$26, US$32 and US$63, on par with the White Swan Hotel. The general sales agent in Hong Kong is the Hong Kong and Yaumati Ferry Company.

**Things to See**
Looking out from the upper storeys of the Zen Hai Tower, Canton appears as a rather nondescript jumble of drab buildings stretching into the haze.

Canton was originally three cities. The inner city was enclosed behind sturdy walls and was divided into the new and old cities. The outer city was everything outside these walls. The building of the walls was begun during the 11th century and completed in the 16th. They were 15 km in circumference, eight metres high and five to eight metres thick. The two main thoroughfares of today, Jiefang Lu (Liberation Rd) and Zhongshan Lu, running north-south and east-west respectively, divided up the old walled city. They met the walls at the main gates.

The city in its present shape began to take form in the early 1920s. The demolition of the walls was completed, the canals were filled in and several km of motorways were built. This parallelled an administrative reorganisation of the city government that produced China's first city municipal council. The city's first mayor was Sun Fo, the son of Sun Yat-sen (Sun Fo, by the way, initially denounced Chiang Kai-shek as an 'usurper' who had 'ruined the party' and declared that under Chiang 'every local government, every provincial and municipal government is rotten to the core'. Despite these accusations and Chiang's massacre of the Communists in 1927, Sun made up with Chiang and once again took office in the Kuomingtang government).

Outside the city walls to the west lies the **xiguan (western quarter)**. Wealthy Chinese merchants built their residences the same distance from the centre of the city as the foreign enclave of Shamian Island. The thoroughfare still known as Shihbapu became the street of millionaires in the 19th century and remained the exclusive residential district of the well-to-do class. It was these people who patronised the famous old restaurants of the area.

In the north-east of the city is the **xiaobei (little north)** area. During the late dynastic times it was inhabited mainly by out-of-town officials as it was close to the offices of the bureaucracy. It was later developed into a residential area for civil servants, which it remains today.

At the western end of Zhongshan Lu is a residential district built in the 1930s, using modern town-planning methods. It's known as **Dong Shan (East Mountain)**. Part of the Dong Shan residential area is called **Meihuacun (Plum Blossom Village)** which is a 'model village' laid out in the 1930s with beautiful residences constructed for the high-ranking officials.

Before the Communists came to power the waterfront on the south side of the Pearl River was notorious for its gambling houses and opium dens. The area became increasingly integrated into the life of the city with the completion of the first suspension bridge in 1932 and it was then developed as a site for warehouses and factories.

Although it pales in comparison with Hong Kong, Canton remains one of the liveliest towns in China and it's not hard to imagine that this is probably what Hong Kong looked like before all those gleaming skyscrapers sprouted. In summer the older areas make interesting street walking, but there are a number of 'sights' worth checking out, including revolutionary pilgrimage spots, temples, churches, mosques and parks.

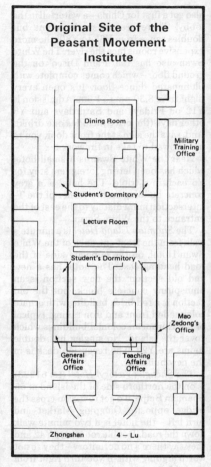

Original Site of the Peasant Movement Institute

## Peasant Movement Institute

The Institute was founded in 1924 on the site of a Ming Dynasty Confucian temple. The institute was used by the fledgling Communist Party as a school to train cadres from all over the country. It was set up by Peng Pai, a member of the Communist Party Central Committee, who believed that if a Communist revolution was to succeed in China then the peasants must be its main force. Mao Zedong took over as director of the institute in 1925 or 1926. Zhou Enlai lectured here and one of his students was Mao's brother, Mao Zemin. Apparently a large percentage of the students in the institute were from Hunan Province, probably recruited by Mao Zedong's provincial party committee. Peng was executed by the Kuomintang in 1929, and Mao Zemin was executed by a warlord in Xinjiang in 1942.

The buildings were restored in 1953 and they're now used as a revolutionary museum. There's not a great deal to see at the institute; a replica of Mao's room, the soldiers barracks and their rifles, and various photographs. The institute is at 42 Zhongshan 4-Lu, and is open daily from 8.15 to 11.30 am and 2.30 to 5.30 pm each day.

**Memorial Garden to the Martyrs** This memorial is within walking distance of the Peasant Movement Institute, east along Zhongshan Lu. It was officially opened in 1957 on the 30th anniversary of the December 1927 Canton uprising.

In April, 1927, Chiang Kai-shek had ordered his troops to massacre Communists in Shanghai and Nanjing. On May 21 the Communists led an uprising of peasants on the Hunan-Jiangxi border, and on August 1 they staged another in Nanchang. Both uprisings were defeated by Kuomingtang troops.

On 11 December 1927 the Communists staged yet another uprising in Canton but this was also bloodly suppressed by the Kuomintang. The Communists claim that over 5,700 people were killed during or after the uprising and the memorial garden is laid out on Red Flower Hill (Honghuagang) which was one of the

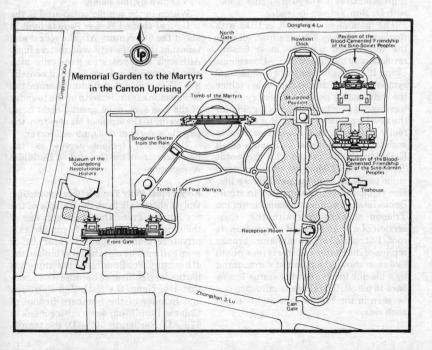

Memorial Garden to the Martyrs in the Canton Uprising

execution grounds.

There's nothing of particular interest here, though the gardens are quite attractive. You'll also find the **Pavilion of Blood-cemented Friendship of the Sino-Soviet Peoples** and the **Pavilion of Blood-Cemented Friendship of the Sino-Korean Peoples** in the park.

## Mausoleum of the 72 Martyrs and Memorial of Yellow Flowers

This memorial was built in memory of the victims of the unsuccessful Canton insurrection of 27 April 1911. (It was not until October of that year that the Qing Dynasty was overthrown and a Republic of China declared). The uprising was organised by the China Revolutionary League, a grouping of different Chinese organisations which opposed the Qing Imperial government. These organisations had formally unified at a meeting of representatives in Tokyo in August, 1905, with Dr Sun Yat-sen as leader.

The monument was built in 1918 with funds provided by Chinese from all over the world, and was the most famous revolutionary monument of pre-Communist China. It's a conglomeration of architectural symbols of freedom and democracy (since the outstanding periods of history in the west were going to be used as a guide for the new Republican China). But what that really means is that it's an exercise in architectural bad taste. In front, a small Egyptian obelisk carved with the words 'Tomb of the 72 Martyrs' stands under a stone pavilion. Atop the pavilion is a life-size replica of the Liberty Bell in stone. Behind stands a miniature imitation of the Trianon at Versailles, with the cross-section of a huge pyramid of stone on its roof. To top it all off is a miniature bronze replica of the Statue of Liberty (one photo I've seen shows the pyramid surmounted by a blazing torch – but the statue is now back in place). The Chinese influence can be seen in the bronze urns and lions on each side.

## Temple of the Six Banyan Trees (Liu Rong Si)

This is one of the most significant in Canton. The history of the temple is a bit vague but it seems the first temple on this site, called the 'Precious Solemnity Temple', was built during the 6th century AD, but ruined by fire in the 10th. The temple was rebuilt at the end of the 10th century and renamed the 'Purificatory Wisdom Temple' since the monks worshipped Hui Neng, the sixth patriarch of the Zen Buddhist sect.

The temple received its name from Su Dongpo, a celebrated poet and calligrapher of the Northern Song Dynasty who visited the temple in the 11th or 12th century. He was so enchanted by the six banyan trees growing in the courtyard (no longer there) that he wrote two large characters 'Six Banyans' as his imaginative inscription to the temple, and from then on the temple was known by this name.

Within in the temple compound is the octagonal-shaped **Flower Pagoda** built in about the 6th century AD, the oldest and tallest in the in the city at 55 metres high. Although it appears to have only nine storeys from the outside, inside it actually has 17. It is said that Boddhidharma, the Indian monk considered to be the founder of the Zen sect, once spent a night here, and owing to the virtue of his presence the pagoda was rid of mosquitoes forever.

Today the temple serves as the headquarters of the Guangzhou Buddhist Association.

## Bright Filial Piety Temple (Guangxiao Si)

Only a short walk from the Temple of the Six Banyan Trees, this building is one of the oldest in Canton and began life as a private residence in the 2nd century BC or even earlier. The main hall was built in the 4th century. For Buddhists the temple has particular significance because it was here that Hui Neng, the sixth Zen Patriarch and founder of the Southern School of Chinese Buddhism, was a novice monk in 676 AD. Earlier, in 502 AD, the temple had been visited by Boddidharma, while another Indian monk brought with him a bodhi tree which was planted in the grounds.

The two iron pagodas flanking the entrance to the main hall antedate the buildings which were destroyed by fire in 1665. These pagodas were presented to the monastery by a viceroy in 951. On each pagoda are a thousand miniature representations of the Buddha. The Hall of the Sleeping Buddha was added in 684. It was commonly held that women could become fertile through its intercession, by sheets that were draped over the figure being used on their beds.

It appears to be closed to tourists, at least to individuals – in any case the guards at the gate wouldn't let me in. A section of the temple complex is now used as the Guangdong Antique Store.

### Five Genies Temple (Wuxian Guan)

This is a Taoist temple held to be the site of the appearance of the five rams in the myth of the foundation of the city. The stone tablets, flanking the forecourt, commemorate the various restorations that the temple has undergone. The present buildings are comparatively recent; the earlier buildings that dated from the Ming dynasty were destroyed by fire in 1864.

The large hollow in the rock in the temple courtyard is said to be the impression of a genie's foot (the Chinese refer to it by the name of 'Rice-Ear Rock of Unique Beauty' – hmmh) and is supposed to be one of the eight 'great' sights of Canton. The great bell which weighs five tonnes was cast during the Ming Dynasty – it's three metres high, two in diameter and about 10 cm thick, probably the largest in Guangdong Province. It's known as the 'calamity bell', since the sound of the bell, which has no clapper, is a portent of calamity for the city. The temple is at the back of a laneway off Xianyang 4-Lu.

### Roman Catholic Church

This impressive edifice is known to the Chinese as the 'house of stone', as it is built entirely of granite. Designed by the French architect, Guillemin, the church is an imitation of the Gothic structures prevalent in Europe in the Middle Ages. The two towering steeples symbolise 'Ascending to Heaven' and 'Converting to God'. Engraved on the foundation stones to the east and west of the church are the Latin words 'Jerusalem' and 'Rome' which means that Catholicism may have had its origins in the east, but rose in Rome in the west.

Four bronze bells suspended in the building to the east of the church were cast in France; the original coloured glass was also made in France, but almost all of this has gone. The church is about 31 metres wide and about 79 metres long, and 58 metres from the ground to the top of the spires.

The site was originally the location of the office of the governor of Guangdong and Guangxi Provinces, but the building was destroyed by British and French troops at the end of the Second Opium War in the early 1840s. The area was leased to the French following the signing of the Sino-French 'Tianjin Treaty', and construction of the church began in 1863, not being completed until 1888. The church is normally closed, except on Sundays when masses are said. All are welcome.

### Zion Christian Church

This is a large church in a sort of hybrid European and Chinese style with a traditional European Gothic shape and Chinese eaves. It's at 392 Renmin Zhonglu and is still functioning; Sunday services at 12 noon and 7.30 pm and choir-practice on Fridays at 7.30 pm.

### Huaisheng Mosque

Built in 627 AD by the first Muslim missionary to China, the name means 'Remember the Sage' in memory of the prophet Mohammed. Inside the mosque is a minaret, which because of its flat, even appearance, has come to be known as the 'Guang Minaret' or 'Smooth Tower'. The mosque stands on Guangta Lu which runs off Renmin Lu.

### The Waterfront

The northern bank of the Pearl River is the most interesting part of Canton; filled with people and markets and dilapidated buildings it's a stark contrast to the greyness of the northern part of the city.

Just before you reach the end of Renmin Lu, **Liuersan Lu** leads off westwards. 'Liu er san' means '6 2 3', referring to 23 June 1925, when British and French troops fired on striking Chinese workers during the Hong Kong-Canton Strike of that year.

Liuersan Lu runs parallel to the northern bank of **Shamian Island**. The island is separated from the rest of Canton by a narrow canal to the north and east, and by the Pearl River to the south and west. Two bridges connect the island to the city. At the side of the bridge leading on to the island in the east, stands a **Monument to the Martyrs of the Shaji Massacre** as the 1925 massacre was known.

A short walk down Liuersan Lu takes you to the second bridge which connects the city to the north side of Shamian Island. Directly opposite the bridge, on the city side, is one of Canton's prime, but lesser known tourist, attractions, **Qingping Market** on Quingping Lu. If you want to buy, kill, cook it yourself, this is the place to come, since the market is more like a take-away zoo. Near the entrance you'll find the usual selection of medicinal herbs and spices, along with such delectables as dried starfish, snakes, lizards and deer antlers. Further up you'll find the live ones waiting to be butchered; sad-eyed monkeys rattle at the bars of their wooden cages; tortoises crawl over each other in shallow tin trays; owls sit perched on boxes full of pigeons; half-alive fish swim around in tubs whilst being squirted with jets of water to keep them aerated. You can also get pangolins, dogs and raccoons, either alive or in a variety of different positions of recent violent death – which may just swear you off meat for the next few weeks. Anyway, it's a great place to get a feel for China and is probably the best market in the country. The market spills out into Tiyun Lu which cuts east-west across Qingping Lu. Further north is another area supplying sedate little vegetables, flowers, potted plants and goldfish.

There is a tourist boat-ride down the Pearl River which goes from 3.30 pm to 5 pm and costs Y10. Boats leave from the pier just east of Renmin Bridge. They take you down the river as far as Ershatou and then turn around and head back towards Renmin Bridge.

### Shamian Island

Head back to Liuersan Lu and cross the bridge opposite Qingping Lu to **Shamian Island**. 'Shamian' means 'sand flat' which is all the island was until foreign traders were permitted to set up their warehouses (factories) here in the middle of the 18th century. Land reclamation increased its area to its present size; 900 metres from east to west, and 300 metres from north to south. The island became a British and French concession after they defeated the Chinese in one of the Opium Wars and is covered with old colonial buildings which housed the trading offices and the residences of the foreigners. Today, most of these are used as offices or apartment blocks and the area still retains a quiet residential atmosphere, rather detached from the bustle just across the canals.

In the last two or three years, 30,000 square metres of land were added to the south bank of the island and the 35-storey, snow-white, White Swan Hotel was built here. It's worth having a look in; you'll find a hotel like this on every street corner of Hong Kong Central and Tsimshatsui in Kowloon, but it's interesting to see one

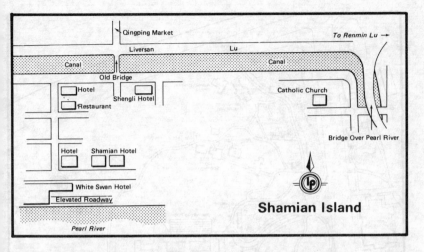

Qingping Market

Liversan        Lu        To Renmin Lu →

Canal                Canal

Old Bridge

Hotel

Shengli Hotel

Restaurant        Catholic Church

Hotel    Shamian Hotel            Bridge Over Pearl River

White Swan Hotel

Elevated Roadway

Shamian Island

Pearl River

transplanted to the Peoples Republic. It was built by foreign firms. The White Swan is an indication that the Chinese are coming (slowly) to the realisation that they have to provide value for money if they want to attract tourists to the country; which means better quality hotels and better service. It also means prices are being pushed even higher. The most staggering feature of the hotel is the giant lobby complete with its own waterfall – certainly a first for China. And like Chinese anywhere, the Hong Kongers stand in front of this thing to have their photos taken! Wandering around to the lush sounds of muzak, you'll find a horrendously-priced Japanese Restaurant on the 3rd floor, a ground-floor cafe called the 'River Garden' where a sandwich will cost you a mere mountain of fen, and an assortment of plush little shops selling some of the most extravagantly-priced tourist rubbish I've ever seen . . . get your fat Buddha statue with kiddies crawling all over him for just Y216. One of the shops sells 'Pien Tze Huang' which is supposed to stop 'all pains due to hepatitis and other inflammatory diseases' and is composed of 3% musk, 5% cow bezdar, 85% pupalia geniculata and 7%

snakes gall. There's a disco on the ground floor, a swimming pool at the back and 1000 rooms to choose from, including a couple of Presidential Suites.

From the White Swan to slightly more dilapidated surroundings, it's worth a walk along the north bank of Shamian Island to get a view of the houses on Liuersan across the canal. These are all ramshackle three and four storey terrace houses which make quite a sight in the setting sun.

The **Cultural Park** has its main entrance on Liuersan Lu. The park was opened in 1956 and is the Chinese equivalent of Coney Island. Inside are fair ground amusements like merry-go-rounds and swirling planes, a roller-skating rink, exhibition halls, an aquarium which exhibits aquatic products from Guangdong Province and theatres for film and opera. It's usually open until 10 pm – not a bad place to drop into. The park backs onto **Shisanhang Lu** – 'Shisanhang' means '13 Factories'; the name is a reminder that this is where the infamous opium warehouses were located. Nothing remains of the original buildings, which were completely destroyed in 1857, and the area was developed into a busy trading

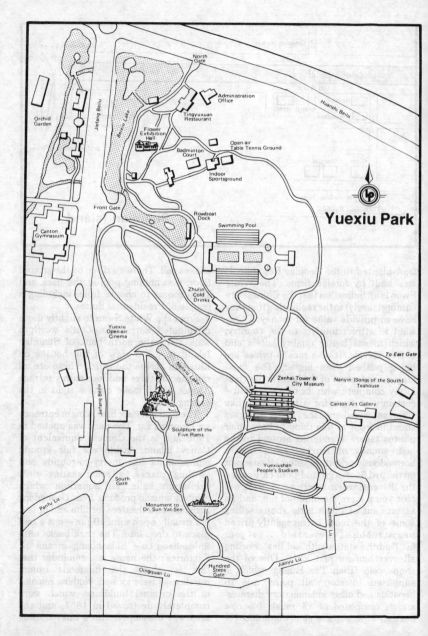

Orchid Garden

North Gate

Administration Office

Tingyuxuan Restaurant

Flower Exhibition Hall

Open-air Table Tennis Ground

Badminton Court

Indoor Sportsground

Huanshi Beilu

Jiefang Beilu

Baiau Lake

Front Gate

Rowboat Dock

Swimming Pool

Canton Gymnasium

Zhulin Cold Drinks

**Yuexiu Park**

Yuexiu Open-air Cinema

Nanxiu Lake

To East Gate

Zhenhai Tower & City Museum

Nanyin (Songs of the South) Teahouse

Canton Art Gallery

Sculpture of the Five Rams

Yuexiushan People's Stadium

South Gate

Jiefang Beilu

Pantu Lu

Monument to Dr. Sun Yat-Sen

Zhenhai Lu

Jiaoyu Lu

Qingquan Lu

Hundred Steps Gate

centre. By the 1930s it housed the leading banks and exchange houses, and so became known as Bankers Street.

## Across the Pearl River

Renmin Bridge stands just to the east of Shamian Island and runs over the Pearl River to the area of Canton known as **Honan**. Here you'll find **Haichuang Park** which would be nondescript but for the remains of what was once Canton's largest monastery, the **Ocean Banner Monastery**. It was founded by a Buddhist monk in 1662, and in its heyday covered 2½ hectares. Soon after 1911, part of the temple became a school and part was used as a soldiers barracks (another common fate of temples). It was opened to the public as a park in the 1930s. Though the three colossal images of the seated Buddha have gone, the main hall still remains.

The entrance to the park is on Xiangqun Lu. The large stone which decorates the fish pond at the entrance is considered by the Chinese to look like a tiger struggling to turn around. The stone came from Lake Tai in Jiangsu Province, some 1800 km north of Canton. During the Qing Dynasty the wealthy used these rare, strangely shaped stones to decorate their gardens; many are found in the gardens of the Forbidden City in Beijing, though none as large as this. This particular stone was brought back by a wealthy Cantonese merchant in the last century. The Japanese took Canton in 1938 and plans were made to ship the stone back to Japan, though this did not eventuate. After the war, the stone was sold to a private collector for five million yuan and it disappeared from public view. It was finally returned to the park in 1951.

## Parks and Gardens

Chinese make a great thing of their parks and gardens with their neat little gardens littered with pavilions and bridges. Most of them turn out to be fairly disappointing, though the ones in Canton are worth a look.

For the Chinese, along with films and restaurants, parks are a major source of leisure. It's worth getting up early (around 7 am) to see the young and old come out to exercise; jogging, tai-chi and calisthenics are the usual activities, but you'll often find old women swinging on tree branches and old men running slower than they could walk. Others go out to walk their pet birds. The parks are also sites for minor exhibitions of painting, photography or flower shows (notably chrysanthemums in December).

**Yuexiu Park** is the biggest park in Canton, covering about 93 hectares, and here you'll find the **Zenhai Tower**, the **Sun Yat-sen Monument** and the large **Sculpture of the Five Rams**. The sculpture by the way, is the symbol of the city; the foundation of Canton goes back to the time when history dissolves into myth. It is said that five genies, wearing robes of five colours, came to Canton riding through the air on rams. Each carried a stem of rice, which they presented to the people as an auspicious sign from heaven that the area would be free from famine forever. Guangzhou means Broad Region, but from this myth it takes its other name, City of Rams or just Goat City.

The **Zen Hai Tower**, also known as the **Five Storey Pagoda** is the only part of the city wall that remains. From the upper storeys it commands a view of the city to the south and the White Cloud Hills to the north. The present tower was built during the Ming Dynasty, on the site of a former structure. Because of its strategic location it was occupied by the British and French troops at the time of the Opium Wars. The 12 cannon in front of the tower date from this time (five of them are foreign, the rest were made in Foshan).

The Zen Hai Tower now houses the **City Museum**. The collection is quite interesting, though all the captions are in Chinese. The exhibits tend to fall into two parts; the first part describes the history of Canton from Neolithic times to the later period of the Qin Dynasty. The second part covers the Opium War of the 1840s, the 1911 Revolution and the May 4 Movement of 1919. Admission to the tower is 25 fen.

The **Sun Yat-sen Monument** is south of the Zenhai Tower. This tall obelisk was constructed in 1929, four years after Sun's death, on the site of a temple to Guanyin. The obelisk is built of granite and marble blocks and there is a staircase inside leading to the top. There's nothing to see inside though there's a good view of the city from the top. On the south side of the obelisk the full text of Dr Sun's last testament is engraved in stone tablets on the ground:

For forty years I have devoted myself to the cause of national revolution, the object of which is to raise China to a position of independence and equality among nations. The experience of these 40 years has convinced me that to attain this goal, the people must be aroused, and that we must associate ourselves in a common struggle with all the people of the world who treat us as equals. The revolution has not yet been successfully completed. Let all our comrades follow the principles set forth in my writings 'Plans for National Renovation', 'Fundamentals of National Reconstruction', 'The Three Principles of the People' and the 'Manifesto of the First National Convention of the Kuomintang' and continue to make every effort to carry them into effect. Above all, my recent declaration in favour of holding a National Convention of the People of China and abolishing unequal treaties should be carried into effect as soon as possible.

This is my last will and testament.

(Signed) Sun Wen

11 March, 1925

West of the Zenhai Tower is the **Sculpture of the Five Rams** erected in 1959, and south of the tower is the large **sports stadium** with a seating capacity of 40,000. The park also features a **roller-coaster**. There are three artificial lakes; **Dongxiu, Nanxiu** and **Beixiu** – the last has rowboats which you can hire; the boats cost only 40 fen per hour, plus a Y5 deposit which is refunded when you sail safely back into port.

Lying south of Yuexiu Park is the **Sun Yat-sen Memorial Hall** on Dongfeng Lu. The hall was built with donations from Overseas Chinese and from Canton citizens; construction began in January 1929 and finished in November 1931. It's built on the site of the residence of the governor of Guangdong and Guangxi during the Qing Dynasty, which was later used by Sun Yat-sen when he became President of the Republic in 1922. The memorial hall is an octagonal Chinese monolith 47 metres high and 71 metres wide; inside it's a concert hall (nothing to see) with a seating capacity of about 4,800.

The **Canton Orchid Park**, also on Jiefang Lu, was built in 1957 and expanded in 1963. This pleasant little park is devoted, as the name suggests, to orchids – over a hundred varieties are on display here. The Y1 admission fee effectively excludes the locals, which is why it's a good place to avoid the proletariat. The admission charge also includes tea, which you can have in the rooms by the small pond. Except Wednesdays, the park opens daily from 7.30 to 11.30 am and 1.30 to 5.00pm.

The **Mohammedan Tomb and Burial Ground** can be found in the Orchid Park. It may be the tomb of the same Moslem missionary who built the Huaisheng Mosque – who may have been the maternal uncle of the prophet Mohammed. There are two other Moslem tombs outside the town of Quanzhou on the south-east coast of China; these may be the tombs of Arab traders, but it's also suggested that they may be the tombs of missionaries who were sent to China by Mohammed with the one who is now buried in Canton. In any case, the tomb in Canton is one of the oldest Moslem tombs in China, dating from the time of the introduction of Islam into the country in the 7th century AD. For Chinese Moslems it is one of the most sacred sites in China. The tomb is in a secluded bamboo grove, behind the Orchid Garden; continue past the entrance to the garden, through the narrow gateway ahead and take the narrow stone path on the right. Behind the tomb compound are individual Moslem graves of stone, as well as a large monumental stone arch. The tomb came to be known as the 'Tomb of the Echo' or the 'Resounding Tomb' because of the noises that reverberate in the inner chamber.

**Other Parks** The **Liuhua Park** spreads over 75 hectares and contains the largest artificial lake in the city. Built in 1958 – a product of the Great Leap Forward – the main entrance, on the north side, is decorated with two examples of Chairman Mao's calligraphy. The metre-high characters are reproduced in relief. On the left, 'A single spark can start a prairie fire' and on the right 'The east wind prevails over the west wind' – apt expressions of the enthusiasm of the time. There is an entrance to the park on Renmin Lu, south-west of the Dong Fang Hotel.

Just east of Beijing Lu, on the north side of Zhongshan Si-Lu is a **Childrens Park** where parents bring their tiny tots to play on the swings and slides. The **Canton Zoo** was built in 1958 and is one of the better zoos you'll see in China. It's located on Xianlie Lu, northwest of the Huanghuagang Mausoleum of the 72 Martyrs.

**Other Sights**
A couple of things worth noting about Canton are the billboards that line Renmin Lu all the way from the railway station to the Dong Fang Hotel and Trade Fair Exhibition Hall; you'll find them advertising such products as 'Moon Rabbit' brand batteries, 'Long March' car tyres (how crass!) and 'Shaolin Tonic Water (Packed by China National Native Produce and Animal By-products Import and Export Corporation)'.

Next to the Dong Fang Hotel is an enormous building called 'Loupa Mansions' – construction of which should have been completed by the time this book is out. The building is intended for use as a residence for foreigners doing business with China.

**Guangdong Provincial Museum** is situated on Yan'an Er-Lu and houses exhibitions of archeological finds from Guangdong Province. Also on Yan'an Er-Lu is Canton's **Zhongshan University** which houses the **Lu Xun Museum**; China's No 1 thinking-man's revolutionary taught at the university between January and September 1927. According to the Chinese he 'experienced a critical period in his life during which he changed from a revolutionary democrat to a great communist fighter'. In 1958 his bedroom, the bell tower and something called the 'urgent meeting room' were turned into a museum.

Down the road from Canton is the site of a proposed commerical **nuclear power reactor**, on the Leizhou Peninsula near Daya Bay. Daya Bay is just northeast of Mirs Bay which borders Hong Kong's New Territories. British and French firms are likely to build the plant, which will also provide power to Hong Kong, and construction is expected to be completed by 1991. Another nuclear plant is to be built at Qinshan in Zhejiang Province. I guess it goes to show that Socialist reactors are safer than Capitalist reactors?

**Places to Eat**
There is an old Chinese saying that to enjoy the best that life has to offer, one has to be 'born in Suzhou, live in Hangzhou, eat in Canton and die in Liuzhou' (Suzhou is renowned for its beautiful women, Hangzhou for its scenery, and Liuzhou for the finest wood for making coffins). Well, I did not go to Suzhou, I was not terribly impressed by Hangzhou and I have no wish to die in China, but Canton isn't a bad place to stuff your face.

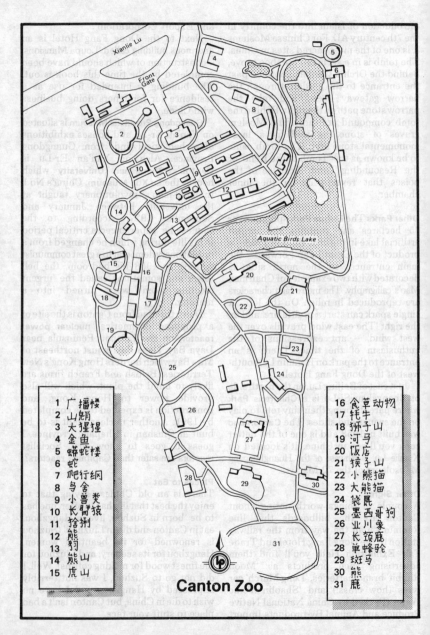

Xianlie Lu

Front Gate

Aquatic Birds Lake

1 广播楼
2 山猯
3 大猩猩
4 金鱼
5 蟒蛇楼
6 蛇
7 爬行纲
8 鸟舍 鸟兽禽类猿
9 小兽
10 长臂捌
11 捨猂
12 熊猫
13 熊狗
14 熊山
15 虎山

16 食草动物
17 牦牛子山
18 狮子山
19 河马
20 饭店
21 猴子山
22 小熊猫
23 大熊猫
24 大袋鼠
25 墨西哥狗
26 业川象
27 长颈鹿
28 单峰驼
29 斑马
30 熊
31 鹿

Canton Zoo

| | | | |
|---|---|---|---|
| 1 | Broadcasting Room | 17 | Yak |
| 2 | Baboon, Mandrill | 18 | Lion Hill |
| 3 | Gorilla | 19 | Hippopotamus |
| 4 | Goldfish | 20 | Restaurant |
| 5 | Boa House | 21 | Monkey Hill |
| 6 | Snakes | 22 | Lesser Panda |
| 7 | Reptiles | 23 | Panda |
| 8 | Birds | 24 | Kangaroo |
| 9 | Smaller Animals | 25 | Mexican Dog |
| 10 | Gibbon | 26 | Asian Elephant |
| 11 | Lynx | 27 | Giraffe |
| 12 | Bear | 28 | Bactrian Camel |
| 13 | Leopard | 29 | Zebra |
| 14 | Bear Hill | 30 | Bear |
| 15 | Tiger Hill | 31 | Deer |
| 16 | Herbivores | | |

The big advantage in Canton is that there are more restaurants to choose from ... dozens of famous old establishments along with heaps of smaller places, so eating out is not to be passed up. All the restaurants of any size have private rooms or partitioned areas, if you want to get away from the hoi-polloi – and since restaurants tend to be crowded this is a distinct advantage. If you can speak Chinese you can book tables over the phone. If there's a group of you with no particular preference or aversions to what you eat, then you could try stipulating how much you want to pay and let the staff do the rest; it doesn't always work – you may get a great meal or a heap of nastiness. Remember also that what the restaurant specialises in is not necessarily what you'll be able to get if you just walk in off the street; the exquisite stuff will *probably* have to be ordered in advance or may not be available to miscellaneous wanderers.

Normal service hours in Canton's restaurants are usually around 5 to 9 am for breakfast, 10 am to 2 pm for lunch and 5 to 8 pm for dinner. Several places have longer hours, but remember that China wakes up early and goes to sleep early; no use wandering into a restaurant late at night and expecting to be served.

There are a couple of worthy places close to the riverfront. Foremost is the *Datong Restaurant* (tel 86396 or 86983) at 63 Yanjiang Lu, just around the corner from Renmin Lu; it occupies all of an eight-storey building overlooking the river. The sixth floor has the cheaper dining rooms. Specialities of the house are crisp fried chicken and roast suckling pig. The skin of the pig is the delicacy; crisply roasted, dipped in bean sauce, salt and sugar, and served with a spring onion in a steamed roll.

Close to the Datong Restaurant is the *Yan Yan Restaurant*. It's on a sidestreet which runs east from Renmin Lu; look for the pedestrian overpass which goes over Renmin Lu just up from the intersection with Yanjiang Lu – the steps of the overpass lead down into the side street and the restaurant is opposite them. The restaurant is easily recognisable by the fish tanks in the entrance; get your turtles, catfish as well as roast suckling pig here. It's also fantastically well air-conditioned.

At 54 Renmin Lu, you'll find the

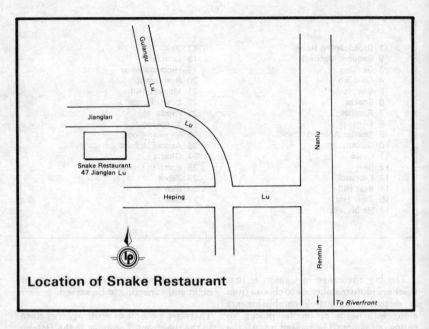

Jianglan Lu

Gulangu Lu

Snake Restaurant
47 Jianglan Lu

Heping Lu

Nanlu

Renmin

To Riverfront

**Location of Snake Restaurant**

*Seafood Restaurant* (sign in English), which serves what appear to be giant salamanders around 80 cm long and about 20 cm wide.

Further north and to the west of Renmin Lu are two other restaurants worth trying. At 43 Jianglan Lu is the *Shecanguan* or the *Snake Restaurant* (tel 23424). It was being renovated in mid-1983, but they usually have their selection of snakes on display in the window. To get to the restaurant you have to walk down Heping Lu which runs west from Renmin Lu. After a few minutes you come to Jianglan Lu; turn right and follow the road around to the restaurant which is on the left-hand side of the road. The restaurant was originally known as the 'Snake King Moon' and has a history of 80 years. The Chinese believe that snake meat is rather effective in curing diseases; snake meat is supposed to be good for dispelling wind, promoting blood circulation and to be

useful in treating anaemia, rheumatism, arthritis and asthenia. Snake gall bladder is supposed to be even more effective in dispelling wind, and promoting blood circulation, dissolving phlegm and soothing ones breathing. Some of the more creative snake recipes around are: Fricasseed assorted snake and cat meats, snake breast meat stuffed with shelled shrimp, stir-fried colourful shredded snakes, and braised snake slices with chicken liver. These dishes may be available in the restaurant.

One of the city's best known restaurants is the *Guangzhou* (tel 87136 or 87840) at 2 Xiuli 2-Lu on the corner with Wenchang Lu. It boasts a 70-year history and in the 1930s came to be known as the 'first house in Canton'. Its kitchens were staffed by the city's best chefs and the restaurant was frequented by the most important people of the day. It serves about 7000 to 8000 people a day, and about 10,000 in the busy season. The four storeys of dining halls and private rooms (some of them being renovated in mid-1983) are built around a central garden courtyard, with potted shrubs and flowers and landscape paintings, designed to give the feeling (at least to the people in the dingy ground floor rooms) that they're 'eating in a landscape'. Anyway, the food at this self-proclaimed illustrious restaurant ain't bad and it's cheap. Specialities of the house include sharkfin soup with shredded chicken, chopped crabmeat balls, and braised dove. The staff here treat you like an idiot.

There are a couple of places on Zhongshan Lu in the section between Renmin Lu and Jiefang Lu which are worth a try. The *Moslem Restaurant* is at 326 Zhongshan Lu, on the corner with Renmin Lu – look for the Arabic letters above the front entrance. It's an OK place, but go upstairs since the ground floor is dingy.

The *Tsaikenhsiang* is at 167 Zhongshan Lu. It's a vegetarian restaurant. It's dingy and depressing downstairs but upstairs is OK; they have private rooms too.

The *Xiyuan* is further up from the vegetarian restaurant and on the other side of the road at No 46. It's OK for basic food, but nothing amazing. Eat upstairs, since the ground floor is just a grotty canteen.

North of Zhongshan Lu is Dongfeng Lu which runs east-west across the city. At No 320 Dongfeng Beilu is the *Beiyuan Restaurant* (tel 33365 or 32471). This is another of Cantons 'famous houses' – a measure of its success being the number of cars and tourist buses parked outside. Inside is a courtyard and garden, from which the restaurant takes its name, *North Garden*. Specialities of the house include stewed pork, roast duck, barbecued chicken liver, steamed chicken in huadiao wine, stewed fish head with vegetables, fried crab, steamed fish, fried boneless chicken (could be a first for China), fried

snow-white shrimp, and stewed duck legs in oyster sauce.

In the west of Canton, the *Banxi Restaurant* (tel 85655 or 88706) at 151 Xiangyang 1-Lu is an enormous place and the biggest restaurant in the city. It's noted for its dumplings, stewed turtle, roast pork, chicken in tea leaves, and a crabmeat-sharkfin consomme.

Off in the same general direction is the *Tao Tao Ju (Abode of Tao Tao)* (tel 87501) at 288 Xiulu 1-Lu. Originally built as a private academy in the 17th century, it was turned into a restaurant in the late 19th century. Tao Tao was the name of the wife of the first proprietor. 'Yum cha' is the speciality here; you choose sweet and savoury snacks from the selection on trolleys that are wheeled around the restaurant. Tea is the preferred beverage ('Yum cha' means 'drink tea', but it also means to have dim sum – the two go together). The tea, apparently, is made with Canton's best water – transported (so the story goes) from the Nile Dragon Well in the White Cloud Hills.

Not far from Tao Tao Ju is a mooncake bakery, the *Lianxiang Lou (Lotus Fragrance Pavilion)*. Traditionally, mooncakes were eaten at the mid-autumn festival when the moon was brightest. The soft, golden-coloured crusts are stuffed with sweet and savoury fillings like pieces of fruit, nuts, lotus seeds and red beans. They're also used for weddings and receptions and are exported from here to Hong Kong.

Beijing Lu, serves both western and Chinese food. The roast pigeon here is *(Wild Animals Restaurant)* (tel 30997) is at No 247. This is where you can feast on dogs and cats, deer, bear paws, and snake. Once upon a time they even served tiger.

*Taiping House* (tel 35529) at 344 Beijing Lu, serves both Western and Chinese food. The roast pigeon here is supposed to have been a favourite of no less a personage than Zhou En-lai.

When the missiles start firing you can eat your way into oblivion at Canton's underground restaurant, the *Diaxia Canting*, a short walk from the Dong Fang Hotel down Jiefang Lu. From the street only a concrete archway topped by a green neon sign is visible. The entrance is through the archway and along the laneway. This structure was originally built as a bomb shelter, but today some of the corridors are hung with exhibits of local art works, while the rooms have been turned into games rooms and dining halls. The place is very popular with Canton's youth and was one of the first of its kind in China (bomb-shelter restaurants are now a common sight in China). The restaurant is open for lunch and dinner and the fried rice is excellent.

A few other restaurants worth mentioning include the *Xiyuan (West Garden) Teahouse* on Dongfeng 1-Lu. It's popular with the more well-heeled young people. The teahouse is set in a large garden with lots of bonsai on display. The *Nanyuan (South Garden Restaurant)* (tel 50532 or 51576) is at 120 Qianjin Lu. The specialities include pigeon in plum sauce and chicken in honey and oyster sauce. Qianjin Lu is on the south side of the Pearl River. To get to it you have to cross over Haizhu Bridge and go down Yuejin Lu. Qianjin Lu branches off to the east.

There are a couple of restaurants on Shamian Island which are OK for a meal. There is an excellent restaurant a short walk from the White Swan Hotel. Turn right from the entrance of the White Swan, and then left at the first T-intersection. The restaurant is two streets up on the right-hand side of the road. Friendly staff, and good and cheap food. The *Shengli Hotel* on the north bank of the island has an OK restaurant, which is open 5.30 to 9 am, 11.30 am to 2 pm and 5.30 to 8 pm.

Good though fairly mundane food is served in the little restaurants in the laneway alongside the Liu Hua Hotel. A few of these places are marginally better than the others; look around until you see something you like. Some of the restaurateurs have an aggravating habit of trying to snatch you off the street and some charge ridiculous prices, like Y1 for a small bowl of soupy noodles! But in general, you should be able to get a sizeable helping of meat, rice and vegies and beer for a few yuan. Try to avoid the Double Happiness brand beer which is commonly sold here; it tastes like a sickly-sweet soft drink.

There are innumerable street restaurants open at night in the vicinity of the Renmin Daxia Hotel; If you walk around the streets, and particularly along Changdi Damalu on the north side of the hotel, you'll find quite a few culinary delights; such delectables as frogs, toads and tortoises kept in buckets on the side of the road. At your merest whim these will be summarily executed, thrown in the wok and fried. It's a bit like eating in an abattoir, but at least there's no doubt about the freshness.

If you're staying off in oblivion at the Bai Yun Hotel there's a cheap little restaurant close by; walk out the front gate and turn left – the restaurant is about five minutes walk up the road. Good, though fairly ordinary food, for about Y2 to Y3 a plate and the people are friendly. They seem to stay open fairly late.

The food in the tourist hotels tends to be safely ordinary. The main advantage of eating in the hotels is that you can escape from the proletariat for a while.

The *Lui Hua Hotel* restaurant is OK, but rather expensive; you'd be looking at Y7 to Y10 for a decent meal that's only marginally better than the small restaurants in the laneway at the side of the hotel. They serve an approximation to a western breakfast but the bread is either sweet or has the texture of chipboard.

The Chinese restaurant on the 8th floor of the *Dong Fang Hotel* has been recommended by a travelling couple; it's open 6.30 to 9 am, 11.30 am to 2 pm and 5.30 to 9 pm. The *Bai Yun Hotel* may be expensive to stay in, but the restaurant is cheap – though I wouldn't go all the way there just to eat.

Mention has to be made of the food in the *White Swan Hotel* if only for interest. At the River Garden Cafe on the ground floor you can get a cup of coffee or tea (hot or iced) for just Y2, a milkshake (vanilla, pineapple, coffee or mango) for Y3, a 'tuna fish delight' sandwich for just Y4.50, spaghetti and meatballs for only Y6.50, and a roast beef sandwich with watercress, tomato, mustard and mayonnaise dressing for a mere Y9.50. If that's not enough, then try a hamburger with a quarter-pound of US ground meat – that will set you back another Y9.50. For dessert there's creme caramel for Y1.50 The hotel even has a *Japanese Restaurant* on the 3rd floor with rooms where you can sit on the floor with your shoes off. It's horrendously priced and is open daily from 11 am to 2.30 pm and 5 to 9.30 pm.

Back in the 1320s the Franciscan Friar Odoric visited China and commented on the culinary delights of the country. In Canton he noted the fat, pure white Guinea geese and the ducks and hens which were twice as large as those in Europe, as well as the habit these southerners had of eating snake 'There be monstrous great serpents likewise, which are taken by the inhabitants and eaten. A solemn feast among them without serpents is thought nothing of. To be brief, in this city there are all kinds of victuals in great abundance.'

In Zaiton, the present-day port of Quanzhou in Fujian Province, he described the feeding of the Chinese gods by the monks. 'These religious men every day feed their idol gods; whereupon at a certain time I went to behold the banquet and indeed those things which they brought to them were good to eat, and fuming hot, and when the steam ascended up to their idols they said that their gods

were refreshed. Howbeit, all the meat they conveyed away, eating it up themselves, and so they fed their dumb gods with the smoke only.'

## Getting Around

The city proper extends for some 60 square km, with most of the interesting sights scattered throughout. Hence, seeing the place on foot is quite impractical. Just the walk from the railway station to the Pearl River is about six km – not recommended for beginning each day's sightseeing.

There are electric-powered trolley-buses and ordinary motor-buses trundling the streets. They're reasonably frequent and the service is extensive but they can be *tediously* slow and extremely crowded – a bus terminus is definitely the best place to get on board if you can. They're slightly more civilised about getting on board then they are in other parts of China, but there's still a lot of pushing to contend with and you may find you'll just give up and walk a lot of the time.

Taxis are available from the major hotels 24 hours a day, from outside the railway station, and they can be hailed in the streets – which is a first for China. Demand for taxis is great, particularly during the peak hours; mornings from 8 to 9 am, and lunchtime and dinnertime. Flagfall is Y1.80 and the rate is about Y0.20 per quarter km.

Minivans which seat about a dozen people ply the streets on set routes. If you can find out where they're going they're a good way to avoid the crowded buses.

## Shopping

Canton's main shopping areas are Beijing Lu, Zhongshan Lu, the downtown section of Jiefang Lu and Xiuli 1-Lu and Xiuli 2-Lu. Beijing Lu is a most prestigious thoroughfare by Chinese standards – probably because it's the location of the Seiko Store. Several of the large cinemas are to be found here as are a couple of Canton's renowned restaurants. On the north-west corner of the Zhongshan/ Beijing Lu intersection, is the Zhongshan Department Store. Canton's main department store is the Nan Fang which is situated opposite the Cultural Park on Liuersan Lu. The store is popular with Hong Kongers and there's a currency exchange counter at the rear of the ground floor. The Friendship Store is right next to the Bai Yun Hotel.

For arts and crafts and antiques try the Friendship Store and the other major tourist trap the Guangdong Antique Store at 575 Hongshu Bei Lu, in front of the Guangxiao Temple.

East along Zhongshan Lu, across Beijing Lu and opposite the entrance to the Childrens Park, is the South China Specialities Store which specialises in regional handicrafts.

Continuing east along Zhongshan Lu, turn right at the next intersection into Wande Lu. Not far down on the left side of the road at No 146 is the Canton Antique Store – not as large as the Guangdong Antique Store, but worth a look in. The Jiangnan Native Product Store at 399 Zhongshan Lu has a good selection of bamboo and baskets.

On Beijing Lu, next door to the Foreign Languages Bookstore at No 326, is Canton's main art supply shop, the Sanduoxuan. Apart from art materials it also sells original paintings.

For Books and Magazines try the Foreign Language Bookstore at 326 Beijing Lu – almost directly opposite the Seiko Store. As well as translations of Chinese books and magazines, foreign magazines like *Time, Newsweek, Far Eastern Economic Review* and even the *Readers Digest* are sold here.

The Classical Bookstore at 338 Beijing Lu specialises in pre-1949 Chinese string-bound editions.

The Xinhua Bookstore is at 336 Beijing Lu, and is the main Chinese bookstore in the city. If you want to investigate the state of the pictorial arts in the country today, then this is a good place to come; there are lots of wallposters as well as sets of reproductions of Chinese paintings. They also sell children's comic books, voraciously read by young and old alike.

For Theatre Costumes then drop into the Theatre Shop almost next door to the Zhongshan Department Store. Here you can pick up Chinese opera costumes, masks and swords. Part of the shop specialises in Chinese musical instruments.

## AROUND CANTON

### Baiyun Shan (White Cloud Hills)

These hills are situated in the north-eastern suburbs of Canton. The hills are an offshoot of **Dayu Ling**, the chief mountain range of the province. From its summit, known as **Moxing Ling (Star Touching Peak)**, (which only rises 382 metres, but anything that's higher than a mound of dirt is a mountain in eastern China) there is a panorama of the city below, the **Xiqiao Hills** to one side, the **North River** and the **Fayuan Hills** on the other side, as well as the sweep of the Pearl River.

The Chinese rate the evening view from **Cheng Precipice** as one of the eight sights of Canton. The precipice takes its name from a story from the Qin Dynasty. It is said that the first Qin Emperor, Qin Shi Huang, heard of a herb which would confer immortality on whoever ate it. Cheng On Kee, a minister of the Emperor, was dispatched to find it. Five years of wandering brought Cheng to the White Cloud Hills where the herb grew in profusion. On eating the herb, the rest of it disappeared. In dismay and fearful of returning empty-handed, Cheng threw himself off the precipice. But assured immortality since he had eaten the herb, he was caught by a stork and taken to heaven. The precipice, named in his memory, was formerly the site of the oldest monastery in the area.

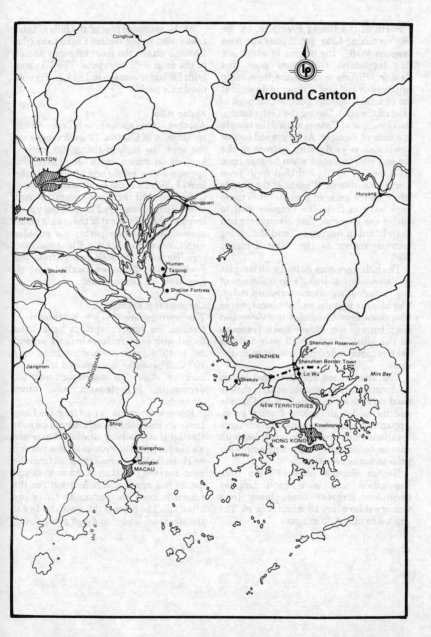

North of the Cheng Precipice, on the way up toxing Ling, you'll pass the **Nine Dragons Well** – the origins of which are also legendary. One story goes that Canton officials would come to worship twice yearly and also at times of drought at the Dragon Emperor Temple that used to exist on the spot. During the 18th century, the Governor of Canton visited the temple at a time of drought. As he prayed he saw nine small boys dancing in front of the temple, who vanished when he rose from his knees. A spring bubbled forth from where he had been. A monk at the temple informed the amazed governor that these boys were in fact nine dragons sent to advise the governor that his prayers had been heard in heaven ... and the spring became known as the 'Nine Dragons Well'.

The hills were once dotted with temples and monasteries, though no buildings of any historical significance remain today. The hills are popular with the local people who come here to admire the views and slurp cups of tea; **Cloudy Rock Teahouse** on the hillside by a small waterfall has been recommended if you want to do the same.

The **Shanzhuang** and **Shuangxi Hotels** are located on the mountainside – they're used exclusively by high-ranking Chinese and the odd high-ranking foreign guest. Apparently they're made up of large luxurious villas which come complete with sunken baths, private gardens and other proletarian necessities.

Baiyun Shan is about 15 km from Guangzhou and is a good half-day excursion. Express buses leave from Guangwei Lu every 15 minutes or so. The trip takes about 30 minutes.

At the southern foot of the hills is **Luhu Lake** – also called **Golden Liquid Lake** (the Chinese attach the most fabulous names to the most ordinary spots) The lake was built for water storage in 1958 and is now used as a park.

### Xiqiao Hills

Another scenic spot, these hills are 68 km south-west of Canton. 72 peaks make up the area, the highest rising 400 metres, keeping company with 36 caves, 32 springs, 28 waterfalls and 21 crags. At the foot of the hills is the small markettown of Guanshan, and there are several ancient stone villages scattered around the upper levels of the hills. Most of the area is made accessible by stone paths; it's popular with Chinese tourists but Europeans are rare. Buses to the hills depart from the Foshan Bus Station on Daxin Lu which runs west off Jiefang Nanlu.

### Conghua Hot Springs

The springs are 81 km north-east of Canton. So far, 12 springs have been found with temperatures mostly around 30° to 40° C, with the highest being over 70° C. The water is supposed to have a curative effect on neuralgia, arthritis, dermatitis, hypertension and other ailments.

Buses to Conghua depart from the Long Distance Bus Station on Hongyun Lu near Canton East Railway Station. There are also buses from the Provincial Bus Station on Huanshi Xilu, across the road from the long-distance bus station. As soon as you get to the springs, buy a ticket for the return journey to Canton as buses are often full. The place is thick with bodies at the weekend, so try to avoid going then.

# Guangdong

While the Han Chinese were carving out a civilisation in the north, the southern region, now known as Guangdong Province, remained a semi-independent tributary peopled by native tribes who still exist today as a minority groups. It was not until the Qin Dynasty that the Chinese finally conquered the area, but revolts and uprisings were frequent and the Chinese settlements remained small and dispersed amongst a predominantly aboriginal population.

Guangdong was reconquered by the Song after a brief period of independence towards the end of the Tang Dynasty and Han Chinese emigration to the region began in earnest, acceleration after the 12th century. The original native tribes were killed by Chinese armies, isolated in small pockets or pushed further south like the Li and Miao peoples who now inhabit the mountainous areas of Hainan Island. By the 17th century the Han Chinese had outgrown Guangdong and pressure of population forced them to move into adjoining Guangxi Province, and into Sichuan which had been ravaged and depopulated after the mid-17th century rebellions.

It was Guangdong which first made contact with both the merchants and the armies of the modern European states, and it was the people of this province who spearheaded the Chinese emigration to America, Australia and South Africa in the mid-19th century. The move was spurred on by the gold rushes in those countries, but it was mainly the wars and the growing poverty of the century which caused the Chinese to leave in droves. The image which most westerners have today of a 'Chinatown' is based on Canton; it is Cantonese food which is eaten and the Cantonese dialect which is spoken amongst the Chinese populations from Melbourne to Toronto to London.

## THE SHENZHEN SPECIAL ECONOMIC ZONE

The Shenzhen municipality stretches right across the northern border of Hong Kong from **Daya Bay** in the east to the mouth of the **Pearl River** in the west. Though it's hardly a place to linger, it's worth stopping off for a few hours to look around Shenzhen town since this is the centre of one of China's major Special Economic Zones.

China's economic policies have undergone a radical change since the death of Mao Zedong and the fall of the so-called 'Gang of Four'. Under Mao, China had largely isolated itself economically from the rest of the world, apprehensive that economic links with other countries would make China dependent on them. Although the country was opening up in the later years of Mao's life, this was only on a limited basis.

With the rise of Deng Xiao-ping to No 1 in the Chinese government, economic policy has turned away from the narrow path of self-reliance advocated by the Maoists. The post-Mao period is characterised by what is referred to as the 'Four Modernisations' – the modernisation of agriculture, industry, defence, science and technology. The present leadership believes that China can be modernised faster and more easily by importing foreign technology and management techniques.

The Special Economic Zones have

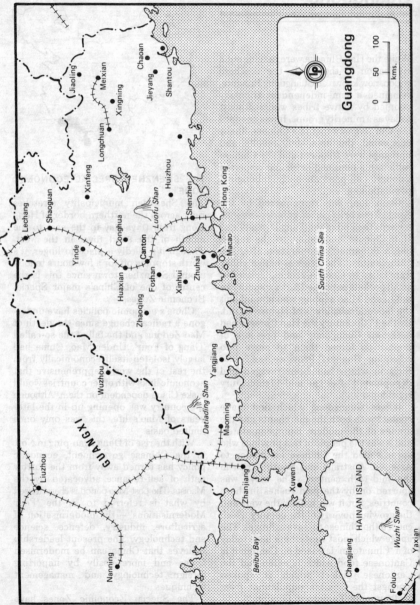

been set up to promote foreign and Overseas Chinese investment in China using reduced taxation, low wages, abundant labour supply and low operating costs as encouragement. They're a sort of geographical laboratory where western capitalist economic principles can be tested using cheap Socialist labour. These zones are not a new idea; they bear some resemblance to the Export Processing Zones to be found in almost 30 countries around the world.

The SEZ was set up in a small part of the Shenzhen municipality in 1979. The area was chosen for several reasons; it is adjacent to Hong Kong, thus allowing easier access to the world market, most Hong Kong businessmen speak the same dialects and maintain kinship relations with Shenzhen and other parts of southern China. There is easy access to the port facilities of Hong Kong, lastly, the area itself has enough level land suitable for settlement and the construction of industrial plants and a ready supply of raw materials suitable for use in the construction industry.

## SHENZHEN TOWN

The town of Shenzhen is the showpiece of the municipality. The modern world is establishing itself here in the form of several enormous high-rise blocks. These are scattered in the area immediately north of the railway station, and the place is beginning to look like some sort of embryonic Hong Kong.

The main road runs parallel to the railway tracks, east of the railway station. Walk out of the station and turn left. About 10 minutes walk up the road you'll come to the **Friendship Restaurant and Buying Centre**. This is followed by several high-rise blocks and a crossroads; on the corner is the *Pan Hsi Restaurant* which looks like it's been lifted lock stock and barrel out of Hong Kong; the locals often stand around outside the door to catch the air-conditioning. Right next to the restaurant is the large **Friendship Store**.

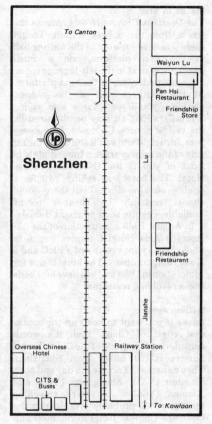

Shenzhen

### Information
**CITS** (tel 2151 or 2149) has its office inside the Shenzhen Railway Station.

If you want to know more about the region, particularly its economic set-up, get a copy of *Shenzhen Special Economic Zone – China's Experiment in Modernization* published by the Hong Kong Geographical Association, and available from the Hong Kong Government Bookstore in the GPO Building, Connaught Place, Central, Hong Kong Island.

## Places to Stay

The *Overseas Chinese Hotel* is across the tracks from the railway station. To get there you have to go out of the waiting hall to the first platform, via a small passageway next to the left-luggage room. Take the underpass to the next platform. At the southern end of this second platform, you'll see a large sign saying 'Travellers Exit' (it may be obscured by the yellow horde). Go down the subway here, turn right and you'll end up on the far side of the railway tracks. Immediately in front of you is the Overseas Chinese Hotel. The hotel was asking Y45 for a double room (no singles) but there would almost certainly be cheaper rooms available, despite their adamant denials.

In August 1983 construction of the 33-storey(!) Asia Hotel Complex began in Shenzhen, a joint venture of a PRC and a Hong Kong company. The hotel is due for completion in 1985 and will have 600 beds and a revolving restaurant.

## Getting Away

**Buses** If you want to head up the south-east coast of China, then it's worth considering taking one of the China Travel Service (CTS) buses from Shenzhen. They depart at 12 noon each day and go to Shantou (Y37), Zhangzhou (Y60) and Xiamen (Y65) - if you're travelling through you'll probably overnight at the Overseas Chinese Hotel in Shantou and the bus fare includes the cost of accommodation. In Shenzhen tickets for the buses can be bought from the office in front and just off to one side of the Overseas Chinese Hotel. You should also be able to book at the CTS offices in Hong Kong.

The CTS buses are comfortable and air-conditioned; what you spend on the bus, you'll save on the train fare from Shenzhen to Canton, the hotel bill in Canton, and your bum on the road to Shantou (which has got to be one of the roughest rides in China!)

**Trains** After you've been through customs on the Chinese side, you wind up in Shenzhen Railway Station's crowded waiting room. Considering the multitude that crosses the border every day, a new building is long overdue.

At one end of the waiting room (that close to the border) you'll see a white and blue illuminated sign, with red Chinese characters and 'Booking Office' in English - this is where you buy your tickets to Canton.

The following trains go to Canton:

| No | dep. Shenzhen | arr. Canton |
| --- | --- | --- |
| 98 | 9.33 am | 12.54 am |
| 100 | 11.33 am | 2.29 pm |
| 96 | 1.00 pm | 3.00 pm |
| 102 | 3.02 pm | 5.50 pm |
| 502 | 4.30 pm | 9.42 pm |

Remember that all train timetables in China change every six months or so, and the Shenzen-Canton timetable changes even faster, so check the departure times when you're there. During the holiday periods, particularly Chinese New Year and Easter), there will probably be extra trains, but try to avoid going at this time because the crowds that flood over from Hong Kong are truly horrendous.

**CANTON** For a complete description of Canton, see the previous chapter.

## FOSHAN

Just 28 km south-west of Canton is the town of Foshan. The name means 'Buddha Hill'. The story goes that a monk travelling through the area enshrined three statues of Buddha on a hilltop. After the monk left, the shrine collapsed and the statues disappeared. Hundreds of years later, during the Tang dynasty (618-907 AD), the Buddha figurines were suddenly rediscovered, a new temple was built on the hill and the town renamed.

Whether the story is true or not, from about the 10th century onwards the town became a well-known religious centre -

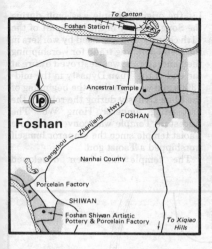

and because of its location in the north of the Pearl River Delta with the Fen River flowing through it, and its proximity to Canton, Foshan was ideally placed to take off as a market town and a trade centre.

Since the 10th or 11th centuries it's been notable as one of the four main handicraft centres of old China; the other three were Zhuxian in Henan Province, Jingdezhen in Jiangxi and Hankou in Hebei. The nearby town of Shiwan (which is now virtually an extension of Foshan) became noted for its pottery and the village of Nanpu (which is now a suburb of Foshan) developed the art of metal casting. Silk weaving and paper-cutting also became important industries and today Foshan paper-cuts are one of the commonly sold tourist souvenirs in China.

If you're going to be in Canton for any length of time, then Foshan is worth a day trip.

## Information & Orientation

The bus from Canton heads into Foshan from the north; first stop is Foshan Railway Station (the railway line starts in Canton, passes through Foshan and heads west about 60 km to the town of Hekou The bus then passes over the narrow Fen River, with a few decaying barges huddled nearby, and a few minutes down the road pulls into the long-distance bus station.

Walk out of the station and turn left; you're on the Canton-Zhanjiang Highway and that's no respite from the bustle of Canton! Turn left again down any one of the side streets. Walk for about 10 minutes and you'll come to one of Foshan's main streets, Song Feng Lu. A right turn into Song Feng Lu will point you in the direction of the town centre.

Continue down Song Feng Lu and you'll come to the junction with Kuaizi Lu; another minute's walk is a T-intersection where Kuaizi Lu meets Lianhua Lu, the town's main street.

Turn left into Lianhua Lu and there's a bustling little fruit, meat and vegetable market. If you head up Lianhua Lu in the opposite direction you go down the main shopping street and eventually come to a roundabout. Across the road, diagonally on your left is the big *Pearl River Hotel*. A hard left turn here takes you into Zumiao Lu and down to the CITS Office, the Foshan Museum and the Foshan Hotel.

**CITS** is at 64 Zumiao Lu (tel 87923 or 85775)

**Public Security** is at 10 Fumin Lu, just down from the intersection with Lixin Lu.

### Lianhua Market

This market on Lianhua Lu can't compare to Qingping Market in Canton, but it's worth a wander through if you're in Foshan. Here you can stock up on fish that have been sliced in half but with the heart still intact and pumping, or on turtles, crabs or skinned and roasted dogs. A few shops up from the Lianhua/Kuaizi Lu intersection is one selling snakes, and across the road from it is a building housing the main meat, fish and poultry market. At the far end of the street are a few miscellaneous stalls selling clothes, oddments, furniture, flowers, birds and goldfish. (Pets are back in favour in the People's Republic; during the Cultural Revolution the keeping of goldfish and birds was regarded as a bourgeois pursuit and activists tried to wipe out the hobby. Come the end of the Cultural Revolution even the animals had to be rehabilitated.)

### Ancestors Temple

Located at the southern end of Zumiao Lu, the original temple was built during the Song Dynasty in the later part of the 11th century, and was used by workers in the metal-smelting trade for worshipping their ancestors. It was destroyed by fire at the end of the Yuan Dynasty in the mid-1300s and was rebuilt at the beginning of the Ming Dynasty during the reign of the first Ming emperor Hong Wu. The Ancestors Temple was converted into a Taoist temple since the emperor himself worshipped a Taoist god.

The temple has been developed

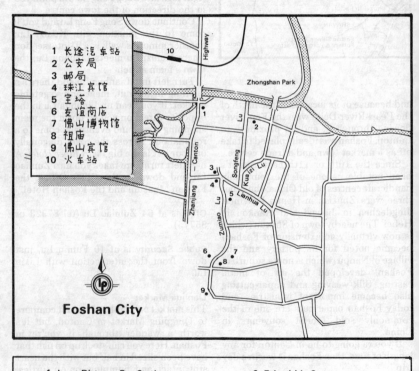

1 长途汽车站
2 公安局
3 邮局
4 珠江宾馆
5 宝塔
6 友谊商店
7 佛山博物馆
8 祖庙
9 佛山宾馆
10 火车站

**Foshan City**

| 1 Long Distance Bus Station | 6 Friendship Store |
| 2 Public Security Office | 7 Fosham Museum |
| 3 Post Office | 8 Ancestral Temple |
| 4 Pearl River Hotel | 9 Fosham Hotel / CITS |
| 5 Pagoda | 10 Railway Station |

through renovations and additions in the Ming and Qing Dynasties. The structure is built entirely of interlocking wooden beams, with no nails or other metal used at all. The temple is roofed with coloured tiles made in Shiwan.

The main hall contains a 2,500 kg bronze statue of a god known as the Northern Emperor (Beidi). He's also known as the Black Emperor (Heidi) and rules over water and all its inhabitants, especially fish, turtles and snakes. Since South China was prone to floods, people often tried to appease Beidi by honouring him with temples and carvings of turtles and snakes. In the courtyard is a pool containing a large statue of a turtle with a serpent crawling over it and the Chinese throw one, two and five fen notes – plus the odd soft-drink can – onto the statue.

The temple also has an interesting collection of rather ornate weapons used on ceremonial occasions during the imperial days; the **Foshan Museum** is in the temple grounds and is OK if you're there, but there's nothing of special interest. The **Foshan Antique Store** is also here and is open 9am to 4pm, and there is also an **Arts and Crafts Store**. Entry to the temple is 10 fen and it's open daily 8.30am to 4.30pm

## Zhongshan Park

The other much-touted tourist attraction is this park on the north side of the Fen River. It's a pleasant enough place, but not really worth the effort, especially if you've already been to the parks in Canton.

## Places to Stay

The *Foshan Hotel* is the town's tourist-joint. Single rooms are Y20 and doubles Y28. The staff are friendly, and it would probably be a nice place to stay in summer, but it looks miserably cold and empty in winter. The restaurant here is open from 6.30 to 8.30 am, 10.30 am to 1.30 pm and 5 to 8 pm. The hotel is located at the far end of Zumiao Lu. It's too far to walk to the hotel from the bus station –

there might be a bus but even the staff at the hotel don't know which one to get, and a taxi back to the city centre would cost you about Y4.

Much better located is the big *Pearl River Hotel* (tel 86481 or 87512) in the centre of town. Doubles for Y28, but there'd almost certainly be cheaper accommodation in a place this size! It seems to be primarily for Chinese, but the staff are friendly (though they don't speak any English) and they should let you stay.

The *Overseas Chinese Mansion (Huaqiao Daxia)* is at 14 Zumiao Lu – it's a good central location and could be worth trying.

## Places to Eat

There are cheap canteens in front of the bus station serving rice-noodles and meat, and soup for about 50 fen a plate. There's also a cheap canteen on the road when you turn left out of the bus station; nothing special, just cheap. There are lots of cheap places with similar canteen-style food on Lianhua Lu down from the market, but nothing particularly worth recommending.

You might give the *Qunyingge (Heros Pavilion) Restaurant* in Zhongshan Park a shot, or the *Meiyuan (Plum Garden) Restaurant* near the Temple of the Ancestors. In Shiwan you might try the *Taodu* across the road from the bus station.

## Getting There

Buses from Canton leave from the Foshan Bus Terminal at the corner of Daxin Lu and Jiefang Nanlu. You can buy your ticket on the bus, but it's probably better to get it beforehand so you can be sure of a reserved seat; the ticket office is on Daxin Lu just a few minutes walk down from Jiefang Nanlu. The fare to Foshan is Y0.55 and the trip takes 50 to 60 minutes. The buses park out in the street and have a sign (in Chinese) on the front showing their destination. A wooden board with the departure time of the bus is hung on the side facing the footpath.

The bus heads west out of Canton, over Zhujiang Bridge. The countryside is dead flat rice-paddies the whole way; not really anything to see, though if you're only up from Hong Kong for a few days then it at least gives you a glimpse of the countryside and the odd few old villages along the way. You pass through the very small town of **Dali** on the way. Foshan lies on the main Canton-Zhanjiang Highway and there are numerous trucks and buses on the road; and a great number of bicycles as well, their pack-racks holding bales of grass, tubs of water and even dead pigs.

## THE PEARL RIVER DELTA

The Pearl River Delta is the large , fertile and heavily populated territory immediately south of Canton. Apart from Canton the delta has several towns and places of interest.

**Zhuhai** is the stretch of land immediately to the north of Macau, and was set up as a Special Economic Zone in 1979. The principal town is **Xiangzhou**, just nine km north of Macau. **Gongbei** is the border town with Macau and from here you can get buses to various places in Zhuhai.

**Zhongshan County** is immediately to the north of Zhuhai. The administrative centre is **Shiqi**. Zhongshan is the birthplace of one of China's great notables, Dr Sun Yat-sen who was born in the village of **Cuiheng**, 29 km from Macau. His former house, which still stands in the village, was built in 1892 with money sent back from Honolulu by his elder brother. There is also a Sun Yat-sen Museum which was set up in 1966. South-west of Cuiheng are the **Zhongshan Hot Springs** which have been turned into a tourist resort and three km away are the **Yungmo Hot Springs**. Again, all these places can be reached by bus from Gongbei.

**Jiangmen** is an old town in the west of Zhongshan County, and there are buses from Canton's long-distance bus station on Huanshi Lu, west of the railway station. There are four buses a day, with departures at 7.30 am, 11.30 am, 1.30 pm and 2.30 pm; the fare is Y2.55. Stay at the *Jiangmen Mansions* which is right next to Jiangmen's bus station.

**Humen** is a small town about 100 km south-east of Canton, and is noted by the Chinese as a centre of resistance during the Opium Wars. According to one information booklet:

Humen was the place where the Chinese people captured and burned the opium dumped into China by the British and American merchants in the 1830s and it was also the outpost of the Chinese people to fight against the aggressive opium war. In 1839, Lin Zexu, the then imperial envoy of the Qing government, resolutely put a ban on opium smoking and the trade of opium. Supported by the broad masses of the people, Lin Zexu forced the British and American opium mongers to hand over 20,285 cases of opium ... and burned all of them at Humen beach, Dongguang County. This just action showed the strong will of the Chinese people to resist against the imperialist aggression ...

Today there is a 'Museum of the Humen People's Resistance Against the British in the Opium War', a monument and a memorial statue in the town 'to extol the Chinese people for their tenacious spirit in fighting against the foreign aggression during the Opium War'.

**Sanyuanli** is on the outskirts of Canton and is also noted for its role in the first Opium War. The story – which I find a bit hard to believe – goes like this:

In 1840, the British imperialists launched the opium war against China. No sooner had the British invaders landed on the western outskirts of Guangzhou on 24 May 1841 than they started to burn, slaughter, rape and loot the local people. All this aroused Guangzhou people's great indignation *[not to mention that they got slightly annoyed?]*. Holding high the great banner of anti-invasion, the heroic people of Sanyuanli together with the people from the nearby 103 villages took an oath to fight against the enemy at Sanyuan Old Temple. On 30 May, they lured the British troops to the place called Niulangang where they used hoes, swords and

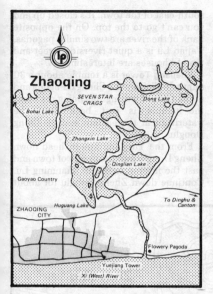

were actually seven stars that fell from the sky to form a pattern resembling the Big Dipper – hence the name 'Seven Stars'. In keeping with their celestial origin they've been given exotic names like 'Hill Slope' and 'Toad'. The lakes are artificial and were built in 1955, and the park is adorned with concrete pathways, arched bridges and little pavilions.

Amongst Zhaoqing's other more notable visitors was the defunct Song Dynasty which set up shop here on their flight from the Mongol invaders. Later, in 1583, foreign devils in the guise of the Jesuit priests Matteo Ricci and Michael Ruggieri came here and were allowed to establish a church. Marshal Ye Jianying trundled through in 1966 and composed some inspired verse:

> With water borrowed from the West Lake,
> Seven hills transferred from Yangshuo,
> Green willows lining the banks –
> This picturesque scenery will remain forever!

If you're going to Guilin or Yangshuo it's not worth coming here just to see them, but the ride out to Zhaoqing from Canton and the town itself are interesting. The town lies 110 km west of Canton on Xi (West) River.

### Information & Orientation

The town itself is bounded to the south by the West River and to the north by Duanzhou Lu which runs parallel to the river. It's a small place and a good deal of it can be seen on foot.

The long-distance bus station is on Duanzhou Lu; turn left out of the station and walk for a few minutes to the traffic circle where the multi-storey Zhaoqing Mansion and the entrance to Seven Star Crags Park are located. Make a hard left turn into Tianming Lu – this is the main street, lined with shops, cheap little restaurants and noisy canteens. Streets to the right lead off into the older part of Zhaoqing. It's a 20-minute walk down to Jiangbin Donglu which hugs the north

spears as weapons and annihilated over 200 British invaders armed with rifles and cannons. Finally the British troops were forced to withdraw from the Guangzhou area.

There is a museum and a monument here commemorating the struggle.

Forty km north of Canton is the village of **Guanlubu** where Hong Xiuquan, the leader of the Taiping Rebellion, was born in 1814 and lived in his early years. His house has been restored, and the Hong clan temple is now used as a museum.

### ZHAOQING

For almost a thousand years people have been coming to Zhaoqing to scribble graffiti on its cliffs or inside its caves, often poems or essays describing how much they like the rock formations they were drawing all over.

Zhaoqing is noted for the Seven Star Crags, a group of limestone towers – a peculiar geological formation that is abundant in the paddy fields of Guilin and Yangshuo. Legend has it that the crags bank of the West River. A right turn at the river will lead you to the ticket office for boats to Canton or Wuzhou.

### Things to See

Zhaoqing is a town for street-walking. It's a place where the peak-hour bicycle crush goes hand-in-hand with quiet side-streets and where dilapidated houses come complete with colour TVs and outdoor communal toilets.

Apart from the Seven Star Crags there are a couple of sights scattered about. The **Chongxi Pagoda** is a sadly dilapidated nine-storey structure on Tajiao Lu in the south-east of the town. It's closed up and you can't go to the top. On the opposite bank of the river are two similar pagodas. Tajiao Lu is a quiet riverside street and the old houses are interesting.

**Yuejiang Tower** is a temple about a 30 minute walk from the Chongxi Pagoda and at the time of writing was being restored; the temple is just back from the waterfront at the eastern end of Zheng Donglu.

From the Yuejiang Tower, head down Zheng Donglu into the centre of town and past the intersection with Tianming Lu. Continue down Zheng Donglu for about

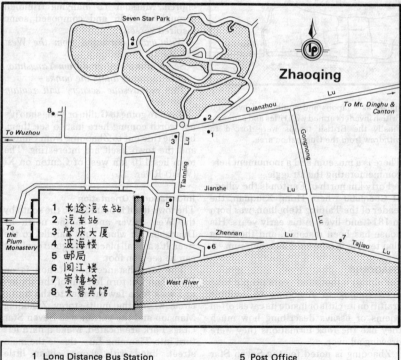

| | |
|---|---|
| 1 长途汽车站 | |
| 2 汽车站 | |
| 3 肇庆大厦 | |
| 4 波海楼 | |
| 5 邮局 | |
| 6 阅江楼 | |
| 7 崇禧塔 | |
| 8 芙蓉宾馆 | |

| | | | |
|---|---|---|---|
| 1 | Long Distance Bus Station | 5 | Post Office |
| 2 | Local Bus Station | 6 | Yuejiang Tower |
| 3 | Zhaoqing Mansions | 7 | Chongxi Pagoda |
| 4 | Bohailou Hotel | 8 | Furong Hotel |

10 minutes; on your left you'll come to an interesting street market where bicycles, people and hand-drawn carts all compete for space.

At the western end of town is the **Plum Monastery** and to get here you have to continue to the end of Zheng Donglu and turn right. Although one building appears to have been recently restored, the rest are dilapidated and overgrown with moss. The monastery compound is closed up but you can climb over the wall and have a look through, though there's not much of interest unless you're an enthusiast.

**Mount Dinghu** is 20 km east of Zhaoqing and is another 'scenic beauty spot' – and a summer resort for the Chinese. Apart from its streams, brooks, pools, hills and trees, the mountain is noted for the Qingyuan Temple built towards the end of the Ming Dynasty.

## Places to Stay

There are a couple of places to stay in Zhaoqing but the only convenient place is the *Zhaoqing Mansion (the Overseas Chinese Hotel)* on the corner of Duanzhou Lu and Tianming Lu. Turn left out of the bus station and walk down Duanzhou Lu for 10 minutes; the hotel is a multi-storey tower and you can't miss it. Big, beautiful double rooms here for Y26, but there would almost certainly be cheaper rooms available in a place this size. If you take the expensive rooms then you discover that someone in China *does* pay attention to their interior-decoration classes.

The *Bohailou Hotel* is on the north side of Zhongxin (Central) Lake in the Seven Star Crag Park. It's a concrete block with a Chinese-style roof, slightly more attractive than other Chinese hotels but no less cold and dreary inside. It does have one advantage; if you're here in the off-season it's extremely quiet with farms to the rear and the lake to the front. Double rooms are Y10, but it's a long way from the town.

There is another hotel in the town for foreign tourists, the *Furong* but it's out of the way and difficult to get to. Doubles go for around Y24.

## Places to Eat

One can only hope that the Song and the Jesuits ate somewhat better. There's nothing remarkable to be had here, just the usual plates of noodles, meat and vegies in the cheap restaurants along Tianming Lu, but nothing worth noting. There's a reasonably decent restaurant right around the corner from Zhaoqing Mansions on Tianming Lu. It stays open until around midnight, by which time the streets are almost deserted.

## Getting Around

The local bus station is on Duanzhou Lu, a few minutes walk east of the intersection with Tianming Lu. Bus No 1 starts at the Langfeng Crag in the Seven Star Park, goes down Duanzhou Lu, Tianming Lu, Zheng Dong and Renming Lu terminating at the corner of Renming Lu and Jiangbin Donglu on the riverfront. Bus No 4 departs from the local bus station, goes down Tianming Lu and then down Zheng Donglu most of the way to the Plum Monastery.

Auto-rickshaws with tray and bench seats ply the streets and there's a stand right across from the long-distance bus station. If you catch one in the street beware of overcharging.

## Getting Away

**Buses** Buses to Canton take about 3½ to 4 hours; the fare is Y2.80 and there are several buses each day. The road to Zhaoqing will lift you off your seat! There seems to be some roadwork in progress, so things may have improved by the time this book is available.

There's one river crossing and if you don't have to wait too long for the barge you will probably make it to Canton in just three hours.

**Boats** The ticket office for boats upriver to Wuzhou or downriver to Canton is at 3

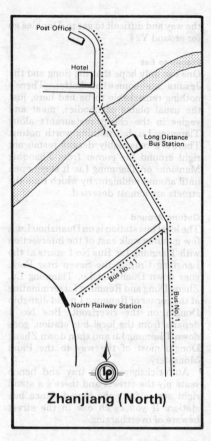

Zhanjiang (North)

## CHAOZHOU

Chaozhou is an ancient commercial and trading city dating back 1700 years situated on the Hanjiang River and surrounded by the Golden and Calabash Hills. One of the major 'sights' is the **Kaiyuan Temple** which was built in 738 AD during the Tang Dynasty and houses a large collection of Buddhist scriptures sent there by the Emperor Qian Long. The cliffs at the foot of Calabash Mountain and on the shore of the West Lake are the **Moya Carvings** depicting the local landscapes and the customs of the people, as well as poems and examples of calligraphy; they date back 1000 years. South-east of Chaozhou is the seven-storey **Phoenix Pagoda** built in 1585.

There are frequent buses to Chaozhou from the nearby town of Shantou; see the Shantou section for details. There is an *Overseas Chinese Hotel* in the town.

## ZHANJIANG

Zhanjiang is a major port on the southern coast of China, and the largest Chinese port west of Canton. It was leased to France in 1898 and remained under French control until World War II. Today the French are back here, but this time Zhanjiang is a base for their oil-drilling projects in the South China Sea. Perhaps more importantly, Zhanjiang is a naval base and part of China's southern defences against the Vietnamese.

You're most likely to come to Zhanjiang if you're on your way to Haikou on Hainan Island. The bus ride from Canton is a fascinating trip (see the Canton section for details) and it may be worth coming here just for that, though Zhanjiang is one of the greyest towns in China.

### Information & Orientation

Zhanjiang is divided into two separate sections with a stretch of countryside several km long between them. The northern section is a nondescript collection of concrete buildings. The bus from Canton pulls in here and the hotel is close

Jiangbin Donglu. Take bus No 1 or No 2 to the corner of Jiangbin Donglu and Renming Lu, and walk west along Jiangbin Donglu. The office is easily identifiable since there's a sign in English Above the entrance saying 'Rong Hotel'. It's office is open 6 to 11.30 am, 12 to 5.30 pm and 6 to 7 pm. The scenery along the river is supposed to be fairly impressive and the boat passes through Zhaoqing Gorge which is 11 km long and has cliffs that rise to 1000 metres.

to the bus station. It's a good place to wander around at night when the crowds are out on the streets, but it's rather dusty and boring during the day. The southern section is littered with more concrete buildings and there's also an Overseas Chinese Hotel here. The harbour area is a collection of drab streets, grotty slum buildings and dilapidated junks –and *everything* is an intense grey! There are two railway stations and two long-distance bus stations, one each in the northern and southern parts of town.

### Places to Stay

There is one hotel you can stay at in the northern part of town. When you come out of the long-distance bus station, turn right, look straight ahead and a 10-minute walk up the road is a building with large black Chinese characters on it. Single rooms here are Y3.50, doubles are Y6, dormitory beds are Y1.80 and the beds have mosquito nets. Use a phrase-book since there's almost nobody here who

speaks any English. It's basically OK if you don't mind the warehouse-palatial style of accommodation – the main problem being the noise! You won't want to hang around here for very long.

There is an *Overseas Chinese Hotel* in the southern section of town where you can stay. Double rooms are Y18, but you may be able to get a cheaper price if you say you're a student. They also have a dormitory. To get there, take bus No 10 from Zhanjiang South Railway Station. It puts you off right beside the hotel.

### Getting Around

Bus No 1 runs between the two sections of the town. To get to Zhanjiang South Railway Station you have to take bus No 1 to the southern part and then change to bus No 2 – see the bus map in this book. There are lots of motorcycles-with-sidecars plying the roads; agree on a price beforehand, otherwise they'll charge you the earth.

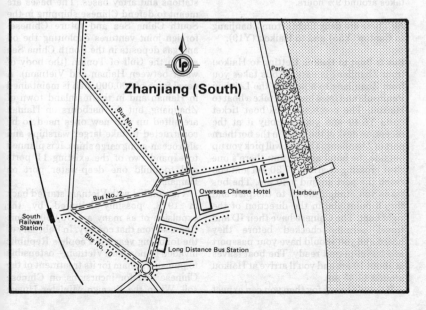

## Getting Away

**Bus** There is a long-distance bus station in the northern section of the town just near the hotel. There is another in the south mid-way between the railway station and the Overseas Chinese Hotel. The northern bus station is a peculiar sight at night. Masses of people sleep in the waiting hall on bunks (presumably waiting for morning buses?) guarded by a guy wielding a machine-gun!

Buses for Canton ·depart from the northern and southern stations at 5.30 am and 5.50 am. The trip takes about 13½ hours.

**Train** Trains to Guilin and to Nanning leave from Zhanjiang South Railway Station. The trip to *Guilin* takes about 13 hours; hard seat is Y12 and hard sleeper is Y20.30 (local prices). As you approach Guilin in the early morning you pass through some stunning scenery with huge limestone peaks that push up out of the flat countryside. The trip to *Nanning* takes around 9½ hours.

**Air** There are daily flights from Zhanjiang to Canton (Y55) and to Haikou (Y19).

**Bus & Boat to Haikou** Getting to Haikou from Zhanjiang is easy. A bus takes you from Zhanjiang to a port on the Leizhou Peninsula and from here you take a boat to Haikou. The combined bus/boat ticket costs Y6.40 and you can buy it at the reception desk of the hotel in the northern part of Zhanjiang. The bus will pick you up outside the hotel at 5.30 am; there's one river crossing at around 7.30 am and you reach the port around 9.30 am. The bus takes you straight down to the pier and they'll point you in the direction of the right boat. The Chinese have their ID and travel permits checked before they board and you should have your passport and travel-permit ready. The boat leaves at about 10 am and you'll arrive at Haikou around 11.45 am.

If there's heavy fog then you can expect the boat to be delayed or even cancelled. When I returned from Haikou, the boat was due to leave at 7.30am and finally got under way at 12 noon. It stopped midway for three hours until some of the fog had cleared, and didn't reach the Leizhou Peninsula until 5pm.

**Boat to Hong Kong** There is a direct boat to Hong Kong, departing Zhanjiang once-a-week at 5.30 pm and arriving in Hong Kong at 9 am the next day.

## HAINAN ISLAND

Hainan is a large tropical island off the south coast of China which is administered by the government of Guangdong Province. The island lies close to Vietnam and its military importance has increased over the past few years since China and Vietnam locked themselves into permanent war.

Consequently, the west coast of Hainan Island is dotted with naval bases, aircraft and missile bases, radio towers and radar stations and army bases. The bases are meant to defend Chinese shipping in the South China Sea and future Chinese-foreign joint ventures exploiting the oil and gas deposits in the South China Sea and in the Gulf of Tonkin (the body of water between Hainan and Vietnam). A naval force of 300,000 men is maintained in Hainan and in the mainland town of Zhanjiang, but the harbours on Hainan are silted up and new ones need to be constructed to take larger warships and also ocean-going cargo ships. It is planned to expand two of the existing 11 ports and to build one deep-water port on Hainan.

The conflict with Vietnam started back in 1978, possibly initiated by the expulsion of as many as 250,000 ethnic Chinese from that country. In February of the following year the People's Republic invaded by northern Vietnam – ostensibly to punish Vietnam for its treatment of the Chinese and for incursions on Chinese soil. When the Foreign Minister Huang

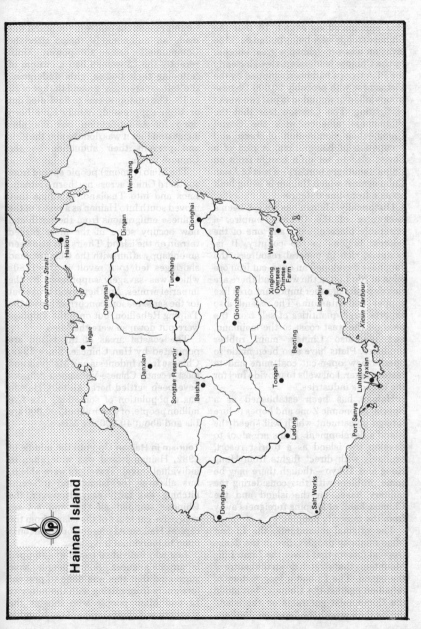

Hainan Island

Hua announced on March 16 that the Chinese troops were being pulled back the invasion was proclaimed a great success by the Chinese leadership, though clearly the PLA troops had been whipped by the Vietnamese with probably 20,000 Chinese troops killed or wounded in just two weeks of fighting. The Chinese fear that the Vietnamese alliance with the Soviet Union, their domination of Laos and occupation of Kampuchea, is part of a Soviet plan to set up a hostile front on China's southern borders – a sort of Asian Cuba against which Hainan is being built up as a front-line defence.

Historically, Hainan has always been a backwater of the Chinese empire, a miserable place of exile and one of the poorest regions in the country. It is, however, rich in mineral resources; the Japanese developed an open-cut iron ore mine at Shi Lou in the west and there are rich deposits of other important ores like copper and titanium. The island also exports large quantities of salt from the pans on the west coast to the mainland, and it's also China's main rubber producer. Plans have also been made to open a new open-cut coal mine and to restore several oil wells to provide fuel for the island's industries.

Hainan has been established as a Special Economic Zone and hopes to lure foreign investment which will speed the island's development. Plans are afoot to develop the island as a tourist resort, probably with direct flights from Hong Kong and Tokyo – though there may be some problem with this considering the military bases on the island and the Chinese habit of keeping foreigners away from the minority peoples.

The original inhabitants, the Li and Miao minority peoples, live in the dense tropical forests that cover the Limu Ling Mountains that stretch down the centre of the island. The Li had a long history of rebellion against the Chinese, but aided the Communist guerrillas on the island during the war with the Japanese. Perhaps for this reason the centre of the island was made an 'autonomous' region after the Communists came to power. Until recently the Li women had a custom of tattooing their bodies, girls undergoing the 'tattoo ceremony' around the age of 12 or 13. The custom seems to have died out or been suppressed; it may have been done for beautification but it's also suggested that it was done to mar the girls and prevent their abduction by the Chinese rulers.

The Miao (Hmong) people spread from southern China across northern Vietnam, Laos and into Thailand. In China they moved south into Hainan as a result of the Chinese emigrations from the north and now occupy some of the most rugged terrain on the island. Theirs has also been an unhappy affair with the Chinese; land shortages led to a revolt in the 1780s which was savagely suppressed by the imperial armies. Another revolt broke out for the same reason, concurrently with the Taiping Rebellion, but once the Taipings were put down so were the Miao.

The coastal areas of the island are populated by Han Chinese. Since 1949, Chinese from Indonesia and Malaysia and most recently Chinese-Vietnamese refugees have been settled here. All told, Hainan has a population of something like five million people, of which about 700,000 are Lis and about 40,000 are Miaos.

**Tourism in Hainan** Up until the middle of 1982, Hainan Island was wide open to individual travel. Travellers were able to bus all over the island and it seems hitching was fairly easy. However, the Chinese stopped all this and set up expensive car tours of the island from the capital, Haikou. At present, only Haikou is open to individual travellers.

Just why individual travel was stopped is anyone's guess. Some people have suggested that this was done to prevent foreigners from mixing with the minority Li and Miao people who inhabit the southern and central areas of the island; it

Haikou (Central)

1 Terminus of Buses 1, 2, 3, 4
2 Terminus of Buses 5, 6, 7
3 Post Office
4 Post Office
5 Public Security Office
6 Bookstore
7 Dept. Store
8 Cinema
9 Overseas Chinese Hotel
10 Booking Office for Boats to Zhanjiang & Guangzhou (Canton)
11 Long Distance Bus Station

might be because there are a military bases on the island. Or it might simply be because the Chinese know that tours rake in more money.

The long-distance bus station in Haikou will *not* sell you tickets to travel outside Haikou unless you have a permit from Public Security, and of course Public Security will not give you a permit. The other alternative would be to try hitching, cycling or walking, but in all probability you'll be turned back to Haikou by the first policeman who spots you.

Tours can be booked from the Hainan Travel Service Corporation office just inside the gate of the Overseas Chinese Hotel in Haikou. For a car, driver, interpreter, meals and accommodation it's Y320 each for a four-day and five-night tour, and they'll only take two people per car (you may be able to persuade them otherwise). They also have Kombi van tours which are cheaper but you'd have to get a group of maybe eight or ten people together. There are several places on the island which are open to foreigners on tours, and these inclue Jiaji, Sanya and Tongzha.

**Haikou** is the capital of Hainan. On the east coast of the island is the **Xincun** commune populated almost solely by Danjia (Tanha) minority people who are employed in the fishing and pearl cultivating industry. Also on the east coast is **Xinglong Overseas Chinese Farm** inhabited largely by Overseas Chinese and refugee Chinese-Vietnamese. On the southern coast is the port of **Sanya** and nearby is the holiday resort of **Luhuitou** with a beach and guest houses and bungalows – the area is noted for what are supposed to be some very beautiful tropical beaches. About 40 km west of Sanya is the town of **Baoting,** the administrative centre of the Li and Miao autonomous regions. **Dongfang** is a port on the west coast.

## HAIKOU
Haikou is the capital of the island, and lies on the northern coastline at the mouth of the Nandu River. It's a port town and handles most of the island's commerce with the mainland.

### Information & Orientation
Haikou is split up into three fairly separate sections. The western section is the port area and a long road connects it to the northern section which is the centre of Haikou. You'll find the tourist facilities in this northern section. Another road connects this central section to a smaller urban area to the south.

**CITS** All enquiries and tickets at the offices on the ground floor of the Overseas Chinese Hotel.

**Public Security** is a short walk from the Overseas Chinese Hotel. Turn right out of the hotel and walk down the road until you come to a traffic circle with a small obelisk. Turn right again; the office is a short walk further up the road on the right-hand side of the road. They're a friendly lot here and they do have an interpreter on call.

**CAAC**(tel 515) is at 50 Jiefang Lu.

**Bank** The Bank of China is at No 1 Fangxiu Lu.

**Post** There is a post office in the foyer of the Overseas Chinese Hotel. There's another on the same street as the Public Security Office, but on the opposite side of the road and further west. There's another on the corner of the main intersection immediately east of the Public Security Office.

**Maps** There *is* a good map of Haikou – in Chinese and showing the bus routes – but it's hard to come by. You may find someone outside the harbour hawking them. Maps of Hainan Island, in Chinese, are available from the shop at the Overseas Chinese Hotel.

### Things to See
There's not really anything to see, as such, in Haikou. The Overseas Chinese Hotel is a good starting point for a walk around the town. Turn right out of the hotel and walk for about 15 minutes down to the traffic circle marked by an obelisk. Turn hard right here and then right at the second major intersection. A few minutes walk down is a jam-packed street market, with the usual array of culinary delicacies that would normally end up in a zoo in other countries. It's one of the best markets you'll see in China and almost on par with the Qingping Market in Canton. It's notable for the snug-fitting tube-shaped bamboo cages that live pigs are kept in. It's a fairly grotty area with old buildings which look like they haven't been cleaned for about 30 years, but it's quite a change from the usual array of drab concrete blocks that you see in other Chinese cities.

If you continue south along the street which the market runs off you come to a T-intersection. Immediately to the left is the large booking hall for boats to Canton and Haikou. Further up is the long-distance bus station – and on the street directly in front of the bus station are slum houses as bad as anything you'll see in Asia. If you turn right at the T-intersection, you go past a small park and lake. Follow this road and after about 15 minutes you'll come to the road with the Overseas Chinese Hotel.

The riverfront in the northern part of town is lined with decaying buildings and wall-to-wall junks; an oddly picturesque sight.

## Places to Stay

The *Overseas Chinese Hotel* is in the middle of town. It's a vast, cavernous construction built by the Chinese to undertake echo research in the corridors and currently entering the first stages of transformation into an archaeological ruin. The best thing that can be said about it is that it's a cheap place to stay – and unfortunately the only place to stay. Single rooms here are Y5, or Y10 with a shower. Double rooms are Y12, or Y16 with a shower. Rooms with four beds are Y16.

To get to the hotel from the harbour where the boats from Zhanjiang pull in, take a motorcycle-and-sidecar for Y1 (although you'll probably end up paying Y2). A pedal-rickshaw should only cost about Y0.50.

If you're coming in from Canton on the ship, take bus No 3 as far as the obelisk in the centre of town and then walk the last 15 minutes to the hotel.

## Places to Eat

There's nothing to make your mouth water. The *Overseas Chinese Hotel* has a restaurant on the ground floor which serves cheap food – it's OK. There's another restaurant on the second floor which has slightly less of a canteen atmosphere about it. There are a number of cheap places in the vicinity of the main market and along the road leading to the main post office – the usual rice, meat and vegetable fare for Y1 or Y2.

## Getting Around

The central area of Haikou is quite small and easy to walk around, but there are motorcycle-and-sidecars trundling the streets which are quite cheap and the buses are useful. The separate sections of Haikou are connected by bus.

## Getting Away

**Air** There are daily flights from Haikou to Canton (Y74) and daily flights to Zhangjiang (Y19).

**Boats** Boats leave Haikou at 7.30 am and 12 noon for the Leizhou Peninsula where you get a connecting bus to Zhanjiang; the combined bus/boat ticket is Y7. There are direct boats from Haikou to Canton and tickets start at Y12. There is also a direct boat to Hong Kong. Tickets can be bought from the booking office on the ground floor of the Overseas Chinese Hotel.

## SHANTOU

Considering the length of the southern and south-eastern coasts of China, they are remarkably deficient in sea-ports. The main problem has been the constant accumulation of silt and mud which has rendered the natural harbours cramped and shallow. Only a few, like Xiamen and Hong Kong have been fortunate enough to have unlimited deep-water accommodation. On top of that, the mainland ports have been further handicapped by the mountainous country which surrounds many of them, making communication and transport of goods difficult – the predominance of Canton is partly due to the delta waterway system which gives it a better communication and transport system than any of its rivals.

Shantou is the chief port of eastern Guangdong. As early as the 18th century the East India Company had a station on an island outside the harbour, at a time when the town was little more than a fishing village on a mud-flat. The port was officially opened up to foreign trade in 1860, with the Treaty of Tianjin which ended another Opium War. The British were the first to establish themselves here – though their first projected settlement fell through due to the hostility of the local populace and they had to clear off to a nearby island; but before 1870 foreigners were freely living and trading in the town itself.

Today the town is the first major stop on the long haul along the coast road from Canton to Fujian, a rather colourful, lively place that's well worth a visit.

## Information & Orientation

Most of Shantou lies on a sort of peninsula, bounded in the south by the ocean and separated from the mainland in the west and the north by a river and canals. Most of the tourist facilities (CAAC, the Friendship Store, the Overseas Chinese Hotel ... ) are located in the western part of the peninsula along Jinsha Lu and Shanzhang Lu. From Shanzhang Lu two main arteries, Zhongshan Lu and Waima Lu lead westwards to the town centre – the area around Minzu Lu and Shengping Lu.

**CITS** seem to have disappeared into a black hole. Chinese treasure maps have got them located at the Overseas Chinese Hotel on Shanzhang Lu.

**Public Security** is at 11 Yuejin Lu, near the intersection with Nanhai Lu. Look for the big grey concrete entrance-way, with the glass display cases at the front.

**CAAC** is on Shanzhang Lu, just a few minutes' walk south of the intersection with Jinsha Lu. The office is a nondescript grey building with light-green window frames and doors – nothing to indicate its function. Opening hours seem to be almost non-existent and you might be better off booking through CITS (if you can find CITS).

**Bank** There's a foreign exchange counter in the North Building of the Overseas

Chinese Hotel (through the front gate and turn left), but it never seems to be open.

**Post** There's a post office at 415 Zhongshan Lu, near the intersection with Shanzhang Lu. There's another at the intersection of Guoping Lu and Shengping Lu on the north-western side of the roundabout.

**Maps** Excellent maps of Shantou, showing the bus routes, are available from the stalls at the front entrance of the long-distance bus station. They also sell a couple of sketch maps of the town, which aren't very good but might help you find your way around if you can't find a copy of the detailed map. The detailed map is also available from the shop on the ground floor of the big Chinese hotel next to the Friendship Store.

## Things to See

There's nothing in Shantou 'to see' as such, but there's an intrinsic interest which makes it worth a visit. The town is quite small and you could do a long sight-seeing circuit around it in a day. The best area for exploring is the south-western section, around Anping Lu, Xidi Lu and Shangping Lu. If I had to live in this area I'd call it a slum, but since I don't I'll refer to it as a picturesque, bustling, dilapidated harbourside suburb, full of old two and three-storey buildings with colonnaded verandahs. Most of the buildings are now falling to bits and alot are making way for new concrete apartment blocks, but the old area is still largely intact. Streets like Yuejin Lu are lined with ugly little slum shacks, ramshackle mud and wood constructions.

Near the intersection of Minzu Lu and Zhongshan Lu is a medium-sized temple now falling into ruins. Further down Minzu Lu from the temple is a shop where you can stock up on cobras and large lizards.

Waima Lu is also worth exploring; at 243 is the 'China Practional Horsepower

Motor Corpeation' which sells electrical motors and various other electrical oddments.

The eastern section of the town is mainly big concrete apartment blocks. There's quite a bit of agricultural land on the outskirts here if you want to stare at a few peasants breaking their backs in the field. It's a long walk to get to the waterfront in the east, but if you do you'll find a large breakwater and shelter for boats, several slummy little fishermen's hovels, and the odd lean-to enclosing little altars with statues of the fishermen's gods.

## Places to Stay

The *Overseas Chinese Hotel* is on Shanzhang Lu and is one of those places where no one really seems to know anything. No single rooms, but doubles for Y14 and triples for Y16.50 (you should be able to pay for just one bed).

There's another hotel on Shanzhang Lu, about 10 minutes walk north of the Shanzhang/Jinsha intersection – see the map in this book for directions. I was probably the first foreigner ever to front up at this place and they gave me an enormous room which was divided into a separate bedroom, bathroom and livingroom, for just Y8! Extremely friendly staff.

To get to the hotels from the long-distance bus station, turn left out of the main entrance to the station and walk up to the traffic-circle where there's a No 3 bus stop. Take bus No 3 to the stop just after the intersection of Shanzhang Lu and Jinsha Lu – this puts you off right outside the CAAC office. Walk south along Shanzhang Lu to the Overseas Chinese Hotel, or north to the Chinese hotel.

## Places to Eat

The restaurant in the *Overseas Chinese Hotel* is a good place to eat; try the octopus. They'd almost finished building a new restaurant and it should be open by the time this book is out.

There is a restaurant on Zhongshan Lu just near the corner with Congyuan Lu – a great place to eat (go upstairs as the ground floor is pretty dingy). They serve big plates of eels, frogs and prawns here, but be sure to specify how much you want – if you're by yourself they still bring out as much as they would for a group – which means you end up paying a fortune for food you can't possibly stuff away. Friendly staff.

No 51 Guoping Lu, in the western part of town, is a former temple – nothing of note and fairly dingy, but could be worth checking out.

The restaurant on the corner of Yongyi Lu and Yuejin Lu could be worth a try (go upstairs), though it's a bit out of the way. Note the signboards diagonally across the road showing happy Commies going wild.

There's no worries about getting the little pleasures of life in Shantou; bottles and cans of Coca-cola, Pepsi and Sunkist are sold on the streets, as are western cigarettes like Camel Filters and State Express 555's.

## Getting Around

There are incredibly dilapidated-looking pedal-rickshaws and motorised trishaws outside the long-distance bus station; say about Y1 to either of the two hotels. Other than that there are the local buses, although Shantou is quite small and a good deal of the town can be seen on foot.

## Getting Away

**Bus** The long-distance bus station is in the northern part of Shantou. From here you can get buses westwards to Canton and Shenzhen, or eastwards into Fujian Province.

There are daily buses to Canton leaving at 5 am and two at 5.10 am The fare is Y11.70 and the trip takes 15 to 16 hours over one of the roughest roads in China. It's pot-holes almost the whole way (see the Canton section for details).

There is only one bus a day to Shenzhen, leaving at 5 am; the fare is Y9.55.

There are buses to Zhangzhou at 6.40 am, 6.50 am, 7 am; the fare is Y5.60.

There are buses to Xiamen leaving at 6.10 am, 6.20 am and 6.30 am. The fare is Y7.40 and the ride takes about nine hours. It's fairly dull scenery the whole way; hilly rice and sugar-cane fields. The bus stops briefly at Zhangzhou around 1.30 pm.

There are regular buses throughout the day to Chaozhou, the first at 6 am and the last at 8 pm. The fare is Y1.

**CITS Buses** There are comfy CITS buses running from Shantou to Shenzhen (Y37) and to Zhangzhou and Xiamen in Fujian Province. Book at the CITS office (if you can find it) or at the Overseas Chinese Hotel also.

**Plane** There are daily flights from Shantou to Canton (Y56).

**Boats** There are boats from Shantou to Canton and to Hong Kong.

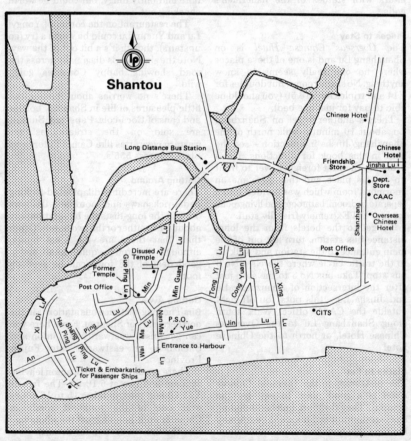

# Fujian

Fujian is an odd place. The coastal region has well-established trading ports which for centuries have enjoyed substantial contact with the outside world. Early on the great seaports developed a booming trade which transformed the region from a frontier into one of the centres of the Chinese world.

But the Fujianese were also the emigrants of China – packing up in droves and leaving the Middle Kingdom and heading to the countries of South-East Asia. Exactly why this happened is debatable. One suggestion is that the population of Fujian exploded on the basis of rampant prosperity spurred on by the internal and international trade which the ports developed – the land simply ran out and the only direction to take was out of China. The other suggestion is that the money never got beyond the ports, the interior remained poor – but the ports provided a means of escape and the people took the opportunity and left.

Whatever the reason ports like Xiamen were stepping stones for droves of people heading for Singapore, the Philippines, Malaysia and Indonesia. The Manchus had attempted to put a halt to Chinese emigration with an Imperial edict of 1718 which recalled all subjects who were in foreign lands. Finding this ineffectual the court issued another proclamation in 1728 which declared that anyone who did not return to China would be banished and those captured would be executed. Chinese emigration was made lawful only by the Convention of Beijing, which ended the Fourth Opium War in 1860.

Even now many of the descendants of the original emigrants still remit money back to Fujian, and the Chinese government is also trying to build up a sense of patriotism in these Overseas Chinese aimed at getting them to invest even more money in the 'motherland'.

Fujian is a lush, attractive piece of real estate, inhabited by almost 26 million people. The rugged, mountainous interior of the province is closed to tourists and is said to be very poor (suggesting that the Fujianese left for this reason, not because of rampant prosperity) and only the lively and prosperous port towns on the narrow coastal strip are open.

## XIAMEN

Xiamen began life sometime around the middle of the 14th century, in the early years of the Ming dynasty. There had been a town here since the Song dynasty two or three hundred years earlier, but the Ming built the city walls and established it as a major seaport and commercial centre. In the 17th century Xiamen became a place of refuge for the Ming rulers fleeing from the Manchu invaders; and it was from here that their armies fought their way north again under the command of the Pirate-General Koxinga.

The Portuguese traded here surreptitiously for a period of 50 years from 1516 onwards (based on an island close to Xiamen), but the government is supposed to have finally discouraged the Chinese traders by lopping off 90 heads. The Spaniards first arrived from Manila in the Philippines in 1575 and succeeded in building up a substantial trade in raw silk which was shipped to Manila and then to Mexico, but that also eventually came to an end. The Dutch arrived in 1604 but

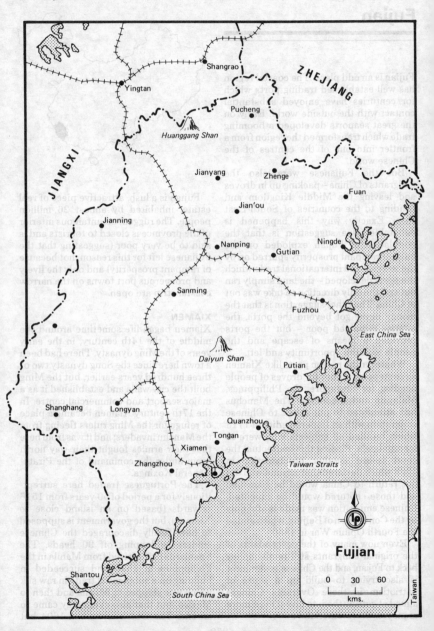

failed to gain a footing in Xiamen. After seizing Taiwan they maintained a secret trade base on the island of Quemoy, until Koxinga came into the picture and put an end to their commercial aspirations. The British took the opportunity offered by the Dutch expulsion and opened up trade with the new regime on Taiwan, and even established a base in Xiamen. But by the early 1700s trade with westerners was carried on only intermittently and secretly.

Things changed very dramatically with the Opium Wars of the 19th century. In August 1841 a British naval force of 38 ships carrying artillery and soldiers sailed into Xiamen harbour, forcing the opening of the port which was formalised by the Treaty of Nanjing. Xiamen was to come under the control of an assortment of foreigners, mainly the 'round-eye' British and the 'dwarf-barbarian' Japanese. And by the early part of this century the Belgians, Danes, French, Germans, Dutch and Americans all had consulates here and Gulangyu Island, just offshore, was established by the European settlers as a foreign enclave.

Most people would be better off if armies and navies would just go away. Unfortunately for Xiamen when Chiang

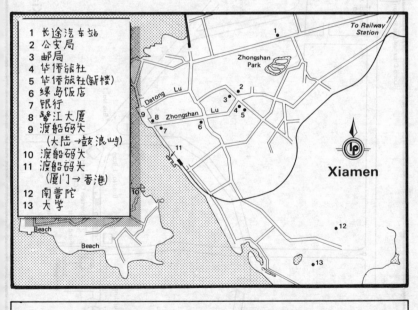

1 长途汽车站
2 公安局
3 邮局
4 华侨旅社
5 华侨旅社(新楼)
6 绿岛饭店
7 银行
8 鹭江大厦
9 渡船码头
　(大陆 →鼓浪屿)
10 渡船码头
11 渡船码头
　(厦门 → 香港)
12 南普陀
13 大学

1 Long Distance Bus Station
2 Public Security Office
3 Post Office
4 Overseas Chinese Hotel (OCH)
5 New Wing of the OCH
6 Ludao Restaurant
7 Bank
8 Lujiang Hotel
9 Ferry Pier
　(Mainland — Gulangyu)
10 Ferry Pier
　(Mainland — Gulangyu)
11 Xiamen — Hong Kong
　Ferry Pier
12 Nanputuo Temple
13 Xiamen University

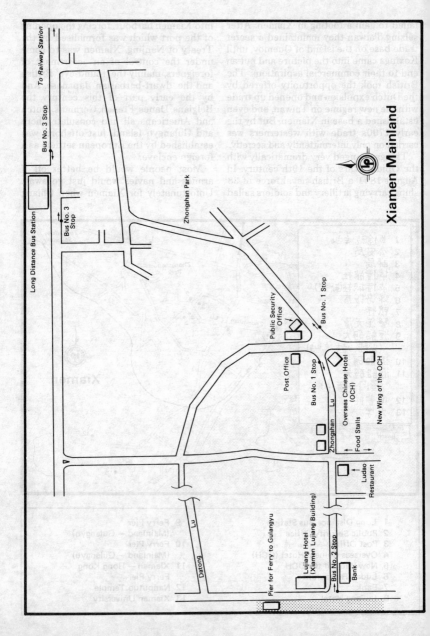

Kai-shek went away to Taiwan in 1949 he left the nearby Quemoy and Matsu Islands armed to the teeth with Kuomintang troops. In 1958 the PLA started bombarding the Kuomintang on the islands with artillery shells lobbed across the straits. In the west the crisis is only dimly remembered, but at the time the US and Taiwan had a Mutual Security Treaty and it seemed that the Americans might be about to enter another miserable Asiatic war for the sake of Chiang's pathetic regime. The Kuomintang troops still occupy the islands.

Today, Xiamen appears to be a peaceful place. Still a thriving port, it was opened to the tourist dollar in 1980 and the following year became a Special Economic Zone – added potential for rapid economic development. With the similar, though less derelict architecture of the mainland buildings, the city is something of an 'up-market' version of Shantou.

### Information & Orientation

The town of Xiamen is situated on an island of the same name, just offshore from the mainland.

The island is connected to the mainland by a long causeway which carries a railway, road and footpath. The first section of the causeway connects the town of Xinglin on the mainland to the town of Jimei which is at the tip of a peninsula due east of Xinglin. The second section connects Jimei to the north of Xiamen Island. The town of Xiamen lies in the south-western corner of the island and Gulangyu is a small island which lies directly opposite the town.

The railway station is at the far eastern side of Xiamen town and the long-distance bus station is in the northern part of the town. The main street is Zhongshan Lu which starts at the south-western shoreline; at this end you'll find the pier for the ferry to Gulangyu, the Lujiang Hotel, the Bank of China and a short walk away is the wharf for the ferry to Hong Kong. Scattered along the length of Zhongshan Lu, which cuts through the centre of town, are most of the restaurants, shops, the Overseas Chinese Hotel and other facilities. At the far southern end of the town is the Nanputuo Temple and Xiamen University.

**CITS** (tel 4398) is on the ground floor of the Overseas Chinese Hotel. They don't speak any English which means they're not of much help.

**Public Security** (tel 2329) is near the Overseas Chinese Hotel. Across the road from the OCH is a large, red-brick building. There is a wide footpath running alongside it on the right-hand side as you face the building; this pathway leads to the gateway of the Public Security Office.

**CAAC** does not have an office in Xiamen and there are no flights to the town. Quanzhou has the nearest airport. This situation is likely to change quite soon, since an international airport is presently being constructed and may even be completed by the time this book is out. The airport is expected to handle flights from both Hong Kong and Manila.

**Post** There is a large post office across the road from the Overseas Chinese Hotel. There's also a post office on Gulangyu at 102 Longtou Lu, a few minutes walk up from the ferry pier.

**Bank** The Bank of China is at No 10 Zhongshan Lu, just near the Lujiang Hotel. The bank is open Monday to Saturday from 8.30 to 11.30 am and 3 to 5.30 pm, and on Sundays from 8.30 to 11.30 am.

**Maps** in Chinese are available from the ground floor shop of the Lujiang Building; they show the bus routes, but other than that they're almost useless for finding your way around, particularly on Gulangyu.

There is a larger, better map at the reception desk of the Lujiang Hotel which is worth having a look at.

## Things to See

Back in 1912 an American missionary, Reverend Pitcher described Xiamen in the following terms:

A city! But not the kind of city you have in mind. There are no wide avenues, beautiful residences, magnificent public and mercantile buildings. All is directly opposite to the condition of things. The streets are narrow and crooked . . . ever winding and twisting, descending and ascending, and finally ending in the great nowhere. The wayfaring man, tho' wise, is bound to err therein. There is no street either straight, or one even called 'Straight' in Amoy. Then in addition to the crookedness, they must add another aggravation by making some of them very narrow. There are streets in Amoy so narrow that you cannot carry an open umbrella, but there are others ten, twelve and fifteen feet wide. Of course they are crowded . . . alive with a teeming throng . . . Here every aspect of Chinese life passes before you, presenting grotesque pictures. Here goes the motley crowd, from the wretched beggar clothed in filthy rags to the stately mandarin adorned in gorgeous array.

Today, the streets are wider and something less of a concentrated maze. They still teem with people, but the beggars whom Pitcher described as 'spending idle hours picking out the vermin from their dirty and ragged garments' are conspicuous by their absence. Every so often some parody of humanity does drag itself into a Chinese city and is instantly surrounded by an audience of staring locals. At the other end of the scale the post-imperial mandarins have been replaced by privileged Red cadres or a bus-load of occidentals down from Quanzhou airport for the day. Xiamen conveys the impression of prosperity, a lively colourful place of 260,000 people with a couple of reminders of bygone turmoils still littering its premises.

## Gulangyu Island

Neither Gulangyu nor Xiamen were considered much of a paradise when the westerners landed here in the 1840s. But by about 1860 they had well-established residencies on Gulangyu, and as the years rolled by, put up a couple of churches, hospitals, post and telegraph offices, libraries, hotels and consulates. The island was officially designated an International Foreign Settlement in 1903 and a municipal council was set up to govern the place, with a police force made up entirely of Sikhs under its control. Today the only reminders are the

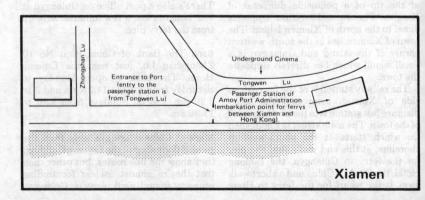

charming old colonial buildings which blanket the island. Dominating the skyline of Gulangyu, and seen on just about every leaflet and postcard, is a huge red-domed colonial building which faces the Xiamen mainland; it now houses – so the sign says – the 'Department for the Development of New Technology – Chinese Association of Micro-computer Applications'.

There is a ferry to Gulangyu which leaves from the pier just north of Xiamen's Lujiang Hotel. You don't pay anything to go from the mainland to the island – but on the way back you buy a counter at the pier on the Gulangyu side and drop into a box at the barrier gate before going down the ramp to the ferry; the fare is 10 fen. The ferries start running at around 5.10 am and the last is at about 12.30 am. Transport around Gulangyu is by foot; there are no buses, cars or rickshaws. It's a small island and the sights are within easy tramping of each other. There is no good map of the island except for the one I drew myself.

It may (or may not be) appropiate for the ironies of China to be discovered in a former bastion of foreign imperialism. From the Gulangyu ferry pier head straight up the road in front of you; this is Longtou Lu, the main shopping street. A short way up on the left is a 'Camel Filters' sign in English and Chinese and on either side are the culprit merchants who sell plaster statues, including gross little renditions of Santa Claus! The *Underground Restaurant* is a short walk away and was originally built as a bomb shelter. There's a sign in English advertising its existence and a long flight of steps from the street leads down to the depths which would otherwise protect a small number of the minions from shrapnel. Around the corner from the restaurant is a soccer field and behind that a group of colonial buildings which now serves as the *Gulangyu Guest House*.

I really didn't believe it when a Chinese guide-book described the emanations of the 'sweet music of pianos coming from

the villa-style houses' – for connoisseurs of music or for people who have been in China for too long, you can hear classical piano (played or practised) coming from several houses around the island. It probably seems a trivial observation except when you consider that Beethoven, along with all other decadent western music was banned during the Cultural Revolution; though the irony of Madame Jiang Qing's cultural renaissance Chinese-style was the introduction of western instruments and musical constructions into her revolutionary operas. With her demise, western music has been undergoing a resurgence – although songs like 'Jingle Bells' that squeak out through the speakers in your train carriage are hardly likely to crack the revolutionary fibre.

**Sunlight Rock** The highest point on Gulangyu is this rocky outcrop. It's an easy climb up the steps to the top of the rock where there's an observation platform and a great view across Gulangyu and the harbour.

### Zheng Chenggong (Koxinga) Memorial Hall

When the Ming Dynasty collapsed under the weight of the Manchu invasion in 1644 the court fled to the south of China. One after the other a melange of Ming princes assumed the title of emperor in the hope of driving out the barbarians and ascending the Dragon Throne. One of the more successful attempts focused on the port of Xiamen, and an army led by Zheng Chenggong.

Known to the west as Koxinga, Zheng's origins are a mystery. His father is said to have run away to Japan and married a Japanese woman who gave birth to Koxinga. The father returned to China as a pirate, raiding the coasts of Guangdong and Fujian, even taking possession of Amoy (the present-day Xiamen). Exactly how and why Koxinga came to be allied with the defunct Ming princes is unknown;

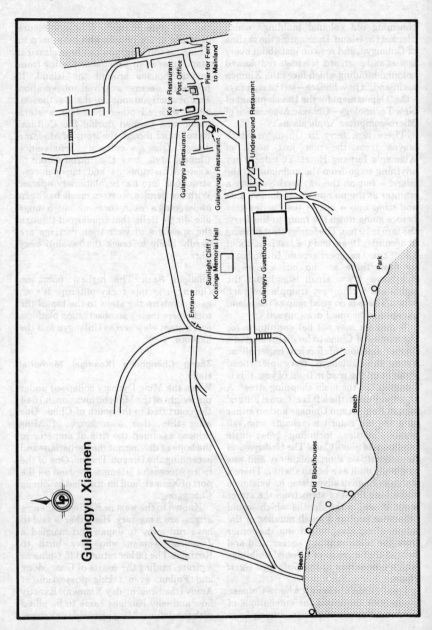

Gulangyu Xiamen

Pier for Ferry to Mainland
Post Office
Ke Le Restaurant
Gulangyu Restaurant
Gulangyugu Restaurant
Underground Restaurant
Entrance
Sunlight Cliff / Koxinga Memorial Hall
Gulangyu Guesthouse
Park
Beach
Old Blockhouses
Beach

one story goes that a prince took a liking to Koxinga when he was still young and made him a noble, and another goes that Koxinga was a pirate like his father, a local warlord who for some reason teamed up with one of the refugee princes.

Koxinga used Xiamen as a base for his attacks on the Manchus to the north. He is said to have had a fleet of 8000 war junks, 240,000 fighting men, and all the pirates who infested the coast of southern China under his command – in all, a combined force of 800,000. He is supposed to have used a stone lion weighing 600 pounds to test the strength of his soldiers, and those who were strong enough to lift and carry it were enlisted in the vanguard of the army. They wore iron masks and iron armour, and carried long-handled swords used to cut and maim the legs of the horses of the enemy cavalry.

Koxinga's army fought its way to the Grand Canal, but in the end was forced to retreat to Xiamen. In 1661 he set sail from there with his army for Taiwan which was then held by the Dutch. He attacked the Dutch settlement at Casteel Zeelandia, not far from present-day Taiwan on the west coast and after a six month siege the Dutch surrendered. Zheng hoped to use Taiwan as a stepping stone from which to invade the mainland and restore the Ming to power, but it was not to be. A year or two later Koxinga died, but it was not until the early 1680s that the Manchus finally conquered the island.

In China, those who live in major places seem to have had a precarious existence. Like the inhabitants of other Chinese cities the people of Xiamen probably didn't aspire to having an army of 800,000 swarming over them, though it was probably good for business and brothels before the killing commenced.

Whilst Koxinga may have been a pirate and a running-dog of the feudal Ming princes, he is regarded in China as a national hero because he recovered Taiwan from the Dutch; it's a rough analogy to the mainland's ambition to recover the island from today's Kuomintang regime. Those in China who rewrite (reinterpret?) history have decided to forget that Koxinga was forced to retreat to Taiwan after his defeats on the mainland and that the 'liberation' of the island was completely superfluous to the story. In any case, the story more closely parallels the Kuomintang defeat – a regime which fled to Taiwan but awaits the day when it will invade and sieze control of the mainland.

The memorial hall is in the same park as Sunlight Rock. It's a large colonial building and the verandahs of the upper storeys afford a good view across the island. Part of the exhibition is dedicated to the Dutch in Taiwan and the rest to Koxinga throwing them out. There are no captions in English, though it's still worth a look in. The hall is open daily around 8 to 11 am and 3 to 5.30 pm.

### The Beaches

'In the past few years' says one of the tourist leaflets 'many foreign visitors . . . plunged into the sea, indulging themselves in the waves, or lay on the golden sandy beach, being caressed by the sunshine, and made friends with the young people of Gulangyu. When the foreigners go away, they say: I am sure to come back again'. China is not a sun-worshippers paradise; there are two beaches on Gulangyu, the East Beach and the West Beach. The first is overpopulated, with placid and scungy water; the second belongs to the Army and is off-limits, as I discovered when three PLA guards armed with machine-guns picked me up and escorted me back to base where my bag was checked. There's a number of old, disused and overgrown concrete blockhouses on the beaches, and they appear to have ringed the entire island at one time.

### Nanputuo Temple

On the southern outskirts of Xiamen town, the Nanputuo Temple is a Buddhist temple built during the Tang Dynasty more than a thousand years ago. It was ruined in a battle during the Ming dynasty but was rebuilt during the Qing.

You enter the temple through Tian Wang (Heavenly King) Hall, where the welcoming Maitreya, the fat Buddha, sits cross-legged exposing his protruding belly. On either side are a pair of guardians which protect the Buddha. Behind Maitreya is Wei Tuo, another Buddhist diety who safeguards the Buddhist doctrine. He stands holding a stick which points to the ground – traditionally, this indicates that the temple is rich and can provide visiting monks with board and lodging (if the stick is held horizontally it means the temple is poor, a polite way of saying find somewhere else).

Behind Tian Wang Hall is a courtyard and on either side are the Drum and Bell Towers. In front of the courtyard is Daxiongbao (Great Heroic Treasure) Hall, a two-storey building which houses three Buddhas which may represent Sakyamuni Buddha in his past, present and future lives. On the lotus-flower base of the Buddha figure the biography of Sakyamuni and the story of the monk Xuan Zhuang (the monk who made a pilgrimage to India to bring back the Buddhist scriptures) have been carved.

On the buildings to the left and right of Daxiongbao, are eight inlaid stone tablets, and the inscriptions on them are carved in the handwriting of Emperor Qian Long of the Qing dynasty. Four tablets are inscribed in Chinese and the others in the peculiar Manchu script; both record the suppression of the uprisings of the 'Tian Di Society' by the Manchu government. The tablets were originally erected in front of the temple in 1789, but were inlaid in the walls when the temple was enlarged around 1920.

The Dabei (Great Compassion) Hall contains four Bodhisattvas, a multi-armed standing figure and three seated figures. The worshippers throw divining sticks at the feet of the statues in order to seek heavenly guidance.

At the rear of the temple complex is a pavilion built in 1936 which stores Buddhist scriptures, as well as as specimens of calligraphy, wood carvings, ivory sculptures and other works of art – unfortunately it appears to be closed to visitors. Behind the temple is a rocky outcrop gouged out with poetic grafitti; the big, red solitary character carved on the large boulder simply means 'Buddha'.

To get to the temple, take bus No 1 from the stop outside the Overseas Chinese Hotel, or bus No 2 which leaves from the intersection of Zhongshan Lu and Lujiangdao Lu; both of these put you down right outside the temple. Admission to the temple is only a few fen, and at the time of writing you could take photos of anything you wanted to.

## Xiamen University

The university is next to the Nanputuo Temple, and was established with Overseas Chinese funds. The older buildings facing the shoreline are not without a certain charm, though most of the campus is a scattered collection of brick and concrete blocks. The entrance to the campus is next to the No 1 bus-stop.

The Museum of Anthropology is worth a visit if you're down this way. There's a large collection of prehistoric stone implements and pottery from China, Taiwan and Malaya as well as human fossil remains (particularly rooms 103 and 105); a collection of porcelains, bronzes, jade and stone implements, coins, inscriptions on bones or tortoise shells of the Shang dynasty; calligraphy, paintings (in particular the exquisite paintings of royal women in room 215), glazed clay figurines (rooms 19 and 106), sculptures, clothing and ornaments from the Shang and Zhou through to the Ming and Qing dynasties. To get to the museum from the Nanpoutuo bus stop, go through the entrance to the campus and turn right at the first crossroads. Walk until you come to a roundabout; the museum is the old stone building with the cannon at the front, over on the left.

*If* you can find it, there is a museum located on the 2nd floor of the 'Jimei Building' dedicated to Lu Xun, China's No 1 Thinking-man's Revolutionary. Lu Xun only taught at Xiamen University between September 1926 and January 1927 and the museum was set up in 1952, a tribute to the type of mentality that likes to collect fragments of Paul McCartney's old socks.

### Jimei School Village

This much-touted tourist attraction is across the causeway on the mainland north of Xiamen island. The school is a conglomeration and expansion of a number of separate schools and colleges which were set up here by Tan Kah Kee (1874-1961). Tan was a native of the area who migrated to Singapore when he was young and rose to become a rich industrialist, setting a fine example to other Overseas Chinese by returning some of that wealth to the mother country (which is not to deny the value of the school which now numbers 20,000 students). The Chinese-style architecture has a certain appeal which may make a trip worthwhile.

### Fat Buddhas, Ballerinas and Subterranean Flicks

Zhongshan Lu is the main street of Xiamen and harbours some peculiar shops. At No 54 is the Narcissus Tea Store (in the ancient Greek myth, Narcissus was a youth who pined away for love of his own image and was transformed into a flower; 'narcissism' is sensual gratification found in one's own body. Exactly what either of those has to do with tea is beyond me). Further down the road at No 66 is the Huichen Chemists Shop selling medicinal herbs and spices; No 150 is the Arts and Crafts Service of Amoy which has some *unbelievably* ugly plaster statues, including a golden-coloured fat Buddha with kiddies

crawling all over him, tugging at his navel, licking his ear and sucking one of his nipples – a mere Y3.17. No 396 is the Dried Aquatic Products Retail Department which smells like a can of fish food. Across the road is the Xiamen Antique Store where you can buy a fat Buddha for only Y100; further down at No 351 is a small shop with a wide range of revolting plaster statues, including ballerinas and abstract nude women.

### Places to Stay

Probably the best place to stay is the *Xiamen Lujiang Building* (tel 2212) on Xiamen Island right near the Gulangyu ferry pier. It's a rather run-down though clean building, a great location looking out over the harbour, and the staff are friendly. There are no singles but air-con double rooms are Y16 for those facing the sea and Y14 for those facing the city. A bed in a triple is Y4 and a bed in a four-bed room is Y3. Bus No 3 from the railway station terminates at the Gulangyu ferry pier right outside the hotel. From the long-distance bus station take bus No 3, or alternatively take a rickshaw for Y1.

The *Overseas Chinese Hotel* (tel 2729) is centrally located at 444 Zhongshan Lu. I don't know what it is about the place but the air hangs heavy here and the place reeks of depression. A bed in a triple is Y4. From the railway station take bus No 1. From the bus station it's probably better to walk – it takes about 20 minutes. There is also a new multi-storey hotel just a few minutes walk from the Overseas Chinese Hotel. No single rooms, but doubles go for Y30, Y35 and Y40. Dorm beds go for Y12, or Y14 with air-con.

The *Gulangyu Guest House* on Gulangyu is made up of a number of old colonial buildings. It's occasionally used for conferences at which time it's closed to foreign tourists.

### Places to Eat

The restaurant on the 7th floor of the *Xiamen Lujiang Building* is a great place to eat and watch the sunset over Gulangyu. The chef speaks communicable English and you can try prawns, frogs, fish and squid – it's a bit expensive at around Y5 or Y6 for a proper meal, but it's quite good food and the view makes it all worth it. (If you order vegetables, specify what you want or you may just end up with a plate of boiled cabbage).

On a side street which runs off Zhongshan Lu about mid-way between the harbour and the Overseas Chinese Hotel, are a number of street stalls where you can get good, cheap seafood and frogs usually cooked with green and red peppers. They also sell a lot of fresh pineapples and bananas.

There are a couple of places on Zhongshan Lu which are worth investigating, although most of them are pretty drab to say the least. The upstairs part of the *Guangfeng Restaurant* at 40 Zhongshan Lu was being renovated and may turn out to be an OK place. The *Ludao Restaurant* at No 230 Zhongshan Lu sells slightly banana-flavoured vanilla ice-cream on the ground floor and the fare upstairs looks OK. The cake shop at No 122 Zhongshan Lu is forgettable but there's nothing else around. The air in the *Overseas Chinese Hotel Restaurant* hangs as heavy as in the rest of the hotel.

Offshore on Gulangyu, try upstairs at the *Gulangyu Restaurant* for some tasty seafood – and don't be put off by the grotty ground floor. Near the ferry pier is the *Seaside Ice-Pub* (sign in English) which is more memorable for the name than its cold drinks. There's a rather good ice-cream shop close to the East Beach.

Vita Ginseng is worth trying as an alternative to Coca Cola – its's sold widely on the streets in Xiamen, though you might decide it tastes more like cough mixture. Across the road from the wharf for the boats to Hong Kong is the *Tong Wen Soft Drinking Room* which sells bottles of alcholic drinks.

**Getting Around**

Much of the town can easily be seen on foot. The bus service is quite extensive but the buses always seem to be extremely crowded. Pedal and motorised rickshaws congregate outside the railway station, the long-distance bus station and the Gulangyu ferry pier on the mainland side. The only means of moving on Gulangyu is by walking; there are no buses, cars or rickshaws.

**Getting Away**

**Buses** From the long-distance bus station there are buses to *Fuzhou* departing at 6 am, 6.05 am, and 6.10 am; the fare is Y7.60.

Buses to Quanzhou depart at 6.20 am, 6.50 am, 7.25 am, 8 am, 1.15 pm, 1.35 pm, 2 pm, 2.30 pm, 3.30 pm and 3.50 pm; the fare is Y2.65.

Buses to Shantou depart at 6.10 am, 6.25 am and 6.30 am; the fare is Y7.50.

There is one bus a day to Guangzhou departing at 7.50 am; the fare is Y20.60 and you'll probably overnight in Shantou.

There is apparently only one bus a day to Zhangzhou, departing at 6.15 am and the fare is Y1.80. Buses to Shantou go through Zhangzhou and there is also a train.

There doesn't seem to be a direct bus to Chaozhou. You'll have to go to Shantou first and change buses.

**CITS Buses** There are two CITS buses a week to *Shenzhen* departing on Tuesdays and Fridays. The fare is Y66 and you'll probably overnight in Shantou. Tickets can be booked at CITS in the Overseas Chinese Hotel. Although more expensive than the local buses, the CITS buses are air-con and the comfy seats are far easier on your bum – something worth considering because the road between Shantou and Canton is very poor.

**Trains** The railway line from Xiamen heads north and connects the city with the main Shanghai-Canton line at the Yingtan junction. A branch line splits off from the Xiamen-Yingtan line and goes to Fuzhou. From Xiamen there are direct trains to nearby Zhangzhou and to Yingtan, Shanghai, Fuzhou, and possibly to Canton. The train to Fuzhou runs by a circuitous route and unless you want to travel by night you're better off taking the bus.

**Plane** There are flights from Xiamen to Shanghai, Fuzhou, Canton and possibly Beijing. Xiamen's is a recently opened airport and is expected to handle direct flights to Manila and Hong Kong.

**Boats** Ships to Hong Kong depart from the Passenger Station of Amoy Port Administration which is on Tongwen Lu, about 10 minutes' walk from the Lujiang Hotel. The gateway to the station is on Tongwen Lu and a long flight of steps leads up to the ticket and booking-office; there is also a bank and a China Travel Service office in this building but they probably only open when passengers are boarding or disembarking. Ships to Hong Kong depart on Tuesdays and Fridays at 12 noon. Ticket prices depend on which boat you take and the cheapest ticket available is Y65.

### QUANZHOU

Long before the large port of Xiamen became a centre for both domestic and foreign trade, there was another city in the vicinity known as Zaiton, which held that distinction until the end of the 14th century. There is some debate as to the site of this port but it's generally accepted to be the present-day city of Quanzhou, to the north-east of Xiamen.

The port was probably one of the greatest commercial centres in the world from which Chinese silks, satins, sugar and spices were exported to India, Arabia and western Asia. And it was from here that Kublai Khan's invasion fleets set sail for Japan and Java. Marco Polo visited the port and raved about it as 'a great resort of

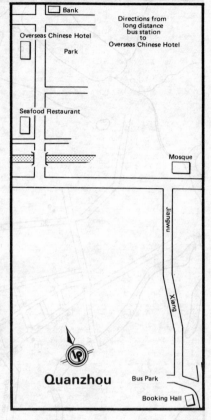

ships and merchandise ... for one spice ship that goes to Alexandria or elsewhere to pick up pepper for export to Christendom, Zaiton is visited by a hundred. For you must know that it is one of the two ports in the world with the biggest flow of merchandise'. (Alexandria was the other.) And with tariffs imposed on all imported goods the city was an important source of refills for the Great Khan's treasury.

Marco noted Zaiton as a place where many people came to have figures 'pricked out on their bodies with needles'. Marco had seen the master craftsmen at

**Quanzhou**

1 清真寺
2 寺
3 华侨旅行社
4 长途汽车站
5 海味业饭店
6 中国民用航空总局
7 银行
8 钟楼
9 开元寺
10 公安局
11 邮局

| | |
|---|---|
| 1 Mosque | 8 Clock Tower |
| 2 Temple | 9 Kaiyuan Temple & |
| 3 Overseas Chinese Hotel | Museum of Overseas |
| 4 Long Distance Bus Station | Communications History |
| 5 Seafood Restaurant | 10 Public Security Office |
| 6 CAAC | 11 Post Office |
| 7 Bank | |

work elsewhere on his travels; the 13th century method involved being tied hand and foot and held down by two assistants whilst the tattooist pricked out the images and then applied ink to the incisions, during which time the victim 'suffers what might well pass for the pains of Purgatory. Many even die during the operation through loss of blood'.

The prosperity of Zaiton began to decline as a result of fierce fighting in the middle of the 14th century, towards the end of the Yuan Dynasty. When the first Ming emperor, Hong Wu, came to power his isolationist policies reduced foreign trade to a trickle, and as if that wasn't enough the fate of Quanzhou was finally sealed by the silting up of the harbour. Today there are few reminders of its former glory. Nevertheless, it's a lively little town of narrow streets and wooden houses and the main streets, with their numerous shops and restaurants, radiate an air of prosperity.

### Information & Orientation
Quanzhou lies on the northern bank of the Jin River. The main street is Zhongshan Lu which runs north-south and cuts the town roughly in half. Down the length of this street or in the immediate vicinity you'll find most of the shops, restaurants, the long-distance bus station, the hotel and the tourist facilities. The Kaiyuan Temple, which is the main sight of Quanzhou, lies in the north-western part of the town and there's a scattering of sights in the hills to the north-east of the town.

CITS is on the ground floor of the Overseas Chinese Hotel. Friendly people, but they don't speak much English.

**Public Security** is at 334-336 Dong Jie (East Road), a five minute walk east of the intersection with Zhongshan Lu.

**CAAC** is in the park opposite the Overseas Chinese Hotel. Enter the park through the gateway opposite the hotel and cross the pond on the zig-zag bridge; turn right and walk straight ahead until you come to a pavilion which sits in the lake. Turn left into the road leading from the pavilion; this will take you to the CAAC office which is a red brick building on the right-hand side of the road.

**Post** There is a post office at 75 Xiamen Jie. If you only need stamps for letters or postcards, the shop on the ground floor of the Overseas Chinese Hotel sells them.

**Bank** The Bank of China, where you can change money, is at the corner of Jiuyi Lu and Zhongshan Lu, a few minutes' walk north of the hotel.

**Maps** are available from the little book and magazine shop next to the ticket hall in the long-distance bus station; not very good but they're helpful. Some of the street names on the map differ from those on houses and other buildings in Quanzhou.

### Things to See
### Kaiyuan Temple
This temple is the main attraction of Quanzhou and is noted for its pair of large

pagodas. The temple was founded in the 7th century during the Tang Dynasty and reached its peak under the Song when a thousand monks lived here. The present buildings only date from the 13th or 14th centuries, including the pagodas and the main hall. The main hall contains five large golden, seated Buddhas – which were being restored at the time of writing. Protruding from the eaves of the roof above them are peculiar winged figures. Behind the large Buddhas are several other smaller Buddha figures. Behind the main hall stands the Guanyin Temple. Inside, a canopy shelters a saffron-robed golden Buddha who sits on a lotus flower supported by a stone pillar. The pillar sits on top of a large platform on which stand several other figures. In front of the platform is a 1000-armed statue of Buddha and guardians surround the complex.

The temple is on West Road (Xi Lu) in the north-western part of the town. From the Overseas Chinese Hotel it's a lengthy but interesting walk – or you could take a rickshaw.

**Museum of Overseas Communications History**

This museum is in the grounds of the Kaiyuan Temple behind the eastern pagoda. It contains one of *the* attractions of Quanzhou: the enormous hull of a Song Dynasty Chinese sea-going junk. The hull was excavated near Quanzhou and there is a display featuring photos of the excavation, as well as coins, an axehead, ropes and other objects found in the wreck. There's a display of maps showing the routes taken by Chinese junks and their points of contact with foreign countries, extending all the way from Japan to the east coast of Africa and as far south as Madagascar. A number of Arab tombstones are on display here, probably those of Arab traders who lived here when Quanzhou was a booming seaport.

The remains of the ship display the characteristic features of Chinese ship construction; square bow and stern and flat bottom (no keel) and the division by bulkheads into many watertight compartments (the Quanzhou wreck has at least 11 – the technique was still unknown in Europe at the time). An efficient stern rudder had been developed several centuries before and a mariner's compass was in widespread use by the 11th century. Both the compass and the rudder had had a long period of development in China from the Han period onwards. The earliest record of the rudder (in northern Europe) and the compass (in southern Europe) are at the end of the 12th century.

The overseas trade of the late Tang and of Song China was closely tied to the river trade. Ocean-going ships brought goods to the great ports to be carried by the inland river and land routes – the river routes were slower but also cheaper than the land routes and ideal for heavy loads like grain and salt. Canals were built and existing ones extended to link up the major river systems, which made possible the nationwide trade of the Song period. So much trade developed that certain cities along the water routes developed into big consumer and commercial centres in their own right – like Yangzhou on the Grand Canal. Zaiton became the major seaport of the Song period.

Overseas trade revolved around the import and export of luxury goods. The chief imports were aromatics, spices, dyes, cotton fabrics, gold, swords, rhinoceros horn, ivory, ebony, precious stones, peacock and kingfisher feathers for use as insignia of rank – and slaves. Slaves were mainly Africans, usually employed as domestic servants in wealthy households. The central government encouraged the export of the highly-prized Chinese silk and porcelain but was unsuccessful in halting the drain of precious metals, mainly gold, silver and copper. By the second decade of Southern Song rule a fifth of government revenue came from taxes on overseas trade. That gave even greater encouragement to continue and expand the trade; the Chinese now took it on themselves to take an active part in long-distance trade instead of depending on foreign traders coming to China. Chinese-built ships had been used on long-distance voyages for centuries but it was mainly Arabs, Persians and other foreigners who manned them.

The Southern Song government encouraged the overseas trade to replace revenue which was no longer obtainable from the north – the Song having fled from an invasion from the northern steppes. It offered rewards for new inventions in ship-building, and used the tax on sea trade to develop a navy which would protect merchant shipping along the coast and at the entrance of the Yangtse – mainly against the northern invaders who had been halted at the Yangtse. Southern Song China became a sea power, both in the sense of its ocean-going trade and its effective naval defence.

Chinese sea power effectively came to an end with the establishment of the Ming Dynasty under the Emperor Hong Wu in the 14th century. Foreign trade was banned – possibly because the emperor feared conspiracies carried out under the guise of trade. Some trade did continue, but in an illicit form, and the government lost the customs revenue it might have had.

The great exception to the isolationist policies of the Ming period was the second Ming Emperor Yong Le. He re-established the Superintendencies of Merchant Shipping which had been set up under the Song to oversee the maritime trade and collect customs duties and taxes. Between 1405 and 1433 he dispatched seven enormous maritime expeditions led by the palace eunuch Zheng He. The expeditions were court enterprises, not government ventures, and Zheng was the personal representative of the emperor. The purpose of the expeditions was complex; possibly to impress the southern Asian countries with Chinese power, to expand the maritime trade, to extend Chinese knowledge of the outside world possibly with the intention of one day founding colonies or a commercial empire. The fleets sailed to South-East Asia, Sumatra and Java, India, the Persian Gulf, up the Red Sea and the east coast of Africa.

These expeditions came to an end with the death of Yong Le – only 64 years before Vasco da Gama finally sailed around the tip of Africa in 1497 on his way to India. One reason may have been the expense, another the government bureaucrats who were jealous of the power the eunuchs had in the imperial court – so much so that in the 1470s the official records of the voyages were burnt. Another reason for the neglect of the navy may have been the restoration and improvement of the Grand Canal – with the inland trade route reopened the coastal trade dropped off and a powerful naval escort no longer needed to be maintained; one by one the shipyards closed down and China's days as a maritime power came to a halt.

### Streetwalking
Zhongshan Lu is the main street of Quanzhou and the location of most of the shops. The intersection of Zhongshan Lu with Xi Lu and Dong Lu is distinguished by a grotesque clock tower. Walking south from the clock tower down Zhongshan Lu takes you past some interesting shops; No 424 is the 'Candy Tobacco and Liquor Shop'. No 192 is a large bookshop (open 8.30am-6pm) with one of the best selections of western titles I've seen, including *The Island of Doctor Moreau, Jonathon Livingston Seagull, Black Beauty, Alice in Wonderland* and *The Caine Mutiny* to mention a few. No 303 is a bicycle repair shop, No 149 sells musical instruments including some made with cobra skin and No 509 is full of Chinese lanterns and things which look as if they might be used as Xmas decorations ... if the Chinese celebrated Xmas.

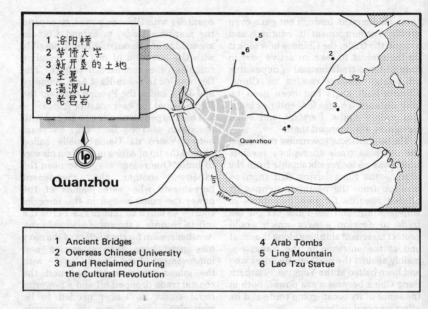

1 洛阳桥
2 华侨大学
3 新开垦的土地
4 圣墓
5 清源山
6 老君岩

**Quanzhou**

| 1 Ancient Bridges | 4 Arab Tombs |
| 2 Overseas Chinese University | 5 Ling Mountain |
| 3 Land Reclaimed During the Cultural Revolution | 6 Lao Tzu Statue |

Just to the south of the Overseas Chinese Hotel is another interesting street where you'll find the shell of a mosque built during the Song Dynasty to serve Quanzhou's large Moslem population. This street is lined with shops; No 210 is the 'Printing and Cooking Services Department' and No 188 is the 'Clock Work Repair Shop'.

The town also has its share of derelict temples, most ransacked during the Cultural Revolution. There is one, now being restored, just inside the gate of the park opposite the Overseas Chinese Hotel. Another is on Zhenfu Si, a side street which runs west off the square at the north end of Zhongshan Lu; it's also been restored and is now used as a middle-school library.

### Around Quanzhou

There are a number of sights around Quanzhou worth noting.

To the north of the town is an unusual stubby statue of Lao Tzu, the legendary founder of Taoism. The Chinese say that Kuomintang soldiers used the statue as target practice but there's no sign of any bullet holes.

To the north of the statue is Ling Mountain. On top of the mountain is a guarded communications base – the Chinese say they get TV broadcasts from here, which may be so, although it may also have some military use. There are Buddhist caves here but they were destroyed during the Cultural Revolution, though some people still come and pray in front of the empty spaces where the statues used to be. According to an old woman who lives on the mountain, two Red Guard factions fought each other here during the Cultural Revolution using mortars!

The 'Rock that moves' is situated on the mountain (there's a large painting of it hanging in the dining room of the Overseas Chinese Hotel). It's one of these nicely shaped and balanced rocks which wobbles when you give it a nudge – but I'm told that to see it move you have to place a stick or a piece of straw lengthwise between the rock and the ground and watch it bend as someone pushes on the rock.

To the east of the town are a number of Arab tombs. It's been suggested that the tombs are of two of Mohammed's disciples, sent here to convert the Chinese to Islam. Another tomb in Canton is said to be that of a third disciple.

To the east of the tombs is a peninsula of land built by hand during the Cultural Revolution. The land is now used for agriculture. A village on the northern side of the peninsula used to be a separate island before the reclamation of the land. 7000 mu (about 467 hectares) of land are said to have been reclaimed.

Due north of the peninsula is the Overseas Chinese University which was originally built to attract Hong Kongers and Taiwanese (only the first group came) to study in China. Like universities elsewhere in China it was closed down during the Cultural Revolution. North-east of the university are two bridges which were built several hundred years ago and are still intact.

### Places to Stay

The *Overseas Chinese Hotel* is conveniently located close to Zhongshan Rd. There are no single rooms but doubles are Y18 and triples are Y21 (with toilet and shower). A bed in a triple (without toilet or shower) is Y3. The hotel is an easy 15 minute walk from the long-distance bus station. Turn hard left out of the bus station and walk to the end of the narrow Jiangwu Xiang; a left turn takes you past the old mosque and a right turn at the next T-intersection will point you in the direction of the hotel a few minutes' walk up ahead. Or if you prefer, take a rickshaw. Most of the hotel's front courtyard has been turned into a popular cafe.

### Places to Eat

Quanzhou is a great place for seafood –

perhaps better than Xiamen. The best place to eat is a little restaurant a few minutes' walk south down the road from the Overseas Chinese Hotel. It's run by an elderly couple who serve shellfish, crab, prawns, octopus and cold beer.

Around the corner on the same street as the Song Dynasty mosque is a restaurant (at No 215) serving exceptionally large crabs. There's another seafood restaurant on this street at No 243.

No 382 Zhongshan Lu is a rather dingy seafood restaurant that may be worth a try, as is the *Guoying Madang Fandian* on the corner of Zhongshan Lu and Xiamen Lu. Food at the *Overseas Chinese Hotel* is OK though nothing to rave about.

### Getting Around

There are no city buses in Quanzhou. Buses to places outside of Quanzhou leave from the square at the north end of Zhongshan Lu. Transport within the city is by rickshaw and in this town the rickshaws are ordinary bicycles with little wooden sidecarts tacked on which seat two people. The drivers are getting fairly predatory and you may be leapt on as you clamber off the bus.

### Getting Away

**Buses** The long-distance bus station is in the south-eastern part of town.

Buses to Xiamen depart at 7 am, 7.20 am, 7.50 am, 8.20 am, 8.40 am, 11.40 am, 12.40 pm, 1.30 pm, 2 pm and 3.25 pm. The fare is Y2.75 and the trip takes 2½ to 3 hours. It's an interesting ride notable for the profusion of large colonnaded stone houses in the villages, ostentatious enough to suggest that these places are being built with Overseas Chinese money.

Buses to Fuzhou depart at 6 am, 6.05 am, 7.10 am, 7.30 am, 8.30 am, 9 am, 9.30 am, 9.50 am, 12.30 pm and 12.40 pm. The fare is Y4.95. After leaving Quanzhou you'll see more of these large stone houses going up at a furious rate. You stop for lunch at a small town, and soon after you

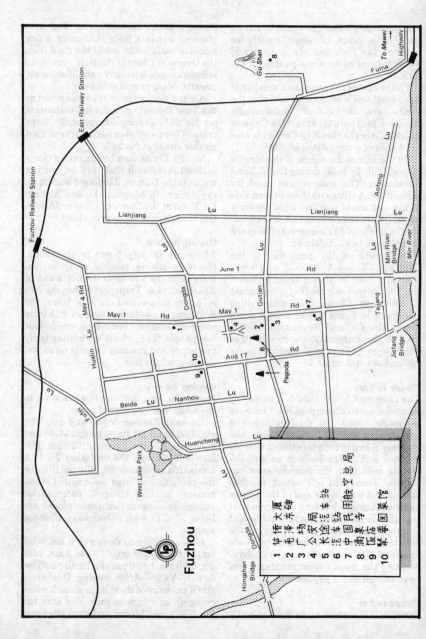

go through an area which is dotted with numerous two-storey sprawling mansions with ornate curved roofs seemingly big enough to accommodate an entire clan. The trip takes about six hours, including the half-hour stop for lunch.

**CITS** has buses running from Quanzhou to Shenzhen (Y66) probably overnighting in Shantou. Book at the CITS office in the Overseas Chinese Hotel.

**Train** The nearest railheads are at Xiamen and Fuzhou; see those sections for details.

**Plane** The only flights out of Quanzhou are to Canton(Y96).

## FUZHOU

In the 1320s the Franciscan Friar Odoric spent three years in China on a missionary venture. He came via India and after landing in Canton he travelled eastwards and 'came unto a city named Fuzo, which contains 30 miles in circuit, wherein are exceeding great and fair cocks, and all their hens are as white as the very snow, having wool instead of feathers, like unto sheep. It is a most stately and beautiful city and stands upon the sea'. Odoric's woolly hens are in fact what poultry-breeders call Fleecy Persians, though the Chinese call them Velvet-Hair Fowls.

Whilst the Chinese still breed chickens in makeshift pens in their backyards, Fuzhou seems to have lost both its fame as a poultry farm and as a stately and beautiful city. Though it's the capital of Fujian Province, the city is a let-down after other colourful and lively south-east coasal towns like Xiamen and Quanzhou.

Although Fuzhou's economy was – and largely still is – based on agriculture, with rice, sugar-cane, tea and oranges being the main crops, and fishing a thriving pursuit, Fuzhou looks very much like the dull industrial towns of the north, with long avenues, concrete block buildings and expansive suburbs.

Fuzhou was founded in the 6th century AD and rapidly became a thriving commercial port (the name means 'wealthy town') second only to Quanzhou. Marco Polo passed through the city of Fuzhou towards the end of the 13th century, several years before Odoric's visit, and described the town as an important commercial centre, full of merchants and craftsmen and a centre of distribution of goods from India. Polo decribed the city as as:

an important centre of commerce in pearls and other precious stones, because it is much frequented by ships from India bringing merchants who traffic in the Indies. Moreover it is not far from the port of Zaiton (Quangzhou) on the ocean, a great resort for ships and merchandise from India; and from Zaiton ships come . . . as far as the city of Fu-chau (Fuzhou). By this means many precious wares are imported from India. There is no lack here of anything that the human body requires to sustain life. There are gardens of great beauty and charm, full of excellent fruit. In short, it is a good city and so well provided with every amenity that it is a veritable marvel.

Yet, despite it's prosperity, Fuzhou had a reputation for revolt. Marco also noted that the city was garrisoned by a large number of soldiers as the district was one in which there were frequent rebellions of cities and towns . . .

| | |
|---|---|
| 1  Overseas Chinese Hotel / CITS | 6  Buses to Mawei |
| 2  Mao Statue | 7  CAAC |
| 3  Square | 8  Yongquan Monastery |
| 4  Public Security Office | 9  Restaurant |
| 5  Long Distance Bus Station | 10  Juchunyan Restaurant |

This is because . . . the natives hold life very cheap, believing that they will enjoy an honoured existence in the next world and also because their dwellings are in fastnesses among the mountains. So, when they are intoxicated with the spirit of revolt, they kill their rulers, and troops have to be called in to take their strongholds and crush them. That is why several armies of the Great Khan are stationed in this city'.

Fuzhou's status as an important trading centre and port continued over the centuries and quickly drew the attention of the western traders who began to arrive in the area in the 16th century. It was to be 200 years before they could set up shop here. That was achieved by the Treaty of Nanjing which ended the Second Opium War and opened Fuzhou to foreign traders in 1842.

One of the peculiarities of Fuzhou is its position as a centre of Chinese Christianity. Marco Polo describes a Christian sect who worshipped here. They . . .

enquired from what source they had received their faith and their rule, and their informants replied: 'From our forefathers'. It came out that they had in certain temples of theirs three pictures representing three apostles of the 70 who went through the world preaching. And they declared that it was these three who had instructed their ancestors in the faith long ago, and that it had been preserved among them for 700 years . . .

The Christians that Polo met were probably Nestorians, descendants of a Syrian sect whose religion had been carried into China via the Silk Road. What eventually happened to the Nestorian Christians in Fuzhou is unknown, although Marco claims there were 700,000 such households in southern China – probably an exaggeration. A more recent addition to the Christian community were the converts made by the westerners during the 19th and 20th centuries, since this was a centre of both Catholic and Protestant missionary activity. After being suppressed and forced underground during the

Cultural Revolution, at least one nondenominational Protestant Church, the 'Flower Lane Church' originally built by American Methodist missionaries in 1938, was reopened in the last few years in accord with the government's more lenient policy on religious worship.

## Information & Orientation

Most of Fuzhou lies on the northern bank of the Min River, sprawling northwards in a roughly rectangular shape. The railway station lies on the far north-eastern outskirts of the city and the long-distance bus station lies towards the southern end. The few tourist attractions are scattered about. Most of the activity is in the central part of town, roughly between the bus and railway stations, and here you'll find the hotel and tourist facilities.

There are three main arteries running north-south and approximately parallel to each other. August 1st Rd cuts Fuzhou in half and crosses the Min River over an ancient stone bridge. To the east is June 1st Rd which crosses the Min over a second stone bridge. In between them is May 1st Rd, where you'll find the long-distance bus station, the CAAC office and the Overseas Chinese Hotel. Running east-west and cutting across all three roads is Gutian Lu – here you'll find the large town square and a pair of ancient pagodas. Further north is Dongda Lu which is the main shopping and restaurant street and the centre of activity at night.

**CITS** is in Room 119 on the ground floor of the Overseas Chinese Hotel. They speak communicable English and are friendly and efficient.

**Public Security Office** is a short walk southwest of the intersection of Dongda Lu and May 1st: see the sketch map for directions.

**CAAC** is on May 1st Rd. Flight tickets can be bought here or at the efficient CITS office in the Overseas Chinese Hotel.

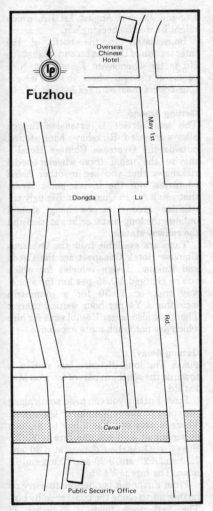

**Fuzhou**

Overseas Chinese Hotel

May 1st

Dongda Lu

Rd

Canal

Public Security Office

There's a reassuring sign outside Fuzhou airport which says that 'It is our CAAC's supreme responsibility to ensure the safety of our passengers'.

**Post** There is a post office on the ground floor of the Overseas Chinese Hotel.

**Bank** There is a money exchange counter on the ground floor of the Overseas Chinese Hotel.

**Maps** Good maps, in Chinese and showing the bus routes, are available from a small magazine and book shop near the railway station. The shop is on the left, a few minutes' walk down May 4th Rd which leads from the railway station – look for the pinyin sign 'Beifang Fandian'. There's also a not-very-good map available from the shop on the ground floor of the Overseas Chinese Hotel, but it's in English. Available in some of the bookstores is a booklet of detailed maps of the counties and towns of Fujian Province; it costs around Y2.30 and includes an excellent map of Fuzhou showing the bus routes.

### Things to See

In terms of sights there's not a great deal. The northern and southern sections of the town are separated by the Min River. Two old stone bridges link the two halves of the city but these have lost their former charm. Much of the riverfront is a ramshackle collection of dilapidated brick and wood houses probably awaiting demolition, though on a good day it can be interesting to watch the junks or to observe the squadrons of sampans dredging the bottom of the river for sand. Across the Min River is Nantai Island where the foreigners set themselves up when Fuzhou became a treaty port.

In the centre of town is a wind-swept square presided over by an enormous statue of Mao Zedong. The statue was erected to commemorate the Ninth National Congress of the Communist Party in which Maoism was enshrined as the new state religion and Lin Biao officially declared Mao's successor. In the north-western part of the town is West Lake (Xi Hu) Park on Hubin Lu, the site of the Fujian Provincial Museum.

## Hualin Temple

This ancient temple is supposed to be just north of Hualin Lu in the northern part of Fuzhou, but it seems to have disappeared. The original temple was built during the Tang Dynasty, though the present structure (if there still is one) only dates from the Qing.

## Yongquan Monastery

This thousand-year-old monastery was built in the early part of the 10th century, and is said to house a collection of 20,000 Buddhist scriptures of which 675 are written in blood! The monastery is located on Drum Hill (Gu Shan) immediately to the east of Fuzhou. The hill takes its name from a large drum-shaped rock which lies at the summit. There is a hot springs spa next to the monastery.

## Places to Stay

The *Overseas Chinese Hotel* is the best place to stay. It's a hotel with its act together too! Shops are open, services actually service you, staff are friendly – it's got to be one of the best hotels in China! No single rooms, but doubles with air-conditioning are Y20 (and if you don't think you'll want air-conditioning just try coming here in summer!). There is cheaper accommodation available.

The hotel is on May 4th Rd which runs into May 1st Rd. From the railway station take bus No 2 (the bus stop is on the right-hand side, a few minutes' walk down the road directly in front of the railway station). From the long-distance bus station take bus No 2 (there is a stop across the road from the station).

## Places to Eat

The best place to eat is the *Overseas Chinese Hotel* which has a restaurant on the ground floor serving *big* helpings of good food. There's also a cafe on the ground floor serving cakes, shishkebab, Coke, Fanta and tsingtao beer.

There's a big restaurant in a large neon-decorated building on the corner of Dongda Jie and August 1st Rd, which might be worth checking out.

Immediately to the north of the intersection of Dongda Lu and August 7th Rd is the *Juchunyan Restaurant*. Nice rooms at the rear where you can have a four-course meal with tea for just Y6.50

## Getting Around

The bus service is extensive though always crowded. Rickshaws hang around outside the Overseas Chinese Hotel – they're the usual three-wheeler pedal rickshaws that you see in other Asian countries, not the bicycle-and-sidecars that you'll see in Quanzhou. Big ugly tri-wheeler green tempos hang around outside the long-distance bus station and the railway station.

Taxis are available from the Overseas Chinese Hotel. Cheapest are the Czech and Russian design vehicles for which you're charged Y0.65 per km for a one-way trip, or Y0.50 for a round-trip including a Y4 per hour waiting charge. There are also larger Kombi vans for hire which are not much more expensive.

## Getting Away

**Buses** The long distance bus station is towards the southern part of town on May 1st Rd.

From Fuzhou you can head south along the coast to either Xiamen or Quanzhou. There is only one bus a bay to Xiamen departing at 6.10 am; the fare is Y7.70. Buses to Quanzhou depart at 6.30 am, 7.10 am, 8.20 am, 9.20 am, 10 am and 12 noon. The fare is Y4.95.

From Fuzhou it is possible to carry on further north along the coast road by bus. The next open town is Wenzhou in Zhejiang Province. There is no direct bus from Fuzhou to Wenzhou and you have to change buses at Fuan. The daily bus to Fuan departs Fuzhou at 6.50 am and the fare is Y5.10.

**Train** The railway line from Fuzhou heads north and connects the city with the main

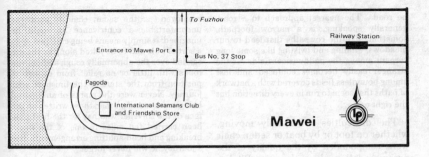

Shanghai-Canton line at the Yingtan junction. A branch line splits from the Fuzhou-Yingtan line and goes to Xiamen. There are direct trains from Fuzhou to Beijing, Shanghai, Nanchang and Xiamen. The rail route to Xiamen is circuitous and you'd be better off taking the bus.

Fuzhou railway station provides another fine example of how the Chinese concoct English sentences. One at the information desk says:

INFORMATION DESK ITEMS OF
SERVICE
TRAIN TICKET SIGNING TRAIN
CHANGING
PLATFORM TICKET BOOKING

**Plane** Fuzhou is connected by air to Beijing (Y255), Canton (Y106), Hangzhou (Y85), Nanchang (Y61), Shanghai (Y105). There are also flights to Xiamen.

**Boats** Passenger ships out of Fuzhou actually depart from the nearby port town of Mawei, which lies to the south-east of Fuzhou. Don't go to Mawei expecting to find a bustling harbour full of ships and junks. The port is a boring, sprawling town of concrete blocks. The only attraction (for enthusiasts only) is the pagoda. The Mawei Friendship Store and the International Seamen's Club are next to the pagoda.
either by bus or train. Bus No 37 leaves regularly from the stop at the western end of Gutian Lu near the corner with August 1st Rd. The fare is 48 fen and the ride

takes about an hour. The bus terminates outside Mawei port, just near the pagoda.

Trains to Mawei depart Fuzhou at 7.50 am and 1.20 pm The fare is 30 fen and the conductor comes around selling tickets on the train. It's a 45-minute ride. To get to the port from Mawei railway station, turn right and head along the road running parallel to the tracks; this takes you down to the pagoda and to the road which runs alongside the port. Trains depart Mawei for Fuzhou at 11.42 am and 5.20 pm.

From Mawei you can take a ship to Shanghai. CITS does not handle tickets and you have to buy them at the booking office which is supposed to be *somewhere* on Dongda Jie – again you're a genius if you can find it! Fares are Y82.00 Special Class, Y68.30 1st class, Y54.70 2nd class, Y27.30 3rd class, Y20.20 4th class, Y15.60 5th class, Y12.10 deck class. Timetables vary but these boats usually go twice a week. CITS in Fuzhou can also book you a ticket for the Xiamen to Hong Kong boat.

**Footnote**
Even in the early years of this century communications across Fujian Province were at best difficult. In 1912 Reverend Philip Pitcher, an American missionary in Xiamen described travelling in the district as:

a slow process, more wearisome than otherwise – a peculiar wearisomeness of its own ... So far as South China is concerned there are no roads. The nearest approach to a road, generally speaking, is a narrow footpath, something like the cowpaths that lead to our meadows, winding and twisting like some long serpent among the paddy (rice) fields . . . the stranger easily becomes confused and lost among boundless fields covered with a network of paths that seem to run in every direction but the right one . . .

The difficulties of actually moving, whether on foot or by boat or sedan chair were compounded by the quality of the accommodation along the way. Pitcher says it is:

an almost hopeless task to describe these places as they really are. For, there are sights and sounds, conditions and smells, that no pen can adequately describe, nor any camera even fully portray . . . the wayside inns you will find on the streets of the cities, on the outskirts of the towns, and sometimes far out in the country . . . are disreputable looking affairs, consisting of little more than a dirty old burlap or plaited bamboo mat fastened to a single pole in some instances. Sometimes they are more dignified when they are enclosed, with sheds made of mud walls on three sides, with a tile (or thatched) roof, open in the front. There may be a few stone slabs, or a single board bench, three or four inches wide, for the weary traveller to rest his weary bones on . . . The regular inns found in towns, villages and sometimes out in the hills . . . are places of real horror, enough to give one the nightmare at the very threshold, to say nothing about passing the night in one of them. Of all the filthy places in China, there are none that can equal these inns.

In 1912 Reverend Pitcher listed the sedan chair as one of the principal ways of getting around the district of Xiamen. He describes the sedan chair as

an instrument of torture to the uninitiated. It consists of a box-like contrivance swung on two long poles each about fifteen feet in length. It is usually carried on the shoulders of two men, unless the person occupying it weighs more than 175 pounds, when three men are employed . . . the sedan chair is about as uncomfortable a contrivance as could be imagined. It simply means being cramped up in a sort of box, and to be jolted along as you are carried over the abnormally rough and uneven roads with little or no relief from change of position from the start to the finish of your journey. Never were the marks of an 'injured being' more manifest than those written on the face of the traveller who has for the first time been carried ten miles in one of the back-breaking and head-splitting arrangements. It is a journey he will never forget.

Travelling through the province the ever tolerant Reverend struck the same problem which afflicts present-day travellers to Asia and particularly China – staring. Of the regular inns he says that:

sometimes there are smaller rooms partitioned off, but rarely having doors to screen you from other guests. Privacy therefore is out of the question. If you chance to have a spare sheet . . . and you can manage to hang it up on some friendly peg or nail, you may succeed in shutting yourself off from the staring, gaping crowd, and secure such privacy as that article can afford. And you may be assured that there will be a crowd around when a foreigner is on exhibition. They never tire of looking, and they are bound to force their company upon you whether it is agreeable or otherwise, and watch you, if possible, with eager attention to the very last act in your preparation for bed – and apparently enjoy it to the fullest. The early morning will find some watchers ready for your next appearance. At all times, so long as you are a guest in the inn, you will be the great attraction, the centre of an ever inquisitive, never tiring, multitude. As they stand gazing at you sleeping or awake, they will be making all sorts of remarks concerning you, speculating about this and that, about your dress, from your shoes to your hat, categorically and in detail, your age (not a pleasant thing to hear always), your looks (not agreeable at times), your country, your motives in being there, and a hundred other questions that only a Chinaman thinks out loud.

# Hunan

Hunan Province lies on some of the richest land in China. It's main period of growth occurred between the 8th and the 11th centuries when the population increased five-fold, spurred on by a prosperous agricultural industry and by migrations from the north. Under the Ming and the Qing it was one of the empire's granaries, and vast quantities of Hunan's rice surplus were shipped to the depleted regions to the north.

But by the 19th century it was beginning to suffer from the pressure of population; land shortage and landlordism led to widespread peasant unrest, amongst both the Chinese farmers the hill-dwelling minority peoples. The southern regions of China have always had their own strong local identities, a sense of independence from northern rule – couple this with an increasingly more desperate economic situation and the result was the massive Taiping Rebellion of the mid-19th century. But the culmination was the Communist movement of the 1920s which found a base here amongst the poor peasantry, and a refuge for the first Communist armies on the mountainous Hunan-Jiangxi border in 1927. It was also in Hunan that some of the more prominent Communist leaders were born; Mao Zedong, Liu Shaoqi, Peng Dehuai and Hu Yaobang – and it was in Hunan that Hua Guofeng (a native of Shanxi) became an important provincial leader.

Fifty four million people live in Hunan, most of them Han Chinese. The hill-dwelling minorities can still be found today in the border regions of the province. They include the Miao, the Tujia, the Dong (a Thai people who have assimilated Chinese culture), the Yao, and oddly enough in the far north of the province is a little pocket of Uygurs.

In his book *One's Company*, the young English traveller Peter Fleming describes a train trip which he made through Hunan in 1934. He wrote that:

There are two classes of passenger accommodation, Goods and Cattle; between these the chief difference in comfort is that Goods is open, whereas Cattle has a roof. In the latter class we were fortunate enough to secure a corner seat. The truck was very full, and its passengers made, as always in China, a pattern of humanity so intricate and so seemingly well-established, with their babies and their bundles and their bowls of rice, that one thought of them rather as a community than as a carriage full of strangers.

Next to me there was a woman with a baby. The babies who were my neighbours in public conveyances in China all fell into one of two categories: babies who appeared to be dead, and babies who appeared to be dying. This one belonged to the former, and preferable, category . . . there were three fat schoolgirls on their way back to college in Changsha. They wore European dress and clearly belonged to rich families. At one station a special meal had been ordered for them in advance, and our average rate of progress can be gauged from the fact that, when we started again with unexpected punctuality, the man who had brought the meal on board was able, without mishap, to leave the train half a mile further on, holding a tray piled high with bowls.

There were the usual quarrels, the usual gambling games, the usual children being sick . . . At every station hawkers came on board with fruit and tea and cakes and less edible delicacies; they generally travelled on with us as far as the next station, and, when unable to force their way through the crowded carriages or alternately when approached by the ticket-

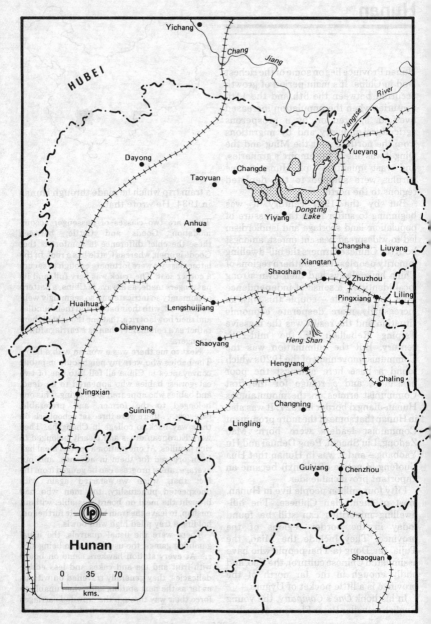

collector, would climb up on to the roof of the carriage and thus pass unchallenged up and down the train.

## SHAOSHAN

The village of Shaoshan is so small it doesn't even appear on many large-scale maps of China. But its importance to the Communist movement far surpasses its physical dimensions since this is the birthplace of Mao Zedong.

The village is about 131 km south-west of Changsha. During the height of the Cultural Revolution it was said to have been visited by around 3,000,000 pilgrims a year, and a railway line and a paved road were built from Changsha to transport them here.

Mao was born here in 1893 (probably on December 26). His father was a poor peasant who had been forced to join the army because of heavy debts. After several years of service he returned to Shaoshan and by careful saving and gathering together money through small trading and other enterprises he managed to buy back his land. As 'middle' peasants they owned enough land to produce a surplus of rice. Using the surplus, Mao's father was able to buy more land and this gave them the status of 'rich' peasants. Mao's father began to deal in grain transport and selling, buying grain from the poor farmers and taking it to the city merchants where he could get a higher price for it. As Mao told Edgar Snow 'My family ate frugally, but had enough always'.

Mao began studying in the local primary school when he was eight years old and remained at school until the age of 13, as well as working on the farm and keeping the accounts for his father's business. Of his parents, Mao described his father as 'a hot-tempered man who frequently beat both me and my brothers ... I learned to hate him' and his mother as 'a kind woman, generous and sympathetic'.

Mao's father continued to 'amass wealth', or what was considered a fortune

in the little village, by buying mortgages on other people's land; creditors of other peasants would be paid off in lump sums, and these peasants would then have to pay back their loans to Mao's father who would profit from the interest rates charged over a long period.

When Mao left school he worked on the farm, but continued to read as much as possible, except the Confucian classics, which he disliked. But, as he told Edgar Snow, he found that all the old tales of Chinese literature glorified soldiers and rulers who did not have to work the land because they owned it and had the peasants to work it – there were no peasant heroes.

Apart from his reading, there were several incidents which influenced Mao around this time. A famine in Hunan and a subsequent uprising in Changsha of starving people ended in the execution of the leaders by the Manchu governor, and this left an everlasting impression on Mao who ' ... felt that there with the rebels were ordinary people like my own family and I deeply resented the injustice in the treatment given to them'. He was also influenced by a band of rebels who had taken to the hills around Shaoshan to defy the landlords and the government and by a radical teacher in the local primary school who opposed Buddhism and wanted people to convert their temples into schools. When there was a food shortage in the area, one of his father's consignments of grain to the city was seized by poor farmers – and although Mao thought the villager's methods were wrong, he did not sympathise with his father.

At the age of sixteen, Mao left Shaoshan to enter middle school in Changsha. At this time he was not yet an anti-monarchist ' ... indeed, I considered the emperor as well as most officials to be honest, good and clever men ... ' but that the country was in desperate need of reform. He was fascinated by stories of the ancient rulers of China, and he also learned something of foreign history and geography.

## Information and Orientation

There are two parts to Shaoshan, the railhead and the village several km away.

The railhead is characterised by its over-sized railway station, built to accommodate the hordes that pilgrimaged here while Mao was still alive. Immediately outside the station is a square where the bus to the village meets the daily train from Changsha and in front of the square is a gleaming white statue of Mao and a park. Follow the road up the right-hand side of the park to the main street, where you'll find a large bookshop, foodstalls and the long-distance bus station. At the intersection of the main street and the road leading up from the train station you can catch the irregular local buses which trundle down to Shaoshan village. There's also a large post office on the main street notable for its big portrait of Mao and Zhu De meeting Zhou En-lai at the airport –

with an enormous blank where Liu Shao-qi is supposed to stand!

The bus which connects with the train at the railhead drops you off at the northern end of Shaoshan Village, at the pathway which leads up to Mao's house. Follow the road down from the bus stop and you come to a large traffic circle; here you'll find the bus stop where the local bus from the railhead pulls in and there is a pathway which leads up to the Chinese hotel. Further down from the bus stop is the Mao Museum. On the opposite side of the traffic circle is a small post office. To get to the Shaoshan Guest House follow the pathway from alongside the post office, cross the bridge and follow the path straight ahead to the gateway in the hotel compound.

## Things to See

Shaoshan is hardly typical of Chinese villages, considering the number of tourists and their money that have passed through the place since it was established as a national shrine. It is, however, a rare

### Shaoshan (Mao's Village)

1 韶山宾馆
2 汽车站
3 毛泽东展览馆
4 旅社
5 邮局
6 汽车终点
7 毛泽东旧居

1 Shaoshan Guesthouse
2 Local Bus Station
3 Mao Exhibition Hall
4 Chinese Hotel
5 Post Office
6 Terminus of Buses from Shaoshan Railway Station
7 Mao's House

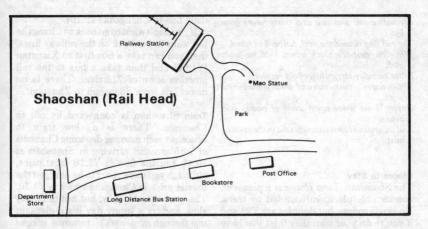

Shaoshan (Rail Head)

Railway Station

Mao Statue

Park

Post Office

Bookstore

Department Store

Long Distance Bus Station

opportunity to get something of a look at the Chinese countryside. It's a beautiful valley and you could probably wander off for days exploring the sleepy little villages in the surrounding area. Apart from its historical significance, it's a great place to get away from those grim, grey cities.

### Mao Zedong's House

This is the principal shrine of Shaoshan. It's a fairly large building with mud-walls and thatched roof. There's not a great deal to see; a few utensils in the kitchen, the beds and some sparse furnishings, as well as a photo of his mother and father. In front of the house is a pond, and on the other side a pavilion where the Chinese pose to have their photo taken with the house in the background.

**Mao Zedong Exhibition Hall** is a museum entirely devoted to the life of Mao. Opened in 1967 during the Cultural Revolution the museum originally had two wings, exact duplicates of each other, so that more visitors could be accommodated at the same time. Today there is only one set of exhibits, mostly of paintings, photos, books and statues. There are no captions in English, but a few of the guides speak a little English and are quite helpful.

On the top floor of the museum there is

(at the time of writing) a large room which houses another exhibition of photos; according to one of the guides it has been closed for two years because of 'many mistakes'. Standing on a chair and peering in over the papered-up lower windows, the only recognisable photos were those of Mao and Hua Guo-feng. Presumably the 'mistakes' are those which refer to Hua as the 'wise-leader' and quote Chairman Mao as saying 'With you in charge, I am at ease'. Another photo showed Mao and Zhu De welcoming Zhou En-lai at Beijing Airport on Zhou's return from Moscow. It's a picture seen all over China but this particular version still hadn't been altered to include Liu Shao-qi. One hates to think how many times the exhibits here have to be altered to keep them up-to-date with ever-changing Communist history.

There's a souvenir shop here where you can buy pin-on badges showing Mao's house, and also little stand-up flat plastic relief models of Mao's profile showing rays of sunshine emanating from behind his head.

Mao, by the way, revisited Shaoshan in June 1959, after an absence of 32 years. The visit inspired this poem:

*Like a dream recalled, I curse the long-fled past,*

*My native soil and two and thirty years gone by.*

*The red flag roused the serf, halberd in hand,*
*While the despot's black talons held his whip aloft.*

*Bitter sacrifice stregnthens bold resolve*
*Which dares to make sun and moon shine in new skies.*

*Happy, I see wave upon wave of paddy and beans,*
*And all around heroes homebound in the evening mist.*

## Places to Stay

The *Shaoshan Guest House* is a pleasant, comfortable place, surrounded by trees. No single rooms, but doubles are Y24 and if you're on your own they'll let you have the double for Y12. The staff here are exceptionally friendly. The Guest House is about a 15 minute walk down from the bus stop. There is a large Chinese hotel in the village, but it's unlikely you'll be able to stay here.

## Places to Eat

The hotels seem to be the only places to eat at. The *Guest House* serves three good meals a day, at Y3.80 each, and Tsingtao beer for an extra Y1.14 per bottle. You may have to tell them you want Chinese food; at my first meal all that initially landed on the table was some fried beef, chicken, rice and a knife and fork — possibly an imaginary approximation to western food. Once you've worked that one out though you'll be served up a huge bowl of rice plus plates of meat, vegetables, beancurd, fish, buns and maybe some sort of dessert such as canned mandarins. For breakfast you get eggs, meat, and *real* porridge (not rice-porridge). There's also a large canteen-style restaurant at the Chinese Hotel.

## Getting Away

**Bus** The long-distance bus station is on the main street at the Shaoshan railhead. The ticket booth is open 6.40 to 7.30 am and 8 am to 5.10 pm. From here there is a daily bus to Changsha (Y2.10).

If you don't want to go back to Changsha but want to get back on the railway lines, then you can take a bus first to Xiangtan (Y1.00) and then take a bus to the rail junction town of Zhuzhou. There is no direct bus from Shaoshan to Zhuzhou.

**Train** Shaoshan is connected by rail to Changsha. There is a slow train to Shaoshan each morning departing Changsha at 7.35 am and arriving in Shaoshan at 10.42 am; the fare is Y2.10 local price, although you can expect to be charged the tourist price in Changsha which is Y3.70. The train may be slow, but not tediously slow, and on a sunny day it's a pleasant trip through numerous picturesque villages and attractive countryside. The train back to Changsha departs Shaoshan at 4.30 pm and arrives in Changsha at 8.05 pm, so you can make the village a day trip if you want to.

## CHANGSHA

The site of Changsha has been inhabited for 3000 years and by the Warring States Period (770-221 BC) a large town had grown up here. The town owes its prosperity to its location on the fertile Hunan plains of central China and on the Xiang River, where it rapidly grew as a major trading centre of agricultural produce.

In 1904 the city was opened up to foreign trade as the result of the 1903 Treaty of Shanghai between Japan and China. The 'most favoured nation' principle allowed all and sundry foreigners to set themselves up in Changsha and large numbers of Europeans and Americans came to live here, building factories, churches and schools (including a college set up by Yale University, now used as a medical centre). Today Changsha is the capital of Hunan Province and has a population of around 2.6 million people.

Changsha's most famous import/export was, in fact, Mao Zedong. This city was the first stop on his footpath to power; it took him in, gave him an education, and churned him out a considerably less naive country lad. Later, the city became a transit point for pilgrims on their way to Shaoshan village, the holy place of the Maoist nativity.

It was in Changsha that Mao was first exposed to the ideas of revolutionaries and reformers who were active in China. It was here that he first heard of Sun Yat-sen's revolutionary secret society, and read about the abortive Canton uprising of 1911. Later that year there was an army uprising in Wuhan which quickly spread and the Qing Dynasty collapsed. Then Yuan Shi-kai made his grab for power and the country appeared to be slipping into civil war; Mao joined the regular army but resigned six months later, thinking the revolution was over when Sun handed the Presidency to Yuan and the war between the north and south of China did not eventuate.

At this time Mao became an avid reader of newspapers and from these he was introduced to socialism. He enrolled and studied at the the First Provincial Middle School after leaving the army but left after six months, finding the curriculum limited and the regulations objectionable. He seems to have been a voracious reader, studying books on world geography and history. He decided to become a teacher and enrolled in the Hunan Provincial First Normal (Teachers' Training) School where he was a student for five years.

During his time at the Teachers' Training School, he inserted an advertisement in a Changsha newspaper 'inviting young men interested in patriotic work to make contact with me ... ' Gradually Mao did manage to build up a group of students around himself which in 1917 became the 'New People's Study Society' with about 70 to 80 members in Changsha and in other towns and cities. Amongst them was Liu Shao-qi, who later became President of the People's Republic, and Xiao Chen later a founding member of the party. Among the four who initially replied to

the advertisement was Li Lisan, later responsible for the 'Li Lisan Line' which advocated an urban-based rather than a rural-based revolution, a line which Mao bitterly opposed. 'At this time' says Mao 'my mind was a curious mixture of ideas of liberalism, democratic reformism and utopian socialism ... and I was definitely antimilitarist and anti-imperialist'.

Mao graduated from the Teachers' Training School in 1918, and went to Beijing where he worked as an assistant librarian at Beijing University. In Beijing he met future co-founders of the Chinese Communist Party; the student leader Zhang Guodao (who threw his lot in with the Kuomintang in 1938) and Professor Chen Duxiu and University Librarian Li Dazhao (executed by the Kuomintang in 1927), regarded as the two founders of Chinese Communism. It was Li who gave Mao a job and also first introduced him to the serious study of Marxism.

Mao was very much the perplexed convert, a Nationalist who found in Marxist theory a programme for reform and revolution in China. He did not found Chinese Communism but was introduced to it by Beijing intellectuals, and on returning to Changsha became increasingly active in Communist politics. At this time, says Mao, ' ... I became more and more convinced that only mass political power, secured through mass action, could guarantee the realisation of dynamic reforms'. He became editor of the *Xiang River Review*, a radical Hunan students' newspaper. He continued working in the New People's Study Society and also took up a post as a teacher. In 1920 he was organising workers for the first time and from that year onwards he considered himself to be a Marxist. In May of 1921, Mao went to Shanghai to attend the founding meeting of the Chinese Communist Party. The following October he helped to organise the first provincial branch of the Party in Hunan and by the middle of 1922 the Party had organised trade unions among the workers and students.

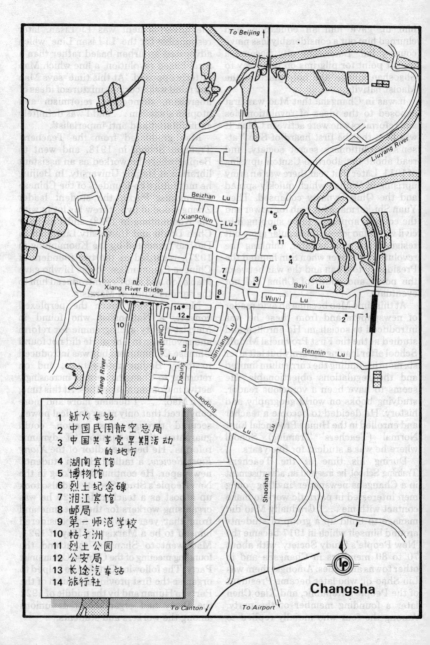

1 新火车站
2 中国民用航空总局
3 中国共产党早期活动
  的地方
4 湖南宾馆
5 博物馆
6 烈士纪念碑
7 湘江宾馆
8 邮局
9 第一师范学校
10 桔子洲
11 烈士公园
12 公安局
13 长途汽车站
14 旅行社

**Changsha**

To Beijing

Liuyang River

Beizhan Lu

Xiangchun Lu

Xiang River Bridge

Wuyi Lu

Bayi Lu

Renmin Lu

Chenghan Lu

Daqing Lu

Jianxiang Lu

Laodong Lu

Shaoshan Lu

Xiang River

To Canton

To Airport

Orthodox Marxist philosophy saw revolution spreading from the cities as it had in the Soviet Union. The peasants, ignored through the ages by poets, scholars and political soothsayers had likewise been ignored by the Communists. But Mao took a different stand and saw the peasants as the life-blood of the revolution. The Party had done very little work among the peasants but by the latter half of 1925 Mao was beginning to organise peasant trade unions. This aroused the wrath of the landlords and Mao had to flee to Canton where the Kuomintang and the Communists held power and were in alliance with each other. He returned to Hunan in 1926 to inspect the peasant organisations and political conditions in Changsha and other counties. He proposed a radical redistribution of the land to help the poor peasants and supported (and probably initiated) the demands of the Hunan Peasants Union to confiscate large land-holdings, and probably at this stage he foresaw the need to organise and arm them for a struggle against the landlords.

In April 1927, Chiang Kai-shek launched his massacre of the Communists. In the autumn of that year Mao was sent by the Party to Changsha to organise what became known as the 'Autumn Harvest Uprising'. By September the first units of a peasant-worker army had been formed, with troops drawn from the peasantry, the Hengyang miners and rebel Kuomintang soldiers. Mao's army moved south through Hunan and climbed up into the Jinggang Mountains to embark on a guerilla war against the Kuomintang.

**Information & Orientation** Most of Changsha lies on the eastern bank of the Xiang River. The New Railway Station is at the far east of the city; from here, the main artery Wuyi Lu leads down to the river, neatly separating the northern and southern sections of the city. From Wuyi Lu you cross the Xiang Bridge to the western bank, passing over Long Island which lies in the middle of the river. Most of the sights and the tourist facilities are on the eastern side of the river.

**CITS** (tel 24845) looks like it has been sited with a view to making it as hard to find as possible. It is on a small street running south from Wuyi Lu, the first one west of Daqing Lu. There is no sign. You have to go through a gateway into a courtyard; the office is up the stairs through a doorway on your left as you enter the courtyard.

**Public Security** (tel 24898) is on Daqing Lu, about 10 minutes' walk south of the intersection with Wuyi Xilu, and just before you get to Pozi Lu. Friendly lot here and one of the guys speaks good English. They didn't really seem to know what was open and what wasn't, but they're careful about what permits they issue. You may be able to get a permit for a few obscure towns, but nothing exotic.

**CAAC** (tel 23820) is at 5 Wuji Donglu on the left-hand side of the road as you walk down from the New Railway Station. Watch for it; it's only a small building and is marked only by very small signs.

| 1 | New Railway Station | 8 | Post Office |
|---|---|---|---|
| 2 | CAAC | 9 | Hunan No. 1 Teachers Training School |
| 3 | Former Headquarters of Hunan Communist Party | 10 | Long Island |
| 4 | Hunan Guesthouse | 11 | Martyrs Park |
| 5 | Hunan Provincial Museum | 12 | Public Security Office |
| 6 | Monument to the Martyrs | 13 | Long Distance Bus Station |
| 7 | Xianjiang Hotel | 14 | CITS |

**Post** There is a post office in the Xianjiang Guest House, open weekdays 8 am to 8.30 pm and on Saturdays and Sundays 7.30 to 11.30 am and 3.30 to 7 pm There is also a large post-office at the corner of Wuji Xilu and Dazhai Lu in the centre of town.

**Bank** You can change money at the bank in the Xiangjiang Guest House, open weekdays and Saturdays from 7.30 to 9.30 am and 5.30 to 7.30 pm, and on Sundays from 5.30 to 7.30 pm.

**Friendship Store** is in the Xiangjiang Guest House.

**Maps** There's usually a hawker or two outside the New Railway Station selling very good maps (in Chinese), with the bus routes marked, for 20 fen.

### Things to See

Most of Changsha's sights are related to Mao Zedong and the Communist Revolution, but don't miss the mummified remains of the Han Dynasty woman in the Hunan Provincial Museum! The Hunan Provincial Museum, the Hunan No 1 Teachers' Training School and the former HQ of the Hunan Communist Party are all open Monday to Saturday, 8 to 11 am and 2 to 5 pm, and are closed on Sundays.

### Hunan Provincial Museum

If you're an archaeological buff or only in Changsha for a very short time then the Hunan Provincial Museum is not to be missed. The chief attraction is the preserved body of a royal woman from a 2100– year-old Han tomb excavated a few km east of the museum at Mawangtui.

The only sign of the tombs which could be seen above ground were two earthen mounds of similar size and height standing close together. The body was found in the eastern tomb in a chamber 16 metres underground and approached from the north by a sloping passageway. The walls of the tomb were covered in a thick layer of charcoal surrounded by a layer of compact clay, which appears to have kept out moisture and prevented the decay of the body and other objects in the tomb.

At the bottom of the tomb was a chamber made of wooden planks, containing an outer, middle and inner coffin. In the coffin was the corpse of a woman of about 50 years of age, wrapped in more than 20 layers of silk and linen, and the outer layer bound with nine bands of silk ribbons.

Large quantities of silk garments and fabrics were found in the tomb as well as stockings, shoes and gloves and other pieces of clothing. One of the most interesting objects found in the tomb, and now on display in the museum, is a painting on silk depicting the underworld, the earth and heaven. The tomb also contained lacquerware, pottery containing food, musical instruments (including a 25-stringed wooden instrument called a *se zither*, a set of reed pipes and a set of bamboo pitch-pipes) as well as a collection of wooden tomb figurines. Other finds included bamboo boxes containing clothing and fabrics, vegetables and grain seeds, straw mats, medicinal herbs, seals and several hundred pieces of money made of unbaked clay with clear inscriptions. There were numerous bamboo slips with writing on them, listing the name, size and number of the objects.

The woman's body is housed in the basement of the museum and is viewed from the floor above through perspex. Her organs have been removed and are laid out on display for the appreciation of the masses.

To get to the museum from the Xiangjiang Guest House, take bus No 3 north along Jianxiang Zhonglu. It goes straight past the museum.

### Maoist Pilgrimage Spots

Scattered about the city are a number of spots associated with the time Mao ate, worked and slept here.

The **Hunan No 1 Teachers' Training School** is where Mao attended classes between 1913 and 1918, and where he returned as a teacher in 1920-1921. The school was destroyed during the civil war, but has since been restored. Although of historical interest, there's not really anything to see; the main attraction is a sort of Mao 'shrine' with banners, his photo, candles and black arm-banded attendants. To get there, take bus No 1 from outside the Xiangjiang Guest House; it goes straight past the school.

The **Former Office of the Hunan (Xiang District) Communist Party Committee** is now used as a museum and includes Mao's living quarters and an exhibition of photos and historical items from the 1920s. Some of it harks back to the time when the Mao cult was a little more intact; apart from the larger-than-life statues, the front of the museum is decorated with a large portrait of the man himself in his younger days, beams of sunshine emanating from behind his brain. Inside the museum there are a couple of paintings of the great man surrounded by grovelling mortals and some interesting photos from the time that he spent here. Another hall is devoted to an exhibition of archaeological relics, mainly pottery, tools, weapons and coins, but all the captions are in Chinese. The Monument to the Martyrs is in the grounds of the museum but it's just a spire and there's nothing to see.

About 60 km from Changsha is the **Home and Tomb of Yang Kaihui.** Yang was Mao's first wife (discounting an unconsummated arranged childhood marriage) and is being built up by the present regime as his favourite, as a counter to the vilified Jiang Qing. Yang was the daughter of one of Mao's teachers at the First Teachers' Training School in Changsha, a member of a wealthy Hunanese land owning family. Mao seems to have influenced Yang Kaihui towards radicalism, and also to marriage in 1920 when she was 25 years old. She was arrested by the Kuomintang in 1930 and executed after she refused to denounce the Communist Party and Mao. Yang had two children by Mao, Mao

Anqing who escaped to Russia after his mother's arrest and the elder son Mao Anying who was arrested with his mother but later released. Mao Anying was killed in the Korean War in 1950.

## Other Attractions

A few other notables of Changsha are the **Loving Dusk Pavilion** situated on Yuelu Hill on the west bank of the Xiang River, from where you can get a good view of the town. **Long Island** or Long Sandbank, from which Changsha takes it's name, lies in the middle of the Xiang River. The only part of the old city walls which still remains is the **Tianxin Tower** in the south of the city – the walls were built during the Tang Dynasty.

The **New Railway Station** is a tourist attraction in itself; it's one of those massive concrete blocks with a huge foyer and giant waiting rooms, all of which are kept immaculately clean. It's probably got the most sparkling floor in China, regularly polished by little motorised vehicles resembling golf-carts.

If you're looking for some innocent night-time entertainment then there's a video game shed just down the road from the Xiangjiang Hotel; turn right at the front entrance of the hotel and after about ten minutes you'll come to a large building with columns at the front. The machines are in a lane on the right side of the building.

## Places to Stay

The *Xiangjiang Guest House* (tel 26261) is the only tourist hotel in town and is another enormous, cold, grey concrete construction. Take a Bus No 1 from the New Railway Station – it drops you off right outside the hotel. There are double rooms for Y34 and there may be some for Y32 – no single rooms. If you're on your own you should be able to pay half price, though that may depend on who's sitting behind the reception desk. They also have beds for Y10 in triple rooms on the ground floor, but you may have to argue before you'll get them. There is said to be a cheaper dormitory. The hotel is at 267 Zhongshan Lu; when you come out of the railway station the ticket hall is on your left and bus No 1 leaves from behind it. railway station the ticket hall is is on your left and bus No 1 leaves from behind it).

The *Hunan Guest House* (tel 26331) used to take foreigners but it doesn't any longer. If you can force your way past the frantically waving guards at the gate, this hotel has single rooms for Y22 and doubles for Y36. It's also permanently 'full' – which is hard to imagine since it's literally big enough to be a palace with 250 rooms and enough beds for 600 people! The hotel is at 9 Yingbin Lu and is a bit out of the way in any case.

## Places to Eat

Hunanese food, like that of the neighbouring Sichuan province, is characterised by a liberal use of hot chili pepper and spices.

The best place to eat is about 10 minutes' walk from the Xiangjiang Hotel on Jianxiang Zhonglu, south of the intersection with Zhongshan Lu. It's a tiny restaurant serving good, non-greasy, spicy food for only Y1 or Y2 a plate. Look for a light blue board with white Chinese characters hanging above the pavement in front of the restaurant.

The much-touted *Youyicun Restaurant* (tel 22797) is at 116 Zhongshan Lu, about 15 minutes' walk west of the Xiangjiang Hotel; the restaurant's sign is spelt Yu Yi Tsun. It's worth eating here if you know what to order, or so I'm told, and is probably worth a shot, though I never saw anything I'd be game to try. There are probably private rooms in a restaurant

this size – otherwise be prepared for an audience of about 200 people per floor whilst you stuff your gut.

The food at the *Xiangjiang Hotel* is OK, but it's an incredibly dreary place to eat.

## Getting Around

The city is much too spread out to walk around. Buses are fairly frequent though as usual, crowded. If you get into Changsha late at night when the buses have stopped, there are bicycle rickshaws and motorised rickshaws outside the railway station which will take you down to the hotel but you'll have to bargain hard for a decent price. (The hotel is locked up late at night; if you can't wake up the gate keeper, you'll probably have to climb over the wall and camp out for the night, or else stay at the railway station until morning).

## Getting Away

**Bus** There are buses to Shaoshan departing from the long-distance bus station which is just to the north of the New Railway Station. The bus departs daily at 12.45 pm and the fare is Y2.10; buy your ticket at window No 2 in the booking hall.

**Train** Changsha is on the main Canton-Beijing line. There are also direct trains to Guilin. Shanghai-Kunming trains pass through the railway junction of Zhuzhou just south of Changsha.

From Changsha there is a branch line out to the village of Shaoshan, the birthplace of Mao Zedong. There is a slow train to Shaoshan each morning departing Changsha at 7.35 am and arriving in Shaoshan at 10.42 am; the fare is Y2.10

| | |
|---|---|
| 1 Railway Station | 6 Ticket Office for |
| 2 Tourist Hotel |    Boats to Junshan |
| 3 Chinese Hotel | 7 Street Market |
| 4 Chinese Hotel | 8 Park & Temple |
| 5 Yueyang Tower | |

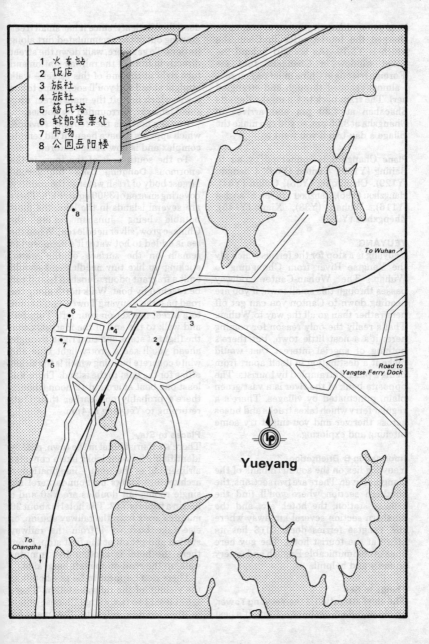

1 火车站
2 饭店
3 旅社
4 旅社
5 慈氏塔
6 轮船售票处
7 市场
8 公园岳阳楼

To Wuhan

Road to
Yangtse Ferry Dock

**Yueyang**

To
Changsha

local price, although you can expect to be charged the tourist price in Changsha which is Y3.70. (As the girl behind the ticket window in Changsha told me 'Foreign friends in China must pay more' – I almost reached through and strangled her). The train back to Changsha departs Shaoshan at 4.30 pm and arrives in Changsha at 8.05 pm, so you can make the village a day-trip if you want to.

**Plane** Changsha is connected by air to Beijing (Y179), Canton (Y68), Chengdu (Y129), Chongqing (Y95), Guilin (Y54), Hangzhou (Y96), Lanzhou (Y208), Shanghai (Y116), Wuhan (Y38), Xian (Y145), Zhengzhou (Y98).

## YEUYANG

Yeuyang is a stop for the ferries which ply the Yangtse River from Chongqing to Wuhan. The Wuhan-Canton railway passes through this small town; if you are heading down to Canton you can get off here rather than go all the way to Wuhan. That's really the only reason for coming here; it's a neat little town, but there's nothing of special interest that would make it a destination in itself apart from being a place untrampled by tourists. The opposite bank of the river is a vast green plain, punctuated by villages. There's a regular ferry which takes trucks and buses across the river and you might try some hitching and exploring.

### Information & Orientation

Yeuyang lies on the southern bank of the Yangtse River. There are two sections; the southern section where you'll find the railway station, the hotel, etc, and the northern section several km away where the Yangtse ferries dock. CITS has its office at the tourist hotel. The guy here speaks communicable English and is very friendly and helpful.

### Things to See

The chief attraction is the **Yeuyang Tower**, an old pagoda near the riverfront. It's best described as 'leafy' since it has small trees growing out of the accumulated dirt along its tiers. To get there, walk down the street directly in front of the railway station and turn right at the end of this street – walk straight ahead and you'll soon come to the tower which lies off the main street up a small laneway, surrounded by houses.

Further north is the **Yeuyang Pavilion**, which appears to have been an old temple complex and is now being restored.

To the south-west of the town is the enormous **Dongting Lake**, the second largest body of fresh water in the country, covering an area of 3900 square km. There are several islands in the lake, the most notable being Junshan where the Chinese grow 'silver needle tea'. When the tea is added to hot water it's supposed to remain on the surface of the water, sticking up like tiny needles and should emit a fragrant odour. Junshan Island can be reached by boat. Walk north along the road past the Yeuyang Tower; you'll come to a street market on your left. Turn left and walk to the end of the market, down the flight of steps and turn right. Straight ahead you'll see a grotty light blue and white concrete building which is the ticket office for the boat to the island. There's at least one boat at around 12 noon (though there's probably one earlier than that) returning to Yeuyang at 4pm.

### Places to Stay

There's a tourist hotel in the town, readily identifiable by what looks like a concrete airliner tail at the front – imagination in architecture knows no bounds here! No single rooms but doubles are Y30 and a bed in a triple is Y12. The hotel is about 20 minutes' walk from the railway station, or else take bus No 4 from the railway station and get off at the first stop. From there the hotel is another five minutes walk up the road on the left-hand side.

There don't appear to be any hotels in the vicinity of the railway station. There are at least two fairly large Chinese hotels in the town – refer to the map for directions – and these may be worth trying if you're on a tight budget.

## Places to Eat

The tourist hotel has a good restaurant, though quite expensive at Y6 per meal; you get little plates of vegetables, fish, meat and rice. Open 7.30 to 8.30 am, 12 noon to 1 pm and 5.30 to 6.30 pm.

Less expensive and somewhat more imaginative food is available at the little food stalls along the market street which leads down from the railway station. A bottle of *Changsha Piju* is Y1 and it's a fine brew.

## Getting Away

**Train** Yeuyang is on the main Canton-Beijing railway line. It's a four hour trip by express train to Wuhan, to Changsha it's two hours, and to Canton about 13 hours.

**Boat** The Yangtse ferries dock at the pier in the northern section of the town. There may be buses at the pier which meet the boat, but if not the bus stop is nearby; walk out of the booking hall, turn right and follow the road around for about 10 minutes and this will take you straight to

the bus stop. The bus fare to the southern section of Yeuyang is Y0.30 and it's about a 35 to 40-minute ride.

## ZHUZHOU

Unlike nearby Changsha, Zhuzhou is an entirely modern town and owed its sudden development to the completion of the Canton-Wuhan railway line back in 1937. Formerly a small market town it became a river port for the shipment of coal, later becoming an important rail junction town and a centre for the manufacture of railway equipment, locomotives and rolling stock.

It's still a major rail junction, the Beijing-Canton and the Shanghai-Kunming rail lines intersect here. There's nothing of particular interest but you may come here to change trains.

There is at least one hotel in Zhuzhou which you can stay in. Leaving the railway station, turn right along the small road in front of the station and then right again at the first intersection. Cross over the bridge – the hotel is a big grey concrete building a few minutes' walk down on the right-hand side. Single rooms are Y10 and doubles are Y20. A bed in a four-bed room is Y8.

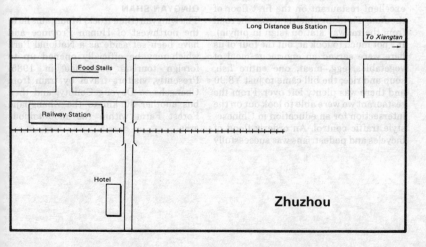

Zhuzhou

Best places to eat are the small food stalls just near the railway station. Walk down the main street directly in front of the railway station; on the right is a small side-street, lined with stalls where you can get some excellently-cooked food. But agree on the price beforehand or they'll charge you the earth.

If you're coming into Zhuzhou by bus from Xiangtan, the bus terminates on Zhuzhou's main street; continue straight ahead to the railway station, a half-hour walk or you can take the local bus.

## HENGYANG

Hengyang is the major town of southern Hunan, and like Zhuzhou grew rapidly after the construction of the Canton-Wuhan railway line in 1937. The town became a major lead and zinc mining centre. Its industry was badly damaged during the later stages of World War II and though it was restored after 1949, the town was overshadowed by the growth of Zhuzhou and Changsha. Today it's a rather dull industrial town on the Beijing-Canton rail line. Travellers who take the train from Canton to Guilin have to stop here for a couple of hours waiting for a connection.

One of the delights of Hengyang is the excellent restaurant on the first floor of the *Jiang Fandian* which is across the road from the railway station (sign in pinyin). It's not much to look at, but the four of us here were served an enormous meal of vegetables, egg, meat, one entire fish, soup and rice; the bill came to just Y8.90 and there was plenty left over. From the restaurant we were able to look out on the intersection for an education in Chinese-style traffic control. An orderly flood of bicycles and pedestrians was successfully maintained by an elderly but energetic official who simply harangued anyone who didn't obey the road rules.

There's at least one hotel in Hengyang which may take you; it's about a 10-minute walk directly down the street in front of the station and a bed in a triple is Y10. There are two town centres, one close to the hotel and one across the river. There's a small but interesting street market off to the side of the Jiang Fandian.

## XIANGTAN

Once a river port and market centre, Xiangtan stagnated early this century when the railway took away much of its trade. The Kuomintang gave it a kick by getting its industry going in the late 1930s and this was expanded by the Communists. Today, Xiangtan is a rather flat, hot, drab town of 300,000 people lying on the Shanghai-Kunming rail line. From the long-distance bus station there are buses to Shaoshan, a 1½ hour ride passing by several small villages located in some neat countryside. There are regular buses from Xiangtan to Zhuzhou, a 1¼ hour ride costing Y0.65. There are also buses to Changsha.

## QINGYAN SHAN

The Qingyan (Blue Rock) Mountains lie in the northwest of Hunan Province and have been set aside as a National Park which may be officially opened up to foreign tourists sometime in 1985. Presently, visitors travel by train from Changsha to Dayong County, and then bus another 30 km to the Zhangjiajie Forest Farm within the mountainous area.

# Jiangxi

Jiangxi was incorporated into the Chinese empire at an early date, but it remained sparsely populated until the 8th century. Before this the main expansion of the Han Chinese had been from the north into Hunan and then into Guangdong. But the building of the Grand Canal from the 7th century onwards opened up the south-eastern regions and Jiangxi became an important transit point on the trade and shipment route overland from Guangdong. Before long the human traffic diverted into Jiangxi and between the 8th and 13th century the region was rapidly settled by Chinese peasants; the development of silver mining and tea growing also allowed the development of a wealthy Jiangxi merchant class. But by the 19th century its role as a major transport route from Canton was much reduced by the opening of coastal ports to foreign shipping – which also helped the Chinese junk trade into a steady decline. Jiangxi also bears the distinction of having been one of the most famous of the Communist guerilla bases – and it was only after several years of war that the Kuomintang were able to drive the Communists out on their 'Long March' to Shaanxi.

## NANCHANG

The capital of Jiangxi Province, Nanchang is largely remembered in modern Chinese history for the Communist-led uprising of 1 August 1927. After Chiang Kai-shek staged his massacre of Communists and other opponents in March 1927, what was left of the Communist Party fled underground and a state of confusion reigned. It was a time when the Chinese Communist Party was dominated by a policy of urban revolution, believing that victory could only be won by organising insurrections in the cities. Units of the Kuomintang Army led by Communist officers happened to be concentrated around Nanchang at the time, and there appeared to be an opportunity for a successful insurrection.

On 1 August, a combined army of 30,000 under the leadership of Zhou Enlai and Zhu De siezed the city and held it for several days until they were driven out by troops loyal to the Nanjing regime. The revolt was largely a fiasco, but it is marked in Chinese history as the beginning of the Red Army. The Army retreated from Nanchang south to Guangdong. But part of it, led by Zhu De, circled back to Jiangxi and joined forces with the rag-tag army that Mao Zedong had organised in Hunan and led up into the Jinggangshan Mountains. Still locked into policies of urban insurrection, Nanchang was one of the cities which the Communists (unsuccessfully) attacked, along with Changsha, until Mao and Zhu broke with the Party leadership and shifted the focus of the revolution to the countryside and the peasants.

Not all of Nanchang's history has been so tumultuous – in fact, the name means 'southern prosperity'. It was founded back in the Eastern Han Dynasty and became a busy trading city, a major staging post on the trade route from Guangdong to Beijing, and also a major distribution point for the kaolin pottery of nearby Jingdezhen. Since 1949 it has grown into another of China's multi-purpose industrial urban organised sprawls with something like 2½ million inhabitants.

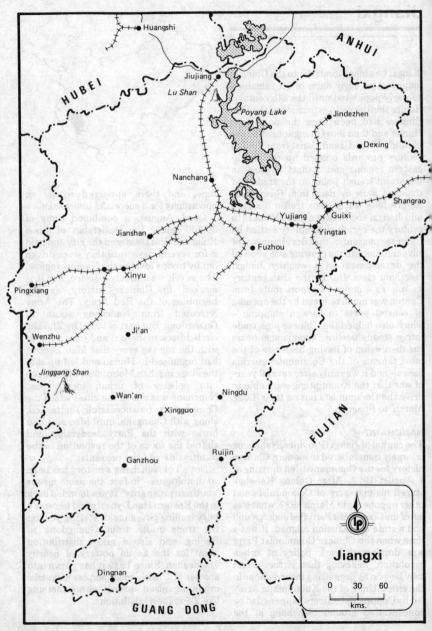

Map labels:

ANHUI

HUBEI

Huangshi

Jiujiang

*Lu Shan*

*Poyang Lake*

Jindezhen

Dexing

Nanchang

Shangrao

Yujiang

Guixi

Yingtan

Jianshan

Fuzhou

Xinyu

Pingxiang

Ji'an

Wenzhu

*Jinggang Shan*

Wan'an

Ningdu

Xingguo

FUJIAN

Ganzhou

Ruijin

Dingnan

GUANG DONG

Jiangxi

0    30    60
kms.

## Information & Orientation

Nanchang is bounded to the north by the Gan River and to the west by the Fu River which branches off the Gan. The railway station is in the south-east of the city; Dongfeng Lu runs westwards from the station and into Bayi Lu. Bayi Lu is the main artery and cuts a circuitous route through the centre of town, finally leaving the north-west over the Bayi Bridge across the Gan River. Most of the 'sights' and the tourist facilities are scattered along or are in the immediate vicinity of Bayi Lu; the centre of town is the ugly People's Square at the intersection of Bayi Lu and Renmin Lu.

**CITS** have their office at the Jiangxi Binguan. As you face the main gateway, the office is just over on the right in a small building outside the hotel compound – it's readily identifiable by a sign that looks like two seagulls. Friendly people here, and one speaks good English and is quite helpful.

**Public Security** is located on Bayi Lu a short distance east of the Hongdu Hotel in a walled-in government compound (look for the PLA guard at the gate).

**CAAC** is on Dongfeng Road, approximately 10 minutes' walk westwards from the railway station.

**Post** There is a post office on the ground floor of the Jiangxi Guest House. There is another on Bayi Lu just south of the Exhibition Hall opposite the People's Square.

**Maps** Good maps in Chinese showing the bus routes are available from the reception desk in the Jiangxi Guest House. There are larger maps available from the bookstore next to the large Exhibition Hall on Bayi Lu, opposite the People's Square.

## Things to See

The poor man's Beijing; the mattest of greys, the most depressing of all Chinese cities. This is colour deprivation at its worst, the whole length of Bayi Lu stricken with drab concrete blocks.

The People's Square is the heart of it all. A dismal sort of piazza built in the Mussolini Modern style. It's too small to be monolithic and too big to be comfortable. The Monument to the Martyrs stands here – stone pillar and gun atop what looks like a ship's funnel but is probably a flag. Opposite, on Bayi Lu, stands the immense off-yellow Exhibition Hall capped with red flags and a beaming portrait of a younger Chairman Mao. On the other side of the square stands a pavilion of petrified red flags. Across the narrow street from the martyr's monument is a grey building (the Jiangxi Provincial Museum?) slowly transforming itself into an archaeological site – in front of it stands a hideous petrified stone garden. Once you've fled the piazza you might try some street-walking around the old residential districts down near the river – the houses are built for mere mortals though they're equally as drab.

Most of the sights are reminders of the Communist Revolution and include the **Memorial Hall to the Martyrs of the Revolution** on Bayi Lu to the north of the People's Square; the **Residence of Zhou En-lai & Zhu De** on Changzhang Lu and the **Former Headquarters of the Nanchang Uprising** near the corner of Shengli and Zhongshan Lu which has now been converted into a museum.

## Places to Stay

The best place to stay is the *Hongdu Hotel* a pleasant place with exceptionally friendly staff. They don't really seem to want foreigners, but if enough show up they'll probably reconcile themselves to accepting us – certainly give this place a try before you go to the Jiangxi Hotel. Room prices seem a bit variable, but I got a double room (with toilet and shower) for just Y10. Take bus No 2 eight stops from the railway station – the hotel wil be just a few minutes' walk further up the road.

The *Jiangxi Guest House* is the big tourist joint – it's one of the most depressing hotels I have ever had the good fortune not to have to stay in. The ultimate in ugliness, sterility – a matt grey/brown tower set in a dismal walled-in compound, the interior simply reeks *cold*. Cheapest rooms are Y30 for a double, and it's very unlikely you'll get a discount if you're on your own. The front entrance to the hotel faces out onto Bayi Lu but this is now closed up. To get into the hotel you have to walk down the street on the side of the compound and enter through the main gate.

### Places to eat

The *Hongdu Hotel* is probably the best place to eat. You can get three meals per day here for just Y3 – nothing spectacular but it is decent food. The *Jiangxi Guest House* has a restaurant which should be worth checking out. Other than that there's not much to recommend; the food in the many small restaurants near the train station looks positively poisonous, though you might give the street stalls a try.

### Getting Around

You're reliant almost exclusively on buses – but one advantage is that the people here seem to be a bit more civilised about loading themselves on board the things than in other Chinese cities. There are pedal rickshaws and three-wheeler scooters which hang around the railway station, but I never saw any on the streets. You should be able to hire taxis from the Jiangxi Guest House.

### Getting Away

**Bus** The long-distance bus station is on Bayi Lu, midway between the People's Square and the railway station. The ticket office is open 5.10 am to 7 pm.

From here you can take the early-morning bus to Guling the main hill-station astride beautiful Lu Shan. The fare is Y5.30 and the bus *might* take you on a tour of some of the sights around Lu Shan before reaching Guling.

There are also buses from Nanchang to Juijiang on the Yangtse River (Y4.85), and to Jingdezhen (Y6.35).

**Train** Nanchang lies just off the main Canton-Shanghai rail but many trains make the short detour north and pass through the city. There is also a railway line from Nanchang heading north to the Yangtse river port of Jiujiang.

**Air** Nanchang is connected by air to Beijing (Y189), Canton (Y81), Changsha (Y37), Fuzhou (Y61), Ganzhou in southern Jiangxi (Y44), Hangzhou (Y59), Jingdezhen (Y23), Shanghai (Y79).

### JINGDEZHEN

Jingdezhen is an ancient town that was once famous for the manufacture of much-coveted porcelain. Earthenware production has a long history in China, beginning with the primitive pottery of prehistoric times. As much as 8000 years ago primitive Chinese tribes were making earthenware artefacts with clay. The primitive 'Yangshao' culture (so named because the first example of the earliest agricultural villages was excavated near the village of Yangshao, near the confluence of the Yellow, Fen and Wei Rivers) is noted for its distinctive painted pottery, with flowers, fish, animals and sometimes human faces and geometric designs painted on by brush. Around 3500 BC the 'Lungshanoid' culture (so named because it was near the village of Lungshan in Shandong Province that the first evidence of this ancient culture was excavated) was making egg shell thin black pottery, as well as a type of white pottery.

Pottery-making was well advanced by the Shang period, and the most important advance occurred around the middle of the dynasty with the manufacture of a high-fired greenish glaze applied to stoneware artefacts. It was during the Han Dynasty that the custom of glazing pottery became fairly common. A yellowish-grey glaze applied to a reddish surface, for example, resulted after firing in a pale shade of green. The production of terracotta pottery – made of a mixture of sand and clay, fired to produce a reddish-brown colour and left unglazed – continued, however.

During the Southern and Northern

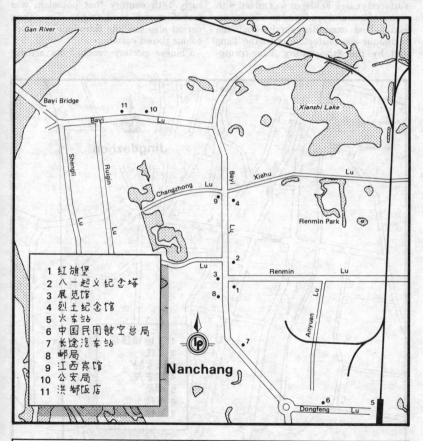

Gan River

Bayi Bridge

11
10

Bayi    Lu

Shengli    Lu

Ruijin    Lu

Changzhong    Lu

Xianshi Lake

Xiahu    Lu

Bayi    Lu

9
4

Renmin Park

2

Lu

Renmin    Lu

3

8
1

Anyuan    Lu

7

**Nanchang**

6
5

Dongfeng    Lu

1 红旗堡
2 八一起义纪念塔
3 展览馆
4 烈士纪念馆
5 火车站
6 中国民用航空总局
7 长途汽车站
8 邮局
9 江西宾馆
10 公安局
11 洪都饭店

| 1 Monument to the Matyrs | 6 CAAC |
| 2 Red Flag Pavilion | 7 Long Distance Bus Station |
| 3 Exhibition Hall | 8 Post Office |
| 4 Memorial Hall to the Matyrs of the Revolution | 9 Jianxi Guest House |
| 5 Railway Station | 10 Public Security Office |
| | 11 Hongdu Hotel |

Dynasties period a type of proto-porcelain was developed. This is a type of pottery halfway between Han glazed pottery and true porcelain. The proto-porcelain was made by mixing clay with quartz and the mineral feldspar to make a hard smooth-surfaced vessel. Feldspar was mixed with traces of iron and produced an olive-green glaze. Few examples survive but the technique was perfected under the Tang and by the 8th century Tang proto-porcelain and other types of pottery found an international market – and were exported as far afield as Japan and the east coast of Africa. Chinese porcelain did not find its way into Europe until the Ming period and it was not until the 17th or early 18th century that porcelain was manufactured in Europe. The Tang period also saw the introduction of tri-colour glazed vessels.

Chinese pottery reached its artistic

| 1 | Jingdezhen Hotel | 5 | Post Office |
| 2 | Jingdezhen Guesthouse | 6 | Street Market |
| 3 | Railway Station | 7 | Long Distance Bus Station |
| 4 | Public Security Office | | |

peak under the Song. During this time true porcelain was developed; made of fine gaolin clay, white, thin, transparent or translucent. The art of the Song is generally regarded as the finest China has ever produced. The production of porcelain continued under the Yuan but gradually lost the delicacy and near-perfection of the Song period; nevertheless it was probably during this time that the 'blue and white' porcelain – as it became known under the Ming – made its first appearance.

The blue and white type, blue decoration on a white background, was obtained from the gaolin clay quarried near Jingdezhen coupled with a type of cobalt imported from Persia. Also produced during this period were the three-colour and five-colour porcelain (the former usually green, yellow and violet, the latter with light blue and red as well) with floral decorations on a white background. Another notable invention was mono-coloured porcelain, in ferrous red, black or dark blue.

The tradition continued under the Qing with the addition of new colours and glazes and more complex decorations. This is the age of true painted porcelain, decorated with delicate landscapes, birds and flowers –though at the same time a range of new monocolour vessels was being developed.

Today Jingdezhen still makes porcelain and other ceramics and the smoke-stacks litter the town, but the quality is not what it once was. The town took off in the 12th century when the Song Dynasty fled south in the wake of the Jurchen invasion from the north of China. The Song court moved to Hangzhou and the imperial potters moved to Jingdezhen, near Gaolin village and the rich supply of gaolin clay. Today 30,000 of Jingdezhen's 250,000 people are employed in the Jingdezhen ceramics industry.

## Information & Orientation

Jingdezhen lies mostly on the eastern bank of the Chang River. The main arteries are Zhongshan Lu and Jiushan Lu, and the area between the river and Zhongshan Lu is the older part of town and the more interesting. The long-distance bus station is inconveniently located on the western bank of the river, and the railway station is in the south-eastern part of town. Various travellers' survival facilities, restaurants, hotels, etc, are all located in the central city area and are all within fairly easy walking distance of each other.

**CITS** appears to have gone into hiding – but you might try the Jingdezhen Guest House for enquiries, tickets, etc.

**Public Security Office** is about a 15-minute walk from the Jingdezhen Hotel. Turn right at the front entrance and then turn right again at the first intersection. The PSO is about a five-minute walk up this road in a walled in compound. Amiable lot, and they have one or two people around who speak very good English.

**Post** There is a post office on Jiushan Donglu, west of the Jingdezhen Hotel.

**Maps** There are very good maps (in Chinese and showing the bus routes) available from the Jingdezhen Guest House.

## Things to See

The town is littered with pottery factories, many of them cottage industries carried on behind enclosed courtyards. The government showpiece factory is the Jingdezhen People's Porcelain Factory at 54 Fengling Lu (tel 498) and you'll also find the Jingdezhen Porcelain Friendship Store at 13 Zhushan Lu (tel 231).

The best parts of the town to wander around are the little side streets which lead off Zhongshan Lu, particularly those between Zhongshan Lu and the river. Tiny streets, barely 1½ metres wide are flooded with washing strung out between the houses. The washing is particularly preponderant along the river bank where there's a solid wall of it stretching along the entire street. They're all old houses in this area, with large wooden doors that are removed in summer so that the whole house is ventilated.

## Places to Stay

Centrally located is the *Jingdezhen Hotel*. It's a big building and almost looks imposing the way it's set up on its little mound of dirt above the main street. But the rooms are as basic as any other Chinese hotel. There's a great range of rooms here, but you may have to fight for a decent price. You should probably expect them to charge you around about Y18 for a double room. They also wanted payment for the room in FECs, though their restaurant readily accepted RMB. To get to the hotel take bus No 2 from either the bus station or the railway station; it goes straight past the hotel.

The *Jingdezhen Guest House* is the tourist joint about a 15-minute walk from the Jingdezhen Hotel. The guest house is a pleasant building surrounded by trees, and the compound is next to a lake. Single rooms are Y16, doubles are Y32 and they say there is no dormitory.

## Places to eat

There's an excellent restaurant at 496 Zhongshan Beilu where you can get a *big* meal for around Y6, including beer – good food and they may have a few oddities. People are friendly here too. Eat upstairs since the ground floor is dingy. The *Jingdezhen Hotel* has an OK restaurant.

## Getting Around

The central part of town is small enough to walk around. Bus No 2 runs between the long-distance bus station, through the centre of town, and out to the railway station.

## Getting Away

**Bus** The bus to Yingtan departs at 10 am; the fare is Y3.75.

There are buses to Juijiang departing at 6.40 am and 7.25 am, the fare is Y4. There are also buses to Nanchang and the fare is around Y6.

There is a bus from Tunxi at 7.10 am; the fare is Y4.85. From Tunxi you can take a bus to Huang Shan; there is no direct bus from Jingdezhen.

**Train** Jingdezhen is connected by a branch line to the railway junction of *Yingtan* and there are two trains a day, around 6.05 am and 2.17 pm. You can expect to be charged tourist-price which is Y4.90 for a hard seat. It's a beautiful ride past lush paddy fields, and takes about 4½ hours. Heading north there are trains to Wuhu via Tunxi.

**Air** Jingdezhen is connected by air to Nanchang (Y23).

## JIUJIANG

Jiujiang has been a river port on the Yangtse for over a thousand years, and a treaty port from 1862 onwards. Situated near the Poyang Lake which drains into the Yangtze, Jiujiang has been a natural outlet for Jiangxi's trade. After it was opened to foreign trade it became a port not only for Jiangxi but also for eastern Hubei and Anhui.

Today Jiujiang has taken on another role as the transit station for hordes of Chinese tourists on their way to nearby Lu Shan. The done thing in Jiujiang seems to be to buy a notched walking-stick and a unisex, ribboned sun-bonnet, and then parade around in front of everyone else. When they're not strutting around they're inevitably having photos of themselves taken in front of anything that remotely resembles a 'sight'.

## Information & Orientation

Jiujiang is stretched out along the south bank of the Yangtse River. The long-distance bus station is in the eastern part of town and the railway station is at the western end; the harbour is located

1 上海客轮码头
2 轮度码头
3 长途汽车站
4 南湖宾馆
5 塔
6 火车站
7 博物馆
8 东风饭店

*Yantse River*

*To Shanghai*

*To Wuhan*

**Jiujiang**

| | |
|---|---|
| 1 Yangtse River Ferry Dock | 5 Pagoda |
| 2 Local Ferry Across River | 6 Railway Station |
| 3 Long Distance Bus Station | 7 Museum |
| 4 Nanhu Guesthouse | 8 Dong Fang Hotel |

midway between the two in a narrow urban neck squashed between the river and the lake. In between the harbour and the lake are the hotels, restaurants, shops and other facilities vital to the living organism – all within easy tentacle distance of each other.

### Things to See

Apart from the yellow hordes who are a day's entertainment in themselves, there's a seven-storey pagoda in the south-east of the town which is worth a look. The Museum is in a quaint old temple offshore in the lake near the centre of town and connected by a zig-zag bridge. There's an interesting collection of prehistoric tools and weapons (no captions in English

though) and the building itself is a quaint structure. It's open 8 to 10.45 am and 2 to 5 pm.

### Places to stay

The *Dong Fang Hotel* is a 10-minute walk from the boat dock and is situated on Xunyang Lu. They may try and send you off to the Nanhu Hotel, but hold your ground since they are allowed to take foreigners. It's not a bad hotel if you don't mind the warehouse-palatial style. A bed in a triple starts at around Y2.50; they gave me a room to myself for just Y7.50. Try to avoid the rooms facing the street though, as it's very noisy. To get to the hotel from the dock walk straight up Jiaotong Lu and then turn left when you reach the intersection with the road which fronts the lake and turn left for the hotel. To get to the hotel from the long-distance bus station or the train station, take bus No 1 and get off at the stop out front of the museum (that's the old building sitting offshore in the lake – you can't miss it) and then walk the last few minutes to the hotel.

The *Nanhu Guest House* is the tourist hotel. It's a big, hotel set next to the lake and very inconveniently located on the eastern side of it. Double rooms are Y16 (possibly more). There doesn't appear to be a bus out here; it's a long walk from the station but you may find an autorickshaw around the dock or the train or bus station which could take you there.

### Places to Eat
There are a couple of places around the dock and on the streets close to the Dong Fang Hotel – most of them OK but not memorable. One fairly good place is right on the corner of Jiaotong Lu and the road which runs parallel to the river – but be persistent as it's rather difficult to get served here. Two plates of meat and vegetables and a huge bowl of rice for about Y1.60 is more than enough for two people.

### Getting Around
Bus No 1 runs the length of Jiujiang from the long-distance bus station in the east past the South Lake to the railway station in the western part of the town. Other than that there may be autorickshaws around the train and bus stations and the dock.

### Getting Away
**Bus** Buses to Jingdezhen depart around 6 am and the trip takes about 5½ hours, including one river crossing by barge – you may get to Jingdezhen a bit earlier if you don't have to wait too long at the river. A good part of the road is unsurfaced, but the last half of the trip is interesting since

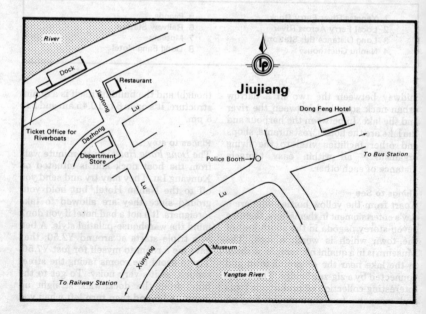

you pass through a number of small villages and there's a rest stop for about half an hour in one of them. It's neat, rolling countryside. The fare is Y4.

The earliest buses to Lu Shan depart around 5.45 am with several departures in the early morning and possibly some in the early afternoon; the fare is Y1.30.

**Train** Jiujiang is connected by rail southwards to Nanchang and there are several trains per day. There is also a 216 metre span railway bridge being built across the Yangtse River at Jiujiang and presumably this will eventually link Juijiang (and Nanchang) with Hefei, the capital of Anhui.

**Boats** Juijiang lies on the Yangtse, and from here you can get boats to Wuhan or to Shanghai, stopping off at various ports in between.

## LU SHAN

Every so often China throws up something that takes you completely by surprise. A village lifted lock stock and barrel out of Switzerland and grafted onto a Chinese mountain top is just about the last thing you'd expect – but here is Lu Shan and its humble chunks of European architecture pitted amongst the foliage.

Situated at the very north of Jiangxi Province, this mountain is regarded as one of the most beautiful in China. Established as a hill resort by the foreign settlers in China in the 19th and 20th centuries, the top of the mountain is dotted with European-style stone cottages, churches and hotels. The bus ride up from the plains of Jiangxi to the top of Lu Shan is equally dramatic; the road winds its way around the mountainside looking down on sheer cliffs and over the long drop below you can look out over immense terraced plains.

The mountain belies its significance in the destiny of a billion Chinese. It was here in 1959 that the Central Commitee of the Communist Party held its fateful meeting which eventually ended in the dismissal of Peng Dehuai, sent Mao almost into a political wilderness and provided the seeds of the rise and fall of Liu Shaoqi and Deng Xiaoping. Then in 1970 another meeting was held in Lu Shan, this time of the Politburo –exactly what happened is shrouded in as much mist as the mountain itself, but it seems that Lin Biao clashed with Mao, opposed his policies towards rapprochement with the USA and probably proposed the continuation of the xenophobic policies of the Cultural Revolution. Whatever, Lin was dead the next year.

## Information & Orientation

The bus puts you off at Guling, the main hill station. The hill station is scattered right out across the mountain top, and the 'centre' of Guling is little more than the street where the buses pull in and where many of the larger restaurants, shops and long-distance bus station are lined up. The Lu Shan Hotel and the various tourist facilities are either here or within easy walking distance.

**CITS** (tel 2275, and ask for Liu) The office is located at one of the gateways to the Lu Shan Hotel. Liu speaks good English and is very friendly and helpful. The office is open 7.30 to 11.30 am, 2.30 to 6 pm and 7.30 to 9.30 pm.

**Public Security** is located a short walk from the bus station – see the map in this book for directions. The office is open 9 am to 5 pm (probably closed for a few hours in the middle of the day and probably all day Sunday).

**Maps** There are excellent maps available from the shops in Guling; they show all the tracks and roads and are very accurate and detailed. They're also available from the counter in the dining room of the Lu Shan Hotel.

## Things to See

The best thing to do here is take off along the innumerable paths and tracks and just explore; the houses are beautiful, tasteful affairs and it's not hard to get away from the crowds (and their numbers in this hill resort – a favourite with the Chinese – are quite phenomenal).

There are a couple of designated 'sights' which are OK – but be warned that the route is trampled *en masse*. You can do the circuit from the hotel to **Dragon Head Cliff** via **Three Ancient Trees**, then follow the road to the **Fairy Cave** and back to the hotel via the lake in around five to six hours of easy walking; even less if you don't stop or detour.

The best views out on the plains of Jiangxi below are from the track which leads out from the Fairy Cave; there's a rugged, rocky cliff face with a sheer drop below, and the plains outstretched beyond. Three Ancient Trees are little more than three rather largish trees each with a low fence around them – but that doesn't deter the old Chinese men from climbing high into the branches to – yes, you guessed it – have their photo taken at this 'sight'.

### Places to Stay

The *Lu Shan Hotel* is the main tourist hotel and is an old colonial building. One person said it was German-built, another that it used to be the old British hospital circa 1930. Double rooms here are Y30. There are no singles but they'll readily give you a double for Y15 if you're on your own. They also have dormitory beds for Y4 in a room with four beds, but there's nowhere to wash. The hotel is about a 15-minute walk from the bus terminus; go straight ahead from where the bus pulls in to where the road curves around. On your left you'll see a long flight of steps leading down to another road – turn right and this will take you to the hotel which is a 10-minute walk down on the right-hand side.

The *Luling Binguan* sits beside beautiful Luling Lake. The hotel is stunning though the rooms are spartan. Double rooms are Y30, or Y15 if you're on your own. They don't have a dormitory.

The *Yuzhhong Hotel* is a much smaller hotel than the first two and is down the road from the Lu Shan. Singles Y16 and Doubles Y32.

### Places to Eat

There are a number of large restaurants along Guling's main street near the bus station, but nothing I'd really recommend. Food at the Lu Shan Hotel is nothing amazing either; meals are Y2 per person and helpings tend to be on the small side. There is another restaurant at the Luling Hotel.

### Getting Around

The central area of Guling is very compact and you can see quite a lot on foot. The surrounding area is dotted everywhere with old houses and there are well-defined tracks and narrow roads everywhere. Watch out for some low-slung power lines in the bushy areas between the tracks.

There are bus tours which take you down to Juijiang via some of the sights on Lu Shan. The tours cost Y6; one goes to Juijiang via the sights on the eastern side of the mountain and one via the western side. Apparently there's more to see on the eastern side. Tickets from the little shed on the same street as the bus station.

### Getting Away

The only way out of Lu Shan is by bus. Book ahead for all buses if possible, since Lu Shan is crowded with tourists and there are constant hordes of Chinese coming and going.

The bus to Nanchang departs at 6.30 am; the fare is Y6.05.

Buses to **Jiujiang** depart at 7.30 am, 8 am, 8.05 am, 8.50 am, 1.10 pm, 3.05 pm and 3.10 pm; the fare is Y1.30.

## YINGTAN

Yingtan is a major rail junction. Nanchang is north of the main Shanghai-Canton line and though most trains make the short

Jiangxi 293

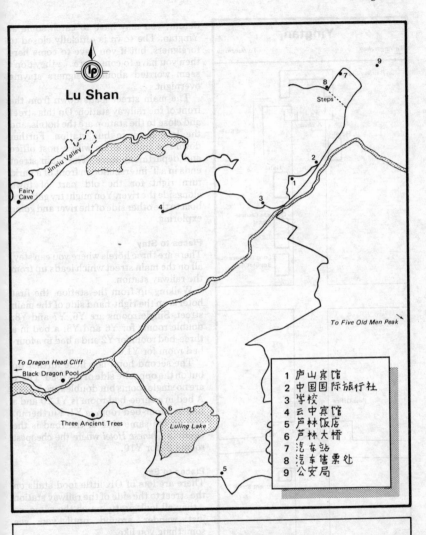

1 庐山宾馆
2 中国国际旅行社
3 学校
4 云中宾馆
5 芦林饭店
6 芦林大桥
7 汽车站
8 汽车售票处
9 公安局

1 Lushan Hotel
2 CITS
3 School
4 Yunzhong (Yunchung)
  Guest House
5 Luling Hotel
6 Luling Bridge
7 Buses to Jiujiang & Nanchang
8 Booking Office for Bus Tours
9 Public Security Office

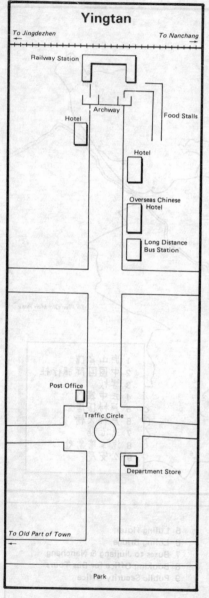

**Yingtan**

To Jingdezhen — To Nanchang

Railway Station

Archway

Hotel

Food Stalls

Hotel

Overseas Chinese Hotel

Long Distance Bus Station

Post Office

Traffic Circle

Department Store

To Old Part of Town

Park

detour, you may have to catch some at Yingtan. The town is officially closed to foreigners, but if you have to come here then you have to come here . . . they don't seem worried about foreigners staying overnight.

The main street leads down from the front of the railway station. On this street and close to the station are the hotels, and the long-distance bus station. Further down is a traffic circle with a post office and department store. The main street ends in a T-intersection in front of a park; turn right for the old part of town alongside the river. You might try getting a boat to the other side of the river and going exploring.

### Places to Stay

There are three hotels where you can stay, all on the main street which leads up from the railway station.

Walking up from the station, the first hotel is on the right-hand side of the main street. Single rooms are Y6, Y7 and Y8; double rooms for Y6 and Y8; a bed in a three-bed room for Y2 and a bed in a four-bed room for Y1.6

The second hotel is a little further up but on the opposite side of the road. There are no single rooms but doubles are Y3.60. A bed in a three-bed room is Y1.20 and a bed in a four-bed room is Y1. Further up and on the same side of the road is the *Overseas Chinese Hotel* where the cheapest rooms go for Y10.

### Places to Eat

There are lots of OK little food-stalls on the street to the side of the railway station – they all look pretty much the same, so just wander around until you see something you like.

### Getting Away

**Bus** The long-distance bus station is right next to the Overseas Chinese Hotel. The ticket office is open 5 to 7 am, 8 to 11.30 am and 1 to 7 pm. The bus for Jingdezhen departs at 7 am.

**Trains** Yingtan is a rail junction and from here you can catch trains to Fuzhou, Xiamen, Shanghai, Canton and Kunming.

**To Jingdezhen** – there is a line which stretches northwards to Jingdezhen, a 4½-hour ride through beautiful, rolling green paddy fields. Hard seat is about Y2.80.

**To Hangzhou** – a long trip. Hard seat is Y10.20 (local price) and hard-sleeper is Y17.00 (local price).

## THE JINGGANG MOUNTAINS

Located in the middle of the Luoxiao Range on the Hunan-Jiangxi border, the Jinggang Mountains are a remote region famed for their connection with the early Communist movement. It was into these hills that the Communist leaders led their rag-tag armies to begin the struggle against the Kuomintang and it was from here that the Long March began. The main township in the area is Ciping, surrounded on all sides by the hills, 320 km south-west of Nanchang. There are probably buses here from Nanchang.

# Zhejiang

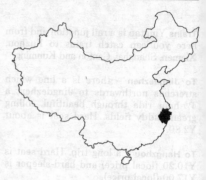

Thirty-nine million people squash into one of China's smallest provinces. The importance of Zhejiang has always been out of proportion to its size and the province has traditionally been considered one of the most prosperous in China.

The region falls into two distinct parts. The area north of Hangzhou is part of the lush Yangtse River delta, similar to the southern region of Jiangsu Province. The south is mountainous, a continuation of the rugged terrain of Fujian Province. Intensely cultivated for a thousand years, northern Zhejiang has lost most of its natural vegetation cover; a flat, featureless plain with a dense network of waterways, canals and irrigation channels, this is also the end of the Grand Canal. Zhejiang was part of the great southern granary from which food was shipped to the depleted areas of the north.

The growth of Zhejiang's towns was based on their proximity to the sea and their location in some of China's most highly productive farmland. Hangzhou, Ningbo and Shaoxing have all been important trading centres and ports since the 7th and 8th centuries, and their growth was accelerated when the Song Dynasty moved court to Hangzhou in the wake of a northern invasion in the 12th century. Silk was one of the popular exports and today Zhejiang is known as the 'land of silk' producing one-third of China's raw silk, brocade and satin.

Hangzhou is the capital of the province, and to the south-east of the city are several places you can visit without backtracking; a road and railway line runs east from Hangzhou to Shaoxing and Ningbo. From Ningbo you could take a bus to Tiantai Shan and from there either bus back to Hangzhou or continue south to Wenzhou and down the coast road into Fujian Province. Jiaxing on the Hangzhou-Shanghai railway line is also open, as is

Huzhou in the far north of Zhejiang Province on the shores of Lake Taihu.

## HANGZHOU

When Marco Polo passed through Hangzhou in the 13th century he described it as one of the finest and most splendid cities in the world. Though Hangzhou had risen to prominence when the southern end of the Grand Canal reached here at the start of the 7th century, Hangzhou really came into its own after the Song Dynasty was overthrown by the Jurchen – northern invaders, the ancestors of the Manchus who were to conquer China five centuries later. The Song capital of Kaifeng, along with the emperor and the leaders of the imperial court, were all captured by the Jurchen in 1126. The rest of the Song court fled south, finally settling at Hangzhou and founding the Southern Song Dynasty.

Whilst the north remained in the hands of the northerners – who rapidly became Sinicised anyway – the hub of the Chinese state in the south was Hangzhou. The court, the military and civil officials and merchants all congregated here and the population rose from half a million to 1¾ million by 1275. The large population and its proximity to the ocean promoted the growth of the river and sea trade, and of the navy and ship-building industries. China had gone through an economic revolution during the 8th and 12th centuries, producing huge and prosperous

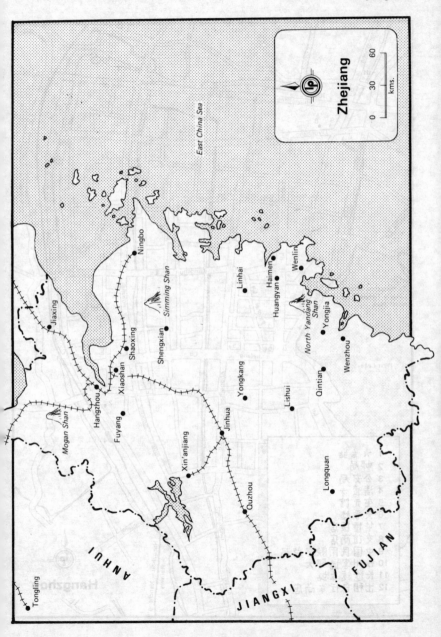

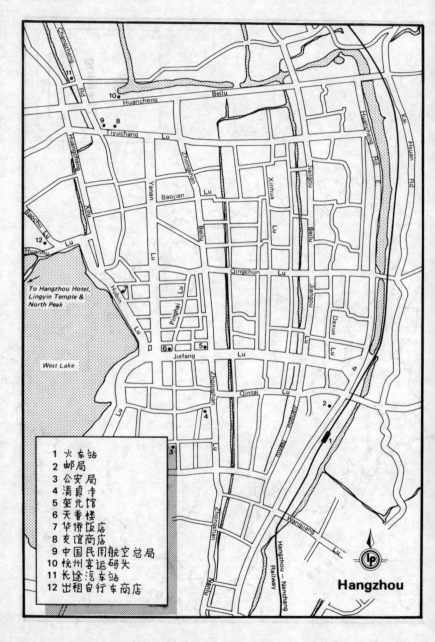

To Hangzhou Hotel, Lingyin Temple & North Peak

West Lake

1 火车站
2 邮局
3 公安局
4 清真寺
5 玺元馆
6 天香楼
7 华侨饭店
8 友谊商店
9 中国民用航空总局
10 杭州客运码头
11 长途汽车站
12 出租自行车商店

Hangzhou

cities, an advanced economy and a flourishing inter-regional trade. With the Jurchen invasion, the centre of this revolution was pushed south from the Yellow River Valley down to the lower Yangtse Valley and the sea coast between the Yangtse and Canton, and as the seat of the imperial court Hangzhou was now at the hub of it all.

When the Mongols swept into China they established their court at Beijing – but Hangzhou retained its status as a prosperous commercial city. The Franciscan Friar Odoric visited it in the 1320s and described it as follows:

Never in my life did I see so great a city. It contains in circuit a hundred miles. Neither saw I any plot thereof, which was not thoroughly inhabited. I saw many houses of ten or 12 storeys high, one above the other. It has mighty large suburbs containing more people than the city itself. Also it has twelve principal gates, and about the distance of eight miles, in the highway to every one of theses gates stands a city as big, by estimation as Venice... In this city there are more than eleven thousand bridges ... I marvelled much how such an infinite number of persons could inhabit and live together.

The city is famous in Chinese tourism for its West Lake, a large freshwater lake surrounded by hills and gardens, its banks dotted with pavilions and temples. It gives rise to what must be one of China's oldest tourist blurbs 'Above there is heaven, below there is Suzhou and Hangzhou'. Life has not always been so peaceful – in 1861 the Taipings lay siege to and captured the city and two years later the imperial armies took it back. These

campaigns reduced almost the entire city to ashes, annihalated or displaced most of the population, and finally ended Hangzhou's significance as a commercial and trading centre. Few monuments survived the devastation and those that did became victims of the Red Guards a hundred years later.

Located in the area known as 'Jiangnan' or 'South of the River' which covers southern Jiangsu and northern Zhejiang provinces, Hangzhou lies in one of the most prosperous regions of China and at first glance seems a century away from the austerity of other Chinese cities. Permanent residents only number 750,000 but on weekends they're flooded out by Chinese who day-trip down from Shanghai, Suzhou or Wuxi, and daily with tour buses carrying their cargoes of westerners Hangzhou is one of China's great tourist attractions, popularity on par with Guilin.

## Information & Orientation

Hangzhou is bounded to the south by the Qiantang River and in the west by a range of hills. Between the hills and the urban area is the large West Lake, the city's most famous tourist attraction. To the north of the city and to the south of the river are the fertile plains of Jiangnan.

The vicinity of Jiefang Lu, Zhongshan Lu and Yanan Lu is the main all-purpose shopping, restaurant, focus-of-activity, bustling-streets section of town. The local sights are scattered around the lake or in the hills to the west of the urban area. The tourist hotels, public security office, CAAC etc are scattered around the town.

1 Railway Station
2 Post Office
3 Public Security Office
4 Mosque
5 Restaurant
6 Restaurant
7 Overseas Chinese Hotel

8 Friendship Store
9 CAAC
10 Embarkation Point for Boats up the Grand Canal
11 Long Distance Bus Station
12 Bicycle Hire

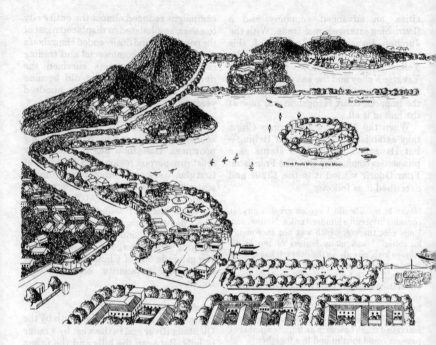

Su Causeway

Three Pools Mirroring the Moon

The older areas of Hangzhou lie back from the lake in the eastern and southern parts of town, around the small canals which cut their way through the town.

**CITS** (tel 22921) is on the ground floor of the Hangzhou Hotel at 2 Yuefen Jie. They're not very useful for information, but they're OK if you want to book tickets or get info about train, plane and bus timetables.

**CAAC** (tel 24259) is at 304 Tiyuchang Lu. The booking desk is open 8 to 11.30 am and 1.30 pm to 5 pm. A taxi from the Hangzhou Hotel to the CAAC office will cost about Y5, and about Y15 from the hotel to the airport.

**Public Security** (tel 22401) is at the junction of Dingan Lu and Huimin Lu. It's open every day except Sunday, from 8 to 11.30 am and 2 to 5 pm. The guy here speaks good English.

**Bank** There is a money-exchange counter on the 2nd floor of the Hangzhou Hotel.

**Post** There is a post office in the foyer of the Hangzhou Hotel. There is a large post office on Huancheng Lu, about 10 minutes' walk north of the railway station.

**Maps** There are some excellent maps of Hangzhou available. In Hong Kong some of the bookshops sell a map (in both Chinese and English) which covers Hangzhou, Huang Shan and Mogan Shan and has quite a bit of background information. China Travel Service in Hong Kong stocks a leaflet which shows an isometric perspective of the West Lake with the individual sights and buildings

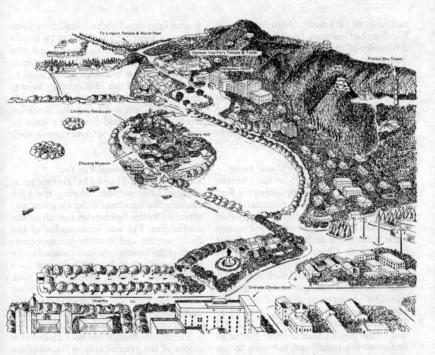

labelled in English and Chinese – quite useful for orientating yourself. In Hangzhou there are maps in Chinese, showing the bus routes, available from a shop near the bus No 7 terminus across the road from the railway station.

**Temple of Inspired Seclusion (Lingyin Si)**
Lingyin Si, roughly translated as the Temple of Inspired Seclusion or the Temple of the Soul's Retreat, should rate as Hangzhou's No 1 attraction. The temple was originally built in 326 AD, but it has been devastated and restored no less than 16 times throughout its history due to war and calamity.

The Cultural Revolution might have seen it razed for good but for the intervention of Zhou En-lai. Accounts vary as to what exactly happened, but it seems there was a confrontation between

those who wanted to save the temple and those who wanted to destroy it; the matter eventually went all the way up to Zhou, who gave the order to save both the temple and the sculptures on the rock face opposite. The monks however were sent to work in the fields. In the early 1970s a few of the elderly and invalid monks were allowed to come back and live out their last few years in a small outbuilding on the hillside behind the temple.

The present buildings are restorations of Qing Dynasty structures. At the front of the temple is the Hall of the Four Main Guardians. A statue of Maitreya, the coming Buddha, sits on a platform in the middle of the hall flanked by two dragons. At either corner of the hall are the statues of the guardians, the protectors of the Buddha.

Behind the Hall of the Four Main Guardians is the Great Hall where sits the magnificent 20-metre high statue of Siddhartha Guatama, resculptured out of 24 blocks of camphor wood in 1956 and based on the Tang Dynasty original. Behind this giant statue is a startling montage of 150 small figures.

To get to the temple, take bus No 7 to its terminus at the foot of the hills to the west of Hangzhou. It's also a pleasant, though rather lengthy, walk from the Hangzhou Hotel.

## Peak That Flew From Afar (Feilai Feng)
Congratulations must go to the Chinese (or the Indians) for accomplishing the first successful solo flight of a mountain! The story goes that an Indian monk who visited here in the 3rd century said the hill looked exactly like one in India and asked when it had flown to China. The hill faces the Lingyin Temple and its rocky walls and cliffs have been indented with about 330 sculptures and multiple acts of graffiti chiselled in between the middle of the 10th century to the beginning of the 14th. The earliest sculpture dates to 951 AD and comprises a group of three Buddhist deities at the right-hand entrance to the Qing Lin Cave. More interesting are the droves of Chinese who clamber up all over the sculptures and inscriptions to have their photo taken; the most popular backdrop is the laughing Maitreya, the fat Buddha at the foot of the ridge.

## Northern Peak (Bei Feng)
Behind the Lingyin Temple is the Northern Peak. Cable cars climb to the base of the summit and you get a sweeping view across the lake and city below. The cable car leaves from Lingyin Lu, east of the bus No 7 terminus.

## Zhejiang Provincial Museum
This interesting museum is located a short walk from the Hangzhou Hotel on Solitary Hill Island. The main atractions are the preserved bodies of a man and a woman excavated from a tomb in what is now Xinjiang. The rest of the exhibits are mainly concerned with natural history and there's a large whale skeleton (a female Rhachianectos glaucus cope) and the skeleton of a dinosaur. The museum is housed in some buildings which used to make up part of the 18th century holiday palace of the Qing Emperor Qianlong. It's open 8 to 11 am and 1 to 5 pm. Someone wrote to us and said that you should be sure to have the Ming Dynasty eye wash bowl demonstrated(?!)

## Mausoleum of General Yue Fei
General Yue Fei (1103-1141) is held up as a great Chinese hero. During the 12th century the Southern Song kingdom was attacked by the Jurchen invaders from the north. Yue Fei was commander of the Song armies and despite his successes against the invaders he was recalled to the Song court where he was executed by a treacherous court official, Qin Gui. Twenty years later in 1163 the Song Emperor Xiao Zong rehabilitated him and had his corpse reburied at the present site. Yue was eventually deified.

The mausoleum contains a glazed clay statue of the general and on the walls are paintings of scenes from his life, including one of his back being tattooed, supposedly with the words 'Loyal to the Last'. The mausoleum of this soldier/patriot/nationalist is just a few minutes' walk west of the Hangzhou Hotel on Huanhu Lu, located in a compound bounded by a large reddish-coloured brick wall. The mausoleum was ransacked during the Cultural Revolution but has now been restored.

## Protect Shu Tower (Baoshu Ta)
Looking something like a stone age rocket ship, this tower was erected during the Song Dynasty on the top of Jewellery Hill (whoever gave it that name should be arrested for false advertising). First built in 938 AD, the present tower is a 1933 reconstruction, 45.3 metres. The original tower was built to assure the safe return of Hangzhou's Prince Qian Shu from an audience with the emperor. The tower lies

just to the north of Huanhu Lu on the northern side of the lake, but if you can find the track, path, road or tunnel which leads up to the pagoda then you're a genius.

### Six Harmonies Pagoda (Liuhe Ta)

To the south-west of the city stands an enormous rail and road bridge which spans the Qiantang River. Close by is the huge Six Harmonies Pagoda. As a legacy of the feudal past it was cited for demolition during the Cultural Revolution, but since it would have required an army of experts to demolish it the project had to be called off. The pagoda was built in 970 AD as a lighthouse for river shipping. Its cosmic force was also supposed to be able to deflect the 'bore' – a tidal wave which thunders up the Qiantang River in mid-September of each year.

The name refers to the six codes of Buddhism: to observe the harmony of the body, of speech, of thoughts, to resist temptation, to refrain from uttering opinions and from accumulating wealth. It's a 60-metre high octagonal structure of brick and wood; from the outside it appears to have 13 storeys and from the inside only seven.

### The West Lake

There are 30 lakes in China called Xi Hu but this one is by far the most famous. Again, if you travel a thousand km just for the water you'll probably be disappointed. The lake was originally a lagoon off the Qiantang River, and in the 8th century the governor of Hangzhou had it dredged and later a dyke was built which cut it off from the river completely.

The lake is about three km long and a bit under three wide. Two causeways, the Bai Ti and the Su Ti, split the lake into sections. The causeways each have a number of arched bridges, large enough for small boats and ferries to pass under. The sights are scattered around the lake, though most of them are little more than fancy names attached to rather uninspiring

pavilions or bridges . . . though the whole being greater than the sum of the parts it is a pretty place to wander around.

The largest island in the lake is **Solitary Hill (Gu Shan)** at its northern edge, the location of the Provincial Museum, the Louwailou Restaurant and Zhongshan Park. Zhongshan Park was once part of an imperial palace during the 18th century, but was renamed after 1911 in honour of Sun Yatsen. The Bai causeway connects the island to the mainland and bus No 7 runs across the causeway and the island.

Most of the other sights have some story behind them and are named after some famous poet who once lived there, some alchemist who bubbled up longevity pills, or the private garden of some emperor who rolled around there with his palace whores. One such is the **Pavilion for Releasing Crane** on Solitary Hill Island, built in memory of the Song poet Lin Hejing, of whom it is said 'refused to serve the emperor and remained a bachelor his whole life. His only pastime was planting plum trees and fondling his crane'. A more notable sight is the **Three Pools Mirroring the Moon (Santanyinyue)**, an island in the middle of the West Lake with *four* of its own lakes. There are boats to the island from Solitary Hill Island or from Huagang Park. Hangzhou's botanical gardens even have a sequoia presented to China by Tricky Dickie on his 1972 visit. If you want to contemplate the water in the privacy of your own boat there are a couple of places around the lake where you can hire paddle boats and go for a slow spin; they charge around 80 fen per hour.

### Other

Some of the more interesting areas for street walking are in the easterly part of town, around the scungy canals which cut through the urban areas. The houses out here are all one or two storey brick and wood constructions with the washing (and drying boots) slung out on lines hung across the narrow laneways.

The Hangzhou zoo is notable for its

Manchurian tigers, but to my untrained eye they look indistinguishable from any other tigers. It's a pleasant place set amidst thickly-wooded hills.

About 60 km north of Hangzhou is Mogan Shan, noted for its scenery. Pleasantly cool at the height of summer it was developed as a hill resort for Europeans living in Shanghai and Hangzhou back in the International Settlement days.

### Places to Stay

The *Hangzhou Hotel* (tel 22921 or 25828) is a huge palatial building set on the northern bank of the West Lake. It's one of the best hotels in China and dorm beds are readily given – if they say the dorm is full then it is full. Double rooms here for Y40, Y36 and Y32. Beds in the very comfortable dormitory in the main building are only Y6. They also have another building where there are dorm beds for Y5. A bed in a triple is Y8. Bus No 7 from the railway station will take you straight to the hotel. Forget the rickshaws, as they'd take forever to cover the distance. Worth checking out is the band which plays every night in the hotel's coffee lounge on the ground floor of the main building; if you can cope with the 'Blue Danube' followed by 'YMCA' then this is for you. The band varies from five to 12 players, dominated by the piano-accordionist; fun if you're drunk. A comfy hotel, combined with the rather pleasant surroundings of the city, makes Hangzhou a good place to rest for a few days.

The *Huagang Hotel* (tel 24001) is the other tourist joint. Double rooms here are Y40 but there are supposed to be cheaper rooms in building No 6. It's a nice location as far as the scenery goes, being situated on the western bank of the lake, but it's isolated and I wouldn't recommend it. Take bus No 7 from the railway station and then change to bus No 4. The last bus No 4 runs at about 9.30 pm which is another problem if you're staying here.

The *Overseas Chinese Hotel* (tel 23401) at 92 Hubin Lu is conveniently located, but it's almost impossible for big-noses to get into. Double rooms are Y22 and there are dorm beds for Y5.

### Places to Eat

There are a couple of places close to the Hangzhou Hotel which are worth investigating. Just past the entrance to General Yue Fei's Mausoleum, but on the other side of the road, is a mouthful in itself called the *Xihuyuefendianxiadian* which has been mentioned in the Michelin guide as having 'Good service, good food and prices', and has a sign to that effect hung up inside. Directly opposite the entrance to the mausoleum is a little street leading to the banks of the lake, and there are one or two good restaurants here. To get to the *Louwailou Restaurant* turn left at the end of this little street and continue down the side path. Walk over the bridge and down Gushan Lu on Gushan Island and after a few minutes you'll come to a medium-sized building which harbours the restaurant.

There are some good places on the eastern side of the lake. The first is on Jiefang Lu just east of the intersection with Yanan Lu (see the map for directions). The top floor here is expensive (around Y7 to Y10 per plate) but very pleasant, but on the lower floors you'll get OK meals for around Y2 to Y3.

The other restaurant is further east on the corner of Jiefang Lu and Zhongshan Lu. The ground floor is a canteen but upstairs is quite pleasant.

The restaurant in the Hangzhou Hotel varies from good to awful – sometimes excellent food, sometimes lathered in oil. But it's a nice place to have breakfast.

### Getting Around

Bicycle is the best way of getting around Hangzhou. There are two places which rent them. The nearest place to the Hangzhou Hotel is a restaurant on Beishan Lu. Look for the sign *Cha Shi Leng Yin Shi Pin* – ask in here and they'll take you to the bikes. Beishan Lu continues down to a large square at the rear of which is a platform with a large hammer and sickle; the second rental place is a little cabin to the left of the platform with a row of bikes out the front. The cabin is open until 5 pm. The bikes are rented for Y0.20 per hour plus a Y20 deposit and you might have to leave some identification.

### Getting Away

**Bus** The long-distance bus station is on Changzheng Lu just north of the intersection with Huancheng Lu.

Buses to Shanghai depart at 5.50 am, 6 am, 12.30 pm and 12.40 pm The fare is Y5.

Buses to Huang Shan depart at 6.10 am, 6.40 am, 7.20 am and 7.30 am The fare is Y6.90.

There is a bus to Tunxi at 6.30 am. The fare is Y5.80.

There is a bus to Nanjing at 6 am. The fare is Y7.65.

Buses to Shaoxing depart at 9.10 am, 9.20 am, 11.50 am, 12.50 pm and 2.50 pm The fare is Y1.60.

Buses to Ningbo depart at 6.40 am and 2.30 pm The fare is Y4.

Buses to Tiantai Shan depart at 7 am and 8 am. The fare is Y5.35.

**Train** There are direct trains from Hangzhou to Shaoxing and Ningbo, to Shanghai (always crowded and sometimes impossible to get a seat – fortunately the trip is only three hours long) and to Canton (which can take between 29 to 38 hours depending on the train). CITS in Hangzhou only sells soft sleeper tickets and if you want hard seat or hard sleeper you'll have to buy it from the railway station.

**Plane** There are flights from Hangzhou to Beijing (Y150), Canton (Y135), Changsha (Y96), Fuzhou (Y85), Guilin (Y148), Hefei (Y73), Shanghai (Y20), Tunxi (Y30). There are also flights from Hangzhou to Hong Kong five days a week, costing Y237.

**Boat** You can take a boat up the Grand Canal from Hangzhou to Suzhou (oddly enough, in Suzhou they won't sell you a ticket to do the trip to Hangzhou). Boats depart Hangzhou at 5 am and at 5 pm and it's a 12-hour ride costing Y5 with a sleeper. The boat leaves from the dock near the corner of Huancheng Lu and Changzheng Lu in the northern part of town. Tickets can be bought from CITS in the Hangzhou Hotel or at the Booking Office at the dock which is open 5 am to 6 pm.

### SHAOXING
Shaoxing is situated in the middle of the waterway system of the northern Zhejiang plain. It's been a major administrative town since early times and an agricultural market centre, though it never attained the same heights as neighbouring Hangzhou and Ningbo. Shaoxing is connected by train and bus to Hangzhou (see Hangzhou for details) and there are buses from Shaoxing to Tiantai Shan and to Wenzhou.

### NINGBO
Like Shaoxing, Ningbo rose to prominence in the 7th and 8th centuries as a trading port from which ships would sail to Japan and the Ryuku Islands and up and down the Chinese coast, carrying the exports of Zhejiang Province. By the 16th century the Portuguese had established themselves here, working as middlemen in the Japan-China trade since Chinese were forbidden to deal with the Japanese; the British East India Company even gained a brief foothold here in the 17th century. Although Ningbo was thrown open to western traders after the First Opium War, its flourishing trade gradually declined as the title of premier port was usurped by a booming Shanghai. By that time the Ningbo traders had put their money into banking, taken it to Shanghai and founded the basis of the Chinese business community in that city. Today Ningbo is a city of 250,000 with fishing, salt production, textiles and food processing

being the primary industries.

Ningbo is linked to Hangzhou by rail and bus (see Hangzhou for details) and by ship to Shanghai (see Shanghai for details). There are daily buses from Ningbo to Tiantai Shan and to Wenzhou.

## TIANTAI SHAN

One of the sacred mountains of China, Tiantai is notable not so much for its beautiful scenery as for a lack of the trampling hordes who are gradually pounding places like Emei Shan and Huang Shan into dust. The Buddhist monasteries of Tiantai Shan date back to the 6th century and the Tiantai sect, heavily influenced by Taoism, seems to be going strong.

The mountain lies in the central-eastern region of Zhejiang. There are buses linking Tiantai with Hangzhou, Shaoxing, Ningbo and Wenzhou.

## WENZHOU

Wenzhou is an ancient city, founded at the end of the 4th century. It's an ocean port and was opened up to foreign trade in 1877 as the result of another treaty with Britain, though no foreign settlement developed. The few foreigners that did come here were missionaries and trade officials – the former concerned with saving souls and the later mainly with the once-profitable tea trade.

The town lies on the far south-eastern coast of Zhejiang. From here you could continue south into Fujian Province by taking a bus to Fuan and from there onto the capital of Fuzhou. There are also ships linking Wenzhou and Shanghai (see the Shanghai section for details).

## CHUNAN COUNTY

Chunan County is known as the Lake of 1000 Islands and lies in the west of Zhejiang Province. It should be open to foreigners by the time this book is out.

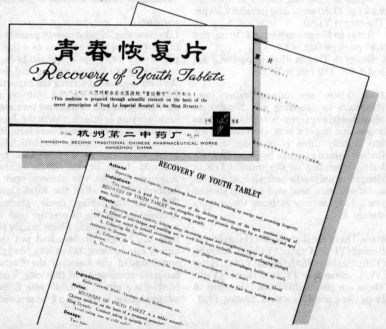

青春恢复片

*Recovery of Youth Tablets*

(根据明朝御水乐太医院的"富廷秘方"研制而成)
(This medicine is prepared through scientific research on the basis of the secret prescription of Yong Le Imperial Hospital in the Ming Dynasty.)

杭州第二中药厂 杭州
HANGZHOU SECOND TRADITIONAL CHINESE PHARMACEUTICAL WORKS
HANGZHOU CHINA

RECOVERY OF YOUTH TABLET

**Actions:**
Improving mental capacity, strengthening bones and muscles, building up energy and promising longevity.

**Indications:**
This medicine is good for the treatment of the declining functions of the aged, constant taking of RECOVERY OF YOUTH TABLET can strengthen vigour and promise longevity for a middle-age and aged man, build up health and maintain youth for young people.

**Effects:**
1. Improving mental capacity, helping sleep, decreasing dream and strengthening vigour of thinking.
2. Effects of anti-fatigue and enabling one to work long hours tirelessly, maintaining unflagging strength and making one suited to natural environment.
3. Enhancing the faculties of nonspecific immunity and phagocytosis of macrophages, building up one's resistance to diseases.
4. Enhancing the function of the heart, increasing the nourishment to the heart, promoting blood circulation.
5. Promoting sexual function, increasing the metabolism of protein, deferring the hair from turning grey.

**Ingredients:**
Radix Ginseng, Radix Asparagi, Radix Rehmanniae, etc.

**Notes:**
RECOVERY OF YOUTH TABLET is a tablet scientific Chinese medicine on the basis of a treasured prescription of the Ming Dynasty. Constant taking is suitable f...
Avoid eating raw or cold radi...

**Dosage:**
Two time...

# Anhui

The provincial borders of Anhui were cut out by the Qing government and except for a few changes to the boundary with Jiangsu have remained pretty much the same. The north of the province forms part of the North China Plain and the Han Chinese settled here in large numbers during the Han Dynasty. The southern area, below the Yangtse River was not settled until the 7th and 8th centuries. Today Anhui has a population of almost 50 million.

The Yangtse cuts straight through the middle of this province, and since there are no bridges between the two halves transport is rather difficult. Most of Anhui's tourist attractions are in the southern part of the province, and you can get to them more easily from either Hangzhou or Shanghai than from the provincial capital of Hefei. There is, however, a rail line from Hefei to Wuhu. Cross the river at Wuhu and you can then take another train to Yingtan, via Tunxi (the jumping-off point for Huang Shan) and Jingdezhen.

Notable amongst the sights open to foreigners are the impressive Yellow Mountains (Huang Shan) in the far south of the province, and close by the Nine Flowers Mountains (Jiuhua Shan). On the eastern edge of the province, on the south bank of the Yangtse River, are the Maan Shan. The Yangtse River ports of Guichi and Wuhu, whilst not officially open to foreigners, have been visited by several travellers and are convenient jumping-off points for the Jiuhua and Huang Mountains.

## HUANG SHAN (YELLOW MOUNTAIN)

Li Bai whom the Chinese tell us was 'a great poet who was deep in love with the beautiful landscape of his motherland' once took a trip to Huangshan and wrote:

*Huangshan is hundreds of thousands of feet high,*
*With numerous soaring peaks lotus-like,*
*Rock pillars shooting up to kiss empryrean roses,*
*Like so many lillies grown amid a sea of gold.*

Li got the altitude wrong since most people climb Huang Shan without oxygen masks. It probably doesn't measure up to the mountains of Europe, and don't expect the Himalayas, but by any standards the view from the top is worth the effort to get there. There's some pretty rugged scenery, and the sunrise from the top really is a spectacular sight. But don't expect any man in the wilderness stuff; there are stone steps the whole way to the top of the mountain and concrete paths connect the sights – and the Chinese clamber up and down these paths *en masse!*

Huang Shan is the collective name of a range of 72 peaks lying in the south of Anhui Province, 280 km west of Hangzhou. The highest peak is Lotus Flower Peak (Lianhua Feng) at 1800 metres, followed by the slightly lower Bright Summit Peak (Guangming Ding) and Heavenly Capital Peak (Tiandu Feng). In all 30 peaks rise above 1500 metres.

The area has been a famous scenic spot for at least 1200 years, since the Tang Dynasty emperor Tian Biao gave it its' present name in the middle of the eighth century. Over the centuries the range has

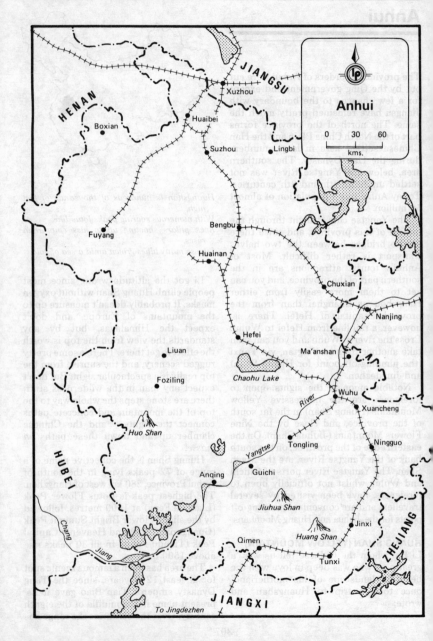

been an inspiration for Chinese poets and painters (though perhaps some of the poetry leaves something to be desired) and the four great attractions have been the jagged rocks, the 'sea of clouds' swirling around the peaks, the hot springs and the ancient pines clinging to the rockface.

## The Base Camp

Buses pull into the Huang Shan 'base camp' at the foot of the range. The base camp is really an overgrown tourist resort with a couple of hotels, a hot springs public bath and two Friendship Stores.

## Information and Orientation

The base camp is split down the middle by a narrow stream and the tourist facilities are all congregated in a small area on either side.

The bus pulls into the long-distance bus station which is immediately in front of the CITS hotel. Also in front of the hotel is the post office and one of the Friendship Stores. The CITS has a desk in the foyer of the CITS hotel –they speak little English and are not terribly helpful.

There is another Friendship Store on the opposite side of the stream, and this one has a cute little sign which says that *Friendship flowers are in full bloom all over the world.*

## Places to Stay

The *CITS Hotel* is the only hotel you'll be able to stay at in the base camp. It's Y28 for a double (with private shower and toilet), though if you're on your own they'll probably let you pay just Y14. A bed in a triple is Y8, though they may not let you use these rooms unless you show up with two other people. If you take the triple, then you'll have to use the communal showers in the basement of the hotel, which are very clean and very hot. The shower, by the way costs a penny-pinching 20 fen! The hotel has a storeroom where you can leave your excess baggage for Y1 whilst you climb the mountain.

## Places to Eat

There's a restaurant in the rear building of the CITS hotel. The food is good though the restaurant itself is a bit of a dreary place. There is another restaurant to the rear of the long-distance bus station notable for the loud disco tapes which are played here.

## Getting Away

There are buses from the Huang Shan base camp to numerous destinations. The office at the bus station is open 5 to 7.30 am, 8 am to 5 pm and 6 to 7 pm.

Buses to Hangzhou depart at 6.20 am, 6.30 am and 6.50 am The fare is Y6.90 and it's about an eight or nine hour trip.

Buses to Tunxi depart at 5.45 am, 7 am, 1.20 pm and 1.30 pm The fare is Y1.95.

Buses to Wuhu depart at 6.25 am, 6.40 am, and 7 am. The fare is Y5.35.

The bus to Shanghai departs at 5.30 am. The fare is Y11.40.

The bus to Jiuhua Shan departs at 5.55 am. The fare is Y4.05.

The bus to Guichi departs at 6.50 am. The fare is Y4.30.

Buses to Nanjing depart at 5.50 am and 6.05 am and the fare is Y7.80.

## Scaling the Heights

There are two ways to get to the top of the mountain; the long way and the short way.

The short way is to take the bus along the eastern road to the *Yonguzhi Hostel* which is half-way up the mountain. The bus leaves from beside the *Hot Spring Guest House* on the opposite side of the stream to the CITS hotel. Tickets are bought from the small booth next to the Hot Spring Guest House. The fare is Y0.80. From the hostel you gasp up a steep flight of steps to the top of the mountain, a distance of 7½ km. This can be done in two hours, though more comfortably in three. There's very little to see on the way up. At the top of the mountain you'll find the *Beihai (North Sea) Guest House.*

From the Behai Guest House you can make your descent via the western flight of steps which are incredibly long and incredibly steep – if you come up this way don't say I didn't warn you! The western path has some spectacular scenery, which will be much more enjoyable if you're clambering down the steps rather than gasping your way up them. The western path leads you down to the Yupinglou Hostel and the Mid-level Monastery and back to the base camp.

If you take the eastern route up and the western route down then you could do the whole circuit comfortably in about 10 hours, although you could take several hours off that if you want to rush. On the other hand, if you want to spend a night on the mountain, then you've got plenty of time for interesting side-trips.

Guides aren't necessary for the climb up the mountain; everything is along concrete paths and steps and the place is crawling with people so you can't get lost. But if you want one then CITS charges Y14 per day per group. There are a couple of private entrepreneurs around who'll do it for half that price, but you probably won't find them if you don't speak Chinese as they're not supposed to be competing with CITS.

If you want to be carried up the mountain, then you can get two coolies to carry you in a chair slung between two bamboo poles. I've been told that they charge Y300 for the round trip, of which Y150 goes to the government to pay insurance in case they drop someone. They carry you up one day and bring you down the next. And if you think it's hard going up the mountain then spare a thought for the army of coolies who carry

supplies up it each day; they rasp their way up the steps with crates of drink bottles, baskets of food and even armchairs strung on bamboo poles held across the shoulder.

By the time this book is out there should be a cable car operating between the Yunghuzhi Hostel and White Swan Peak on the top of the mountain, a distance of almost three km which would be covered by the cable car in just eight minutes.

## Things to See

Wang Ch'ao-wen, said to be China's 'famous critic of art and literature' had this to say about Huang Shan:

The Huangshan beauties are manifold – pines, clouds and rocks all possess their respective charms. Nevertheless, if one does not view them from various angles and in a different light, and if one doesn't employ one's own imagination, such an inviting scenic marvel as 'The Squirrel is jumping to Heavenly Capital' is nothing but a common squirrel-shaped rock. If that is the case, how is it possible that the more I look at it, the more it arouses my interest and the more I feel that it presents a lifelike figure of a squirrel on the point of jumping?

I firmly believe that the Huangshan tourist must use his own imagination. If you approach those picturesque sights with borrowed vision, the Huangshan pines, thousands upon thousands in number and so beautifully varied in shape, will not be able to catch your eye and strike your fancy.

It seems to me that the tendency toward formularization exists not only in artistic and literary creation but also in sight-seeing recreation. Although the Huangshan beauties will never be diminished by stereotyped formularisation on the part of the tourist, yet the existence of such stereotypes reflects that even in tourism there exists an ideological conflict between independent thinking and

| | | | |
|---|---|---|---|
| 1 | CITS / Hotel | 6 | Beihai Guesthouse |
| 2 | Long Distance Bus Station | 7 | Rock—that—flew |
| 3 | Hot Spring Guesthouse | 8 | Restaurant |
| 4 | Bus to Yunguzhi Hostel | 9 | Yupinglou Hostel |
| 5 | Yunguzhi Hostel | 10 | Mid-level Monastery |

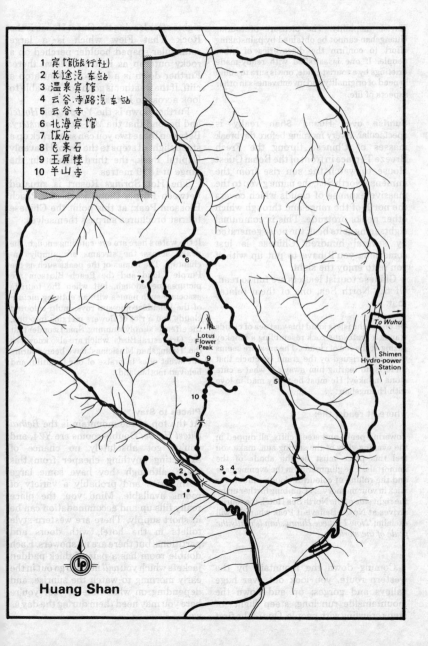

1 宾馆(旅行社)
2 长途汽车站
3 温泉宾馆
4 云谷寺路汽车站
5 云谷寺
6 北海宾馆
7 饭店
8 飞来石
9 玉屏楼
10 羊山寺

Lotus
Flower
Peak

To Wuhu

Shimen
Hydro-power
Station

**Huang Shan**

slavish mentality. The pleasure of touring Huangshan cannot be obtained by painstaking effort to confirm the discoveries of other people. If one is satisfied with ready-made briefings by a tourist guide, one is sure to stand in need of originality and inventiveness in other aspects of life.

**Sunrise over Huang Shan** really is spectacular. Every morning before daybreak masses of Chinese throng the Fresh Breeze Terrace in front of the Behai Guest House to watch the sun rise from the immense North Sea, the name given to the massive expanse of clouds which covers the north of the range and through which other peaks protrude. This is communal sightseeing at its best; the noise generated by several hundred Chinese is just something you'll have to put up with if you're to enjoy the sight.

Chinese tourist leaflets are fun to read. Of the North Sea, one of them relates that:

On one of the islets amid this vast sea of clouds stands a grotesque rock resembling a monkey gazing at the sea of clouds. The creature seems to be so intrigued by the grand spectacle that there is no tearing him away . . . what a cute stone monkey! He must be really mad in love with Huangshan . . .

where, it reads, the:

towering peaks and steep cliffs, all dipped in the evening glow of the setting sun, make you feel this place must be the abode of the immortals. The glimmering in the evening haze and the rolling of colourful clouds will forever stick in your memory . . . Climbing further up by the right side of the North Sea Hotel, the tourist arrives at Now-I-Believe-it Peak where he will exclaim; '*Now I believe Huangshan is really the pride of the world*'.

Coming down the mountain by the western route, you look out over huge valleys and gorges; up and down the mountainside run long, steep flights of steps crawling with people. One of the first sights after leaving the Guest House is the Rock That Flew which is a large retangular-shaped boulder perched on a rocky outcrop · as if it had flown there. Further down is a look-out point atop a cliff. If the weather is good you'll be able to look across to Lotus Peak.

Further down is the *Youpinglou Hostel* and beyond that the *Mid-level monastery*. Between these two you can side-track up a steep flight of steps to the top of Heavenly Capital Peak, the third highest in the range at 1829 metres.

The Hot Springs Resort is situated between Purple Cloud Peak and Peach Blossom Peak; at this point the Chinese tourist brochures surpass themselves:

If the waters here are eye-catching enough, the peaks across the streams are simply enchanting. The names of the peaks such as the Purple Cloud and the Peach Blossom are picturesque enough, but when the tourists associate such names with an enticing picture of the kaleidoscopic sun rays, multi-coloured clouds and a riot of flowers merging into one, the effect is simply stunning. Small wonder that the 'Orchestral Birds' which are also known as the 'Huangshan Musicians' have been pouring out sweet odes in praise of our beautiful and beloved motherland.

**Places to Stay**

At the top of the mountain is the *Beihai Guest House*. Double rooms are Y24, and you've got absolutely no chance of extracting anything cheaper from this place, although they have some large dormitories and probably a variety of rooms available. Mind you, the place really fills up and accommodation can be in short supply. There are western-style toilets in the hotel, with doors and partitions, but there are no showers. Each double room has a pair of thick padded jackets which you *will* need to go out in the early morning to watch the sunrise, and depending on what time of year you're here you may need them during the day as well.

'The masses' can't afford to stay at the Beihei, and even if they were willing to pay they wouldn't be permitted to stay here since the rooms are reserved for ranking Chinese. The common horde is accommodated in large blue barracks which hold at least 100 people each on bunk beds. You'll see some of these just in front of the Guest House, but the really crowded ones are a 10 minute walk from the Guest House on the downward descent.

Mid-way down the mountain, taking the long path from the top, is the *Yupinglou Hostel* and further down is the *Mid-level Monastery* which used to be a monastery but is also being used as a hotel.

### Places to Eat

The *Beihai Guest House* has two restaurants on the ground floor; Chinese pay Y3 for a set meal, westerners pay Y12! To avoid this, walk out the front entrance of the hotel, turn left and go down the short flight of steps and you'll see a small blue building. Behind this is a bamboo walled building with a greenish-coloured roof; you can get OK meals here for about Y2 or Y3 each. There's usually someone at the front of the Beihai selling bowls of soupy noodles for 20 or 30 fen.

The *Yupinglou Hostel* has a restaurant, and there is a small restaurant just before the hostel on your way down the mountain.

### TUNXI

South of Huang Shan is the old trading town of Tunxi which may make a worthwhile stopover if you're heading out to Huang Shan. Tunxi is connected by bus to Huang Shan, Hangzhou and Jingdezhen. There are also planes from Tunxi to Hangzhou (Y30), Hefei (Y43), Shanghai (Y53). Heading south there is a rail line to Yingtan via Jingdezhen. Heading North there is a rail line to Wuhu.

### JIUHUA SHAN

One way to escape the trampling hordes of Huang Shan is to head north-west to Jiuhua Shan, the Nine Flowers Mountains. The mountains take their name from the Tang poet Li Bai who wrote:

*Looking far ahead from Juijiang,*
*I saw the peaks of Mount Jiuhua*
*Emerging from the Heavenly River*
*Like nine beautiful lotus flowers.*

Jiuhua Shan is regarded as one of the sacred Buddhist mountains of China (just how many sacred mountains there are in China depends on which book you read but the other sacred Buddhist mountains are Pu Tuo in Zhejiang, Emei in Sichuan and Wutai in Shanxi). There are buses from Huang Shan to Jiuhua Shan and the fare is Y4.05, and there may be buses from Guichi.

### WUHU

Wuhu is one of the Yangtse River ports. Rail lines branch off here southwards to Tunxi, and east to Shanghai via Nanjing. From the northern bank of the river another line heads north to Hefei, the provincial capital of Anhui. There are also buses to Huang Shan. Wuhu is not officially open to foreigners but several people have gone there on their way to Huang Shan.

### GUICHI

Further west along the Yangtse River from Wuhu is the port of Guichi, again officially closed to foreigners but also a convenient jumping-off point for heading down to Huang Shan. There are buses to Huang Shan from Guichi.

### HEFEI

This nondescript industrial city is the capital of Anhui but has little to recommend it to tourists. It used to be a quiet market town but after 1949 was built up as an industrial centre and now has a population of about 500,000. The only real attraction is the local Provincial Museum whose prize possession is a 2000-year-old jade burial suit made of pieces of jade sewn with silver thread.

314 Anhui

Hefei is connected by direct trains northwards to Jinan, Beijing and Zhengzhou, southwards to the port of Wuhu on the Yangtse River, and westwards to Xian. There are also flights from Hefei to Beijing (Y119), Fuyang (Y26), Hangzhou (Y73), Jinan (Y67), Shanghai (Y51), Tunxi (Y43), Wuhan (Y49), Xian (Y125) and Zhengzhou (Y69). There are probably buses from Hefei to Nanjing.

# Hubei

Hubei Province comprises two quite different areas. The eastern two-thirds is a low-lying plain drained by the Yangtse and its main northern tributary the Han Shui. The western third is an area of rugged highlands with small cultivated valleys and basins dividing Hubei from Sichuan. The plain has been settled by the Han Chinese since 1000 BC. Around the 7th century it was intensively settled and by the 11th it was producing a rice surplus. In the late 19th century it was the first area in the Chinese interior to undergo considerable industrialisation. Site of the great industrial city and river port of Wuhan, slashed through by the Yangtse River and its many tributaries, and supporting a population of almost 48 million, Hubei is still one of China's most important provinces.

## WUHAN

With a population of three million, Wuhan is one of the largest cities in China. It's actually made up of a conglomeration of what were once three independent cities; Hankou, Hanyang and Wuchang.

Wuchang was established during the Han Dynasty, became a regional capital under the Yuan and is now the seat of the Provincial government. It used to be a walled city – alas, no longer.

Hankou, on the other hand, was little more than a village until the Treaty of Nanjing opened it to foreign trade. Within a few years it was divided into British, French, German, Russian and Japanese concessions, all grouped around present-day Zhongshan Lu north of the Xuangong Hotel. It was with the building of the Beijing-Wuhan railway in the 1920s that Hankou really began to expand and became the first major industrial centre in the interior of China.

Hanyang has been outstripped by neighbouring Hankou and today it's the smallest municipality. It dates back to around 600 AD when a town first started to develop on the site. During the second half of the 19th century it was developed as a site for heavy industry – the first modern iron and steel complex in China was built here in 1891 and by the early 1900s a string of factories had been set up along the waterfront. The 1930s depression and the Japanese invasion led to the collapse or destruction of Hanyang's industry and since 1949 only light industry has operated here.

Not many people go out of their way to get to Wuhan, but a lot of people pass through the place since this is the terminus of the Yangtse ferries from Chongqing. Rather livelier, less grimy, more modern than Chongqing, it's almost something of a transit-warp on the trip down to the – by comparison – sparkling, cosmopolitan citadels of Nanjing and Shanghai. Like those cities, Wuhan has been a fortunate metropolis in unfortunate times; it was here in 1911 that an army revolt led to the downfall of the Qing Dynasty. The fighting here almost totally burnt Hankou to the ground, except for the foreign concessions along the river front. The city was the centre of the bloodily-suppressed February 7th 1923 strike of the workers building the Wuhan-Beijing railway line. It was here that the Kuomintang government first retreated from Nanjing in the wake of the Japanese invasion, until bombing and the advance

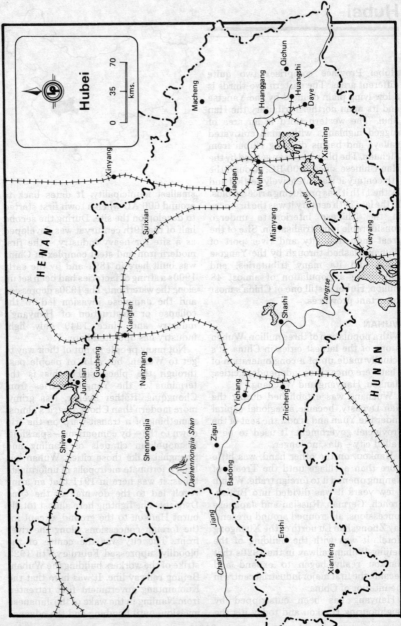

of the Japanese army forced them further west to Chongqing.

## Information & Orientation

Wuhan lies on both sides of the Yangtse River. Wuchang lies on the east bank; on the west bank lie Hankou and Hanyang, separated from each other by the Han River. Hankou is the centre of things and here you find the dock for the Yangtse ferries, the hotels and other tourist life support systems. The main artery is Zhongshan Dadao (Zhongshan Boulevard) which cuts through Hankou roughly parallel to the Yangtse River and is the main shopping street. Most of the trains into Wuhan stop at both Hankou and Wuchang but it's more convenient to get off at Hankou.

**CITS** (tel 23505) is at 1395 Zhongshan Dadao, Hankou, in a rather nondescript building to the north around the corner from the Jianghan Hotel. They're amiable but not overly helpful.

**Public Security** (tel 25129) is at 206 Shengli Lu, a 10-minute walk north of the Jianghan Hotel. They're quite friendly and helpful.

**CAAC** (tel 51248 and 52371) is at 209 Liji Beilu, Hankou.

**Post** There is a post office near the Aiguo Hotel (refer to the map for directions) which is open from around 7.30 am to around 9 pm or 9.30 pm.

**Maps** You may find hawkers near the Yangtse ferry dock selling maps in Chinese with the bus routes. Otherwise they're available from the shop in the Jianghan Hotel.

## Things to See

Hankou is the centre of Wuhan. Zhongshan Lu is the main thoroughfare with the shops, department stores, restaurants and several market streets branching off

it. Jiefang Lu is a market street but a better one, where food and live animals are sold, is a cobbled street lined with old houses south of Jiefang Lu. The north of Hankou, around the Shengli Hotel, is a quiet residential area full of old colonial buildings. Since Hankou was the foreign concession area, you'll find quite a few European-style buildings littering other parts of the municipality, particularly along Yanjiang Lu which runs parallel to the Yangtse in the north-east part of town; government offices now occupy what were the foreign banks, department stores and palatial residences. There were five foreign concession areas in Hankou; the first was set up by the British in 1861, then the German in 1895, the Russian in 1896, the French in 1896 and finally the Japanese in 1898. Wuchang is a modern district with long wide avenues lined with drab concrete blocks; the Hubei Provincial Museum can be found here, and the remarkable Guiyan Temple can be found across the river in Hanyang.

## Guiyan Temple

The Number 1 attraction of Wuhan is this Buddhist Temple with buildings dating from the late Ming and early Qing dynasties. The temple is located in Hanyang and is slowly being restored and even appears to be returning as an active place of worship – at least for the elderly. The chief attraction is the main hall with numerous seated statues of Buddha's disciples, lined up in an array of comical poses, including one with a bird perched on his head, another with a head growing out of his own head, another gazing at a Buddha seated on a lotus flower growing from a pot. In the courtyard of the building there's a large metal urn which is partly magnetised and the Chinese stand around it trying to get coins to stick on the magnetised points.

## Yangtse River Bridge

Prior to the construction of the Yangtse Bridge, all traffic on the north-south route had to be ferried across the river. This 1156-metre long and 80-metre high road and rail bridge was completed in 1957, and like the one in Nanjing it's regarded as a symbol of China's industrial progress. The bridge connects Wuchang to Hanyang, and a shorter bridge spans the Han River to link Hanyang with Hankou.

### Hong Shan (Red Hill)
East of the Yangtse Bridge in Wuchang, the hill is noted for its nine-storey 1000-year-old Buddhist pagoda. Next to it stands the ruins of an old temple, with its walls falling in and the roof ready to cave in completely.

### Hubei Provincial Museum
The museum is a must if you're interested in archaeology. There's a large collection of artefacts uncovered from the Zhenghouyi Tomb which was unearthed in 1978 on the outskirts of Suizhou City. The tomb dates to the Warring States Period, around 433 BC or a little later. The male internee was buried with about 7000 of his favourite artefacts including bronze ritual vessels, weapons, horse and chariot equipment, bamboo instruments and utensils and gold and jade objects. But most impressive are the massive set of bronze bell chimes that would make Mike Oldfield's eyes water. Other musical instruments were excavated from the tomb, including a wooden drum set on an ornate stand,

stringed instruments and a kind of flute similar to pan-pipes.

### Wuhan University
In the northern part of Wuchang, the campus consists of traditional-style buildings which are not without a certain charm. Most of them date from 1913 when the university was established.

### Places to Stay
All the tourist hotels are located in the Hankou region. Apart from the Xuangong Hotel these are all within easy walking distance of Hankou railway station. From the Yangtse ferry dock take bus No 30.

The *Aiguo Hotel* is on Zhongshan Dadao, a 10 minute walk from the Hankou Railway Station. Prices at the hotel are a bit confusing, but you shouldn't end up paying more than Y10 for a double room. The hotel is quite a pleasant little place, unlike the monolithic concrete echo-chambers you generally end up staying in. The toilets on the ground floor reek; don't use them. Upstairs on the 2nd and 3rd floors there are private bathrooms which you can use with bathtubs and toilets. There's hot water, but it probably only runs at night. People seem to go to sleep fairly early, and the staff are friendly.

The *Jianghan Hotel* (tel 23998) is a 15 minute walk from the Hankou Railway Station. The woodwork is one of the last reminders of pre-1949 China, a nice place

| | |
|---|---|
| 1 Xuangong Hotel | 10 Hangyang Railway Station |
| 2 Jianghan Hotel | 11 Wuchang Railway Station |
| 3 Aiguo Hotel | 12 Hankou Railway Station |
| 4 Shengli Hotel | 13 Railway Ticket Office |
| 5 Guiyan Temple | 14 Dock for Yangtse Ferries |
| 6 Hong Shan | 15 Booking Office for Yangtse Ferries |
| 7 Wuchang Bridge | 16 Public Security Office |
| 8 Laotongchang Restaurant | 17 CITS |
| 9 Sijimei Restaurant | 18 CAAC |

1 璇宫饭店
2 江汉饭店
3 爱国旅行社
4 胜利饭店
5 归元禅寺
6 洪山
7 武汉长江大桥
8 笔涌城酒楼
9 四季美饭店
10 汉阳火车站
11 武昌火车站
12 汉口站
13 汉口站售票处
14 长航客运站
15 港务局售票处
16 公安局
17 中国国际旅行社
18 中国民用航空总局

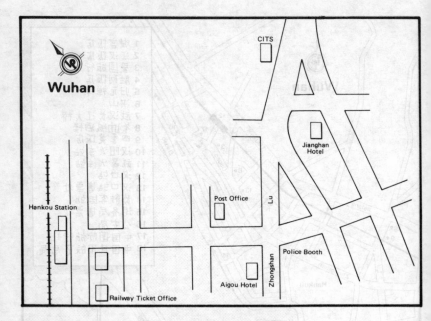

to stay if you can afford it. Double rooms, with bath, on the 4th floor for Y24. Other doubles for Y34. The 5th floor has four-bed dormitories on the roof at Y6 per bed, but you may have to jump up and down to get them. If you're on your own it's absolutely impossible to extract a discount on the cost of a double room.

The *Shengli Hotel* (tel 22531) is a dreary place rather inconveniently located. Singles for Y20 and doubles for Y34. They say there's no dormitory but apparently they've given some travellers beds for just Y6.

The *Xuangong Hotel* (tel 24404) has singles for Y24 and doubles for Y34. There are cheaper rooms in the wing directly across the street for Y6. They say they have no dormitory. To get there from Hankou station you must first walk down to Zhongshan Dadao, and take trolley bus No 2 as far as Jianghan Lu and then walk to the hotel. From the Yangtse ferry dock you'd be best off taking a rickshaw.

**Places to Eat**

The *Laotongchang Restaurant* (tel 24559) at 1 Dazhi Lu on the corner with Zhongshan Dadao, serves a delicious snack called

# 豆皮

which appears to be made up of some sort of soft flavoured bread encasing a mixture of rice, meat, egg and vegetables; great for breakfast. The *Sijimei Restaurant* (tel 22842) at 888 Zhongshan Dadao is full of dumplings, but there's more elaborate food up on the 3rd floor. There are a couple of restaurants in the vicinity of Hankou railway station and on the street leading down from it which may be worth trying. The *Jianghan Hotel* has a good restaurant and they serve the very tasty Wuchang fish here which is dragged up from Wuhan's East Lake.

Top: The poeple's transport – Red Flag limo, Beijing [AS]
Bottom: The people's transport – parking lot, Hohhot [MB]

Top: Transport (continued) – rubbish removal, Hangzhou [AS]
Bottom: Furniture removalist, Shanghai [MB]

## Getting Around

Wuhan has an extensive bus network but you may have to take two or even three to get to where you want to go. There are ferries across the river from Hankou to Wuchang which are more convenient than the buses. Rickshaws hang around outside of Wuchang Station and the ferry dock. Autorickshaws in Wuhan are decrepit blue and white machines which rattle and vibrate in the best traditions of Asian travel. They can also be found outside of Wuchang Station and the ferry dock. Bargain hard.

## Getting Away

**Train** Wuhan is on the main Beijing-Canton railway line. Express trains to Kunming and to Xian also pass through here. The most sensible way of heading east to Nanjing and Shanghai is by river, not by the circuitous rail route.

Hankou station is almost impossible to extract local-priced tickets out of; however the railway booking office on Zhongshan Dadao (see the map for location) was selling local-price tickets and should be worth a try. A hard seat ticket to Yeuyang is around Y4.90.

**Plane** Wuhan is connected by air to Beijing (Y142), Canton (Y106), Changsha (Y38), Chengdu (Y147), Chongqing (Y110), Enshi (Y67), Hefei (Y49), Nanjing (Y57), Shanghai (Y88), Shashi (Y28), Shenyang (Y222), Yichang (Y39), Zhengzhou (Y60).

**Boats** You can take ferries from Wuhan along the Yangtse River either west to Chongqing or east to Shanghai – see the section on tripping off down the Yangtse from Wuhan for details.

## UP & DOWN the YANGTSE RIVER – WUHAN TO CHONGQING & SHANGHAI

Ferries continue down from Wuhan to ports further east on the Yangtse River, and ultimately as far as Shanghai which lies on the Huangpu, which branches off

the Yangtse. You can also take the ferry west from Wuhan to Chongqing – not very advisable, since it's a five day trip.

The Chinese are planning to set up a hydrofoil service which will carry passengers along the Yangtse River between Wuhan and Nanjing. The hydrofoil is expected to make the 730 km trip in just 10 hours (as opposed to the 40 hours that it now takes on the boat) and will carry 100 to 110 passengers.

In Wuhan, you can buy tickets for the river ferries from CITS, the booking office at the river port or through the tourist hotel service desks. There are 2nd, 3rd and 4th class tickets, but if you buy through the hotel or through CITS you may have to argue to get a 4th class ticket as they don't seem too keen on selling them.

On the ferry 2nd class is a two-person cabin, 3rd class is an eight-person room and 4th class is a 16-person room.

Listed below are approximate durations and ticket prices (yuan).

|          |         | 2nd class | 3rd class | 4th class |
|----------|---------|-----------|-----------|-----------|
|          |         | Y         | Y         | Y         |
| Juijiang | o'night | 12.20     | 4.90      | 3.40      |
| Wuhu     | 30 hrs  | 26.10     | 10.40     | 7.10      |
| Nanjing  | 36 hrs  | 29.23     | 11.70     | 8.00      |
| Shanghai | 48 hrs  | 41.24     | 16.60     | 11.20     |

Heading downriver on leaving Wuhan, the steamer passes through the town of **Huangshi** in the east of Hubei Province. The town lies on the southern bank of the river and is being developed as a centre for heavy industry. Nearby an ancient mining tunnel was discovered, dating back to the Spring and Autumn Period, which contained numerous mining tools including bronze axes. Near the border with Jiangxi is the town of **Wuxue** on the north bank, which is noted for the production of bamboo goods.

The first major town in Jiangxi is **Juijiang**, the jumping-off point for nearby **Lu Shan** – for details, see the separate sections in this book. The mouth of **Lake**

**Poyang** is situated on the Yangtse River, and just here on the southern bank of the river is **Stone Bell Mountain**, noted for its numerous Tang Dynasty stone carvings, and also as the site where Taiping troops were garrisoned for five years defending Jinling, their capital.

The first major town in Anhui Province is **Anqing**, on the north bank, in the foothills of the Dabie mountains. Next comes the town of **Guichi** from which you can get a bus to **Huang Shan**. The town of **Tongling** lies in a mountainous area in central Anhui on the southern bank, west of Tongguan Shan. Tongling has been a copper mining centre for 2000 years, and is a source of copper for the minting of coins. Still in Anhui Province, and at the confluence of the Yangtse and Qingyi River, is **Wuhu** which is also a jumping-off point for Huang Shan. Just before leaving Anhui Province is the city of **Mannshan**, the site of a large iron and steel complex.

The first large city in Jiangsu Province is **Nanjing** followed by **Zhenjiang** (see the separate sections in this book for details) and the port of **Nantong** at the confluence of the Tongyang and Tonglu Canals. The ferry then proceeds down the Yangtse and then down the Huangpu to **Shanghai**. The Yangtse itself empties into the East China Sea.

## WUDANG MOUNTAINS

The Wudang Mountains (otherwise known as the Canshang or the Taihe Shan) stretch for 400 km across northwestern Hubei Province. The highest peak rises 1600 metres, and was known as the 'pillar propping up the sky' or 'Heavenly Pillar Peak'. The Wudang Mountains are a sacred range to the Taoists and a number

of Taoist temples were built here during the construction sprees of the Ming Emperors Cheng Zu and Zhen Wu. Notable temples include the Golden Hall on Heavenly Pillar Peak which was built entirely of gilded copper in 1416; the hall contains a bronze statue of the Ming Emperor Zhen Wu, who became a Taoist deity. The Purple Cloud Temple stands on Zhanqifeng Peak, and the Nanyan Temple perches on the South Cliff.

## SHENNONGJIA

This is an inaccessible mountain area in north-western Hubei, 160 km to the north of the Yangtse River gorges. The area is distinguished by the sightings of wild apemen, a sort of Chinese equivalent of the Himalayan Yeti or the North American Bigfoot. Well, it's an interesting story, but the creatures seem to be able to distinguish between peasants and scientists – molesting the former and evading the latter. Graham Earnshaw's guidebook *On Your Own in China* gives a lengthy account of the apemen and some of the reported sightings.

## YICHANG

Yichang is a port on the Yangtse River and a stopping point for the Chongqing-Wuhan boats. There is a railway line heading north from here to the town of Xiangfan, where you change trains and carry on to Luoyang. Yichang is regarded as the gateway to the Upper Yangtse and was once a walled city dating at least as far back as the Sui Dynasty. The town was opened to foreign trade in 1877 by a treaty between Britain and China and a foreign concession area was set up along the river front to the south-east of the walled city.

# Shanghai

Shanghai, Paris of the East, Whore of China, Queen of the Orient; city of bums, adventurers, pimps, swindlers, gamblers, sailors, socialites, dandies, drugrunners. Humiliation, indignation, starvation, back alley corpses, coolies, rickshaw drivers, deformed beggars, child prostitutes, scab-ridden infants, student activists, strikers, intellectuals, communist activists, rebels, foreign armies supporting foreign business interests. Trend-setter, snob, leader, industrial muscle, the name that keeps the Beijing bureaucrats awake at night . . . a hybrid of Paris and New York in the 1930s with millions trampling the streets where the millionaires once trod . . . one way or another Shanghai has permeated the Western consciousness.

To seize the tail end of this leviathan you have to go back to the 1840s. At that time Shanghai was a prosperous weaving and fishing town – but not an important one – and walled to keep out the Japanese pirates that roamed the China coast. The British forcibly opened up a concession here in 1842 after the First Opium War; the French followed in 1847, an International Settlement was established in 1863 and a Japanese enclave in 1895 – each completely autonomous and immune from Chinese law.

Lying just off the sea and just upstream from the Yangtse, a river that could be navigated several hundred km into the interior by ocean-going vessels – Shanghai provided a gateway to a vast internal market. Spurred on by massive foreign investment, coupled with an inexhaustible supply of cheap Chinese labour, Shanghai quickly became a booming port and industrial city. In the mid-18th century it had a population of a mere 50,000 – by 1900 it had reached its first million, partly caused by the flood of refugees who came here when the Taipings took Nanjing in 1853. As for the foreign population, from a few thousand adventurers in the 1860s

there were some 60,000 by the 1930s.

The International Settlement had the tallest buildings in Asia in the 1930s, the most spacious cinemas, more motor vehicles than any eastern metropolis or in all other Chinese cities combined. Powerful foreign financial houses had set up here; the Hong Kong & Shanghai Banking Corporation, the Chartered Bank of India, Australia & China, the National City and Chas Manhattan Banks of New York; there were the blue-blood British firms of Jardine & Matheson, Sassoons and others that got their start with the opium trade; and there were the newer but aggressive American firms, representing American factories that had *everything* for sale. Guarding it all were the American, French and Italian marines, British Tommies and Japanese Blue-jackets; foreign ships and submarines patrolled the Yangtse and Huangpu Rivers and the coasts of China. They maintained the biggest single foreign investment anywhere in the world – the British alone had 400 million pounds sunk into the place. After Chiang Kai-shek's coup against the communists in 1927, the Kuomintang closely co-operated with the foreign police and with Chinese and foreign factory owners to suppress the labour unrest; the Settlement police, run by the British, arrested Chinese labour leaders and handed them over to the Kuomintang for imprisonment or execution and the Shanghai gangs were repeatedly called in to 'mediate' disputes inside the Settlement.

So if you were rich – and preferably foreign – you could get anything in the Shanghai of the 1920s and 1930s; dance halls, opium dens, gambling halls, flashing lights and great restaurants, and the dimmed lights of the brothels and your choice of 30,000 prostitutes. Supporting it all were the Chinese who provided the muscle in Shanghai's port and factories; beasts of burden possibly worse off than beasts. Shanghai was the largest manufacturing city in Asia, with more than 200,000 workers employed in the many factories.

Edgar Snow, who came to Shanghai in the late 1920s wrote of

hundreds of factories where little boy and girl slave workers sit or stand at their tasks twelve or thirteen hours a day, and then drop, in exhausted sleep, to the dirty cotton quilt their bed, directly beneath the machine.

I remembered little girls in silk filature factories – all of them, like most contract labour in Shanghai, literally sold into these jobs as virtual slaves for four or five years, unable to leave the heavily guarded, high-walled premises day or night, without special permission.

And I remembered that during 1935 more than 29,000 bodies were picked up from the streets and rivers and canals of Shanghai – bodies of the destitute poor, and the starved or drowned babies or children they could not feed.

When the Communists came to power in 1949 one of the first things they wanted to do was turn Shanghai into a showcase of how communism really worked. Today, whilst housing, sanitation, water supply and pollution are still serious problems in Shanghai, it should be remembered that the housing developments, the eradication of the slums, the rehabilitation of the city's hundreds of thousands of opium addicts, the elimination of child and slave labour, are staggering achievements.

Today, Shanghai has a population of 11.85 million people – but that figure is deceiving since it takes into account the whole municipal area of 6100 square km. Nevertheless, the central core of some 220 square km has 6.3 million people, which must rate as some of the densest living in China, if not in the world. In 1955 a plan was announced to reduce the city's population by one million. Some estimates put the number of people moved out of Shanghai at two million since 1949; perhaps as many as 1½ million were young people 'sent down' to the countryside during the Cultural Revolution (although at the same time Shanghai's birthrate rose). Whatever the actual figure Chinese officials will tell you that the professionals and technicians were 'persuaded' to go to the interior to start new schools, colleges and hospitals. Meanwhile, many of the 'exiled' young people who try to creep back are nabbed and shipped out again.

Population and unemployment are severe problems in Shanghai; some economists claim that China's switch to light industry over the last five years or so is due to the fact that it can absorb up to three times the number of workers that heavy industry can – and at the same time increase the general standard of living. A 1982 estimate of the number of private businesses operating in Shanghai was 12,500 – and there must be thousands more if you include the roving pedlars and free-marketeers. People are so numerous in Shanghai that the weekly day off is staggered – so shipyard workers don't rub shoulders with textile workers on the streets. Overcrowded as it is, Shanghai still enjoys a high living standard in comparison with the rest of China, at least in terms of wages, the availability of consumer goods and educational opportunities.

Shanghai continues to play an enormous role in the national economy; when the Communists came to power they set about downplaying this role and priority of industrial development (under the first five Year Plan launched in 1953) was given to the strategically less vulnerable and poorer cities and towns of the interior.

In 1956 the coastal regions were again reaffirmed as logical places for an industrial base, possibly because of the ease of import and export of goods by ship. That resulted in another burst for Shanghai and in the late 1950s the city's limits were extended to encompass the surrounding counties, giving the city more control over its supply of food and raw materials. In 1963 Zhou Enlai put his personal seal of approval on the city and output for certain facets of the city's economy was given priority. Today, the city accounts for 15% of China's total industrial output and 20% of its exports. Shanghai is now being looked upon as a source of technical expertise, the weak link in China's modernisation drive.

Foreign business is also back in business in Shanghai; some US$200 million has been invested by foreign companies in the city, like the massive Baoshan steelworks (aided by the Japanese) and a giant petro-chemical works. But Shanghai still lags behind developments like the Shenzhen Special Economic Zone. There are plans for a satellite city to accommodate 100 new foreign enterprises, joint ventures are being boosted (the key foreign investor in these enterprises so far are the Japanese) and in 1983 the State Council announced that Shanghai would become the hub of a new economic zone in the Yangtse Delta. The new zone would cover 84,000 square km of Jiangsu and Zhejiang farmland, with 50 million people and 10 major urban centres (Suzhou, Wuxi, Changzhou, Nantong, Hangzhou, Jiaxing, Huzhu, Ningbo and Shaoxing). Economic development has been hampered by different regulations in these areas, so the idea is to give Shanghai overall control of the region and greater autonomy in decision-making, which will most certainly allow it to lead the way for the rest of the country.

Shanghai is also one of the most politically important centres in China – and one of the political hot spots. The meeting which founded the Chinese Communist Party was held here back in 1921. It was an important centre of Communist activity when the Party was still concentrating on organising urban workers – a disastrous policy as it turned out. It was also in this city that Mao threw the first stone of the Cultural Revolution, a piece of political rhetoric that he had failed to get published in any of the newspapers or journals in Beijing.

Most extraordinary, it was in Shanghai during the Cultural Revolution that a 'Peoples Commune' was set up, modelled on the Paris Commune of 19th century. The Paris Commune was set up in 1871 and was made up of municipal councillors elected by universal suffrage. The commune controlled Paris for two months, attempting reforms aimed vaguely at achieving socialism. It abolished state support for religious organisations, resumed church property and excluded religious teaching and services from the schools. It planned to take over workshops and factories not in production and turn over their management to the workers associations. But the propertied classes of France, whose representatives dominated the National Assembly, organised an attack on Paris in an effort to destroy the commune; in a week of street fighting – the 'Week of Blood' from May 22 to May 28 – 30,000 Parisians died and another 45,000 were arrested, later to be exiled, executed or imprisoned. 'Now we have finished with socialism for a long time' declared Adolph Thiers, a royalist and Chief Minister of the National Assembly. It seems the Shanghai Red Guards misinterpreted the Chairman and got the idea that the Cultural Revolution was all about introducing true Socialism to China – they lasted three weeks before Mao ordered the army in to put an end to the People's Commune.

It was in Shanghai that the 'Gang of Four' had their power base; the campaign to criticise Confucius and Mencius was started were in 1969, before it became nationwide in 1973 and was linked to Lin Biao. In 1973 an influential journal called

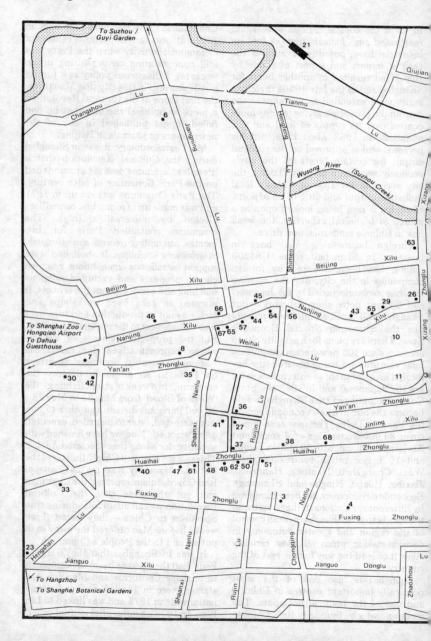

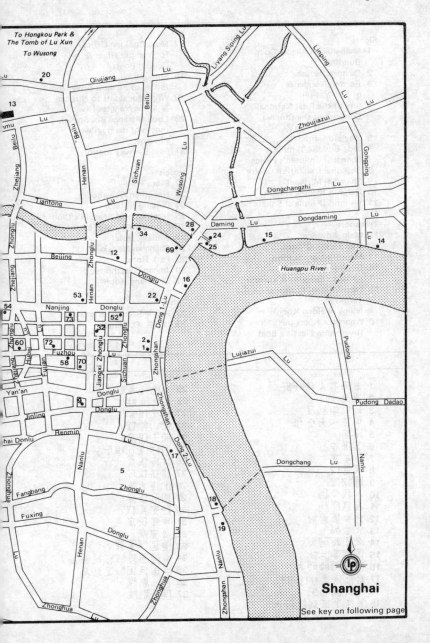

To Hongkou Park &
The Tomb of Lu Xun

To Wusong

20

13

Qiujiang Lu

Lu

Beilu

Beilu

Zhejiang

Henan

Sichuan

Wusong

Zhoujiazui

Gongping

Lu

Tiantong Lu

Beilu

Lu

Dongchangzhi Lu

Zhongmu

Zhongmu

Zhejiang

Beijing Lu

Zhonglu

Henan

Zhonglu

Donglu

28

34

69

12

24

25

15

14

Daming Lu

Dongdaming Lu

Huangpu River

53

16

Nanjing Donglu

22

54

73

52

Zhonglu

2

1

Zhongshan

60

32

72

Fuzhou

Jiangxi Zhonglu

Sichuan

58

70

Lujiazui Lu

Pudong

Yan'an

Donglu

Zhongshan

Dong 1 Lu

Jinling

Donglu

Pudong Dadao

hai Donlu

Renmin

Lu

17

Zhongshan

Nanlu

Dong 2 Lu

Dongchang Lu

Nanlu

5

Zhonglu

Fangbang

Nanlu

18

Fuxing

19

Donglu

Henan

Lu

Zhongshan

Zhonghua Lu

Nanlu

**Shanghai**

See key on following page

Sights
1 Shanghai Municipal Govt. Building
2 Customs House
3 Former Residence of Sun Yat-sen
4 Site of the First National Congress of the Chinese Communist Party
5 Yuyuan Garden
6 Jade Buddha Temple
7 Shanghai Children's Palace
8 Shanghai Exhibition Centre
9 Shanghai Museum
10 Renmin (People's) Park
11 Renmin (People's) Square

Transport
12 Main Advance Rail Ticket Office
13 Main Railway Station
14 Gongpinglu Wharf (ships to Qingdao & Dalian)
15 International Passenger Terminal (ships to Hong Kong)
16 Wharf for Huangpu Rivercruise Pleasure Boat

17 Main Booking Office for Yangtse River & Coastal Boats
18 Shiliupu Wharf (boats to Fuzhou & Wenzhou)
19 Wharf for Boats to Ningbo & Along Yangtse River
20 Long Distance Bus Station (north of main railway station)
21 East Railway Station

Hotels
22 Peace Hotel
23 Hengshan Guesthouse
24 Pujiang Hotel
25 International Seamen's Club
26 Overseas Chinese Hotel / CTS
27 Jinjiang Hotel
28 Shanghai Mansions
29 Park Hotel
30 Jingan Guesthouse
31 Shenjiang Hotel

Other
32 Public Security Bureau
33 U.S.A. Consulate

1 上海市人民政府
2 海关
3 孙中山故居
4 中共一大会址
5 豫园
6 玉佛寺
7 少年宫
8 展览馆
9 博物馆
10 人民公园
11 人民广场
12 火车售票处
13 火车站
14 公平路码头
15 国际客运站
16 浦江游船码头
17 轮船售票处(长江)
18 十六铺码头
19 长江,宁波轮船码头

20 长途汽车站
21 东火车站
22 和平饭店
23 衡山宾馆
24 浦江饭店
25 国际海员俱乐部
26 华侨饭店
27 锦江饭店
28 上海大厦
29 国际饭店
30 静安宾馆
31 申江饭店
32 公安局
33 美国领事馆
34 中国国际旅行社总局
35 中国民用航空总局
36 艺术剧院
37 国泰剧院

34 CITS Head Office
(all dealings to be done
at the counter in Peace Hotel)
35 CAAC

Entertainment
36 Shanghai Art Theatre
37 Guotai Theatre
38 Shanghai Art Academy
Exhibition Hall
39 Workers Cultural Palace
40 Conservatory of Music
41 Jinjiang Club
42 International Club
43 Shanghai Acrobatics Ground

Snackshops & Foodstores
44 Kaige Coffeeshop
45 Children's Foodstore
46 Shanghai Cafe
47 Shanghai Bakery /
Confectionary
48 Gongtai Fruit Store
49 Laodachang Bakery /
Confectionary
50 Haiyan Bakery /
Confectionary
51 Tainshan Moslem Foodstore

Restaurants
52 Deda
53 Yangzhou
54 Xinya
55 Renmin
56 Luyangcun
57 Meilongzhen
58 Xinghualou
59 Moslem
60 Dahongyun
61 Meixin
62 Chengdu

Shopping
63 24-Hour Dept. Store
64 Chinese-style
Clothing Store
65 Dongfang Furs &
Leather Shop
66 Fuli Silk Store
67 Jingdezhen Porcelain Shop
68 Huaihai Secondhand Shop
69 Friendship Store
70 Shanghai Antique &
Curio Store
71 Shanghai No. 1 Dept. Store
72 Foriegn Languages Bookstore
73 Xinhua Bookstore

38 画院美术馆
39 工人文化宫
40 音乐学院
41 锦江俱乐部
42 国际俱乐部
43 杂技场
44 凯歌咖啡总店
45 儿童食品店
46 上海咖啡分店
47 上海食品店
48 公泰水果店
49 老大昌食品店
50 海燕食物厂
51 天山回民食品店
52 德西餐社
53 扬州饭店
54 新雅饭店
55 人民饭店

56 绿阳香饭店
57 梅龙镇酒家
58 杏花楼
59 回民饭店
60 大泸运饭店
61 美心饭店
62 成都饭店
63 二十四百货商店
64 龙凤中式服装厂
65 东方毛服装厂
66 富丽绸布商店
67 景德镇艺术瓷器服务部
68 淮海旧惯商店
69 友谊商店
70 文物商店
71 第一百货商店
72 外文书店
73 新华书店

*Study & Criticism* appeared in the city – the calligraphy on the covers of the first issues is believed to be that of Mao himself, and the journal is thought to have been the mouthpiece of the 'Gang of Four'.

Shanghai's history as the most radical city in China, the supporter of dogmatic Maoism, one of the focuses of the Cultural Revolution, and the power base of Mao's ridiculous widow is rather ironic when you consider that the city is now, perhaps with the exception of Canton, the most capitalist and the most consumer-orientated in China.

### Climate

The best time to visit Shanghai is in spring and autumn. Winters can drop well below freezing and are blanketed in drizzle. Summers are hot and humid with temperatures as high as 40°C.

### Information & Orientation

Landmarks are a good way to navigate in Shanghai. The Peace Hotel at the intersection of the Bund and Nanjing Lu is just about the closest thing to a centre – it's the chief tourist crossroads. On the Bund the easy direction finder is the Customs House (with its large red star and clock tower) and the Communist Party HQ – both of these are to the south of the Peace Hotel. To the north is the unmistakable looming slab known as Shanghai Mansions.

From the strip of the Bund near the Peace Hotel you can get a bus in almost any direction. Heading west along Nanjing Lu you'll come to the futuristic facade of the Park Hotel which roughly marks the division between Nanjing Donglu and Nanjing Xilu. From here you can easily spot the TV Tower, which is a good intermediary point to aim for when heading to the area of the old French Concession (Frenchtown). The heart of Frenchtown is marked by the colossal wings of the Jinjiang Hotel.

The oldest part of the city is at the Wuxinting Teahouse, something of a city

symbol but very low-rise. Other destinations are a little awkward to get to on foot. Shanghai is a big place. It covers an area of 6100 square km, with the city proper estimated at 220 square km. Some of the sights are right off the map – the zoo, for example, is right near the airport.

Street names are in Pinyin which makes navigating easy, and many of the streets are named after cities and provinces. In the central district (around Nanjing Lu) the provincial names run north-south, and the city names run east-west.

There are three main areas of interest in the city; the Bund from the Friendship Store to the Dongfeng Hotel; Nanjing Donglu from the Peace to the Park Hotels – as well as the sector to the south of this strip which is the downtown sector; Frenchtown which is the strip of Huaihai Zhonglu from Shaanxi Nanlu to Chongqing Nanlu, plus the adjoining Jinjiang Hotel area; and the Jade Buddha Temple and the side trip along Suzhou Creek.

**CITS** (tel 217117) does its dealings from the ground floor of the Peace Hotel. Trains, planes and boats can be booked here; standard markups on planes and trains and a surcharge on boats out of Shanghai. They also have astronomically priced tours to Suzhou, Wuxi and the rest of the wonders as far as Nanjing. One thing they are good for is arranging trips to factories, and you could also enquire about visits to other places, such as schools, hospitals, film studios . . .

There are two factories you can get into by yourself – a jade carving factory and a carpet factory, next door to each other at 25 & 33 Caobao Lu in the Xuhui District on the south-western outskirts of Shanghai. However, CITS may be able to organise visits to various other factories – a toothpaste factory? a neon signs factory? a chocolate factory?

They'll also get you tickets for the theatre, opera, acrobatic shows, etc – at a markup on what you'd pay at the door but at least you'll be sure of a seat; they also handle tickets for the Huangpu River trip, but these will also be cheaper at the source which is virtually across the road.

It's better set up than the Beijing CITS – more people to do the work and more space to work in – but they're a fairly tired, inundated looking lot, on the phones constantly, so you'll just have to be patient getting information from them; various bits and pieces of useful info (such as the trains to Hangzhou and back, directions to the Shanghai-Hong Kong ferry booking office) are laid out on the desk under the glass. The office is open 8.30 to 11.30 am and 1.30 to 5.30 pm

**Other Travel Services** China Travel Service (CTS) and the Overseas Chinese Travel Service (OCTS) operate out of the Overseas Chinese Hotel and seem to be better for boat bookings than CITS, if you can use their services. Another travel and touring service operates out of the Seaman's Club (across the road from the Pujiang Hotel); they'll book theatre tickets, and will organise visits to factories and places of interest, and also conducted shopping – could be worth checking out.

**Public Security** (tel 211997) is located at 210 Hankou Lu. It's difficult to locate the exact building and totally useless when you do. They will not give you even the standard alien permit additions that are easily obtainable elsewhere. The office is open 8.30 am to 12 noon, and 1.30 to 5.30 pm. It's near the bus No 49 stop.

**CAAC** (tel 532255 international passengers, 535953 domestic) is at 789 Yanan Zhonglu; the office is open 8.30 am to 12 noon, and 1 pm to 5 pm. The enquiry office at Hongqiao Airport can be reached on tel 537664.

**Post & Communications** The larger tourist hotels have post offices from which you can mail letters and packages. The Express Mail Service(tel 245025) is at 276 Bei Suzhou Lu – letters to London in

just two days, so they advertise. To receive letters, address them c/o the Peace Hotel; there is a counter on the ground floor where incoming letters are held.

Shanghai phones are busy during the day; the city has four phones to every 100 people, some 5000 'phone stations' and an equal number of private telephones – over 100 million calls were made in 1982! Long distance calls can be placed from hotel rooms and do not take long to get through. The International Telegraph Office, from which you can make long distance phone calls, is on Nanjing Donglu, right next to the Peace Hotel.

There are telex machines at the Jinjiang Club's business building and in the Jinjiang Hotel.

**Bank** There are money exchange counters in the premises of the larger tourist hotels, such as the Peace Hotel, the Jinjiang Hotel and the Seamen's Club. Credit cards are more readily accepted in Shanghai than in other parts of China. Most tourist hotels will accept the main ones like Visa, Amex, Mastercharge, Diner's, JCB, as will banks and Friendship Stores (and related tourist outlets like the Antique & Curio Store). Value is good to Y1500 with a 4% surcharge added. American Express will allow encashment of personal cheques up to US$1500 at no surcharge at selected counters of the Bank of China (this service now operates in 17 Chinese cities).

**Maps** There are quite a few variations around and lots of sources of them. For starters get one from the hawkers outside the railway station. Other places to try are the bookstores in the tourist hotels, which are usually well stocked.

Good maps in English get snapped up fast – so if you find one elsewhere during your travels before you get to Shanghai, it would be wise to get it there and then while you have the chance.

The best Chinese-language map is a

small foldup one with a picture of the Peace Hotel and the Bund on the cover, costing 14 fen; it's a masterpiece of map-making – though the heap of detail squashed into it may well require a magnifying glass. There is a larger bus map with Shanghai Shi on the cover which is easier to follow for the buses, but it does not include the location of the autorickshaw ranks (it does, however, include public toilets).

English maps are hard to get hold of – there's one called a 'Map of Shanghai Proper' which does not have bus routes and everything is in Wade-Giles spelling so it won't match the Pinyin street name signs – and the map is outdated.

There are two excellent large foldout maps, one in English called the 'Shanghai Tourist Map' and one in Chinese called 'Shanghai Daoyoutu', put out by the Cartographic Publishing House in Beijing. On the rear of the Chinese map is a simplified run-down of the bus system.

Probably the best English map is 'A Tourist Map of Shanghai' published by China Travel & Tourism Press; it's readily identifiable by the large advertisements for American Express, Remy Martin and Shanghai Arts & Crafts Jewellery. It tends to fall apart easily, you'll need a bus map anyway, but it's probably one of the best, if not the best English map of a city in China.

**Consulates** The United States Consulate (tel 379880) is at 1469 Huahai Zhonglu. The French Consulate (tel 371414) at 1431 Huaihai Zhonglu. The Japanese Consulate (tel 372073) is at 1517 Huaihai Zhonglu.

**Foreign Airlines** Cathay Pacific (tel 534242) is in room 123 of the Jinjiang Hotel. Japan Airlines (tel 378467) is at 1202 Huaihai Zhonglu. Pan Am (tel 563050 for the city office, and 536530 for the airport office) is in room 103 of the Jingan Guest House.

**Hospitals** Shanghai is credited with the best medical facilities and most advanced medical knowledge in China. Shanghai No 3 Hospital (tel 289930) is at 145 Shandong Zhonglu and offers outpatient services. Shanghai Huadong Hospital (tel 523125) at 257 Yanan Xilu, west of the Jingan Guest House, has round the clock service. Western medicines are sold at the Shanghai No 8 Drugstore at 951 Huahai Zhonglu.

**Film** Shanghai is a good place to stock up on film. Limited repairs to Japanese brand cameras are available at Seagull Photo Supplies, 471 Nanjing Donglu (tel 221004). The shop also sells Japanese cameras – who buys them? E4 and C41 film can be developed in Shanghai – enquire through your hotel reception desk or bookstore in the hotel; prints are around Y0.55 to Y1 each, and judging from the sample prints on display in the windows of the Nanjing shops, it's on a par with the west. Sanyo and Olympus have service stations in the city, but replacement parts must be ordered from Hong Kong, and sometimes goods have to be sent to Japan.

Olympus is at 38 10th Lane, Shaanxi Beilu (tel 534839) and 850 Yanan Zhonglu (tel 565222). Sanyo is at 159 Yanan Donglu (tel 2822906).

**Books** There are numerous foreign language outlets in Shanghai, if you take the tourist hotel bookshops into account. The main Foreign Language Bookstore is at 390 Fuzhou Lu (tel 224109). Next door is a stationery shop if you need writing supplies as well. Of special interest is the branch at 201 Shandong Zhonglu which sells old books in foreign languages. At 424 Fuzhou Lu is the Classics Bookshop. There are other specialist bookshops around Shanghai, if you can read Chinese. Fuzhou Lu is the bookstore hunting ground – it always has been that way – back in 1949 the bookshops removed the porn from the shelves and set up displays of Marx and company overnight.

There is a largish range of foreign newspapers and magazines available from the tourist hotels, from the *Wall Street Journal* to the *International Herald Tribune*, as well as *Time* and *Newsweek*. The latter two are the most valued by Chinese comrades and would make excellent gifts.

The biggest selection of Chinese periodicals is found at 16 Sichuan Beilu – and whilst the lingo might not make these seem worth browsing through, there are oddities like the comic book rental section to dive into. The Xinhua Bookstore at 345 Nanjing Donglu has kids books, lots of posters, some maps, and a foreigners' section on the 2nd floor.

For information on Shanghai, get a copy of Pan Ling's *In Search of Old Shanghai* for a run down on who was who back then. Another glossy that's produced in Hong Kong by the South China Morning Post is *Shanghai Hotels & Tourism* – it's designed for businessmen, comes out quarterly, and you'll find it around the major hotels.

## Things to See

Shanghai's thrills and spills are in the streets. If the world ran out of gasoline tomorrow it would hardly make any difference to the noise level in Shanghai – but even despite the lack of motorised traffic the place still has some of the most insane collections of hybrids on two, three and four or more wheels. Coming through the insectoid rush-hour is a legless rider using his hands to crank up the rear bike drive, then a truck-class tricycle with the rider pedalling backwards (using a rear sprocket and chain arrangement) walls of pedestrians spill over into the vacant bike lanes of Nanjing Rd, whilst retired men with 'serve the people' armbands hurdle the railings to try and nail jaywalkers. As early as 5 am the city is alive; mass taichi in the parks, whilst the younger set go for the more exotic martial arts, and there's the inevitable jogging and even playing

frisbees. Covered food markets out in the neighbourhoods are readily identified by the mounds of fresh cabbage, or the halved pig carcasses thrown on the sidewalk nearby, or simply by the queues for eggs and slabs of bean curd. It's difficult to haul yourself out of bed at these hours, but Shanghai is a place for doing things and watching people – the sort of place where unobtainable Japanese products dangle on the billboards, and strips of pigs' innards hang from a dim doorway that smells of herbs and incense . . .pedlars materialise on street corners with their shady wares and cooks pound dough behind steamy windows, while outside a shoe repairer sets up shop on the sidewalk . . .

## What Was What

Time to engage in the hobby of determining what building was what, when, how, and why. It's a bit like a giant game of Monopoly: Jimmy's Kitchen, St Petersburg Restaurant, Delmonte's Casino, the Lido, Roxy's, Kabul Rd, Oxford St, Singapore Park. Most of the taller structures are dead wood from the 1930s and the buildings rapidly changed function after the Japanese invasion of 1937; the westerners got a brief respite from 1945 to 1949, but then the game was up.

The old **Chinese city** is now identified by the Zhonghua-Renmin ringroad, which encloses a shoddy maze of cobbled alleyways, with some newer buildings to the south. Old walls used to be surrounded by a moat, but these walls were torn down in 1912.

The **International Settlement** started off as small tracts of land on the banks of the Huangpu, north of the old Chinese city – and eventually snowballed to roughly the area shown by the map in this text. The British-dominated Settlement was a brave new world of co-operation by European and American powers (the Japs were also included but were suspect). It's fairly easy to discern. If you draw a line directly north from the Jingan Guest House to Suzhou Creek, then the area is everything from Yanan Lu up to Suzhou Creek in the north, and to the Huangpu River in the east. The ritziest place to live was west of today's Xizang Lu – villas spread this way as far as the zoo (now the Jingan district). The foreign embassies were grouped on either side of the Waibaidu Bridge; the Friendship Store now occupies some of the buildings of the old British Consulate, and the Seaman's Club used to be the Soviet Consulate.

Throwing a pincer around the top of the Chinese city and lying on the southern flank of the International Settlement, was the **French Concession**. The east-west dividing line between the French Concession and the International Settlement is the present-day Yanan Lu (previously known as Avenue Foch in the west, and Avenue Edward VII in the east). The French strip of the Bund (south of Yanan) was known as the Quai de France. Roughly, the boundaries of Frenchtown can be drawn by heading south from the Dahua Guest House on Yanan Lu to the Xujiahui Traffic Circle, east along Zhaojiabang Lu and Xujiahui Lu to the Hunan Stadium, then up alongside the western border of the Chinese city as far as Yanan Donglu – and then tack on the pincer between Yanan Donglu and the northern rim of the Chinese city. Not all of Frenchtown was densely inhabited back then, and in any case the name is a bit of a misnomer as there weren't too many French there to begin with – like the other concessions it was 90% Chinese, and the most numerous foreign residents in Frenchtown were White Russians. Vietnamese troops were used by the French as a police force (just as the British used Sikhs in their concessions). For villa and mansion architecture the French concession holds the most surprises – a rather exclusive air to the elegant townhouses and apartment blocks. The core of things is around the present Jinjiang Hotel and Huaihai Lu.

The original **central district** was bounded by today's Xizang Lu, Yanan Lu, Suzhou Creek and the Huangpu River. If you bisect that with Nanjing Lu then the key wining and dining, shopping and administrative/hotel area is the slab south of Nanjing as far as Yanan, with Nanjing Donglu being the chief culprit. This is today's Huangpu District.

The area north of the central district and up as far as Suzhou Creek used to be the **American Settlement**. The area on the other side of the creek, east of the Main Railway Station and along the banks of the Huangpu, used to be the **Japanese Concession**. These areas eventually became a Chinese industrial suburb, the **Hongkou District** and are not of great interest, although the bridges above the polluted sections along Suzhou Creek are good for observing tugs and barges – there's a great deal of industry and warehouses along these banks. The major universities, Tongji and Fudan, are right up north. The main factory zones, shipyards, warehouses and new high rise housing developments are in the sector northeast of here.

Over on the other side of the railway tracks to the west and the north of the city, are rings of new industrial suburbs – **satellite towns** where the workers live in highrises adjacent to their factories and plants – the Soviet model. This also includes the area due south of the old Chinese city and Frenchtown. The housing projects sprang up, as they did in other Chinese cities, in the 1950s, and were erected outside the original city limits. Ten thousand dwelling units were concentrated in north-east Shanghai, and another 10,000 in southern, northern and western Shanghai in the initial building programme. These satellite towns are about eight km from the centre of Shanghai, and they have their own schools, day-care centres, markets, hospitals . . .

Beyond the industrial zones are the **market gardens** that feed the Shanghai dynamo – a long way out there from

downtown, but very close if you head due east. Directly east of the Bund, on the eastern banks of the Huangpu is an area which was barely worked on by the western powers. There is now a mixed residential, industrial and warehousing strip running along the eastern bank, but immediately beyond it are farming areas. There are no bridges over the Huangpu, since it would disturb the heavy shipping, but lots of ferries do the job.

**The Bund**

The Bund is an Anglo-Indian term for the embankment of a muddy waterfront – in Chinese it's referred to as 'Waitan' and on the map it's Zhongshan Donglu (Zhongshan Road East). The Bund is an apt description; between 1920 (when the problem was first noticed) and 1965 the city of Shanghai sank several metres; correction of the problem involved pumping water back into the ground, but the Venetian threat is still there. Concrete rafts are used as foundations for highrises in this spongy mass.

The Bund is a great meeting place for local Chinese and foreigners alike – people stroll up and down in search of vicarious excitement, often provided by street performers or free-marketeers.

Pedlars sell anything from home-made underwear to naughty pictures. In the morning it's taichi and the martial arts exercises on display; at night it's a lovers lane.

Though startling to behold in a Chinese city, the edifices that line the Bund are no special wonder; the exteriors are a solemn mix of neo-classical 1930s Chicago with a bit of monumental Eygptian thrown in for good measure. To the Europeans, the Bund was from Shanghai's Wall St, and it saw a fever of trading as the city's fortunes rose and fell with each impending crisis. The buildings changed function several times as the crises got the better of traders, but originally they were banks, trading houses, hotels, residential buildings, commercial buildings and clubs.

One of the most famous traders was Jardine Matheson and Co, occupying a building about half-way between the present Friendship Store and the Peace Hotel. They registered in Canton in 1832, and dug into the China trade two years later when the British parliament abolished the East India Company's monopoly of the place. In 1848 Jardine's purchased the first land offered for sale to foreigners in Shanghai and set up shop shortly after dealing in opium and tea. Today, Jardine

Matheson just about owns half of Hong Kong – and they're not finished with Shanghai either – they have an office across the way at Shanghai Mansions. (James Matheson's nephew Donald, who inherited most of the Matheson side of the fortune, served in China from 1837 to 1849. By the age of 30 he'd had it, went to England, and later became the chairman of the Executive Committee for the Supression of the Opium Trade).

At the northwest end of the Bund were, or are, the British Public Gardens (now Huangpu Park) which was off-limits to Chinese during the colonial era – a sign at the entrance listed regulations, which included the prohibition of Chinese and dogs from the park. A Sikh guard stood at the gateway – part of the Indian force the British had brought in to protect themselves after the Boxer Uprising of 1900. Part of the British Consulate grounds has now become the Friendship Store, now guarded by plain-clothes Chinese policemen.

Whilst the Bund may no longer be full of noisy hawkers, tramcars, Oldsmobiles, typists, blackmarketeers, sailors, taipans and rickshawmen, its function is still very much the same – only this time it's the foreigners who come to kowtow to the Chinese trading establishments now set up here. There are a few alterations; the Customs House (built in 1927) is still a customs house, but the clock chime now plays 'The East is Red' at 6 am and 6 pm. A readily identifiable exterior by the dome on top is the Hong Kong & Shanghai Bank, completed in 1921 and one of the most impressive hunks of granite in colonial Asia. The rowdy RAF Club used to be up in the dome. Today the bank houses the Shanghai People's Municipal Government (City Hall, CCP and PLA HQ) – so there's little chance of seeing the interior. As for the HK & Shanghai Bank, they have a more modest office now nearing the Bund further north.

The statues that lined the Bund were stripped, the whereabouts of the pair of bronze lions that once stood outside the HK & Shanghai Bank a mystery. It was first thought that they were melted down for cannons by the Japanese – but later the Chinese claim they found them, and several western sources mention seeing the lions in the early 1970s – possibly brought out for the making of a movie.

One interior that you can visit is the Dongfeng Hotel; as you sweep through the double doors, over the marble paving and bump into what looks like a railway concourse, you get an idea of how the Dongfeng started life – this was the Shanghai Club, the snootiest little gang this side of Trafalgar Square. Membership was confined to high-brow Brits, men only. To the left of the entrance is a Suzhou-style restaurant where you'll find the Long Bar, a 33-metre span of thick wood now hacked into three separate pieces. Opposite was the smoking room, now a Cantonese style restaurant, where the members, stomach replete, would doze with their copies of the Times, freshly ironed by the roomboys. There is a story (another one!) which underlines just how exclusive the Shanghai Club was in 1949; it goes that a westerner was caught in some polite crossfire between Communist and Kuomintang troops along the Bund – he made for the nearest shelter which just happened to be the Shanghai Club. His boss peered out from the window, then opened the door and barked 'You can't come in here. You're not a member'. He eventually let the poor sod in, but only after he'd been proposed for temporary membership.

## Nanjing Lu & the Downtown District

Nanjing Donglu (or Nanjing Rd East), from the Peace to the Park Hotels, is the golden mile of China's commerce. There are display windows here which will even stop you in your tracks! Just about everything can be found here (though back in Hong Kong it'd be cheaper). Before 1949 Nanjing Lu was a mixture of restaurants, nightclubs – and coffin makers. The most prestigious department stores were there, and still are – Wing On's (now the No 10 Department Store), Sun Sun's (now No 1 Food Store), and The Sun (now the No 1 Department Store). It's rather entertaining to drag yourself through these places where the escalators no longer function – the stores used to be exclusive, but now they are used by eager patrons clamouring for the latest things in short supply. The one practical souvenir that travellers like to get is a black vinyl carry bag, with 'Shanghai' embossed on it – proves you've been there.

A stroll down Nanjing Lu at night is neat, the window displays are eye catching, as are the bits of neon. Shanghai has the best reputation in China for the art of hairdressing (considered yet another facet of decadence back in the '60s and early '70s) – the Xinxin Beauty Salon at 546 Nanjing Donglu is for both men and women.

By day, from 9 am to 6 pm, only buses are allowed on Nanjing Lu and the rest turns into a pedestrian thoroughfare – you'll see why there's such a keen one-child-only campaign in Shanghai; the human tide on Nanjing Lu has to be seen to be believed.

At the end of Nanjing Donglu you come to another shopping drag, Nanjing Xilu (once called Bubbling Well Rd, before the well was sealed over). Dividing the sections for a bit of a breather is Renmin Square and Renmin Park, once the Shanghai Racecourse. The old Racecourse Clubhouse is now the Shanghai Municipal Library – the building is amongst the oldest in the city. The nondescript parkland and the desert-like expanses of paving at Renmin Square are where all those large meetings and rallies were held back in the '60s and '70s. In April 1969, 2.7 million people poured in here to demonstrate against the Soviet Union after clashes on the border (though even that figure didn't top the peaceful 10 million who'd gathered for the May Day celebrations in Beijing in 1963). The area

is also used for paramilitary training; under Renmin Square is a large air raid shelter.

An interesting store at the dividing line of Nanjing Donglu and Nanjing Xilu is the Shanghai Plants & Bird Shop, at 364 Nanjing Xilu. It sells bonsai plants, pots, tools, birdcages, goldfish and funeral wreaths. Related to hobbies, such activities (with the possible exception of the last) were suppressed during the Cultural Revolution. This is possibly one of the few places in the city where you'll find fresh flowers for sale. Most Shanghainese will queue up to buy plastic flowers – they last longer and are cheaper than the real thing.

The downtown area, bounded by Yanan Donglu, Xizang Zhonglu, Jinling Donglu and Sichuan Zhonglu, is a good place to rummage around. A lot of it is administrative, as it was under the International Settlement. Fuzhou Lu is an alleyway to explore, with bookshops, small restaurants . . . once a collection of teahouses covering for brothels.

## Shanghai Museum

On Henan Nanlu, just off Yanan Donglu, is the Shanghai Museum. It's said to be one of the best in China – perhaps so if you knew what you were looking at. There's a fair collection of bronzes (graduated bells, knives, axeheads, chariot ornaments), ceramics (blue and white Ming wares, black and cradle-glazed pottery), paintings and some terracotta figures from Xian. And, according to the museum itself, the opening hours are 9 to 10.30 am (closing 11.45 am) and 1 to 3.30 pm (closing 4.45 pm), and closed Sundays. There is a shop on the 2nd floor where bronzes, scrolls and ceramics can be bought.

## Frenchtown

Take a No 26 bus from the downtown area to land yourself in the general vicinity of Frenchtown, the former French concession. The lengthy walk out there is also worthwhile. The core of Frenchtown is the area around Huaihai Lu and the Jinjiang Hotel. The area was mainly inhabited by White Russian emigres who numbered up to a third of the foreign population in the 1920s and 1930s. They ran cafes and tailoring businesses along Huaihai, and took jobs as riding instructors, bodyguards – and prostitutes.

The cafes and tailoring outlets in today's Shanghai still centre around Huaihai, and there are excellent bakeries and shopping (mainly shoe stores, household decorations and some second-hand shops). The Parisian touch is about as chic as China will get – the architecture is still standing from the 1930s . . . more spacious, more parkland. The street leading west off the northwestern tip of the Jinjiang Hotel is intriguing for its squat double-storied architecture where underwear flaps from the former residences of the rich, or a duck on a pole hangs out to dry.

Back in the bad old days the French Concession had a different set of laws from the International Settlement. The French licensed prostitution and opium smoking (whilst the Internationals just turned a blind eye). With such laws, and because of its proximity to the old Chinese city, a number of China's underworld figures were attracted to the French side of things. On Xinle Lu, a kind of cul-de-sac which is the first diagonal street to the west of Xiangyang Park, is the Donghu Guest House (at No 167). This used to be the headquarters of the Great Circle Gang. Chief mobster was Du Yuesheng. After a career as a sweet-potato vendor, Du got his start in the police force of the French Concession, where he used his position to squeeze money out of the local opium merchants. In 10 years he had risen to a high position in the Chinese gangs that controlled the opium trade in the Yangtze Valley – they were said to contribute the equivalent of 20 million American dollars, annually, to the French authorities – and in return the French allowed them to use the concession as a

base for their operations. By the 1930s Du was on first-name terms with the Nanjing government leaders, and Chiang Kai-shek even appointed him 'chief of the bureau of opium suppression'. In March 1927, as the Kuomintang troops approached Shanghai on their Northern Expedition, the Communist-led workers rose in revolt and took over the Chinese part of Shanghai as planned. But Chiang had different ideas; financed by Chiang's supporters among the Chinese bankers in Shanghai, escorted by foreign police, and provided with rifles and armoured cars by the International Settlement, Du Yuesheng's gangs launched an attack on the workers, killing between five and 10 thousand people, many of them Communists and left-wing Kuomintang. The attack wiped out the Shanghai communists in a single stroke, and was followed by further massacres in Canton, Changsha and Nanchang, forcing the Communists to move the focus of their movement to the countryside.

## Site of the First National Congress of the Communist Party

One activity which the French, and later the Kuomintang, did not take to, were political meetings – these were illegal. The Chinese Communist Party was founded in July 1921 at a meeting held in a building in the French Concession of delegates from the various Communist and Socialist organisations around China. This building is usually recorded as being at 76 Xingye Lu – but according to the street signs in the area it stands at the corner of Huangpi and Ximen Lu, furthur south of Xingye Lu – see the map for directions.

We don't really know if the 'First Supper' was as cool, calm or collected as the present museum makes out. We don't even know if this really was where the meeting took place, exactly who was there, how many were there, the actual date or even what happened. Nevertheless, the Museum has been organised here in what is supposed to be the house of one of the delegates, Li Hanjun. There are also said to have been two foreigners in attendance.

Simon Leys in his book *Chinese Shadows* drops 12 names in the attendance list – and according to him, what happened to them afterwards didn't bode too well for Communist history. Only two, Mao Zedong and Tong Biwu (elder statesman of the Party and a remarkable political all-rounder) survived in good standing until their natural deaths – Tong in 1975 and Mao in 1976. As for the others, four were executed by the Kuomintang or provincial warlords; four defected to the Kuomintang (like Zhang Guodao who left after losing in the power struggle to Mao) – and of these four, two went over to the Japanese. Another delegate (Li Da) remained loyal to the Party and eventually became President of Wuhan Univerity after Liberation – he is supposed to have died of injuries inflicted on him by the Red Guards in 1966. The host, Li Hanjun, appears to have left or to have been excluded from the Party early on, but his execution by the Kuomintang in 1927 rehabilitated him.

The story continues that the delegates were disrupted in their meeting by the intrusion of an outsider – presumably a spy – and fearing a raid by the French police, they left the premises and later continued their meeting on a houseboat in Jiaxing, halfway to Hangzhou. The building is supposed to have been damaged during the massacre of 1927, and again at the hands of the Japanese.

So who and how many were actually there? The Mao Zedong Museum down at his birthplace in Shaoshan seems to mention only seven; Mao, Tong, Li Da, and the four who remained loyal and died martyrs. There probably wouldn't have been more than 16 – there aren't enough seats in the meeting room – in fact, just for the record, the meeting room contained (when I saw it in, um, was it August 1983?), 12 stools, four chairs, two small tables, one large table, 16 tea cups, two teapots, and one medium sized table.

## Sun Yat-sen's Residence

7 Xianshan Lu (formerly the Rue Moliere) is the former residence of Dr Sun Yat-sen. He lived not far from Fuxing Park for six years in this house, supported by Overseas Chinese funds. After Sun's death, his wife, Soong Qingling continued to live here until 1937, constantly watched by Kuomintang plain-clothes men and French police. Her sister had married Chiang Kai-shek in 1927, and her brother T V Soong was on-and-off Finance Minister to Chiang, and a wheeler and dealer in banking fortunes. Soong Qingling was a Communist – so it must have made for interesting dinner conversation. The house is set back from the street, furnished the way it used to be (it was looted by the Japanese) – however, admission is screened to save wear and tear on the floorboards and furnishings. Fuxing Park is also worth a stroll if you're in the area; locals airing the kids off, playing chess . . .

## Arts & Crafts Research Institute

A villa of the bourgeois French class is worth delving into; it's now the Arts & Crafts Research Institute at 79 Fenyang Lu. The mansion is magnifique, and the institute has something like 15 specialities – woollen embroidery, boxwood carving, lacquerware inlay, paper-cutting. The faculty here creates the prototypes for small factories and workshops around China, examines the traditional arts, and acts as technical adviser to the specialist factories in Shanghai. The first of its kind in the PRC, the institute was created in 1956. The Conservatory of Music is on the same street – for more details see the section on Nightlife.

## Huangpu River Trip

There are three main perspectives of Shanghai – from the gutters, from the heights (747 views from the battlements of the tourist fortresses), and from the waters. The Huangpu River has some remarkable viewing of the Bund and the riverfront activity. There's something historical about doing this joy ride – the junks that cut in and out of the harbour bring back memories so old you probably last saw them in some pirate movie. Boat is the way you would have arrived in Shanghai back in the 1920s, and today's touring vessels seem to ham it up for the colonial style of that era.

Tour boats down the Huangpu depart from the dock on the Bund, slightly north of the Peace Hotel. There are several decks on the boat, and foreigners are expected to take the upper deck, with tea service in the cabin, deckchairs, and beer galore. Upper deck is Y12 for special service, and Y8 for ordinary service (not much difference between them, apart from subtle distinctions in the teaware) and you may be able to get a boat ride for Y2 (student price) if you're persistent. Locals pay less than that for lower deck. Departure time is 1.30 pm daily, with possible extra departures at 8.30 am and 7 pm in the summer, and possibly an extra departure on Sunday. The schedule may become erratic in winter due to worsening weather. Tickets can be purchased in advance from CITS at the Peace Hotel, or at the boat dock – but there's no real need if you're taking upper deck since it probably won't be full. If you roll up at the boat dock attendants will take your case in hand, usher you to the front of the queue and through elaborate sets of doors to the privacy of your deck. The boat takes you on a 3½ hour ride, 60 km round-trip, northward up the Huangpu to the junction with the Yangtse River, to Wusongkou and takes the same route back. There's usually a mini-acrobat show on the Chinese deck below on the return run (highly rated!).

Shanghai is one of the world's largest ports; 2000 ocean-going ships and 15,000-odd river steamers load and unload here every year. Coolies used to have the backbreaking task of loading and unloading, but these days the ports are a forest of cranes, derricks, conveyor belts and forklifts. The tour boat passes by all sorts of shipping, freighters, bulk carriers, ro-ro ships, sculling sampans, the occasional junk – and Chinese navy vessels (which aren't supposed to be photographed).

The boat turns around before you get wind of what is happening at the giant steel works under construction at Baoshan. The Baoshan works were designed at a projected cost of US$13.3 billion, the largest single project undertaken since the founding of the PRC, planned to yield 6.7 million tonnes of steel per year, using the most advanced technology imported from Japan, West Germany and the USA. It was going to be a centrepiece of the modernisation programme, and when the ground-breaking ceremony was held a plane load of Politburo members flew down from Beijing for the occasion. Exactly what state the steelworks are in now is anyone's guess, but in 1980 and 1981 the government slashed its expenditure on its over-ambitious building programme and work on Baoshan was suspended. There had been a number of problems with the plant; Chinese ore was too low-grade for the sophisticated Japanese blast furnaces, so higher grade ore had to be bought from Australia, but that was too expensive; the location of the steel mill was on swampy ground, requiring 300,000 tonnes of steel supporting piles, some of which sank out of sight; the shallow Yangtze River Estuary could not accommodate the 100,000-tonne freighters bringing the ore from Australia, so new port and storage facilities had to be built 209 km south and the ore shipped to Baoshan in smaller vessels. The real cost of building the steel works looked like running up to US$27 billion, an astronomical 40% of China's national budget of US$65 billion for 1981. Chinese fascination with heavy industry perhaps stems back to the 19th and early 20th centuries, when they were repeatedly defeated by industrialised Japan and the western nations. Modernisation was associated with heavy industry and a famous Mao thought was 'Make steel the key link' . . . thus from 1949 to 1980, 50% of all government investment went into heavy industry and only 5% into the consumer-goods-producing light industry, and 8% to agriculture. The trend now is away from heavy industry and more to light industry and the production of consumer goods.

## Yuyuan Bazaar

At the north-eastern end of the old Chinese city, this centres on what is known as Yuyuan or Mandarin Gardens, and combines the Temple of the Town Gods (Chenghuangmiao). The place gets some 200,000 visitors daily, so try and stay out of it on weekends! There's nothing of historical interest left – people just come here to gawk at each other, mix, buy, sell and eat (see the Places to Eat section) – it's all entertaining enough.

**Yu Gardens** were built for the Pan Family, rich Ming Dynasty officials, and took 18 years to throw together (from 1559 to 1577) and much less time to destroy. It was bombarded during the Opium War in 1842 – somewhat ironic since the deity lurking in the Temple of the Town Gods is supposed to guarantee the peace of the region. In the mid-19th century the gardens became the home-base of the 'Society of Small Swords' who joined with the Taipings and wreaked considerable casualties on the adjacent French Concession – the French responded promptly with thorough destruction. There's a museum devoted to the uprising and demise within the gardens. The area was again savaged during the Boxer Rebellion.

The **Temple of the Town Gods** first appeared in the Song Dynasty, and disappeared somewhere in the last paragraph. The main hall was rebuilt in 1926 with reinforced concrete and has recently undergone renovation after being used as a warehouse.

Fanning out from the temple and the gardens is the Yuyuan shopping area – a Disneyland version of what the authorities think tourists might think is the real China. You enter the main action area via the **Wuxinting Teahouse**, a five-sided job set in a pond and looking as old as tea itself (pleasant to sit on the upper floor over a 60 fen pot of chai, but stay clear of the coffee and cocoa!). The zigzag bridges leading to the teahouse were once full of misshapen beggars at every turn, something to try and visualise as you take in the present scenery. The surrounding bazaar has something like 100 small shops selling the tiny, the curious and tourist junk. Lots of places for Chinese snacks. You can get hankies emblazoned with Chinese landmarks – every time you blow your nose it will remind you of China. You can get antiques, fans, scissors, bamboo articles, steamed ravioli, vegetarian buns, wine and meat dumplings, chicken and duck blood soup, radish-shred cakes, shell carvings, paintings, jigsaws . . .

The strangest thing about Yuyuan Bazaar is that you get past the 'reception centre' and the stage shows and further into the cobbled alleyways, you strike near poverty. The slums have been cleared, and newer housing blocks exist to the south, but the back alleys are certainly lower-end living. There's no sanitation – everything's done with buckets and public toilets. Notices in Chinese warn residents not to eat too much at the height of summer because disease spreads faster. Group tours that have requested a bit more of an in-depth visit have been somewhat misled – word goes out to the area to be visited ahead of time, and the sick and disabled are told to stay off the streets. The maze of alleys is best explored early in the morning (5 am to 8 am), when gutter teeth-cleaning and other ablutions are underway . . . a group of tourists remarked on the 'healthy' rouged cheeks of the children down this way – it was winter, and the red cheeks came from windchill.

## Jade Buddha Temple & Suzhou Creek

From the Yuyuan Bazaar you can hop on a

bus No 16 and ride all the way out to the Jade Buddha Temple (Yufosi). The ride takes in half of Shanghai en route, and most likely half the population will get off the bus too.

The temple is an active one, with 70 resident monks at last count. It was built from 1911-18; the exterior is readily identifiable by the bright saffron walls. Inside, the centre piece is a 1.9-metre high white jade Buddha (some say it's alabaster), brought back by a monk from Burma to Zhejiang Province in 1882 and finding its final resting spot here. This seated Buddha, encrusted with jewels, is said to weigh 1000 kg. A smaller, reclining Buddha, from the same shipment, lies on a redwood bed – suspiciously adopting the reclining pose of an opium smoker?

In the large hall are three gold-plated Buddhas, and other halls house ferocious looking deities. Artefacts abound, not all on display, and some 7000 Buddhist sutras line the walls. Should your timing coincide, there may be a ceremony of some description in progress. Also in the precincts is a vegetarian restaurant, and a branch of the Antique & Curio Store that sells miniature sandalwood drums and gongs, replicas of the larger ones used in ceremonies.

The temple was largely inactive from 1949 to 1980, as the monks were disbanded and the temple used for other functions. During the Cultural Revolution the place was only saved from destruction by a telegram (so the story goes) direct from the State Council. No doubt the recent picking up of activity is partly due to the tourist trade – the fact is that Shanghai, being so young, has almost no temples to show off. Yufosi is popular with Overseas Chinese.

No photography is permitted. The temple is open daily from 8 am to 5 pm, but closed on some special occasions such as the Lunar New Year in February–that's when Chinese Buddhists, some 20,000 of them, descend on the place.

An interesting route to the Jade Buddha Temple is along Suzhou Creek. It's a long walk there, and you may prefer to bus it part of the way. The creek (water and banks heavily polluted) is home to sampans, small craft and barges, with crews delivering goods from the Yangtse reaches. There are stacks of bridges along the route and from these you'll get a decent view of the river life – walking direct along the banks at times is not possible due to warehouses blocking the paths. Along the way is a former church with an interesting twist – it's now a research institute for the electric light industry.

## Events

There are three events of significance. The Mid-Autumn Festival is held in October when they lay on the mooncakes–the festival recalls an uprising against the Mongols in the 14th century when plans for the revolt were passed around in cakes. Mooncakes are usually filled with a mixture of ground lotus, sesame seed and dates, and sometimes duck egg. The Shanghai Music Festival is in May. The Shanghai Marathon Cup is in March and is one of the top sporting events in the country. The latter two, if not the first one, were suspended during the Cultural Revolution. Hotel space may be harder to come by at these times, also at Lunar New Year in February.

## Kids

Chinese kids are the most baffling part of the population; diaperless, never crying, never looking worried – who knows what goes on inside their heads? Around the city are Children's Palaces, where extra-curricular activities take place and special interests are pursued. In theory this supplements regular schooling–but it has overtones of an elitist educational system. The one most visited by group tours (you can get in by yourself if you push) is on Yanan Zhonglu, just west of Jingan Park. The building really is a palace – once belonging to the Kadoorie family, and was then known as Marble House. The children here make model aeroplanes, play video games, attend classes in drawing, drama, music – and practise how to love their country and impress tourists.

A stark contrast to the kids palace is the Peiguang Middle School early in the morning – drop down here in the early morning when the kids are doing their exercises in the courtyard just off the street (to the sound of 'Oh Canada'). The school is along Xizang Lu, cornering Jiujiang Lu, which is one block south of Nanjing Donglu – the school used to be the notorious Laozhu Police Station in the concession days.

Children's stores are some of the places that parents and their (usually one) offspring gather. Try the bookstore at 772 Nanjing Xilu, the Xiangyang at 993 Nanjing Xilu (toys, clothing and furniture), the foodstore at 980 Nanjing Xilu (cakes and cookies), the shoe and hat shop at 600 Nanjing Donglu, and the clothing store at 939 and 765 Huaihai Zhonglu.

In the entertainment line the much-publicised child prodigies pop up at the Conservatory of Music (see the Nightlife section). Shanghai has its own film animation studio – China's Disneyworld products. There's also a troupe called the Children's Art Theatre, and acrobat shows are superb.

### Tomb of Lu Xun (in Hongkou Park)

Lu Xun (1881-1936) was a novelist and essayist, and was regarded as the founder of modern Chinese writing. He was revered as a scholar and a teacher – he was not a Communist, but most of his books were banned by the Kuomintang and he had to stay in hiding in the French Concession. His message to Chinese youth read 'Think, and study the economic problems of society ... travel through the hundreds of dead villages, visit the generals and then visit the victims, see the realities of your time with opened eyes and a clear mind, and work

for an enlightened society, but always think and study'.

Lu Xun is best remembered for *The True Story of Ah Q* – the story of an illiterate coolie whose experiences through the first revolution of 1911 show the utter failure of that event to reach down to the ordinary people. Constantly baffled, seeing everything through a fog of ignorance and susperstition, knowing words but not their meaning, he goes from one humiliation to the next, but each time rationalises his defeats into moral victories. Even when he is executed for a crime he did not commit, he goes cheerily to his death singing from a Chinese opera he does not understand 'After 20 years I will be reborn again a hero'.

Lu Xun's tomb is within easy reach of the Bund, and is located in Hongkou Park. There's a pompous statue of the writer which would have horrified him. The statue was cast in 1961 and replaces an earlier concrete model, which would also have horrified him. His brother in Beijing wrote to another writer in Hong Kong 'I have just seen a photograph of the statue they put up in front of Lu Xun's tomb in Shanghai; really, this is the supreme mockery! How could this personage sitting as on a throne be the effigy of someone who hated all solemn attitudes?' A museum in Hongkou Park tells the story of Lu Xun from the Communist point of view.

### Around Shanghai

A further 20 km north of Hongkou Park, towards the banks of the Yangtse and requiring a longer distance travel suburban bus, is Jiading County, with a ruined Confucian temple and a classical garden.

Southwest of central Shanghai and nearing a bend in the Huangpu River (within reach of Frenchtown) is the Longhua Pagoda. This fell into disrepair, was used by the Red Guards as an advertising pole, and has since undergone renovation for the tourist trade. The surrounding temple is largely concrete restructured, but the statuary of ferocious figures is impressive. The temple was once famous for its peach blossoms which have now disappeared. The pagoda is 40 metres high, octagonal with upturned eaves, said to date to the 10th century, but probably rebuilt a couple of times.

The Xijiahui area bordering the western end of Frenchtown once had a Jesuit settlement, with an observatory (still in use!). The St Ignatius Cathedral, whose spires were lopped off by Red Guards, has been restored and is open once again for Catholic services. It's at 158 Puxi Lu, Xujiahui District. Further south-west of the Longhua Pagoda are the Shanghai Botanical Gardens. They're open daily from 8.30 am to 4 pm, and have an exquisite collection of 9000 miniatures and 100 species.

On the way to the town of Jiaxing, by rail or road, is Sonjiang County 20 km south-west of Shanghai. The place is older than Shanghai itself. On Tianma Shan, in Sonjiang County, is the Huzhou Pagoda, built in 1079 AD. It's the leaning tower of China, with an inclination now exceeding the tower at Pisa by 1.5 degrees. The 18.8-metre high tower started tilting 200 years ago.

Heading in a westerly direction from the centre of Shanghai is the Industrial Exhibition Hall – you can drop in here for a mammoth view of some Soviet palace architecture. There are irregular displays of industrial wares and handicrafts from Shanghai. Out near the airport is Xijiao Park, a zoo with a roller skating rink, children's playground and other recreational facilities. To the west of that is the former Sassoon Villas. At Qingpu County, 25 km west of Shanghai, they're creating a new scenic area for tourists to visit, to make up for the dearth of real antiquities and temples that tourists go for.

## Places to Stay – the Mansions of Shanghai

Shanghai hotels are sights in their own right, a trip back to the 20s and 30s when the city was the most sophisticated of travellers' destinations. Furnishings and art decor opulence have survived quite well, considering what has passed. Add to this the strange armoury of electronic gadgets like closed-circuit TV, air-con, video games – all those creature comforts for today's visitor. A fair amount of renovation has been done on the buildings in the interest of tourism, though socialist plumbing is not always as successful as the western.

Apart from being navigation landmarks the lofty upper floors of the downtown hotels offer stupendous views, day or night. These can also be combined with a trip to restaurants serving great Chinese and western food (the latter sometimes linked with pre-Liberation chefs and usually excellent). Shanghai's relatively decadent nightlife also happens within the walls of the hotels (those mainly guilty of this are the Peace Hotel, the Jinjiang Club and Jinjiang Hotel, and to some extent Shanghai Mansions and the International Seaman's Club – see the Nightlife section).

Shanghai is a headache for the low budget traveller. Like Beijing there is simply a chronic lack of space and a lot of what's available is permanently occupied by businessmen, foreign dignitaries or resident foreign experts. The one established dorms have shown up in the *Jinjiang* and *Shenjiang* Hotels, but not on a regular cheapest available accommodation. Other dorms have shown up in the Jinjiang and the Shenjiang Hotels, but not on a regular basis – ask other people who have come from Shanghai, they may be able to fill you in on the situation. If you can't get cheap accommodation at one hotel then try and get the staff to telephone another hotel and see what's available – much better than tramping from hotel to hotel (the Jinjiang for example is six km from Shanghai Mansions). One thing worth thinking about – this is Shanghai and the history and the character of the Bund is one of the reasons to come here – a nice wood panelled room in the Park or the upper storeys of the Peace Hotel would be worth the splurge . . .

*Shanghai Mansions* (tel 246260) is at 20 Suzhou Beilu, near the Pujiang Hotel on the same side of Huangpu River at the junction with Suzhou Creek. Rooms are Y42 for a single (Y29 for a foreign expert) and Y140 for a double (Y82 for foreign experts) and there are 250 rooms and suites to choose from. For a suite toward the top of the hotel with a waterfront view and balcony and perhaps a grand piano – well, if you've got that sort of money then there's no need to ask . . . the Mansions are rather dull compared to other Shanghai hotels but try and make it to the rooftop because the views are stunning! The Mansions is a 20 storey brick building constructed in 1934 as a posh British residential hotel. Since it was on the fringes of the International Settlement near the Japanese side of town it was quickly taken over at the outset of the Sino-Japanese war in 1937. The Japanese stripped the fittings (like the radiators) for scrap metal, as they did with other Shanghai hotels during the occupation. As for the billiard tables, these were sawn off at the legs to suit the small Japanese stature. The place used to be known as Broadway Mansions; after the Japanese surrender and before 1949, the US Military Advisory Group to the Kuomintang set up shop on the lower floors, whilst the upper section was used by the foreign press and one floor was devoted to the Foreign Correspondents Club.

The *Jinjiang Hotel* (tel 534242) is at 59 Maoming Lu. Its so vast you need a map of the place to find your way around – there's a brochure on the hotel with a map available in the north building. The colossus stretches north-south along an entire block with two gates on the western side. The middle building is an 18-storey highrise and is mainly used by group tours; rooms start from Y40 for a single,

Y48 a double, Y52 for a triple, and Y68 for a room with four people in it. This includes nice old plumbing and excellent radiators; there are also rarer doubles for Y38 with a shared bathroom adjoining two rooms. Most rooms have a video hookup. The west wing, along Maomong Lu, has cheaper rooms and may have a dormitory. Back in the days when there were established dorms here an American traveller rolled in and when he was refused a dorm bed, he went off, found the dormitory and took over one of the three empty beds within; next day he went back to reception and enquired if there was a bed – he was told no, but stayed on regardless. About three days later they finally gave him a bed in the dorm! To get to the Jinjiang take bus No 41 from the North Railway Station; bus No 26 goes there from the Bund area.

If you don't stay at the Jinjiang you should at least drop down and have a look at it; it's located in what used to be the old French Concession, an interesting alternative to the area near the Bund, since the surrounding area is now entirely residential. The residents of the hotel though need never venture out – this fortress-like building has all you need to survive. Foreign heads of government are lodged here to impress them; at the same time the cockroaches scamper over the floor boards of the middle wing. The hotel pioneered close-circuit TV but the staff have no idea who's in what room at what time. Nixon stayed here if that's any recommendation, and in 1972 he and Zhou Enlai signed the 'Shanghai Communique' which set about normalising relations between China and the USA. The Presidential suite on the 16th floor of the middle wing goes for a modest Y500 a day. Other illustrious members of the human race who have passed through here are President Tito of Yugoslavia, Presidents Ford and Carter of the USA, Prime Minister Thatcher of the UK, Nehru of India and Tanaka of Japan. Apart from their fingerprints, check out the North building, a 14-storey block once called the Cathay Mansions and built as an exclusive French apartment block; amazing wood-panelling and iron chandelier period pieces – and the elevator men with grubby white gloves.

The *Peace Hotel (Heping Fandian)* (tel 211244 for the northern highrise wing, and 218050 for the south building). This hotel is on the corner of the Bund and Nanjing Donglu. Room rates vary from Y42 to Y48 for a double and then spiral rapidly upwards through the ceiling (though Y29 for a foreign expert may be possible); some travellers have managed Y12 and lower for a bed, but that's difficult and may only apply to foreign students in China. On the ground floor of the 12-storey edifice is the sumptuous lobby, shops, bookstore, bank, CITS office, barber, video games, snooker tables, cafe, etc – and the scalp massage service has a good reputation. To get to the hotel take bus No 65 from the railway station.

The Peace is a prize location for businessmen since it is adjacent to the Chinese trading corporations along the Bund. Copious space is taken up by the likes of Sanyo, Hitachi and the Banque Nationale de Paris, amongst others. In addition, Chinese move in during the winter months, conferences are rife and its a mite difficult to get in here. Drop in and examine the decor; staggering! High ceilings, chandeliers, brass door plates, ornate mirrors, art-deco lamps and fixtures – and 1930s calligraphy to be found around the place. Go up to the *Dragon & Phoenix Restaurant* on the 8th floor for great views across the Bund and the Huangpu River. The south wing has an elaborate lobby and magnificent staircase – the building used to be the Palace Hotel and was built in 1906 – and the brass plumbing and red carpets within are the originals.

The Peace is a ghostly reminder of the immense wealth of Victor Sassoon, from a Baghdad Jewish family; he made millions out of the opium trade and then ploughed it back into Shanghai real estate and horses. Sassoon's quote of the day was 'There is only one race greater than the Jews, and that's the Derby'. His office-cum-hotel was completed in 1930 and was known as Sassoon House, incorporating the Cathay Hotel. From the top floors Victor commanded the real estate – he is estimated to have owned 1900 buildings in Shanghai. As for the Cathay Hotel, that fell into the same category as the Taj in Bombay, the Stanley Raffles in Singapore and the Peninsula in Hong Kong as one of – or was it *the* place to stay. Sassoon himself resided in what is now the VIP section below the green pyramidal tower, complete with Tudor panelling – he also maintained a Tudor-style villa out near Hongqiao Airport just west of the zoo – it's now called the Hongqiao Club and is leased long-term by businessmen at Y1500 per day. Anyone who was anyone could be seen dancing in the Tower Restaurant; the likes of Noel Coward (who wrote *Private Lives* in the Cathay) entertained themselves in this penthouse ballroom – Noel himself being particularly taken with the gracious ladies who could argue with each other in six languages.

Back in 1949 the Kuomintang strayed into the place and set up their machine gun posts awaiting the arrival of the Communists. A western writer of the time records an incident where 50 Kuomintang arrived carrying their pots and pans, vegetables and firewood, and one soldier was overheard asking where to billet the mules. After the Communists took over the city, the troops were billeted in places like the Picardie (now the Hengshen Hotel on the outskirts of the city) where they spent hours experimenting with the elevators, used bidets as face-showers, and washed rice in the toilets – which was all very well until someone pulled the chain. In 1953, foreigners tried to give the Cathay to the CCP in return for exit visas – the government refused but finally accepted after the payment of 'back taxes'.

The *Overseas Chinese Hotel (Huaqiao Fandian)* (tel 226226) is at 104 Nanjing Xilu – it's easily recognisable by the distinctive clock tower with the big Red Star on it. The price range is Y39 to Y44 and up, with little chance you will get in since there are only 95 rooms and Overseas Chinese outnumber westerners by at least 10 to one (Shanghai is a prime OC destination – many being attracted by the city's reputation for advanced medicine).

The *Park Hotel* (tel 225224) is at 170 Nanjing Xilu and overlooks Renmin Park. The rooms have some old-world furnishings (the place went up in 1934) and prices are a drop lower than most hotels at Y29 a single (one on each floor); Y44 a double (10 on each floor, and you may be able to negotiate to price to Y36); Y52 a triple (two on each floor, negotiable to Y46) and Y120 for a four-bed room (two in the whole hotel but you may be able to get them to move in extra beds). A bus No 18 from the railway station will get you there; a bus No 65 will also, but it takes the long way around. The hotel is 24 storeys and was the tallest in Shanghai until the Shanghai Hotel topped it by eight metres in 1983 – the top floors have nice views.

The *Shenjiang Hotel* (tel 225115) is at 740 Hankou Lu, down an alley facing south off Renmin Park, and best approached from this direction. It's ostensibly for Chinese and Overseas Chinese only, but some travellers have got in. Double rooms are Y35 with bath; there is cheaper dormitory accommodation though the management will inform you otherwise and they may not want to talk about any sort of accommodation. Beds are designed for short legs. The hotel was built back in 1934 – a nine-storey block with no distinguishing features. Take bus No 18 from the railway station or bus No 65, but that goes around the long way.

The *Pujiang Hotel* (tel 246388) at 15 Huangpu Lu is near Shanghai Mansions, and caters to a mixed Chinese and western clientele. The dormitories here are the main attraction at Y6 per bed – readily given if beds are available. If the dorm is full then enquire about the rooms. The Pujiang used to be the Astor House Hotel, one of the most elegant in the early concession days, before it was dwarfed by Shanghai Mansions. Today the Pujiang is run down and can get cold and clammy in winter – otherwise it's nice enough. Take bus No 65 from the north railway station (or from the Qingdao boat dock) – the bus stop is further south over Waibaidu Bridge, so you'll have to walk back across the bridge.

The *Jingan Guest House* (tel 563050) is at 370 Huashan Lu; double rooms are Y36 to Y48 and may go lower. It's a suburban location but within reach of Nanjing Xilu. From the railway station take bus No 65 to Huangpu Park, then change to bus No 48 which starts at Huangpu Park. The hotel was formerly a German residential apartment building, constructed in 1925, nine storeys high, with traces of Spanish style in the balconies – the hotel faces onto a small park and has an outdoor cafe.

The following two hotels are far out from the centre of things and best avoided if you want to use public transport; the *Dahua Guest House* (tel 523079) at 914 Yanan Xilu has doubles from Y40 and up. It was built in 1937, a nine-storey building with 90 rooms and suites. The *Hengshan Guest House* (tel 377050) is at 534 Hengshan Lu and has 180 rooms in a 15-storey block. Doubles start from Y50 – enormous bathrooms and an enormous distance from the Bund.

Opened in mid-1982 is the *Longpoai* one km from Hongqiao Airport; this highrise has two wings, tennis courts, swimming pool and 162 rooms – modern and lacking character. The *Shanghai Hotel* is due to open in 1984 and stands at 460 Huashan Lu, near the Jingan Guest

House; 26 storeys, 600 rooms, sound system, computerised reception, 16 dining halls including European and Japanese, indoor gardens ... Ground has been broken for the *Huating Hotel* which will be 29 storeys, 1000 rooms, indoor swimming pool, tennis courts, gym, sauna, roof garden – the completion date is 1986 and is financed jointly by China and the USA.

## Places to Eat

Shanghai has a couple of its own specialities and is noted for its seafood (such as the freshwater crab that appears around October to December). Sampling the fare in the major restaurants can be an abysmal experience, due to the competition for seats and tables from the masses; restaurants are forever packed in Shanghai and you really need some local help to overcome the language problems. Lunch (around 11.30 am to 2 pm) is OK but dinner (5 pm to 7 pm) is a rat race. In these busy restaurants the waiters will try and get rid of you by either telling you that there are no tables, or by directing you to the cadre and foreigners rooms – more elegant decor and beefed-up prices (if it eases your digestion, back in the inflation-ridden China of 1947, a couple had dinner one evening in a Shanghai hotel and found their bill came to 250 million yuan!)

If you want to spend more time eating, and at local prices, then try restaurants a bit off the track, perhaps around the old French Concession area. You could also try the smaller places on Fuzhou Lu, where the greasy-spoon prices drop to around Y3 to Y4 per head and a large plastic mug of beer is 20 fen. On the other hand, if it's good food (either Chinese or western) you want, in surroundings that echo the days of the foreign concessions, then splash out on the restaurants in the old colonial hotels – details at the end of this section – it's one aspect of Shanghai not to be missed.

Not to be missed in Shanghai is the ease and delight of snack-eating. You get waylaid for hours trying to make it along the length of Nanjing Lu, stumbling into pastry shops and wiping off the smudges of lemon meringue pie, chocolate and cream, leaving only to fall immediately into the sweet store next door. In 1982 there were some 8500 workers in 75 bakeries – so there is a lot of the stuff around. The tourist hotels have a good range of cakes, chocolate eclairs and icecream sundaes to get you started (try the 8th floor of the Peace Hotel). The offerings for breakfast from the Chinese snackshops are so good you may be converted yet! (Common Chinese breakfast fare is the *youtiao*, a disgustingly greasy doughnut stick – but there are deep fried variations in the dough line that are smaller and much more palatable). Western snacks are a fad amongst the young of Shanghai; sandwiches are awful, coffee is terrible, creamcakes are fair to good, cocoa is disgusting, cold drinks are erk, but pastries are top notch. These snack hangouts have lots of character and there are lots of characters to be observed.

One thing worth noting – if you wander into a Nanjing Lu restaurant and see a couple in matching suits, a red rose in the lapel, and orange soft drinks on every table – then forget it, it's a wedding party. Around dinner time all the Nanjing Lu restaurants seem to be occupied by them.

### Restaurants on Nanjing Donglu

The *Deda Western Restaurant* (tel 214588) at 390 Sichuan Zhonglu on the corner of Nanjing Donglu, is of German origin; they serve western meals upstairs, and in winter you can get the Nippon sukiyaki cooked at the table. The ground floor of the Deda is a hang-out, open until 10 pm – a shocking contrast to the Peace Hotel Jazz Bar at this hour, and a sobering experience to visit both within the same hour.

The *Yangzhou* (tel 226174) at 308 Nanjing Donglu has fast food and jiaozi downstairs, and Yangzhou-style food upstairs. Coloured pictures outside and greasy spoons within. The *Sichuan* (tel 221965) at No 457 has hot and spicy food, including camphor-tea duck and some rather strange-tasting chicken. The *Minjiang* (tel 241009) at No 679 is a Fujianese-style establishment.

The *Xinya* (tel 223636) at No 719 has foreigners cubicles on the 3rd floor with rail-car wood panelling and Cantonese food at Y10 to Y20 per head. On the ground floor is a marvellous pastry shop featuring lemon and coconut tarts and cream-filled cones. Across the road is an enormous sweet and cake store the size of a department store.

For snacks and pastries try the *Donghai Fandian* at No 145; it was once known as the Chez Sullivan and is now full of bicycle punks. The *Xinjian* wineshop at No 547 has cold dishes and peanuts and you can get Chinese wines (including warm Shaoxing rice wine) by the glass – and in season they also have crab banquets.

## Restaurants on Nanjing Xilu

The *Renmin Fandian* (tel 537351) at No 226 serves Xinjiang-style food at around Y8 for three large shared dishes. The *Luyangcun* (tel 539787) at No 763 has snacks downstairs; upstairs is Sichuan and Yangzhou style chicken and seafood. The *Meilongzhen* (tel 532561) at No 1081 also deals in Sichuan and Yangzhou styles (the upper floor is for banquets).

For snacks, try the *Wangjiasha Snackbar* at No 805, off Shimen Lu; chicken, shrimp in soup, sweet and salty glutinous dumplings. The *Shanghai Children's Foodstore* is at No 980 and is good for cakes, candies and cookies. The *Kaige Coffeeshop* is at No 1001 and is a cafe and bakery; there's a branch at No 569 which used to be Kiesling & Bader's Shanghai establishment. The *Shanghai Coffeebar* at No 1442 is near the Exhibition Hall and is open until 10.30 pm – go upstairs for cakes, coffee (Y1 per head) and atmosphere.

## Restaurants on Fuzhou Lu

This street provides the best chance of getting a feed at low prices – try other places than those listed; there's enough around. The *Xinghualou* (tel 282747) at No 343 has snacks, cakes and refreshments downstairs from 9 am to 7 pm, including a kind of dimsum at 2.30 pm; upstairs you'll get Cantonese food, including 'stewed wild cat' and snake . . .

The *Meiweishi* (tel 221705) at No 600 serves Suzhou and Wuxi styles, as does the *Dahongyun* (tel 223176) at No 556. The *Moslem (Qingzhen Fandian)* (tel 224876) at No 710 has beefsteak, mutton and toffee apple. Also in the area is the *Hunan Restaurant* (tel 285454) at 28 Xizang Nanlu – for hot and spicy food and dongan chicken.

For Chinese-style snacks there's no better than the *Yuyuan Bazaar*; Nanxiang dumplings (served in a bamboo steamer); pigeon-egg dumplings (shaped like a pigeon egg in summer); vegetarian buns; spicy cold noodles . . . In the area, the *Olde Town Restaurant* (tel 282782) at 242 Fuyou Lu is a major restaurant specialising in 'Shanghai cuisine' and has been around since day 1 – it's now housed in a new building – the second floor is air-conditioned and mainly used for banquets, but you might try lunchtimes. The *Green Wave Gallery (Lubolang)* serves main courses and more expensive snacks; a seafood dinner here will cost around Y16 per head and may consist of black carp raised in the Lotus Pond under the winding bridge. Snacks include crabmeat buns, lotus root and bamboo shoot shortbread, three-shred eyebrow crisp-cakes and phoenix-tail dumplings (whatever they are).

## Restaurants in the Old French Concession Area

Try the *Shanghai Western Restaurant* (tel 374902) at 845 Huaihai Zhonglu, and the *Chengdu* (tel 376412) at No 795 – the latter is air-conditioned and has good Sichuan food. The *Meixan* (tel 285454) at

314 Shaanxi Nanlu, near Huaihai Zhonglu, serves Cantonese crisp duck and chicken. The *Red House* (tel 565748) at 37 Shaanxi Nanlu was formerly the Chez Louis and things haven't gone so well since Louis left; the food is generally terrible, but the snacks are better so long as they've got the right liqueur (baked Alaska and Grand Marnier souffle); foreigners are expected to use the top floor where meals are around Y15 a head, with wine included. The ground floor is cheaper and ostensibly for Chinese only.

Along Huaihai Zhonglu is a string of confectioneries that will drive you bonkers! The *Canglangting* at 10 Chongqing Nanlu south of Huaihai, has glutinous rice cakes and Suzhou-style dumplings and noodles. The *Tianshan Moslem Foodstore* at 671 Huaihai has Moslem delicacies, sweets and cakes. The *Haiyan Bakery* at 789 has brown bread(!) in the morning. The *Guoqiao Bakery* opposite the Haiyan at the corner of Ruijin Lu and Huaihai Lu, specialises in shortcake with red beans and osmanthus among the ingredients. The *Laodacheng Bakery & Confectionery*

at 875 has a downstairs bakery with superb ice cream in season; upstairs is a cafe where they spray ice cream over everything, and has meringues and macaroons – open until 9.30 pm. The *Shanghai Bakery* at No 979 has French bread, wholemeal bread(!), cream cakes and chocolate. The *Tianjin* at 1029 has Tianjin-style dumplings. The *Shanghai Dairy* at 1568 has milk, yoghurt and ice cream.

### Hotel Food

The big tourist hotels have excellent Chinese and western food. Dining hours are 7 am to 9 am for breakfast, 11.30 am to 2 pm for lunch and 5.30 pm to 8 pm for dinner. Whilst some of the offerings in the ritzier parts of the hotels are on the expensive side, a western breakfast is unbeatable and should cost no more than Y3.

*Shanghai Mansions* has a great dining hall on the 3rd floor overlooking Suzhou Creek and the sound effects at breakfast include the hoots of tugs and barges. There is another dining hall near the top,

mainly for foreign experts and banquets.

The restaurant on the 11th floor of the north building of the *Jinjiang Hotel* serves great western breakfasts (including yoghurt) and the bill should be around Y3, though you may even bargain a student rate. It's open 7 am to 8.30 am for breakfast and has some of the most opulent surroundings and incredible views to be found in Shanghai. The banquet room seats 1000; dinner dishes range from Y1 to Y20 each and include both European and Chinese – Sichuan food is a speciality. In the west buildings the *Bamboo Restaurant* serves reasonable fare at reasonable prices at dinner time but it closes at 7 pm. There is another restaurant in the vicinity that stays open until 9.30 pm but it's a total ripoff and serves (badly) 20 boring variations on steamed bread and noodles.

The *Dragon & Phoenix Restaurant* on the 8th floor of the *Peace Hotel* has western, Shanghainese, Sichuan and Cantonese food (breakfasts are amazingly excellent but stay away from the T-bone steak at dinner!). If you examine the tableware closely you might find original Cathay crests. Whilst the exotic seafood is expensive (Y9 for a seaslug) there are vegetable and pork dishes for around Y2.50 at dinner – on the other hand, if you've never eaten a seaslug then this might be the time to spend some money and find out what it's like . . . Breakfast is 7 to 9 am, lunch is 11.30 am to 2 pm, and dinner is 5.30 to 9.30 pm. Staff are attentive – they even have their courtesy rules posted up (smiling face, proper posture).

The *Overseas Chinese Hotel* has a few restaurants and Fujianese food is a speciality in the restaurant near the top of the nine-storey block; there's also a quaint little coffee bar to the left as you enter on the ground floor.

The *Park Hotel* has several restaurants; on the 14th floor (that's actually the 12th since two of the floors are below ground) is a restaurant that used to be called the Sky Terrace – a section of the roof could be rolled back to allow patrons to dine under the stars. Apparently the gizmo is still in place though we haven't heard of anyone getting the planetarium effect. Towards the top is the *Four Seasons Banquet Room* where extensive imperial banquets can be ordered in advance – it costs around Y50 per head for an eight-course dinner and that includes Beijing Duck.

The *Shenjiang Hotel* has some good, cheap restaurants – including Sichuan, Cantonese and Yangzhou fare. The *Jingan Guest House* has three restaurants; Sichuan, Yangzhou and French cuisines.

The *International Seamen's Club* (tel 242808) is at 20 Huangpu Lu, opposite the Pujiang Hotel. This is one of the favourites of travellers from across the road, particularly those who haven't had a western meal since they left Hong Kong. At the Seamen's you'll get beef steak with eggs for Y2.80, or with mushrooms for Y3.50; pork chop and onion Y1.80; mushroom omelette Y2.20, eggs and chips Y1.40; bacon and eggs Y1.80 – and their chips are nice and not the least bit greasy. Exotic drinks in the ground floor bar include Club Cocktail at Y2.50; Million Dollar Y2.50; Bloody Mary Y2.50; Brandy Egg Nogg Y2.50; and Screwdriver Y2.00 – and if you're hungry you can even order a Peach 'Mall Ba' for Y2.00. The ground floor restaurant also serves Cantonese, Yangzhou and western food.

### Vegetarian Food

Vegetarianism became something of a snobbish fad in Shanghai at one time; it was linked to the Taoist and Buddhist groups, then to the underworld, and surfaced on the tables of restaurants where creations shaped like flowers or animals appeared. Khi Vehdu, who ran the Jingan Temple in the 1930s, was one of the most celebrated exponents. The 1.9 metre tall abbot had a large following – and each of his seven concubines had a house and car. (The Jingan Temple was eventually turned into a factory.)

Materials for vegetarian fare include bean products, dried mushrooms, fungus, bamboo shoots, noodles, seaweed – and vegetables. It should be possible to arrange for a more elaborate presentation and quality by phoning in advance and booking a vegetarian banquet.

The *Jade Buddha Temple Vegetarian Restaurant* (tel 535745) is inside the temple, and serves bamboo shoots, bean curd, mock ham and mock eel shreds. The *Gongdelin* (tel 531313) at 43 Huanghe Lu has mock crab and other mock seafood, and mock duck and roasted bran-dough. Banquets can be arranged. The *Lixin* (tel 284433) is at 324 Huaihai Zhonglu.

A couple of shops specialise in vegetarian food; these include the *Hongkouqu Grain Store* at 10 Bei Haining Lu, and is good for fresh peanut butter, taihini, grains, beans and vegetable oils. The *Sanjiaodi Vegetable Market* is at 250 Tanggu Lu in the Hongkou District, north of the Bund – it's a large indoor market selling fresh vegetables and bean curd products (and also ready-to-cook dinners, fish and meat). The *Yuyuan Bazaar* area has snackbars serving vegetarian food.

### Night Owl Food

Food can be bought fairly late in Shanghai; The *Hongjia Eating House* (tel 660598) at 976 Piaoyang Lu, opposite Zhexing Market, is open until 4 am – get there on bus No 55. The *Kaifu Restaurant* (tel 244492) at 878 Sichuan Beilu has Beijing and other cuisines and is open until 10 pm. The *Hongkouqu Moslem Restaurant* (tel 462233) at 2033 Sichuan Beilu has beef, lamb, baozi and jiaozi dumplings, and is open until 11 pm – take trolley bus No 21 to get there.

### Nightlife

There's a bite-sized chunk of nightlife to be had here – like elsewhere in China it proceeds in fits and starts, mostly fits, and whilst it's pretty tame by pre-1949 standards it's rewarding enough . . . back in the bad old days the missionaries just didn't know where to start firing in this Sodom of the east; the acrid smell of opium hung in the streets, bevies of bar girls from the four corners draped themselves over the rich; there were casinos, greyhound and horse-racing tracks, strings of nightclubs, thousands of brothels, lavish dinners, several hundred ballrooms. The Kuomintang dampened the nightlife by imposing a curfew – the patrons just couldn't get it up in the daylight. When the Communists took over they wiped out in a year what the missionaries had failed to do in a hundred years. Since the average Chinese has to get up at the crack of dawn there's a self-imposed curfew of around 10 pm – nevertheless there are Chinese couples lolling about on the walkways and park benches of the Bund late into the night. Decadent foreign devils can rage on (as much as this place will allow) until around midnight.

Before the Communist takeover one of the major sources of diversion was the Great World Amusement Centre, offering girls, earwax extractors, magicians, mah-jong, jugglers, freak shows, dancing, slot machines, story-tellers, barbers, shooting galleries and pickpockets – and a bureau for writing love letters. Today the place has been turned into the Shanghai Youth Palace and stands at the corner of Yanan and Xizang Lu. Since 1983 the place has been hosting 'Youth Evenings' where 30-year-olds come in the hope of finding a husband or wife – match making is back in vogue in the PRC.

**Peace Hotel Jazz Bar** From 8 pm to 11 pm nightly they wind up the 1930s music machine here. Up front are two survivors of the 1940s pumping out polite renditions of 'Tea for two' or 'Gypsy Rag' or 'When the Saints . . .' or 'I Wonder Who's Kissing her Now?' and a sprinkling of Hong Kong pop tunes – no singing but these old timers do a splendid job with their piano, horns and drum smashes. Elderly foreign guests are so inspired as to leap to the dance floor

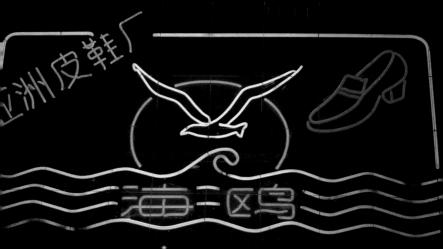

Top: Neon sign for Seagull shoes, Shanghai [MB]
Left: The Bund, Shanghai's main drag [MB]
Right: Laundry drying in back street of Shanghai [MB]

Top: Sunrise from Huang Shan [AS]
Bottom: On the Grand Canal [AS]

but I couldn't tell if it was a foxtrot or a rhumba – before my time. It's time to clean out the eardrums too – what's this, they *can't* be playing Waltzing Matilda! It's a good place to meet the rest of the foreigners in the woodwork. In the background, waiters with starched napkins over their arms glide between the tables ready to dispense Hot Toddies, Manhattans, Russian Bears, Rusty Nails and Shanghai Cocktails (a mix of gin and Chinese white wine). Ice cream sundaes and other delectables can be procured. All this takes place on the ground floor of the Peace Hotel; cover charge is Y1.

**Jinjiang Club** Located on Maoming Lu, opposite the main gates of the Jinjiang Hotel. You can't pass this one up – it's the most extraordinary nightlife museum in the PRC, if not Asia, and the emphasis is on 'museum'. The dazzling collection of interiors was thrown up in the 1920s and was then known as the Cercle Sportif Francais – the French Sporting Club. It closed its doors in 1949, underwent a 30-year silence (rumoured to be either a military training centre or Mao's Shanghai residence) and was reopened in 1979 for foreigners and high-ranking Chinese. For a Y2 entrance fee (temporary membership) you can dig some jaded glory out of this overgrown piece of bacchanalia. If it's real entertainment you want then the Jinjiang Club has only a few partial answers – it reeks of the exclusive club it once was.

On the ground floor is a vast dining room where patrons perform delicate surgical operations on their filet mignon Monte Carlo, digestion eased by the mellow tones of a grand piano and a weeping violin. Down the hall is a grandiose ballroom with the original Steinway piano and fittings, magnificent overhead lighting and a sad dixieland band that outnumbers the audience. Video games and pinball machines are stabled in a side room; a billiards room with overhanging lamps; and a six-lane

freeway of bowling shoved through the art-deco bric-a-brac (automatic US equipment). The Club is said to be the only place in the PRC where mah-jong is still alive. For the ultimate, try the teak-panelled bar at the far end, and get drunk by the deserted pool (Y5 for the pool and a rented swimsuit if needed – you may be asked for a swimming license). The pool is the original Olympic-sized one and it's heated. A table-tennis room (free) leads out into the gardens, which are theoretically not accessible at night.

Next floor up is mainly high brass get-togethers, banquet rooms, conference rooms, and Japanese business offices. There is apparently a suite on this floor with four bedrooms and adjoining bathrooms, which, if not used for 'official purposes' runs to something like Y1500 a day.

Up on the top floor the Japanese have installed a sushi bar – perhaps they just can't hack that gourmet French cuisine on the ground floor. The sushi bar looks like it stepped straight out of the Ginza, the tuna is flown in from Tokyo, the chefs are re-educated Chinese – and all this, of course, is ultra-expensive.

Most Jinjiang facilities are open 11 am to 11 pm, with prime time from 7 pm onwards. The pool is open 9 am to 10.30 pm. Out through the fancy gardens are two tennis courts, open 8 am to 6 pm if the weather is kind – racquets can be rented. It's business as usual at the Club – the Service Centre for Overseas Chinese (SCOT) is located in the Club's second building and provides interpreters, guides, telex, consulting services, daily overseas financial information and current newspapers for foreign businessmen. Some foreign offices are located in the gardens.

**Jinjiang Hotel**, across the road from the Jinjiang Club, has a bar and disco at the south end of the West Building No 1, open 4 pm to midnight.

There are some 70 cinemas and theatres and 35 performing troupes in Greater

Shanghai – with a little help from the numerous English-speakers in this place it should be possible to delve into the local listings which may include top notch travelling troupes. This is probably the best place in China to get a look at the local entertainment scene, acrobatics, ballet, music, burlesque, opera, drama, puppets, sporting events . . . a couple of venues are listed below to give you some idea of what's in stock here.

The **Shanghai Art Theatre** is just down the road from the Jinjiang Club, and is housed in what used to be the Lyceum Theatre. The theatre was completed in 1931 and was used by the Shanghai Amateur Dramatic Society – a favourite haunt of the Brits (the barman probably had a lot to do with it). The theatre company of the same name started up in 1929, the first drama troupe of the Communist Party.

The **Shanghai Film Studio** continues to produce some of the better material in China – although no one won the 1983 Golden Rooster Award (well, in the USA you've got the Oscars, in Australia you've got the Logies and the Penguins) for best leading male actor – in fact the award hasn't been given out for the last three years. Film making in Shanghai has a long tradition – or as old as movie making can be – and one of the starlets of the B-grade set back in the 1930s was Jiang Qing. It's pot luck whether you'll find a good movie or not, but it won't cost more than a few fen to find out. A good gauge of a film's popularity is to check the bike parking outside – if it spreads for two blocks then it must be a hit!

The **Conservatory of Music** (tel 370137) at 20 Fenyang Lu off Huahai Zhonglu in Frenchtown, is a treat not to be missed by classical music lovers. The conservatory was established in 1927 and its faculty members were mainly foreign – post World War I Shanghai was a meeting place for talented European musicians. The most enthralling aspect of the conservatory is the child prodigies; back in 1979 Yehudi Menuhin was passing through here and picked 11 year-old violinist Jin Li for further instruction in England; the kid enthralled audiences in London in 1982 with his renditions of Beethoven. Other wonders, products of the special training classes set up in the 1950s, have gone to the west on cultural exchange visits. The conservatory was closed during the Cultural Revolution, but Beethoven et al have now been rehabilitated along with the conservatory. Performances take place on Sunday evenings at 7 pm – tickets are usually sold out the previous Thursday, but if you roll up early on a Sunday evening a foreigner always rates 'special' seats.

There are several professional orchestras in Shanghai – the Shanghai Philharmonic and the Shanghai National Orchestra (the latter specialising in native instruments).

The largest indoor sports venue in Shanghai is the **Shanghai Gymnasium** at the southwest corner of the city. It's airconditioned, has computer-controlled score boards and seats 18,000.

Shanghai's cafes are open until around 10 pm and sometimes until 10.30 pm – just follow the neon. These are meeting and gossip hangouts – coffee and cakes cost around Y2 for two people, dreadful coffee and lousy cakes, but if you've wondered what it must have been like in a Parisian cafe in the 1930s then the ambience is definitely there. The **Deda** near the Peace Hotel is one of these coffee shops. It's as dead as a dodo. Further west, on Nanjing Xilu is the **Shanghai Cafe**, an upstairs venue which is worth a try. After they get booted out of all the shoe stores along Huaihai Zhonglu, young and old folk head for the upstairs section of the **Laodacheng Bakery** which is open until around 10 pm – you can choose cakes downstairs first if you want to. In case things get a bit out of hand there are little round coasters under the glass tops of the tables upstairs at the Laodacheng, reminding people of the one-child policy – with graphics of a lady feeding rabbits.

## Acrobatics

Acrobats are pure fun and they're China's true ambassadors. Donating a panda may soothe relations but it's the acrobats who capture the international imagination. The Shenyang Acrobatic Troupe toured the USA before the two countries established diplomatic relations, and Chinese troupes have gone to 30 countries with not a dud response.

Circus acts go back 2000 years in the Middle Kingdom; effects are obtained using simple props, sticks, plates, eggs, chairs, and apart from the acrobatics there's magic, vaudeville, drama, clowning, music, conjuring, dance and mime thrown into a complete performance. Happily it's an art which gained from the Communist takeover and which did not suffer during the Cultural Revolution. Performers used to have the status of gypsies, but now its 'people's art'. Most of the provinces have their own performing troupes, sponsored either by government agencies, industrial complexes, the army or rural administrations. About 80 troupes are active in China, and they're much in demand with scalpers being able to get Y5 for a Y0.40 ticket. You'll also see more bare leg, star-spangled costumes and rouge in one acrobat show then you'll see anywhere else in China – something of a revelation to see dressed-up and made-up Chinese!

Acts vary from troupe to troupe – some traditional acts haven't changed over the centuries – whilst others have incorporated roller skates and motorcycles. A couple of time-proven acts that are hard to follow include the 'balancing in pairs' with one man balanced upside down on the head of another mimicking every movement of the partner below, mirror image – even drinking a glass of water! Hoop-jumping is another. Four hoops are stacked on top of each other; the human chunk of rubber going through the very top hoop may attempt a backflip with a simultaneous body-twist. The 'Peacock Displaying its Feathers' involves an array of people balanced on one motor-bike – according to the Guinness Book of Records a Shanghai troupe holds the record at 13, though apparently a Wuhan troupe has done 14. The 'Pagoda of Bowls' is a balancing act where the performer, usually a woman, does everything with her torso except tie it in knots, all the while casually balancing a stack of porcelain bowls on foot, head or both – and perhaps also balancing on a partner.

The **Shanghai Acrobatics Dome** on Nanjing Xilu has shows most evenings. It's one of the best equipped in China for these acts. Sometimes performing tigers and pandas (not together) show up as an added bonus. Tickets for the regular shows are 80 fen – but try and get them ahead of time from the office to the side of the Dome. CITS will also book seats. Or you could try your luck and roll up when performances start (around 7 pm nightly.)

## Shopping

Good buys in Shanghai are clothing (silks, down jackets, traditional Chinese clothing, stencilled T-shirts, embroidered clothing), antiques, tea (Chrysanthemum tea from Hangzhou), stationery . . . the list goes on and on, so just regard this place as one big department store. All consumer urges can be catered for here. Other major, but less crowded than Najing Donglu, shopping areas in Shanghai are Huaihai Zhonglu, Sichuan Beilu, Jinling Donglu and Nanjing Xilu. There are some smaller streets in Shanghai that seem to run specialities – one is Shimen Yilu which has clothing and houseware stores. At No 323 Shimen Yilu there are silk blouses, kimonos, scarves and silk pyjamas. Over in Frenchtown – now we're getting specialised – is the Gujin Brassiere Store at 863 Huaihai Zhonglu. You can shop around the clock in Shanghai should the urge take you – for example, the Caitongde Traditional Chinese Medicine Shop at 320 Nanjing Donglu is open 24 hours a day. The Friendship Store is on Zhongshan Lu and stocks *everything* – it's open 9 am to 11 pm.

## Getting Around

Distances are far between the sights in Shanghai. Not only that, but the place is a menagerie of vehicles with a host of noise generators to announce their oncoming right of way; buses and traffic police have megaphones, bells, buzzers, hooters, honkers, screechers, flashing lights; taxis may as well just have a permanent siren attached; pedestrians have no early warning system and just rely on fast legs. If you've got the energy, then walking through Shanghai's various neighbourhoods is fascinating. If not . . .

**Buses** Often packed to the hilt and at times impossible to board – the closest thing to revolutionary fervour in Shanghai today is the rush-hour bus ambushes . . . once on a bus, keep your valuables tucked away since pickpocketing is easy under such conditions, and foreigners are not exempt as targets.

Contrary to popular belief, buses are not colour coded. The bus map is. The bus map coding for trolley buses is prefixed by the symbol which roughly means 'electricity'.

电

Routes 1-30 are trolley buses. Those numbered 31-99 are city buses. Routes 201-220 are peak hour city buses, and 301-321 are all-night buses. Buses operate from 4 am to 10 pm. Suburban and longer distance buses don't carry numbers – the destination is in characters. Some useful buses:

**North-South** No 18 runs from the front of the Main Railway Station (it originates further north-east at Hongkou or Lu Xun Park) and proceeds straight south down Xizang Lu, and then straight south to the banks of the Huangpu.

No 65 runs from behind the Main Railway Station, goes past Shanghai Mansions, crosses Waibaidu Bridge, then heads directly south along the Bund (Zhongshan Lu) as far as the Bund can go.

**East-West** No 37 comes in from the north side of the Huangpu River, along Daming Lu to Shanghai Mansions, over the bridge, south along the Bund, then directly west for the whole length of Nanjing Lu.

No 49 from the Public Security terminus heads west along Yanan Lu. No 48 and No 42 follow similar routes from Huangpu Park, south along the Bund, west around the Donfeng Hotel, then link westbound along Yanan Lu. No 26 starts downtown a few streets west of the Bund, drops to the Yuyuan Bazaar, then west along Huaihai Lu.

**Tours** A good linking bus for all those awkward destinations is the No 16, running from the Jade Buddha temple to Yuyuan Bazaar, then on to a ferry hop over the Huangpu River. The No 11 bus travels the ring road around the old Chinese city.

**Autorickshaws** These things leave not much between you and the road, as they dart through impossible holes in the traffic and cut blithely in front of buses. They will get you there fast, carry two passengers and luggage, and you can pay in renmibi – the fare will be considerably less than taxis. Fares work out around Y0.30 per km (or less) and there is no flagfall. For covering longer distances you might work out a deal with the driver and pay him a flat sum for a given number of hours. Bargaining is essential! The Shanghai Taxi Service has a telephone number if you want an autorickshaw – it's 213090 – but they usually don't go into hotels, just near them. Otherwise, they have parking ranks and these are marked on the bus maps – they can be found at major transport junctions like the CAAC office, the Qingdao boat dock, the railway station, the north side of the People's Park (near Nanjing Lu), and on Jiangxi Lu (between Hankou Lu and Fuzhou Lu, and just east of Henan Zhonglu not far from Public Security).

## Other Wheels

Friendship Taxis operate out of all the tourist hotels in Shanghai, and they're expensive. Flagfall is Y3 (air-con) which is good for five km, and then it's Y0.60 per km after that. If you stray too far out of the metropolitan region then the rate goes up to Y0.90 per km. Waiting time is Y2.40 per hour (calculated to the nearest 15 minutes). Cost for all-day hire is Y30 – but the catch is that its a maximum of 40 km and 10 hours. Rates are payable only in FECs.

The gun metal grey Shanghai Saloons, resembling vintage Mercedes are beautiful cars and worth a few rides – but hang on to your wallet. Check the odometer – some of these things have been on the road since the 1950s!

If you want to let go, then get one of those plush hearses, the Red Flags; they start at Y5 flag fall, and then cost Y1 per km after the flag falls. You can pretend you're the would-be President of Namibia for the day. And it's still cheaper than hiring a Rolls in Hong Kong! All-day rate on a Red Flag is Y50.

On the streets you can pick up cheaper models and makes. Shanghai Taxi Service (tel 564444 for cars and minibuses, and 215555 for coaches) has its headquarters at 816 Beijing Donglu and is one of the cheaper companies. Other companies and taxi ranks can be located from the bus maps – ask your hotel reception desk for help translating. There are some Datsun and Russian-built cars as well as some non-aircon Shanghais around for Y2.50 flag fall and Y0.50 per km (or Y25 for the whole day). There are also minibuses available.

## Getting Away

**Bus** There are two major long-distance bus stations. For destinations to the north and north-west go to the station behind

the North (Main) Railway Station. For destinations to the south-west of Shanghai, there is a station just below the Shanghai Gymnasium in the Xujiahui District. There are long-distance buses to Hangzhou (a beautiful ride on the right kind of day) and the fare is Y5.

**Train** Shanghai's main station is a dilapidated old structure, too small to really cope with the hordes – quite a surprise after the vast modern stations you find in other Chinese cities – though there seems to be some new building in progress.

Getting Chinese-priced tickets is difficult but not impossible, though the main station is very resistant. You could go as far as, say, Suzhou or Jiaxing, and try getting a Chinese-price ticket there – it may be easier. You might also try buying tickets from one of the smaller railway stations, such as Xujiahui Station in the western suburbs of Shanghai, rather than from the main station.

There are five advance ticket offices in Shanghai; the main one is at 230 Beijing Lu and handles all destinations north of the Yangtse and south of Jinhua (Jinhua is beyond Hangzhou to the south-west, 373 km from Shanghai). Departures for these trains are from Shanghai North (Main) Station (tel 242299) on Tianmu Donglu.

Shanghai is at the junction of the Beijing-Shanghai and the Beijing-Hangzhou lines, both of which branch off in various directions, so many parts of the country can be got to by direct train. Not all trains originate in Shanghai; there is one, for example, which starts in Beijing and winds up in Fuzhou; others like the train bound for Urumqi do start in Shanghai.

**Ticket Prices** To calculate approximate ticket prices, see the distance tables in the 'Getting Around' section of this book. Some sample *Chinese-priced* fares are given below. Travelling time is given for express trains.

| | Time hrs | Hard-seat Y | Hard-sleep Y |
|---|---|---|---|
| Suzhou | 1¼ | 2 | |
| Wuxi | 1¾ | 3 | |
| Zhenjiang | 3½ | 6 | |
| Nanjing | 4 | 7.50 | |
| Hangzhou | 3 | 4.50 | |
| Nanchang | 16½ | 13 | 23 |
| Zhuzhou | 23¾ | 19 | 32 |
| Guilin | 28½ | 29.50 | 46 |
| Kunming | 61½ | 49.50 | 77.50 |
| Canton | 33 | 32 | 50 |
| Fuzhou | 22½ | 23 | 36 |
| Beijing | 19¼ | 27.50 | 43 |
| Qingdao | 24 | 22.50 | 36 |
| Zhengzhou | 15¼ | 21 | 33 |
| Xian | 26 | 24.50 | 40 |

**Plane** Something like 160 domestic flights a week take off from Shanghai, with 707s and Tridents operating on the Shanghai-Beijing and Shanghai-Canton routes daily. Hongqiao Airport is 15 km from the downtown district, and there is a free airport bus from the CAAC office on Yanan Zhonglu. There are flights to Beijing (first class Y195, second class Y150), Canton (Y155), Changsha (Y116), Chengdu (Y250), Chongqing (Y213), Dalian (Y283), Fuzhou (Y105), Guilin (Y167), Hangzhou (Y20), Harbin (Y290), Hefei (Y51), Jinan (Y105), Kunming (Y284), Lanzhou (Y226), Nanchang (Y79), Nanjing (Y36), Qingdao (Y118), Shenyang (Y225), Tunxi (Y53), Urumqi (Y452), Wuhan (Y88), Xian (Y164), Zhengzhou (Y107). There are also flights to Xiamen.

For details of international flights out of Shanghai, including direct flights to Hong Kong, see 'Getting There' and 'Getting Away' in the introductory sections of this book.

**Boats**

Boats are definitely one of the best ways of leaving Shanghai – they're also the cheapest. For destinations on the coast or inland on the Yangtse, they may even sometimes be faster than trains which have to take rather circuitous routes. Smaller, grottier boats handle numerous inland shipping routes – if you're going to try using these make sure that 'Ship' hasn't been struck off your travel permit. Tickets for larger boats (like the Hong Kong-Shanghai ferries) are handled by CITS which charges a commission (anything from Y3 to Y8 for a ticket to Qingdao, for example). There are also various ticket offices scattered around the city, and business is more than brisk. Considering how cheap boats are you ought to consider taking a class or two above the hordes – it won't cost you that much more to do so.

**Ship from Shanghai to Hong Kong**

This route was reopened in 1980 after a gap of 28 years. Two passenger ships now ply the route; the *Shanghai* and the *Haihing*. A lot of travellers leave China this way and the trip gets rave reviews. The booking office (tel 225674) is the China Ocean Shipping Agency at 255 Jiangxi Lu and there are sailings four times a month. The Shanghai to Hong Kong leg can be advance booked in Hong Kong (see 'Getting There' in the introductory section of this book for details) and also at CITS in Beijing. Ships depart from the International Passenger Terminal to the east of Shanghai Mansions, and the trip to Hong Kong takes 60 hours.

When you take into account the luxurious living, the boat is cheap. Both ships come complete with dance floor, library, swimming pool . . . just about the classiest thing sailing regularly around Chinese waters. The *Haihing* sounds like it's the better of the two boats.

The fares below are from CITS in Shanghai – there is some discrepancy between them and the fares and type of cabin accommodation listed in 'Getting There' in the introductory section – but hopefully it will give you some idea of what's available. You may find in Hong Kong that if you buy through an agent (such as one that also issues visas) there may be a hefty commission tacked on to the fare – perhaps as much as 25% – which may account for the discrepancy in the figures listed in this book.

Special Class: a two-berth cabin that can only be booked on a full cabin basis. Prices quoted are Y234 and Y216 per person – may depend on the boat.

1st Class: one-berth cabin Y198 per person, three-berth cabin Y180 per person.

2nd Class: three-berth cabins and two-berth cabins for Y170 per person: four-berth cabins for Y156 per person.

3rd Class: two-berth cabin Y143 per person: four-berth cabin Y130 per person.

General Class: a large dormitory with upper and lower berths, and lights that stay on all night. Tickets for around Y90 to Y100 per person. Strongly recommend that you at least take 3rd Class.

Children below four years of age travel free, children four to 10 years old are half fare. There's a 20% discount if you buy your round trip ticket in Hong Kong.

### Boats Along the Yangtse River

The main destinations of ferries up the Yangtse River from Shanghai are: Nantong, Zhenhai, Nanjing, Maanshan, Wuhu, Tongling, Chizhou, Anqing, Huayang, Jiujiang, Wuxue, Huangshi, Wuhan. From Wuhan you can change to another ferry which will take you all the way to Chongqing. Boats vary in quality with their size – for more details of the Yangtse ferry trips, see the sections on the Yangtse River.

Tickets can be bought from the booking hall at 222 Renmin Lu (it's a large whitewashed building that looks like it was once used as a warehouse). The boats leave Shanghai from just south of Shilipu Wharf, and there are departures every day. Tickets, per person, are:

| | 1st class Y | 2nd class Y | 3rd class Y | 4th class Y |
|---|---|---|---|---|
| Nanjing | 35.60 | 18.00 | 6.90 | 5.80 |
| Wuhan | 42.30 | 21.80 | 8.70 | 5.60 |
| Guichi | 52.20 | 26.10 | 10.40 | 7.10 |
| Jiujiang | 66.10 | 35.00 | 13.20 | 9.00 |
| Wuhan | 82.80 | 41.40 | 16.60 | 11.20 |

Unless you can afford to fly, the most sensible way of heading due west from Shanghai is along the river. Wuhan, for example, is 1545 km by rail from Shanghai, so you'd be looking at something in the vicinity of Y40 for a hard sleeper on the train, if you could get Chinese price, if you could even get a sleeper! For just a quarter of that you can get a berth in the 4th class on the boat. For just a bit more than a tourist-priced hard sleeper ticket on a train you'd probably be able to get a bed in a two-person cabin on the boat.

Other inland shipping routes have been little explored by westerners. One possible route is a boat to Huzhou from Shanghai; Huzhou is on the southern shore of Lake Taihu and was officially opened to foreigners in late 1983.

### Coastal Boats

Tickets for the coastal boats can be bought from the booking hall at 222 Renmin Lu. Frequency of coastal shipping varies according to destination, from daily departures to once every two to six days. Some of the 5000-tonne liners on the coastal routes have staterooms with private bath in first and special classes – panelling, red velvet curtains, the works. The run of the ship should have a restaurant, bar, snackshops ... depends on the boat.

There are several offices around Shanghai that sell tickets for the coastal boats in advance, but which handles what I don't know. At 1 Jinling Donglu is another ticket office, with a branch at 59 Jinling Donglu. The rail advance ticket office at 230 Beijing Donglu also appears to handle advance boat tickets. You could buy tickets the same day (or the night before) at the relevant wharf –though you may only be able to get the unsold, more expensive tickets. Fares are:

|  | 1st class Y | 2nd class Y | 3rd class Y | 4th class Y |
|---|---|---|---|---|
| Ningbo | 30.00 | 15.00 | 5.70 | 5.00 |
| Wenzhou | 45.60 | 22.80 | 8.70 | 7.60 |
| Fuzhou | 68.30 | 54.70 | 27.30 | 20.20 |
| Qingdao | 51.60 | 25.80 | 9.80 | 8.60 |

Boats to Fuzhou and Wenzhou leave from Shilipu Wharf. Boats to Ningbo leave from the dock just south of Shilipu Wharf (the same dock from which the Yangtse ferries depart). Most other boats to southern destinations also leave from Shalipu Wharf.

Boats to northern destinations (Qingdao, Dalian) leave from Gongpinglu Wharf, which is to the east of Shanghai Mansions. The boat to Qingdao departs daily, with the exception of a few odd days of the month. It takes about 26 hours, whilst the train takes 24 hours. Second class on liner is roughly equivalent to the price of a hard-seat on a train (if you get the Chinese price) and the boat would be incomparably more comfortable. Boat connections like Shanghai to Dalian, and then Dalian to Tianjin can be made, though you may find the huge number of passengers using the cheaper services a problem getting tickets.

There may be other boats from Shanghai to points along the coast – possibly to Haimen, Dinghai, Putuo Shan.

## FLOWERS FROM HORSEBACK

HE is cycling along the Bund, I am puzzling over a Shanghai busmap – we meet on a streetcorner. His name is Wang – he speaks very good English, not the kind that comes from parroting phrasebooks. Within a short time we have struck up a bizarre deal. I express my loathing for packed buses, he expresses his loathing for his dismal heap of a bike – it all clicks. I will buy a bike, use it for my stay in Shanghai, and sell it to him. The same afternoon we are down at the Friendship Store, and he is selecting 'my' bike. It's a handsome black tank – I take it for a spin around the grounds of the old British Consulate, pay for it, and we coast off into the streets. Wang waves at me to slow down, but I'm off like a rocket getting my revenge on the buses – overtaking everything in sight, revelling in this newly-acquired freedom. I have joined the orchestra – the crescendo of bells – what a blast! Dodging the heavy-laden tricycles and streams of bikes, we ride all the way out to Frenchtown. I give the bell one final flick before going into a cafe with Wang, and the top-part shoots clear off the handlebar into the gutter. Wang jumps down to retrieve it, giving me a startled look – for me it's just a bike, for him it's a status symbol. Instead

of going to the cafe we go to a bikeshop where all the nuts and bolts on this factory-fresh job are tightened.

The bike suits my own brand of random access tourism – but much more than a deal now, it has sparked a tour-guide on wheels. Wang can give me the rat's eye view of Shanghai – the gutters and drainpipes. He manages some time off, takes me round the restaurants, the back-alleys, the old Chinese sector. For the reduced amount he can get a meal, I figure he's not an extra expense when I foot the bill. He insists, at least, on paying all parking bills – 2 fen a time – and dives in with coupons at cafes.

Thunk! Pow! Boom! Kerrash! 'This is most interesting!' shouts Wang. 'Watch out! Hey!' He has just smashed up again – in a racing-circuit video game. Never having been at the driver's wheel, he is gaining the wrong impression of driving – yelps of delight and frustration – and I glance around quickly to see if anyone has noticed the imposter in their midst. It could only be possible at the Jinjiang Club – I try and steer Wang away from Space Invaders, lest he attract more attention. At table-tennis he is on more familiar ground – slaughters me. Our roles are reversed now – I am his guide to the hallowed sections of the city where he is normally forbidden. But what a contrast – here at the silent cavernous tables of the tourist hotels, the Chinese food is tasteless – while out there in Shanghai's backalleys, excitement is the forbidden fruit – western video, jazz, pool, video-games, opulent decor – fuel for his insatiable curiosity. The guy is bored out of his mind. We'd long cancelled the English lesson component – nobody, however, had taught him any table manners, and it was with considerable embarrassment that I rushed him out of an elegant hotel dining room after attempting breakfast. To my horror he had leaned over and stuck his face right into the fried egg – and with one almighty slurp, polished it off. Still recovering from this, I gazed in wonder as he proceeded, egg all over his grinning face, to spoon jam on the toast, and then coat it with butter – using a left-handed knife.

'During the Cultural Revolution,' explains Wang, 'we had a lot of trouble even to go to the barber. There are wallpaper slogans in red over the shop windows, and your memory must be good to find the place. After you find him, the barber says – Serve the People! And then you reply – Heart and Soul, Brother! And then he gives you the haircut.' Such are China's great secrets – I promptly lost Wang in the sea of blue jackets and black bikes after the stop-light. I still had no idea where Wang lived, and he wasn't about to invite me home – our only method of contact was pre-arranged meetings at a cafe. He was growing more confident in his research into western mores and values – myself being the source. He enquires a lot about sexual customs – did people live together? What did the government do about it? The reason for this was related to his present dilemma – 'My girlfriend and I would like to conduct sexy experiment,' he told me, 'to see if we fit, and if possible to achieve the orgasms. But if the government finds out, I will get the criticism, so my girlfriend does not want the experiment yet – but we hear that there are others who do.' This is actually a build-up to his next topic – will I assist in purchasing a pair of leather high-heel shoes from the Friendship Store? We leave the cafe, rip down to the 'Embassy', and I smuggle Wang in – he looks like he could be some official translator. 'These ones,' he whispers. Feeling very foolish, I pick up a pair of high-heels with furry backs and look the saleslady in the eye. As we exit the store, walking back down the Bund to the cycle-parking, Wang takes my hand. Here I am with a pair of high-heel shoes in a box, Wang holding my hand – a most peculiar feeling – holding hands is common amongst Chinese, men or women, but not men *and* women!

'We are good friends now,' beams Wang. This time he is riding the bike, still in mint condition. He has paid for it, at a reduction – in amongst other deals like shoes, cigarettes and train-tickets. The time has come for me to leave – he wants to escort me to the station. I really can't face a bus after all that biking freedom – I get the hotel desk to arrange a taxi. We stroll to the front of the hotel – and find a sleek Red Limo in wait. Not what I have in mind – but all the other taxis are out on patrol. The cost isn't too damaging, so what the heck . . . Wang puffs up like a general, strutting around like he owns Shanghai, finally getting into the vehicle and lighting up a cigarette. 'Look at the police!' he yells triumphantly – I peer through the curtained windows at the poles mounted over the street – the crow's nest for manual light operation. Each time we pass a policeman, orders come booming down from the crow's nest for cyclists to stop as we whizz by – and the policeman frantically phones the next crow's nest along the route. Lights green all the way. Feeling rather VIP-ish myself by the time we reach the station, I emerge with my backpack to find a crowd of several hundred have gathered round the Red Flag. Wang takes it all in his stride and hustles me through to the station. On the platform he tells me that the high-heel shoes don't fit his girlfriend – but she'll wear them anyway – 'she is used to the tight shoe' . . .

Much later, I returned to Shanghai – it hadn't really occurred to me until I arrived *how* I would find Wang again. I had his address on a scrap of paper, but knew I could not visit. By devious means, I got a call placed through to the man in the phone-booth that served Wang's neigh-bourhood, and we arranged a meeting. Wang never got any letters I sent – and I never got any he sent – but there was something else in the air. I was looking forward to this meeting – he, obviously, was not. He wouldn't tell me what had happened – I guessed that his privileges and opportunities had been derailed for being in touch with foreigners. When I broached the subject, he shrugged and looked away. He didn't want to discuss it. It was risky enough that he'd come to see me. There was nothing to be salvaged in this friendship any more. I had lost a comrade.

It took a convoluted messing-around with coupons and other deals to get me another bike – the Friendship Store stock was locked away and only for foreign experts. Finally got what I wanted – a brand-new Feng Huang, a Phoenix. Shoved together some saddlebags, loaded up with cakes, nougat, chocolate and Cokes – and headed out, still brooding over the extent of government influence in the choice of friends. Five-thirty in the morning – I had a vague idea of how to get out of the metropolis; there weren't any decent roadmaps to show me.

Anyhow, there's always plenty to distract one in Shanghai. As I picked my way through the morning rush, my attention became rivetted to a man with a large-wheel tricycle-carrier bearing a heavy load – a phantom thrown up by the traffic. He had fitted an ingenious bell to the front hub, which was operated by a string from the handlebar. When he tugged it, the bell at the forks came into contact with the spokes and made an absolutely deafening clatter that surprised even the most seasoned earholes – and they all allowed him to pass. I followed in the slipstream, past joggers, people brushing their teeth in the gutters, washing cabbages, an old man spearing cigarette butts with a bamboo skewer.

Two hours later, I begin to wonder if I'll ever get out of Shanghai. Magically, I round a corner and there it is – the countryside, but not from the cage of a train. Beautiful, disturbingly beautiful. Fields of yellow rapeseed, brilliant greens, the smell of manure, waterways. Up ahead is a countdown milestone in Chinese li, along with the relevant destination – Suzhou – in characters. I follow a farmer with a dead pig slung over his rack for a few miles. He takes a small earphone from his pocket and plugs it in – a hearing-aid? What would he want to listen to the noisy trucks for? No, it's a small radio he's tuned into. Modernisation! The man has achieved rightist nirvana – two of the most treasured possessions, radio and bicycle, combined with a freemarket pig. Suddenly the pig falls off the rack – and I dismount to assist recovery.

The farmer is due to turn off – I give him a cigarette – we must part company. He gives me

some final directions, pats his bum and grimaces. My destination is several sore bums away. Is this actual farming jargon? (Ah, yes, Nanjing – 100 sore bums to the north!). In quick succession, the oncoming traffic throws up a Shanghai sedan with drawn curtains, a droning three-wheel samlor with passengers and luggage piled to the canvas roof, and two PLA punks at the helm of a Harley-sized Xingfu motorcycle. In the sidecar of this speedy number is a very pale-looking grandmother.

Bikes break the ice – lost in Wuxi I struck up a conversation in the traffic with a young Chinese, and before I knew it I was on the seventh floor of a grey concrete apartment block – and his dad was drinking me under the table. 'I hate factory!' my new-found friend proclaimed. 'Me too,' I responded. What he meant was that he worked in a hat factory. His girlfriend was a truck driver; his sister was in the army – arrived home in her khakis to prove it. Before I could protest, mum was up barbecuing dinner on the charcoal burner on the balcony – and dad was refilling my glass with a powerful brandy steeped in herbs. A resounding 'ganbei!' for every glass I knocked back. The walls were bare concrete – six people living in two tiny rooms. At dinner, an amazing bunch of dishes just kept rolling through – duck-eggs, fish, snails, crispy chicken-skin . . . All entirely spontaneous, it spoke volumes for the state of the culinary arts – they hadn't gone down the drain in the Cultural Revolution, far from it. Feeling the effects of the alcohol, I got up to go to the toilet. Toilet!?? We don't have things like that! Out, down seven floors, follow your nose, no lights – a communal one. I staggered back – and there was some more of that evil brandy waiting for me, along with some delicious shrivelled coconuts. The family insisted that I stay the night, but there didn't seem to be even floorspace for me to do so. My 'friend' escorted me, considerably under the weather, to the gates of my hotel, where he could go no further . . .

Off the main drag. It still doesn't get me away from the trucks that come roaring down the centreline at breakneck speeds, but it does get me closer to villages. A different vehicle commands the roads – the walking-tractor – little more than an engine with an easy-rider crossbar attached to it. I pull up as one lumbers past. In the open driver's seat is a man whose gaping lower mandible is stuffed full of rice; in the back, atop a load of produce is his wife in haircurlers and a surgical mask, and a kid with a toy binoculars filled with blue lollywater – hard to say which party looks more stupefied . . .

My automatic reaction to any sound of double-barrel throat-clearing is to speed up – when the sound came on my left flank, I was surprised to find the same farmer I'd seen 15 km back. He is waving as he lobs a big number into the side of the road. I smile back, we ride on a bit further – suddenly he cuts me off, dismounts, motions with a gnarled hand at a roadside farmhouse. We trundle off down a dirt path – seconds later I am guest of honour in his dark dank hovel. Quaint from the outside, bare table, mud-floor and chickens inside. And a giant cassette player. I don't think the farmer quite understands that my command of Chinese is about 30 words, and I'd get the tones on those wrong anyway. He keeps writing things down on the palm of his hands – hieroglyphics to me. I search through my phrasebook in vain – 'Do you take credit-cards?' – 'Can I make a reservation?' Who writes this crap? The farmer brings out a book, a broken pair of glasses, and his daughter. She touches my curly hair – I guess to find out if it's real or not. The neighbours quickly crowd into the hovel – filling every square inch – and the farmer offers me a sickly mixture of hot water in a grossly dirty jamjar. Then some cooked eggs – which I refuse. He can ill afford to waste eggs over a stranger. An argument breaks out between him and his wife. I throw in some shortcake from my saddlebags, and before the man can claim me as his long-lost grandson, I decide to retreat. I give the farmer my phrasebook – won't do me much good anyway – he'll get many years of amusement out of it . . .

In Yixing, cinema-sized staring-squads trail my every step down the main street. By lunchtime I've had enough and shoot off on the bike – to the nearby village of Dingshu, famed for its teapots. I arrive at what must be *xiuxi*-time – hardly a soul in sight, probably all dozing away in dormitories. Out of a factory comes a man who speaks fairly good English: he escorts me back through the factory to the lab, where he brews up some tea. He then opens up a small kiln – which reveals not a scientific experiment in progress, but his lunch being heated at 200°. This he shares with me, then takes me on a tour of the idle factory, and out to the canal markets.

Enthused from a great day in Dingshu, I moseyed back to Yixing, looking forward to a hot bath in the tourist and cadre hotel. Rooms aren't locked at Yixing Guesthouse – I turned the door handle, saw four people in the room and closed the door again, thinking it was the wrong room. It was the right room all right – full of the wrong people. Two were public security, one was a CITS man with a good command of English, and the fourth was the hotel manager. I offered them a cup of tea – they barked an instant refusal, in unison. Formalities over, PSB swung into full stride with interrogation – a fixed bitchy face on the woman who directed it. As angelic as I could make myself out, it got me nowhere. They weren't even concerned about the cycling – though this, they claimed, was much too dangerous, for a foreigner – what riled them up was the visit to the farmer's hovel. Bicycle breakdown, I explained – the wheel was wonky. 'You left the highway – someone telephoned us' – the phrase was repeated over and over again.

Took them a while to nail me with a technicality. 'You haven't got a bicycle licence' said the CITS man. 'Don't need one,' I told him bluntly. 'It's the same as ration coupons.' 'Your alien-permit isn't valid for travel by road,' said the CITS man. 'Car' had been struck off. How then was I supposed to have gotten to Yixing, which was on my permit, if there was no train? By taxi, of course. By this stage we'd estabished that 'car' was the same as 'bicycle', meaning 'road', but not the same as 'taxi', and I'd given up on the logic of the situation.

They wanted two things – to post me back to Wuxi where the 'mistake' had been made, and a written guarantee that I would not do the same thing again. The 'mistake' would cost 90 kuai – the fee to transport myself and bike for 40-odd km in a minibus. I bargained this ridiculous amount to a still-hefty 50 yuan, and immediately shoved the figure on my 'confession'. The PSB woman screamed that I shouldn't have done that, naughty boy . . .

On a northbound train from Wuxi – the bike stashed in the baggage-car, myself demonstrating zips, velcro, runners and webbing to the assembled curious crammed into the aisle of a rail car. In Changzhou, a short run from Wuxi, I rescue the bike and roar off from the station, free to roam again. I seem to have mislaid my travel-permit – oh well, never was attached to it anyway. It will take more than slips of paper to dampen my zest for the highway. There is a saying in Chinese that what the tourist sees is 'looking at flowers from horseback'. The surface meaning is that the tourist doesn't see things as they really are – just gets fleeting impressions. If you stopped the scenery long enough, maybe things would come out much better – or maybe much worse. The days of 'flowers from horseback' are over in the main cities that China has opened up – the warts and pimples are there for the freelance traveller to see. But in the countryside and the backwaters, glossed over by comfortable expanses of train-glass, travellers haven't even started . . .

– michael buckley

# Jiangsu

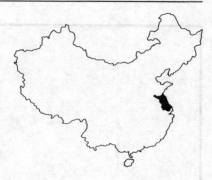

The southern part of Jiangsu lies in the rich Yangtse Basin, an incredibly beautiful tapestry of greens, yellows and blues, offset with whitewashed farm housing. Since the 12th century it's been the economic heart of China; it has the densest population of any province, the highest land productivity, an above-average educational level, and mellow people. Woven into this land of 'fish and rice' is a concentration of towns and cities, with the third highest industrial output in the land (Shanghai and Liaoning being greater).

As far back as the 16th century, the towns on the Grand Canal set up industrial bases for silk production and grain storage, and they still have the jump on the rest of the nation. Heavy industry is located in Nanjing and Wuxi; the other towns lean more to light industry, machinery and textiles. They're what you might term 'hi-tech canal towns' –they're major producers of electronics and computer components and haven't been blotted out by the scourges of coal mining or steel works.

From Nanjing down to Hangzhou in Zhejiang Province the area is heavily touristed, full of Japanese Hino tour buses, and pock-marked with luxury hotels. But north of the Yangtse there's not really much to talk about; it's a complete contrast, decayed, backward and has always lagged behind the rest of the province; the major port is at Lianyungang and there's a big coal mess in Xuzhou.

**Weather** Hot and humid in summer, overcoat temperatures in winter (and visibility can drop to zero in January). Rain or drizzle can be prevalent – but it's nice rain, adding a misty soft touch to the land, and the colourings in spring can be spectacular. Heavy rains come in spring and summer but there's little rain in autumn.

## THE GRAND CANAL

The original Grand Canal (Da Yunhe), like the Great Wall, was not one but a series of interlocking projects from different eras. The earliest parts were dug 2,400 years ago in the north to facilitate troop movements. During the Sui Dynasty (581-618 AD), the ruthless Emperor Yang Di conscripted a massive workforce to link his new capital of Luoyang to the older capital of Changan (Xian). Then he extended the project down to Hangzhou in less than a decade, making it possible for junks to go along the Yangtse, up the Canal, and on to ports along the Yellow River –a trip that might take up to a year.

The canal at that time linked up four major rivers; –the Huang (Yellow), Yangtse, Huai and Qiantang, which all run east-west. It thus gave China a major north-south transport route, and linked the compass points. This feat, the construction of the longest man-made waterway in the world, was accomplished by a million men with teaspoons, some estimate closer to five million. By even the crudest mathematics, the cost in lives must have been enormous.

The Emperor was not so much interested in unification as subjugation; grain from the rich fields of the south was appropriated to feed the hungry armies in

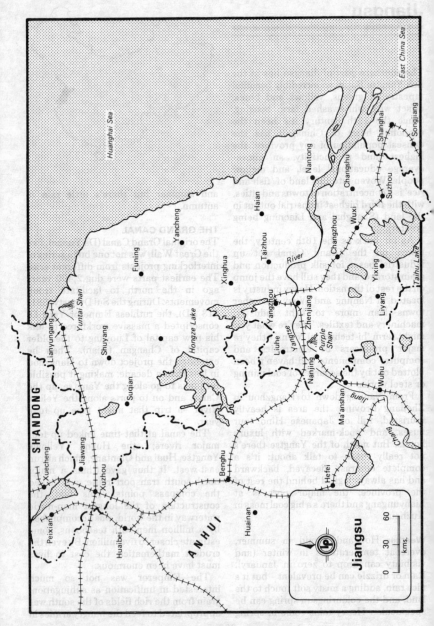

East China Sea

Huanghai Sea

SHANDONG

ANHUI

Lianyungang
Yuntai Shan
Xuecheng
Peixian
Huaibei
Jiawang
Xuzhou
Shuyang
Funing
Yancheng
Hongze Lake
Xinghua
Huainan
Bengbu
Hefei
Taizhou
Haian
Nantong
Changshu
Suzhou
Wuxi
Changzhou
Yixing
Taihu Lake
Liyang
Zhenjiang
Yangzhou
Liuhe
Nanjing
Purple Shan
Yangtse
Wuhu
Ma'anshan
Chang Jiang

Shanghai
Songjiang

River

kms.
0   30   60

Jiangsu

the northern capitals. In the Tang Dynasty 100,000 tons of grain were transported annually to the north; long chains of imperial barges loaded with tax grain plied the waterways.

In the 13th century, Kublai Khan used the work of his predecessors for much the same purpose, and he did a bit of remodelling to bring the northern terminus up to Beijing, his capital. Marco Polo noted that boats were pulled along by horses, which walked along the banks of the canal pulling the boats with long harnesses and in this way large quantities of corn and rice were shipped northwards. 'This magnificent work (the canal) is deserving of admiration; and not so much from the manner in which it is conducted through the country, or its vast extent, as from its utility and the benefit it produces to the cities which lie in its course'. Apart from bringing prosperity to the towns along its course, the canal was also a means by which the sybaritic emperors would move from point A to point B; at one point, in Emperor Qianlong's reign, it was suggested that the grain fleets be removed from the canal so as to allow the imperial pleasure-cruisers a freer passage.

As time went by, sections of the Canal fell into disuse, or were engulfed by Yellow River flooding; in this century the railways eclipsed the need for water transport. By 1980, internal waterway mileage in China had been reduced to one third of the 1960s due to silt, poorly planned dams, watergates and irrigation systems, or plain atrophy.

**The Imperial Revival** Suddenly in 1980 the Grand Canal became a tourist attraction. A flat-bottomed cruiser, with air-conditioning and all mod cons, materialised out of Wuxi, and passengers coughed up several thousand dollars for a week-long run from Yangzhou to Suzhou, including overnight stopovers at the towns along the way. Since the 'opening' over 400 groups have made the trip, which adds up to over 10,000 tourists, and quite a lot of money.

At its disposal in Wuxi, CITS has a new concept – the Dragon Boat, a replica of an imperial barge, with carvings, antique furniture, and a high-class restaurant on board. Tourists can dress up like emperors and strut about nibbling at the delicacies served on imperial tableware. Since then, several more boats have been added, and more are planned.

The Beijing-Hangzhou canal meandered almost 1,800 km. Today perhaps half of it remains seasonally navigable. The Party claims that, since liberation, large scale dredging has made the navigable length 1,100 km, but this is an exaggeration – 100 cm of water might qualify as 'seasonally navigable'. Canal depths are up to three metres and canal widths can narrow to less than nine metres; put these facts together, add the fact that there are old stone bridges spanning the route, and you come to the conclusion that it is restricted to flat-bottom vessels up to 600 tons. The section from Beijing to Tianjin has been silted for centuries; a similar fate has befallen most sections from the Yellow River to Tianjin. From the Yellow River to Peixian (in northern Jiangsu Province) is highly dubious and is most likely silted from Yellow River flooding. Jining, which lies between those two points, was once a prosperous cloth producer, now lying idle, and is served by rail.

The canal itself is polluted with oil slicks, and doubles as the local garbage bin, sewer and washing machine. There's still plenty to look at on the water; moss-stricken canal housing, barges laden with toothpaste by the ton, houseboats, fishermen. It's quite stunning what's floating around out there – even more stunning that it hasn't sunk. And there are glimpses of life at the water's edge, like women pounding their washing to a pulp.

Heading southwards from the northern Chinese plains, the canal really picks up at **Peixian**. There are two Peixians – this one is in the far north of Jiangsu province near the border with Shandong. It lies east of the town of Xuzhou and there is a railway line linking Xuzhou and Peixian. Peixian itself is closed, but a tributary canal runs past Xuzhou, feeding into the Grand Canal.

Continuing south you come to **Huaian** which is open with a permit (no rail link). It's open not because of the canal but because it's beloved Zhou En-lai's home town. Tourists (mostly Overseas Chinese) usually only stop to visit his former residence, but there are a couple of other places of interest – pavilions, pagodas, and the plaster and tile housing typical of area south of the Yangtse now gives way to mud and thatched buildings. The canal runs deep here and is eminently navigable.

Further south is **Yangzhou** and below Yangzhou the canal passes through locks into the Yangtse. The section from Peixian to Yangzhou is part of a bold plan to divert water from the Yangtse and the rainy south to the arid (drought-wrecked) provinces of Shandong, Hebei, Henan and Anhui. The route is also needed to ship coal to energy-hungry Shanghai from major coal producer, Xuzhou. The plan, with a tentative completion date of 1990, calls for dredging the Yangzhou-Xuzhou section to a depth of four metres and to a width of 70m at the bottom, so that 2000-ton vessels can pass. A double ship lock is being built at Huaian. So it seems the old canal still has its major uses. The water, it seems, will be provided for irrigation as far north as Jining in Shandong province.

**South of the Yangtse** the picture is much brighter, with year-round navigation. The Jiangnan Section of the Canal (Hangzhou-Suzhou-Wuxi-Changzhou-Danyang-Zhenjiang) is a skein of canals, rivers and branching lakes. It's often difficult to tell where the Grand Canal flows since people are in the habit of pointing at any old canal and calling it that. Just as interesting as the Grand Canal are the feeder canals, many of them major thoroughfares in their own right.

**Cruising the Canal** Travellers have done the route from Hangzhou to Suzhou on overnight passenger boats (with sleeping berths) or on daytime 150-seater ferries. They've found the boats dirty, crowded, uncomfortable, and a fair percentage of the trip taken up by high canal banks. Some words of advice for this trip: you need a good bladder (the toilets are terrible), you need some food, try and get a window seat (lots of smokers on the boat, scenery), and you must not have 'Ship' struck off your permit.

Going the other way, Suzhou to Hangzhou, is not so easy. Even travellers with their papers in order (ie 'Ship' unstruck) have been told by the Suzhou boat dock to see Public Security, and that means impossible. In such situations, it's better not to ask – get the nearest Hong Konger or friendly local to buy you a ticket and keep your face out of it. What officialdom is worried about is the present condition of the passenger boats – they'd much rather you took the train (though that still doesn't really explain why you can go in one direction and not the other).

to ride in air-conditioned luxury waving at the natives as they speed along, you fall into a totally different category because you make some kind of contact. CITS policy has been to inform travellers that there are *no* passenger boats on the canal (what canal?) except, of course, for their dragon cruisers. You can prove them wrong, but expect slow trips and a number of hassles. Estimated times for the sections south of the Yangtse is:

Hangzhou-Suzhou, 14 hours, overnight berth or day boat
Suzhou-Wuxi, 5 to 6 hours, early morning day boat
Wuxi-Changzhou, 4 to 5 hours
Changzhou-Zhenjiang, 8 to 9 hours (possible break in Danyang)

It's possible to break the Hangzhou-Suzhou journey at the superb canal town

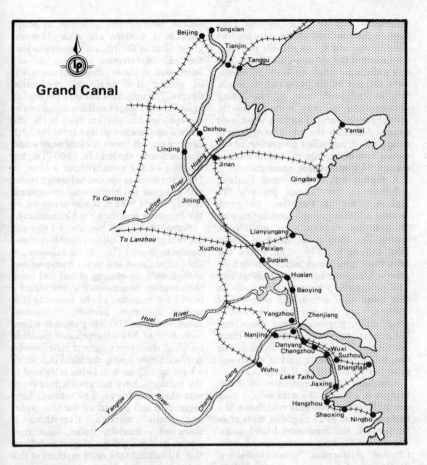

**Grand Canal**

Beijing · Tongxian · Tianjin · Tanggu · Dezhou · Yantai · Linqing · Jinan · Qingdao · To Canton · Jining · Lianyungang · To Lanzhou · Xuzhou · Peixian · Suqian · Huaian · Baoying · Yangzhou · Zhenjiang · Nanjing · Danyang · Changzhou · Wuxi · Suzhou · Shanghai · Wuhu · Lake Taihu · Jiaxing · Hangzhou · Shaoxing · Ningbo · Huang He · Yellow River · Huai River · Jiang · Chang · Yangtse River

of **Jiaxing** around the half-way mark (linked by rail to Shanghai or Hangzhou). Needless to say, Jiaxing is not where your journey is officially permitted to be broken. Jiaxing has textile and food-processing factories, and deals in silk and rice; the pavilion to the south-east of the town, on an island lake, is reputed to be the site that gave shelter to CCP members disturbed by Shanghai police in 1921.

There are other connections running through Lake Taihu. Fares are negligible (Hangzhou-Suzhou, Y4 berth, Y2 seat).

## SUZHOU

Suzhou's history reaches back 2500 years, give or take a hundred – it is one of the oldest towns in the Yangtse basin. Credit for its foundation is given to the King of the State of Wu, who made it his capital in the 6th century BC. With the completion of the Grand Canal in the Sui Dynasty (589 – 618 AD), Suzhou found itself strategically sited on a major trading route, and the city's fortunes – and size – rose rapidly. It flourished as a centre of shipping and grain storage, bustling with merchants and artisans. By the 12th century the town had attained its present dimensions, and if you consult the map, the layout of the old town is distinct. The city walls, a rectangle enclosed by moats, were pierced by six gates (north, south, two in the east, two to the west). Crisscrossing the city were six north-south canals, and fourteen east-west canals. Although the walls have largely disappeared, and a fair proportion of the canals have been plugged, central Suzhou retains its 'Renaissance' character.

A legend was spun around Suzhou, reflected in the famous proverb "In Heaven there is Paradise, on earth Suzhou and Hangzhou" – and in the tales of beautiful women with mellifluous voices. The story picks up when Marco Polo arrived in 1276 – he added the adjectives 'great' and 'noble', though he reserved his finer epithets for Hangzhou. The peripatetic's keen memory tells us that there were astonishing numbers of craftsmen and rich merchants, as well as great sages, physicians and magicians. "Moreover I tell you quite truly that there are six thousand bridges of stone in this city, below the greater part of which one galley or two could well pass ... '

Although Polo's estimate of 6000 bridges is a bit on the wild side, a map made 150 years before his visit shows 359 bridges, as well as 12 pagodas, more than 50 temples and numerous bath-houses. The town became a nesting spot for the Chinese aristocracy, pleasure-seekers, gentlemen of leisure, famous scholars, actors and painters – who set about constructing villas and garden retreats for themselves. At the height of Suzhou's development in the 16th century, the gardens, large and small, numbered over a hundred. If we mark time here, we arrive at Suzhou's tourist formula today – 'Garden City , Venice of the East' – a medieval mix of woodblock guilds and embroidery societies, whitewashed housing, cobbled streets, treelined avenues and canals.

This basically holds true; strangely

enough Suzhou has managed to adapt itself to a modern era with old-world grace. Part of the reason perhaps is that the silk merchants in days of old succeeded, at the expense of commoners, in getting the maximum production figures. The wretched workers, protesting against paltry wages and the injustices of the contract hire system used in the silk sweatshops, staged strikes from the 15th century on – at times, violent ones – and the landlords shifted. In 1860 Taiping troops took the town without a blow; in 1896 Suzhou was opened to foreign trade, with Japanese and international concessions. During World War II, it was occupied by the Japanese and then the Kuomintang.

Somehow Suzhou has slipped through the ravages of the Cultural Revolution and 'modernisation'. Though its reliance on the Grand Canal and water transport has shifted with the coming of rail and road, the common denominator – sericulture – is still the mainstay of the economy (the worms are now partially computer-assisted). Some 600,000 people live here now. Around 500 enterprises – machine building, electronics, optical instruments, ferro-concrete boats, chemical industries – have sprung up but, being relegated to the outskirts, have not greatly interfered with the central core. The artisans have regrouped and geared up for the export and tourist markets. Everything is absorbed – tourists, trains, silkworms, wheat, gardens, galleys, digital watches – they all melt into the calm rhythms of this ancient water-town.

**CITS** will materialise in either the Nanlin or Suzhou Hotels in response to a request at the desk, and are believed to live in the old wing of the Suzhou Hotel.

**Public Security** (tel 5661) is at 7 Dashitou Lane.

### Things to See
Suzhou is one of those towns where walking becomes a pleasure, and where

you get to do most of the staring. The solid French plane trees that canopy the avenues set the tone; for canal-side residents it's a two-way street, with boats gliding past their lounge rooms. Once you discern the lines of the inner town canals, it's easy to work out walking routes to destinations, and you will probably find the canals themselves of more interest than the destination. And the chance perspectives – a weary boatman sculling his sampan under a humpback bridge – an old woman nimbly bouncing over the cobblestones with two laden baskets slung over a bamboo pole – a gentleman stepping out of his rickety cottage to clean his teeth, his eye catching the lady opposite about to heave a nightsoil bucket into the canal – a street artist putting some final touches to a one-child-only mural . . . the local talent for drawing perspectives never stops – night, rain, moon, winter – the arched bridge and double-pagoda combination viewed along a canal off Ganjiang Lu (the temple no longer exists but the pagodas poke into the skyline) and Panmen Gate with its juxtaposed bridges, old city walling, interlocking housing and the ruins of the pagoda in the background. The canal housing around the Suzhou Hotel is delightful, with low, tiled dwellings hugging the banks.

For some lively action you can't really miss the bridges over the main moat, which offer great vantage points and are often host to impromptu markets. Because of their proximity to the Grand Canal, the six bridges to the west and south (Diaoqiao, Nanxin, Hongqi, Wannian, Wumen and Renmin) are especially rewarding. Two of these bridges face docks where barges from other villages come to unload produce. Wumen Bridge is the largest single-arched stone bridge in Suzhou. Next to it is the best-preserved city gate, Panmen, along with surviving fortifications; the dilapidated Ruigang Pagoda, once attached to a temple, adds a fitting dimension to the scene. To get away from it all, the two parks bordering the moat at the north-east end (Dongyuan and Ouyuan) are not noted for their layouts, but they are uncrowded, ideal for a quiet cup of tea.

### North Temple (Bei Si)

The North Temple has the tallest pagoda south of the Yangtse – nine storeys – you can climb it for a superb aerial view of the town. You can see the farmland beyond, used for growing tea, rice, wheat . . . the mere fact that you can see this in the first place means you're in a medium-sized city (less than one million!). The chimney factories, the new pagodas of Suzhou, loom on the outskirts.

### Suzhou Museum

Situated some blocks east of the pagoda, near the humble administrator's garden, the museum was once the residence of one of the Taiping leaders, Li Xiucheng. It's a good place to visit after you've seen something of Suzhou – it helps fill in the missing bits of the jigsaw, retracing Suzhou's history.

### Suzhou Bazaar

The area surrounding Guanqian Lu is riddled with restaurants, speciality shops, theatres, street-vendors, hairdressing salons, noodle dispensaries, silk merchants and sweet shops. This maze of back alleys, the main shopping thoroughfare of Suzhou, is a strolling area – with neither bicycles nor buses allowed on Guanqian by day.

The heart of Suzhou Bazaar is the Taoist **Temple of Mystery (Xuanmiao Si)**. It was founded in the third century (Jin Dynasty, laid out 275-279 AD), with additions from the Song. From the Qing Dynasty on, the bazaar fanned out from the Temple, with small tradesmen and travelling performing troupes using the grounds. The enormous Sanqing Hall, supported by 60 pillars and capped with a double roof with upturned eaves, dates from 1181 – it was burned and seriously damaged in the 19th century.

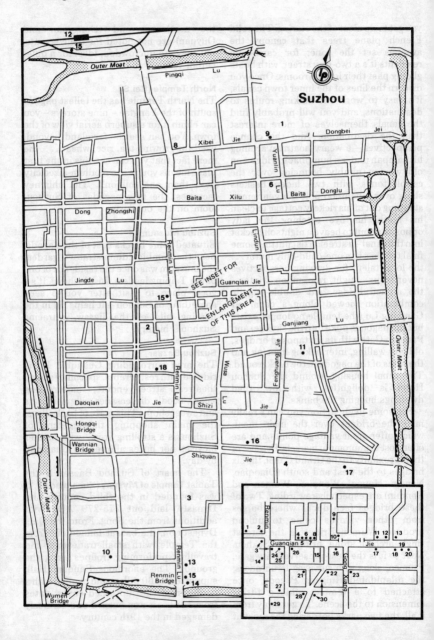

**Suzhou**

Outer Moat

Pingqi Lu

Dongbei Jei

1

Xibei Jie

8

9

Yuanlin Lu

6

Baita Xilu

Baita Donglu

Lindun Lu

Dong Zhongshi

Dong

7

5

Renmin Lu

Jingde Lu

SEE INSET FOR

Guanqian Jie

ENLARGEMENT OF THIS AREA

15

2

Ganjiang Lu

11

18

Wusa Lu

Fenghuang Jie

Guangji Jie

Renmin Lu

Daoqian Jie

Shizi Lu

Hongqi Bridge

16

Wannian Bridge

Shiquan Jie

4

17

3

Outer Moat

Renmin Lu

10

13

Renmin Bridge

15

14

Wumen Bridge

Renmin Lu

Guanqian

1 2

9

3

14

4 6 8

24 5 7

25 26

15

10

11 12 13

Jie

16

17 18 19 20

Gong Xiang

27

21

22

23

29

30

28

| | | | |
|---|---|---|---|
| | | 1 | 拙政园 |
| 1 | Zhuozheng Garden | 2 | 怡园 |
| 2 | Yiyuan Garden | 3 | 沧浪亭 |
| 3 | Canglangting Garden | 4 | 网师园 |
| 4 | Wangshi Garden | 5 | 耦园 |
| 5 | Ouyuan Garden | 6 | 狮子林 |
| 6 | Shizilin Garden | 7 | 东园 |
| 7 | Dong Garden | 8 | 北寺塔 |
| 8 | North Temple (Bei Si) Pagoda | 9 | 博物馆 |
| 9 | Suzhou Museum | 10 | 盘门/瑞光塔 |
| 10 | Pan Gate Area / Ruigang Pagoda | 11 | 双塔 |
| 11 | Twin Pagoda Temple | 12 | 火车站 |
| 12 | Suzhou Railway Station | 13 | 长途汽车站 |
| 13 | Long Distance Bus Station | 14 | 轮船运输公司 |
| 14 | Grand Canal Boat Ticket Office & Dock | 15 | 出租汽车站 |
| 15 | Taxi, Autorickshaw & Pedicab Stand / CAAC Booking Office | 16 | 南林饭店 |
| 16 | Nanlin Hotel | 17 | 苏州和姑苏饭店 |
| 17 | Suzhou I, Suzhou II & Gusu Hotels | 18 | 公安局 |
| 18 | Public Security (On Daishitou Xiang) | | |

| | | | |
|---|---|---|---|
| | | 1 | 工艺美术服务部 |
| | Suzhou Centre (Insert) | 2 | 邮电大楼 |
| 1 | Arts & Crafts Shop | 3 | 展销商店 |
| 2 | Main Post Office | 4 | 广州食品商店 |
| 3 | Suzhou Underground Store Entrances | 5 | 食品商店 |
| 4 | Guangzhou Food Shop | 6 | 旅社 |
| 5 | Food & Sweet Shop | 7 | 新华书店 |
| 6 | Chinese Hotel | 8 | 久泰绸布店 |
| 7 | Xinhua Bookstore | 9 | 玄妙观点心店 |
| 8 | Silk Merchant / Cloth Shop | 10 | 土特产商店 |
| 9 | Snack Bar | 11 | 黄天源糕粿店 |
| 10 | Suzhou Speciality Shop | 12 | 女用商店 |
| 11 | Huangtianyuan Cakeshop | 13 | 海鸥照相馆 |
| 12 | Ladies Clothing Shop | 14 | 出租汽车站 |
| 13 | Seagull Photo Service | 15 | 松鹤照相馆 |
| 14 | Taxi, Pedicab & 3-Wheeler Station | 16 | 面馆 |
| 15 | Songhelou Restaurant (Front & Back Entrances) | 17 | 采芝斋糖果店 |
| 16 | Oodles of Noodles | 18 | 苏州糕店 |
| 17 | Caizhizhai Confectionary | 19 | 稻香村糖果店 |
| 18 | Suzhou Pastry Shop | 20 | 新乐面店 |
| 19 | Daoxiangcun Cake & Candy Store | 21 | 人民商场 |
| 20 | Xinle Noodles Restaurant | 22 | 上海老正兴菜馆 |
| 21 | Renmin Dept. Store | 23 | 餐厅 |
| 22 | Shanghai Laozhenxin Restaurant | 24 | 春风饭店 |
| 23 | Masses Restaurant | 25 | 绿阳馄饨店 |
| 24 | Chunfeng Restaurant | 26 | 火车售票处 |
| 25 | Luyang Soup Dumpling Restaurant | 27 | 乐乡饭店 |
| 26 | Advance Rail Ticket Office | 28 | 书场 |
| 27 | Lexiang Hotel | 29 | 南门商业大楼 |
| 28 | Suzhou Story-telling House | 30 | 电影院 |
| 29 | Telecom, Building | | |
| 30 | Theatres & Cinemas | | |

## Silk Factories

CITS tours are really your only option if you want to get into a silk-reeling, silk-weaving or silk-printing mill – it's unlikely you'll get in there by yourself. The silkworms are hand-fed by peasants on bamboo trays. When their cocoons are spun, these are sent off to the factories where the larva cases are boiled and the filament unwound in long strands. There is also an embroidery factory, a jade-carving factory and a sandalwood fan factory – all within the central area. A guide will cost at least Y15 per half day and a taxi will take a maximum of three passengers – so you're looking at a minimum of Y25 for a half-day tour, probably more.

## The Gardens

Suzhou's gardens are looked upon as works of art – a fusion of nature, architecture, poetry and painting designed to ease the mind, move it, or assist it. Unlike the massive imperial gardens, the classical landscaping of Suzhou reflects the personal taste of officials and scholars south of the Yangtse. A rich official, his worldly duties performed, would find solace here in his kingdom of ponds and rockeries. The gardens were meant to be enjoyed in solitary contemplation, or in the company of a close circle of friends – a glass of wine, a concert, reciting of poetry, a discussion about literature.

The key elements are rocks and water – surprisingly few flowers and no fountains, just as the Zen gardens of Japan give one an illusion of a natural scene with only moss, sand and rock. These microcosms were laid out by master craftsmen and changed hands many times over the centuries. The gardens suffered a setback during the Taiping Rebellion in the 1870s, and under subsequent foreign domination of Suzhou. Efforts were made to restore them in the 1950s but during the so-called Horticultural Revolution gardeners downed tools as flowers were frowned upon. In 1979 the Suzhou

Garden Society was formed, and an export company was set up to promote Suzhou-designed gardens. A handful of the gardens have been renovated and opened to the public.

It's best not to run around knocking off every garden on the list – this will swiftly turn Suzhou into weeds. Each garden is meant to be savoured at snail's-pace – the thing to do is take along a Sunday newspaper, a pot of tea, a deckchair, sketch pad and bath sponge. Having said that, let me add that it is very hard to wax contemplative when there are thousands of other visitors – mostly Chinese – examining every nook and cranny. The size of the crowds depends on the weather, which day of the week it is, and which garden. They're an amiable enough lot – mostly taking photos of each other, or sketching the foliage – old-timers come to relax. Gardens are open early morning to dusk (7.30 am to 5 pm, admission Y0.20).

A footnote on gardening in Suzhou: the common people, not having the resources for larger gardens, work at arranging miniatures (potted landscapes, courtyard cultivation). Suzhou, in fact, is the one place in China where you can count on real flowers instead of plastic – if there are any artificial ones, they will at least be silk. As you're strolling the streets, it is worthwhile looking for plebeian miniatures. Potted landscapes are sold in various shops, so you can actually buy a piece of Suzhou – but what are you going to do with it?!

## Zhuozheng (a humble administrator's garden)

Built in the early 1500s, this was a private garden belonging to Wang Xianchen, a censor with a chequered history. Some say he was demoted to Suzhou, some claim he extorted the money to have the garden constructed, others that the garden was lost as a gambling debt by his son.

The garden is also known as the 'Plain Man's Politics Garden' deriving from the quotation 'to cultivate one's garden to

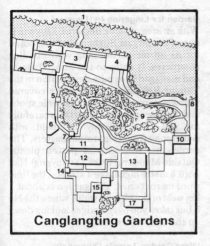

| | | | |
|---|---|---|---|
| 1 | Canglangshengji | **1** | 沧浪胜蹟坊 |
| 2 | Lotus Waterside Pavilion | **2** | 公厕 |
| 3 | Steles | **3** | 碑记 |
| 4 | Waterside House | **4** | 面水轩 |
| 5 | Pavilion of Imperial Stele | **5** | 御碑记 |
| 6 | Toilet | **6** | 公厕 |
| 7 | Buqi Pavilion | **7** | 步碕亭 |
| 8 | Pavilion for Admiring Fish | **8** | 观鱼处 |
| 9 | Canglangting Garden | **9** | 沧浪亭 |
| 10 | Wenmiaoxiang House | **10** | 闻妙香亭 |
| 11 | Qingxiang Hall | **11** | 清香馆 |
| 12 | Shrine of 500 Sages | **12** | 五百名贤祠 |
| 13 | Mingdao Hall | **13** | 明道堂 |
| 14 | Yangzhi Pavilion | **14** | 仰止亭 |
| 15 | Cuilinglong Houses | **15** | 翠玲珑 |
| 16 | Kanshen Tower | **16** | 看山楼 |
| 17 | Yaohuajingjie House | **17** | 瑶华境界 |

**Canglangting Gardens**

meet one's daily needs, that is what is known as the politics of the plain man'. The garden contains a five hectare water park, streams, ponds, bridges, islands of bamboo – and you can sense the painter's hand in its design, meant to mimic parts of rural South China – strong emphasis in Suzhou gardens is given to scenery not found locally. The garden is divided into East, Middle and West sections. Avoid the East Garden – nothing of great interest in it. The Middle Garden is the best, and from the Ming Dynasty Distant Fragrance (Yuanxiang) Hall, you can get a view of the entire works through lattice windows. In the same area is the Suzhou Museum, and several silk mills.

### Lion Grove (Shizilin)

Just up the street from the humble administrator's garden, this grove was constructed in 1350 by the Monk Tian Ru and his disciples as a memorial to their master Zhi Zheng. Zhi Zheng, it appears, was some kind of cave dweller, and his last fixed address was c/o 'Lion Cliff', Tianmu Mountains, Zhejiang Province. The garden has rockeries that evoke leonine forms, and a labyrinth of tunnels, the walls of which bear calligraphy

from famous chisels. It's one hectare, on the dull side.

### Garden of Harmony (Yiyuan)

A small Qing Dynasty garden owned by an official called Gu Wenbin, this one is quite young for a Suzhou garden. It's assimilated many of the features of other gardens and blended them into a style of its own. It's divided into eastern and western sections linked by a covered promenade with lattice windows. In the east are buildings and courtyards; the western section has pools with coloured pebbles, rockeries, hillocks and pavilions. The garden is off Renmin Lu, just south of Guanqian.

### Surging Wave Pavilion (Canlangting)

A bit on the wild side with winding creeks and luxuriant trees. It is one of the oldest gardens in Suzhou, completed in the 11th century, destroyed and reconstructed more than a few times. Originally the villa of a prince, it passed into the hands of a scholar, Su Zimei, who gave it the poetic name. One hectare in size, the garden attempts to create illusion between outside and inside scenery by stealing scenes from the surroundings – from the pool immediately outside to the distant hills. Enlightened Way (Mingdao) Hall, the largest building, is said to have been a site for delivery of lectures in the Ming Dynasty. On the other side of Renmin Lu, close by, is the former Confucian Temple.

## Master of the Nets (Wangshi)

This is the smallest garden in Suzhou – half the size of Canglangting, and one tenth the size of Zhuozheng. In fact, so small, it's hard to find. But it's well worth the trouble since this micro outstrips the others combined. It was laid out in the 12th century, abandoned, then restored in the 18th century as the residence of a retired official. One story has it that he announced he'd had enough of bureaucracy and would rather be a fisherman; another explanation of the name is that it was simply near Wangshi Lu.

The eastern part of the garden is the residential area – originally with siderooms for sedan-chair lackeys, guest receiving halls and living quarters. The central part is the main garden. The western part is an inner garden where a courtyard contains the Spring-Rear (Dianchun) Cottage, the master's study. This section – the study with its Ming-style furniture and palace lanterns – was duplicated and unveiled at the Metropolitan Museum of Art in New York in 1981. A miniature model of the whole garden, using Qingtian jade, Yingde rocks, Anhui paper and Suzhou silk – incorporating the halls, kiosks, ponds, blossoms and rare plants of the original design – was produced especially for a display at the Pompidou Centre in Paris in 1982.

The most striking feature of Wangshi is its use of space. Despite its size the scale of the buildings is large, but nothing appears cramped. A section of the buildings is used by a co-operative of woodblock artists who find the peaceful atmosphere congenial to work. One should not spoil this garden's surprises any further – the entrance is a narrow alley-way just west of the Suzhou Hotel.

## Garden for Lingering In (Liuyuan)

With an area of three hectares, Liuyuan is one of the largest Suzhou gardens, noted for its adroit partitioning with building complexes. It dates to the Ming Dynasty and managed to escape destruction in the Taiping Rebellion. A 700 metre covered walkway connects the major scenic spots, and windows select perspectives carefully for you. The walkway is inlaid with calligraphy from celebrated masters. The garden has a wealth of potted plants. Outside Mandarin Duck (Yuanyang) Hall is a 6.5 metre high Lake Tai piece, the final word on rockeries. The garden is about 1 km west of the old city walls, where the No 5 bus takes you over bridges looking down on the busy water traffic.

## West Garden Temple (Xiyuansi)

500 metres west of Liuyuan (take bus No 5,) this garden was built on the site of a garden laid out at the same time as Liuyuan and then donated to the Buddhist community. The temple was destroyed in the 19th century and entirely rebuilt; it contains some expressive Buddhist statues.

## Cold Mountain Temple (Hanshansi)

1 km west of Liuyuan (take bus No 4 to the terminus, cross the bridge and walk to the No 6 bus route; or take bus No 5 and then connect with bus No 6). This temple was named after the poet monk Hanshan, who lived in the 7th century. It was repeatedly burned down and rebuilt, and holds little of interest except for a stele immortalising Maple Bridge (nearby) and the temple-bell (removed to Japan) by poet Zhang Ji. The fine walls, however, and the humpback bridge are worth it. The temple was once the site for lively local trading in silk, wood and grain; not far from its saffron walls lies the Grand Canal.

## Tiger Hill

Located at the No 5 bus terminus, I counted 15 Chinese tour buses, six minibuses, five Toyotas, three Shanghai taxis and two Kingswoods (modified with drawn curtains) in the parking lot here, so it must be good. Actually, it's below average to boring.

It's an artificial hill, 36 metres high, set in a park of 20 hectares. Near the top of the hill is buried King He Lu, founding father of Suzhou, who died in the 6th century BC. A white tiger is said to have appeared to guard the tomb; hence the name.

Arthurian-type legends abound on Tiger Hill. There's a Sword-Testing Stone with a crack on it, split by He Lu. The old boy, according to legend, is buried with his 3,000 swords – and 1,000 builders were reputedly bumped off after making the tomb so that its secrets would not be revealed. It is apparently booby-trapped with spring water; any attempt at digging would be bad news for the pagoda further up.

Tiger Hill Pagoda, which was finished in 961 AD, has been leaning for several centuries. This century the thing split, and had to be restabilised (since it is the symbol of Suzhou!). Work has been in progress to reinforce the foundation now that the tilt has reached over two metres – concrete piles have been driven into the ground around the base, rather like planting it in a flowerpot.

## Places to Stay

There are two hotel locations; the Lexiang Hotel (near Guanqian) is central but lacking in ambience. The Gusu, Suzhou and Nalin Hotels are grouped at the southeast end of town – further out, more spacious, more amenities, and preferable. Price range is much of a muchness, with the Lexiang being cheaper. Take bus No 1 from the railway station to the Lexiang. For the other three, a few options on the buses – you can take bus No 1 straight down Renmin, alight at Shiquan and walk east; or take No 1 to Baita Lu, change to No 4 and take it direct (eastwards) to the hotels; bus No 2 also passes close (north side) to Nalin Hotel.

The Lexiang Hotel (tel 2815) is at 18 Dajing Xiang – down an alley near the Guanqian markets. Both the Lexiang and the Suzhou Hotels have things called 'TV-rooms' which are lined with plush couches – one is tempted to say 'couchettes' – available only when the house is full and under extreme pressure at midnight (Y5 per person). Otherwise the Lexiang is Y40 for a triple room including bath; Y24 for a triple, no bath; Y20 for a four-bed room, no bath.

The Suzhou Hotel (tel 4616) is at 115 Shiquan Jie. There are two wings, a three-storey old wing with 120 beds and a nine-storey new wing with 300 beds. Both are aircon luxury, with a full range of services – Friendship Store branch, theatre, extensive gardens. The restaurant has excellent though pricey Suzhou cuisine, as well as western pastries; there's a penthouse bar on the highrise wing with late-night music and intoxicating views. The average room rate is Y36 double, including fridge and bath. Old wing dormitory beds are Y6.50 for men, Y8 for women (the women's dorm is in bad shape – so therefore it's more expensive!). The desk staff just know you'd love the two-hour argument for a dorm, and you'll get it just about every time. Ah well, you know the old proverb. 'An argument in Suzhou is more pleasant than praise in Guangzhou'. Some travellers have marched in and scored a dorm-bed straight off; others have spent hours arguing over whether in fact the dorm exists – depends who's on the desk and what they had for breakfast.

The Guzou Hotel is in the same enclosure as the Suzhou, and is an Australian prefab. Doubles Y40, triples Y52 and full of electronics and outback creature comforts, angled towards Overseas Chinese. Bar, cafe, dining rooms.

Nanlin Hotel (tel 4641) at Gunxiufang offset from Shiquan Jie. Very pleasant gardens with a small section with outdoor ceramic tables and chairs. Doubles Y36, Y8 dorm beds and a full range of facilities and a dining hall. The hotel is not to be confused with the Nanyuan Guesthouse across the way, where they'll chase you around the gardens till you find out where the Nanlin is. The mysterious Nanyuan is most likely a cadre/VIP hotel.

### Places to eat

Suzhou Bazaar is the restaurant centre of the city. If there's pleasure in anticipation, then westerners who are used to seeing items on the supermarket shelves all year round will perhaps not be too disappointed to learn that food in Suzhou is greatly dependent on the seasons. Towards autumn, the residents start salivating for a dish of a strange hairy crab, steamed with soy sauce and ginger. The crabs are caught at a freshwater lake seven km north-east of Suzhou in early autumn. The resulting feast is an annual event; Nanjingers and Shanghainese make the trip to Suzhou to sample it. There are prices around the area to suit all wallets – you can stuff your gills for 30 fen in a noodle shop, or blow your inheritance in the Songhelou Restaurant.

The *Songhelou Caiguan* (tel 2066) is the most famed in Suzhou – several centuries old – so old that Emperor Qianlong is supposed to have eaten there. Perhaps it's been on the map too long. Large variety of dishes – squirrel fish, plain steamed prawns, braised eel, pork with pine nuts, butterfly-shaped sea-cucumber, watermelon chicken, spicy duck ... and the waiter will insist that you be parcelled off to the special 'tour bus' cubicle at the back where an English menu awaits. The Songhelou runs through from Guanqian to an alley behind, where tour minibuses pull up. If you refuse to budge from the front (Guanqian) section, the waiter will simply rush out to the back for an English menu and the surly service and high prices will remain the same. Count on Y7 per head minimum, unless you can negotiate steamed dumplings or sweet taro (on the other hand there's not much point coming here if all you're going to eat is dumplings!).

In the same alley at the back of the

Songhelou are two large, crowded prole restaurants – the *Shanghai Laozhenxin* is one and the other is at No 19 on a corner further east of the Shanghai. The Shanghai Laozhenxin serves pot-stewed food, cold dishes, and smoked fish.

There are lots of other small places to explore – pick the most crowded, wheel in and see what's cooking (unfortunately the most crowded will mean longer waits). Another indicator is the noise level – if it's over 100 decibels, it's a thumping good restaurant by Chinese standards – they like plenty of shouting, clatter and mayhem at the tables. The inner alley sections of Guanqian have a grand, almost homely feel to them, with palace lanterns hung off some restaurants, narrow doorways, and ornamental windows. Some of the restaurants have food pictures outside – the *Chunfeng* at 213-215 Guanqian has some – you have to get tickets first, so lead the cashier out to the pictures and point out what you want.

A pot of tea is the correct way to lubricate your repast: Suzhou has two native teas – Biluochun Green (Snail Spring Tea) and Jasmine Scented. This consumed, the next correct thing to do is belch heartily, march outside, spit into the gutter, and hang about with a toothpick.

For snacks there are loads of shops and vendors. Right on the corner of Renmin Lu and Guanqian Lu at night are market-stalls with sizzling tasty fare. The *Luyang Soup-Dumpling Restaurant* specialises in *hundun*, *jiaozi* and *baozi* – it's just around the corner from Renmin and Guanqian Lu. In the soup line it's worth investigating a regional speciality made from Lake Taihu aquatic plants – you might find it in a larger restaurant. Around Xuanmiao Temple you can find snackshops selling dough-cakes, cream cakes, square cakes, meat dumplings and steamed buns by day. In the late spring, fruit from the shores of Lake Taihu comes to the Guanqian markets – loquats and strawberries.

Suzhou is famous for its sweets, candied fruits and pastries – some 170 varieties, depending on the stuffing. At the far end of Guanqian Lu is a concentration of the better-known shops. The *Huangtianyun Cake-shop* at 88 Guanqian Lu has been in business for over a century, serves steamed leaf-wrapped dumplings and savouries, and pastries with ingredients like cabbage juice, cocoa, walnuts and preserved fruits. Almost opposite is the *Caizhizhai Confectionery*, equally as ancient and equally as grubby. It sells pine nut candy and sweetened flour-cakes and a real treat here, in season, are the candied strawberries. Down the road is the *Suzhou Pastry Shop* and nearby at No 35 is the *Daoxiangcun Cake & Candy Shop* which, you must agree, is already a strain on the tooth-enamel.

You will undoubtedly be asked in these cake shops for grain-flour coupons – being a foreigner means never having to say 'sorry', but it allows the shopkeeper the discretion to jack up the prices of the 'ration'. Having been asked the question innumerable times, I got round to learning the Chinese for 'coupon' which is *liangpiao* – not only that, I managed to procure some of the correct ones. Just for kicks, I went into one of the candy stores, and when the dreary automatic question came, I produced my 'stamps' – the lady behind the counter almost died of fright. Well, bless me boots, don't the tourists come well equipped these days?

Other than in the bazaar, a couple of other places worth trying are the *Xinjufeng Restaurant* at 657 Renmin Lu, which serves variations on duck and chicken and regional specialities; and the restaurants in the *Suzhou* and the *Nanlin Hotels* which serve all of the local delicacies like Suzhou almond duck, and phoenix shrimp – try for student price.

**Shopping**

Along Guanqian, and in the alleys behind it, you can find Suzhou-style embroidery, calligraphy, painting, sandalwood fans, writing brushes, or silk by the metre – it may be hard to find what you want, but it

sure beats dowdy Friendship Stores where the staff sit around all day swatting flies and polishing Coca-Cola bottles. Rummaging around the smaller shops is far more fun. The Friendship Store, by the way, is on the 3rd floor of 604 Renmin Lu (north of Guanqian).

A curious store is Suzhou Y – no, not a dormitory, but a good place to spend WW III. This is a mini underground department store that runs five blocks north-south on the west side of Renmin Lu, with Guanquin Lu at the northern end. It's about three metres wide (the store, not the silk) and has entrances that look like subway exits on the street. I thought they were WCs, but figured the place couldn't be *that* clean.

On Jingde Lu, which runs west from the Renmin/Guanqian Lu intersection, is the Arts & Crafts Store stocking, among other handicrafts, clay figurines, traditional painting, calligraphy, musical instruments, jade carving. Never tried embroidery myself, but the Suzhou pieces look nearly impossible to have been done with single filaments of silk. The double-sided hand embroidery, with its dazzling colours and striking patterns, is especially nifty.

It's worth tracking down to the National Embroidery Institute display, which is in the same area as the Arts & Crafts Store. The institute specialised in hair-embroidery and the art is supposed to have been revived in Jiangsu Province since the Communists came to power. The technique uses human hair worked onto a silk backing. Suzhou is ranked among the top four needle-styles in China. Another Suzhou speciality is *Kesi*, which mixes raw and boiled-off silk and is known as 'carved silk'. It was once reserved for imperial robing and can be bought in painting-scrolls, waistbands and other items.

A little further afield at 344 Renmin Lu is an Antique Shop where a funny old man shuffles around after you to make sure you don't pocket anything. The shop has some antique hardwood furniture, and you might delve into sandalwood fans (sandalwood is scarce – the fans are now made of other kinds of wood, like oak).

Though not open to tourists there is some fascinating activity going on at the Arts & Crafts Research Institute in Suzhou. In 1981 32 year-old Shen Weizhong carved the world's smallest Buddha – 3 mm tall, fingers as thin as hair, and a smiling face that can only be seen through a microscope. Another worker carved words onto the hair of a panda. Now you know how they come up with those bus maps!

## Entertainment

Try the barber shops and hairdressing salons on Guanqian Lu. I kid you not – these places have the brightest lights and the most action in the early evening. Anyway, as you're walking along, do peep over the curtains of the salons to discover China's great beauty secrets. Suzhou does have night life, with over a dozen theatres and some story-telling houses. Suzhou Pingtan (ballad singing and story telling) is where you can hear those sweet voices worked to their fullest. Most of the after hours activity takes place south of Guanqian.

Late nights can be spent at the penthouse of the *Suzhou Hotel* (new wing) with bright lights, big-city views, jazz, coffee, brandy – you name it. It's open until midnight by which time the buses will be long gone. The 570 seat theatre at the Suzhou Hotel has occasional live shows.

## Getting Around

The main thoroughfare is Renmin Lu with the railway station off the north end, and a large boat dock and long-distance bus station at the south end.

Bus No 1 runs the length of Renmin Lu. Bus No 2 is a kind of round-the-city bus; No 5 is a good east-west bus. The No 4 bus runs from Changmen directly east along Baita, turns south and runs past the east end of Guanqian and then on to the Suzhou Hotel. The high-numbered buses

are long-run suburban routes (No 11, 12, 13, 14, 15, 16); they all terminate around the intersection of Renmin and Guanqian.

Taxis and autorickshaws can be found ranked at the Renmin and Guanqian intersection, outside the main railway station, down by the boat dock at the southern end of Renmin Lu and at Jingmen (Nanxin Bridge) at the western end of Jingde Lu.

## Getting Away

**Bus** There are bus connections between Suzhou and just about every major place in the region.

**Train** Suzhou is on the Nanjing-Shanghai line. It's 1¼ hrs to Shanghai, 40 minutes to Wuxi and 3¼ hrs to Nanjing. There are frequent expresses on this line. If you're thinking of day-tripping this line is ideal for 'rail-hopping' – get a through ticket from say Nanjing to Shanghai and break the journey in Suzhou (your ticket will *probably* be good for two days).

You'll most likely have trouble getting Chinese prices in Shanghai – the solution to this is to take the tourist price to Suzhou which will only be a small markup, then try and get Chinese price in Suzhou (remember that if you want a sleeper reservation it will be difficult to get it in Suzhou)

In Suzhou the advance booking office for the trains is at 203 Guanqian Lu (tel 6462).

**Boat** Boats along the Grand Canal to Wuxi (6 hours) and to Hangzhou (14 hours). Getting to Suzhou may be easier than getting out of Suzhou by boat; while getting out is not impossible from Suzhou, it will take a good deal of perseverance and ingenuity, and your permit must be valid for 'Ship'. The situation may change by the time this book is out but at the time of writing foreigners were not allowed to go down the Grand Canal from Suzhou to Hangzhou – but we were allowed to go from Hangzhou to Suzhou! Makes sense.

The main boat dock is at the south end of Renmin Lu where there's a large ticket office.

**Plane** There is no airport at Suzhou but CAAC has a booking office on Renmin Lu.

## AROUND SUZHOU

While you may be right on track in Suzhou, go 20 kms in any direction and you'll be off the record. The further out you go, of course, the less likely you should be there in the first place. Some of the local buses, it should be added, go for a considerable distance, No 11 for example – you could hop on one for a ride to the terminus to see the enchanting countryside.

### The Grand Canal

The canal proper cuts to the west and south of Suzhou, within a 10 km range of the town. Suburban bus routes No 13, 14, 15, 16 will get you there, and No 11 bus tracks the canal a fair distance in the north-west. Once you arrive, it's simply a matter of finding yourself a nice bridge, getting out your deckchair and watch the world go by.

### Precious Belt Bridge (Baodai Qiao)

Welcome to the bridge club! This is one of China's best – it has 53 arches, with the three central humpbacks being larger to allow boats through. It straddles the Grand Canal, and is a popular spot with fishermen (the bridge is not used for traffic – a modern one has been built alongside). Disconcertingly, the disused bridge has been planted with telegraph poles along its length that mar its ancient grace. The bridge is thought to be a Tang Dynasty construction and is said to be named after Wang Zhongshu, a local prefect who sold his precious belt to pay for the bridge's construction for the benefit of his people. Precious Belt Bridge is about five km south-east of Suzhou; bus No 13 will set you on the right track.

### Lake Taihu Hangouts

The following places can all be reached by long-distance buses from the station at the south end of Renmin Lu.

**Lingyan Shan** is 15 km south-west of Suzhou with its weirdly-shaped rocks, a temple and pagoda (molested by Red Guards), panoramas of mulberry trees and fertile fields and Taihu in the distance.

**Tianping Shan** 18 km south-west is more of the same – plus some medicinal spring waters. **Guangfu** 25 km south-west, bordering the lake, has an ancient seven-storey pagoda, and is dotted with plum trees.

**Dong Shan** is 40 km south-west and is noted for its gardens and the Purple Gold (Zijin) Nunnery which contains 16 coloured clay arhats and is surrounded by Lake Taihu on three sides.

**Xidongting Shan Isle** is a large island 60 km south-west of Suzhou – and getting there also involves a 10 km ferry ride. Eroded Taihu rocks are 'harvested' here for landscaping.

**Changshu** is 50 km to the north-east of Suzhou and the town is noted for its lace-making. To the north-west of the town is Yu Shan with historical/scenic spots including a nine-storey Song pagoda. Both these places were opened to foreigners in late 1983.

**Luzhi** is 25 km east and is a town on the water: the canals in fact are the main form of commuting (in concrete flat-bottom boats). The town has an old temple, Baosheng, with old arhats – but that is probably not why you should come here. You could try your luck getting to places like this via canals from Suzhou (the smaller boat docks) – the connections exist as does the red tape.

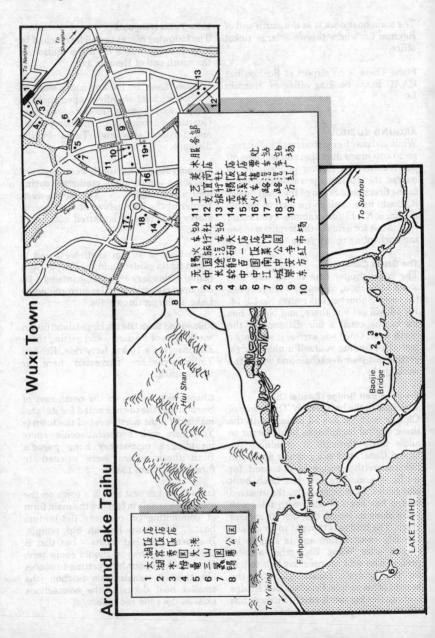

# Wuxi Town

## Around Lake Taihu

**Wuxi Town** map legend:

1 无锡饭店
2 湖滨饭店
3 水秀饭店
4 梅园大洗
5 电毫大山
6 三国城
7 三国城
8 锡惠公园

**Legend (right panel):**

1 无锡火车站
2 中国旅行社
3 水途活车站
4 轮船码大
5 中百一店
6 中国饭店
7 江南饭莱馆
8 城中公园
9 崇安寺
10 东方红市场
11 工艺谊美术服务部
12 支谊商店
13 版行社
14 无锡饭店
15 深溪饭莱处
16 火车站与汽车站
17 一路与二路汽车站
18 二路汽车站
19 东方红广场

Map labels: To Nanjing, To Shanghai, To Suzhou, To Yixing, Hui Shan, Grand Canal, Renmin Lu, Zhongshan Lu, Xin Lu, Gongnong Lu, LAKE TAIHU, Fishponds, Baojie Bridge

## WUXI

Just up the line from Suzhou is Wuxi, a name that means 'tinless' – the local mine was exhausted. Not that the locals especially cared – a stone tablet dug out of Xishan Hill is engraved 'Where there is tin, there is fighting; where there is no tin, there is tranquillity'. And indeed there was tranquillity –like Suzhou, Wuxi was an ancient silk producer, but it remained a sleepy backwater town little altered by the intrusion of the Grand Canal (though it did once or twice come into the spotlight as a rice-marketing centre).

In this century Wuxi made up for the long sleep. In the 1930s Shanghai businessmen, backed by foreign technicians, set up textile and flour mills, oil-extracting plants, and a soap factory. After liberation, textile production was stepped up considerably, light and heavy industry boomed, and monstrous housing developments were flung up to accommodate a population that had surpassed Suzhou's and which today stands at 800,000. The town is now ranked among the top 15 economic centres in China, with 600 factories and an emphasis on electronics, textiles, machine building, chemicals, fishing, and agricultural crops serving the Shanghai market.

### Information & Orientation

Wuxi is divided into two sections, five to 10 km apart, and the hotel situation is not good in either. Because of Wuxi's earlier stunted growth, there are few 'historical relics' and the main attraction is a natural one – Lake Taihu – which is clear out of town. Tourist land is out by the lakeside: if you want to observe the locals then the water life around town holds interest.

CITS (tel 22951) has its office in the south-eastern corner of the town near the Friendship Store. However the CTS office is conveniently located at 55 Chezhan Lu (tel 3024) right near the railway station, and harbours several English-speakers. Wuxi is being promoted as a resort area, and if you have resort-type money the programme consists of cooking classes, fishing, 10-day acupuncture and massage courses, sanitorium treatments, and taijiquan lessons (the base for operations seems to be the more isolated

---

Around Lake Taihu
1 Taihu Hotel
2 Hubin Hotel
3 Shuixiu Hotel
4 Meiyuan (Plum Garden)
5 Yuantouzhu
   (Turtle Head Isle)
6 Sanshan (Three Hills Isle)
7 Liyuan Garden
8 Xihui Park

Wuxi Town
1 Wuxi Railway Station
2 China Travel Service (CTS)
3 Long Distance Bus Station
4 Canal Boat Dock
5 First Department Store
6 Zhongguo Fandian
   (China Restaurant)
7 Jiangnan Restaurant

8 Chengzheng Park
9 Free Markets
   (Chongansi People's Market)
10 Dongfanghong Emporium
11 Arts & Crafts Store
12 Friendship Store
13 China International Travel
   Service
14 Wuxi Hotel / Restaurant
15 Liangxi Hotel / Restaurant
16 Advance Bus, Rail, & Boat
   Ticket Office
17 Bus No. 2 Stop
   (To Xihui Park & Taihu
   Starts at Station)
18 Bus No. 1 Stop
   (Starts Near Wuxi Hotel &
   Goes to Hubin & Shuixiu
   Hotel)
19 Dongfanghong Square

Taihu Hotel). Also at CITS' command is a small fleet of power craft that cruises the Grand Canal and Lake Taihu. You might like to investigate the T.S. Taihu, a 33 metre motor boat which carries 30 passengers. Then there are the new 'dragon boats', imperial replicas. Either of these, if they are not requisitioned by group tours, will cost you a bundle for a cruise so try your luck on the local boats first. Factory visits can no doubt be arranged through CITS (guides don't ride in buses!) and the No 1 Silk Filature or an embroidery factory may be of interest; from May to October group tours are taken to see silkworm breeding on a people's commune outside Wuxi.

## Things to See

Wuxi is shaped like a heart, with the Grand Canal at its aorta, and loads of capillary canals. To this we add two valves of concrete and factories. To finalise this simile, or metaphor, whatever it is by now, some might say that the heart has been carved right out of Wuxi and what you're looking at is a transplant. Apartment block building has been going on at a furious pace – in the last five years almost doubling the number of living quarters built from 1949 to 1978. Never mind – vestiges of Wuxi's former charm remain. The main street of Wuxi is, in fact, the old Grand Canal which sees plenty of bottlenecks and frenzied activity. There are numerous waterways cutting into the Canal, and more than a fair share of bridges to observe from.

Just down from the train station is Gongyun Bridge with a passenger and loading dock close by – well worth your attention. In the north-west of the city is an older bridge, Wuqiao, which has a great view of canal traffic and overlooks an ancient pavilion stranded on tiny Huangbudun Isle. Traffic will, in fact, come at you from all directions. For an insider point of view, try zipping around in a small boat yourself – there are at least three boat stations within the city.

## Free markets

Not far from the corner of Renmin and Zhongshan Lu. Go south on Zhongshan, turn left at Renmin, walk along a bit and you'll find the market entrance leading north again. This is about the most exciting thing in Wuxi. Be prepared to bargin for foodstuffs as the prices suddenly rocket when they see your face. There's a restaurant located in the food markets area, and an antique store. If you follow the alleys in, you will eventually arrive at the delightful Chengzhong Park, a small retreat from the traffic noise and hoi-polloi. It's not a park to look at (thank heavens) – more one to observe the Chinese at leisure, at your leisure. Old men gather at the back of the park sipping tea at ceramic tables, smoking pipes, eyes and ears glued to their caged birds. If you wait long enough a man will truck in, sweating, with a large lozenge-shaped barrel on wheels (fresh tea water). Tai Chi in the early morning.

## Xihui Park

By contrast, Xihui Park is enormous, nebulous, and hard to pin down as an attraction. It's located to the west of the city on a No 2 or No 10 bus route. The peak of the park, Hui Hill, is 75 metres above sea level; if you climb the Longguang (Dragon Light) Pagoda, the seven-storey octagonal structure at the top, you'll be able to take in comprehensive panoramas of Wuxi and Lake Taihu. The brick and wood pagoda was built in the Ming, burned down in the Qing, and rebuilt in the Spring (many years later). For sunrises, try the Qingyun Pavilion, just to the east of the pagoda.

The park has a motley collection of pavilions, snack-bars, and teahouses; a small zoo, a large artificial lake, and a cave that burrows for half a km from the east side to the west. The western section of the park rambles off into Huishan Hill, where you'll find the famous Ming Dynasty Jichang Garden (Ming refers to the garden layout – the buildings are recent), and the remaining Huishan Temple nearby, once a Buddhist monastery. What follows for this area is the standard catalogue of inscribed stones, halls, gates and crumbled villas – Ming, Song, Qing, Tang – what is this, an antique store? Sometimes you have to wonder who is pulling whose leg – there are so many copies, permutations and fakes in the PRC, it's hard to know exactly which year you're looking at. Still, the copies are nice. Speaking of Tang, the 'Second Spring under Heaven' is sited here – bring your tea mugs, or try the local teahouse brew. The Chinese patronise this watering hole

to indulge in the ancient hobby of carp watching. From the Second Spring you can scale to vantage points and pavilions higher up: a major detour leads to the 329 metre peak in the north-west called Sanmao.

## Lake Taihu

Lake Taihu is a freshwater lake with a total area of 2,200 sq km; 58 km wide and 68 km long. Average depth of the lake is two metres; there are some 90 islands, large and small, within it. Junks with all sails set ply the waters – the winds of nostalgia make them a magnificent sight,

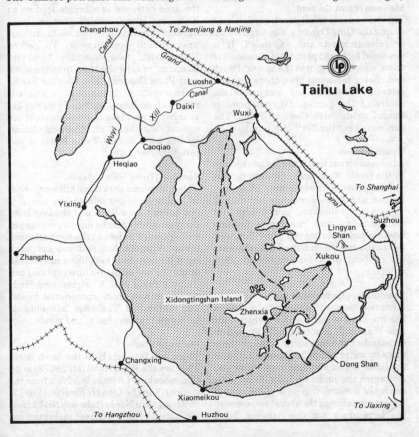

gracefully clipping across the waters. The fishing industry is very active – over 30 varietes caught; there's fish breeding in the shoals; you can see women floating around in eooden tubs harvesting water-chestnuts. And the shores, rice, tea, mulberry trees, citrus fruits. Suitably grotesque rocks are submerged in the Lake for decades – when sufficiently weathered, they are prized for classical garden landscaping. To the north-west of the lakes are hilly zones, to the south-east is a vast plain; the whole area is referred to as 'the land of fish and rice'.

### Meiyuan (Plum Garden)

This was once a small *peach* garden built during the Qing Dynasty, since renovated or relandscaped, and expanded. It is renowned for its red plum trees, thousands of them, which blossom in the spring. Peach and cherry blossoms grow there too, and grotesque rockeries are arrayed at the centre of the garden. Highest point is Plum Pagoda, with views of Taihu. The garden is near the No 2 bus terminus.

### Liyuan Garden

A hideous circus that is always packed out by the locals. As Chinese gardens go, this one is a goner. The whole tatty affair goes beyond bad taste – a concrete labyrinth of fishponds, walkways, mini-bridges, a mini-pagoda, and souvenir vendors hawking garish plaster and gilded figurines. Inside the garden on Lake Taihu shores is a tour boat dock for cruises to other points.

### Yuantouzhu (Turtle-Head Isle)

So named because it appears to be shaped like the head of a turtle. Elementary, my dear Watson. It is not actually situated on an island – but being surrounded on three sides by water makes it appear so. This is the basic scenic strolling area where you can watch the junks on Lake Taihu. You can make a round-trip walk of the area: if you continue along the shore, you come to the ferry dock for the Sanshan Isles,

passing Taihujiajue Archway and Perpetual Spring (Changchun) Bridge. A walkway leads to a small lighthouse, near which is an inscribed stone referring to the island name, and several pavilions. The architecture here is mostly, like Liyuan Garden, copies of the classical. Inland a bit from the lighthouse is Clear Ripples (Chenglan) Hall, a very nice teahouse where you get a view of the lake. Further along the south coast are similar vantage points: Jingsong Tower, Guangfu Temple, and the 72-Peaks Villa. The highest point of Yuantouzhu is the Guangming (Brightness) Pavilion with all-round vistas. Back past the area entrance is a bridge leading to Zhongdu Island, which has a large workers' sanatorium – no visits without prior (CITS) appointment. To get to Yuantouzhu, take bus No 1 to its terminus, or take the ferry from the dock near Plum Gardens. The Chinese like to make a cycling trip out of it – a pleasant road with no heavy traffic, if you can lay your hands on a bike. A possible short cut around the back of Zhongdu Island leading back toward Taihu Hotel, if you care to investigate.

### Sanshan (Three Hills) Isles

This is an island park three km south-west of Yuantouzhu (20 minutes by ferry). If you haven't seen Wuxi and the lake from every possible angle by now, try this one as well. Vantage points at the top look back toward Yuantouzhou and you can work out if it really does look like a turtle-head or not. As one of the picture captions in a Chinese guide puts it: 'sightseeing feeds chummies with more conversation-topics'. The Three-Hill Teahouse has outdoor tables and rattan chairs, and views.

### Places to Stay

There are two hotels in the town itself. They are the *Wuxi Hotel* (tel 26678) at 26 Gongnongbing Lu (take bus No 2 from the station); and the *Liangxi Hotel* (tel 26812) on Zhongshan Nanlu (take bus No 12 from the station). Both of these hotels start out at Y20 a double but will undoubtedly go lower. They don't speak English and the only Chinese they seem to know is 'mei-o' in a rising whining tone. It's an all-purpose Chinese word meaning 'nothing, not available, sold out, all gone' – a very useful phrase in what has always been a land of perpetual shortages – but when applied to hotels can usually be taken as 'get lost'. It's highly unlikely you'll be able to stay in the Wuxi Hotel or the Liangxi Hotel. CITS is rumoured to have a dorm very near the station, going cheap.

The tourist hotels are around the lakeside. The *Taihu* (tel 23001 or 26389) on Meiji Lu has a large restaurant, telecom office, bank and souvenir shop. It overlooks Lake Taihu and has air-con dining rooms serving Taihu seafood and Wuxi specialities. Three special lakeside villas are for foreign convalescents receiving treatment. The hotel is one of the key centres for group tour activity, and has some boat touring (and luxury bus) itineraries. Varying reports – some travellers have got the rates down to Y12 a double (from the Y30 and up double range); others have paid Y12 each in a 3-bed room. Probably the best of a rum bunch, a little awkward to get to (Bus No 2 to terminus, then walk about 20 minutes).

The *Hubin Hotel* (tel 2258824) on Liyuan Lu is a highrise tour bus hotel. Y36 a double minimum, and stiff prices elsewhere in the building for a dead and dull atmosphere. There are 356 beds, air-con, and a full range of facilities including a bar. Take bus No 1 from the train station.

The *Shuixiu Hotel* (tel 22985) is next to the Hubin Hotel. It's a squat Australian prefab with koalas and kangaroos crawling all over the curtains and rooms full of refrigerators, phones, digital devices – you get the picture, yes, it's very expensive. Prices from Y40 double which can be knocked down to Y30 double after a good arm wrestle with the manager – if you're on your own you might get a bed for Y15. There are rooms with views over the lake

(Take bus No 1 from the train station).

The three above hotels (the Hubin was built 1978, the Suixiu was assembled 1980) are designed for the group tours – nothing remotely close to them in the way of shops or anything else. Anglers can drop out of the hotels, toting fishing licences, tackle and bait, cruise around Lake Taihu and have their catches cooked back at the hotel (a rubbing made first as a memento – have your fish and eat it too!). Amateurs are parcelled off to fish ponds in communes for an easy catch.

### Places to Eat

The *China Restaurant*, just down from the station, is one of the better ones. It does not have a pinyin sign – the 'Gong Ying' refers to the opening hours, 6 to 12 am and 1.30 to 5.30 pm; this is the ground floor of a Chinese hotel. Straight ahead from the station, across the bridge, and it's on your left, second block down.

Eating places can be found in the markets off Renmin, and the stretch along Zhongshan Lu (from First Department Store to Renmin Lu) has lots of restaurants such as the *Jiangnan Restaurant* at 435 Zhongshan Lu. Otherwise, the more established restaurants in town are at the Wuxi Hotel and the Liangxi, which have large, quiet dining halls (they will try and detour you to private sections which are deadly quiet).

Out in the boondocks, Lake Taihu, it's the hotel dining rooms, or whatever you can scrounge from stalls or teahouses at the tour attractions out that way. One discovery that was particularly fortifying was a packet of Huishan shortcake cookies (delicious) continuing a tourist tradition that dates back to the 14th century when Buddhist monasteries from Huishan hillsides doled the stuff out to vegetarians in transit. There's seasonal seafood – crab, shrimp, eel, fresh fish. Wuxi specialities include pork ribs in soy sauce, beancurd, and a kind of pancake padded out with midget fish from Lake Taihu. Honey-peach in season.

### Shopping

The Arts & Crafts Store is at 192 Renmin Lu; the Dongfanghong Emporium is nearby; the Friendship Store is at 8 Zhongshan Lu; the First Department Store is at the top end of Zhongshan Lu; the Huishan Clay Figurine Factory is near Xihui Park.

Silk products and embroidery are good buys. Apart from the places already mentioned, try the merchants in the side streets (Dongfanghong Square is the busiest shopping area). There are some remarkably ugly clay figurines for sale around the place. A peasant folk art, they were usually opera stars, and after a little diversion into revolutionary heroes, are back to opera figures and story figures (Wuxi has its own form of opera deriving from folk songs). The 'Lucky Fatties' are obese babies – symbols of fortune and happiness. Just the thing to fill up your mantelpiece with and forget about.

### Getting Around Wuxi

There are about 15 local bus lines. An alternative for faster connections is to grab a 'rocket' (autorickshaw) – there are ranks at the main station, the Wuxi Hotel, and a third near the Friendship Store.

Bus No 2 runs from the railway station, along Jiefang Lu, across two bridges to Xihui Park, then way out there to Plum Garden, which is short of the Taihu hotel.

Bus No 1 almost crosses the No 2 bus route at Gongnongbing Square. No 1 starts near Wuxi Hotel on Gongnongbing Lu, and runs to the other acupuncture point for ferries and hotels, Liyuan Gardens. There is a bus depot at Liyuan Garden – the actual terminus of No 1 bus is further on across a bridge to the scenery on Turtle-Head Island.

A good tour bus is No 10, which does a long loop around the northern part of the city area, taking in four bridges, Xihui Park, and the shopping strip of Renmin Lu (passes to the south of the station). Bus No 10 runs late and No 1 & 2 finish early.

There's a special tour boat that runs from the pier near the railway station. It cuts down the Liangxi River (through the city), under Ximen Bridge, south to Liyuan Garden. The boat then continues on to Turtle-Head Island and finally the Sanshan Isles. Enquire at CITS. Local boat routes duplicate this idea – leaving from wharves marked on the map. There's a ferry running from the south of Plum Garden to Turtle-Head Island. Liyuan Garden is a major touring junction with a boat dock – 1, 2, 3 and 12-hour cruises (motorboats) around Lake Taihu for prices ranging from Y2.50 to Y32.

### Getting Away

The advance ticket office for boat, bus and train in Wuxi is at 224 Renmin Lu (Tel: 26340). Some boats require one or two day's advance booking.

**Bus** There are long-distance buses to Nanjing, Shanghai and Suzhou.

**Train** Wuxi is on the Beijing-Shanghai line, with frequent express and special express trains. There are trains to Suzhou (40 minutes, 42 km); to Shanghai (1¾ hrs, 128 km); and to Nanjing (2¾ hrs, 177 km).

If you're day-tripping get a through ticket from, say, Nanjing to Suzhou, alight at Wuxi and continue the same evening to Suzhou – it doesn't matter about reserved seating because of the short distances between cities; you can dump your bags at the railway station in Wuxi.

**Boat** With such a large lake there is a wealth of scenery and some fascinating routes out of the town. Yixing and Suzhou lie almost on the lake, Changzhou lies north-west of Wuxi on the Grand Canal and Hangzhou lies inland but is accessible from Wuxi.

From Wuxi there are at least 10 boat routes running along smaller canals to outlying counties as well as boats across Lake Taihu and along the Grand Canal. There are six boats a day to Yixing and around 15 a day to Changzhou; there is another route through the Wuxi canals, across Lake Taihu and down south through a series of canals to Hangzhou. Alternatively you can take a boat across Lake Taihu to Huzhou on the southern side and then take a bus to Hangzhou. Huzhou and also Jiaxing which is near the lake, are both open to foreigners – with a permit.

Huzhou lies at the junction of routes to Shanghai, Hangzhou and Huang Shan (Yellow Mountain) and there is a tourist service set up in Huzhou. Just north of Huzhou is Xiaomeikou, the ferry dock, and to the north-west of Huzhou is Changxing, a branch-line railway running to Hangzhou. Another interchange point for boating is at Zhenxia on the east side of Xidongtingshan Isle; from Zhenxia there are connections to Wuxi, and to Xukou near Suzhou.

Since Wuxi itself covers an area of 400 sq km, open without a permit, day-tripping along the canals is not technically out-of-bounds – there's no reason to stop you running between Hangzhou, Yixing, Jiaxing, Huzhou Wuxi and Suzhou on the canals. A variety of motor boats ply these routes including 2-deck motor-barges (air-con, soft seats, restaurant, space for over 100 passengers); the latest word is the introduction soon of a Chinese-designed hovercraft which will carry up to 40 passengers and scurry across the lake at 43 km/hr.

## CHANGZHOU

Changzhou is overlooked by the guidebooks, and the CITS offices in Wuxi and Suzhou will tell you it's not worth a visit. The former is oversight and the latter is regional jealousy – Changzhou has zero unemployment, and is doing very well economically, thank you.

Changzhou is the largest textile producer in Jiangsu Province after Shanghai. The population is around half a million and the city's history is linked with the ancient canal. Industries include textiles, food-processing, machinery, chemicals, building materials, locomotives and diesel engines. They also produce integrated circuits and electronic parts: large digital clocks around the place will tell you the time from Moscow to Canberra.

It's a delightful mix of old and new: Changzhou has managed to retain its timeless canal housing by placing new residential areas outside the old city core. If you look at the bus map, you'll see these dotted around the perimeter. It is very much a back-alley town, with some interesting sorties on foot. Tourism is only just getting off the ground, so at least for the moment the natives are very friendly. If you want to avoid the crush at Wuxi or Suzhou, Changzhou is a good place to go.

**CITS** will make 'house calls' at the Changzhou Hotel.

### Things to See
Changzhou has a skein of canals and is an excellent place to observe canal life. There are quite a few archaic bridges which are good vantage points: these are easily picked on the bus map. Some of the bridges shelter interconnected time-worn housing that melts in – if you took the older housing away the bridges would probably fall down (or vice-versa!). Small markets take place on occasion along canal banks near bridges.

### Mooring Pavilion
This is a small park in the south-east of Changzhou sited right on the Grand Canal. You can sit here and watch rusty hulks drift by or the oil and pollution being churned up by the rusty hulks. There's a boat dock here, and much hooting and honking on the water. The park was set up in remembrance of Su Dongpo, a great poet. Take bus No 3 or bus No 7 to Mooring Pavilion. If you take bus No 7 further, it runs clear out of town south-eastwards along the banks of the canal past dry-dock repair zones. In the north-

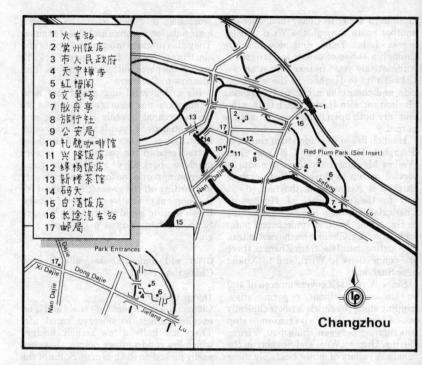

1 火车站
2 常州饭店
3 市人民政府
4 天宁禅寺
5 红梅阁
6 文笔塔
7 舣舟亭
8 旅行社
9 公安局
10 礼貌咖啡馆
11 兴隆饭店
12 绿杨饭店
13 新桥茶馆
14 码头
15 白荡饭店
16 长途汽车站
17 邮局

Park Entrances

Red Plum Park (See Inset)

Changzhou

| | |
|---|---|
| 1 Railway Station | 9 Public Security Bureau |
| 2 Changzhou Hotel | 10 Courtesy Cafe |
| 3 Municipal Government Building | 11 Xinglong Restaurant (down sidestreet) |
| 4 Temple of Heavenly Tranquility (Tianning Si) | 12 Luyang Restaurant |
| 5 Red Plum Residence | 13 Xinguiao Chadian (Teahouse) |
| 6 Literary Lion Tower | 14 Boat Dock |
| 7 Mooring Pavilion & Boat Dock | 15 Baidung Hotel |
| 8 CITS | 16 Long Distance Bus Station |
| | 17 Post Office |

west bus No 4 does a similar job (No 4 and No 7 meet at a city centre terminus).

### Xinqiao Chadian (Teahouse)

Perched off to one side of a very old bridge in the western part of the city is the Xinqiao Chadian, a decrepit old teahouse full of men who seem to have been sitting there since the Opium Wars. It's a pleasant location to watch activity on the canal and commands a great view. It's near a boat dock at the intersection of two canals (marked with an anchor on the city bus map). Bus No 3 will land you in the general vicinity and you can then explore on foot. For a totally different perspective, try to jump a boat from dock to dock within Changzhou, or day-trip on the canal.

### Red Plum Park

North of Mooring Pavilion is Red Plum Park. It's large (very large), has a pagoda (small), a teahouse (nicely-sited) and boating on the lake (nearby). There are one or two structures of significance – Qu Qui Bai's house, now a museum, and Red Plum Pavilion. Qu was a literary man and an early member of the Chinese Communist Party. The park itself is nondescript, and sits plum in an area that looks like the tail end of the Industrial Revolution hit it – at the back of the park and around it are shanty housing and dark, gloomy housing. The Temple of Heavenly Tranquillity (Tianning Si), levelled, rebuilt, destroyed, renovated – ah yes, being renovated – is below the park at the south-west corner.

### Danyang

Danyang is another canal town, situated between Changzhou and Zhenjiang. On the banks of the Danyang main canal are some 20 stone animal statues, 1500 years old.

### Places to Stay

The *Changzhou Hotel* – central, de luxe accommodation, large grounds, gardens, dining halls. Y34 a double, which can be knocked down to Y12 or less per head, depending on how poverty-stricken you look. Surprisingly so, bargaining is more difficult in places like Changzhou where they have little experience with individual travellers. Take bus No 2 three stops from the railway station. (Don't walk into City Government HQ! – it's around the corner and down an alley from the Big Red Star.)

*Baidung Guesthouse*, on the southern edge of town, is more difficult to get to as some hiking is involved. This is a TV-tourbus hotel, like the Changzhou, with similar rates and a dining hall. It's also on the bus No 2 route.

### Places to Eat

*Xinglong Restaurant* – noise level at 80 decibels, frozen pigs at the back near the kitchen and a huge painting of a dam on the wall – atmosphere! Gluey, gooey Jiangsu food – if you want to mail a letter, this is the place to seal it – just use the sauce.

The *Luyang Fandian* gets a Four Red Star rating. A full tasty meal can be had for Y5 a head. They'll probably try to shuffle you away from the noisy plebs and take you upstairs where it's quieter, the furniture is plusher, the food more expensive, and you get a tablecloth, a white one. It's not far from the Changzhou Hotel – if you take the alley that leads off the Changzhou and follow it south through a vegetable market, you'll hit the main street – the Luyang is to the left, opposite the Red Star Theatre.

The *Courtesy Cafe* is a small cafe serving drinks and pastries – quaint atmosphere, remarkably like that of a western coffee shop, and there is a courtesy award framed on the wall – so they have to live up to it. Easily spotted at night by its neon sign. There are several bakeries along the same stretch. It's on the bus No 2 route south of the Changzhou Hotel.

### Shopping

Wooden combs with imaginative designs – fish, butterflies, bottles or standing figures – are a Changzhou folk art. There's a comb factory in the western suburbs, and an Arts/Fine Arts Workshop downtown.

### Getting Away

**Bus** There's a direct bus from Changzhou to Dingshu (thus skipping Yixing town). The fare is Y1.65; the first bus leaves at 6 am and the last returning bus is at 5 pm. There are also buses from Changzhou to Wuxi, Zhenjiang, Suzhou and Nanjing, but they take longer than the fast trains.

There are three long-distance bus stations in Changzhou – the main one is near the train station; another is in the north-west sector, and the third in the south-west sector near the Baidung Hotel.

**Trains** Changzhou is on the Shanghai-Nanjing line. One hour from either Wuxi or Zhenjiang, two hours from Suzhou or Nanjing.

**Boat** A more interesting route is along the Grand Canal; Wuxi, the closest major town, is five hours away by boat.

## ZHENJIANG

Zhenjiang takes its character not from the Grand Canal but from the Yangtse, which it faces. In other words, it's large, murky and industrial. The old silk trade still exists, overshadowed by auto and ship-building, textiles and food-processing plants. It's a medium-sized place, population 320,000, 300 factories. Attempts have been made to 'humanise' the city with tree-planting along the streets. The sights are pleasant enough since they're removed from the industrial eyesores; to the south are densely wooded areas, mountains and temples tucked away in bamboo groves (difficult to get there by local bus). The city's history goes back some 2,500 years: its strategic and commercial importance – as the gateway to Nanjing – is underlined by the fact that the British and the French established concessions here.

### Information

**CITS** (tel 23281) is, for a change, quite helpful – take any bus going to the right from the train station (or walk) and get off at the first bridge you see. The CITS office is inside the Jingkou Hotel (Jingkou Hotel is Y10 a bed, but only for Chinese).

### Things to See

The 'three mounts of Zhenjiang', vantage points strewn along the Yangtse, are the principal sights.

### Jiao Shan

Also known as 'Jade Hill' because of its dark green foliage – cypresses and bamboo. It is to the east on a small island. Good hiking here – there are a number of pavilions along the way to the top of the 150 metre high mount, where Xijiang Tower gives a good view of activity on the Yangtse. At the base of the mount is an active monastery – some 200 pieces of tablet engravings, gardens and bonzai displays. Take bus No 4 to the terminus, a short walk and a little boat ride.

### Beigu Shan

Also on the No 4 bus route, this hill has a temple complex (Ganluosi) featuring a Song Dynasty Pagoda, which was once six storeys, now four.

### Jin Shan

This hill has a temple arrayed tier by tier with connecting staircases on a hillside – a remarkable design. Right at the top is the octagonal Cishou Pagoda, which gives an all-embracing view of the town from the seventh storey, and also the fishponds immediately below and the Yangtse beyond. There are four caves at the mount: Fahai (Buddhist Sea), Bailong (White Dragon), Zhao Yang (Morning Sun), and the Luohan (Arhat). The first two are immortalised in the Chinese fairytale, 'The Story of the White Snake'. Take bus No 2.

### Museum

A fourth 'mount' of interest between Jin Shan and the downtown area is the old British Consulate, which is now a museum and display gallery. It houses pottery, bronzes, gold, silver, paintings of the Chao and Tang Dynasties, and a separate section with photographs and memorabilia of the anti-Japanese campaign. It has a retail outlet selling calligraphy, rubbings and paintings. It's on the bus No 2 route.

### Places to Stay

For foreign devils the hotel is the *Jin Shan*

*(Golden Hill)*(tel 24962) which more resembles a motel – an indication of its genesis as an Australian pre-fab. Y40 a double, but you can get that down to Y12 a bed, student rate. It's a ten minute walk around the artificial lake near Jinshan Temple, at the bus No 2 terminus.

## Places to Eat

There's a restaurant near the Number One Lifespring and some in town located in the Chinese hotels. There's a pastry shop near the central town crossroads and dumpling houses and noodle shops near the railway stations. The *Jinjiang Hotel*, at the city centre, is reputed to have the best food in town.

## Getting Around

The city is ideal for day-tripping – all the transport is conveniently close to the railway station (local buses, long-distance buses, taxis, 3-wheelers).

Bus No 2 is a convenient tour bus – it

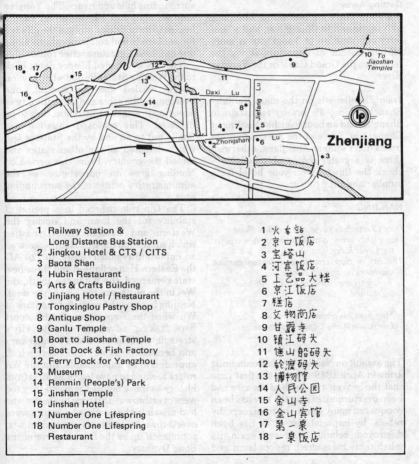

| | | |
|---|---|---|
| 1 | Railway Station & Long Distance Bus Station | 火车站 |
| 2 | Jingkou Hotel & CTS / CITS | 京口饭店 |
| 3 | Baota Shan | 宝塔山 |
| 4 | Hubin Restaurant | 河宾饭店 |
| 5 | Arts & Crafts Building | 工艺品大楼 |
| 6 | Jinjiang Hotel / Restaurant | 京江饭店 |
| 7 | Tongxinglou Pastry Shop | 糕店 |
| 8 | Antique Shop | 文物商店 |
| 9 | Ganlu Temple | 甘露寺 |
| 10 | Boat to Jiaoshan Temple | 镇江码头 |
| 11 | Boat Dock & Fish Factory | 焦山船码头 |
| 12 | Ferry Dock for Yangzhou | 轮渡码头 |
| 13 | Museum | 博物馆 |
| 14 | Renmin (People's) Park | 人民公园 |
| 15 | Jinshan Temple | 金山寺 |
| 16 | Jinshan Hotel | 金山宾馆 |
| 17 | Number One Lifespring | 第一泉 |
| 18 | Number One Lifespring Restaurant | 一泉饭店 |

goes east from the station along Zhongshan Lu to the downtown area where Friendship Store, department stores, antique shop and post office are located. It then swings west into the older part of town where some speciality and second-hand stores are to be found, goes past the former British consulate, and on to Jin Shan, the terminus. Bus No 4, which crosses No 2 downtown on Jiefang Lu, runs to Ganlu Temple and Jiao Shan in the east.

### Getting Away

**Bus/Ferry** There are buses from Zhenjiang to Nanjing and to Changzhou, and a bus/ferry combination to Yangzhou. A more off-beat means of departure is via the ferries on the Grand Canal or the Yangtse River.

**Train** Zhenjiang is on the main Nanjing-Shanghai Line; 3½ hrs by fast train to Shanghai and an hour to either Nanjing or Changzhou. Some of the special express trains don't stop at Zhenjiang, otherwise there is a grand choice of schedules – check the timetable in your hotel for a number and time to suit.

## NANJING

*Over Chungshan swept a storm, headlong*
*Our mighty army, a million strong, has crossed*
  *the Great River.*
*The city, a tiger crouching a dragon curling,*
  *outshines its ancient glories;*
*In heroic triumph heaven and earth have been*
  *overturned.*

  *Mao from his poem 'The People's*
  *Liberation Army Captures Nanjing'*

The assault on Nanjing by the Communist army in April 1949 was not the first time that the heaven and earth of the city had been overturned. In fact, the city has been conquered many times –by foreigners, by rebels, by imperial armies; it has been destroyed, rebuilt, destroyed again, its inhabitants massacred, repopulated and rebuilt . . . only to be decimated by the occasional natural disaster.

Though often not the choicest piece of real estate to own, the area has been inhabited for about 5000 years, and there have been a number of prehistoric sites discovered either in Nanjing or in the vicinity. There are also sites which date back to the Shang and Zhou Dynasties.

It is the city's location which is both the source of its prosperity and of its troubles. It has a strategic position, guarded by the surrounding hills and rivers. The Yangtse narrows here and a little further east it begins to form a delta, so thus the city is a focus of trade and communications along one of China's greatest water routes.

The city's recorded history dates back to the Warring States Period when several states battled for its control, one overcoming the other and using the city as a bastion to attack a third state, only to be defeated. This confused situation was finally put to an end by the State of Qin which defeated all the other states and united the country. From this period on Nanjing grew in importance as the administrative centre of the surrounding area.

The Qin rule ushered in a period of stability for the town and during the Western and Eastern Han Dynasties which succeeded the Qin, Nanjing grew as an important regional centre. In 220 AD the Eastern Han collapsed and three new states emerged, the Wu in the south, the Wei in the north and the Shu in the west. Nanjing became the capital of the state of Wu when the emperor moved his court here, taking advantage of the city's strategic position on China's waterways and because there was a fort here which appeared to be impregnable. But the Wu rulers seemed to have learnt as little from history as those before them and they too were overthrown–this time by the Jin who had arisen in the north, who in turn were overthrown by a military strongman who set himself up as the first emperor of the Song Dynasty.

The early part of the 6th century was an inauspicious time to be in Nanjing. There was a terrible flood in 507, a great fire in 521 which destroyed a huge section of the Imperial Palace, a pestilence in 529 and another flood in 533. There were peasant rebellions in 533, 541, 542 and 544, and this was compounded by the strains imposed by large numbers of refugees and immigrants from the north. If that wasn't enough, in 548 AD the army of General Hou Jing, who was originally allied to but now plotted to overthrow the southern emperor, attacked Nanjing and in a wave of gratuitous violence looted the city, raped the women and killed or conscripted the other inhabitants. Hou Jing took the city but after a series of palace intrigues wound up dead; another general seized power and founded his own dynasty, the Chen, which lasted a mere 32 years.

Meanwhile in the north another general, Wen Di, had usurped the throne of the reigning Northern Zhou dynasty, established himself as the first emperor of the Sui Dynasty and set out on a war on the south. Nanjing fell to his army in about 589. It was a bad century for Nanjing all round; Wen Di chose to establish his capital at Xian and to eradicate once and for all any claims of the south to the throne of a now united China. Wen had all the important buildings of Nanjing, including her beautiful palaces, completely demolished. Every trace of the city's former magnificence was destroyed and the city ceased to be important. Although it enjoyed a period of prosperity under the succeeding and long-lived Tang Dynasty, it gradually slipped back into obscurity.

Nanjing's brightest day came in the 14th century with the overthrow of the Yuan Dynasty by a peasant rebellion led by Zhu Yuanzhang. The rebels captured Nanjing in 1356 and went on to capture the Mongol capital at Beijing in 1368. Zhu took the name of Hong Wu, and set himself up as the first emperor of the Ming Dynasty.

Under Hong Wu, Nanjing was established as the capital partly because it was far from the north and safe from sudden barbarian attacks and partly because it was located in the most wealthy and populous part of the country. A massive palace was built, huge walls were built around the city, and construction of other buildings proceeded at a furious pace. The city became a manufacturing and administrative metropolis and a centre of learning and culture.

Nevertheless the city seemed inextricably locked in a cycle of fortune and misfortune; the next Ming emperor Yong Le moved his capital to Beijing in 1420 and Nanjing was kept only as a secondary capital. The population was halved and the city declined in importance. It was another bad century for Nanjing – the city suffered a succession of fires, famines, floods, typhoons, tornadoes and even a snow-storm said to have lasted 40 days.

But if Nanjing was down then the Manchus to the north were coming up fighting. In 1644 the Ming Dynasty in Beijing fell to the rebel Li Zicheng, who then found himself under attack from a Manchu invasion. The north of China was conquered by the invaders, and though various Ming descendants tried to hold out in Nanjing and in other places in the south, in time they were all overcome.

Although Nanjing continued as a major centre under the Qing, nothing much of note happened here until the 19th century when China once again began its cyclic decline into chaos. The country was torn apart by the foreign powers, the Taiping rebellion, the warlords, an unstable republican government, the civil war between the Communists and Kuomintang and the Japanese invasion. For Nanjing it was not a happy time, and the city was ravaged by all the forces which afflicted China from the mid-19th to mid-20th centuries.

The Opium Wars were carried right to Nanjing's doorstep. The first war had broken out in Canton in 1841; the second started in 1842 when Sir Henry Pottinger and his British naval task force of 80 ships sailed up the Yangtse River, took the city of Zhenjiang and arrived at Nanjing in August. Pottinger threatened to bombard Nanjing, forcing the Chinese to sign the first of the 'Unequal Treaties' which opened several Chinese ports to foreign trade, forced China to pay a huge war indemnity and officially ceded the island of Hong Kong to Britain.

Just a few years later, one of the most dramatic periods in China's history focused on Nanjing – the Taiping Rebellion of 1851-1864. It was one of the most dramatic, most bizarre, most unlikely revolutions which has ever swept China – or for that matter any part of the world.

Its founder and leader was Hong Xiuquan, born in Guangdong Province in 1813. Unsuccessful in the Imperial examinations, Hong turned to the study of Christianity. Convinced that he was on a mission from God and professing to be the younger brother of Jesus Christ he began preaching Christianity in Guangxi and Guangdong. Gathering around him a band of followers which gradually grew in size and strength they proceeded to preach Christianity whilst destroying Buddhist, Taoist and Confucian idols and razing their temples to the ground.

The Qing government decided to suppress the movement, but this only caused the Taipings to declare open rebellion in 1851 and before long town after town was falling to their army. Hong called his movement the 'Taiping Tianguo' or the 'Heavenly Kingdom of the Great Peace' with himself as Heavenly King. His four main disciples/assistants became known as the Princes of the North, South, East and West.

Marching north from Guangdong, the Taipings captured numerous towns on the Yangtse River. By now their army had increased to a phenomonal 600,000 men and 500,000 women. In 1853 they were powerful enough to attack and capture Nanjing, storming in after a 10-day siege and massacring the Manchu part of the population. Nanjing was made the capital of the Heavenly Kingdom.

A month after capturing Nanjing they had also captured several towns further east, giving them control over both the Yangtse and the Grand Canal. During the next few years the rebels waged a highly successful war against the Qing, conquering most of southern China; the dynasty seemed set to topple to their onslaught.

The Taipings were highly organised and strictly disciplined. They were mono-gamists, adhering to none other than the Christian God. Gambling, opium, tobacco and alcohol were forbidden. Women were appointed as administraters and officials, and the practice of foot-binding was abolished. Slavery, prostitution, arranged marriages and polygamy were also abolished. What attracted the peasants was their policy of agrarian reform and lighter and more equitable taxation in the areas they controlled, as well as a policy of public instead of private ownership. In many ways the movement was a forerunner of the Communist movement of the following century.

Internal dissensions in the Taiping leadership in 1856 seriously weakened the rebels. The Qing might have been able to use this to their advantage but they were locked in yet another war with the Western powers from 1856 to 1860. By the end of that war the internal conflicts amongst the Taipings had been resolved and the rebels were at the height of their power.

But the Taipings had failed to gain the support of the western powers, who up until now had remained neutral. Reports of a Chinese Christian army defeating the Imperial army had gained attention in the west, but eventually it was probably the success of the Taipings which worried the western powers. Far better for the west to deal with a corrupt and weak Qing government than with the united and strong Taipings, so after 1860 the western powers allied with the Qing and the counter-offensive began. By 1864 the Taipings had been encircled in their capital of Nanjing. A Qing army under General Tseng Kuo-fan, helped by British army regulars like General Charles Gordon (of Khartoum fame) and mixed European and American mercenaries besieged and bombarded the city for seven months, finally capturing it on July 19 and slaughtering the Taiping defenders. Hong Xiuquan committed suicide and the rebellion was ended.

The Manchus were overthrown in 1911 and a republic established, first with its capital at Beijing but later moved to Nanjing. Nanjing continued its reign as one of China's great abattoirs. In 1927 Chiang Kai-shek ordered the extermination of the Communists and Yuhuatai Hill to the south of the city bears the distinction of being one of the great execution sites. In 1937 the Japanese captured the city and set about butchering the population. Just how many died in what became known as the 'Rape of Nanjing' is unknown. One estimate was 400,000 while another writer gives a figure of 100,000 and a *People's Daily* article in June 1981 claims 300,000 were killed.

With the Japanese defeat in 1945 the Kuomintang government moved back to Nanjing and between 1946 and 1947 peace talks were held here between the Kuomintang and the Communists, but when these broke down the civil war resumed and Nanjing was captured in that great turning over of heaven and earth in 1949.

Today, Nanjing is an industrialised city of around three million people. It looks little different from other Chinese cities which have been ploughed under and rebuilt by the Communist government. Its broad boulevards and concrete blocks however are laid down in the midst of thousands and thousands of trees, alleviating the heat for which this city was justifiably known as one of the 'Three Furnaces' of China. With the Communist victory in 1949 the cycle of turmoil

completed a turn and the last 35 years have been one of relative stability and prosperity for the city.

But true to its past, the city has not remained outside conflicts. On March 25 1976, 2½ months after the death of Zhou En-lai, the 'radicals' inflamed public opinion by publishing an article in two of Shanghai's mass-circulation newspapers that the late Premier had been a 'capitalist-roader'. It was the time of the Qing Ming Festival when the Chinese traditionally honoured their dead. The first reaction to the article was in Nanjing where large crowds gathered and speeches were made and wreaths laid in honour of Zhou; slogans and posters were put up, a protest march took place through the streets of the city and Zhang Chunqiao was named and attacked. The story goes that the carriages of Beijing-bound trains were daubed with messages and slogans so that people in the capital would know what was happening in Nanjing, and that these contributed to the memorable 'Tiananmen Incident' a week later.

### Information and Orientation

Nanjing lies on the eastern bank of the Yangtse River, bounded in the west by the Purple Hills. The centre of town is a traffic circle and from this run Zhongshan Bei, Nan, Xi and Dong Lu.

Zhongshan Beilu heads north to another traffic circle; Daqing Lu branches off here and heads up towards the long-distance bus station and train station in the far north of the city. Meanwhile Zhongshan Beilu turns northwest and heads up towards the CITS office, the Dingshan and Shengmenlou Hotels, the dock for the ferries to Shanghai and Wuhan, and the massive Yangtse River Bridge. The other tourist hotels, CAAC, the post office and bank, and Public Security are located at or are close to the central traffic circle. Many of the major restaurants are also here or close by on Taiping Lu to the east of the traffic circle.

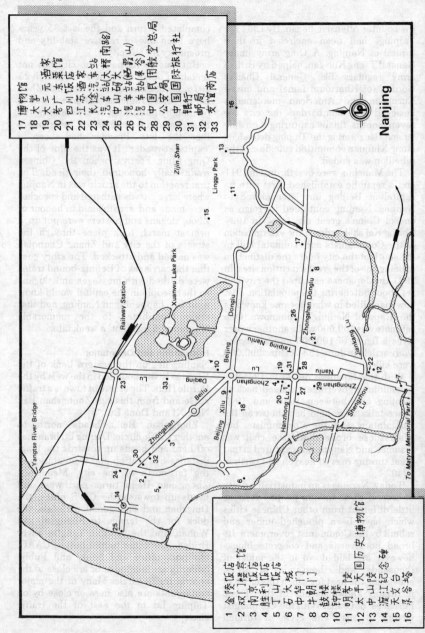

Nanjing

17 博物館
18 大学三元
19 大大老广
20 四川飯店
21 江苏飯店
22 长途汽车站
23 汽车站大碼大
24 中山碼大
25 汽车站(栖霞山)
26 汽车站(栖霞)
27 汽车站
28 公安局
29 中国民用航空总局
30 中国国际旅行社
31 中银行
32 邮局
33 友谊商店

1 金陵飯店
2 双门楼飯店
3 南京飯店
4 丁山飯店
5 石头城
6 中华门
7 牛朝楼
8 鼓楼
9 钟楼
10 明孝陵
11 太平天国历史博物館
12 中山陵
13 渡江胜利纪念碑
14 天文台
15 灵谷塔

Zijin Shan

Lingu Park

Xuanwu Lake Park

Railway Station

Yangtse River Bridge

To Matyrs Memorial Park

Most of the 'sights' are to the east of Nanjing, in or around the Purple Mountains; these include the Sun Yat-sen Memorial, Linggu Park, the tomb of the first Ming Emperor Hong Wu and the astronomical observatory. Other sights are scattered about throughout the city.

**CITS** (tel 86968) is at 313 Zhongshan Beilu, close to the Shuangmenlou Guest House. They're not extraordinarily helpful; someone said they spoke English, French, German, Japanese and Russian. If they do then they're very modest about it. They don't book air tickets, you'll have to go direct to the CAAC office. There is another CITS office in the Jingling Hotel but they only handle bookings for hotel guests – nevertheless the guy here speaks excellent English and is a good information source.

**Public Security** is a ten-minute walk up a side street which runs off Zhongshan Nanlu. For directions refer to the map in this book; look for a walled compound with a grey metal gate and a sign in English, Russian and Chinese.

**CAAC** (tel 43378) is just ten minutes walk up from the central traffic circle at 76 Zhongshan Donglu. It's open 8 to 11.30 am and 2.30 to 5 pm.

**Post** There is a post office in the Shuangmenlou Guest House and another in the Nanjing Hotel.

**Bank** The Bank of China is near the central traffic circle at 3 Zhongshan Donglu; it's open daily 8.30 to 11.30 am and 2 to 5 pm, and is closed on Sundays and Wednesday mornings. There is also a money-exchange counter at the Jingling Hotel.

**Maps** There are excellent maps of Nanjing. Maps in English are available from the reception desk of the Shuangmenlou

Hotel for 50 fen each – they show the bus routes and also list and give a brief description of the major sights both in the city and the surrounding area. Maps in Chinese which also show the bus routes are available from the shop in the Nanjing Hotel. Similar, though not so detailed, maps are available from the counter in the waiting hall of the railway station.

### Things to See

Before embarking on a tour of the remains of 3000 years of history, go and see Nanjing's prime tourist attraction, the *Jingling Hotel*. This 36-storey tower is currently the tallest building in China and was (so I'm told) designed by a Japanese architect and built by a Singapore firm. With the exception of the White Swan Hotel in Canton this is an undreamt-of structure for the Chinese. Only high-ranking Chinese and those who work there are allowed in. The proletariat forms a perpetual audience on the other side of the fence, gazing up at this thing and taking each other's photograph in front of the gate.

The **Sky Palace** is a revolving restaurant (the only one in China) on the top of the hotel. You can sit here in palatial surroundings and look out on the streets of Nanjing 36 storeys below; in the distance you can spot the Yangtse Bridge, the observatory, the Linggu Pagoda and the Sun Yat-sen Mausoleum. The waiters and waitresses actually come and serve you, and everyone here and in other parts of the hotel speaks at least communicable English. As you wander out of the elevator to the 36th floor you're greeted by a young girl in a long Chinese dress, collared to the neck and split up the side – enough to turn Mao in his sarcophagus! Drinks in the restaurant are pricey, but it's a small amount to pay for a breath of civilisation. They've also put together their own cocktails; 'East Meets West', 'Sky Lounge' and the 'Panda', all Y4.50 each.

If you think this monument to Singapore-Japanese-western luxury and decadence

**Garbage Man** — 6 a.m., the sun & workmen are rising as the neighbourhood trash collector comes down the street, ringing his bell and leading his stunted stallion...

Cartoon by Tony Jenkins

was bad enough, then you'll be horrified to learn that Donald Duck has made it to the People's Republic. Take a walk from the the hotel east along Zhongshan Lu; the Xinhua Bookstore is at 130 Zhongshan Lu and right next to it is a billboard, with Donald, Minnie Mouse and 'Three Hairs' advertising a TV set! 'Three Hairs' is the name given to a cartoon character invented by Zhang Leping. This 'half-starved orphan child' was based on the Dickensian life of his creator. The character first made his appearance in 1935 in a cartoon satirising the puppet-emperor Pu Yi of Manchukuo(?). In the next 48 years Three Hairs fled the Japanese, joined the Communist Party, was suppressed by the Gang of Four, but later rose as a student of Lei Feng, and became an exponent of learning and sport who hopes that under the care of the Communist Party all Chinese children will grow healthy and strong, and contribute to the economy by buying TV sets.

In 1983 you could see it all over China – but how appropiate to see it in Nanjing – a new film from the August 1st Film Studios called *The Liberation of Nanjing* which follows the People's Liberation Army across the Yangtse River in April 1949 to capture the city. Much of the film is concerned with dialogue between the top Communist leaders of the time (or at least those who are still held in favour), played by a bunch of remarkable look-alikes; Mao, Zhou, Zhu Teh, Ren Rishi and Chen Yi. Not only do they talk they also laugh – in fact there is so much laughter in the Communist camp that it looks like some sort of Chinese 'Hogans Heroes'. The high point of the film is the rumbling in the audience when a chain-smoking Mao suddenly turns to Lui Shao-qi(!) for Lui's dispensation of wisdom. Meanwhile, off in the Kuomintang camp the generals and their hangers-on wine and dine while the air hangs heavy with oncoming defeat, and American ambassador John Leighton Stuart dispenses advice to a distraught Chiang Kai-shek.

Apart from gleaming hotels, incongruous billboards, and comical movies, there are quite a few 'sights' to be seen. Like Xian, Nanjing doesn't drip with history, but it is pock-marked with it. Within the city and on the surrounding plains are an extra-ordinary number of reminders of the city's splendid and not-so-splendid imperial past. Not always a happy place to live, the city has nevertheless also enjoyed long periods of prosperity and this is evident in the numerous buildings which successive rulers have built here –if only for the sake of giving the next ruler something to loot, burn and pillage. There is a phenomenal quantity of tombs, steles, pagodas, small temples, Buddhist niches, and government buildings scattered around Nanjing. For complete description get a copy of *In Search of Old Nanking* by Barry Till and Paula Swart. Unfortunately much of what was built has been destroyed or allowed to crumble into ruins.

### Prehistoric Remains

The remains of a prehistoric culture called Beiyinyang have been found at the site of today's Drum Tower in the centre of the city. The remains of Xiacanwan man, which date back tens of thousands of years have been found 150 km north of Nanjing, in a place called Hongzu Hupan in Sihong County. The bones and artefacts of prehistoric people dating back 10,000 years have been found in a cave 50 km southeast of Nanjing, in Huifeng Mountain in Lishui County.

### Shang and Zhou Dynasty Sites

About 200 sites of small clan communities dating back to the late Shang and Zhou Dynasties have been found on both sides of the Yangtse, mainly pottery and bronze artefacts. But no one actually sat down and wrote anything about the place until the Spring and Autumn period of the 8th-3rd centuries BC.

### Remains of the Han Dynasty Wall

At the end of the Eastern Han period the

military commander in charge of the Nanjing region built a citadel on what is today called Qingling Mountain in the west of Nanjing. At that time the mountain was referred to as Shitou Shan (Stone Mountain) and so the citadel became known as the Stone City. The wall measured over 10 km in circumference, and was built in about 212 AD. Today, some of the red sandstone foundation blocks of the wall can be seen in the west of Nanjing.

### Remains of the Southern Dynasties

The most interesting remains of the Southern Dynasties are the **Tombs of the Qi emperors** (the dynasty which followed the Song) and the **Qixia Shan Buddhist Grottoes**.

The tombs are located near the town of **Danyang** 70 km east of Nanjing. Danyang was the original home of the Qi royal family and so they chose to be buried here. There are two groups of tombs; one to the north-east of Danyang and one to the east. Some of these tombs are surmounted by stone chimeras, ferocious looking one or two-horned beasts, often depicted with wings, which symbolise the power and majesty of the emperors.

The Buddhist grottoes lie about 20 km east of Nanjing; the earliest caves date from the Qi dynasty though there are others from a number of succeeding dynasties right through to the Ming. There are over 300 caves or niches here. The grottoes are on a much smaller scale though along the same lines as the Yugang Caves in Datong or the Longmen Caves in Luoyang. There are several steles and small stone tablets, including some inscribed in Tibetan, which can be found in and around the grottoes. The caves were badly damaged during the Cultural Revolution, but the real damage had already been done in 1924 when the Buddhist monks of Qixia Temple carried out restoration work and covered many of the statues with cement to make a smoother surface.

### The Tang Dynasty Pagoda at Niutou Shan

The most impressive monument from the Tang dynasty lies 12 km south of Nanjing on Niutou Shan, and is a large rust-coloured pagoda built in 774. The inside of the pagoda is destroyed and you can't climb to the top. There used to be several temples here but these have vanished.

### The Ming Dynasty

Since it was under the Ming that Nanjing enjoyed its golden years there are numerous reminders of the period to be found.

One of the most impressive remains is the **City Wall**. It is the longest city wall ever built in the world, measuring 33.4 km. About two-thirds of it is still standing. It took 21 years to build (1366-1386) and involved a labour force of over 200,000. The layout of the wall is irregular, an exception to the usual square-shaped walls of these times. This is because much of the wall is built on the foundations of earlier walls, and also takes advantage of strategic hills. The wall is an average of 12 metres high and on average is seven metres wide at the top. It was built of bricks supplied from five Chinese provinces. Each brick had stamped on it the place it came from, the overseers name and rank, the brickmaker's name and sometimes the date. This was to ensure that the bricks were well made, and if they began to break apart they would have to be replaced. On some parts of the wall stone bricks are used, but on the whole it was mainly clay bricks.

Only two city gates remain, the **Heping Gate** in the north and the **Zhonghua Gate** in the south. Originally there were 13 gates. The city gates were heavily fortified, and rather than being the weak points of the defences as they usually are, they were defensive strongholds. Zhonghua Gate has four rows of gates, making it almost impregnable, and could be garrisoned by 3000 soldiers who lived in vaults in the front building of the gate. Today some of these vaults are used as souvenir shops

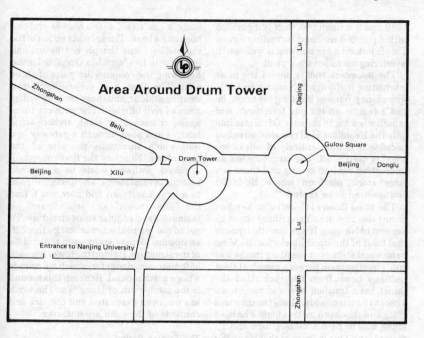

Area Around Drum Tower

and cafes and are wonderfully cool in summer. Zhonghua Gate can be visited, but Heping Gate is now used as a military barracks. The canal to the south of Zhonghua Gate is almost pitch black!

The **Ming Palace** built by Hong Wu is said to have been a magnificent structure and the Imperial Palace in Beijing was modelled after it. Almost nothing remains of the Nanjing palace, except for five marble bridges lying side by side known as the Five Dragon Bridges, the old ruined gate called Wu Men, and the enormous column bases of the palace buildings. There are also some stone blocks with animals and scenery carved on them and a little stone screen with animal carvings. The palace suffered two major fires in the first century after it was built, and it was allowed to fall into ruins after the Ming court moved to Beijing. The Manchus looted it, and during the Taiping rebellion the bombardment of Nanjing by Qing and

western troops almost completely destroyed the palace.

The **Drum Tower** lies roughly in the centre of Nanjing in the centre of a traffic circle on Beijing Xilu. It was built in 1382. Drums were usually beaten to give directions for the change of the night watches and in rare instances to warn the populace of some impending danger. The Nanjing tower originally contained numerous drums and other instruments used on ceremonial occasions, though now only one large drum remains. On the top floor of the tower is a tearoom housing a stone steele set on a tortoise (vicious teeth and head poised to snap) dating from the 17th century. The ground floor is used for exhibitions of paintings and calligraphy.

The **Bell Tower** is north-east of the Drum Tower and houses an *enormous* bell dating from 1388. The bell was originally in a pavilion on the west side of the Drum Tower. The present tower dates only from

1889 and is a small two-storeyed pavilion with a pointed roof and turned-up eaves. This is indeed a big bell and is well worth wandering up to have a look at.

The **Beamless Hall** is one of the most interesting buildings in Nanjing. In 1381, when Hong Wu was building his tomb, he had a temple on the site torn down and rebuilt a few km to the east. Of this temple only the Beamless Hall remains, so called because it is built entirely of bricks; no wood is used at all. The structure has an interesting vaulted ceiling and there is a large stone platform where Buddhist statues used to be seated.

The **Ming Quarry** is located at Yanmen Shan (also known as Yang Shan) about 15 km east of Nanjing. It was from this quarry that most of the stone blocks for the Ming palace and statues of the Ming tombs was cut. The attraction here is a massive tablet partially hewn from the rock. Had the tablet been finished it would have been almost 15 metres wide, almost four metres thick and almost 45 metres high! The base stone was to be 6.5 metres high and 13 metres long. One story goes that Hong Wu wished to place the enormous tablet on the top of Zijin (Purple) Mountain; the gods had promised their assistance to move it, but when they saw the size of the tablet even they gave up and Hong Wu had to abandon the project. It seems however that it was Yong Le, the son of Hong Wu, who ordered the tablet to be carved, planning to erect it at his father's tomb. When the tablet was almost finished he realised there was no way it could be moved and had to abandon the project.

The **Tomb of Hong Wu** is located east of the city on the southern slope of Zijin Mountain. The construction of the tomb began in 1381 and was finished in 1383. The emperor died at the age of 71 in 1398. The first section of the avenue leading up to the mausoleum is lined with stone statues of lions, camels, elephants and horses as well as a mythical animal called a *xiezhi* which has a mane and a single horn on its head, and a *qilin* which has a scaly

body, a cow's tail, deer's hooves and one horn on its head. The second section of the tomb alley turns sharply northward and begins with two large hexagonal columns. Following the columns are pairs of stone men. The first pair are military men wearing armour, and these are followed by pairs of civil officials. The pathway turns again, crosses over some arched stone bridges and goes through a gateway in a wall which surrounds the site of the mausoleum. Entering the first courtyard, a paved pathway leads to a pavilion housing several steles. The next gate leads to a large courtyard and here you'll find the 'altar tower' or 'soul tower' –a mammoth rectangular stone structure. To get to the top of the tower you go through an upward sloping stairway in the middle of the structure. Behind the tower is a wall, 350 metres in diameter, which surrounds a huge earth mound. Beneath this mound is the tomb-vault of Hong Wu. The tomb has not been excavated and the size and contents of the vault are unknown.

### The Taiping Period

Although Hong Xiquan, the leader of the Taipings, had a palace built in Nanjing the building was completely destroyed when Nanjing was taken in 1864. All that remains is a stone boat located in an ornamental lake in the Western Garden, inside the old KMT government buildings on Changjiang Lu, east of Taiping Lu.

There is a **Taiping Museum** housed in the former mansion of the Hong's Eastern Prince Yang Xiuqing. The garden next to the mansion is called **Zhan Yuan** and originally belonged to the first Ming emperor. The Taiping Museum is fairly interesting with a large collection of documents, books and artefacts relating to the rebellion. Most of the literature is copied, the originals being kept in Beijing. There are maps showing the northward progress of the Taiping army from Guangdong, Hong Xiuquan's declaration made when he entered Nanjing, his seals and those belonging to his sons, Taiping coins, cannon balls, rifles and other weapons, texts which describe the Taiping laws on agrarian reform, social law and cultural policy. There are also texts which describe divisions in the Taiping leadership, the attacks by the Manchus and foreigners and the fall of Nanjing in 1864. A notable stone tablet is also here, its inscription reading *In memory of the organiser and leader of the ever-victorious army, erected by Frederick Ward Post, American Legion, May 27 1923.*

### The Republic of China

The **Sun Yat-sen Memorial Hall** is the chief attraction of this period. Some people admire its passive symmetry, others say it lacks imagination and falls far short of the possibilites that the expenditure would have allowed.

The man who is regarded as the father of modern China (by both the Communists on the mainland and the Kuomintang on Taiwan) died in Beijing in 1924, the 13th year of an unstable Chinese republic. Sun had wished to be buried in Nanjing, but whether he quite meant his successors to build him a Ming-style tomb is another matter. Nevertheless less than a year after his death construction of his immense mausoleum began.

The tomb lies at the southern foot of Zhongmao Peak in the eastern Purple Mountains which ring Nanjing. The tomb itself lies on the mountain slope at the end of a 323 metre long and 70 metre wide pathway. At the start of the pathway is a stone gateway built of Fujian marble, and a roof of blue glazed tiles. The blue and white of the mausoleum was meant to symbolise the Kuomintang flag of the white sun on a blue background. At the top of the steps is a platform and here you'll find the memorial ceremony chamber and the coffin chamber. Across the threshold of the memorial ceremony chamber hangs a tablet inscribed with the 'Three Principles of the People' as formulated by Dr. Sun; reading left to right the characters say 'Nationalism, Democracy and People's Livelihood'. Inside is a seated statue of Dr Sun, and on the walls is carved the complete text of the 'Outline of Principles for the Establishment of the Nation' put forward by the Nationalist government. Behind the hall is a crypt; inside is a prostrate marble statue of Sun, beneath which lies his body.

Other sights of more historical interest are the buildings which housed the **Foreign Consulates** during the Kuomintang rule. These are mainly mainly found on Beijing Xilu, the street west of the Drum Tower; the numerous brothels that existed before 1949 were mostly found in the southern part of the city near the Qinhuai River. The old **Kuomintang Government Buildings** were located on the same spot as the ancient palace of the Taiping ruler, Hong Xiuquan, on Changjiang Lu. Chiang Kai-shek lived and worked here until 1938 when he was forced to flee the Japanese. He returned in 1945 only to be driven out again by the Communists four years later.

After the defeat of the Japanese in 1945 the Communists and the Kuomintang opened peace talks in Chongqing. The talks moved to Nanjing in May 1946, but finally broke down in March 1947. The houses occupied by the top Communist negotiators have been turned into museums which are found on Meiyuan Xincun in the vicinity of the Taiping Museum. Zhou Enlai and his wife Deng Yingchao lived at No 30, Dong Biwu and Li Weihan at No 35 and other staff at No 17. Lu Dingyi was also at the negotiations.

### The People's Republic of China

One of the great achievements of the Communists, and one of which they are justifiably proud is the **Yangtse River Bridge** at Nanjing which was opened on December 23rd 1968. Currently it's the longest bridge in China and is a double-decker bridge with a roadway(4500 metres long) on top and a railway(6700 metres long) on the lower level. The story

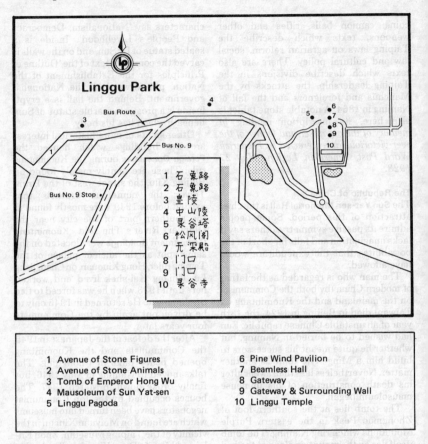

```
1 石象路
2 石象路
3 皇陵
4 中山陵
5 灵谷塔
6 松风阁
7 无梁船
8 门口
9 门口
10 灵谷寺
```

1 Avenue of Stone Figures
2 Avenue of Stone Animals
3 Tomb of Emperor Hong Wu
4 Mausoleum of Sun Yat-sen
5 Linggu Pagoda
6 Pine Wind Pavilion
7 Beamless Hall
8 Gateway
9 Gateway & Surrounding Wall
10 Linggu Temple

goes that the bridge was designed and built entirely by the Chinese after the Russians withdrew with both their expertise and blueprints in 1960. Given the immensity of the construction it really is an impressive engineering feat, before which there was no direct rail link between Beijing and Shanghai.

A **Monument to the Crossing of the Yangtse River** stands in the north-western part of the city in Zhongshan Beilu. The monument, erected in April 1979, commemorates the crossing of the river on 23rd April 1949 and the capture of Nanjing from the Kuomintang by the million-strong Communist Army. The characters on the monument are in the calligraphy of Deng Xiao-ping.

### Other Sights

The **Zijin Shan Observatory** was founded in 1934 and is today the largest in China. There's also a collection of ancient astronomical instruments originally designed in the Han and Yuan Dynasties, but the ones now on display are reproductions made during the Ming and Qing periods.

To the east of the city is **Soul Valley**

(Linggu) Park with its assortment of sights which include the Beamless Hall. A road leads either side of the Beamless Hall and up two flights of steps to the Pine Wind Pavilion. The pavilion was originally dedicated to the Goddess of Mercy as part of the Linggu Temple, but today houses a small shop and teahouse. The Linggu Temple and memorial hall to Xuan Zhang is close by; after you pass through the Beamless Hall, turn right and follow the pathway. Xuan Zhang was the Buddhist monk who travelled to India and brought back the Buddhist scriptures. Inside the memorial hall is a model 13-storey wooden pagoda which contains part of his skull. In front of this pagoda is a sacrificial table and on the wall is a portrait of the monk. Close by is the Linggu Pagoda which was built in the 1930s under the direction of an American architect. It's an octagonal-shaped building, 60 metres high and has nine storeys.

A good way to combine the Linggu Park with the Ming Tomb and the Sun Yat-sen Memorial is to take bus No 9 as far as the avenue of stone animals and the avenue of stone figures; at the end of the second avenue you'll come to the three bridges over the moat which surrounds the tomb. From outside the tomb there is a bus which goes to the Sun Yat-sen memorial. Another bus leaves from the opposite the gateway to the memorial, and this takes you up to Linggu Park.

Nanjing Museum is just east of Zhongshan Gate on Zhongshan Lu. This interesting museum houses an array of artefacts from Neolithic times through to the Communist period. The main building of the museum itself was built in 1933 with yellow-glazed tiles, red-lacquered gates and columns in the style of an ancient temple. Amongst the more interesting items on display are the fragments of skull, jawbone, teeth, and bone of primitive men, as well as primitive stone tools. Particularly notable is the burial suit made of small rectangles of jade sewn together with silver thread, dating from

the Eastern Han Dynasty (25-220 AD) and excavated from a tomb discovered in the city of Xuzhou in northern Jiangsu province. Other exhibits include bricks with the inscriptions of their maker and overseer from the Ming city wall; a large iron pan from the late Qing period used for evaporating salt; drawings of old Nanjing; an early Qing mural of old Suzhou; a large statue (Ming or Qing period) of a man showing the acupuncture points; Rooms 5 and 6 have displays relating to the Opium Wars and the Treaty of Nanjing, and contain relics such as cannon and muskets from the Taiping rebellion. Just east of the museum is another section of the Ming city wall; there are steps leading up from the road and you can walk along the top of this heavily overgrown wall.

A mosque stands at 298 Taiping Nanlu; it was damaged and closed during the Cultural Revolution but was reopened in 1980. At Yuhuatai Mountain are found the beautiful multi-coloured pebbles which are sold in Nanjing as tourist souvenirs; the colour of these pebbles is enhanced if they're placed in water. (Yuhuatai Mountain also bears the distinction of being one of the execution grounds where Chiang Kai-shek had thousands of Communists and other opponents massacred). In the northeast of Nanjing is the Xuanwu Lake Park with its five islets connected by bridges in the midst of large lake; you'll also find the zoo here and the seven-storey Nuona Pagoda built in 1937. Nanjing University is a 15 minute walk from the Drum Tower.

## Places to Stay

Most of the accommodation in Nanjing is expensive and cheaper accommodation is in short supply. One consolation: the hotels in this city are excellent and if you end up paying a lot you at least get your money's worth.

The *Jingling Hotel* (tel 41121 or 44141) is Y80 a night for a double room, which is cheap compared to what you'd pay for similar accommodation in a major city in the west. This gleaming monument is accessible by trolleybus No 33 from the long-distance bus station or the train station. You can't miss the place; it stands at the intersection in the centre of town. If you arrive by helicopter there is, apparently, a pad on the top of the tower just metres above the revolving restaurant.

The *Sheungmenlou Guest House* (85584) mainly caters for tour groups. Double rooms here for Y36 and you can even get a massage for Y15. Their cafe serves 'female panda cocktails' and 'male panda cocktails' –the first is sweet, the second is dry. The hotel is in the north-west part of town and is rather inconveniently isolated except for the CITS office which is nearby. Probably the easiest way to get there is to take trolleybus No 33 from either the train station or long-distance bus station to the traffic-circle just east of the Drum Tower and then change to trolley bus No 31.

The *Nanjing Hotel* (tel 34121) has excellent double rooms for Y36. The hotel is situated in a large, well-kept garden setting, and even if you're not staying here it's worth a wander up to sit around and do nothing. The hotel is at 259 Zhongshan Beilu within a large walled compound. Take trolleybus No 32 from the long distance bus or from the train station.

The *Shengli Hotel* (tel 42217) is the cheapest place to stay. Double rooms go for Y42, Y36, Y32, Y30 though there are supposed to be cheaper ones. The men's dormitory charges about Y4 a bed, and Y6 in the air-conditioned dormitory, and it's in not bad condition. The women's dormitory is Y8 and is in bad condition . . . work that out. The hotel is centrally located at 75 Zhongshan Lu. From the long distance bus station or the train station take trolleybus No 33.

The *Dingshan Hotel* (tel 85931) is a good place but inconveniently located at the oblivion end of Nanjing on top of (as the name implies) a hill. Double rooms are between Y28 to Y36 and they have dorm beds for Y8. The hotel is at 90 Chahaer Lu; take trolleybus No 32 from the long

distance bus station or train station; you have to walk the last km or two.

## Places to Eat

Despite the size of this city the restaurants have short opening hours. Most of them have stacked their chairs on the tables by 8 pm, so remember to eat early. They're all pretty much the same; food tends to be fairly oily and there really isn't anything to rave about and you'll probably find yourself fleeing to the hotel restaurants.

The *Dasunyuan* (tel 41027) at 40 Zhongshan Lu looks like the best bet for a decent meal. It's a large restaurant and doesn't smell, but go upstairs since the ground floor is a divey noodle canteen.

The *Laoguangdong* at 45 Zhongshan Lu, approximately across the road from the Dasunyuan, is nothing special but might be OK if you see a good dish that you can point out to one of the staff.

The *Sichuan Restaurant* (tel 43651) is at 171 Taiping Rd; downstairs is a dive, but you may find something you like upstairs. The food looks extremely oily, though at least the place doesn't smell. The *Luliuju Vegetarian Restaurant* (tel 43644) at 248 Taiping Lu is much the same as the Sichuan Restaurant.

Recommended is the *Jiangsu Restaurant* at 26 Jiankang Lu, not far from the Taiping Museum. Three floors of increasing excellence. Nanjing Duck is the speciality – you can have it with a dish of pork and bamboo shoots, and vegetables with shrimp and rice for just Y3.20 in the best room on the 3rd floor.

You can get fairly high-priced drinks in the revolving restaurant of the *Jingling Hotel*, but think of it more as an opportunity to have some relief from the proletariat. 'Jingling Beer' which is commonly sold in the city is great, perhaps the equal of Tsingtao. The ground floor restaurant in the Jingling Hotel also serves approximations of hamburgers at Y3.50 each and you can dine to muzak.

At the *Nanjing Hotel* you can get an excellent western-style breakfast. The restaurant is open 7 to 8.30 am, 11.30 am to 1 pm and 6 to 8.30 pm.

The *Shengli Hotel* restaurant serves both western and Chinese food and is generally not bad – but you have to watch what you order otherwise you could end up paying five or six yuan for two plates of oil and a fizzy drink. They actually serve chips (french fries to Americans) here – good ones too.

The *Dingshan Hotel* is a good place to eat with both western and Chinese food on the menu –though you may find prices a bit on the expensive side. Nanjing Salted Duck is the speciality here with 'Tender meat beautiful smell, fat but not greasy, with first-rate cooks, orders welcome . . .' The duck is salted with roasted salt, steeped in clear brine, baked dry and then kept under cover for some time; the finished product should have a creamy-coloured skin and red, tender flesh. You'll probably have to order this dish in advance.

## Getting Around

Rickshaws hang around outside the railway station and taxis are available from the tourist hotels. Buses and trolleybuses are the main means of transport.

When you leave the railway station turn right and walk for a few minutes to the terminus of trolleybuses No 32 and No 33. These buses head west along Shaoshan Lu to the long-distance bus station and then turn south down Daqing Lu towards the city centre. If you're taking one of these buses from the long-distance bus station into the centre, the busstop is diagonally across the traffic circle on the northern side of Shaoshan Lu.

There are buses from Hanzhong Lu, just west and on the other side of the road of the Jingling Hotel, which will take you to the Sun Yat-sen Memorial. There are shuttle buses between the Sun Yat-sen Memorial and the Ming Tombs and the Linggu Pagoda.

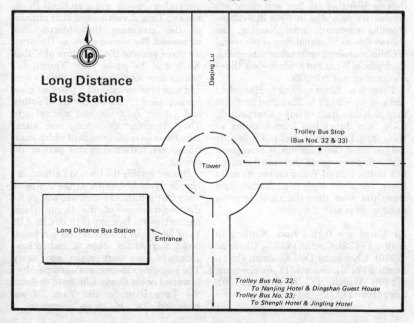

## Getting Away

Nanjing is escapable by bus, train, plane and boat.

**Bus** The long-distance bus station is at the northern end of town to the west of the train station; it stands on an intersection which is readily identifiable by a tall white column on top of which is a silver sphere with little satellites orbiting around it.

There is one bus a day to Huang Shan departing at 5.40 am and the fare is Y7.80.

There is one bus a day to Hangzhou departing at 6 am and the fare is Y7.65.

Buses to Yangzhou depart at 6 am, 7 am, 8 am, 9 am, 12.40 pm, 2 pm, 3 pm, 4 pm, 4.30 pm and 5 pm.

There are also buses from Nanjing to Wuxi, Changzhou, Zhenjiang, Yixing town, possibly to Suzhou – see those sections for details.

**Train** Nanjing is a major stop on the Beijing-Shanghai rail line and there are several trains a day in both directions. Heading eastwards from Nanjing, the railway line to Shanghai connects several of China's notable tourist towns; Zhenjiang, Changzhou, Wuxi and Suzhou – see those sections for more details.

There is no direct rail link to Hangzhou and you have to go to Shanghai first and then pick up a train or bus – alternatively there is a direct bus from Nanjing to Hangzhou. Likewise, to get to Canton by rail you must change trains at Shanghai.

Heading westwards, there is a direct rail link to the port of Wuhu on the Yangtse River, but if you want to go further west along the river then the most sensible thing to do is take the ferry.

**Air** There are flights from Nanjing to Beijing (Y123), Canton (Y153), Chengdu (Y210), Chongqing (Y173), Jinan (Y71), Lanzhou (Y191), Shanghai (Y36), Shenyang (Y190), Wuhan (Y57), Xian (Y128), Zhengzhou (Y71).

**Boat** Ferries ply the Yangtse River from Nanjing eastward to Shanghai and westward to Wuhan; they leave from the dock at the western end of Zhongshan Beilu.

There are two boats each day to Shanghai. The first departure is at 5 pm and it arrives in Shanghai next day at 12 noon. The second departure is at 11.20 pm and it arrives in Shanghai at 2.20 pm next day. Fares are Y17.20 each in a two or four-bed cabin, Y6.90 each in an eight-bed cabin, and Y4.70 in a large dormitory.

There are two boats each day to Wuhan; the first departure is at 2 pm and the next is at 3.30 pm. The trip takes 38 to 48 hours, depending on which boat you're on. Fares are Y29.30, Y11.70 and Y8.00.

## YANGZHOU

Yangzhou, at the junction of the Grand Canal and the Yangtse, was once an economic and cultural centre of Southern China. It was home to scholars, painters, storytellers, poets and merchants in the Sui and Tang dynasties, but little remains of the greatness that Marco Polo witnessed. He served there as Governor for three years at the invitation of Kublai Khan and he wrote that 'Yangui has twenty-four towns under its jurisdiction, and must be considered a place of great consequence . . . the people are idolators, and subsist by trade and manual arts. They manufacture arms and other munitions: in consequence of which many troops are stationed in this part of the country.'

Buried outside the town at Leitang, in a simple mound of earth, is the Emperor Yang Di, the ruthless tyrant who completed the construction of the Grand Canal during the Sui Dynasty (518 to 618 AD). Yang Di is said to have levied exorbitant taxes, starved his subjects, and to have generally been very mean and nasty. The emperor's throne was unsurped by a powerful noble family who were to found the Tang Dynasty, and Yang Di was strangled by his own generals at

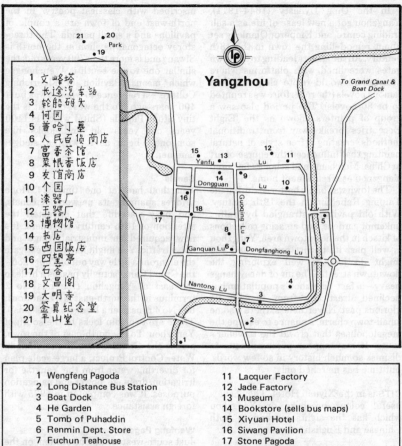

**Yangzhou**

To Grand Canal &
Boat Dock

Park

15 Yanfu
13
12
11

Lu

14
Dongguan
9
10

Lu

16
18
Guoqing Lu

17

8

Ganquan Lu 6
Dongfanghong Lu

Nantong Lu
4

3

1

2

| 1 文峰塔 |
| 2 长途汽车站 |
| 3 轮船码头 |
| 4 何园 |
| 5 普哈丁墓 |
| 6 人民百货商店 |
| 7 富春茶馆 |
| 8 菜根香饭店 |
| 9 友谊商店 |
| 10 个园 |
| 11 漆器厂 |
| 12 玉器厂 |
| 13 博物馆 |
| 14 书店 |
| 15 西园饭店 |
| 16 四望亭 |
| 17 石塔 |
| 18 文昌阁 |
| 19 大明寺 |
| 20 鉴真纪念堂 |
| 21 平山堂 |

| 1 Wengfeng Pagoda | 11 Lacquer Factory |
| 2 Long Distance Bus Station | 12 Jade Factory |
| 3 Boat Dock | 13 Museum |
| 4 He Garden | 14 Bookstore (sells bus maps) |
| 5 Tomb of Puhaddin | 15 Xiyuan Hotel |
| 6 Renmin Dept. Store | 16 Siwang Pavilion |
| 7 Fuchun Teahouse | 17 Stone Pagoda |
|   (off Guoqing Lu) | 18 Pavilion of Flourishing |
| 8 Caigenxiang Restaurant |     Culture (Wenchangee) |
|   (off Guoqing Lu) | 19 Daming Monastery (Fajingsi) |
| 9 Friendship Store | 20 Jiazhen Memorial Hall |
| 10 Ge Garden | 21 Pingshan Hall |

Yangzhou in 618. To the northwest of Yangzhou once stood the Maze Palace, a labyrinth of bronze mirros, couches and concubines, in which Yang Di is supposed to have torn about in a leopard-skin outfit, turning one night into ten before he finally emerged to deal with affairs of state (or maybe he just couldn't find his way out again). The building was burned down, and on the ruins was erected a structure called Jian (Warning) Building, a reminder for future generations. That building is still there, near Guanyin Hill, and is now used as a museum of Tang relics.

In the Qing Dynasty (1644-1911), Yangzhou got a new lease of life as a salt trading centre, and Emperor Qianlong set about remodelling the town in the 18th century. All the streets leading to the town gates were lined with platforms where storytellers would recite chapters from famous novels (the repertoire was reputed to be 30 novels). The period also saw a group of painters known as the 'Eight Eccentrics' break away from traditional methods, creating a free style of natural painting that influenced the course of art in China. Merchants and scholars favoured Yangzhou as a retirement home.

The town was badly battered during the Taiping Rebellion in the 19th century. With old pavilions strangled by traffic, unkempt gardens, and amazing collections of kitsch in the downtown area, Yangzhou is well past its tourist prime – and you might do just as well exploring the downtown streets. The air of decay hangs heavy – in fact Yangzhou's population has declined drastically from that of its glorious past. Nevertheless, there's some small-town charm, a chance to escape the megalopolises that crowd the traveller's route. It may appear presumptuous to dismiss so much history in so few words, but time has marched on!

**CITS** is in the Xiyuan Hotel. They have a useful colour brochure on Yangzhou which has the sights marked in both Chinese and English.

**Maps** Yangzhou has China's messiest bus maps which can only be bought in the bookstores.

### In Town

The Ge Garden on Dongguan St was landscaped by the painter Shi Tao for an officer of the Qing court. Shi Tao was an expert at making artificial rocks; the composition here suggests the four seasons. He Garden (alias Jixiao Mountain Villa), built in the 19th century, has rockeries, ponds and pavilions, and walls inscribed with classical poetry. In the north-west end of town are a couple of pavilions and a small pagoda. The three-storey octagonal pavilion at the north is Siwang and is more than 700 years old; the similar one to the south is Wenchangge which means 'Pavilion of Flourishing Culture' – a reference to when it was built 400 years ago. To the west of that is the tiny Stone Pagoda (Shita) which is 1100 years old years old and looks like someone's been at it with a sledge-hammer.

### Canals

Yangzhou had, at one time, 24 stone bridges spanning its network of canals, and busy waterlife that attracted the attention of 18th century travellers. It's now acquired an industrial fringe and noisy traffic. You might like to investigate the environs a little way out of Yangzhou – the Grand Canal actually passes a little to the east of Yangzhou (the bus No 2 terminus in the north-east is a boat dock; bus No 4 runs over a bridge on the canal). There are two ship locks to the south of Yangzhou. To the north-east of the town, across the Grand Canal, is the Jiangdu Water Control Project, a large-scale plan for diverting water from the Yangtse for irrigation, drainage, power and navigation purposes. It was completed in 1975 with foreign assistance.

### Wenfeng Pagoda

Just south-west of the bus station, on the bus No 1 route, this pagoda can be scaled to the seventh level (get out your grappling-hooks, assemble at 0900 hours, highly recommended). It offers a bird's-eye view of the flotsam, jetsam and sampans along a canal, as well as an overview of the town. Made of brick and wood, it's been rebuilt several times.

### Shouxi Hu (Slender West Lake)

This is the top scenic spot in Yangzhou, located in the western suburbs on the bus No 5 route. 'Shouxi' means 'slender west' as opposed to the 'fat west' lake in Hangzhou (fat signifies happy, slender means beautiful – but this park verges toward the emaciated, desperately in need of rejuvenation). It has boating (with an imperial dragon boat ferry), a restaurant, a white pagoda modelled after the one in Beihai Park in Beijing. The highlight is a triple-arched five-pavilion bridge (Wutang Qiao) built in 1757 – and for bridge connoisseurs is rated as one of the top ten ancient Chinese bridges. Emperor Qianlong's fishing platform is in the park – the local divers used to attach fish to the poor man's hook so he'd think it was good luck and cough up some more funding for the town. **Fajingsi (Daming Monastery)** The temple complex was founded over 1,000 years ago, subsequently destroyed and rebuilt. Then it was *really* destroyed during the Taiping Rebellion, and what you see today is a 1934 reconstruction. Nice architecture, even so, and if you time it right you'll find the shaven-headed monks indulging in mysterious ritual.

The original temple is credited to Tang Dynasty monk Jianzhen, who made profound studies in sculpture, architecture, fine arts and medicine as well as Buddhism. In 742 AD two Japanese monks invited him to Japan for missionary work. It turned out to be mission impossible – Jianzhen made five attempts, failing due to storms – the fifth time he ended up in Hainan. On the sixth trip, at the age of 66, he finally arrived, stayed in Japan for 10 years, and died there in 763 AD. Sometime after, the Japanese made a lacquer statue of Jianzhen, and in 1980 the statue made a homecoming tour to Yangzhou. The Chinese have a wooden copy of this statue on display at the Jianzhen Memorial Hall. Modelled after the chief hall of the Toshodai Temple in Nara (Japan), the Jianzhen Memorial Hall was built in 1974 at Fajingsi, and was financed by Japanese contributions. There are special exchanges between Nara and Yangzhou and even Deng Xiaoping, returning from a trip to Japan,

came to the Yangzhou monastery to add some cement to renewed links between the two countries.

West of Fajingsi is Pingshan Hall, the residence of the Song Dynasty writer Ouyang Xiu, who served in Yangzhou. West of that is Number Five Lifespring Under Heaven (in the Western Gardens).

## The Tomb of Puhaddin

This tomb has documents regarding China's contacts with the Moslems. It's on the east bank of a canal on the bus No 2 route. Puhaddin came to China during the Yuan Dynasty to spread the Moslem faith, spent ten years in Yangzhou, and died there. There is a mosque in Yangzhou.

## History Museum

The museum lies to the north of Guoqing Lu, in the vicinity of the Xiyuan Hotel. It's housed in a temple which was originally dedicated to Shi Kefa, a Ming Dynasty official who refused to succumb to his new Qing masters and was executed. The museum contains items from Yangzhou's past. A small collection of calligraphy and paintings of the 'Eight Eccentrics' is displayed in another small museum just off Yanfu Lu near the Xiyuan Hotel.

## The Place to Stay

The *Xiyuan Hotel* is the only one open to foreigners and was obviously built to impress VIPs; it's said to have been constructed over the site of Qianlong's imperial villa. Prices for this sprawling deluxe hotel range from Y30 to Y60 a double, but you can wangle a bed for Y7 or less, minus the TV. There are lots of rooms with three beds and some with no bath (technically that is a dormitory). Take bus No 3 or No 5 from the bus station alight at the Friendship Store (near a bridge) and walk uphill to the left about 60 metres; the hotel is on your right. If arriving late, grab an autorickshaw for around Y1 (buses stop early in the evening). The hotel can arrange onward long-distance buses.

## Places to Eat

The big wining, dining (but no dancing) area is the crossroads of Guoqing Lu (which runs north from the bus station) and Ganquan. Yangzhou has its own cuisine – bar a special banquet, you might have trouble finding it. Try the *Caigenxiang Restaurant*, 115 Guoqing Lu, inset off the road through a blue gate. How about buns with crab-ovary stuffing? Along Guoqing Lu and Ganquan Lu are small bakeries and cafes which sell steamed dumplings, noodles, pastries and other goodies – you can see the stuff being kneaded right behind the counter.

The *Fuchun Teahouse* has the best snack reputation in town. A bit hard to find at 39 Deshengqiao Lu, off Guoqing Lu. Has baozi and dessert dumplings, ham, and, of course, green tea.

## Getting Around

The sights are at the edge of town: if you're in a hurry you might consider commandeering a 'turtle' (autorickshaw) – they can be found outside the bus station.

Bus Nos 2, 3, 5, 6, 7 terminate near the bus station, and bus No 1 passes by it. Bus No 5 is a handy tour bus and runs from the bus station, across the canal and on to the Grand Canal boat dock in the north-east end of town. Bus No 1 runs from the Wenfeng Pagoda past the bus station, up Guoqing Lu and then loops around the perimeter of the inside canal, returning just north of the bus station. Bus No 4 is an east-west bus and cuts its way along Ganquan Lu. The downtown area can easily be covered on foot.

## Shopping

Downtown is full of shoe shops and housewares, but no sign of the lacquerware, jade, papercuts, woodcuts, embroidery or painting that Yangzhou is supposed to be famous for. So investigate the following if that's what you're after: Arts & Crafts Factory, west of Xiyuan Hotel; Friendship Store; Lacquer Factory, making inlaid lacquer screens with translucent properties, due east of Xiyuan Hotel; Jade Factory at 6 Guangchumenwai Jie; Block Printing Co-op (woodblock printed classics, handbound); and possibly the Renmin Department Store.

## Getting Away

The rail line gave Yangzhou a miss, the steam locos just didn't give her the magic kiss – one of the main reasons that this flower has wilted. Unless you're lucky enough to engineer a boat ride from Nanjing or Zhenjiang, that leaves a bus from either of those places.

The bus to Nanjing takes about 2½ hours, and costs Y2.30, passing over the stunning Yangtse River Bridge. The last bus to Nanjing leaves Yangzhou around 4.30 pm. There are nine buses per day.

To Zhenjiang, 1½ hours, Y1.05, 15 buses a day, amphibious crossing at the Yangtse. The last bus departs Yangzhou around 4.40 pm.

It's possible to day-trip from Nanjing or Zhenjiang; more comprehensive routes would be Nanjing-Yangzhou-Zhenjiang-Nanjing or Changzhou-Zhenjiang-Yangzhou-Nanjing, where you could juggle with trains also. Allow an overnight stop for such a routing.

There are two buses a day from Yangzhou to Wuxi; the fare is Y4.10. There is one bus a day from Yangzhou to Suzhou; the fare is Y5.50.

## YIXING COUNTY

Yixing County, to the west side of Lake Taihu, has enormous touring potential, and is a chance to get out of the cities. There are fertile plains, tea and bamboo plantations, undulating mountains with large caves and grottoes. The spectacular potteries of Dingshu village are, however, the real prize. Though busloads of Chinese tourists descend daily on the County from Wuxi, Nanjing and Shanghai, along with the day-tripper western group tours, Yixing Country has seen very few individuals.

| | |
|---|---|
| 1 Shanjuan Cave | 1 善卷洞 |
| 2 Linggu Cave | 2 灵谷洞 |
| 3 Zhanggong Cave | 3 张公洞 |
| 4 Yunu Pool | 4 玉女潭 |
| 5 Aquatic Breeding Farm | 5 养鱼场 |
| 6 Purple Sandware Factory | 6 紫砂工艺厂 |
| 7 Yangxian Tea Plantation | 7 茶场 |
| 8 Chuanbu Tea Plantation | 8 川埠茶场 |
| 9 Furongsi Tea Plantation | 9 芙蓉寺茶场 |

The town of Yixing is *not* the place to go – you're likely to end up being the main attraction yourself. It's a small town of about 50,000 where the main business of selling noodles, zips, steamed bread, pigs' feet, pots and pans, tools and sunglasses, is all done out on the main street which terminates at the forbidding gates of the Yixing Guest House. You'll probably end up in Yixing town one way or another since the only tourist hotel is there and the buses pass through the town. The attractions of Yixing County are all within a 30 km range of the town.

### Information & Orientation

**CITS** Their bunker is located in the north of the town somewhere – if you pick up the phone in the Yixing Guesthouse they will suddenly materialise, the fairy translators. They will then set about organising you into a taxi or a minibus with a guide (Y4 per hour; taxi costs at least Y20 to

Dingshu). They'll tell you that there are no buses to the caves or Dingshu, and they seem to be under the impression that all foreigners really *are* millionaires, since all they've come across is group tours. Best to avoid them altogether.

### Things to See

If you have time, explore the north-east end of Yixing town with its heavy concentration of comic-book rentals (and not just kids doing the reading) and all manner of strange transactions down side streets. This and more can be seen in Dingshu. The Confucius Temple at the north-west end of Yixing town was closed at the time of writing due to poor condition, though it's being renovated.

### Karst Caves

There are a number of these to the south-west of Yixing township, and they're a cut above average. The drab interiors are lit by the standard Chinese selection of coloured neon, but you may wish to supplement this with a torch for navigation. The caves slobber a lot, so take your raincoat, too. The countryside around the caves is excellent, and actually worth more time than the underground.

### Shanjuan Cave

This cave is embedded in Snail Shell Hill (Luoyan Shan), 27 km south-west of Yixing. It covers an area of roughly 5,000 sq metres, with passages of 800 metres – enough to make any speleologist delirious. It's divided into upper, middle and lower reaches, plus a water cave. An exterior waterfall provides special sound effects for this weird set. Entry is via the Middle Cave, a stone hall with a 1,000 metre floor space. From here you can mount a staircase to the snail's shell, the Upper Cave, or wander down to the lower and water caves. In the Water Cave, you can jump in a rowing boat for a 120-metre ride to the exit, called 'Suddenly-see-the-Light', where a restaurant, hotel, teahouse, Zhuling Village and goodness knows what else awaits you. Good luck! There are, of course, many legends associated with the caves – mostly to do with past hermits in residence. One was the hermitess Zhu Yingtai; at the exit is a small pavilion which she used as her 'reading room'. Zhu, as the story goes, being a Jin Dynasty lass was not permitted to attend school, so she disguised herself as a male student and took up residence in the caves which must have been tough without electricity. Every piece of stalagmite and stalactite in the cave is carefully catalogued – whether it be a moist sheep, a soggy plum, a cluster of bananas or an elephant. If the commentary is in Chinese, just exercise your imagination – that's what they did.

Nine buses a day run to Shanjuan from Yixing bus station – the first is at 6 am and the last is at 4.20 pm. The trip takes one hour and the fare is peanuts.

## Zhanggong Cave

19 km south of Yixing town are three score caves-within-caves, large and small, divided into upper and lower reaches. It's about the size of Shanjuan, but different layout. This is up-down caving; what you do is scale a small hill called Yufeng Shan from the inside, and you come out on the top with a splendid view of the surrounding countryside with hamlets stretching as far as Lake Taihu. There are two large grottoes in this bunch of caverns – the more impressive is the Hall of the Dragon King, with a ceiling that definitely isn't sprayed-on stucco. The place would make a perfect disco! From the Hall of the Dragon King you make your way through the Dry Nostril Cave, pause to clear your sinuses, and work up to the afore-mentioned exit.

A little further south of Zhanggong is the Yunutan, or Jade Maiden Pond, which was being 'renovated'.

Buses to Zhanggong run at 8.40 am, 10 am, 12.10 pm and 2.30 pm (Y0.45, takes half and hour from Yixing town). From Zhanggong you can pick up a passing bus to Linggu – the terminus of the line. If you're stuck on transport, try to get to Dingshu Village, where bus connections are good.

## Linggu Cave

Eight km down a dirt road from Zhanggong, Linggu is the largest and least explored of the three caves. You could easily get lost in this one and not because of the scenery either. The cave has six large halls arrayed roughly in a semi-circle, and it's a long, deep forage.

Near the Linggu Caves is the Yanxian Tea Plantation, with bushels laid out like fat caterpillars stretching into the horizon, and the odd tea villa in the background. The trip is worth it for the tea fields alone.

There are buses to Linggu from Zhanggong; see the section above on Zhanggong for details.

## Dingshu

In Yixing County they not only grow tea, they make plenty of pots to put it in. Small towns in China can be utterly engrossing if they specialise in some kind of product and such is the case with Dingshuzhen. The town has a history of bulk pottery output since the Qin and Han Dynasties (221 BC to 220 AD), and some of the scenes you can witness here, especially at the loading dock that leads into Lake Taihu, are timeless. Almost every family is engaged in the manufacture of ceramics, and at the back end of town half the houses are made of the stuff. Dingshu is *the* pottery capital of China. There are also important porcelain-making plants in Jingdeshen, Handan, Zibo and parts of Guangzhou, but few that handle the wide range of ceramics that Dingshu does.

Dingshu is about 25 km from Yixing town and has two dozen ceramics factories producing more than 2,000 varieties of pottery – quite an output for a population of 100,000. Among the array of products are the ceramic tables and trash-cans that you find around China, huge jars used to store oil and grain, the famed

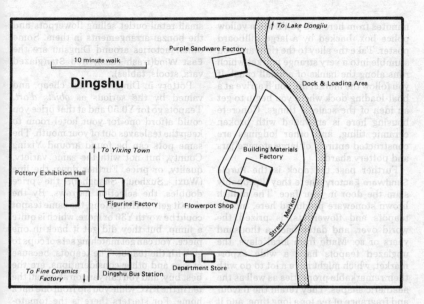

Within the map:
**Dingshu**
10 minute walk
↑ To Lake Dongjiu
Purple Sandware Factory
Dock & Loading Area
To Yixing Town
Building Materials Factory
Pottery Exhibition Hall
Figurine Factory
Flowerpot Shop
Street Market
To Fine Ceramics Factory
Department Store
Dingshu Bus Station

---

Yixing teapots, and the glazed tiling and ceramic frescoes that are desperately needed as spare parts for tourist attractions (the Forbidden City in Peking is one of the customers).

The back end of Dingshu is a good Chinese hour away (40 minutes) from the local bus station, but there's plenty to amuse you along the route. You *can* get into the factories if you persist. If you act like a bigshot buyer, all doors will automatically swing open, as far as the showrooms anyway. Each factory in theory has a retail outlet, so you can march in and say you're looking for the shop. Unfortunately, bigshots don't walk but arrive in big taxis. Perhaps an eccentric millionaire? If you have the bucks to sling around, CITS in Yixing town can get you into the factories of your choice at a price of their choice. A suggested three-hour walking tour is:

**The Pottery Exhibition Hall** is the logical first step to get your bearings in Dingshu. Turn leftish from the bus station and veer right past a small corner store. The

Exhibition is the large solid building, five minutes up the street on your left. You can view two floors and several wings of the Dingshu pottery time-line and get a good idea of what might be a good purchase. The exhibits are well presented; they don't like photos. Opposite the Hall is a **Figurine Factory** which produces absolute kitsch, lampstands and the like, but even they are experimenting with glazes like tigerskin and snowflake, which is the secret of Dingshu. Technology got off to a great start here when they introduced the new improved Dragon Kiln over a thousand years ago. Some distance north of the Exhibition Hall is the **Ceramics Research Institute**.

Backtrack to the bus station. By now you're an expert on Dingshu pots, so ignore the little retail shop on the corner! If you go straight down the street past the bus station, you'll get to the centre of town. En route, you pass two retail outlets – the second one has celadon-ware on the top floor, but you're better off loading up on the way back. Proceed about ten minutes from here and you'll see a yellow police box, backed by a large billboard poster. Take the alley to the right and you stumble into a very strange market which runs along the banks of a small canal. If you follow the market up, you'll arrive at a boat-loading dock where you begin to get an idea of the scale of things. Concrete housing here is enlivened with broken ceramic tiling, and other lodgings are constructed entirely of large storage jars and pottery shards.

Further past the dock is the **Purple Sandware Factory** where they'll probably slam the door in your face. The dullish brown stoneware produced here, mostly teapots and flowerpots, is prized the world over, and dates back a thousand years or so. Made from local clays, the unglazed teapots have a wide export market, which might have a lot to do with their remarkable properties as well as the aesthetic shapes. They retain the flavour and fragrance of tea for a long time, and it is said that after extended use with one type of tea, no further tealeaves are necessary. The teapots glaze themselves eventually, a darker silkier brown – well, you've heard of tea stains. And it's claimed that the Purple Sands pots can be placed over a direct flame or shoved in boiling water without cracking (though it's a different story if you drop one on the floor).

From the Purple Sands you can return to town by a different route. Go back to the dock and take a right fork. This brings you down to another road, and if you look left, you will spot the **Building Materials Factory**, a large operation which makes glazed tiles, garbage bins, ceramic tables and pottery pavilions. The production of pottery for civic and military use was what really got Dingshu off the ground, and is still the mainstay. Pottery is now produced for sanitation, construction, daily use – and that all-important spin-off, the tourist industry, chuck up a pavilion here, re-tile a temple there. Near the gates of the Building Materials Factory is a

small retail outlet selling flowerpots and the bonzai arrangements in them. Some other factories around Dingshu are the **East Wind**(trash cans); **Red Star**(glazed vats, stools, tables).

Pottery in Dingshu is dirt cheap, and valued by the serious as *objets d'art*. Teapots go for Y0.50 and at that price you could afford one for your hotel room to keep the tealeaves out of your mouth. The same pots can be found around Yixing County, but not with the same variety, quality, or price. Further down the line (Wuxi, Suzhou, Shanghai), the price doubles, the selection narrows. By the time it gets to Hong Kong, the same teapot could be worth Y30 or more, which is quite a jump, but they did get it back in one piece. You can get matching sets of cups to go with the teapot. The teapots, because of size and other considerations, are the best buy, and you can yarn on about all the tea in the PRC while you sip from one back home. For starters there is the tomato-shaped dragon teapot, the lid of which has a free-rolling dragon's head embedded in it – this amazing pot costs Y1. Indeed, Dingshu is the home of the world's most surprising teapots – with ingenious musical properties involving nipples of clay in the lid – or, for the purist, no lid! Teapots range from Y0.50 to Y2.50 for a simple model, and climb high into the yuans after that. There is a complicated ritual that should be followed for breaking in a new teapot, depending on what kind of tea is to be brewed (oolong, black or green). Check for tight lids when purchasing and test the pouring lip by transferring water from one pot to another. Also look for the small squarish teapots – they're lighter and they pack better, travel easier. The two retail outlets along the road from the bus station are the best places to stock up but you may spot a better deal at a factory outlet. Anyway, at Y1 you're not about to lose on the deal. Some of the locals sell on the free market – they make the pots up, then get them fired at local factories.

Also on sale, and something that can be lugged out, are flowerpots (Y0.75 to Y3.50), figures and casseroles, all of them imbued with magical properties (the casseroles are supposed to make the meat tender). In the kitsch-en-ware department are ceramic lampshades (let's see – they must make the bulbs shine brighter!).

## E.T. Extraordinary Touring

For the adventurous, there are a number of unexplored routes once you're on the loose in Yixing County. A suggestion is to get there in the conventional manner, and try your luck on a different route out. Pottery is transported through canals and across Lake Taihu to Wuxi and it might be possible to transport yourself likewise. Highways skirt Lake Taihu, eventually running to Suzhou, Shanghai and Hangzhou. If you took a bus to Changxing, a slow branch line railway leads from there to Hangzhou. At the southern end of the lake is a cross-over point: Huzhou. A little way north of this, right on Lake Taihu is Xiaomeikou, where ferry routes are marked on the map leading to Wuxi (right across the lake), and Suzhou via Yuanshan and Xukou.

## The Place to Stay

The *Yixing Guesthouse* caters chiefly to cadres holding meetings. The Guesthouse is at the end of Renmin Rd on the southern edge of Yixing town. Y30 double or Y12 per bed, student price, after a good tussle. If there's not a rash of meetings, or a rare tour bus assault, the hotel will be empty. It's a large building, with gardens and luxury living, in stark contrast with the rest of the town, which has nothing.

The hotel is a half-hour walk from Yixing bus station: turn right from the station, follow the main road south along the lakeside, across three bridges, then turn left, and the hotel is close by. The long stretch across the bridges is the same road that runs to Dingshu, so if your bus goes to Dingshu, ask the driver to let you off closer to the hotel. If you don't mind the stroll, and want to see the main drag of Yixing town, another way of getting to the hotel is to walk three blocks straight ahead of the bus station, turn right into Renmin Lu, and keep walking till you hit the hotel.

## Places to Eat

The *Yixing Guesthouse* has set menu meals, and they expect you to take full service (three meals, Y15 a day). Dinner alone is Y7.50 and before you can say 'a la carte', the waitress plonks six or seven dishes in front of you – and an apple signifies the end of the production line. If you don't mind 500 people at your table (staring at you, not their food), there's a restaurant opposite the bus station, and several along Renmin Lu, and along here you'll find some baked food, and dumplings also.

## Getting Around

There are no local buses in Yixing. There are longer-run buses to the sights out of town and all of them end up in the bus stations of either Yixing town or Dingshu. There are frequent connections between the two stations with buses every 20 minutes and the fare is Y0.40. Hitchhiking is a possibility.

## Getting Away

There are buses from Yixing town to Changzhou and Wuxi. The fare is around Y1.40 and the trip takes about 2½ hours; there are 10 buses a day on the Yixing-Wuxi route.

There's a direct bus from Dingshu to Changzhou (skipping Yixing town). The fare is Y1.65 and there are regular buses throughout the day.

There are buses direct to Shanghai, Nanjing, and possibly Suzhou.

## XUZHOU

Xuzhou does not fall into the category of a canal town though a tributary of the Grand Canal passes by the north-east end of Xuzhou; the history of the town has little to do with the canal. The colour brochure for Xuzhou shows the marshalling yard of the railway station as one of the sights and that, perhaps, is more to the point. If you're a rail buff there are plenty of lines to keep you happy since the town is at the intersection of China's two main railways: the Beijing-Shanghai line, and the Longhai line which runs from Kaifeng, Luoyang and Xian in the west to the coastal town of Lianyungang in the east. Still, the place has 12 cinemas, 16 bus lines, and an airport, so there must be something more – the coal mines.

### Information & Orientation

The city centre is straight ahead of the railway station, at the intersection of Huaihai and Zhongshan Lu (note that there are two stations, north and main, and these directions are for the main station). Take bus No 1 two stops west of the main station and you'll get to the main roundabout.

**CITS** is in the Nanjiao Hotel. Take bus No 2 from the main railway station.

**Maps** There is a Chinese hotel on the right as you come out of the main railway station; maps in Chinese showing the bus routes are sold here. CITS sells an English/Chinese map.

### Things to See

The main railway station houses a collection of beggars and vagrants. Meanwhile, there are a number of sights around town.

### Yunlong Shan (Dragon in the Clouds Hill)

This hill has half the sights of Xuzhou; the Xinghua Temple, several pavilions, and a stone carving from the Northern Wei Dynasty (386-534 AD). If you climb to the top of the hill, where the Xinghua Temple is located, there's a magnificent panorama of the concrete boxes that compose the Xuzhou valley and the mountains that ring it. Yes, there are even orchards out

there somewhere. Set in a grotto off the mountainside is a giant gilded Buddha head, the statue of the Sakyamuni Buddha. The park itself is circus-land with an outdoor BB shooting gallery (good practice for nailing those sparrows!), beggars, peanuts and popsicles littering the slopes. The hill is a 10-minute walk west of the Nanjiao Hotel, or take bus No 2 or bus No 11.

### Monument to the Martyrs of the Huaihai Campaign

A revolutionary war memorial and obelisk monument opened in 1965, set in a huge wooded park at the southern edge of town. The Huaihai battle was a decisive one fought by the PLA from November 1948 to January 1949. The obelisk, 38.5 metres high, has a gold inscription by Chairman Mao and a grand flight of stairs leading up to it. There is a Memorial Hall close by which has an extensive collection of weaponry, photos, maps, paintings and memorabilia, over 2,000 items altogether, as well as inscriptions from important heads of state from Zhou Enlai to Deng Xiaoping. The grounds, 100 acres of pines and cypresses, are meant to be 'symbolic of the evergreen spirit of the revolutionary martyrs'. The park lies on the bus No 11 route.

### Places to Stay

The *Nanjiao (South Suburbs) Hotel* is on Heping Rd, three km from the main railway station. This is a TV Hotel since most of the staff are permanently glued to the box downstairs. The rooms also have TVs but there are some without so you can knock the standard Y34 double down to Y12 double or Y6 a person. Take bus No 2 from the main railway station.

### Places to Eat

There's not much food in the vicinity of the Nanjiao Hotel, apart from the hotel dining room.

*Huaihaifandiancaiguanbu* is the Huaihai Hotel, which is on Huaihai Donglu between the main station and the large roundabout, south side of street. The best eating in town is found in this hotel and in the *Pencheng Hotel* which is close by. The Pencheng is located on a corner after an overhead bridge. It has a section with noodles, icecreams, drinks and bakery. Further west of Zhongshan Rd, north-west side of large roundabout, is a busy noodle shop.

There are noodle shops on the right when you come out of the main railway station.

### Getting Around

The local bus station is straight across the square in front of the main railway station. There are also autorickshaws parked to the left as you leave the main railway station.

### Getting Away

Xuzhou lies on the junction of the main Beijing-Shanghai and the Longhai lines. The Longhai line runs from Xian, Luoyang, Zhengzhou and Kaifeng in the west to the town of Lianyungang in the east.

### LIANYUNGANG

From Xuzhou, a branch line runs east to the major coastal port of Lianyungang (a six-hour ride). The town is divided into port and city sections. Yuntai Hill is the 'scenic spot' overlooking the ocean and there are some salt mines along the shores, topped with a Taoist monastery. The mountain is reputed to be the location or the inspiration for the Flowers and Fruit Mountain in the Ming Dynasty novel 'Pilgrimage to the West' (three other places in the PRC lay the same claim). Other sights include the 2,000-year-old stone carvings at Kung Wang Mountain. There's an International Seamen's Club, Friendship Store, CITS office and several hotels. A possibility of boat connections on the east coast, but no details at hand.

### NANTONG

Nantong only opened to foreign tourists in late 1983. It's an industrial city of 210,000 and an important textile and shipping centre for routes along the Yangtse and the canals running inland. The old walled city was on an island in the Hao River – there are no walls left, but the city administration is still on the island. There are three satellite towns outside the city core.

Boat would be the most sensible way of getting to Nantong – it's only six hours upriver from Shanghai. It's a long way round by road, but a possible land/boat route might be via Suzhou and Changshu, both of which are open to foreigners.

### Footnote

With one small exception, Zhou En-lai was one of the few in the Communist hierarchy who did not use his position to have his poems published. A recent translation of the poems which Zhou wrote in his youth suggests why – they are incredibly bad! Perhaps the translation was a poor one, perhaps the poems simply don't translate well into English or maybe I'm just picking out the worst, but one poem *Bon Voyage to Li Yu-ju with Rememberances to Shu-ti* written in 1920, stands out:

*An absence of three months*
*And how you have progressed!*
*Nien-chiang came the other day*
*Saying that you meant to go to England.*
*I thought you were only talking.*
*A couple of days later, Tan-wen told me*
*You were going to France.*
*I took it again as jesting.*
*Not many days had passed*
*When surprisingly enough*
*You came to bid me good-bye*
*And told me in person*
*That you were to go.*
*So you are really going!*

# Henan

Henan is where it all began. The Yellow River cuts its way across the north of the province and 3500 years ago the Chinese were turning their primitive settlements into an urban-centred civilisation governed by the Shang Dynasty.

Excavations of the ancient towns of the Shang Dynasty have shown that these were built on the sites of ancient settlements. The Shang civilisation had not been founded by people migrating from Western Asia as was once thought but had grown on the spot, another phase in a continuous line of development which had been going on here since prehistoric times.

The Shang was the second dynasty to rule over the Han Chinese. Before the Shang there was the Xia Dynasty, but the last Xia emperor was so cruel that his subjects revolted. The noble who led the revolt, said to be a descendant of China's legendary Yellow Emperor, founded the Shang Dynasty which ruled from the 16th to the 11th century BC. They controlled an area which included parts of what is today Shandong, Henan, and Hebei Provinces. But to the west of their territory the powerful Zhou people arose and conquered the Shang, and the last Shang emperor supposedly hurled himself into the flames of his burning palace.

The first Shang capital is believed to be the site of Yenshih, west of modern-day Zhengzhou, and dating back maybe as much as 3800 years. The capital was moved to Zhengzhou, where the walls of the ancient city are still visible, around the middle of the 16th century BC. Later the capital moved to Yin near the modern town of Anyang in the north of Henan.

The only clues as to what Shang society was like are drawn from the remnants of their cities, the divining bones which have been unearthed and which are inscribed with a primitive form of Chinese writing,
and from the texts of ancient Chinese literary works. Apart from the walls at Zhengzhou, all that has survived of their cities are the pounded earth foundations of the buildings, stone-lined trenches where wooden poles once stood supporting thatched roofs and pits used for storage or as underground houses.

Today Henan is one of the smaller of the Chinese provinces but also one of the most densely populated, with 74 million people squashed in here. Once the centre of Chinese civilisation, political power moved away from the region once and for all when the Song Dynasty fled south from its capital at Kaifeng, in the wake of an invasion from the north in the 12th century. Nevertheless, with such a high population and its location on the fertile (through periodically flood-ravaged) plains of the Yellow River it remained an important agricultural area. Henan's urban centres rapidly diminished in size and population with the demise of the Song, and it was not until the Communist takeover in 1949 that they once again expanded; places like Zhengzhou and Luoyang in particular being transformed into great industrial cities, and others like Kaifeng and Anyang also being industrialised. Off on the Henan-Shandong border of the province, a 10 km-long bridge is being built across the Yellow River, and will be the longest bridge in China.

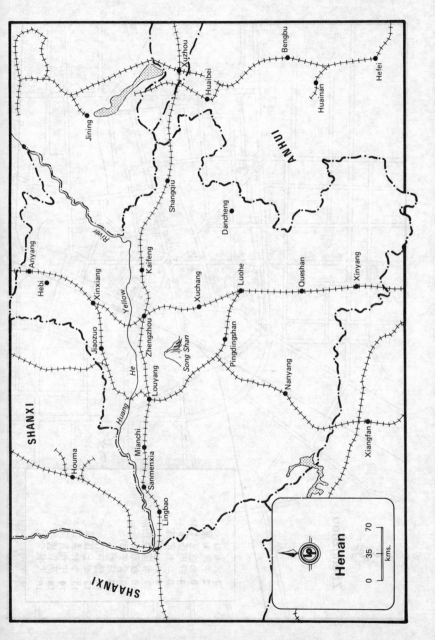

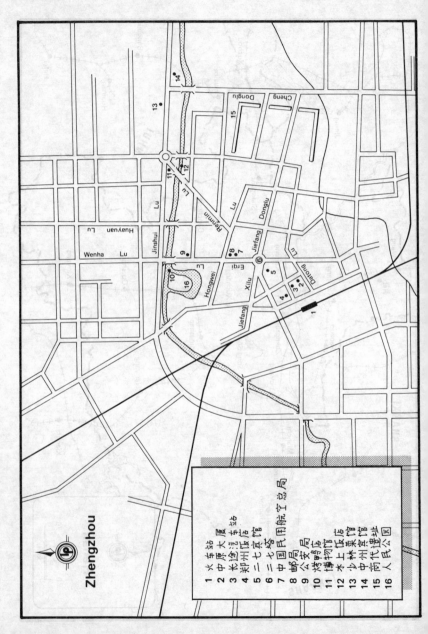

Zhengzhou

1 火车站
2 中原大厦
3 长途汽车站
4 郑州饭店
5 二七塔宾馆
6 二七塔
7 中国民用航空总局
8 邮电局
9 公安局
10 游乐庭
11 博物馆
12 木上饭店
13 少林饭店
14 中州宾菜宾馆
15 中尚代遗址
16 人民公园

## ZHENGZHOU

Zhengzhou is a twelve hour train ride and a couple of psychological decades from Shanghai and Beijing where most foreigners spend their time. Because of its' importance as a railway junction, the city was made the capital of Henan Province after 1949. Since 1950 the population has increased ten-fold from around 100,000 people, and may even have passed the million mark. It is the city itself, not the individual sights which is the reason for coming here; with Zhengzhou the Communists had a chance to build an entire city from the ground up in whatever style they saw as the ideal, or as close as resources would allow, and this is what they came up with.

Seen from the top floors of the Henan International Hotel, Zhengzhou's No 1 tourist joint, the city stretches into the distance, a sea of near-identical red-brick low-rise residential blocks interspersed with factories and smokestacks. The whole lot is plonked down like lego blocks on an orderly grid network of tree-lined roads, wide enough to hold their own against the onslaught of hundreds of thousands of bicycles.

A typical group of apartment buildings consists of eight or ten four-storey brick rectangles arranged in rows. The dirt courtyard in front of the building is a play and gossip area, and the rear is divided amongst tenants and used for vegetable plots and makeshift chicken coops. The whole complex, which might include the factory or office block where the tenants work and a hospital, is surrounded by a 12-foot wall, often topped with barbed wire or broken glass. There is only one entry gate per complex, two at the most, sometimes there is a gatekeeper and sometimes not.

Inside the apartments, everything is concrete; floors, walls and ceilings. Often there is white or cream paint, seldom plaster and never wallpaper. The rooms are small but the ceilings are high at 10 or 11 feet. Furnishings are sparse; no rugs or carpets, a few chairs or wooden stools, a table, bed, a desk lamp. In crowded China, happiness is having your own apartment and a four-person family would be privileged to have two rooms to themselves. Two families of four in a three-room apartment and sharing the kitchen and toilet would be the more common situation.

### Information & Orientation

Most of the tourist facilities and sights are located in the south-eastern and eastern sections of the city.

The city centre is a traffic circle on the intersection of Erqi Lu and Jiefang Lu, readily identifiable by the large February 7th Monument there. South-east of the monument is the railway station and directly opposite the railway station is Zhongyuan Mansions (one of Zhengzhou's major hotels) right next to the long-distance bus station. The area between the railway station and the February 7th Monument is the location of many shops and restaurants.

Erqi Lu runs northwards from the monument and along here can be found the CAAC office, Public Security, the post

| | |
|---|---|
| 1 Railway Station | 9 Public Security Office |
| 2 Zhongyuan Mansion | 10 'Restaurant Over The Water' |
| 3 Long Distance Bus Station | 11 Henan Provincial Museum |
| 4 Zhengzhou Hotel | 12 'Restaurant Over The Water' |
| 5 February 7th Hotel | 13 Restaurant |
| 6 February 7th Monument | 14 Zhongzhou Guesthouse |
| 7 CAAC | 15 Shang City Walls |
| 8 Post Office | 16 People's Park |

office and the February 7th Hotel. Jingshui Lu runs east-west and intersects with Erqi Lu; it's the site of the Provincial Museum and the Zhongzhou Guest House (otherwise known as the Henan International Hotel).

**CITS** (tel 5578) is supposed to be at 8 Jinshuihe Lu and you're a genius if you can find it. They have a desk on the ground floor of the Henan International Hotel but it never seems to be manned.

**Public Security Office** is in a government compound at 113 Erqi Lu. It's open 8 am to 12 noon and 2.30 to 6 pm Monday to Saturday, and is closed on Sundays.

**CAAC** (tel 4339) is at 38 Erqi Lu. You'll have to look for it – it's a nondescript building with nothing to suggest an association with aeroplanes.

**Post** There is a post office on the ground floor of the Zhongzhou Guest House. There's another at the corner of Hongwei Lu and Erqi Lu immediately to the north of the CAAC office.

**Maps** Excellent maps are available from an information window in the railway station; the window faces out onto the square in front of the station. The maps cost 20 fen, are in Chinese and have the bus routes marked.

### Things to See

The streets which branch off from the February 7th Monument are worth a wander. One that will always stick in my mind is Dahua Lu, memorable as the first street I ever saw in China with houses decked out in something other than grey. One was actually painted green, another yellow and the rest in green, light blue, crimson, yellow and aqua! As for the red-brick lego blocks, they go on endlessly but there are a couple of sights scattered about.

### Shang City Ruins

On the eastern outskirts of Zhengzhou city lie the remains of an ancient city from the Shang period of the 16th to 11th century BC. All that remains are the long, high mounds of earth which indicate where the city walls used to be, now bisected by a couple of modern roads. Nevertheless, this is probably one of the earliest relics of Chinese urban life.

The first archaeological evidence of the Shang period was discovered near the town of Anyang in northern Henan.

The city at Zhengzhou is believed to have been the second Shang capital, and many Shang settlements have been found outside the walled area. Excavations here and at other Shang sites suggest that a 'typical' Shang city consisted of a central walled area containing large buildings (presumably government buildings or the residences of important people, and used for ceremonial occasions) surrounded by a ring of villages each specialising in a particular occupation, such as pottery, metal-work, wine or textile making. The village dwellings were mostly semi-underground pit houses, whilst the buildings in the centre were retangular and above ground.

Excavations at various Shang sites have also uncovered tombs, rectangular pits with ramps or steps leading down to a burial chamber in which the coffin was placed and surrounded with funeral objects such as bronze weapons, helmets, musical instruments, oracle bones and shells with inscriptions, silk fabrics and various jade, bone, and ivory ornaments. And amongst those, depending on the wealth and status of the deceased, could also be found the skeletons of animals and other humans – sacrifices meant to accompany their masters to the next world. Many of the skeletons of the sacrificial victims were of a different ethnic origin from the Shang – possibly prisoners of war. This, and other evidence, has suggested that Shang society was not based on the slavery of its own people, but was ruled over by a sort of benevolent dictatorship of the aristocracy with the emperor/father-figure at the apex.

## Henan Provincial Museum

There's an interesting collection of artefacts discovered in Henan Province, including some from the Shang period. Unfortunately, the collection suffers from a lack of English captions. The museum is located on Renmin Lu, at the intersection with Jinshui Lu and is readily identifiable by the large white Mao statue at the front.

## February 7th Monument

This monument in the centre of Zhengzhou commemorates the 1923 strike organised by workers building the Wuhan-Beijing Railway, and which was bloodily suppressed.

## The Yellow River

The Yellow River is just 24 km north of Zhengzhou and the road leads to a point near the village of Huayuankou, where Kuomintang troops blew up the dykes of the river in April 1938. It was an ingenious tactic ordered by Chiang Kai-shek, who must have thought that halting the Japanese advance for a few weeks was worth drowning maybe a million Chinese and making another 11 million homeless and starving. The dyke was repaired with American help in 1947 and today the point where it was breached has an irrigation sluice gate and Mao's instruction 'Control the Yellow River' etched into the embankment.

The river has always been regarded as 'China's sorrow' because of its propensity to flood. It carries masses of silt from the loess plains which is deposited on the river bed, causing the water to overflow the banks. Consequently the peasants along the riverbank have had to build the dykes higher and higher each century. As a result parts of the river flow along an elevated channel which is often as much as 1½ km wide and sometimes more than seven metres high!

## People's Park

One of the few parks I'd recommend, not for scenic beauty but for the entranceway which looks like someone's attempt to recreate either the Lunan Stone Forest or an embryonic Tiger Balm Gardens. Family circuses sometimes set up shop here, performing such feats of strength as wrapping wire around their torsos or getting dogs to jump through hoops. You can also play that venerated Chinese sport of ping-pong on the concrete tables in the park if you've got some bats and a ball. The entrance to the park is on Erqi Lu.

## Places to Stay

Directly across the road from the Zhengzhou Railway Station is the *Zhongyuan Mansion*, a big white tower. Prices are a bit confusing, but they seem to charge around Y20 for a double room (with bath and toilet) or Y5 or Y6 for a bed in a four-bed room. It's a run-down place, but OK and convenient for everything.

The long-distance bus station is next to Zhongyuan Mansions, and across the road from the bus station is the *Zhengzhou Hotel* which will probably take you. They charge Y1.40 for a bed in a four-bed room, and single rooms seem to start from around about Y6.50.

The *February 7th Hotel* is adjacent to the February 7th Monument, a very convenient location and they'll probably let you stay here. Double rooms are Y8.30 and there may be singles for half that price. They also have four-bed rooms.

The best place to stay is the *Zhongzhou Guest House* (tel 4255) which is otherwise known as the *Henan International Hotel*. It's Zhengzhou's big tourist joint but is rather inconveniently located in the distant eastern outskirts of the city on Jinshui Lu. Despite the hotel's great size the rooms are pleasantly small and have comfy beds. There are no single rooms; double rooms are Y30, but if you can convince them you're a student then you should be able to get the room for Y20, and if you're on your own you might get it for Y10 (as I did). A bed in a triple is Y10. A bus No 2 from the railway station will take you straight to the hotel. Cute signs in the rooms: 'Please keep cleaness and no birds, animals or anything with a strange smell in the room' and 'Please inform the attendent for leaving beforehand and helps will come to you for all the things undone'.

### Places to Eat

There's not much to recommend in this city. Available from the foodstalls around the central part of town is a tasty little dish which seems to be made out of what looks like gelatinised potato and fried in a wok. It goes for 20 fen a plate. It's called

凉粉

There's a good restaurant on the corner of Jinshui Lu and Jingsi Lu, a ten minute walk west of the Zhongzhou Guest House. It is readily identifiable by a large painting of the Shaolin monastery above the entrance.

There are two *Restaurants Over the Water* but don't expect tranquil pavilions on a pleasant lake. Both restaurants are built above oversized creeks. The first one, near the intersection of Erqi Lu and Jinshui Lu, is OK upstairs though downstairs is just like any other Chinese canteen. There's another on Renmin Lu, just south of the Provincial Museum, but it's even uglier than the first.

### Getting Around

Transport is almost exclusively by bus; walking is only recommended for the relatively narrow confines of the central city area.

### Getting Away

**Bus** The long-distance bus station is across the road from the railway station.

There are frequent buses to Kaifeng, the earliest at 5.30 am and the last at 7 pm. The fare is Y1.70.

There are buses to Dengfeng every hour

from 5.30 am until 10.30 am. The next is at 1 pm and then every hour until the last at 6 pm. The fare is Y1.90 and you buy tickets at window No 7 of the bus station.

There are buses to Luoyang every hour – the first at 5.30 am and the last at 5 pm. The fare is Y3.60 and you buy tickets at window No 11. The ride to Luoyang is an interesting one which takes about 4½ hours. You go past long stretches of terraced wheat fields, through drab, dusty little towns, and you'll even see people living in dwellings cut into dry embankments, or where the hillside makes up one of the walls of the house.

There are buses to the Shaolin Monastery from Zhengzhou. You can take a local bus from Zhengzhou to Dengfeng and then walk or hitch. Alternatively, you can take a tour bus which leaves from outside the railway station each morning. You buy your ticket from the small white booth across the road from the railway station directly in front of Zhongyuan Mansions. A round-trip ticket is Y5.

**Train** Zhengzhou is on the main Beijing-Canton line. It's a major rail junction and you may have to stop here overnight to take a train east towards Shanghai, west towards Xian, or north to Taiyuan and Datong. There is a train to Urumqi which originates in Zhengzhou. If you're heading north from Canton to Taiyuan then you have to change trains at Zhengzhou.

**Plane** Zhengzhou is connected by air to Beijing (Y82), Canton (Y166), Changsha (Y98), Hefei (Y69), Lanzhou (Y120), Nanjing (Y71), Nanyang (Y28), Shanghai (Y107), Wuhan (Y60), Xian (Y56).

### KAIFENG

One of the favourites of travellers – though not that many people go there –is Kaifeng, a medium sized city east of the provincial capital of Zhengzhou. Its size belies the fact that this was once the imperial capital of China, prosperous centre of the Middle Kingdom during the

Northern Song Dynasty. That was put to an end by the invading Jin in 1127 – the Song fled south, where their poets wrote heart-wrenching verse as their beautiful capital was pillaged. Kaifeng never recovered from the assault and was never restored; all that remains today of the imperial splendour is a scroll painting in the Forbidden City in Beijing which depicts the bustling town centre.

Kaifeng's population has grown little in the past 60 years – from just 280,000 in 1923 to about 300,000 today – which makes it something of an odd-man-out in China's urban population boom. The most peculiar members of Kaifeng's population are the Chinese Jews – though they still consider themselves Jewish (or Israelites) the religious beliefs and the customs associated with Judaism appear to have completely died out. Just how the Jews came to China is unknown; the story of the scattering of the 'ten tribes' is one possibility, but more likely they may have come as traders and merchants along the Silk Road when Kaifeng was the capital, or they may have emigrated from the Jewish populations of the south-western coast of India. A prominent short-lived member of Kaifeng's population was Liu Shaoqi, who is supposed to have ended his days here in 1969.

Chief among the 'sights' is the **Xiangguo Monastery** in the centre of town, originally founded in 555 AD, rebuilt several times over the next thousand years and then completely destroyed in the flood of 1644 (when the city leaders opened the dikes on the Yellow River in a disastrous attempt to halt the invading Manchu armies) – the current buildings only date from 1766. Also on the tourist-route is the 11th century **Iron Pagoda** – made of normal bricks but covered in specially coloured tiles to make it look like iron.

### Getting There

Kaifeng lies on the railway line from Zhengzhou to Shanghai. There are regular buses from Zhengzhou (see the Zhengzhou section). There are no flights to Kaifeng and the nearest airport is at Zhengzhou.

Father Nicola Trigault translated and published the diaries of the Jesuit Priest Matteo Ricci in 1615, and based on these diaries he gives an account of a meeting between Ricci and a Jew from Kaifeng whilst Ricci was living in Beijing. The Jew was on his way to Beijing to take part in the Imperial examinations and Trigault writes that 'Being a Jew and having read . . . that our Fathers were not Saracens and that they believed in only one God of heaven and earth, he concluded that we must be believers in, and followers of, the Mosaic Law . . . His whole external appearance, nose, eyes, and all his facial lineaments, were anything but Chinese. Father Ricci took him into the church and showed him a picture above the high altar, a painting of the Blessed Virgin and the child Jesus, with John the Precursor, praying on his knees before them. Being a Jew and believing that we were of the same religious belief, he thought the picture represented Rebecca and her two children, Jacob and Esau and so made a humble curtsey before it . . . each one was mistaken as to what the other had in mind. When he (Ricci) brought the visitor back to the house and began to question him as to his identity, it gradually dawned upon him that he was talking with a believer in the ancient Jewish law. The man admitted that he was an Israelite, but he knew no such word as Jew . . . '

Ricci found out from the visitor that there were ten or twelve families of Israelites in Kaifeng. A 'magnificent' synagogue had been built there and the five books of Moses had been preserved in the synagogue in scroll form over five or six hundred years. The visitor was familiar with the stories of the Old Testament and some of the followers, he said, were expert in the Hebrew language. He also told Ricci that in a province which Trigault refers to as 'Cequian' at the capital of 'Hamcheu' there were a far greater number of Israelite families than at Kaifeng and that there were also others scattered about. Ricci sent one of his Chinese converts to Kaifeng who confirmed the visitor's story.

Today there are still descendants of the original Jews living in Kaifeng, and though they still consider themselves Jewish (or Israelites) the religious beliefs and the customs associated with Judaism appear to have completely died out.

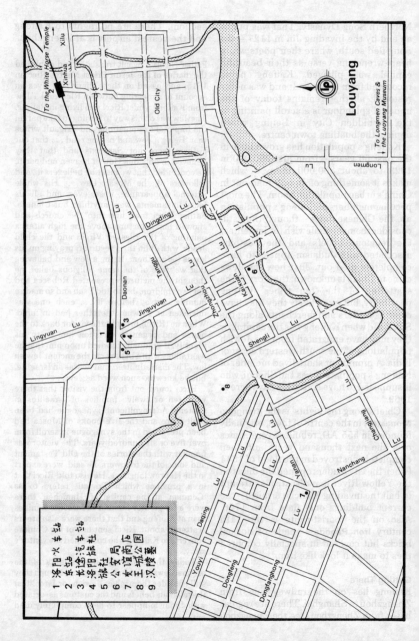

Louyang

Old City

To the White Horse Temple

To Longmen Caves & the Louyang Museum

1 洛阳火车站
2 车站
3 水塔;汽车站
4 洛阳旅社
5 旅社
6 公交谊社
7 友谊局/商场
8 友谊王城公园
9 汉陵墓

## ANYANG

Close to this small town is the site of Yin, the last capital of the ancient Shang Dynasty and one of the first centres of an urban-based Chinese civilisation.

In the last few decades of the 19th century, peasants working near Anyang began unearthing pieces of polished bone which were inscribed with specimens of an ancient form of Chinese writing – these turned out to be divining bones with questions addressed to the spirits and ancestors. Other inscriptions were found on the undershells of tortoises as well as on bronze objects, and these suggested that the last capital of the Shang Dynasty had once stood here. The discoveries attracted the attention of both Chinese and western archaeologists, though it was not until the late 1920s that work began on excavating the site. These excavations uncovered ancient tombs, the ruins of a royal palace, workshops and houses – proof that the legendary Shang Dynasty had indeed existed.

Anyang is in the far north of Henan Province, not far from the border of Hebei Province. It lies on the main Zhengzhou-Beijing railway.

## LUOYANG

Luoyang is one of the richest historical sites to be found in all of China; founded in 1200 BC it was the capital of 10 dynasties before losing its rank in the 10th century AD when the Jin moved their capital to Kaifeng. In the 12th century Luoyang was stormed and sacked by Jurchen invaders from the north and never really recovered from the disaster; for centuries it

remained a squalid little town vegetating on the edge of a vanished capital. By the 1920s it had only 20,000 inhabitants. It took the Communists to shake the lethargy out of the area; they built a new industrial city at Luoyang, similar to Zhengzhou, a vast expanse of wide avenues and endless red-brick and concrete apartment blocks now housing around 900,000 people.

Looking at it today it's hard to imagine that Luoyang was once the centre of Buddhism in China. When the religion was introduced from India this was the site of the Baima (White Horse) Temple, the first Buddhist temple to be constructed in the country and it was here that the first translations into Chinese were made of Indian Sanskrit scriptures. When the city was the imperial capital under the Northern Wei Dynasty there were supposed to be 1300 Buddhist temples operating in the area, and at the same time work was begun on the magnificent Longmen Buddhist Cave Temples outside the city.

### Information & Orientation

Luoyang spreads across the northern bank of the Luo River, most of it a vast but organised urban sprawl. The main railway station is Luoyang West Station which is located in the central-northern area of the city. The city centre gravitates around the main axis of Jinguyyuan Lu which runs roughly south-east from the railway station and is criss-crossed by a couple of major arteries like Zhongzhou Lu. The old city is in the eastern part of Luoyang and some of the old walls can still be seen. The

| | |
|---|---|
| 1 Luoyang West Railway Station | 6 Public Security Office |
| 2 Luoyang East Railway Station | 7 Friendship Guesthouse |
| | 8 Royal Town (Wangcheng) Park (also known as the Working People's Park) |
| 3 Long Distance Bus Station | 9 Han Dynasty Tombs |
| 4 Chinese Hotel | |
| 5 Chinese Hotel | |

various sights and the tourist facilities are scattered around the city or outside it. The tourist hotel is a long bus ride out the western part of town and the Longmen Caves lie to the south of the city.

**CITS** Rumour has it that CITS is somewhere to be found in the Friendship Hotel, and that their office is supposed to be open 8 am to 12 noon and 2 to 5 pm.

**Public Security** (tel 7423) is on Kaixuan Lu, close to the centre of town; it stands opposite a large government building which lies in a compound at the southern terminus of Jinguyuan Lu. They're quite friendly and helpful.

**CAAC** There are no flights to Luoyang. The nearest airport is at Zhengzhou.

**Post** There is a post office in the Friendship Hotel.

**Money** There is an exchange counter in the Friendship Hotel.

**Maps** are hard to come by. You may find someone outside the railway station selling maps with the bus routes on them which are useful although not very detailed. The Friendship Hotel also sells maps, but they're not very helpful. The hotel does have a good bus map up on the wall just inside the main entrance.

## Things to See
The chief attraction of Luoyang are the Longmen caves, but scattered around the city are a number of sights worth checking out.

### White Horse Temple (Baima Si)
One of the most venerable Buddhist shrines in China, the present Ming and Qing buildings are built on the site of the original temple which dates back 2000 years and was the first Buddhist temple to be built in China. In front of the temple are two Song Dynasty stone horses, and to the

east is a 13-storey pagoda built sometime between the 10th and 12th centuries. Legend has it that two Buddhist monks from India, riding a white horse, delivered the Buddhist scriptures to Luoyang – hence the name of the temple.

The temple stands 13 km north-east of the city. To get there take bus No 8 from near the Friendship Hotel to the bus terminus outside the west gate of the Old City, and then take bus No 6 to the end of the line.

### Wangcheng (Royal Town) Park
Wancheng Park on Zhongzhou Lu contains two subterranean tombs dating from the Han Dynasty. Although the coffins have been removed the wall paintings and bas-reliefs on the stone doors still remain.

### Luoyang Museum
The Luoyang Museum was set up in 1958 and is housed in the Guandi Temple. The temple is a 16th century Taoist construction dedicated to the Three Kingdoms hero Guan Yu, who was later canonised as the god of war. The museum is south of the town on Longmen Lu on the way to the caves; bus No 10 will take you there.

### East is Red Tractor Plant
It might be possible to go on a tour of the East is Red Tractor Plant, a model factory which opened in 1959 and provides social services for its workers and families, including a hospital, schools and day-care centres. Enquire at CITS or the Friendship Hotel.

### The Longmen Caves
In 494 AD the Northern Wei Dynasty moved its capital from Datong to Luoyang. At Datong the dynasty had built the impressive Yungang Caves and now at Luoyang they began work on the Longmen Caves. Over the next 200 or so years, more than 100,000 images and statues of Buddha and his disciples were carved into the cliff walls on the banks of the Yi River,

16 km south of the city.

It was an ideal site; as at Datong the rock was hard-textured and took well to being carved. Together with the caves at Dunhuang and Datong, the Luoyang caves are one of the high points of Buddhist cave art. Although there has been some natural erosion at Luoyang since ancient times, most of the damage done to the sculptures has been through western souvenir hunters during the 19th and early 20th centuries who beheaded just about every figure they could lay their saws on. These now grace the museums and private paperweight collections of Europe and North America. Two murals depicting religious processions were cut off the rock face in their entirety and can be found today in the Metropolitan Museum of Art in New York and in the Nelson Gallery of the Atkinson Museum in Kansas City. Oddly enough the caves appear to have been spared the ravages of the Cultural Revolution. Even during the most anarchic year of 1967 the caves were reported to be open, no one was watching over them and anybody could go in and have a look.

In Buddhist art the Buddha is frequently displayed in a basic triad, with a bodhisattva on either side. The latter are Buddhist saints who have arrived at the gateway to nirvana but have chosen to return to earth to guide lesser mortals along righteous paths. Their faces tend to express joy, serenity and compassion. Sometimes the statues of the bodhisattvas are replaced by those of Buddha's first two disciples, the youthful Ananda and the older Kasyapa.

The art of Buddhist cave sculpture largely came to an end around the middle of the 9th century as the Tang Dynasty sunk into the depths. A persecution of foreign religions in China was begun. Buddhism was the Number 1 target. Although Buddhist art and sculpture continued in China it never reached the heights it had enjoyed previously.

The major caves of the Longmen group are on the west bank of the Yi River. They stretch out along the cliff face on a north-south axis. The three **Pingyang Caves** are at the northern end, closest to the entrance. All were begun under the Northern Wei, and though two were finished during the Sui and Tang Dynasties the statues all display the benevolent saccharine expressions which characterised the Northern Wei style. The central Pingyang cave, carved in 500 AD, contains 11 large figures of Buddha and a number of smaller sculptures of Buddha and his disciples.

The **Ten Thousand Buddha Cave** is several minutes walk south of the Pingyang Caves. In addition to the legions of tiny bas-relief Buddhas which give the cave its name, there is a fine big Buddha and noteworthy bas-reliefs of celestial maidens.

**Lotus Flower Cave** was carved in 527 during the Northern Wei and has a large standing Buddha, now faceless. On the ceiling are sinuous, whispery figures drifting around a central lotus flower. The lotus flower is a common symbol in Buddhist art and represents purity and serenity.

The **Fengxiansi Cave** is a misnomer since the roof is gone and the statues lie exposed to the elements. It's the largest structure at Longmen and was built during the Tang Dynasty from 672 to 675. The Tang figures tend to be more three-dimensional than the Northern Wei figures, standing out in high relief and rather freer from their stone backdrop. Their expressions and poses also appear to be more natural, but unlike the other-wordly figures of the Northern Wei the Tang figures are built with a monolithic sense of overpowering awesomeness.

The seated central Buddha statue is 17 metres high and is believed to be Vairocana, the supreme, omnipresent divinity. As you stand facing the Buddha, to the left is a statue of a disciple, followed by a bodhisattva wearing a crown, a tassel and a string of pearls. To the right of the Buddha are the remains of a statue of another disciple, followed by a bodhisattva. The next figure on this side appears to be a divine general, a protector of heavenly order, trampling on a spirit and this is followed by a guardian of the Buddha. Both of these statues are about 10 metres tall.

South of Fengxiansi is the tiny **Medical Prescription Cave** whose entrance is filled with 6th century stone steles inscribed with remedies for common ailments.

Adjacent is the much larger **Guyang Cave**, cut between 495 and 575. It's a narrow high-roofed cave featuring an elongated Buddha statue and a profusion of sculpture, particularly of flying apsaras (apsaras are celestial beings, similar to Christian angels; they're often depicted as musicians or bearers of flowers and incense).

The **Shikusi Cave**, also a Northern Wei construction, is the last major cave and has carvings depicting religious processions.

The best way to get to the caves is on bus No 10 from the stop near the Friendship Hotel. It's a half-hour ride and costs 40 fen. Admission to the caves is 5 fen for Chinese and Y3 for foreigners, a mark-up of 6000%! There's a good view of the Juxiansi Cave from the eastern bank of the river. Also on this side of the river are another group of caves dating from the Tang period, but they're not worth seeing unless you're an enthusiast – plus it's another Y3 entrance fee.

### Places to Stay

The *Friendship Guest House* (tel 21392) is the only place taking foreigners. It's good and also cheap; double rooms are Y12 and if you're on your own they'll readily give you the room for Y6. Dormitory-accommodation is Y5 for a bed in a three-bed room, and apparently they also have six-bed dorms at Y4 each. Most of the rooms and dormitories are air-conditioned.

The hotel is on Dongfanghong Lu in the western part of town. To get there take bus No 2 from Luoyang West Train Station or from the long-distance bus station (the long-distance bus station is opposite this train station). Stay on the bus until you see the enormous Friendship Store on your left and then get off at the next stop. The hotel is about a 15 minute walk further up the road.

The hotel even has its own air-raid shelter. When you walk out of the rear entrance of the ground floor shop over to the dining hall, you'll see a tin platform. The platform rolls back to reveal a long flight of steps down into the shelter, which is a passageway with small rooms attached. It's very cool down here and they use the rooms to store soft drinks.

There are two Chinese hotels directly across the road from the railway station, where you might try staying if you arrive in town late at night. The first hotel is called the *Luoyang Lushe* and the second is a few minutes walk further west and is identifiable by the large red characters on the front of the building.

### Places to Eat

The best place to eat is the restaurant in the *Friendship Hotel* – not the slightest touch of excess oil, a real treat in this country! Western breakfasts are a flat Y3. Lunch and dinner hover around the Y5 or Y6 mark, depending on how much you eat – they give you little plates of fish, vegetables, pork, etc, and it's definitely worth it. Student price for dinners is Y3.50.

There is a restaurant at No 12 Guangzhou Lu, near the Friendship Hotel. Turn right out the front entrance of the hotel, then right again at the first street. The restaurant is on the left-hand side of the street in a grey brick building with green window frames. It's cheerily located next to a store selling funeral wreaths.

There are lots of little food stalls set up outside the West Railway Station at night, with some OK food.

### Getting Away

**Bus** The long-distance bus station is

across the road from Luoyang west Railway Station.

Buses to Dengfeng depart at 6 am, 9 am, 1.30 pm and 2 pm.

There are regular buses to Zhengzhou during the day, about every hour.

There are no buses to Xian or Sanmenxia; you have to take the train.

**Train** Trains run east from Luoyang to Zhengzhou, west to Xian, north to Taiyuan and south to Xiangfan.

In Xiangfan you can change trains and carry on to Yichang on the Yangtse River, which is a stopping point for the Chongqing-Wuhan ferries. If you're heading up to Luoyang from Yichang, be warned Xiangfan may not be an easy railway station to get out of. It seems there are two trains to Luoyang – one to Luoyang East Station and one to Luoyang West – each requiring a different ticket, although the stations are only a few kilometres apart. Hard to believe – but at least one person was stopped from boarding a train in Xiangfan because he had a ticket for one station whereas the train was going to the other – you may have this problem, you may not.

**Plane** The nearest airport is at Zhengzhou.

### Cave dwellings

On the road from Zhengzou to Luoyang you'll see some of China's most interesting cave dwellings. These are not peculiar to Henan Province as over 100 milion people live in caves cut into dry embankments, or in houses where the hill makes up one or more walls and a third of these are in the dry loess plateau.

The floors, walls and ceilings of these cave dwellings are all made of earth – that is, loess, a fine yellowish-brown soil which is soft and thick and makes good building material. The front wall may be made of loess, adobe (a mixture of mud and straw made into bricks and hardened in the sun or fired in kilns), concrete, bricks or wood depending on the availability of materials.

Ceilings are shaped according to the quality of the loess; if the loess is hard then the ceiling may be arched, if not then the ceiling may rise to a point. Besides the doors and windows in the front wall, cave dwellings often have additional vents to let in light and air. There are three main groups of cave dwellings; some communities use both caves and houses, since the former is warmer in winter and cooler in summer, but also tends to be darker and less ventilated than houses. Sometimes a large square pit is dug first and and then caves are dug into the four sides of the pit. A well is dug in the middle of the yard to prevent flooding during heavy rains. Sometimes caves such as those at Yanan are dug into the side of a cliff face.

### SHAOLIN

David Carradine never actually trained here, but at the Shaolin monastery 80 km west of Zhengzou a form of unarmed combat was indeed developed by the Buddhist monks.

Separating myth from history is hard enough in China – Shaolin is no exception. It is said to have been founded by an Indian monk in the 5th century and stories are told of how the fighting monks fought against invaders and led rebellions against foreign rulers. Perhaps as a result they had their monastery burned down several times – the most recent in 1928 when a local warlord had a go, and that was topped off with some more vandalism by the Red Guards.

The Chinese come here in droves – spurred on by a People's Republic movie which actually used the monastery as a set and features innumerable impossible high-flying unarmed gladiators inflicting punches and kicks that would wind an elephant. As a result Shaolin is a booming tourist mecca. Despite the fires and the vandalism many of the monastery buildings still stand, and most impressive is the 'forest of stupas' outside the walls, each built in remembrance of a monk.

The monastery lies on Song Shan, a

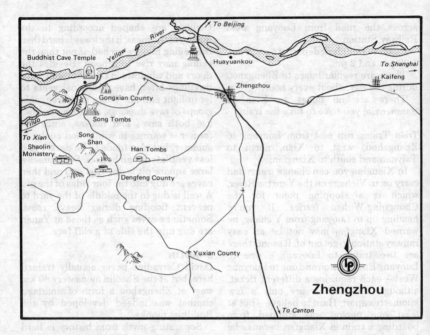

mountain sacred to the Taoists, and close by is the Zhongyue Temple, one of the few Taoist temples in China open to tourists, built in the 9th century.

Shaolin is accessible by bus from Zhengzhou. Tour buses leave from outside the Zhengzhou railway station each morning. You buy your ticket from the small white booth across the road from the railway station directly in front of Zhongyuan Mansions. A round-trip ticket is Y5. Apparently there are similar tours available from Luoyang.

## LINXIAN COUNTY

Linxian County is a rural area which rates with Dazhai and Shaoshan as one of the holy places of Maoism, since this is the location of the famous Red Flag Canal. To irrigate the district a river was rerouted through a tunnel beneath a mountain and then along a new bed built on the side of steep cliffs. The Communists insist that this colossal work, carried out during the Cultural Revolution, was done entirely by the toiling masses without the help of engineers and machines. The statistics are quite impressive; 1500 km of canal was dug, hills levelled, 134 tunnels pierced, 150 aqueducts constructed and enough earth displaced to build a road one metre high, six metres wide and 4000 km long; all supposedly done by hand and a tribute to Mao's vision of a self-reliant China.

Critics have called it an achievement worthy of Qin Shi-huang who pressed millions into building the Great Wall, and that this sort of self-reliance only projected a China in which the peasants and workers would be subjected to endless back-breaking toil; it would have made more sense to put the energy to some productive use and use the profit to buy a pump and lay a pipeline that would bring the water straight over the hill.

Linxian County lies to the west of Anyang in the north-west corner of Henan Province close to the junction of the border with Shanxi and Hebei.

## GONGXIAN COUNTY

Gongxian County lies on the railway line which runs west from Zhengzhou to Luoyang. During the Northern Wei Dynasty a series of Buddhist caves were cut and a temple built on the bank of the Yiluo River. But the main attractions of the area are the great tombs which were built here by the Northern Song emperors.

The county is bounded in the south by Mount Song and in the north by the Huang (Yellow) River; the Yiluo River is a branch of the Yellow River and cuts through the centre of the county.

The **Buddhist Cave Temples** are at the foot of Mt Dali on the northern bank of the Yiluo River. Construction of the caves began in 517 AD and additions were made during the Eastern and Western Wei, Tang and Song Dynasties. There are now 256 shrines containing over 7700 Buddhist figures.

The **Song Tombs** are scattered over an area of about 30 sq km. Seven of the nine Northern Song emperors were buried here; the other two were captured and taken away by the Jin armies who overthrew the Northern Song in the 12th century.

After the vicissitudes of more than 800 years history and repeated wars all that remains of the tombs are the ruined buildings, the burial mounds and and the statues which line the sacred avenues leading up to the ruins. There are 700 or so remaining stone statues, and these have a simple and unsophisticated imposing manner about them.

Some of the earlier statues such as those on the Yongan Tomb and on the Yongchang Tomb utilise very plain lines and are characteristic of the late Tang Dynasty style. The statues of the intermediate period, the Yongding Tomb and the Yongzhao Tomb, are carved more exquisitely with harmonious proportions. Later statues, such as those leading to the Yongyu Tomb and the Yongtai Tomb, tend to be more realistic and lifelike. The statues of humans include civil officials, foreign envoys and military leaders. There are also numerous statues of animals including a *jiaoduan*, a mythical animal which symbolises luck.

## AROUND HENAN PROVINCE

There are several other places officially open to foreigners in Henan Province. Heading south from Zhengzhou, **Xinyang** is on the main Wuhan-Zhengzhou railway line just near the Henan-Hubei border. In the far west of the province, on the railway line from Zhengzhou to Xian, is **Sanmenxia**. **Xinxiang** is a large industrial city on the railway line just north of Zhengzhou. **Yuxian** is about 70 km south-west of Zhengzhou, on the Yinghe River.

# Shaanxi

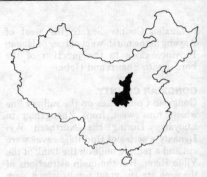

The northern part of Shaanxi is one of the oldest settled regions of China, with the remains of human habitation dating back to prehistoric times. This was the homeland of the Zhou people who eventually conquered the Shang and established their rule over much of northern China. It was also the homeland of the Qin who ruled from their capital of Xianyang near modern-day Xian – the first dynasty to rule over all of eastern China. Shaanxi remained the political heart of China up until the 9th century; the great Sui and Tang capital of Xian was built here from the ground up, and the province was a crossroads on the trading routes from eastern China out to Central Asia. Today, Xian is the highlight of Shaanxi, flooded with reminders of the time when it was the hub of the empire.

With the migration of the imperial court to pastures further east, Shaanxi seemed to become a rather less attractive piece of real estate. Rebellions afflicted the territory from 1340-68, again in 1620-44, and finally in the mid-19th century when the great Moslem rebellion started here leaving maybe 60,000 of the province's original 700,000 or 800,000 Moslems dead. Five million died in the famine of 1876-78 and another three million in the famines of 1915, 1921 and 1928. It was probably the dismal condition of the Shaanxi peasant that gave the Communists such a willing base in the province in the late 1920s and during the ensuing civil war; it was from their base at Yanan that the Communist leaders directed the war against the Kuomintang and later against the Japanese before being forced to evacuate in 1947 in the wake of a Kuomintang attack.

Almost 29 million people live in Shaanxi, mostly in the central and southern regions. The north of the province is a plateau covered with a thick layer of wind-blown loess soil which masks the original landforms. In turn it's been deeply eroded, forming a characteristic landscape of deep ravines and almost vertical cliff faces; the Great Wall in the far north of the province is something of a cultural barrier, beyond which agriculture and human existence was always a precarious venture. Yet like so much of China, this depleted region is rich in natural resources, particularly coal and oil. The Wei River, a branch of the Yellow River, cuts across the centre of the province and it was this fertile belt that became a centre of Chinese civilisation. The south of the province is quite different from the north; it's a comparatively lush mountainous area with a subtropical climate similar to Sichuan or the Yangtse Valley.

## XIAN

Once the focus of China, Xian vied with its contemporaries, Rome and later Constantinople, for the title of greatest city in the world. Over a period of three thousand years Xian has seen the rise and fall of numerous Chinese dynasties, and the archaeological sites that pock mark the city and the surrounding plain are a reminder that once upon a time Xian was a booming cosmopolitan metropolis.

The earliest evidence of human habitation dates back 6000 years to Neolithic times, when the plain was lush and green and primitive Chinese tribes established their

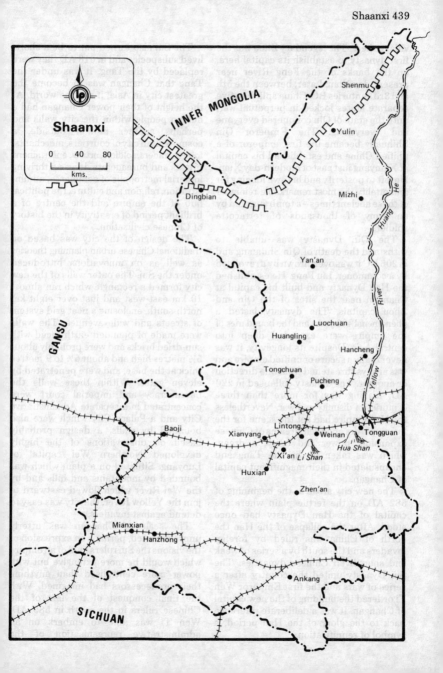

villages here. The legendary Zhou was the first dynasty to establish its capital here, on the banks of the Feng River near present-day Xian. Later, between the 5th and 3rd centuries BC, China split into five separate states locked in perpetual war, until the state of Qin conquered everyone and everything. The Emperor Qin Shihuang became the first emperor of a unified China and established his capital at Xianyang just east of modern-day Xian. He left to posterity and his own longing for immortality the most remarkable reminder of these ancient times – a tomb guarded by an army of thousands of terracotta soldiers.

The Qin Dynasty was unable to withstand the death of Qin Shihuang and in 206 BC it was overthrown by a revolt led by a commoner, Liu Pang. He established the Han Dynasty and built his capital at Changan near the sites of the Qin and Zhou capitals. The dynasty lasted a phenomenal 400 years and the boundaries of the empire were extended deep into central Asia. Despite its longevity, it was never really a secure or unified empire and was always threatened from one direction or another. The dynasty collapsed in 220 AD, making way for more than three centuries of disunity and war. Nevertheless the Han empire had set the scene for the Sui emperors and their dreams of Chinese expansion, power and unity, a dream which was taken up by the Tang and encapsulated in their magnificent capital of Changan.

The new city arose at the beginning of 582 AD on the fertile plain where the capital of the Han Dynasty had once stood. After the collapse of the Han the north of China was ruled by foreign invaders and the south by a series of weak and short-lived Chinese dynasties. The Sui Dynasty united the country after a series of wars and the first Emperor Wen Ti ordered the building of the new capital of Changan. It was a deliberate reference back to the glory of the Han period, a symbol of reunification.

The Sui also turned out to be a short-lived subspecies and in 618 AD they were replaced by the Tang. It was under the Tang that Changan was to become the greatest city in Asia, if not the world. At the height of their power Changan had a million people within the city walls and perhaps another million outside, a cosmopolitan city of courtiers, merchants, foreign traders, soldiers, artists, entertainers, priests and bureaucrats. It was a thriving imperial metropolis of commerce, administration, religion and culture, the political hub of the empire and the centre of a brilliant period of creativity in the history of Chinese civilisation.

The design of the city was based on traditional Chinese urban planning theories as well as on innovations introduced under the Sui. The outer walls of the new city formed a rectangle which ran almost 10 km east-west and just over eight km north-south, enclosing a neat grid system of streets and wide avenues. The walls were made of pounded earth faced with sun-dried bricks and were probably about 5½ metres high and about 5½ to 9 metres thick at the base, and were penetrated by eleven gates. Within these walls the bureaucracy and imperial court were concentrated in a separate Administrative City and a Palace City which were also bounded by walls, a design probably based on observations of the highly developed Northern Wei capital of Luoyang. Situated on a plain which was bounded by mountains and hills and by the Wei River which flowed eastward to join the Yellow River, the city was easy to defend against invaders.

The scale of Changan was utterly unprecedented, perhaps an expression of the visions the Sui rulers held of an empire which would be more extensive but with power more centralised than anything their predecessors had imagined. With the final conquest of the last of the Chinese rulers in the south in 589 AD, Wen Ti was able to embark on an administrative reorganisation of the empire. A nationwide examination system enabled more people from the eastern plains and the increasingly populous southern regions to serve in the government bureaucracy in Changan, thus ensuring that the elite were drawn from all over the country, a system continued and developed by the Tang. Communications between the capital and the rest of China were developed, mainly by the construction or reconstruction of canals which would link Changan to the Grand Canal and to other strategically important parts of the empire – another system also developed and improved by the Tang. Roads were built radiating from the capital, with inns for officials, travellers, merchants and pilgrims. Changan was thus the centre of two communication and transport systems which enabled it to make its power felt and draw in taxes and tribute.

These two communications systems radiated out to the sea ports and to the caravan routes which connected China to the rest of the world, allowing Changan to import the world's ideas and products. The city became a centre of international trade and a large foreign community established itself here. Numerous foreign religions built temples and mosques here including the Moslems, the Zoroastrians of Persia, and the Nestorian Christian sect of Syria. The growth of the government elite and the evolution of a more complex imperial court drew in vast numbers of people to serve it; merchants, clerks, artisans, priests and laborers all came to Changan, and by the 8th century the city had a phenomenal population of two million!

The Tang system of government was to have a profound influence on future dynasties, particularly the Ming who modelled themselves on the Tang and who were scrupulously copied by the Manchus who set up the Qing Dynasty. At the apex of the social order was the emperor and his entourage whose lives were shaped by the triple responsibilities of ceremonial duties, political administration

and the pursuit of pleasure. The Tang emperors had inherited the traditional ideology of kingship and the rituals and roles attached to it; not only was the emperor the Son of Heaven who maintained the balance between the world of men and the forces of nature, he was also the first farmer of a peasant empire, the ceremonial head of a ruling class and the guardian of the state ideology of Confucianism and now the patron and devotee of the popular religions of Buddhism and Taoism. He presided over government policy and state affairs with his ministers and other high officials, honoured officials and foreign dignitaries with audiences and banquets, and in wartime took part in devising strategy and issued orders and commissions to his officers. The unfortunate man was also the prize stud and impregnator of the inmates of his ever well-stocked harem. The day-to-day task of government was handled by the emperor's personal staff, the palace eunuchs and the huge government bureaucracy; religious and ceremonial decrees, imperial appointments, promotions or demotions, amnesty proclamations, dealings with tributary rulers, treaties and judicial decrees were just some of the things that were handled by the elite of the administrative apparatus. But whilst the bureaucratic process occupied much of their time, politics occupied most of their attention; their position depended on the life-span of their superiors, on whether a successor would reverse the policies of the previous administration and sack those connected with it, on who was rising in the emperor's favour. Changan was the place for ambitious administrators to either rise or fall, the centre of position, power and wealth.

The city remained through the second half of the eighth and most of the ninth centuries by far the greatest city in Asia, but towards the end of the eighth century the Tang Dynasty, and consequently its capital, was starting to decline. From 775 onwards the central government was

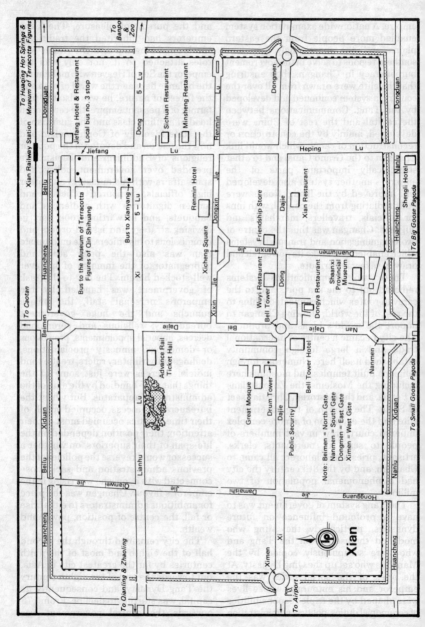

**Xian**

Note: Beimen = North Gate
Nanmen = South Gate
Dongmen = East Gate
Ximen = West Gate

suffering reverses at the hands of provincial warlords and Tibetan and Turkish invaders. The setbacks exposed weaknesses in the empire and though the Tang still maintained overall supremacy they gradually began to lose control of the the transport networks and the tax collection system on which their power as well as the prosperity of Changan depended. Perhaps as an indication of the increasingly dismal state of the dynasty, between 841-5 the government went on a wholesale destruction of Buddhist temples and of temples belonging to other non-Chinese religions. The dynasty finally fell in 907 AD and China once again broke up into a number of independent states. Changan eventually found itself relegated to the role of a regional centre, never to regain its former supremacy.

The modern-day city of Xian stands on the site of Changan. In the 19th century Xian was a rather isolated provincial town, a condition which persisted until the completion of a railway line from Zhengzhou in 1930. After 1949 the Communists started to industrialise the city and it now supports a population of 2½ million people. It's the capital of Shaanxi Province and is something of an example of the government's efforts to create new inland industrial centres to counterbalance the traditional dominance of the large industrial cities on the coast. At first glance the city looks little different from other modern Chinese industrial cities, but scattered about both within and outside the city limits are the reminders of several thousand years of history. Today, Xian is one of the biggest museums in China.

## Information & Orientation

Xian retains the same rectangular shape that characterised Changan, with streets and avenues laid out in a neat grid pattern. The central block of the city is bounded by the old city walls (built during the Ming period on the foundations of the walls of the Tang Forbidden City). Not all of the

wall is intact and some sections have completely disappeared, though they're still shown on the maps.

The centre of town is the enormous Bell Tower, and from here run Xian's four major streets; Bei, Nan, Xi and Dong Dajie. The railway station stands at the north-east edge of the central block and Jiefang Lu runs south from the station to intersect with Dong Dajie. Many of the city's sights, as well as most of the restaurants, tourist hotels and facilities can be found either along or in the vicinity of Jiefang Lu or Xi and Dong Dajie. There's a scattering of sights outside the central block, like the Big Goose and the Small Goose Pagodas. Other sights, like the terracotta soldiers and the remains of the Banpo Neolithic Village can be found on the plain which surrounds Xian.

**CITS** (tel 21190) has its office on the ground floor of the rear building of the Renmin Hotel. The guy here speaks excellent English and also has a wall poster listing all the trains out of Xian together with their departure and arrival times and the cost of tickets (both tourist and local prices). The office is open 8 am to 8 pm.

**Public Security Office** (tel 25121) is a ten minute walk west of the Bell Tower at 138 Xi Dajie. One of the female staff speaks good English and is extremely helpful. The office is open Monday to Saturday 7 to 11.30 am and 2.30 to 6 pm, closed on Sundays.

**CAAC** (tel 41989 or 40281) is said to be at 296 Xishaomen, somewhere to the west of the West Gate of the old city. If you can find the office you're a genius; if you want air tickets go to CITS.

**Bank** There is a money exchange counter in the front building of the Renmin Hotel.

**Post** There is a post office in front of the

main building of the Renmin Hotel and the rear building has an office from which you can make long-distance phone calls.

**Friendship Store** is east of the Bell Tower. The store is on Nanxin Jie just north of the intersection with Dong Dajie. It's open 10 am to 9.30 pm. It's one of the few places I've seen in China selling Kodachrome 35 mm film.

**Maps** Chinese maps with the bus routes are available from hawkers at the railway station, and these were also being sold at the shop on the ground floor of the Bell Tower Hotel. The supply of other maps is probably a bit variable, but you should be able to get large maps in English from the CITS office and the shop in the Renmin Hotel is also worth trying.

## Things to See

Xian is a city of wide dusty avenues and regimented modern housing. The chief attraction is, of course, the tomb of the Emperor Qin Shihuang and his army of terracotta soldiers. Bell Towers, Drum Towers, pagodas and revolutionary history museums can be found in just about every Chinese city; Xian offers an opportunity to see the whole lot in one go.

## The Bell and Drum Towers

The Bell Tower is a huge building at the very centre of Xian. The original tower was built in the late 14th century, but was rebuilt at the present location in 1739 during the Qing Dynasty. There used to be a large iron bell hung in the tower for marking the time each day, and hence the name. It's usually possible to go to the top of the tower. The Drum Tower is a smaller building which stands to the west of the Bell Tower and marks the Moslem quarter of Xian.

## The City Walls

Xian is one of the few old cities in China where the original city walls are still visible. The walls were built on the foundations of the walls of the Tang Forbidden City during the reign of the Emperor Hong Wu, first emperor of the Ming Dynasty. The wall forms a rectangle with a circumference of 14 km. On each side of the wall is a gateway, and over each stands a series of three towers. At each of the four corners stands a watch-tower and the top of the wall is punctuated with defence towers. The wall is 12 metres high, with a width at the top of 12-14 metres and 15-18 metres at the base. It was originally covered in grey brick although a lot of this has been removed and in parts only the earthen rampart remains. Some sections of the wall have completely disappeared.

## Big Goose Pagoda

Located in the south of Xian, this pagoda stands in what was formerly the Temple of Great Maternal Grace. The temple was built around about 648 AD by the Emperor Gao Zong (the third emperor of the Tang Dynasty) when he was still Crown Prince, in memory of his deceased mother. The buildings that stand today only date from the Qing dynasty and were built in a Ming style.

The original pagoda was built in 652 AD and only had five storeys, but has been renovated, restored and added to many times. It was built to house the Buddhist scriptures brought back from India by the travelling monk Xuan Zang, who then set about translating them into 1335 Chinese volumes. It's an impressive, fortress-like wood and brick building which rises 64 metres up out of the surrounding wheat fields. You can climb to the top for a view of the surrounding countryside and the city.

The pagoda is at the end of Yanta Lu at the southern edge of Xian. Take bus No 5 down Jiefang Lu to the end of Yanta Lu and get off when it turns right into Xiaozhai Donglu. The entrance to the compound is on the southern side of the pagoda. On the western side of the pagoda compound is a former air-raid shelter which is now used as an amusement centre with video games and made-in-China (Taiwan?) one-armed bandits!

### The Little Goose Pagoda

The Little Goose Pagoda is situated in the grounds of the Jianfu Temple. The top of the pagoda was shaken off by an earthquake in the middle of the 16th century but the rest of the structure, 43 metres high, is intact. The Jianfu Temple was built in 684 AD as a site to hold prayers to bless the after-life of the late Emperor Gao Zong. The pagoda, a rather delicate building of 15 tiers, was built in 707-709 AD and also housed Buddhist scriptures brought back by another pilgrim to India. You can get to the pagoda on bus No 3; it runs from the railway station through the south gate of the old city and down Nanguan Zhengjie. The pagoda stands on Youyi Xilu just west of the intersection with Nanguan Zhengjie. It's open daily from 7.30 am to 6.30 pm.

### The Great Mosque

This is one of the largest Islamic mosques in China. Just when it was built is debatable; the present buildings may only date back to the middle of the 18th century, though the mosque might have been established several hundred years earlier. The mosque is built in a Chinese architectural style and most of the grounds are taken up with gardens. It's still an active place of worship and several prayer services are held each day. You may not be allowed in during these times, otherwise the mosque is open to all. It stands to the north-west of the Drum Tower. To get to the mosque, walk west along Xi Dajie and turn right at the Drum Tower. Go through the tunnel that passes under the tower; at the second street on your left you'll see a small sign in both English and Chinese pointing the direction to the mosque which is down a small side-street five minutes walk away. This is the large Moslem quarter of Xian where the narrow streets are lined by old mud-brick houses. While you're in the mosque check out the toilet – it's a large wooden seat complete with armrests and a bowl complemented by a roll-back cover!

### The Shaanxi Provincial Museum

Once the Temple of Confucius, the museum houses a large collection of relics from the Zhou, Qin, Han, Sui and Tang Dynasties, including a collection of rare relics unearthed in Shaanxi Province.

One of the more extraordinary exhibits is the Forest of Steles, the name given to the collection of the heaviest books in the world. The earliest of these 2300 large engraved stone tablets dates as far back as the Han Dynasty and the collection spans a 2000 year period.

Most interesting is the 'Popular Stele of Daiqin Nestorianism'. It's inscribed in both Chinese and Syrian and stands just to the left of the entrance of the hall containing the collection of tablets; it's recognisable by the small cross which is inscribed at the top. The Nestorians were a Syrian Christian sect whose disciples spread eastwards to China via the Silk Road; Marco Polo mentions making contact with members of the sect in Fuzhou in the 13th century. The tablet in the Xian museum was engraved in 781 AD to mark the opening of a Nestorian church. It describes how a Syrian named Raban came to the Imperial court of Xian in 635 and presented Christian scriptures which were translated and then read by the emperor. The emperor, says the stone, was impressed and ordered that a monastery dedicated to the new religion be established in the city. The Nestorians believed that Jesus was actually two people, one divine and one human, as opposed to the orthodox Christian view which regards him as one person who takes the three forms of the father, son and holy spirit.

Other tablets in the museum include the 'Ming De Shou Ji Stele' which records the peasant uprising led by Li Zhicheng against the Ming and the 'Stone Classics of Kaichen' which are 114 tablets made during the Tang Dynasty inscribed with 13 ancient classics and historical records.

The 'rare relics' exhibition is in another building. There's an interesting collection of artefacts including a tasteful gold-plated bronze horse of the Western Han Dynasty. Another interesting exhibit is a tiger-shaped tally from the Warring States Period, inscribed with ancient Chinese characters and probably used to convey messages or orders from one military commander to another.

The museum is open 8 am to 5.30 pm. It's 10 fen to get into the museum but an additional Y3 (or Y1 if you convince them you're a student) for the 'rare relics' section. The rare relics section has captions in English; the other sections have the odd English caption but they're mostly in Chinese. The entrance to the museum is on a side street which runs off Baishulin Lu, close to the South Gate of the old city wall.

## Banpo – the Neolithic Village

The ruins of this 6000 year-old village represent the earliest signs of human habitation around Xian. The village was discovered in 1953 and is situated on the eastern bank of the Chan River in a suburb of Xian. A large hall has been built over what was part of the residential area of the village.

The earliest known agricultural villages in China have been uncovered North of the Qinling Mountains near the eastward bend of the Yellow River where it is joined by the Fen and the Wei Rivers. Since the first example to be found was near Yangshao Village, the term 'Yangshao Culture' has been used as a type name. The oldest Yangshao-type village is that of Banpo, and it appears to have been occupied from 4500 BC until around 3750 BC. Pottery found south of the Qinling mountains has suggested that even earlier agricultural villages may have existed there, but this is only speculation at present.

The Banpo ruins are divided into three areas: a residential area, a pottery-manufacturing area and a cemetery. These include the remains of 45 houses or other buildings, over 200 storage cellars, six pottery kilns and 250 graves (including 73 for dead children who were buried in earthen jars).

The earlier houses are half underground, in contrast to the later houses which were built using a wooden framework and stand on ground level. Some huts are round, others square, with doors facing south in both cases. There is a hearth or fire-pit in each house. The main building materials were wood for the framework and mud mixed with straw for the walls.

The residential part of the village is surrounded by a man-made moat, 300 metres long and about two metres deep and two metres wide, protecting the village from attacks from wild animals and from the effects of heavy rainfall in what was originally a hot and humid enviroment. Another trench, about two metres deep, runs through the middle of the village. To the east of the residential area is the pottery kiln centre. To the north of the village lies the cemetery where the adult dead were buried along with funerary objects like earthen pots. The children were buried in earthen pots close to the houses.

The villagers lived by hunting, fishing and gathering, but had also started farming the surrounding land and kept domestic animals. The tools and utensils used by the villagers were made of stone and bone and included stone axes, chisels, knives, shovels, hewing instruments, millstones, arrowheads, and fishing-net sinkers. The bone objects included needles and fish hooks. Earthenware pots, bowls, basins and jars were used for the storage of food and water, cooking, or storing utensils. There was even a simple earthen vessel for steam cooking. The materials vary from fine clay to clay mixed with fine or coarse sand. Much of the pottery is coloured and illustrated with geometric patterns as well as a few zoomorphic figures like fish with gaping mouths or galloping deer. Personal ornaments like hairpins, beads, rings, earrings and other artefacts are made of bone, stone, animal tooth or shell and there's even a carved pottery whistle. Some of the pottery vessels have symbols carved on their outside edges -these consist of simple strokes, but in regular shapes and appear to be some primitive form of writing.

There's a museum at the site which displays the artefacts excavated from the village and there's a book on sale here entitled *Neolithic Site at Banpo Near Xian* which describes the objects on view. The site is open daily 8.30 to 11.30 am and 2 to 5 pm. Admission is 20 fen. To get there take bus No 8 from the stop on Dong Dajie immediately to the east of the Bell Tower. This bus stops short of the village; about five minutes walk further up the road is the stop for trolleybus No 5 and this will take you the last stretch to the village. Alternatively, take trolleybus No 5 from the stop on Bei Dajie just north of the Bell Tower. This bus heads out of Xian via the gate on Dong 5-Lu and goes past the village. There are also tours to Banpo– see the section on 'Getting Around' for details.

**Huaqing Pool**

At the foot of Li Shan, 30 km from Xian, is the Huaqing Pool, where water from hot springs is funnelled into public bath-houses where 60 pools can accommodate 4000 people. At the summit of the mountain are beacon towers built for defence during the Han Dynasty, and there is a temple on the mountain dedicated to the 'Old Mother' Nu Wa who created the human race and even patched up cracks in the sky after a catastrophe.

Li Shan is hardly worth the effort of going there but one person who did probably regretted it. 12 December 1936 was not a happy day for Chiang Kai-shek; he was arrested here by his own generals,

supposedly clad only in his pyjamas and dressing gown on the slopes of the snow-covered mountain up which he had fled. A pavilion marks the spot and there's a simple inscription 'Chiang was caught here'.

In the early 1930s General Yang Huzheng was the undisputed monarch of those parts of Shaanxi which were not under Communist control. In 1935 he had been forced to divide his power in the north-west when General Zhang Xueliang arrived with his North-Eastern troops from Manchuria, and assumed the office of 'Vice-Commander of the National Bandit Suppression Commission'.

In October and November 1935 Chiang's army had suffered severe defeats at the hands of the Communists and thousands of soldiers had gone over to the Reds. Captured officers had been given a period of 'anti-Japanese tutelage' and were then released. Returning to Xian they brought back to Zhang reports of the Red Army's sincere desire to stop the civil war and unite to oppose the Japanese, a policy which appealed to the Manchurians whose homeland was now occupied by the invader. But Chiang Kai-shek had stubbornly refused to turn his forces against the Japanese and continued his war against the Communists. On 7 December 1936 he flew into Xian to oversee yet another of his 'extermination' campaigns against the Reds. But Chiang now had too many enemies within his own troops.

Zhang Xueliang had actually flown to Yanan, met Zhou Enlai and had become convinced of the sincerity of the Red's anti-Japanese policies and a secret truce was established. On the night of 11 December, Zhang met the divisional commanders of his Manchurian army and the army of General Yang, and a decision was made to arrest Chiang Kai-shek. The mutiny of 170,000 troops had become a fact. The following night the commander of the bodyguard led the attack on Chiang Kai-shek's residence at the foot of Li

Shan, and took Chiang prisoner. Most of Chiang's General Staff were taken prisoner at the residence, and in the city the 1500 'Blueshirts' – the police force controlled by Chiang's nephew, which was credited with numerous abductions, killings and imprisonments of Chiang's opponents – had been disarmed and arrested, as had the local police force.

A few days later, Zhang sent his plane to collect three representatives of the Red Army and bring them to Xian: Zhou En-lai, vice-chairman of the military council; Ye Jianying, commander of the eastern front army; and Bo Gu, chairman of the north-west branch of the Communist government. Chiang Kai-shek had feared he was going to be given a trial and executed, but instead the Communists and the Manchurian leaders told him what they thought of his policies and the changes they thought were necessary to save the country. Whatever Chiang did or did not promise to do, the practical result of the 'Xian Incident' was the end of the civil war. It's probable that the government of the Soviet Union had influenced the decision of the Reds and the Manchurians to restore Chiang Kai-shek to power as quickly as possible. The Russians may have feared that without Chiang the country would continue a protracted civil war and the Japanese might work out an alliance with the Kuomintang regime which would turn China into a potential belligerent against the Soviet Union.

Zhang released Chiang Kai-shek on Christmas Day and flew back with him to Nanjing to await punishment! It was a face-saving gesture for Chiang. Zhang was sentenced to ten years imprisonment and 'deprivation of civil rights for five years' and was pardoned the next day. But the extermination campaign aginst the Reds was called off and the Kuomintang announced that their first task now was to recover the territory lost to Japan, whereas before it had been 'internal pacification' – the elimination of the Communists.

Nevertheless, Chiang began organising what he hoped would be a quiet decimation of the Communist forces. By June 1937 the negotiations with the Communists had reached a stalemate. But by then Chiang had moved the sympathetic Manchurian army out of Shaanxi and replaced it with loyal Kuomintang troops, and he now planned to disperse the Communists by moving the Red Army piece-meal to other parts of the country supposedly in preparation for the war against the Japanese. The Communists were only extricated from their precarious position by Japan's sudden and all-out invasion of China in July 1937; Chiang was forced to leave the Red Army intact and in control of the north-west.

Chiang never forgave Zhang Xueliang and never freed him. Thirty years later he was still held prisoner on Taiwan. As for General Yang he was eventually arrested in Chongqing and towards the end of the Second World War was secretly executed.

There is another reminder of this period in Xian itself. After the Xian Incident the Communist Party set up an office to liaise with the Kuomintang. The office was disbanded in 1946, and after 1949 it was made into a memorial hall to the Eighth Route Army. The hall is on Beixin Lu in the north-eastern part of the central city block.

## The Tomb & Terracotta Warriors of Qin Shihuang

The history of Xian is inextricably linked to the first emperor of a unified Chinese people, Qin Shihuang. In the 3rd century BC China was split into five independent and perpetually warring states. In the year 246 BC, at the age of 13, Ying Zheng ascended to the throne of the state of Qin. One by one the Qin defeated the other states, and by 222 BC all had fallen to the Qin armies.

With the country now united the emperor moved to break the power of the aristocratic families of the other states.

These families were forced to move either to the Qin capital at Xianyang near present-day Xian or to the isolated border regions. Their control of land was broken by apportioning it to private owners who could buy and sell it, but heavy taxation ruined the poorer farmers enabling the land to be bought up by rich farmers, merchants and officials. This generated a landlord class based on the private ownership of land rather than on aristocratic inheritance and a serf population, as during the Zhou Dynasty. Landless peasants became labourers or were drafted into the work gangs which the emperor used to build his fortifications and his monuments.

Centralised control was assisted by the destruction of fortifications of the other states, by the building of roads from the capital to other parts of the empire and by the introduction of a national currency and writing system. To hold out the troublesome nomadic tribes to the north, and to occupy the unemployed armies and the vast numbers of prisoners and criminals convicted under Qin law, the emperor ordered the building of the Great Wall, an enormous defensive wall which linked smaller walls which had already been built.

To silence the critics of the new regime the emperor embarked on his own 'Cultural Revolution' and ordered all books other than those on subjects like medicine and agriculture to be burned. All histories and writings other than the official Qin histories were destroyed, including works by Confucius, many of which are only known today because they were written from memory once the Qin Dynasty fell. He is even said to have had Confucian scholars put to death along with the makers of immortality pills (often Taoists) whose ineffective alchemy had displeased him – another act aimed at terrorising members of the aristocracy who opposed his rule. The emperor is said to have become secretive and suspicious in his last days, fearing assassination and

searching for an elixir of immortality. His tyrannical rule lasted until his death in 210 BC and his son lasted just four more years until the Dynasty was overthrown by the revolt which established the Han Dynasty.

### The Tomb of Qin Shihuang

When Qin Shihuang ascended the throne of Qin, construction of his final resting place began immediately. But when the emperor had conquered the other states construction was expanded on an unprecedented scale and continued for 36 of the 37 years of his reign. Today the tomb of the Emperor is *the* reason to come to Xian.

The tomb itself is covered by a huge mound of earth and is situated 1 km north of Mt Lishan. The tomb has not been excavated and there is no clear knowledge as to what is inside. But the *Historical Records* of Sima Qian, a famous historian of the 2nd century BC, relate that the tomb contains palaces and pavilions filled with rare gems and other treasures and equipped with crossbows which could shoot automatically at intruders. The ceiling was inlaid with pearls to simulate the sun, the stars and the moon; gold and silver cast in the form of wild geese and ducks were arranged on the floor, and precious stones were carved into pines. The walls of the tomb are said to be lined with plates of bronze to keep out underground water. Mercury was pumped in to create images of flowing rivers and the surging oceans. At the end of the internment rites, all the artisans who worked inside and all the palace maids who had no children were forced to remain in the underground palace – buried alive so that none of its secrets could be revealed.

As to the size of the entire necropolis, a Ming dynasty author in *Notes about Mount Lishan* states that the sanctuary of the mausoleum has four gates and a circumference of 2½ km, and that the outer wall has a perimeter of six km. Modern surveys of the site show that the necropolis is indeed divided into an inner sanctuary and an outer city, and measurements of the inner and outer walls closely match the figures of the Ming author. The southern part of the complex is marked by a large mound of rammed earth below which the emperor is buried. The mound is 40 metres high and at the bottom measures 485 by 551 metres. It's now planted with low trees and surrounded by fields.

## The Entombed Warriors

Just how far the necropolis actually extends is anyone's guess. In 1974 peasants digging a well about 1500 metres east of the tomb uncovered one of the greatest archaeological sites in the world. They uncovered an underground vault of earth and timber and subsequent excavation revealed thousands of terracotta figures, life-size warriors and their horses all in battle formation – a whole army which would follow its emperor into immortality! In 1976, two other vaults were discovered close to the first one, but each of these was refilled with soil after excavation. The first and largest pit has been covered over with a roof to become a huge archaeological exhibition hall.

The underground vault measures 210 metres east to west and 62 metres from north to south. The bottom of the pit varies from five to seven metres below ground level; walls were built running from east to west at intervals of three metres, forming corridors in between. In these corridors, on floors laid with grey brick, are arrayed the terracotta figures, and pillars and beams support a roof.

Buried in the vault were a total of 6000 terracotta figures of soldiers and horses. The figures all face east and form a rectangular battle array. The vanguard appears to be three rows of 210 crossbow and longbowmen who stand at the easternmost end of the army. Close behind is the main force of armoured soldiers, holding spears, dagger-axes and other long-shaft weapons, and these

soldiers are intermingled with 35 horse-drawn chariots. Every figure differs in facial features and expressions. The figures of the horsemen show them wearing tight-sleeved outer robes, short coats of chain mail and wind-proof caps. The archers are sculptured with their bodies and limbs positioned in strict accordance with an ancient book on the art of war.

Many of the figures originally held real weapons of the day and over 10,000 pieces have been sorted out to date. Bronze swords were worn by the figures representing the generals and other senior officers; surface treatment made the swords resistant to rust and corrosion so that after being buried for more than 2000 years they were still sharp. Arrow-heads were made of a metal alloy containing a high percentage of lead, making them highly lethal.

The second vault, excavated in 1976 but refilled, contains about 1000 figures. The third vault contained only 68 soldiers and one war chariot and appears to be the command post for the soldiers in the other vaults. Presumably the soldiers represent the army which is meant to protect the necropolis. These are probably just a beginning and excavation of the entire complex and of the tomb itself could take decades.

The warriors are located 30 km east of the present city of Xian. You can get there on the bus which leaves from Xi Balu, which is a small street which runs off Jiefang Lu just near the railway station. There are lots of buses here and you'll have to keep asking until you find the right one. Buy your ticket on the bus; it takes you out to a small bus station about a 40 minute drive from Xian (the fare is 80 fen) and from here you must get another bus which will take you the last few km to the warriors (the fare on this last stretch is 20 fen). Admission to the warriors is 20 fen. Alternatively you can go on a tour; see the 'Getting Around' section for details.

It is forbidden to take photos at the site

(partly to prevent damage to the figures from flashes, though they won't even let you take a time-exposure) and if you infringe that rule you can expect to have your film confiscated. A few people have sneaked a few shots (including Michael Buckley who took about two dozen) but I wouldn't advise it unless you start with a blank roll of film ... and if you do get caught try and remember that the attendants are just doing their job.

## Places to Stay

Although Xian's hotel accommodation is rather less than fabulous, it's worth remembering that this is a tourist city and possibilities for entertainment are relatively great; while I was in Xian I saw a stunning rendition of Chinese music and singing in a show staged for an audience of mainly western tourists. You can find out what's happening around town by watching the notices in the tourist hotels or asking CITS.

The *Renmin Hotel* (tel 25111) is one of the big tourist hotels, a palace-like structure opened for business in 1953. There are two-room 'suites' here with four beds apiece and shared bathroom. You can pay for just one bed, which is Y10. Despite the word 'suite' don't expect anything luxurious; the place is entering the first stages of decay and the rooms are basic, but there's a certain character to this immense concrete block and its dim, cold interiors. There's a bar on the 3rd floor of the front building (open at night) and another on the roof of the rear building, but the former is the meeting place. To get to the hotel take bus No 3 (*not* trolleybus No 3) from the railway station; it goes straight down Jiefang Lu and turns right into Dong Dajie. You get off at the first stop on Dong Dajie and the hotel is a five minute walk up ahead. The hotel is notable for its two decaying signs at the front with their quotations from Chairman Mao slowly turning into rubble.

The *Bell Tower Hotel* is diagonally opposite the Bell Tower in the centre of town. Y30 for a double, Y19 a single. Student price is Y18 and Y10.80 respectively. The place resembles a large compartmentalised aircraft hangar. Take bus No 3 from the railway station and get off at the Bell Tower.

The *Jiefang Hotel* is the large red brick building on Jiefang Lu, diagonally across the road from the railway station. Doubles are Y12. If you're on your own they'll let you pay Y6 for just one bed, but the staff have been known to try and charge Y8, or even to make individuals pay Y12. It probably rates as one of the most unpleasant hotels in China, mainly because of the staff who seem to loathe foreigners and go out of their way to be unfriendly. One or two people have described them as 'bastards' and there's been the odd story of theft from the rooms. It's also been described as 'absolutely abominable'. You're better off going to the Renmin.

*Shengli Hotel* (tel 23184) may or may not let you stay, though some people have done so for Y6 for a dormitory bed. It's a rather inconveniently located hotel and lies just outside the city walls south of Heping Gate. A bus No 5 from the railway station will take you there.

## Places to Eat

There *are* a few good places to eat in Xian. The main problem is that many of the restaurants are gifted with that foul and repugnant odour that afflicts many northern Chinese eating establishments.

The *Xian Restaurant* (tel 22037) is definitely the place to eat in the city; four levels in a huge grey building, with excellent food and the place doesn't smell. The original Xian Restaurant was located elsewhere and was an establishment dating back 50 years. The modern restaurant is on Dong Dajie near the corner with Juhuayuan Lu.

The *Wuji Restaurant* (tel 23824) is on Dong Dajie, near the corner with Nanxin Jie and next to the Foreign Languages

Bookstore. Eat in the the large hall at the back, not in the front.

If you want to escape the hordes then try the *Dongya (East Asia) Restaurant*. This used to be an established hotel/restaurant in Shanghai, founded in 1916 but moved to Xian in 1956. The top floor looks like it's reserved for tourists and it might only serve groups, not individuals. The food is supposed to be very good and they even have a souvenir shop here. The restaurant is south-east of the Bell Tower, on Luoma Shi which is a small street which runs off Dong Dajie.

The *Jiefang Fandian* is the restaurant in the Jiefang Hotel; it's nothing special, but the food is simple and cheap (rice and meat and bamboo shoots for 80 fen) and the place doesn't smell.

The *Sichuan Cuisine Restaurant* on Jiefang Lu is a bit grotty and also smells so give it a miss. The *Heiping Restaurant* at the corner of Jiefang and Dong Daijie is small, crowded and odorous. The *Misheng Restaurant* on Jiefang Lu has better food than the Jiefang Restaurant and is not as odorous as the Sichuan Restaurant.

## Getting Around

Transport around the city is almost entirely by bus. Taxis can be hired from the tourist hotels. There are local buses out to the major sights around the city such as Banpo Village and the terracotta warriors. To get to some of the more distant sites you may have to take a tour bus.

There are daily bus tours which take you to the Neolithic village, the entombed warriors and the Huaqing Hot Springs. Buses leave from the Bell Tower Hotel at 7.15 am each morning, returning at 4 pm and all-inclusive tickets are Y6 from the Bell Tower Hotel or Y5 from the Jiefang Hotel. There is a small booth outside the Bell Tower Hotel where you can buy tickets for bus tours to the tomb of Prince Zhanghuai and the tomb of Princess Yongtai – the Jiefang Hotel might also sell tickets for this tour.

## Getting Away

Train and plane are the usual means of leaving Xian. Centrally located and a major tourist city it's a convenient jumping off point for any number of destinations.

**Train** There are direct trains from Xian to Urumqi, Beijing, Shanghai, Chengdu, Taiyuan, Hefei, Qingdao and Wuhan. For Datong change at Taiyuan; for Chongqing change at Chengdu; for Guilin change at Wuhan; for Canton change at Wuhan; for Kunming change at Chengdu. A lot of people are taking the train straight through from Xian to Urumqi – a 2½ day trip – and then working their way back down the railway line.

If you're buying tickets more than one day in advance before departure, you have to go to the booking office on Lianhu Lu. This booking office is open 7 to 11.30 am,

**Distance by Rail (km)**

| | Bei | Jin | Qing | Hef | Shan | Zhe | Wuha | Cant | Xia | Chen |
|---|---|---|---|---|---|---|---|---|---|---|
| Beijing | | | | | | | | | | |
| Jinan | 494 | | | | | | | | | |
| Qingdao | 877 | 393 | | | | | | | | |
| Hefei | 1107 | 613 | 1006 | | | | | | | |
| Shanghai | 1462 | 968 | 1361 | 617 | | | | | | |
| Zhengzhou | 695 | 666 | 1059 | 645 | 1000 | | | | | |
| Wuhan | 1229 | 1200 | 1593 | 1179 | 1545 | 534 | | | | |
| Canton | 2313 | 2284 | 2677 | 2263 | 1811 | 1618 | 1084 | | | |
| Xian | 1165 | 1177 | 1570 | 1156 | 1511 | 511 | 1045 | 2129 | | |
| Chengdu | 2048 | 2019 | 2412 | 1998 | 2353 | 1353 | 1887 | 2544 | 842 | |
| Taiyuan | 514 | 529 | 922 | 1142 | 1497 | 643 | 1177 | 2261 | 651 | 1493 |

12.30 to 2 pm, 2.30 to 8 pm. Tickets for same-day or day-after departure can be bought from the railway station.

Distances by rail (in km) from Xian to destinations around China are shown below. This distance table can be used with the price table in the Getting Around section of this book to calculate the approximate cost of train tickets. For destinations in the north-west, there is an additional table in the Getting Around section.

**Plane** Xian is connected by air to; Ankang in southern Shaanxi (Y29), Beijing (Y132), Canton (Y221), Changsha (Y221), Chengdu, (Y145), Chongqing (Y81), Golmud (Y190), Hanzhong in southern Shaanxi (Y46), Hefei (Y125), Kunming (Y149), Lanzhou (Y63), Lhasa (Y390), Nanjing (Y128), Shanghai (Y164), Shenyang (Y212), Taiyuan (Y69), Urumqi (Y289), Xining (Y87), Yanan (Y39), Yinchuan (Y97), Yulin in northern Shanxi (Y66), Zhengzhou (Y56).

## AROUND XIAN
### Xianyang

This is a dusty little town a half-hour's bus ride from Xian. The chief attraction of Xianyang is the museum which houses a remarkable collection of 3000 minature terracotta soldiers and horses, discovered in 1965. Each figure is about half a metre high. They date back about 1000 years but their origin is unknown.

To get to Xianyang from Xian, take bus No 59 from the corner of Xi 5-Lu and Shangde Lu, just west of Jiefang Lu. The fare is 70 fen. Get off at the final stop in Xianyang. Up ahead on the left-hand side of the road you'll see a clocktower. Turn right at this intersection and then turn left at Xining Jie. The museum is on Zhongshan Jie which is a continuation of Xining Jie. The museum appears to have

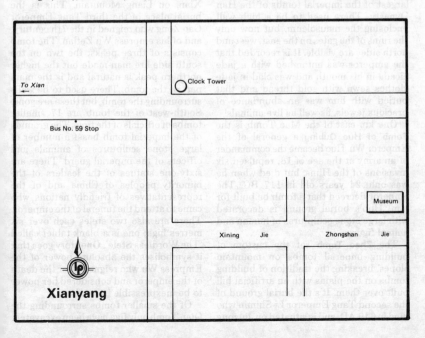

been a monastery or a temple and the entrance is flanked by two stone lions; it's about a 20 minute walk from the bus stop.

## The Imperial Tombs

Apart from the tomb of Qin Shihuang, there are a large number of other imperial tombs which dot the Guanzhong Plain surrounding Xian. In these tombs are buried the emperors of numerous dynasties, as well as their empresses, concubines, government officials and high-ranking military leaders. Construction of an emperor's tomb would often begin within a few years of him assuming the throne, and often would not finish until he died.

The **Mao Tomb** is 40 km from Xian to the west of Xianyang. It's the resting place of the Emperor Wu, the most powerful ruler of the Han Dynasty who died in 87 BC. It's a cone-shaped mound of rammed dirt almost 47 metres high and is the largest of the imperial tombs of the Han Dynasty. There used to be a high wall enclosing the mausoleum, but now only the ruins of the gates on the east, west and north sides are visible. It is recorded that the emperor was entombed with a jade cicada in his mouth and was clad in jade clothes sewn with gold thread and that buried with him was an abundance of precious jewels, as well as live animals!

One km east of the Mao Tomb is the **Tomb of Huo Qubing** a general of the Emperor Wu. Huo became the commander of an army at the age of 18, repulsed six invasions of the Huns, but died when he was onlu 24 years old in 117 BC. The emperor decreed that a tomb be built for him. Huo's burial ground is decorated with large stone sculptures of human and animal figures.

The **Zhao Tomb** set the custom of building imperial tombs on mountain slopes, breaking the tradition of building tombs on the plains with an artificial hill built over them. It's the burial ground of the second Tang Emperor Li Shimin who died in 649 AD, and is situated on Jiuzong

Mountain 70 km north-west of Xian. Of the eighteen imperial mausoleums on the Guanzhong Plain, this is probably the most representative. With the mountain at the centre, the tomb fans out to the south-east and south-west in the form of a fan. Within its confines are 167 lesser tombs of the emperor's relatives as well as high-ranking military and government officials. Burying other people in the same park as the emperor's mausoleum was a custom dating back to the Han Dynasty. Li Shimin used it to win support and loyalty from his ministers and officials by bestowing on them the great favour of being buried in attendance of the son of Heaven. Buried in the sacrificial altar of Li's tomb were six statues known as the 'Six Steeds of Zhao Ling', representing the horses which Li Shimin used during his wars of conquest; four of the statues are now in the Shaanxi Museum.

The **Qian Tomb** is 85 km north-west of Xian, on Liang Mountain. This is the burial place of the third Tang Emperor Gao Zong who reigned in the 7th century, and of his empress Wu Zetian. The tomb consists of three peaks; the two on the south side are man-made but the higher northern peak is natural and is the main part of the tomb. There used to be walls surrounding the tomb, but these are gone. South-west of the tomb are 17 smaller tombs of officials of the time. The grounds of the imperial tomb boast a number of large stone sculptures of animals and officers of the imperial guard. There are sixty-one statues of the leaders of the minority peoples of China and of the representatives of friendly nations who came to attend the funeral of the emperor. There are also two steles each over six metres high; one is a blank tablet called 'The Wordless Stele'. One story goes that it symbolises the absolute power of the Empress Wu who reigned after the death of the emperor and considered her power to be inexpressible in words.

Of the smaller tombs surrounding the Qian Tomb only five have been excavated.

The **Tomb of Prince Zhanghuai** and the **Tomb of Princess Yongtai** are adorned with well-preserved frescoes.

## Ancient Ruins

Scattered around the plain are the ruins of several ancient cities and palaces.

The site of the Zhou capital of Feng-Hao has not been found, although concentrations of settlements from that period have been found on the banks of the Feng River.

The ruins of the **Han City Wall** lie about 10 km north-west of the present city of Xian. The walls surrounded the Han capital of Changan, a circumference of 65 km. They stood 12 metres high and were five metres wide at the base and three at the top, and were made entirely of earth rammed so well that it was comparable with the strength of brick walls.

The ruins of two Han Palaces are visible today. The Changle and Weiyang Palaces were built during the reign of Emperor Gao Zu (about 206-195 BC). The ruins of Changle Palace lie in Gelaomen village in the north-western suburbs of Xian. The ruins of Weiyang Palace lie in Ximazhai village. A third Han palace, the Jianzhang, was built by Emperor Wu outside Changan near the Weiyang Palace. When Wang Mang upsurped the Han throne in 9-24 AD, he had several buildings of this enormous palace complex demolished to make way for his ancestral temple.

The ruins of the Anfang Palace built by Qin Shihuang lie between the villages of Zhaojiabu and Dagucun in the western suburbs of present-day Xian. The remains of the rammed earth for the foundations of the palace hall measure 2.5 km from east to west and 1 km from north to south. The palace was so big that it was not even completed when it was destroyed by the armies which overthrew the Qin Dynasty.

The Daming Palace was built by the Tang Emperor Li Shimin in 634 AD as a summer residence for his father who had abdicated the throne. The palace lay to the north-east of Changan, and later Tang emperors moved their court here from the old Taiji Palace. The main throne hall of the Daming Palace was called Hanyuandian and its ruins lie in today's Hanyuandian Village. All that remains of the palace are the foundations of the walls, the bases of the pillars and the ruins of the gates.

## Temples

Not only was Changan the political and economic centre of China, it was also a religious centre. Except for Taoism, all the religions of China like Buddhism, Nestorianism and Islam have been imported. All of them have left some sort of mark in Xian and the city and the surrounding plain are littered with temples and monasteries. Of the 10 major Buddhist sects which have operated in China, five originated in Xian.

The **Xingjiao (Let Religion Thrive) Temple** lies 20 km to the south-east of Xian. Most of Xuan Zang, the famous monk who brought back the Buddhist scriptures from India and who died in 664 AD, is buried here. Other bits and pieces of him have ended up in various other temples around China.

The **Caotang Temple (Temple of the Thatched Cottage)** lies 50 km south-west of Xian and was built in the middle of the 9th century to house the relics of the Indian monk Kumarajiva. He came to Changan in the 5th century to teach Buddhism and presided over a large-scale translation of Buddhist texts until his death in 413 AD. The original buildings were burnt down during the wars at the end of the Tang Dynasty and the present buildings are comparatively modern. Another temple, the **Daxingshan Temple** was built just south of Changan in the 3rd century. During the 6th century and the 8th century, Buddhist monks from India lived here while they translated their scriptures into Chinese.

The **Xianji Temple** lies 17 km southwest of Xian. Originally built in the 8th century, the present buildings only date to the Qing Dyansty. This temple was the birthplace of the Jingtu or 'Pure Land' sect of Buddhism, now popular in Japan.

The **Huayuan Temple** is the birthplace of the Huayuan Sect of Buddhism, and was built in the 7th century. All that remains of the temple are two dagobas. The larger dagoba is dedicated to the monk Du Shun, the founder of the sect. The other is dedicated to its fourth patriarch Chengguan, who is said to have died at the age of 100 in 838 AD. The remains of the temple lie south of Xian.

### Morning Exertions

Apart from the historical relics, it's worth noting that Xian could very well be the tai chi centre of China, that is if the number of practitioners on the streets is any indication. A ten minute walk west of the Renmin Hotel is Xinchang Square where you can see individual and mass-choreographed exercises every morning and evening. There's even one old man who looks like he just dropped out of an episode of *Kung Fu* teaching martial arts to his young students, watched by an audience of fascinated Chinese and stray westerners. It's fairly debatable whether most people are getting any value from their exertions, but that doesn't stop the old women swinging on tree branches or rotating their torsos and twisting their necks, and so far the the elderly joggers who jog at a deathly slow pace haven't dropped yet. Perhaps the benefits are more a state of mind?

### HUANGLING

Mid-way between Xian and Yanan is the town of Huangling, and the tomb on nearby Mount Qiaoshan is said to be that of the Yellow Emperor Huang Di. Huang is said to be the father of the Chinese people – one of the 'Five Sovereigns'; and to have reigned about 5000 years ago; and by wars of conquest to have unified the Chinese clans. He is credited with numerous inventions and discoveries; the cultivation of silkworms, weaving, writing, the cart and the boat, the compass,

building bricks and musical instruments. You can overnight in this town if you're taking the bus up from Xian to Yanan.

### HUA SHAN

Hua Shan (Flower Mountain) is one of the sacred mountains of China, 2200 metres high, 120 km east of Xian.

The mountain is just south of the Xian-Luoyang railway line and the nearest train station is Huayin. At present the mountain is not open to foreigners, but one guy dumped his bags at the left-luggage room in the railway station and climbed to the top of the mountain, no questions asked.

There is only one route to the top, a north-south path about 15 km long. There is a hotel near the railway station in Huayin and another on the mountain summit.

### YANAN

This town is 270 km from Xian in the far north of Shaanxi Province. Although just a small market town of 30,000 people, it vies with Mao's birthplace at Shaoshan as the No 1 Communist pilgrimage spot. Between the years 1936 to 1947 this was the headquarters of the Chinese Communists. The 'Long March' from Jiangxi had ended in 1936 when the Communists reached the northern Shaanxi town of Wuqi; the following year they moved their base to Yanan.

The town lies on the Yan River, which cuts a deep path between the surrounding hills. There are numerous caves here which the Communists built and the main sights are those caves in which the Chinese leaders lived . and worked. Dominating the area is the Baota (Precious Pagoda) built during the Song Dynasty.

Yanan is connected by bus from Xian. There are also flights from Taiyuan (Y42), Beijing (Y111), and Xian (Y39).

### Footnote

When the Manchus invaded China in

1644, they not only conquered what their predecessors had acquired but set about expanding that territory. It was in the north-west that the Manchus met their strongest resistance and it was not until the late 1750s that the last resistance was crushed. Eighty per cent of the 600,000 strong Dzungarians, a Mongolian tribe who inhabited the northern part of Xinjiang, were wiped out. The rest were captured or fled to Russia. In the south of Xinjiang the final resistance amongst the Moslem Uygurs finally collapsed when the Chinese captured Yarkand and Kashgar in 1759.

The near-total destruction of the Dzungarians had left northern Xinjiang open. Towards the end of the 18th century the Han Chinese and the Dungans (Chinese Moslems) from Gansu and Shaanxi were encouraged to migrate to the depopulated areas; Uygurs from southern Xinjiang were also moved in.

The Uygurs are believed to have entered China during the Tang Dynasty; they speak a Turkish-related language, use Arabic script, and are probably of mixed descent, their features combining Caucasian and Mongoloid characteristics though many can easily be mistaken for southern Europeans.

The Dungans are believed to be descendants of the Uygurs, and with the exception of their Moslem religion and the accompanying traditions the Dungans had long assimilated the Chinese language, dress and customs. Because of this they were known to the Chinese as *Han Hui* or 'Chinese Moslems'. A term which is quite misleading. They are not Han Chinese who believe in the Moslem religion but a group of mixed-blood Uygur descendants who assimilated Chinese culture. The Chinese distinguished the Hui from the Uygur by referring to the latter as *Chan Hui*, 'turban-bearing Moslems', because they used to wear turbans on their heads. Whereas the Uygurs were found mainly in Xinjiang, the Hui could be found all over China, in Yunnan, Shaanxi, Gansu,

Xinjiang and what is now Qinghai and Ningxia.

The Manchus considered it safer to defend the empire west of Xinjiang, where a mountain range forms a natural defence, than at the doorsteps of Beijing. Exploitation of the resources of the 'New Dominion' could maintain the frontier army and migration of Han Chinese into the region would also relieve economic and population pressure on Eastern China. Migrations of different people into the region also evened out the balance of power between the inhabitants and helped the Manchus maintain overall control by exploiting differences and suspicions between the various groups.

The policy worked well so long as the Manchu rulers treated the different groups equally , and so long as it was backed up by a powerful army which could defend the frontier and maintain internal order, but within a hundred years the Manchu warriors had been softened by Chinese civilisation, just like the Mongols before them. Military power declined rapidly and by the 19th century the empire was racked by the Taiping and Niem Rebellions, the Moslem rebellions in Yuannan, as well as the intrusions of the western powers.

When the Manchus conquered Xinjiang they behaved like a common master to Moslems and Chinese; because they were foreigners themselves they treated both Chinese and Moslems in the same way. But by the 19th century the Manchus had become thoroughly assimilated into Chinese culture, indistinguishable from their Chinese subjects, adopting Chinese philosophy, religion and anti-Moslem prejudices. The Manchus ceased to be fair rulers and the dissatisfaction of the Moslems grew.

In 1862 the Taipings invaded Shaanxi; the Moslems and the Chinese of the region had been organised into defence corps, but the Moslems and Chinese started to fight each other and before long an all-out Moslem rebellion ensued. Gansu and

Xinjiang were quiet, but the government failed to extinguish the fire immediately and it spread from town to town.

In Shaanxi the government lacked the military strength to suppress and execute the rebels. It was forced into a wavering policy of fighting inferior Moslem forces and making gestures of reconciliation to superior ones, which failed to establish peace. The rebellion across northwest China was put down in each region, one by one, by the imperial armies. When the first of these armies arrived in Shaanxi government policy ceased to be wavering; bitter and bloody battles were fought, numerous Moslems were killed and their bases destroyed. The Moslem rebels never did make any substantial comeback in Shaanxi. In Gansu the situation in the early days of the rebellion was much the same as in Shaanxi; military weakness on the part of the Manchu rulers leading to widespread rebellion and a government that was too weak to fight but would make no serious attempt at reconciliation. In what is now Ningxia the Manchus eventually embarked on an all-out policy of suppressing the rebels by force, but the best they could achieve was stalemate. The war exhausted both sides and due to the shortage of food the Moslems negotiated a peace with the Chinese and the area returned to 'normal'. Meanwhile, in Gansu initial Chinese successes came to a grinding halt with the shortage of food and shortage of funds, leading to mutinies in the Chinese armies. By this time the rebellion was no longer the only problem in Gansu; famine, refugees and mutinous Chinese soldiers complicated the situation. It was only with the final suppression of the rebels in Gansu that the imperial armies were able to move into Xinjiang - but it was not until 1878 that the northwestern rebellion was finally crushed.

The rebellion had lasted 16 years and had spread across a quarter of China's territory. The toll on lives was incredible; Gansu had its population reduced from 15 million to just a million; nine out of ten Chinese were killed and two out of three Moslems; in Shaanxi perhaps only 60,000 of the original 700,000 or 800,000 Moslems survived. Villages were laid in ruins and huge tracts of cultivated land were deserted.

# Shanxi

Shanxi Province, especially the southern half, was one of the earliest centres of Chinese civilisation and formed the territory of the state of Qin. After the first emperor, Qin Shihuang, unified the Chinese states, it was the northern part of Shanxi which became the key defensive bulwark between the Chinese and the nomadic tribes to the north. Despite the Great Wall, the nomadic tribes still managed to break through and used Shanxi as a base for their conquest of the Middle Kingdom.

When the Tang Dynasty fell the political centre of China moved away from the north-west and the province went into a rapid economic decline, though its importance in the northern defence network remained paramount. Strategically important, but economically backward and rather isolated, was not unusual for any of China's border regions –then or now. It was not until the intrusion of the western powers into China that any industrialisation got under way; when the Japanese invaded China in the 1930s they carried out further development of industry and coal mining around the capital of Taiyuan. True to form, Shanxi was a bastion of resistance to this invasion from the north, this time from the Communist guerillas who operated in the mountainous regions. After 1949 the Communists set about a serious exploitation of Shanxi's mineral and ore deposits, and the development of places like Datong and Taiyuan as major industrial centres. Some of the biggest coal mines can be found near these cities, and the province accounts for a third of China's known coal deposits.

Shanxi means 'west of the mountains' and is named after the Taihing range which forms its eastern border. To the west it is bordered by the Yellow River. The province has a population of about 25 million people, relatively light by Chinese standards unless you take into consideration that almost 70% of the province is mountains. The Taihing range, which also includes the Wutai Mountains, runs north-south, and separates the province from the great North China Plain to the east. The Central Shanxi Basin crosses the central part of the province from north to south in a series of valleys. This is the main farming and economic area. Most of the farmland is used to grow crops, though the north-west is the centre of the province's animal husbandry industry.

Despite its intended future as an industrial bastion, Shanxi is hardly one big quarry. The province is literally a gold-mine of temples, monasteries and cave-temples, a reminder that this was once the political and cultural centre of China. The Number One attraction is the Yugang Caves at Datong, but there are monuments scattered throughout the region.

## TAIYUAN

The first settlements on the site of modern-day Taiyuan date back something like 2500 years. By the 13th century it had developed into what Marco Polo referred to as 'a prosperous city, a great centre of trade and industry'.

Like Datong, Taiyuan rose to become an important frontier town, and because of, or despite, the prosperity the city has been the site of constant armed conflict. The trouble with Taiyuan was that it was

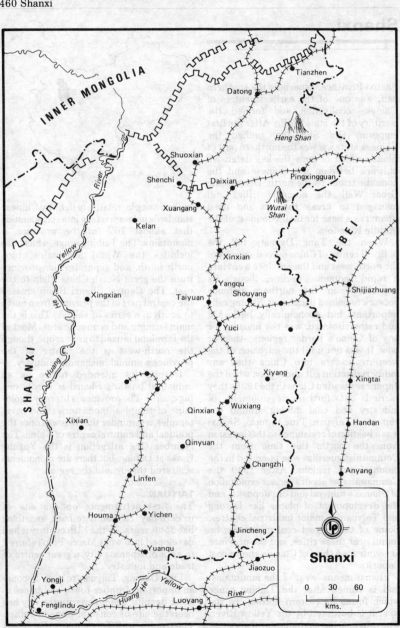

Shanxi

0    30    60
kms.

always in somebody else's way, situated on the path which successive northern invaders have repeatedly entered China intent on conquest. As some indication of the importance of bloodshed in the city's life, there were once 27 temples dedicated to the God of War in the city and its environs. The Huns, the Tobas, the Jin, Mongols and Manchus, amongst others, all took turns to sweep through the city. If it wasn't foreign invasion which afflicted the city then it was the rise and fall of various Chinese dynasties during periods of disunity, the town passing from one army to another as different rulers vied for power. It was a scene repeated in many of China's cities which either stood in the path of advancing armies or even found themselves targets. Nevertheless they and Taiyuan somehow managed to survive.

In the later part of the 19th century, Taiyuan moved rapidly towards industrialisation. It was spurred on by the city's location on some of the largest coal and iron ore deposits in the world. It started to develop as a modern city between 1889 and 1909 when the western powers built a railway line linking Taiyuan with Hebei province, introduced electricity, installed a telephone and telegraph system and established a military academy and university. It was pushed along by the warlord Yan Xishan who ruled Shanxi virtually as his own private empire after the fall of the Manchu Dynasty, and the coal mines around Taiyuan were also developed by the Japanese invaders during the 1930s and 40s.

The Communists began the serious industrialisation of Taiyuan, along with other regions of Shanxi, after 1949. Today the city looks very much like its modern counterparts, Zhengzhou and Luoyang; with wide avenues, extensive areas of residential blocks interspersed with numerous factories, a vast sea of apartment blocks, factories and innumerable smoke stacks. The industrial debris now makes up the capital of Shanxi Province, but scattered amongst it are some of the finest examples of Chinese Buddhist temples and artwork in the country, which makes Taiyuan eminently worth visiting.

### Information & Orientation

Much of Taiyuan stretches out along the eastern side of the Feng River. The main road is Yingze Dajie which leads down from the railway station and cuts its way through the centre of the city in an east-west direction. Most of the tourist facilities and many of the sights are along this road or lie in the immediate vicinity. The centre of town is the former Red Guard Review Platform on Yinze Lu, opposite which is the large May 1st Square.

**CITS** (tel 29155) is on the ground floor of the Yingze Guest House. They don't speak much English but they're reasonably friendly and helpful, though not overly so.

**Public Security** is in a walled compound on a street running parrallel and just north of Yingze Lu. Refer to the map in this book for directions. The gateway is flanked by two signs with white characters, and there's a sign in English.

**CAAC** (tel 29903) is in a large building right next to the Chinese hotel which lies diagonally across the road from the Yingze Guest House.

**Friendship Store** is on Yingze Dajie in a walled compound a few minutes walk east from the Yingze Guest House.

**Bank** There is a Bank of China in the same compound as the Friendship Store, where you can change money and travellers cheques. It's open daily 8.30 to 11.30 am and 2.30 to 5.30 pm.

**Post** There's a post office in the Yingze Guest House and there's another one right next to the hotel.

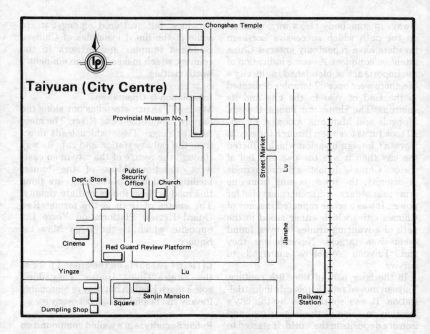

**Taiyuan (City Centre)**

Chongshan Temple

Provincial Museum No. 1

Street Market

Lu

Jianshe

Public Security Office

Church

Dept. Store

Cinema

Red Guard Review Platform

Yingze

Lu

Dumpling Shop

Square

Sanjin Mansion

Railway Station

**Maps** Excellent maps of Taiyuan, in Chinese and showing the bus routes, are available from the ground floor shop of the Yingze Guest House.

### Things to See
### Jinci Temple

The No 1 attraction of Taiyuan is this ancient Buddhist temple, located at the source of the Jin River by Xuanwang Hill 25 km south-west of Taiyuan. It's not known for sure when the original buildings were constructed but there have been numerous additions and restorations over the centuries right up to the Qing Dynasty, though the temple probably dates back at least a thousand years and probably more.

A number of the major buildings of the temple and the gateway to the compound are situated on an east-west axis. Entering the compound the first major building is

the Mirror Terrace, a Ming building used as an open-air theatre. The name is used in the figurative sense to denote the reflection of life in drama.

Zhibo's Canal cuts through the temple complex and lies west of the Mirror Terrace. Spanning this canal is the Huixian (Meet the Immortals) Bridge which provides access to the Terrace for Iron Statues. At each corner of this platform stands an iron figure, each cast in 1097 AD and carrying very little rust.

Immediately behind the statues is Duiyuefang Gate fronted by two iron statues. The Offerings Hall stands behind the Duiyuefang Gate and was built in 1168 for the display of offerings to the temple. On the side of the offerings hall is a pavilion housing a large drum and on the other side is another which houses a large bell.

Behind the Offerings Hall is the Fish Pond with Flying Beams – one of those quaintly named mediocrities the Chinese are so fond of. The pond is one of the springs from the Jin River and has 34 small octagonal stone pillars planted in it, on top of which are brackets and cross-beams supporting a bridge in the shape of a cross. The other spring is Nanlao Spring – Nanlao means 'everlasting' in Chinese. The pond was full of rubbish and the fish must have expired long ago.

The bridge connects the Offerings Hall with the Goddess Mother Hall, otherwise known as the Sacred Lady Hall. The Sacred Lady Hall was originally constructed during the Northern Wei and rebuilt during the Northern Song. It's the oldest wooden building in the city and one of the most interesting in the temple complex. The temple is fronted by large wooden pillars supporting the roof, and around each pillar are wrapped wooden carvings of bizarre dragons, their claws outstretched and their teeth ready to attack. On either side of the temple stand two weapon-wielding guardians encased in armour. Inside the Sacred Lady Hall are 42 Song Dynasty clay figures of maid-servants standing around a large seated statue of the Sacred Lady herself. The Sacred Lady is said to be the mother of Prince Shuyu of the ancient Zhou Dynasty, and the temple was built in her memory during the Northern Song period – though it's suggested that the original building was constructed by the prince as a place to offer prayers and sacrifices to his mother. Today, people still throw money on the altar in front of the statue of the Sacred Lady. Next to the Sacred Lady Hall is the Zhou Cypress, a rather unusual tree which has chosen to grow at an angle of about 30° for the last 900 years.

On the northern side of the Sacred Lady Hall is a long flight of steps leading to a building which houses a hideous god with red eyebrows, black eyes, and screaming mouth, and flanked by two dragons.

South of the Sacred Lady Hall is the Nanlao (Forever Young) Spring over which stands a pavilion –the spring is the chief source of the Jinshui River. To the west of the spring is the two-storeyed Shuimou Lou (Water Goddess House) constructed in 1563. Otherwise imaginatively entitled the Crystal Palace, it's a two-storey building. On the ground floor is a statue of the goddess cast in bronze; she sits in front of a stone urn into which people have thrown money, food coupons and even cigarettes! On the upper storey is a shrine with a seated statue of the goddess surrounded by eight statues of her female servants.

There are several places of note in the northern part of the temple grounds. The Zhenguan Baohan Pavilion houses four stone steles inscribed with the hand-writing of the Tang Emperor Tai Zong. Nearby is a small pavilion with a sign 'Service Centre of the Locust of Tang Dynasty'. No comment.

The Memorial Halls of Prince Shuyu stand in the northern part of the temple grounds. In one of these halls is a shrine containing a seated figure of Prince Shuyu surrounded by 12 Ming Dynasty female attendants, some holding bamboo flutes, some pipes, and others stringed instruments. The halls are located in the northern part of the temple compound.

The Sacred Relics Pagoda juts up in the southern part of the temple grounds; it's a seven-storeyed, octagonal building constructed at the end of the 7th century. The pagoda is currently being restored. Close by is a large bell.

To get to the temple, there is a bus which leaves regularly from the large square in front of the Red Guard Review Platform. The fare is 45 fen and the ride takes about 45 minutes to an hour. The bus is always crowded, but coming back is the worst part; that placid gathering of the Asian horde makes a rampaging frontal assault on the bus as it pulls up at the temple bus stop. Photographs are not permitted inside the buildings of the temple complex.

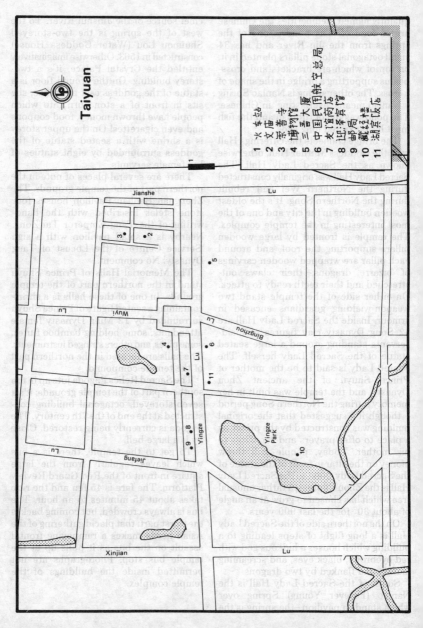

Taiyuan

1 火车站
2 文庙书院
3 崇善寺
4 博物馆
5 三晋中国民俗商店
6 友谊商店
7 迎泽大厦
8 邮局
9 藏经楼
10 湖滨宾馆饭店
11

Jianshe Lu

Wuyi Lu

Bingzhou Lu

Yingze Park

Yingze

Jiefang

Xinjian

Lu

### Ming Library & Yingze Park

The Ming library is a rather ornate building in Yingze Park and is worth wandering in to have a look. Turn right out of the Yingze Guest House; the entrance to the park is a ten minute walk west and on the other side of the road.

### Chongshan Monastery

This Buddhist monastery was built towards the end of the 14th century on the site of an even older monastery, said to date back to the 6th or 7th centuries. The interior of the main hall is one of the the sights of Taiyuan. It contains three large statues, the central figure representing Guanyin, the Goddess of Mercy, with a thousand hands and a thousand eyes. Apart from the statues, they also have beautifully decorated and illustrated book covers showing scenes from the life of Buddha. Also preserved here are Buddhist scriptures of the Song, Yuan, Ming and Qing periods.

Unfortunately the only time the temple seems to be open is when a tour group is visiting, so you'll probably have to try and tag on to one. The monastery is in the eastern part of town on a sidestreet to the west of Jianshe Beilu.

### Yongzhuo Monastery

The Yongzhuo or 'Eternal Blessing' Monastery was built during the Ming Dynasty, in the late 16th and early 17th century. It's usually referred to as the 'Twin Pagoda Monastery' since it has two identical pagodas as part of the complex, which are now regarded as the symbol of Taiyuan.

Each of these octagonally-shaped, 50 metre high pagodas has thirteen storeys, and is built entirely of bricks. In imitation of wooden pagodas, the bricks are carved with brackets and cornices. The pagodas are currently being restored – they're in great disrepair, cracked and corroded, and one of them is defintely leaning. The main hall in the monastery contains three golden Buddha statues, two seated in meditation and the third standing. Restoration work is currently being carried out on some of these buildings.

There are no buses which even come close to the monastery and you'll have to walk most of the way. Walk for 15 minutes southwards from the railway station and turn left at Chaoyang Jie. Turn right again at Shuangta Beilu; walk almost to the end and turn left up the road which runs roughly parallel to the river. There is a small bridge further up which leads over to the monastery. In all, it's about a 45 minute walk from the railway station.

### Provincial Museums

The Shanxi Provincial Museum is housed in two separate complexes. The No 1 Museum is housed in an old Confucius Temple on Dilianggong Lu. The No 2 Museum is in Chunyang Palace, west of May 1st square, and used to be a temple for offering sacrifices to the priest Lu Dongbin who lived in the Tang Dynasty. The temple was built during the Ming and extended during the Qing.

| | |
|---|---|
| 1 Railway Station | 7 Friendship Store & Bank |
| 2 Provincial Museum No. 1 | 8 Yingze Guest House |
| 3 Chongshan Temple | 9 Post Office |
| 4 Provincial Museum No. 2 | 10 Ming Library |
| 5 Sanjin Mansions | 11 Hubing Hotel |
| 6 CAAC | |

The No 2 Museum has an interesting collection and though none of the captions are in English, and you can't take photos, it's definitely worth checking out. Just inside the main entrance on the right is a grotesque statue of the laughing Buddha with a huge head, and behind it is a long row of inscribed tablets and Buddhist carvings, as well as five large standing Buddhas. The tablet supported by a turtle shows the dead Buddha. Other exhibits in the museum include copper vessels, stele rubbings, inlaid mother-of-pearl ornaments, paintings and examples of calligraphy.

### Places to Stay

The *Yingze Guest House* is the tourist hotel and will probably irritate you no end. Room-rates seem to depend on which side of the communal kang the desk-clerk got out on. I fronted up here with two people; at first they were going to put two of us in one room for Y12 each, and give a separate room to the third for Y32! Finally they put all three of us in a three-bed room and charged us Y12 each. A few days later, after the others had checked out, two more westerners came and were given the same beds for just Y8 each! Good luck. The hotel is a cavernous monstrosity with a vast gloomy foyer. The shops on the ground floor hardly ever seem to be open. You'll probably have to herd the staff into your room to get the sheets changed, the thermoses filled, the teacups emptied, the towels replaced and the water mopped off the floor of the bathroom. The guest house is on Yinze Dajie. It's a 20-minute quick walk from the railway station.

The **Hubing Hotel** is a Chinese abode diagonally across the road from the Yingze Guest House. You might get a cheaper room here if they let you stay, but most likely you'll be sent off to the Yingze.

will probably let you stay, but they were asking Y30 for a double room. It may be worth dropping in on your way down to the Yingze to see what sort of price you can extract.

### Places to Eat

If nothing else the *Yingze Guest House* is a good place to eat. Breakfast is Y2 for western food, though it's a bit dreary, but lunch and dinner at Y2.50 each is quite good!

The road which runs along the western side of the Hubing Hotel supports a flourishing collection of night-time food stalls and eating places. You can get cheap bowls of noodles and hard-boiled eggs. An especially tasty morsel is the little stuffed pancake fried up in the wok by an elderly couple. OK food and friendly people.

Other than that there's not a great deal to recommend; there's a number of evening food-stalls set up along Bingzhou Lu which runs south from the Red Guard Review platform, but nothing particularly memorable.

### Getting Around

Buses and feet. If you're interested then the Friendship Store sells 'Flying Pigeon' bicycles. Bicycles in China go for about Y150 and you could buy one and resell it before you leave the country.

### Getting Away

**Train** Taiyuan is connected northwards by rail to Beijing via Datong. There are trains east to Shijiazhuang, and this will put you on the main Canton-Beijing railway line. Alternatively, you can go south to Zhengzhou and then change trains and head either south towards Canton, west towards Xian or east towards Shanghai. There are also direct trains from Taiyuan to Xian.

**Plane** There are planes from Taiyuan to Beijing (Y63), Changzhi (Y25), Chengdu (Y145), Lanzhou (Y129), Xian (Y69), Xining (Y153) and Yanan (Y42).

## AROUND TAIYUAN
### Shuanglin Monastery

This monastery is a must; the interior walls of its buildings are covered in the most exquisite painted-clay figurines and statues, dating from the Song, Yuan, Ming and Qing Dynasties. The monastery is 97 km south of Taiyuan and is well worth the effort to get to. Most of the present buildings date from the Ming and Qing Dynasties, while the majority of sculptures are from the Song and Yuan Dynasties. There are something like 2000 statues and figurines in all.

To get to the temple you have to take a train from Taiyuan to the town of Qiatou, a 2½ hour journey. The fare is Y1.90 (hard seat, local price).

When you arrive at Qiatou you can get a rickshaw to take you from the station to the temple. The ride to the temple takes about 30 minutes and will probably cost you Y2 oneway. There are several trains a day between Taiyuan and Qiatou, and if you leave early in the morning you should be able to spend a couple of hours at the temple and return on one of the afternoon trains to Taiyuan.

**Tianlong Shan (Celestial Mountain) Caves**
These Buddhist caves are 40 km south-west of Taiyuan. Some of them pre-date the earliest of the Yungang Caves at Datong. The caves at Tianlong were built during the Eastern Wei, the Northern Qi, Sui and Tang Dynasties. The chief carving is the large seated statue of Maitreya, the coming Buddha.

**Tianning (Heavenly Tranquillity) Temple**
60 km south-west of Taiyuan is the town of Jiaochang. 2 km north of Jiaochang is Gua Shan (Divination Mountain), the site of Tianning Temple. This is a Buddhist temple first built during the Tang Dynasty 1300 years ago, though most of the present buildings belong to the Ming period; it's noted for its painted clay sculptures and figures.

**Xuanzhong (Stone Wall) Monastery**
This monastery is 70 km south-west of Taiyuan in the mountainous area around

Jiaochang. It's so named because the rocky hills around it look like its walls. It dates back 1500 years and was a Buddhist centre in northern China during the Tang Dynasty.

**Juwei Monastery**
Also known as the Duofu Monastery, this monastery lies on top of Juwei Shan 24 km north-west of Taiyuan. It was originally built towards the end of the 8th century, destroyed during war at the end of the Song and then rebuilt under the Ming; the murals and clay figures in the monastery all belong to the Ming period.

**Jinying Temple**
Jinying Temple is located at Tutang Village at the foot of Juwei Shan, 20 km north-west of Taiyuan. The temple was originally built during the Northern Qi Dynasty back in the 6th century, rebuilt and added to through the ages – the present buildings all date from the Ming and the Qing. The chief attraction is the nine metre high seated figure of Sakyamuni in the main hall. All the clay figures in the temple date from the Ming Dynasty.

**Walls of Pingyao**
90 km south-west of Taiyuan are the remains of the wall of the ancient Zhou dynasty town of Pingyao. The town dates back at least as far as the 8th and 9th centuries BC when the original walls were built. These walls were expanded during the reign of the first Ming Emperor Hong Wu, constructed of rammed earth wrapped in bricks, almost 11 metres high and an average of five metres.

**Other sights in Shanxi Province**
Shanxi is a treasure trove of temples and archaeological sites. Scattered around the province are a number of ancient temples and monasteries. Amongst them is the **Wooden Pagoda** south of Datong in Ying County, the oldest and highest wooden pagoda still standing in China. It was built in 1056 during the Liao Dynasty. West of

Datong is the **Xuankong Monastery**. In southern Shanxi you'll find **Guangsheng (Temple of Little Western Paradise)**. In the far south of the province is the **Temple of the Wargod** and the **Yangle Palace**.

### Taiyuan experiences

There's a peculiar sign in the Taiyuan Friendship Store:

The Tatung copper chafing dish is a famous traditional handicraft in Shanxi Province with a long history and it is well known over the world. As the old saying goes *Go to Watai Mountain for sightseeing, and go to Tatung for buying copper chafing dish*. The Tatung chafing-dish is engraved finely with vivid and gorgeous patterns on its surface. The dishes cooked by delicacies. Entertaining intimate friends with chafing-dish makes both host and guests happy, and bringing something unique about the dinner style.

Buying train tickets at Taiyuan railway station is an exercise in mental torment. I went to the enquiry window on the 16th of the month and said I wanted a ticket for the 18th; but sorry, tickets are only sold one day in advance and I'd have to come back the next day. I returned the next day and was suddenly taken in tow by a policeman; an English-speaking person was found and he went to buy the ticket for me, but the window will only take RMB not FECs, so I change some with my interpreter and he goes back to buy the ticket. He returns with a ticket to leave on a train that very night. But I don't want to go tonight, and he returns to get a refund.

It turns out that if I want to go on the 18th I have to wait at window No 19, which is conveniently shut. But window 19 will open at 2.30 pm, so I venture out to get something to eat and return at 2 pm to wait in front of the window. Another window opens a few feet away which is also selling tickets for the train I want and I try that one, but I'm told to go to window No 5.

At window No 5 another policeman takes me in tow, reads my scrawled Chinese note explaining what I want, and a debate ensues between him and half a dozen other people about what I want. They question the ticket seller behind window No 5, and through an interpreter I am told that I must come back tomorrow to buy the ticket. My reaction is SCREAM, EXPLODE and SHOUT things like 'I WANT MY TICKET AND I WANT IT NOW!!!' This scene goes on for several minutes, attracting a crowd of several dozen curious Chinese who have never seen a rabid foreigner. I'm led back to the window, the clerk pulls out his little book, makes a few calculations on his abacus and sells me a ticket for the 18th . . . the finishing touch is added when I'm led around to yet another office and someone glues on a little tag with the number of the train and the time of departure. It was not a good day.

### DATONG

In 220 AD the Han Empire fragmented into three separate kingdoms. Rivalry between them left China open to invasion from the north, and though the other kingdoms were subjugated by the Wei Kingdom (who took the dynasty name of Jin) it was a shaky unification. The nomads to the north were waiting for an opportunity to invade. A series of kingdoms rose and fell in the north until the Toba, a Turkish-speaking people, rose at the end of the 4th century and by the middle of the 5th had conquered all of northern China, taking the dynasty name of Northern Wei.

The success of the Tobas in ruling the northern Chinese was not due to numbers, which were relatively small, but to adopting a Chinese style of administration and by the intermarriage of the Chinese gentry and the Toba aristocracy. The dynasty appears to have been a very active period of development, particularly in agriculture, irrigation and trade, as well as being a high point culturally, despite the continuing wars and social instability. It was during this time that the Buddhist teachings of personal salvation and nirvana began taking root amongst the Chinese population and Buddhism was made a state religion.

The Northern Wei established their capital at Datong. The town had long been an important centre, strategically located just south of the Great Wall and near the border with Inner Mongolia. The town had been fortified under the Han and when the Wei set up their capital here it became the political hub of the dynasty until the court moved to Luoyang a hundred years later in 494 AD. Outside the modern-day city is the greatest legacy of the period, the Yugang Buddhist Caves.

Apart from the caves there are few reminders today that Datong was once northern China's imperial city. This city of 700,000 is a rather uglier version of the post-1949 Beijing prototype but it does have one of the largest and most intact old sections left in any Chinese city. It's one of the most interesting Chinese cities for street-walking, particularly in the north. It's also one of the few places left in the world which is still building steam engines, and the city is also Shanxi's leading coal producer.

## Information and Orientation

Datong is divided into an old city and the modern post-1949 construction. The centre of town is the intersection of two main roads, in the immediate vicinity of which is the bus station, the public security office, the main department store, and the Exhibition Hall. Heading north from the intersection takes you to the railway station, heading south to the Datong Guest House. Heading east leads you through the old city, with such attractions as the Huayuan Monastery and the Dragon Screen. Various other attractions, like the Yungang Caves, are

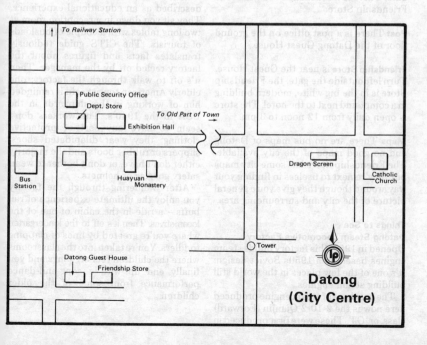

To Railway Station

Public Security Office

Dept. Store

To Old Part of Town →

Exhibition Hall

Bus Station

Huayuan Monastery

Dragon Screen

Catholic Church

Datong Guest House

Friendship Store

Tower

**Datong
(City Centre)**

scattered around the outskirts of the city.

**CITS** This slothful band of useless individuals may be found in Room 111 on the ground floor of the Datong Guest House. It's useless trying to get any correct information out of them so try to avoid any dealings with them at all.

**Public Security Office** is a 10 minute walk from the long-distance bus station. Turn right out of the station and left at the crossroads; the office is on the opposite side of the road just a few minutes walk down from the cross-roads. Friendly people here. They used to give permits for Lhasa but no longer.

**CAAC** There are no civilian flights to Datong.

**Bank** There is an exchange counter in the Friendship Store.

**Post** There is a post office on the ground floor of the Datong Guest House.

**Friendship Store** is near the Guest House. Turn left outside the gate; the Friendship Store is in the big white, modern building in a compound next to the hotel. The store is open daily from 12 noon to 3 pm.

**Maps** There are no bus maps of Datong and no good maps of the city available. The Friendship Store has some city maps but they're next to useless in finding your way around though they give you a general picture of the city and surrounding area.

### Things to See
### Datong Steam Locomotive Factory
Opened in 1959, this factory builds steam engines based on a 1950s Soviet design. It's one of the few places in the world still building steam engines.

The only type of steam engine produced here now is the 2-10-2 Qianjin (Forward) class, or 'QJ'. These were first produced in 1965 and production is scheduled to continue until 1985. Figures of 300 QJs produced annually have been mentioned, but the number is probably around 200 to 250. The works are the only place in China producing (main) railway line engines – up until 1976 the works at Tangshan were producing the Shangyang (Aiming at the Sun) or 'SY' class loco, but the Tangshan works were devastated by the earthquake of that year.

The factory is only open to visitors on Tuesdays and Saturdays but the only way you'll get to see this place is to arrange a tour with CITS. Even then you can only go if there's a spare seat on one of the tour buses; the factory won't let individuals in, even if you front up at the gate at the same time as the tour group. To go on the bus will cost Y8 per person, or Y4 if you're a student in China – but they *do* scrutinise student cards.

The tour of the factory can be best described as an educational experience. They sit you down in a reception room at two long tables with a couple of busloads of tourists. The CITS guide tediously translates facts and figures about the factory reeled off by the manager. Then it's off to walk through the factory; one elderly American tourist said it reminded him of working in the shipyards in the USA in the 1940's. The workers don't seem to have any sort of protective clothing; they wear dilapidated shoes, slippers or rubber boots and the majority either don't have, or don't bother to wear, safety goggles or helmets.

After wandering through the factory you enjoy the ultimate experience of rail buffs – a ride in the cabin of one of the locomotives. Then it's off to the kindergarten where you're greeted by lines of clapping toddlers. You're taken into the classrooms where the children reel off songs and you finally end up with a song-and-dance performance from some of the older children.

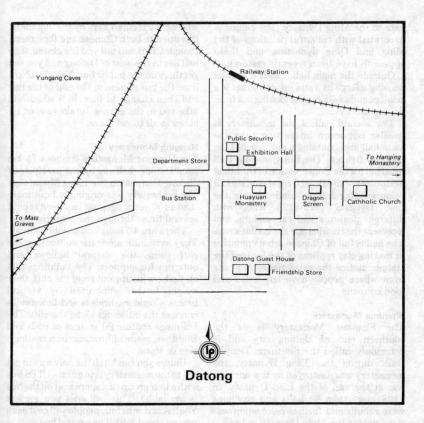

**Datong**

## Dragon Screen

Situated in the old part of Datong, the Dragon Screen is said to have faced the mansion of the thirteenth son of the first emperor of the Ming Dynasty. The screen is eight metres high, 45.5 metres long and 2.02 metres thick. On the main part of the screen, in relief, are nine stylised dragons. The screen stands on Dadong Avenue and the compound is open 9 am to 4 pm. It is, unfortunately, very badly deteriorated.

## The Huayuan Monastery

The Huayuan Monastery is located on the outskirts of the old city, close to Datong's main intersection.

Built in 1140 during the reign of Emperor Tian Juan of the Jin Dynasty, the Mahavira Hall is the main building in the monastery; it's one of the largest Buddhist halls still standing in China today. In the centre of the hall are five gilded and multicoloured Buddhas seated on lotus thrones. The three statues in the middle are carved out of wood whilst the other two are made of clay. These are interspersed with standing boddhisattvas, and at either end of the hall are a number of standing figures leaning forward dressed as soldiers and mandarins. The roof is supported by massive red columns. It appears that the five large Buddhas only date to the Ming Dynasty. The ceiling is decorated with colourful paintings of the Ming and Qing dynasties, and these appear to have been recently restored.

Outside the main hall stands a pagoda housing a large bell and opposite that is a small pagoda with monks looking out from the top storeys.

The second hall of the monastery is smaller but more interesting than the main hall and contains a number of Liao Dynasty figures. The Bojiajiaocang Hall (the Hall for the Conservation of Buddhist Scriptures of the Bojia Order) contains 29 coloured clay figures made during the Liao Dynasty (916-1125 AD), with different postures and expressions, and represent the Buddha and the bodhisattvas. The hall is full of Chinese artists painting or making clay replicas of the faces of the statues; notice the small pedestal at the front where people have left notes and food coupons.

### Shanhua Monastery

The Shanhua Monastery is at the southern end of Datong city and is commonly called the Southern Temple. Built during the Tang Dynasty, the monastery was destroyed by fire during a war at the end of the Liao Dynasty. In 1128 more than 80 halls and pavilions were rebuilt and further restoration was done during the Ming Dynasty in 1445.

### Roman Catholic Church

There is a Roman Catholic Church further down past the Dragon Screen and on the right-hand side of the road. You'll see the church from the main street, and the entrance to the compound is on a sidestreet on the right. Look for the gateway with a small wire cross above it. The church has been fully renovated and appears to be an active place of worship.

### The Mass Graves Class Education Exhibition Hall

This rather depressing structure is dedicated to the 10,000 or more people who were executed here by the Japanese. It *is* open to both Chinese and foreigners, though CITS will tell you it's closed. The hall lies to the west of Datong and you can get there on the public bus. Take bus No 6 from the bus station to the end of the line and then change to bus No 5 which will take you to the graves. It takes about 1½ hours in all to get there.

### Hanging Monastery

The Hanging Monastery is about 75 km from Datong, halfway up the precipice of Jinlong Canyon on the Heng Mountains. The monastery was originally built more than 1400 years ago, but has been rebuilt several times through the centuries.

There are 40 halls and pavilions in all. They were built along the contours of the cliff using the natural hollows and outcrops for support. The buildings rest on timbers jutting out from the cliff, their weight further supported by vertical beams. Corridors, bridges and broadwalks connect the buildings along the cliff. The buildings contain 80 statues of gods and Buddhas, made of bronzem iron castings, clay or stone.

Unless you can hitch the only way to get out to the monastery is to go on a CITS bus with a tour group (if a spare seat on the bus is available). This will cost you a mere Y35!! A taxi with four people will cost each person about Y40. The central bus station in town will *not* sell you a ticket to take the local bus out to the monastery.

### Yungang Caves

The main attraction of Datong is these caves, cut into the southern cliffs of Wuzhon Mountain, 16 km west of Datong. The 53 caves and niches containing over 50,000 statues stretch for about one km east to west. Most of the Datong caves were carved under the Northern Wei Dynasty between 460 and 494 AD. Work on the caves fizzled out when the Northern Wei moved its capital to Luoyang in 494, and Datong itself also declined in importance. In comparison with the caves at Luoyang the Datong caves are probably the more impressive, if only because they've suffered slightly less of the vandalism which beheaded most of the Luoyang statues.

The art of building cave temples originated in India and some of the earliest examples in China are the caves of Dunhuang in Gansu Province. The Dunhuang statues are terracotta since the rock was too soft to be carved, whereas the Datong caves are some of the earliest Chinese examples of stone sculpture.

A number of different influences can be seen in the Yugang caves; Persian and Byzantine weapons, lions and beards, Greek tridents and curling acanthus leaves and Hindu Indian images of Vishnu and Shiva. The Chinese style is reflected in the bodhisattvas, the flying apsaras (celestial beings) and dragons.

From east to west the caves fall into four major groups.

**Caves 1 to 4** At the far eastern end, separated from the rest of the caves, is this first group. Caves 1 and 2 each contain carved pagodas and the former is presently being restored. The square floor plan indicates that these caves were built early on. Cave 3 is the largest in this first group, though it contains only a seated Buddha flanked by two boddhisattvas, the rest of the cave being mostly empty space.

Between this group of four caves and the other caves is a monastery which dates back to 1652, its pavilions hugging and climbing up the face of the cliff.

**Caves 5 to 13** Caves 5 and 6 are the high point of Yungang art, both richly carved with episodes from religious stories and processional scenes.

Cave 5 contains an almost 17 metre high colossal seated Buddha which may give you some idea of the original colour schemes used here; the face is bronze, the lips red and the hair is blue. Many of the smaller images in the caves have been beheaded. On the whole the sculptures and paintings in Caves 5 and 6 are better preserved than those in other caves since they've been protected from the elements by the wooden towers at their entrances. Cave 5 also contains a five-storey pagoda perched on the back of an elephant, carved on the upper part of the south wall.

Cave 6 contains a richly-carved pagoda, covered with scenes from religious stories and the entrance is flanked by fierce guardians. The floor plan of the cave is approximately square and each side is about 13 metres long. In the centre of the rear chamber stands a two-storey pagoda-pillar about 15 metres high. On the lower part of the pagoda are four niches with carved images including one of the Maitreya Buddha. The life story of Buddha from birth to his attainment of nirvana is carved in the east, south and west walls of the cave as well as on two sides of the pagoda.

Cave 7 is in an advanced state of decay, but it's notable for the wispy, flying apsaras carved on the roof.

Cave 8 contains carvings in very poor condition, but it indicates a number of Hindu influences that found their way into Buddhist mythology. Lord Vishnu, with eight arms and four heads and seated on a bull is on the right-hand wall of the entrance of the cave as you walk in. Below him is a trident-bearing figure – probably Lord Shiva. On the other side of the entrance is a six-armed, five-headed figure perched on what may be an eagle, which might also represent Vishnu seated on his carrier Garuda, though the figure appears to be female. In one hand the figure holds a bow, in another a small bird and in another what appears to be an orb. Below the figure is a second trident-bearing figure. Flying apsaras hover above each of these figures.

Caves 9 and 10 are fronted by pillars. The caves are notable for the considerable amount of colour which is still left in them. Inside, just above the entrance to the inner chamber of one of the caves are winged figures with unusual bodies and beards. Many of the smaller figures in these caves have humorous faces and some carry musical instruments.

Cave 11 also has a number of wall paintings. The roof has strange serpent-like creatures carved on it. Cave 12 has interesting carvings of apsaras with musical instruments. Cave 13 has a colossal seated Buddha, its right arm supported by a small figure which stands in its lap.

**Caves 14 to 20** are badly corroded and the only features are small Buddhas in niches around the walls.

The next five caves were all carved in 460 AD. Caves 16, 17, 18, 19 and 20 have oval-shaped floors and the roofs are dome-shaped to make room for the huge Buddha statues with saccharin-sweet expressions in these caves, some standing and some sitting.

The Buddha figure in Cave 18 is in good condition. The walls are covered with sculptures of Buddha's disciples and an interesting one is to the right of the main figure's elbow; a head with a long nose and distinct Caucasian features.

The sitting statue of the main Buddha in Cave 20 is 13.7 metres high. The front wall and the wooden structure which stood in front of it are believed to have crumbled away very early on, and the statue now stands exposed to the weather.

**Cave 21 onwards** Cave 21 and onwards are all small caves and in poor condition. Cave 51 contains a small carved pagoda.

To get to the caves take bus No 3 from the bus station in the centre of town to the terminus. The caves are just a few minutes walk from the terminus and there are regular buses every day. The bus fare is 25 fen; admission to the caves is 10 fen and at the time of writing you can take as many photos as you want.

**Places to Stay**

The *Datong Guest House* is the only hotel in Datong taking foreigners. Somewhere off in the distance a thoughtful soul has set up a set of speakers which allow you to awake every morning to the blissful strains of 'The East is Red'.

The hotel is OK by budget standards, but if you're on an expensive tour then this is likely to be one of the worst hotels you'll stay at in China. You'll stand ankle deep in water in the bathroom and the staff haven't quite learnt the necessity to change the sheets once in a while. Nevertheless room prices here are almost as high as you would pay for good accommodation in a place like Nanjing or Canton. The cute notice in the dormitory (Rm 403) may cheer you up:

Welcome to Datong Hotel
I hope you have a good time in our hotel
Everythings wonderful with you!

Double rooms are Y32. Dormitory beds are readily given and cost Y6, or Y4 for 'students in China'. To get to the hotel, take a long double-segmented bus No 2 from the railway station to the central bus station and then change to bus No 1 take this three stops. Get off and continue walking up to the crossroads, turn left and the hotel is a five minute walk down the road on the left. Alternatively, an ordinary bus No 2 should take you directly from the railway station to the hotel.

**Places to Eat**

The Guest House is a good place to eat. If you can convince them you're a student then each meal is only Y2.50 and the food is good, though the portions could be larger! The beer here is permanently flat and the food may be substantially better when there's a tour group in town. Around town there's little worth risking.

**Getting Around**

Transport around town is primarily by bus though there are the odd few rickshaws and autorickshaws around the railway station. Taxis can also be hired from the Guest House. If you have to catch a train or a long-distance bus I suggest you give yourself plenty of time to get to the station.

### Getting Away

Datong is a major junction on the north-central China railway network. There are daily express trains to Taiyuan, to Beijing, and to Lanzhou via Hohhot and Baotou; there are no planes, no boats, probably no buses to anywhere you'd want to go to, and no transporter beams. There are daily express trains to Taiyuan (7 to 9 hours, hard seat Y7.20 local price), to Beijing (7 to 8½ hours), to Hohhot (5 to 6 hours), to Baotou (8 to 9½ hours).

### WUTAI SHAN

Wutai Shan is one of the sacred Buddhist mountains of China. It's actually a cluster of five peaks of which the northern peak, Yedonfeng, is just over 3000 metres high and is known as the roof of northern China.

The temples of Wutai Shan are concentrated at Taihuai. The **Tayuan** Temple is the most prominent with its large white bottle-shaped pagoda, 63 metres high, built during the Ming Dynasty. Other temples include the **Xiantong Temple** with its seven rows of halls totalling over 400 rooms; the **Nanshan Temple** built during the Yuan dynasty on the slopes of Nan Mountain to the south of Taihuai, which contains frescoes of the fable *Pilgrimage to the West*. Not far from the Nashan Temple is the **Fuguang Temple** originally built during the Northern Wei Dynasty but rebuilt during the Tang at the end of the 9th century. Other sights are the marble archway of the **Longquan Temple**, the 26 metre high Buddha statue in the **Shuxiang Temple** and the carving on its ceiling of 500 arhats crossing a river. The **Lohou Temple** contains a large wooden lotus flower with eight petals, on each of which sits a carved Buddhist figure; the big flower is attached to a rotating disk and the structure is designed so that when the flower turns the petals open up and the Buddhas appear.

At the present time Wutai Shan is officially closed to westerners – for what reason nobody knows.

# Shandong

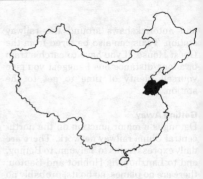

Shandong, the turtle-head bobbing into the Yellow Sea, is a slow starter. The province is relatively poor and beset by economic problems, not the least of which is the rotten Yellow River which can't make up its mind where to void itself. The river has changed direction some 26 times in its history, flooded many more times; six times it has swung its mouth from the Bohai Gulf (North Shandong) to the Yellow Sea (South Shandong), and wreaked havoc on the residents.

Back in 1899 the river flooded the entire Shandong plain; a sad irony in view of the two scorching droughts which swept the area that same year and the year before. Add to that a long period of economic depression; also a sudden influx of demobilised troops in 1895 after China's humiliating defeat in the war with Japan and droves of refugees from the south moving north to escape famines, floods and drought. Then top it off with an Imperial government in Beijing either incapable or unwilling to help the local people, and foreigners whose missionaries and railroads had disregarded and angered the gods and spirits. It added up to a province which was a perfect breeding ground for a rebellion and in the last few years of the 19th century the 'Boxers' arose out of Shandong and set all of China ablaze. Entering into an anti-foreigner alliance with the Qing, the Boxers began the massacre of Chinese Christians, missionaries and foreigners in general, as well as destroying churches and ripping up railroads. Moving out of Shandong, they converged on Beijing in the middle of June 1900 and laid siege to the foreign legations compound and the Imperial government declared war on the foreign powers. The siege of the legations lasted for two months until a relief force of 20,000 Western and Japanese troops marched on Beijing and ended the rebellion.

Work on controlling the monstrous river that started it all is still going to take a fair bit of dykemanship. The other major problem is over population. Shandong comes third to Henan and Sichuan for the title of most populous province; at the 1982 census 74.4 million were squashed into an area of just 150,000 sq km. And just to make matters harder, about two-thirds of Shandong is hilly, with the Shandong massif (its highest peak is Taishan) looming up in the south-west, and another mountain chain over the tip of the Shandong peninsula. The rest is fertile plains sprouting grain, potatoes, cotton, peanuts, soybeans, fruit and tobacco.

The Germans got their hands on the port of Qingdao in 1898 and set up a few factories. Shandong subsequently took a few quantum leaps towards industrialisation. The leading industrial town today is still Qingdao, with the capital Jinan in second place. Zibo is the major coal-mining centre, and is also noted for its glassworks and porcelain output. The Shengli Oilfield in northern Shandong, which opened in 1965, is the second largest crude oil source in China. As for rail lines, you can count them on the fingers of one hand, but the Shandong peninsula has some first class harbours with good passenger links, and there is a dense road network.

Travellers tend to gloss over this province and lest it be forgotten the Shandong tourist authorities are trying to tizz it up with special-interest group tours

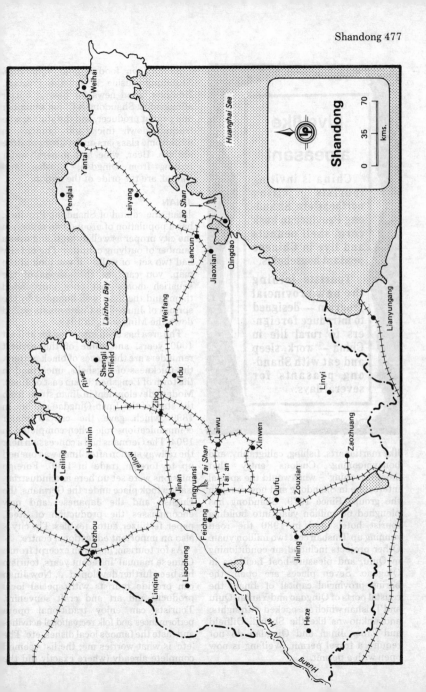

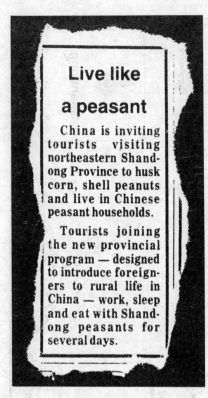

## Live like a peasant

China is inviting tourists visiting northeastern Shandong Province to husk corn, shell peanuts and live in Chinese peasant households.

Tourists joining the new provincial program — designed to introduce foreigners to rural life in China — work, sleep and eat with Shandong peasants for several days.

like martial arts, fishing, calligraphy, and honeymooning. Curious entry that 'honeymooning' – what would the special interest be in Shandong and how many in the group? Since 1979, Shandong has ploughed 60 million yuan into building tourist hotels and in 1980 the road running up Taishan cost two million yuan. Other projects included air-conditioning in Qufu, and pleasure-boat facilities in Qingdao. Seven places are open; the boring provincial capital of Jinan, the coastal ports of Qingdao and Yantai, Qufu and Taishan which are packed with sights; and unknowns like the Shengli Oilfield and Zibo. Jinan and Qingdao do not require a travel permit. Weifang is now open with a permit.

A word on food – hold your guts. Shandong cuisine is not the greatest. However, good news for peanut butter aficionados: Shandong is China's number one peanut producer, and the stuff can be tracked down thick and crunchy in wholesome glass jars on department store shelves. Beer, wine and mineral water coming from Qingdao, Laoshan and Yantai, are the pride of the nation.

### JINAN

Jinan, the capital of Shandong Province, has a population of around two million in the city proper as well as presiding over a number of outlying counties. The old city had two sets of walls – if you look at the map, you can see the shapes of the squarish moats that once surrounded them, and the inner wall bounded by the springs of Jinan. The Communists pulled down the Ming walls in 1949.

The area has been inhabited for at least 4000 years, and some of the earliest reminders are the pieces of black pottery the thickness of eggshells, unearthed in the town of Longshan 30 km east of Jinan. Modern development in Jinan stems from the start of the Jinan-Qingdao rail line in 1899 which gave the city a major communications role when completed in 1904. The Germans had a concession near the railway station after Jinan was opened up to foreign trade in 1906. Foreign missions were set up here and industrialisation took place under the Germans, the English and the Japanese, and now encompasses the production of steel, paper, fertilizer, autos, textiles. The city is also an important educational centre.

As for tourism, here's an excerpt from a Chinese manual 'In recent years, tourism has been further developed... Now Jinan can provide tourists with special local products and art and craft souvenirs. Tourists can enjoy traditional opera performances and folk recreational activities and taste the famous local dishes, etc' The 'etc' is what worries me; the list seemed complete already (where exactly did the souvenir industry come from?). On closer examination, the manual reveals that a four-day tour to Jinan consists of six hours in Jinan and the rest of the time in Qingdao, Taishan, etc. Not a bad idea since Jinan is really the kind of place where you go about your business, like the locals. Go to the post-office, the bank, Public Security, then back to the rail station, etc.

**CITS** (tel 35351) has an office at the Jinan Hotel. Take bus No 9 from the railway station.

## Things to See

Go no further than the railway station. I am deadly serious. The further you go, the worse it gets. Wandering Jinan for two days, I could find absolutely nothing to better that quaint piece of German railway architecture and its surreal clock gazing sternly down. Oh yes – there was something else – a safety display board just up the street with mangled bodies amid twisted bits of truck and bicycle, several photos in full gory colour. After a battle with the hotel, I headed back into the streets, dropped into Public Security and got a month's extension on my visa – the highlight of the day. Luckily I met the son of a cadre who asked me if I had any foreign video tapes. No, I didn't – how silly of me not to have stocked up in Hong Kong. He shuffled me round to a few dreary tour spots, offered me a place to stay for the night. Took me to dinner with his girlfriend – quite a treat, don't get to talk to those shy Chinese women very much. He was, I guess, trying to impress her with his broken English – he certainly impressed her with the price of the meal. I stayed the night in his spacious apartment finding out how cadre's sons live – high! They have enough money or access to it to create a generation gap between themselves and parents, something that I had unwittingly been incorporated into.

The next day I set off in search of the *real* Jinan. This is the capital! There's got to be more out there. I eventually headed off to the Foreign Language Institute on the edge of the city. I asked the first white man I saw 'What is there to see in Jinan?'. 'Nothing', came the blunt answer. This from an English teacher who'd been stationed in this dump for two years, and who was nearing the end of his sentence. How he'd managed that long was beyond me. Two years, two days, it made no difference. The impression was the same. Walking around the Institute area, the English teacher pointed out an old German church which had been converted into a sandpaper factory. Now *that* sounded interesting. My ears pricked up – the poetry of the situation was irresistible. I could just picture the manager at the altar, the workers bowing down to the machinery, the supervisor delivering sermons on production figures, the whole scene illuminated by shafts of sunlight filtered through stained-glass windows. 'Have you tried to get inside?', I asked with bated breath. 'Yes', said the English teacher. 'Did you succeed?' The English teacher looked at the ground. 'No', he said, 'not a peek'. Sandpaper production was obviously a state secret.

## Miscellaneous Wonders

Jinan isn't worth much time (if any) in the way of sights and the outside locations are slightly better. You could make the trek south to **Thousand Buddha Mountain** which is only worth it for the views since its statues were disfigured or just disappeared during the Cultural Revolution. Up the opposite end of town, past **Golden Ox Park** (a zoo) is the dyke of the Yellow River, a few km north of the No 4 bus terminal. That's on the dull side but you pass by some dusty villages where the locals are engaged in interesting permutations on back-breaking labour. There's the **Shandong Provincial Museum** sited in an old temple that turns out to be more impressive than the contents of the museum itself. The museum is divided into history and nature sections – tools, objets d'art, pottery,

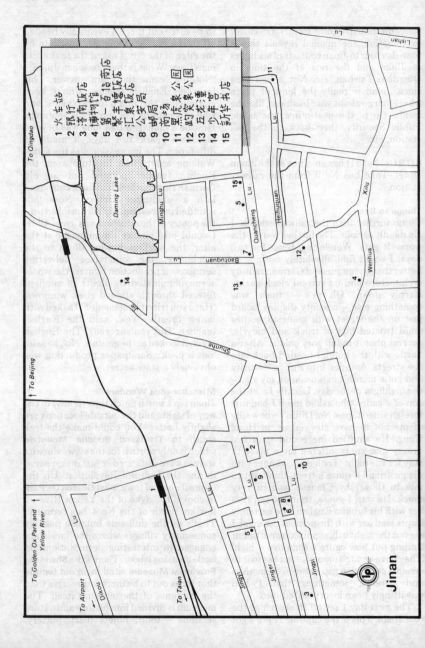

1 火车站
2 银行
3 济南饭店
4 博物馆
5 聚丰德饭店
6 汇泉饭店
7 公安局
8 邮局
9 商场
10 黑虎泉泉公园
11 趵突泉公园
12 趵突泉宾馆
13 五龙潭
14 少年宫
15 新华书店

Jinan

To Qingdao
To Beijing
To Golden Ox Park and Yellow River
To Airport
To Tai'an
Daming Lake
Dikou

musical instruments etc. Otherwise, there's always **Daguanyuan Market** to browse around.

### The Mystery of the Springs

Jinan's hundred-plus springs are often quoted as the main attraction, so let's set the record straight on this one. The four main parks cum springs are Black Tiger, Pearl, Five Dragon, and Gushing-from-the-Ground, all marvellous names but hardly accurate as adjectives. Twenty years ago they might have sprung but now they've virtually dried up. Reasons given vary – droughts, pollution from factories, increased industrial and domestic use, and, more quietly, the digging of bomb shelters outside the city. Daming Lake, covering one quarter of the city area, is also affected by this malaise which the authorities are attempting to 'correct'. Daming Lake has several minor temples, a few teahouses and a restaurant. At Baotu Spring Park there is a small memorial museum dedicated to the 11th century patriotic poetess Li Qingzhao.

### Simenta (Four Gate Pagoda)

33 km south-east of Jinan, near the village of Liu Bu, are some of the oldest Buddhist structures in Shandong. There are two clusters, one a few km north-east of the village, and the other to the south. Shentong Monastery, founded in the 4th century AD, holds the Four Gate Pagoda (Simenta), which is possibly the oldest stone pagoda in China and dates back to the 6th century. There are four beautiful

light-coloured Buddhas facing each door. The Pagoda of the Dragon and the Tiger (Longhuta) was built during the Tang Dynasty. It stands close to the Shentong Monastery and is surrounded by stupas. Higher up is the Thousand Buddha Cliff (Qianfoya), with grottoes carved with some 200 small Buddhas and half a dozen life-size ones. There are local long-distance buses from Jinan to Simenta. There are also daily tourist buses which depart Jinan at 8 am and return at 3 pm.

### Lingyansi (Divine Rock Temple)

Located in Changqing County, 75 km from Jinan, this temple is set in mountainous terrain. Lingyan Temple was a large monastery that served many dynasties, the Tang, Song, Yuan, etc, and had 500 monks in its heyday. On view is a forest of stupas, 200 of them commemorating the priests who directed the institution. There's also a nine-storey octagonal pagoda, and Thousand Buddha Temple (Qianfodian) which contains 40 fine, highly individualised clay arhats – the best Buddhist statues in Shandong. There are local long-distance buses from Jinan to Lingyansi, but these would take about three hours to get there so it's better to approach the town from Wan De station (which is south of Jinan and 10 km from Lingyansi). Tourist buses from Jinan depart at 7.30 am and return at 4 pm.

### Places to Stay

The sombre Russian-style *Jinan Hotel* (tel

| | |
|---|---|
| 1 Main Railway Station | 10 Daguanyuan Market |
| 2 Bank | 11 Black Tiger (Heihu) Park & |
| 3 Jinan Hotel | Spring |
| 4 Provincial Museum | 12 Gushing from the Ground |
| 5 Dept. Store | (Baotuquan) Spring |
| 6 Chufengde Restaurant | 13 Five Dragon (Wulongquan) |
| 7 Huiquan Restaurant | Spring |
| 8 Public Security | 14 Children's Palace |
| 9 Post Office | 15 Bookstore |

35351) has some sobering prices: Y30 double and no deals. A foreign expert says he got it down to Y7 a bed, but that was on the second night – so that must be the record. You might manage Y12 a bed at a student rate. Take bus No 9 from the railway station.

The *Nanjiao Guest House* (tel 23931) is a similar establishment to the Jinan Hotel, and is Y32 a double. But to get there requires more effort; a bus No 2 from the railway station and then a hike of one kilometre. It was, as the story goes, flung up for an impending visit by Mao, who then decided to skip Jinan.

### Places to Eat

A blank – there's nought really worth recommending. You can try the ones on the map – the *Chufengde*, etc – but the best thing is to get yourself a bottle of 16% proof Tsingtao Red and hope you'll be too far gone to notice the food. There's a sizeable Moslem population in Jinan, and there's a Moslem restaurant located near the Provincial Museum (lamb and mutton, pancakes, sesame bread – not clean, but cheap). The *Yuji Paji*, at the corner of Jingsan and Weiyi Rds, serves boneless braised chicken.

### Getting Around

There are about 25 urban and suburban bus lines in Jinan, running from 5 am to 9 pm, and two late-night lines (east-west, north-south) finishing at midnight. There are plenty of 3-wheeler autorickshaws around the train station.

### Shopping

Shopping territory is mostly in the area of the Jinan Hotel, with another strip in the older town section along Quancheng Ave. Indigenous artefacts for sale include feather paintings, inlaid mahogany boxes, gear from other parts of Shandong, dough and wooden figurines. The Arts & Crafts Service Dept is at 3 Nanmen St. There are a couple of antique stores, including the ones at 321 Quancheng, and 28 Jingsan Lu.

### Getting Away

**Train** Jinan is a major link in the east China rail system, with over 30 trains passing through daily. From Jinan there are direct trains to Beijing (6 hours) and to Shanghai (13 hours). The Qingdao-Shengyang trains which pass through Jinan side step Beijing and go through Tianjin instead. There are direct trains from Jinan to Qingdao and to Yantai in Shandong Province, and to Hefei in Anhui Province. There are also direct Qingdao-Jinan-Xian-Xining trains.

**Plane** There are flights from Jinan to Beijing (Y52), Hefei (Y67), Nanjing (Y71) and Shanghai (Y105).

## ZIBO

Zibo is a major coal-mining centre, on the railway line east of Jinan. The city has a population of two million, and is also noted for its glassworks and porcelain. Not far from Zibo, at Linzhi, a pit of horses dating back some 2500 years has been excavated, older than those at Xian and with one big difference – the horses are real. So far, 600 horse skeletons have been discovered, probably linked to the state of Qi. Horses and chariots indicated the strength of the state, so it's not unusual that they'd be buried with their master. About 90 horse skeletons are on display side by side in the pit.

## QINGDAO

Qingdao is a remarkable replica of a Bavarian village plonked on the Bohai Gulf. Like Shanghai it evokes an eerie feeling – have you passed this way before? A city of red-tiled roofs, European angles, shapes and echoes, right down to the gardens.

It was a simple fishing village until 1897 when German troops landed – the killing of two German missionaries gave them sufficient pretext. In 1898 China ceded Qingdao to Germany for a 99 year period, along with the right to build the Shandong railways and to work the mines for 15 km on either side of the tracks. The Germans developed Qingdao as a coaling station and a naval base and when the Jinan-Qingdao rail line was finished in 1904, harbour facilities blossomed, electric lighting appeared, the brewery (established 1903) was belching beer, and a modern town had risen. It was divided into European, Chinese and business sections. The Germans founded missions and a university, and before long Qingdao rivalled Tianjin as a trading centre, its independence from China maintained by a garrison of 2000 soldiers.

For a city with such a short history, Qingdao has seen a lot of ping-pong: in 1914 the Japanese occupied it, in 1922 the Chinese wrested it back, it fell to the Japanese again in 1938, and was recaptured by the Kuomintang. The official version is that the people of Qingdao engaged in heroic struggles against the imperialists and the Kuomintang, and that industrial production has increased 10-fold since 1949. The latter claim, it would seem, is not exaggerated: behind the innocuous facade of a beach resort is a monstrous mess of factories brewing up the nation's drinking supplies. Qingdao is the largest industrial producer in Shandong, concentrating on diesel locomotives, automobiles, generators, machinery and light industry (watches, cameras, TVs, textiles). It has a population of 1.5 million – though its jurisdiction spreads over 5900 sq km and another 3½ million people.

If you ignore the megalopolis behind it – and most do – Qingdao has a distinct charm, and is colourful for a Chinese city (irony intended). One can indulge in the guessing-game of who once occupied these well-preserved mansions, or what the function of the larger edifices was. The present function is a combination of naval base, cadre playground and sanatorium. The town is a favourite for rest and recuperation, and top-level meetings.

The German presence lingers strongly in Qingdao – in the famous beer, in the villas stretching along the beaches, in the rail station where the vintage clocks have stopped. At night you seem to travel further back in time to the pages of a Gothic novel. In the old German quarter, low-powered street lamps, dimly-lit apartments, smoke rising from chimneys, chinks of light in a turret or attic window, the outlines of a cathedral, the hoot of a passing train – all you need is a heavy fog. Only the shapes of cyclists, hurtling out of the darkness, break the spell – meaning that they almost run you over. For a town that produces such copious quantities of beer, wine and spirits, Qingdao is pretty dead at night – not a drunk in sight, and lights out at nine.

**CITS** is located in the Huiquan Hotel and they're fairly relaxed.

### Things to See & Do

'Qingdao' means 'green island', and the waterfront promontory, backed by undulating hills, is a true garden city. The misty beauty of the place is unmistakable – the visual stimulation of sea, parks, patterns of boats and mansions. Heavy traffic is absent, no sign of strenuous labour, or pollution. Sauntering along the esplanade is the thing to do in Qingdao and, of course, sunbaking.

### Beaches

There are six beaches along the coast with fine white sand. Taking the setting into account, they're hard to beat. The swimming season is June to September, when the beaches are crowded, but there's also the possibility of fog and rain from June to August. Water temperature is soupy, and sea breezes are pleasant. Beaches are sheltered, have changing sheds (you can rent demure swimsuits), shower facilities, photo booths, stores, snackbars. Swimming areas are marked off with buoys and Bondi Beach style shark-nets, lifeboat patrols and lifeguards (plus medical stations). Your chances of

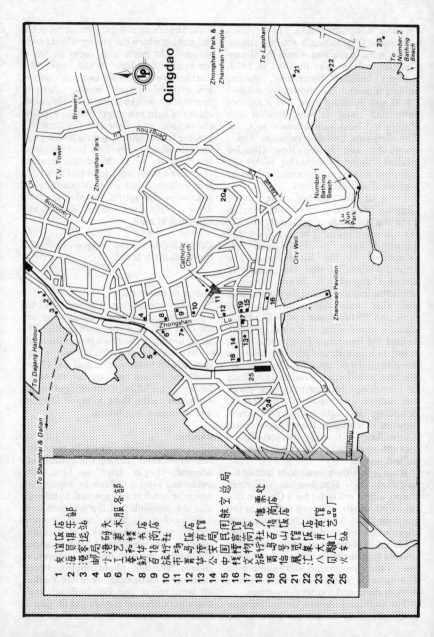

Qingdao

Brewery

T.V. Tower

Zhushaishan Park

Dengzhou

Liaoning

Zhongshan Park &
Zhanshan Temple

Daxue

Number 1
Bathing Beach

To Laoshan

To
Number 2
Bathing Beach

Lu Xun
Park

City Well

Catholic
Church

Zhongshan

Lu

Zhanqiao Pavilion

To Dagang Harbour

To Shanghai & Dalian

Guizhou

| | |
|---|---|
| 1 | 友谊饭店 |
| 2 | 海员俱乐部 |
| 3 | 港客运站 |
| 4 | 邮局 |
| 5 | 小港码头 |
| 6 | 工艺美术楼 |
| 7 | 春和木服务部 |
| 8 | 新华书店 |
| 9 | 百货行社 |
| 10 | 市场 |
| 11 | 青岛饭店 |
| 12 | 华侨宾馆 |
| 13 | 公安局 |
| 14 | 中国民用航空总局 |
| 15 | 栈桥宾馆 |
| 16 | 文物商店 |
| 17 | 新华书社/唐商店 |
| 18 | 信号山饭店 |
| 19 | 百货店 |
| 20 | 展览馆 |
| 21 | 汇泉宾馆 |
| 22 | 八大关宾馆 |
| 23 | 贝雕工艺厂 |
| 24 | 火车站 |
| 25 | |

drowning at Qingdao, in other words, are absolutely nil. Don't pass up Qingdao in other seasons – spring and fall bring out the best in local foliage and there's some spectacular flowering.

## The Esplanade

Just around the corner from the railway station is the **No 6 Bathing Beach**. This strip is particularly lively early in the morning when joggers, fencers, tai chi exponents, old men reading newspapers and a few frisbee players turn out. Streetstall breakfast queues form, and there's a busy cottage industry of picking over the rocks and beach at low tide. Most of the people are on (privileged) vacation and it's quite an eye-opener to see such relaxed Chinese in such a relaxed setting.

**Zhanqiao Pavilion**, on a jetty thrusting into the sea, holds occasional art and craft exhibitions – worth the stroll, anyhow. Continuing east along the esplanade, you pass **City Hall** and around the headland past the lighthouse is **Lu Xun Park** which has the combined **Marine Museum and Aquarium**. The Marine Museum has stuffed and pickled sea life; the Aquarium has sea life that would be better off stuffed or pickled, or in someone's soup. These tiny buildings are billed as the most famous of the kind in China; I'd hate to see the other ones.

Never mind, since you're now at the start of the **Number I Bathing Beach**. While it's no Cable Beach (Western Australia), it's certainly flash for China and bodies of all shapes and sizes jam the sands in the summer. It's a 580 metre stretch of fine sand with multicoloured bathing sheds – the largest beach in Qingdao, and a refreshing sight. The best facilities are grouped around it.

Past the Huiquan hotel and the Ocean Research Institute you come to the **Badaguan (Eight Passes Area)**, well-known for its sanatoriums, and exclusive guest houses. The spas are scattered in lush wooded zones off the coast, and the streets, named after passes, are each lined with a different tree or flower. On Jiayuguan St it's maples and on Zheng-yangguan it's myrtles. The locals simply call them Peach St, Snowp ine St or Crab-apple St. Gardens here are extremely well-groomed. In amongst this lot is the one true sight of Qingdao, the former **German Governor's Residence**. This castle-like villa, made of stone, is a replica of a German palace. It is said to have cost 2,450,000 taels of silver – when Kaiser Wilhelm II got the bill, he immediately recalled the extravagant Governor and sacked him.

Heading out of the Eight Passes Area **Bathing Beaches 2 and 3** are just east, and the villas lining the headlands are

---

1 Friendship Store / Friendship Hotel / Peace Hotel
2 International Seaman's Club
3 Boat Station
4 Main Post Office
5 Local Ferry
6 Arts & Crafts Services Dept.
7 Chunhelou Restaurant
8 Xinhua Bookstore
9 Dept. Store
10 Travel Agent
11 Local Markets
12 Qingdao Restaurant
13 Overseas Chinese Hotel
14 Public Security Bureau
15 CAAC & Seafood Restaurant
16 Zhanqiao Hotel
17 Antique Store
18 Travel Agent / Booking Office
19 Qingdao Dept. Store
20 Xinhao Hill Hotel
21 Trade Centre & Trade Exhibit Centre
22 Huiquan Hotel
23 Badaquan Guest House
24 Seashell Carving Factory
25 Main Railway Station

exquisite. Number 2 Beach is smaller, quieter and more sheltered than Number 1, and is preferred when Number 1 is overloaded. Facing Number 2 are sanatoriums – at the western headland is a naval installation, so don't take short cuts!

## The Brewery

No guide to Qingdao would be complete without a mention of the brewery, tucked into the industrial part of town, east of the main harbour. The brewery was established early this century by the Germans, who still supply the parts for 'modernisation' of the system. The finest brew in Asia, its flavour comes from the mineral waters of Laoshan close by. It was first exported in 1954 and in 1979 it received the national silver medal for quality in China (as judged by the National Committee on Wines and Liquors). Pilgrimages to the brewery are reserved for tour groups, but if you care to try then I suggest you approach CITS at the Huiquan Hotel and organise a guide and taxi. Otherwise, it's on tap in town, or cheap enough in the stores and in any case is sold all over China.

## Other Sights

There are numerous parks in Qingdao. **Zhongshan (Sun Yatsen) Park** is north of the Huiquan Hotel, covers 80 hectares, has a teahouse and temple and is a heavily wooded profusion of flowering shrubs and plants in springtime.

Further west of the park, at Daxue St, is the **Qingdao Museum** with a collection of Yuan, Ming and Qing paintings. Crossing the map north-west of that is an impressive piece of architecture, the **Xinhao Hill Hotel** at the edge of a park.

Off Zhongshan Rd, up a steep hill, is a structure now simply known as the **Catholic Church** –its double spires can be spotted a long way off. The Church is active and services are held on Sunday mornings. On the sidestreets around the church are some lively street markets with birds, bonsais and poultry for sale.

Tours can be organised through CITS to the Qingdao locomotive factory, as well as to the shell-carving factory.

## Places to Stay

The top end of the accommodation spectrum goes through the roof, with the *Badaguan Guesthouse* at Y100 per night, and the *Zhanqiao Guesthouse* at Y60 a double. These are very classy villas with an atmosphere of total exclusion.

The *Overseas Chinese Hotel* (tel 27738) on Hunan Lu is a budget possibility, but you may get knocked back due to your prominent facial features. That leaves three hotels.

*Huiquan Binguan* (tel 25216) at 9 Nanhai Lu, presides over the No 1 Beach; this highrise 10-storey could be a Hilton anywhere. Y32 double is the lowest rate (prices go to Y60 double); travellers have managed to get it down to Y12 a bed, and one hard-core bargainer claims he got a bed for Y6. There are also cheaper TV-less rooms. Another tactic is to take a Y32 room, add an extra bed for Y5 and split the cost between three people. The hotel serves a passable western breakfast. To get there take a bus No 6 from near the railway station.

The *Heping (Peace)* and the *Friendship Hotel* are both located in the complex around the Friendship Store and the boat station in the north-west end of town, and both are difficult to get into. The Friendship Hotel(tel 27778) is at 12 Xinjiang Lu on the right-hand side of the Friendship Store and double rooms go for Y14, Y20 and Y40 depending on the rooms. Plumbing is very weird in this hotel! Try for Y20 double (Y10 a person). There's some English spoken here. The Peace Hotel is located behind the Seamen's Club and Friendship Store, through a small alley to the right of the boat station. Rooms start from Y24 a double.

If you arrived by boat, these two hotels are just a step away. If you arrive by train then it's a little complicated – take bus No

6 to northern terminus, where it turns around. Then walk back under an overhead bridge near the terminus, turn right, and take No 20 or No 21 bus for one stop north.

## Places to Eat
The end of town with the boat station, Seamen's Club, Friendship Store, a cinema and the two hotels thrown in together, has the best restaurant and most of the nightlife. The restaurant serves both the Friendship Store and the Seamen's Club, and is located between the two on the second floor. There's a large range of seafood (swordfish, red snapper, scallops, shellfish in season – more in autumn) all at very fishy prices, and higher for private booths. A bar attached – cold dishes like jellyfish and cucumber served for drinking with. Facilities in the Seamen's Club are open till 10 or 11 pm; No 6 bus runs until 10.30 pm.

If you want some cheaper fare, and are staying at either the Peace or the Friendship hotels it's a long way to the nearest decent noodle-shop – your best advised to do your eating along Zhongshan on the way back, or buy a roasted chicken or something (from the markets near the Catholic Church). Otherwise, it's canned food from the Friendship Store.

Zhongshan Lu has several restaurants. The top one is the *Chunhelou* towards the north end of Zhongshan on the western side of the street. Pricey seafood, and Tsingtao beer served in real pint beer mugs. Further down Zhongshan, at the railway station end, is a cheap seafood restaurant close to the CAAC office – look for a glassed-in building with a corrugated green roof on the corner opposite an antique store. The restaurant sells ice cream, steamed buns, seafood, soup, duck eggs, and various other dishes. You can get a snack for next to nothing, or pig out for Y2 – recommended, cheap, tasty, friendly.

There are some cafes and sidewalk stalls in the Huiquan Hotel vicinity; you could also chase up the menus in the Chinese hotels, the *Overseas Chinese Hotel* for one. Alcohol in this town is plentiful and cheap – a bottle of Tsingtao Red is Y3.30; a good addition to a meal – there's a huge stock in the department stores on Zhongshan Lu.

## Shopping
The busiest shopping area is the length of Zhongshan Lu, which has an antique store at No 40, and the Arts & Crafts Service Department at the north end. Good buys are straw-plaited wares (hats, mats), shell carvings (there's a small retail shop on a side street leading from Zhongshan Rd to the station) – and for instant consumption, good cheap grog. The Friendship Store is mammoth but for more personalised shopping head up to the markets around the Catholic Church – very pleasant to wander this sector of the city, which is the old German quarter. The section of the market selling bird cages is the best part.

## Getting Around
Most transport needs can be catered for by the bus No 6 route, running from the north end of Zhongshan Lu down within a few blocks of the train stations, then east to the area above Number 3 beach. If you're stuck for transport then an autorickshaw from outside the railway station may help.

## Getting Away
**Train** All trains from Qingdao go through the provincial capital of Jinan, except for the direct Qingdao-Yantai trains.

There are direct trains to Beijing (17 hrs). Direct trains to Shenyang (about 26 hrs) pass through Jinan and Tianjin side-stepping Beijing. There are direct trains to Xian (about 31 hrs) and these carry on to Lanzhou and Xining.

Trains to Dalian and to Shanghai (about 24 hrs) will take almost the same time as the boats. But the train is much more expensive and there's no foreigners mark-up on boat fares as there is on train fares. The fare to Shanghai is Y36.20 hard-sleeper, Chinese price; the the fare to Dalian is Y46 hard-sleeper, Chinese price.

**Boat** The boat to Dalian on the Liaoning Peninsula, across the Bo Sea, is the best way of getting there from Qingdao – it's a long way there by train. The boat takes 26 hours and leaves every four days, but sometimes there could be gaps of up to eight days. It departs Qingdao at 4 pm and arrives in Dalian at 6 am. It's a comfortable boat and fares are Y84 special class; Y42 first; Y21 second; Y8 third and Y7 fourth class. You could also take a train from Qingdao to Yantai and catch the Yantai-Dalian boat.

The Qingdao-Shanghai boat departs Qingdao every four days and the trip takes about 27 hours. Fares are Y103 special; Y51.60 first; Y25.80 second (four-berth); Y9.80 third (six to eight berth); Y8.60 fourth. There's not much difference between second and third classes apart from the wash basin in the second class cabins.

Tickets in Qingdao can be bought at the boat station near the Friendship Store. The ticket office in Shanghai is at 222 Renmin Lu; if you buy your tickets from Shanghai CITS they charge an extra Y3 (for details see the section on Shanghai).

**Plane** There are flights from Qingdao to Beijing (Y110), Dalian (Y65), Shanghai (Y65) and Shanyang (Y111).

## AROUND QINGDAO

40 km east of Qingdao is Laoshan Mountain, covering some 400 sq km. It's an excellent place to go hiking or climbing – the mountain reaches an elevation of 1133 metres. Historical sites and scenic spots dot the area and the local product is Laoshan mineral water. The Song Dynasty Taiqing Palace (a Taoist monastery) is the central attraction; there are paths leading

to the summit of Laoshan from there. With such a large area, there's plenty to explore. Due north of the Taiqing Palace is Jiushui, noted for its numerous streams and waterfalls. A special early morning bus runs there from Qingdao rail station to Taiqing Palace and the fare is about Y4. Other travel agents around Qingdao have more extended itineraries including an overnight stop in Laoshan, but it's probably hard to crash these tours unless you speak Chinese.

And a mystery tour; there's a local ferry to the west of the top end of Zhongshan Rd shown on the bus map as running either to a large island off the coast or to a piece of mainland across the bay from Qingdao. Well, it won't cost you much to find out. There are also several new tourist boats that have been launched for harbour cruising in Qingdao.

## TAINAN

Tainan is the gateway town to the sacred Tai Mountain. Apart from this it's notable as the home town of Jiang Qing, Mao's fourth wife, ex-film-actress, notorious spearhead of all-purpose villains the 'Gang of Four', which is neither here nor there but it's something to bring up anyway. She's since been airbrushed out of Chinese memory and is now serving a life sentence, last heard of making stuffed dolls.

### Information

**CITS** lies within the Tai Shan Guest House, awaiting your dollars.

### Places to Stay

The tourist HQ is the *Tai Shan Guest House*. The guest house is a five-storey complex with souvenir shops, telecommunication services, bank, dining halls, 250 beds, and a roof garden snack bar in summer. There are 10 deluxe suites; double rooms go for Y24; a bed in 6-bed dorm is Y8 and there's a massive 20-bed dorm on the second floor which is Y6 a bed.

The guest house is four km from the station and just a short walk from the start of the central route trail up Tai Shan – and its position near the Daimao Temple makes it convenient. To get to the guest house, take bus No 3 from the railway station to the second last stop.

Tai Shan Guest House will hold your bags for you while you climb the mountain (note that the station is cheaper, but we won't quibble over a few fen).

### Places to Eat

Visitors generally keep to the set menus in the dining hall which is not too shabby. There are a couple of other restaurants around town but after Tai Shan your legs may not let you go hunting (if in need, there's a roaring trade in Tainan selling walking sticks – many neatly crafted from gnarled pieces of wood).

### Getting Around

Getting around is easy. The long-distance bus station is near the train station, so all the local transport is directed toward these two termini. There are three main bus routes; bus No 3 runs from the central route trailhead to the western route trailhead via the train station, so that just about covers everything. Buses No 1 and 2 also end up near the station. Auto-rickshaws and pedicabs can be found outside the train station.

### Getting There

There are more than 20 express trains daily running through Tainan with links to Beijing, Harbin, Shengyang, Nanjing, Shanghai, Xian, Zhengzhou, Qingdao and Jinan. Trains go through Jinan and the station you want is Tainan, about 1¼ hours from Jinan. Note that some special expresses don't stop at Tainan. The town is nine hours from Beijing (Y18.40 hard-sleeper, Chinese price), 11 hours from Zhengzhou and nine from Nanjing. Arrival times in Tainan are impossible, with trains pulling in during the early hours of the morning.

Tainan is also approachable by road from either Jinan (50 km) or Qufu (80 km); it is often combined with a trip to Qufu (see the Getting There section for Qufu for buses and more train details).

## TAI SHAN

Tai Shan is the most revered of the five sacred mountains of China, adopted in turn by Taoists, Buddhists, Confucians and Maoists, and from its summit imperial sacrifices to Heaven and Earth were offered. In China's long history, only five emperors felt confident enough to dare the celebration. Emperor Qianlong scaled Tai Shan 11 times; from the heights Confucius uttered the dictum 'the world is small'. Mao lumbered up it – his comment on the sunrise from the top: 'The East is Red'. Poets, writers and painters have found it a great source of inspiration, and extolled its virtues, but one is left wondering now what natural beauty is left. A long string of worshippers have laid their wreaths on the slopes – calligraphy cut into rock faces, temples, shrines, stairs – to which modern history has added revolutionary memorials, guest houses, soft drink and food vendors, photo booths, a weather and radio station, and, the final insult, a cable-car.

No matter, the pull of the supernatural (legend, religion and history rolled into one) is enough. The Princess of the Azure Clouds, a Taoist deity whose presence permeates the temples dotted along the route, is a powerful cult figure for the peasant women of Shandong and beyond. Tribes of wiry grandmothers come each year for the ascent, a journey made difficult by bound feet. Their target is the main temples at the summit, where they can offer gifts and prayers for their progeny; it is said that if you climb Tai Shan you'll live to be 100, and some of the grandmothers look pretty close to that already. For the younger set, Tai Shan is a popular picnic destination; tourists – foreign and Chinese – gather on the cold summit at daybreak in the hope of catching a perfect 747 sunrise. In ancient Chinese tradition, it was believed that the sun began its westward journey from Tai Shan.

As the adage goes: 'the journey of a thousand miles begins with a single step' – on Tai Shan there are some 6000 of them that you'll remember clearly. The mountain is relatively small, but the steps are the kind that get your blood pounding. You and 5000 other climbers, that is: after a while you realise that what you're looking at is not the mountain but the pilgrims toiling up it. The hackwork of China – the carting of concrete blocks, water, produce, goods – is a common sight on the streets, but nowhere does it appear more painful than on the sheer slopes of this mountain.

Porters with weals on their shoulders and misshapen backs plod up the stairway to heaven with crates of drinks, bedding and construction materials – supplies for the hotels and dining halls further up. It's a time-honoured tradition, a job passed from father to son, and most likely the cable-car will do little to alter it (it is planned that the cable-car will transport passengers by day, and cargo by night: graveyard shift?). One wonders how many backs were broken in the building of the temples and stone stairs on Tai Shan over the centuries – a massive undertaking accomplished without mechanical aids.

All in all, as you may have surmised, Tai Shan is not the mountain climbing you might expect it to be, but if you accept that

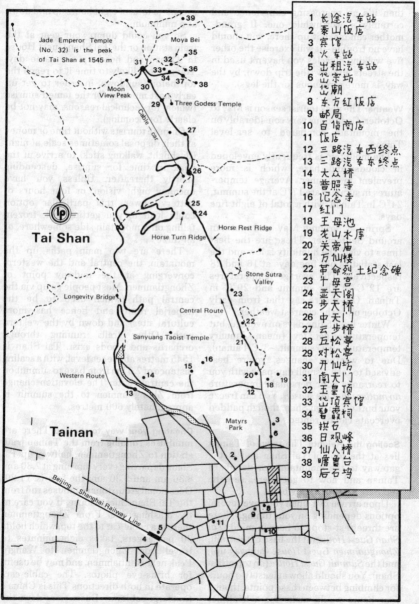

| | |
|---|---|
| 1 | 长途汽车站 |
| 2 | 泰山饭店 |
| 3 | 宾馆 |
| 4 | 火车站 |
| 5 | 出租汽车站 |
| 6 | 岱宗坊 |
| 7 | 岱庙 |
| 8 | 东方红饭店 |
| 9 | 邮局 |
| 10 | 百货商店 |
| 11 | 饭店 |
| 12 | 三路汽车西终点 |
| 13 | 三路汽车东终点 |
| 14 | 大众桥 |
| 15 | 普照寺 |
| 16 | 记念寺 |
| 17 | 门 |
| 18 | 王母池 |
| 19 | 龙山水库 |
| 20 | 关帝庙 |
| 21 | 万仙楼 |
| 22 | 革命烈士纪念碑 |
| 23 | 斗母宫 |
| 24 | 壶天阁 |
| 25 | 步天桥 |
| 26 | 中天门 |
| 27 | 云步桥 |
| 28 | 五松亭 |
| 29 | 对松亭 |
| 30 | 开仙坊 |
| 31 | 南天门 |
| 32 | 玉皇顶 |
| 33 | 岱顶宾馆 |
| 34 | 碧霞祠 |
| 35 | 拱石 |
| 36 | 日观峰 |
| 37 | 仙人桥 |
| 38 | 曜鲁台 |
| 39 | 后石坞 |

**Labels on map:**

Jade Emperor Temple (No. 32) is the peak of Tai Shan at 1545 m

Moya Bei

Moon View Peak

Three Godess Temple

Cable – car

**Tai Shan**

Horse Rest Ridge

Horse Turn Ridge

Stone Sutra Valley

Longevity Bridge

Central Route

Sanyuang Taoist Temple

**Western Route**

**Tainan**

Matyrs Park

Beijing – Shanghai Railway Line

then it's an engrossing experience and certainly a worthwhile one. If grandmother can make it up there, you should have no trouble – it will exercise the other five walking muscles you haven't used in the streets already (the trip down, by the way, is more strenuous for the legs).

**Weather** The peak tourist season is May to October. Conditions vary considerably on the mountain compared to sea-level Tainan.

The mountain is frequently enveloped in clouds and haze, which is more prevalent in summer. Average temperatures in summer are 17°C at the summit, 24°C in Tainan, with a total of eight fine days.

Spring is around May and autumn around September. These are the best times to visit, the humidity is low and the last statistics put fine days at 16 and 28 respectively. The average temperatures are 12°C at the summit and 20°C in Tainan. Old-timers say that from early October on is the clearest weather.

Winter has 35 fine days on average, but temperatures get icy (mean January temperature –9°C summit, –3°C Tainan). Due to weather changes, you're best advised to take a small day-pack with you to rearrange your personal temperature *no matter what the season*. You can freeze your butt off on Tai Shan, though padded overcoats can be rented.

**Scaling the Heights** The town of Tainan lies at the foot of Tai Shan and is the gateway to the mountain. For details of Tainan and how to get there, see the separate section in this book.

Upon arrival in Tainan you have several options depending on your timing. There are three rest-stops to bear in mind: *Tai Shan Guest House* (at the base of the trail), *Zhongtianmen Guest House* (midway up), and the *Summit Guest House* (on top of Tai Shan). You should allow at least two hours for climbing between these points, though four hours would make for a healthier

ascent – a total of eight hours up and down at a minimum.

So you could dump your gear at the train station or the Tai Shan Guest House in Tainan and head up the same day. You're most likely to time it to reach the top before sundown, in order to get up early next morning for the famed sunrise (which, for technical reasons, may not be clearly forthcoming).

Chinese tourists without time or money at their disposal sometimes scale at night (flashlight, walking stick) to arrive at the peak in time for sunrise, descending shortly thereafter. Unless you have uncanny night vision, or four hours of battery power, this particular option could lead to you getting lost, frozen, falling off a mountain side somewhere, or all three . . . .

There are two main paths up the mountain, the central and the western, converging at the midway point of Zhongtianmen. Most people go up via the central path (which used to be the imperial route and hence has more cultural sites) and down by the western path. Other trails running through orchards and woods exist. Tai Shan is 1545 metres above sea level, with a scaling distance of 7.5 km from base to summit on the central route. The elevation change from Zhongtianmen to the summit is approximately 600 metres.

**Cheating your way to the top** There are minibuses running from the Tainan train station to Zhongtianmen, halfway up Tai Shan, departing every morning at 7.30 am, 8.30 am and 9.30 am; the fare is Y1.20. Occasional group tour minibuses run from the Tai Shan Guest House, if you care to try crashing one. From Zhongtianmen there is a cable-car to the top, which holds 30 passengers, takes eight minutes to travel from Zhongtianmen to Wangfu Peak near Nantianmen, and may be useful for birds-eye photos. The cable-cars operate in both directions This is China's first large cableway. Buses come down the mountain hourly between 1 pm and 5 pm, but don't count on the schedule or the seats.

**Central route** A bewildering catalogue of bridges, trees, towers, inscribed stones, caves, pavilions, temples complex and simplex (!). Half the trip, for the Chinese at least, is the colossal amount of calligraphy scoring the stones en route (can they still *read* the old characters?). Tai Shan in fact functions as an outdoor museum of calligraphic art, with the prize items being the Diamond Sutra (or Stone Valley Sutra) and the Moya Bei at the summit which commemorates an imperial sacrifice.

The climb proper begins at **Number One Archway Under Heaven** at the mountain base. Behind that is a stone archway overgrown with wisteria and inscribed 'the place where Confucius began to climb'. **Red Gate Palace**, standing out with its wine-coloured walls, is the first of a series of temples dedicated to the Princess of the Azure Clouds (Bixia), who was the daughter of the God of Tai Shan. It was rebuilt in 1626. **Doumu Hall** was first constructed in 1542 and has the more poetic name of Dragon Spring Nunnery; there's a teahouse within. Continuing through the tunnel of cypresses known as **Cypress Cave** is **Horse-Turn Ridge** where Emperor Zhen Zong had to dismount and continue by sedan-chair because his horse refused to go further. Smart move on the part of the horse: another Emperor rode a white mule up and down the mountain and the beast died soon after the descent (it was posthumously given the title of general and its tomb is on the mountain).

**Zhongtian Men** is the second celestial gate. Beyond **Cloud Bridge** and to the right is the place where Emperor Zhen Zong pitched his overnight tents. A little way on is **Five Pine Pavilion** where one day back in 219 BC, Emperor Qin Shi Huang was overtaken by a violent storm and was sheltered by the kind pines. He promoted them to the 5th rank of Minister though the three you see are, understandably, not

the same ministers. On the slopes higher up is the **Welcoming Pine** with a branch extended as if to shake hands. Beyond that is the **Archway to Immortality** (the belief was that those passing through it would become celestial beings). From here to the summit, emperors were carried in sedan-chairs – eatcha heart out! The third celestial gate is **Nantian Men** –that, and the steep pathway leading up to it are symbolic of Tai Shan, and of Shandong itself and the picture pops up on covers of books and on Shandong maps.

**Dalding (The Summit)** On arrival you see the **Wavelegnth Pavilion** (radio and weather station) and the **Journey to the Stars Gondola** (cablecar) and if you continue along Paradise road, you'll come to **Sunset Statue** (frozen photographer slumped over table, with view beyond dutifully recorded in sunrises, clipped in front of him).

So welcome to Tai Shan shopping centre. Fascinating Chinese antics on the precarious rock lookouts – go and check the **Bridge of the Gods** which are a couple of giant rocks trapped between two precipices. Grandma's epic journey ends at the **Bixia (Azure Clouds) Temple** where small offerings of one sort or another are made to a bronze statue, once richly decorated. The iron tiling on the buildings is intended to avoid damage by strong wind currents and on the bronze eaves there are 'chiwen', ornaments meant to protect against fire. The temple is absolutely splendid, with its location in the clouds, but its guardians are a trifle touchy about you wandering around and parts are inaccessible. Little is known of its history – what is known is that it cost a fortune to restore it or make additions, as was done in the Ming and Qing dynasties. The bronze statuette of the Princess of Azure Clouds is in the main hall.

Perched on the highest point of the Tai Shan plateau is **Jade Emperor Temple** with a bronze statue of a Taoist deity. In the courtyard is a rock inscribed with the elevation of the mountain. In front of the temple is the one piece of calligraphy that you can really appreciate –the **Wordless Monument**. This one will leave you speechless; one story goes that it was set up by the Emperor Wu 2100 years ago – he wasn't satisfied with what his scribes came up with, so he left it to the viewers' imagination.

The main sunrise vantage point is a springboard-shaped thing called **Gongbei Rock** and if you're lucky visibility could be over 200 km, as far as the coast. Sunset slides over the Yellow River side. On the backside of the mountain is **Rear Rocky Recess** which is one of the better-known spots for pine viewing and there are some ruins tangled in the foliage. It's a good place to ramble and lose the crowds for a while.

**Western Route** There's nothing of note in the way of structures, but there's a considerable variation in scenery – orchards, pools, flowering plants. The major scenic attraction is **Black Dragon Pool** which is just below Longevity Bridge (between that and West Brook Pavilion) and fed by a small waterfall. Swimming in the waters are some rare red-scaled carp which are occasionally cooked for the rich. Mythical tales revolve around this pool, said to be the site of underground carp palaces and of magic herbs that turn people into beasts. Worth looking into along the base of the mountain is the **Puzhao Monastery**, founded in 1500 years ago.

**Daimaio (Tai Shan Temple)** is at the foot of the mountain, south of the hotel. This was the pilgrim's first stopover and an ideal place to preview or recap the journey. It once functioned solely for that purpose, being a resting spot for the hiking emperors. The temple is a very large one, 96,000 square metres, enclosed by high walls. The main hall is the Temple of Heavenly Blessing (Tiankung) which towers some 22 metres, constructed of wood with double-roof yellow tiling, and dates to 1009 AD.

The Tiankung was the first built of the 'big three' (the others being Taihe Hall at the Forbidden City, and Dacheng Hall at Qufu). The Tiankung was restored in 1956 and inside is a 62-metre long fresco, running from the west to east walls, depicting the God of Tai Shan on his outward and return journeys. In this case 'God' is Emperor Zhen Zong who had the temple built (Zhen Zong raised the God of Tai Shan to the rank of Emperor – there is a seven-metre high stele to this effect in the western courtyard). The fresco has been painstakingly retouched by artisans of succeeding dynasties, and though recently restored somewhat, it is in poor shape – majestic concept nonetheless.

The temple complex here has been repeatedly restored; in the late 1920s, however, it was stripped of its statues and transmogrified into offices and shops – and later suffered damage under the Kuomintang. It is gradually coming back together, not as a temple but as an open-air museum. There is a forest of 200-odd steles. One inscribed stone, originally at the summit of Tai Shan, is believed to be over 2000 years old (Qin Dynasty) and can be seen at the Eastern Imperial Hall (along with a small collection of imperial sacrificial vessels). Out-of-towners flock to Tai Shan Temple to copy the styles of calligraphy and poetry, of which there is a masterly range. Some have been removed from Tai Shan; also removed from the summit is a beautiful bronze pavilion.

Around the courtyards are ancient cypresses, gingkos and acacias; at the rear of the temple is a bonzai garden and rookery. The cypress in front of Tiankung Hall is amusing: locals and visitors can indulge in a game of luck. A person is blindfolded next to rock, has to go around the rock three times anti-clockwise, then three times clockwise, and try and grope toward the cypress which is 20 steps away. They miss every time. Outside the main temple gates, if it's the right season, street hawkers sell watermelons, with the display pieces cut into the shape of roses.

**Places to Stay & Eat – on the Mountain**
**Zhongtianmen Guest House** is a half-way house with little in the way of food, but there are food stalls nearby. Doubles start at Y18, possibly Y7 per bed. It's very quiet, lacking in water and atmosphere, but if you're tired you probably won't notice.

The **Summit Guest house** has no water except washbasins, is spartan but only costs Y6 per person. It's a Chinese-style squat building with enough space for almost 200 people, and also has a dining hall. If you get the rooms in the right places then you get excellent views. The hotel provides extra blankets and rents out heavy padded cotton overcoats, PLA-type, in lieu of heating. There's even an alarm bell which tells you when to get up for sunrise.

If you wonder where all those amazing grannies go, it seems that there are lodgings tucked off down side trails, possibly former monasteries.

As for other sustenance, there are snacks and drinks and the like sold on the mountain trail.

## YANTAI

Yantai, alias 'Chefoo', is a busy ice-free port on the northern coast of Shandong Peninsula. Like Qingdao it grew from a defence outpost and fishing village, but although it was opened for foreign trade in 1862, it had no foreign concessions. Several nations, the Japanese and the Americans among them, had trading establishments there and Yantai was something of a resort area at one time. About 60 km east of Yantai by road, the British had a concession at Weihaiwei around the turn of the century – it's now a major port. Since 1949, the port and naval base at Yantai have been expanded and apart from fishing and trading, the town is a major producer of wines, spirits and fruits.

**CITS** has an office near the Overseas Chinese Hotel. They're set up to handle stray seamen and the tourist ships – as when a Scandinavian liner disgorges 500 passengers for five hours on their shores. CITS can be summoned over the phone and will arrive pronto in the lobby of the Overseas Chinese Hotel, and that's when your problems begin – they're not terribly helpful.

## Things to See and Do

Apart from getting drunk and building sand-castles, there's very little. Group tours are corralled off to a fish-freezing factory, a brandy distillery, or to the orchards behind the town. Yantai's beaches are not the greatest – they're unsheltered and prone to heavy wind-lashing. The main one is hemmed in at the south-west side by an industrial complex and a naval establishment. Beach Number 2, out by the Chefoo Guesthouse, is small, more likeable, but difficult to get to.

A convenient tour of the town can be had on local bus No 3 which leaves from the square near the train and boat stations – it takes half an hour to get to Yantai Hill. The bus cuts through Yantai, taking in the older parts of town that are being eaten away by apartment blocks and chimney factories, and past the odd colonial edifices, and the newer sections. The bus turns around at the Yantai Hill terminus. If you get off at the terminus and follow a stone wall from there up to the headland, you get a nice view of the naval dockyards, heavy shipping and even navy manoeuvres. 'Yantai' means 'smoke-terrace': wolf dung fires were lit on the headland to warn fishing fleets of approaching pirates, a practice that continued into the Opium Wars. If you continue round the headland, you hit the esplanade for Number l Beach, where there is some distinctively European architecture – former foreign trading or resort housing. You can continue along to the bus No l route which will take you back into town.

## Around Yantai

About 75 km north-west of Yantai by road

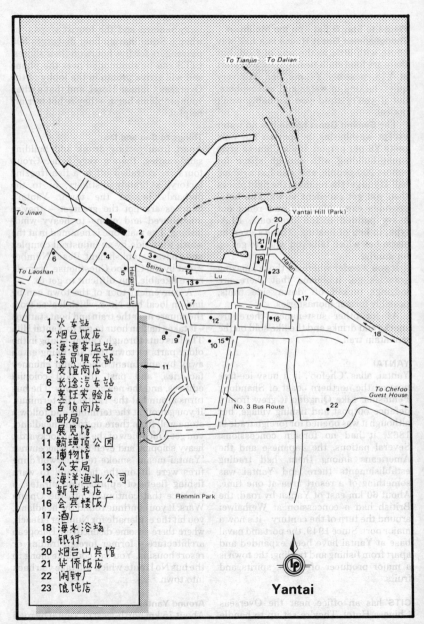

1 火车站
2 烟台饭店
3 海港客运站
4 海员俱乐部
5 友谊商店
6 长途汽车站
7 烹饪实验店
8 百货商店
9 邮局
10 展览馆
11 毓璜顶公园
12 博物馆
13 公安局
14 海洋渔业公司
15 新华书店
16 会宾楼饭厂
17 酒厂
18 海水浴场
19 银行
20 烟台山宾馆
21 华侨饭店
22 闹钟厂
23 馄饨店

To Tianjin
To Dalian
Yantai Hill (Park)
To Jinan
To Laoshan
Haigang Lu
Beima
Lu
Haian
Lu
To Chefoo
Guest House
No. 3 Bus Route
Renmin Park

Yantai

is the coastal castle of Penglai, a place of the gods often referred to in Chinese mythology. The castle is perched on a clifftop overlooking the sea, and is about a thousand years old. The last full mirage seen from this site was in July 1981 when two islands appeared, with roads, trees, buildings, people and vehicles – this phenomenon lasted about 40 minutes (if it lasted any longer, little red flags and factory chimneys would, no doubt, have appeared!). There are some pebbly beaches in the area and a seafood restaurant. Penglai is a two-hour bus ride from Yantai and costs Y1.40, the last bus returning from Penglai at 2.30 pm.

## Places to Stay

I was hoping you wouldn't ask. The bad news: a new highrise, the *Chefoo Guesthouse* has gone up about eight km from the station. It's a nice place but a transport disaster. You need three buses to get there (Nos 3, 4 and 5), and the last one is a rare species indeed, if not extinct. In other words you'll most likely end up commuting by taxi (Y4 to Y8 one way). Otherwise it's hitching or jumping the laundry bus which runs into town from the hotel every morning. As for accommodation, the base rate is Y32 for a double with TV, Y24 a double without TV (or Y12 per person). The main gate closes at 10 pm. There's nothing out in the vicinity of the hotel except the Number 2 Beach which is about ten minutes walk away, a set menu in the dining hall and a conference room for 200 which is set up for reclusive meetings (with participants ferried in by minibus).

The alternative is to try and worm your way into the *Yantai Hill Hotel*, a beautiful villa overlooking the sea – it used to be a tourist hotel but suddenly turned Chinese only. Y30 double (Y14 double negotiable). Some tactics to work on: say you're only staying one night, leaving by train or boat next day and the Chefoo is too far out; or install yourself in the nearest *Chinese* hotel and wait for CITS to come and haul you off to the Yantai Hill Hotel after a good wrangle over hotel rates. Both the Yantai Hill Hotel and the Overseas Chinese Hotel are at the No 3 bus terminus.

## Things to Eat & Wash Down

Cheap meals in the dining rooms of the *Yantai Hill* and the *Overseas Chinese Hotel* for Y2 to Y4. Try also the *Yantai Cooking School* and the *Huibin* both on the bus No 3 route.

The *Yantai Restaurant* is a large eatery between the rail station and the boat station: three rooms – the central one, the cheapest, has a mass of proletarian

| 1 | Railway Station |
|---|---|
| 2 | Yantai Restaurant |
| 3 | Boat Ticket Office & Departures |
| 4 | Seamen's Club |
| 5 | Friendship Store |
| 6 | Long Distance Bus Station |
| 7 | Yantai Cooking School (Restaurant) |
| 8 | Dept. Store |
| 9 | Post Office |
| 10 | Exhibition Hall |
| 11 | Jade Emperor Taoist Temple |

| 12 | Museum |
|---|---|
| 13 | Public Security Office |
| 14 | Ocean Fishing Company |
| 15 | Bookstore |
| 16 | Huibin Restaurant |
| 17 | Wine Distillery |
| 18 | Beach & Esplanade |
| 19 | Bank |
| 20 | Yantai Hill Hotel |
| 21 | Overseas Chinese Hotel CITS / Bus No. Terminus |
| 22 | Alarm Clock Factory |
| 23 | Soup Dumpling Snackshop |

clientele with about four chairs between them, so it's stand-up noodles, dumplings, beggars and bowls of hot water. The other two sections have beer, and bigger, meatier dishes – and chairs.

As for alcohol, you can buy the stuff anywhere, including the train station. It's mostly under Y4 a bottle, and there's some evil-looking substance that retails as low as Y0.80. Yantai is famous for rose-petal wine (meiguijui), brandy (bailandi), and red/white wines. Renowned brands are Yantai Red, Weimeisi Wine, and Jinjiang Brandy.

### Getting Away

**Train** There are two lines to Yantai, one from Jinan and one from Qingdao, joining at Lancun. There are express trains to Beijing (about 19½ hours) and a direct but slow train to Shanghai. There are direct trains to Jinan (about 12 hours).

Of interest to rail buffs is the slow train from Qingdao – hard wooden seats, steam, a magnificent dining car with genuine lamps, curtains and fittings – and beautiful woodwork. This is train No 506; it departs Qingdao at 8.50 am and arrives in Yantai at 3.15 pm (Y4.10 hard-seat, Y7.10 soft-seat). The return train is No 508, which departs Yantai at 12.18 pm.

**Boats** The trip to Dalian on the Liaoning Paninsula cuts a circuitous route by rail to that city. There are daily boats from Yantai and the ticket office in Yantai is open 6am to 8pm. Yantai to Dalian is Y26.40 first class; Y13.20 second (two-bed cabin); Y5 third (four-bed cabin); Y4.40 fourth (eight to 10-bed) and another class that you'd rather not know about, even cheaper. The boat leaves Yantai 8 pm and arrives in Dalian at 6 am the next day. There are other boats between Yantai and Tianjin (berthing at Tianjin's Tanggu Harbour) which run only once every five days. Fare in 2nd class is Y9.10.

### QUFU

Qufu is the birth and death place of Confucius (551-479 BC). The sage's impact was not felt in his own lifetime: he spent his years in abject poverty and hardly put pen to paper. His teachings were recorded by dedicated followers (in the *Analects*), and his descendants, the Kong family, fared considerably better. Confucian ethics were adopted by subsequent rulers to keep the populace in line – there were temples in numerous towns run by officials. Qufu acquired the status of a holy place, with the direct descendants as its guardian angels. The original Confucian Temple at Qufu (dating from 478 BC) was enlarged, remodelled, added to, taken away from, rebuilt . . . . the present buildings are from the Ming Dynasty. In 1513, armed bands sacked the temple and the Kong residence, and walls were built around the town to fortify it (1522-1567). The walls were recently removed, but vestiges of Ming town planning, like Drum and Bell Towers, remain.

More a code that defined hierarchical relationships than a religion, Confucianism has had great impact on Chinese culture: it teaches that son must respect father, wife must respect husband, commoner must respect official, officials must respect their ruler, and vice versa. The essence of the teaching is obedience, respect and selflessness – working for the common good. One would think that this code would have streamlined nicely into the new order of Communism. The values, however, were swept aside because of their connections with the past: Confucius was seen as a kind of misguided feudal educator, and the clan ties and the worship of ancestors were seen as a threat. In 1948 Confucius' direct heir, the first-born son of the 77th generation of the Kong family, fled to Taiwan, breaking a 2500-year chain of Kong residence in Qufu.

In the Cultural Revolution, the emphasis shifted to the youth of China (even if they were being led by an old man). A popular anti-Confucian campaign was instigated and Confucius lost face, and many of the statues at Qufu lost face also amidst cries of 'Down with Confucius, down with his wife!' In the late 60s, a contingent of Red Guards descended on the sleepy town of Qufu burning, defacing and destroying. Other Confucian edifices around the country were also attacted. The leader of the Guards who ransacked Qufu was Tan Houlan; she was jailed for that in 1978, and was not tried until 1982. The Confucius family archives appear to have survived the assaults intact.

Confucian ethics have made something

of a comeback, presumably to instil some civic-mindedness where the Party has (miserably) failed to. Confucianism is finding its way back into the Shandong school system, though not by that name – students are encouraged once again to respect their teachers, their elders, their neighbours and their family. If there's one thing you discover quickly travelling in China, it's that respect amongst the Chinese has fallen to pieces. With corruption at the top of the system, the cynical young find it difficult to reciprocate respect; the elderly remain suspicious of what has passed, untrusting of the attention paid to finding jobs for the young, afraid of the street fights and arguments.

In 1979 the Qufu temples were reopened – millions of yuan were allocated for renovations, or Red Guard repairs. This is Confucius Country – tourism is the name of the game, and 'Confucius' is an excellent name to drop. If a temple hasn't got a fresh coat of paint, new support pillars, replaced tiling or stonework, a souvenir shop, or a photo merchant manning a Great Sage cardboard cut-out, they'll get round to it soon. Some of the buildings are even electrified, with speakers hooked up to the eaves playing soothing flute. Emanating from the eaves is some real music – you have to stop and listen twice to make sure – yes, real birds up there! Perhaps Qufu Department Store doesn't stock BB guns?

Fully one-fifth of Qufu's 50,000 residents are again claiming to be descendants of the Great Sage, though incense-burning, mound-burial and ancestor-worship are not consistent with the Party line. Walk into the local bookstore in Qufu and you'll get another story. If you ask for the works of Confucius, they'll look at you like you're crazy. The walls are lined with the overprinted works of Marx, Mao and company; the locals thrive on a steady diet of comic books. New editions of Confucian texts and some 18th century classics are planned, but like most editions they will be sold out the minute they hit the shelves (due to paper shortages, editions are small, often 20,000) and highly unlikely that they will hit the shelves of Qufu at all.

Whether Confucianism can take fresh root in China is a matter for conjecture – something is needed to fill the idealist void. A recent symposium held in Qufu by Chinese scholars, resulted in careful statements reaffirming the significance of Confucius' historical role, and suggesting that the 'progressive' aspects of his work were a valuable legacy (a legacy cited in the writings of Mao Zedong). It's simply a matter of picking Confucian hairs out of Marxist soup.

There are two fairs a year in Qufu, in spring and autumn. The place comes alive with craftsmen, medicine men, acrobats, pedlars and poor peasants. The fair has a 2000 year old tradition.

**CITS** is at the gate of Confucius Mansions. They're useful, speak English and are well-organised. Help is not really needed as Qufu is a small place – but they have all the bus schedules written up in English and will buy bus tickets for you (there's no mark-up for bus travel). CITS sell a local map showing the temple and residence plan and there is also other literature available from them.

## Things to See

With its marriage of stone, wood and fine imperial architecture, Qufu is a treasure house dripping with culture, second only to the Forbidden City. It's an excellent stopover, worth one or two days. Quiet, real quiet, birds – real birds – and some real grass. Plenty to see, a Ming Dynasty manor for a hotel, no hassling with transport or big-city complications –a good place for traveller R & R.

## Kong Miao (Confucius Temple)

The Temple started out as a simple memorial hall and mushroomed to a complex one-fifth the size of Qufu. It is laid on a north-south axis, over one km long; the main entrance is **Lingxingmen (Star Gate)** at the south, which leads through a series of portals emblazoned with calligraphy. The third entrance gateway, with four bluish characters, refers to the doctrines of Confucius as being heavenly bodies which move in circles without end; it is known as the **Arch of the Spirit of the Universe**.

Throughout the courtyards of the Kong Miao, the dominant features are the clusters of twisted pines and cypresses, and row upon row of steles. The **tortoise tablets** record temple reconstructions, a great ceremony, or perhaps a tree planting: if you could read archaic Chinese they would act as your guide. There are over 1000 steles in the Temple grounds, with inscriptions from the Han to Qing Dynasties – the largest such collection in China. The creatures bearing the tablets of praise are not actually tortoises but 'Bixi', dragon-offspring legendary for their strength. The tablets at Qufu are noted for their fine calligraphy and a rubbing once formed part of the dowry for a Kong lady.

At roughly the mid-way point along the north-south axis is the **Guiwenge (Great Pavilion of the Constellation of Scholars)**, a triple-roofed wooden structure (Jin Dynasty, 1190) of ceremonial importance. Further north through **Dacheng Gate** and to the right is a juniper planted by Confucius – or so claims the tablet in front of it (root-regeneration). The small **Xingtan Pavilion** up from that commemorates the spot where Confucius is said to have taught under the shade of an apricot tree.

The core of the Confucian complex is **Dacheng Hall**, towering 31 metres, on a white marble terrace. The reigning sovereign permitted the importation of glazed yellow tiling for this Hall (as well as the others in the Kong Miao) and special stones were brought in from Xishan. The craftsmen did such a good job on the stone dragon-coiled columns gracing the Hall

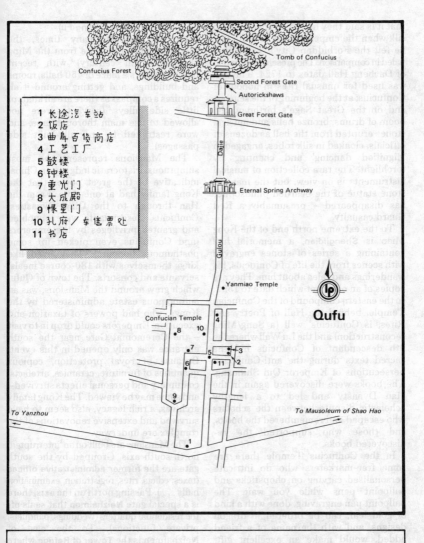

1 Long Distance Bus Station
2 Restaurant
3 Qufu Dept. Store
4 Arts & Crafts Factory
5 Drum Tower
6 Bell Tower
7 Ceremonial Gate
8 Dacheng Hall
9 Lingxing Gate
10 Confucious Mansions /
   CITS / Bus Ticketing Office
11 Bookstore

that it is said they had to be covered with silk when the emperor came to Qufu lest he felt the Forbidden City's Taihe Hall paled in comparison. The present incarnation of Dacheng Hall dates to 1724. The hall was used for unusual rites in honour of Confucius; at the beginning of the seasons and on the Great Sage's birthday, the boom of drums, bronze bells and musical stones erupted from the hall as dozens of officials, cloaked in silk robes, engaged in 'dignified dancing' and chanting by torchlight. The rare collection of musical instruments is on view, but the massive stone statue of the bearded philosopher has disappeared – presumably a Red Guard casualty.

To the extreme north end of the Kong Miao is **Shengjidian**, a memorial hall containing a series of stones engraved with scenes from the life of Confucius, his wanderings and tales about him. They are copies of an older set which date to 1592. In the eastern compound of the Confucian Temple, behind the Hall of Poetry and Rites, is Confucius' well (a Song/Ming reconstruction) and the Lu Wall where the 9th descendant of Confucius hid the sacred texts during the anti-Confucian persecutions of Emperor Qin Shihuang. The books were discovered again in the Han Dynasty and led to a lengthy scholastic dispute between the scholars who escaped and remembered the books, and those who supported the rediscovered books.

In the Confucius Temple there are some free-marketers who do intricate personalised carving on chopsticks and ballpoint pens while you wait. The ballpoint pen engraving, done with a kind of gold leaf, can be ordered in dragon designs, and with the name of a friend added, would make an excellent gift. These vendors will do a chopstick with an English name that the top shops in Shanghai refuse to do (because it's not 'art'). The Friendship Store is also to be found in the Confucius Temple and sells stele-rubbings for calligraphy lovers.

## Confucius Mansions (Kong Fu)

Built and rebuilt many times, the Mansions presently date from the Ming Dynasty (16th century) with recent patchwork. It's a maze of 450 halls, rooms and buildings, and getting around it all requires a compass as there are all kinds of little side alleys (servants were not allowed to use main thoroughfares, and were restricted to specially-built side passages).

The Mansions represent the most sumptuous aristocratic lodgings in China, indicative of the great power that the Kong family had at one time. From the Han through to the Qing Dynasties, Confucius' descendants were ennobled and granted privileges by the emperors (and Confucius even picked up some posthumous honours). They lived like kings themselves with 180-course meals, servants and consorts. The town of Qufu, which grew around the Mansions, was an autonomous estate administered by the Kongs, who had powers of taxation and execution. Emperors could drop in to visit – the Ceremonial Gate near the south entrance was only opened in this event. Because of royal protection, copious quantities of furniture, ceramics, artefacts, costumery and personal effects survived – and some may be viewed. The Kong family archives, a rich legacy, also seem to have survived and extensive renovations of the complex are underway.

The Mansions are built on an 'interrupted' north-south axis. Grouped by the south gate are the former **administrative offices** (taxes, edicts, rites, registration, examination halls . . . ). Passing north on the axis, there is a special gate **Neizhaimen** that seals off the residential quarters (weddings, banquets, private functions). To the east of Neizhaimen is the **Tower of Refuge** where the Kong clan could gather in case the peasants turned nasty. It has an iron-lined ceiling on the ground floor, and a staircase that is removable to the first floor. Grouped to the west of the main axis are former recreational facilities (studies, guest rooms, libraries, small temples). To the east, the odd kitchen, ancestral temple, family branch apartments. Far north, a spacious garden with rockeries, ponds and bamboo groves. Kong Decheng, the last of the line, lived in the Mansions until the 1940s when he hightailed it to Taiwan.

### Kong Lin (Confucian Forest)

North of Confucius Mansions, about 2½ km up on Drum Tower Rd, is the Confucian Forest, the largest man-made park and best-preserved cemetery in China. A time-worn route, it has a kind of 'spirit-way' lined with ancient cypresses. It's about a 40-minute walk or 10 minutes in an autorickshaw. On the way, look into the **Yanmiao Temple** off to the right which has a spectacular dragon head embedded in the ceiling of the main hall, and a pottery collection. The route to the forest passes through the **Archway of Eternal Spring**, its stone lintels decorated with coiled dragons, flying phoenixes and galloping horses (Ming, 1594). At the **Forest Gates** visitors had to dismount and permission was required to enter. The Forest covers 200 hectares and is bounded by a wall 10 km long. Buried here is the Great Sage himself, and all his descendants; the trees, numbering over 20,000, are pines and cypresses planted by followers of Confucius. Flanking the approach to **Confucius' Tomb** are a pair of stone panthers, griffins and larger than life guardians. The Confucian tumulus is a simple grass mound, six metres high, enclosed by a low wall, and faced with a Ming Dynasty stele. Nearby are buried his immediate sons; scattered through the Forest are dozens of temples and pavilions, and hundreds of sculptures, tablets and tombstones . . .

### Places to Stay

Stay at the *Confucius Mansions* – not often will you get to stay in such labyrinthine splendour. For genuine classical architecture, this is the finest hotel in China and is

cheap to boot. There are no TVs or carpets, but the rooms are comfortable and have baths. The starting price is Y12 per bed and up though you can knock it down to Y6 a bed. There is a new, traditional-style hotel under construction in the town.

### Places to Eat

The *Confucius Mansions* dining hall has western breakfast for Y1.20 and lunch Y2.30. The alternative, if you need one, is a restaurant near Qufu Department Store. There are snack stalls in and around the main attractions and these have good fare.

### Getting There

There's no direct railway to Qufu. When the project to have a railway station at Qufu was first brought up, the Kong family petitioned for a change of routes, claiming that the trains would disturb the great sage's tomb. They won in the end – the clan still had pull in those days – and the nearest the tracks go is Yanzhou, 13 km to the west of Qufu. The railway builders haven't given up and the next in line to disturb the sage's tomb is CAAC with an airport planned at Qufu.

Yanzhou is on the Beijing-Shanghai line with a fair selection of trains. Try and get one that arrives at Yanzhou before 4 pm, since the last bus from Yanzhou to Qufu is at 5 pm. Some special express trains don't stop at Yanzhou and others arrive at inconvenient times like midnight. Yanzhou is two hours by train from Taian, three hours from Jinan, about seven hours from Nanjing, and about nine hours from Kaifeng.

Leaving Yanzhou is less of a problem – but again you have to make an early evening bus connection. Check the rail timetable at the CITS office in Qufu. There are about 20 Qufu-Yanzhou buses a day with with a frequency of half an hour or less. The last bus departs Yanzhou for Qufu at 5 pm. The last bus to Yanzhou departs Qufu at 5.40 pm with a possible bus at 6.40 pm. The fare is Y0.40. Buses start running at 6.30 am. The bus station in Yanzhou is 100 metres from the Yanzhou Hotel (see below). There are also direct buses from Qufu to Taian, a three-hour trip which costs Y2.10; there are three or four buses a day (two continue to Jinan), departing 7 am, 1 pm, 1.30 pm.

If you get stuck in Yanzhou on your way to Qufu then this is your big chance to stay in a Chinese hotel. The *Yanzhou Hotel* is right near the station; go straight ahead from the station and the hotel is on your left. They'll start off at around Y12 but you can get that down to Y5 or less per bed. Not even the mirrors work here – bare bulbs dangling from the ceiling, towels all over the furniture, washing up and down the corridors, and no curtains. Follow your nose to the washroom; you can cook your own food downstairs out the back. Zero items of interest in Yanzhou town.

## AROUND QUFU

Four km east of Qufu is the **Mausoleum of Shao Hao**, one of the five legendary emperors supposed to have ruled China 4000 years ago. It's the only pyramidal tomb in China. It dates from the Song Dynasty and is made of large blocks of stone, 25 metres base width, six metres high, with a small temple on top.

To the south of Qufu, a short hop on the rail line from Yanzhou is **Zouxian**, which is the home town of Mencius. Mencius (372-289 BC) is regarded as the first great Confucian philosopher – he developed many of the ideas of 'Confucianism' as they were later understood.

# Hebei

Wrapping itself around the centrally-administered municipalities of Beijing and Tianjin is the province of Hebei. The province is often viewed as an extension of Beijing or Tianjin, the red tape maker and the industrial giant respectively. This is not far off the mark since, geographically speaking, they take up a fair piece of the pie anyway. In fact, Tianjin used to be the provincial capital, but when that came under central government administration the next largest city, Shijiazhuang replaced it. The population of Hebei is 53 million.

The relief map of Hebei falls into two distinct parts – the mountain tableland to the north, where the Great Wall runs (and also to the western fringes of the province), and the monotonous southern plain. Agriculture, mainly wheat and cotton, is hampered by dust storms, droughts (five years in a row from 1972 to 1977) and flooding –which will give you some idea of the weather. It's scorching and humid in summer, freezing in winter, dust fallout in spring, with heavy rainfall in July and August. Coal is the main resource and most of it is shipped through Qinhuangdao, an ugly port town with iron and steel and machine industries secondary.

As far as tourist sights go the pickings in Hebei are slim, and if I were you, I'd make a wide detour around the capital, Shijiazhuang. Down that way also is Handan, an industrial city and one of the oldest in Hebei with an iron and steel plant, coal mining, textiles, a fair number of historical sites, production of imitation Song dynasty glazed pottery and porcelain - and you can forget all that because the place is closed.

On the other hand, there's still Beidaihe, the weirdest summer resort you'll ever visit, and Chengde with its memories of palaces and temples. And there's Tangshan, the city that disappeared in a few minutes when an eight-on-the-richter-scale -earthquake struck it on 28 July, 1976. The big attraction here is going to be the casting section of a rolling stock plant, with rubble of wall, steel, cement and rusted equipment – officials in Tangshan say there are no plans to clear it up – rather it will be left for future generations to dwell on. Apart from that the greatest thing to see is the Wanli Changcheng, the Great Wall, which makes everything else look insignificant. Whilst the rest of Hebei may not paint much of a pretty picture, the wall makes it all worthwhile.

## CHENGDE

Chengde is an 18th century imperial resort area, also known as 'Jehol'. It's billed as an escape from the heat (and now the traffic) of summers in the capital and boasts the remnants of the largest regal gardens in China.

Chengde remained an obscure town until 1703, when Emperor Kangxi began building a summer palace – with a throne room and the full range of court trappings. More than a home away from home, Chengde turned into a sort of government seat, since where the Emperor went, his seat went too. Kangxi called his summer creation 'Bihushanzhuang' (Fleeing the heat Mountain Hamlet); by 1790, in the reign of his grandson Qianlong, it had grown to the size of Beijing's Summer Palace and Forbidden City combined – a

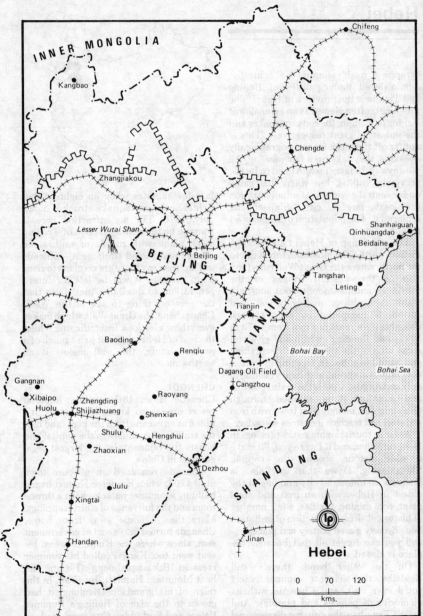

Hebei

0        70      120

kms.

vast park bounded by a 10 km wall. Qianlong extended an idea that Kangxi had started, which was to build replicas of minority architecture to make envoys feel comfortable. In particular he was keen on promoting Tibetan and Mongolian Lamaism, which had proved to be a useful way of debilitating the meddlesome Mongols. The Mongolian branch of Lamaism required one male in every family to become a monk – a convenient method of rechannelling manpower and ruining the Mongol economy. This serves to explain the Tibetan and Mongolian features of the monasteries north of the summer palace, one of them a replica of the Potala.

So much for business – the rest was the Emperor's pleasure. The usual bouts of hunting, consorts and feasting. Occasionally the outer world would make a rude intrusion into this dream-life: in 1793 along came British emissary Lord Macartney, seeking to open the China trade. Qianlong dismissed him with the statement that China possessed all things and had no need of trade.

Chengde has very much slipped back into being the provincial town it once was, its grandeur long decayed, its monks and emperors long gone. The population, over 150,000, is engaged in mining, textiles, light industry, canned food and tourism. The Qing court has left them a little legacy, but one that needs working on. The palaces and monasteries are not what they're cracked up to be, or, alternatively, more cracked up than you'd expect them to be. The Buddhist statues are disfigured, on occasion beyond recognition, or else locked up in dark corners; windows are bricked up; columns are reduced to stumps; the temples are facades, impressive from the outside but shells on the inside. All this is currently being restored, in some cases from the base up, in the interests of a projected increase in tourism. On the cards is the addition of Chinese and western restaurants, high-class shops, evenings of traditional music (with instruments rescued and copied from tombs around China), horse riding . . . meanwhile there's absolutely nothing wrong with ruins, just a matter of changing your expectations. Chengde has nothing remotely approaching Beijing's temples, if you were expecting something along those lines (Chinese photography of the place is more a tribute to the skills of the photographers and lab technicians than anything else).

The dusty small-town ambience of Chengde is nice enough; there's some quiet hiking in the rolling countryside and Chinese speakers, apparently, are delighted with the clarity of the local dialect (is that because they can actually hear it in the absence of traffic?)

## Bihushanzhuang

The park is 590 hectares, bounded by a 10 km wall. Emperor Kangxi decreed that there would be 36 'beauty spots' in Jehol; Qianlong delineated 36 more. That makes a total of 72 but where are they? At the north end of the gardens the pavilions were decimated by warlords and Japanese invaders and even the forests have suffered cutbacks. The park is on the dull side, not much in the way of upkeep. With a good deal of imagination, you can perhaps detect traces of the original scheme of things with borrowed landscaping from southern gardens (Suzhou, Hangzhou, Jiaxing) and Mongolian grasslands. There is even a feature for resurrecting the moon should it not be around – there is a pool that shows a crescent moon created by reflection of a hole in surrounding rocks.

Passing through Lizhengmen, the main gate, you arrive at the Front Palace, a modest version of Beijing's Palace. It contains the main throne hall, the Hall of Simplicity and Sincerity, built of an aromatic hardwood called nanmu. The hall now functions as a museum, with displays of royal memorabilia, arms, clothing and other accoutrements, and the emperor's bedrooms are fully furnished. Around to the side is a door without an exterior handle, through which the lucky bed partner for the night was ushered and stripped and searched by eunuchs.

The double-storeyed Misty Rain Tower, on the north-west side of the main lake, was an imperial study; further north of that is the Wenjin Chamber, built in 1773 to house a copy of the Sikuquanshu, a major anthology (classics, history, philosophy, literature) commissioned by Qianlong. The anthology took 10 years to put together; four copies were made of which three have disappeared, and the fourth is in Beijing.

Ninety per cent of the compound is taken up by lakes, hills, mini-forests and plains, with the odd vantage point pavilion. At the northern part of the park, the emperors reviewed displays of archery, horsemanship or fireworks. Horses were also chosen and tested here before hunting sorties. Yurts were set up on the mock-Mongolian prairies (a throne, of course, installed in the Emperor's yurt) and picnics were held for minority princes. So, good idea, pack a lunch, take your tent, and head off for the day ... the yurts are back again for the benefit of weary tourists.

### Waibamiao (Outer Temples)

To the north and north-east of the imperial garden are former temples and monasteries. Well, what *is* the count? They started off at 11 many years ago, plummeted to five (Japanese bombers, Cultural Revolution), and now the numbers given vary from five to nine. I make it 4.5 and some heavy socialist

reconstruction – by the time you get there, it might even be five. The outer temples are about three to five km from the garden front gate; a bus No 6 taken to the north-east corner will land you in the vicinity.

The surviving temples were built 1750 to 1780. The Chinese-style Purensi and the vaguely Shanxi-style Shuxiangsi are undergoing total rebuilding. Clockwise, the temples are:

**Putuozongsheng** is the largest of the Chengde temples, and is a mini-facsimile of Lhasa's Potala. It was built for the chieftains from Xinjiang, Qinghai, Mongolia and Tibet to celebrate Qianlong's 60th birthday and was also a site for religious assemblies. It's a solid-looking fortress, but no guts and in bad shape, parts inaccessible or boarded up and gutted by fire.

**Xumifushou** was built in honour of the sixth Panchen Lama, who visited in 1781 and stayed here. It incorporates elements of Tibetan and Han architecture and is actually an imitation of a temple in Xigaze, Tibet. At the highest point is a hall with eight gilded copper dragons commanding the roof ridges and behind that sits a glazed-tile pagoda.

**Puning** is also modelled on a Tibetan temple, built to commemorate Qianlong's victory over Mongol tribes – the subjugated leaders were invited to Chengde. A stele relating to the victory is inscribed in Tibetan, Mongol, Chinese and Manchu. The main feature is an Avalokita, towering 22 metres; this wooden Buddha has 42 arms with an eye on each palm.

| | |
|---|---|
| 1 Jiaodaichiu Hotel | 11 Anyuan (Distant Tranquility) Temple |
| 2 Outdoor Markets | 12 Puning (Universal Peace) Temple |
| 3 Chengde Dept. Store | 13 Ximifushou (Mount Sumeru) Temple |
| 4 Arts & Craft Store | 14 Putuozhongsheng (Potala) Temple |
| 5 Chengde Hotel | 15 Shuxiang (Wenshu Image) Temple |
| 6 Renmin Restaurant | 16 Lizhengmen (Main Gate) |
| 7 Long Distance Bus Station | 17 Front Palace |
| 8 Puren (Universal Love) Temple | 18 Misty Rain Tower |
| 9 Hammer Rock | 19 Wenjin Chamber |
| 10 Pule (Universal Joy) Temple | |

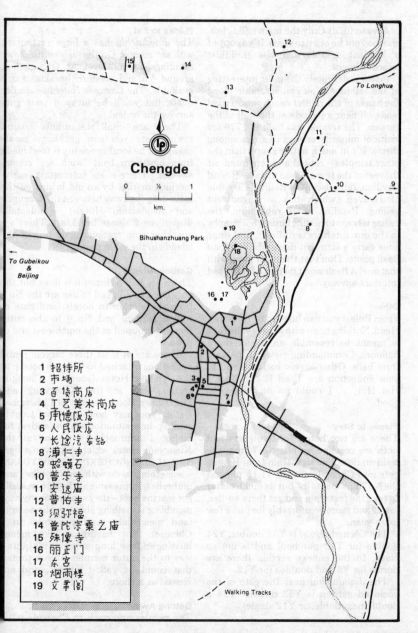

To Longhua

To Gubeikou
&
Beijing

**Chengde**

0    ½    1
km.

Bihushanzhuang Park

Walking Tracks

1 招待所
2 市场
3 百货商店
4 工艺美木商店
5 承德饭店
6 人民饭店
7 长途汽车站
8 溥仁寺
9 磬锤峰石
10 普乐寺
11 安远庙
12 普佑寺
13 须弥福
14 普陀宗乘之庙
15 殊像寺
16 丽正门
17 东宫
18 烟雨楼
19 文拿阁

**Anyuan** (0.5!) Only the main hall is left, and may not be open to visits. It's a copy of a Xinjiang temple and has Buddhist frescoes inside.

**Pulesi** is definitely the most interesting of the temples. You can scramble along the banks of the rivulet nearby and a road leads off near a pagoda at the wall of the garden. The temple was built in 1776 for visits of minority envoys (Kazaks among them). It's in much better shape than the other temples – retiled and repainted. At the rear of the temple is an unusual Round Pavilion, reminiscent of Beijing's Temple of Heaven, which has a magnificent ceiling. Pending total rebuilding, the ceiling is home to nesting birds. Photography in the dim interiors is difficult, and some sites carry a sign that demands Y10 for a flash photo. Don't let them get away with that one! A flash won't do much for the sad interiors anyway.

### Other

From Pulesi you can hike up to Hammer-Head. Nothing to do with sharks – the rock is meant to resemble an upside-down hammer. Commanding views of the area from here. Other scenic rocks to add to your collection are Toad Rock, Monk's Hat Hill ... I could go on. Hiking is good.

### Places to Stay

There are two hotels for foreigners and both are reached by bus No 7 from the train station. The slow train from Beijing gets into Chengde around 11.15 pm and the No 7 bus meets it – but its much better to take the fast train and get there earlier, faster and more comfortably for just a few extra yuan.

The *Chengde Hotel* is Y32 double, Y24 double (or Y12 per bed) and is not so clean. In the annexe section there are dorms for Y5 and doubles for Y12.

The *Jiaodaichiu* near the gate of the enclosed garden is Y32 double (Y24 a double negotiable, or Y12 single).

### Places to Eat

The *Jiaodaichiu* has a large restaurant with set menus. Go through to the inner buildings, second level. An OK lunch is around Y5 and western breakfasts are available. The *Chengde Hotel* has similar deals, but you'll be lucky if your guts survive the ordeal.

There are small restaurants around town where you can get huge meals cheaply. The local speciality is food made from hawthorn fruit (wine, ice cream sweets). There's an interesting early morning market by an old bridge on the main drag (halfway between the Chengde and Jiaodaichiu Hotels) – sidestalls dispensing Chinese breakfast. There's a snackbar cum restaurant on one of the islands in the main park.

### Getting Around

There are half a dozen bus lines but the only ones you'll need to use are the No 7 from the station to hotels (and gate of walled garden) and No 6 to the outer temples grouped at the north-east end of town.

There are at least three bicycle rental operations attached to Chinese hotels; at the Xinhua Hotel (south of Chengde Hotel), and at the Xiangyang and Lizhengmen Hotels (vicinity of Lizhengmen Gate). You may however have trouble renting, in a situation which is ideal for biking. I approached the one at the Xiangyang Hotel, which displayed a sign 'CHUZUZIXINGCHEXINGLIYUYIYUSAN – something to do with renting bikes and umbrellas. Impressive as the sign was, all I got was the boot – they sent me on my way mumbling something about public security (and meanwhile renting a bike to a Chinese). Not having a bike meant bussing and the 'long march' as it's quite a way to the outer temples. If you prefer that could be called 'hiking', and not viewed as a chore.

### Getting Away

The regular approach to Chengde is by

train from Beijing; an unexplored route is the train from Jinzhou which is in Liaoning Province on the way to Shenyang. There are also long-distance buses plying the road between Chengde and Beijing. There is an airport at Chengde but this is used by CITS charter flights and there is no regular passenger service.

The fastest trains to Beijing take about five hours (Y5.30 hard seat, Chinese price). Slow trains take about seven hours, Y4.40 on a hard *wooden* seat, Chinese price. These trains have one sleeper car and it's an extra Y9.80 for a berth.

## BEIDAIHE-QINHUANGDAO-SHANHAIGUAN

The Beidaihe-Qinhuangdao-Shanhaiguan district is a 35 km stretch of coastline on China's east coast, bordering the Bo Sea (Bo Hai).

The three stations of Beidaihe, Qinghuangdao and Shanhaiguan are all accessible by train from Beijing, Tianjin

1 Beidaihe Railway Stn 北戴河饭店
2 Liangfeng Park / Sea Facing Pavilion 连蓬山公园
3 Western Hills (Xi Shan) Hotel 西山宾馆
4 Central Beach (Zhongaitan) Hotel 中海滩宾馆
5 Bus Terminus / Free Market Area 汽车终点
6 Broadcasting Tower 广播楼
7 Eastern Hills (Dong Shan) Hotel 东山宾馆
7 Pigeon's Nest 鸽子窝
9 Eagle Pavilion 鹰角亭
10 Tiger Rocks 老虎石
11 Seamen's Club & Hotel 海员俱乐部
12 Oil Wharf 油码头
13 Great Wall Museum 文物保管所
14 'First pass under Heaven' 天下第一关
15 Great Wall Souvenir Shops 旅游纪念品服务部
16 Trade Service Hotel 商业饭店
17 Jiangnu Temple 孟姜庙
18 Old Dragon Head (where the Great Wall meets the sea) 老龙头
19 Yansai Lake 燕塞湖

Bus routes
Rail routes

or Shengyang. There are frequent trains but they don't always stop at all three stations (they usually stop at Shanhaiguan but several skip Beidaihe), and they don't always arrive at convenient hours. The major factor to consider is that the hotel at Shanhaiguan is within walking distance of the train station, whereas at Beidaihe the nearest hotel is at least 10 km from the station (you can't count on a connecting bus after 6 pm and a taxi would cost Y10 or so). So if you're going to arrive in the early hours of the morning it's better to do so at Shanhaiguan.

It takes the fastest trains five hours to make it to Beidaihe from Beijing, and an it's an extra 1½ hours to Shanhaiguan. Shenyang to Shanhaiguan is a five hour trip. On a special express train, hard-seat (Chinese price) will cost you Y8.70 (Beijing-Beidaihe) and Y11.20 (Shenyang-Beidaihe).

Alternatively you could get a train that stops at Qinhuangdao and then take a bus from there to Beidaihe. Or you could jump a midnight train from either Beijing or Shenyang, arrive early in the morning, day-trip, and go on to the next place. One rail route to consider is the connection from the city of Jinzhou to Chengde. The resorts of Chengde and Beidaihe are usually considered separate round trips from Beijing, but by going through Jinzhou (which lies between Shanhaiguan and Shenyang), it might be possible to do an all-embracing round trip.

There are some dubious maritime links between Qinhuangdao and Dalian, Shanghai, Qingdao and Tianjin. But it's unclear whether these are freight or passenger boats. If they are passenger, then the journey will be cheaper than rail and in the case of Dalian the trip could be shorter.

Buses connect Beidaihe, Shanhaiguan and Qinhuangdao, and these run from 6.30 am to 6.30 pm (not guaranteed after 6 pm), generally every 30 minutes. Fares are nominal, 20 to 30 fen. Some of the important routes are:

Beidaihe Station to Beidaihe Beach, takes 30 minutes, bus No 5. Beidaihe Beach to Qinghuangdao, takes 40 minutes, bus No 4. Qinghuangdao to Beidaihe Station , takes 45 minutes, bus No 6. Qinghuangdao to Shanhaiguan, takes 30 minutes, bus No 3.

## BEIDAIHE
Beidaihe is a seaside resort opened to foreigners in 1979. It was in fact built by westerners: the simple fishing village was transformed when English railway engineers stumbled across it in the 1890s. Diplomats, missionaries and businessmen from the Tianjin concessions and the Beijing Legations set about throwing up villas and cottages to indulge in the new fad of bathing. The original golf courses, bars and cabarets have disappeared. In the interests of the nouveau bourgeoisie, there are signs that these will be revived: a recent article in the People's Daily suggested: 'It does much good to both body and mind to putt and walk under fresh air'. There are plans afoot to construct golf courses in the suburbs of Beijing and Guangzhou. Meanwhile, back in Beidaihe, what is more desperately needed than a golf course is a coat of paint since the architecture is monumentally drab. Something jars – the setting is right enough – hills, rocks, beaches, pine forests, a sort of Mediterranean flavour – but the buildings appear too heavy to the modern eye, and lacking in glass.

But really, who gives a damn about the architecture? Then, as now, Beidaihe is an escape from the hassles of Beijing or Tianjin – the Beijing International Club runs its own villas there, with package tours from the capital. Kiesslings, the former Austrian restaurant, sells excellent pastries and seafood in the summer. The cream of China's leaders congregate at the summer villas, also continuing a tradition (Jiang Qing, Mao's wife, had a large villa here, and so did Lin Biao). Both the foreign diplomat and the Party compounds are guarded by rifle-toting soldiers in

Top: The Terracotta Army, Xian [MB]
Left: Pollution in the Yangtze River at Nanjing [MB]
Right: Author and friend, Datong [AS]

Top: Front gate (Qianmen), Beijing [AS]
Bottom : A night at the opera, Beijing [MB]

sentry boxes. Just to make sure nothing nasty comes by in the water, there are shark nets (dubious whether sharks would approach at this latitude) –or maybe they're submarine nets. Army members and working heroes are rewarded with two-week vacations at Beidaihe; there are large numbers of sanatoriums where patients can get away from the honking of cars, the screech of traffic and machinery, and, more importantly, breathe some fresh air.

That's about all you need to know about Beidaihe. The Chinese have worked the place over trying to categorise the rocks and deciding whether they're shaped like camels or tigers or steamed bread (or immortalising the rocks where Mao sat and wrote lines about fishing boats disappearing). Nobody gives a hoot – they come for the beaches. For the Chinese that could mean indulging in the new fad of bathing all over again, and bare thighs are in style.

The village only comes to life in the summer (June to September) when it's warm, fanned by sea breezes, and the beaches are jammed. Average June temperature is 21°C. In January, by contrast, temperatures rest at minus 5°C.

**Beaches** All right, where's your swimming licence? Doesn't appear that you need one for the open sea, and in case you forgot your bathers, they'll fix you up with a set. Class divisions, however, still extend to the seaside. There are three beaches at Beidaihe. The foreign stretch of sand is the West Beach, in front of the International Club complex: marked off, rattan chairs and CITS beach umbrellas. Lifeguards shoo away Chinese curious about western shapes and sizes, especially if the shapes come packaged in bikinis. The smaller middle beach is used by cadres, state guests and high officials. The East Beach, stretching half a dozen km from Beidaihe toward Qinghuangdoa, is for privileged Chinese vacationers and the sanatorium

patients. This beach is the finest in terms of sand. As an individual, it's not clear where the class system places you – so you might as well take advantage of the situation and swim where you like.

## Miscellania

There's various hikes to vantage points with expansive views of village villas or seaside, notably the pavilion at Lotus Rock Park. For early morning strollers the tide at the East Beach recedes dramatically and tribes of kelp and shell-pickers descend upon it. You can even be photographed with amusing cardboard cut-out racing boats with the sea as a backdrop. There may be some nightlife at the International Club complex or Xishan Beach Club. The free market behind the bus terminus has the most amusing high-kitsch collection of sculpted and glued shellwork this side of Dalian – go see. Handicrafts such as raffia and basketware on sale in stores.

## Places to Stay

Three possibilities for travellers: the *Xishan (Western Hills) Hotel,* the *Zhonghaitan (Central Beach) Hotel* and *Dongshan (East Hills) Hotel*, all located exactly where the names suggest. Prices are in the Y34 double category, though you may negotiate it to Y24 or less for a double.

If you're aiming for the *Xishan* (tel 2018) and arriving by bus from Beidaihe Station, get the driver to drop you off on the way in – it's a reasonable distance to walk back there from the bus terminus.

Though comfortable, the *Zhonghaitan* (tel 2445) has an atmosphere that is a cross between a hospital, a prison and a Jacques Tati movie set. It's just around the corner from the bus-terminus. CITS is located near the gates of this hotel.

There are other villas but they're generally only for tour groups.

## Places to Eat

In season, seafood is dished up in various restaurants. There's the *Beihai Fandian* near the markets and the *Haibin Fandian* near the Bank of China (Broadcasting Tower area). Near the Haibin is *Kiesslings* which is a relative of the Tianjin branch and only operates June to August. You can haggle for crabs in the markets, then take them over to Kiessling's for crab au gratin. There are other restaurants inside the hotels, as well as a couple of ice cream parlours scattered about.

### Getting Around

Turn left out of the gates of the Zhonghaitan and go about 70 metres, there's a small green building on the left that rents bicycles – not many available. There are also taxis and minibuses for hire, but bicycles are the best transportation. There are a couple of short-run buses in Beidaihe, such as from the centre of town to Pigeon's Nest (summer only) but the area is small enough to walk around, or you can stick to the longer-route buses and alight where you want. Unlike Shanhaiguan and Qinhuangdao, the buses in Beidaihe don't connect around the train station. Take bus No 5 from Beidaihe train station to Beidaihe beach; a half-hour trip.

### QINGHUANGDAO

Qinghuangdao is an ugly port city that you'd have to squeeze pretty hard for signs of life, and even harder if you wanted to see something. It has an ice-free harbour and petroleum is piped in from the Daqing oilfields to the wharves. Pollution on both land and sea is incredible – like the chemical fumes from the glass factory. This is *not* the place to visit; the locals will be the first to suggest that you move along to Beidaihe or Shanhaiguan.

No permit is needed as Qinghuangdao is one of the 29 cities open with passport only, and Shanhaiguan and Beidaihe fall under its jurisdiction.

If you do get stuck here most needs are catered to on a No 2 bus route from the train station. This runs the short distance to the port area where the Seamen's Club

has a hotel, restaurant (some seafood) and bar/store. The Seaman's Club is only a 15 minute walk from the station if you can't nail a No 2 bus. Rooms in the hotel there are Y8 single, Y22-24 double, Y23 triple.

### SHANHAIGUAN

Shanhaiguan is where the Great Wall meets the sea, or, should we say, crumbles into it. The Wall, what's left of it, is in poor shape, but Shanhaiguan is well worth your time. It was a garrison town, with a square fortress, four gates at the compass points, and two major avenues running between the gates. The present village is within the substantial remains of the old walled enclosure, making it a rather picturesque place to wander around. Shanhaiguan has a long and chequered history –nobody is quite sure how long or what kind of chequer. Plenty of pitched battles and blood, one imagines.

### East Gate

The main attraction is the magnificent east gate, topped with a two-storey double-roofed tower (Ming Dynasty, rebuilt 1639). The calligraphy at the top (attributed to the scholar Xiao Xian) reads: 'The First Pass Under Heaven'. The words reflect the Chinese belief that divided the world into civilised China and the 'barbarians'. The barbarians got the better of civilised China when they stormed this gate in 1644. There's an intriguing mini-museum in the tower, displaying armour, dress, weaponry and pictures. A short section of the Wall attached to the east gate has been rebricked; from this vantage point you can see decayed sections trailing off into the mountains. There's a snack bar right on top of the wall at the tower; souvenir shops selling First Pass Under Heaven tablecloths, and a parked horse waiting for photos.

**Side trips** A visit to the seaside to see Old Dragon Head (the legendary carved dragon head that once faced the sea) will end in disappointment. It's a four km hike, and there's nothing much there although there is a beach. A more viable route is to follow the Wall north (by road) to the first beacon tower. You can get part way by bicycle on a dirt road, and pass a small village with some pleasant countryside. On the north road, toward the town exit, is the one restaurant of note in Shanhaiguan, simply called the 'North Road' (serves mutton and other dishes). Six kilometres north-west of Shanhaiguan is Yansai Lake, an artificial reservoir 45 km long with tourist boating – give them a few years and they'll make a Guilin out of it yet.

Six km east of Shanhaiguan (with regular bus service from the south gate) is the **Temple of Mengjiangnu**, a Song/Ming reconstruction with coloured sculptures of Lady Meng and her maids, and calligraphy by the famous inscribed on 'Looking for Husband Rock'. Meng's husband, Wan, was pressganged into Wall building because his views conflicted with those of the Emperor Qin Shi-huang. As winter approached, the beautiful Meng Jiang set off to take warm clothing to her husband, only to discover that he had perished from backbreaking labour. Meng tearfully wandered the Wall, thinking only of finding the bones to give Wan a decent burial. The Wall was very moved and a long section suddenly crumbled, revealing the skeletons entombed within. Overcome with grief, Meng climbed to the top of a boulder and then threw herself into the sea . . .

### Places to Stay & Eat

The *Shanhaiguan Trade Service Hotel* is a TV-type hotel with three classes – special, first and second (Y30 double, starting price). The hotel restaurant is passable. Opposite the hotel, by the south gate wall, is the bus station with a snack bar.

### Getting Around

The town is easy to get around on foot: there are two key points to bear in mind, the south gate (just up from the railway station), and the east gate. At the south gate, as you walk up from the station, there's a bicycle-rental on your left (old hulks) and another in the Shanhaiguan Trade Service Hotel, the large building on the right. The S.T.S. Hotel will rent bikes and raingear – good bikes for Y1.60 a day. Like Beidaihe there are some short-route buses, but again you can easily walk around much of the area. Buses in Shanhaiguan all connect near the train station.

### SHIJIAZHUANG

The odd man out in Hebei, Shijiazhuang is a rail junction about 250 km south-west of Beijing. At the turn of the century the place had a population of 500, a few roads and a couple of wells. With the building of the Beijing-Wuhan Line in 1905 (financed by a Belgian company) and the Shijiazhuang-Taiyuan Line which was finished in 1907 (a Russian/French project), the town rapidly expanded to a population of 10,000 in the 1920s. It is now the capital of Hebei Province, and has a population of 900,000.

It serves as the centre of Hebei cotton production, and is a major producer of textiles, machinery (cars, diesel engines, mining equipment), petrochemicals and electronics equipment. It has the largest pharmaceutical plant in north China; the plains around it are used for the cultivation of wheat and cotton. To the west of the city, in the Taihang mountains, is a mining area for coal, iron ore and limestone. Perhaps this is why Shijiazhuang is euphemistically subtitled a 'developing city'. What that means is that it is a boring sprawl of factories and railway lines.

The tomb of Dr Norman Bethune is just about all there is to see in Shijiazhuang – otherwise the city itself is only useful as a transit point or a staging area to sights within the region.

### Revolutionary Martyr's Mausoleum

The guerilla doctor Norman Bethune

(1890-1939) is interred here, together with a photo/drawing display depicting his life and works, and a white memorial. Bethune is the most famous *waigoren* in China since Marco Polo (actually most Chinese don't know who Polo is, but they all know Bethune – or 'Baiqiuen' as pronounced in Chinese). He goes down in modern history as the man who fought alongside Mao, serving as a surgeon with the Eighth Route Army in the war against Japan, having previously served with Communists in Spain against Franco and his Nazi and Facist allies.

Bethune is eulogised in the compulsory reading of Mao Zedong Thought: 'We must all learn the spirit of absolute selflessness from Dr Norman Bethune'.

'Bethune' is synonymous with 'Canada' in China –it's about all they know about Canada, and bringing up the name makes for instant friendship if you're Canadian. There are more than 700 army cadres and heroes buried in the cemetery who died during the Resistance against Japan, the War of Liberation and the Korean War. The area is a large park and in the central alley of the cemetery is a pair of bronze lions from 1185 (Jin Dynasty). The Martyr's Mausoleum is located on Zhongshan Lu, west of the railway station. There is another Bethune statue located in the courtyard of the Bethune International Peace Hospital of the PLA, which is a bit further west of the cemetery.

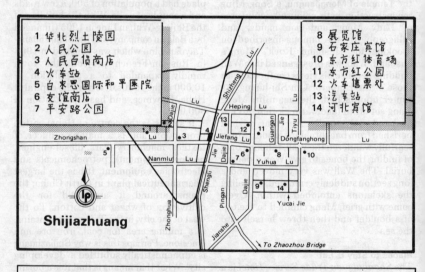

| | |
|---|---|
| 1 华北烈士陵园 | 8 展览馆 |
| 2 人民公园 | 9 石家庄宾馆 |
| 3 人民百货商店 | 10 东方红体育场 |
| 4 火车站 | 11 东方红公园 |
| 5 白求恩国际和平医院 | 12 火车售票处 |
| 6 友谊商店 | 13 汽车站 |
| 7 平安路公园 | 14 河北宾馆 |

| | |
|---|---|
| 1 Cemetry of Revolutionary Matyrs | 8 Provincial Exhibition Hall |
| 2 Renmin (People's) Park | 9 Shijiazhuang Guest House |
| 3 Renmin Dept. Store | 10 Dongfanghong Stadium |
| 4 Railway Station | 11 Dongfanfhong Park |
| 5 Bethune International Peace Hospital of the PLA | 12 Advance Railway Booking Office |
| 6 Friendship Store | 13 Bus Station |
| 7 Pingan Lu Park | 14 Hebei Guest House |

### Zhengding

10 km north of Shijiazhuang, Zhengding is a town which has several temples and monasteries. Largest and oldest is the Longxing Monastery which is noted for its immense, 20-metre high, bronze Buddha dating from the Song Dynasty almost a thousand years ago. The multi-armed statue is housed in the Temple of Great Mercy, an impressive structure with red and yellow galleries. The trip to Zhengding can be done in first class comfort in 20 minutes; there's a blue and silver air-conditioned Hino that loops around Shijiazhuang collecting passengers. Scheduled departures are at 7.30 am and 1.30 pm. You can pick the bus up on the south side of Jiefang Lu near the station at 7.40 am and 1.40 pm – look for special bus stops. Buses return at 9.40 pm and 3.40 pm, but there seem to be extra buses running, though you'll have to check.

### Zhaozhou Bridge

There's an old folk poem about the four wonders of Hebei which goes:

The Lion of Cangzhou
The Pagoda of Dingzhou
The Buddha of Zhengding
The Bridge of Zhaozhou

The Bridge is located in Zhaoxian County, about 40 km south-east of Shijiazhuang, two km to the south of Zhaoxian town. It spans the Jiao River, and has done so for 1300 years. It is possibly the oldest stone-arch bridge in China (another, believed older, has recently been unveiled in Linying County, Henan Province).

The Book of Records aside, the Zhaozhou Bridge is remarkable in that it still stands. It is 50 metres long, 9.6 metres wide, with a span of 37 metres; the balustrades are carved with dragons and mythical creatures. Credit for this daring piece of engineering is disputed – according to legend the master mason Lu Ban constructed it overnight. The astounded immortals, refusing to believe this was possible, arrived to test the bridge. One immortal had a wagon, another a donkey, and they asked Lu Ban if it was possible for them both to cross at the same time. He nodded; halfway across, the bridge started to shake and Lu Ban rushed into the water to stabilise it. This resulted in donkey-prints, wheel-prints and hand-prints being left on the bridge. Several more old stone bridges are to be found in Zhaoxian County.

### Cangyan Shan

78 km south-west of Shijiazhuang is a scenic area dotted with pagodas and temples – woods, valleys and steep cliffs. The novelty here is a bizarre double-roofed hall sitting on a stone arch bridge spanning a precipitous gorge. It is known as the Hanging Palace, and is reached by a 300-step stairway. The palace dates back to the Sui Dynasty. On the surrounding slopes are other ancient halls.

### Xibaipo

In Pingshan County, 80 km north-west of Shijiazhuang, was the base from which Mao Zedong, Zhou Enlai and Zhu De directed the northern campaign against the Kuomintang from 1947-1948. The original site of Xibaipo Village was submerged by Gangnan Reservoir and the present village has been rebuilt close by. In 1977 a Revolutionary Memorial Museum was erected.

### Places to Stay

The *Hebei Guest House* (tel 6351) is a modern eight-storey block with a bar, restaurant and store. Bus No 6 will take you from the station to the south-east of the city –alight at Yucai Jie and walk five minutes south to the Guest House. Rooms are Y18 double, or Y12 student rate. You can get any information you need there. A few blocks west of the Hebei Guesthouse is the **Shijiazhuang Guest house** – it's a possibility for lodgings but there's no English spoken.

## Places to Eat

The main drag runs east-west just below the station. On the west side it's Zhongshan Rd, on the east side of the station it's Jiefang Rd which merges into Dongfanghong Rd. There are some eateries along this strip, bland stuff and all much of a muchness. Bethune certainly had no effect on the level of hygiene in Shijiazhuang – the restaurants and snackbars in the station vicinity come straight from Dante's Inferno – thick layers of dirt on the tables, greasy to disgusting food, and bodies littering the alleys waiting for one train connection or another.

## Getting Around

The long-distance bus station is within walking distance north-east of the rail station – from there you can get buses to sights outside Shijiazhuang. Within the city there are 10 bus lines.

## Getting Away

Shijiazhuang is a major rail hub with comprehensive connections: there are lines to Beijing (about four hours) and to Canton, to Taiyuan (about five hours) and to Dezhou (also about five hours).

## TANGSHAN

To the north of Tianjin is the major industrial town of Tangshan. On 28 July 1976, Tangshan disappeared in a few minutes, demolished by an earthquake registering around 8 on the Richter scale, the equivalent to 20 megatons of TNT. The official death toll is now stated at 148,000 (and 81,000 seriously injured); if the casualties from Beijing and Tianjin are added, the toll is 242,000 killed though western estimates place the toll as high as 800,000.

Earthquakes in China traditionally herald the downfall of dynasties; this one was unnervingly accurate. In September 1976, Mao Zedong died; in October the Gang of Four were arrested. Some 300,000 people, roughly a third of Tangshan's present population, still live in temporary hovels, waiting for new housing to be constructed away from the fault lines. This is scheduled to be done in 1985. Meanwhile a new Tangshan has arisen from the ashes, just as polluted as before, and touted as a model of efficiency by Beijing; rows of apartment blocks, giant factories. As early as 1978 it was claimed that industrial output (steel, engineering, cement) was back to 1976 figures and it wasn't until 1978 that the People's Daily finally got round to reporting the catastrophe, in a small article that didn't even make the front page.

# Beijing

Beijing; home to stuffy museums and bureaucrats, puffy generals and backdoor elitists, host to disgruntled reporters and diplomats – a labyrinth of doors, walls, gates and entrances, marked and unmarked. As far away as Urumqi they run on Beijing's clock; around the country they chortle in *putonghua*, the Beijing dialect; in the remote foothills of Tibet they struggle to interpret the latest directives from the capital. In 1983 the Chinese government announced that if the Dalai Lama were to return he'd be posted – where else? – to a desk job in Beijing. This is where they make the book and move the cogs and wheels of the Chinese universe, or try to slow them down if they're moving in the wrong direction.

Beijing is like a spoilt brat – it has the best of everything in China bar the weather – the best food, the best hotels, the best transport, the best temples – but its vast squares, its vast boulevards, its cavernous monoliths and its vast numbers of tourists will leave you cold. It's a weird city, one that has lost its energy and character, traces of which may be found down the back alleys where things are a little more to human scale. Stepping off a train at Beijing Main Station and driving up to Tiananmen Square in a bulbous Russian Warszawa, you would be forgiven if you were under the delusion that you'd strayed into the Red Square in Moscow, especially if you came face to face with a giant portrait of Stalin.

In 1981, Beijingnese were gazing at imported TV sets displayed behind plate glass at the Main Department Store on Wangfujing; in 1983 the same window sported a fashion-display direct from Paris. Pierre Cardin had been and gone, Arthur Miller had drifted through, the Italians had done a video remake of Marco Polo, and Elton John dropped in to pose for photographers in a Mao jacket.

Upstairs in the Department Store a western mannequin models a see-through top, nipples clearly visible, which sets passing Chinese (excuse the phrase) tittering. Outside the store a worker is stopped and fined for gobbing on the footpath, part of another cleanup campaign – most likely to prevent tourists being grossed out than as an attack on a health hazard. Further up Wangfujing, 6 pm and there's a parking problem: embassy cars and cadre limos have congregated at a restaurant for a banquet and there's nowhere to go except up on the footpath. For all its seeming liberalism, Beijing keeps an iron fist on its residents – and the premiere of Opium Wars IV (drug addicts) is a little way off yet.

It's actually the foreigners who add the colour to dull, grey Beijing. The outskirts of town where the old walls used to stand are now ringed by four-lane highways with spaghetti-like flyovers and devoid of the heavy traffic they were built for. Sprinkled around the perimeter are drab housing blocks. Is this *it*? Is this the *capital*? Tourists are often disappointed with Beijing, seeing it as a third-rate European city divested of its energy; others, having passed their time in the westernised bits of town come away with the impression that everything is hunky dory in the PRC and that the Chinese are living high. The Chinese they encounter may, in truth, be doing so. Group tourists are processed through Beijing in much the same way the ducks are force-fed on the outlying farms—the two usually meet on the first night over the dinner table where the phenomenon known as the Jetlag Duck attack overtakes the bowels and other organs of the unwary. Meanwhile, out in the embassy ghettoes long-term foreigners complain that they're losing their Chinese language skills due to lack of contact. I asked a foreign journalist what she thought was the greatest sight in Beijing; without hesitation, and in all seriousness, she replied 'The sauna at the Finnish Embassy'.

Whatever impression you come away with, Beijing is not a realistic window on China. It's too much of a cosmetic showcase to qualify. It is, however, a large city, and with a bit of effort you can get out of the make-up department. Better still, try and get out of Beijing. At least once.

## History

Beijing is a time-setter for China, but it actually has a short history as Chinese time spans go. Although the area southwest of the city was inhabited by cave dwellers some 500,000 years ago, the earliest records of settlements date from around 1000 BC. It developed as a frontier trading town for the Mongols, Koreans and the tribes from Shandong and Central China. By the Warring States Period (475-221 BC) it had grown to be the capital of the Yan Kingdom and was called Ji – a reference to the marshy features of the area. The town underwent a number of changes as it acquired new warlords, the Khitan Mongols and the Manchurian Turchen tribes among them. What attracted the conquerors was the strategic position of the town on the edge of the North China Plain.

History really gets under way in 1215 AD, the year that Genghis Khan thoroughly set fire to the preceding paragraph and slaughtered everything in sight. From the ashes emerged 'Dadu' the Great Capital, alias 'Khanbaliq', the Khan's town. By 1279 Genghis' grandson Kublai had made

himself ruler of all China and Khanbaliq was his capital. Until this time attempts at unifying China had been centred around Luoyang and Changan(Xian). With a lull in the fighting from 1280 to 1300 foreigners managed to drop in along the Silk Road for tea with the Great Khan – Marco Polo even landed a job. The Mongol emperor was informed by his astrologers that the old city site of Beijing was a breeding ground for rebels, so he shifted it slightly north. The great palace he built no longer remains, but here is Polo's description:

Within these walls ... stands the palace of the Great Khan, the most extensive that has ever yet been known ... The sides of the great halls are adorned with dragons in carved work and gold, figures of warriors, of birds and of beasts ... On each of the four sides of the palace there is a grand flight of marble steps ... The new city is of a form perfectly square ... each of its sides being six miles. It is enclosed with walls of earth ... the wall of the city has twelve gates. The multitude of inhabitants, and the number of houses in the city of Kanbula, as also in the suburbs outside the city of which there are twelve corresponding to the twelve gates, is greater than the mind can comprehend ... corresponding to the twelve gates, is greater than the mind can comprehend ... '

Oddly enough, Polo's description could well have been applied to the later Ming city, and the lavish lifestyle of the great Khan set the trends for the Ming emperors. Polo goes on to recount what happens on Tartar New Years Day:

On this occasion, great numbers of beautiful white horses are presented to the Great Khan ... all his elephants, amounting to 5000, are exhibited in the procession, covered with housings of cloth, richly worked with gold and silk ...

Polo was equally dazzled by the innovations of gunpowder and paper money. These were not without their drawbacks; in history's first case of paper-currency inflation the last Mongol emperor, Shun-ti, flooded the country with worthless bills. This, coupled with a large number of natural disasters, provoked an uprising led by Zhu Yanhang, a mercenary who took Beijing in 1368 and ushered in the Ming Dynasty. The city was renamed 'Beiping' (Northern Peace) and for the next 35 years the capital was shifted to Nanjing. To this day the Kuomintang regime on Taiwan refers to the city as 'Beiping' and recognises Nanjing as the capital.

In the early 1400s, Zhu's son son Yong Le shuffled the court back to 'Beiping' and renamed it 'Beijing'(Northern capital). Millions of taels of silver were spent on refurbishing the city – many of the structures like the Forbidden City and the Temple of heaven were first built in Yong Le's reign. In fact, he is credited with being the true architect of the modern city. The Inner City moved to the area around the Imperial City and a suburban zone was added to the south, a bustle of merchants and street life. The basic grid of present-day Beijing has been laid and history became a question of who rules the turf. The first change of government came with the Manchus who invaded China and established the Qing Dynasty – under them, and particularly during the reigns of the emperors Kangxi and Qianlong, Beijing was expanded and renovated and summer palaces, pagodas and temples were built. In the last 120 years Beijing and subsequently China had been subjected to the afflictions of power-struggles, invaders and the chaos created by those who held or sought power; the Anglo-French troops who marched in in 1860 and burnt the summer palace to the ground; the corrupt regime under the Empress Dowager Cixi, the Boxers, General Yuan Shikai, the warlords, the Japanese who occupied the city in 1937 followed by the Kuomintang after the Japanese defeat. A century of turmoil finally ended in January 1949 when PLA troops entered the city, and on 1 October of that year Mao proclaimed a 'People's Republic' to an audience of some 500,000 citizens in Tiananmen Square.

Post-1949 was a period of reconstruction. While the centre of power, the area around the Forbidden City has remained in the same location, the CCP has significantly altered the face of Beijing. Like the warlords of bygone eras they wanted to leave their mark. Under the old city planning shemes high-rises were verboten – they would interfere with the emperor's view and lessen his sunlight. It was also a question of rank – the higher the building the more important the person within. The aristocrats got decorations and glazed tiling and the plebs got baked clay tiles and grey brick squats. This building code to some extent prevailed over the 'house that Mao built'. Premier Zhou suggested that nothing higher than 45 metres be built within the old city wall limits and that nothing higher than Tiananmen Gate be erected in that area.

In the 1950s the urban planners got to work. Down came the commemorative arches, blocks of buildings were reduced to rubble to widen Changan Avenue and Tiananmen Square; from 1950 to 1952 the outer walls were levelled in the interests of traffic circulation. Russian experts and technicians poured in, which may explain the Stalinesque features on the public structures that went up. Meanwhile industry, negligible in Beijing until this time, was rapidly expanded; textiles, iron and steel, petrochemicals, machine-making factories and plants were set up and Beijing became a major industrial city. Complicated by the fact that most of the city's greenery had been ripped up, this led to serious pollution problems. Five and six-storey housing blocks went up at a brisk pace but construction was of poor quality and it still didn't keep pace with the population boom. Communes were established on the city outskirts to feed the influx of people.

By 1960 the Great Leap Forward had bombed, the Russian experts withdrawn, there was a backlash against Mao and his response in 1966 was to launch ten years of utter madness – there is still no head count of those tortured, killed or humiliated though the *People's Daily* has now put the figure at 100 million who 'suffered' from harassment over the decade. In 1976 the 'Gang of Four' were disposed of and the nation entered a period of slow recovery.

In 1982 the Central Committee of the Party adopted a new urban construction programme for Beijing, a revised version of the 1950s one. They faced tremendous challenges: on the one hand they wanted to continue the building of new roads and the widening of old streets and preserve the character of the old city and the historical sites. The new 20 metre wide ring road is in place and there are two more ring roads planned, the last one passing through the Summer Palace. The population of the Beijing area, already 9.23 million, is to be limited to 10 million by the year 2000, with four million in the metropolis, 2.5 million in satellite towns and 3.5 million in farming areas. Thirty-four new residential zones have been constructed in 12 to 16-storey blocks, but the workmanship is shoddy, facilities have to be bargained for (in some cases the water pressure does not go above the third storey). Other parts of the plan call for a limitation on industrial construction, a halt to the growth of heavy industry and a shift to self-sufficient food production in the outlying counties. For the moment the self-sufficiency program appears to be working, with extended use of greenhouses for the winter months. Another major priority shift is enviromental – a massive tree-planting campaign is underway to make Beijing green again with a goal of turning some 50% of the metropolitan area into landscaping and recreational zones. This, however, will mean the mushrooming of buildings in satellite locations which means less farmland.

Small businesses have re-emerged, an about-face to the days when they were the mainstay of Beijing's economy. They were wiped out in the craze to nationalise. To solve a huge unemployment problem (no figures were released) the government has offered incentives for the self-employed such as tax exemptions and loans. By the end of 1982 about 10,000 Beijingers were self-employed, of which about a third fell into the category of 'jobless youths' – meaning dislocated and returned Cultural Revolutionaries. Those with initiative are faring better than average – some make incomes above Y200 a month, and repair services such as those for bicycles, shoes and watches run by individuals now outnumber state and collective-owned ones in Beijing.

## Climate

The city is not blessed with congenial weather. Autumn September-October is the best time to visit – little rain, not dry or humid, pleasant cloak of foliage. Winter isn't bad if you're used to the cold – although the temperature can dip as far as $-20°C$ and you freeze your butt off, parts of the capital appear charming in this season. The subdued winter lighting makes the place very photogenic. Winter clothing is readily available – the locals wear about 15 layers. If the wind races down the wide boulevards like Changan there's a particularly nasty windchill factor. Spring is short, dry and dusty – in April-May a phenomenon known as 'Yellow Wind' plagues the capital when fine dust particles are blown in from the Gobi Desert in the north-west, sandpapering everything in sight including your face. The locals run around with mesh bags over their heads. In the 1950s the government ordered the extermination of the citys birds, which led to an insect uprising. So then they ordered the insects' habitats (grass and other greens) to be dug up which led to even more dust being set loose. In summer (June, July, August) the average temperature is $26°C$ – very hot, humid, semi-tropical weather, with mosquitoes and heavy rains in July.

## INFORMATION & ORIENTATION

Though it may not appear so on the

shambles of arrival, Beijing is a place of very orderly design. Long straight boulevards and avenues are criss-crossed by a network of lanes: places are either very easy to find (especially if high-rises) if situated on the avenues – or impossible to find when buried down the narrow alleys (the *hutongs*). This refers to the chessboard of the downtown core, once a walled enclosure. The symmetry folds on an ancient north-south axis passing through Qianmen Gate; the major east-west road is Changan (Avenue of Eternal Tranquility).

As for the street names: *Chongwenmenwai Dajie* means the avenue (dajie) outside (wai) Chongwen Gate (Chongwenmen); whereas *Chongwenmennai* means the street inside Chongwen Gate (ie inside the old wall). It's an academic exercise since the gate and the wall in question no longer exist. Streets are also split by compass points; Dongdajie (East Avenue), Xidajie (West Avenue), Beidajie (North Avenue)

and Nandajie (South Avenue) – and these streets head off from an intersection, usually where a gate once stood.

A major boulevard can change names six or eight times in its length, so intersection points become important (the buses are also routed through these points). It therefore pays to study your gates and intersection points, and familiarise yourself with the high-rise buildings, often hotels, which serve as useful landmarks to gauge your progress along the chessboard. Other streets are named after bridges, also long gone, like the Bridge of Heaven (Tianqiao), and old temple features or attractions which are still there.

The city limits of Beijing extend some 80 km – the urban, the suburban, and the nine counties under its administration. With a total area of 16,800 square km, it is roughly the size of Belgium. At July 1982 census, the urban and suburban population

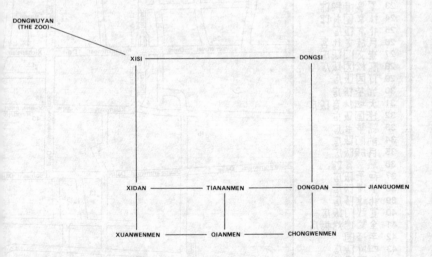

To Friendship Hotel

1 天安门广场
2 毛主席纪念堂
3 中国历史博物馆
4 人民大会堂
5 前门
6 天安门
7 鼓楼
8 北京观象台
9 白塔寺
10 雍和宫
11 孔庙
12 白塔
13 牛街礼拜寺
14 广济寺
15 法源寺
16 天宁寺
17 天主教堂东堂
18 天主教堂南堂
19 鲁迅博物馆
20 中国美术馆
21 农业展览馆
22 北京展览馆
23 军事博物馆
24 北京图书馆
25 北京饭店
26 民族文化宫
27 崇文门饭店
28 庞松园饭店
29 竹园饭店
30 光华饭店
31 天坛体育饭店
32 建国饭店
33 新华书店
34 前门饭店
35 民族饭店
36 燕京宾馆
37 和平饭店
38 华侨饭店
39 北纬饭店
40 宣武门饭店
41 全聚德烤鸭店
42 丰泽园
43 四川饭店
44 曲园酒楼
45 东来顺饭店

To Badaling Ming Tombs

Xinjiekouwai Dajie

Xizhimen Railway Station

Deshengmen Xidajie

Xinjiekou

Beidajie

Xinjiekou Nandajie

Zoo

Xizhimennei Dajie

Xizhimenwai Dajie

Xizhimen Nandajie

Fuchengmen Beidajie

Xisi Beidajie

Di'anmen

Chegongzhuang Dajie

Yeutan Park

Fuchengmennei Dajie

Wenjin

Fuchengmenwai Dajie

Yuetan Dajie

Fuchengmen Nandajie

Telegraph Building

Fuxingmen Beidajie

Fuxingmennei Dajie

Xidan Beidajie

Xichang'an

Fuxingmenwai Dajie

Fuxingmen Nandajie

Xuanwumen Dongdajie

Xuanwumen Xidajie

Xuanwumennei Dajie

Guang'anmenwai Dajie

Guang'anmennei Dajie

Luomashi Daj

Taoranting Park

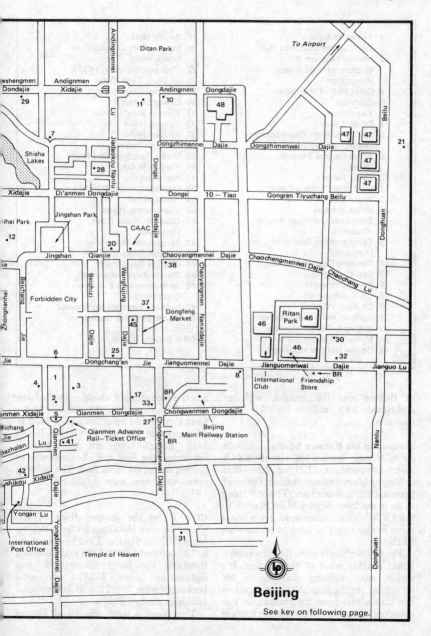

To Airport

Ditan Park

Andingmennei

Andingmen

Xidajie

Andingmen    Dongdajie

eshengmen
Dondajie
• 29

• 7

Shisha
Lakes

Xidajie

Di'anmen Dongdajie

Jiadaokou Nanlu

Dongsi

• 28

• 11

• 10

48

Dongzhimennei    Dajie

Dongzhimenwai    Dajie

47    47

47

47

21

• 12

Jingshan Park

Jingshan    Qianjie

Dongsi    10 — Tiao

Gongren Tiyuchang Beilu

Chaochengmenwai Dajie    Chaochang Lu

ihai Park

Zhongnanhai

Forbidden City

CAAC

• 20

Beidajie

Wangfujing

Beichizi

• 38

Chaoyangmennei    Dajie

Chaoyangmen Nanxidajie

Ritan
Park    46

46

46

• 30

Jie

Beichang    Jie

• 6

Dongchang'an    Jie

Dajie

• 25

• 45

• 37

Dongfeng
Market

Jianguomennei    Dajie

• 32

Jianguo Lu

Jie

• 4

1

2

• 3

5

Qianmen

• 17

33 •

• 8

International
Club

Jianguomenwai

BR
Friendship
Store

ichang
Jie

Qianmen Xidajie

Qianmen    Dongdajie

BR

• 27

Chongwenmen Dongdajie

Beijing
Main Railway Station

Donghuan

azhalan

• 41

BR

Lu

42

Xidajie

ushikou

Yongan Lu

Yongdingmennei    Dajie

International
Post Office

Temple of Heaven

• 31

Chongwenmenwai Dajie

Nanlu

Donghuan

lp

Beijing

See key on following page.

| | |
|---|---|
| 1 Tianamen Square | 25 Beijing Hotel |
| 2 Mao Zedong Memorial Hall | 26 Nationalities Cultural |
| 3 History Museum & | Palace Hotel |
| Museum of the Chinese | 27 Chongwenan Hotel / CITS |
| Revolution | 28 Lu Song Yuan Hotel |
| 4 Great Hall of the People | 29 Bamboo Garden Hotel |
| 5 Qianmen | 30 Guanghua Hotel |
| 6 Tiananmen | 31 Tiantan Sports Hotel |
| 7 Drum Tower | 32 Jianguo Hotel |
| 8 Beijing Ancient Observatory | 33 Xinqiao Hotel |
| (Jesuit Observatory) | 34 Qianmen Hotel |
| 9 White Dagoba Temple | 35 Minzu (Nationalities) Hotel |
| (Baitasi) | 36 Yanjing Hotel |
| 10 Lama Temple | 37 Peace Hotel |
| 11 Confucian Temple Complex | 38 Overseas Chinese Building |
| 12 White Dagoba (Baita) | 39 Beiwei Hotel |
| 13 Nuijie Mosque | 40 Xuanwumen Hotel |
| 14 Temple of Universal Rescue | 41 Qianmen Roast Duck |
| (Guangjisi) | Restaurant |
| 15 Temple of the Source of Law | 42 Fengzeyuan Restaurant |
| (Fayuansi) | 43 Sichuan Restaurant |
| 16 Tianning Temple Pagoda | 44 Quyuan Restaurant |
| 17 East Cathedral | 45 Donglaishun Restaurant |
| 18 South Cathedral | 46 Jianguomenwai Embassy |
| 19 Lu Xun Museum | Compound |
| 20 China Art Gallery | 47 Sanlitun Embassy Compound |
| 21 Agricultural Exhibition Hall | 48 Soviet Embassy Compound |
| 22 Beijing Exhibition Centre | |
| 23 Military Museum | BR = Bicycle Rental |
| 24 Beijing National Library | |

of Beijing was 5.6 million, with an additional 3.63 million in the nine counties.

**Evacuating the Railway Station** Latitude 39°56'N, map-section 5E, elevation 44.8 metres; you surface at Beijing Zhan – that is, Beijing Main Railway Station. For most people, Beijing starts here. The first thing to do is get from Beijing Main Station to the CITS office, because to get a hotel room in this city you have to go through CITS.

The CITS office is in the Chongwenmen Hotel roughly west of the station. It's within easy walking distance – for directions see the map. Alternatively, you can take a taxi from the station; as you come out of the front of the station there is

a taxi depot straight ahead – you have to get tickets first from the old bus that's been turned into an office and parked in the square in front of the station. If you keep going there are two subway entrances, the best and cheapest way ot getting out of the area fast. The subway taken one stop west will land you at CITS.

**CITS** is on the ground floor of the Chongwenmen Hotel not far from Beijing Main Railway Station. They're open 9 am to 12 noon and 1.30 to 5 pm and closed on Sundays. For hotel reservations and sightseeing phone 755374, domestic bookings phone 755272, and international bookings phone 755276.

They keep a tight rein on all tourist

affairs in the capital – hotels, train tickets, even permits. You can shake off this yoke, and get things done considerably faster – CITS is not, after all, the police force. But they do come in very handy if you want tickets to things like the Beijing Opera, acrobatic shows, the theatre – costs a bit more than you'd pay at the door but at least you'll be sure of a seat.

Tempers and Basil Fawlty blood pressures run high in this tiny little office, which it should be kept in mind, caters to the full onslaught of foreign tourists with an onsite staff of maybe three to six. Tourists have just stepped off a plane from Frankfurt or wherever, and they're not used to the surly CITS style. Some maps and general information in pamphlet form at the desk. If you have the money and the patience, CITS can probably arrange mini-group visits (factories, schools etc) Your best idea with CITS is to get what you have to from them, and then get the hell out of there before you drive each other up the Great Wall!

**CITS Railway Booking Office** is on the third floor of the Chongwenmen Hotel; you get there via a flight of stairs which is accessible from the southern gate of the hotel – there should be a sign at the front entrance of the hotel pointing the way. It's open 9 am to 12 noon and 2 to 5 pm. Bookings for the Trans-Siberian railway are done here, and in theory all other train departures from Beijing. Separate from CITS, the railways have an information number (tel 554866/5576851/5582042) though you'll probably need one of your hotel staff to place the call for you – it *may* be possible to book a ticket over the phone.

**CITS Advance Boat Bookings** (for the Shanghai-Hong Kong ferry for example) can be made through the CITS office. You could also try the CTS (China Travel Service) office at the Overseas Chinese Hotel (tel 558851) – they have the same office hours as CITS. There is another CTS office at the Xuanwumen Hotel (tel 755448).

**Public Security Bureau** (tel 553102) is located on the street running north-south at the east side of the Forbidden City, about half-way along. The address is 85 Beichizi Dajie. They're open 8 to 11.30 am and 1.30 to 5 pm, closed Saturday and Sunday.

CITS claims you must go through them to get places added to your permit or a new permit issued – if so, then this is the only place in China where such a situation exists, as there is not supposed to be a link between the two. CITS will surcharge for the service, and it will take longer. Permits issued at PSB take up to one day – don't expect unusual additions. If in doubt, just collect enough permits to get you on your way and do your shopping elsewhere. The last thing to expect of Beijing PSB is a visa extension.

**CAAC** (tel 558861 for enquiries and 557319 for international flight information) is at 117 Dongsi Xidajie.

**Bank** Exchange counters in many of the tourist hotels; conveniently located is the Beijing Hotel which has an exchange counter on the ground floor.

**Post & Communications** Most of the tourist hotels have post offices. You can send packages overseas from these post offices as long as they contain printed matter only. All other parcels to be sent overseas have to be taken to the International Post Office which is at 121 Yongan Lu, a fifteen minute walk east of the Qianmen Hotel.

Patience is necessary when making long distance phone calls – the exchanges are overworked and the lines can be bad. Long distance phone calls can be made from your hotel room if you have a phone in it, or at major hotels, or at the Telecom Office west of the Beijing Hotel. For the Overseas Operator phone 337431. For long distance information phone 116.

Letters from the folks back home can be received at the following places:

– Beijing Hotel, Changan Dongjie
– one of the embassies listed below (see the 'General Information' section). Short opening hours and long way out.
– Clients' Mail, American Express, Room 1527, Beijing Hotel, 15th floor. Open 9 to 5. This is the only American Express office in China.
– Poste Restante, Beijing (this will arrive at 121 Yongan Lu, the International Post Office, east of the Qianmen Hotel).

**Maps** Until about 1978 there was no detailed English map of the capital. Now Beijing is thoroughly mapped out – a pretty horrendous job I wouldn't wish on anyone.

A good sightseeing map is the *Beijing Tourist Map* – one of the series issued by the Cartographic Publishing House of Beijing and available in both Chinese and in English. You may have trouble finding an English copy so if you see one being sold in another city on your way up to Beijing I suggest you snap it up. Another excellent map is available in Hong Kong but nowhere to be found in Beijing – *Map of Beijing* – which shows the sights and the bus routes and is bilingual throughout.

The main problem is showing transport routes on maps – the regular English bus map is extremely difficult to follow – there's so much information squashed into a small space that you need a magnifying glass.

There are two maps which make life easier – unfortunately they're both in Chinese, but if you follow some of the graphics and identify some landmarks, it's much clearer. *Beijing Luyou Jiaotongtu* with a yellow cover is a small booklet with a foldout map in the middle showing buses, sights, taxis, etc. The second map is *Beijingshi Chenqujiedaotu* and is the best bus map of the capital – shows multi-coloured bus route lines and buses to destinations outside Beijing. It's a large

foldup map with a small brown and blue cover and an illustration of a totem-like structure from the Forbidden City. These maps cost 30 fen each. There's an English version of the second map produced in Hong Kong, but doesn't show all the routes, and none of the bus stops are shown, a major drawback.

If you have some time, try and get down to Number 3 Baizhifang Xijie (in the south-west corner of Beijing) where the Cartographic Publishing House is located – there's a retail outlet on the corner that sells not only the best general map of Beijing (no bus information, but good for restaurants etc), as well as excellent maps of other cities and areas you may wish to visit. They may run out of English stock.

Finally, for those staying longer, and aware of the lingo, there's a quarto-sized Michelin-type bundle of 32 section maps that even gets down to the nitty-gritty of the hutongs. It's called *Beijing Shiqu Dituce* and goes for Y0.92.

**Books & Information** Good selection of paperbacks, magazines and other saddlebag material can be found at the Foreign Languages Bookstore on Wangfujing near Beijing Hotel – also try the ground floor of the Friendship Store, the lobby of the International Club (surprisingly good), the Beijing Hotel and other tourist hangouts. Recent copies of western magazines are treasured by Chinese comrades – good gifts (if it's a novel, pick the raciest one you can!). If going on the Trans-Siberian, pick the dreariest covers and contents you can – the Outer Mongolians and Russians may confiscate them otherwise.

The China Travel & Tourism Press is located on the 3rd floor of the Chongwenmen Hotel – use the elevator – it's the unmarked office directly across from the elevator. They don't exactly advertise their presence, but they will if you prod them produce a wonderful array of maps and tourist literature at hefty prices, and may still have items that other places have

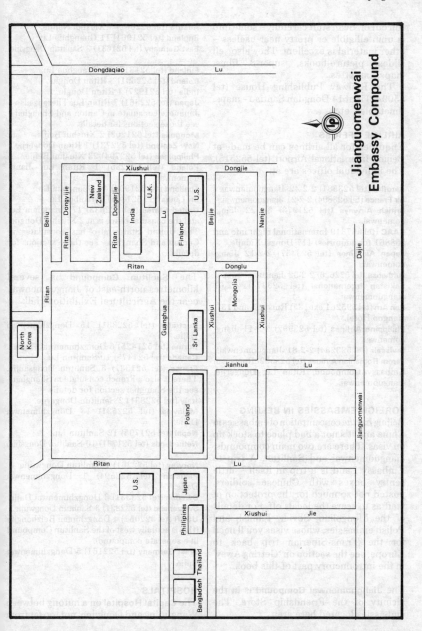

Jianguomenwai Embassy Compound

Dongdaqiao Lu

Xiushui

Dongjie

Beiju

Ritan
Dongyijie

New Zealand

Dongerjie

Ritan

India

U.K.

Lu

Finland

U.S.

Beijie

Nanjie

Dajie

Ritan

Dongli

Guanghua

Sri Lanka

Dongliu

Mongolia

Xiushui

Xiushui

North Korea

Ritan

Jianhua

Lu

Poland

Jianguomenwai

Ritan

Lu

U.S.

Japan

Philipines

Xiushui

Jie

Bangladesh Thailand

run out of. Scan stuff carefully – some info is unintelligible or pretty near useless – other material is excellent. They also sell slides, picture-books, super-8 films, maps, cassettes.

The Railway Publishing House (tel 550942) is at 14 Dongdan Santiao – maps, timetables, etc . . .

## AIRLINE OFFICES

Enquiries for all airlines can be made at Beijing International Airport (tel 552515). The individual offices are at:

Aeroflot (tel 523581) 2-2-42 Jianguomenwai.

Air France (tel 523894) 2-2-21 Jianguomenwai.

British Airways (tel 521973) 3-1-22 Jianguomenwai.

CAAC (tel 557319 International flight info and 558861 for enquiries) 117 Dongsi Xidajie.

Japan Air Lines (tel 523457) 2-2-12 Jianguomenwai.

Lufthansa (tel 522626) 2-2-52 Jianguomenwai.

Pakistan International (tel 523274) 2-2-61 Jianguomenwai.

Pan Am (tel 595261 ext 135) Rms 135 and 137, Jianguo Hotel.

Philippine Airlines (tel 523992) 2-2-11 Jianguomenwai.

Swissair (tel 523284) 2-2-81 Jianguomenwai.

Tarom Romanian Airlines (tel 523552) Romanian Embassy Compound, Ritan Lu, Dongerjie, Jianguomenwai.

## FOREIGN EMBASSIES IN BEIJING

Beijing has *the* concentration of embassies in China and it's not a bad place to stock up on visas. There are two main compounds: Jianguomenwai and Sanlitun. A trip to Embassy Land is a trip in itself – little sentry boxes with Chinese soldiers, posted not so much for the protection of staff as to scare the locals off. For details of the Mongolian, Soviet, Finnish and Polish embassies, whose visas you'll need for the Trans-Siberian trip back to Europe, see the section on 'Getting Away' in the introductory part of this book.

The **Jianguomenwai Compound** is in the vicinity of the Friendship Store. The embassies located here are:

Austria (tel 522061) 5 Xiushui Nanjie.

England (tel 521961) 11 Guanghua Lu.

East Germany (tel 521631) 3 Sanlitun Dongsijie.

Finland (tel 521817) 30 Guanghua Lu.

Ireland (tel 522691) 3 Ritan Donglu .

India (tel 521927) 1 Ritan Donglu.

Japan (tel 522361) 7 Ritan Lu. There is also a Japanese consulate in Canton and Shanghai – see those sections for details.

Mongolia (tel 521203) 2 Xiushui Beijie.

New Zealand (tel 522731) 1 Ritan Dongerjie.

Philippines (tel 522794) 23 Xiushui Beijie.

Poland (tel 521235) 1 Ritan Lu, Jianguomenwai.

Thailand (tel 521903) 40 Guanghua Lu.

Sri Lanka (tel 521861) 3 Jianhua Lu.

United States (tel 522033) 17 Guanghua Lu, and the consular office is at 2 Xiushui Dongjie. The United States also has consulates in Canton and Shanghai – see those sections for details.

The **Sanlitun Compound** is several kilometres north-east of Jianguomenwai, near the Agricultural Exhibition Hall:

Australia (tel 522331) 15 Dongzhimenwai Dajie.

Burma (tel 521425) 6 Dongzhimenwai Dajie.

Canada (tel 521475) 10 Sanlitun Lu.

France (tel 521331) 3 Sanlitun Dongsanjie. There is also a French consulate in Shanghai – see the Shanghai section for details.

Italy (tel 522831) 2 Sanlitun Dongerjie.

Malaysia (tel 522531) 13 Dongzhimenwai Dajie.

Nepal (tel 521795) 12 Sanlitun Lu.

Netherlands (tel 521731) 10 Sanlitun Dongsijie.

Norway (tel 522261) 1 Sanlitun Dongwujie.

Pakistan (tel 522504) 1 Dongzhimenwai Dajie.

Sweden (tel 523331) 3 Dongzhimenwai Dajie.

Switzerland (tel 522831) 3 Sanlitun Dongwujie.

USSR (tel 522051) 4 Dongzhiman Beizhongjie (this is actually west of the Sanlitun Compound in a separate compound).

West Germany (tel 522161) 5 Dongzhimenwai Dajie

## HOSPITALS

The **Capital Hospital** on a hutong between Wangfujing and Dongdan, not too far from

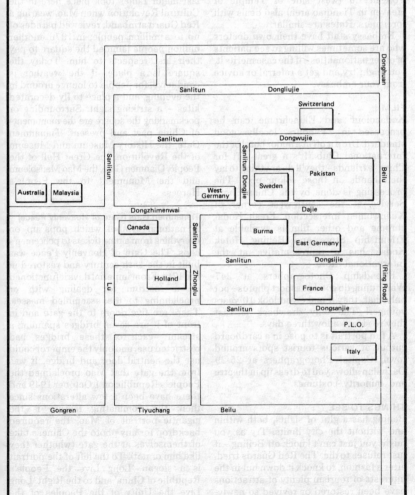

# Sansitun Embassy Compound

Beijing Hotel, has a section for foreigners. Telephone 553731 ext 274; home calls on the same number, ext 222. The hospital also has a 24-hour emergency service, and there are facilities for western and traditional Chinese treatment.

**Friendship Hospital** (tel 3331631) at 95 Yongan Lu (west side of Temple of Heaven in Tianqiao area) also deals with foreigners. Rates are similar.

Embassy staff have their own doctors who are sometimes willing to see patients of other nationalities – if the case merits it, you might try and get a referral or advice from your embassy.

## FILM

Kodacolour and Ektachrome can be processed in 24 hours, locally, good standard. Drop it off at a major hotel or the International Club (It's a great gift for Chinese friends – they'll do anything to lay their hands on those colour pix!). The processing is done by the China Photo Service at the south-west corner of Xuanwumen intersection. Fresh Kodachrome and other film is available at Friendship Store and Beijing Hotel; Kodak has a representative at the International Store.

Friendship Photographers at 247 Wangfujing do good passport photos – not only that, they'll make you look 10 years younger! The only drawback is that they're slow – allow three days.

A fun portrait is to pose in a cardboard cutout at various tourist spots around town; Capital Photographers at 25-29 Dazhalan allows you to dress up in theatre and minority costumes.

## THINGS TO SEE

Beijing has a glut of sights, both within and without the city limits. Try as you might you just can't knock off Beijing – it just refuses to die. The Red Guards tried, after a fashion, to knock it down but in the interests of tourism plenty of attractions have been restored or revived so newly-spruced sites are becoming available.

## TIANANMEN SQUARE

Though it was a gathering place and the location of government offices in the imperial days, the square is Mao's creation, as is Changan Avenue leading onto it. It is the heart of Beijing, a vast desert of paving and photo-booths. The last major rallies took place here in the Cultural Revolution when Mao, wearing a Red Guard armband, reviewed parades of up to a million people; in 1976 another million people jammed the square to pay their last respects to him. Today the square is a place, if the weather is conducive, for people to lounge around in the evening, and a place to fly decorated kites – a striking sight. Surrounding or pockmarking the square are the monuments of China past and present: Tiananmen Gate, the History Museum and Museum of the Revolution, the Great Hall of the People, Qianmen Gate, the Mao Mausoleum and the Monument to the People's Heroes.

### Tiananmen Gate (Gate of Heavenly Peace)

A national symbol which pops up on everything from airline tickets to policemen's caps. The Gate of Heavenly Peace was built in the 15th century and restored in the 17th. From imperial days it functioned as a rostrum for dealing with or proclaiming to the assembled masses. There are five doors to the gate and in front of it are seven bridges spanning a stream –each of these bridges had restricted use, and only the emperor could use the central door and bridge. It was from the gate that Mao proclaimed the People's Republic on 1 October 1949 and there have been a few alterations since then; the dominating feature is the gigantic portrait of Mao, the required backdrop for any photo the Chinese take of themselves at the gate (whether they like him or not). To the left of the portrait is a slogan 'Long Live the People's Republic of China' and to the Right 'Long Live the Unity of the Peoples of the World'. Grandstands with a capacity of

20,000 dignitaries were added for reviewing purposes. Photography is big at Tiananmen – the Chinese aspire to visiting the heart of the nation almost like the Muslims aspire to visiting Mecca and Chinese schoolkids grow up singing 'I Love Tiananmen'. If you venture a little way into the Forbidden City through Tiananmen you will find all kinds of bizarre photo-props such as cardboard cut-outs of opera stars or a car provided by the state.

## History Museum & Museum of the Revolution

Housed in the same sombre building on the east side of Tiananmen Square, it's difficult to decide where one museum ends and the other begins. Museums hold a rather odd position in relation to tourism in China, if not in relation to the Chinese themselves. Access to both of these was long thwarted by special permission requirements; from 1966-78 the Museum of Chinese Revolution was closed, so some claimed, that history could be reassessed in the light of recent events. The presentation of history indeed poses quite a problem for the CCP. While the Maoist factions did their level best to destroy thousands of years of history and literature, they declined to publish anything of note on the history of their own party after it had gained power, before, during or since the Cultural Revolution. This would require reams of carefully-worded revision according to what tack politics (here synonymous with history) might take – so better left unwritten.

Explanations throughout the museums are, unfortunately, entirely in Chinese, so you won't get much out of this labyrinth unless you pick yourself up an English-speaking student, but there is an English text relating to the history museum available inside at Y2. The History Museum has artefacts and cultural relics (many are copies) from Day 1 to 1919, subdivided into areas of primitive communal man, slavery, feudalism and capitalism/imperialism – all laced with Marxism.

Without a guide you can discern ancient weapons, inventions and musical instruments. The Museum of the Revolution is split into five sections: the founding of the CCP(1919-21); the first civil war(1924-27); the second civil war(1927-37); resistance against Japan(1937-45) and the third civil war(1945-49).

In 1978 a permanent photo-pictorial exhibit of the life and works of Zhou En-lai became a star attraction and in 1983 there was an exhibit tracing the life of Liu Shao-qi. PLA soldiers are occasionally taken through the museums on tours; they snap to attention, open portable chairs and sit down in unison for explanations of each section – whatever spiel they're given would probably be engrossing if you had someone to translate for you.

The museums are open 8.30 am to 3 pm except on Sundays when they're closed. No photos permitted.

## Monument to the People's Heroes

On the southern side of Tiananmen, this monument was completed in 1958 and stands on the site of the old Outer Palace Gate. The 36 metre obelisk, made of Qingdao granite, bears bas relief carvings of key revolutionary events as well as appropriate calligraphy from Mao Zedong and Zhou En-lai. In 1976 it was the focus of the 'Tiananmen Incident' when thousands gathered here to protest the tyranny of the Gang of Four, and to mourn the death of Zhou En-lai.

## Mao Zedong Mausoleum

Behind the Monument to the People's Heroes stands this giant mausoleum built to house the body of Chairman Mao. It was constructed over a period of ten months in 1976-77. At the end of 1983 the mausoleum was reopened as a museum with exhibitions on the lives of Zhou En-lai, Zhu De, Mao and the man he killed, Liu Shao-qi. Mao's body still remains in its place.

Whatever history will make of Mao, his impact on the course of history will remain unchanged: enormous. Easy as it now is to vilify his deeds and excesses, there is a good measure of respect when confronted with the 'physical' presence of the man. Shoving a couple of museums into the mausoleum was meant to knock Mao another rung down the divine ladder; nevertheless the atmosphere in the inner sanctum itself has been one of hushed reverence, with a thick red pile carpet muting any sound.

Only the upper part of the body is visible – draped in a red flag and encased in a crystal sarcophagus. We haven't heard what the situation on visiting the place is since the museums were added: previously you had to line up four abreast in Tiananmen Square, march into the first hall which displays a large white statue of Mao, then two go to the left of the body and two to the right. Admission was by group-tour (for westerners) or work unit (for Chinese) – though a few individual travellers managed to get in by tagging onto the end of tour groups. The body is apparently lowered into the ground for the winter months, and not on view.

The CITS guides freely quote the old 7/3 ratio on Mao that first surfaced in 1976 – that Mao was 70% right and 30% wrong (what, one wonders, are the figures for CITS itself?), which is now the official party line. His gross errors in the Cultural Revolution, it is said, are far outweighed by his contributions. Mao died in September 1976, and the Memorial Hall was erected shortly after – it occupies a prominent position on the powerful north-south axis of the city, but against all laws of geomancy, faces north.

### Qianmen Gate (Front Gate)

Silent sentinel to the changing times, the Front Gate has had its context removed. It is one of the few old gates left, and a great landmark to get around by. It guarded the wall-division between the ancient Inner City and the outer suburban zone, and dates back to the reign of Emperor Yong-le in the 15th century.

### Great Hall of the People

This is the venue of the National People's Congress. You can get into this building – for a price. The entrance fee is Y5 for foreigners, Y3 for foreign students and Y0.20 for Chinese, which is quite a mark-up. A passport is necessary (don't ask me why!). You tramp through the halls of power, many of them named after provinces and regions of China and decorated appropriately; you get to see the 5000-seat banquet room where Nixon dined in 1972 and the 10,000-seat auditorium with the familiar red star embedded in a galaxy of lights in the ceiling There's a sort of museum-like atmosphere in the Great Hall, with objets d'art donated by the provinces, and a snack bar and restaurant at the end of a brief escorted tour. The Hall was completed over a 10-month period in 1958-59.

### THE FORBIDDEN CITY

The Forbidden City, so-called because it was offlimits for 500 years, is the largest and best-preserved cluster of ancient buildings in China. It was home to two dynasties of emperors, the Ming and the Qing, and they didn't stray from this pleasure-dome unless they absolutely had to.

The Forbidden City is open daily 8.30 am to 4.30 pm but entry is not permitted after 3.30 pm. Two hundred years ago the admission price would have been instant death, but this has dropped considerably to just 10 fen.

The basic layout was built between 1406 and 1420 by Emperor Yong-le, commanding battalions of laborers and craftsmen – some estimate up to a million of them. From this palace the emperors governed China, often rather erratically as they tended to become lost in this self-contained little world and allocated real power to the court eunuchs. One emperor devoted his entire career to carpentry – when an earthquake struck, an ominous sign for the emperor, he was delighted since it gave him a chance to renovate.

The buildings now seen are mostly post-18th century, as with a lot of restored or rebuilt structures around Beijing. The palace was constantly coming down in flames – a lantern festival combined with a sudden gust of Gobi wind would easily do the trick – as would a fireworks display. There were also deliberate fires lit by court eunuchs and officials who could get rich off the repair bills. The moat around the palace, now used for boating, came in handy since the local fire brigade was considered too common to quench the royal flames. Some of the emperors enjoyed the spectacle of fires, whilst the Emperor Jiajing was so disturbed by them that he ordered a hall built in honour of the 'Fire-Pressing God'. Three fires caused by lightning broke out during his reign including the biggest bonfire of the lot in 1557. A century later, in 1664, the Manchus stormed in and burned the palace to the ground.

It was not just the buildings that went up in smoke; rare books, paintings, calligraphy, anything flammable. In this century there have been two major lootings of the palace, first by the Japanese forces, and secondly on the eve of the Communist takeover in 1949 by the Kuomintang, who removed thousands of crates of booty to Taiwan. The gaps have been filled by bringing treasures, old and newly-discovered, from other parts of China.

The palace is so large (720,000 sq metres, 800 buildings, 9000 rooms) that a permanent restoration squad moves around repainting and repairing. It's estimated to take about ten years to do a full renovation, by which time the starting end is due for repairs again. The complex was opened to the public in 1949 and it's hoped that by the late 1980s all the buildings will be accessible. For the moment, most of the buildings which are open are grouped at the northern end.

The palace was built on a monumental scale, one that should not be taken lightly. Allow yourself a full day for exploration or perhaps several separate trips. The information given here can only be a skeleton guide and if you want more detail then tag along with a tour group for explanations of individual artefacts. There are plenty of western tour groups around and overall the Forbidden City gets 10,000 visitors a day. Tour buses drop their groups off at Tiananmen and pick them up again at the north gate; you can also enter the palace from the east or west gates. Even if you had a separate guide-book on the Forbidden City, it would be rather time-consuming to match up and identify every individual object, building and so forth – a spoken guide has more immediacy.

On the north-south axis of the forbidden City, from Tiananmen at the south to Shenwumen at the north, lie the palaces ceremonial buildings, the most holy of routings.

The **Meridian Gate (Wumen)** was restored in the 17th century. This massive portal was reserved for the use of the emperor and gongs and bells would be sounded upon royal comings and goings. Lesser mortals would use lesser gates – the military used the west gate, civilians used the east gate. The emperor also reviewed his armies from here, passed judgement on prisoners, announced the new year calendar and surveyed the flogging of cheeky ministers.

Across **Golden Stream** which is shaped to resemble a tartar bow and is spanned by five marble bridges, is **(Taihemen) Supreme Harmony Gate** which overlooks a massive courtyard that could hold up to 100,000 in imperial audience.

Raised on a marble terrace with balustrades are the **Three Great Halls**, the heart of the Forbidden City. The **Taihedian (Hall of Supreme Harmony)** is the most important and the largest structure in the Forbidden City. Restored in the 15th century, it was used for ceremonial occasions such as the emperor's birthday, the nomination of military leaders, and coronations. Flanking the entrance to the

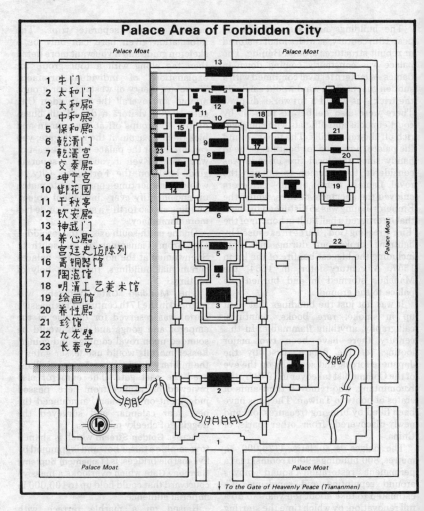

## Palace Area of Forbidden City

Palace Moat

Palace Moat

1 午门
2 太和门
3 太和殿
4 中和殿
5 保和殿
6 乾清门
7 乾清宫
8 交泰殿
9 坤宁宫
10 御花园
11 千秋亭
12 钦安殿
13 神武门
14 养心殿
15 宫廷史迹陈列
16 青铜器馆
17 陶瓷馆
18 明清工艺美术馆
19 绘画馆
20 养性殿
21 珍馆
22 九龙壁
23 长春宫

Palace Moat

Palace Moat

Palace Moat

↓ To the Gate of Heavenly Peace (Tiananmen)

hall are bronze incense burners; the large bronze turtle in the front is a symbol of longevity and stability – it has a removable lid and on special occasions incense was lit inside so that smoke billowed from the mouth. To the west side of the terrace is a small pavilion with a bronze grain-measure and to the east is a sundial, both symbolic of imperial justice. On the corners of the roof, as with some other buildings in the city, you'll see a mounted figure with his retreat cut off by mythical and real animals, a story that relates to a cruel tyrant hung from one such eave. Inside the hall is a richly-decorated Dragon Throne where the emperor would preside (decisions final, no correspondence entered into) over trembling officials. The

1 Meridian Gate (Wumen)
2 Gate of Supreme Harmony (Taihemen)
3 Hall of Supreme Harmony (Taihedian)
4 Hall of Middle Harmony (Zhonghedian)
5 Hall of Preserving Harmony (Baohedian)
6 Gate of Heavenly Purity (Qiangingmen)
7 Palace of Heavenly Purity (Qianqinggong)
8 Hall of Vigorous Fertility (Jiaotaidian)
9 Palace of Earthly Tranquility (Kunninggong)
10 Imperial Garden
11 Thousand Autumns Pavilion
12 Hall of Imperial Peace
13 Gate of Divine Military Genius (Shenwumen)

14 Hall of Mental Cultivation (Yangxindian)
15 Western Palaces
Nos. 16, 17 and 18 were formerly the residential palaces and are now used as museums;
16 Exhibition of Bronzes
17 Exhibiton of Ceramics
18 Exhibition of Arts & Crafts of the Ming & Qing Dynasties
19 Exhibiton of Paintings (formerly the Hall of Imperial Supremacy)
20 Palace of Peaceful Old Age
21 Exhibition of Jewellery (formerly the Hall of the Cultivation of Character)
22 Nine Dragon Screen
23 Palace of Eternal Spring (Changchungong)

entire court had to hit the floor nine times with their foreheads, combine that with thick veils of incense and battering of gongs and it would be enough to make anyone dizzy. At the back of the throne is a carved Xumi Mountain, the Buddhist paradise, signifying the throne's supremacy.

Behind Taihedian is a smaller hall, the **Zhonghedian (Hall of Middle Harmony)** which was used as a transit lounge for the emperor. Here he would make last-minute preparations, rehearse speeches and receive close ministers. There are two Qing Dynasty sedan chairs displayed, the emperor's mode of transport around the Forbidden City. The last of the Qing emperors, Pu Yi, used a bicycle and altered a few features of the palace grounds to make it easier to get around.

The third hall is the **Baohedian (Hall of Preserving Harmony)** used for banquets and later for imperial examinations. It now houses archaeological finds. The Baohedian has no support pillars, and behind it is a 250-ton marble block carved with dragons and clouds which was moved from its location near Beijing by sliding it over an

ice path. The outer housing surrounding the Three Great Halls was used for storing gold, silver, silks, carpets and other treasures.

The basic configuration of the Three Great Halls is mimicked by the next group of buildings, smaller in scale but more important in terms of real power. In China, real power traditionally lies at the back door, or in this case, the back gate. The first structure is the **Qianqinggong (Palace of Heavenly Purity)**, a residence of Ming and early Qing emperors, and later an audience hall for receiving foreign envoys and high officials. Immediately behind it is the **Hall of Union** which contains a clepsydre – a water clock with five bronze vessels and a calibrated scale. Water clocks date back several thousand years but this one was made in 1745. There's also a mechanical clock on display, built in 1797, and a collection of imperial jade seals.

At the northern end of the Forbidden City is the **Imperial Garden**, a classical Chinese garden of 7000 sq metres of superb landscaping, with rockeries, walkways and pavilions. A good place to take a breather; snack bars, WCs and souvenir shops. Two more gates lead out through the large **Shenwumen (Gate of Divine Military Genius)**.

North of Shenwumen and outside the present confines of the Forbidden City, is **Jing Shan (Coal Hill Park)**, an artificial mound made of earth excavated to create the palace moat. If you clamber to the top pavilions of this regal pleasure garden you get a magnificent panorama of the capital and a great overview of the russet roofing of the Forbidden City. On the east side of the park is a locust tree where the last of the Mings, the Emperor Chongzhen, hanged himself (after slaying his family) rather than see the palace razed by the Manchus. The hill supposedly protects the palace from the evil spirits – or duststorms – from the north, but didn't quite work for Chongzhen. The park is open to the public 6 am to 9 pm.

**Other sections of the palace** are the former palatial living quarters, once containing libraries, temples, theatres, gardens, even the tennis court of the last emperor. These buildings now function as museums and often require separate but nominal admission fees, have irregular opening hours and no photos allowed without prior permission. Special exhibits sometimes appear in the palace museum halls – check *China Daily* for details.

On the western side of the Forbidden City, towards the north exit, are the six **Western Palaces** which were living quarters for the empress and the concubines. These are kept in pristine condition, displaying furniture, silk bedcovers, personal items, and fittings such as cloisonne charcoal burners. Of particular interest is the **Changchunggong (Palace of Eternal Spring)** decorated with mural scenes from the Ming novel *A Dream of the Red Mansions*. This is where the Empress Dowager Cixi lived when she was still a concubine. Nearby is **Yangxindian (Hall of Mental Cultivation)**, a private

apartment for the emperors; it was divided into reception rooms, a study where important documents were signed and a bedchamber at the rear.

On the eastern side of the city, six more palaces duplicate the rhythms and layout of those on the west. There are more museums here – for Bronzes (open Thurs/Fri), Ceramics (open Sat/Sun), Ming Dynasty Arts and Crafts (open Tues and Thurs). Further east is a display of gold and jade artefacts and Ming and Qing paintings – the latter is augmented from October to November with Song and Yuan paintings. Just south, protecting the gateway to two of the palaces, is the polychrome **Nine Dragon Screen** built in 1773.

**Other features** of the Forbidden City worth noting are the **Watchtowers** at the four corners of the city which stand atop the walls; structural delights, they have three storeys, are double-roofed and 27.5 metres high. **Zhongshan Park**, otherwise known as Sun Yat-sen Park is in the southwest of the city and was laid out at the same time as the palace; here you'll find the **Altar of Land and Grain**, which is divided into five sections, each filled with earth of a different colour (red, green, black, yellow and white) to symbolise all the earth belonging to the emperor. There is also a concert hall and a 'modernisation' playground in the park. The **Worker's Cultural Palace** is in the south-east sector of the city and is a park with halls dating from 1462 which were used as ancestral temples under the Ming and Qing; they come complete with marble balustrades, terraces and detailed gargoyles. The park is now used for movies, temporary exhibits and cultural performances, and the odd mass wedding (there's a waiting list of 5000 couples) – there's boating at the north end and skating in winter on the frozen moat.

Four hundred years ago the Jesuit priest Matteo Ricci, who spent 20 years in

China, much of that time at the Imperial court in Beijing, recorded in his diary:

Just as this people is grossly subject to superstition, so, too, they have very little regard for the truth, acting always with great circumspection, and very cautious about trusting anyone. Subject to this same fear, the kings of modern times abandoned the custom of going out in public. Even formerly, when they did leave the royal enclosure, they would never dare to do so without a thousand preliminary precautions. On such occasions the whole court was placed under military guard. Secret servicemen were placed along the route over which the King was to travel and on all roads leading into it. He was not only hidden from view, but the public never knew in which of the palanquins of his cortege he was actually riding. One would think he was making a journey through enemy country rather than through multitudes of his own subjects and clients.

If ceremonial and administrative duties occupied much of the emperor's time, then behind the high walls of the Forbidden City it was the pursuit of pleasure which occupied much of his attention. One of the imperial bedtime systems was to keep the names of royal wives, consorts and favourites on jade tablets near the emperor's chambers – sometimes as many as 50 of them. By turning the tablet over the Emperor made his request for the evening, and the eunuch on duty would rush off to find the lucky lady. Stripped naked and therefore 'weaponless' she was wrapped in a yellow cloth, and the little bound-footed creature was piggybacked over to the royal boudoir and dumped at the feet of the emperor; and the eunuch recorded the date and time to verify legitimacy of a possible child.

Financing the pleasure-drome was an arduous affair that drew on the resources of the empire. During the Ming Dynasty there were an estimated 9,000 maids of honour and 70,000 eunuchs serving the court. Apart from the servants and the prize whores there were also the royal elephants to upkeep. These were gifts from Burma and were stabled south-west of the Forbidden City. Accorded rank by the emperor, when one died a period of mourning was declared. Periodically the elephant keepers embezzled the funds intended for elephant chow. When this occurred, the ravenous pachyderms went on a rampage. While pocketing this cash was illegal, selling elephant dung for use as shampoo was not, and it was believed to give the hair that extra sheen. Back in the harem the cosmetic bills piled up to 400,000 taels of silver and supplies cost several million. Rather than cut back on expenditure, the emperor sent out eunuchs to collect emergency taxes whenever the money ran short.

As for the palace eunuchs, the royal chop was administered at the Eunuch Clinic near the Forbidden City, using a swift knife and a special chair with a hole in the seat. The candidates sought to better their lives in the court – half of them died after the 'operation'. Mutilation of any kind was considered unsuitable for entry to the next life, so many eunuchs carried their appendages around in pouches, believing that at the time of death the spirits might be deceived into thinking of them as whole.

## MUSEUMS & LIBRARIES
The best museums are located in the Forbidden City, and the biggest are the combined Historical and Revolutionary Museums in Tiananmen Square. The most interesting are the temporary exhibits held in parks or places like the Nationalities Cultural Palace. Museums in Beijing are poorly maintained, poorly presented and little research work is done.

### Military Museum
Perhaps more to the point than the Museum of the Chinese Revolution, this traces the genesis of the PLA from 1927 to present and has some interesting exhibits: pictures of Mao in the early days, US planes the Chinese shot down and

Russian tanks they'd captured and trophies from India and Vietnam. The fourth floor has documents relating to the war with Vietnam and arms captured from Vietnam; it's only open to Chinese. The museum is on Fuxing Lu on the western side of the city, and to get there take the subway to Junshibowuguan. It's open 8.30 am to 5 pm, the last entry at 4 pm. Entry is free, but bring your passport with you as you may be asked for ID.

## Lu Xun Museum

Dedicated to China's No 1 Thinking Man's Revolutionary, this museum contains manuscripts, diaries, letters and inscriptions by the famous writer. To the west of the museum is a small Chinese walled compound where Lu Xun lived from 1924 to 1926. The museum is west of the Xisi intersection and is open 8.30 to 11 am and 1.30 to 4 pm and is closed on Sundays.

## Beijing National Library

This holds around five million books and four million periodicals and newspapers, over a third of which are in foreign languages. Access to books is limited and access to rare books is even rarer though you might be shown a microfilm copy if

you're lucky. The large collection of rare books includes surviving imperial works such as the *Yong Le Encyclopedia* and selections from the old Jesuit library. Of interest to Ming-Qing scholars is the special collection, the *Shanbenbu*. The library is near Behai Park on the south side and is open 8 am to 8 pm, closed on Saturdays. Beijing University Library also has a large collection of rare books.

## Capital Museum & Library

Formerly a Confucian Temple, the museum houses steles, stone inscriptions, bronzes, vases and documents. It's near the Lama Temple and is open 9 am to 5 pm, closed on Mondays.

## China Art Gallery

Back in the post-Liberation days one of the safest hobbies for an artist was to retouch classical-type landscapes with red flags, belching factory chimneys or bright red tractors. You can get some idea of the state of the arts in China at this gallery and at times there are very good exhibitions of current work held in an adjacent gallery (including photo displays) – check *China Daily* for listings. The Arts and Crafts Shop inside has an excellent range of woodblock prints and papercuts. The gallery is west of the Dongsi intersection and is open 9 am to 5 pm though the last tickets are sold at 4 pm. It's closed on Mondays.

## Xu Beihong Museum

Here you'll find traditional Chinese paintings, oils, gouaches, sketches and memorabilia of the famous artist, noted for his galloping horse paintings. Painting-albums on sale, reproductions and Chinese stationery. It's at 53 Xinjiekou Beidajie, Xicheng District and is open 9 am to 5 pm, closed on Mondays.

## Song Qingling Museum

Madam Song was the wife of Sun Yat-sen, the founder of the Republic of China and held the position of Vice-Chairperson of the State. After 1981 her large residence was transformed into a museum dedicated to her memory and to that of Sun Yat-sen.

BEHAI PARK

The original layout of the residence is unchanged and on display are personal items and pictures of historical interest. It's located to the north of Lake Shishahai.

## ZHONGNANHAI

Situated just to the west of the Forbidden City is China's new forbidden city, Zhongnanhai. The name means 'the central and south seas' and takes its name from the two large lakes which are enclosed in the compound. The southern entrance is via Xinhuamen (The Gate of New China) which you'll see on Changan Avenue, the entrance guarded by two PLA soldiers and fronted by a flagpole with the Red Flag flying. The gate was built in 1758 and was then known as the **Tower of the Treasured Moon**.

The compound was first built between the 10th and 13th centuries as a sort of playground for the emperors and their retinue. It was expanded during the Ming but most of the present buildings only date from the Qing Dynasty. After the overthrow of the imperial government and the establishment of the republic it served as the site of the presidential palace. Since the founding of the People's Republic in 1949, Zhongnanhai has been the residence and offices of the highest ranking members of the Communist Party: the Central Committee of the Communist Party of the State Council, the Central People's Government and the Military Commission of the Party Central Committee all have their offices here. People like Mao Zedong, Zhou En-lai, Lui Shao-qi and Zhu De and others all lived and worked here.

Prior to the arrival of the new batch of tenants **Zongnanhai** had been the site of the emperor's ploughing of the first symbolic furrow of the farming season and the venue for imperial banquets as well as the highest examinations in martial arts. The Empress Dowager Cixi once lived here; after the failure of the 1898 reform movement she imprisoned the Emperor Guangxu in the Hall of Impregnating Vitality, where, rather ironically, he later died. Yuan Shikai used **Zongnanhai** for ceremonial occasions during the few years of his presidency of the Chinese Republic and his vice-president moved into Guangxu's death-house.

## BEIJING PARKS
### Beihai Park

Approached by four gates, and just north-west of the Forbidden City, Beihai Park is the former playground of the Emperors – and rumoured to have been the private pleasure domain of the great dragon lady/wicked lady/white witch Jiang Qing, widow of Mao and now serving a life sentence as No 1 of the 'Gang of Four'.

The park covers an area of 68.2 hectares, half of which is a lake. The island in the lower middle is composed of heaped earth dug to create the lake – some attribute this to the handiwork of Kublai Khan. The site is associated with the Great Khan's Palace, the belly-button of Beijing before the creation of the Forbidden City. All that remains of the Khan's court is a large jar, made of green jade, in the **Round City** near the south entrance. A present given in 1265, and said to contain the Khan's wine, it was later discovered in the hands of Taoist priests who used it to store pickles. In the **Light Receiving Hall**, the main structure nearby, is a 1½-metre high white jade Buddha inlaid with jewels – a gift to Empress Dowager Cixi, from Burma

From the 12th century on, Beihai Park was landscaped with artificial hills, pavilions, halls, temples and covered walkways – culminating in the present era when the structures were massively restored. It is one of the best examples of a classical garden now found in China.

Dominating Jade Islet on the lake is the **White Dagoba**, a pop-art 'Peppermint Bottle' about 36 metres high, built in 1651 to commemorate the visit of a Dalai Lama, and rebuilt in 1741. It is believed that Lamaist scriptures, robes and other

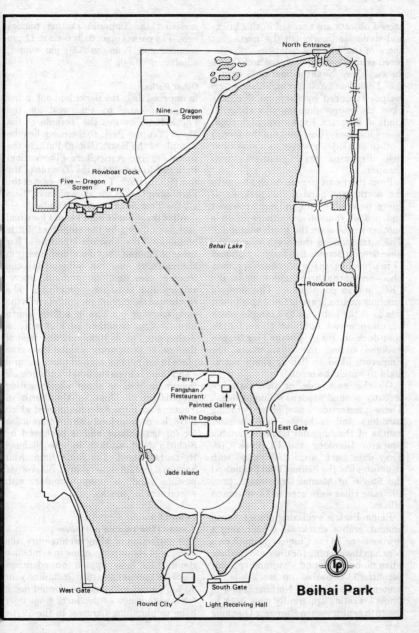

North Entrance

Nine – Dragon
Screen

Rowboat Dock

Five – Dragon
Screen

Ferry

*Behai Lake*

Rowboat Dock

Ferry

Fangshan
Restaurant

Painted Gallery

White Dagoba

East Gate

Jade Island

West Gate

South Gate

Round City

Light Receiving Hall

**Beihai Park**

sacred objects are encased in this brick-and-stone landmark. On the north-east shore of the islet is a handsome double-tiered **painted gallery** – unusual architecure for a walkway. Near the boat-dock here is the *Fangshan Restaurant*, dishing up recipes favoured by Empress Cixi; she liked 120-course dinners with about 30 kinds of desserts. Expensive, high class, reservation only (but check out the decor!) – off to one side, however, is a snack bar that dispenses royal pastries, much cheaper.

From this point you can catch a barge to the north-west part of the park, or, if energetic, double back and rent a rowboat and propel yourself over there (there's another rowboat on the north-west side). The attraction on the north side is the **Nine-Dragon Screen**, five metres high and 27 metres long, made of coloured glazed tiles – one of the three famous ones in the PRC, and in good shape. The screen's function was to scare off evil spirits – it stands at the entrance to a temple which has disappeared. To the south-west of the boat-dock on this side is the **Five Dragon Pavillion** dating to 1651, where the Emperors liked to fish or camp out at night to watch the moon.

On the east side of the park are recently-opened 'gardens within gardens'. These waterside pavilions, winding corridors and rockeries were summer haunts of the imperial family – notably Emperor Qianlong and Empress Cixi. They date back some 200 years, with structures like the **Painted Boat Studio** and the **Studio of Mental Calmness** – until 1980 the villas were used as Government offices.

Beihai Park is a relaxing place to stroll around, grab a snack, sip a beer, rent a rowboat – or, as the Chinese do, neck on a bench in the evening (or dive into the lake when no-one's around – swimming is not permitted). Crowded on weekends. In winter there is skating. Nothing is new in China – skating apparently goes back to the 18th century when Emperor Qianlong

reviewed the imperial skating parties here. The park is open daily 6 am to 11 pm summer and 7 am to 8.30 pm winter; admission Y0.50.

## Other Parks

In imperial days the parks laid out at the compass-points; to the west of the Forbidden City lies the Temple of the Moon (Yeutan) Park, to the north lies the Temple of the Earth (Ditan) Park, to the south lies the Agriculture (Taoranting) Park and to the east is the Temple of the Sun (Ritan) Park. To the south-east of the Forbidden City is the showpiece of them all, the Temple of Heaven (Tiantan).

All of these parks were venues for ritual sacrifice offered by the emperors. Little remains of the shaman structures, bar those of Tiantan – but if you arrive early in the morning you can witness tai chi, fencing exercises, or perhaps opera-singers and musicians practising. The rhythms of the city are very different in the early morning – a hive of activity worth investigating. (Another park of note is Zizhuyuan, Purple Bamboo Park, west of the zoo.) Temporary exhibitions take place in the parks – horticultural, cultural – and there is even the odd bit of open-air theatre as well as some worthy eating establishments. Just to the north of Yeutan Park is the *Emei Restaurant* which serves hot Sichuan food with no compromise for foreign palates and is preferred by Sichuan food addicts to the Sichuan Restaurant itself. The *Ritan Restaurant* has *jiaozi* (for foreigners) in an older-style pavilion and is very popular with westerners for snacks.

## TEMPLES
### Tiantan (The Temple of Heaven)

The perfection of Ming architecture, the Temple of Heaven has come to symbolise Beijing. Its lines appear on countless pieces of tourist literature (including your 50-fen tourist bill), and as a brand name for a wide range of products from tiger balm to plumbing fixtures. In the 1970s

Top: Tiananmen Square, Beijing [AS]
Left: Ceiling of Temple of Heaven, Beijing [MB]
Right: Lama Temple, Beijing [MB]

Top: Walking the Great Wall at Badaling, near Beijing [AS]
Bottom: . . . and buying antique T-shirts nearby [AS]

the complex got a facelift and was freshly painted after pigment research. It is set in a 267 hectare park, with four gates at the compass points, and bounded by walls to the north and east. It originally functioned as a vast stage for solemn rites performed by the Son of Heaven who came here to pray for good harvests, seek divine clearance, and to atone for the sins of the people.

With this complicated mix in mind, the unique architectural features will delight numerologists, necromancers, and the superstitious – not to mention acoustic engineers and carpenters. Shape, colour and sound take on symbolic significance: the temples, seen in aerial perspective, are round, and the bases are square, deriving from the ancient Chinese belief that heaven is round, and the earth is square. Thus the north end of the park is semicircular and the south end is square (remember that the layout of the Beijing parks places the Temple of Earth on the northern compass point and the Temple of Heaven on the southern compass point).

In October, just before the winter solstice, the Emperor and his massive entourage used to burst through the five gates at Tiananmen and make their way down toward Qianmen. The procession included elephant chariots, horse chariots and long lines of lancers, nobles, officials and musicians, dressed in their finest, flags fluttering. The cortege passed the length of present-day Qianmen Street in total silence – commoners were not permitted to view the ceremony and remained behind shuttered windows. The Emperor meditated in the Imperial Vault of Heaven, and passed the night at the Hall of Prayer for Good Harvests. The next day he waited in a yellow silk tent at the south gate while officials moved sacred tablets to the Round Altar. Finally, amid burning of incense, peals of gongs and bells, and incantations by priests, he would ascend the Round Altar and make offerings. The least hitch in any part of the proceedings was regarded as an ill omen, and it was thought that the nation's future was thus decided. This was the most important ceremony – other excursions to the Temple of the Earth (Ditan Park) also took place.

The five-metre-high **Round Altar** was constructed in 1530 and rebuilt in 1740. It is composed of white marble arrayed in three tiers, and its geometry revolves around the imperial number 9. Odd numbers were considered heavenly, and 9 is the largest single-digit odd number. The top tier, thought to symbolise Heaven, has 9 rings of stones, each ring composed of multiples of 9 stones, so that the 9th ring has 81 stones. The middle tier – Earth – has the 10th to 18th rings, and the bottom tier – Man – has the 19th to 27th rings, ending with a total of 243 stones in the largest ring, or 27 times 9. The number of stairs and balustrades are also multiples of 9. If you stand in the centre of the upper terrace there is an acoustic effect where sound waves are bounced off the marble balustrades, making your own voice appear louder. (Nine times?)

Just north of this, surrounding the entrance to the Imperial Vault of Heaven, is the **Echo Wall**, 65 metres in diametre. A vast improvement over the Chinese telephone, this enables a whisper to travel from one end to your friend's ear elsewhere, clearly – that is, if there's not a group tour in the middle. In the courtyard are the **Triple Echo Stones** – if you stand on Number One and clap or shout, the sound is echoed once, on the second stone twice, and on the third, three times. Should it return four times, you will almost certainly not get a railway ticket that day, or any other day that is a multiple of three.

The octagonal **Imperial Vault of Heaven** was built at the same time as the Round Altar, and is structured along the lines of the older Hall of Prayer for Good Harvests, though it is smaller. It used to contain tablets of the emperor's ancestors, which were used in the winter solstice

# Tiatan (Temple of Heaven) Park

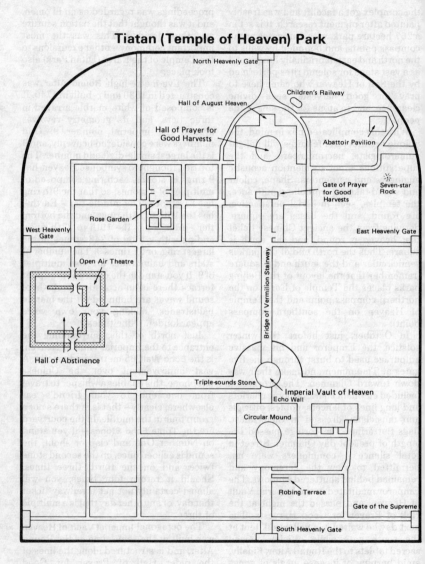

North Heavenly Gate

Children's Railway

Hall of August Heaven

Hall of Prayer for
Good Harvests

Abattoir Pavilion

Gate of Prayer
for Good
Harvests

Seven-star
Rock

Rose Garden

West Heavenly
Gate

East Heavenly Gate

Open Air Theatre

Bridge of Vermilion Stairway

Hall of Abstinence

Triple-sounds Stone

Imperial Vault of Heaven

Echo Wall

Circular Mound

Robing Terrace

Gate of the Supreme

South Heavenly Gate

ceremony. Proceeding up from the Imperial Vault is a walkway: to the left is a molehill composed of excess dirt dumped from digging air-raid shelters and to the right is a rash of souvenir shops.

The main structure of the complex is the **Hall of Prayer for Good Harvests**, a magnificent piece mounted on a three-tiered marble terrace. It was built in 1420 – in 1889 it was burnt to cinders, and heads rolled in dispensing blame. The supposed cause was lightning – no good harvests that year! A faithful reproduction, based on Ming architectural methods was erected the following year, using Oregon fir as the support pillars. The four pillars at the centre represent the seasons, the twelve ringing those denote the months of the year, and the twelve outer ones are symbolic of the day, broken into twelve 'watches'. Embedded in the ceiling is a carved dragon, symbol of royalty. The patterning, carving and gilt decoration of this ceiling and its swirl of colour is a dizzy sight – enough to carry you into the Seventh Heaven. In fact it looks peculiarly modern – like a graphic from a science-fiction movie of a spaceship about to blast into hyperspace. All this is made more amazing by the fact that the wooden pillars ingeniously support the ceiling without nails or cement – for a building 38 metres high and 30 metres in diameter, a stunning accomplishment of carpentry. Capping the structure is a deep blue umbrella of tiles with a golden knob and two complementary eaves.

Tiantan, it should not to be forgotten, is also a park and a meeting place. Tai chi enthusiasts assemble at the gates in the morning and head off for their favourite spots, some practising snatches of opera en route. There are also nice floral exhibits; along the east wall is a poultry and food market. The park is open 6.30 am to 6 pm daily, admission 10 fen; bus 116 terminates at the south gate – other buses run past the east, north and west gates.

## Yonghegong (Lama Temple)

By far the most pleasant temple in Beijing – beautiful gardens, stunning frescoes and tapestries, incredible carpentry. Get to this one before you are 'templed out' – it won't chew up your day.

Yonghegong is the most renowned Tibetan Buddhist temple within China outside Tibet itself (a carefully worded statement!). Located toward Andingmen, it became after extensive renovation the official residence of Count Yin Zhen. Nothing unusual in that – but in 1723 he was promoted to Emperor, and moved to the Forbidden City. His name was changed to Yong Zheng, and his former residence became Yonghe Palace. The green tiles were changed to yellow, the imperial colour, and – as was the custom – the place could not be used except as a temple. In 1744 it was converted into a lamasery, and became a residence for monks from Mongolia and Tibet, large numbers of them.

In 1792, Qianlong, having quelled an uprising in Tibet, instituted a system whereby the government issued two gold vases. One was kept at the Jokhang Temple in Lhasa for determining the reincarnation of the Dalai Lama (under the supervision of the Minister for Tibetan Affairs), and the other was kept at Yonghegong for the lottery for the Mongolian Grand Living Buddha. The Lama Temple thus assumed a new importance in minority control

The lamasery has three richly-worked archways, and five main halls strung in a line down the middle, each taller than the preceding one. Styles are mixed – Mongolian, Tibetan and Han, with courtyard enclosures and galleries. The first hall, **Lokapala**, houses a statue of the Maitreya (future) Buddha, flanked by celestial guardians; the statue facing the back door is Weituo, guardian of Buddhism, made of white sandalwood. Beyond, in the courtyard, is a pond with a bronze mandala depicting Xumi Mountain, the Buddhist paradise.

The next hall, **Yonghedian,** has three figures of Buddha (past, present, future); the third hall, **Yongyoudian** has statues of the Buddha of Longevity, and the Buddha of Medicine (to the left). The courtyard following has galleries with some Nandikesvaras – joyful Buddhas tangled up in multi-armed close encounters. These are coyly draped lest you be corrupted by the sight, and are to be found in other esoteric locations.

**The Hall of the Wheel of Law,** further north, contains a large bronze statue of Tsongkapa (1357 to 1419), founder of the Yellow Sect, and frescoes depicting his life. This Tibetan-style building is used for study and prayer. The last hall, **Wanfu Pavillion,** has an 18-metre high statue of the Maitreya Buddha in his Tibetan form, sculpted from a single piece of sandalwood and clothed in yellow satin. The smoke curling up from the yak-butter lamps transports you momentarily to Tibet, from where the log for this statue came.

In 1949 the Lama Temple was declared protected as a major historical relic – miraculously it survived the Cultural Revolution without scars – and was closed. In 1979 large amounts were spent on repairs and it was restocked with several dozen novices from Inner Mongolia, a token move on the part of the government to back up its claim that the Lama Temple is a 'symbol of religious freedom, national unity and stability in China'. The novices study Tibetan language and the secret practices of the Yellow Sect. The temple is very much active again – prayers take place early in the morning, not for public viewing, but if you enquire discreetly of the head-lama, you might be allowed to return the following morning. No photography is permitted in any part of the temple – tempting as it is – in part due to the monkish sensitivity to the reproduction of Buddha images, and in part perhaps to the postcard industry. The temple is open 8.30 am to 5.30 pm, closed Tuesdays and Thursdays, Y0.50 entrance fee but free from 4.30 to 5.30 pm.

## Confucian Temple Complex

Just down the hutong opposite the gates of the Lama Temple is the former Confucian Temple (Kongmiao) and Imperial College (Guozijian). The Confucian Temple is the largest in the land after the one at Qufu. The temple was reopened in 1981 after some mysterious use as a high-official residence and is now used as a museum – in sharp contrast to the Lama temple. The forest of steles in the temple courtyard look very forlorn. The steles record the names of those successful in the civil service examinations (possibly the world's first) of the Imperial court. To see his name engraved here was the ambition of every scholar – but it wasn't made easy; candidates were locked in cubicles (about 8,000 of them) measuring roughly 1½ by 1½ metres for a period of three days. Many died or went insane. The museum is open 9 am to 5 pm, closed Mondays.

The Imperial College was the place where the Emperor expounded the Confucian classics to an audience of thousands of kneeling students, professors and court officials – an annual rite. Built by the grandson of Kublai Khan in 1306, the former College was the only institution of its kind in China – it's now the Capital Library. Part of the 'collection' is the stone tablets commissioned by Emperor Qianlong. These have 13 Confucian classics engraved on them – 800,000 characters (twelve years' work for the scholar who did it). There is an ancient 'Scholar-Tree' in the courtyard.

## Celestial Potpourri

There are heaps of temples and other divine edifices scattered around the capital – in varying states of preservation, decay or renovation. These have been put to various uses as warehouses, residences, schools, army barracks, factories . . : . they may even be open to visitors or quick peepers. Some are listed below and others in the Bicycle Tour section.

### Wutasi

This is an Indian-style temple with five pagodas, first constructed in 1473 from a model presented to the court. It's difficult to find but it's been restored and reopened. It's north-west of the zoo; take Bashiqiao Lu north for almost one km to a bridge, turn east to the temple which lies in the middle of a field.

### Dazhongsi (Big Bell Temple)

This temple is almost two km due east of the Friendship Hotel, and has an enormous bell weighing 46 tons with Buddhist sutras inscribed on it. The bell was cast during the reign of Ming Emperor Yong Le in 1406 and the tower was built in 1733. This monastery is one of the most popular in Beijing and was reopened in 1980.

### Baitasi (White Dagoba Temple)

The Dagoba can be spotted from the top of Jingshan Hill, and is similar (and close to) the one in Beihai Park. Occupied by factories during the Cultural Revolution but reopened in restored state since 1980. The dagoba dates back to Kublai Khan's days, and was completed with the help of a Nepalese architect though the halls date only from the Qing Dynasty. It lies off Fuchengmennai Dajie.

### Guangjisi (Temple of Universal Rescue)

This temple is on the north-west side of Xisi intersection, and east of the White Dagoba Temple. It's in good shape and is headquarters of the Chinese Buddhist Association. It is said to contain some of the finest Buddhist statues in China and there are plans to open it to the public 'soon'.

### Huangsi (Yellow Temple)

The Yellow Temple can be sighted from Beihuan Donglu ringroad (south side). The temple lies north-west of the intersection of Andingmen and Andingmenwai Dajie. The temple has a distinctive gold and white dagoba and was once used as the residence for visiting Panchen Lamas from Tibet in the 17th century. Today it's occupied by a school but is being rebuilt. Try Sundays if you want to visit.

### Niujie District (Ox Street)

in the south-west sector of Beijing, south of Guanganmennai Dajie, is a Moslem residential area with a handsome mosque facing Mecca. It's an area worth checking out – a different feel for many-mooded Beijing. In a lane further east of the mosque is the Fayuansi, the Temple of the Source of Law. The temple was originally constructed in the 7th century and is still going strong – it's now a Buddhist College, open to visits 8.30 to 11.30 am and 1.30 to 4.30 pm (not Wednesdays).

### Baiyunguan (White Cloud Temple)

This is in a district directly south of Yanjing Hotel and west of the moat. It was once the Taoist centre of North China and the site of of temple fairs. There are plans afoot to restore it. Further south of that sits Tianningsi pagoda, looking pretty miserable in a virtual industrial junkyard (the temple once attached has disappeared).

### Cathedrals

Dongtang (East Cathedral) at 74 Wangfujing, was built on the site of the Jesuit Priest Adam Schall's house, founded 1666 and later used by the Portuguese Lazarists. It has been rebuilt several times. It's now used as a primary school during the week, Catholic services early Sunday mornings. Nantang (Southern Cathedral) on Qianmen at the Xuanwumen intersection (north-east side) is built on the site of Matteo Ricci's house (first built 1703 and destroyed three times since then).

### Mahakala Miao

The monastery here is dedicated to the Great Black Deva, a Mongolian patron saint. It's located on the hutong running east from Beichizi Dajie (approximately in line with the south moat of the Forbidden City).

## Zhihuasi (Black Temple)

So nicknamed because of its deep blue tiling this is a pretty example of Ming (dating to 1443) but there's nothing else of note. If you strain at the bus map, looking north of the main railway station, you will find a hutong called Lumicang, which runs east off Chaoyangmen Nanxidajie (about 1½ km north of the station). The temple is at the east end of Lumicang hutong. The coffered ceiling of the third hall of the 'Growth of Intellect Temple' is not at the east end of Lumicang – it's in the USA. Lumicang hutong had rice granaries in the Qing Dynasty.

## The Underground City

With a Soviet invasion supposedly hanging over them in the late 60s, the Chinese built huge civil defence systems, especially in northern China. This hobby started before 1949 when the PLA used the tunnelling technique to surprise the enemy. Pressed for space, and trying to maximise the peacetime possibilities of the air-raid shelters – apart from being useless against nuclear attack – Beijing has put them to use as warehouses, factories, shops, restaurants, hotels, rollerskating rinks, theatres, clinics.

CITS has a tour to the Underground City which is worth considering (Y5, Tuesdays, Thursdays and Saturdays, 8.30 to 10.30 am, guide but no food, 8-seater minibuses) and which is sometimes combined with a visit to the Mao Zedong Mausoleum – costs Y8.

The section you see on the brief tour is about 270 metres long with tunnels at the 4, 8 and 15 metre levels. It was constructed by volunteers and shop assistants living in the Qianmen area – about 2,000 people and 10 years of spare-time work with simple tools – the shelters planned and construction supervised by the army. The people reap a few benefits now – preferential treatment for relatives

and friends who can stay in a 100-bed hotel (see on the tour), use of the warehouse space, and there's a few bucks to be made off tourists. Some features of the system are viewed: telecommunications room, first-aid room, ventilation system. There are roughly 90 entrances to this particular complex – the guide claims that 10,000 shoppers in the Dazhalan area can be evacuated to the suburbs in five minutes (what about the other 70,000?!) in the event of an attack. Entrances are hidden in shops – the one you descend by is an ordinary-looking garment shop (ordinary, that is, until the entrance is revealed). It's got the flavour of a James Bond movie with a bit of Dr Strangelove thrown in on the side. A short terse lecture is given by a Civil Air Defence man at the end, complete with fluorescent wall map – oh, and a cup of tea before you surface.

If you want to give the CITS tour a miss then there are two bits of the underground city that are easy to get to yourself – the subway and the Dongtian Underground Restaurant.

The **Dongtian (Cave Heaven) Restaurant** is just north of Changan on Xidan St, east side – look for a display of pictures of subterranean scenes that mark the entrance. Descending 60 steps you'll come to four small dining rooms, all served by the same restaurant. They have the decor of an American greasy-spoon truck-stop as interpreted by a crazed neoclassical Sino-Italian decorator. The chambers are The Plum Blossom, the Orchid and Chrysanthemum Rooms, and the Bamboo Chamber – three of them serve spaghetti, pork cutlets, sausages, quasi-French and Italian dishes (no hamburgers yet, but close). The fourth section, Chinese-style decor with ceramic tables and stools, is an icecream parlour. The restaurant is jointly managed by the People's Defence Administration and a food company; it caters for some 4,000 customers per day with a staff of 100 and western food which is a bit off – but then it's the ambience you go for. Eating western style with western utensils is chic in Beijing (leaving half of it on the plate is also chic), and good practice for that tiny, tiny possibility that our Chinese friend may end up in Paris on vacation. The customers are therefore amenable to the stray European face that wanders in. Dongtian is one of about a dozen underground restaurants operating in Beijing, and it's open 10 am to 8 pm, continuous service. What better way to get there than by subway? Take the tube to Xuanwumen, then hop a bus north about two stops.

Next to the Dongtian, but not accessible to the public (you can try) is the **Changan Inn** with its 400 beds. There are some 100 underground hotels in Beijing with a total of 10,000 beds. While the views may not be great, the rooms are insulated by several metres of earth from traffic noise, dust, wind and pesky mosquitoes. Young Chinese honeymooners to the capital can rent one of the Changan Inn's special Double Happiness rooms, decorated with bright red calligraphy wishing them joys when they surface and re-enter the real world. As the Chinese saying goes 'Make one thing serve two purposes' – come a long way from bomb-shelters ...

Walking along the hutongs kind of destroys the advantage of a lightning visit, and may well lead to you accumulating a Chinese entourage – charging off on a bicycle is the only way to go. If you see an interesting compound, you can stop and peer in – maybe even be invited in. With a bike you have the option cruising past the duller bits. There are two basic styles for this fine sport: the random tour and the semi-controlled tour. The random tour consists of ceremonially ripping up your bus map and, letting loose a loud roar, flinging yourself and bicycle down the nearest hutong (preferably together). An hour before sundown you start asking around for a BIG street, if you haven't stumbled across one lately, in order to find the bigger streets that might lead back to your hotel. The semi-controlled method is

to pick larger hutongs running east-west between major streets (a lot of them do), so you know where you are at any given point, provided you have a magnifying glass for the bus map and a bit of luck navigating by a jumble of bus numbers.

## Beijing Buster Bicycle Tour

Lama Temple – Confucian Temple – Bamboo Garden Hotel – Drum Tower – Northern Lakes – Jingshan Park – Forbidden City – Beihai Park – Zhongnanhai – Tiananmen – Qianmen – Dazhalan.

Obviously this is far too much to attempt in one day, and it's not recommended that you *see* everything unless you have only one whirlwind day to dive-bomb the capital. The Forbidden City alone is worth a full day's exploration. Attractions like this, however, can be visited several times rather than cased in one fell swoop. This bike tour takes in some of the many moods of Beijing – not, one hopes, just the temples. Mainly, however, there is little chance of getting lost on the route described! Note that the Lama Temple is closed Tuesdays and Thursdays: in this case the Temple of Heaven would make a good substitute at the end of the tour.

Non-stop cycling time is about 80 minutes, Chinese bike, western legs, average pace – add half an hour if you rented from opposite the Friendship Store. Bike repair shops: if you have trouble, there are two on Dongdan (112 Dongdan Beidajie and 247b Dongsi Nandajie); another just west of Jingshan Park near intersection, and one at 107 Qianmen Jie.

Starting point is outside the CITS office at the Chongwenmen Hotel – what better place to start a self-guided tour that will cost you all of two yuan? Launch yourself into the sea of cyclists, throw your legs into cruising speed, and cycle the length of Dongdan north to the Lama Temple – about a 20-minute haul. Dongdan is a mildly busy shopping area, and this

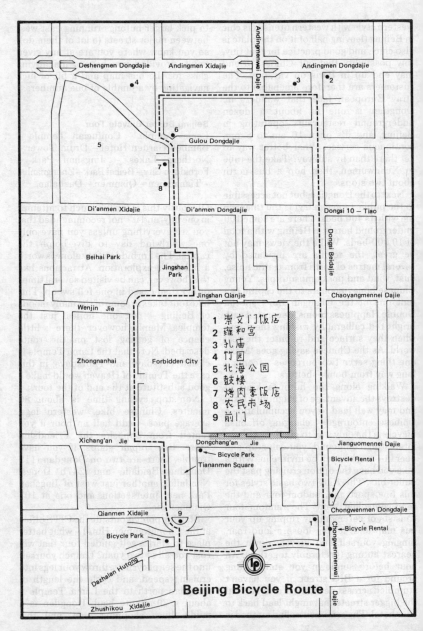

Deshengmen Dongdajie
Andingmen Xidajie
Andingmen Dongdajie
Andingmenwai Dajie

4
3
2

6

Gulou Dongdajie

5

7

8

Di'anmen Xidajie
Di'anmen Dongdajie
Dongsi 10 – Tiao

Beihai Park

Jingshan Park

Dongsi Beidajie

Jingshan Qianjie
Chaoyangmennei Dajie

Wenjin Jie

Zhongnanhai

Forbidden City

| 1 | 崇文门饭店 |
| 2 | 雍和宫 |
| 3 | 孔庙 |
| 4 | 竹园 |
| 5 | 北海公园 |
| 6 | 鼓楼 |
| 7 | 烤肉季饭店 |
| 8 | 农民市场 |
| 9 | 前门 |

Xichang'an Jie
Dongchang'an Jie
Jianguomennei Dajie

Bicycle Park
Tiananmen Square
Bicycle Rental

Qianmen Xidajie
Chongwenmen Dongdajie

9
Bicycle Rental

1

Bicycle Park
Chongwenmenwai Dajie

Dazhalan Hutong

Dajie

**Beijing Bicycle Route**

Zhushikou Xidajie

straight stretch is a good way to find your Beijing bicycle-legs – watch for Chinese cyclists and buses cutting you off. The Lama Temple is the most refreshing temple you'll see in Beijing – extremely well-groomed.

Take the hutong running west opposite the gates of the Lama Temple – there are several decorated lintels that you pass through. These graceful pailous (triumphal archways), which commemorate mandarin officials or chaste widows, were ripped out of the thoroughfares of Beijing in the 1950s – the reason given was the facilitation of traffic movement. Some have been relocated in parks. The ones you see in this hutong are rarities. On your right, a short way down the hutong are the former **Confucian Temple** and **Imperial College**, now a museum/library complex. Unless you can read stele-calligraphy, not of great interest (one of the steles, standing in the hutong, ordered officials to dismount at this point).

Continue direct west on this hutong – on your right, further down, you will spot a charcoal briquette factory – if you peer in, you will see, and hear, the grimy production of these noxious bricks, which are the major heating and cooking source for Beijing residents, and the cause of incredible pollution in winter. In imperial days, 'Fuel-Saving Lane', down by the Palace, supplied the court with charcoal and firewood – 400 years later, it seems this factory is performing a similar task. Marco Polo marvelled at the black lumps that produced heat; you may feel otherwise.

The hutong eventually runs into a smaller one – continue straight on until it ends at Jiugulou Dajie. A small detour here – if you go north on Jiugulou and take the first hutong to the left, you will arrive at the **Zhuyuan (Bamboo Garden Hotel)**, which is a wonderful illustration of the surprises that hutongs hold. It was originally the personal garden of Sheng Xuanhuai, an important Qing official. Exquisite gardens, beautiful courtyards and compound architecture (renovated), and expensive restaurant (English menu, al fresco in summer). A quiet place to sip a drink.

Go back to Jiugulou Dajie, head south following the bus No 8 route; follow Jiugulou to a dead end, turn left and you will come to the **Gulou (Drum Tower)**. It was built in 1420 and has several drums which were beaten to mark the hours of the day – in effect the Big Ben of Beijing (time was kept with a water clock). It's in pretty sad shape, but an impressive structure nonetheless (solid brick base). Occasional exhibitions take place here – the Tower is connected with local artisans. Behind the Drum Tower, down an alley directly north, is the Bell Tower (Zhong Lou) – originally built at the same time as the Drum Tower, but it burnt down. The present structure is 18th century; the gigantic bell which used to hang there has been removed to the Drum Tower. Legend has it that the bellmaker's daughter plunged into the molten iron before the bell was cast – her father only managed to grab her shoe as she did so, and the bell's soft sound resembled that of the Chinese for 'shoe' (*xie*). *Xiuxi*, dingdong, time for lunch. The same story is told about a couple of other bells in China.

---

1 Chongwenan Hotel / CITS
2 Yonghe Lama Temple
3 Confucious Complex
4 Bamboo Garden Hotel
5 Northern Lakes

6 Drum Tower (Gulou)
7 Kaorouji Restaurant
8 Farmer's Market
9 Qianmen

Heading due south of the Drum Tower, the first hutong to the right provides a very interesting excursion into the **Northern Lakes** area. This district is steeped in history: if you consult a Beijing map you will see that the set of lakes connects from north to south. In the Yuan Dynasty, barges would come through various canals to the top lake (Jishuitan), a sort of harbour for Beijing. Later the lakes were used for pleasure-boating; at the lakeside were the residences of high officials.

The larger lake to the north-west is the **Shisha Houhai (Lake of the Ten Back Monasteries)**; below that is the **Shisha Qianhai (Lake of the Ten Front Monasteries)**. Little evidence of the splendour left, but check out the **Shoudu Karouji Restaurant** which has balcony dining in summer – buried down a hutong. For those with some more time, it's possible to circumnavigate the lakes – a peaceful area – good to see what the locals are up to, and you can't really get lost – just keep the lakes in sight. **Gongwangfu** is a huge compound with traditional housing behind high walls, lying more or less at the centre of the arc created by the lakes running from north to south. It's reputed to be the model mansion for Cao Xueqin's 18th century classic, *A Dream of Red Mansions* (translated as the *The Story of the Stone* by David Hawkes, Penguin ,1980).

Back on track – back to the Drum Tower. Looking south from the Drum Tower you can see the outlines of pavilions on **Jing Shan (Jing Hill)** which is where you're heading. From this point, you are tracing the historic north-south axis, travelling the ancient hour-glass that filters into Qianmen Jie (too bad they won't let you ride through the centre of the Forbidden City!). Continuing south of the Drum Tower, you come into a fairly busy shopping street – about halfway down you cross a small stone bridge (now with buildings around it). If you turn right immediately after the bridge you'll arrive at a farmer's market on the shores of **Shisha Front Lake** – explore!

Continuing down Dianmen Dajie, you'll bump into the backside of Jing Shan Park – proceed to the front, where there is bicycle parking. Jing Shan Park is a splendid place to survey the smog of Beijing and get your bearings – 360° views, and a good overview of the russet roofing of the Forbidden City, directly opposite. Snack bars in both the park and the north end of the Forbidden City.

Hop back on your trusty hulk – follow the moat west. Just beyond the traffic lights is the entrance to **Beihai Park**, where you can exercise your arms as well as your legs – rent a rowboat. There's a cafe near the south gate overlooking Beihai Lake, where you can get beer, coffee, tea or cold drinks.

Back-pedal a bit to the traffic lights, hang a right, you're heading into the most sensitive part of the capital – the **Zhongnanhai Compound**. On the left, going down Beichang Jie you pass some older housing that lines the moat and on the right is a high wall that shields from view the area where top Party members live and work (it was decided not to rip down this section of the old walls). Mao and other members of the Communist hierarchy lived here in this huge compound. In 1973 when the new wing of the Peking Hotel shot up, the Public Security Bureau suddenly realised that guests with binoculars could observe activity in Zhongnanhai, so a fake building was erected along the western wall of the Forbidden City to short-circuit that possibility. Mysterious buildings, indeed, abound in this locale (also the strip back at the traffic lights along to Jingshan Park) – private theatres for viewing foreign films and so on. On the flank of **Zhongshan Park** (ie on your left), there's a rounded hole-in-the-wall entrance that leads to the **Tai Sam Yuen Restaurant** serving jet-set food, incredible range of liquors – for cadre clientele.

At the end of the street is an archway that brings you into Changan Boulevard and **Tiananmen Square**; traffic is one way for north/south avenues lining the square. If you want to go to Tiananmen Gate, dismount after the archway and wheel the bike to the parking areas (along the sidewalk). Cycling across Tiananmen Square is a no-no, but you can walk the bike.

From Tiananmen it's a short ride to **Qianmen Gate**, and if you continue down Qianmen St, you'll see a large bike-parking lot on your right, open to 9 pm. It's right at the entrance to Beijing's most fascinating hutong **Dazhalan**. Here your bicycle is absolutely useless – park it. From Dazhalan, you're within reach of good restaurants, and there's an acrobat theatre on Dazhalan itself.

The fast route back to the Chongwenmen Hotel is to go back to Qianmen Gate and take the wide avenue to the right; more interesting, but slower, is to take the eastern extension of Dazhalan – this hutong will run you right back to your starting point. You have to wheel your bike for the first 50 metres or so, then the crowds thin out. Ride slowly – this is a market-type hutong and a shopping area (it's called Fishmouth Lane) – things can jump out at you.

Weary legs? Why not try the public baths – there's one located at the Qianmen entrance side of the hutong. The baths are a bit like the Japanese communal tubs in concept, but split into men's and women's sections, with a variety of services (massage, foot-treatment, hair cut) and different temperature tubs – lukewarm, hot, and searing. The locals are unabashed – and a hairy, sweaty cyclist is bound to attract attention. The baths are nowhere near Japanese hygiene standards – try and get there early in the day before the water thickens. Private rooms may be possible and prices are low. There are different temperature tubs – the public sections are hot and searing.

## OTHER SIGHTS IN BEIJING
### Jesuit Observatory
One of the newer perspectives on Beijing is the Observatory mounted on the battlements of a watchtower, once part of the city walls. The observatory was recently reopened after 25 years, presumably for safety reasons (it stands right above the subway). Dwarfed by embassy housing blocks, it lies in a no-man's land of traffic loops and highways just west of the Friendship Store – the views themselves are worth the visit. This is one of the sights that you can safely say you've seen – small in scope, interesting, some English explanation. The observatory dates back to Kublai Khan's days when it was north of the present site, and Marco Polo writes:

There are in the city of Khanbalu ... about five thousand astrologers and soothsayers ... They have their astrolabes, upon which are described the planetary signs, the hours and their several aspects for the whole year ... They write their predictions for the year upon for the year upon certain small squares ... and these they sell, for a groat apiece, to all persons who are desirous of peeping into the future ...

Likewise, the Ming and Qing Emperors relied heavily on astrologers before making a move. The present Beijing Observatory was built in 1437 to 1446, not only to facilitate astrological predictions but to aid seafaring navigators.

Downstairs are displays of navigational equipment used by Chinese shipping (the explanations are only in Chinese). On the first floor are replicas of five 5000-year-old pottery jars, unearthed from Henan province in 1972 and showing painted patterns of the sun. There are also four replicas from the Han Dynasty – eave tiles representing east, west, north and south. There is a map drawn on a wooden octagonal board with 1420 stars marked in gold foil or powder – it's a reproduction of the original, which is said to be Ming Dynasty but is based on an older Tang map. Busts of six prominent astronomers are also displayed.

On the 'roof' are a variety of astronomical instruments designed by the Jesuits. The Jesuits, scholars as well as proselytisers, found their way into the capital in 1601 when Matteo Ricci and company were permitted to work with Chinese scientists (the Jesuits were eventually suppressed in 1773). The Emperor was keen to find out about European firearms and cannons from them.

The Jesuits outdid the resident Moslem calendar-setters and were given control of the observatory, becoming the Chinese court's advisors. Of the eight bronze instruments on display (including an equatorial armilla, celestial globe and altazimuth) six were designed and constructed under the supervision of the Belgian priest Ferdinand Verbiest, who came to China in 1659 to work at the Qing court. The instruments were built between 1669 and 1673, and are embellished with sculpted bronze dragons and other Chinese craftwork, a unique mix of east and west. The azimuth theodolite was supervised by Bernard Stumpf, also a missionary; the eighth instrument, the new armilla, was completed in 1754. It's not known which of the instruments on display are the originals.

During the Boxer Rebellion, the instruments disappeared into the hands of the French and the Germans – some were returned in 1902, others came back under the provisions of the Treaty of Versailles (1919). Bertrand Russell's comment: 'This was probably the most important benefit which the treaty secured to the world.' The observatory the Jesuits set up in Shanghai was used for meteorological predictions – and still used for that purpose. They even had some influence over architecture in Beijing, and designed the Italian rococo palaces at Yuanmingyuan (the Old Summer Palace, destroyed in 1860) using Versailles as a blueprint.

The Jesuit Observatory is open 9 am to 5 pm, closed Friday mornings. The only thing that isn't astronomical is the entry fee; Y0.10.

**Gong Wang Fu (Prince Gong's Residence)**
This is one of the largest private residence compounds in Beijing, with a nine-courtyard layout, high walls and elaborate gardens. Prince Gong was the son of a Qing Emperor. The residence has been selected or identified, as the locale for the classic Ming novel *A Dream of Red Mansions*, written by Cao Xueqin in the 18th century. The temple is on Qianhai Xilu, in the vicinity of the north end of Beihai Park at the west end of Shishahai Lake. It's currently being renovated and is now used by government departments. If it is opened to tourists it will probably be tacked onto tours of the Forbidden City (complete with souvenir-shops, no doubt flogging English copies of the novel).

**The Zoo**
The zoo is the pits – after you've been there you'll probably look as pissed off as the animals do. No attempt has been made to recreate their natural environments – all concrete and cages, little shade or water. The Panda House, right by the gates, has four dirty specimens with very little drive left. The site of a former Ming Dynasty garden, this place was converted to a zoo in 1908. It now contains 400 species – the largest zoo in China. Some rare species reside here; golden monkeys from Sichuan, Yangzi alligators, wild Tibetan donkeys, snow-leopard, black-necked crane. The zoo lies in the north-west corner of the city. Open 7.30 am to 6 pm (5 pm winter) daily, admission Y0.10, free on public holidays. Feeding times: summer 9.30 am to 10 am and 4.30 to 5 pm; winter 9 to 10 am and 4 to 4.30 pm.

Nearby are the **Beijing Planetarium** and the **Exhibition Hall** (irregular industrial displays, theatre, Russian restaurant).

**PLACES TO STAY**
Beijing has chronic overbooked hotel space, aggravated in peak seasons. New hotels *are* going up to alleviate the problem, but if you want a bed for the night there are going to be problems for

some time. Hotels in Beijing fall into different categories; those permanently occupied by foreign businessmen, diplomats and visiting dignitaries; those used by foreign experts; the group tour hotels; the Overseas Chinese Hotels; the 'cadre' hotels; and the scarcer budget-hotels. Theoretically CITS controls all the strings,but since they're not computerised there is general chaos of who to put where and how and when. Last-minute changes by CITS are legendary and even group-tours don't know where they're going to be lodged even if they're booked well ahead – some have been known to land up in Tianjin!

At present, CITS is responsible for finding hotel rooms for stray travellers. You can't just front up at a hotel and expect to be given a room, so when you get into Beijing, go straight to the CITS office – it's within walking distance of the railway station. The system may not apply in the off-season during winter when there's more accommodation available, but certainly in the spring and summer seasons the system makes sense and will at least save you tramping from hotel to hotel in search of elusive accommodation.

Unfortunately, since CITS is set up for group tours their solution to the refugee problem is to evacuate you to the countryside (e.g. the Sports College). If you approach a hotel downtown the manager will send you back to CITS for a referral (Yl charge). Try CITS first, but if you don't get what you want, try the hotels anyway – you can get round managers by arriving late at night when CITS is closed, or by saying that you're only staying one night (next day you try and find out which rooms are empty). The manager will ask you how long you intend to stay – the best response to this is to pocket the key, head off early in the morning and forget the whole shemozzle!

Hotels perform a number of functions other than lodging, so this listing provides a sampling of what those functions might be. The listing is by no means complete,

nor are your chances of getting into these hotels. Even if you have the money and you look like the kind of person the hotel deems acceptable you could be turned away for any number of reasons or whims. Those who have the correct ID (like foreign experts) can usually get much cheaper prices; the *Xinqiao Hotel* for example, which usually charges Y50 a double minimum, will give the same room to a foreign expert couple for only Y28.

## Top End Accommodation

The *Xiangshan (Fragrant Hills Hotel)* (tel 819242 – switchboard) is in the north-west of Beijing in the forested grounds where Emperor Kangxi had his summer villas. It's a joint-investment project financed with US loans and designed by Guangdong-born American architect I.M. Pei – world famous for his creations. Pei travelled the length and breadth of China in his search for architectual forms and this 'palace' has its fair share of them; northern-style courtyards, Suzhou-style gardens and landscapes (including a mini stone-forest imported from Yunnan) and a layer of electronics and 'modernisation'. The western facilities include paging and security systems, gym, sauna, swimming-pool, restaurants and a main lobby-courtyard crowned with a glass roof. The hotel opened in 1983 and has 300 rooms – you can get one of them for a mere Y140-Y250 per night. If you want to see what a well-behaved, well-dressed Chinese hotel-staffer looks like, then go and visit this place. The locals stand at the gate and have their picture taken against this wonder of the western world.

The up-and-coming *Great Wall Hotel* is located near the Agricultural Exhibition Centre in embassy-land, north-east Beijing. When completed the hotel will have 22 floors, 1007 rooms, a staff of 1300, foreign management team of 14 and the cost will be US$87 million. Room rates vary from US$90 to US$800 per night . . .

The *Jianguo* (tel 595261) is just east of the Friendship Store. The hotel was opened in 1982 and has the distinction of being China's first joint-venture hotel. San Francisco architect Clement Chen, who fled Shanghai in 1949, came back for his magic 49% share of the Jianguo. The place is managed by the Hong Kong based Peninsula group which has a ten-year contract and is responsible for the spiffy-green uniforms that the Chinese maids wear. They must be doing something right; in the first ten months of operation the hotel turned over a profit of US$1 million with an occupancy rate of 98%. The Chinese staff of about 600 have no spittoons and are thoroughly trained not to bite the tourists – they're not allowed newspapers, cigarettes, naps or even chairs. As a compensation prize they rake in Y50 to Y150 per month, an astronomical wage for the Beijing hotel-worker or any worker for that matter. Facilities include three restaurants, swimming pool, disco, cocktail lounge and late-night coffee-bar and health club. The Jianguo is the height of bourgeois decadence, computerised cash registers, ultra-suede walls, muzak, hamburgers, the works. This place could be anywhere, which is part of the idea and it sets up a wall (airport-jianguo-friendship store-jianguo-airport) over which tourists see little of China. Meanwhile more than a few goggle-eyed Chinese cyclists have come crashing down along Jianguomenwai, engrossed in the 20th century opulence clearly visible through the plateglass windows. The toilets in this hotel are a *must* – scented and spotless. Major credit-cards are accepted and the price range is Y110-120 a single with bath, and Y120-140 a double with bath.

The *Beijing Hotel* (tel 552231 or 558331) on East Changan Avenue has the most central location of any hotel in the capital and is therefore prized by businessmen, embassy staff and dignitaries (prices range from Y60 single and Y140 double, to Y180 a suite in the new wing). The hotel is split into three wings; the middle and west wings, though cheaper, are more difficult to get into as Chinese officials and businessmen lodge there. The new 17-storey east wing is for foreigners with air-con, electronic hookups – rooms here are also used on long-term basis. There are lots of other reasons to visit this hotel; the roof of the west wing commands a great view of Tiananmen Square and the Forbidden City – take an elevator to the top floor. There's a selection of services and shops that makes the ground floor stretch between the wings something of a mini-Friendship Store. The whole hotel is riddled with restaurants and banquet rooms – different styles (Sichuan, Beijing Duck, Japanese . . . ) and some of the specials are worth chasing. The main attraction of the Beijing, however, is that it has great temperature-control (and it's a meeting place for a great cross-section of foreigners). In the lobbies of the middle and east wings are cafes – the one in the east wing is nicknamed 'The Zoo' (a reference to the selection of stuffed animals on a souvenir shop shelf surveying the exotic humans stuffed into easy-chairs opposite). All kinds of drinks, liquors, icecream sundaes, apple pie and it's open throughout the day to 11.30 pm. You can get yourself some excellent postcards (made in Japan), copies of *China Daily*, and forget you're in the capital for a while.

Two other top-range hotels worthy of your attention as sights are the *Bamboo Garden Hotel* and the *Diaoyutai State Guesthouse*. The latter, off Sanlihe Lu north of Muxudi, was formerly an exclusive cadre residence, now opened up for 'special' foreigners due to lack of hotel space. The site was linked with emperors and top officials and the gardens are immense (rockeries, pavilions, lake). Other exclusive hotels are tucked into places like the Summer Palace.

### Mid-range

The price of mid-range hotels varies from Y40 to Y100 a double, and Y120 and up for suites. The rooms are usually air-con with colour TV, phone, bath, desk.

The *Xinqiao* (tel 557731) at Chong-wenmen intersection, north-west side, was built in the 50s, Soviet-style, and used to be a favourite hangout for foreign journos and businessmen until the Beijing Hotel drew them away. The Xinqiao has some rarer rooms for Y30 double; foreign experts can wrangle cheaper rates. The main attraction of the Xinqiao is its western food. The top floor restaurant has the best chocolate sundae in China – icecream smothered in a rich chocolate sauce with shavings of chopped nuts and chocolate. This item goes for Y2.10, and icecream addicts visit only for that purpose. The top-floor restaurant has much more to offer; dishes with Russian, Italian, French and Pakistani influences, open 6 to 9 pm. Not all the items are listed on the English menu – two different ethnic dishes are produced as specials each day (Chicken Normandy or Jewish-style beef, for example). Meats are especially good – fillet mignon, lamb curry, shashlik, schnitzel: a popular off-the-menu dish is chapatis in butter. Strawberries available in season. You can get a reasonable meal for Y4, or splurge a bit and go for several courses – Y8 including wine. For that special romantic occasion this is the place to go – great views, candle-lit tables. The restaurant is actually open to midnight, but quality and variety of food is not guaranteeed after 8.30 pm. To one side of the restaurant is a bar where you can indulge in a game of billiards. Downstairs, ground floor, around the back of the staircase, is a Chinese restaurant, not of great interest. If you go out of the Xinqiao to the back of the building (ie facing the Chongwenmen Hotel), there is a western-style restaurant patronised entirely by Chinese; this is a very curious affair – nobody taught them any western table manners. You can see jam applied with a spoon to a piece of bread, butter on top of that, and the whole assembly speared with a fork! The restaurant serves cold cuts, breaded shrimps (Y3.20), chicken hotpot (Y2.40), icecreams, liqueurs, and other western trappings at prices much lower than you'll find in regular western-patronised places. It's heavy on the cheese sauces, not a chopstick in sight, gets crowded and there's no English menu.

The *Friendship Hotel* (tel 890621), was also built in the 50s to house Soviet experts, and is now primarily used by western experts and their families, though it does have some tourist accommodation. Decor and fittings are Sino-Russo, facilities are legendary, including full-size swimming pool, theatre, tennis courts and a foreign experts' club. It's a long way out – up past the zoo in the Haidian area, but runs its own bus service to the downtown area, which may be of use to those staying in locations outside Beijing. The nightlife here is worth checking out, with movies and dances. The hotel has the staggering number of 2,600 rooms – and prices are a touch lower than those of downtown hotels.

Other hotels in the mid-ranges are useful to navigate by as landmarks, – and difficult to get into since they're either reserved for group-tours or are permanently occupied by businessmen. These hotels include;

The *Minzu* (tel 668541) west of Xidan intersection on Fuxingmennei. It's a dark, sombre 11-storey Russian monolith and has a 200-room extension in progress. Double rooms start from around Y40.

The *Yanjing* (tel 868721) near Muxudi subway on Fuxingmenwai. The hotel was formerly called the 'Fuxing', which came across rather strongly when pronounced with a thick Scottish accent. It's a 20-storey hotel which was opened in 1981. Doubles start from around Y55 and Y60, suites are Y115. The hotel has some impressive modern murals within, and the one on the first floor is a glazed ceramic fresco with the theme of the Silk Road.

*Peace* (tel 551031) on Jinyu hutong, which is the eastern continuation of Donghuamen (perpendicular to Wangfujing). A modern group-tour hotel with 91 double rooms and 23 suites. Doubles range from Y55 to Y85, and suites are Y100.

*Qianmen* (tel 338731) at the corner of Yongan Lu and Hufang Lu, south-west of Qianmen Gate; an 8-storey mid-50s block. Doubles range from Y40 to Y70, suites are Y80, and four-bed rooms go from Y30 to Y60.

*Huadu* (tel 475431) at 8 Xinyuannan Lu, in eastern suburbs near Dongzhimen Gate. Six and five-storey blocks, managed by CITS and opened in 1982.

*Huaqiao Daxia (Overseas Chinese Building)* (tel 558851) at the corner of Wangfujing and Chaoyangmennei. Clientele as the name suggests housed in an 8-storey block. Doubles are Y24, suites are Y50, dormitory beds (for Overseas Chinese only) are Y6.5.

*Xiyuan* (tel 890721) in Erligou area near zoo. Slated for expansions with plans for revolving restaurant atop 26-storey block.

*Yanxiang* (tel 471131) en route to the airport. 144 single rooms.

## Bottom End

The bargaining position for travellers is weak. Basically, dorms are few – the *Guanghua* the travellers' cheapie, was put out of action for renovation and may not be cheap when reopened. There are a few routes to pursue – the most important is to ask every traveller you meet on the way to Beijing what the latest hangout is, and what steps 1,2,3 and 4 might be for getting in. At the time of writing travellers were getting 'reasonable' rates at the *Tiantan Sports Hotel*, the *Beiwei*, the *Lu Song Yuan* and some wormed their way into the *Qianmen* (previously listed), but this situation could change at any time.

Rockbottom in Beijing are the dorms of the *Xuanwumen* (alias Xiangyang No 2 on Xuanwumen Dongdajie) with a dorm for Y6 (double room for Y20, triple Y25, 4-bed Y36). The *Chongwenmen* (Xiangyang No 1), housing the CITS office, has a 12-bed dorm for Y6 per bed (regular rooms Y32 to Y63). Both of these are pretty

unassailable and for Overseas Chinese only.

*Tiantan Sports Hotel* (tel 752831), 10 Tiyuguan Rd. The hotel derives its name from its position between the Temple of Heaven and the Gymnasium. It hosts sports-minded group tours (offices of the Chinese Mountaineering Association and the Cycling Association are in the hotel). Dorms Y10/bed; doubles Y28 to Y36 depending on size, air-con, TV etc; triples to Y41; rare singles Y22. Some other deals: Y28 double and one person on the floor for Y5 extra; Y32 and two on the floor Y5 apiece. With its sporting links the hotel has a YMCA tinge to it: certain combinations (two guys, one girl) are considered kinky (two girls, one guy is not!) – also depending on whether they met in the lobby or not. To get there take the subway one stop from Main Station to Chongwenmen, then bus No 39, 41 or 43.

*Beiwei* (tel 338631) west side of the Temple of Heaven on 13 Xijing Rd. It caters to a similar clientele to the Sports Hotel but it's got a snottier reception. Y33 for three people; Y24 a double, and other doubles for Y27, Y45 and suites for Y55. Take the subway two stops from the Main Railway Station, then bus No 5 south. It's also approachable from Xinhuajie subway stop (then No 25 or 15 south) or you can take bus No 20 direct from the Main Station.

*Lu Song Yuan* (tel 442352), No 22 South Eight Lane, Jiao Dou Kou St – difficult to find – directly north of China Art Gallery, second hutong north of Dianmen, turn left. A very pleasant place with a laid – out courtyard style with compound architecture. There's no highrise and there's plenty of sunlight. Bar, dining hall (don't expect gourmet treats), has connections with China Youth Travel Service (CYTS). About three dozen rooms, Y25 single, Y30 double, Y35 triple, Y50 for a 4-bed. Accessible by bus No 104 from the railway station.

Try also the *Guanghua Hotel (Beijing hostel for Foreign Trainees* (tel 592931) 38

Donghuan Beilu. It's undergoing renovation at the time of writing, fate not known.

A recent addition to the beleagured budget ranks is the *Chaoyuhan Hotel* which has a dorm for Y6 – men only. It's in a quiet location by the canal near Yondingmen Railway Station (the hotel also serves reasonable vegetarian food). Take trolley bus No 106 to the intersection of the canal and a bridge; there is a sign in English here. Walk from there for about half a kilometre along the towpath – the hotel is on the left. CITS knows about the hotel ('Chaoyuhan' is most likely misspelt).

### In the Countryside

*Beida (Beijing University) Hostel* has some accommodation for short-term travellers. Theoretically you can only stay there for two nights but I stayed longer. Double rooms are Y20, though if you're on your own you may get it for Y10. There are communal showers (partitioned off) down the end of the hallways, the rooms are nice, the setting pleasant, and you can later mix with the foreign students. To get there take bus No 103 from the main railway station to the zoo, and then change to bus No 332 (the last of these runs at around 10.30pm) A taxi from the Beijing Hotel out to the university will cost you around Y14 – though there's often someone else hanging around outside the hotel also waiting for a taxi to Beida, so you can split the cost. A lot of students ride their bicycles into the city-centre and that takes about an hour.

The *Sports College* at the Beijing Institute of Physical Education, in the Tiyu Xueyuan area, past Beida. Pleasant rooms, quiet, garden, swimming pool, sauna – the Institute hosts foreign sportsmen studying taijiquan and other arts. Y12 for a room, Y6 for dorm bed. Take bus No 103 to the zoo, and then No 332 to Zhongguancun where you change to bus No 365 and take it to the terminus. An alternative route is to connect with bus No 302 running from Nongzhanguan (just south of the Agricultural Exhibition Centre) to Zhongguancun, then change to No 365. Those buses give you some idea of how far out the place is: connections take about two hours from Main Station to Sports College, and the last set of changes takes place around 8.30 pm. Otherwise a taxi costs Y16 – split between four people it's not too painful. If you're staying at either Beida or the Sports College, take advantage of the situation by covering the sights up that end like the Summer Palace and the Western Hills, which are within biking range and served by local buses; there are some decent restaurants in the Haidian and zoo areas.

### The Temple of Heaven Crashpad

A short aside on the creation of dormitories, since I happened to witness such a transition.

Scene 1: the meeting room ground floor Tiantan Sports Hotel. I roll in at 11 pm – good timing – the next hotel is miles off, and the manager knows even before he picks up the phone that everything else in town is chockablock. After a laborious wait, he allows me a couch in the meeting room. Two more travellers, I discover, are already snoozing on the couches within. Cost is Y3 per night per couchette. Three days later, travellers discover another meeting room on the fourth floor.

Scene 2: a traveller strides straight past the manager, backpack on. 'Where are you going?' he demands. 'To the meeting room', she answers, taking the stairs three at a time, not looking back, unrolls sleeping bag on arrival. Manager scratches head – she didn't even bother to ask if there were any rooms free. Manager, driven crazy by travellers' preference for the low-priced meeting rooms, transforms the one on the fourth floor into a dorm with camp beds, Y8, men only. Female travellers quickly point out injustice – a conference is held, where else, in the ground floor meeting room, and, amazingly enough, a third meeting room is found (second floor) and designated a women's dorm. These former meeting rooms, now established dorms, are large and filled with camp beds surrounded by armchairs, a somewhat surreal decor.

Scene 3: word has spread along the travellers' grapevine as far as Hong Kong, but CITS has received neither news nor reservations. A fresh group of travellers steps into the Tiantan off the Trans-Siberian and head straight for the dorms – later they set up a disco. The manager has given up denying that the dorms exist: the campbeds are given a shakedown, spruced up, and the price jumps to Y10.

Scene 4: much later. The dorms are full, *really* full. I am sharing a room with two people, one sleeping on the floor. I pass the desk as two travellers argue with the manager, refusing to believe the dorms are really really full, otherwise known as 'aw-full'. The room I'm in is large – space for two more on the floor, so I offer the travellers the option if they get stuck and tell them the room number. When I return in the evening, there are about seven travellers in the room arguing with the manager about floor space, and I quietly slip back out again. Ah yes, time to leave Beijing before another crashpad is created . . .

## PLACES TO EAT – PIGGING IT OUT IN BEIJING

In 1949, Beijing had the incredible number of 10,000 snack bars and restaurants; by 1976 that number had dwindled to less than 700. Restaurants, a nasty bourgeois habit, were at one time planned to be replaced by revolutionary dispensaries dishing out rice. We could hazard some wild guesses about what happened to all the restaurants – the chefs were allocated jobs as bus drivers, the bus drivers were given jobs as chefs. Anyhow the number of eateries is well on the rise again. While they're not enough to cater to the million-odd Chinese customers, they certainly present ample choice for the average gastronome (there's no way you'll get through them all). Most of the regional styles are represented in the capital.

Northern cuisine specialities are Beijing Duck, Mongolian Hot Pot, Moslem Barbecue, and Imperial Food. Imperial cuisine is served up in the restaurants of Beihai Park, the Summer Palace and the Western Hills – very expensive, but attempt the cheaper snacks. Mongolian Hot Pot is a winter dish – a brass pot with charcoal inside it is placed at the centre of the table and you cook thick strips of mutton and vegetables yourself, fondue fashion, spicing as you like. Moslem Barbecue uses lamb, a Chinese Moslem influence – and you can sometimes grill your own shish kebabs (called shashlik) at the Kaorouwan Restaurant south of Xidan intersection. Beijing Duck is the capital's famous invention, now a production-line of sorts. Your meal starts at one of the agricultural communes around Beijing where the duck is pumped full of grain and soya bean paste to fatten it up. The ripe duck is lacquered with molasses, pumped with air, filled with boiling water, dried, and then roasted over a fruitwood fire. The result, force-fed or not, is delicious. (I forgot to mention that the poor duck is killed somewhere along the line – the story goes that the original Roast Duck was not killed. In Changan, where the dish is said to have been devised 1200 years ago, two nobles placed live geese and ducks in an iron cage over a charcoal fire, and as the heat increased the thirsty birds would drink from a bowl filled with vinegar, honey, malt, ginger and salt until they expired).

**Table manners** Forget those! We speak here of the popular prole section of a restaurant – waiters have a nasty habit of intercepting foreigners and detouring them to private cubicles where the furniture is plusher, crowds non-existent, the prices sky-rocket and the kitchen is exactly the same. Any number of tactics will be employed to steer you away. Never mind – throw yourself in there anyway – there's a lot to be said for fighting for your supper (increases the appetite!), and your table company will be congenial enough once you manage to land a seat.

Order by pointing to your neighbour's dishes – make sure your finger gets within an inch of the food and make sure you didn't order three of that dish. Beer is usually obtained with tickets at a separate counter but you can solve that one by arriving with your own beer from a nearby store. At the established places you can reserve tables by phoning ahead – this will mean cubicles, banquet-style and more expensive (it should be noted that some dishes can only be obtained by phoning ahead with a group order). Food, like the trains, comes in different classes: if you want to get more out of a restaurant, you'll have to pay more.

**When & Where** Location and timing have a lot to do with whether you get your meal. At around 5 pm, a strange eating hour for westerners, the internal alarm clock hasn't got the message yet – dinner is under way, and the panic is on. Where's the nearest hotpot? Which bus? Listed below are seven favoured restaurants and attached to each is a brief rundown of others in the same area. It's an indication of what's out there – the tip of the epicurean iceberg – go and hunt for more. Eating out in the capital is a true adventure, one that should be seized with both chopsticks. Dining hours are 5 to 7 pm sharp – try and get there by 6 pm. Lunch is 11 am to 1 pm and is less crowded. If you miss out, there's always, of course, predictable hotel food.

*Qianmen Roast Duck* (tel 751379) at 32 Qianmen, east side, near Qianmen subway – one of the oldest in the capital, goes back to 1864. Also known as 'Big Duck' to distinguish it from other restaurants in the Quanjude state-owned duck chain. Split into several sections: prices for foreigners range Y20 and up per head, but the cheap section, through the right-hand doorway, is Y5 to Y8 per head (Y12 will get a whole duck, enough for two

very greedy souls). Same duck, same kitchen. Cheap section is very crowded – if you don't get there by 6 pm, forget it. Beer brewed on premises Y1.35 a jug (deposit on jug). The duck is served in stages – boneless meat and crispy skin with a side dish of shallots, plum sauce and crepes, followed by duck soup made of bones and all the other parts except the quack. Language is not really a problem as one basic dish is served – what you have to do is negotiate half or whole ducks, and the locals will show you the correct etiquette – like when it's the right time to spit on the floor. Open 4 to 6.30 pm (lunch possible). Transport: buses 2, 5 and 20; trolleys 110, 116; or subway.

In the same area you'll find the *Lili* at 30 Qianmen – Sichuan style, spicy chicken, hot noodles, peanuts and chilis – very good. The *Duyichu* is at 36 Qianmen and is good for shaomai (Cantonese-style dumplings). The *Laozhengxing* at 46 Qianmen is Shanghai-style with a range of seafood, fish, eel, and hairy crabs when in season. The *Jianchun* at 6 Liangshidian is in an alley off the beginning of Dazhalan – it's a very small place and serves Mongolian hot-pot, but in winter only. One subway stop west of Qianmen is *Super-Duck* or *McDonald's Duck*, a 6-storey version of the one at Qianmen – a rather impersonal duck factory with modern gas ovens and seating for 2000. It's open 10.30 am to 1.30 pm and 2.30 to 7.30 pm and has skyscraper prices.

*Fengzeyuan* (tel 332828) at 83 Zhushikou Xidajie serves Shandong-style cuisine – highly rated by gourmets – famous for seafood and soups. This 'cornucopia' is famous for another reason – in 1980 a young cook, Chen Aiwu, announced that the Minister of Commerce, Wang Lei, had often dined here on the best food at low prices. The minister wrote a self-criticism. Then in 1983 a muncipal delegation inspected the restaurant and later dined there at much reduced prices. Up shot Chen, dashed a letter off to the *China*

*Youth* newspaper, and the delegation had to pay up and make a personal critique. Well, if you can't have a sex scandal you may as well have a food scandal. There doesn't seem to be a way round the high prices, unless you're a minister – or if you stay away from the seafood. Specialities include sea-cucumber braised with scallion, snowflake prawns, chicken puffs with sharkskin. Duck and crisp chicken, duckmarrow soup, turtle soup with egg. For dessert there's 'silver-thread rolls', toffee apples, and almond beancurd with pineapple. It's open 4 to 7 pm and is accessible by bus Nos 2, 5, 6, 20, 23.

In the same area is the *Jinyang* at 241 Zhushikou, a red-fronted building west of the Fengzeyuan. Shanxi-style – salty duck, squirrel fish, noodles, onion cakes and a pleasant atmostphere.

*Sichuan* (tel 336356) – to get here go south from Xidan intersection (where Xidan meets Changan), turn left into a hutong marked by traffic lights and a police-box, continue along the hutong till you find a grey wall entrance, number 51 Rongxian hutong. In contrast to the bland interiors and peeling paint of most of the capital's restaurants, this one is housed in a sumptuous old mansion, in fact the residence of Yuan Shikai (the general who tried to set himself up as an emperor in 1914).

Spectacular compound decor – and several dining rooms which will clean out your wallet very fast. For cheaper food continue to the back of the courtyard, veer right, and there's a dining room where you can get a good meal for Y6 per head if you're sharing dishes. You'll need some drinks for this one! It's a good idea to bring your own in case they've run out (or better still a flask of yoghurt to cool the flames). The food is out of this world – highly recommended. Side dishes (cucumber, bakchoi) run to about Y0.60 each; fiery pork Y1.50, explosive prawns Y6 and worth it. Also bamboo shoots, beancurd, beef dishes, some seafood. In the more expensive bits of the restaurant (Y20 to Y50 per head), variety is greater, but the back dining room will sate the appetite. Overcrowding is not a problem. Lunch 10.30 am to 1.30 pm; dinner 4.30 to 7.30 pm. Transport: trolley-bus Nos 102, 105, 109; you can also get there via the Xuanwumen subway and bus north.

In the same area is the *Vegetarian* (tel 334296) at 74 Xuanwumennai, just around the corner from the Sichuan (north of Xuanwumen intersection). Downstairs for cold dishes and beer, jiaozi and baozi. Upstairs for a wider selection; fungus, beancurd, nuts, fresh vegetables, cauliflower soup – Y4 per person for a bloated serving. Things come shaped like fish, chicken (vegetarian duck!), except that they're made of soya meat or dofu. Get there early for fresh stuff – they turn out better fare for pre-ordered banquets.

The *Kaorouwan* at 102 Xuanwumennai, south of Xidan intersection, east side of street, serves Moslem Barbeque and you can do your own skewers if the wind is blowing the right direction. The *Hongbinlou* at 82 Xi Changan, just east of Xidan intersection serves shashlik, Beijing Duck and Mongolian Hot Pot. It has a cheap section downstairs but the waiters are difficult to get round. Upstairs you can get a Bejing Duck for Y20. They also serve *guotie* (dumplings) and toffee apples too. On special order, a lamb banquet can be had – three days advance notice needed – and you get every part of the lamb including the eyes.

*Quyuan* (tel 592648) at 133 Xidan Lu north of Changan, west side, in a red fronted building by an overhead bridge. If the French can do it with frogs, how often do you get a chance to digest dog? Hunan food is one of the major tasty styles in China, largely unknown in the west – hot and spicy like Sichuan. Anyone for hot-dog? On the menu is Onion Dog, Dog Soup (reputed to be an aphrodisiac) and Dog Stew. For those with canine sensibilities, perhaps a switch to Hunan-style duck, spiced with hot pepper, some seafood, and several styles of noodles. Good desserts with lychee nuts – can be varied or custom-made if you phone in advance. Management is nice, food is cheap. Take bus Nos 22, 102, 105, 109.

In the same area is the *Dongtian Underground Restaurant*(for details see the section on touring Bejing by bicycle). The *Huaiyang Fanzhuang* at 217 Xidan Beidajie has a Jiangsu cuisine section serving hairy crab when in season. The *Shagouju* at 60 Xisi Nandajie is further north toward the Xisi intersection. Pork in many forms, some served in earthenware pots, tacky building but cheap. The *Tongheju* near the Xisi intersection at No 3 Xisi Nandajie, serves Shandong-style crispy spiced duck, seafood and a renowned pudding *san bu zhan* (made of eggs, lard and flour).

*Shoudu Karouji* (tel 445921) at 37 Shichahai is difficult to find but worth it in summer; go to the Drum Tower (Gulou) area, take a hutong to the left immediately before the Drum Tower as you go north, and follow it down to the lakeside. The dowdy interiors of most Chinese restaurants make you feel boxed in – no windows – but here you've got a view of the lake, the alleys and activity in the area. In summer tables are moved onto the balcony. This is a place for potless hotpot and Moslem Barbecue. Open 10.30 am to 2 pm and 4.30 to 8pm. Take buses 5, 8 and 107.

In the same area but further north of the Drum Tower, down a hutong (follow the signs on the bus No 8 route) is another al fresco dining experience (summer only) in the *Bamboo Garden Hotel*. Extra-expensive Cantonese (for example shark fin with chicken sauce is Y200) but you can get a pork dish for Y2.40, and the garden is very pleasant. The *Kangle* at 259 Andingmenwai is further east of Drum Tower near the Jiaodaokou intersection. This place serves up Fujian and Yunnan styles. 'Across-the-bridge-noodles' must be ordered in advance, minimum four people, and

expensive. Also try Yunnan-style steamed chicken, seafood and *san bu zhan* (sweet sticky pudding).

*Donglaishun* (tel 551098) at 16 Donghuamen, north entrance to Dongfeng Market. This is actually a minorities restaurant with a variety of Xinjiang Moslem and other foods. On the ground floor is the masses section (dumplings); second floor is either Mongolian Hotpot (only from October to April – group tours, however, get it year-round in special closeted sections) or it's greasy and gluey fare for around Y3 per head; top floor is duck and pancake, shashlik with sesame bread (try and order one day ahead). Open 10 am to 2 pm, 4 to 7 pm. Take buses Nos 2, 21, 37, 103, 104.

The *Xiangshu Canting* is on the Wangfujing side of Dongfeng Market – Sichuan and Hunan mixture – highly recommended. You may find the Donglaishun a disappointment in summer – try the Xiangshu which has 'silver-thread rolls' (Beijing's best pastry). The *Cuihailou* at 60 Wangfujing (north of Dongfeng Market) – Shandong-style – seafood, velvet chicken, toffee apples and crowded. The *Sick Duck Restaurant* – nickname conjured up by its location close to the Capitol Hospital – is on the Shuaifuyuan hutong – and as the name implies it's a Beijing duck venue.

The *Beijing Hotel* has a number of top-class restaurants. Of interest is the one on the seventh floor west wing dining room where you can get painless Peking Duck for Y10 a head including beer (and other gourmet novelties like bear's paw if you have the bucks). The Beijing Hotel also has the best buffet lunch you could hope to get – stuff your face for around Y6!

The *Shuxiang Canguan* at 40 Chongwenmennei is near the Xinquiao Hotel and dishes up Sichuan-style food. The *Xinqiao Hotel*, sixth floor, has good western food (see the Places to Stay section). The *Bianyifang (Small Duck)* at 2 Chongwenmenwai Dajie is just east of CITS and has been in business for donkey's years. It uses a slightly different method of preparation (closed oven).

*Russian Restaurant* (tel 893713) is nicknamed 'The Moscow' and is on the west side of the Exhibition Centre in the zoo district. A vast interior in the Russian-designed Exhibition Centre – chanderliers, high ceiling, fluted columns. Foreigners are shuffled to a side room overlooking the zoo (there is, by the way, no connection with the menu). What you could do is grab the English menu from the side room and run back to the central section which has the cavernous decor. Borscht for Y2 to Y4, cream prawns au gratin Y6.10, pork a la Kiev Y2.80, beef stroganoff Y3.40, roast duck and apple Y4.40, black bread Y0.06, soups Y1.30 to Y2.40, black caviar Y10.80. Also has good vegetable dishes and coffee with icecream. Y10 a head should get an excellent meal, wine included. Open 11 am to 1.30 pm lunch, 4.30 to 7.30 pm dinner. Bus Nos 7, 15, 16, 19, 22, 102, 103, 111.

In the same area is the *Xijiao Huimin Canting* in the Xijiao market area opposite the zoo, south side. Beijing duck, shashlik, and in winter they have hotpot. The *Guandong Canting* in the Xijiao market serves up Beijing Duck and Cantonese-style cuisine (turtle, snake). The *Xinjiang Fandian* at 42 Erligou is opposite the zoo – shashlik, Beijing duck, good desserts.

**Haidian Area** The *Zhenxing Fanguan* near Beida gates for cheap Mongolian hotpot. The *Youyi Canting* next to the Friendship Hotel for low-priced hotpot, apple pie and other Chinese and western meals. The *Zhenjing Mianguan* on Haidian south of Zhongguancun intersection for Sichuan and Korean-style noodles.

**Western Breakfast** So much for the X, Y and Z of restaurants – what about petit dejeuner? Travellers pining for a croissant or a strong coffee will be pleased to know that Beijing is the best place in China to find such delicacies.

*Friendship Store* – best place to assemble breakfast, a mite on the expensive side. The deli next to the supermarket has sliced ham, bread rolls, scotch eggs and sausages. It also has a range of pastries and croissants that can be heated up in a microwave. The cakes are supplied by BACL (CAAC catering) which has connections with the International Club across the way. You can get yoghurt in ceramic flasks (works of art) for 20 fen plus deposit – both the yoghurt and the pastries can be found in other locations around Beijing. Fresh milk, fruit juice and other delectables in the supermarket. Occasionally the deli stocks an excellent Heilongjiang cheese, comparable to Gouda: look for a red cannonball. This is one of the very few places in China where you can get those cheese-enzymes working again. Atmosphere is zilch, open 9 am.

*Beijing Hotel* has Y4 breakfast buffet – meats, toast, eggs, jam, passable coffee – 7 to 9 am. Nice spread, help yourself and come back for more.

*Xinqiao Hotel*, sixth floor, has an elaborate omelette menu – from chicken to cheese and everything else in the omelette alphabet. Around Y1.30 each.

*Minzu Hotel* is reputed to have some of the best western food in the capital – German cuisine a speciality – they serve a Viking-sized omelette.

*Jianguo Hotel* – Holiday Inn, California home-style cooking at greater-than-Californian prices. Y3 for cereal, cornflakes; Y6 for two eggs plus ham, bacon or sausages; Y6.50 for three-egg omelette (ham, cheese or mushroom); Y2 for German-imported coffee. Also cheese, yoghurt, pancakes, waffles (bakery). Open 6.30 to 9 am approximately.

The *Huadu Restaurant* at 76 Dongdan Beidajie is a small place that serves pizzas! The dish was first introduced by tourists.

For some light relief try *Maxim's* somewhere within the precincts of the Chongwenmen Hotel – it's a joint Sino-

French venture initiated by Pierre Cardin. The Paris-trained and French-speaking staff have picked up some strange habits from the capital, and will knock back those wearing shorts and runners. The place is a copy of Maxims in Paris and was opened in October 1983. Dinner for two – sacre bleu – is a cool Y200 or so, excluding that Bordeaux red or the Alsatian Gewurtztraminer; crepes for Y16 are a bargain. The pissoir is reputed to be the best in China. No vegemite.

**Snacks off da trax** Beijing has a fair number of snack bars, noodle bars, dumpling shops and cake shops – nowhere near the number it used to have, but sufficient to sate the curiosity. A Beijing newspaper suggested there weren't nearly enough snack bars and that the locals should resort to selling hot dogs. Snacks can be found at roadside stalls (especially around breakfast), in market areas, and often on the ground floor of restaurants (the masses section). Small vendors are making a comeback, ever since the return of the icecream soda in 1980 after an absence of 14 years: in fact a health problem exists with the random production of popsicles by home entrepreneurs.

In 1982 a group of Beijing chefs set about reviving the imperial pastry recipes – they even went so far as to dig up the last emperor's brother to try their products out on. The same year, an Overseas Chinese outfit was permitted to start up a snack bar specialising in South-East Asian snacks. Snacking is where you may meet the free market – jobless youths have carved out small businesses for themselves, and there are some licensed family-owned restaurants (35% profit allowed). The other person you'll meet is the snacker, someone who can't afford a full-course meal. In winter I hit a bakery to get out of the cold for a moment – I gathered 99% of the clientele was in there for the same reason, a group huddled round a woodburner clutching bowls of hot water (good way to warm up the hands!) It will cost you next to nothing to sample these places, all highly educational.

Historically, the different varieties of snack (some 200 survive) were trotted out with the changing of the seasons, or at temple fairs. In winter it was *wonton* or quick-boiled tripe; in summer jellied cheese or almond-curd; and in the spring it was *aiwowo* (glutinous rice stuffed with sesame and sugar) – a dish of Mongolian origins. This still holds true to some extent – at Chinese New Year moonshaped *jiaozi* (meat-filled ravioli) are consumed for five days solid. A few suggestions for snacktrackers are given, but you're better off thinking of it as 'chance-food' – when you see something you like, jump it – you've got nothing to lose but your taste-buds.

The Qianmen area in bygone Beijing had the largest concentration of snack bars, and is a good place to go hunting. Down Qianmen Lu is the *Zhengmingzhai Cake shop*; the *Duyichu* at No 36 Qianmen and close to Dazhalan is an ancient restaurant serving *shaomai* (steamed dumplings). Off the beginning of Dazhalan on Liangshidian alley is *Zhimielou* which sells dragon-whisker noodles – strands as fine as silk, an old Qing recipe. The *Fangshan Restaurant* snack bar outlet in Beihai Park also doles out imperial cakes.

For *baozi* and *jiaozi* try the *Hongxinglou Jiaooziguan* at 1 Beiiwei St (west side of the Temple of Heaven) which serves jiaozi, shaomai and noodles – three floors of the stuff. Twenty different kinds of jiaozi (in season) can be ordered and there's even frozen take-home. Prices rise as you go up – crowded ground floor has two kinds of jiaozi, beer and cold cuts. Next floor has jiaozi and 60 Shandong seafood/pork dishes. The seafood is not cheap, but if you stick to jiaozi this place can be very cheap (scallops Y9 a dish, roast chicken Shandong-style Y8, prawns Y12). The *Jinfeng* at 157 Qianmen sells Beijing-style baozi-dumplings. The *Ritan Park Restaurant* to the north of the Friendship Store has classy jiaozi and western snacks (full courses also, but not so interesting). It's patronised by westerners and housed in a classical-style building. It's open 4.30 to 8 pm but closed on Fridays.

## NIGHT LIFE AND ENTERTAINMENT

La Dolce Vita is non-existent in Beijing, but in a city of museums, red tape and paperwork hacks what did you expect? The town goes to bed early – most cultural events start around 7 pm and are finished by 9.30 pm, when transport becomes infrequent (buses that run after 11 pm are Nos 20, 201, 202, 203 and 204). The Chinese mostly stick to restauranting or playing chess in the gutters at midnight.

### Discos

Back in the late 70s, Saturday Night Fever (1940s style) hit Beijing. Discos popped up in various hotels and more notably in the Nationalities Cultural Palace on Changan Avenue where it was punctuated by a floor show with minority groups. The authorities reasoned that the high admission price of Y10 would keep the locals out, but they misjudged the craze for the (illicit) joys of dancing. Due to problems of mixing and drinking, the music died, and even the Life Disco at the Jianguo Hotel had trouble getting started. The latter is open 9 pm to 1 am with an entry fee of Y17 (includes two drinks) and at that price it will do no more than keep the locals away. Considerably cheaper is the disco at the Overseas Chinese Building near CAAC Office. It's an erratic schedule of around 8 pm to midnight and entry is Y3. The *Friendship Hotel* holds a combination dance-acrobat show, and being close to Beida University and Beijing Languages Institute, it attracts the younger foreign set. They even have movies there also. It's best to check which dance floor is still operating by phoning ahead from your hotel.

### Fun with the Foreign Community

Embassy staff and journalists, bored with Peking's 'night life', have created their own. At one time in the 70s the sole source of decadence in Beijing was the 'Down Under Club' in the basement of the Australian Embassy, which got such a reputation that taxi drivers refused to collect passengers late at night (this problem was overcome by summoning a taxi to the Malaysian Embassy next door!). Anyway, they started something of a precedent, which has evolved into a Friday night get-together at varying embassies or residences – keep your ear to the ground, the news sometimes hits the lobby of the Beijing Hotel and the fun usually gets underway around 5.30 pm. The Brits have imported their night life – there's a British pub located inside the grounds of the UK Embassy, called The Bell. Beer is Y1.50 a pint but the place is not exactly open to the public.

### Local Cafes

Very few in number. The one 'hot spot' is the *Peace Cafe*, much publicised in the foreign press for the shady deals that take place in its gloomy interior. It's down 'Goldfish Alley', the hutong that leads to the Peace Hotel – try and find the Peace Hotel first. The cafe serves beer and icecream (some have been noted to combine the two), main courses (including a Chinese approximation to a hamburger) and snacks, and is open till the outlandish hour of 9 pm. The clientele is very different from the polite Chinese – there are 'punks' who can swear in English, claim they're flying off to Switzerland next day and are preoccupied with how to get the next status symbol, be it a digital wrist watch, a pair of cowboy boots or a Walkman.

Just inside the gates of Beida (Beijing University) is a student canteen open to 10.30 pm, serves food, beer, wonton and baozi.

Near Xisi, on Xianmen Dajie, is a genuine coffee and teahouse, a private business called the *Daoshanzhuang* – and there's a sign in pinyin and 'Welcome' under it. It's open from 9.30 am to 9.30 pm, with a two hour break in the afternoon. Refreshments are served, music by Chopin, Mozart and Schubert, light foreign and Chinese music. Art on the walls is by the manager-owner, Su Daoshan, who is in his 20s.

## Clubbing

Sporting, recreational and club facilities are to be found in the Friendship Hotel, the International Club and the Minority Nationalities Cultural Palace. The International Club is pretty lifeless, patronised by dozy diplomats and has signs around the place telling you what not to do. There are tennis-courts (dusty), billiard tables (in bad shape), full-sized swimming pool (you need a swimming licence), bowling alley (a bummer – you have to set up your own pins), and a bar/restaurant (it's debatable whether the chef isn't in fact a can opener).

The Nationalities Cultural Palace is a toffee-nosed Chinese and foreign hangout with a large range of amenities – bowling alley, pingpong, bar, restaurant and ballroom, banquet rooms – and a sentry at the gate. Of interest here might be minority singing and dancing events by night, and occasional exhibitions featuring minority wares by day. If you get to the upper floors of this massive group of buildings there are some very nice views.

## What's On

China Daily carries a listing of cultural evenings recommended for foreigners. Offerings include concerts, theatre, minority dancing and some cinema. There are about 35 theatres and 50 cinemas in the capital – you can reserve ahead by phoning the box office via your hotel, or pick up tickets at CITS for a surcharge -or take a risk and just roll up at the theatre (seats are always held for surprise visits by cadres and dignitaries, and you rate as one).

Entertainment is dirt cheap, one to two yuan at most. Beijing is on the touring circuit for foreign groups, and these are also listed in China Daily. They're somewhat screened for content, but lately they've been beefing up what's available. In 1983 Arthur Miller's Death of a Salesman was acted out by Chinese at the Capital Theatre, and held over for two months by popular demand. The same theatre staged some avant-garde Chinese theatre; it put on two plays by Gao Zingjian, incorporating theatre of the absurd and traditional Chinese theatrical techniques. One of the plays Bus-stop is based on eight characters who spend ten years at the bus stop to discover that the service was cancelled long ago – which is either a vicious comment on the Beijing bus service, or a sly reference to Gao's stint in re-education camp during the Cultural Revolution, or else it is a direct steal from Sam Beckett or Luigi Pirandello (both of whom would be unknown in China).

In the concert department, a recent offering was Beethoven's Ninth played on Chinese palace instruments such as tuned bells, found and copied from an ancient tomb. Other classical instruments are being revived for dance-drama backings.

Film is out of the boring stage and starting to delve into some contemporary issues – even verging on Cultural Revolution after-shock in a mild manner. Television, if you're that kind of addict, brings a lot of different types of Chinese entertainment direct into your hotel room, if you have that kind of room. There are three channels – and if you have the right kind of electronic hookups, perhaps some naughty Hong Kong video. Programmes are listed in China Daily. TV is actually a good way of studying Chinese, especially the kids' programmes with fascinating forms of Chinese animation.

As for other events, you might also like to delve into items not listed in China Daily but listed in the local newspapers (if you can read Chinese or get a translation) – sporting events, puppet theatre, story-telling and local cinema. These are bound to be sold out, but scalpers exist.

## A night at the Opera

It used to be the Marx Brothers, the Gang of Four and the Red Ballet – but it's back to the classics again these days. Beijing Opera is one of the many forms of the art and the most famous, but it's only got a short history; 1790 is the key date given, the year that a provincial troupe performed before Emperor Qianlong on his 80th birthday. The form was popularised in the west by the actor Mei Lan-fang (who played 'dan' or female roles) and who even influenced, it is claimed, Charlie Chaplin.

Earlier in the century teahouses, wine shops and opera were the main nightlife in Beijing and of these, only the opera has survived (just). The opera bears little resemblance to its European counterpart. It's a mixture of singing, dancing, speaking, mime, acrobatics and dancing, and a traditional opera performance would go on for five or six hours. An hour is usually long enough for a westerner. Plots are fairly basic so the language barrier is not really a problem – the problem is the music, which is searing to western ears, and the acting which is heavy and stylised.

Beijing Opera is usually regarded as the *creme de la creme* of all the opera styles prevalent in China. Traditionally it's been the opera of the masses. In some ways it's very similar to the ancient Greek theatre, with its combination of singing, dialogue, acrobatics and pantomine, the actors wearing masks and the performance accompanied by loud and monotonous rythms produced with percussion instruments. The themes are usually inspired by disasters, natural calamities, intrigues or rebellions, and many have their source in the fairy tales and stock characters and legends of classical literature and myth- logical themes of love, villainy or heroism – titles like *The Monkey King*, *A Drunken Beauty* or *A Fisherman's Revenge*.

The music, singing and costumes are very much a product of the origins of the opera; formerly, Beijing opera was performed mostly on open-air stages in the markets and streets, in the teahouses or the courtyards of temples. The orchestra had to play loud and the performers had to develop a piercing style of singing which could be heard over the throng. The costumes are a garish collection of sharply contrasting colours because the stages were originally lit by oil lamps.

The origins of Bejing opera may be traced as far back as the Tang Dynasty; the movements and techniques of the dance styles of the time are similar to those of today's Beijing Opera. Provincial opera companies were characterised by the dialect and style of singing of the regions where they originate, but when these companies converged on Beijing they brought together a style of musical drama called *kunqu*. This developed during the Ming Dynasty, with a more popular variety of play-acting with pieces based on legends, historical events and popular novels which had developed simultaneously. These styles gradually merged by the late 18th and early 19th centuries into the Beijing opera as we know it today.

The musicians usually sit on the stage, in plain clothes and play without written scores. The *erhu* is a two-stringed fiddle which is tuned to a low register, has a soft tone and generally supports the *huqin* another two-stringed fiddle tuned to a high register. The *yueqin*, a sort of moon- shaped four-stringed guitar, has a soft tone and is used to support the *erhu*. Other instruments are the *sheng* (reed pipes), the *pipa* (lute), as well as drums, bells and cymbals. Last but not least is the *ban*, a time-clapper which virtually directs the band, beats time for the actors and gives them their cues.

There are four types of actor's roles; the *sheng*, *dan*, *jing* and *chou*, and each is subdivided; the *sheng* are the leading male actors and they play scholars, officials, warriors, etc. They are divided into the *laosheng* who wear beards and represent old men, and the *xiaosheng* who represent young men. The *wensheng* are the scholars and the civil servants. The *wu sheng* play soldiers and other fighters and because of this are specially trained in acrobatics.

The *dan* are the female roles; the *laodan* are the elderly, dignified ladies – the mothers, aunts and widows. The *qingyi* are aristocratic ladies in elegant costumes. The *huadan* are the ladies' maids, usually in brightly-coloured costumes. The *daomadan* are the warrior women and the *caidan* are the female comedians. Traditionally, female roles were played by male actors.

The *jing* are the painted-face roles, and they represent warriors, heroes, statesmen, adventurers and demons. The counterparts are the *fu jing* – ridiculous figures who are anything but heroic. Lastly, the *chou* are basically the clowns, often performing as servants or peasants. The *caidan* are sometimes the female counterparts of this male role.

Apart from the singing and music, the opera also uses acrobatics and mime. Few props are used so each move, gesture or facial expression is symbolic; a whip with silk tassels indicates an actor riding a horse, lifting a foot means going through a doorway. Language is often archaic Chinese, music is earsplitting (bring some cotton wool), but the costumery and makeup are magnificent. The only action that really catches the western eye is a swift battle sequence – the women warriors involved are trained acrobats, who leap, twirl, twist and somersault into attack.

When you get bored after the first hour or so, and are sick of the high-pitched whining, the local audience is with you all the way – spitting, eating apples, breastfeeding an urchin on the balcony, or plugging into a transistor radio (important sports match?!) – it's a lively prole audience viewing entertainment fit for kings. Major Beijing Opera theatres are the Capital (22 Wangfujing); Erqi (Fuxingmenwai Dajie); Tianqiao (near the Temple of Heaven); Renmin (Huguosi Dajie); Jixiang (14 Jinyu Hutong, off Wangfujing) and the Changan (Xi Changan Jie). The oldest in Beijing is the Guanghe at 24-26 Qianmen Lu. Most performances start around 7 or 7.30 pm.

There are numerous other forms of opera apart from the Beijing variety. The Cantonese variety is more 'music hall' often with 'boy meets girl' themes. Gaojia opera is one of the five local opera forms from Fujian province and is also popular in Taiwan, with the singing based mainly on songs in the Fujian dialect but influenced by the Beijing opera style.

### Acrobatics

2000 years old, and one of the few art forms condoned by Mao, it's the best deal in town. For the mere sum of 50 fen, you can forget CITS, forget train stations, forget hotels, forget language problems, in fact forget all your China problems. Magic! Acts take place in various locations – for authentic atmosphere, try the Acrobat Rehearsal Hall on Dazhalan, once the major theatre location in Beijing. There's a ticket office past the theatre down Dazhalan on your left. CITS sells the same seats for Y2. You can forget both of those if you want – roll up, roll in, and count on your facial features to land you a cadre seat. The show starts at 7.15 pm and acts change nightly. Dazhalan is a hutong off the subway end of Qianmen St.

### SHOPPING

In China they say you get what you pay for, a double-edged pun – if the man says it's top quality jade, it *is* top quality jade and you'll pay through the nose for it. Therefore, although prices are lower for items like this in other parts of Asia, there's no need for paranoia about being ripped off by fakes. Bargains are to be had on certain goods, prices are lower than in the west, but you may have to take into account the sometimes outrageous tariffs for shipping items. It therefore makes sense to go for smaller or lighter items that you can carry yourself.

Fast shopping can be done at the Friendship Store which stocks most items that you will want, and also carries luxury items not available elsewhere. More fun and a bit cheaper, for hard-to-find items you want, is to rummage around with the Chinese. Shopping is concentrated on three busy areas: Wangfujing, Qianmen (Dazhalan) and Liulichang (antiques). Other mildly interesting shopping streets are on Xidan and Dongdan, north of Changan. Inside various tourist attractions such as the Temple of Heaven, as well as in the major hotels, are some garish souvenir shops stocking arts and crafts. Otherwise, speciality shops are scattered around the city core. Stores are generally open 9 am to 7 pm seven days a week, some are open 8 am to 8 pm. Good buys are stationery items (chops, brushes, inks), prints, handicrafts, clothing (fur, silk, down jackets), and antiques. Small or light items to buy are silk scarves and T-shirts, embroidered purses, papercuts, wooden and bronze buddhas, foldup paper lanterns and kites. Bargaining is not a way of life – but on the free market it certainly is.

## Friendship Store

This is the largest in the land, detectives posted near the entrance to keep the Chinese out. Top floor: furniture, carpets, arts & crafts (stones, paintings, carvings, cloissone etc). Middle floor: clothing items, fabrics, cosmetics, toys, 'daily necessities'. Ground floor: tinned and dried imported/local foods, tobacco wines and spirits, Chinese medicines, film, foreign books and magazines. To the right: supermarket, deli and florist.

The Friendship Store caters to the embassy mob. If they're out of the food you want and you just have to have that cheese or whatever, try the branch up in Sanlitun. The Friendship Store has two tailors (numbers 1 and 2 and count on a long wait for alterations or made-to-

measures) taxi service, bank, and a section that handles packing clearance and shipping. The Friendship Store is at 21 Jianguomenwai (tel 593531).

## Wangfujing

This street, just east of Beijing Hotel, is lined with a number of speciality stores. At No 120 is Beijing's second largest department store. Opposite the department store is the Dongfeng, a covered market with a similar selection of dry goods. It's the classiest shopping area in the capital with largest-of-the-kind stores and parallel-size crowds on weekends and holidays. In pre-49 days it was known as Morrison Street, catering largely to foreigners and still does so with it's snooty Friendship Store atmosphere to it. Swiss and Seiko have moved in – among the first foreign businesses to set up shop in Beijing. The name Wangfujing derives from a 15th century well, the site of which is now occupied by offices of *The People's Daily*, about mid-way between East Changan Avenue and Donghuamen Lu, where 600 reporters toil to put out an eight-page newspaper. A branch of the foreign languages bookstore is at 179, a shop that will stencil Chinese or English motifs on your T-shirt is at 155, chop shop at 162, chopstick and fan shop at 160.

## Qianmen Area

If Wangfujing is too sterilised for you, the place to go and rub shoulders is Dazhalan, a hutong running west from the top end of Qianmen. It's a heady jumble of silk shops, department stores, theatres, herbal medicines, food and clothing specialists, and has some unusual architecture. It's really more of a sight than a place to shop but you might find something that catches your eye. Dazhalan has a definite medieval flavour to it, a look back to the days when hutongs sold specialised products – one would sell lace, another lanterns, another jade. This one used to be called Silk Street – the name 'Dazhalan' refers to a wicker-gate that was closed at night to keep undesirable prowlers out. In imperial Beijing, shops and theatres were not permitted near the city centre, and the Qianmen-Dazhalan district was outside the gates – many of the city's oldest shops can be found along or near this crowded hutong.

Just off the beginning of Dazhalan (3 Liangshidan Jie) is Liubiju, a 400-year old pickle and sauce emporium patronised by discriminating housewives. Nearby is the Zhimielou Restaurant which serves imperial snacks. On your right going down Dazhalan is a green concave archway with columns, number 5, which is the entrance to Ruifuxiang, one of the better-known material and silk stores and a century old. Its unusual interior amazed visitors then and now. Next door to that is the entrance to the Acrobat Rehearsal Hall – you can get advance tickets further down the street on the left at No 36. Dazhalan at one time had five opera theatres – the place used to be thronged with theatre-goers by day (cheap rehearsals) and at night (professionals). The night life lingers on with two performing theatres, and rickshaw men still wait for the post-theatre crowds. No 1 Dazhalan was once a theatre.

Other famous shops are the Tongrengtang at No 24, selling Chinese herbal medicines. It's been in business since 1669 though it doesn't appear that way from the renovations. It was a royal dispensary in the Qing Dynasty, and derives its pills and potions from secret prescriptions used by royalty. All kinds of weird mixtures – tiger-bone, rhino horn, snake-wine – will cure you of anything from fright to encephalitis, or so they claim. Traditional doctors on the spot for consultation – perhaps ask them about fear of railway stations (patience pills?).

Neiliangshang at No 34 are the former royal shoemakers, and sell leather shoes and handmade cotton-cloth slippers. If you're into bound feet, just the place for you – custom-made sizes are possible. A century ago, Manchu court officials bought shoes here as 'bribes' for superiors – records were kept of patrons' foot-sizes.

Dazhalan runs about 300 metres deep off Qianmen. At the far end where the hubbub dies down is a bunch of Chinese hotels and if you sense something here . . . yes, you're right, Dazhalan was the gateway to Beijing's red-light district. The brothels were shut down in 1949 and the girls packed off to factories to make wares instead of plying them.

Qianmen Lu, down and into Zhushikou Lu (and along to Caishikou intersection to the west) is an interesting place to meander: pottery stores at No 99 and 149, minorities musical instruments at 104 (another at No 18), and a nice secondhand shop at 117. Zhenyunge, a shop just west of Zhushikou intersection at No 86 Xi Zhushikou, sells furniture and porcelain.

## Antiques

The most illustrious chain of antique shops in Beijing is in Liulichang, a hutong south-west of Tiananmen. In the Yuan Dynasty this street had a kiln and later supplied tiling for the Forbidden City; in the Qing Dynasty it had a number of booksellers and became a scholars' meeting place. In 1983 the ancient street was getting a classical-style facelift in preparation for slicker dealings, and the 60 odd curio-shops were scattered around places like the Beijing Hotel and Temple of Heaven. Sold on Liulichang are cloisonne, antique reproductions, bronzes, stones, rare books and modern editions of ancient books. Some of the shops are: Rongbaozhai (brushes, inkstones, paper, paints and paintings, woodcuts, calligraphy materials, seals and chops – cards, chops and mounting done to order); Yunguzhai (porcelain, jade); Qingyuntang (old books, seals, rubbings); Wenshengzhai (palace lanterns). Most antiques have been produced within the last 185 years (with the exception of one shop, the Yueyatang which sells government-authorised pre-1795). Anything over 100 years old needs a red wax seal on the object or the price-tag. Prices on Liulichang are inflated – an institutionalised approach to antique-selling with only tourists in mind, but whether you want to spend Y2 or Y20,000 it does no harm to browse. Shops will mail purchases for you.

## Second-Hand Shopping

Second-hand shopping is one of the favourite pastimes of embassy staff in Beijing – this is reputedly worked on a rota system so that anything of real value can be snapped up the moment it hits the shelf. Most of the second-hand or commission shops sell recycled radios, TVs and household goods, but some are specialised (unmarked, hard to find). Here are a few:

Arts & Crafts Trust Company, 12 Chongwenmennei, just north of Xinqiao Hotel and CITS, has a very pleasant atmosphere. Sells theatrical costumes, used furs and clothing, jewellery, a large selection of antiques including a wonderful array of clocks (not necessarily Chinese – could be European or Japanese). A separate section next door sells furniture, carpets and embroidery.

Beixinqiao Second-hand, 30 Dongsi Bei Dajie, old chests of all shapes and sizes, some made of camphor and mahogany. Furniture can be restored at No 38 Dongsi Nan Dajie (takes a long time) and mailing goes through the Friendship Store (which will also identify antiques). Other second-hand furniture can be found at 128 Dianmenwai, 32 Chongwenmenwai, 101 Xuannei, and 56 Wangfujing. It's all expensive stuff.

Qianmen Commission Shop 117 Qianmen – furs and fur-lined coats and jackets. The older style of wealth was having it, not to display it, so long coats look cheap from the outside but have a 'silver lining' – and expensive skin, like fox.

## Markets

With the resurgence of individual trading, going to market is a good way of observing some lively interaction between locals. Markets are a bit difficult to locate – the area at lower Qianmen (West Zhushikou Lu and the Tianqiao area) is pretty brisk, and the north-east wall section of the Temple of Heaven is very busy (poultry, gardening supplies). 'Market' on the bus map basically means Department Store: the People's Market on a hutong near the CAAC building, however, may be worth a visit for another reason – the newer store is in an old area once occupied by the Longfusi Temple, the remains of which are still visible.

In the vicinity of the zoo, there's a bird and fish market west of Pinganli intersection. There's a large fruit and vegetable market near Beitaipingzhuang intersection (north-west of Deshengmen, follow Xinjiekouwai Dajie). Pigeon racing is coming back into style in China and there is a pigeon market on Changping Lu (about 3 km north of Deshengmen en route to Ming Tombs).

## GETTING AROUND

### Buses

Sharpen your elbows, chain your money to your underwear and muster all the patience you can – you'll need it. Overstuffed buses are in vogue in Beijing – and can be particularly unpleasant at the height of summer when passengers drip with nausea and perspiration. Cosy in winter if you haven't frozen to the bus stop by the time the trolley arrives, but difficult to exit from – try the nearest window.

There are about 140 bus and trolley routes, which makes navigation rather confusing, especially if you can't see out of the window in the first place. For a good, clear bus map refer to the section on 'Information & Orientation'. Buses run from 5.10 am to 11 pm and four lines run all night. Fares are based on distance – Y0.05 to Y0.20 – a minor compensation is that the conductor rarely gets through to you. Bus stops are few and far between – it's important to work out how many stops to go before boarding. Avoid these horrors during rush hours or holidays.

Buses are routed through landmarks and key intersections, and if you can pick out the head and tail of the route, you can get a good idea of where the monster will travel. Major termini occur near long-distance junctions: Beijing Main Station, Dongzhimen, Tianqiao, Yongdingmen, Qianmen. The Zoo (Dongwuyuan) has the biggest pile-up with about 15 lines since it's where inner and outer Beijing get together. One or two-digit bus numbers are city core, 100-series buses are trolleys, and 300-series are suburban lines. If you can work out how to combine bus and subway connections, the subway will speed up part of the trip (eg: subway to Lishilu, then bus No 15 or bus No 19 to the Zoo). All-night buses are Nos 201, 202, 203, 204 and No 20. Some useful buses:

**No 1** travels across the city east-west straight along Changan, from Jianguolu (east) to Fuxinglu (west). **No 5** travels north-south axis, from Deshengmen/Gulou (north) down the west side of the Forbidden City then to Qianmen/Tianqiao (south) and ending at Youanmen. **No 44** follows the Circle Line subway in a square on the ring road. **No 15** zigzags from Tianqiao area to the Zoo (passes several subway stops). **No 7** runs from the west of Qianmen Gate to the Zoo. **No 20** zigzags Main Station to Yongdingmen Station and runs late night (goes via Changan and Qianmen streets). **No 103** (trolley) Main Station to Zoo via Chongwenmen, Wangfujing, Art Gallery, Jingshan and Beihai Parks (south side). **No 111** (trolley): similar route, but goes via Dongdan and north side of Beihai Park (starts at Chongwenmen). **No 116** (trolley): good sightseeing bus – travels from south entrance of Temple of Heaven up Qianmen to Qianmen Gate, then Tiananmen, east along Changan to Dongdan and direct north on Dongdan to Lama Temple. **No 332** is a useful suburban route, starting from the Zoo. There are two kinds of 332: regular and express – the express buses (fewer stops) are at the head of the queue near the zoo. **No 332** route: Dongwuyuan (Zoo) – Minzuxueyuan (Institute for Nationalities) – Weigongcun – Renmindaxue (People's University) – Zhongguancun – Haidian – Beijingdaxue (Beijing University) – Yiheyuan (Summer Palace).

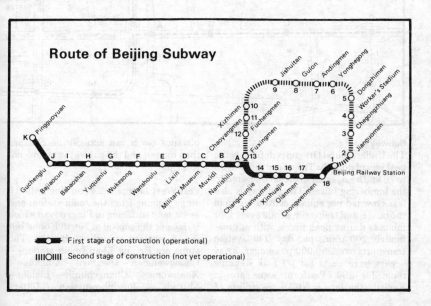

## Route of Beijing Subway

First stage of construction (operational)

Second stage of construction (not yet operational)

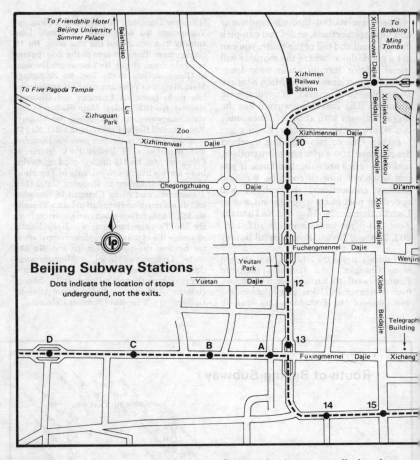

To Friendship Hotel
Beijing University
Summer Palace

To Five Pagoda Temple

To Badaling
Ming Tombs

Xinjiekouwai Dajie
Xinjiekou
Xinjiekou Nandajie
Beidajie

Xizhimen Railway Station

9

Baishiqiao Lu

Zizhuguan Park

Zoo

Xizhimenwai Dajie

Xizhimennei Dajie

10

Di'anme

Chegongzhuang Dajie

11

Xisi Beidajie

Yeutan Park

Fuchengmennei Dajie

Wenjin

**Beijing Subway Stations**

Dots indicate the location of stops underground, not the exits.

Yuetan Dajie

12

Xidan Beidajie

Telegraph Building

D            C            B            A

13

Fuxingmennei Dajie

Xichang

14      15

## Subway

The Underground Dragon is definitely the best way of doing it. Trains can move at up to 70 km/h – a jaguar on heat compared to the lumbering buses. The subway is also less crowded per square centimetre than the buses, and trains run at one every four minutes during peak times, with approximately 200 trains per day. The system transports over 250,000 passengers a day – cars have seats for 60 and standing room for 200. Platform signs are in English; the fare is Y0.10 regardless of distance (so it can actually be cheaper than buses); and the subway is open 5 am to 11 pm.

**East-West Line** is a 24 km line with 17 stops running from the main station and eventually surfacing in Pingguoyan which is, no, not the capital of North Korea, but yes, a western suburb of Beijing. The stops are Beijing Zhan (main station) – Chongwenmen – Qianmen – Xinhuajie – Xuanwumen – Changchunjie – Lishilu – Muxudi – Junshibowuguan (Military

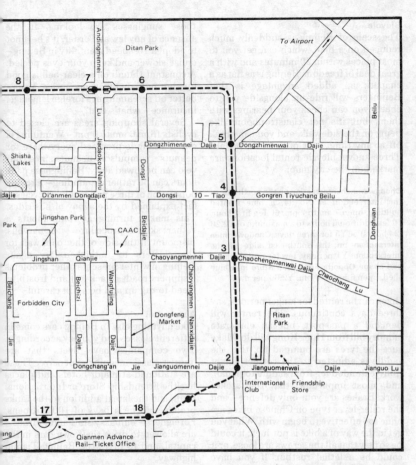

Museum) – Lixinzhan – Wanshoulu – Wukesong –Yuquanlu – Babaoshan – Bajiaocun – Guchenglu – Pingguoyan. It takes 40 minutes to travel the length of the line.

**Circle Line** This 16 km long line is only partially open but also partially computerised. It loops around the city on the western, northern and eastern sides and is extremely useful for sightseeing destinations. It is not known exactly how this section operates – or if it is yet open to tourists. It will be very popular and is expected to handle around 500,000 people a day. It probably connects to the East-West line with a transfer system. The Circle Line has 13 stations: Beijingzhan – Jianguomen – Chaoyangmen – Dongsi 10 – Dongzhimen (the subway here tunnels right around the Russian Embassy!) – Yonghegong (Lama Temple) – Andingmen – Gulou – Jishuitaan – Xizhimen (North Station & Zoo) – Chegongzhuang – Fuchengmen –Fuxingmen.

### Bicycle

The scale of Beijing is suddenly much reduced on a bike, which can get you to most places within 20 minutes and with a great deal of freedom. Beijing is as flat as a chapati; an added advantage is that Beijingers will ride up alongside you to chat – you can check your bearings with them, but it's not claustrophobic like being on the sidewalk, and you can break off at any time. Just push those pedals! Three known bicycle-rental locations are marked on the city map:

**Chongwenmen intersection** on the north side of the intersection at No 94, a blue fronted building; open 7 am to 7 pm, 60 fen first hour, 10 fen additional hours to a maximum of Y2.20 (24 hours) or Y5 for three days. **Chongwenmen Intersection** on the south-east side of the intersection; Y1 per day, few for rent, hulks in bad shape **Oppoite Friendship Store** in a blue shed, open 6 am to 6 pm, Y2.60 per day.

Bikes can be rented for longer periods, say three days continuous. The renter will demand a passport, but an elaborate laundry bill from Hong Kong will do. Make sure the tyres are pumped up, that the saddle is adjusted to the correct height (fully-extended leg from saddle to pedal), and, most important, that the brakes work. Brakes are your only defence – and the roller-lever type on Chinese bikes are none too effective to begin with. What you get in the way of a bike is pot-luck; it could be so new that all the screws are loose, or it could be a lethal rustbin. If you have problems later on, adjustments can be made at any bike shop – dirt cheap. The locations listed are often out of bikes – if this happens, don't despair – walk into every bike shop you see and ask.

Traffic rules for bikes: none. Cyclists pile through red lights, buses sound a warning horn and scatter a slew of bikers over a bus stop, taxis zip past the mess and policemen look the other way. Traffic policemen have no power to fine cyclists, and if they stop one, everybody will gather to jeer the cop. Who knows which way those sunglasses are looking. In the absence of any law and order, it's best not to adopt a 10-speed mentality in Beijing – cruise slower and keep your eyes peeled. A constant thumb on a clear bell is good fun, but nobody takes any notice. You're better off screaming in a foreign language. Insurance – what's that?

Several shopping areas are closed to cyclists from 6 am to 6 pm – Wanfujing is one. Parking is provided everywhere for peanuts – compulsory peanuts since your velo can be towed away. Beijingnese peak hours can be rather astounding – a roving population of three million plus bicycles, a fact explained by the agony of bus rides. This makes turning at roundabouts a rather skilled procedure – if nervous, dismount at the side of the road, wait for the clusters to unthicken, try again. Beijing in winter presents other problems – slippery roads (black ice) and frostbite. Need to rug up and be extra careful.

### Auto rental

Like anything else in Beijing cars come in different classes and you pay accordingly. Two companies have fleets that are 'tourist class', meaning expensive. These are stationed at major hotels and places like the Friendship Store or International Club, and the latest addition to the ranks promises to be a bevy of 100 Citroens. Foreigners – embassy staff and journos – are allowed to drive their own cars in the capital, and to drive the Beijing-Tianjin highway.

The American rental company, National, is moving in. Their boast is that they're the only foreign car rental company in the PRC – they run sizes from Toyotas to 40-seater buses on an 8-hour basis, and you can reserve one for a client by dialling a toll-free number in the USA before the person arrives in Beijing. All vehicles are chauffeur-driven.

Coming down to earth; the Car Co (tel 557661) has a fleet of older East European cars and lesser-known models which lurk down hutongs, at hospitals, near major restaurants and theatres, also main station and zoo – and a lot cheaper. You can pick these off the bus map –look for any taxis marked that aren't at a hotel or tourist spot.

## Taxis & Mini-buses

Taxi rates are Y0.60 per km, minimum charge Y2.40. Few meters – pricing depends on size, make, age of car, backway subsidy, air-con, heating, waiting time – I could go on. Taxis can be hired from the major tourist hotels or by phoning 557461 (English service). There are also minibuses available for hire – Y1.40/km, Y10 minimum. De luxe buses with heater/air-con Y2.60/km, Y20 minimum (tel 444468). If price is of no concern then you can even hire a Red Flag Limo (tel 863664).

In general, if you want a cheap ride, search for the oldest, smallest, most decrepit-looking bomb you can. The light brown Russian Warszawas (known as Huashache) are not only half the price of regular cabs but you're riding an antique. Taxis can be summoned to a location of your choosing, but the older ones are embarrassed to go to your hotel – perhaps rendezvous with these vintages elsewhere. At certain hours such as drivers' dinner time (6 to 8 pm) or the sacred lunch time siesta, taxis are scarce.

Award for the most memorable taxi ride: stuck out at the Summer Palace on a public holiday with 5,000 people clawing at the buses, four of us hijacked a Shanghai, the Chinese Mercedes. Boy could she drive! She shot down those hutongs and boulevards like a champion – chickens, cyclists, jaywalkers, policemen, flying past – we arrived with mouths open and hands riveted to the seats. Taxis don't carry insurance, so they drive cautiously – after that ride, I dunno . . . .

## Autorickshaws

Far cheaper than cars and good to get your adrenalin up. They can be summoned by phone – but they will not enter foreign

enclaves and take ages to arrive anyway. Some of their congregation points can be discerned from the bus map: some rough locations are the main station (tel 555661), Qianmen Gate, and halfway up Wangfujing Jie and to the right.

## GETTING AWAY

Getting there is no problem – one of those rail or air lines will suck you into the capital sooner or later. The real problem is getting *out* of Beijing, and your departure is best planned well in advance. There are planes from Beijing to numerous destinations – see below for details – but most people will probably leave the city by train. Beijing is the magnet for all rail lines – the trouble is that once you've hit the magnet it's hard to come unstuck again.

## CITS Railway Booking Office

The CITS rail-booking office (in the Chongwenmen Hotel, open daily 9 am to noon and 2 to 5 pm) carries a sign demanding four or five days' notice for tickets. What they do is run down to the station the day before to buy your ticket – which will, of course, be tourist-priced. If you have ID as a student *in China* you can get Chinese prices from them. Even with four days' notice they're prone to balls-ups: wrong date, wrong class, no reservations. If you're going to pay 75% extra, and a Y2 service charge on top of that, don't let them string you out with the 'waiting game' – you're paying extra for the privilege of not waiting. Double check your tickets, make sure everything you paid for has full official stamped receipts (including service charge) – pocketing extras has been known to happen.

## Beijing Main Station

You can do what CITS does but faster by going to the Foreigners' Ticketing Office at Beijing Main Station. They will charge tourist price, and other windows may direct you back there, though some travellers have managed to get Chinese prices right at the regular ticket windows (usually using a student I.D.) These ticket windows, two dozen of them, often can't be seen half the time for the crowds and even if they have electronic ticket machines it can still be a real battle to get that piece of cardboard.

Beijing Main Station sells same day tickets. It's unlikely that you'll be able to get a sleeper on a same-day ticket, but that can depend on the route – you could jump the train and try your luck with the conductor. Main Station also sells next day tickets after 7 pm (these are unsold tickets from advance ticket offices scattered around the city). For departures allow plenty of time to get to your train – sometimes it can take 15 minutes to get from the entrance to the correct platform. If you're early then there are plenty of first-class and foreign waiting rooms.

| *Destination* | *Rail distance km* | *Fastest time hours* | *Train number* | *Hard-seat fare Y* | *Hard-sleeper fare Y* |
|---|---|---|---|---|---|
| Tianjin | 137 | 1¾ | 11/12 | 3.50 | |
| Shijiazhuang | 283 | 3¼ | 9/10 | 7 | |
| Jinan | 494 | 6¼ | 13/14 | 12 | |
| Datong | 382 | 7¼ | 43/44 | 9.50 | |
| Taiyuan | 514 | 9 | 35/36 | 12 | 18.50 |
| Hohhot | 668 | 12¼ | 43/44 | 14.50 | 22.50 |
| Zhengzhou | 695 | 8½ | 1/2 | 15 | 23.50 |
| Shenyang | 738 | 9¾ | 11/12 | 15.50 | 24.50 |
| Qingdao | 887 | 17½ | 139/140 | 16 | 26 |
| Changchung | 1043 | 13½ | 17/18 | 21 | 33 |
| Hefei | 1107 | 18½ | 127/128 | 19 | 32 |
| Nanjing | 1157 | 15¼ | 13/14 | 23 | 36 |
| Xian | 1206 | 18½ | 35/36 | 24 | 37 |
| Wuhan | 1229 | 16¼ | 5/6 | 24 | 37 |
| Dalian | 1238 | 18¾ | 130/131 | 20.50 | 34 |
| Harbin | 1285 | 16¾ | 17/18 | 24.50 | 38.50 |
| Yinchuan | 1343 | 25 | 43/44 | 25.50 | 40 |
| Shanghai | 1462 | 19¼ | 13/14 | 27.50 | 43 |
| Changsha | 1587 | 21¼ | 1/2 | 29 | 45 |
| Hangzhou | 1651 | 23¾ | 45/46 | 29.50 | 46 |
| Lanzhou | 1882 | 34 | 43/44 | 32.50 | 51 |
| Nanchang | 2005 | 35¾ | 146/147 | 29.50 | 48.50 |
| Chengdu | 2048 | 37¼ | 7/8 | 35 | 55.50 |
| Xining | 2098 | 44 | 121/122 | 31 | 51 |
| Guilin | 2134 | 31¼ | 5/6 | 36 | 56 |
| Guangzhou | 2313 | 33½ | 15/16 | 39 | 60.50 |
| Chongqing | 2552 | 44¾ | 9/10 | 43 | 67 |
| Nanning | 2565 | 39 | 5/6 | 43 | 67 |
| Fuzhou | 2623 | 43¼ | 45/46 | 44 | 69 |
| Kunming | 3179 | 59 | 61/62 | 52 | 81 |
| Urumqi | 3774 | 74¼ | 69/70 | 60.50 | 94.50 |

## Fares out of Beijing

As a rough guide to timing and prices, the table shows the fastest trains between Beijing and various cities. Fast trains have one- or two-digit numbers; trains with three-digit numbers are slower and cost a little less. Hotel desks will have time-tables. Remember that train numbers – and timetables – can change.

Prices given are all *Chinese* prices, so add 75% to get the price that CITS charges. For journeys of under eight hours only the hard-seat price is listed; for longer journeys the hard-seat (middle berth) price is also given. Express charges are included.

For example, from Beijing to Canton (Guangzhou) is 2313 km by rail; the trip takes about 33½ hours by the fastest express train (No 15/16). The Chinese price for a hard seat is Y39, for a hard sleeper Y60.50. The CITS tourist prices are 75% extra – about Y68 and Y106 respectively.

## Advance Ticket Offices

These are scattered around Beijing. The following offices sell hard-seat and hard-sleeper for one, two or three days in advance of intended departure:

**Qianmen ticket office** east side of loop at top end of Qianmen Lu. Sells tickets to Kunming, Chongqing, Urumqi, Canton, Baotou, Chengde, Shijiazhuang, Tiayuan, Chengdu, Lanzhou.

**Xizhimen ticket office** on the approach to Xizhimen Station (north). Tickets to Nanchang, Qingdao, Suzhou, Shanghai, Xiamen, Hohhot. Also non-express to Baotou and regular Chinese trains to Great Wall.

**Dongdan ticket office** on Dongdan Beidajie, third block north of Changan up Dongdan, on the left-hand side. Tickets to all of the north-east lines (Shenyang, Harbin, etc). Go to window number 5 for your ID clearance.

**Beixinqiao ticket office** on Dongsi Beidajie, north of Dianmen Lu. Tickets for any destination from Beijing Main or Yongdingmen Stations. However this office only sells hard-seat tickets, no sleepers available. It also sells some boat tickets such as the Tanggu-Dalian boat.

**Yongdingmen ticket office** near Yongdingmen Station – sells tickets for the suburban lines and for very slow trains heading out of Beijing for the southern part of the country – not very useful.

Rail time tables are sold by street hawkers outside Xizhimen and Dongdan ticket offices. If all else fails, hop a train out of Beijing to, say, Datong, and get another ticket there.

**Plane** Beijing Capital Airport, operational since 1980, was built as part of the 'Four Modernisations' drive, and is modelled on Paris' Orly Airport. It's 29 km north-east of the city – you can take the CAAC bus which leaves the downtown office at irregular times for Y1.60 – likewise coming in from the airport. It's not a free bus as in most cities. A one-way taxi (with back-way subsidy) costs around Y22 – split between a maximum of four passengers is not too bad – plus the taxi leaves from your hotel, an important consideration if your plane leaves at 6 am. There's the local bus No 359 that runs to the airport from Dongzhimen. Regular taxis take half an hour for the journey.

The partially computerised CAAC ticket office is at 117 Dongsi Xi Dajie; telephone 550497 (domestic reservations), 552945 (international reservations), 558861 and 553245 (enquiries). Over-booking does occur with flights – as with everything else in Beijing – but standby does exist.

Aerial umbilical cords shoot off in every conceivable direction – over 500 domestic and 70 international flights are scheduled out of Capital Airport every week. For

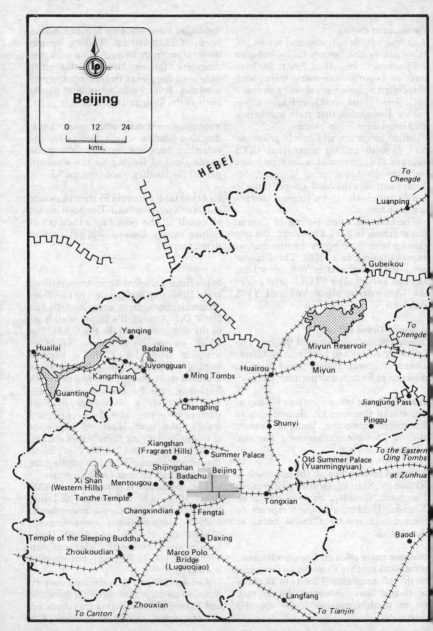

Beijing

0    12    24
kms.

HEBEI

To Chengde

Luanping

Gubeikou

To Chengde

Yanqing

Miyun Reservoir

Badaling

Huailai

Juyongguan

Ming Tombs

Huairou

Miyun

Kangzhuang

Jiangjung Pass

Guanting

Changping

Pinggu

Shunyi

Xiangshan
(Fragrant Hills)

Summer Palace

Old Summer Palace
(Yuanmingyuan)

To the Eastern
Qing Tombs
at Zunhua

Shijingshan

Badachu

Xi Shan
(Western Hills)

Mentougou

Beijing

Tongxian

Tanzhe Temple

Changxindian

Fengtai

Temple of the Sleeping Buddha

Daxing

Zhoukoudian

Marco Polo
Bridge
(Luguoqiao)

Baodi

Zhouxian

Langfang

To Canton

To Tianjin

international flights out of Beijing see 'Getting Away', chapter earlier in this book. There are domestic flights from Beijing to Baotou (Y74), Canton (Y179 first class and Y244 second class), Chanchun (Y115), Changsha (Y179), Chengdu (Y226), Chifeng (Y43), Chongqing (Y200), Dalian (Y80), Fuzhou (Y255), Guilin (Y232), Guiyang (Y254), Hangzhou (Y150), Harbin (Y144), Hefei (Y119), Hohhot (Y55), Jinan (Y52), Kunming (Y361), Lanzhou (Y198), Nanchang (Y189), Nanjing (Y123), Nanning (Y280), Qingdao (Y110), Shanghai (Y195 first-class, Y150 second class), Shenyang (Y80), Taiyuan (Y63), Tianjin (Y24), Tongliao (Y86), Urumqi (Y541 first class, Y416 second class), Wuhan (Y142), Xian (Y132), Xining (Y222), Yanan (Y111), Yinchuan (Y124), Zhengzhou (Y82).

**Boat** Shanghai to Hong Kong boats can be booked in Beijing at CITS (see the 'Information & Orientation' section for details).

**Bus** Beijing is approachable by bus from outlying locations – bumpy roads except for the highway from Tianjin which is in good nick. Long-distance bus lines within Beijing are located on the perimeter: at Dongzhimen (north-east); Guangqumen (south-east); Tianqiao (near the theatre on the west side of the Temple of Heaven). There are two bus stations near Yongdingmen Station, another at the Ganjiakou intersection (south of the Zoo) and one more off Deshengmenwai Dajie. Usually the bus stations are located part-way along the direction you want to travel. These bus stations also have cheaper alternatives to tour buses (going to out-of-town locations like the Ming Tombs).

## AROUND BEIJING

Northern China is blotted with the huge municipal areas of Beijing and Tianjin – and in theory both of these areas are open without special permits. In the past individual travel has been restricted to a

20 km radius from the city centres, with 'corridors' beyond that limit (airport, highway to Tianjin, Great Wall, Summer Palace and Western Hills). If you trundle out and around on a bicycle you occasionally stumble across signs in Chinese, Russian and English stating 'Restricted Area – no foreigners beyond this point'.

Three further corridors will be added by 1990: the south-west route (Lugoqiao, Zhoukoudian, Qingxiling), east route (Jixian, Panshan Hills, Zunhua County) and the more interesting north-east route (Miyun Reservoir, Jinshanling Great Wall, Huarou Reservoir, Mutianyou Great Wall).

There are also plans for a tourist 'satellite city' in Changping County on the route to the Ming Tombs (2000 rooms) – perhaps a visit to the top security prison near Changping will be on the itinerary. Eastern routes are also approachable from Tianjin, which is developing into another staging area, but doesn't have the facilities that Beijing does.

**Transport & Touring** CITS operates a number of high-priced tours to various destinations outside Beijing (Great Wall and Ming Tombs, Y50, including guide and lunch). You can dispense with the guides and food and go for the Chinese tour bus operators that offer Y3 to Y10 day-trips (designed more for Overseas Chinese since there are ticketing offices in the Xuanwumen Hotel and Overseas Chinese Building).

There are two inner city operators; all buses leave from across the road from the Chongwenmen Hotel (with possible pick-up spots), and most return by 5 or 6 pm. The operator most commonly used by travellers is the blue booth ticketing office opposite the Chongwenan Hotel (north-west side of Chongwenmen intersection). The other ticket office used by Chinese, which involves some translation problems, is at 2 Qianmen Lu, north-east side of the loop below Qianmen Gate –look for a

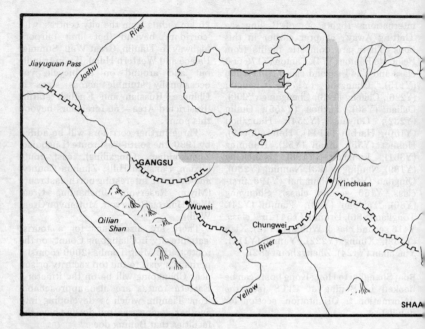

Map labels: River, Jiayuguan Pass, Joshui, GANGSU, Qilian Shan, Wuwei, Yinchuan, Chungwei, River, Yellow, SHAA

small billboard with a picture of the Great Wll. This ticket office offers a wider selection than the one at Chongwenmen. The touring schedule (with departure times) run thus:

### Route 1
Great Wall & Ming Tombs, daily, 7.30 am summer, 8 am winter, Y7 return.

### Route 2
Western Hills & Summer Palace, daily 8 am summer, 8.30 winter, Y3.5 return.

### Route 2
Western Hills & Sleeping Buddha Temple, Thursday, 7.30 am, Y3.5 return.

### Route 3
Tanzhe Temple, Wednesday, Friday, Sunday, 9 am, Y4 return.

### Route 4
Yunshui Caves, Wednesday, Friday, 8 am, Y5 return.

### Route 4
Zhoukoudian, Sunday, 8 am, Y4 return.

### Route 5
Zunhua (Eastern Qing Tombs), Tuesday, Thursday, Sunday (summer), 7.30 am, Y8 return.

Not all of these departures and frequencies are available from the Chongwenmen ticket office. In summer the same bus operators run Chinese-only packages to Chengde (3 day) and Beidaihe (5 day). The international club has expensive packages for foreigners.

Local transport, though it will not offer the same comfort (and timing) is available at a fraction of the cost – some options are listed with the attractions. Try and get your destinations written in Chinese to save time.

### The Great Wall at Badaling
Known to the Chinese as the *10,000 li Wall* (5000 km), the Great Wall stretches from Shanhaiguan Pass on the East Coast to Jiayuguan Pass in the Gobi Desert,

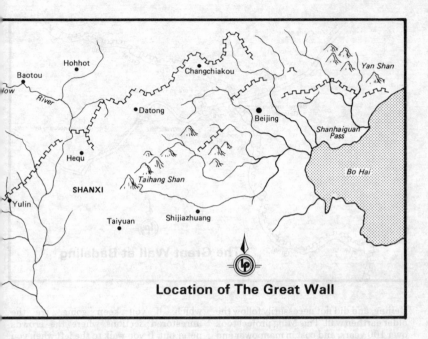

**Location of The Great Wall**

crossing five provinces and two autonomous regions.

The undertaking was begun 2000 years ago during the Qin Dynasty (221-207 BC), when China was unified under Emperor Qin Shihuang. Separate walls, constructed by independent kingdoms to keep out marauding nomads were linked up. The effort required hundreds of thousands of workers, many of them political prisoners, and 10 years of hard labour under General Meng Tian. An estimated 180 million cubic metres of rammed earth were used to form the core of the original wall – and legend has it that some of the building materials used were the bodies of deceased workers.

The wall never really did perform its supposed function as a defence line to keep invaders out – as Genghis Khan noted 'the strength of a wall depends on the courage of those who defend it' (sentries could be bribed). But it did work

very well as a kind of elevated highway – transporting men and equipment across mountainous terrain. Its beacon tower system, using smoke signals generated by burning wolves' dung, transmitted news of enemy movements quickly back to the capital. To the west was Jiayuguan Pass, an important link on the Silk Road where there was a customs post of sorts –and where unwanted Chinese were ejected through the gates to face the terrifying wild west.

Marco Polo makes no mention of China's greatest tourist attraction. Both sides of the wall were under the same government at the time of his visit – but the Ming Great Wall had not been built. In the Ming Dynasty (1368-1644) a determined effort was made to rehash the whole project– this time facing it with bricks and stone slabs, some 60 million cubic metres of them. They created double-walling running in an elliptical shape to the west of

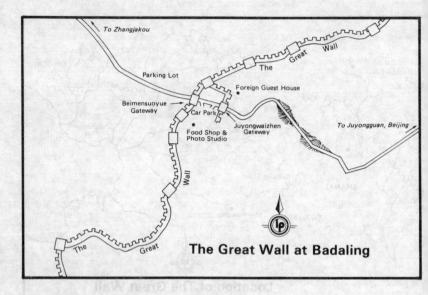

**The Great Wall at Badaling**

Beijing, and did not necessarily follow the older earthen wall. This Ming project took over 100 years, and cost in manpower and resources was phenomenal.

The Wall was largely forgotten after that – now it's reached its greatest heights as a tourist attraction. Lengthy sections of it have been swallowed up by the sands, returned to the mountains, intersected by road or rail, or simply returned to dust. Other bits were carted off by local peasants to construct their own walls – four of them usually – a hobby that no-one objected to in the Cultural Revolution. The depiction of the Wall as an object of great beauty is a bizarre one – like the hated Berlin Wall it is really a symbol of tyranny.

The section at Badaling is the one that most travellers see – 70 km north-west of Beijing at an elevation of 1000 metres. It was restored in 1957 with the addition of guard rails to prevent slippages. This section runs 7.8 metres high with a base of 6.5 metres and a width at the top of 5.8 metres – for several hundred metres, after

which, if you keep going, are the unrestored sections where the crowds peter out. If you walk to the left when you mount the Wall, you can go a long way along the unrestored bits (in the direction of Beijing). Originally the section seen could hold five horsemen riding abreast – nowadays it's about 15 tourists walking abreast.

Unfortunately, if you take a tour bus or train from Beijing you hit peak-hour, and it is only a touch over an hour that you actually get there. Many are dissatisfied with such paltry time at the wall, which is by far and away one of the most spectacular sights in the PRC. The solution to this is to take one-way tours or public transport, spend the time you want, and then figure out a way to get back. If you're found wandering in the vicinity late in the afternoon, the locals and public security will be only too pleased to get rid of you and will speed up your return to Beijing. There's no hotel as yet, but there is Badaling Railway Station, and there are lots of watch towers! Take some food along – there's a restaurant but it's slow, mediocre, and crowded.

For Y5 or so you can get your snapshot taken aboard a camel and pretend to be Marco Polo – though he wasn't tethered to a wall. There's a story attached to the camel – in 1981 when director Labella was filming the travels of Polo, the commune that owned the camel refused to move it from the camera's field of view unless they were paid the day's lost earnings. The bill came to 2000 yuan!

**Getting There** Most travellers get to the Great Wall via the tour buses from opposite the Chongwenmen Hotel, which take in the Ming Tombs and Juyong Pass as well – you're left to your own devices at the Wall, and the antics of the Chinese on the tour bus are worth observing. There are several other options worth considering.

Local buses ply the route to the wall; take bus No 5 or bus No 44 to Deshengmen; then No 345 to terminus (Changping); then a non-numbered bus to the Wall (alternatively bus No 357 goes partway along the route and you then hitch). The cost is less than Y1 in fares. Another route is bus No 14 to Beijiao Market, which is north of Deshenmen, then a non-numbered bus to the wall (hourly departures, the last bus is around 2 pm and the last bus coming back from Badaling is around 5 pm).

A taxi to the wall and back will cost at least 75 yuan for an 8-hour hire – and a maximum of four passengers.

There is a special tourist train, the T1, that leaves Beijing Main Station at 8.05 am (no service on Wednesdays). The cost is Y11.50 air-con soft-seat return, and that includes a packed lunch. Tickets through CITS – and the train is booked well in advance by tour groups. The back of the train is hard-seat, Chinese only. The train arrives at Badaling at 10.25; the

return trip is on the T2, leaving Badaling at 12.36 pm and arriving back at Beijing at 3.15 pm (the tour groups get off at Nankou on the way back and go by coach to the Ming Tombs). Badaling Station is one km from the Wall. The Badaling Line is quite a feat of engineering, built 1909 – it tunnels under the Wall.

Two local trains run from Xizhimen (north railway station) in Beijing, stop at Badaling and continue to Kangzhuang. The fare is Y1.60 return and the trains follow the T1, leaving Beijing around 8.18 am and 8.34 am (no service on Wednesdays). You're not likely to get tickets on Chinese trains the same day – try and get them in advance.

It's also possible to reach the wall by express train from Beijing, getting off at Qinglongqiao which is the station before Badaling. Several express trains leaving Beijing Main Station stop at Qinglongqiao, but not at Badaling. The wall is an easy one km hike from Qinglongqiao. One day train is the No 44 Special Express, leaving Beijing 11 am, arriving Qinglongqiao 12.58 pm. If you are coming from the direction of Hohhot or Datong you could get out at Qinglongqiao, look around the wall and then continue same day to Beijing (for example Train No 170

departs Hohhot at 9 pm and arrives at Qinglongqiao at 7.54 am – your ticket will still be valid for travel to Beijing and you can dump your bags in the left-luggage room at Qinglongqiao station whilst you look around). Qinglongqiao station is recognisable by its statue of Chian Tianyu, the engineer in charge of building the Beijing-Baotou Line.

### Juyongguan Pass
About 10 km south-east of Badaling, Juyong Pass was a garrison town dating back to the Mongol period. There remains a solid stone and marble gateway, Cloud Terrace, built in 1345 and is now being entirely rebuilt. The vault of the archway bears superb bas-reliefs of the four Celestial Guardians, and on the walls are incantation inscriptions in six different languages – Sanskrit, Tibetan, Mongolian (Phagspa script), Uygur, Chinese and Tangut (a rare language from a 13th century Gansu kingdom) – all of which drive philologists crazy!

### Other Walls
Other bits of the wall open to foreigners are those stretches at Jiayuguan in Gansu Province and Shanhiaguan in Hebei Province. Other bits and pieces are scattered around.

To ease the squeeze on Badaling, another section is being renovated at Jinshanling (Shalinkou), 130 km north-east of Beijing on the bus route to Chengde. It's 10 km east of Gubeikou Pass – with a combined package to Chengde it will be a real money-raker. This section of the wall dates from the Ming Dyansty and has some unusual features like 'obstacle walls', which are walls-within-walls used for defending against enemies who'd already scaled the Great Wall. Small cannon have been discovered here (as well as evidence of rocket-type weapons such as flying knives and flying swords).

An early western visitor was Lord Macartney, who crossed Gubei Pass on

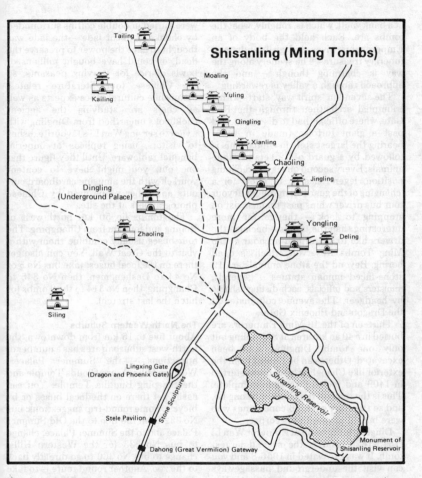

Shisanling (Ming Tombs)

Tailing

Moaling

Yuling

Qingling

Kailing

Xianling

Chaoling

Jingling

Dingling
(Underground Palace)

Zhaoling

Yongling

Deling

Siling

Lingxing Gate
(Dragon and Phoenix Gate)

Shisanling Reservoir

Stone Sculptures

Stele Pavilion

Dahong (Great Vermilion) Gateway

Monument of
Shisanling Reservoir

his way to Chengde in 1793. His party, at a wild guess, calculated that the Wall contained almost as much material as the total dwelling houses of England and Scotland. In the early 1970s a PLA unit stationed at Gubeikou destroyed about three km of the Wall to build barracks, setting an example for the locals who did likewise. In 1979, the same unit was ordered to rebuild the section torn down. Isn't tourism wonderful?

Along the route to Jinshanling, another

plus, is the Miyun Reservoir, a huge artificial lake which is slated to become a holiday resort for foreigners. It already has five touring vessels but they're limited to group tours. Trains running to Chengde stop at Miyun (which is 90 km from Beijing); Gubeikou is on the Beijing-Tongliao Line.

## Shisanling (Ming Tombs)
The general traveller's consensus on the tombs is that you'd be better off looking

at a bank vault, which is, roughly, what the tombs are. Each held the body of an Emperor, his wives and girlfriends, and funerary treasures. The scenery along the way is charming though – and the approach through a valley is rewarding.

The seven km 'spirit way' starts with a triumphal arch, then through the Red Gate, where officials had to dismount, and past a giant tortoise (made in 1425) bearing the largest stele in China. This is followed by a guard of 12 sets of stone animals. Every second one is in a reclining position, legend has it, to allow for a 'changing of the guard' at midnight. If your tour bus driver whips past them, insist on stopping to look – they're far more interesting than the tombs – because the drivers like to spend half an hour at the Ming Tombs Reservoir which is dead boring. Beyond the stone animals are 12 stone-faced human statues – generals, ministers and officials, each distinguishable by headgear. The avenue culminates at the Dragon and Phoenix Gate.

Thirteen of the 16 Ming Emperors are buried in a 40 sq km area at Shisanling but only one tomb, Dingling, has been excavated. Others can be viewed from the exterior like Changling, which was started in 1409 and took 18 years to complete. This is the tomb of the Emperor Yong Le, and so the story goes, 16 concubines who were buried alive with his corpse.

Dingling is the tomb of Emperor Wan Li (1573-1620) and is the second largest tomb. It was excavated in 1956-8 and you can visit the underground passageways and caverns. The emperor used half a million workers, a heap of silver and six years to build his necropolis and then held a wild party inside the completed chambers. The underground covers 1195 sq metres, entirely built of stone, and sealed with an unusual lock stone. The tomb yielded 26 lacquered trunks of funerary objects, some of which are displayed on-site; others have been removed to Beijing Museums and replaced with copies. Wan Li and his royal spouses

were buried in double coffins surrounded by chunks of uncut jade – the jade was thought to have the power to preserve the dead, or could have bought millions of bowls of rice for starving peasants, so the Chinese tour literature relates. Meanwhile cultural relics experts as well as chefs are studying the ancient cookbooks unearthed from Dingling with a view to serving Wan Li's favourite dishes to visitors, using replicas of imperial banquet tableware. Until they figure that one out, you might have to content yourself with the amusing cardboard cut-outs and other props used by Chinese photographers at the site.

The tombs lie 50 km north-west of Beijing and four km from Changping. The tour buses usually combine them with a visit to the Great Wall. You can also get there on the local buses; take bus No 5 or No 44 to Deshengmen, then No 345 to Changping, then No 314 to the Tombs (or hitch the last stretch).

## The North-Western Suburbs

About five to 15 km from downtown, the north-west suburban area has a number of attractions – the Summer Palaces, Western Hills, Azure Clouds Temple and the Sleeping Buddha Temple. You can easily get there on the local buses or by bicycle. Some round-trip suggestions: bus No 332 from the Zoo to the Old Summer Palace and to the Summer Palace; change to bus No 333 for the Western Hills; change to bus No 360 to go directly back to the zoo. Another round route is to take the subway to Pingguoyan (the last stop in the west) and then take bus No 318 bus to the Western Hills, change to No 333 for the Summer Palace, and then to No 332 for the zoo.

## Beida Daxue (Beijing University)

Beijing has about 50 Colleges and Universities – a curious one is the Minorities Institute (Minzuxueyan), just north of the Zoo. The institute trains cadres for the minority regions.

Beijing University (Beida) and Qinghua University are the most prestigious institutes in China. Beida was founded at the turn of the century – it was then called Yanjing University and was administered by the Americans. Its students figured prominently in the May 4th 1919 demonstrations, and the later resistance against the Japanese. In 1953 the University moved from Coal Hill to its present location; in the 1960s the Red Guards first appeared here and the place witnessed some scenes of utter mayhem as the persecutions of the Cultural Revolution took place. Today there are about 200 foreign students at Beida, studying a range of subjects. The shopping district for Beida is the Haidian area to the south, where students congregate in the small restaurants and locals from surrounding communes come in to stock up on provisions. Beida is on No 332 bus route from the Zoo, or about 45 minutes cycle from downtown. Further east, past Qinghua University, is the Beijing Languages Institute (B.L.I.) with about 400 foreign students. The institute is on the No 331 bus route.

### Yuanmingyuan (Old Summer Palace)

The original Yuanmingyuan was laid out in the 12th century. By the reign of the Emperor Qianlong, it developed into a set of interlocking gardens. Qianlong set the Jesuits to work as architects for a set of European palaces for the gardens – elaborate fountains, baroque statues, kiosks included. In the second Opium War (1860), foreign troops destroyed the place and sent the booty abroad. Since the Chinese pavilions and temples were made of wood they did not survive fires, but a marble facade, some broken columns and traces of the fountains stick out of the rice paddies. The ruins are a favourite picnic spot for foreigners living in the capital and for Chinese couples seeking a bit of privacy. The ruins can be reached on foot (about half an hour) or by bike from Beida – the ruins aren't signposted and they're easy to miss; go north from Beida, turn right along the road to Qinghua University, detour left into the ricefields – and then ask whoever happens to be wandering by.

### Yihuyuan (Summer Palace)

This is an immense park containing some newish Qing architecture. The site had long been a royal garden and it was considerably enlarged and embellished by Emperor Qianlong in the 18th century. He deepened and expanded Kunming Lake with the help of 100,000 labourers – and reputedly surveyed Imperial Navy drills from a hilltop perch. In 1860 Anglo-French troops gutted and looted the place during the Opium War. Empress Dowager Cixi began rebuilding in 1888 using money that was supposedly reserved for the construction of a modern navy – but she did restore a marble boat that sits immobile at the edge of the lake. She had this ugly thing fitted out with several large mirrors and used to dine at the lakeside. In 1900 foreign troops, annoyed by the Boxer Rebellion, had another go at roasting the Summer Palace – restorations took place a few years later, and a major renovation occurred after 1949 (by which time the palace had once more fallen into disrepair).

The original palace was used as a summer residence, an escape from the ferocious heat. The Forbidden City packed up and decamped here for their holidays, so the emphasis is on cool features –water, gardens, etc. It was divided into four sections – court reception, residences, temples and strolling or sightseeing areas. Three-quarters of the park is occupied by Lake Kunming, and most items of structural interest are located toward the east gate or the north gate. The main building is the **Hall of Benevolence and Longevity**, just off the lake toward the east gate. It houses a hardwood throne, and has a courtyard with bronze animals; it was used by the emperor-in-residence for handling state

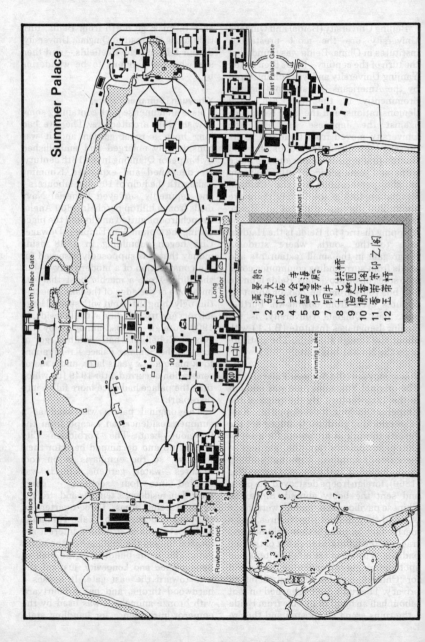

# Summary Palace

East Palace Gate

Rowboat Dock

North Palace Gate

Long Corridor

West Palace Gate

Tong Corridor

Rowboat Dock

Kunming Lake

1 涵虚堂
2 砭大会寺
3 饭会寺
4 云和慧海
5 和慧海
6 仁寿殿
7 祠牛
8 十七拱桥
9 谐趣园
10 佛香阁
11 香岩宗印之阁
12 玉带桥

affairs and receiving envoys. Along the north shore of the lake is the 7228 metre **Long Corridor**, which is decorated with mythical scenes – if the paint looks new it's because a lot of pictures were whitewashed during the Cultural Revolution.

On man-made **Longevity Hill** are a number of temples. The **Pavilion of Precious Clouds** is on the western slopes and is one of the few structures to escape destruction by the Anglo-French forces. It contains some elaborate bronzes. At the top of the hill sits the Buddhist **Temple of the Sea of Wisdom**, made of glazed tiles: good views of the lake can be had from this spot.

Other buildings are largely associated with Empress Cixi like the place where she kept Emperor Guangxu under house arrest, the place where she celebrated her birthdays, and exhibitions of her furniture and memorabilia. It's a very Disneylandish atmosphere that pervades this 'museum': tourists can have their photos taken, imperial dress-up fashion, down by the lakeside just east of the marble boat. In the same vicinity is the *Tingliguan Restaurant* serving banquet imperial food on regal tableware look-alikes (fish from Lake Kunming, velvet chicken, dumplings). Splendid al fresco location, exorbitant prices, housed in what was once an imperial theatre, and has souvenir shops attached.

Other noteworthy features of the Summer Palace are the seventeen arch bridge spanning 150 metres to South Lake Island – on the mainland side is a beautiful bronze ox; the **Jade Belt Bridge**

down the mid-west side of the Lake; and the **Garden of Harmonious Interest** at the north-east end (a copy of a Wuxi garden). You can get around the lake to the bridges by rowboat: boating and swimming are popular pastimes for the locals (windsurfing for the richer) – in winter it's skating. As with the Forbidden City Moat, slabs of ice are cut out of the lake in winter and stored for summer use.

The Park is open 7 am to 6 pm, admission Y0.10. It's about 12 km north-west of the centre of Beijing. Take bus No 332 from the Zoo. You can can also get there by bicycle – it takes about 1½ to 2 hours from downtown (if you consult a bus map, you'll see the Beijing-Miyun Irrigation Canal feeding from Yuyuan Lake to Kunming Lake – good route for biking, although it's a dirt road – the bus map will show which side of various sections of the canal is bikeable).

### Western Hills

Within striking distance of the Summer Palace, and often combined on a tour, are the Western Hills, another former villa-resort area. On the approach is the **Temple of the Sleeping Buddha (Wofosi)**. During the Cultural Revolution the Buddhas in one of the halls here were replaced by a statue of Mao (since removed). The drawcard is the huge reclining Buddha, 5.2 metres long, cast in copper. The history books place it in the year 1331 but it is most likely a copy. Its weight is unknown but it could be up to 50 tons. It's also barefoot and pilgrims used to make offerings of shoes.

A short distance from the North Gate of Western Hills Park is the **Azure Clouds Temple (Biyunsi)** whose landmark is the **Diamond Throne Pagoda**. Of Indian design, it consists of a raised platform with a central pagoda and stupas around it. The temple was first built in 1366, expanded in the 18th century with the addition of the Hall of Arhats (containing 500 statues representing disciples of Buddha). Dr Sun Yatsen's coffin was placed in the temple in 1925 before being moved to Nanjing: in 1954 the Government renovated Sun's memorial hall which has a picture display of his revolutionary activities.

Like the Summer Palace, the Western Hills area was razed by foreign troops in 1860 and 1900 but a few bits still poke out. A glazed tile pagoda and the remains of the **Zhaomiao** a mock Tibetan temple built in 1780, are both in the same area. The surrounding, heavily-wooded park was a hunting ground for the Emperors, and once contained many pavilions and shrines. It's a favourite strolling spot for the Beijingers, many of whom go to gaze through the gates of the new **Xiangshan Hotel**, the best in Beijing. There is a crowded cable-car to the top of **Incense-Burner Peak** or you can scramble up the

**Xiangshan Park**

Vajra Throne Pagoda

Temple of Azure Clouds (Biyun Si)

Sun Yat-sen Memorial Hall

North Gate

*Spectacles Lake*

Stele of Western Hills Shimmering in Snow

Unbosoming Chamber

Glazed-Tile Pagoda

Temple of Brilliance

Incense Burner Peak

Tiered-Cloud Villa

Fourth Jade Flower Villa

Hibiscus Hall

Pavilion of Scattered Clouds

East Gate

Pavilion of Varied Scenery

Jade Flower Villa

*Jingcui Lake*

Sun-Facing Cave

Moonlight Villa

Eighteen turns

Xiangshan Hotel

Jade Scepter Cliff

Temple of Red Glow

Halfway Pavilion

Jade Fragrance Hall

White Pine Pavilion

Site of Xiangshan Temple

Red-Leaf Grove

Twin Lakes Villa

slopes. From the peak you can get an all-embracing view of the countryside. You might also like to hunt for a restaurant (called the Xiangshan, but not linked with hotel) serving excellent spring-rolls, fried duck liver, spiced pork and fried noodles – service is said to be slow so some people place their orders, ramble off around the 150 hectares of parkland, and come back to the table.

To get to the hills take bus No 333 from the Summer Palace; bus No 360 from the zoo; bus No 318 from Pingguoyan (the last stop in the west on the subway).

Directly south of the Western Hills is *Badachu*, the 'Eight Great Sites', which is a Chinese tourist destination. It has eight monasteries or temples scattered in wooded valleys. The 'Second Site' has the Buddha's tooth pagoda, built to house the sacred fang and accidentally discovered when the allied army demolished the place in 1900. Badachu is a military zone – you might accidentally end up there on a magical mystery tour from Qianmen ticket/tour office; otherwise take bus No 347 which runs there from the Zoo (it crosses the No 318 route).

## The Outlying Areas
### Tanzhe Si (Tanzhe Temple)
South-west of Badachu, or 45 km directly west of Beijing, is Tanzhe Si, the largest of all the Beijing temples, occupying an area of 260 metres by 160 metres. It's a Buddhist complex with a long history – first mentions place it as early as the 3rd century (Jin Dynasty) and it has structural modifications from Liao, Tang, Ming and Qing Dynasties. It therefore has a number of features – dragon-decorations, mythical animal sculptures, grimacing gods – no longer found in temples in the capital. The temple takes its name from its proximity to the Dragon Pool (longtan) and some *Zhe* trees. The Zhe trees nourish silkworms and provides a yellow dye – and the bark of the tree is believed to cure women of sterility, which may explain why there are few *zhe* trees left at the temple

entrance. Locals come to the Dragon Pool to pray for rain during droughts.

Transport: bus No 336 from Zhanlanguan Lu which runs off Fuchengmenwai Dajie north-west of Yeutan Park – take this bus to the terminus at Mentougou and then hitch. A direct route is bus No 307 from Qianmen to the Hetan terminus and then a no-number bus to the temple. Alternatively, subway to Pingguoyan, bus No 336 to Hetan and the no-number bus to the temple.

### Lugouqiao (Marco Polo Bridge)
Publicised by the great traveller himself, the Reed Moat Bridge is made of grey marble, is 231 metres long, has over 250 marble balustrades with carved lions – the challenge is to try to add up the number of lions, large and small (allow several days for this task). First built 1192, the original arches were washed away in the 17th century. The bridge is a composite of different eras – lately widened in 1969.

The bridge stands near the little town of Wanping and will probably be most remembered in Chinese history not for its connection with Marco Polo but as the site of an incident which sparked off full-scale war with the Japanese in 1937. On the night of July 7 Japanese troops illegally occupied a railway junction outside Wanping – Japanese and Chinese soldiers started shooting at each other and that gave Japan enough of an excuse (as if they really needed one!) to attack and occupy Beijing.

You can get to the bridge by taking bus No 109 to Guanganmen and then catching bus No 339. Alternatively take bus No 335 to Fengtai and change to bus No 313. By bicycle it's about a 16 km trip.

### Zhoukoudian
Site of those primaeval Chinese the Peking Men; 48 km south-west of Beijing –there's a dig-site here and a fossil Exhibition Hall and you'd have to be a fossil to stay at either for more than 15 minutes. On display are models, stone

tools, the skeletons of prehistoric creatures and laborious explanations about the evolution of Peking Man (basically Darwinian but given a Marxist twist – 'labour created man'). The display was set up in 1953 and expanded in 1972; the cave has suffered serious damage and pollution.

There is an interesting story attached to the Peking Man skull: earlier this century, villagers around Zhoukoudian found fossils in a local quarry and took them to the local medicine shop for sale as 'dragon bones'. This got back to Beijing, and archaeologists – foreign and Chinese – poured in for a dig. Many years later, a molar was extracted from the earth, and the hunt for a skull was on. They found him in the late afternoon on a day in December 1929, *Sinanthropus Pekinensis* – a complete skullcap. The cap was believed to be half a million years old – if so then it rates as one of the missing links in the evolutionary chain. Research on the skull was never carried out; when the Japanese invaded in 1937 the skullcap was packed away with other dig results and the whole lot vanished. The Chinese accused the Americans, the Americans accused the Japanese, and the mystery remains. Other fragments surfaced from Zhoukoudian after 1949, but no comparable treasure was found.

The museum is open 9 am to 4 pm, Wednesday to Sunday. In theory you need a permit; in practice you could get a suburban train (721/724) from Yongdingmen Station, or a bus from the Tianqiao Bus station (near Tianqiao Theatre, west side of Temple of Heaven). The Tianqiao bus station serves the south-west suburbs/areas of Beijing. There may be CITS-organised tour buses to the prehistoric site – ask at the office in the Chongwenmen Hotel.

### Yunshui Caves

In the direction of Zhoukoudian in Fangshan County is a more pedestrian variety of 'cave' – the Yunshui Caves – with coloured lights, passageways and snack bar; some newly-discovered ones in the same area, too.

### Qingxiling (Western Qing Tombs)

Located in Yixian County, 110 km southwest of Beijing. If you didn't see enough at Dingling, Yuling, Yongling and Deling, well, there's always Tailing, Changling, Chongling and Muling – the latter four being part of Xiling. The tomb area is vast and houses the corpses of the emperors, empresses and other members of the royal family. The tomb of Emperor Guangxu (Chongling) has been excavated – his was the last imperial tomb and was constructed between 1905 and 1915.

### Zhuoxian

Along the road to Qingxiling, 60 km from Beiji is Zhuoxian. In 1980 the Zhouxian Travel Hotel went up here – new wave tourist satellite style with courtyards, bamboo groves, 54 air-con double rooms with an extra fleet of caravans parked at the back with what amounts to 50 more rooms. Hong Kong connections handle the management and dining facilities (Northern Cantonese and Sichuan cuisine). It seems that the hotel is designed to take the overflow from the main hotels in the capital when overbooked. It's about two hours from Beijing.

### Qingdongling (Eastern Qing Tombs)

Qingdongling is Death Valley – five emperors, 14 empresses, 136 imperial consorts – and in the mountains ringing the valley are buried princes, dukes, imperial nurses . . . The approach to the tomb area is a common 'spirit way', similar to that of the Ming Tombs but with the addition of marble-arch bridges. The materials for the tombs come from all over China – 20-ton logs pulled over iced roads, and giant stone slabs.

Two of the tombs are open. Emperor Qianlong (1711-1799) started preparations when he was 30, and by the time he was 88 the old boy had used up 90 tons of his silver – his resting place covers half a square km. Some of the beamless stone chambers are decorated with Tibetan and Sanskrit sutras; the doors bear bas-relief Bodhisattvas. Empress Dowager Cixi also got a head start; her tomb, Dingdong, was completed some three decades before her death. The phoenix, symbol of the empress, appears above that of the dragon (the emperor's symbol) in the artwork at the front of the tomb – not side by side as on other tombs. Both tombs were plundered in the 1920s.

The tombs are located in Zunhua County, 125 km east of Beijing. These have more to see in them than the Ming Tombs but after the Forbidden City – who cares? Again, the scenery may make the visit worthwhile. The only way to go is by bus and it's a rough ride, though tour buses are considerably more comfortable. Bureaucratically speaking you need a permit for Zunhua, but if you're on a day-trip bus tour then it's plain sailing. Tour buses take three or four hours to get there, and you have about three hours on site. It may be possible to make a one-way trip to Zunhua and then take off to somewhere else rather than go back to Beijing; there is a road to Chengde and a little way north

along this road on the way to Chengde is a piece of the Great Wall.

### Jixian

Halfway to Zunhua, the tour bus makes a lunch stop at Jixian, more interesting than Zunhua. If you have a permit you could hop a regular long-distance bus from Guangqumenwai bus station, south-east of Beijing Main Station. Jixian is also connected by a direct rail link to Tianjin.

The Jixian area is about 90 km due east of Beijing and is little explored by individuals. In the west gate is the Temple of Solitary Joy (Dulesi); the main multi-storey wooden structure, the Avolokitesvara Pavilion, qualifies for the oldest such structure in China at 1000 years of age. It houses a 16 metre high statue of a Bodhisattva which rates as one of China's largest terracotta statues, and has 10 heads mounted on it. The Buddha is Liao Dynasty and the murals inside are Ming Dynasty. The complex has been recently restored.

To the north-west of Jixian is **Pan Shan**, ranked among the 15 famous mountains of China – wooded hills, springs, streams.

# Tianjin

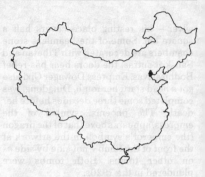

Tianjin is the 'Shanghai of the North' – a reference to its common concession background, heavy industrial output, large port, and direct administration by the central government. In terms of energy and character, however, Tianjin is more like a mongrel cross between Beijing and Shanghai – dowdier than Shanghai, more stimulating than Beijing.

The city's fortunes are, and always have been, linked to those of Beijing. When the Mongols established Beijing as the capital in the 13th century, Tianjin first rose to prominence as a grain storage point. Pending remodelling of the Grand Canal by Kublai Khan, tax-grain was routed along the Yangtse River, out into the open sea, up to Tianjin, and then through to Beijing. With the Grand Canal fully functional as far as Beijing, Tianjin was at the intersection of both inland and port navigation routes. By the 15th century, the town was a walled garrison; in the 17th century Dutch envoys described the city thus – 'The town has many temples; it is thickly populated and trade is very brisk – it would be hard to find another town as busy as this in China – because all the boats which go to Beijing, whatever their port of origin, call here, and traffic is astonishingly heavy'.

For the sea-dog western nations, Tianjin was a trading bottleneck too good to be passed up. Then in 1856 Chinese soldiers boarded the *Arrow*, a boat flying the British flag, obstensibly in search of pirates. This was as much of an excuse as the British and the French needed. Their gunboats attacked the forts outside Tianjin, forcing the Chinese to sign the Treaty of Tianjin (1858). That treaty opened Tianjin up to foreign trade and also legalised the sale of opium. However, the Chinese refused to ratify the treaty immediately, and were none too happy about a concession so close to Beijing.

Finally the French and British bombarded Tianjin in 1860, marched on Beijing, looted it, and coerced another treaty – mainly concerned with opening Tianjin as a concession.

The English and the French settled in; between 1895 and 1900 they were joined by the Japanese, Germans, Austro-Hungarians, Italians and Belgians. Each of the concessions was a self-contained world – its own prison, school, barracks, hospital – and being so close together, it was possible to traverse the national styles of national architecture in the course of a few hours, from Via Vittorio Emanuele to Cambridge Rd. One could cross from the flat roofs and white housing of the Italian concession, past the Corinthian columns of the banks along the Rue de France, down to the manicured lawns of Victorian mansions, and while away the wee hours of the morning dancing at the German Club (now a library). The palatial life was broken only in 1870 when the locals attacked the French-run orphanage and killed, amongst others, ten of the nuns – apparently the Chinese thought the children were being kidnapped. Thirty years later during the Boxer Rebellion the foreign powers levelled the walls of the old Chinese city. Other than that, the European presence stimulated trade and industry – salt, textiles, glass – but heavy silting of the Hai River forced a new port to be built at Tanggu, 50 km downstream.

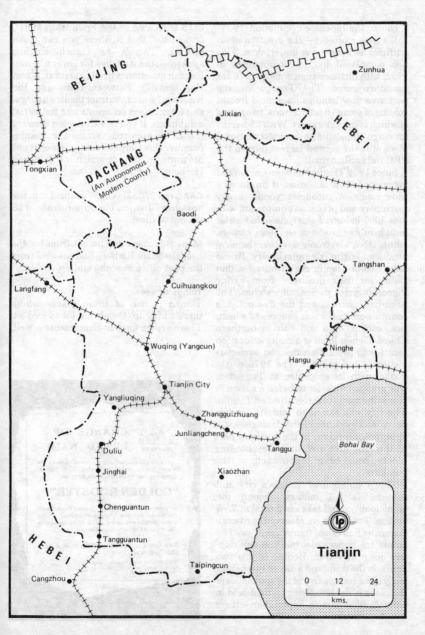

BEIJING

HEBEI

Zunhua

Jixian

Tongxian

DACHANG
(An Autonomous
Moslem County)

Baodi

Tangshan

Langfang

Cuihuangkou

Wuqing (Yangcun)

Ninghe

Hangu

Tianjin City

Yangliuqing

Zhangguizhuang

Junliangcheng

Tanggu

Bohai Bay

Duliu

Jinghai

Xiaozhan

Chenguantun

Tangguantun

Tianjin

HEBEI

Taipingcun

Cangzhou

0       12       24
kms.

During the Japanese occupation (1937-45), a major project – the creation of an artificial harbour – was undertaken. This was completed by the communists in 1952, with further expansions in 1976 for container cargo. The Tanggu-Xingang port area now handles an annual freight volume of some 10 million tons, two thirds of which is import-export. With 25 berths for cargo ships, and several international piers, it is the second largest port in the PRC (after Shanghai).

Since 1949 Tianjin has been earmarked for major industrialisation; it produces a wide range of consumer goods, heavy machinery and precision equipment, with over 3000 industrial enterprises. Industries include rubber products, elevators, carpets, autos, steel, electronic devices, chemical products, engineering machinery. Brand names from Tianjin are favoured within China for their quality – from Flying Pigeon bicycles to Seagull watches. The suburban districts and the five outlying counties are important sources of wheat, rice, cotton, corn and fish in northern China. Tianjin itself is a major education centre with two universities and numerous institutes and colleges. The 1976 earthquake, with its epicentre at Tangshan, (the greatest disaster to befall a nation in recent memory) severely affected Tianjin. The city was closed to tourists for two years, and evidence of the damage is still apparent, especially in the northern part of the city. Five and six-storey housing blocks have been constructed at the outskirts.

The population of Tianjin's city and suburbs is 5.3 million, though the municipality itself takes in a total of 7.76 million. The locals are reserved hard-core starers as individual tourists are few. The hotels are impossible, but you can daytrip down here from Beijing in just two hours on the train, and a day or two here is really quite enough. One of the specialities of the place is the kite-flying festival held in early April or late in September – it's a two-day contest.

**CITS** is located in the Friendship Hotel, or, at least, that is where you can make contact. There's not much English spoken, so the staff dive for cover when an English question is fired (run for it, it's an Englishman!). Between them and the hotel staff you can extract theatre listings, and information on events like industrial exhibitions. If you're well-heeled then try the CITS escorted tour to the Tianjin Number One Carpet Factory, which is out of town in the direction of Xingang Harbour.

**CAAC** (tel 37055) is at 57 Hubei Lu in the downtown district. The airport is about 18 km out of town.

**Maps** Bus maps can be got from booths near the Main Railway Station, and from the post office near the station.

**Things to See**

Tianjin is one of those places where there's little to 'see', but a lot to look at. There are no ancient monuments – well,

there are a few odd ones – so your attention is directed to the streets and to the European structural jigsaws – and there's the back-street sauntering, eating, shopping, and a touch of nightlife.

Quasi-sights fall into two kinds; handicraft factories (cloisonne plant, ceramic workshops and so on) and the odd museum. There is a third variety, the parks, but they're hardly worth the effort.

### Water Park
To the south-west, the Water Park is artificial in more ways than one. It has islands, bridges, a small zoo, boating, a museum with Ming & Qing paintings, and a restaurant. Very large, very boring.

### Friendship Club
Down that way is the Friendship Club where sons of high cadres linger over cues in the oak-panelled billiards room, set up their own bowling pins, or dive into the stagnant swimming pool – what more fitting scene for the old British Country Club? The place does have a posh western-style restaurant . . .

### Industrial Exhibition Hall
In the vicinity of the Friendship Club is the Industrial Exhibition Hall, which shows all the products that Tianjin locals will never get to buy (enquire elsewhere if a trade fair is in progress – otherwise there will be no exhibition).

### Museums
There are five or so in Tianjin. The **Natural History Museum**, down the fossil-end of town near the Friendship Club, should be spared the trouble unless you're a specialist. The **Historical Museum** over the south-eastern side of the Hai River, at the edge of a triangular park, contains 'historical and revolutionary relics of the Tianjin area'. The **Zhou Enlai Memorial Museum** is on the western side of the city on Fourth Avenue, in the Nankai District) – it's situated in the eastern building of Nankai School. Zhou Enlai studied here,

so his classroom is enshrined and there are photos and other memorabilia from his youth, circa 1913-17. If you can't find it, just ask for 'Zhouenlai Tongzhi Qingnianshidai Zai Tianjin Geming Huidong Jinian Guan'. Sorry, just change that to Nankai School.

### Art Gallery
The Art Gallery is at 77 Jiefang Beilu, one stop from the main railway station, easy to get to, and is pleasant to stroll around. It's open 8.30 am to noon, and 2 pm to 6 pm. The gallery is housed in an imposing rococo mansion and has a small but choice collection of brush paintings, painting and calligraphy from bygone eras on the ground floor, folk-art products such as New Year pictures, Zhang family clay figurines and Wei family kites from the Tianjin area on the second floor, and special displays on top floor.

Far more engrossing than any of the preceding is the fact that Tianjin itself is a museum of European architecture from the turn of the century. One minute you're in little Vienna, turn a corner and you could be in a London street, hop off a bus and you're looking at some vintage French wrought-iron gates, or a neo-Gothic cathedral. If you're an architecture student – go no further – Tianjin is a textbook of just about every style imaginable – a draftsman's nightmare or a historian's delight, depending on which way you look at it. Poking out of the post-earthquake shanty rubble could be a high rise castle of glass and steel; and anyone with a sense of humour will be well-satisfied with some of the uses that the bastions of the European well-to-do have been put to.

Tianjin traffic is equally as mixed; horse carts, cyclists with heavy loads struggling to make it across an intersection before an ambush from a changing light cuts them off, a parent with a kid in a bicycle sidecar. Judiciously selected buses will take you through as many former concessions as you want – and presuming that you have a window seat, this kind of random touring will be quite rewarding, architecturally speaking.

There's enough action on the main shopping drags of Tianjin and around the former Chinese city to keep even the most hardened of alley-cats interested. Some of these features are described in the touring section further on, but should one have the time, there's much more that is not described. Coming from Beijing, Tianjin (another megalopolis) is not exactly what you would call a refreshing sight – and the one quality that would make a difference is largely absent. This is a reference to something found very easily in Shanghai – personal local contact. Free-roaming tourists are regarded in Tianjin with a mixture of apathy, suspicion and downright rudeness, which doesn't help. College or university students eager to experiment with their English can provide some relief – and since Tianjin is off the touring track, they're not the kind that breathe down your neck, or corner you. They are, however, hard to find.

**Touring Tianjin**

The following is a combined bus, subway and foot tour which will whip you round the streets, the eating holes and the buy-and-sell stretches – allow at least three hours. The route follows an elliptical shape in a clockwise direction, starting at the Main Railway Station and taking in the Art Gallery, Kiesling's, Arts & Crafts Factory, old Chinese sector, Heping Lu, downtown district. Because opening and closing hours for places mentioned may not fit your own schedule, you might skip some places, or return to them later, or do the route in reverse, or just scrap the whole thing and use the information as you see fit. If you have a bit more time, then more walking is preferable at the beginning and end of the tour.

**Step One – The Main Railway Station** Turn right out of the Main Railway Station;

you'll find the 24-hour-a-day baggage room with its windows facing onto the street – dump your bags here. Get a bus map – they're available from booths near the station and also from the post office near the station. To catch the elusive No 13 bus, continue past the baggage offices to the end of the street, turn left, walk 1½ blocks south and you'll find the terminus queue (the No 13 bus actually goes back towards the station first before heading over Jiefang Bridge into town).

**Step Two – The No 13 Bus Route** First stop is the former French concession and the Art Gallery. The Art Gallery is open 8.30 am to noon and 2 pm to 6 pm. If you're interested in Tianjin folk art in the buying sense, this would be a logical stop-over as the best examples are to be found within.

Second stop – you are now entering the former British concession. The Tianjin No 2 Hotel is on your left.

Third stop – is the park near the Tianjin Hotel, the Tianjin No 1 Hotel and the Friendship Store.

Fourth stop – get off, definitely! This lands you between the Friendship Hotel and Kiesling's. Just ahead of the bus stop is Shengli Lu, a wide boulevard. If you turn left on Shengli and walk about five minutes, you'll arrive at Kiesling's, open 11 am to 1 pm and 5 pm to 8 pm. It's an excellent place to knock off those long overdue postcards in grub-street art-deco splendour. Should Kiesling's not be open at the time, the retail outlet, while not architecturally stimulating, has enough ammunition in it to keep you in dental bills for many years to come – all good high-energy walking food. It's three blocks further east of the restaurant.

**Step Three – The Subway** Go back the same way you came (along Shengli Lu) and go past the fourth bus stop – you will see a subway exit on the north side of Shengli Lu. Tianjin's subway, 5.2 km long, opened in 1982 and can only be described as 'cute'. It has two cars which shuttle back and forth on a single track, serving five stops in all (there are plans to extend it to Tianjin West Station). There's nothing to see down in the depths except the subterranean bathroom tiling, but it saves a lot of paperwork with buses. The subway is open 5.45 am to 7.30 pm. Ride it to the last (fifth) stop. When you surface, there is a bus which will take you to the Arts & Crafts factory, though you may wish to skip this.

**Step Four – The Arts & Crafts Factory** The factory is open 7.30 am to 4.30 pm (and it remains open through the usual lunchtime siesta). It's a bit tricky to find the No 25 bus stop that will get you there – it's just west of the fifth subway exit. Take the bus for seven long stops west – the factory is at the west end of Huanghe Lu, Nankai District. The bus will drop you quite close to the factory; they're used to group tours roving through, so they won't object to you.

The factory has about 20 product lines; feather paintings, paper and silk cuts, shell paintings, embroidery. The main draw is the kites, made of silk paper and bamboo, soft and rigid forms in the shapes of goldfish, frogs, butterflies, birds and dragons, handpainted in vivid colours – prices range from Y10 to Y60 each. Some of the kites have bamboo whistles and musical attachments activated by wind. The retail shop is on the top floor, but on the way you can see the factory workers doing their 'shift' – strange to see an assembly line of artists busily painting their goose eggs.

**Step Five – Chinatown** My apologies in advance for this misnomer – couldn't resist it. If you're returning from the A & C Factory, take bus No 25 back to the subway terminus.

The old Chinese sector can easily be identified on the bus map as a rectangle with buses running around the perimeter. Roughly, the bounding roads are Beima (north horse), Nanma (south horse), Xima (west horse) and Dongma (east horse). Originally there was one main north-south street, crossing an east-west one within that (walled) rectangle.

Within this area you can spend time fruitfully exploring the lanes and side-streets where traditional architecture remains – and perhaps even find a dilapidated temple or two. Basically, though, this is a people-watching place, where you can get snatches of daily life through doorways. There's a good run of shops on Nanma, Dongma and Beima Lu.

**Step Six – Heping Lu** A massive shopping drag extends from the West Station down via Beima Lu, where it meets another shopping drag coming from the North Station (along Zhongshan Lu); both of these snake down the length of Heping Lu as far as Zhongxin Park.

If you make your way on foot along Nanma Lu, the southern fringe of 'Chinatown', you'll arrive at the top end of Heping Lu. As you turn right onto Heping, a little way down, there's a nice *jiaozi* shop upstairs at No 74 – it's a green-fronted building near a musical instruments shop. Open 10.30 am to 1.30 pm and 4.30 pm to 7.30 pm; you can get a large amount of dumplings and a beer for Y0.80.

Going south on Heping, you will find a busy alley, Rongji Jie, leading off to the right – plenty more food, but try to save some space in the lower intestines for the *Goubuli* dumpling shop which is a little way off yet. From Rongjie Jie you can walk on south, or jump a bus several stops down Heping to the heart of the shopping district – Downtown.

**Step Seven – Downtown** Buzzing with activity till late in the evening (8 pm!), crammed with theatres, speciality shops, restaurants, large department stores, icecream parlours. The walking street is Binjiang Dao, with alleyways and other shopping streets gathered around it –

1 艺术博物馆
2 第二饭店
3 第一饭店
4 友谊商店
5 友谊饭店
6 地下铁道第五站
7 荣吉胡同儿
8 狗不理饱子铺
9 劝业场百货商店
10 中国民用航空总局
11 登瀛楼饭店
12 烤鸭店
13 川苏菜馆
14 火车信票处
15 起士林饭店
16 周恩来纪念馆
17 绞子店
18 红旗饭庄
19 红桥饭店
20 天津市百货商店

1 Art Gallery
2 Tianjin No. 2 Hotel
3 Tianjin No. 1 Hotel / CITS
4 Friendship Store
5 Friendship Hotel / CITS
6 5th Subway Exit
7 Rongji Hutong
   (location of restaurants
   in small alley)
8 Goubuli Baozi Shop
   (in alley not marked on map)
9 Quanyechang Dept. Store
10 CAAC
11 Dengyinglou Restaurant
12 Tianjin Roast Duck
   (Tianjin Kaoya) Restaurant
13 Chuansu Sichuan Restaurant
14 Advance Rail Ticket Office
15 Kiessling's Food Restaurant
16 Zhou Enlai Memorial Museum
17 Jiaozi Shop
18 Red Flag Restaurant
19 Red Bridge Restaurant
20 Tianjin Dept. Store

something like eight whole blocks of concentrated shopping. The business volume per square metre here works out to something like Y10,000 a year, so it's as good as gold.

You can find just about anything – from silk flowers to a hot bath – many boutiques, curio stores and emporiums. The area is particularly lively between 5 pm and 8pm, when the streets are thronged with excited shoppers and ingoing theatre fans. The poster shop has a very nice selection of prints and children's books.

Quanyechang (Encouraging Industrial Development Emporium) is the largest department store, with more than 200,000 customers a day and an income in 1982 of Y160,000,000. Besides selling a large variety of consumer goods, the emporium has two theatres and some electronic amusement facilities. The original smaller Quanyechang has a fascinating balcony

interior – if you follow the galleries around they will eventually lead into the main seven-storey block (the older section was founded in 1926).

Some western trends in the downtown district include locals examining public phone boxes (a rare item on the streets of China) and an eyewear shop (next to the second-hand store on Binjiang). At the south-eastern fringes of the downtown district are some street markets, mostly food. Speaking of which, don't miss out on *Goubuli Baozi* restaurant, which is open 10.30 am to 7.30 pm. Justly famous.

**Step Eight – The Home Run** A bus No 24 will get you back to the main station – you can pick it up opposite the Dengyinglou Restaurant on the north section of Binjiang. Alternatively, stroll back along the banks of the Hai River – a popular pastime with the locals – photo booths, fishing, early morning taichi, opera-singer

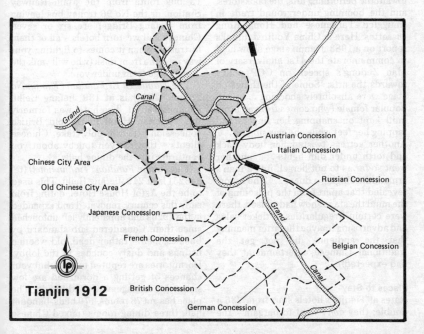

practice and old men toting bird cages. The Hai River esplanades have a peculiarly Parisian touch, in part due to the fact that some of the railing and bridge work is French.

At the north end of town are half a dozen canals that branch off the Hai River – one vantage point is Xigu Park (take bus No 5 running from near the main station and passing by West Station).

### Nightlife

Tianjin is on the nightlife circuit, so to speak, for travelling troupes, and has its own stable of local talent, trained at the Tianjin School of Traditional Opera. There are half a dozen theatres and cinemas in the downtown district; some of them carry display boards with scenes from what's offered. As of mid-1983, a resurgence of the Chinese battle with 'bourgeois ideology' was under way, with a clean up campaign directed mainly toward the performing arts, the bookstores, and the booming underground trade in smuggled Taiwanese and Hong Kong cassettes. Here is China Youth Journal's report on a 1983 Tianjin stage show held to commemorate the 41st anniversary of Mao Zedong's speech on CCP policy towards the arts: 'Some of the things on stage were absolutely shocking . . . One popular female (who comes from an army unit) kept on snapping her fingers and tapping her feet while she was singing . . . Another actress twisted her body back and forth under dim lights . . . another went so far as to put herself into a man's arms while singing a duet . . . ' The report revealed that apart from the poisoning of the mind the stage show had caused, there were certain irregularities in ticket sales and advertising (maybe the latter meaning that the audience did not get the traditional Chinese entertainment they had expected!).

### Places to Stay

Rates at Tianjin's hotels start from Y36 a double; they *don't* want to bargain – the staff will put you on hold pending the arrival of the manager (invariably nowhere to be found) – that is, assuming there are any empty rooms to begin with. Hotels are full of foreign businessmen who stay for one or two months or longer.

Unless you've got the money, or can work your way into a Chinese hotel, or ingratiate yourself into one of the university residences, or the Foreign Language Institute (or a church or bath house?), you may end up back at the station. The Tangshan earthquake of 1976 aggravated an already serious housing shortage so there are no new tourist hotels being built. A smart move is to dump your luggage at the station (there's a 24-hour left luggage) – so if the worst comes to worst, you can stay up late somewhere without having to cart your gear around. Alternatively, make Tianjin a day-trip from Beijing.

Strung along Jiefang Beilu (on the No 13 bus route from the Main Railway Station, or the No 96 trolley bus leaving from Jiefang Bridge) are six or seven Chinese and western hotels – all of them fortresses when it comes to fighting your way past the front desk (who will yank the drawbridge from under you).

The *Tianjin Di Er Fandian (Tianjin No 2)* (tel 32887) is at 189 Jiefang Beilu, Heping District. The hotel was formerly the Victorian Hotel in the old British concession. It will only take Chinese clients – they're even touchy about you venturing into the dining halls.

The *Tianjin Fandian (Tianjin hotel)* (tel 34325) is at 219 Jiefang Beilu. This used to be the Astor House Hotel, dating from early this century, renovated and expanded in the 1920s and apparently left untouched since then. Considered sub-standard by businessmen – rather dead, old wooden fittings and dusty couches in the lobby. Dormitories are reputed to exist, but your chances of getting a dorm bed are low since the management is difficult. The place has got 78 rooms, 170 beds, banquet hall, three dining rooms (mixed Chinese styles). Situated near what was once Victoria Park, take bus No 13 three stops from the Main Railway Station.

The *Tianjin Di Yi Fandian (Tianjin No 1)* (tel 36438) is at 198 Jiefang Beilu. This is a prime businessman location and its got single rooms and suites which are perpetually full. There's zero chance that you will squeeze in. The hotel is close to the Friendship Store – take bus No 13 three stops from the Main Station and walk one block south. The hotel phone number is also the number of CTS, and the hotel has a service counter for Overseas Chinese.

The *Youyi Fandian (Friendship Hotel)* (tel 35663) is at 100 Shengli Lu. It's a nine-storey Holiday Inn-type place, built in 1975 in an air-con deluxe style with 209 rooms and 380 beds. Prices range from Y36 for a double to Y70 for a suite. Take bus No 13 four stops from the Main Railway Station and then walk west on Shengli Lu for about ten minutes.

The *Tianjin Grand* (tel 39613) is on Youyi Lu, Hexi District. And grand it is; 1000 beds in two high-rise blocks built in 1960 in the air-con deluxe style, complete with a four-storey conference building, 1500-seat dining room, and 1000-seat auditorium. Room prices start from Y36 for a double. The hotel is set in the gone-to-seed end of town and is deadly quiet. Take bus No 13 five stops from the Main Station and then change to bus No 26 and take it to the southern edge of town.

Other hotels include the *Tianjin Binguan (Tianjin Guest House)* (tel 24010) at 337 Machang Dao, a VIP landscaped garden, villa-style hotel with about 50 rooms – used for international conferences. Two other hotels, probably Chinese-only, are the *Renmin Fandian (People's Hotel)* (tel 23667) at 52 Chifeng Dao, and the *Huizhong Hotel* (tel 25360) at 14 Huazhong Lu. These are both in the vicinity of the downtown shopping district.

### Places to Eat

There's some wonderful digestibles in Tianjin, which is more than you can say for most places in China. If you're staying longer, you can get a small group together, phone ahead, and negotiate gourmet delights. 'Tianjin flavour' specialties are mostly in the seasonal seafood line with crab, prawns, cuttlefish soup, and fried carp.

**Downtown District** The *Tianjin Kaoya (Tianjin Roast Duck Restaurant)* (tel 23335) is at 142 Liaoning Lu. You can get Beijing Duck here at (negotiable) Y10 a head for the full works, or around Y5 a head if you're keeping to basic duck. This place has Mao Zedong's seal of approval (one doesn't really know if that's positive or positively embarrassing advertising these days) but on the restaurant walls are a couple of black and white photos of a relaxed-looking Mao talking to the chefs and autographing the visitor's book.

The *Chuansu Caiguan* (tel 25142) is at 189 Changchun Dao, and very close to the Tianjin Roast Duck. It serves hot Sichuan food and other styles at around Y6 per head.

The *Dengyinglou* (tel 23594) is at 94 Binjiang Dao; it's one of the best known seafood restaurants and serves Shandong-style seafood (crab in season). Other eateries can be found in this area to suit thinner wallets.

**Rongji Jie** This is an alley running west off the north end of Heping Lu, and has its fair share of restaurants. The *Quanjude* (tel 20046) is just near the alley entrance off Heping; you can't miss it, look for the ducks hanging from the beam outside. The restaurant is open 10.30 am to 2 pm and 4.30 pm to 8 pm. Upstairs are banquet rooms where prices range from Y8 to Y30 per head and upwards. Seafood is expensive (Y14 for a dish of sea-cucumber, a delicacy that chefs love to foist on foreigners, who generally find it alien to their palates). Beijing Duck and Shandong food is served in the restaurant.

Directly opposite the Quanjude is

another duck house, the *Yanchunlou* (tel 22761) at 22 Rongji Jie; Moslem food, lamb dishes, hotpot in winter.

**Western food** The old pre-liberation chefs are still around, or at least they have passed their skills on to a new generation. The famed *Kiesling's* (tel 32030) is at the corner of Xuzhou Lu and Shanghai Lu; it's open 11 am to 1 pm and 5 pm to 8 pm. Pinyinised to Qishilin or Jisiling, and renamed the *Tianjin Restaurant*, it does not disguise the fact that this was the Austrian cafe 'Kiesling and Bader' in the former German concession. On the ground floor there is a bakery and cake shop, and sit-down sundaes, cold drinks, coffee, glacees and floats. Chocolate sundae, with a choice of flavours, is Y1.25 (note the 30 fen deposit on metal spoons!). Upstairs it's full-course meals, a mix of French, British and Italian (hamburger & chips, crab au gratin, wiener schnitzel) but an interesting variation on the cubicle routine has been instituted. A bald-headed pre-liberationer who's been with Kiesling's for 40 odd years will try to shuffle you off to a special section with rattan chairs, silverware, silver service and silver prices (curry beef, usually Y2, costs Y7 in the silver department). Minus the silver service, you could get a meal for Y5 – on the other hand maybe the point of coming here is to get a taste of life in the foreign concessions, not just a taste of the food. One foreigner noted that when the bill came, the price had been jacked up – he happened to read Chinese – when he confronted the waiter, the venerable gentleman demanded to know how the foreigner had noticed the difference – and then made him recite the bits of the menu in Chinese as proof of the error!

As for the hotels, try the ground floor of the *Tianjin No 1 Hotel*; hamburger steak Y1.90; fillet steak & eggs Y3.20; stewed chicken & rice Y2.75; pork chops a la France Y2.20; also cheaper soups, vegetable dishes and dumplings (and there's an English menu). The *Friendship Club* (tel 32465) at the south end of town is reputedly good for western food.

**Finger food** A permanent cake box clipped to a bicycle rack is one of the eccentricities of Tianjin residents – and a pre-requisite for a visit to friends. The best cake boxes come from the direction of Kiesling's retail shop, which is next door to their food factory (three blocks east of Kiesling's Restaurant). Although the restaurant has a shop within selling baked goods, cakes and liqueurs, the retail shop has a superior range of tasty toffees, peanut nougat, pastries and top-notch chocolates. If you have a sweet tooth, it will fall out when you see this place!

Other Tianjin cake varieties: Yangcun rice-flour cake is a pastry produced in Wuqing County in the suburbs, since the Ming dynasty, so they say; it's made from rice and white sugar. Eardrum Fried Sponge cake, made from rice powder, sugar and bean paste, and fried in sesame oil, is so named from the proximity of the shop that makes it to Eardrum Lane (Erduoyan). Another specialty that takes its name from the shop location is 18th Street Sough-Twists, which have a bar inside made of sugar, sesame, nuts and vanilla.

The best area to go snack hunting is in the downtown zone, where you can find both the Chinese and the western varieties – well, mock western. The 'coolest' places to be in Tianjin are the icecream parlours or the sandwich and refreshment hangouts in this district. There's an icecream, cake and cold drink place at 280 Heping Lu, and near the intersection of Binjiang and Heping is the *Cold Comfort Buffet*, a three-storey effort with drink slot-machines (plastic tokens) for the lunch hour rush. Their piece de resistance is a glaceed snowman in a base of fruit salad. This particular place has a window dispensing directly onto the street, which is a practice followed by even some of the major restaurants in the area (roast duck is served this way). As you go south on Binjiang Jie from Heping Lu, you will find some very trendy icecream shops with ghoulish neon and fluorescent interiors – even western music.

King of the dumpling shops is *Goubuli* (tel 23277) at 97 Shandong Lu (down a side street, set back in a courtyard off the street). It's open 10.30 am to 7.30 pm, and is very crowded, it seems, for the whole of that period. Downstairs is cold cuts of meat and vegetables, beer, dumplings and sauces. You have to get tickets first, which makes life complicated for a few greasy *baozi*; you might like to get above the milling crowds and chaos, and try the upper floor where the waiter will run downstairs to purchase tickets for you. This place serves some of the finest dumplings in the nation – so you might as well dine in style, and it won't cost you an arm or a leg to do so. You can back up the dumplings with tea, soup or beer – and you get uppercrust lacquered chopsticks to spear the slippery little devils on your plate. The shop has a century-old history – the staple of the maison is a dough bun filled with high-grade pork, spices and a gravy that disintegrates on contact with the palate. Watch for the baozi with the red dot – this indicates a special filling like chicken or shrimp. Baozi can be ordered by the jin (1 jin = 10 leung = 1/2 kilo = 30 baozi approx). 'Goubuli' has the alarming translation of 'dogs won't touch them' or 'dog doesn't care'. The most satisfying explanation of this seems to be that Goubuli was the nickname of the shop's founder, a man with an extraordinarily ugly face – so ugly that even dogs were turned off by him. The shop turns out about 50,000 buns a day; baozi and jiaozi are Tianjin specialties which are frozen and exported to Japan.

Should you wish to fortify a main meal, an icecream or a coffee, Tianjin produces a variety of liquid substances: there's Kafeijui, which approximates to Kahlua, and there's Sekijiu, which is halfway between vodka and aviation fuel.

## Shopping

The four traditional arts and crafts in Tianjin are New Year posters, clay figurines, kites and carpets. You can also go hunting for antiques and second-hand goods – Tianjin is less picked-over than Beijing. The Quanyechang Dept Store, the Overseas Chinese store and the other department stores are mainly directed toward consumer goods and the craft stocks are low or non-existent, so it's a matter of finding the specialty shops or going to the factory source, where the selection is wider.

**Rugs and carpets** The Friendship Store has a fair stock (Y2080 large woolpile, Y1720 medium silkpile, Y490 small woolpile, Y700 small silkpile), and also has some very intricate 3-D feather paintings (Y1000 apiece) and a big selection of Tianjin medicines. If you're serious about carpets (that's serious money!), the best idea is to get to a factory outlet. There are eight carpet factories in the Tianjin municipality. Making the carpets by hand is a long and tedious process – some of the larger ones can take a proficient weaver over a year to complete. Patterns range from traditional to modern; factory prices are only valid for foreign exporters. The Number One Carpet Factory(tel 49342) is at No 2 Bridge, Jintang Highway, Hedong District and the Number Three Carpet Factory is in the Hexi District. Small tapestries are a side line.

**Kites** are not easily found, and the Friendship Store stock is poor. Again it's better to go direct to the source which is the Arts & Crafts Factory (see the Touring section for directions). The Wei kites were created by master craftsman Mr Wei Yuan Tai at the beginning of the century, although the kite has been a traditional toy in China for thousands of years. One story has it that Mr Wei's crow kite was so good that a flock of crows joined it aloft. The body of this line is made of brocade and silk, the skeleton made of bamboo sticks. Wings can be folded or disassembled, and will pack into boxes (the smaller ones into envelopes). Different kite varieties are made in Beijing, where there is a Kite Arts Company and a Kite Society (Mr Ha Kuiming, the Vice-President of the Society once made a kite with an eight metre diameter – it took two men to hold it back once it got going).

**Clay figurines** The terracotta figures originated in the 19th century from the work of Zhang Ming Shan: his fifth generation descendants train new craftsmen. The small figures take themes from human or deity sources and the emphasis is on realistic emotional expressions. Master Zhang was reputedly so skilful that he carried clay up his sleeves on visits to the theatre and came away with clay opera stars in his pockets. In 1900, during the Boxer Rebellion, western troops came across satirical versions of themselves correct down to the last detail in uniforms. These voodoo dolls were ordered removed from the marketplace immediately! Painted figurines are now much watered down from that particular output; the workshop is at 270 Machang Dao, Hexi District (south end of Tianjin). The Art Gallery on Jiefang Lu has a collection of earlier Zhang family figurines.

**New Year Posters** A batch of these is also on display at the Art Gallery; they first appeared in the 17th century in the town of Yangliuqing, 15 km west of Tianjin proper. Woodblock prints are hand-coloured, and considered to bring good luck and happiness when posted on the front door on Lunar New Year – OK if you like pictures of fat babies done in dayglo colour schemes. Rarer are the varieties that have historical, deity or folk tale representations. There's a salesroom and workshop at 111 Sanheli, Tonglou, Hexi District, and a sales department in the downtown area at 136 Changchun Dao.

**Other** There's a Special Handicrafts Factory at 16 Liuweilu, Hedong District (jade, ivory and wood carving); Cloisonne Factory at Jinggangshandao, Hongxinglou, Hedong District. There are also some second-hand stores selling mostly chintz though some older fur clothing can be found; a few of these stores are downtown, one at 268 Heping, and another at 137 Binjiang. Try Dongma Lu also. The Yilinge Antique Store at 175 Liaoning Lu has bronzes, ceramics, carvings, paintings, calligraphy, and will engrave seals or arrange artist-commission work. The Wenyuange, at 263 Heping Lu, is another curio store, mainly dealing in hardwood furniture, and will arrange packing, customs and delivery.

**GETTING AROUND**
A pox on local transport in this city! It's one of the most confusing places you can take on in China, compounded by the fact that your visit there may turn, by necessity, into a very short one. If your time is indeed limited, refer to the touring section and save yourself the trouble – it's a real mess out there trying to find bus stops. Your chances of getting on a bus at rush-hour are about two per cent – and you'll get a unique chance to find out what it feels like to be buried alive in a pile of people. If you must use a bus then try and ambush it at the point of origin.

Key local transport junctions are the areas around the three rail stations. The Main (that is, the East Station) has the biggest collection: buses 24, 27 and 13, and further out toward the river are numbers 2, 5, 7, 25, 28, 96. At the West Station are buses 24,10 and 31 (numbers 11 and 37 run past West Station); at the North Station are buses 1, 7 and 12.

Another major bus terminus point is located around Zhongxin Park, at the edge of the downtown shopping district. From here you'll get buses 11, 26 and 94, and close by are buses 9, 20 and 37. To the north of Zhongxin Park are buses 1, 91, 92, 93.

A useful bus to know is the No 24, running between Main Station and West Station 24 hours a day. Other bus services run from 5 am to 11 pm.

A few alternatives to the buses are the autorickshaws or the taxis from the railway stations. The 5 km of subway is not greatly useful, but it does get you through some chockablock bits of town. Unfortunately, there doesn't seem to be a bicycle rental. The downtown shopping area can be covered on foot – in fact, some streets are closed to motor traffic.

## GETTING AWAY

**Train** Tianjin is a major north-south rail junction with frequent trains to Beijing, extensive links to the North-Eastern provinces, and southwards to Jinan, Nanjing, Shanghai, Fuzhou, Hefei, Yantai, Qingdao, and Shijiazhuang.

There are three rail stations in Tianjin; Main, North and West. Ascertain the correct station; for most trains you'll want the Main Station; some trains stop at both Main and West, and some go only through the West Station (particularly those originating in Beijing and heading south).

If you have to alight at the West Station, bus No 24 connects the West Station to the Main Station, passing through the downtown shopping district.

The advance rail ticket office in Tianjin is at 284 Heping Lu. After 8 pm you can purchase next day sleeper tickets at one of the windows at the main station; (another window even books advance Chinese hotel reservations for Beijing).

**Trains to/from Beijing** Express trains take just under two hours for the trip between Tianjin and Beijing; normal trains take about 2½ hours. The departure times and train numbers are likely to change, but to give you some idea of the daytripping possibilities, train No 309 departs Beijing at 6.34 am, No 11 at 8 am, No 171 at 8.40 am and No 311 at 9.10 am. Train No 12 departs Tianjin for Beijing at 5.06 pm, No 310 at 6.53 pm and No 172 at 7.47 pm.

Since Tianjin is only two hours from Beijing and three to four hours from Beidaihe/Shanhaiguan, it may be worth buying a through ticket from Beijing to Beidaihe and making Tianjin a stopover; you can then continue on to Beidaihe on the same day using the same ticket. You'll probably have to stand but if you only want to wander around Tianjin for a few hours then it'll be cheaper than buying two tickets. Another rail route worth considering (also served by road) is Tianjin to Beijing via Jixian.

**Plane** Tianjin is connected by air to Beijing(Y24), Canton, (Y265) and Shenyang (Y83). There are twice weekly flights to Hong Kong costing Y330 (HK$1158).

**Boat** Tianjin's port is Tanggu, which was renamed Xingang (New Harbour), so just refer to Tanggu Xingang and everyone will know what you're talking about. The port is 50 km from the centre of Tianjin. There are departures from Tanggu to Dalian and Yantai.

There are boats to Dalian five times a month, departing Tanggu at 12.30 pm and arriving in Dalian about 20 hours later. Fares are Y28.80 de luxe, Y14.90 2nd class and cheaper for 3rd class which should be comfortable enough. There are boats to Yantai about 12 times a month and the trip takes about 30 hours. The 2nd class fare is Y9.10. It is recommended, due to the high volume of passengers on the boats, that the traveller sticks to 4th class and higher. The liners are comfortable, and can take up to 1000 passengers, and are equipped with a bar, restaurant, movies . . .

Tickets for both boats available at Tianjin Gangkeyun Zhan, at 61 Taierzhuang Lu which is in the vicinity of the Friendship Store. Tickets can also be purchased at Tanggu port opposite the Tanggue Theatre, but you'll be best off buying in Tianjin. The embarkation/disembarkation point in Tanggu is opposite Tanggu South Railway Station.

Tickets for either boat can be purchased in Beijing on any day of the month with a 2 or a 7 (I'm not making this up!) eg; 2nd, 7th, 22nd, 27th, at the Qianmen or Yongdingmen ticket offices at the hour of 8 am.

To get to Tanggu from Tianjin take a train from Tianjin South Railway Station. There are also buses. There are also direct trains between Beijing and Tanggu, and Tanggu and Tangshan.

**Bus** There are three long-distance bus stations, with buses running to places that are not in the lexicon of the average traveller's catalogue.

Bus stations are usually located partway along the direction of travel. Nanzhan (Balitai) is on the northeast edge of the Water Park (which is south-west of city centre); Xizhan (Xinqingdao) is outside Tianjin West Railway Station. The bus station of interest is Tianjin Zhan (Dongbei) which has the most destinations and the largest ticket office. It's located just west of the Haihe River, in the north end of Tianjin – a No 24 bus from downtown will land you in the general vicinity. From the Dongbei station you can get buses to Beijing, Jixian, Zunhua and Tangshan and the station also sells advance tickets to many places. The bus station in Beijing for buses to Tianjin is Yongdingmen. Another road route worth considering (also served by rail) is Tianjin to Beijing via Jixian.

**Car** Foreigners with their own cars, ie diplomatic corps or similar, are permitted to drive the Beijing-Tianjin highway with authorisation. Apparently, however, there is no gas station open to foreigners along the route, and no rambling off down the by-ways is allowed.

## EXCURSIONS FROM TIANJIN

Were it not for the abysmal hotel situation, Tianjin would make a fine staging point for trips directly north (to Jixian, Zunhua, Tangshan, Beidaihe), and

a launching pad for roaring into the North-East (Manchuria). Preliminary tour buses have been set up for some northern routes, but it's expensive tour stuff.

### Jixian

Jixian is rated as one of the 'northern suburbs' of Tianjin, though it's actually 125 km from Tianjin City proper. For more details see the section on Beijing.

### Tangshan

Devastated in the earthquake of 1976, Tangshan may be open by now; even if it's not you could drop off there for a few hours en route by train to Beidaihe – or just survey the place from your train window.

### Yangcun and Dagang

It is not clear how much of the actual Tianjin municipality is open – the town of Yangcun (famous for its rice-flour cakes) is listed as open (it's in Wuqing County, about 30 km north-west of Tianjin proper, approachable by rail or road). The Dagang Oilfield is also open; it's to the southeast of Tianjin, approachable by road.

### Tanggu

There are three harbours on the Tianjin municipality stretch of coastline; Hangu (north), Tanggu-Xingang (centre) and Dagang (south). By road or rail you can get to **Tanggu** about 50 km from Tianjin proper (for details, see the 'Getting Away' section) – the road and rail route from Tianjin to Tanggu passes by salt-works which furnish roughly a quarter of the nation's salt. There's a Friendship Store and International Seamen's Club in Tanggu. As for permission to visit, well, the harbour is where 'friends from all over the world' come to drop anchor, and they're used to foreign faces . . . The port is kept open by ice-breakers in winter. The Number One Carpet Factory is in the direction of the port. The factory specialises in cut-pile carpeting and employs about 1,400 people.

# The
# North – East

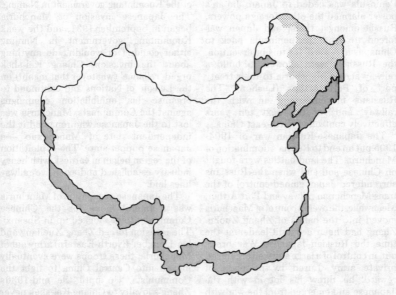

Steam trains, icecream, dusty roads, mud houses, Mao statues, chimney stacks, logging towns, Soviet-clone hotels, red maples, snowcaps ... Manchuria, the north-east, a bleak area that's played more than its fair share in the tumultuous events of 20th century China.

Historically, Manchuria has been the birthplace of the conquerors; maybe there's something about the inhospitable geography of this region that drives successive waves of people southwards, amongst them the Mongols and the Manchus. At the turn of this century Manchuria was a sparsely populated region, but it had rich resources, largely untapped. Both the Russians and the Japanese eyed it enviously. After the Chinese were defeated by the Japanese in the war of 1894-95, the Liaoning Peninsula was ceded to Japan. Japan's power alarmed the other foreign powers, Russia amongst them, and Japan was forced to hand the peninsula back to China; as a 'reward' for this intervention, the Russians were allowed to build a railway across Manchuria to their treaty port of Port Arthur (Lushun). The Russians moved troops in with the railway, and for the next ten years effectively controlled north-east China.

The Japanese-Russian war of 1904-1905 put an end to Russia's domination of Manchuria. The land battles were fought on Chinese soil and when the Russians surrendered Japan gained control of the trans-Manchurian railway and Port Arthur. Meanwhile, the overall control of Manchuria moved into the hands of Zhang Zuolin. Zhang had been a bandit-leader at the time the Russian-Japanese War broke out, in control of a large and well organised private army. Lured by promises of reward, he threw his lot in with the Japanese and emerged from the war with the strongest Chinese army in Manchuria. By the time the Qing Dynasty fell he held the power of life and death in southern Manchuria, and between 1926 to 1928 ran a regional government which was recognised by the foreign powers. He was ousted by the 'Northern Expedition' of the Kuomintang which unified southern and northern China, and forced to retire.

Zhang's policy in Manchuria had been to limit Japan's economic and political expansion, and to break Japan's influence entirely in time. But by the 1920s the militarist Japanese government was ready to take a 'hard line' on China. To them, the advantages of seizing Manchuria were enormous; here was an area of land three times as large as Japan, but with a third of her population; an area of undeveloped mines and timber, and vast agricultural possibilities.

Zhang Zuolin was assassinated (both the Japanese and the Kuomintang were credited); control of Manchuria passed to his son, Zhang Xueliang, with the blessing of the Kuomintang government in Nanjing. The Japanese invasion of Manchuria began in September 1931, and the weak Kuomintang government in Nanjing either couldn't or wouldn't do anything about the invasion. Chiang Kai-shek urged 'reliance' (whatever that meant) on the League of Nations and continued to organise his annihilation campaigns against the Communists. Manchuria was lost to the Japanese who renamed it the independent state of 'Manchukuo' – a Japanese puppet state. The exploitation of the region began in earnest, with heavy industry established and extensive railway lines laid.

The Japanese occupation of Manchuria was a fateful move for the Chinese Communist forces locked up in Shaanxi. The invasion forced Zhang Xueliang and his 'Dongbei' (North-Eastern) army out of Manchuria; these troops were eventually moved into Central China to fight the Communists. Up until the mid-1930s Zhang's loyalty to Chiang Kai-shek never wavered, but he gradually became convinced that Chiang's promises to cede no more territory to Japan and to recover the Manchurian homeland were empty ones. Zhang made a secret truce with the

Communists, and when Chiang Kai-shek flew to Xian in December 1936 to organise yet another extermination campaign against the Communists, Zhang had Chiang arrested. This forced Chiang to call off the extermination campaign and to form an alliance with the Communists to resist the Japanese.

When World War II ended, the north-east suddenly became the focus of a renewed confrontation between the Communist and Kuomintang troops. In February 1945 the meeting of Allied leaders at Yalta discussed the invasion of Japan; Roosevelt was anxious that the Russians should take part, but in return for Soviet support Stalin demanded that Mongolia (part of the Chinese empire until 1911) should be regarded as independent (in fact, a Soviet satellite) and that Russian rights in Manchuria, lost to Japan, should be restored – that meant the restoration of Russian control over trans-Manchurian railways and the commercial port of Dalian and naval base of Port Arthur (Lushun). Chiang Kai-shek wished to keep the Russians favourably disposed and began negotiations for a treaty with the USSR on the basis of the Yalta agreements. A treaty was eventually signed which pledged each side to 'work together in close and friendly collaboration' and to 'render each other every possible economic assistance in the post-war period' – Stalin had sold out the Communists and thrown Russian support behind the Kuomintang. At the Potsdam conference of July 1945 it was decided that the Russians would take the surrender of all Japanese forces in Manchuria and North Korea, and that the Kuomintang would take it elsewhere.

After the A-bombs obliterated Hiroshima and Nagasaki in August 1945 and forced the Japanese to surrender, the Russian armies moved into Manchuria, engaging the Japanese in a brief but bloody conflict before the Japanese surrendered. The Americans started transporting Kuomintang troops by air and sea to the north where they could take the surrender of Japanese forces and regain control of north and central China. The American navy moved in to Qingdao and landed 53,000 marines to protect the railways leading to Beijing and Tianjin and the coalmines which supplied those railways.

The Communists, still in a shaky peace with the Kuomintang also joined the rush for position; although Chiang Kai-shek told them to remain where they were, the Communist troops marched to Manchuria on foot, picking up arms from abandoned Japanese depots as they went. Other Communist forces went north by sea from Shandong. The first Kuomintang attack on the Communists had taken place in November 1945, even while American-organised peace negotiations were taking place between the Communists and the Kuomintang. That attack put an end to the negotiations.

All these moves came within days of the Japanese surrender. The Russian troops established themselves along the railways and the main cities of Manchuria; Harbin, Changchun, Dalian and the like, and since the Kuomintang troops could not move in to replace them by the agreed date of mid-November, Chiang asked the Russians to stay in the cities and prevent the Chinese Communist forces from entering the Russian-controlled zones. The Russians met those requests and did not withdraw until March 1946 when the Kuomintang troops were finally installed. In the mean time the Russians stripped the Manchurian cities of all the Japanese military and industrial equipment; whole factories, machinery, machine tools, even office furniture, was dispatched by train to the USSR, even the railway tracks were taken up and shipped out and gold in the Manchurian banks was taken away. The Russians remained in Port Arthur and Dalian, and the last of the American troops were not withdrawn until March 1947, though Qingdao (in Shandong Province) continued to be used by the American navy.

The Communists, meanwhile, occupied the countryside, and set in motion their land-reform policies which quickly built up their support amongst the peasants. There was a tremendous growth of mass support for the Communists, and the force of 100,000 regulars who had marched into Manchuria rapidly grew to 300,000 as soldiers of the old Manchurian armies that had been forcibly incorporated into the Japanese armies flocked to join the Communists. Within two years the Red Army had grown to 1½ million combat troops and four million support personnel. On the other side, though the Kuomintang troops numbered three million and had Russian and American arms and support, its soldiers had nothing to fight for and either deserted or went over to the Communists – who took them in by the thousands. The Kuomintang armies were led by generals whom Chiang had chosen for their personal loyalty to himself rather than military competence, and Chiang ignored the advice of the American military advisers who he himself had requested.

In 1948 the Communists took the initiative in Manchuria. Strengthened by the recruitment of Kuomintang soldiers and the capture of American equipment, the Communists were both the numerical and material equals of the Kuomintang. Three great battles in Manchuria, led by Lin Biao, decided the outcome; in the first battle of August 1948, the Kuomintang lost 500,000 men. In the second of November 1948 to January 1949 whole Kuomintang divisions went over to the Communists who took 327,000 prisoners. The Kuomintang lost seven generals, dead, captured or deserted, and seven divisional commanders crossed sides. The third battle was fought in the Beijing-Tianjin area; Tianjin fell to on January 15 and Beijing on January 23 – and another 500,000 troops came into the Communist camp. It was these victories which sealed the fate of the Kuomintang and allowed the Communists to drive southwards.

With almost a century of perpetual turmoil behind them, the north-eastern regions are being developed into the backbone of China's industries, and attempts are being made to turn them into a bread-basket with state-run farms out on the prairies – it's the same sort of economic possibility which the Japanese sought to exploit and which the Russians stripped bare. To preserve the ailing forests, the last great timber reserves in the land, zones have been placed off-limits to hunters and lumberjacks, albeit a small area (at the end of 1982, 0.4% of China's total land area had been set aside for nature reserves). A vigorous tree planting campaign is also in progress.

Of the three provinces making up the north-east, Liaoning is China's richest province in natural resources. There are large deposits of coal, and iron ore, as well as magnesium and petroleum. The heaviest industry and the densest rail network is here. While there is much hoopla about this year's production of knitted underwear exceeding that of last year by x per cent, and exceeding that of 1949 by ... per cent, the PRC has kept very quiet on the subject of industrial pollution. But from every direction it glares at you in the cities of the north-east and particularly in Liaoning. This may sound like a sweeping generalisation, but the situation may be more sweeping and more general than at first imagined. A rare snippet on the topic comes from Beijing Review in a 1983 article which says; 'Then in 1949, with the liberation, progress arrived, and with it chimneys belching coal smoke into blue skies, factory sluices emptying into once-clear rivers, and an ever-growing and hungry populace indiscriminately clearing ancient forests in their search for arable land.' Those keen on delving into heavy industry and the accompanying soot, grime and fallout, can find no better place than Liaoning. Seeing this aspect of China is probably as valid as visiting its temples, but success at getting into the factories is not guaranteed. In lieu of an expensive CITS liaison it pays to befriend a ranking factory worker.

The population of the north-east has increased dramatically over the last 35 years: 1982 figures put Heilongjiang at 32.6 million people, Jilin at 22.5 million and Liaoning at 35.7 million. Most are Han Chinese immigrants or their progeny. Of the local minority groups, the Manchus have sunk without a trace, the Koreans are over a million strong (mostly in the south-east of Jilin Province) and, in the freezing far north of Heilongjiang are pockets of Oroqens, few in number, hunters who have only recently been persuaded to give up their nomadic ways.

**Tourism** in the north-east is the proverbial 'good news, bad news'. The good news: the open site listing jumped from eight to 18 in late 1982, with offerings dangled for well-heeled visitors ranging from back-packing, fishing and hunting in Heilongjiang, to skiing in Jilin. The bad news: in a word, monotonous! The industrial city landscapes are supposed to look (starkly) beautiful in winter with photogenic blacks and whites, and some extra-sooty greys. To break up the boredom, a few nature reserves have appeared, accessible in the summer. This is very much a fledgling tourist operation and there are signs that more places will be opened up. Deep in the woods north-east of Harbin, a hunting and winter sport range is being set up, centred around Taoshan Manor, and log cabins are under construction. In Dedu Country, way, way up there north of Harbin, a set of volcano crater lakes and a volcano museum are being 'prepared'. All in all, the north-east is a place of specialised interests; pharmacology, ornithology and metallurgy are among the disciplines that can be catered to. Otherwise, if you go right up north, or way out east, the trip itself is the real reward.

**Climate** There's lots of it in the North-East. Mostly cold. Up in Harbin, come January, they'll all be huddled round their Russian stoves drinking vodka – and so would you be if it was minus 20 outside, with howling Siberian gales. Activity slows to a crunch in this snowflake-spitting weather, while the animals pass the season over altogether and sensibly hibernate. At the higher latitude along the Sino-Soviet border there's a nine-month snow period (September to May); moving south to Harbin it lessens to a November to March cold snap; by the time you get to Dalian, it's about December to February. High points for rain are June to August.

Minimum temperatures (°C):

|  | Jan | Apr | Jul | Oct |
|---|---|---|---|---|
| Harbin | -38 | -13 | 11 | -12 |
| Changchun | -37 | -8 | 11 | -11 |
| Shenyang | -30 | -5 | 16 | -8 |
| Dalian | -20 | -4 | 15 | -2 |

Maximum temperatures (°C):

|  | Jan | Apr | Jul | Oct |
|---|---|---|---|---|
| Harbin | 4.2 | 28 | 36 | 27 |
| Changchun | -1 | 25 | 38 | 26 |
| Shenyang | 3 | 25 | 35 | 25 |
| Dalian | 7 | 28 | 33 | 28 |

For ease of getting around freely, May to September is the best time. This is not to suggest you should avoid winter, merely that it would be a damn good idea! If you can deal with the cold and have a good pair of earmuffs, you may be attracted by winter-sporting activities – at least then all the muck is covered by snow.

Mohe, in northern Heilongjiang, has the record for the coldest temperature – a mere minus 52.3°C.

**Skifields** We have to fuel our travelling fantasies – are there any skiers out there? Some foreign skiers *have* been granted the ultimate sanction to ski the Chinese slopes, and if an individual gets one, we'd like to know about it! There are a number of skifields in Jilin and Heilongjiang – at a guess you'd have to bring your own equipment. The Chinese make wood and fibreglass skis, and there is a possibility of rental, but the quality or size of boots and so on cannot be vouched for.

20 km from Jilin town (in Jilin Province, east of the capital Changchun) are the Songhua Lake Skifields of Daqing Mountain, with a 1700 metre cableway, lounge, drying rooms, and restaurant. Another skifield is at Tonghua, where championships have been held. In Heilongjiang, there's the Qingyun skifield, in Shangzhi County, south-east of Harbin; it has a cableway, guest house for 350, and stone cottages. North of Shangzhi, and approachable by bus, is the Yanzhou County skifield. The snow period is long; the main season is late November to early April.

**Tigers** China has three subspecies of tiger; the Bengal, the South China and the North-eastern or Manchurian. All told there are no more than 400 tigers left in China; the South China subspecies is the most endangered with only about 50 in the wild and about 30 in zoos both in China and abroad. (Even when India launched its Project Tiger in 1973 there were 1800 Royal Bengal tigers left in the territory and that was considered perilously low.) And unlike the Bengal and Manchurian tiger which is found in several countries, the South China tiger is peculiar to China only. The plight of the South China tiger really began in the 1950s, with indiscriminate hunting and deforestation. At that time the tiger was still fairly numerous in many southern provinces, especially in Hunan, Fujian, Guizhou and Jiangxi. But throughout the 50s and the early 60s there were 'anti-pest' campaigns and as a result many areas had their entire tiger populations wiped out, and today the subspecies only exists in the mountainous regions of southwest and southeast Hunan, and in northern Guangdong. The fate of the Manchurian tiger is rather more secure, since it exists in larger numbers both in the wild (about 160 in Jinan and Heilongjiang) and in zoos (about 100) and they're also found in the Soviet Union and North Korea. The exact number of Bengal tigers in China is not known; they live in the Xishuangbanna Autonomous Region and in southern Yunnan near Burma and Laos, a few counties in western Yunnan bordering Burma, and the subtropical mountainous region of south-eastern Tibet and the neighbouring Assam.

Meanwhile, off in Mengxian County on the Yellow River, Henan Province, lives a 74 year-old gent, He Guangwei, who makes a living catching the big cats *barehanded* – with a bit of help from the martial arts. Over the past 50 years he's captured 230 leopards and seven tigers, as well as killing 700 wild boars and 800 wolves. If you do happen to come across one of the beasties his advice is to go for the muzzle 'The most sensitive part of a leopard or tiger is on the muzzle between the eyes and the nose. A quick hard blow there will make its eyes water, and it stops to rub them. But the blow must be sharp and accurate. If several blows aren't effective, you're in trouble. You have to kick the animal quickly and hard in vulnerable places like the ears or the belly. But this usually kills the animal. So I don't do it unless my life is at stake.' Good luck.

**Getting There**

**Bus** Bus travel in the north-east is on poor dirt roads and is best avoided when possible. Apart from rail, the other major approach to the north-east is by boat to Dalian. Some boating information is given in the Dalian section.

**Train** Far flung as the north-east might be, the rail connections on the main lines are very good. Shenyang is the hub of all lines in the north-east.

There are high frequency trains on the Beijing-Tianjin-Shenyang-Changchun-Harbin line and good connections from Beijing to Qiqihar, Dalian, Dandong, Jilin. All other lines are slow and trains are of low frequency.

Approximate cost of rail travel can be calculated using the distance tables in the 'Getting Around' section of this book. A couple of sample fares; Beijing to Jiamusi is Y46.30 hard sleeper, Beijing-Changchun is Y32 hard sleeper, Jilin-Changchun is Y2.80 hard seat (all these are Chinese price – tourist price is an additional 75%).

There is some confusion with the railway stations when you go up to the north-east. While most trains leaving Tianjin will do so from the main station, some leave from Tianjin West Station. Likewise in Harbin there may be departures from Sankeshu Station, while in Shenyang, the slower trains to Jilin may leave from Shenyang North Station.

Some examples of travel time (in hours) by express train: Beijing to Harbin 18 hrs, Beijing to Shenyang 9 hrs, Jilin to Harbin 8 hrs, Changchun to Harbin 3 hrs, Changchun to Jilin 2 hrs, Shenyang to Anshan 1 hr, Shenyang to Dandong 5 hrs, Harbin to Jiamusi 15 hrs, Harbin to Yichun 12 hrs.

**Plane** There are flights to several cities and towns in the north-east; for details, see the individual sections.

## THE EAST IS STEAM
The following article was sent to us by Patrick Whitehouse.

The first railway in China was the line from Shanghai to Woosung, built by foreign capital. Negotiations for its construction began in 1865 and, after fierce opposition, the first eight km out of Shanghai were completed in 1876. The line was pushed on until a Chinese was knocked down and killed, and the resulting riots caused the whole line to close. Subsequently the Chinese Government bought and reopened it but, after completing payments in 1878, they closed the line, took up the permanent way, and sank it in the sea with all the rolling stock and equipment!

A few lines were built within the next decade but it was not until after the Japanese War in 1894 that railway building really got going. With the formation of the Chinese Republic in 1912 came nationalisation and considerable construction took place in the next two decades. The Japanese made their mark on the Manchurian railways after 1931; their influence extended into China as the country was overrun during WW II, and a high proportion of locomotives and rolling stock in operation after the war was of Japanese manufacture or design. During this period a large number of American-built locomotives were sent to China to help rehabilitate the railways, and many of these survive as Class 'KD' 2-8-0s. At the time of liberation China's railways lay in ruins after 15 years of war. Before 1935, the country had approximately 20,000 km of railway, but by 1949 less than half of it was in working order. The new government was faced with the gigantic task of reconstructing its war-torn network. The first five-year plan envisaged the building of 55 new railways and the reconstruction or double-tracking of 29 existing lines. In the first 15 years, to 1964, the length of operating railways was estimated to have reached 35,000 km; today the total length is close to 40,000 km and still expanding – only the province of Tibet is without at least some railway facility. There was hardly any signalling 15 years ago; today, China Railways have some of the most modern and sophisticated signalling. Before WW II, China imported practically all its rolling stock, equipment and supplies; now it manufactures its own. About 500 locomotives of all types are built each year; imported diesels to date have come from France and Romania.

The major development plan calls for main line electrification. Today a small proportion of lines have wire (Baoji to Chengdu; Yangpingquan to Xiangfan). Also being electrified are the Beijing-Baotou and the Guiyang-Kunming lines. Diesel will be kept to a minimum since fuel is deemed too precious for railway combustion; the jump is direct from steam to electric. The system employed is 25,000V AC single-phase 50Hz, with overhead conductor. The French electrical industry has assisted in the initial development of electrification, although the Chinese are becoming increasingly self-reliant in this work.

Three grateful Brits joined a small party of Australians in an official 'rail visit' to Manchuria. As always in China, we were treated as honoured guests – and if our dedication to railways was deemed to be slightly unusual, this was never made known. On this trip everything really begins at Shenyang, the capital of Liaoning Province, and both the largest industrial centre and the communications hub of north-east China. From the rail-fan's point of view, Shenyang is one of the most important rail centres in the country. Six lines converge on the city and with the coal traffic from Fushun and other mines in the area, with the inbound iron ore and outbound steel to and from nearby Anshan, and with the chemical and manufacturing goods flowing from and through Shenyang itself, freight traffic is plentiful – and in China that means steam!

Space forbids a detailed description of the Fushun mine complex with its attendant steam and electrified railway system – except to say that it's immense. The highlight of the visit to Shenyang was Sugintun steam depot, which is all freight and consequently almost 100 percent 'QJ' class 2-10-2s, and 'JS' class 2-8-2s. Like most Chinese depots, Sugintun shed is fully equipped to carry out heavy repair work, but not boiler fitting. The 'two-star' attractions were found hidden away. These were two Japanese Pacifics sitting at the back of the shed – a class 'SL8' No 296 (in steam) and a class 'SL7' (very dead). Both were pre-war Manchurian express classes of note; the former being used on the Port Arthur (Luda, near Dalian) to Harbin overnight service on the South Manchurian Railway, and the latter between Port Arthur and Shenyang. The 'SL7s' made their trip with fully air-conditioned trains (some of the first in the world) and ran at an average speed of 110 km/h (68.75 mph).

From Shenyang we journeyed to Jilin, behind steam 'SL' class Pacifics hauling 12 bogies of about 518 tonnes, which is a good load for these engines over a steeply-graded route. At least eight sizeable rivers are bridged during the trip. As foreign guests we travelled extremely comfortably in a soft-class coach with tea on hand at any time from the blue-uniformed coach attendant. Jilin provided an opportunity for that most relaxing of railway pursuits – railway sauntering, at a place called Dragon Pond Hill station. Locomotive variety here was classes 'QJ' 2-10-2, 'JF' 2-8-2, and, on the passenger runs, 'RM' Pacifics.

At Changchun, further along the line, there are two railway factories: a Locomotive Works and a Passenger Coach Works. The Locomotive Works built the first of the big 'Heping' (Peace) steam locomotives, as well as the power cars for the Peking Metro. The Passenger Coach Works was built in 1957 to help overcome the shortage of passenger stock and today builds lightweight coaches for 160 km/h operation, de luxe coaches and sleeping cars. The plant has been modernised and expanded since 1978; technological aid comes from Japan's largest railway vehicle builders, Nippon Sharyo Seizo Kaisha. The Locomotive Works and the Carriage Works have been visited by foreigners, as have the social complex with its schools, housing and hospital. Other Changchun joys included line-side photography, and an early morning visit to the steam shed. The latter was so fantastic – clean engines, variety and hospitality – that I just stood there in the sunshine for a moment and said out loud, 'I just don't believe it!'. In addition to the usual tender engines, the depot sported two different classes of 2-6-4T Class 'DB2' No 89, a Japanese-built locomotive dating from 1934-36, and 'DB1' No 28, an Alco of 1907. The main classes based here are the 'QJ' 2-10-2 'RM' 4-6-2, and 'SL' 4-6-2 with a shed allocation for around a hundred. As with Sugintun depot, Changchun was equipped for overhauls at 100,000 km intervals. A heavy general on steam locomotives is carried out at the main works after 300,000 km.

Our last stop northwards was Harbin, some 500 km north of Vladivostok and at one time on the Trans-Siberian railway; the Manzhouli to Harbin and Harbin to Mudanjiang lines form most of the original route. Harbin itself is the junction of two major and three secondary lines. Winter comes to Harbin early and line-side photography included snow scenes, albeit dull ones from the weather point of view. Even so, it was impossible not to be thrilled by the sight of heavy double-headed freights hauled by thundering 'QJs', headlights on in the gloom, pounding up the bank at Wang Guang on their way south. Of particular interest was one of China's three named engines – General Zhu De, No 2470. Passenger trains were 'RM' hauled.

At a further shed there was another gem hiding in the yard – a Tangshan-built 2-6-2T of 1949-50, No PL275. Harbin is the area freight depot containing the usual high quota of 'QJs' (still being built at Datong). The shed itself dates from 1899 and has a working staff of some 2,600 for the 100 percent steam allocation of approximately 100 locomotives. Winter is the busy season as the roads become impassable, and 70 locomotives from the shed are in daily service, with an equal number coming in for servicing.

Suffice it to say that our visit covered only a small section of China's rail network, but along the way we saw a great deal of Manchuria. Help was always at hand, and we were fortunate enough to find interpreters and guides who showed a positive interest in our hobby – purchasing technical books and crawling over engines for special identification points. One guide had worked his service out on the installation of the Tan Zam Railway ('Uhuru' or 'Freedom' Railway). The Tan Zam Railway was completed in 1975, linking Zambia's copper mines with Tanzania's ports, thus enabling the two countries to bypass the usual South African export routes. 20,000 Chinese worked on the project alongside 36,000 Africans. That particular guide had some fascinating stories to tell . . .

Patrick Whitehouse
Millbrook House Ltd
England.

# Liaoning

## SHENYANG

The first grey city on the north-east route, Shenyang has the distinction of being the only one to hold historical interest. It is the cradle of the Manchus, starting as a nomad trading centre as far back as the 11th century, and becoming established as the capital in the 17th century. With the Manchu conquest of Beijing in 1644, Shenyang became a secondary capital under the Manchu name of Mukden, and a centre of the ginseng trade.

The city was occupied by the Russians around the turn of the century as part of their 'railway colonialism', and it was a key battleground during the Russian-Japanese War (1904-5). The city rapidly changed hands – dominated by warlords, then the Japanese (1931), the Russians (1945), the Kuomintang (1946), and the CCP (1948). The present population is around five million (for a jurisdiction area of 8500 sq km – the urban population is 2.7 million), which represents something like a 900% increase in population since 1949.

Shenyang is the centre of the Liaoning Province Industrial Effort; six major rail lines converge on Shenyang, including those freight lines from Anshun, the steel giant, and Fushun, the coal capital. Industrial output of Shenyang rivals that of Shanghai and includes machinery, aircraft, tramcars, textiles, pharmaceuticals, rubber products, you name it. The latest products can be viewed at the Liaoning Industrial Exhibition Hall and factory visits are on the group tour agenda.

**CITS** (tel 66265) has an office close to Liaoning Mansions (see under 'Places to Stay' for details.

**CAAC** (tel 33705) is at 31 Dongfeng Dalu Sanduan.

## Things to See

Before thundering off to the sights, it might be worth noting that consumerism is alive and rife in Shenyang. The *Lianying Corporation*, opened in 1983, is an enormous (clean) four floors of glassed-in counters and muzak that is superior to any department store in Beijing. It stocks arts and crafts. Shenyang seems to be one long bout of buy and sell, with a high density of department stores. The main arteries are on Taiyuan Lu and Zhongshan Lu. Taiyuan has a poster shop, arts and crafts store, and an antique shop. The Overseas Chinese come to raid the medicine shops of Shenyang; on the streets there is a rampant population of *binggun* (popsicle) vendors who inexplicably patrol the streets at the height of the bitter winters. The Shenyang Acrobatic Troupe is one of China's best and definitely worth chasing up.

### The Imperial Palace

This is a mini-Beijing model in layout, though the features are Manchu. The main structures were started by Nurhachi, leader of the Manchus, and completed in 1636 by his son, Huang Taiji.

Straight through the main gate, at the far end of the courtyard, is the main structure, the octagonal Dazheng Hall with its caisson ceiling and an elaborate throne. It was here that Emperor Shunzhi was crowned before setting off to cross the Great Wall in 1644. In the courtyard in

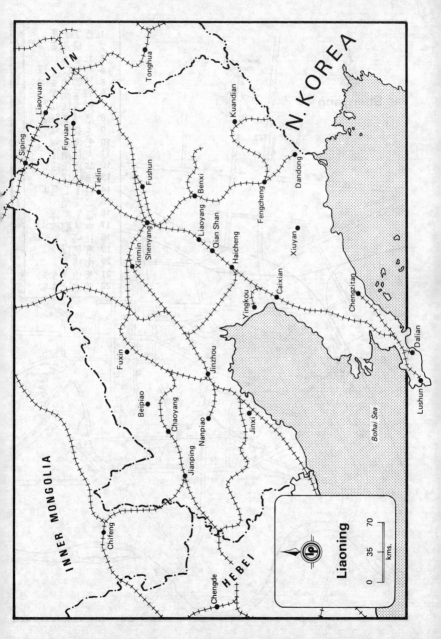

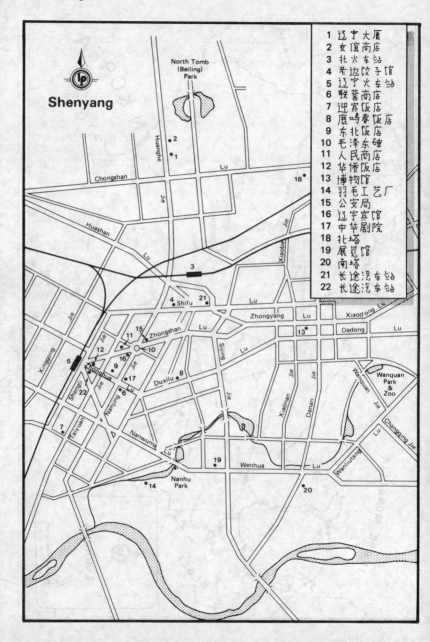

**Shenyang**

North Tomb
(Beiling)
Park

1 辽宁大厦
2 友谊商店
3 北火车站
4 老边饺子馆
5 辽宁火车站
6 联营商店
7 迎宾饭店
8 鹿鸣春饭店
9 东北饭店
10 毛泽东碑
11 人民商店
12 华侨饭店
13 博物馆
14 羽毛工艺厂
15 公安局
16 辽宁宾馆
17 中华剧院
18 北塔
19 展览馆
20 南塔
21 长途汽车站
22 长途汽车站

front of the Hall are the Banner Pavilions, formerly administrative offices used by tribal chieftains. They now house displays of 17th and 18th century military equipment – armour, swords, bows. The central courtyard, west of Dazheng Hall, contains a conference hall, some living quarters, and some shamanist structures (one of the customs of the Manchus was to pour boiling wine into a sacrificial pig's ear, so that its cries would attract the devotee's ancestors). The courtyard to the western fringe is a residential area added on by Emperor Qianlong in the 18th century, and the Wenshu Gallery to the rear housed a copy of the Qianlong anthology.

Like the Forbidden City, the Shenyang Imperial Palace functions as a museum, with exhibitions including ivory and jade artefacts, musical instruments, furniture, and Ming and Qing paintings. The palace is in the oldest section of the city; bus No 10 will get you there.

### North Tomb (called Beiling or Zhaoling)
This is the burial place of Huang Taiji (1592-1643), founder of the Qing dynasty – although he did not live to see its conquest of China. The tomb took eight years to build, and the impressive animal statues on the approach to it are reminiscent of the Ming Tombs. The larger buildings, used as barracks by various warlords are in a state of disrepair,

though some attempt has been made to restore them. The tumulus of the tomb is a grassy mound at the rear. To get to the North Tomb take bus No 6 or bus 20.

### East Tomb (called Dongling or Fuling)
This tomb is set in a forested area eight km from Shenyang. Entombed here is Nurhachi, grandfather of the Emperor Shunzhi who launched the invasion of China in 1644. Nurhachi is entombed with his mistress. Construction of the tomb started in 1626 and took several years to complete, with subsequent additions and renovations. It's similar in layout to the North Tombs, but smaller, and is perched on a wooded hilltop looking over a river. To get to the East Tomb take bus No 18 from the Imperial Palace and then walk.

### Mao Statue
Of all the bizarre statues in the North-East (monuments to Russian war heroes, mini tanks atop pillars . . . ) this one takes the cake. Like some kind of strange machine, it zooms out of Red Flag Square, a giant epoxy-resin Mao at the helm, flanked by vociferous peasants, soldiers and workers. The last word on the personality cult and the follies of the Cultural Revolution, this is a rare item, erected 1969.

### Places to Stay
The *Liaoning Guest House* facing Red Flag

| | | |
|---|---|---|
| 1 | Liaoning Mansions / CITS | |
| 2 | Friendship Hotel | |
| 3 | North Railway Station | |
| 4 | Laobian Dumpling Restaurant | |
| 5 | Main Railway Station | |
| 6 | Lianying Corporation Dept. Store | |
| 7 | YinbinRestaurant | |
| 8 | Lu Ming Chun Restaurant | |
| 9 | Liaoning Dongbei Hotel | |
| 10 | Mao Statue | |
| 11 | Renmin Store / Friendship Store | |
| 12 | Overseas Chinese Hotel / CITS | |
| 13 | Palace Museum | |
| 14 | Feather – picture Factory | |
| 15 | Public Security Bureau | |
| 16 | Liaoning Guest House | |
| 17 | Zhonghua Theatre | |
| 18 | North Pagoda | |
| 19 | Industrial Exhibition Hall | |
| 20 | South Pagoda | |
| 21 | Long Distance Bus Station | |
| 22 | Long Distance Bus Station | |

Square, was constructed in 1927 by the Japanese; it's got 77 suites, billiard room with slate tables, art-nouveau windows – and was closed for repairs at the time of writing.

The *Liaoning Dasha (Liaoning Mansions)* (tel 62536) is at No 2, Sector 6, Huanghe Lu in the direction of the North Tomb. This is an enormous Soviet-style place complete with chandeliers. It's used for meetings and group tours and has double rooms for Y34.

The *Friendship Hotel* (tel 62822) is just north of Liaoning Mansions, and is a villa-type place used for state guests.

The *Overseas Chinese Hotel* (tel 34214) is near the railway station at No 3, Sector 1, Zhongshan Lu. It's difficult to get into – you may get a double room for Y30, but Y7 with your own pet TV is possible. China Travel Service (CTS) is located here.

The *Liaoning Dongbei Hotel* (tel 32031) is at No 1, 7 Li 3 Duan, Taiyuan Lu. It's a difficult place to find: veer left from the station, take Zhongshan Lu toward the Mao statue, turn right into Taiyuan Lu and take the first street, left – you'll find the hotel further down that alley. Beds are Y6 to Y10 a person, Y3 for students – prices negotiable.

### Places to Eat

Can't really say there is anything to recommend. Mouth-watering banquet fare will undoubtedly surface in the classier hotels for a hefty (advance order) price, but on the streets the level of sanitation will quickly cure your hunger pangs without having to eat anything! The local solution to the problems of germs seems to be plenty of vodka, served up in sake-like cups placed in a can of hot water, with a side dish of raw garlic. The *Lao Bian* dumpling restaurant, up in an alley lined with market stalls, has the vodka side drinks, as well as cold cuts (sausage) and trays of jiaozi. North of the Imperial Palace, near the Drum Tower is the *Li Liangui* smoke-cured meat and flat-bread shop, over a century old. Icecream outlets

abound, particularly on Taiyuan Lu – a shovel is used to put the stuff in containers.

The *Overseas Chinese Hotel* and the *Liaoning Dongbei Hotel* both have reasonably clean dining rooms. The *Yingbin* restaurant and the *Lu Ming Chun* are passable, serving northern food, and will dish up regional specialties if there is an advance order and you are willing to fork out. Shenyang's winter speciality is hot-pot.

### Getting Around

There is a bicycle rental to one side of the Liaoning Dongbei Hotel – look for a shed.

### Getting There

**Train** Shenyang is the hub of the north-eastern rail network; for details see the introduction to the north-eastern provinces.

**Plane** Shenyang is connected by air to Beijing (Y80), Canton (Y324), Changchun (Y35), Dalian (Y46), Harbin (Y65), Nanjing (Y190), Qingdao (Y111), Shanghai (Y225), Tianjin (Y83), Wuhan (Y222) and Xian (Y212).

### DALIAN

Dalian is known under a jumble of names – Dalny, Dairen, Lushun, and Luda. Lushun is the part further south (formerly Port Arthur, now a naval base), and Lushun and Dalian comprise Luda. In the late 19th century, the western powers were busy carving up pieces of China for themselves, and to the outrage of Tsar Nicholas II, Japan gained the Liaoning Peninsula under a treaty of 1895 (after creaming Chinese battleships off Port Arthur in 1894). Nicholas II gained the support of the French and Germans and managed to get the Japanese to withdraw from Dalian; the Russians got the place as a concession in 1898 and set about constructing the port of their dreams – as opposed to the only partially ice-free port of Vladivostok.

To Russia's further dismay, however,

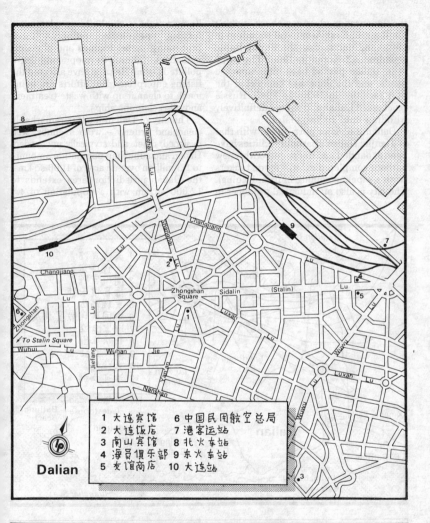

**Dalian**

1 大连宾馆　6 中国民用航空总局
2 大连饭店　7 港客运站
3 南山宾馆　8 北火车站
4 海员俱乐部　9 东火车站
5 友谊商店　10 大连站

1 Dalian Guest House
2 Dalian Hotel
3 Nanshan Guest House
4 International Seaman's Club
5 Friendship Store / Hotel

6 CAAC
7 Harbour Passenger Terminal
8 North Railway Station
9 East Railway Station
10 Dalian Railway Station

the Japanese made a comeback, sinking the Russian East Asia naval squadron in 1902, and decimating the Soviet Baltic squadron off Korea in 1905. The same year, Dalian passed back into Japanese hands, and the Japanese completed the port facilities in 1930. In 1945, Russia reoccupied Dalian and did not definitively withdraw until 10 years later.

Dalian is a major port, on par with that of Tianjin; Dalian's harbour facilities have been expanded and deepened, with a new harbour completed in 1976 for oil tankers (with a pipeline coming in from Daqing). The city is also an industrial producer in its own right – shipbuilding, glassware, textiles, petroleum refinery, food-processing, diesel engines and chemical industries. These developments have polluted Dalian Bay and have affected the fishing enterprises, but efforts are being made to clean it up with waste treatment and oil-reclaiming ships.

The city of Dalian itself is remarkably clean and orderly – wide avenues, well designed, quiet, and atypically uncrowded. Urban and suburban population amounts to 1.3 million over an area of 1000 sq km – the Dalian jurisdiction area extends to 12,000 sq km with a population of 4.4

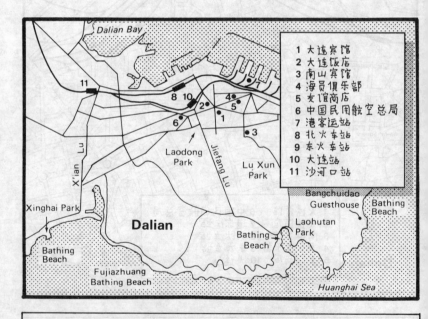

| | |
|---|---|
| 1 | 大连宾馆 |
| 2 | 大连饭店 |
| 3 | 南山宾馆 |
| 4 | 海员俱乐部 |
| 5 | 友谊商店 |
| 6 | 中国民用航空总局 |
| 7 | 港客运站 |
| 8 | 北火车站 |
| 9 | 东火车站 |
| 10 | 大连站 |
| 11 | 沙河口站 |

| | | | |
|---|---|---|---|
| 1 | Dalian Guest House | 7 | Harbour Passenger Terminal |
| 2 | Dalian Hotel | 8 | North Railway Station |
| 3 | Nanshan Guest House | 9 | East Railway Station |
| 4 | International Seaman's Club | 10 | Dalian Railway Station |
| 5 | Friendship Store / Hotel | 11 | Shahekou Railway Station |
| 6 | CAAC | | |

million, including five counties. It's also a prime apple-growing region.

**CITS** has a small office in the Nanshan Guest House (see the 'Places to Stay' section for details).

**CAAC** (tel 52334) is at 12 Dagong Jie.

### Things to See
Access to the port facilities, probably one of the top sights of Dalian, is limited for the individual traveller. You'll have to be content with the large **Natural History Museum** with its stuffed sea-life behind the station; open Tues/Thur/Sat/Sun, 8 am to 4 pm. **Laodong Park** at the centre of town offers good city views. There's also an assortment of handicraft factories, including glasswork and shell mosaic.

Dalian is actually a health resort of a kind, so beaches with their attached parks are the attraction. The beach five km to the south-east is for western VIPs and is bordered by the exclusive Bangchuidao Guest House. **Tiger Beach (Laohutan)** is rocky and poor for swimming (you can get there on bus No 102 from the city centre). **Fujiazhuang Beach** is the best – it's small, has fine sand, surreal rock outcrops in the deep bay, excellent for swimming, few facilities. Like the other beaches, this one has a sanatorium nearby, and the patients sometimes venture out in their pyjamas to assist rubber-booted fishermen hauling in their catch. The beach is a fair way out of town – take bus No 102 and then change to bus No 5. **Xinghai Park & Beach** is five km to the south-west – it's crowded and a little on the slimey side, but it's got a good seafood restaurant (take bus No 2, or else take a tramcar No 201 and then change to tramcar No 202). There is another shallow beach called **Xiajiahezi**, to the northwest of Dalian. July and August are the hottest months.

### Places to Stay
Dalian sees few individual travellers – mostly cruise-ship passengers or seamen.

Here's a quick summary of the hotel battlefield:

The seven-storey *Dalian Hotel* (tel 23171) is at 6 Shanghai Lu. Double rooms go from Y20 to Y70 – it's an Overseas Chinese hangout.

The *Dalian Guesthouse* (tel 23111) is at 7 Zhongshan Square and is of similar size and similar difficulty to the Dalian Hotel. Double rooms start at Y28.

The *Dalian Friendship Hotel* (tel 23890) is above the Friendship Store at 137 Stalin Lu. It's got 27 rooms and prices start at Y50 for a double. The Dalian Guesthouse, the Friendship Hotel, and the Seamen's Club are used by local businessmen and incoming sailors, and will supply a rousing round of rejection when called upon to provide accommodation. One traveller did make it into the hallowed doors of the *Seamen's Club* (opposite the Friendship Store) at Y10 for a single room.

The *Nanshan Guest House* (tel 25103) is at 56 Fenglin Lu, and has a dozen villas tucked into very pleasant gardens. It's got the atmosphere of a country club, but it's on the expensive side at Y40 a double. There's a pleasant outdoor section with beach umbrellas, portico and wicker-cane chairs. CITS has a small office in this hotel, and English-language teachers are also accommodated here. To get there take the round-the-city unnumbered bus; alternatively take a tramcar No 201 and then change to bus No 12 or walk uphill.

Another possibility is the *Bangchuidao Guest House* to the east of the town on the coast. It's next to an exclusive beach.

### Places to Eat
People make the trip to Dalian to gorge themselves on seafood, and let's face it, you could use a change of diet. The *Haiwei Seafood Restaurant* (tel 27067), near the railway station at 85 Zhongshan Lu, will begrudgingly serve up prawns and other sea urchins once you demonstrate that not all foreigners are imbeciles.

Tianjin Jie is the wining-dining-shopping

street. It's within walking range of the station, and boasts a number of restaurants and snackbars. Opposite the Tianjin Department Store (No 199), nearing the east end of Tianjin Jie, is the *Shanshui Restaurant* which serves Jiangsu-style seafood. The hotels around town dish up more expensive clams and scallops – the dining rooms of the *Dalian Guesthouse* are noted for this. The *Seamen's Club* has several dining sections on the second floor, not cheap, but you can get plates of *guotie* (dumplings) in peace and quiet. Xinghai Park, out by the beachfront, has a kind of elevated club house with beach umbrellas – it will cost you about Y15 a head for giant prawns, fish and beer, which is not bad for an al fresco location overlooking windsurfers and sunbathers.

### Entertainment

The Copacabana of Dalian is the International Seamen's Club, open until 10.30 pm, with dining and banquet rooms, a bar where sailors doze with their stale beers to the chirp of video-game machines, and a disco. It has a full-size theatre with weekend offerings – Beijing Opera or perhaps a film or an acrobat show. One of the innovations at the acrobat show is half a dozen Chinese grinding away to the strains of 'YMCA', followed by 'Hawaii Five-0'.

### Shopping

The Friendship Store has stock that rivals Beijing's. Handicrafts such as glassware, feather paintings and shell mosaics can also be found in the Tianjin Department Store at 199 Tianjin Jie. There's an antique store at 229 Tianjin Jie.

### Getting Around

Bus No 13 runs from the railway station area, along behind the Friendship Store, and to the boat terminal. Tramcar No 201 starts from the railway station, heads in the same direction as bus No 13, but turns south before the Friendship Store and proceeds east (it's good for getting partway to the Nanshan Guest House). There is a round-the-city bus, with no number but a character destination sign, which would be useful for a tour through Dalian.

### Getting Away

**Train** There are direct trains from Dalian to Shenyang, Beijing, Harbin and Jiamusi. For more details, see the introduction to the north-eastern provinces.

**Air** Dalian is connected by air to Beijing (Y80), Qingdao (Y65), Shanghai (Y283) and Shenyang (Y46).

**Boat** There are boats to Yantai or Shanghai daily; to Qingdao once every four days; to Tanggu (the port of Tianjin) every four to six days. There are other departures to Weihai, Longkou, Shidao, and possibly Dandong or Yingkou. The booking office is at the boat terminal, east of the Seamen's Club, and it has a left-luggage office (modern facilities, too). Boat rides are very cheap (for example, 3rd class to Qingdao is Y8, takes about 28 hours; 3rd class to Yantai is Y5, takes about eight hours) and comfortable, but avoid cargo class. Since the rail lines from Dalian have to go all the way round the peninsula before proceeding south, boats can actually save you time as well as money.

## ANSHAN

South of Shenyang is Anshan, the largest iron and steel complex in the land, responsible for 25 per cent of the nation's output. It is a massive vista of factories, blast furnaces, converters, rolling mills, metallurgy labs, refractories and chemical plants. The plant started under the Japanese, was taken apart by the Russians, revived by the Chinese, and now employs over 130,000 workers. Outside the town are five iron-ore mines, and to the south is a bunch of scenery and sanatoriums; Qian Shan is 25 kms to the south-east and has a motley scattering of

Tang, Ming and Qing dynasty temples, as well as the Tanggangzi Hot Springs. Tanggangzi has hot springs piped into ordinary baths, and a sanatorium for chronic diseases – there is some hotel accommodation here.

## LIAOYANG
South of Shenyang and just north of Anshan is Liaoyang – the scene of lighter industry, such as textiles, food-processing and machine tools.

## BENXI
Southeast of Shenyang is Benxi, a combination of iron and steel, and coal mining town, with a cement works thrown in for good measure. Liaoning accounts for some 10 per cent of national coal production, with eight large-scale mining areas.

## FUSHUN
Fushun, on the railway line to the east of Shenyang, is presently the largest open-cut coalmine in China; the city also has a sideline in specialised steel, heavy machinery, cement and petrochemicals. In the souvenir line, products from Fushun include cigarette holders, coal sculptures and amber ornaments (especially valued are the pieces with imprisoned insects). Better examples of these art forms are displayed in the city's Exhibition Hall.

## YINGKOU
Yingkou is a port city recently opened to the foreign touring public. It is south-east of Shenyang at the end of a railway line which branches off the main Shenyang-Dalian line.

## DANDONG
Dandong lies at the border of Liaoning Province and North Korea. Along with Dalian and Yingkou, this is one of the three key trading and communication ports for the whole north-eastern area.

Dandong offers a tourist hotel, a couple of Korean noodle houses, some seafood, and a hilltop hike where one can peer across the Yalu River at the city of Sinuiju in North Korea. One historical relic is a steel span bridge full of shrapnel holes, 'accidentally' strafed by the Americans in 1950 (who also accidentally bombed the airstrip at Dandong). Presently the city is being revamped for greater light industry production, like wrist watches, knitwear, printing and foodstuffs. There is a temple in Dandong, which I am told has a sign 'Let there be no photos' – God speaks! There are direct trains to Dandong from Shenyang and Changchun; the trip from Shenyang takes five hours.

# Jilin

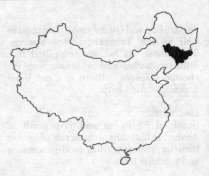

## CHANGCHUN

Changchun, with its broad leafy avenues, is a well laid-out city, and an exceedingly dull one. Those responsible for the uninspiring militaristic structures are the Japanese who developed it as the capital of 'Manchukuo' from 1933 to 1945. In 1945 the Russians arrived in Changchun on a looting spree; when they departed in 1946, the Kuomintang moved in to occupy the cities of the north-east, only to find themselves surrounded by the Communists in the countryside (roving around blowing up railway lines). The Communists had assembled a formidable array of scrounged and captured weaponry from ex-Japanese tanks to US jeeps, and Changchun saw more than a few of them in action. The city was taken over by the Communists in 1948.

China's first autoplant was set up here in the 1950s with Soviet assistance, starting with 95 hp Jiefang (Liberation) Trucks, and moving on to bigger and better things like the Red Flag limousines. Changchun's other claim to fame – the Film Studios – got their start in the civil war, making documentaries.

You might try and arrange a visit via CITS to the Film Studios or the Number One Auto Plant (both are on the No 2 tramcar route). Lesser factories (tractor, rail-car, carpet, fur, woodcarving . . . ) may be accessible. Otherwise, there are numerous wooded parks in the city, a reservoir 20 km to the south, and perhaps a chance to see a deer farm or ginseng garden. The former administrative buildings of the Japanese are now used by the university.

One building with an interesting background is the Provincial Museum, located in the former palace of Puyi. Henry Puyi, by the way, was the last person to ascend the dragon-throne. He was two years old at the time and was

forced to abdicate just six years later when the 1911 Revolution swept the country. He lived in exile in Tianjin and in 1935 was spirited away to Changchun by the Japanese invaders and set up as the puppet-emperor of Manchukuo. Puyi was captured by the Russians in 1945 and was only returned to China sometime in the late 1950s, and was allowed to work as a gardener in one of the colleges in Beijing. He died of cancer in 1967; thus ended a life largely governed by others.

**CITS** is located in the Chunyi Guest House. They have a useful bilingual bus map of Changchun plus other literature.

**CAAC** (tel 39772) is at 2 Liaoning Lu.

### Places to Stay

The *Chunyi* (tel 38495) is at 2 Stalin Boulevard, just across from the railway station. It's got Stalin period decor, old-world opulence, and double rooms at Y40 to Y50. In a similar class of exclusivity are the *Nanhu Guesthouse* (tel 53571) and the *Changchun Guesthouse* (tel 26771) at 128 Changchun Lu.

The *Changbai Shan* (tel 52003) is at 12 Ximen Lu, and is a new highrise with topnotch plumbing, luxury accommodation at reasonable prices. Doubles are Y34, but you can get in at Y8 per person by gazing longingly at the furniture near the reception desk. Take trolley-bus No 62 from the railway station.

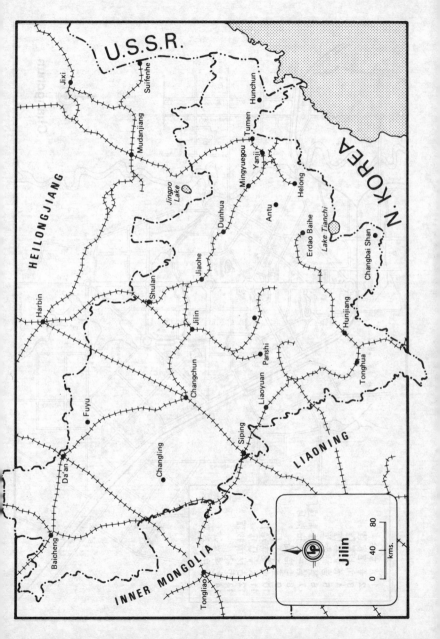

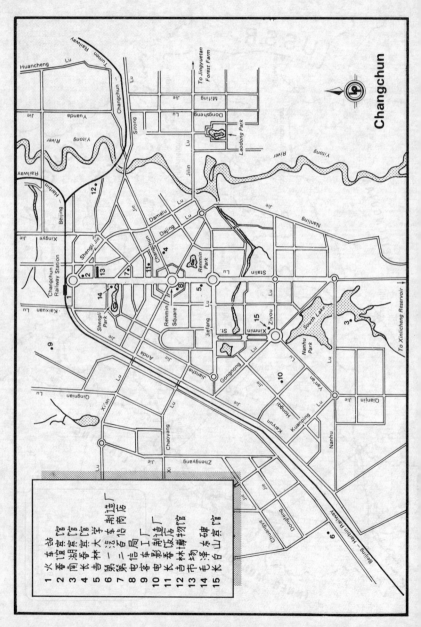

Changchun

1 火车站
2 春谊宾馆
3 南湖宾馆
4 吉林大学
5 第一汽车制造厂
6 第二汽车制造厂
7 春城饭店
8 电信局
9 长春电影制片厂
10 吉林省博物馆
11 市百货商店
12 春城饭店
13 长春饭店
14 毛泽东纪念碑
15 长白山宾馆

| | |
|---|---|
| 1 Changchun Railway Station | 8 Changchun Telecom— |
| 2 Chunyi Hotel | munication Bureau & |
| 3 Nanhu Guest House | Public Security Bureau |
| 4 Changchun Municipal | 9 Changchun Railway |
| Guest House | Carriage Factory |
| 5 Jilin University | 10 Changchun Film Studio |
| 6 Changchun No. 1 | 11 Changchun Restaurant |
| Automobile Plant | 12 Jilin Provincial Museum |
| 7 No. 2 Dept. Store | 13 Shopping / Market Street |
| (Friendship Store is on | 14 Mao Statue |
| the Top Floor) | 15 Changbaishan Guesthouse |

## Getting There

For details of trains, see the introduction to the north-eastern provinces. Changchun is connected by air with Beijing (Y115), Harbin (Y29) and Shenyang (Y35).

## JILIN

East of Changchun is the city of Jilin. A Chinese pamphlet puts it in a nutshell: 'Under the guidance of Chairman Mao's revolutionary line, it has made rapid progress in industrial and agricultural production... From a desolate consumer city, Kirin (Jilin) has become a rising industrial city with emphasis on chemical and power industries'.

Three large chemical plants were built after 1949. The Fengman Hydroelectric Station, built by the Japanese, disassembled by the Russians and put back together by the Chinese, fuels these enterprises, and provides Jilin with an unusual tourist attraction; water passing from artificial Songhua Lake through the power plant becomes a warm steamy current that merges with the Songhua River and prevents it from freezing. Overnight, vapour rising from the river meets the minus 20 Celsius weather, causing condensation on the branches of pines and willows on a 20 km stretch of banks. In the Spring Festival (January 25), hordes of Japanese and Overseas Chinese come for the resulting icicle and spraypaint show. The phenomenon also acts as a kind of snow-machine that creates drifts over a ski-ground some 20 km outside Jilin, at Daqing Shan.

Jilin, like Harbin, has an ice-lantern festival, held at Beishan Park. Other points of interest are a meteorite exhibition hall, and a possible visit to the Jilin Special Products Research Centre, where there is a deer park, ginseng garden, and a collection of sables.

## Places to Stay

Hotels open to foreigners in Jilin are the *Xiguan Guest House* (tel 5645) at 661 Songjiang Lu and the *Dongguan* (tel 3555) at 223 Songjiang Lu. Both these hotels are by the river and CITS is located in the Dongguan.

## CHANGBAI NATURE RESERVE

The Changbai (Ever-White) Nature Reserve is China's largest, covering 210,000 hectares of dense virgin forest. The forest is divided into a semi-protected area where limited lumbering and hunting is permitted, and a protected area where neither is allowed. Because of elevation changes, there is wide variation in animal and plant life. From 700 to 1000 metres above sea level there are mixed coniferous and broad-leaf trees (including white birch and Korean pines); from 1000 to 1800 metres are cold-resistant coniferous trees such as dragon spruce and fir; from 1800 and 2000 metres is another forest belt; above 2000 metres it is treeless and windy with alpine tundra. For the budding

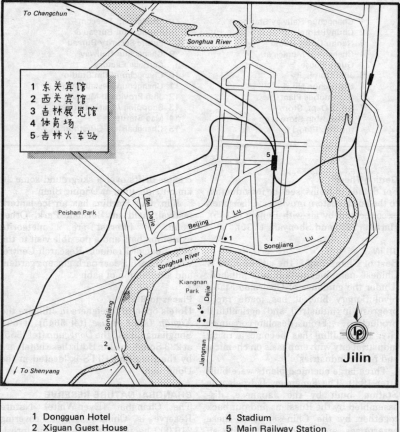

```
1 东关宾馆
2 西关宾馆
3 吉林展览馆
4 体育场
5 吉林火车站
```

To Changchun

Songhua River

Peishan Park

Bei Dajie

Beijing Lu

Songjiang Lu

1

Songhua River

Kiangnan Park

Jiangnan Dajie

3
4

2

To Shenyang

Jilin

1 Dongguan Hotel
2 Xiguan Guest House
3 Jilin Exhibition Hall
4 Stadium
5 Main Railway Station

geologist and botanist there's plenty to investigate. There are some 300 medicinal plants within the reserve (including winter daphne, asiabell and wild ginseng); some very shy animal species make their home in the mountain range (the rarer ones being the protected cranes, deer and Manchurian tiger).

The reserve itself is a recent creation, first designated in 1960. During the Cultural Revolution all forest and conservation work was suspended, and technical and scientific personnel were dispersed to menial jobs. Locals had a free-for-all season on the plant and animal life during this period.

**Lake Tian**, the Lake of Heaven, is the prime scenic spot. It's a volcanic crater-lake, five km from north to south, 3½ km from east to west, 13 km in circumference, and sits at an elevation of 2194 metres. It's surrounded by jagged rock outcrops and peaks; three rivers run off the lake, with a rumbling 68 metre waterfall identified as the source of the Songhua and Tumen Rivers. Down the slopes from the waterfall is a hot-spring bath-house, where water from lake and underground sources are mixed. Authorities have been constructing roads and bridges in the Tianchi area to ease access for tourism and forestry (and meteorological) stations. A vehicle route runs to the top of one of the peaks overlooking the lake; there is a stone path (hiking route) leading from the foothills to the lake level. It's about 1½ km from the hot springs to the lake level. Hiking at the lake itself is limited by the sharp peaks and their rock-strewn debris, and by the fact that the lake actually overlaps the Chinese/North Korean border – there's no tourist build up yet on the Korean side. Cloud cover starts at 1000 metres and can be prevalent. The highest peak in the Changbai Shan range is 2700 metres.

Enchanting scenery like this would not be complete in the Chinese world without a legend or mystique of some sort. Of the many myths, the most intriguing is the origin of the Manchu race. Three heavenly nymphs descended to the lake in search of earthly pleasure. They stripped off for a dip in the lake; along came a magic magpie which deposited a red berry on the dress of one of the maidens. She picked it up to smell it; the berry flew through her lips into her stomach. The nymph became pregnant; she gave birth to a handsome boy with an instant gift of the gab. He went on to foster the Manchus and their dynasty.

Dragons, and other things that go bump in the night, are believed to have sprung out of the lake. In fact, they're still believed to do so. There have been intermittent sightings of unidentified swimming objects – China's own Loch Ness Beasties or aquatic Yetis or what have you. Lake Tian is the deepest alpine lake in China – plumbed to a depth estimated between 200 and 350 metres. Since it is frozen over in winter, and temperatures are well below zero, it would take a pretty hardy sort of monster to survive (even plankton can't). Sightings from the Chinese and North Korean sides point to a black bear, fond of swimming, and oblivious to the paperwork necessary for transiting these tight borders. On a more profound note, Chinese couples throw coins into the lake, pledging that their love will remain as deep as Tianchi, and as long lived.

## Places to Stay

There are two guest houses; the *Baishan* which is near the hot springs, and the *Changbaishan*. Both of these are small (less than 100 beds), rudimentary, and prices are low (Y8 to Y12 starting price for a double).

## Getting There

The Changbai area is remote, and a journey there is somewhat expeditionary: you're advised to bring loads of ginseng, frog-tonic oil and other supplies and refreshments with you, plus good hiking gear (due to high elevations, flash thunderstorms are not uncommon).

The *only* season in terms of transport access is late June to September, when snow and ice cover drop. The road from Erdao to Changbai is only open for this period. Autumn colourings are the goal of Chinese hikers – so the peak season is mid-July to mid-August with a high local turnover. Although Changbai was only opened to foreigners in 1982, it has been on the Chinese tour map for some time, with something like 30,000 visitors from north-eastern provinces over the July to September period.

There are two 'transit points' to Changbai, Mingyuegou (old Antu) and Erdao. Before you go, get a weather forecast from someone in Jilin, Changchun or Shenyang (July/August will be no problem). Allow about five days for the round trip from, say, Shenyang. Tour buses go up the mountain in the July/August period, but in other periods you may have trouble finding a bus from Erdao. The only other local transport is logging trucks and official jeeps – the latter are expensive to rent, the former are very reluctant to give rides.

**Mingyuegou route** There are trains to Mingyuegou from Shenyang North Railway Station; the trip takes about 16 hrs. If you arrive in Mingyuegou at night you can sleep in the station waiting room. There is also a small hotel in Mingyuegou which charges Y3.50 per person. Buses for Erdao depart from 7.20 am to 10.30 am. The one-way trip costs Y4.30 and takes nine hours to trundle the 125 km. But the next hurdle is how to get from Erdao to Changbai, a further 40 km. Special tourist buses run from Mingyuegou to the Changbai hot springs area in July and August; these cost Y20 return for a three-day package. There are also trains from Changchun to Mingyuegou.

**Erdao route** Erdao is the end of the line as far as trains go – a scrap yard for locos. There's no hotel for foreigners yet, but there's a first-class waiting room at the station. To get to Erdao from Jilin, Changchun or Shenyang, you must take a train to Tonghua and then change to a train for Erdao. The two daily trains between Erdao and Tonghua have no sleepers, only cars with soft seats (green velvet) and real hard wooden benches (ouch!). The 500-series trains take nine hours of chuggalugging to make the trip between Tonghua and Erdao. If you're overnighting then it's preferable to take soft seat in lieu of sleeper. Connections in Tonghua may take several hours to come through.

**BACKWOODS**
The Changbai Shan region presents some possibilities for shaking off the cities and traipsing through the wastelands – and gives you some good reasons for doing so. Rough travel, rough places, rough toilets – if you can find one.

A permit for Changbai Shan is good for Antu County, the boundaries of which are unclear. In case there is some confusion, there are two Antus – old Antu and new Antu. Old Antu is to the north (renamed Mingyuegou during the Cultural Revolution), and new Antu is closer to Changbai. Both of them are ragged heaps of mud, littered with pigs, howling dogs and shanties. The whole zone is the Yanbian (Chaoxian) Korean Autonomous Prefecture, which is populated by people of Korean descent – often indistinguishable in dress from their Chinese counterparts. The Koreans are a fairly lively lot, given to spiced cold noodles, dog meat, song and dance – and hospitality. They can also drink you under the table. Yanbian has the greatest concentration of Korean and Korean-Han groups in China, and they mostly inhabit the border areas north and north-east of Erdao, extending up to Yanji.

Yanji is the capital of the autonomous zone – both Korean and Chinese languages are used there, and some semblance of traditional costume and custom is maintained. The countryside around Yanji is sprinkled with clusters of thatched cottages. Since Yanji lies on the rail line between Mingyuegou and Tumen (and thence to Mudanjiang in the southeast of Heilongjiang Province) it should be not too difficult to drop in for a visit, except that rail frequencies are low along this route. Ah well, we all make mistakes, don't we?

Transport is faster by rail, as opposed to spine-jangling dirt roads. There are only jeeps or logging trucks, apart from public buses. Off the main track, the trains are puffing black dragons, possibly of Japanese vintage, not crowded, old fittings, no sleepers, and some surprises in the dining-car – one old gentleman was observed opening a bottle of spirits with chopsticks and downing the whole thing.

Food in general leaves a lot to be desired – in the Korean places you can get by on cold noodles with a pile of hot spices or some meat and egg on top. In a Tonghua restaurant I was rather relieved when two beggars fought it out and wolfed down the remaining grey dumplings on my plate – I was feeling off-colour from the ones I'd already eaten. A bus lunch-stop along the way yielded a hell's kitchen, with pig's heads bloodying the floor, fires going in corners, and concoctions bubbling away in cauldrons. Getting there is half the fun: an English traveller headed off for Dandong (in Liaoning) from Tonghua by bus, a 14-hour trip with an overnight stop. He was chased around various bus stations by a variety of policemen, and arrived hungover from a night carousing with the other passengers.

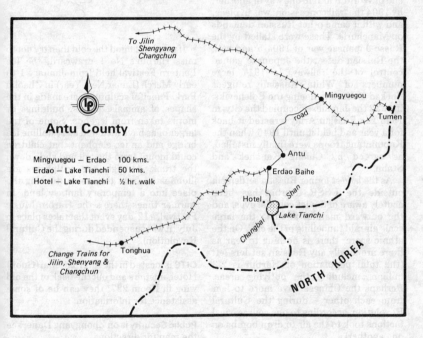

To Jilin
Shengyang
Changchun

**Antu County**

Mingyuegou – Erdao     100 kms.
Erdao – Lake Tianchi     50 kms.
Hotel – Lake Tianchi     ½ hr. walk

Mingyuegou

Tumen

road

Antu

Erdao Baihe

Hotel

Shan

Lake Tianchi

Changbai

NORTH KOREA

Change Trains for
Jilin, Shenyang &
Changchun     Tonghua

# Heilongjiang

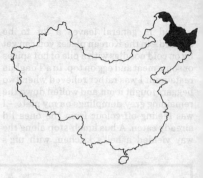

## HARBIN

Harbin was a fishing village until 1896, when the Russians negotiated a contract for shoving a rail line through it to Vladivostok (and Dalian). The Russian imprint on the town remained until the end of World War II in one way or another; by 1904 the 'rail concession' was in place, and with it came other Russian demands on Manchuria. These were stalled by the Russo-Japanese war of 1904-5 and with the Russian defeat the Japanese gained control of the railway. In 1917 large numbers of White Russian refugees flocked to Harbin, fleeing the Bolsheviks; in 1932 the Japanese occupied the city; in 1945 the Russian Army wrested it back for a year and held it until 1946 when the Kuomintang troops were finally installed, as agreed by Chiang Kai-shek and Stalin.

As the largest former Russian settlement outside the USSR, Harbin has been acutely aware of Soviet colonial eyes, and the outward manifestation is the large scale air raid tunnelling in the city. On the ethnic score, there is nothing to fear as there are hardly any Russian settlers left (the total population of Harbin is 2.3 million, including the outlying areas. Perhaps the Chinese have more to fear from each other – during the Cultural Revolution, according to one source, rival factions took to the air to drop bombs on one another).

Harbin's industry grew with its role as a transport hub. Predominant production includes foodprocessing, machinery, tools, cement, paper, pharmaceuticals, electric motors and steam turbines. Output has taken its toll on the Songhua River where the fish population has been decimated (some reports of mercury poisoning) and the water level has declined. As the provincial capital, Harbin is the educational, cultural and political centre of Heilongjiang.

If you don't mind the cold then try not to miss Harbin's No 1 drawcard, the Ice Lantern Festival held from January 1 to early March (Lunar New Year) in Zhaolin Park. Fanciful sculptures are made in the shapes of animals, plants, buildings or motifs taken from legends. Some of the larger ones have included a crystalline ice bridge and an ice elephant that children could mount from the tail and slide down the trunk. At night the sculptures are illuminated from the inside, turning the place into a temporary fantasy land. In warmer times there's the Harbin Music Festival, a 12-day event that takes place in July (it was suspended during the Cultural Revolution).

**CITS** is located in the International (Guoji) Hotel, upstairs and out the back of the old wing in Room 227; they can be of some assistance for information.

**Public Security** is on Zhongyang Dajie; see the map for directions.

**CAAC** (tel 52334) has its office at 87 Zhongshan Lu.

## Things to See

Put wandering around the market areas and the streets high on your list. There's a very different kind of architectual presence in Harbin, with Soviet spires, cupolas and scalloped turreting; Zhongyang Lu and Sun Island are good to investigate.

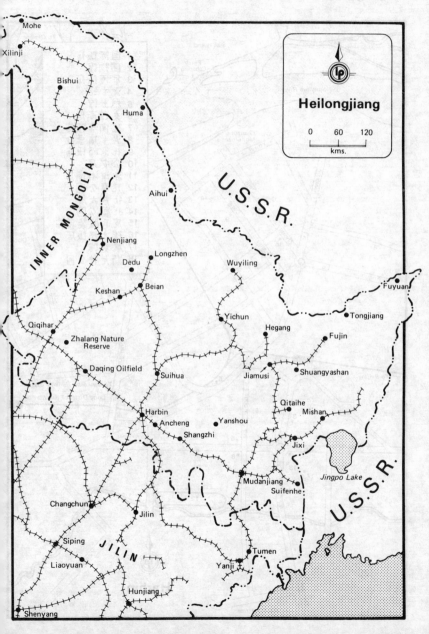

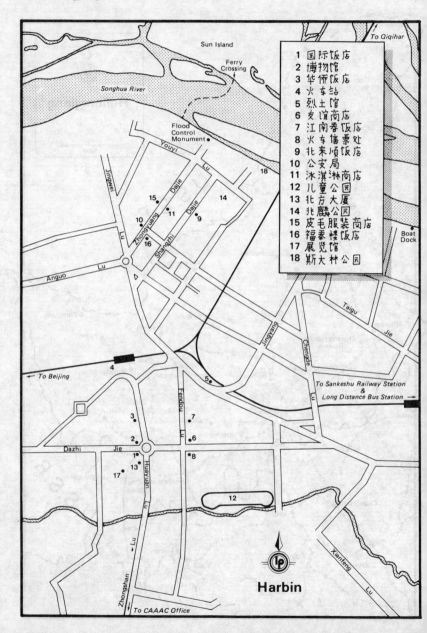

To Qiqihar

Sun Island

Ferry
Crossing

Songhua River

Flood
Control
Monument

Youyi Lu

Jingwei Lu

Daije

Daije

Zhongyuang Lu

Shangzhi

Anguo Lu

15

10

11

16

14

9

18

Boat
Dock

Taigu Jie

Jingyang Lu

Chende Lu

← To Beijing

4

5

To Sankeshu Railway Station
&
Long Distance Bus Station →

3

7

Fendou Lu

2

6

Dazhi Jie

1

8

17

13

Huanyuan Lu

12

Zhongshan Lu

Xianteng Lu

**lp**

**Harbin**

To CAAAC Office

1 国际饭店
2 博物馆
3 华侨饭店
4 火车站
5 烈士馆
6 友谊商店
7 江南春饭店
8 火车售票处
9 北来顺饭店
10 公安局
11 冰淇淋商店
12 儿童公园
13 北方大厦
14 兆麟公园
15 皮毛服装商店
16 福泰楼饭店
17 展览馆
18 斯大林公园

Harbin has several dozen Orthodox Churches but most were sacked during the Cultural Revolution and have since been boarded up or converted to other uses. A few stray onion-domes punctuate the skyline in the Daoliqu district (the spelling here may not be correct) which is the rectangle bounded by the Flood Control Monument, Zhaolin Park, Public Security Bureau and the railway line.

The Daoliqu district, in the section toward the banks of the Songhua River, has the best specialty-type shops, some market activity, and is worth your time on foot. Another shopping and market area is to be found north-east of the Guoji Hotel, a short walk away at Dazhi Dajie.

### Children's Railway

Located in the Children's Park, this railway was built in 1956. It has two km of track and is plied by a miniature diesel pulling seven cars with seating for 190; the round trip (Beijing-Moscow?) takes 20 minutes. The crew and administrators are kids under the age of 13.

### Stalin Park

Down by the river, this is a tacky strip stacked with statues, and it's the number one perambulating zone, with recreation clubs for Chinese. A 42 km embankment was constructed along the edge to curb the unruly Songhua River – hence the Flood Control Monument which was built in 1958. The sandy banks of the Songhua take on something of a beach atmosphere in summer, with boating, icecream stands,

photo booths. Tour boats arranged through CITS are possible but you might like to investigate local boat docks for a quick sortie down the Songhua.

During winter the Songhua River becomes a road of ice (when it's one metre thick it can support a truck) and the Stalin Park/Sun Island area is the venue for hockey, skating, ice-sailing, sledding and sleighing – equipment can be rented.

### Sun Island

Opposite Stalin Park, and reached by a ferry hop, is Sun Island, a combo sanatorium/recreational zone still under construction. The island covers 3,800 hectares and has a number of artificial features – a lake, hunting range, parks, gardens, forested areas – all being worked on to turn this into Harbin's biggest touring attraction. In summer there's swimming and picnics; in winter it's skating and other sports. There are a number of restaurants on Sun Island and more facilities are planned.

### Other Attractions/Non-Attractions

The Provincial Museum is opposite the Guoji Hotel and has some boring historical and natural history sections; the Industrial Exhibition Hall is dead boring; the Zoo is lukewarm but it does have some Manchurian Tigers and Red-crowned Cranes. The Martyr's Museum in the centre of town, has relics from the anti-Japanese campaign.

| | |
|---|---|
| 1 Harbin Internation Hotel / CITS | 10 Public Security Bureau |
| 2 Natural History & Science Museum | 11 Ice-cream Shop (Run by Harbin Hotel) |
| 3 Overseas Chinese Hotel | 12 Children's Railway Park |
| 4 Main Railway Station | 13 Beifang Mansions |
| 5 Matyr's Museum | 14 Zhaolin Park |
| 6 Friendship Store / Dept. Store | 15 Fur Shop |
| 7 Jiangnanchun Restaurant | 16 Futailou Restaurant |
| 8 Advance Rail Ticket Office | 17 Industrial Exhibition Hall |
| 9 Beilaishun Moslem Restuarant | 18 Stalin Park |

## Places to Stay

There are three hotels all grouped in the same area, and you can take any bus (or even a rickety tram) on the road leading from the railway station to get there – alternatively, it's about a one km walk.

The *Guoji (International)* (tel 31441) is at 124 Dazhi Jie, Nagang District. It's got two wings, a new nine-storey high-rise, and an old wing, but the latter has been renovated. It's a classy place costing Y60 to Y90 a double. For seekers of dormitories, abandon hope all ye who enter here – or bring out your boxing gloves because it's a guaranteed two hour wrangle. Anyway, a foreign expert got a single room for Y12 single – try the old wing.

The *Oversea; Chinese Hotel* is down the street from the International, and will take foreigners. Comfortable double rooms (without TVs) are Y24. The hotel has got 270 rooms and it was undergoing extensive renovation.

The *Beifang Dasha (Beifang Mansions)* (tel 33061) looks like the Kremlin – you can't miss it! Ten floors harbour 350 rooms, but they're not at all interested in foreigners; double rooms are Y36 if you can get one. The Beifang is at 115 Huayuan Lu, Nagang District.

There are also several exclusive villa-style hotels in Harbin with billiards and all other mod cons, but they're meant for foreign heads of government and the like. Some additional tourist accommodation is proposed for Sun Island, and another proposal is a floating hotel – a converted 3000-ton liner.

## Places to Eat

Within easy walking distance of the hotel locations on Dazhi Jie is a large back-street market with lots of snacks – it's big on sausage, bread and noodles. Also in this area is a large dinery, the *Jiangnanchun* (tel 34398) with dumplings downstairs and main fare upstairs including roast duck and braised dishes. It's at 316 Fendou Jie, Nangang District.

There are a couple of places around Stalin Park; on the edge of Zhaolin Park at 113 Shangzhi Lu is the *Beilaishun Restaurant* (tel 45673) serving Moslem beef and mutton dishes upstairs and also hotpot in winter. The *Futailou Restaurant* (tel 47598) at 19 Xi Shisandao serves Beijing Roast Duck and other dishes, but you need to order two days in advance for regional specialties. The *Huamei Restaurant* (tel 47368) at 142 Zhongyang Lu serves western-style food.

For snacks, head to Zhongyang Lu, leading south off the Flood Control Monument. This is a quieter shopping area with pink, cream, mustard and grey Euro-style buildings. It's a quiet street, that is, until you reach *Hongxia Lengshibu*, a few blocks down from the Monument on the west side. Candles, beer, sausage, bread, and crates of bottles are stacked to the ceiling here – aye, matey, it's a Chinese pub! Well, about as close as you'll get to one this side of the Elephant & Castle. There are also several icecream, keke and kafei places along Zhongyang, including a quaint greenhouse-type cafe that abutts the Harbin Hotel (the Harbin is a Chinese-only hotel). The glace variety icecream is quite good.

As for the hotels, the *International* is riddled with dining rooms of all shapes, sizes and prices; anyone for grilled bear paws? Or some stewed moose nose with monkey-leg mushrooms? These and other elaborate delicacies are served up only in the banquet rooms. The front-section ground-floor dining room of the new wing has western breakfast for Y3. The *Beifang Mansion* has several restaurants and banquet rooms within.

## Shopping

The Friendship Store is on the top floor of the Department Store on Dazhi Jie. It is, for a change, open to all and sundry (at least for locals to gaze at, since many items are beyond their pockets) and you can use renmibi. It's got a selection of furs, leather, jade work, paintings, ox and goat-horn carvings. The *Fur Product Shop* on Zhongyang Lu has slightly lower prices and a larger fur selection than the Friendship Store (coats, vests, hats, gloves). Fur overcoats run from Y200 up (fox, squirrel, sable, some otter collars, sheepskin cushions). Harbin is the best place to buy furs.

### Getting Around

There are over 20 bus routes in Harbin; buses start at 5 am and finish at 10 pm (9.30 pm in winter). Bus No 1 or trolley bus No 3 will take you from the hotel area to Stalin Park. CITS has a boat tour along the Songhua River which lasts 2½ hours and costs Y10 per head.

### Getting Away

There is a long-distance bus station near Sankeshu Railway Station which takes care of a large proportion of bus departures.

For details of trains, see the introduction to the north-eastern provinces.

From Harbin there are flights to Beijing (Y144), Canton (Y388), Changchun (Y29), Shanghai (Y290), and Shenyang (Y65). There may also be flights to Jiamusi. The airport is 35 km outside Harbin.

### MUDANJIANG & LAKE JINGPO

Mudanjiang is an industrial city of 700,000 to the south-east of Harbin. The main attraction of the region is Jingpo (Mirror) Lake, 110 km southwest of Mudanjiang. Far-flung as this place might be, do not presuppose it will be devoid of people – the Chinese have an uncanny habit of turning up in remote areas in large numbers! However, those seeking some quiet hiking with some fishing villages thrown in (villagers of Korean descent) should find the Jingpo Lake nature reserve adequate enough.

The lake itself covers an area of 90 sq km; it's 45 km long from north to south, with a minimum width of 600 metres and a maximum of 6 km and it's dotted with islets. The nature reserve encompasses a strip of forest, hills, pools and cliffs around the lake and there is a lava cave in the area. The main pastime is fishing (the season is June to August) and fishing tackle and boats can be rented for Y30 to Y40 a day; different varieties of carp (silver, black, red-tailed, crucian) are the trophies.

The name 'Mirror Lake' comes from a legend about to a wicked king who sent his minister out every week to find a beautiful girl – if the girl wasn't the right material, he'd have her killed. A passing monk gave the king a mirror to aid in the selection, saying that this mirror would retain the reflection of a true beauty, even after she turned away. The minister duly trotted off, found a beautiful girl at the lake, and found that the mirror test worked. The king immediately asked for the lady's hand. 'What is the most precious thing in the world?' asked the girl. The king thought for some time; 'Power' he replied. Upon hearing this, the girl threw the mirror into the lake, a storm broke out, and she vanished. The moral of the story – it's all done with mirrors – perhaps . . .

### Places to Stay

The centre of operations is the *Jingpo Villa*, at the north end of the lake. Double rooms start from Y30. Boat cruises can be arranged here and there is a small beach nearby. The smallish Mansion Falls (20 metres high, 40 metres wide) is north of Jingpo Villa and within easy hiking distance of it.

### Getting Away

Mudanjiang is linked by rail to Tianjin and Beijing (via Harbin) with two or three trains a day. There are also slower connections by rail to Tumen (about six hours, one train a day), and to Jiamusi (about 10 hours, two trains a day). Jingpo Lake is linked by public bus to Mudanjiang – it's a dirt road.

## JIAMUSI

North-west of Harbin is Jiamusi. Once a fishing village, it mushroomed into a city of half a million, and now deals in aluminium smelting, farm equipment manufacture, and sugar refining, and has a paper mill, plastics factory and an electrical appliances factory.

Amongst the sights are **Sumuhe Farm**, located in the suburbs of Jiamusi. This farm grows ginseng and has a deer farm with over 700 head of sika and red deer which are raised for the antlers (they also raise martens here, close kin to the weasel family). It's not really such a strange combination – in fact the 'three treasures' of the North-East are ginseng, deer antlers and sable pelts. (Each of these is well represented further south in Jilin Province where production is largely domesticated. The magic properties of ginseng are peddled in a wide range of Jilin products, from cosmetics to wines). Use of the ginseng root dates back to the Han dynasty, 1700 years ago. It's a general pep-tonic, life-lengthener and also thought to deal with 'women's problems'. Deer pilose antler, cut into wafers or powdered, is claimed to benefit internal organs, and improve horniness and performance. If ginseng and deer antler are combined in tablet form the earth is yours, and it will take care of bladder disorders and nightmares (is there a relation between the two?). Wild ginseng from the Changbei Shan area fetches astronomical sums on the Hong Kong market.

Other curious items in the north-eastern pharmacopoeia include frog oil, taken from a substance in the frog's ovary. These and other entries will arrive in soups or with stewed chicken if a banquet is ordered at a ritzy hotel. (Non-banquet food, on grease-laden dining tables, is abysmal in the north-east, so a visit to the local medicine shop is obligatory for stays of more than a week's duration).

The **New Friendship Farm** is about 110 km east of Jiamusi on the rail line , a state-run frontier enterprise that is the pride of Heilongjiang – the pioneers who built it arrived in the 1950's and now number around 100,000, organised into numerous agricultural brigades.

The **Village of Fools** is not the pride of Heilongjiang; it's located in Huachuan county to the east and northeast of Jiamusi. The cretins and bearers of bulbous goitre are being studied at Jiamusi Medical College – the cause of their problems is suspected to be dietary deficiencies.

### Getting Away

Jiamusi is connected by rail to Harbin (a 15 hour trip), Dalian and Mudanjiang. Steamers ply the Songhua River so it may be possible to travel between Harbin and Jiamusi by water. There may also be flights between Harbin and Jiamusi.

## DAQING

Daqing is an oil boom town which appeared on the swamplands in 1960. This is one of those triumph of the spirit towns, and a demonstration of China's awesome ability to mobilise manpower for *the cause*. The first drilling began in the 1950s with Soviet technical assistance; when the Russians withdrew in 1959, the Chinese decided to carry on alone. Shortly after, the first well gushed, and a community of tents, wooden shanties and mud-housing erupted in the sub-zero wilderness. By 1975, Daqing was supplying 80 per cent of the PRC's crude oil; production has since tapered off to less than 50 per cent. Most of the oil is piped through to the coast near Dalian.

Daqing is an industrial model – 'In industry, learn from Daqing' being one of the oft-repeated slogans – but whether much is being done to alleviate the harsh conditons of the Daqing workers is questionable. In the late 1970s large sums of money were pumped into this vast sprawl of refineries, petrochemical plants and agricultural centres for the construction of apartment blocks. The figure given is that 20,000 families have been accommodated – a drop in the bucket for a population of 760,000. The rest wait out the Manchurian winter in their mud or wood sheds.

There's no downtown in Daqing as such – there are some 8,000 oil wells scattered throughout the 5000 sq km area with small communities attached. Saertu, however, serves as the administrative, economic and cultural sector, with residential and office buildings, library, stores, modernisation playground, exhibition halls and greenhouses. There's a spartan hotel in Saertou, and you may be allowed to view model bits of the Daqing area such as medical facilities, school or recreational props.

## YICHUN

Towns in the north-east are either built of mud, or in transition to brick buildings (minus the plumbing). Yichun falls into the former category, a real frontier town hacked out of the forest in the 1950s, and still in progress. Adobe housing, horse carts, mud and pigs and slime. It's a logging town (pine, maple, oak and birch in the surrounding forest tracts) with a timber-processing plant (some of the timber tracts are protected from logging). Yinchun's population is about 100,000 – the place is actually a number of isolated settlements with Yichun as the focal point.

Yichun is linked by rail to Jiamusi and to Harbin (two trains a day between April and September, and the trip to Harbin is about 12 hrs).

## QIQIHAR & THE ZHALONG NATURE RESERVE

Qiqihar is one of the oldest settlements in the North-East. It's another industrial town, with a population of over a million, dealing with locomotives, mining equipment, steel, machine tools and motor vehicles. There's not much to see here, a zoo, a stretch of riverside and the ice-carving festival from January to March. The *Hubin Hotel* is close to the railway station

and double rooms start from Y20. The town is linked by direct rail to Beijing (about 22 hours) via Harbin (about four hours).

Qiqihar is the gateway to the Zhalong Nature Reserve, 35 km to the south-east, linked by a brand new road – though there's not much traffic along it and you may have to resort to hitching or getting a taxi. The modest *Zhalong Hotel* has double rooms for Y20, and offers touring through the fresh-water marshes of the reserve for Y40 per day, in flat-bottom boats.

The Zhalong Reserve is at the north-west tip of a giant marshland, about 210,000 hectares of reeds, moss and ponds. It lies strategically on a bird migration path from the Soviet Arctic, around the Gobi Desert, and down into South-East Asia. The bird species number some 180 including storks, swan, goose, duck, heron, grebe, egret . . . The tens of thousands of winged migrants arrive in April to May, rear their young June to August, and depart September to October. Birds will be birds – they value their privacy. While some of the cranes are over 1.5 metres tall, the reed cover is taller. The area is mainly of interest to the patient binoculared and rubber-booted ornithologist – or naturalists and conservationists.

The nature reserve was set up in 1979 – one of China's first. In 1981 the Chinese Ministry of Forestry invited Dr George Archibald (Director of the ICF, the International Crane Foundation) and Wolf Brehm (Director of Vogelpark Walsrode, West Germany) to help set up a crane centre at Zhalong. Of the 15 species of cranes in the world, eight are found in China, and six are found at Zhalong. Four of the species that migrate here are on the endangered list; the Red-crowned Crane, the White-naped Crane, the Siberian Crane and the Hooded Crane. Both the Red-crowned and White-naped Cranes breed at Zhalong (as do the Common and Demoiselle Cranes), while Hooded and

Siberian Cranes use Zhalong as a stopover.

The centre of attention is the Red-crowned Crane, a fragile creature whose numbers at Zhalong (estimated to be 100 in 1979) were threatened by drainage of the wetlands for farming. The near-extinct bird is, ironically, the ancient symbol of immortality and has long been a symbol of longevity and good luck in the Chinese, Korean and Japanese cultures. With some help from overseas experts, the eco-system at Zhalong has been studied and improved, and the number of these rare birds has risen. A small number of hand-reared (domesticated) Red-crowned and White-naped Cranes are kept in a pen at the sanctuary for viewing and study. On the eve of their 'long march' southwards in October, large numbers of cranes can be seen wheeling around, as if in farewell. The birds have been banded to unlock the mystery of their winter migration grounds (either Korea or southern China).

Since the establishment of the International Crane Foundation George Archibald and Ron Sauey have managed to create a 'crane bank' in Wisconsin, USA, stocking 14 of the 15 known species. They've even convinced the North Koreans to set up bird preserves in the mine-studded DMZ between North and South Korea and the travel baggage of these two includes suitcases full of Siberian crane-eggs picked up in Moscow (on one trip a chick hatched en route, nicknamed 'Aeroflot'). Last on the egg-list for the ICF is the black-necked crane, whose home is in remote Tibet and for whom captive breeding may be the last hope.

# The
# South – West

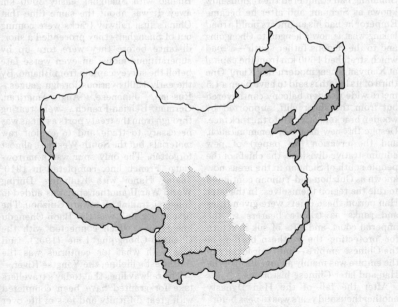

The south-west of China is a tangle of immensely high mountains and precipitous cliffs, cut through by roaring mountain rivers fed by melting snows and covered by dense sub-tropical forests. This is China's backyard jungle, with fertile basins, exotic flora and fauna, rapids, jagged limestone pinnacles, gorges, caverns, and towering peaks that rush up to meet the edges of the Tibetan Plateau. For centuries, communication by river was hazardous because of the rapids, and communication by road assumed heroic feats of human engineering and endurance. A turbulent history lies behind the brooding landscapes, especially in Yunnan and Sichuan where tribal kingdoms have long resisted colonial encroachments.

The ancestors of the Emperor Qin Shihuang had conquered the regions now known as Sichuan, and after he became Emperor he had his engineers build a road linking what is now Chengdu to Chongqing and to the regions futher south – a road which stretched 1600 km from the capital at Xianyang (near modern-day Xian). One third of its length is said to have been a 1.5 metre wide wooden balcony cantilevered out from the sheer cliff, supported by wooden brackets driven into the rock face. Despite this new means of communication, and the creation (on paper) of new administrative divisions, the chiefs of the people south of Sichuan in the areas now known as Guizhou and Yunnan continued to rule the region themselves. In the later Han period these chiefs were given titles and ranks as tribute bearers to the imperial court, and gifts of silk in return for 'protecting' the southern borders of the Chinese empire – but their loyalty to the empire was mainly an invention of the Han and later Chinese historians.

After the fall of the Han Dynasty another thousand years was to pass before much of the south-west could be effectively integrated into the empire, and even then it continued to revert to independence at every opportunity. In the mid-13th century the region was almost finally pounded into submission – this time by the Mongol armies of Mangu Khan. When the Mongol rule collapsed in 1368 the south-western regions once again broke with the north; Sichuan was won back by a Ming military expedition in 1371 and Yunnan the following year. Again, when the Manchus invaded in the 17th century it was the south-western regions which held out the longest – partly due to their geographical location and partly due to inclination. But when the Qing Dynasty collapsed in 1911 the south-west was one of the first areas to break with the central government.

The story of the modern south-west is the story of the railways. In 1875, a British survey team set out from Bhamo, in Upper Burma. The British dream was to link Bhamo with Shanghai, easily 3000 km away. It was about the same time that China's first railway tracks were coming out of Shanghai – they proceeded a short distance before they were torn up by superstitious mobs; an even worse fate befell the survey captain from Bhamo. By the early 1900s various foreign gauges – Russian, Japanese, Anglo-American, German, Belgian-French – were tearing through from the treaty ports as far as was necessary to trade and to exploit raw materials, but the South-West was almost forgotten. The only spur was a narrow-gauge French line, completed in 1910, linking Hanoi with Kunming. During World War II another spur was added in Guangxi, trailing off toward Guizhou. The first major link was the Baoji-Chengdu line (1956), which connected with the Chengdu-Chongqing Line (1952), and thus with what for centuries was the southwest's lifeline, the Yangtse River.

The railway lines that today's travellers take for granted have been completed with great difficulty and loss of life over the past two decades. Over 5000 kms of added track have sliced literally months off travel time in the South-West. The crowning achievement is the Kunming-Chengdu Line, some 12 years in the making (finished 1970), boring through solid rock, bridging deep ravines and treacherous rivers.

Bar Sichuan, the south-west region is relatively underpopulated – and since its (substantial) natural resources remain largely untapped, the mainstay is agriculture – the industrial contribution to China as a whole is negligible. With the opening of the Chengdu-Kunming line there has been a boost in industry, including iron and steel, farm machinery production and the production of chemical fertilisers, in the cities along the path – as well as a gravitation of population to the railway havens. This railway line could actually be added to China's list of impossible projects that have become fact.

## Minority Peoples

Marco Polo has left us some fascinating anecdotes about tribes in the south-west – he arrived in Sichuan after Mangu Khan's armies had laid the place waste, leaving its temples and towns in ruins. The currency used at the time was salt, since the Khan's paper money had not yet come into force. Tigers and wild beasts were such a problem that travellers heaped green bamboo in their campfires – the joints would explode, thus scaring away animals. Marco Polo wrote:

Upon the arrival of a caravan of merchants, as soon as they have set up their tents for the night, those matrons who have marriageable daughters conduct them to the place and beg the strangers to lie with them ... Such as have the most beauty to recommend them are of course chosen, and the others return home disappointed. The chosen continue with the travellers until the point of departure, at which time they restore them to their mothers, and never attempt to carry them away.

Times have changed, as can be imagined, and you will be lucky to get a few lines in a notebook about the curious minority habits. The basic problem is that the minorities who have not been irretrievably Sinicized (loss of original language, customs life, dress, consciousness) are located in remote areas, or toward the sensitive border areas, or both. The south-west groups are mainly of Thai, Burmese and Tibetan origin, ranging in numbers from the 5.4 million Yi to just 4,700 Drung. In Yunnan, 22 of China's official total of 55 minorities are represented, the largest number of any province – and extremely difficult to either see or visit. One case in point are the Miao (Hmong) who number five million and are spread out through the south-west, Hunan, Guangdong and Hubei, as well as through Vietnam, Thailand, Laos and the Golden Triangle – theirs is a sad history of exploitation and disdain by other cultures.

It would be of little relevance here to pinpoint where exactly one might see genuine minority life, since very few westerners have actually seen it. In the north of Thailand you can get yourself a guide that speaks the language and trek off into the Golden Triangle to see different designations of hill-tribers growing opium poppies (and staying in villages along the route). Not so in China, even minus the opium – and supposedly the risk.

Special permission trekking tours have gained access to remote parts, as have mountaineering groups. On an individual basis, chances are slim – progress in remote terrain would be poor or non-existent, and would lead to substantial odds of being stopped. I met a photographer from Hong Kong who'd been given a go-ahead from his liaison with a Chinese photography association. With an escorted jeep, guide and porter he had spent some time running around the mountains of the south-west, using the jeep as far as the roads went, and then trekking into villages. He showed me some of the photos – fantastic stuff – tribespeople laden with kilos of silver jewellery and so on – but there was something terribly disturbing about the shots. They had no soul – they were staged. A pair of tennis shoes, a perfect set of teeth, stilted slow-motion posing, fingernails that looked like the lady had just stepped out of the manicurist. With startling regularity, the same smiling faces would appear engaged in different activities, as if pre-arranged – with a musical instrument or two added into the photo as if to remind the viewer that the minorities are fond of singing. If these people come from rough terrain, it didn't show in those pictures.

This is the picture-perfect world of the minorities that China would like to advertise, but the truth lies elsewhere. Many have suffered and still do – there are enormous hardships in isolation. Minorities are not exotica from the zoo, or part of a fashion parade – but lucky (some would have it 'colourful') survivors of different cultures. I did manage to slip into a stray piece of market-day tribal life – which revealed a totally different picture – like a town gone mad in the streets, giant water pipes, flashes of embroidered belts and head gear, bedraggled clothing, gnarled hands, donkey dung throughout, the weirdest industries in progress – and it sure was one hell of a lot of fun!

Points where one can, with official sanction, venture into minority areas are at the Huangguoshu Falls (Guizhou), the Stone Forest (Yunnan) and possibly Xishuangbanna (Yunnan). From those points, it may just be a case of venturing a little further – and there are other stepping stones right under your nose also. You would feel very awkward arriving in a remote village with no introduction – even the Chinese are wary of the 'rules' (the Han bow to seniors; shaking hands is regarded as rude or humiliating by some minorities). This assumes that you know what the customs are to begin with. Some minorities may be hostile to foreigners, and unpredictable reactions would ensue if a stranger talked to an unmarried woman – even more unpredictable reactions if a stranger attempted to photograph unmarried women. Combine this with a probable severe language and culture gap, as well as shyness – and things might not turn out as pleasant as the postcards make out. Then again, what makes minorities interesting is their very evasion of dreary Chinese rules and bureaucracy – if the ice was broken, you could be treated like a king, who knows?

The best approach, from all sides, is to time yourself for market day in a more obscure town – when tribespeople of various persuasions are bound to drift into town in their finery. This renders mission impossible to the mountains unnecessary, and in the chaos a foreigner can remain in the wings to witness some very lively interaction. Best of all, people expect weird things to surface on market day, and you, being one, tend to blend in – or at least they're a bit more primed for culture shock. The next step, or the one previous to this, is to find out when and where such a market day takes place in a small town and how to get there without attracting attention from the Chinese authorities. Apart from market day, minority wardrobe comes out for festival days, which would be the jackpot – bullfighting, dragon-boat racing, whatever – these occasions, however, attract large crowds of bored Chinese, and this severely impedes bus seat space to the region.

## TRAVEL IN THE SOUTH-WEST
### Trains – the horrors of hard-seat travel
Trains in the south-west are a pain in the arse. The problems arise, as they always do, with hard class seating. No person in his or her right mind would want to endure hard-seat for more than 12 hours – although some masochistic travellers have survived 48-hour ordeals and arrived somewhat dazed to put it mildly. Hard-sleeper is very comfortable (no crowding permitted), but the tickets may require as much as four days of waiting to get. In a place like Kunming, where you're likely to spend several days anyway, this is OK – just book a ticket out of the place immediately upon arrival.

If you wish to speed things up and carry on regardless, there are very *low* chances of upgrading your hard-seat to a hard-sleeper once on the train – this is eminently possible in northern China but not in the south-west. Soft-class sleepers will be available, but most low-budget travellers find them prohibitively expensive. You could try for a soft-seat, which is about the same price as a hard-sleeper ticket, but the trains in the south west don't seem to carry this class very much.

Apart from lack of sleepers, crowding is another *big* problem; Sichuan has the highest population of any province in China and Yunnan has the fewest rail lines: at times it seems that the whole quarter of mankind is hurtling down those tracks. Often the train is packed out before it even *gets* to the south-west, having loaded up in Shanghai (the No 79 Shanghai-Kunming express is a good example – if you get on board at Guilin you have about zero hope of getting a hard-sleeper, and you may not even get a soft-sleeper). On some trains hard-seat carriages have people hanging from the rafters, watering their turtles in the wash basins, spitting everywhere – absolutely crammed. On one train I travelled two westerners almost came to fisticuffs with locals over musical chairs (unreserved section). If a foreigner got up to go to the can, a local would bag the seat and refuse to budge; if the same displaced foreigner tried to pull the same stunt, all hell would break loose. At night, people are toe to toe in the aisles, or sprawled in foetal positions over the furniture. Hong Kongers refer to a phenomenon known as 'fishing' – which is where your head bobs up and down all night, with intermittent jerks. A jerk of a ruder nature – an Australian, supine under a hard seat, woke up in the middle of the night, to his horror, to discover that some Yellow River flooding was coming his way from the child above.

One has to retain one's sense of humour in such situations – it pays to distract yourself somehow. Compensation can be found in the scenery, which is sheer magnificence for much of the route – you should try and travel by day as much as possible to downplay the discomfort of night. The Chengdu-Baoji train, for my money, was one of the most scenic rides. The Kunming-Chengdu route I found to be a disappointment: engineering marvel that it is, it has tunnels every few metres (427 tunnels and 653 bridges to be exact, 40 per cent of the route) – and these plunge one into deafening darkness that precludes any attempt to talk, read, or even view the landscape. I made good use of the tunnels, however. I had gained some facility at Chinese chess on my travels, and had ingratiated myself into a window seat. My opponent had the largest tea mug I'd ever seen – it must've held a gallon – and he kept foisting food on me at an alarming rate. It's rude to say no – but the peanuts were the kind that break on your teeth, and the gray dumplings had fingerprints all over them. Each time we hit a tunnel, I simply hurled the dumplings over my shoulder and out the window – and spilled the peanuts to the floor.

Since the actual act of travelling in the south-west eats up so much of your time there, some strategy is called for. It's better to stop in fewer places, get to know people, leave time for decent train reservations (intermediary stations are not empowered to issue hard-sleeper tickets). If you're really in a bind in hard-class seating, and you've had all you can take, consider getting off at some intermediary station – tickets can be valid for up to seven days, and no re-purchase is necessary – you just use the same ticket to hop back on the next train heading in your direction. You'll be back in the same situation on the next train, but at least you'll get a refreshing night's sleep out of the stop (the first-class waiting room at the station can be wonderfully comfortable upon a midnight arrival). Another booster is to hang out in the dining-car after the rabble has been through – the staff may let you stay or they may kick you out, but it's worth a try – regale the staff there with English lessons on food terminology.

Provisioning on south-west trains is not the greatest – you should stock up like a squirrel for the long journey ahead where possible (coffee, fruit, bread, chocolate?).

### Itineraries

Distances are stretched in the south-west (Guangzhou to Kunming is 2216 km by rail) and the only way to speed it up is to shove an aeroplane in there somewhere or cut out destinations. The well-worn (and proven) route is take a boat from Canton to Wuzhou, then a bus to Guilin, and then travel by train Guiyang-Kunming-Emei-Chengdu-Chongqing. From Chongqing people usually take the Yangtse ferry to Yichang or further. You can also proceed direct from Guiyang to Chongqing, and another option is to bypass the Yangtse trip and head direct to Xian from Chengdu.

Approximate rail prices can be calculated using the distance tables in the 'Getting Around' section of this book.

A favourite plane trip is Canton to Kunming; it costs only Y60 (and the cost can be made up anyway by changing money on the black market in Guilin), and gives you an amazing view of the landscape as you fly in. The view is virtually guaranteed since CAAC will not take off if there is a rain cloud in the sky (though that can lead to lengthy delays of course). One of the newer services for tourists in Guilin is a flight over the karst formations – but you can get an aerial tour by flying there in the first place. You should also remember that the train from Canton to Guilin takes 20 hours(!) whilst flying takes 1½. The other useful flight is Guilin-Kunming, which costs Y109, and takes 1½ hours as compared with 33 hours on the railways. A hard-sleeper ticket will cost you around Y40 (Chinese price) – *if* you can get Chinese price, *if* there are any hard sleepers available.

Unexplored options are boating – the hovercraft from Hong Kong considerably speeds up the trip to Wuzhou, and from Wuzhou it should be possible to navigate to Nanning (this would be a very slow trip, but possibly a scenic one – larger boats anchor in midstream due to difficulties with rapids). An exit to consider is the flight from Kunming to Rangoon (see Getting Away in the 'Facts for the Visitor' section of this book for details).

# Guangxi

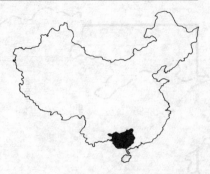

Guangxi first came under Chinese sovereignty when a Qin army was sent southwards in 214 BC to conquer what is now Guangdong Province and eastern Guangxi. Like the rest of the south-west the region was never firmly under the Chinese foot; the eastern and southern parts of Guangxi were occupied by the Chinese, while a system of indirect rule through chieftains of the aboriginal Zhaung people prevailed in the west.

The situation was complicated in the northern regions by the Yao and Miao tribespeople, who had been driven there from their homelands in Hunan and Jiangxi by the advance of the Han Chinese settlers. Unlike the Zhuang who easily assimilated Chinese customs, the Yao and Miao remained in the hill regions, often cruely oppressed by the Han. There was continuous trouble with the tribes, with major uprisings in the 1830s and another coinciding with the Taiping Rebellion. Today China's largest minority, the Zhuang, totalling 13.3 million people is concentrated in Guangxi. They're virtually indistinguishable from the Han Chinese – the last outward vestige of their original identity being their linguistic links with the Thai. Back in 1955 Guangxi Province was reconstituted as the Guangxi Zhuang Autonomous Region; the total population numbers 36.4 million.

The province remained a comparatively poor one until the present century; the first attempts at some modernisation of Guangxi were made during 1926-1927 when the 'Guangxi Clique', the main opposition to Chiang Kai-shek within the Kuomintang, controlled much of Guangdong, Hunan, Guangxi and Hubei. After the outbreak of war with Japan the province was the scene of major battles and substantial destruction. The fighting hasn't ceased either, it's just changed direction; the Chinese and Vietnamese have been sporadically exchanging cannon shells across Vietnam's border with Yunnan and Guangxi for the last few years – ever since yet another Communist fraternal relationship fell through.

A long way from the fighting is Guilin, Guangxi's No 1 attraction and one of the great drawcards of all China – this is the jumping off post for exploring the bizarre landscape for which the region is famous – and if Guilin seems too congested there's always Yangshuo a couple of hours down the Li River.

## WUZHOU

Sited at major and minor river junctions, Wuzhou was an important trading town in the 18th century. In 1897 the British dived in there, setting up steamer services to Canton, Hong Kong and later to Nanning. A British consulate was established – which gives some idea of the town's importance as a trading centre at the time – and the town was also used by British and American missionaries as a launching pad to convert the heathen Chinese.

Post-1949 saw some industrial development with the establishment of a paper mill, food processing factories, and machinery and plastics manufacturing amongst others. During the Cultural Revolution, Guilin and the nearby towns appear to have become battlegrounds for rivals, both claiming loyalty to Mao, and in what must have been more like civil war

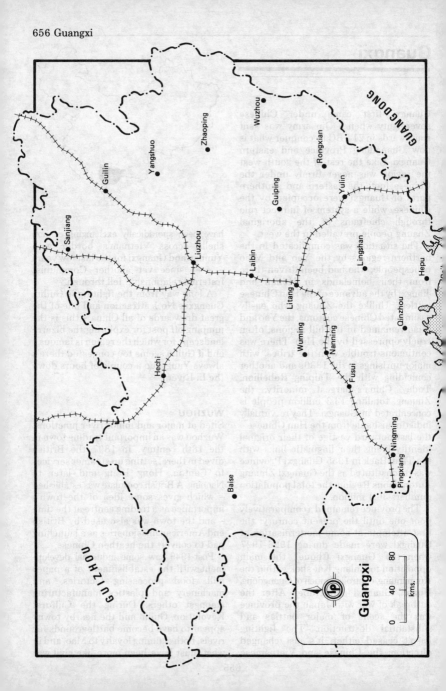

half the town of Wuzhou was reportedly destroyed – maybe, maybe not.

Today, Wuzhou has large snake depositories, probably the one sight of interest, but it's unknown if you can see these. More than one million snakes are transported annually to Wuzhou (from places like Nanning, Liuzhou and Yulin) for export to the palates of Hong Kong, Macao and other countries. The place has also got some street markets, tailors, tobacco, herbs, roast duck and some riverlife to explore.

## Places to Stay

The hotel is a 15 minute walk from either the bus station or the boat dock (if arriving by bus, check with the driver if the hotel is on his route – he could drop you off there). The hotel is on the sleazy side; a bed in a four-bed room is Y4 at the student rate; better rooms are available. The hotel has reasonable food and cold beer; if you don't have a permit for Wuzhou the hotel staff generally overlook it.

## Getting There

The main reason to go to Wuzhou is as a transit point to Guilin and Yangshuo. The easiest way to get to Wuzhou is on the hovercraft from Hong Kong; for details see the section on Getting There in the introductory part of this book. From Canton there are long distance buses, or an overnight boat – see the Canton section for details. From Wuzhou you can take a bus to Yangshuo and Guilin; the local bus to Yangshuo leaves the bus station at 6.30 am and costs Y8.20 – book early or it will be full. There is also an aircon bus leaving at 6.50 am which costs Y14 to Yangshuo. Bookings for it can be made at the ferry wharf, the bus station or the hotel. You'd be looking at about a seven hour trip to

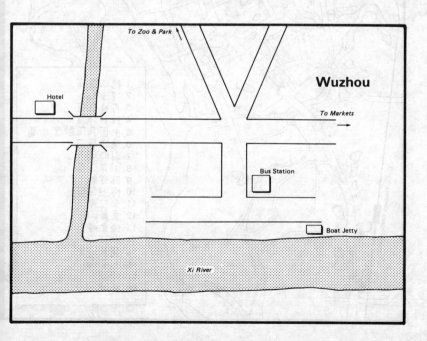

# Guilin

1 隐山饭店
2 汽车站
3 丹桂饭店
4 桂林饭店
5 中国民用航空总局
6 漓江船码头
7 游船码头
8 湖宾饭店
9 旅行社
10 榕湖饭店
11 公安局
12 象鼻山
13 独秀峰山
14 伏波山
15 叠彩山
16 七星山
17 榕湖
18 杉湖

Yangshuo and another two to Guilin, perhaps more depending on the bus. For more details on transport along this route, see the section on Yangshuo.

## GUILIN

Guilin has always been famous in China for its scenery and has been eulogised in innumerable literary works, paintings and inscriptions since its founding. The image that most westerners have of Chinese landscape is the landscape of Guilin. For the Chinese it's *the* tourist resort, the most beautiful spot in the world – the world of course meaning China.

The town sits in the midst of huge limestone peaks which haphazardly jut up out of the plains. Except for these, the town looks little different from other modern Chinese towns with its long wide streets lined with concrete blocks and factories scattered about. The whole town bursts at the seams with a flood of both Chinese and western tourists.

It's worth going to Guilin, but not for the scenery. Rather it's an education in the gestation of a 'tourist scene' which makes the town interesting. In spite of 35 years of Communism and the Cultural Revolution the Chinese didn't forget the meaning of private enterprise; It's a good place to come to learn about Capitalism. Already there's been a proliferation of privately-run shops with souvenirs and exorbitant prices catering for the foreign horde. There's a sort of travellers hangout-coffeeshop, a couple of places to rent

bicycles, a substantial black-market and one or two shonky discount tour-ticket operators. It probably won't grow much bigger than it is now (I may be underestimating Chinese ingenuity) since the tour-groups are going to remain within the official tourist setup and the individual travellers have been giving Guilin the big zero and moving off down to Yangshuo in droves. Nevertheless, Guilin is an interesting indication of just how fast the private entrepreneurs can get their act together given a chance.

The town, by the way, was founded during the Qin Dynasty and developed as a transport centre with the building of the Ling Canal which linked the important Pearl and Yangtse River systems. Under the Ming it was a provincial capital, a status it retained until 1914 when Nanning became the capital. During the 1930's and throughout World War II Guilin was a Communist stronghold and its population expanded from about 100,000 to over a million as people sought refuge here. Today it's the home of 300,000. There's another good reason to come here – the food rates as some of the most bizarre in China.

### Information and Orientation

Most of Guilin lies on the west bank of the Li River. The main artery is Zhongshan Lu which runs roughly parallel to the river on its western side. At the southern end of Zhongshan Lu (Zhongshan Nanlu), is Guilin South Railway Station where most

| 1 | Hidden Hill Hotel | 10 | Banyan Lake Hotel |
| 2 | Buses to Yangshuo | 11 | Public Security Office |
| 3 | Osmanthus Hotel | 12 | Elephant Trunk Hill |
| 4 | Kweilin Hotel | 13 | Solitary Beauty |
| 5 | CAAC | 14 | Fubo Hill |
| 6 | Lijiang Hotel | 15 | Decai Hill |
| 7 | Pier for Tour-boats Down the Li River | 16 | Seven Star Park |
| 8 | Hubin Hotel | 17 | Banyan Lake |
| 9 | CITS | 18 | Fur Lake |

trains pull in. The length of Zhongshan Lu is a hodge-podge of shops and tourist-hotels and a gourmet's delight of restaurants featuring a menagerie of culinary exotica.

Closer to the centre of town is Banyan Lake on the western side of Zhongshan Lu and Fur Lake on the eastern side. Further up is the main Zhongshan Lu/Jiefang Lu intersection. In this general area you'll find the CITS office, Public Security, places to rent bicycles, as well as Guilin's No 1 crash-pad, the large Li River Hotel.

Liberation Lu runs east-west across Zhongshan Lu. Heading east it runs over Liberation Bridge to the large Seven Star Park, one of the town's chief attractions. Most of the limestone pinnacles form a circle around the town though a few pop up within the city limits.

**CITS** (tel 2648) is at 14 Ronghu Beilu, fronting the northern bank of Banyan Lake on the western side of Zhongshan Lu. Friendly people and reasonably helpful.

**Public Security** (tel 3202) is on Sanduo Lu, a side-road which runs westwards off Zhongshan Lu, in between Banyan Lake and Jiefang Lu. Head south from the Zhongshan/Jiefang Lu intersection and turn right at the first street after Liberation Lu; the office is a few minutes walk down this road on the left. It's open daily 8 am to 5 pm but probably closed on Sundays; they're a friendly lot but don't expect any exotic permits.

**CAAC** (tel 2740) is at 144 Zhongshan Lu, just to the south of the intersection of Zhongshan and Shahu Beilu.

**Post** There's a post office in the Li River Hotel open 7.30 to 9 am, noon to 2.30 pm and 6 to 8 pm.

**Bank** There's a money-exchange counter at the Hidden Hill Hotel on the second floor, and another on the ground floor of the Li River Hotel. Both of these are open 8 to 9.30 am, 12.15 to 1.45 pm and 6 to 8 pm. There's a substantial black market in the town for Foreign Exchange Certificates. The 'change-money' women are lined up for the whole length of Zhongshan Lu and Shahu Beilu. The going rate is 120 RMB for 100 FEC, although one person actually got 130 RMB.

### Things to See

The best of Guilin's scenery is outside the town itself, although there are a few sights within the town limits. For the best views of the surrounding karst formations you either have to climb to the top of the hills or get out of the town altogther; the peaks are not very high and they often get obscured by the buildings – the best view of all can be had from the top of the Li River Hotel. Guilin is also an education in how to conjure up extraordinary names for lumps of rock.

### Duxiu Feng (Solitary Beauty)

This is a 152 metre pinnacle rising at the centre of the town. There's a steep climb to the top and a good view of the town, the Li River and surrounding hills. The nephew of a Ming emperor built a palace (the Wang Cheng) at the foot of the peak in the 14th century though only the gate remains. The site of the palace is now occupied by the Guangxi Provincial Teacher Training College. There are a couple of small pavilions at the top of the peak which look like they may have been public dunnies at one time. Bus No 1 goes up Zhongshan Lu past the western side of the peak, or you can take bus No 2 which goes past the eastern side along the river. Both buses leave from Guilin South Railway Station.

### Fubo Hill

Close to Solitary Beauty and standing beside the west bank of the Li River, this peak offers a better view of the surrounding countryside. Beside the steps leading to the top of the hill is an enormous cooking pot as well as a cast-iron bell weighing 2.5 tons. On the southern slope of the hill is **Huanzhu Dong (Returned Pearl Cave)** which takes its name from a local legend. The story goes that the cave was illuminated by a single pearl and inhabited by a dragon; one day a fisherman stole the pearl but returned it when he found himself filled with shame. Near this cave is **Qianfo Dong (Thousand Buddhas Cave)** where there are over 300 statues dating back to the Tang and Song Dynasties. Admission to the hill is 50 fen, and there's a bicycle park at the entrance. Bus No 2 goes straight past the hill.

### Qixing Gongyuan (Seven Star Park)

Seven Star Park is on the eastern side of the Li River; cross over **Liberation Bridge** and the Ming Dynasty **Hua Qiao (Flower Bridge)** to the park. The park takes its name from its seven peaks which are supposed to resemble the star pattern of the Ursa Major (Big Dipper) constellation. There are six caves in the park of which **Long Yin Yan (Dragon Hiding Cave)** and **Qi Xing Yan (Seven Star Cave)** are the most impressive. Visitors have been coming here for centuries and leaving inscriptions (graffiti) on their walls, including a recent one which says *The Chinese Communist Party is the core of the leadership of all the Chinese People.* It takes a lot of imagination (or maybe a lot of drugs) but you can gawk at stalacmites and stalactites with names like 'Monkey Picking Peaches' and 'Two Dragons Playing Ball'. There's also a children's playground in the park; cross Flower Bridge and turn left. The playground is a short walk down and off to the left of the track, but you'll have to look for it since it's obscured by trees and shrubs. To get to the park take bus No 9, 10 or 11 from the railway station. From the park, bus No 13 trundles back across across the Li River, past Fubo Hill and down to Reed Flute Cave.

### Ludi Yan (Reed Flute Cave)

Ironically, the most extraordinary scenery Guilin has to offer is underground, in this cave; if you see nothing else try not to miss it since the cave is a bit like a gaudily lit version of *Journey to the Centre of the Earth.* At one time the entrance to the cave was distinguished by clumps of reeds used by the locals to make musical instruments, and hence the name. Inside you enter a 'palace of natural art' or an 'abode of the immortals' (though how immortal you would remain living in a damp, dark cave . . . )

One grotto, the **Crystal Palace of the Dragon King** can comfortably hold about 1000 people, though many more crammed in here during the war when the cave was used as an air-raid shelter. The dominant feature of the cave is a great slab of white rock hanging down from a ledge like a cataract, while opposite stands a huge stalactite resembling an old scholar. The story goes that a visiting scholar wished to write a poem worthy of the cave's beauty. After a long time he had composed only two sentences lamenting his inability to find the right words, whereupon his uninspired writing career suddenly came to an end and he rather pointlessly turned to stone. The other story is that the slab is the Dragon King's needle, used as a weapon by his opponent the Monkey King. The Monkey King used the needle to destroy the Dragons' army of snails and jellyfish, leaving their petrified remains scattered around the floor of the cave.

The cave is on the north-western outskirts of town. You can take bus No 3 from the railway station which goes along Zhongshan Lu and then turns into the road which runs past Hidden Hill and Western Hill. Reed Flute Cave is the last stop. Bus No 13 will take you to the Cave from Seven Star Park. Otherwise, it's an easy bicycle ride. For a free guided tour, try tagging on to one of the innumerable western tour groups.

## Ling Canal

The Ling Canal is situated in Xingan County, 64 km north of Guilin. It was built during the 2nd century BC in the reign of the first Qing emperor Qin Shihuang to transport supplies to his army. It links the Xiang River (which flows into the Yangtse) and the Tan River (which flows into the Pearl River), thus connecting two of the major waterways of China.

You can see the Ling Canal at **Xigan**, a market town of about 28,000 people, two hours by road from Guilin. The town is also connected to Guilin by rail; a local train leaves Guilin in the morning and another returns in the afternoon. Two canals flow through the town, one at the north end and one at the south; the total length of the canal is 34 km. The local sights include **Feilaishi (Flying In From Elsewhere Rock)**, the **Su Bridge** and something called the **Memorial Hall of the Four Local Worthies**.

## Other Sights

**South Park** is a pretty place at the southern end of Guilin, where there are some caves in South Creek Hill, but if you've seen Reed Flute Cave give these a miss. There's another cave here where Liu the Immortal is said to have concocted his pills, and there are carvings of him in the cave. Admission to the park is 50 fen, but to the caves it's Y5 which is a bit ridiculous.

There are two lakes near the city centre, **Rong Hu (Banyan Lake)** on the west side and **Shan Hu (Fur Lake)** on the east side. Banyan Lake is named after an 800 year-old Banyan tree on its shore – the tree stands by the recently restored South City Gate (Nan Men) built during the Tang Dynasty.

Further north of Solitary Beauty is **Decai Shan (Folded Brocade Hill)**. Climb the stone pathway which takes you through the **Wind Cave** with walls covered with inscriptions and Buddhist sculptures. Some of the smashed faces on the sculptures are a legacy of the Cultural

Revolution. Great views from the top of the hill. Bus No 1 will take you past the hill.

West of the Li River, and across the railway line about 20 minutes walk from the Banyan Hotel are **Xi Shan (West Hill)** and **Yin Shan (Hidden Hill)**. Hidden Hill was named by the Tang Dynasty poet Li Bai (Li Po) who built a pavilion here, which was surrounded by water until drained in the 16th century. There are a couple of caves here. Bus No 3 from Guilin Station will take you to these hills. **Old Man Hill** is a curiously shaped hill to the north-east; there's a good view of it from Fubo Hill and the best way to get there is by bicycle – buses don't go near it.

At the southern end of town, one of Guilin's best-known sights is **Xiang Bi Shan (Elephant Trunk Hill)** which stands next to the Li River and is a lump of rock with a large hole in it.

**Zhuan Shan (Tunneled Hill)** and **Baota Shan (Pagoda Hill)** are a bit out of the way in the southern part of town on the east bank of the Li River. They can be reached by bicycle.

## Places to Stay

Most of Guilins major hotels are laid out along Zhongshan Lu. First up from Guilin South Railway Station is the *Hidden Hill Hotel*. Walk across the large square in front of the station and then head north up Zhongshan Nanlu; the hotel is a few minutes walk up ahead on the left. There are no single rooms, but doubles are Y30 and Y33 and an extra bed in the room is an additional Y10. They also have a dormitory for Y7 per bed. It's a tourist hotel, but it's not vast and cavernous like most other Chinese hotels. Friendly staff, comfortable rooms with private shower and toilet – if you can afford to stay here then it's probably the best place in town. They also have a money-exchange counter, restaurant and a massage service.

The *Osmanthus Hotel* is next up from the Hidden Hill, and is on your left just

Beijing Review, March 21. 1983

# ART PAGE

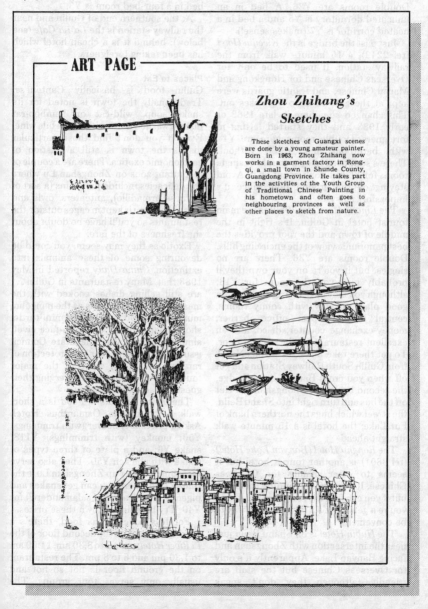

## Zhou Zhihang's Sketches

These sketches of Guangxi scenes are done by a young amateur painter. Born in 1963, Zhou Zhihang now works in a garment factory in Rongqi, a small town in Shunde County, Guangdong Province. He takes part in the activities of the Youth Group of Traditional Chinese Painting in his hometown and often goes to neighbouring provinces as well as other places to sketch from nature.

before the first bridge on Zhongshan Lu. Double rooms are Y36. A bed in an unheated dormitory is Y5 and a bed in a heated corridor is Y7 (makes sense!)

Just past the bridge is the *Kweilin Hotel* (tel 2249), a 15 minute walk from the railway station. It used to be only for Overseas Chinese and for Hongkong and Macau Chinese, and frantic guards were kept at the gate to keep big-noses out. This changed sometime in late 1982 or early 1983 and they started letting in foreigners. Double rooms here are Y14 with bathroom and Y9.60 without. There's supposed to be a couple of single rooms for Y6 but don't count on it. Avoid staying on the ground floor since it's impossibly noisy!

The *Lijiang Hotel* (tel 3050) is the main tourist hotel in Guilin. It's right in the middle of town and the roof provides the best panoramic view of the encircling hills. Double rooms are Y36. There are no singles, but if you're on your own they'll probably give you the room for Y18, although you may have to argue a bit. It's a good place to stay with comfy rooms, central location, post office, barber, money-exchange counter, disco, and an excellent restaurant on the second floor. To get there take bus No 1 or bus No 11 from Guilin South Railway Station and get off when you cross Banyan Lake Bridge, the second bridge on Zhongshan Lu. Get off the bus and turn right into Shahu Beilu, the street which hugs the northern bank of Fur Lake; the hotel is a 15 minute walk straight ahead.

The *Ronghu Hotel (Banyan Lake Hotel)* (tel 3801) is another tourist hotel but it seems to cater mainly for Overseas Chinese. It's no trouble finding the hotel, but if you can find the reception desk then you're a genius! It's a bit out of the way to be convenient.

The *Hubin Hotel* is on Shahu Beilu just near the intersection with Zhongshan and facing Banyan Lake. Apparently it's only for Overseas Chinese but the staff are friendly (although they don't speak English) and you may get a bed here. A bed in a four-bed room is Y3.

At the southern end of Guilin and near the railway station is the *La La Cafe* (see below); behind it is a cheap hotel which has been taking foreigners.

### Places to Eat

Guilin food is basically Cantonese. Traditionally the town is noted for its snake soup, wild-cat or bamboo-rat dishes, washed down with snake bile wine. Even if you don't find those particular dishes the town is still a bastion of gastronomic exotica. There are a couple of restaurant-zoos on Zhongshan Lu where the delicacies include pangolins (a sort of Chinese armadillo), anteaters, owls and cats. The menu is kept in cages outside the restaurants so you'll have no doubt about the freshness of the fare.

Exotic as they may seem, you could be devouring some of these animals into extinction. *China Daily* reported in May 1983 that 'Many restaurants in Guilin . . . are still selling dishes cooked with the meat of such rare animals as the pangolin, muntjac horned pheasant, mini-turtle, short-tailed monkey and gem-face civet, almost a month after the State Council issued a public order for the protection of rare wildlife. Even some of the major tourist hotels in the city are serving their guests these wildlife dishes'.

The *Jiang Pan Game Food* is a short walk north of the Osmanthus Hotel. Asking prices are; beaver (with trimmings) Y50; monkey (with trimmings) Y118; snake Y6; and a plate of three types of snake with chicken Y50. They also serve raccoons. Further up Zhongshan Lu is the *Guang Hua* where you can get snakes and pigeons, as well as giant salamander(?) for Y40. Try bargaining down these prices.

For less adventurous food, there's a good restaurant on the second floor of the *Li River Hotel*, open 7 to 8.30 am, 11.30 am to 1.30 pm and 6 to 8 pm. The restaurant on the ground floor is not so hot and usually only serves tour groups. The

*Hidden Hill Hotel* is good but not so commendable with their western dishes – whatever you do avoid their rice-porridge which is poisonous!

At night there are quite a few little stalls set up outside Guilin South Railway Station, serving cheap but well-cooked Chinese food and you'll probably attract quite a crowd if you eat here. Straight across from the Kweilin Hotel is a cheap place serving delicious dumplings.

The *La La Cafe* is one of the first traveller's hangouts in China, where trendy back-packers go to see and be seen. It's between the railway station and the Hidden Hill Hotel but on the *opposite* side of the road and has its name printed in English on the side of the building. It's run by a guy named Chen who speaks excellent English and serves excellent coffee.

## Getting Around

Bicycles are definitely the best way to get around Guilin! There are a couple of places where you can hire them. The first rental shop is on Zhongshan Lu just north of Banyan Lake Bridge; you'll see a small sign advertising bikes for rent on the right-hand side of the road as you walk northwards from the bridge. Charges are Y4.80 per day or Y0.60 per hour. You have to leave your passport or Y100 as security on the bike. For an extra Y2 you can keep the bike overnight. The shop is open 8 am to 6 pm. The second renter is the oddly-named 'Charlie's Cousins Co-op' situated across from Fur Lake just near the intersection of Shahu Beilu and Zhongshan Lu. Charges are Y5 per day or Y0.70 per hour and you probably won't have to pay a deposit. It's more expensive but they're good bikes. Further up Shahu Beilu outside the gate of the Li River Hotel another entrepreneur charges Y1 per hour and there's no deposit.

Taxis are available for hire from the major tourist hotels. Most of the town buses leave from the terminus at Guilin South Railway Station and will get you around to most of the major sights, but a bicycle is definitely better. You can make bookings at the tourist hotels for bus tours of the city and you're taken around with an English-speaking guide. A tour of Guilin city costs only Y10, the Li River trip costs Y40 (but it is possible to get this one cheaper), and a three-day tour which takes in Guilin, the Li River and Yangshuo costs Y60.

## Getting Away

Guilin is connected to various bits of the country by bus, train, boat and plane. Give serious thought to flying in or out of this place as train connections are not good.

**Bus** The long-distance bus station is on Zhongshan Lu, in between Guilin South Railway Station and the first bridge on Zhongshan Lu.

From here you can get buses to Yangshuo which depart at 6.50 am, 8.20 am, 10 am, 10.40 am, 1.30 pm, 2 pm, 3 pm, 4 pm, 5 pm, and 6 pm. The fare is Y1.65 and the ride takes about two hours through some absolutely stunning scenery!

Buses to Wuzhou depart each day at 6.20 am and 6.30 am. The fare is Y11.20 . There is also a direct bus to Canton which takes two days and you probably overnight in Wuzhou.

**Train** Train connections between Guilin and the rest of the country are not particularly wonderful and it tends to be a long haul getting to or from the place.

There are direct trains to Beijing (about 31 hrs), to Kunming (about 33 hrs), to Guiyang (18 hrs), to Zhanjiang (about 13 hrs), Liuzhou (3 hrs) and to Nanning. For Chongqing change trains at Guiyang.

The train to Kunming via Guiyang, takes about 36 hours. The express train is No 79 which runs Shanghai-Kunming and is *always* crowded and it's virtually impossible to get a seat, let alone a sleeper if you pick it up mid-way – though you might be able to get a soft-sleeper. If you're going to take a soft-sleeper or want to retain your sanity then consider flying – which is only Y109. If you do take the train then its suggested that you avoid the rush for non-existent seats by catching bus No 1 to Guilin North Railway Station – the train will *probably* stop here before carrying on to Guilin South Station – but check this out first.

There is no direct train to Canton; you have to stop at Hengyang and change to another. The entire trip takes 24 hours, including the stopover in Hengyang. If you're charged tourist-price (which you most likely will be in Guilin) than a hard-sleeper ticket will cost you Y40; for an extra Y20 you can fly and save all that time.

In 1983 Guilin railway station started clamping down on people who hadn't paid tourist price for their tickets. If you arrive from somewhere and you've only paid the local price, you may be stopped at the station and made to pay the full tourist price. (Fair enough – it's their job!)

**Plane** There are flights from Guilin to Beijing (Y232), Canton (Y60), Changsha (Y54), Chengdu (Y141), Chongqing (Y104), Hangzhou (Y148), Kunming (Y109), Nanning (Y48), Shanghai (Y167).

**Boat** It's possible to go the entire way from Guilin to Canton by water; see the section on Yangshuo for details.

## YANGSHUO

With Guilin transformed into a grey industrial town and populated with hordes of western and Chinese tourists, backpackers -incorporated have been evacuating the place in droves and heading down to Yangshuo, 80 km to the south. Yangshuo remains a tiny country town, set right in the midst of the limestone pinnacles, and from here you can get right out into the countryside and explore the small villages which litter the area. In fact, the scenery at Yangshuo makes giving Guilin a complete miss no hardship at all.

Chinese tourist leaflets have a peculiar way of plugging the place . . . 'the peaks surrounding the county town are steep and delicate, rising one higher than another like piled up petals. Their inverted images mirrored in the river are just like green lotus shooting up from the water, elegant and graceful. The sceneries in Yangshuo will make you enjoy the beauty of the natural world whenever you come. On fine days they bathe in the sunlight; in the rainy season they are in the misty rain; in the morning the glory casts upon them; at dusk the mountain haze enwraps them – all in all, they are colourful and in different postures, and make you feel intoxicant'.

### Information and Orientation

Yangshuo is a tiny town which lies entirely on the west bank of the Li River. The long-distance bus station is at the southern end of the town on the Guilin-Yangshuo road. Turn left out of the bus station and after a few minutes walk you'll come to the T-intersection with Yangshuo's main street. There's a post office at the intersection. Two minutes walk down the main street and on the left is the tourist hotel; fifteen minutes walk further down is the river, the Friendship Store and the wharf where the tour boats from Guilin dock.

### Things to See

Most people don't see enough of Yangshuo. They usually arrive on the Li River tour boats from Guilin, spend enough time on the wharf to buy some fruit and a few souvenirs and are whisked back to Guilin on the bus.

Yangshuo is a laid-back town if ever there was one in China, and it's one of the few opportunities to relax and explore the villages and countryside. Take off along the main roads and head off down the tracks which lead to old settlements. A lot of people have stayed overnight in the villages, and if you want to go camping on the mountains you shouldn't have any problem doing that either. It's probably not permitted to camp out but who's going to climb a 200 metre peak to bring you down?

The town itself is a pleasant place but there's nothing to see, although there's an old temple on the main street now being used as offices. The peace is disturbed only once a day when the tour buses burn up the main drag from the wharf on the

way back to Guilin. The hills in the immediate vicinity of the town have been given some cute names; **Green Lotus Peak** is the main peak in Yangshuo and stands next to the Li River in the south-east corner of the town. It's also called Bronze Mirror Peak because it's got a flat northern face which is supposed to look like an ancient bronze mirror. **Yangshuo**

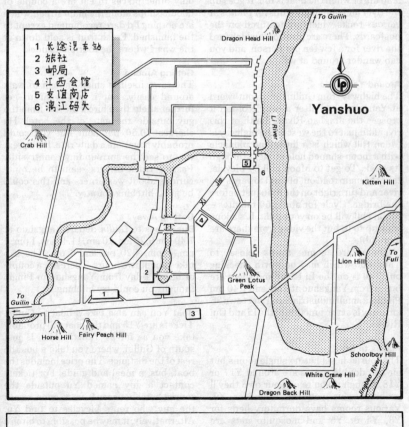

1　长途汽车站
2　旅社
3　邮局
4　江西会馆
5　友谊商店
6　漓江码头

Yanshuo

To Guilin
Dragon Head Hill
Li River
Crab Hill
Kitten Hill
To Fuli
Lion Hill
To Guilin
Green Lotus Peak
Horse Hill
Fairy Peach Hill
Schoolboy Hill
White Crane Hill
Dragon Back Hill
Jingbao River

1  Long Distance Bus Station
2  Hotel
3  Post Office
4  Temple
5  Friendship Store
6  Pier for Li River Tour Boats

Park is in the west of the town and here you'll find **Man Hill** which is supposed to resemble a young man bowing and scraping to a shy young girl represented by **Lady Hill**. The other hills are named after animals; **Crab Hill, Swan Hill, Dragon-head Hill** and **Dragon Back Hill, Kitten Hill, Lion Hill**, and **White Crane Hill**.

There is a mini boat trip down the Li River for Y3 per person, and it departs at 9.30 am or when the boat is full. It goes up the river and obligingly stops for photos at various rocks which are featured on the postcards. There are also boats which ford the river for a few fen per person, and you can wander around at will.

### Around Yangshuo

The highway from Guilin turns southward at Yangshuo and after a couple of km it crosses the Jingbao River. South of this river and just to the west of the highway is **Moon Hill** which is a limestone pinnacle with a moon-shaped hole straight through its peak. To get to Moon Hill by bicycle, take the main road out of town towards the river and turn right on the road just before the bridge. Cycle for about 50 minutes – Moon Hill will be on your irght. It's a long walk up to it, but the views from there are incredible.

There are some towns close to Yangshuo which may be worth checking out. **Fuli** is on the Li River and there are buses from Yangshuo at 8 am and 1.40 pm **Pinglo**, a small industrialised river town 35 km away is at the junction of the Li and Gui Rivers.

### Places to Stay

The tourist hotel has no single rooms but air-con double rooms are around Y17 or Y18, though if you're on your own they'll probably give you the room for Y9. Various rooms have dormitory beds for Y3, Y4 or Y5 and mosquito nets are provided. It's a pleasant hotel with a small lake and a desirable quantity of trees scattered about the compound, set back from the main road and should be quiet.

### Places to Eat

The restaurant at the hotel is certainly the best place to eat. You have to tell them a few hours in advance how much you want to pay for your meal (Y1, 2 or 3) and when you sit down in the dining hall they bring out plates of food for you; set menu, and no choice. If you refuse a dish they'll usually take it back and bring out something else – but it's good food. The only other places to eat are a couple of noodle shops along the main street, which are nothing I'd dare recommend except to the famished. Fresh fruit is sold down at the wharf where the tour boats dock.

### Getting Around

The town itself is small enough to walk around easily, but if you want to get further afield then hire a bicycle from the guy outside the gate of the hotel. He charges Y0.50 per hour but you could probably negotiate a daily rate. It's a great way to see the surrounding countryside. Passing truck drivers seem to be quite curious about westerners and this could be good hitching country.

### Getting Away

**Bus** Buses to *Guilin* depart Yangshuo at 7.40 am, 9.20 am, 10 am, 11.40 am, 1 pm, 2 pm, 4 pm, 4.20 pm and 6 pm. The trip takes about two hours. There are a couple of buses a day from Yangshuo to Pinglo though you could try hitching.

**Boat** You can also take a boat to Guilin. Tickets are Y15 and the boat will probably take you as far as Yangti which is just south of Guilin, where you take a bus the rest of the distance. The price includes the boat, bus, a meal and guide. For tickets contact a guy named Yu outside the tourist hotel between 9 am to noon, or ask the guy who rents bicycles to find Yu. Alternatively, it may be possible to hitch a ride on one of the Li River tour boats, which return to Guilin empty. Successful hitching varies from boat to boat as some will take back stray westerners and some won't. They usually charge Y10 for this trip. If you go back this way you'll have to overnight in Yangti where there's a cheap hotel, and take the morning bus to Guilin.

It is possible to go by boat all the way to Wuzhou and Canton. There is no boat from Yangshuo, but at the town of Pinglo there is a tug-towed barge which goes to Wuzhou. The boat leaves Pinglo on Tuesdays, Thursdays and Saturdays at 6.30 am. The fare is Y4.80, buy your ticket at the town's concrete loading ramp where the barge docks. There is a hotel about one km further up the road (upstream) from the loading ramp which costs only Y1.80 and has a restaurant and friendly people.

The barge is towed downstream through a rugged, forested valley which gradually opens up into riverside farming communities; the mountains remain massive but by now they've lost their vertical faces. The barge stops frequently along the way for small boats to pick up passengers with exotic indigenous animals on the way to the markets. Inside the barge are two-tiered wooden bunks. Fibre-filled quilts rent for 30 fen. Bowls of noodles sell on the boat for 20-30 fen.

You travel for 12 hours on the first day, and at dusk tie up on the bank to sleep. At around 6.15 am the next day the boat gets going and you arrive in Wuzhou at 10.15 am. At Wuzhou you can connect to Canton either by the regular river service or bus. In the opposite direction it appears that the barge departs Wuzhou for Pinglo on Wednesdays, Fridays and Sundays around 12.30 pm.

## THE LI RIVER

The Li River is the connecting waterway between Guilin and Yangshuo and is one of the main tourist attractions of the area. A thousand years ago a poet wrote of the scenery around Yangshuo that 'the river forms a green gauze belt, the mountains are like blue jade hairpins'. The 83 km stretch of fluid between the towns is

hardly a green gauze belt, but a boat ride down its length provides a view of some extraordinary peaks, sprays of bamboo lining the river banks, fishermen in small boats and picturesque little villages.

The tour boats depart Guilin from a jetty adjacent to Elephant Trunk Hill each morning at 7.30 am. Tickets usually cost Y40 and you can buy them from the major tourist hotels, though if you're a student in China then the official price is Y25. A couple of local entrepeneurs have been selling tickets for only Y28 which covers the boat, lunch and bus back to Guilin from Yangshuo. The Chinese pay Y10 and there are lots of booths on the streets selling tickets though it's highly unlikely they'll sell one to a westerner.

The trip takes about six hours and most people find it too long and by the end a bit dragging. It's probably not worth it if you're going to be spending any length of time in Yangshuo. For Y28 it's probably OK, but you should probably regard it as a nice way of getting from Guilin to Yangshuo. Lunch is not too substantial; rice with bean shoots, egg and pork, but you can buy an extra bowl for Y1. Tea is also provided. There are a fair few factories belching smoke close to the banks of the river on the outskirts of Guilin, and it's not until the third hour of the voyage that you pass by the most impressive limestone pinnacles – far better than anything near Guilin. There's nothing to see in the last two hours.

As is the Chinese habit, every feature along the route has been named. **Paint Brush Hill** juts straight up from the ground with a pointed tip like a Chinese writing brush. **Cock-fighting Hills** stand face to face like two cocks about to engage in battle. **Mural Hill** is just past the small town of Yangti; the hill is a sheer cliff rising abruptly out of the water and there are supposed to be the images of nine horses in the weathered patterns on the cliff face. Further on is the old town of Xingping, where the river widens and meanders around to Yangshuo.

The boat arrives in Yangshuo around 1.30 pm; the wharf is a hive of souvenir shops and stalls. The buses back to Guilin leave at around 2 pm and they stop for a short time at a tourist market (notable for the old coins on sale) and also stop for photos near Moon Hill. In all, it's about a 2½ hour drive back to Guilin, and it's a beautiful trip! You'll get back to Guilin around 5 or 5.30 pm.

## NANNING

By way of introduction, a few statistics to dwell upon about Nanning. According to Chinese sources, the number of factories in the city shot from four in 1949 to four hundred by 1979; from 1949 to 1981 the area of Nanning city increased twelve-fold; from 1976 to 1983 it appears that the population doubled (from 1949 to 1979 it quadrupled) and now stands at 650,000. A prestigious list of light and heavy industry could be rattled off here, but perhaps you already have a picture in mind.

At the turn of the century Nanning was a mere market town; now it's the capital of Guangxi. Apart from the urban expansion that the post-1949 railway induced in the south-west, Nanning became important as a staging ground for shipping arms to Vietnam – the rail line to the border town of Pingxian was built in 1952, and was extended to Hanoi, giving Vietnam a lifeline to China. In 1979 with the invasion of Vietnam by China, the train services were suspended indefinitely – the border with Vietnam in Guangxi and Yunnan is a hot one these days and the Vietnamese are also seen as a threat to Chinese oil exploration in the Gulf of Tonkin.

At street level, the town of Nanning is a poor one, with a promise of progress in the solid-looking department stores – whilst elsewhere the city is a motley collection of cracked, peeling, stained, crumbled, worn, seedy, ramshackle walls, facades and fittings. The population in the Nanning region is mostly a Zhuang-Han mix, though the rest of the Zhuang are scattered over Guangxi's rural areas.

Nanning is also a jumping off place for visits to Wuming, Yiling, Binyang, Guixian, Guiping and Beihai.

**CITS** (tel 2986) is in the Mingyuan Hotel.

**CAAC** (tel 3333) is at 64 Chaoyang Lu.

### Things to See

There's a plethora of free markets in Nanning; you can follow a series of different outdoor markets (spices, medicinal herbs and potions, clothing, sunglasses, housewares, eating stalls ... ) by taking the route marked on the map in this book. There are food stalls at the northern and southern sections of the route. Check out the unusual street commerce in progress – strips of car tyre, dead rats, desiccated cockroaches, dried snake skins. And for the rice-weary there's an abundance of subtropical fruit in season. Another market strip is along Fandi Lu, the road leading diagonally to the north-east toward Renmin Park. If you happen to be a

| | |
|---|---|
| 1 Yongjiang Hotel | 10 Foriegn Language Bookstore |
| 2 Nanning Restaurant | 11 CAAC Office |
| 3 Bike Rental | 12 Chaoyang (Chinese) Hotel & |
| 4 Friendship Store | Travel Agency |
| 5 Guangxi Museum | 13 Arts & Crafts Service Dept. |
| 6 Chaoyang Dept. Store | 14 Bailongdong Restaurant |
| 7 Mingyuan Hotel (CIT) | 15 Boat Dock |
| 8 Yongzhou Hotel | 16 Exhibition Hall |
| 9 Long Distance Bus Station | |

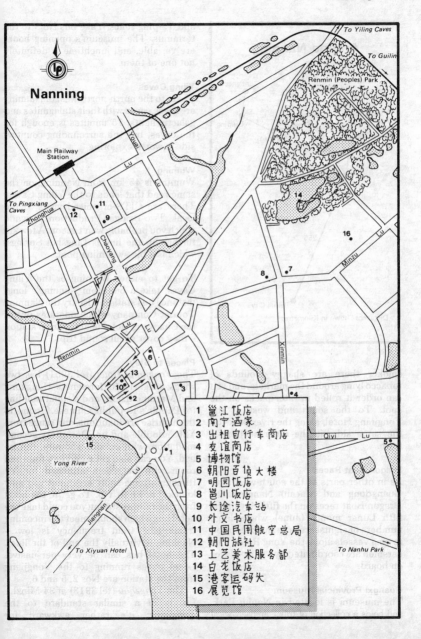

**Nanning**

To Yiling Caves

To Guilin

Renmin (Peoples) Park

Main Railway Station

To Pingxiang Caves

Zhonghua

Youai Lu

Chaoyang Lu

Renmin Lu

Minzu Lu

Xinmin Lu

Qiyi Lu

Jiangnan Lu

Yong River

To Xiyuan Hotel

To Nanhu Park

1 邕江饭店
2 南宁酒家
3 出租自行车商店
4 友谊商店
5 博物馆
6 朝阳百货大楼
7 明园饭店
8 邕川饭店
9 长途汽车站
10 外文书店
11 中国民用航空总局
12 朝阳旅社
13 工艺美术服务部
14 白龙饭店
15 港客运码头
16 展览馆

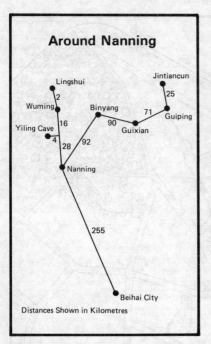

**Around Nanning**

Lingshui

Jintiancun

Wuming

Binyang

Yiling Cave

Guixian

Guiping

Nanning

255

Beihai City

Distances Shown in Kilometres

and Taiping relics. Take bus No 3 to the terminus. The museum's opening hours are variable, and lunchtime is definitely not one of them.

### Yiling Caves

25 km to the north-north-west of Nanning are these caves with their stalagmites and galactic lights; 15 minutes is enough for the caves, but the surrounding country-side is worth exploring.

### Wuming

Wuming is 45 km from Nanning, on the same road that leads to the Yiling Caves. There are CITS-organised visits to the local Two-Bridge Production Brigade which you probably won't get on. A few km further up the line is Lingshui Springs, which is a big swimming pool.

To get to either Wuming or the Yiling Caves, take a bus from Nanning's long-distance bus station. Also try the Nanning Tourist Company which operates out of the Chaoyang Hotel near the train station – they cover small round trips.

### Places to Stay

The *Yongjiang Hotel* (tel 3951) has two wings; a highrise for foreigners, Hongkong and Macau citizens, and a squat building for People's Republic Chinese. Rooms in the highrise are luxurious, and range from Y26 a double and up. Dormitory accom-modation, with outside showers, can be had. You can also get a bed in a four-bed room with bathroom attached for Y9 (though after a short argument you may knock it down to Y6). To get to the hotel from the railway station you could take the hotel bus which should meet the incoming trains (the train frequency is low – Nanning is virtually the end of the line). The hotel bus can be very persuasive! Local buses running to the Yongjiang from the station are Nos 2, 5 and 6.

The *Yongzhou* (tel 3913) at 34 Minzhu Lu, is of a similar standard to the Yongjiang; it's rather awkward for

smoker there are shaggy mounds of tobacco lying around the markets, and you can order it rolled in filter packs on the spot. To the south and west of the Yongjiang Hotel, along the riverbanks on the same side, is the older section of town.

### Dragon Boat Races

As in other parts of the south-west (and Guangdong and Macau) Nanning has Dragon Boat races on the fifth day of the fifth Lunar month (June) where large numbers of sightseers urge the decorated rowing vessels along the Yong River. The oarsmen are coordinated by a gong-player on board.

### Guangxi Provincial Museum

The museum is located in Nanhu Park, and holds a collection of tribal, archaeological transport – you take bus No 2 one stop from the railway station, alight and walk left to the next big intersection, and then take bus No 1 for two stops.

Close to the Yongzhou is the CITS hide-and-seek hotel, the *Mingyuan* (tel 2986) on Xinmin Lu, which starts at Y30 double.

You may or may not be able to get into the *Xiyuan Hotel* down by the riverside (take bus No 5 from the railway station). As for the *Nanning Hotel*, that will only take albino Chinese with Albanian passports.

### Places to Eat

Market stall food is good – snails, glazed chicken, roast duck, and fruit all part of the menu. Opposite the foreign language bookstore is a large speciality restaurant where the specialities include turtle, snake, ants and fruit-eating fox. Snakes and snails and puppy dogs tails can be found at the restaurant in the *Xijiao Park Zoo* which is on the north-west edge of town at the terminus of bus No 6. In *Nanhu Park* there's a fish-speciality restaurant where the creatures are taken from tanks and not too expensive (take bus No 2 to the terminus). The penthouse dining room in the highrise block of the *Yongjiang Hotel* is a bit pricey, but nice views. Renmin Park, with a market run leading up to it (Fandi Lu), has a tea house and restaurant, the *Bailongdong*.

### Getting around

There are at least two bicycle rental places, but they're difficult to find. The one marked on the map in this book is obscured by a (crowded) bus stop – look for a batch of numbered bikes inside a small doorway near the bus stop. The lady wants to know which hotel you're staying at if you rent a bike.

### Getting Away

**Train** Plan your rail trips ahead of time, as the choice of departures is not great. There are direct trains to Zhanjiang

(about 9½ hours), and to Guilin (about nine hours). The Nanning-Guilin trains travel via Liuzhou; if you are continuing from Nanning to Guiyang you have to change at Liuzhou. There are special express trains direct from Nanning to Beijing.

There are direct trains from Nanning to Zhanjiang on the coast of Guyangdong Province; from Zhanjiang you can get a ferry to Haikou on Hainan Island, a direct bus to Canton, or a direct boat (once a week) to Hong Kong. The boat to Hong Kong is an overnight trip taking about 15½ hours.

**Plane** Nanning is connected by air to Beijing (Y280), Canton (Y75), Guilin (Y46) and Kunming (Y88).

**Boat** Boating out of Nanning is unexplored – there are links downstream to Wuzhou via Guixian and Guiping that would be worth checking out. Guixian can be reached by rail or bus in four hours and there *may* be a boat from Guixian to Wuzhou, taking about 12 hours and leaving Guixian in the early afternoon.

**Other** The Binyang-Guixian-Guiping route, going north-east from Nanning, is useful for getting to Wuzhou cross-country. The roads are rough, the areas backward, and it's a sugarcane/grain basin. It's 90 km by road from Nanning to Binyang; 90 km by road from Binyang to Guixian; and 70 km by boat from Guixian to Guiping. From Guiping there are boats to Wuzhou, a ten hour trip. Guixian can also be reached by rail from Nanning – the line continues to Zhanjiang.

There are a couple of cultural sights along the way, but nothing of note. 25 km north-west of Guiping is Jintiancun where one of the weirdest chapters in Chinese history got under way. A schoolmaster, suffering from hallucinations generated by an illness, declared himself the brother of Jesus Christ, and took upon himself the mission of liberating China from the

Manchus – the seeds of the Taiping Rebellion (1850-64).

Another approach to Hainan Island is via Beihai, which is 255 km from Nanning. Beihai is a port town and a very sensitive naval base. The bus trip from Nanning takes eight hours and costs around Y8. From Beihai you might be able to get a boat to Haikou, but if this doesn't work out then continue to Zhanjiang and get a boat there.

## LIUZHOU

Liuzhou, with a population of 500,000, is the largest city on the Liu River. The place dates back to the Tang dynasty, at which time it was a dumping ground for disgraced court officials. The town was largely left to its mountain wilds until 1949 when it was transmogrified into a major industrial city. Both light and heavy industry are engaged in; it's also known for its medicinal herbs, coffins and fruit. Liuzhou is the only place in China where you can buy an exquisitely-wrought wooden coffin (ashtray-sized) – but then, who needs one?

Karst scenery, similar to that of Guilin, can be found on the outskirts of Liuzhou, making this cave-lake-park sightseeing. River transport would be the best way of viewing the karst landscaping and mountainous areas.

### Places to Stay

*Liuzhou Hotel* is the centre of tourist operations: it's down by the Liu River and charges Y32 a double, which can be got for Y6 per bed if you can convince them you're a student, or even Y3.

Women of the Dong minority are known to serve *youcha* or oil-tea (actually a kind of soup) within the confines of the hotel. The ladies seem to be a bit far from home, since the heartland of the Dongs is 200 km or more north of Liuzhou, in Songjiang County (the areas around where the borders of Guizhou, Guangxi and Hunan meet).

### Getting Away

Liuzhou is a railway junction which connects Nanning to Guilin. Guilin to Kunming trains pass through Liuzhou, and if you're coming up from Nanning you'll probably have to change trains here to get to Kunming.

## FANGCHENG

The 'Fangcheng Multi-national Autonomous County' lies on the southern coast of the Guangxi Autonomous Region. The Chinese started building a deep-water harbour here in 1968 and the port has recently been opened. It was annnounced in the middle of 1983 that the harbour would also take foreign ships, so it may be opened to foreign tourists as well – a possibility but not very likely as the Vietnamese border is too close for comfort. Apart from the obvious military uses, it's planned to use the harbour to speed exports from Yunnan, Guizhou, Sichuan, Hunan and some north-western provinces of goods which normally go through the ports at Zhanjiang or Canton.

# Guizhou

Until recent times Guizhou was one of the most backward and sparsely populated areas in China. Although the Han Dynasty set up an administration in the area, the Chinese merely attempted to maintain some measure of control over the non-Chinese tribes who lived here, and Chinese settlement was confined to the north and east of the province; the eastern areas were not settled until the 16th century, forcing the native minorities out of the most fertile areas. Another wave of Chinese immigration in the late 19th century brought many settlers in from overpopulated Hunan and Sichuan. But Guizhou remained poor and backward, with poor communications and transport.

When the Japanese invasion forced the Kuomintang to retreat to the south-west the development of Guizhou began; roads to the neighbouring provinces were built, a rail link was built to Guangxi, and some industries were set up in Guiyang and Zunyi. Most of the activity ceased with the end of World War II; it was not until the construction of the railways in the south-west under Communist rule that some industrialisation was revived.

Today the population of Guizhou is 28.5 million. If the capital of Guiyang is any indication, Guizhou could still be one of the most backward areas of China – certainly the capital has little to recommend it. However, close by are the Huangguaoshu Waterfalls, China's biggest – and the neighbourhood presents some opportunities for hiking and stumbling around some of China's all-too-little visited villages.

## GUIYANG

Guiyang, the capital of Guizhou Province, is a dump. Stronger words could be used; one would not want to inflict this unfortunate place on the rail-weary traveller, or any traveller for that matter.

It is incredibly poor, and has always been that way. Even the weather has turned against it – the drizzle gives it the name of Guiyang, which translates as 'Precious Sun'. A besotted rush of post-liberation factories including the manufacture of diesel engines, machinery, textiles and the like has added a polluting dimension; rapid population expansion has created nightmares in concrete and brick over the top of what was formerly little more than a village. Down dark streets, lie some grimy markets in progress in the vestiges of the older town, and along the murky river that threads through the city are one or two dilapidated temple structures. On paper, Guiyang bristles with societies and educational and military institutes – in reality it's backward to the extremes.

The only reason you'd really want to come here is to go somewhere else (if you're on your way to Chongqing from Guilin, for example, you'll have to change trains at Guiyang) or as a jumping off post for the Huanggushuo Waterfalls – China's biggest – or other places which may open up to foreigners in the future.

**Permits** Guiyang requires a permit. It is not necessary to get a permit in Guiyang for the Huangguoshu Falls – it can be got elsewhere. If you have the Huangguoshu permit, you can bypass Guiyang altogether and get off the train at Anshun, which is closer to the falls and still on the main rail line.

675

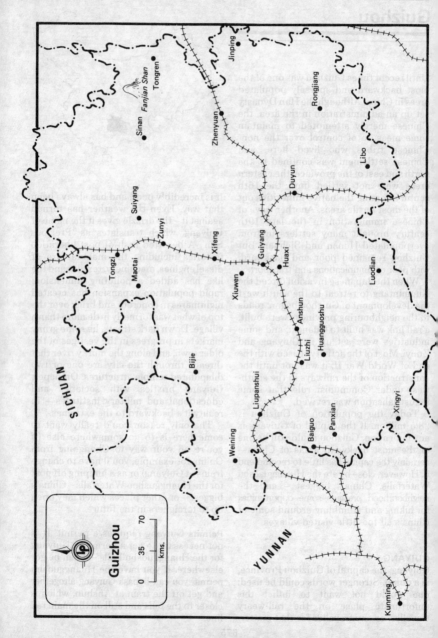

Guizhou

0    35    70
kms.

CITS (tel 25121) is manned by two extremely friendly and helpful gentlemen; one speaks good English and the other speaks French – exactly why their talents have been placed in Guiyang, where there's really nothing to see, is one of the ironies of the China International Travel Syndrome. Bus No 2 or bus No 1 from the railway station will get you to the office; it's in a government compound of colonnaded buildings – the CITS office is in a building on the right of the main gateway to the compound.

CAAC (tel 23000) is at 170 Zunyi Lu.

## Things to See

The distinctive architectural characteristic of Guiyang's handful of Mussolini-modern buildings is the columns -- like the Provincial Exhibition Hall. The main street leading down from the railway station harbours one of the largest glistening white statues of Mao Zedong in China. For details on the scenic bus loop around the city, see the 'Getting Around' section.

Sights on the edges of the city are of the dreary cave-lake-park type – but the Huaxi Caves in Huaxi Park did yield a surprise – photocells along the underground path are activated by the guide's flashlight, triggering a new string of coloured bulbs and neon signs, as well as some musical effects. This electronic wizardry will cost Y1.40 entrance fee for a foreigner, and Y0.10 for a local. Other sights that may (or may not) be worth checking out are the late Ming Dynasty Hongfu Monastery in Qianling Shan Park to the north-west of the city; the Kanzhu Pavilion atop the mountain is the vantage point overlooking the city. Five km to the southwest of Guiyang is Nanjiao Park noted for its caves.

Out at the Huaxi Hotel, I was approached by a lady (not sure of her credentials – PSB? CITS? maid?) who tried to rope me into a minibus tour of Guiyang at Y100 for four passengers for the day, including a transfer to the railway station – having given up on that she proceeded to tell me I was not to wander around Guiyang on foot, and not to use the local buses. I suppose there might have been a connection between the offering and the warning – since I had looped around the city on the buses for Y0.15, a substantial saving. What a load of rubbish some of these tourist authorities come up with!

One thing we were in agreement on, though for different reasons, was that one should gloss over the town and stick to the countryside periphery. I headed straight for the rice paddies near the Huaxi Hotel, where mud can only look like mud. The Huaxi's one saving grace is that right outside the front gates is a Bouyei village, with tattered new-year posters plastering the wooden doors. Nothing to get excited about, but a bit of rural living (the Bouyei are one of China's minority peoples – they number about 2.1 million and appear to live exclusively in Guizhou). Further away, across the rice paddies at the edge of Huaxi Park, is another village with TV antennae poking through stone-slate roofing. The rural aspects are better viewed at Huangguoshu, although if one were to continue further south of the Huaxi Hotel, one would be right in the hamlet zones.

## Places to Stay

If you're changing trains and stranded (going to Chongqing, for example), or attempting to get to the Huangguoshu Falls, and in need of overnight lodgings, then try and use the first-class waiting room at the rail station. It's on the upper floor; on the ground floor there's a 24-hour baggage cage.

There are two hotels open to foreigners in Guiyang. The *Zhao Yan Lushe* is a large building on the main street leading down from the railway station; walk across the square in front of the station – the hotel is just after the square on the left hand side of the main street. It's actually a Chinese hotel and is super-filthy; you can probably get a bed here for Y4, a single room for Y5, doubles Y5.70, rooms for four people at Y7.40, rooms for five at Y7.75. If you have trouble getting in then phone CITS (tel 25121) and tell them that you only intend to overnight for a train connection. According to CITS you can stay in the Zhao Yan if you're only going to be around for one or two nights – but I tend to think that once you're in no one is going to come along and extricate you if you stay longer.

Further into town on the No 1 bus route is the *Jinqiao Hotel* – it's Y9 a double but hard to get into. Some students hang around here waiting to catch a glimpse of the outside world, and you're a prize catch.

The official tourist hotel is the *Huaxi Binguan*(tel 225973) which is 20 km southwest of the city, half-way to the airport. The dun-coloured buildings are on a hill in a landscaped and mini-forest area. Single rooms go for Y10, doubles Y17, and there are dormitory beds for Y7 (although Y5 is possible). The problem is that this hotel is a logistical disaster for transport; from the railway station it requires a bus No 2 to Xinanmen (south-west bus depot), then a no-number bus (it's sometimes identified as a No 16) to Huaxi Park, then a two km walk – by this time you're almost in the countryside so it's not a bad two km walk. But the last bus connection to Huaxi Park is around 6 pm. A taxi from the railway station would cost at least Y15 – taxis and minibuses are available for hire at the Huaxi and if you're in town CITS should be able to get you one. The other problem is that there's little chance of an early morning bus connection from the Huaxi to Guiyang long-distance bus station to catch an early morning bus to Huangguoshu– that would require a taxi also.

### Places to eat
Food in the local restaurants is abominable – one attempt to get into the cleaner-looking *Jinqiao Hotel Restaurant* was summarily rejected by the doorman, who appeared to be under the impression that Guiyang was still closed. (Guiyang opened in late 1982). For munchies try the one or two restaurants on the perimeter of the square around the railway station. The *Huaxi Hotel* has a dining room, not too bad – at least it's clean.

### Getting Around
If you want to do a city-loop tour then straight, across the square from the railway station are two round-the-city buses, Nos 1 and 2. They follow the same route but No 2 goes clockwise while No 1 goes anti-clockwise. These will get you to most places (bar the Huaxi Hotel) – the round trip from the station takes about 45 minutes for the grand sum of Y0.15. You can get a good window seat since you get on at the terminus; the same cannot be said if you choose to alight at random for a foot-sortie into the grisly. The main shopping street is on the No 1 bus route heading north.

### Getting Away
**Bus** Buses to Huangguoshu Falls depart from the long distance bus station in the northwest of the city. The bus station is a distinctive building, an old temple-like structure. For details, see the section on Huangguoshu.

**Train** Direct trains to Kunming, Guilin, Chongqing and Nanning. For Zhanjiang you may have to change trains at Liuzhou. Some sample times and fares (*Chinese price*), for hard sleeper are:

- Guilin, 18 hours, Y26;
- Liuzhou, 15 hours, Y20.50;
- Kunming, 15 hours, Y20;
- Chongqing, 11 hours, Y14.70;

**Plane** Guiyang is connected by air to Beijing (Y254), Canton (Y117), Kunming (Y52) and Wuhan (Y124).

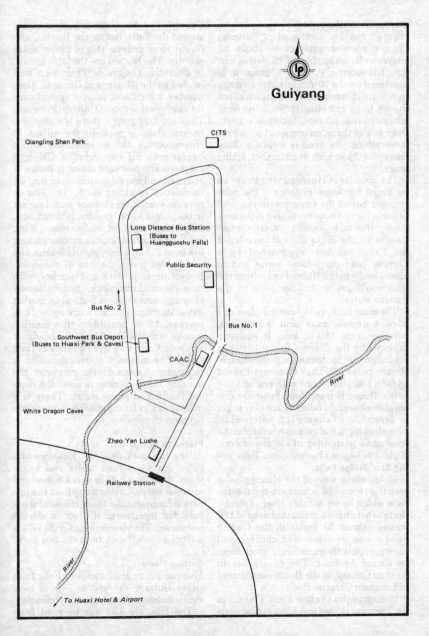

**Guiyang**

CITS

Qiangling Shan Park

Long Distance Bus Station
(Buses to
Huangguoshu Falls)

Public Security

Bus No. 2

Bus No. 1

Southwest Bus Depot
(Buses to Huaxi Park & Caves)

CAAC

White Dragon Caves

River

Zhao Yan Lushe

Railway Station

River

To Huaxi Hotel & Airport

## HUANGGUOSHU FALLS

Located 155 km southwest of Guiyang, China's premier cataract is about 50 metres wide, with a drop of 70 metres into the 'Rhinoceros Pool' – a preview is contained on the 10-fen foreign exchange certificate. Huangguoshu is an excellent chance to go rambling through the rural minority areas on foot; hiking is superb. Once you're there, no transport problems – everything you need is within walking range – or if you wish to go further, hiking range.

The thunder of Huangguoshu Falls can be heard for some distance – the mist churned out of the impact with the pool below is carried over to villages in the area during the rainy season. **Water Curtain Cave** is a niche in the cliffs at the edge of the Falls, which is approached by a slippery (and dangerous) sortie wading across rocks in the Rhino Pool – from the cave you'll get an interior view of the gushing waters.

The main falls are the central piece of a huge waterfall, cave and karst area, covering some 450 sq kms. It was only explored by the Chinese in the 1980s as preliminaries to harnessing the hydro-electric potential. They discovered about 18 falls, four subterranean rivers, and 100 caves. **Doupo (Steep Slope Falls)** are one km above the main falls and are easy to get to. Steep Slope Falls are 105 metres wide, 23 metres high, and gets its name from the criss-cross patterning of sloping waters. Eight km below Huangguoshu Falls are the **Star Bridge Falls**.

10 km north-west of the Huangguoshu area (there may be a bus) are the **Gaotan Falls** which lie on another river system – the falls here have a graduated drop of 120 metres. About 30 km from the Gaotan Falls is a newly-discovered underground cavern, reputedly quite large, which must be toured by boat. The cavern lies in Anshun County, at the Bouyei settlement of Longtain (Dragon Pool).

Huangguoshu (Yellow Fruit Tree) is in the Zhenning Bouyei and Miao Autonomous County. The Miao are not in evidence around the Falls, but for the Bouyei, who favour river valleys, this is prime water country. The Bouyei are the 'aboriginals' of Guizhou. They're of Thai origin and related to the Zhuangs in Guangxi. They number 2.1 million, mostly spread over the southwest sector of Guizhou Province. They are very poor – there is something human about a visit to the village at Huangguoshu, like an encounter with a beggar on a big city street in China; it contrasts the postcard minority image of starched and ironed costumes, or ring-of-confidence sparkling teeth. The Bouyei here are everything that one would expect tribespeople to be: grubby, tattered, shy, suspicious, signs of malnutrition, dank mud and concrete floors, a mother picking lice from a child's hair, pigs, chickens, and rabid dogs given the run of the town. Bouyei dress is dark and sombre, with more colourful trimmings – better (cleaner) clothing comes out on festival or market days. Marriage is at an early age – 16 is average, 12 is possible – the married women are distinguished by headgear symbols. Cloth wax-dyeing is one of their skills. The masonry at Huangguoshu is intriguing – stone blocks comprise the housing, but no plaster is used; the roofs are finished in stone slates. There is a market day in Huangguoshu, if your time happens to coincide.

### Places to Stay & Eat

At the bus park near the Huangguoshu Falls, are some food stalls and below them, down the cliff is a tea house and souvenir shop. Further away from the bus park is *Huangguoshu Guest House* which is only for foreigners; it's got a decent restaurant. The viewing area for the falls is a short downhill walk from the bus park.

### Getting There

You can get to Huangguoshu Falls from either Guiyang or Anshun – both have logistical obstacles but Anshun is preferable.

The falls are 150 km by road from

Guiyang. There's a bus leaving Guiyang's long-distance bus station at 7 am; the fare is around Y4 or Y5, and the trip takes four to five hours. Buses depart the falls for Guiyang at around 3 pm or 4 pm.

Guiyang CITS has minibus tours to the falls, departing from the Huaxi Hotel in Guiyang. Prices are in the region of Y0.50 to Y0.80 per km, dependent on the size of the group and vehicle. For a same-day return trip to the falls you'd be looking at, say, Y230 – no food, no guide. The same deal, but considerably cheaper, can be got in Anshun.

Anshun lies on the Guiyang-Kunming railway line, about two hours from Guiyang. Anshun is 50 km from the falls, and it takes a local bus about 1½ hours to get to Huangguoshu; the fare is Y1.30. If you arrive in Anshun by train you may have problems with a bus connection to Huangguoshu, so you may have to overnight in Anshun and take a bus out the next morning. Buses between Anshun and the falls are sporadic; on weekdays there are buses at 7.40 am and noon and there *may* be one as late as 2 pm – bus frequencies on weekends are higher than on weekdays.

Alternatively, you could go from Anshun to Zhenning which is near the falls; there are five morning buses from Anshun to Zhenning and five afternoon buses.

Buses for Anshun depart Huangguoshu at 10.30 am, 2 pm, 3 pm, 4 pm and 4.30 pm – some of those might continue to Guiyang. These will *probably* connect with trains departing Anshun for Guiyang or Kunming.

## ANSHUN

Anshun was once an opium-trading centre – it remains the commercial hub of western Guizhou but is now known for its wax-dyed fabrics. At the north-east end of town is a large Confucian temple. The town lies on the Guiyang-Kunming railway line, a two hour ride from Guiyang.

You can make Anshun a jumping off point for the Huangguoshu Falls. However, everything in Anshun except the hotel, train and bus station is closed, and they probably won't let you leave the hotel. If you don't get intercepted at the train station, you may be able to get down to Huangguoshu on the same day. Walk straight ahead from the railway station about one km to a major road (with striped police box), turn left and walk on – the bus station is in that direction and from here you can get buses to the falls. The bus station is about two kms from the railway station. If you intend coming back on the same day, then dump your bags at the left-luggage room in Anshun Train Station.

### Places to Stay

There is at least one hotel to stay at in Anshun, the *Kungshan*; undernourished in the electricity and plumbing departments, but solid. The hotel gardens overlook an artificial lake, leaving the mud of Anshun town behind. You should be able to get a bed here for Y10, negotiable to Y6. The hotel is completely isolated but the dinner-bell of the hotel dining-room is loud enough to warn of impending food shortages should you miss the occasion.

The hotel is four km from the bus station and three kms from the train station. The bus station is about two kms from the train station; it's a rough triangle between the three places. Transfer from the train station to the hotel in a minibus costs Y5.

# Sichuan

There is a Chinese saying that the real riches in life are not jade or pearls, but the five grains (rice, soybeans, wheat, barley and millet). These are well represented in the fertile Sichuan Basin, under irrigation since the 3rd century BC, and the PRC's greatest rice producer.

Sichuan is the largest province in China but also the most heavily populated, with almost 100 million people. It is the eastern region of Sichuan, the great Chengdu plain, that supports one of the densest rural populations in the world – whilst the regions to the west are mountainous and sparsely populated, mainly by Tibetans.

Back in the Maoist era birth control was a pair of dirty words, a capitalist plot to make China weak. Mao believed in strength in numbers – much the mentality of a peasant who needs many children to work the fields – and anyone who opposed him was put out to pasture. Today, Sichuan has a determined birth control campaign which is attempting to reduce the birth rate to less than half – a huge billboard spells it out (inexplicably in English) in the centre of Chengdu, the provincial capital. That is not the only Maoist policy which is being debunked in Sichuan. Possibly because this is the home of Deng Xiaoping (who was born here in 1904), Sichuan has become a testing ground for the debunking of the commune system; he has called the commune a utopian dream of 'reaching heaven in one step'. The efforts now are towards decentralisation of agriculture, greater autonomy of decision making, establishment of free markets at which peasants can sell their produce, and greater individual incentives. Xindu County, outside Chengdu, is one of the first experimental stations; farms are state-owned, but if a peasant meets the required quota, any surplus is his – he also decides what to plant and when. If the streets of Chengdu are any indication, the 'responsibility system' is a howling success.

Roughly the size of France, give or take Luxembourg, Sichuan has rich natural resources. Wild mountainous terrain and fast rivers blocked access until the present era, and much of the western fringe is still remote. The capital is Chengdu, the largest city is Chongqing which is also the stepping-stone for the ferry ride down the Yangtse River.

The remote mountain area of Sichuan, Gansu and Shaanxi provinces is the natural habitat of the Giant Panda. China's wildlife population includes 1174 species of birds, 420 species of mammals and some 500 species of reptiles and amphibians, but among this free-range menagerie the one animal which most westerners automatically bring to mind when they think of China is the Giant Panda. Just as the koala and kangaroo are synonymous with Australia, so it is with the panda. This mental association is probably due in large measure to the Chinese fondness several years ago of giving them away as presents to foreign governments.

## CHENGDU

Chengdu is Sichuan's capital, and the administrative, educational and cultural centre, as well as being a major industrial base. It boasts a 2500 year history, linked closely with the art and craft trades. In the

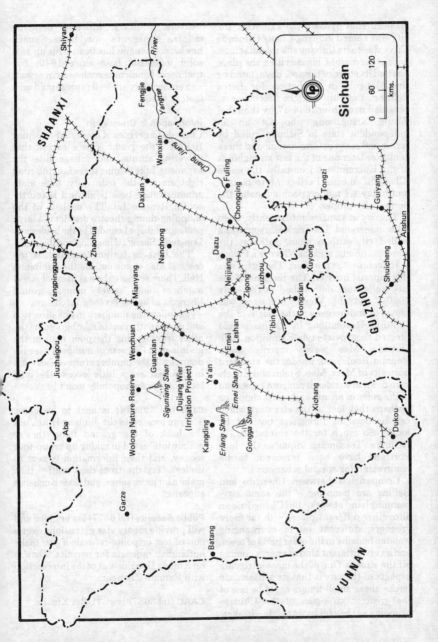

Eastern Han dynasty (25-220 AD), the city was named Jinjiang Cheng (Brocade City), due to its thriving silk manufacture. Like other major Chinese cities, the place has had its share of turmoil; devastated by the Mongols in retaliation for fierce fighting put up by the Sichuanese; presided over from 1644-47 by the rebel Zhang Xiangzhong who set up an independent state in Sichuan, ruled by terror and mass extermination; and three centuries later one of the last strongholds of the Kuomintang. Ironically, the name 'Chengdu' means Perfect Metropolis – and today 1.4 million people inhabit the perfect city proper.

The city was square until recently, when it became round. The original layout was a walled city with a moat, gates at the compass points, and the Viceroy's Palace (14th century) at the heart. The latter was the imperial quarter. The remains of the city walls were demolished in the early 1960s, and the Viceroy's Palace was blown to smithereens at the height of the Cultural Revolution. In its place was erected the Soviet-style Exhibition Hall. Outside, Mao waves merrily down Renmin Boulevard; inside, the standard portraits of Marx, Mao, Stalin and Engels gaze down in wonder at rampant capitalism in the guise of an arts and crafts shop – or perhaps they leer at the elevators which can be used by foreigners but not by locals. So much for the revolution. (In Beijing's Tiananmen Square, the four Portraits have been removed, to be resurrected for special occasions.)

Comparisons between Chengdu and Beijing are tempting – the same city-planning hand at work – but Chengdu is an altogether different place, with far more greenery, different set of overhanging wooden housing in the older parts of town, and a very different kind of energy coming off the streets. One of the most intriguing aspects of the city is that its artisans are back – these small-timers could be one of the greatest strengths of the Chinese economy as they fill basic needs – basket-weavers, cobblers, itinerant dentists, tailors, houseware merchants, snack hawkers. Chengdu has been built up as a solid industrial base since 1949, but traditional handicrafts such as lacquerware and embroidery are well represented on a factory basis.

### Information & Orientation

Chengdu has echoes of boulevard-sweeping Beijing – the grand scale – except that flowering shrubs and foliage line the expanses. Like Beijing there is a ring-road right around the outer city. The main administrative-type boulevard is (north-south) Renmin Lu. The nucleus of the shopping-dining-theatre district is a large pentagonal shape bounded by the boulevards Dongfeng, Shengli, Hongxing and Jiefang.

The best navigation landmark is the colossal Mao statue outside the Exhibition Hall. There seems to be a shifting of street numbers and street names around Chengdu, as well as boulevard reconstruction – you follow the numbers in one direction and meet another set of numbers going the other way, leaving the poor man in the middle with five sets of numbers over his doorway. If the numbers (or even streets) in this text are a little askew, the map locations given hopefully won't be . . .

**CITS** (tel 125914) is next to hopeless. They're located in the Jinjiang Hotel, out the back of the ground floor: they're mainly interested in raking up group-tour money, and their information is next to useless. Try the front-desk staff – they make a lot more sense, and their English is superior.

**Public Security** (tel 6577) is very nice and will provide meaty visa extensions over a cup of tea, or polite refusals if you make outlandish requests for permits. They're on Xinhua Donglu, east of the intersection with Renmin Zhonglu.

**CAAC** (tel 3087) is at 31 Bei Xin Jie.

**Maps** City bus maps can be found at train stations, Jinjiang Hotel and Xinhua bookstores. A rarer item was being sold by a hawker outside the People's – a Sichuan Province Map, not accurate for scale or features, but it showed the roads and the distances.

**Other Information** The Foreign Language Bookstore has mildly captivating tourist literature and general data. And while you're here, there's a counter selling watery versions of western music and traditional Chinese music in cassette form (the store shares the same corner as a Xinhua Bookstore).

### Things to See

Free-markets, flea-markets, black markets, pedlar markets – whatever they are – Chengdu is cooking with them. Each twist and turn down the back alleys seems to reveal a new specialty. Around the corner comes a florist shop on wheels – a bicycle laden with gladioli – or you chance upon a butcher market, a vegetable market, spice market, or a side street devoted to a species of repairman. Add to this the indoor food markets, and you're looking at a thriving small business economy.

There is a busy poultry market a short walk from the Jinjiang Hotel – cross the bridge to the south and turn left – amusing for reasons that will quickly become apparent (not amusing for the animals). In a northerly direction (go to the Furong Restaurant, take an alley to the left after that, off Renmin) is an outdoor factory of sorts – the street is lined with women at their sewing machines. Further west (bordering the south-east edge of Renmin Park) is a small strip devoted entirely to the sale of eggs.

Engrossing to stroll through is the tinker and tailor free market – for lack of better terminology – which runs north from near Chengdu Restaurant, and then turns east along another alley leading to Chunxi Lu – this one is a local mecca for clothing and on-the-spot tailoring. It appears that the market is not affected by cotton-ration coupons, and it also appears that those with fast scissors can earn double what a factory worker gets.

### Renmin Park

I am not a fan of Chinese parklands – but this one I will recommend. The teahouse there is excellent (see the Places to Eat section), and just near the entrance is the candyman. This fascinating hawker was put out of business during the Cultural Revolution – producing as he does the molten versions of butterflies, birds and fish. That sort of thing was associated with hobbies, a big no-no during the Cultural Revolution. The candyman's masterpiece is a toffee dragon in bug-eyed splendour, whipped up before your eyes on a marble tablet. You may not get this, as a kind of roulette-wheel selects items (needless to say, these wheels were not the thing to be seen with during the Cultural Revolution– what a complicated snare these innocent hawkers had become entangled in!). If you go for the toffee, the locals will look at you rather strangely, as the wares are intended for wide-eyed children (extra children were only recently banned in China). Works of art in toffee: China's backstreet merchants can be truly amazing.

While most of the action, or relaxation, is around the entrance to Renmin Park, the rest of it is not too shabby – a bonzai rockery, a kids' playground, a few swimming pools (for locals), and the Monument to the Martyrs of the Railway Protecting Movement (1911). Apparently this obelisk, decorated with shunting and tracks, marks an uprising of the people against officers who pocketed cash raised for the construction of the Chengdu-Chongqing Line. Since Renmin Park was also at the time a private officer's garden it was a fitting place to erect the structure.

### Temple Parks

Of perhaps more middling interest are the temple parks of Chengdu. These are all a fair distance from the Jinjiang Hotel,

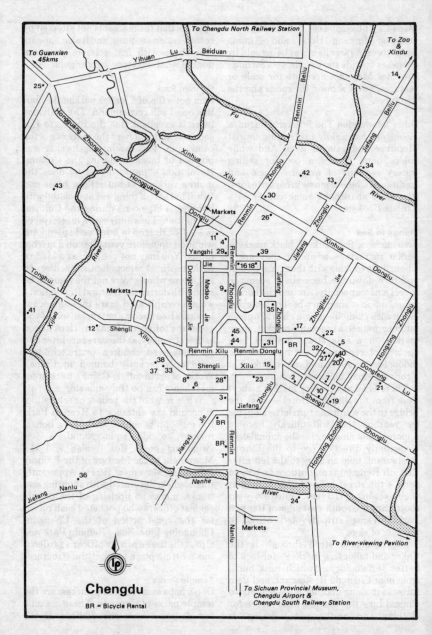

To Chengdu North Railway Station

To Zoo & Xindu

To Guanxian 45kms

Yihuan Lu Beiduan

Renmin Beilu

Jiefang Beilu

25

14

Hongguang Zhonglu

Fu

Xinhua

Xilu

Zhonglu

13

34

Hongguang

Donglu

42

River

43

30

Markets

Renmin

26

Xinhua

Jiefang

River

Tonghui Lu

11 4

Yangshi 29

Rennin

39

Jie

Dongchengen Jie

Madao Jie

Zhonglu

1618

Jiefang

Donglu

Zhonglu

Markets

9

35

17

41

45
44

12 Shengli Xilu

Renmin Xilu

Renmin Donglu

31

22

5

BR

32

40
27

20

Dongfeng Lu

Shengli

Xilu

15

2

1

Hongxing Zhonglu

38
37 33

8 6

28

23

10

21

3

Shengli

19

Jiefang

Zhonglu

Jie

BR

BR

Jiangxi

Rennin

Nanlu

1

36

Jiefang Nanlu

Nanhe

River

24

Markets

Nanlu

To River-viewing Pavilion

**Chengdu**

BR = Bicycle Rental

To Sichuan Provincial Museum, Chengdu Airport & Chengdu South Railway Station

| | | |
|---|---|---|
| 1 | Jinjiang Hotel / CITS | 锦江宾馆 |
| 2 | Chengdu Restaurant | 成都餐厅 |
| 3 | Furong Restaurant | 芙蓉饭店 |
| 4 | Rongleyuan Restaurant | 荣乐饭店 |
| 5 | Dongfeng Restaurant | 东风饭店 |
| 6 | Rongcheng Restaurant | 容城饭店 |
| 7 | Yao Chua Restaurant | 耀华饭店 |
| 8 | Wang Pang Duck Restaurant | 王胖鸭店 |
| 9 | Waisolo Cold Duck Restaurant | 烤鸭店 |
| 10 | Friendship Store | 友谊商店 |
| 11 | Drum & Cymbal Shop | 鼓店 |
| 12 | Lacquer Ware Factory | 漆器厂 |
| 13 | Sichuan Embroidery Factory | 蜀绣厂 |
| 14 | Bamboo Weaving Factory | 门编工艺厂 |
| 15 | Renmin Market | 人民市场 |
| 16 | Soda Bar | 冷饮柜台 |
| 17 | Fuqi Feipian (Husband & Wife Lungs) Snackshop | 夫妻肺片 |
| 18 | Chen Mapo (Granny's Beancurd) Snackshop | 陈麻婆豆腐 |
| 19 | Long Chaoshou Soup Dumplings | 龙抄手饭店 |
| 20 | Lai Tangyuan Rice-ball Restaurant | 赖汤元饭店 |
| 21 | Snackshops (Sweets) | 小吃(东风路) |
| 22 | Zhong Shuijiao Ravioli Restaurant | 钟水饺饭店 |
| 23 | Advace Rail Ticket Office | 火车售票处 |
| 24 | Chengdu Bus Terminal (Xinnanmen Station) | 成都汽车站 |
| 25 | Ximen Bus Station (Buses for Guanxian) | 西门汽车站 |
| 26 | Public Security Bureau | 公安局 |
| 27 | CAAC | 中国民用航空总局 |
| 28 | Xinhua Bookstore | 新华书店 |
| 29 | Foreign Languages Bookstore | 处文书店 |
| 30 | Chengdu Theatre | 成都剧院 |
| 31 | Telecommunications Bldg. | 电讯大楼 |
| 32 | Bank of China | 银行 |
| 33 | Renmin Teahouse | 人民茶馆 |
| 34 | Teahouse | 解放北路茶馆 |
| 35 | Xiao Yuan Teahouse & Bar | 晓园茶馆 |
| 36 | Temple of Wuhou | 武侯祠 |
| 37 | Renmin Park | 人民公园 |
| 38 | Monument to the Matyrs of the Railway – Protecting Movement 1911 | 烈士纪念碑 |
| 39 | Blind Peoples Massage Parlour | 按摩院 |
| 40 | Arcobat Theatre | 杂技场 |
| 41 | Cultural Park & Qingyang Palace | 文化公园 |
| 42 | Wenshu Monastery | 文殊院 |
| 43 | Tomb of Wang Jiang | 王建墓 |
| 44 | Mao Statue | 毛泽东碑 |
| 45 | Sichuan Exhibition Centre | 展览馆 |

although a cycle out to them would be a rewarding exercise in itself. **Du Fu Caotang** is the thatched cottage of celebrated Tang poet Du Fu (712-70 AD). Something of a rover, Du Fu was born in Henan and left his home turf to see China at the tender age of 20. He was an official in Changan (the ancient capital on the site of modern-day Xian) for 10 years, was later captured by rebels after an uprising, and fled to Chengdu, where he stayed for four years. He built himself a humble cottage and penned over 200 poems on the sufferings of the people. The present grounds – 20 hectares of leafy bamboo and luxuriant vegetation – are an expansion over time of the original cottage area. It's also the centre of the Chengdu Du Fu Study Society, houses Chinese and western editions of the poet's works, a Du Fu statue, and miniature calligraphy (a miniaturist might be on hand to engrave rings). From the time of his death in exile (in Hunan), Du Fu acquired a cult status, with the poems themselves being great inspiration for painting (which is displayed on site). Praise for Du Fu comes from the highest source – Chairman Mao. The Great Helmsman seems to have overdone it a bit – the right-hand section of the park is largely devoted to commemorating his visit in 1958. The Park offers tranquil strolling tea gardens – it's about five km west of the city centre.

The **Temple of Wuhou** is in Nanjiao (south Suburb) Park. Wuhou or Zhu Geliang was a famous military strategist of the Three Kingdoms Period (220-265 AD). He was the prime minister of the state of Shu, and shares the tomb space and shrine with his Emperor, Liu Bei. Chengdu was the capital of Shu state. Structures at the site date to the Tang dynasty, with renovations and enlargements in the 17th and 20th centuries. There's some fine stele calligraphy, and statues of military and civic officers. To the west of the temple is a large park with lake, picnicking, nice teahouse, and small antique store at the north end.

**Wanjian Lou (River Viewing Pavilion)**, is as the name suggests. It is located to the south-east of Chengdu, near Sichuan University; a four-storey Qing wooden structure, lush bamboo forests where over 100 types are represented, teahouse, restaurant. The bamboos range from skyscrapers to bonzai-sized potted plants – and this might be a good place to escape the summer heat. The pavilion was built to the memory of Xue Tao, a Tang dynasty poet – nearby is a well, said to be the place where she drew water to dye her writing paper.

These three temple parks are open 7.30 am to 6 pm.

The **Lantern Festival** takes place in Chengdu at Chinese New Year – the main site is Qingyang gong (Cultural Park) where an ancient Taoist temple once stood.

**Tomb of Wang Jian** To the north-west of Chengdu, has an exhibition hall displaying relics (jade belt, mourning books, imperial seals, warrior and musician sculpturing). Wang Jian (847-918 AD) was Emperor of Shu in the 10th century. The hall is open daily except Monday, 9 am to noon and 2 pm to 5.30 pm.

**Sichuan Provincial Museum** Located due south on Renmin Lu, there are relics here relating to the Red Army's Long March, some statues from Mt Emei, and Buddhist statues. Open daily except Monday, 8 to 11.30 am, 2 to 6 pm.

Starting to leave town, but still within easy range is the **Temple of Divine Light** at Xindu, the **Wenshu Monastery** and the **Zoo** – the three together are a guaranteed A-1 excursion. A suggested route is to get to Xindu first in the early morning, then the Zoo, then Wenshu.

**Baoguangsi (The Monastery of Divine Light)**, in the north of Xindu County, is an active Buddhist temple. It comprises five halls and 16 courtyards, surrounded by bamboo. Pilgrims, monks and tourists head for Xindu, which makes for lively proceedings and attracts a fine array of hawkers. The temple was founded in the ninth century, subsequently destroyed, reconstructed in the 17th century.

Among the monastery treasures are a white jade Buddha from Burma, Ming and Qing paintings and calligraphy, a stone tablet engraved with 1000 Buddhist figurines (540 AD), and ceremonial musical instruments. The temple is rich in artefacts, but most of the more valuable items are locked away, and require special permission to view them – you may be able to if you can find whoever's in charge around here.

The Arhat Hall, built in the 19th century, contains 500 two-metre-high clay figurines, representing Buddhist saints and disciples. Well, not all of them: in amongst this spaced-out lot are two earthlings – Emperors Kangxi and Qianlong. They're distinguishable by their royal costume, beards, boots and capes. One of the impostors – Kangxi – is shown with a pockmarked face, perhaps a whim of the sculptor.

The temple has an excellent vegetarian restaurant where a huge array of dishes is prepared by monastic chefs (special requests can be catered for). The temple is open daily, 8 am to 6 pm. The countryside around Xindu is fertile, with bracing farm scenery. About a km from Baoguangsi is Osmanthus Lake – bamboo groves, lotuses, osmanthus trees. In the middle of the lake is a small memorial hall for Ming scholar, Yang Shengan.

Xindu is 18 km to the north of Chengdu: a round trip on a bicycle would be 40 km, or at least four hours cycling time on a Chinese bike. Otherwise, there are buses leaving from the traffic circle south of the main (north) train station. The bus takes about 40 minutes to get to Xindu. Hitching is another possibility, but better done returning from Xindu.

**Zoo** Lush, beautiful grounds – for the humans at least (the animals get the concrete, but some attempt has been made to make them feel at home). Since Sichuan is the largest panda habitat, Chengdu Zoo is the best place to see them in China. There are about eight on hand for observation.

The zoo is about six km from Chengdu centre, and is open 8 am to 6 pm daily. You can hop on a No 9 bus, or drop off the Xindu bus. It's a half-hour by bicycle from Chengdu.

**Wenshu Monastery** Whatever its background, Wenshu (God of Wisdom) Monastery offers a spectacle that few PRC temples do: it's so crowded with worshippers that you may have trouble getting in there on weekends. The object of veneration drawing the burners of incense appears to be a Buddhist statue made in Tibet. Wenshu dates back as far as the Tang dynasty, with reconstruction in the 17th century. Various halls contain Buddhist artefacts – you may not be permitted to view some of these. There is also a teahouse, and a gallery displaying paintings and calligraphy. Open daily, 8 am to 8 pm. The alley on which Wenshu is located is a curiosity in itself – joss-stick vendors, foot-callus removers, flower and fireworks salesmen. The alley runs eastwards off Renmin Zhonglu.

### Places to Stay – Chengdu

The *Jinjiang Guest House*(tel 24481) at 180 Renmin Nan Lu, is the narrow choice at present. This is a 1000-bed mini-state deluxe block with high walls around it and the full works for facilities. At elevator peak hours, backpackers jostle touring Frenchmen, resident foreign experts, businessmen, chirpy Hong Kongers – and a stray Tibetan dignitary with flowing robes may even be caught in the crush. Doubles for Y30 with bath (higher for air-con, TV); Y20 for double room without bath. The cheaper double can be treated as a dormitory and you may be able to wangle a bed for Y6 to Y8 per person.

There are also triple rooms where you may be able to get a bed for a similar rate. Beds in a four-bed room go for Y6 a bed. A footnote on the Jinjiang's socialist plumbing and fixtures: if you're in a room without bath, you are *not* obliged to use the communal facilities on your own floor – should they be substandard, cracked or approaching the swimming pool stage, try the showers on the sixth, seventh and eighth floors.

There's a run of souvenir-type shopping on the ground floor – and a section selling Kodachrome, Nescafe, Johnny Walker and all the other equipment needed for the arduous trip through China. Good film stocks, so load up. On the (British) first floor is an immense dining-room which doubles as an occasional theatre. A student-priced dinner is Y2.50 as opposed to Y6 for a regular – but it's not the same meal – smaller scale, no trimmings or dessert (though you could try pinching it from other tables). The cuisine here hardly matches the quality of spicing in Chengdu's restaurants. Western breakfast inexplicably costs Y2 student, and Y3 regular – and consists of a pot of coffee and some teeth-breaking toast with jam.

Other facilities within this castle: since 99 per cent of externals stay here, all mail (including Poste Restante) will be directed to the front desk, so inquire there. There's a bicycle-rental conveniently located on the wall along Renmin Lu (see Getting Around section). The Jinjiang Penthouse has recreational facilities – billiards, chess, a great outdoor/indoor bar with comfortable seating, views from the south end over the river – and they will crank up the cassette-deck after inserting your western tapes. Normally open to 11 pm, but may continue later for the drunk and obnoxious.

If you're arriving in Chengdu from Leshan or Emei by bus, ask the driver to let you off at the hotel en route to the Chengdu South Bus Station (Xinanmen) – otherwise you'll have to walk back (about 15 minutes). If arriving by train, take a number 16 bus (from either North Station or South Station) – it will deposit you on the hotel doorstep. Everybody knows where the Jinjiang is, so no trouble asking for directions to the hotel (ask for the *Jinjiang Binguan*).

### Places to Eat

Sichuan cuisine is a class unto itself. It emphasises extremities of the taste buds – with an armoury of spicing designed, it seems, to permanently damage them. The art in Chengdu is better represented in the snack line (these are not necessarily tongue-searing – could be sweet or salty). Dishes that won't make your forehead drip or your eyeballs pop out are Sichuan Duck (smoked with camellia and camphor leaves), stuffed fish, and certain chicken dishes. If you head for the Jinjiang dining-halls, of course, you are simply asking for western meals, or else over-priced parodies of local fare – minus the heavy-handed spicing (and minus the grotty table-manner displays that become somewhat amusing after a while). Special dishes may require an advance phone order – get the hotel to ring for you.

**Main Courses** The *Chengdu Restaurant* (tel 7301) at 642 Shengli Zhong Lu, is one of the largest and one of the best in the city, a favourite with travellers. Good atmosphere, decent food, reasonable prices – downstairs is adequate. Try to assemble a party of vagabonds from the hotel before sailing forth – tables are large, and you get to sample more with a bigger group. It's about a 20 minute walk along a side alley opposite the Jinjiang Hotel – arrive early.

The *Furong* (tel 4004) is at 124 Renmin Nanlu. Despite the claim at the front ('Gods will you be if you take meals here'), more than a few travellers have found this place not to their taste, or liking. Well, with items on the English menu such as 'pig's large intestines head fried in lard' what does one expect … the Furong is an easy walk from the Jinjiang.

The *Rong Le Yuan* (tel 24201) is at 48 Renmin Zhonglu. It's hard to find – look for a small red-front doorway that leads to a larger courtyard. It's open for lunch and dinner, and the servings are more than honest here – order dishes one by one. Mapo Dofu Y1; large soups Y0.50; main courses Y1 to Y2. Nice setting – air-con is the outdoor breezes that pass under high roof. The two back rooms are for weddings or special occasions. Examine dishes of other diners carefully – they may not be to your liking if duplicating.

A misunderstanding that turned out for the better: I spotted a mouth-watering mirage at a neighbouring table, dragged the waitress over, almost stuck my finger in the dish in a delirium of anticipation, and, mission accomplished, returned to my seat with a silly grin. Two other foreign devils at the table – we were horrified when the waitress, after the standard time lag, returned with what appeared to be a mere stack of rice bubbles. Once again, we surmised, China had got the better of the salivary glands. We were about to let loose a string of bad words when the lady proceeded to baptise the rice with piping hot soup. The dish erupted in fireworks – when the steam and sizzle had cleared, she had vanished, leaving the mirage on the table. De-licious! The base is a kind of hardened rice-cake, scraped off the bottom of the barrel – crisp and fried. Soupy additions are meat and vegetables, which soften the rice to a crunchy texture. The magic characters for this dish are:

锅炒肉片

**Other** Two Chinese hotel dining-rooms, with unpredictable results, are the *Dongfeng Fandian* (tel 7012) at 147 Dongfeng Lu, and the *Rongcheng Fandian* (tel 22687) at 130 Shaanxi Jie.

Another main course restaurant in the core of downtown is the *Yaohua* (tel 6665) at 22 Chunxi Lu. On the edge of Renmin Park, to the south side of Shengli Xilu, is *Nuli Canting*, which translates to 'Make the Great Effort'. May not be worth doing that, but if you happen to be in the vicinity, drop by and check it out – this small place bears the numbering (or renumbering) 55 57 59 61 63 65 67.

Special treat for ailing vegetarians: take a ride to Xindu Monastery, 18 km north of Chengdu – the bus service is good enough to enable commuting (see the Things to See section for details).

**Duck platters** Chengdu has lots of cold duck places. Some are nondescript, and served in a disappointing fashion – care should be taken because these are not snacks – you are moving out of the pittance price bracket. The next trick is how to get that duck heated up! (it may be possible).

At the foot of Dongchenggen Jie (and south-east of Renmin Park) is *Wang Pang (Fat Mr Wang's Duckshop)*, situated on a corner – it is one of the better-known places. The nicest duck shop sighted is *Weiyuelou* at No 46 Renmin Zhonglu. It's friendly, clean, has brown-tiled frontage, under an apartment block. Inside, marble table-tops, paintings, calligraphy, and WINDOWS! American beer is served in bowls. Y3 for half a chopped stone-cold duck. The restaurant's name translates to 'tasty and delicious chamber' – and the name does not fall short of it.

**Snacks** Many of Chengdu's specialities originated from *xiao chi* or finger food. The snack bars are great fun and will cost you next to nothing. It's not quite clear why there are so few main course restaurants in Chengdu – there are better Sichuan restaurants in Beijing. However, in the snack line, the offerings can be outdone in no other Chinese city – and if you line up several of these places, you will get yourself a banquet in stages. The offerings run through the whole vocabulary – Chengdu won ton, dandan noodles (hot spiced noodles in soup), beef fried in thin pancakes, pearl dumplings, steamed buns, leaf-cakes (wrapped in banana leaves), flower-cakes (made to resemble a white chrysanthemum), water dumplings in hot chilli oil . . . a few of the more renowned snack outlets are listed here.

*Pock-marked Grandma's Bean Curd* serves mapo dofu with a vengeance. Small squares of bean curd, with a fiery meat sauce (laced with garlic, minced beef, salted soybean, chilli oil – enough to make you shut up for a few days). As the story goes, the madame with the pock-marked face set up shop here (reputed to be the same shop) a century ago, providing food and lodging for itinerant pedlars (the clientele look to be roughly the same today, as does the decor). Bean curd is made on the premises, costs Y0.30 a bowl, and a bottle of beer to cool it off is Y0.70 – making Y1 for the right ratio of heater and cooler. The restaurant has grotty, greasy decor – but those spices will kill any lurking bugs, as well as taking care of your sinus problems. Also serves things like spicy chicken and duck, and plates of tripe. Situated at 113 Xi Yulong Jie, it's a small white shop with a green front.

Almost directly opposite (No 90) is the Blind People's Massage Parlour (English sign) where you can rest up after a bean curd – don't expect a massage, all you'll get is a feeble feel-around. Best if you come attired in a minimum of clothing since none is removed. A session lasting twenty minutes costs Y4.10; if you have come to help China's socialist reconstruction as a foreign expert, then it costs Y1.30 (also student rate). The third logical step in the bean curd-massage route is to plunge into a soda bar for an icecream or soft drink – there's one nearby on the corner of Renmin and Xi Yulong.

*Ming Xiao Chi Dian (Chengdu Snack-Bar)* serves noodles, baozi and a kind of jaffle. *Fuqi Feipian (Husband and Wife Lungs)*, at 51 Dongfeng Lu Yi Duan, serves spiced and sliced cow lungs (hot!). *Zhong Shuijiao (Chef Zhong's Ravioli)*, at 107 Dongfeng Lu Yi Duan, is renowned for its boiled dumplings. At the south end

of Chunxi Lu, Nos 6 and 8 are two of the better-known noodleshops – they will also make up sugar jaffles. No 8 is *Cook Long's Soup-Dumpling Restaurant (Long Chaoshou)*.

Off the north end of Chunxi Lu, and situated on Dongfeng, is *Lai's Rice-balls*. Lai started off as a street stall vendor, and has moved up in the world. You get four dumplings in a soup, and a side dish of sesame sauce. Each dumpling has a different sweet stuffing – preserved rose petals or mandarin oranges, for example – and they should be dipped in the sugar-sesame sauce before devouring. This exercise will cost you no more than 30 fen. Further east on Dongfeng, past the intersection with Mangxing Zhonglu a sweet-tooth snack shop, at No 75 – elaborate decor, jaffles, sweet and sticky concoctions.

And one place to investigate is a recent opening in Chengdu – the *Tongrentang Dinetotherapy Restaurant*, whose manager is a traditional Chinese medicine practitioner – among the snacks are ginseng flour dumplings cardamom on steamed bread and tremella soup, all of them low priced.

## Teahouses

The teahouse, or *chadian*, has always been the equivalent of the French cafe or the British pub in China – or at least this was true of the pre-49 era. Activity ranged from haggling over the bride's dowry to fierce political debate. The latter was true of Sichuan, which historically has been one the first to rebel and one of the last to come to heel.

Chengdu's teahouses are thus somewhat special – as in other Chinese cities, they were closed down during the Cultural Revolution as being dangerous assembly places for 'counter-revolutionaries'. With faction battles raging in Sichuan as late as 1975, re-emergence of this part of daily life has been slow – but you can't keep an old tea addict down! Teahouses sprawl over Chengdu sidewalks (in back-alley sections) with bamboo armchairs that permit ventilation of one's back. In the past, Chengdu teahouses also functioned as venues for Sichuan Opera – the plain clothes variety, performed by amateurs or retired workers . There's been a revival of the teahouse opera, but such places (and the times of performances) are difficult to locate, so it's best to find a local to take you there. Other kinds of entertainment include story-telling and musicians; another teahouse caters entirely to chess players.

Most Chinese teahouses cater to the menfolk, young and old (mostly old), who come to meet, stoke their pipes or thump cards on the table. Chengdu, however, offers some family-type teahouses. More in the old-man teahouse variety, with a nice balcony view, is a chadian parked by a bridge (see the map for the location). Downtown is a pleasant interior teahouse, the *Xiao Yuan*. It's very popular and has a certain sophistication.

A more comfortable setting would be the *Renmin Teahouse* in Renmin Park, which is a leisurely tangle of bamboo armchairs, sooty kettles and ceramics, with a great outdoor location by a lake. It's co-ed, a family-type chadian – crowded on weekends. In the late afternoon workers roll up to soothe shattered factory-nerves – and some just doze off in their armchairs. You can do the same – a most pleasant afternoon can be passed here in relative anonymity over a bottomless cup of Stone-flower tea at a cost so ridiculous it's not worth quoting. When enough tea-freaks appear on the terrace, the stray earpicker with Q-tips at the ready, roves through (advertising to improve the quality of conversation?!), and paper profile-cutters with deft scissors also make the rounds.

Another charming indoor co-ed teahouse is to be found within the precincts of Wenshu Monastery – crowded, steamy ambience. Other major Chengdu sights have chadians attached to them – and the back lanes hold plenty more.

## Shopping

Chengdu has a large range of handicrafts of excellent quality – if you want to see an even larger range of a particular output, try and get to the factory source (the Brocade and Filigree Factories are to the west, towards Du Fu Cottage).

Chunxi Lu is the main shopping artery, a walking street lined with department stores, art dealers, secondhand bookstores, stationery, eyeglass shops, photo stores. At No 10 is the Arts & Crafts Service Department Store, dealing in most of the Sichuan specialties (lacquerware, silverwork, bamboo products). This place also has branches in the Jinjiang Hotel, the airport and the Exhibition Centre. At No 13 Chunxi Lu is a musical instrument shop, selling hand-tempered brass gongs and cymbals. At No 14 is a cavernous teahouse for resting weary shopping legs. At No 51 is Shi Bi Jia, specialising in mounting artwork, calligraphy, Chinese stationery. Right at the north end of Chunxi Lu is the Sichuan Antique Store (on Shangyechang Jie), also a largest-of-the-kind, with branches in the Jinjiang and Exhibition Centre, deals in porcelain, jewellery, embroidery, bamboo wares, ivory, jadeite.

At No 22 Chunxi Lu is the Derentang Pharmacy, largest of the kind in Chengdu, a century old, offering, among other elixirs, caterpillar fungus (a mix of the fungus and larva of a moth species – good for TB, coughs, restoring the kidneys, Y250 for 500 g), and the rhizome of chuanxiong (pain reliever, blood purifier).

The Exhibition Hall, which actually does have industrial exhibitions, has Friendship wares with a capital F scattered on the ground floor, 3rd floor and 5th floor. Everything is for foreigners only. Antiques are sold on the 3rd floor. These expanses of counters are staffed by mild-mannered clerks who put in strenuous hours of newspaper-reading in between tour-bus assaults. The largest section is the 5th floor, where you can find anything from a sword to an antique bird cage to your aunt's lost wedding ring. There's double-sided embroidery (Sichuan Shu embroidery is one of the most famous in China), stage costumes, palmwood walking sticks, lacquerware screens, bamboo-thread-covered tea-sets – a list as long as your arm. If you have any further needs, there's always the Friendship Store which stocks Sichuan wines and liquors, tapestries, Kodak film, Kekou Kele, imports and foodstuffs.

Of the Chinese shopping variety are the specialty stores – but they're difficult to locate. There's a very nice place selling drums, cymbals and brass gongs at the eastern end of Hongguang Donglu (near Renmin Zhonglu). At 154 Renmin Nanlu Sanduan is a Household Goods Store, selling cane furniture, baskets, bamboo and porcelain.

Renmin Market is a maze of daily necessity stuff – worth poking your nose into the chaos but not of great interest for purchases – further north of that, along Jiefang Zhonglu, are small shops selling fur-lined and sheepskin coats and jackets

(as well as heavy PLA-type overcoats) – a good selection, not found in too many other places. Although a few Tibetans drift into Chengdu, there's little sign of minority wares from the high plateau, and what there is may be of dubious authenticity.

## Night life & Entertainment

Night life can be fruitful hunting in Chengdu – and you will have to hunt. Delve into local newspaper listings via desk liaison at the Jinjiang. If something strikes your fancy, get it written down in Chinese, and get a good map location – these places are often hard to find, especially at night. If you have more time, try and get advance tickets. Offerings include teahouse entertainment, acrobatics, cinema, Sichuan opera, Beijing opera, drama, art exhibits, traditional music, story-telling, shadow plays, sporting events, visiting troupes.

A rented bicycle is a useful adjunct to night life since bus services are low

**Entertainment**

# Sichuan flood featured in film

The flood that struck Sichuan Province in 1981 gets full dramatic treatment in a locally produced feature film titled "Red Alert 333."

In the film, a flood involves thousands of Jialing County residents in a life or death struggle. In one scene a captain insists that some people must leave his overloaded ship. The first to leave is the county magistrate's wife, who takes her little daughter to the nearby roof of a flooded house. More and more people crowd on to the roof until it collapses. In another scene, thousands of people swarm to a nearby bridge for safety but a floating 20-ton petrol tank threatens to crash into it.

The film is being premiered in Beijing.

*An exhausted messenger brings more bad news to flood headquarters, in a scene from the new feature film "Red Alert 333."*

China Daily. April-July 1983

frequency or unreliable after 9 pm (also packed to the hilt). Chengdu is Sichuan's cultural centre, home of Sichuan opera which has a 200-year tradition, and features slapstick dress-up, eyeglass-shattering songs, and old men dressed as old women. Cinemas abound – there's the Sichuan Cinema a block north of the Jinjiang Hotel (same side of street) – pot luck, but at 30 fen a seat it's not about to break the piggy-bank. Top deck of the Jinjiang has a late-nite bar for decadent carousing.

### Getting Around

**Bus** The most useful bus is No 16 which runs from the North Railway Station to the South Railway Station, passing by Public Security, the Foreign Languages Bookstore and the Jinjiang Hotel. Bus maps carry colour coding for trolleys and ordinary buses – buses 1,2,3,4, and 5 can also be trolleys bearing the same number. Trolleys have wires – it's easy to work out which colour is the wiring – it can only go so far around the city. Trolleybus No 1 runs from Chengdu main bus station (Xinamen) to Chengdu North Railway Station. Ordinary bus No 4 runs from Ximen bus depot (north-west end of town) to the south-east sector, and continues service to 1 am (most others cease around 9.30 to 10.30 pm).

**Bicycles** There are three rental locations (see the map). The one near the Jinjiang Guest House is open from 8 am to 10 pm, costs 30 fen/hr to a maximum of Y4 a day – longer rentals possible. More expensive, but conveniently located – you can whip down there at suppertime, head off to a restaurant on a bike and return by 10 pm. Do not park the bike outside the hotel gates overnight – it may be towed away. One traveller had a rental towed from outside a storefront, and, after a complex inquiry, found the storage yard which turned out to be the police station.

Around the corner from the Jinjiang, No 31-33 on Jiefang Lu, is a rental with an English sign, open 7 am to 6 pm, Y1.80 for half-day; Y2.40 for 24 hours; Y3.60 for 48 hours. In the downtown district at No 105 Jiefang Zhong Lu (a bit difficult to find) there is an even cheaper rental, designed for Chinese – around Y1.40 for 24 hours.

Those who have headed out of Chengdu in a southerly direction will have encountered trilingual signs (how many Russians are there running around Chengdu on bicycles?) that warn foreigners not to proceed further. Going north-east to Xindu is no problem.

Buses are very crowded in Chengdu, and bike rentals come as a relief. More than this, however, they give access to back alleys where thriving markets and strange industries are in progress (comic-book rentals, teahouses, small shops, weathered housing). Some areas are walking streets by day (Chunxi Lu), but otherwise you can use back streets to get to your destination – you may get lost, so best to have the destination written in Chinese.

Wenshu Monastery, itself on an alley, provides an interesting target – if attempting to reach it via back alleys from the Jinjiang Hotel, you can cut a wide circle around the city to get there and back. Head for Chengdu Restaurant, turn right along Shengli Zhonglu, take the alley past Hongxing Zhonglu (left turn), and turn left into the same alley that the Wenshu Monastery is on.

When leaving Wenshu, head north-west along the same alley, cross Renmin Zhonglu, take an alley to the left after that, head down to Hongguang Donglu, turn right, continue north-west on Hongguang till you get to Changshun Jie (which is marked by a cinema on the left-hand side, near the corner) – turn left down this alley and trickle down to Renmin Park. Interesting markets can be found down this alley, plus odd shops like one selling funeral floral wreaths. From Renmin Park you can return to Jinjiang Hotel via

Shaanxi Jie, an alley paralleling Shengli Xilu.

The north-west sector of Chengdu is an interesting area – Tudor-style housing, a Mao statue almost hidden from view inside a military institution (visible from the alley that Wenshu Monastery is on, looking north-west), street stalls and markets tucked down the byways.

If you have good reflexes, good night vision and a strong sense of compass points, night-riding is a dangerous sport that yields a different side of Chengdu. Light-bulbs are at a premium in China – often the street lamps do a better job than house lighting. Back in Beijing, that leads to card players almost being run over by honking taxidrivers. Headlights are only used to warn cyclists that something large is speeding through; no Chinese bikes carry lamps (the cost is too high), very few carry reflectors. Add to this the complete disdain of red lights (manually operated, the police box nearby may be empty), and some accidents are bound to occur.

The back alleys are a little safer in terms of the number of large random objects coming towards you, but more hazardous in terms of the small random objects. With reduced visibility, it is advisable to ride slower. Although Beijing is soundly snoring by 9.30 pm, Chengdu hangs in there for a bit longer – the glow of TV tubes is visible from dark house doorways, the occasional cluster of night-markets, theatre crowds spilling onto the streets, and the brilliant blues, greens and reds of the icecream parlours and soda-bars. The only place seen that outdid the neon fluorescent tubing of the latter was a store selling lamp fixtures and shades. Night-riding is pleasantly cool, and the darkness allows a latitude of creeping up on things without being noticed. Chances of getting lost are quite high.

### Getting Away

Transport connections in Chengdu are more comprehensive than in other parts of the south-west.

**Bus** The main station for buses to and from Emei, Kanding, etc is to the south-east of the Jinjiang Hotel and is called *Xinanmen*. The depot to the north-west of town, called *Ximen*, is mainly for runs to the Guanxian irrigation project and vicinity. There is another long-distance station to the west called *Qinyang Gong*.

**Train** Most rail traffic proceeds from Chengdu main (north) Station. The advance rail ticket office, a smaller building on Shengli Xilu, works OK for the right prices. CITS has also been known to dish out Chinese priced tickets to foreigners (perhaps because they're mixed in with CTS), but you may have to wait longer to get a ticket. For more information on trains in the south-west, see the introductory section.

From Chengdu there are direct trains to Emei (3 hrs, Y3.40 hard-seat Chinese price), to Leshan (4 hrs, Y4.70 hard-seat Chinese price), to Kunming (25 hrs, Y31 hard-sleeper Chinese-price), to Chongqing (11 hrs, Y17 hard-sleeper, Y10.20 hard-seat, Chinese price), and to Xian (about 20 hrs, around Y25.80 hard-sleeper Chinese price), and there are also direct trains to Lanzhou, Hefei, and Beijing. For more information, see the Introduction to the South-West region.

**Air** Chengdu is connected by air with Beijing (Y226), Canton (Y201), Changsha (Y129), Chongqing (Y37), Guilin (Y141), Kunming (Y84), Lhasa (Y322), Nanjing (Y210), Shanghai (Y250), Taiyuan (Y145), Wuhan (Y147), Xian (Y79), Xichang (Y47).

**Combination Tickets** Combination rail/bus/boat tickets are sold at the North Rail Station, window No 14. You may have trouble trying to get one of these – I can't even locate half the places these tickets take you to on my map! There are at least 15 combinations – and some brief details are given here for the sake of interest. There are rail/bus tickets for the route from Chengdu via Jiajiang to Leshan, Wutong Qiao, and Mabian. There is a combine rail/bus ticket from Chengdu via Longchuan to Luzhou, Fushun, Naxi, Xuyong, Gusong, Guilin etc. There is a rail/boat/bus ticket from Chengdu via JiaJing, Leshan and then along the Min River to wherever. There is a combined ticket which will take you by rail to Chongqing, and then by ferry to Shanghai. There is a similar combination ticket service in Chongqing.

## AROUND CHENGDU
### Guanxian

The Dujiangyan Irrigation Project, some 60 km north-west of Chengdu, was undertaken in the 3rd century BC to divert the fast-flowing Min River and rechannel it into irrigation canals. The Min was subject to flooding at this point – when it subsided, droughts could ensue. A weir system was built to split the force of

the river, and a trunk canal (Mouth of Precious Jar) was cut through a mountain to irrigate the Chengdu Plain. Thus the mighty Min was tamed – a temple (Fulong) was erected to commemorate the occasion in the Jin Dynasty (265-420 AD).

The project is ongoing – it originally irrigated some 1.2 million hectares of land, and since liberation this has expanded to 3.2 million hectares. Most of the present dams, reservoirs, pumping stations, hydro-electric works, bridge work, and features are modern: a good overall view of the outlay can be gained from **Two Kings Temple (Er Wang Si)**. The two kings are Li Bing, governor of the Kingdom of Shu and father of the irrigation project, and his son, Er Lang, who were given the titles posthumously – this makes for a rather unusual and dilapidated engineering temple. Inside is a statue of Li Bing, shockingly lifelike; in the rear hall is a standing figure of his son

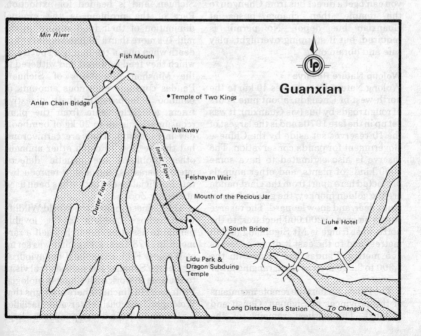

holding a dam tool; there's also a Qing dynasty project map, and behind the temple there is a terrace saying in effect 'Mao was here' (1958).

Guanxian, while of immense importance in the progress of agriculture in China, is of specialist interest – how exciting can dams and irrigation get? Of local flavour, there is precious little. A nice teahouse sited on **South Bridge**, near Lidui Park entrance. The main hotel is about 15 minutes walk from the Guanxian bus station; beds from Y3. You can most likely get into Chinese hotels in Guanxian – regulations appear to be relaxed.

Buses run to Guanxian from Ximen bus depot in Chengdu every half-hour from 7 to 11.30 am, and hourly from 1 to 6 pm, cost Y1, trip takes 1½ hours over bumpy roads. You'd do better to take a bus direct to Two Kings Temple (a further half hour beyond the Guanxian bus station), and work your way back to Guanxian township. If you can't get a direct bus from Chengdu to the temple, then change buses at Guanxian bus depot. No permit is required, but if stopping overnight, play safe and obtain one.

### Wolong Nature Reserve

Wolong Nature Reserve lies 40 km to the north-west of Chengdu, about nine hours of rough roads by bus (via Guanxin). It was set up in the late 1970s and is the largest of the 10 reserves set aside by the Chinese Government for panda conservation. The reserve is also estimated to have some 3000 kinds of plants, and other animals protected here apart from the giant panda are the golden monkey, the golden langur, musk deer, and snow leopard. The reserve covers an area of 200,000 hectares; to the north-west fringe is Mt Siguniang (6,240 metres) and to the east it drops as low as 155 metres. Pandas like to dine in the 2,300 to 3,200 metres zone, ranging lower in winter.

The Panda inhabits the remote mountains of the provinces of Sichuan, Gansu and Shaanxi. The earliest remains of the animal date back 600,000 years. It's stoutly built, rather clumsy, and has a thick pelt of fine hair, a short tail, and a round white face with eyeballs set in black-rimmed sockets. Though it staggers when it walks, the Panda is a good climber, and lives on a vegetarian diet of bamboo and sugar-cane leaves. Mating season has proved a great disappointment to observers at the Wolong Reserve, since pandas are rather particular. Related to the bear and the raccoon, pandas – despite their human-looking shades – can be vicious in self-defence. In captivity they establish remarkable ties with their keepers after a period of time, and can be trained in a repertoire of tricks.

Estimates place the total number of giant pandas at a round figure of 1000, most of which are distributed in north and north-western Sichuan (with further ranges in Gansu and Shaanxi). The giant panda was first discovered in 1896 in Sichuan, and is headed for extinction. Part of the problem is the gradual diminution of their food supply; in the mid-70s more than 130 pandas starved to death when one of the bamboo species on which they feed flowered and withered in the Minshan Mountains of Sichuan. Pandas consume enormous amounts of bamboo – apparently their digestive tracts get little value from the plant (consumption is up to 20 kg of bamboo a day in captivity). They are carnivorous, but they're slow to catch other animals; other problems are genetic defects, internal parasites, and a slow reproductive rate (artificial insemination has been used at Beijing Zoo).

The Chinese invited the World Wildlife Fund (whose emblem is the lovable panda) to assist in research, itself a rare move. In 1978 a research centre was set up at Wolong. Eminent animal behaviourist Dr George Schaller has paid several visits to the area to work with Chinese biologist Professor Hu Jinchu. There are signs that Wolong will establish observation facilities for tourists – half a dozen pandas are kept at the commune for research. At present, access to this small community is limited to trek-type tours – the road in is a treacherous one. There is little chance of seeing a panda in the wild – Dr Schaller spent two months trekking in the mountains before he got to see one.

One of Schaller's research tasks was to fit wild pandas with radio-monitoring devices. In early 1983, the *People's Daily* reported that Hanhan, one of the very few pandas tagged, was caught in a steel wire trap by a Wolong local. The man strangled the panda, cut off its monitoring ring, skinned it, took it home and ate it. I'm not quite sure what the moral of the story is – but the meal earned the man two years in jail. On a brighter note, directives have been issued forbidding locals to hunt, fell trees or make charcoal in the mountainous habitats of the panda. Peasants in the areas are being offered rewards equivalent to double their annual salary if they save a starving panda. In late 1983 more pandas were found dead, but several starving pandas have been rounded up for nursing on special farms.

## EMEI SHAN

Emei is locked in a medieval time warp – a steady stream of happy pilgims with their straw hats, makeshift baggage, walking canes and fans; at the monasteries, sombre Buddhist monks, the tinkle of bells, clouds of incense, firewood and coal lumped in the courtyards for the winter months. It is more or less a straight mountain climb, with your attention directed to the luxuriant scenery – and, as in the Canterbury Tales, to fellow pilgrims. Admirable are the hardened affiliates of Grannies Alpine Club, who slog it up there with the best of them, walking sticks at the ready lest a brazen monkey dare think them easy prey for a food-mugging. They come yearly for the assault, and burn paper money as a Buddhist offering for longevity. The climb, no doubt, adds to their longevity, so

the two factors may be related. For the traveller itching to do something, the Mt Emei climb is a good opportunity to air the respiratory organs, as well as to observe post-76 religious freedoms in action from the inside, since you are obliged to stay in the rickety monasteries along the route.

One of the Middle Kingdom's four famous Buddhist mountains (the others are Putuo, Wutai and Jiuhua), Emei Shan has little of its original temple-work left. The glittering Golden Summit Temple, with its brass tiling engraved with Tibetan script, was completely gutted by fire. A similar fate befell numerous other temples and monasteries on the mount – war with the Japanese and Red Guard looting have taken their toll. The original temple structures dated back as far as the advent of Buddhism itself in China; by the 14th century, the estimated 100 or so holy structures housed several thousand monks. The present temple count is around 20 active after a Cultural Revolution hiatus, bearing traces of original splendour. Since 1976 the remnants have been renovated, access to the mountain has been improved, hiking paths widened, lodgings added, and tourists permitted to climb to the sacred summit.

Hiking is spectacular enough – fir trees, pines, and cedars clothe the slopes; lofty crags, cloud-kissing precipices, butterflies, azaleas . . . a nature reserve of sorts. The major scenic goal of Chinese hikers is to witness a sunrise or sunset over the sea of clouds at the summit. In the afternoon (rarely), there is a phenomenon known as Buddha's Aureole – rainbow rings, produced by refraction of water particles, attach themselves to a person's shadow in a cloud bank below the summit. Devout Buddhists, thinking this was a call from yonder, used to jump off the Cliff of Self-Sacrifice in ecstasy; during the Ming and Qing dynasties, officials set up iron poles and chain railing to prevent suicides. These days the head can be stuck in a cardboard cut-out on the site, and one can

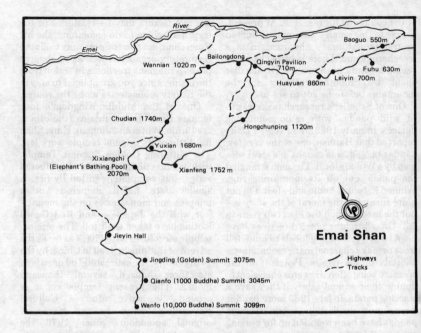

River
Emei
Baoguo 550m
Wannian 1020 m
Bailongdong
Qingyin Pavilion
710m
Fuhu 630m
Leiyin 700m
Huayuan 860m
Chudian 1740m
Hongchunping 1120m
Yuxian 1680m
Xixiangchi
(Elephant's Bathing Pool)
2070m
Xianfeng 1752 m
Jieyin Hall
Jingding (Golden) Summit 3075m
Qianfo (1000 Buddha) Summit 3045m
Wanfo (10,000 Buddha) Summit 3099m

Emai Shan

—— Highways
– – – Tracks

be photographed in that same act of attaining Nirvana.

**Weather** The best season to visit is May to October. Winter is not impossible, but will present some trekking problems – iron soles with spikes can be rented to deal with encrusted ice and snow on the trails. At the height of summer, which is scorching elsewhere in Sichuan, Emei presents cool majesty. Temperate zones start at 1000 metres. Cloud cover and mist are prevalent, and will most likely interfere with the sunrise – if lucky, you can get to see Mt Gongga to the west; if not, you'll have to settle for the telecom tower 'temple' and the meteorological station. Monthly average temperatures in degrees Celsius are:

|  | Jan | Apr | July | Oct |
|---|---|---|---|---|
| Emei town | 7 | 21 | 26 | 17 |
| Summit | –6 | 3 | 12 | –1 |

**Gear** Emei is a tall one at 3099 metres, so the weather is uncertain and you'd be best advised to prepare for sudden changes without weighing yourself down with a huge pack (steps can be steep). There is no heating or insulation in the monasteries – blankets are provided, and you can rent heavy overcoats at the top. Heavy rain is a problem – a good pair of rough-soled shoes or boots is called for, as you can go head over heels on the smooth stone steps further up. Flimsy plastic macs are sold by enterprising vendors on the slopes – these will last about 10 minutes before you get wet. Strange hiking equipment as it may sound, a fixed-length umbrella would be most useful – for the rain, and as a walking stick (scare the hell out of those monkeys by pressing auto-release!). These kinds of umbrellas are not cheap in China, though they may have some resale value. If you want to look more authentic you can get yourself a hand-crafted walking stick, very cheap – and while you're at it, get a fan and a straw hat too. A flashlight would be handy. Food supplies are not necessary, but a pocket of munchies wouldn't hurt. Bring toilet paper with you. Luggage can be left at Emei train station, at the Hongzhushan Hotel, or at one of the monasteries.

**Permits** In theory you need a hiking permit on top of your Emei addition to your normal alien's travel permit. In practice, no one will bother asking. The hiking permit looks like a museum entrance chit, and can be obtained from Baguo Monastery for 30 fen. You will be asked for your alien's travel permit (or your passport) so it's best to have Emei on it.

### Getting Away

The hubs of the transport links to Emei Shan are Baguo Village, and Emei town. Emei town itself is best skipped, though it has markets, a cheap dormitory at the *Emei Hotel*, a good restaurant, and a long distance bus station.

Emei town lies 3½ km from the railway station which is on the Kunming-Chengdu railway line. Baguo is another 6½ km from Emei town. At Emei Station, buses will be waiting for train arrivals – the short trip to Baguo is Y1 in an air-con bus, and Y0.30 in a local bus. From Baguo there are eleven buses a day to Emei town, the first at 7 am and the last at 6 pm – no service during lunch hour.

There are also direct buses running from Baguo to Leshan and Chengdu. There are eight buses a day from Baguo to Leshan, the first at 7 am and the last at 5.30 pm – takes one hour and the fare is Y1.10. There are good bus connections between Leshan and Chengdu. The bus from Baguo to Chengdu costs Y4.60 and takes four hours.

Emei Railway Station is on the Chengdu-Kunming railway line, and the trip to Chengdu takes three hours, costing Y3.40 hard seat (Chinese price). The train from Emei town is actually cheaper than the bus, but does not offer the convenience of leaving Baguo (trains are also less frequent and timing may be off). You can purchase one-day advance train tickets at two little booths by the pavilion in Baguo square.

### Ascending the Heights

Baguo village is the key transport junction; it lies between Baguo Monastery and the Hongzhushan Hotel at the foot of the mountain. You can dump your bags at the Hongzhushan Hotel for a modest charge (and it may be possible to dump them at the Baguo Monastery or the Emei town train station).

Most people start their ascent of the mountain at Wanniansi (Temple of Myriad Ages) and come down through Qingyingge (Pure Sound Pavilion). From Baguo there are buses running close to Wannian and to Qingyin. Buses from Buguo to Wannian leave at 7.10 am, 9 am, 11 am, 1 pm and 2.10 pm and there may be a later bus at 4.30 pm; the fare is Y0.50.

On the return trip, buses from Qingyin depart for Baguo at 8 am, 11 am, 1 pm and 4 pm. The bus depot near Qingyin also has connections back to Emei Town, and to Leshan, but frequencies are much higher from Baguo. If you're stuck for connections when you get back down, you may be able to hitch back to Baguo – otherwise it's a 15 km hike.

**Routes** Most people ascend Emei Shan by the Wanniansi-Chudian-Xixiangchi-Summit route, and descend from the Summit via Xixiangchi – Xianfeng – Hongchunping – Qingyingge. The paths converge just below Xixiangchi, where there are three small restaurants at a fork. A common route is:

Wannian – 15 km – Xixiangchi – 15 km – Jinding – 3.5 km – Wanfo – 3.5 km – Jinding – 15 km – Xixiangchi – 12.5 km – Xianfeng – 15 km – Hongchunping – 6 km – Qingyin – 12.5 km – Leiyin – 1.5 km – Fuhu – 1 km – Baguo.

**Timing** Two to three days on-site is enough for the return climb. Usually one day up and one day down. Enough time should be left for a slow-paced descent, which can be more punishing for the old trotters. A hardy Frenchman made it up and down on the same day, but he must have had unusual legs. A round of applause for the Frenchman – but don't try it unless you're made of rubber.

Chinese and western sources have some wildly misleading figures on the length and difficulty of the Emei climb. These figures can be attributed to geriatrics or Chinese walking times, or ignorance of the buses running to Wannian.

Assuming that most people will want to start climbing from Qingyin or Wannian – buses from Baguo run close to these points, so that knocks off the initial 15 km. Wannian is at 1020 metres, and the Golden Summit is at 3075 metres. With a healthy set of lungs, at a rate of 200 metres elevation gain per hour, the trip up from Wanniansi could be done in 10 hours if foul weather does not start.

Starting off early in the morning from Wannian, you should be able to get to a point below the Jinding summit by nightfall, then continue to the Jinding and Wanfo summits the next day, and descend to Baguo the same day. If you have more time to spare, you could meander over the slopes to villages hugging the mountainsides.

On the main routes described above, in climbing time you'd be looking at:

**Ascent** Qingyin – 1 hr – Wannian – 4 hrs – Xixiangchi – 3 hrs – Jieyin – 1 hr – Golden Summit – 1 hr – Wanfo Summit

**Descent** Wanfo Summit – 45 min – Golden Summit – 45 min – Jieyin – 2½ hrs – Xixiangchi – 2 hrs – Xianfeng – 3½ hrs – Qingyin

**Cheating** There are several minibuses and buses leaving from the square in front of Baguo Monastery very early in the morning, and running along a recently-made dirt road ,round the back of the mountain up to the 2640 metre level. From there, it's only 1½ hours to the top. Minibuses (Y7 to Y9 one-way) and buses (Y4.50) take about three hours to get up the mountain. Minibuses are usually chartered by prior arrangement.

Cheating is a popular pastime on Emei (the name Emei means 'moth-eyebrow mountain' – raised or lowered these days?). Grannies are portered up on the sturdy backs of young men (likewise healthy-looking young women are carried up).

The most spectacular brawl I witnessed in China took place at 2640 metres. The bus was waiting for passengers to go down – well, not exactly waiting ... What had happened was that a group of Hong Kong visitors, easily discernible by their clothing and cameras, had set up a deal with the driver to charter the whole bus back down the mountain, leaving no space for locals. The driver, in his wisdom, did not open the main bus door, but his cabin door – to let the Hong Kongers squeeze onto the vehicle. Pandemonium broke out in the crowd of Chinese onlookers – they burst through the main bus door, and old women were piling through the windows ... Some very nasty scenes ensued as the conductor and the driver rushed back to boot them out again and re-seal the bus. The remaining Hong Kongers, the ones still on terra firma, regrouped. The Charge of the Light Brigade followed as they smashed through the ranks of the locals and were pulled up by the scruffs of their necks through the driver's cabin. Meanwhile, old and young alike, the locals were bashing at the bus with their walking sticks and screaming abuse – finally the bus pulled out, horns blaring, with Chinese running after it, kicking the paintwork for all they were worth, and almost doing in the rear lights with walking sticks.

**Places to Stay & Eat** The old monasteries are food, shelter and sights all rolled into one, and, while spartan, are a delightful change from the regular tourist hotels. They've got maybe as much as a thousand years of character.

For once in your life, you don't have to bargain – room rates are fixed, and reasonably so. Prices range from Y0.80 in a very large dormitory (10 beds or more) to Y5 for a single room. In between are other options like Y2 per person in a four-bed room. Plumbing and electricity are primitive; candles are supplied. The greatest thing is no tussle at the desk – if the man says it's full, then believe him, it's full – (if there's space, they'll give you the price range you want and no questions asked).

There are eight monastery guest houses – at Baguo, Qingyin, Wannian, Xixiangchi, Xianfeng, Hongchunping, Fuhu and Leiyan. There's also a host of smaller lodgings, at Chudian, Jieyin, Yuxian, Bailongdong, the Jinding Summit and Huayan for instance. The smaller places will accept you if the main monasteries are overloaded. Failing those, you can virtually kip out anywhere – a teahouse, a wayside restaurant – if night is descending. Be prepared to backtrack or advance under cover of darkness as key points are often full of pilgrims – old women two to a bed, camped down the corridors, or camping out in the hallowed temple itself, on the floor. Monasteries usually have half-way hygienic restaurants with monk-chefs serving up the vegetarian fare; Y1 to Y2 should cover a meal. There is often a small retail outlet selling peanuts, biscuits and canned fruit within the monastery precincts. Along the route are small restaurants and foodstalls where one can replenish the guts and the tea mug. Food gets more expensive and comes in less variety the higher you mount, due to cartage surcharges and difficulties.

An exception to the monasteries is the *Hongzhushan Hotel*, at the foot of Emei Shan. It's got dreary brick and plaster dorm accommodation at Y3 per person. Better villa-type rooms are available, Y5 per person and up. This hotel has a very pleasant dining section which is a 10 minute walk back into the forest – you can dine on a second-floor balcony, set menu, great food, copious servings, Y2 a head, open 6 pm to 6.30 pm only.

Some notes on the monasteries follow – most of the ones mentioned are sited at key walking junctions and tend to be packed out – if you don't get in, however, do visit and check out the restaurant and its patrons.

**Baguosi (Monastery of Country Rewards)** was built in the 16th century, enlarged in the 17th by Emperor Kangxi, and recently renovated. It's got a 3.4 metre porcelain Buddha, made in 1415 and housed near the Sutra Library. To the left of the gate is a rookery for potted miniature trees and rare plants. Costs Y3 a bed, grubby. Nice restaurant and tearoom with solid wood tables.

**Fuhusi (Crouching Tiger Monastery)** is sunk in the forest. Inside the monastery is a 7-metre-high copper pagoda with Buddhist images and texts inscribed on it. Completely renovated recently – with additional section of bedding for 400 and restaurant for 200. Costs a bit more to stay there (Y4/Y5 a head) but well worth it if you can get in.

**Wanniansi (Temple of Ten Thousand Years)** is the oldest surviving Emei monastery (reconstructed in the 9th century). It's dedicated to the man on the white elephant, the Bodhisattva Puxian, who is the protector of the mountain. This statue, 8½ metres high, cast in copper and bronze, weighing an estimated 62,000 kg, is to be found in Brick Hall, a domed building with small stupas on it. The statue was made in 980 AD. Accommodation in the Wanniansi area is Y1, Y2, Y4 per person. If full, go back towards Qingyingge to Bailongdong, a small guesthouse.

**Qingyingge (Pure Sound Pavilion)** is so named because of the sound effects produced by rapid waters coursing around rock formations in the area. Has a nice temple perched on a hillside, and small pavilions for lounging around in to observe the waterworks and appreciate the natural music. Y3 for a bed here.

**Xixiangchi (Elephant Bathing Pool)** is, according to legend, the spot where the monk Puxian flew his elephant in for the big scrub, but now there's not much of a pool to speak of. Being almost at the crossroads of both major trails, this is something of a hangout and beds are scarce. New extensions are in progress for handling human overload on the trail. Dorm Y1.20, Y6 double, Y5 single.

The monkeys have got it all figured out – this is the place to be. If you come across a monkey 'toll-gate', the standard procedure is to thrust open palms toward the outlaw to show you have no food. The Chinese find the monkeys an integral part of the Emei trip, and like to tease them. As an aside, monkeys form an important part of Chinese mythology – and there is a saying in Chinese 'With one monkey in the way, not even ten thousand men can pass' – which may be deeper than you think!

**Cloud-Reposing Hermitage,** at 3075 metres, is just below the summit – it was built in 1974, a dark, gloomy, primitive wooden structure. A bed in 6-person dorm costs Y1.20, Y2.90 in a 2-bed room and Y3.90 single (another innovation in these 'advanced' hotels – singles!). The hotel will rent padded cotton overcoats for 40 fen a day; there is another shop nearby with the same deal. These are mostly intended for patrons of the sunrise – on a very clear day (rare) the most spectacular sight would not be the sunrise but the Mt Gongga range rising up like a phantom to the west.

**Xianfeng (Magic Peak) Monastery** is a wonderful location – backed into rugged cliffs – loads of character. Try and get a room right to the rear of the monastery where the floors give pleasant views. It's off the main track so not crowded; costs Y2.50 a person in a 4-bed room, Y1.20 dorm, Y4 to Y6 single. Nearby is **Jiulao Cave,** inhabited by big bats.

## LESHAN

The opportunity to delve into small-town life in the PRC should always be followed up. While Leshan is no village, it's on a scale that one can be comfortable with. It's an old town; parts of it have that lived-in-for-a-millennium look, while the trendiest addition from this century is the odd soda-bar with garish fluorescent tubes, disco music, and patrons huddled over sickly sweet fizzy orange drinks. The hotel situation is good, decent food can be unearthed and it's a good resting spot for those Emei-weary legs – and there is a major site, the Grand Buddha.

The **Dafu (Grand Buddha)** is 71 metres high, carved into a cliff-face overlooking the confluence of the Dadu and Min Rivers. It qualifies as the largest Buddha in the world, with the one at Bamian, Afghanistan, as runner-up (besides the Leshan model is sitting down!). Dafu's ears are seven metres long, insteps 8½ metres broad, and a picnic could be conducted on the nail of his big toe, which is 1.6 metres long – the toe itself is 8.3 metres long.

This lunatic project was begun in the year 713 AD, engineered by a Buddhist monk called Haitong who organised fund raising and hired workers – it was completed 90 years later. Below the Buddha was a hollow where boatmen used to vanish – Haitong hoped that the Buddha's presence would subdue the swift currents and protect the boatmen, and Dafu did do a lot of good, as the surplus rocks from the sculpting filled the river hollow. Haitong gouged out his own eyes in an effort to protect funding from disappearing into the hands of officers, but he died before the completion of his

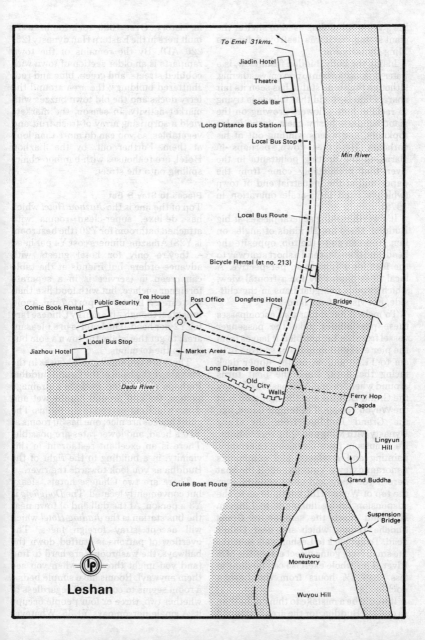

To Emei 31kms.

Jiadin Hotel

Theatre

Soda Bar

Long Distance Bus Station

Local Bus Stop

Min River

Local Bus Route

Bicycle Rental (at no. 213)

Comic Book Rental

Public Security

Tea House

Post Office

Dongfeng Hotel

Bridge

Local Bus Stop

Jiazhou Hotel

Market Areas

Long Distance Boat Station

Dadu River

Old City Walls

Ferry Hop

Pagoda

Lingyun Hill

Grand Buddha

Cruise Boat Route

Suspension Bridge

Wuyou Monastery

Wuyou Hill

Leshan

life's work. A building used to shelter the giant statue, but it was destroyed during a Ming Dynasty war.

Inside the body, hidden from view, is a water-drainage system to prevent weathering, although the stone statue has seen its fair share. Dafu is so old that foliage is trying to reclaim him – flowers growing on the giant hands, a bushy chest, ferns in his topknots, and weeds winding out of his earholes. He gazes down, perhaps in alarm, at the drifting pollutants in the river that presumably come from the paper mill at the industrial end of town (which started large-scale operation in 1979).

It's worth making several passes at big Buddha; there are all kinds of angles on him. You can go to the top, opposite the head, and then descend a short stairway to the feet for a Lilliputian perspective. A local boat passes by for a frontal view, which reveals two guardians in the cliff-side, not visible from land.

To make a round-tour that encompasses these possibilities, take the passenger vessel from the Leshan pier. It leaves from the pier every 40 minutes or so from 6.30 am to 11.30 am; sit on the upper deck facing the dock, since the boat turns around when leaving. You pass in close by the Grand Buddha and the first stop is at the **Wuyou Temple**. The temple dates, like the Grand Buddha, from the Tang Dynasty with Ming and Qing renovations; it's a museum piece containing calligraphy, painting and artefacts, and commands panoramic views. You can get off the boat here if you want and cross-country over the top of Wuyou Hill, continue on to the suspension bridge linking it to Lingyun Hill, and reach the semi-active **Grand Buddha Temple** which sits near Dafu's head. To get back to Leshan walk south to the small ferry going direct across the Min River. This whole exercise can be done in less than 1½ hours from the Leshan dock.

It would be a mistake to think of Leshan as one big Buddha, for the area is steeped

in history. Over 1000 rock-tombs were built here in the Eastern Han dynasty (25-220 AD). By the remains of the town ramparts is an older section of town with cobbled streets, and green, blue and red-shuttered buildings; the area around the ferry docks and the old town buzzes with market activity. In season, the markets yield a surprising array of fresh fruit and vegetables, so you can do more than look at them. Further out, by the Jiazhou Hotel, are teahouses with bamboo chairs spilling onto the street.

## Places to Stay & Eat

Top of the line is the *Jiazhou Hotel* which has de-luxe, super-clean rooms with attached bathroom for Y20 (the best room is Y28) Amazing dinners cost Y4 per head – they're only for hotel guests with advance orders, but friends at the table can creep in (service is in a separate foreigner enclave, but with food like that, who cares!?) Dinner is 6 pm to 7 pm. Avoid breakfast though – it's murky Chinese fare for Y2 per head. The hotel is in a pleasant area; to get there take the town's sole bus line to the terminus.

There are two small guest houses in the area above the head of the Grand Buddha. Perhaps due to the Buddha's drainage system, the cliff around here is wet and damp which can extend to the rooms. The guest houses are nice; one has 30 rooms at Y10 a head, and lower rates are possible. There is an excellent restaurant in this vicinity, in a building to the right of the Buddha as you look towards the river.

There are two Chinese hotels, sleazy but conveniently located. The *Dongfeng* is Y3 a person. At the dull end of town near the bus station is the *Jiading Hotel* which will accept stray foreign faces. The overflow of patrons is stuffed down the hallways, the washrooms are hard to find (and you might throw up when you see them anyway). Rooms have simple beds – a room seems to cost Y3.90 regardless of whether two, three or four people occupy it. A single person pays Y1.35. Whatever the price, it's a pittance, at least for foreign wallets. Make sure you lock your room when you leave it. Down the main street from here there are sidewalk stalls dispensing victuals.

## Getting Around

There is one bus line in Leshan, running from the bus station to the Jiazhou Hotel. The schedule is posted at the Jiazhou bus stop; it runs from 6 am to 6 pm, at roughly 20 minute intervals with no service at lunchtime (11.20 am to 1.20 pm approx). On foot, it's a half-hour walk from one end of town to the other.

You can rent a bike just near the bridge across the Min River (see the map in this book for directions). The price is Y0.50 an hour, which is expensive (for China), and watch out if you rent overnight as charges continue while you snore, unless otherwise negotiated. Bikes are of limited use if visiting the Grand Buddha since uphill work is required, and the track to Wuyou Hill is a dirt one. However, if you wish to explore the surrounding countryside, the bike will be useful – a suggested route is to continue out of town past the Jiazhou Hotel.

## Getting Away

**Bus** From the Leshan long-distance bus station there are five daily buses running to Chengdu (the first at 7.20 am and the last at 1 pm). The 165 km trip takes about four hours; fares are Y4.70 in an ordinary bus and Y6.30 in a soft-seat coach. Get the driver to drop you at the Jinjiang Hotel in Chengdu.

Emei Shan to Leshan is 30 km; buses run to Emei town, Baguosi, or Pure Sound Pavilion. The highest bus frequency is to Baguosi, and there are only two buses a day to Pure Sound.

**Boat** There is a boat to Chongqing, departing Leshan at 5.30 am and another at 7.30 am every few days, but it would be difficult to get aboard. The trip takes 36 hours and costs Y23 in third class. There

is a shorter run to Yibin which departs at 7 am, and costs Y10.20 in third class. Yibin is part-way to Chongqing and has a train station.

## MEISHAN

Meishan, 90 km south-west of Chengdu by road or rail (it's on the Kunming-Chengdu railway line) is largely of interest to those with a savvy of Chinese language, literature and calligraphy. It was the residence of Su Xun and his two sons, Su Shi and Su Zhe, the three noted literators of the Northern Song Dynasty (960-1127). Their residence was converted into a temple in the early Ming Dynasty, with renovations under the Qing Emperor Hongwu (1875-1909). The mansion and pavilions now operate as a museum for the study of the writings of the Northern Song period – historical documents, relics of the Su family, writings, calligraphy – some 4,500 items all told are on display at the Sansu shrine.

## CHONGQING

Chongqing was opened as a treaty port in 1890, but not very many foreigners made it up the river to this isolated outpost and those that did had little impact. A program of industrialisation got underway in 1928, but it was in the wake of the Japanese invasion that Chongqing really took off as a major centre; the city was the war-time capital of the Kuomintang from 1938 onwards and refugees from all over China flooded in, swelling the population to over two million. The irony of this overpopulated, overstrained city with its bomb-shattered houses is that the name means something like 'double jubilation' or 'repeated good luck' – Emperor Zhao Dun of the Song Dynasty succeeded to the throne in 1190, and had previously been made the Prince of the city of Gongzhou; as a celebration of these two happy events, he renamed Gongzhou as Chongqing.

Edgar Snow arrived in the city in 1939 and found it a 'place of moist heat, dirt and

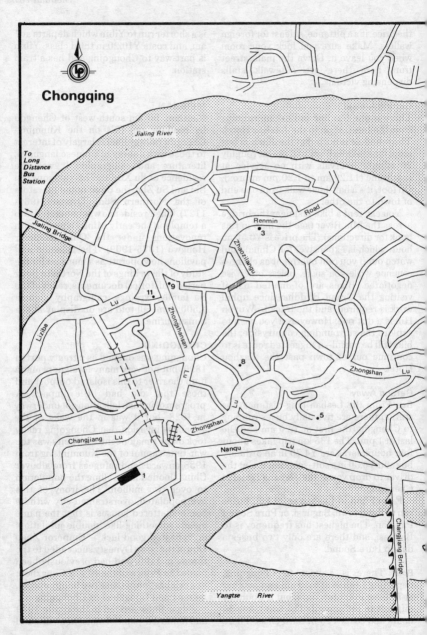

# Chongqing

Jialing River

To Long Distance Bus Station

Jialing Bridge

Lu

Liziba

Zhongshan

Lu

Renmin Road

Zhaoziliangu

11  9

8

5

Zhongshan Lu

Changjiang  Lu

2

Zhongshan

Nanqu  Lu

1

Zhongshan Lu

Changjiang Bridge

Yangtse  River

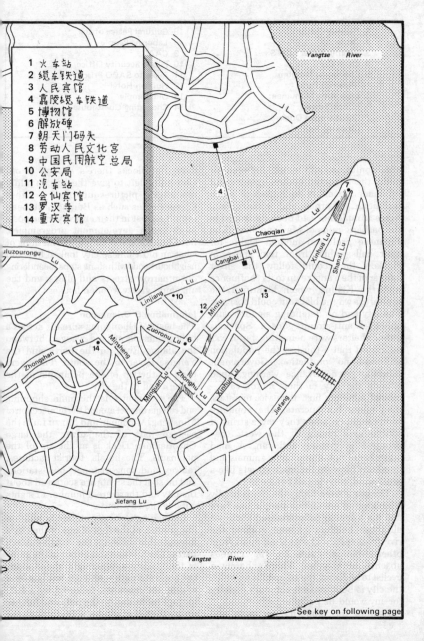

1 火车站
2 缆车铁道
3 人民宾馆
4 嘉陵缆车铁道
5 博物馆
6 解放碑
7 朝天门码头
8 劳动人民文化宫
9 中国民用航空总局
10 公安局
11 汽车站
12 会仙宾馆
13 罗汉寺
14 重庆宾馆

See key on following page

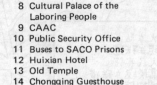

| | |
|---|---|
| 1 Railway Station | 8 Cultural Palace of the |
| 2 Cable Car | Laboring People |
| 3 Renmin Hotel / CITS | 9 CAAC |
| 4 Cable Car | 10 Public Security Office |
| 5 Chongqing Museum | 11 Buses to SACO Prisons |
| (Pipa Hill Park) | 12 Huixian Hotel |
| 6 Liberation Monument | 13 Old Temple |
| (Clock Tower) | 14 Chongqing Guesthouse |
| 7 Chaotianmen Dock | |
| (Booking Hall) | |

wide confusion, into which, between air raids, the imported central government ... made an effort to introduce some technique of order and construction. Acres of buildings had been destroyed in the barbaric raids of May and June. The Japanese preferred moonlit nights for their calls, when from their base in Hankow they could follow the silver banner of the Yangtze up to its confluence with the Kialing, which identified the capital in a way no blackout could obscure. The city had no defending air force and only a few anti-aircraft guns ... Spacious public shelters were being dug, but it was estimated that a third of the population still had no protection. Government officials, given advance warning, sped outside the city in their motor cars – cabinet ministers first, then vice-ministers, then minor bureaucrats. The populace soon caught on; when they saw a string of official cars racing to the west, they dropped everything and ran. A mad scramble of rickshaws, carts, animals and humanity blew up the main streets like a great wind, carrying all before it'.

The war is over, today the city is hardly a backwater; six million people live here and it's a *heavily* industrialised port – as all those belching chimneys along the riverfront testify. It sets itself apart from other Chinese cities by the curious absence of bicycles! There's barely a cyclist to be found, the steep hills on which the city is built make it coronary country for any would-be pedaller.

Despite the modern apartment and industrial blocks there's enough of old Chongqing left to give the city an oddly ramshackle picturesque quality. Other Chinese cities such as Beijing have been rebuilt almost in their entirety in he post-1949 urban development programmes, but Chongqing still conveys something of what an old Chinese city looked like; old neighbourhoods with stone steps meandering down narrow streets and alleys, and the unkempt, grotty wooden houses.

### Information & Orientation
The heart of Chongqing spreads across a hilly peninsula of land wedged between the Jialing River to the north and the Yangtse River to the south. The rivers meet at the tip of the peninsula at the eastern end of the city.

The city centre is the main shopping and cinema district around the intersection of Minsheng, Minchuan and Minzu Lu in the eastern part of the town; the large Chaotianman Dock is at the tip of the peninsula. The hotels, tourist facilities, railway and long-distance bus stations and most of the sights are scattered about the city and there are a number of sights outside the city limits.

Chongqing's railway station is built on low ground, at the foot of one of the city's innumerable hills in the south-eastern part of town. When you go out of the gates of the station walk straight ahead along the concrete path – on your left is a long row of noticeboards, followed by a left-luggage room, and on the right and further up are the ticket windows. Go through the concrete archway at the end of the pathway. On your right is Gaiyuanbazheng Jie. In front of you is Nanqu Lu and on the left is Shahoqingsi Lu.

Over on the left, on the other side of Shahoqingsi Lu is the beginnings of a long flight of steps. About 340 of these will take you up to Changyi Lu, which runs into Zhongshan Lu where you can get buses to the tourist hotels. If you don't feel like walking then beside the steps is a building with the ticket office and cable-car up to Zhongshan Lu – a three fen, 45-degree one-minute ride to the top. Taking the cable-car to the top you exit from a subway; turn right to go to the other side of Zhongshan Lu, or turn left and up the short flight of steps to Changyi Lu. For details of the buses to the tourist hotels, see the section on 'Places to Stay'.

**CITS** (tel 51449) has its office in a building in the *Renmin Hotel* compound. They're a friendly mob but hopelessly disorganised. They have been known to charge 100% extra on the price of train tickets (as against the usual 75%) and they never seem to know what tickets are available on

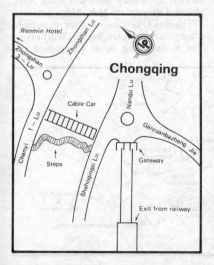

the Yangtse boats – hopefully that situation will change.

**Public Security** (tel 43973) is on Linjiang Lu. A bus No 13 from the front of the Renmin Hotel will take you straight there. They're a friendly lot, but don't expect any permits for strange places.

**CAAC** (tel 52970 or 52643) is at 190 Zhongshan San Lu.

**Bank** There is a money-exchange office in the Renmin Hotel.

**Post** There is a post office in the Renmin Hotel.

**Maps** Good maps in Chinese, one type showing the bus and another without the bus routes, are available from the shop in the Renmin Hotel.

**Things to See**
Chongqing is an enormous industrial city, where the smokes hangs heavily in the air. It's almost what you'd imagine industrial London to look like circa-1890. Some of the old areas of the city are intact, providing something of a ramshackle character to the intrinsic interest of the place. It's not a city of 'sights' but there's a certain picturesque quality to this grey place, situated as it is on the hills surrounding the confluence of two great rivers. The 'sights' are usually connected with the Communist Revolution.

Much of Chongqing makes for good (if uphill) street-walking and the Chaotianmen Dock is a good place to start climbing. Walk up Xinhua Lu past the booking hall for the Yangtse boats and turn into Minzu Lu; from here you can carry on up to Cangbai Lu where you can catch the cable-car which flies over the Jialing River. If you carry on up Minzu Lu you'll eventually see on your left a deteriorated but very ornate gateway which is the entrance to a large temple not visible from the street. You walk through the gateway and past Buddha rock-carvings on either side – at the end of the pathway on the left is the temple which houses a large seated golden Buddha. To the right is another part of the complex now being restored by a team of stone-masons.

Further down Minzu Lu towards the Liberation Monument (the clock tower) is the *Huixian Hotel*. You can take the elevator to the 14th floor where there's a rooftop snack-shop selling plates of cakes and hot milk for Y1. There's a fine view of the city from here and a good place to get it into perspective.

The area around the clock tower is the main shopping area, and also the location of many cinemas, a few street markets, and quite a few bookshops.

### Red Crag Village

During the tenous Kuomintang-Communist alliance against the Japanese during the Second World War, the Red Crag Village outside Chongqing was used as the offices and living quarters of the Communist representatives to the Kuomintang. Amongst others, Ye Jianying, Zhou Enlai and his wife Deng Yingchao lived here. After the Japanese surrender in 1945, it was also to Chongqing that Mao Zedong – at the instigation of American ambassador Patrick Hurley – came in August of that year to join in the peace negotiations with the Kuomintang. The talks lasted 42 days and resulted in a formal agreement which Mao described as 'words on paper'

One of the better revolutionary history museums has now been built at the site, and has a large collection of photos, though none of the captions are in English. A short walk from the museum is the building which housed the South Bureau of the Communist Party's Central Committee and the office of the representatives of the Eighth Route Army –though there's little to see except a few sparse furnishings and photographs.

To get to the Red Crag Village, take the bus No 16 four stops from the main station on Liziba Lu.

### US-Chiang Kai-shek Criminal Acts Exhibition Hall and SACO Prisons

In 1941 the United States and Chiang Kai-shek signed a secret agreement to set up the Sino-American Co-operation Organisation (SACO), under which the United States helped to train and dispatch secret agents for the Kuomintang government. The chief of SACO was Tai Li, head of the Kuomintang military secret service; its deputy chief was a US Navy officer, Commodore M.E. Miles.

The SACO prisons were set up outside Chongqing during the Second World War. The Kuomintang never recognised the

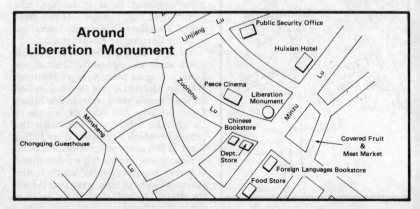

Around Liberation Monument

Communist Party as a legal political entity – it only recognised the army. Civilian Communists remained subject to the same repressive laws, and though these were not enforced at the time, they were not actually rescinded. Hundreds of political prisoners were still kept captive by the Kuomintang in these prisons and others and according to the Communists many were executed.

One of the prisoners held in the Chongqing SACO prisons for five years was General Ye Ding, a Whampoa Military Academy cadet, commander of a Nationalist division during the Northern Expedition of 1926-7 and one of the principal leaders of the Nanchang uprising of 1 August 1927. After the failure of the insurrection Ye retreated to Shantou with part of the Red Army and then took part in the disastrous Canton uprising of December 1927. He escaped to Hong Kong and withdrew from politics for a decade. In 1937, with the anti-Japanese alliance between the Kuomintang and the Communists established, he was authorised by Chiang Kai-shek to reorganise the surviving Red partisans on the Jiangxi-Fujian-Hunan borders, and to create the New Fourth Army – these were soldiers who had been left behind as a rearguard when the main part of the army began its Long March to Shaanxi in 1934. In 1941, Chiang Kai-shek's troops ambushed the rear detachment of the New Fourth Army while it was moving in an area entirely behind Japanese lines to which it had been assigned by Chiang. This non-combat detachment was annihilated and Ye Ding was imprisoned in Chongqing.

Chiang ruled that the massacre was caused by the New Fourth's 'insubordination' and henceforth all aid was withdrawn from that army and also from the Communists' Eighth Route Army; from this time on the Communists received no pay and no ammunition and a blockade was thrown up around their areas to prevent access to supplies. Although the Communists did not retaliate against the Kuomintang – which would have made Japan's task much simpler – clashes between Kuomintang and Communist were continuous, at times amounting to major civil war.

After Ye's release in 1946 he died en route to Yanan, in a plane crash which also killed amongst others Deng Fa (Chief of the Red Army's Security Police) and Bo Gu (General Secretary of the Communist Party from 1932 to 1935 and a supporter of urban-insurrection policies which had cost the Communists dearly in the 1930s).

While the events that surround them are fairly dramatic, the prisons and the exhibition hall are not and you will probably find them fairly boring unless you're an enthusiast. The exhibition hall has lots of photos on display but no English captions. There are manacles and chains but nothing to ghoul over. The hall is open 8.30 am to 5 pm and admission is three fen. To get there take bus No 17 from the station on Liziba Lu. It's about a 20 minute ride and make sure that the driver knows where you want to get off as the place is not obvious. The SACO Prisons are a long hour's walk from the hall (there appears to be no transport, though you could try waving down a truck or jeep), and there's really nothing to see here.

## The Bridges

Worth checking out are the enormous Jialing and Yangtse Bridges. The Jialing Bridge crosses the river to the north of central Chongqing; until the Yangtse Bridge in the south was completed in 1981 this was one of Chongqing's few transport links to other parts of the country. Constructed between 1963 and 1966, the Jialing Bridge is 150 metres long and 60 metres high.

## Chongqing Museum

The museum is a reasonably interesting place, though nothing outstanding. They usually have some dinosaur skeletons on display, unearthed between 1974 and

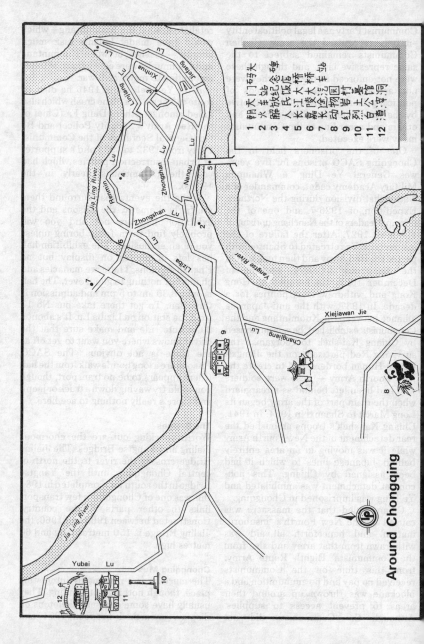

**Around Chongqing**

1 朝天门火车站
2 火车站
3 解放纪念碑
4 人民饭店
5 长江大桥
6 嘉陵江渡大桥
7 水运码头站
8 动物园村
9 红岩村
10 烈士墓
11 白公馆
12 渣滓洞

1977 at Zigong, Yangchuan and elsewhere in Sichuan Province. The museum is located at the foot of Pipa Shan in the southern part of town. It's open 9 to 11.30 am and 2 to 5.30 pm.

The museum is a short walk from the Renmin Hotel. Walk up along Zaozilanyu along the eastern side of the hotel compound; on the right you'll come to a little street market which you walk down and then turn left where it branches into two smaller streets. Follow the street up to the entrance of a park (admission four fen); head through the park, past the 'Cultural Palace of the Laboring People' and at the other end you'll come out on Zhongshan Lu. Directly opposite the entrance to the park, on the other side of the road, is a small street which leads uphill to the Chongqing Museum.

### The Zoo

The zoo is little more than the hideous sight of badly-kept animals in bare concrete cages. There are a couple of slumbering, dirty pandas here. If you come here, whatever you do *don't* come on a Sunday otherwise you'll be the main attraction not the other animals. From near the entrance to the cable-car on Zhongshan Lu, take bus No 3 up Chanjiang Lu to its terminus. From the terminus walk along the road directly in front of you for about ten minutes and this will get you to the zoo.

### Northern Hot Springs

The Northern Hot Springs are located in a large park overlooking the Jialing River to the north-east of the city; they're built on the site of a Buddhist temple of the 5th century AD. The springs have an Olympic-size swimming pool where you can bathe to an audience. There are also private rooms with hot baths – big tubs where the water comes up to your neck if you sit and up to your waist if you stand. They have swim suits for hire here – they're coloured red, symbolising happiness. There's another group of springs 20 km south of Chongqing but the northern group is said to be better.

### Places to Stay

The *Renmin Hotel* is one of the most incredible hotels in China, and if you don't stay here you have got to at least visit the place. It's quite literally a palace, and the design seems to have been inspired by the Temple of Heaven and the Forbidden City in Beijing. Two wings make up the hotel, and these are separated by an enormous circular concert hall. The hotel was constructed in 1953; the concert hall is 65 metres high and seats 4000 people.

For all the grandeur of the facade, the rooms themselves are as basic as in any other Chinese hotel. A close-up inspection of the exterior reveals a certain lack of finesse in the finishing touches to the building. The floor of the concert hall is concrete and the seats are bare wood and metal. The concrete railings on the balconies are sloppily painted, air-cons are tacked on here and there and the backyard is a hodge-podge of tacky little buildings. Nevertheless, there's a certain something about being able to come home to half a palace at the end of the day . . .

Prices at the hotel to suit every pocket; cheapest accommodation is Y5 for a dormitory bed, with common bathroom. A bed in a double room goes for Y6 or Y7 with common bathroom. A bed in a dormitory with attached bathroom is Y8. Various other double rooms go for Y22, Y24, Y30, Y32. A 'double twin room' is Y55. Most of the staff here speak adequate to excellent English, and they're quite friendly.

To get there, take bus No 1 from above the railway station up Zhongshansan Lu as far as the first traffic circle. Then change to bus No 13 or bus No 15 which will take you down past the hotel. It may be as easy just to walk from the traffic circle to the hotel.

The alternative to the Renmin Hotel is the *Chongqing Guest House* on Minsheng Lu, a rather cold dreary hotel. A bed in a dormitory with a TV is Y5, and a bed in the TV-free dormitory is Y4. A single room is Y30 and a double room is Y24 – don't ask me how they work this one out, but *that's what the man said*. The hotel does have the advantage of being rather more centrally located than the Renmin Hotel. A bus No 1 from Zhongshan Lu, above the railway station, goes straight past the hotel.

## Places to Eat

Eating in Chongqing is something of a joke. You've really got the restaurant at the *Renmin Hotel* and not much else if you want a decent meal. Restaurants mentioned in other guidebooks seem to have either gone into hiding or been demolished. For snacks you might try the area around the centre of town, around the corner from Minquan Lu on Zhonghu Lu. On Zhonghu Lu are a number of little street stalls where you can get little plates of vegetable, duck, pork, peanuts and rice for maybe 60 fen to a yuan. OK food but there's nothing particularly worth recommending.

## Getting Around

Buses in Chongqing are tediously slow, and since there are no bicycles they're even more crowded than in other Chinese cities. Taxis can be hired from CITS or the reception desk of the Renmin Hotel.

## Getting Away

**Bus** The long-distance bus station is located on the northern side of the Jialing River, across the Jialing Bridge. Getting to the station isn't so straightforward. Take a bus No 5 from the intersection of Zhongshan Lu and Renmin Lu, across the Jialing Bridge and get off at the terminus. The bus station is further up ahead and you could walk if you're not carrying too much, or alternatively take bus No 10 the last stretch.

There are buses from here to Dazu departing at 7.20 am and 8.00 am; the fare is Y4.50 and the trip takes about eight hours.

**Train** From Chongqing there are direct trains to Beijing, to Chengdu (11 hrs, Y17 hard-sleeper Chinese-price) and to Guiyang (11 hrs, 14.70 hard-sleeper Chinese-price). For Kunming you must change trains at Chengdu and for Guilin you must change trains at Guiyang.

**Plane** Chongqing is connected by air to Beijing (Y200), Canton (Y164), Changsha (Y95), Chengdu (Y37), Guilin (Y104), Kunming (Y86), Nanjing (Y173), Shanghai (Y213), Wuhan (Y110), Xian (Y81).

**Boat** There are boats from Chongqing down the Yangtse River to Wuhan. It's a popular tourist trip and a good way of getting away from the trains –an excellent way to get to Wuhan. For details, see the section in this book on the Yangtse River.

## DAZU

The grotto art of Dazu County, 160 km northwest of Chongqing, is rated alongside the other great Buddhist cave sculpture of

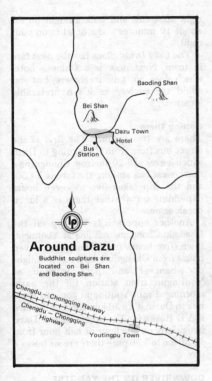

**Around Dazu**

Buddhist sculptures are located on Bei Shan and Baoding Shan.

China, at Dunhuang, Luoyang and Datong. Historical records for Dazu are sketchy; the cliff carving and statues (with Buddhist, Taoist and Confucian influences) amount to thousands of pieces, large and small, scattered over the county in some 40-odd places. The main groupings are at Bei Shan (North Hill) and the more interesting Baoding. They date from the Tang dynasty (9th century) to the Song (13th century).

The town of Dazu itself is a small, dull place, but there are some interesting methods of conveyance to be observed: a child in a bamboo-frame chest carrier; a goose in a wicker backpack; a sick man being ferried around in a wooden sedan mounted on bamboo poles; and four men toting a huge grunting pig lashed to thick poles. It's also been relatively unvisited by westerners (the hotel opened late and the general accommodation situation is inadequate for group tours), and the countryside around is superb.

### Bei Shan

Bei Shan is about a 20-minute hike from Dazu town – aim straight for the pagoda visible from the bus station. There are good overall views from the top of the hill. There are only one or two statues of interest here; dark niches, small statues, many in poor condition.

Niche No 136 depicts Puxian the patron saint (a male) of Emei Shan, riding a white elephant. The same niche has the androgynous Sun and Moon Guanyin. Niche 155 holds a bit more talent, the Peacock King. According to inscriptions, the Bei Shan site was originally a military camp, with the earliest carvings commissioned by a general.

### Baoding

15 km northeast of Dazu town, the Baoding sculptures are definitely more interesting than those at Bei Shan. The founding work is attributed to Zhao Zhifeng, a monk from an obscure Yoga sect of Tantric Buddhism. There's an abandoned monastery here, in good condition with nice woodwork. On the lower section of the hill on which the monastery sits is a horseshoe-shaped cliff sculpted with coloured figures, some of them up to eight metres high.

The centrepiece is a 31 metre long (and five metre high) reclining Buddha, depicted in the state of entering Nirvana, the torso sunk into the cliff face, most peaceful.

Statues around the rest of the 125 metre horseshoe vary considerably; Buddhist preachers and sages, historical figures, realistic scenes (on the rear of a postcard one is described as 'Pastureland – Cowboy at rest'), and delicate sculptures a few centimetres in height. Some of them have been eroded by wind and rain, some have lost layers of paint, but generally there is a remarkable survival rate (fanatic Red Guards did descend on the Dazu area bent on defacing the sculptures, but were stopped – so the story goes – by an urgent order from Zhou Enlai).

Baoding differs from other grottoes in that it was based on a preconceived plan which incorporated some of the area's natural features – a sculpture next to the Reclining Buddha, for example, makes use of an underground spring. It is believed to have taken 70 years to finish the sculptures, completed in 1249 AD. Especially vivid are the demonic pieces: there's an emblem showing the six ways to transmigrate (look for a large dartboard held by the fangs of a Mr Hyde); there is a one-storey section with sobering sculptures on the evils of alcohol and other misdemeanours. Inside a small temple on the carved cliff is the Goddess of Mercy, with a spectacular gilt forest of fingers (1007 hands if you care to check). Each hand has an eye, the symbol of wisdom.

Buses to Baoding leave Dazu town every half hour from 7 am to 3 pm; the fare is 40 fen. The last bus departs Baoding for Dazu at around 5 pm. They probably won't let you take photos at either Bei Shan or Baoding – and Bei Shan is too dark to take photos without a flash anyway. The sites are open from 8 am to 6 pm. It's unknown what the condition of the other 40 sites in Dazu County is like – probably ravaged, but do keep an eye on the cliff-faces as you pass by in the bus for solo sculptures that may occasionally pop up.

### Places to Stay & Eat

The *Dazu Binguan* is Y10 per person (you may get in for Y6) for a room with bath – it's rudimentary but comfortable. The hotel is a major hike from the bus station – turn left from bus station, go straight across a bridge to a place which bears a sign 'Cold Drinks/Dining-room', turn right after this and walk straight on for about 10 minutes – the hotel is on your right.

The *Cold Drink* place has the best fare in town. Next door is a Chinese hotel which does not take foreigners, but you could try anyway as it's a preferable location.

### Getting There

There are two options. The first is the direct bus from from Chongqing to Dazu which leaves at 7.20 am from Chongqing's north-west bus station; the fare is Y4.50, and the trip takes five to seven hours depending on whether there is a lunch break or not.

Another approach is to drop off the Chengdu-Chongqing rail line at Youtingpu town (five hours from Chongqing, seven hours from Chengdu). Arrive at midnight or whenever and park yourself at Youtingpu train station till the early morning. From Youtingpu you can get a bus to Dazu; it's a 30 km ride and the fare is Y1. Buses for Youtingpu depart Dazu irregularly on the hour or half-hour from 11.30 am to 3.30 pm – there are six buses a day.

## DOWNRIVER ON THE YANGTSE: CHONGQING TO WUHAN

Although the scenery and the turbulent waters of China's greatest river have been the inspiration of many poets and painters, for the boatmen who had to ply the waters it was fraught with the perils of dangerous bends, shallows, reefs, strong currents and submerged rocks. A large boat pushing upstream often needed hundreds of coolies ('trackers') who lined the banks of the river and hauled the boat with long ropes against the surging waters. Today smaller boats can still be seen being pulled up the river by their crews.

The Yangtse is China's longest river and the third longest in the world at 6300 km, emanating from the snow-covered Tanggula Mountains in south-west Qinghai and cutting its way through Tibet and seven Chinese provinces before emptying into the East China Sea just north of Shanghai. Between the towns of Fengjie in Sichuan and Yichang in Hubei lie three great gorges, regarded as one of the great scenic attractions of China. The steamer ride from Chongqing to Wuhan is one of the popular tourist trips. It's a nice way to get from Chongqing to Wuhan, a relief from the trains and the scenery is pleasant, but don't expect to be dwarfed by mile-high cliffs! A lot of people find the trip quite boring, possibly because of overanticipation.

The ride downriver from Chongqing to Wuhan takes three days and two nights. Up-river it takes five days. One possibility is to take the boat as far as Yichang which will let you see the gorges and the huge Gezhouba Dam. At Yichang you can take a train north to Xiangfan and another to Luoyang. If you continue you can get off at Yeuyang and take the train to Canton, or you can carry on to Wuhan.

**Tickets** You can buy tickets for the boats from CITS in Chongqing or from the booking office at Chaotianmen Dock. You'll generally have to book two or three days ahead of your intended date of departure, but some people have arrived, got their tickets and left the same day. CITS adds a small service charge to the price of the tickets, but you may wonder where the service went to since they're hopelessly disorganised and never seem to know just what tickets are available. The booking office at Chaotianmen Dock is open daily 9 to 11 am and 2.30 to 5 pm and if CITS doesn't have tickets for the day you want then the booking office is worth trying. You *can* take the boat upriver – see the Wuhan section for details.

Second class cabins get hopelessly overbooked in the middle of the year when tour groups pile into the country, and they can end up being relegated to the third class cabins, so don't be surprised if you can't get a ticket at this time of year.

**Classes** In egaliarian China there is no first class on the boat. Second class is a comfortable two-berth cabin, with soft beds, a small desk and a chair, and a wash-basin. Showers and toilets are private cubicles shared by the passengers. Adjoining the second class deck and at the front of the boat is a large lounge where you can while the time away.

Third class has either four or eight beds depending on what boat you're on. Fourth class is a 24-bed cabin. But toilets and showers are communal though you should be able to use the toilets and showers in second class. If they don't let you into the 2nd class area then have a look around the boat; the one I was on had some toilet cubicles on the lower deck with doors and partitions. There doesn't seem to be any problem just wandering into the lounge and plonking yourself down.

The boat I was on also had a couple of large cabins the entire width of the boat accommodating about 40 people on triple-tiered bunks. There is also deck-class where you camp out in the corridors, but it's highly unlikely you'll be sold tickets for these classes. Remember if you take one of the large dormitories that this part of China is very cold in winter and very hot in summer!

**Fares** CITS in Chongqing charges the following fares per person:

|         | 2nd class | 3rd class | 4th class |
|---------|-----------|-----------|-----------|
|         | Y         | Y         | Y         |
| Wanxian | 35.70     | 25.50     | 8.50      |
| Yichang | 64.70     | 35.50     | 15.20     |
| Shashi  | 74.70     | 39.40     | 17.90     |
| Wuhan   | 102.00    | 51.00     | 27.00     |

If you want to go further down the Yangtse to places like Juijiang, Wuhu, Nanjing or Shanghai, then you have to change boats at Wuhan. CITS in Chongqing can only sell you tickets as far as Wuhan. There is said to be a luxury steamer plying the river, though it's probably only for tour groups and high-ranking Chinese. There will soon be a hydrofoil operating between

Nanjing and Wuhan, which will cut the travelling time down from 40 to just 10 hours – see the Wuhan section for details.

**Departure times** The boat departs Chongqing at 7 am from Chaotianmen. There is a special bus which leaves from the Renmin Hotel at 6 am which will take you straight to the dock. Book a seat on the bus beforehand at the hotel reception desk – it's only Y1.20 per person. Alternatively you can take a taxi. There are probably local buses running at that time, but it's hardly worth the effort.

You're supposed to be able to sleep on the boat the night before departure for Y1 – it's worth asking, but don't be surprised if you're turned away. Perhaps if you have a second class cabin you'll be allowed to.

**Food** There are two restaurants on the boat. The one on the lower deck caters for the masses and is pretty terrible. The restaurant on the upper deck is quite good, but how much you're charged seems to vary from boat to boat. One person was charged Y6 per meal (expensive but worth it considering the alternative) and another Y12. Second class passengers usually get charged either Y10, Y12 or Y15 for three meals each day. It's a good idea to bring some of your own food with you.

**First day** The boat departs Chongqing at around 7 am. For the first few hours the river is lined with factories, though this gives way to some pretty, green terraced countryside punctuated by the occasional small town.

Around 11.30 am you arrive at the town of **Fuling**. The town overlooks the mouth of the Wu River which runs southwards into Guizhou; it controls the river traffic between Guizhou and eastern Sichuan. Near Fuling in the middle of the Yangtse River is a huge rock called Baihe Ridge. On one side of the rock are three carvings

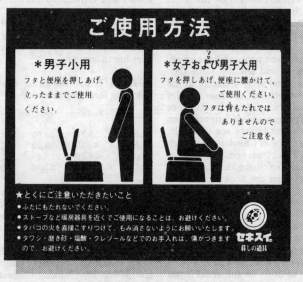

ご使用方法

＊男子小用
フタと便座を押しあげ、
立ったままでご使用
ください。

＊女子および男子大用
フタを押しあげ、便座に腰かけて、
ご使用ください。
フタは背もたれでは
ありませんので
ご注意を。

★とくにご注意いただきたいこと
●ふたにもたれないでください。
●ストーブなど暖房器具を近くでご使用になることは、お避けください。
●タバコの火を直接こすりつけて、もみ消さないようにお願いいたします。
●タワシ・磨き砂・塩酸・クレゾールなどでのお手入れは、傷がつきます
　ので、お避けください。

セキスイ。
暮しの道具

From the toilet on the Yangtse River ferry.

known as 'stone fish' which date back to ancient times and are thought to have served as watermarks –the rock can be seen only when the river is at its very lowest. In addition to the carvings, there are a large number of other inscriptions describing the culture, art, and technology of these ancient times.

**Fengdu** is the next major town. Pingdu Mountain is nearby and this is said to be the abode of devils. The story goes that during the Han dynasty two men, Yin Changsheng and Wang Fangping, lived on the mountain, and when their family names were joined together they were mistakenly thought to be the Yinwang, the King of Hell. Numerous temples containing sculptures of demons and devils have been built on the mountain since the Tang Dynasty, with heartening names like 'Between the Living and the Dead', 'Bridge of Helplessness' and the 'Palace of the King of Hell'.

The boat then passes through **Zhongxian County**. North-east of the county seat of Zhongzhou is the **Qian Jinggou** site where primitive stone artefacts including axes, hoes and stone weights attached to fishing nets were unearthed.

In the afternoon the boat passes by **Shibaozhai (Stone Treasure Stronghold)** on the northern bank of the river. Shibaozhai is a 30 metre high rock which is supposed to look something like a stone seal. During the early years of the reign of the Emperor Qianlong (1736-1797) an impressive red wooden temple, the Landruodian, shaped like a pagoda and 11 storeys high, was built on the rock. It houses a statue of Buddha and inscriptions which commemorate its construction.

Around 7 pm the boat arrives in the large town of **Wanxian** where it ties up for the night. Wanxian is the hub of transportation and communications along the river between eastern Sichuan and western Hubei and has traditionally been known as the gateway to Sichuan. It was opened to foreign trade in 1917. It's a neat, hilly town and a great place to wander around for a few hours while the boat is in port. A *long* flight of steps leads from the pier up the bank of the river to a bustling night market where you can get something to eat or where you can buy very cheap wickerwork baskets, chairs and stools.

**Second day** The boat departs Wanxian at 4 am. Before entering the gorges the boat passes by (and may stop at) the town of **Fengjie**. This is an ancient town which was the capital of the state of Kui during the Spring and Autumn and Warring States Period (770 BC – 221 BC). The town overlooks the Qutang Gorge, the first of the three Yangtse gorges. Just east of Fengjie is a kilometre-long shoal where the remains of stone piles could be seen when the water level was low. These piles were erected in the later part of the Stone Age and during the Bronze Age, possibly for commemorative and sacrificial purposes, but their remains were removed in 1964 since they were considered a danger to navigation. Another set of similar structures can be found east of Fengjie outside a place called Baidicheng.

**Baidicheng** means 'White King Town' and is situated on the river's north bank at the entrance to the Qutang Gorge, 7½ km from Fengjie. The story goes that a high official proclaimed himself king during the Western Han Dynasty, and moved his capital to this town. A well was discovered which emitted a fragrant white vapour, which struck him as such an auspicious omen that he renamed himself the 'White King' and his capital the 'White King Town'.

**Sanxia** The 'Three Gorges', Qutang, Wuxia and Xiling, start just after Fengjie and end near Yichang, a stretch of about 200 km. The gorges vary from 300 metres at their widest section to less than 100 metres at their narrowest. The seasonal difference in water level can be as much as 50 metres.

**Qutang Gorge** is the smallest and shortest gorge (only eight km long) though the water flows most rapidly here. High on the north bank, at a place called Fengxiang (Bellows) Gorge are a series of crevices. There is said to have been an ancient tribe whose custom was to place the coffins of their dead in high mountain caves. Nine coffins were discovered in these crevices; some of them contained bronze swords, armour and other artefacts, but are believed to date back only as far as the Warring States Period.

**Wuxia Gorge** is about 40 km in length and the cliffs on either side rise to just over 900 metres. The gorge is noted for the Kong Ming tablet, a large slab of rock at the foot of the Peak of the Immortals. Kong Ming was the Prime Minister of the state of Shu during the period of the Three Kingdoms (220-280 AD). On the tablet is inscribed a description of his stance upholding the alliance between the states of Shu and Wu against the state of Wei. **Badong** is a town on the southern bank of the river within the gorge. The town is a communications centre and from here roads span out into western Hubei Province, and the boat will usually stop here.

**Xiling Gorge** is the longest of the three gorges at 80 km. At the end of the gorge everyone crowds out onto the deck to watch the boat pass through the locks of the huge **Gezhoura Dam**.

The next stop is at the industrial town of **Yichang**, at about 3 pm if the boat is on time. From here you can take a train north to Xiangfan, where you can catch a train to Luoyang. Yichang is regarded as the gateway to the Upper Yangtse and was once a walled city dating back at least as far as the Sui Dynasty. The town was opened to foreign trade in 1877 by a treaty between Britain and China and a foreign concession area was set up along the riverfront to the south-east of the walled city. After leaving Yichang the boat passes under the immense **Chanjiang Bridge** at the town of **Zhicheng**. The bridge is 1,700 metres long and supports a double-track railway with roads for trucks and cars on

either side. It came into operation in 1971.

The next major town is **Shashi**, a light-industrial town. As early as the Tang Dynasty Shashi was a trading centre of some importance; it enjoyed great prosperity during the Taiping Rebellion when trade lower down the Yangtse was largely at a standstill. It was opened up to foreign trade in 1896 by the Treaty of Shimonoseki between China and Japan, and though an area outside the town was assigned as a Japanese concession it was never developed. About 7½ kms from Shashi is the ancient town of **Jingzhou** which you can get to by bus.

**Third day** There is absolutely nothing to see on the third day; you're out on the flat plains of eastern China, the river widens immensely and you can see little of the shore. The boat continues downriver during the night and passes by the town of **Chenglingji** which lies at the confluence of Lake Dongting and the Yangtse River. East of Lake Dongting is the town of **Yeuyang** which you'll reach at around about 6 am. If the boat is on time then you'll get into **Wuhan** late that afternoon, around 5 pm. (For details of Yeuyang and Wuhan and the Yangtse River between Wuhan and Shanghai, see the separate sections in this book.

## WESTERN & NORTHERN SICHUAN

Literally the next best thing to Tibet are the Sichuan mountains to the north and west of Chengdu – heaps of whipping cream that rise above 4500 metres, with deep valleys and rapid rivers. Tibetans and Tibetan-related peoples (Qiangs) live by herding yaks, sheep and goats on the high-altitude Kangba Plateau Grasslands to the far north-west. Another zone, the Ruoergai Grassland (north of Chengdu, towards the Gansu border) is over 3000 metres above sea level. Closer to Chengdu, the Tibetans have been assimilated, speak Chinese and have little memory of their origins, although they're regarded as a separate minority and are exempt from birth control quotas. Further out, however, Tibetan custom and clothing are much more in evidence.

A theme often echoed by ancient Chinese poets is that the road to Sichuan is harder than the road to heaven. In the present era, with the province more accessible by road, we can shift the poetry to Tibet and the western Sichuan approaches. The roads in these areas are extremely rough, mostly clinging to precarious mountainsides and prone to landslides. Towns on the Kangba Plateau experience cold temperatures, with up to 200 freezing days per year; summers are blistering by day and the high altitude invites mountain burns. Lightning storms are frequent from May to October; cloud cover can shroud the scenic peaks. On a more pleasant note, there appear to be sufficient hot springs in these areas to have a solid bath along the route. Only 150 km a day on a local bus can be counted on – that is, if the bus doesn't break down and your spine doesn't fall out (also assuming that there *is* a bus). Buses won't budge at night – they stop and passengers retire to the same hotel.

A brief idea of what's out on the Kangba Plateau is provided here. It will probably just be armchair reading, because it is almost impossible to get a permit for these places.

## Gongga Shan

At 7556 metres this is a mighty peak – to behold it is worth 10 years of meditation, says an inscription in a ruined monastery by the base. The mountain, apparently, is frequently covered with cloud so patience would be required for the beholding. It sits in a mountain range, with a sister peak just below it towering to 5200 metres. Pilgrims used to circle around the two for several hundred km to pay homage. Gongga Shan is on the open list for foreign mountaineers – in 1981 it buried eight Japanese climbers in an avalanche. Known conquests of this awesome 'goddess' are two Americans in 1939, and six Chinese in 1957.

Both peaks are approached by way of **Kangding**, a small town nestled in majestic scenery. Swift currents from rapids give Kangding (which stands at an altitude of 2620 metres) hydro-power, the source of heating and electricity for the town. The route to Kangding is: Chengdu – Shuangliu – Xinjin – Baizhang – Ya'an – Tianquan (Erlang Shan) – Luding – Kangding.

## Litang

Further west of Kangding is Litang, which at 4700 metres is 1000 metres higher than Lhasa and a few hundred metres short of the world record for high towns (Wenchuan, on the Qinghai-Tibet Plateau). Litang rests at the edge of a vast grassland, and a trading fair and festival lasting 10 days is held annually. The meet is sponsored by the Grand Living Buddha of the Kangba Plateau. Other high altitude towns in the northwest are **Shiqu** and **Sida**, where January minimums can go as low as –37 Celsius.

## Dege

This town lies in the Chola Shan at the north-west corner of Sichuan, and has an extensive Scripture Printing Lamasery, with a 250-year tradition. It has a vast collection of ancient Tibetan scriptures of the five Lamaist sects, and is revered by followers the world over. Under the direction of the Abbot are some 300 workers; housed within the monastery are over 200,000 hardwood printing plates. Texts include ancient works on astronomy, geography, music, medicine, and Buddhist classics. A history of Indian Buddhism, comprising 555 plates, is the only surviving copy in the world (written in Hindi, Sanskrit and Tibetan). Protecting the monastery from fire and earthquake is a guardian goddess, a green Avalokitesvara.

## Jiuzhaigou

In northern Sichuan, close to the Gansu border, is Jiuzhaigou, which has a number of attractive features – it is a nature reserve area (some panda conservation zones) with North American-type alpine scenes (peaks, clear lakes, forests). It consists of valleys in the 2400 to 3600 metre range, and there are stockaded Qiang settlements in the zone. An area called Yellow Dragon is a yellowish earth valley studded with terraced ponds and waterfalls.

Chengdu PSB carries a sign that no permits will be issued for this place – but at least one enterprising traveller has got through. The basic strategy for doing this is to get there as quickly as possible, establish yourself, and then dawdle your way back. In the case of Jiuzhaigou, the bus going directly north of Chengdu takes three days for the 430 km route (stops first night in Maowen, and second night in Sumpan) – which drops you some 15 km short of the nature reserve (the walk there takes four to five hours). This bus leaves every other day from Chengdu, and costs Y13.70.

Michael Gold found a method of defeating the time-and-detection factors by travelling the line with a Hong Kong friend. I met them on a train a little way down the line:

Couldn't get the bus north through Wenchuan and Maowen – booked out seven days in advance due to festival that takes place twice a month Asked around – found out possible to drop off the railway line – landed at the wrong station, backtracked, arrived in Zhaohua (near Guangyuan) in the afternoon. Hotel Y1.50 near station. PSB visit – had to give personal details and then allowed to continue – perhaps confusion because of Hong Kong friend? Bus goes to Nanping, 6.20 am, costs Y7.30, takes 12 hours, needs overnight stop in Nanping – but bus was booked out again. Somehow procured front seat of a truck for a murderous 12-hour ride over dirt track, cutting through Gansu province. Arrived with jangled nerves and bad back. In Nanping, no PSB, cost Y5 each in hotel, locals paid Y0.80. From Nanping to Jiuzhaigou, bus left 7.30 am, took three hours, cost Y2.50, no service Wednesday. Nature Reserve is Y0.50 entrance; hotel cost Y10 for me, and Y6 for Hong Kong friend. Lunch Y5 each. Hiking in reserve excellent – can do 16 km trail to larger lake, passing by small villages with white flags flying over them. Villages are scummy, local groups have grubby costumes but identifiable as Qiangs (Tibetans); copper daggers, special leggings to protect from snakes. Food along the route to Jiuzhaigou terrible. Best part is hiking – crystal sapphire tarns and ponds, fast-flowing rivers, lakes, waterfalls. No snowcaps at the time (summer). Once there, no limit to stay.

From the description given, it appears that Jiuzhaigou has been on the Hong Kong map for at least five years, so there is a hotel setup (and Y10 is not cheap for Sichuan); the Qiang are inured to cameras and starting to get into the souvenir industry.

# Yunnan

When Qin Shihuang and the Han Emperors first held tentative sway over the south-west, Yunnan was occupied by a large number of non-Chinese aboriginal peoples without any strong political organisation. But by the 7th century AD the Bai people had established a powerful kingdom, the Nanzhao (Southern Princedom) south of Dali. Initially allying its power with the Chinese against the Tibetans, this kingdom extended its power until, in the middle of the 8th century, it was able to challenge and defeat the Tang armies. It took control of a large slice of the south-west and established itself as a fully independent entity, dominating the trade routes from China to India and Burma. The Nanzhao kingdom fell in the 10th century and was replaced by the Kingdom of Dali, an independent state which lasted until it was overrun by the Mongols in the mid-13th century – after 15 centuries of resistance to northern rule, this part of the south-west was finally integrated into the empire as the province of Yunnan.

Even so it remained an isolated frontier region, with scattered Chinese garrisons and settlements in the valleys and basins living beside a mixed aboriginal population which occupied the uplands. Like the rest of the southwest it was always one of the first regions to break with the northern government. Today, however, Yunnan looks firmly back in the Chinese fold; a province of 32½ million people, including a veritable constellation of minorities: the Zhuang, Hui, Yi, Miao, Tibetans, Mongols, Yao, Bai, Hani, Dai, Lisu, Lahu, Va, Naxi, Jingpo, Bulang, Pumi, Nu, Achang, Benglong, Jinuo and Drung. Its chief attraction is the provincial capital of Kunming, one of the favourites of many travellers and a delightful city with the flavour of old-fashioned, back street China. For the present Kunming is the only way in to Yunnan, and it's the staging point for trips to the Stone Forest and Xishuangbanna.

## KUNMING

The region of Kunming has been inhabited for the last 2000 years. Tomb excavations around Lake Dian to the south of the city have unearthed thousands of artefacts from that period – weapons, drums, paintings, silver, jade and turquoise jewellery – that suggest a well-developed culture and provide clues to a very sketchy early history of the city. Until the 8th century the town was a remote Chinese outpost, when the Kingdom of Nanzhao, centred to the north-west of Kunming at Dali, captured it and made it a secondary capital. In 1274 the Mongols came through sweeping all and sundry before them. Marco Polo, who put his big feet and top hat in everywhere, gives us a fascinating picture of Kunming's commerce in the late 13th century:

At the end of these five days journeys you arrive at the capital city, which is named Yachi, and is very great and noble. In it are found merchants and artisans, with a mixed population, consisting of idolaters, Nestorian Christians and Saracens or Mohametans ... The land is fertile in rice and wheat ... For money they employ the white porcelain shell, found in the sea, and which they also wear as ornaments about their necks. Eighty of the shells are equal in value to ... two Venetian groats. In this country also there are salt springs ... the duty levied on this salt produces large revenues to the Emperor. The natives do not consider it an

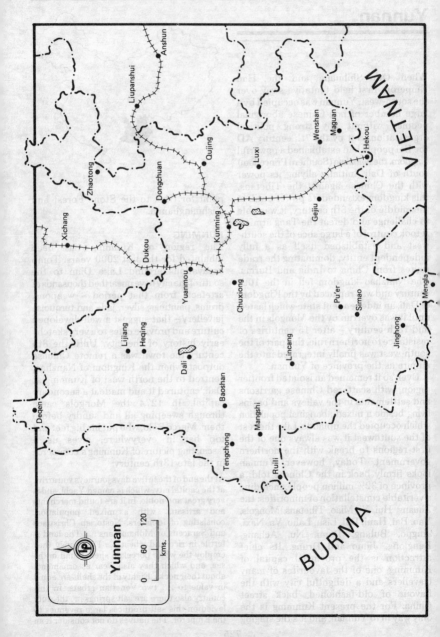

Yunnan

kms.

0    60    120

injury done to them when others have connexion with their wives, provided the act is voluntary on the woman's part. Here there is a lake almost a hundred miles in circuit, in which great quantities of fish are caught. The people are accustomed to eat the raw flesh of fowls, sheep, oxen and buffalo ... the poorer sorts only dip it in a sauce of garlic ... they eat it as well we do the cooked.

In the 14th century the Ming set up shop in Yunnanfu, as Kunming was then known, building a walled town on the present site. From the 17th century onwards the history of this city becomes rather grisly; under the local warlord Wu Sangui the city broke away from Qing control and was not brought to heel until 1681. In the 19th century, the city suffered several blood-baths as the rebel Moslem leader Du Wenxiu, the Sultan of Dali, attacked and besieged the city several times between 1858 and 1868. A large number of buildings were destroyed and it was not until 1873 that the rebellion was finally and bloodily crushed. The intrusion of the west into Kunming began in the middle of the 19th century when Britain took control of Burma and France took control of Indo-China, providing access to the city from the south. By 1900 Kunming, Hekou, Simao and Mengzi were opened to foreign trade. The French were keen on exploiting the region's copper, tin and lumber resources and in 1910 their Indo-China railroad, started in 1898, reached the city.

Kunming's expansion began with World War II, when factories were established here and refugees fleeing the Japanese poured in from eastern China. To keep the Japanese tied up in China, Anglo-American forces sent supplies to Nationalist troops entrenched in Sichuan and Yunnan. Supplies came overland on a dirt road carved out of the mountains in 1937-38 by 160,000 Chinese with teaspoons. This was the famous Burma Road, a 1000 km haul from Lashio to Kunming (today, the western extension of Kunming's Renmin Lu, leading in the direction of

Heilinpu, is the tail end of the Road). Then in early 1942 the Japanese captured Lashio, cutting the line. Kunming continued to handle most of the incoming aid from 1942-45 when American planes flew the dangerous mission of crossing the 'Hump', the towering 5000 metre mountain-ranges between India and Yunnan. A black market sprang up and a fair proportion of the medicines, canned food, petrol and other goods intended for the military were siphoned off into other hands.

The face of Kunming has been radically altered since then – streets widened, office buildings and housing projects flung up. With the coming of the railways, industry has expanded rapidly, and a surprising range of goods and machinery available in China now bears the 'made in Yunnan' stamp. Kunming has a steel plant; the city's production includes foodstuffs, trucks, machine tools, electrical equipment, textiles, chemicals, building materials, plastics. The population of Kunming hovers around the two million mark; minority groups have drifted into the big lights in search of work and some have made their home there. At most the minorities would account for six per cent of Kunming's population – although the farming areas in the outlying counties have some Yi, Hui and Miao groups who are native to the area. Some 150,000 Vietnamese have also called Kunming home, refugees from the Chinese-Vietnamese wars and border clashes that started in 1977.

**Climate** At an elevation of 1890 metres, Kunming has a mild climate, and can be visited at any time of year without need of great clothing adjustments. There's a fairly even spread of temperatures from April till September; winters are short, sunny and dry; in summer (June to August) Kunming offers cool respite although rain is more prevalent then.

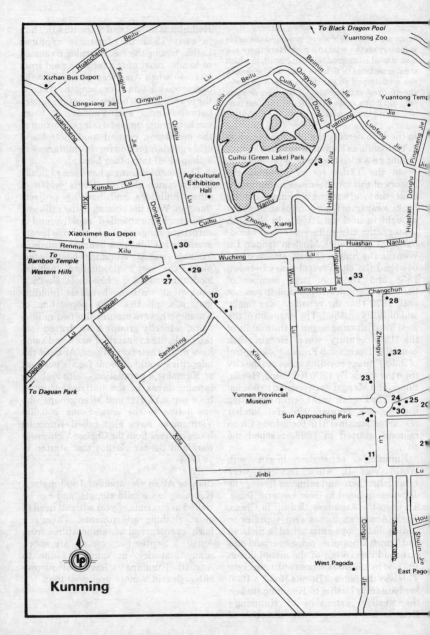

To Black Dragon Pool
Yuantong Zoo

Huancheng Beilu

Xizhan Bus Depot

Fengjian Lu

Longxiang Jie

Qingyun Jie

Qianju Jie

Cuihu Beilu

Beilu

Qingyun Jie

Dongyu

Beimin Jie

Cuihu Beilu

Yuantong Temple

Yuantong Jie

Luofeng Jie

Pinzheng Jie

Cuihu (Green Lake) Park

Xilu

Huashan

Xilu

Huancheng Xilu

Kunshi Lu

Dongfeng Lu

Cuihu Nanlu

Zhonghe Xiang

Nanlu

Agricultural
Exhibition
Hall

3

Huashan Nanlu

Xiaoximen Bus Depot

Renmin Xilu

To
Bamboo Temple
Western Hills

30

Wucheng Lu

Minquan Jie

33

Minsheng Jie

Changchun Lu

28

Daguan Jie

27

29

10

1

To Daguan Park

Daguan Lu

Huancheng Xilu

Sanheying Lu

Wuyi Lu

Xilu

Zhengyi Lu

32

23

Yunnan Provincial
Museum

Sun Approaching Park

24

25

30

4

20

21

11

Jinbi Lu

Dongsi Xiang

Sima Xiang

Houshi

Shulin Jie

West Pagoda

East Pagoda

LP

Kunming

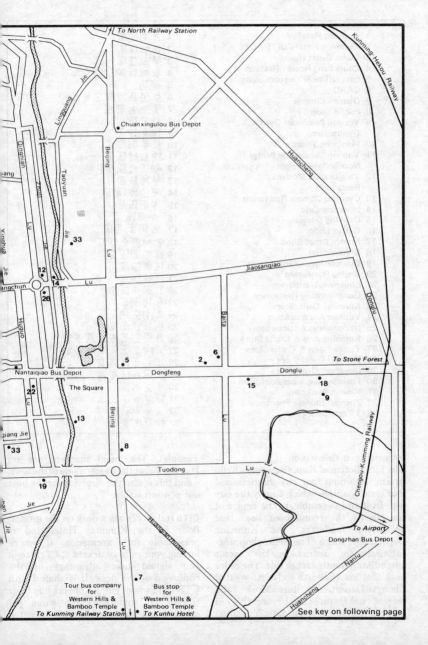

To North Railway Station

Kunming-Hakou Railway

Linguang Jie

Qingnian

Taoyuan Lu

Beijing Lu

Chuanxingulou Bus Depot

Huancheng

Xinhua Jie

• 33

Yanhua Jie

Jie

12
14
26

angchun

Huguo

Baita Lu

Jiaosangiao

Dong123

Lu

To Stone Forest

• 5

• 2  • 6

Dongfeng

Dong123

Nantaiqiao Bus Depot

22

Lu

The Square

• 13

Beijing Jie

qiang Jie

• 33

• 15

• 18

• 9

Chengou-Kunming Railway

• 8

Lu

Lu

• 19

Tuodong

Jie

han Jie

To Airport

Dongzhan Bus Depot •

Nanlu

Huancheng

• 7

Tour bus company
for
Western Hills &
Bamboo Temple
To Kunming Railway Station

Bus stop
for
Western Hills &
Bamboo Temple
To Kunhu Hotel

See key on following page

| | | |
|---|---|---|
| 1 | Yunnam Hotel | 云南饭店 |
| 2 | Kunming Hotel / CITS / CTS | 昆明饭店 |
| 3 | Cuihu Guest House | 翠湖饭店 |
| 4 | Chuncheng Hotel / Restaurant | 春城饭店 |
| 5 | Post Office & Telecom. Bldg. | 邮局 |
| 6 | CAAC | 中国民用航空总局 |
| 7 | Dianchi Cinema | 滇池电影院 |
| 8 | Public Security | 公安局 |
| 9 | Yunnan Provincial Gym. Gymnasium | 体育馆 |
| 10 | Hongxing Theatre | 红星剧院 |
| 11 | Yunnan 'Across the Bridge Noodles' Restaurant | 德胜楼饭店 |
| 12 | Yingjianglou Moslem Restaurant | 映江楼饭店 |
| 13 | Overseas Chinese Restaurant | 华侨饭店 |
| 14 | Riverside Cafe | 河边的饭店 |
| 15 | Cooking School | 学厨饭店 |
| 16 | Coffee Shop | 咖啡馆 |
| 17 | French Bread Shop | 法国面包店 |
| 18 | Olympic Bar | 奥林匹克饭店 |
| 19 | Guanshengyuan Restaurant | 蔚生园饭店 |
| 20 | Beijing Restaurant | 北京饭店 |
| 21 | Chuanwei Restaurant | 川味饭店 |
| 22 | Gongnongbing Restaurant | 工农兵饭店 |
| 23 | Kunming Dept. Store | 百货商店 |
| 24 | Yunnan Antique Store | 云南文物商店 |
| 25 | Nationalities Antique Store | 民族贸商店 |
| 26 | Kunming Arts & Crafts Store | 昆明工艺美术服务部 |
| 27 | Yunnan Arts & Crafts Store | 云南工艺美术服务部 |
| 28 | Zhengyi Dept. Store | 正义百货商店 |
| 29 | Dongfeng Dept. Store | 东风百货商店 |
| 30 | Foriegn Languages Bookstore | 外文书店 |
| 31 | Xinhua Bookstore | 新华书店 |
| 32 | Zhengyi Chinese Pharmacy | 正义中药店 |
| 33 | 3 Teahouses | 桃源街茶馆 |

## Information & Orientation

The jurisdiction of Kunming covers 6200 sq km, including four city districts and four rural counties (which supply the city with fruit and vegetables). The centre of the city is the roundabout near that prominent landmark, the Kunming Department Store. The main shopping-eating-theatre district is the sector immediately south-east of this. The older back alley maze is north and north-west of Zhengyi Department Store. Most of the recreational features are beyond this old quarter (Cuihu Park, the Zoo, Yuantong Temple). The main markets are on Daguan Jie, at the western side of the town – and this is also the direction for the best out-of-town sights.

CITS (tel 3922) has a desk on the ground floor of the Kunming Hotel and is reasonable for information. If you're buying your railway tickets at CITS then you should take advantage of the confusion at the desk. It is shared with CTS from whom Hong Kongers buy their tickets, so sometimes the wires get crossed and you may be able to get a

Chinese price ticket (however, stay away from a rather stout lady who speaks good English – what you're after is a mild-mannered clerk who speaks very little English). Rail tickets generally require about four days notice, so you should book a ticket out as soon as you arrive – there's enough in Kunming and the surrounding area to keep you busy for that long. Otherwise, if your stay may be shorter, seek out the advance railway ticket office in Kunming, or try and get a ticket at the night before departure at the station. CITS also books plane tickets and has tour buses to destinations around Kunming.

**Public Security** is at 525 Beijing Lu. It's most polite (polite refusals to irregular requests like permits to strange places, but good for visa extensions). They're closed on Fridays.

**CAAC** (tel 4270) is at 146 Dongfeng Donglu.

**Maps** The Foreign Language Bookstore at 365 Zhengyi Lu may have large English maps of Kunming. You should also try to pick up two varieties of bus maps; an older one shows longer-distance transport on a side map but doesn't show the connections to the downtown area (except in Chinese writing). The newer bus map shows the connections heading out, but the map is cut at the downtown area. Therefore you may need both maps to work out which tail-end goes where.

**Other** Poste Restante has turned up in several post offices in Kunming, so if you want someone to send you letters here, then you'd best have them addressed c/o Kunming Hotel. The Yanan Hospital is on Jiaosanqiao Lu, about a km north-east of the Kunming Hotel – there's a foreigner's clinic on the first floor of the outpatients building (tel 2184).

**Things to See**
There's very little to see in the way of

temples and such like in Kunming itself. The city is a great place to wander around on foot, once you get off the wide boulevards, and away from the Kunming Hotel end of town.

A suggested walking tour would be to go north on Huguo Lu up to the busy Changchun shopping area, turn left on Changchun and head west to the tea house marked on the map (set in a derelict temple and devoted to bong-smoking chess players). From here you select your own random route through the cobbled back alleys in the general direction of the Cuihi (Green Lake) Guest House – if you get lost, that's the whole point of the exercise. Opposite the Green Lake Guest House is the Green Lake Park; it's pleasantly decked out with foliage and waterways, has several rollerskating rinks and possibility of art exhibitions, floral displays or special shows. The walking distance so far is about two km. From the park you could head up to Yuantong Temple or cross down to Daguan Jie (south) which has an extensive free market (from the southern end of Daguan you can pick up a No 4 bus direct to Yuantong Temple).

In both the north-west sector of Kunming (in the Green Lake vicinity) and along Daguan Jie are green-shuttered, double storey shop fronts – a rarer glimpse of that elusive traditional wooden architecture that Hollywood would have us believe is all over the country. The stretch of Daguan Jie between Dongfeng Xilu and Huancheng is lined with a large range of produce coming from out-of-town farms, along with cobblers and strange merchants.

Another perambulating section to ramble through is the shopping bits south of Dongfeng (east of Zhengyi), around Jinbi Lu – plenty of back-alleys there too.

Keep an eye out for street performers – I am still puzzling over an artiste who stuck knives in his stomach and pulled skewers through his cheeks – he seemed

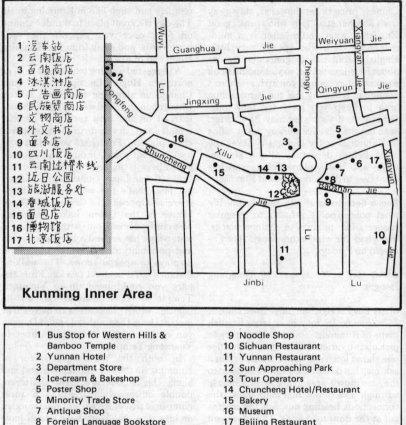

**Kunming Inner Area**

1 汽车站
2 云南饭店
3 百货商店
4 冰淇淋店
5 广告画商店
6 民族贸商店
7 文物商店
8 外文书店
9 面条店
10 四川饭店
11 云南过桥米线
12 近日公园
13 旅游服务处
14 春城饭店
15 面包店
16 博物馆
17 北京饭店

1 Bus Stop for Western Hills &
  Bamboo Temple
2 Yunnan Hotel
3 Department Store
4 Ice-cream & Bakeshop
5 Poster Shop
6 Minority Trade Store
7 Antique Shop
8 Foreign Language Bookstore
9 Noodle Shop
10 Sichuan Restaurant
11 Yunnan Restaurant
12 Sun Approaching Park
13 Tour Operators
14 Chuncheng Hotel/Restaurant
15 Bakery
16 Museum
17 Beijing Restaurant

quite well enough to pass around the hat as he plugged the wounds with a blood-soaked towel.

The relevant bus terminals and depots in Kunming for catching buses to various sites around the city and around the lake are:

**Chuanxingulou** is on the north end of Beijing Lu. Buses to the Black Dragon Pool and the Golden Temple. **Xiaoximen** is on Renmin Lu, just west of Dongfeng Lu. Buses to the Gaoyao terminal at the foot of the Western Hills. **Zhuantang** is

not really a depot, just a terminus for buses to Haigeng Beach. It's on Huancheng Xilu, near Daguan Jie. **Xizhan** the West Bus Terminal is near the Yunnan Hotel. Buses to the Bamboo Temple (these stop short of the temple at the Heilinpu terminal). **Nantaiqiao** is to the west of the Kunming Hotel. Buses to Anning Hot Springs and hosts of other destinations around Kunming, including spots to the eastern and southern sides of Lake Dian.

**Tang Dynasty Pagodas**
To the south of Jinbi Lu are a couple of crumbled Tang pagodas. The East

Pagoda was, according to Chinese sources, destroyed by an earthquake and rebuilt in the 19th century; according to western sources it was destroyed by the Moslem revolt and rebuilt in the 19th century. In any case, the temples once attached are no longer attached.

## Nationalities Institute

Chance spottings of minority groups in town for shopping sprees adds to the spice of Kunming; to the north-west of the city is the Nationalities Institute where minority leaders and trainees struggle to master Marxism and science.

## Kunming Provincial Museum

Located on Wuyi Lu, the museum houses an exhibition on the minorities, as well as a collection of artefacts from tomb excavations at Jinning on the south side of Lake Dian.

## Yuantong Temple

The Yuantong Temple is the largest Buddhist complex in Kunming, and is a target for Buddhist pilgrims. It's located to the north-west of the Green Lake Hotel. The temple is over a thousand years old, and has seen many renovations. Leading up to the main hall from the entrance is an extensive display of flowers and potted landscapes. The central courtyard has a large square pond intersected by walkways and bridges – with an octagonal pavilion at the centre. Art exhibitions and potted landscape miniatures are often to be seen at the temple.

## The Zoo

Behind Yuantong Temple is the Zoo, and as Chinese zoos go it's not too shabby. It's pleasantly leafy, high up, and gives a bird's-eye vista of the city. The zoo and the temple are not linked, and you have to go back out and around the temple to get there.

## The Ancient Mosque

Today, while Kunming's Buddhist shrines, desecrated during the Cultural Revolution, are humming with renovations for the tourist trade, the local Moslem population seems to have been left out of the action. The 400 year-old Ancient Mosque, a ramshackle building at the city centre, was turned into a factory during the Cultural Revolution. In 1977, the machinery was removed and the mosque reopened, but a dozen households remained living in its courtyard. Three other mosques have also been reopened, and the one on Jinbi Lu has had some restoration work done on it. To repair the Ancient Mosque would cost an estimated 350,000 yuan – which would have to be raised by the Moslems themselves. Ten million yuan has been allocated for renovation projects of a historical nature, but the mosque is certainly not on the priority list.

Yunnan's Moslem population seems to be largely a forgotten story – one that includes a dramatic and bloody chapter set in the last century when China was being torn end to end by rebellion. Almost the whole of China was affected by one rebellion or another in the 19th century; the best known of these in the west was the Taiping Rebellion, mainly because it affected areas which were accessible to western observers and because the Christian beliefs of the Taipings attracted western interest. But there were several other major rebellions; the Nien Rebellion which afflicted the Hunan-Hubei-Shaanxi region from 1850-1868, the Moslem Rebellion in the north-west from 1862 to 1873, and the rebellion of the Miao minority in the south coinciding with the Taiping Rebellion. In Yunnan the Moslems rose up in 1855. Their revolt was put down by the imperial armies after years of destruction; untold numbers fled or were massacred, reducing Yunnan's total population from eight million to half or even less.

The Cultural Revolution was the next major assault on the minorities; the rights of the Yunnan minorities were severely curtailed and there was a clampdown on religious activity of any nature. Kunming's Moslems came under much pressure during the Cultural Revolution to change their beliefs and fall in line with the new orders from Beijing; one story goes that a delegation of young Moslems went to Beijing to lodge a protest – they were promptly imprisoned, some for up to 10 years, and accused of being anti-revolutionary and anti-socialist. Punishments included being bound and gagged for up to two days at a time.

Once again the mosques are open, but Kunming's Moslem community is a struggling one, with little access to educational resources to spread their faith – or, in this case, hang on to it – though apparently they have their own underground press.

### Jindian (The Golden Temple)

The Golden Temple is seven km north-east of Kunming. The original model was carted off to Dali; the present one, with bronze pillars, ornate door frames, fittings and roofs, laid on a white marble foundation, dates from the Ming dynasty. It was enlarged by General Wu Sangui, who was dispatched by the Manchus in 1659 to quell the uprisings in the region. Wu Sangui bit the hand that fed him – turned against the Manchus and set himself up as a rebel war lord, with the Golden Temple as his summer residence. The temple is 6.5 metres high, and estimated to weigh more than 200 tons; the roof tiles are covered in copper; in the courtyard are ancient camellia trees. At the back is a 14-ton bronze bell, cast in 1423. To get to the temple take bus No 3 or No 23 to the Chuanxingulou terminal and then take bus No 9 to the temple.

### Heilongtan (Black Dragon Pool)

11 km north of Kunming is this uninspiring garden, with old cypresses and dull pavilions. No bubble in the springs. Within walking distance of this is the **Kunming Botanical Institute**, where the collection of flora is of specialist interest.

From the Chuanxingulou bus terminal take bus No 10. The Golden Temple and the Black Dragon Pool require separate trips from Chuanxingulou.

### Qiongzhu (Bamboo Temple)

12 km north-west of Kunming, this temple dates to the Tang dynasty. Burned down and rebuilt in the 15th century, it was restored from 1883 to 1890 when the abbot employed the master Sichuan sculptor Li Guangxiu and his apprentices to fashion 500 arhats.

These life-size clay figures are stunning – either very realistic or very surrealistic – a sculptural tour de force that will blow your mind. Down one huge wall come the incredible surfing Buddhas, some 70 odd riding the waves on a variety of mounts – blue dogs, giant crabs, shrimp, turtles, unicorns. One gentleman has metre long eyebrows; another has an arm that shoots clear across the hall to the ceiling.

In the main section are housed row upon row of standing figures – the statues have been done with the precision of a split-second photograph – a monk about to chomp into a large peach (the face contorted into almost a scream), a figure caught turning around to emphasise a discussion point, another about to clap two cymbals together or cursing a pet monster. The old, the sick, the emaciated – nothing is spared – the expressions of joy, anger, grief or boredom are extremely vivid.

So accurate are the sculptures that they can be read as an anthropological documentation of the times. The sculptor's work was considered in bad taste by his contemporaries (some of whom no doubt appeared in caricature), and upon the project's completion, Li Guangxiu disappeared into thin air. The temple actually had no bamboo in the grounds till the present, when bamboo was transplanted from Chengdu. The main halls were restored in 1958 and again, extensively, in 1981.

To get there take bus No 5 to Xizhan

and then change to bus No 7 for four stops. It's then a 90-minute hike uphill to the site. Alternatively there is an express bus from the Yunnan Hotel which goes directly to the temple.

### Anning Hot Springs

40 km south-west of Kunming, this is basically a hotel where the waters are piped into baths. Large, private bathrooms are Y5 per person, or Y3 per person if you're sharing – but no mixed couples allowed! The springs themselves are hidden from view. Anning is a bore; it's a sanatorium for privileged Chinese vacationers and there's also a military hospital here.

One km south of the springs is Caoxi Temple, a wooden structure from the Song dynasty; within the region are muddy Miao villages, but they're not overly interesting. If you miss the last bus back to Kunming you might be able to coerce the hotel staff into letting you stay (Y8 double, or Y4 per person in 4-bed dorm).

Several buses run to Anning from Nantaiqiao. The best one to take is the No 18 which departs Kunming at 8 am, 11.30 am, 2 pm and 2.30 pm. It departs Anning for Kunming at 10.30 am, 2 pm and 4.30 pm. Other possible buses (involving a bit of hiking in) are Nos 35, 16, 17 – also departing from Nantaiqiao.

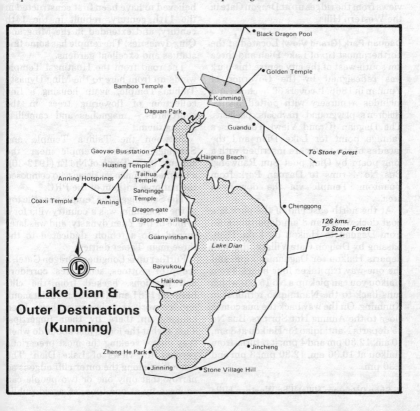

Lake Dian & Outer Destinations (Kunming)

## Lake Dian

Lake Dian, to the south of Kunming, is dotted with settlements, farming and fishing enterprises around the shores; the hilly side is the western, whilst the eastern side is flat country. The southern end of the lake, particularly the south-east, is industrial, but other than that there are lots of possibilities for extended touring and village-crashing. The lake is an elongated one, about 150 km in circumference, about 40 km from north to south, and covering of 300 sq km. Plying the waters are *fanchuan*, pirate-sized junks with bamboo-battened canvas sails. It's mainly an area for scenic touring and hiking, and there are some fabulous aerial views from the ridges up at Dragon Gate in the Western Hills.

**Daguan Park (Grand View)** Located at the northernmost tip of Lake Dian and three km south-west of the city centre this park was redesigned by the Governor of Yunnan in 1866. It covers 60 hectares and includes a nursery with potted plants, children's playground, rowboats, pavilions. The Daguan (Grand View) Tower is a vantage point for Lake Dian and the facades of the tower are inscribed with a long poem by Qing poet Sun Ranweng. Bus No 4 runs to Daguan Park from Yuantong Temple via the downtown area.

At the north-east end of the park is a boat dock where an 8 am departure goes from Daguan to Haikou on Lake Dian, passing by Dragon Gate Village; the boat departs Haikou for Daguan at 2 pm and the one-way trip takes four hours. From Haikou you can pick up a No 15 bus which runs back to the Nantaiqiao terminal in Kunming. On the way back the bus comes close to the Anning Hot Springs. Bus No 15 departs Nantaiqiao for Haikou at 8 am, 10 am, 12.30 pm and 4 pm; it returns from Haikou at 10.30 am, 12.30 pm, 3 pm and 7.30 pm.

**Xi Shan (Western Hills)** The Western Hills spread out across a long wedge of parkland on the western side of Lake Dian; they're noted for a series of temples situated along a path up to the summit. The path up is approached from the north side – and it's steep. At the top point is Dragon Gate situated along a cliffside, from where you'll get a spectacular view of the lake and surrounding countryside. The Western Hills are also known as the 'Sleeping Beauty Hills' – a reference to the undulating contours resembling a reclining woman with tresses of hair flowing into the sea.

At the foot of the climb, about 15 km from Kunming, is the Huatingsi Temple, a country villa of the Nan Zhao kingdom, believed to have been first constructed in the 11th century, rebuilt in the 14th century, and extended in the Ming and Qing dynasties. The temple has some fine statues and excellent gardens.

The road from the Huatingsi Temple winds up from here to the Ming Dynasty Taihua Temple, again housing a fine collection of flowering trees in the courtyards – magnolias and camellias among them.

Between the Taihua Temple and Sanqingge Taoist Temple near the summit, is the Tomb of Nie Er (1912-36), a talented Yunnan musician who composed the national anthem of the PRC.

The Sanqingge, the temple near the top of the mountain, was a country villa for a prince of the Yuan dynasty, and was later turned into a temple dedicated to the three main Taoist deities.

Further up is Longmen (Dragon Gate), a group of grottoes, sculptures, corridors and pavilions, hacked from the cliff between 1781 and 1835 by a Taoist monk and co-workers, who must have been hanging up there by their fingertips. That's what the locals just about do when they visit – seeking the most precarious perches for views of Lake Dian. The tunnelling along the outer cliff edge is so narrow that only one or two people can squeeze by at one time, so avoid public

Top: Up the lazy river in China's South-West [MB]
Left: Fishing in the Li River [MB]
Right: Flooding near Yangshuo [MB]

Top: Poultry market, Chengdu [MB]
Left: Path construction at Emei Shan [MB]
Right: The Stone Forest, Shilin [MB] 15

holidays! One of the last grottoes is dedicated to the deity who assisted those preparing for imperial exams – there is graffiti on the walls from grateful graduates but, nowadays, the Chinese just use it as a urinal. It's a 2½-hour hike from Gaoyao bus depot at the foot of the western Hills to Dragon Gate.

There is a regular bus combination from Kunming to the Western Hills. Take bus No 5 to the Xiaoximen bus depot, and then change to bus No 6 which will take you to the Gaoyao bus depot (terminus) at the foot of the hills. It takes about 2½ to three hours to climb from the Gaoyao terminus up to Dragon Gate. Alternatively, you could take the express bus direct to the Sanqingge temple at the top – though you could get off at, say, the Taihua Temple and do the rest on foot.

From the Dragon Gate area you can scramble directly down to the lakeside by a zigzag dirt path and steps that lead to Dragon Gate Village. There's a narrow spit of land that leads from here straight across the lake. At the western side of the 'spit' is a nice fish restaurant – simple food, wooden hut, fish from the lake – just march into the kitchen and orchestrate the tastey food. Continuing across the land spit, you arrive at a narrow stretch of water which is negotiated by a tiny ferry. It's worthwhile hanging around here to see what comes through – it's the bottleneck of the lake, and junks, fishing vessels and other craft must pass it. Having made the short ferry crossing, you proceed by foot through a village area to **Haigeng Beach**, where you can pick up a No 24 bus for the run back to Zhuantang bus terminal in Kunming. From Zhuantang you can continue touring by jumping on a No 4 bus up to Yuantong Temple and Kunming Zoo (north-east end of the city), or you can stroll along the markets on Daguan Jie to Dongfeng Lu where the No 5 bus runs back into the city centre.

**Baiyukou**, on the south-western side of Lake Dian, is a sanatorium and scenic spot.

Bus No 33 from the Nantaiqiao depot runs via Dragon Gate Village to the sanatorium, departing Nantaiqiao at 8 am, 2 pm and 4 pm and returning at 10 am, 4 pm and 7.30 pm.

**Zheng He Park** at the south-east corner of the lake commemorates the Ming Dynasty navigator Zheng He – there is a mausoleum here with tablets describing his life and works. Zheng He, a Moslem, made seven voyages to over 30 Asian and African countries in the 15th century in command of a huge imperial fleet (for details, see the section on the town of Quanzhou in Fujian Province). Bus No 21 from the Nantaiqiao depot terminates at the Phosphate Fertiliser Factory near Gucheng at the south-west side of the lake, and north-west of Zheng He Park. From here it may be possible to hike along the hills to the No 15 bus terminus at Haikou which will take you back to Nantaiqiao.

**Jinning County** at the southern end of the lake is the site of archaeological discoveries from early Kunming – bronze vessels, a gold seal and other artefacts were unearthed at Stone Village Hill and some items are displayed at the Provincial Museum in Kunming. Bus No 14 runs to Jinning from Nantaiqiao, via Chenggong and Jincheng.

**Chenggong County** is on the eastern side of the lake and is an orchard region. Climate has a lot to do with Kunming's reputation as the florist of China. Flowers bloom year round, with the 'flower tide' in January, February and March – which is the best time to visit. Camellias, azaleas, magnolias, orchids – westerners don't usually associate these flora with China, but many of the western varieties derive from the south-west of China and were first exported to the west by adventuring botanists who carted off samples in the 19th and 20th centuries. Azaleas are native to China – of the 800 varieties in the world, 650 are found in Yunnan. In the Spring Festival (February/March) a profusion of blooming species can be found in temple sites around Kunming – notably Taihua, Huating, and Golden Temples, as well as Black Dragon Pool and Yuantong Hill.

To get to Chenggong County, take bus No 12 from Kunming East Bus Station. Bus No 13 from Kunming's Nantaiqiao depot runs to Chenggong via Jincheng; departures from Nantaiqiao at 7.30 am, 8 am, 2 pm, 2.30 pm, 4.30 pm and 5 pm; the bus departs Chenggong for Nantaiqiao at 9.30 am, 10 am, 4 pm and 4.30 pm. Bus No 14 runs to Jinning from Nantaiqiao, via Chenggong and Jincheng.

**Haigeng Beach** is on the north-eastern side of the lake and has adequate swimming frontage, and a mini resort area (rollerskating, restaurants, snacks, and you can also rent airbeds there for swimming). Take bus No 24 from the Zhuantang terminal. Hiageng Beach is a useful approach to the Western Hills from the eastern side of the lake.

The tour described can easily be done in reverse; start with the No 24 bus to Haigeng Beach, walk to Dragon Gate Village, climb straight up to Dragon Gate, then make your way down through the temples to the Gaoyao bus depot where you can get the No 6 bus back to the Xiaoximen depot. Alternatively, the No 33 bus also runs along the coast through Dragon Gate Village, or you can take the early morning boat from Daguan Park.

**Places to Stay**

The *Kunming Hotel* (tel 5268 and 2240) at 123 Dongfeng Donglu, is split into two wings, a squat older building and a 15-storey newer highrise. The old wing has some excellent dormitories in old-fashioned comfort complete with writing desk, mahogany furniture and mosquito nets; the actual arrangement is five beds in two adjoining rooms, with a shared bath in between. Beds are Y9, and Y8 at the student rate – it might be possible to get a bed for Y6, but the dorms are often full. The de-luxe new wing has comfortable three-bed rooms that include a bath (the plumbing here is top-notch – you'll never see taps like this again) but still function as dorms; beds are Y10 each at the student rate. Reception will usually throw in extra people as they arrive on a male/female basis. If a mixed gender group of three travellers arrives at reception, that would be OK for one room. If a couple, on the other hand, rolled up they would be treated as an independent unit and be asked to take a double room (Y15 a bed). Four travellers can ask for a 3-bed room and then have an extra bed brought in – this will lower the overall price a little. There are higher price ranges for rooms with TVs. To get to the Kunming Hotel, take bus No 23 to the intersection of Dongfeng Lu and Beijing Lu, and then take a bus east or walk.

The *Cuihu Binguan (Green Lake Guest House)* (tel 3514) is at 16 Cuihu Nanlu. It's located at the edge of an older section of Kunming and is quiet and pleasant. It's more in the de-luxe category with closed-circuit TV, heating, air-con, and fridges in special class suites – and some of the staff wear minority dress. Double rooms are Y36 or Y24 for students. Triple rooms are Y36 (although you may be able to negotiate Y10 per bed). A bus No 2 direct from Kunming South Railway Station will get you to the Cuihu.

The *Kunhu Hotel* (tel 7732) is on Beijing Lu close to Kunming South Railway Station. It's a grubby hole, dirty sheets, one shower per corridor if you're lucky (either freezing cold or boiling hot) and the communal bathrooms are full of Chinese washing vegetables. Beds are Y4 each. The hotel is a short bus ride from the station; a bus No 3 is preferable, but No 2 or No 23 will do.

The *Xiyuan (West Garden) Hotel* (tel 9969) is a villa-style hotel. The inner section has rooms with private bath, and the outer section has rooms with a communal bathroom. The hotel is located at the western edge of Lake Dian, on the shores below Taihua Temple. It seems to serve a dual purpose – group tours on the inner section, and convalescing Chinese in the outer section. It's worth keeping the hotel in mind if you're doing an extended tour of Lake Dian, but also keep in mind the low frequency of transport back to Kunming. The outer section of the hotel is said to have cheap rates. To get to the hotel, take a bus No 33 from the Nantaiqiao bus depot in Kunming; it departs around 8 am, 2 pm and 4 pm. (The Nantaiqiao depot is to the west of the Kunming Hotel).

## Places to Eat

Kunming has some great food, especially in the snack line. Regional specialties are ginger chicken in an earthenware pot, Yunnan duck and ham, 'across-the-bridge noodles', Moslem beef and mutton dishes; and there's good western fare to be had. One of the nicest side dishes that can be ordered in the restaurants is a plate of toasted goats cheese – very tasty. For gourmets with money to burn, perhaps a whole banquet based on Jizhong fungus (mushrooms) or 30 courses of cold mutton, not to mention fried grasshoppers or elephant nose braised in soy sauce. Gourmets, or anyone else for that matter, are advised to steer clear of Kunming beer – it's disgusting. Beware of serving sizes – the *Olympic Bar* has teacup-sized versions while the *Overseas Chinese Restaurant* has huge plates – both are called 'small'. It's best to examine the models on neighbouring tables to get your choices together when dining away from the English menu. Y3 a head in the restaurants listed should get you a decent meal – should you be diverted into a foreigner cubicle, the price of course goes up.

There are two places near the Kunming Hotel which are very popular with ravenous travellers; the *Cooking School* on Dongfeng Lu has an English menu,

seafood and vegetable dishes. Across-the-bridge noodles must be ordered one day in advance, costs Y5 and comes with lots of side dishes. The *Olympic Bar* (east of the Cooking School and so named because of its proximity to the gym) serves chicken steampot, toasted goat cheese, vegetable dishes.

Near the Nantaiqiao bus depot is the *Gongnongbing (Worker-Peasant-Soldier Restaurant)* (tel 5679) at 262 Huguo Lu. It's got ratty decor but there are foreigner cubicles on the 2nd floor, and here you'll get northern Chinese food with a touch of south-western spicing. On the ground floor is a lunchtime counter where you can buy tickets and select from cauldrons immediately in front of you. You can also get whole chicken or duck.

North of this is the *Yingjianglou Moslem Restaurant*(tel 5198) at 360 Changchun Jie. This is considered the best Hui food in Kunming – mutton and beef.

To the south of Dongfeng Lu is the *Overseas Chinese Restaurant*. It's on the expensive side but you get large servings of seafood and vegetable dishes. Foreign exchange certificates are required for Coke or imported drinks.

*Guangshengyuan* (tel 2970) on Jinbi Lu has Cantonese-style food including dim sum, fried chicken, sweet and sour pork, fried beef curry. The restaurant has a special section for foreigners.

There is a string of eateries on Xiangyun Jie between Jinbi Lu and Dongfeng Lu. At the Dongfeng end at No 77 is the *Beijing Restaurant*(tel 3214) with northern style seafood, chicken and duck. The service can be annoying here and the restaurant has foreigner cubicles. At the Jinbi end of Xiangyun Jie is the *Chuanwei Restaurant*(tel 3171) which serves Sichuan-style chicken, spicy beancurd, hot pork, duck and seafood. Also located along this alley (close to Jinbi Lu) is a private restaurant operated by a wily gentleman of Burmese descent who speaks good English – don't worry about finding it, he'll find you. Mr Tong has main courses,

Budweiser beer (Y2.20), Coke (Y1.40), and rock music.

Pick of the pleb restaurants is the *Shanghai*(tel 2987) at 73 Dongfeng Xilu. It's a yellow-fronted building – to the left side you'll get cheap noodles, to the right is chicken steampot, cold cuts and dumplings.

Two of the better known places for steampot chicken are the *Chuncheng Hotel* (tel 4154) and the *Dongfeng Hotel* (tel 2905), around the corner of Wuyi and Wucheng Sts, in the direction of the *Cuihu Hotel*. Try the second floor of the Chuncheng Hotel, but service can be bad. Chicken steampot is served in dark brown Jianshui County casserole pots, and is imbued with medicinal properties – depending on the spicing – caterpillar fungus (chongcao), pseudo-ginseng (sanqi), or gastrodia.

**Across-the-bridge-noodles** is Yunnan's best-known dish. You are provided with a bowl of oily soup (stewed with chicken, duck and spare ribs), a side dish of raw pork slivers (in classier places this might be chicken or fish) and vegetables, and a bowl of rice noodles. There is a story to the dish: once upon a time there was a scholar at the South Lake in Mengzi (Southern Yunnan) who was attracted by the peace and quiet of an island there. He settled into a cottage on the island, in preparation for official examinations. His wife, meanwhile, had to cross a long wooden bridge over the lake to bring the bookworm his meals – the fodder was always cold in winter by the time she got to the study bower. Oversleeping one day, she made a curious discovery – she'd stewed a fat chicken and was puzzled to find the soup still hot, though it gave off no steam – the oil layer on the surface had preserved the food temperature. Subsequent experiments enabled her to triumphantly carry food to her husband – with hot results.

You can get hold of the same downtown for less than Y2 where there are two restaurants which serve nothing but the noodles; language is therefore no problem, and all you have to do is get your meal tickets and let the company at the table give you all the necessary instructions for etiquette. The *Guoqiao Mixian (Yunnan Restaurant)* on Nantong Jie asks Y1.20 for a huge helping. Decor is, shall we say, basic – the most predominant noise is a chorus of hissing and slurping; tattered beggars circulate among the stainless-steel-topped tables pursued by management. Never mind the beggars or the decor – the food is absolutely delicious! Atmosphere, as can be imagined, is very different from the Kunming or Cuihu Hotels, where this fare will cost you a good deal more. A second Across-the-Bridge-Noodles establishment is a cheap as the Yunnan but has less space to play around with (try the 2nd floor) – it's at 99 Baoshan Jie.

**Continental Breakfast** Filtered through the cultures of France, Vietnam and Yunnan is this unlikely combination of French bread and Yunnan coffee. The two places selling them are less than a block away from each other on Jinbi Lu. At No 299 is the *Nam Lai Thinh Bread Shop* where a mini French loaf will cost you Y0.08 (the outlet sells another item approaching a Danish loaf). Having loaded up there, you can seek out the wooden benches of the *Coffee Shop* at No 289 where coffee costs Y0.20 a mug (stirred with chopsticks!) and it's excellent quality. Coffee shops are a rarity in China – just as mysterious is where those beans come from, since Yunnan coffee beans are not found in the department stores or shops. For those in search of a western breakfast, this is China's cheapest – 40 fen or so. The bread shop is open 7.30 am to 7.30 pm, and is also worth raiding for train supplies.

**Snack tracking** There are some good bakeries in Kunming – flatbreads, shortbreads and highly edible cakes make a change from those biscuits that are sold on store shelves. For on-the-premises baking go to the Hsing Ho Yoan, near the Provincial Museum on Dongfeng Xilu. Just north of the Kunming Department Store on Zhengyi Lu is a bakery and icecream parlour. A similar but larger concept (nicknamed 'The Neon') is on Dongfeng Xilu near Kunming Bookstore – it's the in place for Kunming nights – and stocks cakes, icecream, fruit sundaes (may be canned) and other gooey desserts.

Some other areas to go snack-hunting are Huguo Lu, north of Nantaiqiao, for simmering noodle bars and a tea shop. The intersection of Changchun and Huguo yields lots of small eateries. Along the canal near the Arts & Crafts Shop is a pleasant riverside cafe with beach umbrellas – for a split second it looks like you got lost and landed up in the wrong country. Also try Baoshan Jie, an east-west street running between Zhengyi Lu and Huguo Lu – Baoshan is known as Number One Food Street because of the retail shops, but it also has noodle bars and eateries. The whole area around here is a hub of restaurant activity. The stretch of Daguan Jie from Dongfeng to Huancheng, is a busy free market, and in season you'll get fruit – mangoes, pineapples, 'ox-belly' fruit from Xishuangbanna, and pears from the Chenggong orchards or from Dali.

**Hotel Food** The *Kunming Hotel* has a restaurant on the ground floor of the old wing which is patronised by Overseas Chinese, so prices will probably be a bit lower. There are other restaurants scattered around on various floors; a student-priced breakfast is Y2 (but their coffee is the pits); across-the-bridge-noodles in the Yunnan-style restaurant is expensive and must be pre-ordered – forget it. On the top floor is a bar, open until late in the evening. At the *Green Lake Guesthouse* there is a bar and cafe on the 3rd floor, a western restaurant on the 5th floor and a Chinese restaurant on the 2nd floor – the food in these has a good reputation.

**Night life & Entertainment** You might be able to chase up minority dancing displays (more often held for the benefit of group tours), passing troupes or Yunnan opera (Hongxing Theatre on Dongfeng Xilu is one of the performing arts venues). The teahouse to the right-hand side of the canal (off Taiyuan Jie), north of Changchun Jie, has plain-clothes Yunnan opera in an old temple structure with fluorescent tubes. It is, however, extremely difficult to locate as the building is not apparent from the front – there's a side entrance.

Other than that it's mostly going to be cinemas. At the Kunming Hotel there's a full-sized theatre and in 1983 one of the showings was a Hong Kong-made feature (*not* a documentary!) on Yunnan minorities – and a happy, smiling, spanking clean bunch they were too – though included in the feature were some more realistic shots of the Third Moon Street market in Dali.

Otherwise drink yourself into a stupor at the penthouse bar of the Kunming Hotel – it's open 1 to 4 pm and 8 to 12 pm – nice views. And recover the next day at the Yunnan Provincial Gymnasium, on Dongfeng Donglu (east of Kunming Hotel), which is open to foreigners and has a tennis court, swimming pool, and volleyball courts.

A stroll around the neighbourhood at night gives a few insights into leisure, Chinese-style – table tennis with brick nets, badminton, TV tubes piercing the night, a little night marketing, chess or cards.

**Shopping**

You have to do a fair bit of digging to come up with inspiring purchases in Kunming. Yunnan specialties are jade (related to Burmese), marble (from the Dali area), batik, minority embroidery (also musical instruments, dress accessories), and spotted brass utensils.

The main shopping drags are Zhengyi Lu which has the Zhengyi Department Store, Overseas Chinese Department

Store and Kunming Department Store, but these mainly sell consumer goods. The Friendship Store is on the top floor of the Kunming Department Store. Other shopping areas are Jinbi Lu around from the Zhengyi Lu intersection, and Dongfeng Donglu, between Zhengyi Lu and Huguo Lu. Along that stretch of Dongfeng Donglu is the Yunnan Antique Store, the Nationalities Trade Store and a poster shop.

The Nationalities Trade Store is mainly intended for the minorities themselves – it's where they pick up their spare parts (beads, cotton and so on) – but it might be worth hanging around to see who rolls up. The Kunming Arts and Crafts Shop, on Qingnian Lu, has some batik, pottery, porcelain, handicrafts – but it's pretty dull. The counters at the Kunming Hotel, and particularly the Cuihu Hotel, look more interesting. Also worthy of your attention is the large range of minority goods on sale at the Green Lake Hotel. Both the Green Lake and the Cuihu Hotels sell batik – something not found elsewhere in China. Delve into the smaller shops around Jinbi Lu if you're into embroidery. Yunnan is also known for its medicines, and there's a large pharmacy on Zhengyi Lu (on the east side, several blocks up from the Kunming Department Store).

Kunming is a fairly good place to stock up on film; Fuji and other film can be bought at the Green Lake Hotel, and the Kunming Hotel has film stocks including Ektachrome.

### Getting Around

Most of the major sights are within a 15 km radius of Kunming. Local transport to these places is awkward, crowded and time-consuming; it tends to be an out-and-back job, with few cross-overs for combined touring. If you wish to take in everything, you'd be looking at something like five return trips, which would consume about three days. You can simplify this by pushing Black Dragon Pool, Anning hot springs and the Golden Temple to the background, and concentrating on the trips of high interest – the Bamboo Temple and the Western Hills – both of which have decent transport connections with special express buses in the mornings. Lake Dianchi presents some engrossing circular tour possibilities on its own.

**Tour buses** There are several outfits that cover the ground faster, but certainly not cheaper. They also include downright boring sights like Black Dragon Pool, and downtown sights like Yuantong Temple (which is not difficult to get to).

The Kunming Bus Service Company at Sun-Approaching Tower (booths opposite main Department Store) caters mainly to locals and Overseas Chinese, and they speak little if any English. They organise a Golden Temple-Black Dragon Pool-Bamboo Temple-Daguan Park tour, leaving Monday, Wednesday or Friday, departing at 8.30 am and returning at 5 pm; the cost is Y5 per person. They also do a Western Hills-Anning hot springs tour (stops at Huating, Taihua Temples and Dragon Gate), leaving Tuesday, Thursday or Saturday; the cost is Y5 per person.

The Yunnan Tourist Bus Co with departures and bookings from the Kunming Hotel, offers a Western Hills-Bamboo Temple-Daguan Park-Yuantong Temple tour for Y5 per person (that's for a group of 10 to 15 people – the price is reduced to Y3 for more than 20 people). Tours depart at 8 am, returning 5 pm. They also have a three-day schedule where they'll throw in the works, as well as the Stone Forest and the airport or train station of your choice for a mere Y35 a person (10 to 15 people, reduced to Y25 for over 20 people). The Kunming Hotel also has taxi-trips to the Stone Forest – inquire at the counter on the ground floor.

The Xiyuan Hotel, at the western shores of Lake Dianchi, has boat touring vessels which can most likely crash. Some tours are operated out of the Kunhu Hotel, such as buses to the Stone Forest (you should at least be able to get tickets for the buses there).

**Express buses** are the best option; they cost only a fraction more than local transport and will save considerable mucking around. There are two routes – to the Bamboo Temple and to the Western Hills. The starting point is the south end of Beijing Lu, where there are specially posted bus stops near Dianchi Cinema (the tour company that operates the buses has an office across the street from the bus stop). No advance booking necessary. The buses make a few stops along the route – the first one is to the left of the Yunnan Hotel in the downtown core, where there are two more special bus stops and the bus will wait here till it fills up before proceeding, so there is little point in trying to board the bus any further down the line than this hotel. Returning buses may not go back to the Dianchi Cinema – they could stop at the Yunnan Hotel, turn around with a fresh load of passengers and head back out again.

Buses from the Dianchi Cinema via the Yunnan Hotel to the Bamboo Temple depart at 8 am, 8.30 am, 9 am. More buses leave from the Yunnan Hotel only at 11 am, 12 noon, 1 pm and 2 pm. Return buses usually go to the Yunnan Hotel only, leaving the Bamboo Temple from 10.30 am to 3 pm at one or half-hour intervals. The one-way fare is 40 fen.

Buses from the Dianchi Cinema, via the Yunnan Hotel, to the Dragon Gate (with stops at the temples going up the mountainside if you want to get off before the top) depart at 7.30 am, 8 am, and 8.30 am (with possible extra departures at 9 am and 9.30 am, probably from the Yunnan Hotel). The bus leaves the Dragon Gate from 2 pm to 4 pm at hourly or half-hourly intervals. The fare is 60 fen.

**Local Transport** There is a bicycle rental

place near the Kunhu Hotel, most likely attached to the hotel. But they refuse to rent to foreigners, maintaining that it's too dangerous. Details of suburban buses are given with the sights and sites in the 'Things to See' section.

### Getting Away
**Train** There are only two rail approaches to Kunming, via Guiyang or Chengdu (a new line is under construction from Nanning to Kunming). There are direct trains from Kunming to Shanghai, via Guiyang, Guilin, Zhuzhou, Nanchang and Hangzhou. There are direct trains from Kunming to Beijing. For Chongqing you must change at Guiyang, and for Canton you must change at Hengyang.

Listed below are some sample times and fares *(Chinese prices)* for hard-sleeper train travel from Kunming:

– Guiyang, 15 hours, Y20
– Anshun, 13 hours, Y19.80
– Emei town, 21 hours, Y28
– Chengdu, 25 hours, Y31

**Plane** Kunming is connected by air to Baoshan (Y51), Beijing (Y362), Canton (Y163), Changsha (Y150), Chengdu (Y84), Chongqing (Y86), Guilin (Y109), Guiyang (Y52), Nanchang (Y192), Nanning (Y88), Shanghai (Y284), Simao (Y42), Xian (Y149), Zhaotong (Y38). There are also international flights to Hong Kong and to Rangoon; see the 'Getting Away' sections in the introductory part of this book for details.

### THE STONE FOREST
The Stone forest (Shilin) is a collection of grey, limestone pillars, split by rain water and eroded to their present fanciful forms, the tallest model standing 30 metres. Marine fossils found in the area suggest that it was once under the sea. Legend has it that the immortals smashed a mountain into a labyrinth for lovers seeking some privacy – and picnicking Chinese couples

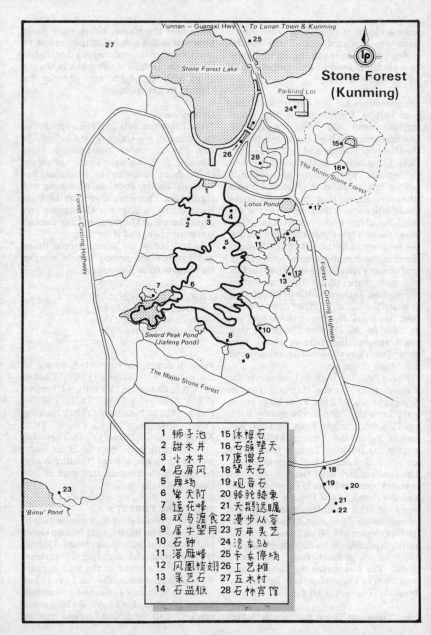

**Stone Forest (Kunming)**

Yunnan – Guangxi Hwy  To Lunan Town & Kunming

Stone Forest Lake

Parkling Lot

The Minor Stone Forest

Forest – Circling Highway

Lotus Pond

Forest – Circling Highway

Sword Peak Pond (Jiafeng Pond)

The Major Stone Forest

'Bimu' Pond

| | |
|---|---|
| 1 狮子池 | 15 沐梳石 |
| 2 甜水井 | 16 石簇擎天 |
| 3 小水牛 | 17 石唐僧石 |
| 4 启屏风 | 18 望夫石 |
| 5 舞场 | 19 观音石 |
| 6 笔天阿 | 20 骆驼骑象 |
| 7 莲花峰 | 21 天鹅远眺 |
| 8 双鸟渡食 | 22 漫步从容 |
| 9 犀牛望月 | 23 万年灵芝 |
| 10 石钟 | 24 汽车停场 |
| 11 落雁峰 | 25 卡车停场 |
| 12 凤凰梳翅 | 26 工艺摊 |
| 13 灵芝石 | 27 五木村 |
| 14 石监狱 | 28 石林宾馆 |

take heed of this myth (it can get busy in there!).

The maze of grey pinnacles and peaks, with the odd pool, is treated as a gargantuan rockery garden, with a walkway here, a pavilion there, some railings along paths, and, if you look more closely, some mind-bending weeds. The larger formations have titles like Baby Elephant, The Everlasting Fungus, Baby Buffalo, Moon-Gazing Rhino, Sword Pond. The maze is cooler and quieter by moonlight, which is the kind of viewing that a surrealist painter would be enthralled by. There are actually several stone forests in the region – the section open to foreign tourists covers 80 hectares. 12 km to the north-east is a larger (300 hectare) rock series called Lingzhi (Fungi Forest) with karst caves and a large waterfall.

The Stone Forest is basically a Chinese tour attraction and it's overrated on the scale of geographical wonders. There are, however, some good reasons for a trip out to the Forest. Lunan County is the home of the Sani branch of the Yi tribespeople. Their craftwork (embroidery, purses, footwear) is sold at stalls by the entrance to the forest and comely Sani maidens act

as tour guides for groups. Off to the side is Five-Tree Village, which is an easy walk, has the flavour of a Mexican pueblo, but the denizens have been somewhat commercialised. For those keen on genuine village and farming life, well, the Stone Forest is a big place – and you can easily get lost. Just take your butterfly net and a box-lunch along and just keep walking – you'll get somewhere eventually.

### Places to Stay

The *Shilin Hotel* is a villa-type place with souvenir shop and dining hall. Double rooms cost Y25, or Y9 per person at the student rate. There are large dorms to the rear; Y6 for a bed in a 6-bed room, and Y4 in an 8-bed room (building No 6). There are no showers, but you can use the public ones in building No 5, or nip into a vacant suite. There's another hotel, a yellow building, ostensibly Chinese only which goes for Y2 per bed, no trimmings, no nothing – just a bed. It's further back from the Stone Forest near the Lake.

### Places to Eat

The *Shilin Hotel* has a western breakfast for Y2, but their other fare (lunch Y4) is under par. Try the outdoor tables just

| | |
|---|---|
| 1 Lion Pond | 16 Rock Arrowhead Pointing |
| 2 Sweet Water Well | to the Sky |
| 3 Stone Buffalo | 17 The Figure of |
| 4 Stone Screen | Monk Tangseng |
| 5 Open Stage | 18 Wife Waiting for Husband |
| 6 Steps to the Sky | 19 Goddess of Mercy |
| 7 Lotus Peak | 20 A Camel Riding |
| 8 Two Birds Feeding | on an Elephant |
| Each Other | 21 Swan Gazing Afar |
| 9 Rhinoceros Looking | 22 Old Man Taking a Stroll |
| at the Moon | 23 Stone Mushroom |
| 10 Stone Bell | 24 Bus Departures |
| 11 Resting Peak for Wild Geese | 25 Truck Stop |
| 12 Phoenix Combing its Wings | 26 Local Handicraft Stalls |
| 13 Stone Mushroom | 27 Five – Tree Village |
| 14 Stone Prison | 28 Shilin Guest House / CITS |
| 15 Inscription of Mao Zedong's Poem | |
| 'Ode to the Plum Blossom' | |

inside the entrance to the Forest – they're open 11 am to 4.30 pm.

## Things to Do
The Shilin Hotel puts on a Sani song-and-dance evening – usually when there are enough tourists around. Surprisingly, these events turn into good-natured exchanges between Homo Ektachromo and Sani Dollari, and neither comes off the worse for wear. Performances are short-lived – costumery, ethnic musical instruments – cost is Y1 a ticket (you must present a Shilin Hotel card to get one, and performances start around 8.30 pm with tickets on sale from 7 pm). The Torch Festival (wrestling, bull fighting, singing and dancing) takes place on 24 June at a natural outdoor amphitheatre by Hidden Lake.

## Getting There
There are a variety of tour options for getting to the Stone Forest. In all cases the trip takes around 3½ hours one way. If you know exactly how long you intend to stay, book return transport in advance in Kunming. It's best to take an overnight stop in the Forest for further exploration – though if you're just looking at the Forest itself then a day trip will do. Departures leave Kunming between 7 am and 8 am; options are same-day return, next-day return, or one-way tickets.

Regular long-distance bus, Y3.50 one way; in theory this bus leaves Kunming West Bus Station (Xizhan) at 7.30 am and 1.30 pm, and passes by the stop outside the Kunming Hotel. In practice some travellers have been left high and dry at the bus stop near the Kunming, so double check arrangements. Y7 return is also possible. There appear to be tickets at Kunming South Station for the bus, and there might be buses leaving from other points than the West Bus Station.

Opposite the Department Store at the centre of Kunming there are two booths selling tickets for buses to the Forest, but these are mainly for Chinese and are difficult to book. Y7 return for bus (leaves 7 am, returns 3 pm), or Y10 for minibus. Getting picked up outside the Kunming could be a problem, so sort out the situation when you buy a ticket.

Other agents operate out of hotels such as the Kunhu and the Kunming. The Kunming Hotel has a minibus at Y5 for a one-way ticket, or Y10 return; tickets can be purchased from the taxi rank inside the front gate. The minibus leaves at 8 am and returns at either 3.30 pm or 5 pm.

CITS and CTS, operating out of the Kunming Hotel, have a three-day trip to the Western Hills, Bamboo Temple, etc, and Stone Forest for Y35 per person, reducible for larger groups. From the Stone Forest there are local buses leaving at 7 am and 3 pm from the bus parking lot, and another departure at 1 pm from Shilin Hotel. These may be pre-booked, but empty seats can be found due to passengers overnighting. You could also try hitching back to Kunming from the Stone Forest.

One other possibility for the trip out to the Stone Forest and/or back is the old French narrow gauge line which runs from Kunming North Railway Station to Kaiyuan, 248 km away. One of the stops is Yiliang, 70 km from Kunming. Yiliang lies on the road from Kunming to the Stone Forest. Timetables are likely to change, but to give you some idea, the fastest trains on this line are Nos 311 and 312. No 311 departs Kunming North Station at 10.10 pm, and arrives in Yilian at 12.23 am and Kaiyuan at 6.25 am. For the return trip, No 312 departs Kaiyuan at 10.30 pm, arrives at Yilian at 4.10 am and Kunming North at 7.05 am – not a terribly convenient schedule. However, if you're hitching back from the Stone Forest, you could check into Yilian Station and enquire about slow train 502, due about 3 pm (the other way, 501 departs Kunming North Station at 8.35 am – there appears to be a special booking office for the train). This line originally made the trip to Hanoi – there's only one class on the 300-trains, and there'll most likely be wooden seats and old fittings on the 500-series.

## LUNAN

Lunan County covers a vast area but the only place open to foreigners is the Stone Forest (the Stone Forest can be visited without a permit). The county seat of Lunan town is closed, but try and make your way there on a Wednesday or Saturday which is market-day. To get to Lunan from the Stone Forest, head back towards Kunming, take the first major crossroads left, and the second crossroads straight on but veering to the right. It's about 10 km; you'll have to hitch a truck or commandeer a 3-wheeler somehow. Plenty of trucks head that way on market day – some from the truck stop near the Forest. Market day is a colossal jam of donkeys, horse carts and bicycles in Lunan, streets are jammed with produce, poultry and wares, and Sani women are dressed in their finest. Public Security will shoo you away if discovered, but they have to find you first.

## DALI

Dali is a town in the north-western sector of Yunnan; it lies at the western edge of Erhan Lake, with an imposing mountain range behind it. The main nationality of the region is the Bai who number about 1.1 million in Yunnan. Probably the time to be here is April during the Third Moon Street Fair, when people come from all over Yunnan for trading and festivities. At other times of the year there's also a Dragon Boat Festival and a Torch Festival.

Dali has a long history. In 126 BC a Han ambassador to Afghanistan was amazed to see bamboo wares and bolts of cloth from Sichuan; the traders were ahead of him and had found a corridor through to India and Burma from Sichuan and Yunnan. Dali lies just off the Burma road and was a centre of the Bai Nanzhao kingdom, and after that the kingdom of Dali which held sway in south-western China up until the 13th century when it was overrun by the Mongols and then by the Chinese. It has long been famous for it's marble, which has been used in temples and palaces around China, although today it's a town of little significance.

There are buses from Kunming to Dali, but palefaces are soon spotted and turned back.

## LIJIANG

North of Dali is Lijiang with its spectacular mountain backdrops (well, in the pictures anyway) – Yulangxue Shan hovers at 5596 metres. Lijiang is the base of the Naxi minority who number about 245,000 in Yunnan and Sichuan; theirs is a matriarchal society where property and children belong to the female. Some of their older customs may have survived in one version or another; thirty years ago it was the custom for a young man to knock at the door of a young woman – if the woman cared to open it then he was the bed partner for the night. There was no limit to the number of door knockings and no marriage as such. To finish off the relationship was a simple matter of slamming the door in the face of the guest!

## XISHUANGBANNA

Located in the deep south of Yunnan Province, next to the Laotian border, is the region of Xishuangbanna. The great attraction of this area are the minority Dai people. They're concentrated in this pocket of Yunnan and number about 840,000 – the rest of them are sprinkled through Thailand, Laos, Burma and Vietnam. The Dais are Buddhists, driven southwards by the Mongol invasion of the 13th century; the Dai state of Xishuangbanna was annexed by the Mongols and then by the Chinese and a Chinese governor was installed in the regional capital of Jinglan (present day Jinghong). Countless Buddhist temples were built in the early days of the Dai state and now lie in the jungles in ruins. During the Cultural Revolution Xishuangbanna's temples were desecrated and destroyed. Some were saved by being used as granaries, but many are now being rebuilt from scratch (although there'll probably be some problem finding the Buddhist monks to staff them). To keep themselves off the damp earth in this tropical rain forest weather the Dais live in wooden houses raised on stilts – the pigs and chickens below. The common dress is sarongs and straw hats and the women have upswept hairstyles.

The region is now being used as a holiday resort. The one time you won't be able to get down here is in April – this is the water-splashing festival time, held on the 13th and 15th of the fourth moon. The festival washes away the dirt, sorrow and demons of the old year and brings in the happiness of the new; it also brings in loads of loaded tourists, so all the planes are booked out . . . as for the Chinese, well, they've got their own myths about the sexual prowess of the minorities, much like white Americans do about blacks – so its debatable whether the holidaying cadres are just down there for some exotic bird-watching.

Jinghong is the tropical tree-lined administrative town of Xishuangbanna. There are things like the Tropical Plant Research Institute, but the main attractions are the Dai villages near Jinghong. Some of these are apparently easy to walk to. If you're lucky there might also be a night-time performance of the Dance of the Peacock, a Dai traditional dance which is sometimes staged for visiting dignitaries at the local theatre. For a while back in 1982 a few travellers managed to get on board the local boats for the ride down the Mekong River from Jinghong to the town of Gan En Bang, staying overnight and returning the next day – but it now looks like tropical PSB models are planted

about every metre of the river to stop people doing this. The hotel in Jinghong is said to be pleasant; prices vary from Y4 per person in an outhouse, to Y12 per person for a carpeted room in the hotel building.

**Permits** To cut a long story short, don't count on getting there – I didn't even make it onto the plane. The place is semi-open; Hong Kong Chinese and group tours can go there any time they like, but individuals got the boot sometime in 1982 or 1983. If you're at the Kunming PSB at the right time of the year you might score a permit and you may even get one in some other part of the country (which does not mean you'll be able to buy a plane ticket when you get to Kunming though). If you do make it down there, at the hotel in Jinghong the hotel staff take your permit to public security and the maximum duration of stay is established; it may be extendable. Travel is restricted to a 20 km radius from Jinghong. Of course, this situation could change at any time.

If it's the minority peoples that attract, you can see groupings of the Dais in upper Burma in the Shan states fringing Mandalay, and in the hills of Thailand – it may be more worth your while going there than hassling around in China.

### Getting There

If you do get a permit there are flights from Kunming to the town of Simao; the fare is Y42 and the planes are scheduled to leave almost daily, though that varies with the tourist volume. Simao has three hotels and prices vary from Y1 per person for the spartan, to Y6 per person for rooms with private bath. You have to stay the night in Simao. Buses to Jinghong leave early in the morning and cost around Y4.50, and the trip takes seven hours; they pass through a roadblock where permits are checked.

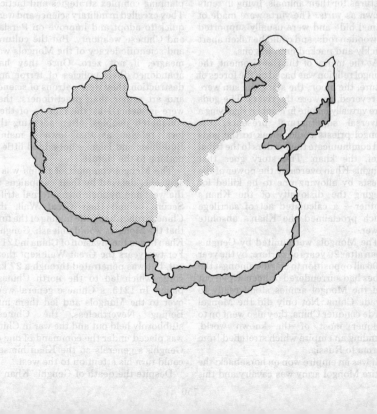

# The
# North
# &
# North – West

# Inner Mongolia

The nomadic tribes to the north of China had always been a problem to China's rulers. The first emperor of the Qin dynasty, Qin Shihuang had the Great Wall built simply to keep them out.

The Mongol homeland was along the banks of the Onon River, a tributary of the Amur, which today forms part of the border between China and the Soviet Union. They inhabited grassland which lay beyond the Great Wall and the Gobi desert and here they endured a rough life as sheep-herders and horse-breeders. They moved with the seasons in search of pastures for their animals, living in tents known as *yurts*. The yurts were made of animal hide and were usually supported by wooden rods, and could be taken apart quickly and packed onto wagons.

At the mercy of their enviroment, the Mongol religion was based on the forces of nature; the moon, the stars, the sun were all revered, as were the rivers. The gods were virtually infinite in number, signifying a universal supernatural presence; the Mongol priests could speak to the gods and communicate their orders to the tribal chief, the khan. The story goes that Genghis Khan overcame the power of the priests by allowing one to be killed for alleging the disloyalty of the Khan's brother – a calculated act of sacrilege which proclaimed the Khan's absolute power.

The Mongols were united by Genghis Khan after 20 years of warfare; by the year 1206 all opposition to his rule amongst the tribes had surrendered or been wiped out and the Mongol armies stood ready to invade China. Not only did the Mongol horde conquer China, they also went on to conquer most of the known world, founding an empire which stretched from Burma to Russia.

It was an empire won on horseback; the entire Mongol army was cavalry and this allowed rapid movement and deployment of the armies. Though the word 'horde' implies a disordered mob, the Mongols were highly organised and expert at planning complex strategies and tactics. They excelled in military science and were quick to adopt and improve on Persian and Chinese weaponry. But the cultural and scientific legacy of the Mongols was meagre, if not zero. Once they had abandoned their policies of terror and destruction, they were patrons of science and art rather than practitioners; they were influenced by the culture of their conquered peoples, often adopting the local religion as their own – mainly Buddhism and Islam – but added little if nothing to the culture.

The Mongol conquest of China was a slow one, delayed by their campaigns in the west and by their own internal strife. Secure behind their Great Wall, the Chinese rulers had little inkling of the fury that the Mongols would unleash. Genghis Khan began the invasion of China in 1211. For two years the Great Wall kept them out, but was penetrated through a 27 km gorge which led to the north Chinese plains. In 1215, a Chinese general went over to the Mongols and led them into Beijing. Nevertheless, the Chinese stubbornly held out and the war in China was placed under the command of one of Genghis's generals so the Khan himself could turn his attention to the west.

Despite the death of Genghis Khan in

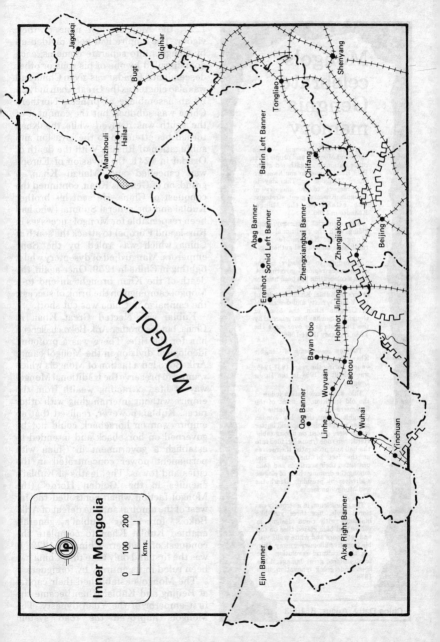

Inner Mongolia

# Mongols celebrate Genghis's memory

HUHEHOT (Xinhua) — One thousand Mongols and people from other nationalities gathered at the Ejin Horo Banner in southwestern Inner Mongolia on Thursday to pay respect to the memory of Genghis Khan, a great strategist who established the Mongol Khanate in 1206.

The memorial ceremony, coinciding with the traditional Inner Mongolian Nadam festival, resulted in an unusual gathering.

According to a leader in the autonomous regional government, such a celebration has been held for several hundred years. On the orders of Kublai Khan, founder of the Yuan Dynasty and descendant of Genghis Khan, the tomb of Genghis Khan has been guarded by the Daerhute tribe ever since the Yuan Dynasty (1271-1368).

The new mausoleum of Genghis Khan, damaged by Japanese invaders during the years 1937-1945, was rebuilt in 1954 in the Ih Ju League.

This week's celebration followed the old tradition. In front of the five-metre-high stone statue of Genghis Khan, three big wooden plates with whole sheep and butter lamps were placed on a long table. Herdsmen rode from afar, filed into the hall and prostrated themselves at the feet of the statue and presented their sacrifices and *hada* among the droning chant of elegiac addresses by presiding Daerhutes and Mongolian lamas.

The mausoleum, in a strongly national style, has three yurt-like buildings with cloud designs in yellow and blue glazed tiles on top and red doors and white walls visible from five kilometres away. During the "cultural revolution" the tomb suffered great damage; it has been undergoing renovation since 1978.

China Daily, August 8, 1983

1227, the Mongols lost none of their vigour. The empire had been divided up by Genghis into separate domains, each domain ruled by one of his sons or other descendents. Ogadai was given China and was also elected as the Great Khan in 1229 by an assemblage of princes. Northern China was subdued but the conquest of the south was delayed while the Khan turned his attention to the invasion and subjugation of Russia. With the death of Ogadai in 1241, the invasion of Europe was cancelled and Mangu Khan, a grandson of Genghis Khan, continued the conquest of China. He sent his brother Kublai and the general Subotai (who had been responsible for Mongol successes in Russia and Europe) to attack the south of China which was ruled by the Song emperors. Mangu died of dysentery whilst fighting in China in 1259. Once again, the death of the Khan brought an end to a Mongol campaign on the brink of success; the campaign in China was cut short.

Kublai was elected Great Khan in China, but his brother Arik-Boko challenged him for the title. There was a profound ideological division in the Mongol camp; Arik-Boko led a faction of Mongols which wanted to preserve the traditional Mongol way of life, extracting wealth from the empire without intermingling with other races. Kublai, however, realised that an empire won on horseback could not be governed on horseback and intended to establish a government in China with permanent power concentrated in the cities and towns. The deaths of Kublai's enemies in the 'Golden Horde' (the Mongol faction which controlled the far west of the empire) and the defeat of Arik-Boko's forces by Kublai's generals enabled Kublai Khan to complete the conquest of southern China by 1279. It was the first and only time that China has been ruled in its entirety by foreigners.

The Mongols established their capital at Beijing and Kublai Khan became the first emperor of the Yuan dynasty. The Mongols improved the road system linking China with Russia, promoted trade throughout the empire and with Europe, instituted a famine relief scheme and expanded the canal system which brought food from the countryside to the cities. It was into this China that foreigners like Marco Polo entered, and his book *Description of the World* revealed the secrets of Asia to an amazed Europe.

But the conquest of China was also the demise of the Mongols. They alienated the Chinese by staffing the government bureaucracy with Mongols, Moslems, and other foreigners. The Chinese were excluded from the government and relegated to the level of second-class citizens in their own country. Landowners and wealthy traders were favoured, taxation was high and the prosperity of the empire did little to improve the lot of the peasant. But even if the Mongols did not intermix with their Chinese subjects, they did succumb to Chinese civilisation; the warriors grew soft. Kublai died in 1294, the last Khan to rule over a united Mongol empire. He was followed by a series of weak and incompetent rulers who were unable to contain the revolts which spread all over China. In 1368, Chinese rebels converged on Beijing and the Mongols were driven out by an army led by Zhu Yuanzhang who then founded the Ming Dynasty.

The entire Mongol Empire had disintegrated by the end of the 14th century, and the Mongol homeland returned to the way of life it knew before Genghis Khan. Once again the Mongols became a collection of disorganised roaming tribes, warring amongst themselves and occasionally raiding China until the Qing dynasty finally gained control over them in the 18th century.

The eastern expansion of Russia placed the Mongols in the middle of the border struggles between the Russians and the Chinese and the Russian empire set up a 'protectorate' over the northern part of Mongolia. The rest of Mongolia was governed by the Chinese up until 1911 when the Qing fell. For eight years it remained an independent state until the Chinese returned. Then in 1924 during the Russian Civil War the Red Army pursued White Russian leaders to Urga (now Ulan Bator), where they helped create the Mongolian People's Republic by ousting the lama priesthood and the Mongol princes – the new republic has remained very much under Soviet domination.

During the war between China and Japan in the 1930s and 1940s, parts of what is now Inner Mongolia were occupied by the Japanese, and Communist guerrillas also operated there. In 1936, Mao Zedong told Edgar Snow in Yanan that 'As for Inner Mongolia, which is populated by both Chinese and Mongolians, we will struggle to drive Japan from there and help Inner Mongolia to establish an autonomous state ... when the people's revolution has been victorious in China, the Outer Mongolian republic will automatically become part of the Chinese federation, at its own will'. But that was not to be. In 1945 Stalin extracted Chiang Kai-shek's full recognition of the Outer Mongolian independence when the two signed an anti-Japanese Sino-Soviet alliance. Two years later, with the resumption of the civil war in China, the Chinese Communists designated what was left to China of the Mongol territories as the 'Autonomous Region of Inner Mongolia'. And with the Communist victory in 1949, Outer Mongolia did *not* join the People's Republic as Mao said it would and the region remained firmly under the control of the Soviet Union.

Around 1½ million people live in the Mongolian People's Republic (Outer Mongolia). Inner Mongolia stretches across half of northern China and is inhabited by almost 19 million people. Perhaps two million of these are Mongols, a predominantly Buddhist people with some Moslems amongst them. The rest of the population is made up of about 16 million Han Chinese who are concentrated in the two large cities of Baotou and Hohhot and the balance is made up of minority Huis, Manchus, Daurs and Ewenkis. That makes the Mongolians very much a minority – in their own land.

Since 1949 the Chinese have followed a policy of assimilation of the Mongols. The Chinese language became a compulsory subject in schools, the populace was organised into sheepfarming co-ops and communes and new railways and roads brought in Chinese settlers. Some of the old nomadic spirit can still be seen at the annual Nadam Fair, held at various grasslands locations sometime between mid-July and early August. The fair has its origins in the ancient Obo-worshipping Festival (an 'obo' is a pile of stones with a hollow space for offerings – a kind of shaman shrine). The Mongolian clans make a beeline for the fairs on any form of transport they can muster and create an impromptu yurt city. It's a splash of colour if you can catch up with it, with competition archery, wrestling, and horsemanship – things the Mongolians excel at, having started learning at an early age. There's also camel racing occasionally. Prizes vary from a goat to a fully-equipped horse. There are signs that the fair may be staged more often with the addition of shooting, motorcycling, storytelling, dancing and more trading. Interestingly enough the cult of Genghis Khan continues in Inner Mongolia today. In 1954 what are said to be the ashes of the Khan were brought back from Qinghai (where they had been taken to prevent them falling into the hands of the Japanese) and a large Mongolian-style mausoleum was built at Ejin Horo Qi, south of Baotou, to house them, faced by a portrait of the Khan.

Much of the Inner Mongolia region comprises vast natural grazing land. The economy is based on stockbreeding of cattle, sheep, horses and camels and the region is the main source of tanned hides, wool and dairy products for China. The Greater Hinggan range makes up about one sixth of the country's forests and is an important source of timber and paper pulp. The region is also rich in mineral reserves, particularly coal and iron ore. As it borders the Soviet Union it is of paramount military importance to the Chinese.

The Mongolians are a fragmented race. They are scattered through China's north-eastern provinces, as well as through Qinghai and Xinjiang. Their 'Inner Mongolia Autonomous Region' enjoys little or no autonomy at all; Outer Mongolia which is ostensibly an independent nation is dominated by the Soviet Union, and then there's a strange little piece of land to the north-west of Outer Mongolia called the Tuva Autonomous Soviet Socialist Republic – originally called Tannu Tuva, it emerged as a semi-autonomous Mongolian state in 1926, and was renamed in 1945. (A smattering of Chinese have also ended on the wrong side of the borders-in-triplicate; by a Beijing count there are 10,000 ethnic Chinese residing in Outer Mongolia, 6000 of them in Ulan Bator. Back in mid-1983 more than 600 were suddenly expelled by the Mongolian government and sent to China.)

Excessive fragmentation has led to a few absurdities; the Mongolian areas remain one of the biggest headaches for cartographers – it was not until 1962 that the border with Outer Mongolia was finally settled though parts of the far north-east were disputed by the Soviet Union. Then in 1969 the Chinese carved up Inner Mongolia and donated bits of it to other provinces – they were reinstated in 1979. The Chinese seem to be suffciently confident about their assimilation of the Mongols to talk about historical absurdities like 'Genghis Khan's Chinese Armies' or the 'minority assistance in building the Great Wall'.

In 1981, when an Italian film crew rented the courtyard of Beijing's Forbidden City as a Marco Polo film location (at a reported cost of US$4000 a day – the Chinese originally wanted US$10,000 a day), a splendid assembly of horses and soldiers was laid on, the soldiers portrayed by PLA troops. The Chinese claimed the money was secondary and that historical accuracy was the thing at stake. This brought some suprising attacks by the Chinese on the script. They didn't like the Mongols being depicted as hated by the Song Dynasty Chinese they overran – after all, that conflicts with the Communist claim that China's minorities get along famously with their Han majority. It's a rather odd claim since the Great Wall was built to keep the 'minorities' out (they were then referred to in a less polite way as 'barbarians'). More predictably, the Chinese vetoed some seduction scenes involving Chinese concubines and Mongol lechers.

**Climate** Inner Mongolia is bleak. Siberian blizzards and cold currents raking the plains in winter – forget it! In winter you'll even witness the curious phenomenon of snow on the desert sand dunes! Summer (June to August) thaws out with pleasant temperatures – but the region is prone to rainfall. May to September is feasible, but pack warm clothing for spring or autumn.

## HOHHOT

Hohhot became the capital of Inner Mongolia in 1952, serving as the administrative and educational centre. It was founded in the 16th century and, like the other towns, grew around its temples and lamaseries, now in ruins. Hide and wool industries are the mainstay, backed up by machine-building, sugar refinery, fertilisers, a diesel engine factory and iron and steel production. The population is around 700,000 – more than a million if the outlying areas are included. Spelling – variants for the town are Huhehaote and Huhehot.

### Information
**CITS** is located in the Hohhot Guest house

Cigarette packet with Mongolian script.

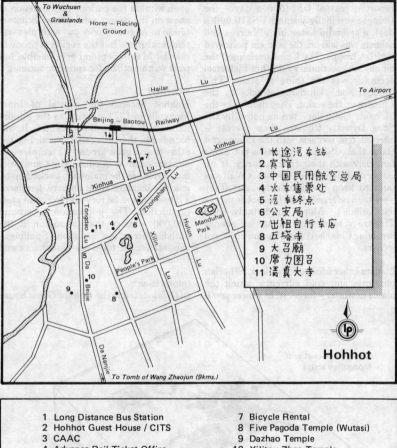

To Wuchuan & Grasslands

Horse – Racing Ground

Hailar Lu

Beijing – Baotou Railway

To Airport

Xinhua Lu

Xinhua Lu

Tongdao Lu

Zhonghan Lu

Xilin Lu

Hulun Lu

Manduhai Park

Da Beijie

Da Nanjie

People's Park

To Tomb of Wang Zhaojun (9kms.)

**Hohhot**

1 长途汽车站
2 宾馆
3 中国民用航空总局
4 火车售票处
5 汽车终点
6 公安局
7 出租自行车店
8 五塔寺
9 大召庙
10 席力图召
11 清真大寺

| 1 | Long Distance Bus Station | 7 | Bicycle Rental |
| 2 | Hohhot Guest House / CITS | 8 | Five Pagoda Temple (Wutasi) |
| 3 | CAAC | 9 | Dazhao Temple |
| 4 | Advance Rail Ticket Office | 10 | Xilitou Zhao Temple |
| 5 | Local Bus Terminus | 11 | The Great Mosque |
| 6 | Public Security | | |

(the guesthouse is built around a quadrangle, and the CITS office is in the buildings on the north side).

CITS turns the tap on culture in Hohhot – from the grasslands tour to the equestrian displays at the horse racing ground. Horse racing, polo and stunt riding is put on for large tour groups, if you latch onto one somehow – otherwise only on rare festive occasions. Likewise, song-and-dance soirees are somewhat academic in nature: you might be able to bypass this by checking out local entertainment, such as events at the Red Theatre near the CAAC office. Other items you might be able to wrangle out of CITS if combining in-town sights with a grasslands sortie are a visit to the carpet works, or to the underground tunnelling system built to evacuate Hohhot residents to the Daqing Mountains in the event of a Russian bear hug. Make all your deals before you set off for the grasslands – it's no use trying to bargain once you get going.

**Public Security** is in the vicinity of the People's Park, near the corner of Zhongshan Lu and Xilin Lu. It's no longer as liberal with visa extensions or permit additions as formerly, and fifth-hand rumours have it that the squad responsible for dishing out Tibet permits in 1982 was bundled off to Xian.

**CAAC** (tel 4103) is located diagonally opposite the People's Park at 6 Zhongshan Donglu. Hohhot airport is about 15 km east of the city.

### Things to See

Don't be in any great hurry to see the historic vestiges of the city – either in bad shape, uninteresting, or inaccessible.

### Wutazhao (Five-Pagoda Temple)

This miniaturised structure, dating back to 1740, is now bereft of its temple, leaving the Five Pagodas standing on a rectangular block. The pagodas are built with glazed bricks; there are inscriptions in Mongolian, Sanskrit and Tibetan. Cut into niches are small Buddhist figures; around the back is a screen wall with an astronomical chart inscribed in Mongolian. The Five Pagodas are on the bus No 1 route.

### The Tomb of Wang Zhaojun

The tomb of this Han Dynasty concubine to the Emperor Yuandi (1st century BC) is a bit of a bore – although it does permit some countryside viewing at the edge of town. The tomb is on the bus No 1 route.

### The old part of town

Directly north of the tomb of Wang Zhaojun are some places of greater interest. The area is the old part of the town. Down some alleys off a main street is the **Dazhao Temple** which has almost fallen apart – a cottage industry clothing concern now occupies the grounds. Not far from it is the **Xilitou Zhao Temple**, which is slated for renovations. It's the stamping ground of the 11th Grand Living Buddha (who dresses in civvies) and is apparently active. The original temple burnt down and the present was built in the 19th century; it's a Chinese-style building with a few Tibetan touches. The swastika symbols on the exterior have long been used in Persian, Indian and Greek and Jewish religions – it symbolises truth and eternity (no relation to the mirror image Nazi swastika). Further north of Xilitou Zhao is **The Great Mosque**, which is not so great and in sad shape; it dates to the Qing Dynasty, with later expansions.

These temples are incidentals: the main action is on the streets. Around the area of the Dazhao Temple are some fascinating adobe houses – low and squat with decorated glass windows – their proximity to the temple structures would explain the preservation of character in the area. Markets in Hohhot are brisk – in summer at least. Recommended is the north-south strip running from west of the bus station (Tongdao Lu) as far as the two temples. It's very busy at the corner of Tongdao Lu and Xinhua Lu, and its a place for a storyteller and the selling of housewares. A food market with a courtyard entrance can be found near the Museum of Inner Mongolia. There's another market on the east side of People's Park.

### Museum of Inner Mongolia

Definitely worth it and well presented! On the lower floor is a large mammoth skeleton dug out of a coal mine; on the upper floor is a fantastic array of Mongolian costumery, artefacts, archery equipment, saddles – and a yurt. The flying horse atop the museum is meant to symbolise the forward spirit of the Mongolian people. The museum is at 1 Xinhua Dajie.

## Places to Stay

The hotel of the day is *Hohhot Guest house* (tel 2838) on Yinbin Lu, which is a solid structure built around a courtyard. Impressive from the outside, nothing fancy inside. Double rooms are Y17, and a bed in a triple is Y6. The hotel is a 15 minute walk from the railway station; there is no direct bus, but you can take an autorickshaw for less than Y1.

The *Xincheng Hotel* (tel 5754) is on Hulunnan Lu at the north-west corner of Manduhai Park, and is a more central location. There is a new tourist hotel being built to the east of the Xincheng.

## Places to Eat

There's one restaurant in the vicinity of the Hohhot Guesthouse – it's down the street (south) and on the corner. Another larger restaurant is on Zhongshan Lu, opposite the People's Park. Neither of these is anything to write home about, and you'd do better with the set menus of the Hohhot Guest house which, at Y2.50 a head for dinner, are adequate. Outside it's better to go snack hunting. Yoghurt in ceramic flasks and some tasty baked goods can be found in the markets scattered around town; there's a dumpling shop (with a red front) next door to the Xilitou Zhao Temple.

## Shopping

Minority handicrafts – there's a store attached to the Hohhot Guesthouse, and you can case the Department Store in town. If you want to get closer to the source of the industry (wider selection), pay a visit to the Minority Handicraft Factory at the south side of town on the No 1 bus route. It has a retail shop for tour visits. Inlaid knife and chopstick sets, daggers, boots, embroidered shoes, costumes, brassware, blankets, curios.

## Getting Around

Directly across from the gates of the Hohhot Guesthouse is a bicycle rental place, renting bikes at 30 fen per hour. Hohhot is reasonably small and you can go a long way on a pair of wheels, weather permitting.

There are 15 bus lines but no bus map. You can get a brochure-type map from CITS with English/Chinese destinations, check with them or the hotel staff for bus numbers for your proposed route. Bus No 1 runs from the railway station to the old part of the city in the south-west corner.

## Getting There

**Bus** There are sporadic bus connections between Hohhot and Datong and Baotou.

**Train** Hohhot is on the Beijing-Lanzhou railway line that cuts a long loop through Inner Mongolia; about 2½ hours out of Beijing you'll pass by fragments of the Great Wall. By the fastest trains Beijing-Hohhot is a 12 hour trip, Datong-Hohhot is five hours, Baotou-Hohhot is three hours, Yinchuan-Hohhot is 12 hours. It would be possible to buy one ticket from Beijing to Lanzhou, get off and have a look at each town and continue on with the same ticket; train frequency is highest between Hohhot and Beijing, lesser between Yinchuan and Hohhot, and low between Lanzhou and Yinchuan so you could be a bit pushed for time to cover all these places on one ticket. There are low-frequency connections from Taiyuan to Datong where a connection to Hohhot can be made.

**Plane** There are flights between Hohhot and Beijing (Y55), Chifeng (Y98), Hailar (Y197), Tongliao (Y141), Ulanhot (Y143), Xilinhot (Y76). One of the Beijing-bound lanes stops off at Chifeng and Tongliao.

**AROUND HOHHOT** 15 km west of Hohhot is the Sino-Tibetan monastery, the **Wusutuzhao** – hardly worth looking at but there are some spectacular arid land-

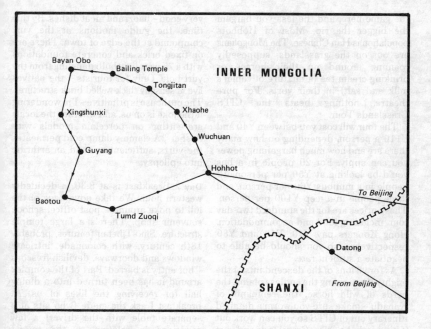

INNER MONGOLIA

Bayan Obo
Bailing Temple
Tongjitan
Xhaohe
Xingshunxi
Wuchuan
Guyang
Hohhot
Baotou
To Beijing
Tumd Zuoqi
Datong
SHANXI
From Beijing

scapes. About 20 km east of Hohhot, along the airport road, is the topless **Wanbuhuayanjing Pagoda**, a seven-storey octagonal tower built with bricks and wood dating from the Liao Dynasty (10th to 12th centuries). The pagoda can be reached by a half-hour suburban train ride.

## THE GRASSLANDS

I must confess I have not the slightest idea where these fabulous grassland communes lie, nor exactly how to get there – not that you will get much chance to do that yourself anyway. Roads turn into arbitrary dirt tracks, buses are few and crowded, and they won't sell you tickets. As for maps, try the KGB office in Moscow – they've probably got some good ones. It is probably due to the military sensitivity of the area that the Chinese don't want you wandering around by yourself.

At present there are three officially open grasslands. About 90 km north of Hohhot (over the Daqing Mountains, through Wuchuan county, veer left) is Ulantuge Commune, alias Wulantuge, or even Ulantoke. In a similar direction, but veer right, is Baiyunhesha Grassland (Baiyinhushao), which lies in Siziwang Banner and is about 180 km from Hohhot (a 'Banner' is a tribal county area). There is a third grassland, Huitengxile, about 120 km from Hohhot, which is managed by China Youth Travel Service whose office is at 9 Zhongshan Donglu, Hohhot – one traveller reports crashing a tour with them – a similar setup to CITS tours but slightly cheaper.

**Tours** Tours to the grasslands are organised by the Hohhot CITS, which has a stable of vehicles ranging from jeeps to buses to take you out there. The rules of the game – negotiate! Cashing in on the magic draw of 'Mongolia' is the name of the game here, and the less you bargain the bigger the rip. Most of Hohhots population is Han Chinese. The Mongolians are out on the grasslands, supposedly roaming around on their horses or drinking cream tea (a mixture of camel's milk and salt) in their yurts. For pure theatre, nothing beats the CITS Grasslands Tour.

The tour will cost you between Y40 and Y110 a person, depending on how many there are and how much bargaining power you can apply. For 20 people in a bus you'd be looking at Y50 per person, 12 people in a minibus Y60 per person, and three people in a jeep Y100 per person. These prices are for the standard two-day tour, including food and accommodation. Hong Kongers pay Y40, Y50 and Y80 respectively – so you should be able to negotiate a student rate.

As for visions of the descendants of the mighty Khan riding the endless plains, the herds of wild horse, the remnants of Xanadu – make sure you worm a detailed itinerary out of CITS so you can work out if it's worth the price. Grasslands and yurt dwellings can be seen in other parts of China – in Xinjiang for example. If you do go on a tour then take warm, windproof clothing – there's a considerable wind-chill factor even at the height of summer.

**Being There** Here's a two-day itinerary to give you some idea of the picnics and outings in Inner Mongolia.

**Day 1** 2.30 pm. We discover the first day is half over – it's calendar days. After a three-hour drive over the mountains to the grasslands plateau we arrive at Ulantuge commune. The major industry here seems to be shepherding tourists. It's the first commune from Hohhot, so lots of groups are processed through this meatworks. On arrival a lady pops out of a door in Mongolian costume to greet us (still, however, wearing slacks underneath and a tell-tale pair of tennis shoes). Dinner is

very good – baozi and meat dishes. By this time, the guide motions at the yurt compound at the edge of town. These are on fixed brick and concrete foundations with a 75 watt lightbulb dangling from the yurt-hole. Only for tourists – the natives live in sensibly thick-walled brick structures. The outhouse is primitive – I'm wondering if the joke is on us, and whether the locals are sitting on porcelain models with flushers. A clammy damp cold permeates the yurts, sufficient to send an arthritic into epilepsy.

**Day 2** Breakfast is at 8.30, a decidedly western hour. We take advantage of the lull to poke around – post office, school, souvenir shop. There's a large temple structure, Sino-Tibetan features, probably 18th century, with colonnade, intricate windows and doorways, devilish frescoes – but entry is barred. Part of the complex around it has been turned into a dining hall for receiving the likes of us. At breakfast I ask the guide (who sits at a separate table with the driver) a few questions in relation to the tourist industry which he either ignores, evades, or pretends not to understand. Back at the yurts are two ruddy-cheeked gentlemen waiting with two moth-eaten animals. The ruddy complexion comes from wind chill – the animals have not weathered it so well. One is, I guess you might call it, yes, a horse. The other is the worst looking excuse for a camel I've seen. I mean, camels are ugly, but this one had just about fallen apart. It's strictly a mounted picture-taking session; the attendants keep these pathetic specimens on leashes, explaining that they're too dangerous to be ridden solo.

At 9.30 am the driver whips over the grasslands – very nice, peaceful, dirt paths – reassuring to see some real grass in China. Hong Kongers get most enthralled about this – there isn't too much of the stuff around Kowloon. We stop to observe a flock of sheep – the shepherd poses for photos. Then, the highlight of the tour – a visit to a typical Mongolian family. They live in a three room brick dwelling, and there, smack on the wall as you enter, is a giant poster of a koala (New South Wales Tourist Authority) which confirms my impression that perhaps I'd be better off on an Australian sheep farm. The typical family is wearing standard Han ration clothing (did we catch them with their pants down?) but they bring out Mongolian garb for dress-up photo-sessions – for us to dress up, that is. They've obviously given up. Parked out the back is their form of transport – bicycles. It puzzled me why we had been brought here when there were yurt dwellers in the area. The only explanation I could think of was that they would be further out from the Ulantuge commune, and the driver was too lazy or had been given other directions. Or perhaps any real Mongolian wanted nothing to do with CITS – a view with which I could sympathise.

Motoring off again we visit an *obo*, a pile of stones in the middle of nowhere. When nomads used to gather for mid-May festivals, each would bring a stone and lay it here. We go back to Ulantuge for a banquet-style lunch; a sheep is slaughtered and barbecued for a surcharge. After lunch, the guide announces that it's time for *xiuxi* – the rest period will be 2½ hours. We wave goodbye to the lady near the yurt compound (as she struggles to get into her Mongolian robes in time), and head back for Hohhot. We arrive around 4.30 that afternoon – the tour is supposed to last until 6 pm and there is a filler of sights around town that I've already seen and which don't require a guide.

In sum, the guides are lethargic and unhelpful; your real time on the grasslands amounts to about two hours, plus the drive there and back. You spend a lot of time sleeping, eating, waiting and taking pictures of each other. I imagine the three and four day itineraries would be much the same, with feeble archery or song-and-dance routines thrown in. It seemed to me that the best part of the trip was, unexpectedly, the food – the meals were banquet-size and tasty, something that the individual traveller is not used to.

I suppose you could try to lose your guides; horse-drawn carts seem to be a common form of transport on the communes – and of course the grassland is perfect horse country – though that later suggestion would probably horrify CITS who'd fear that you'd fall off and break your neck. (I can't get over a Hohhot tourist-leaflet which shows a bunch of foreigners riding in a decorated camel cart with suspension and truck tyres.) Anyway the small Mongolian horse itself is even being phased out – herdsmen can now purchase motorcycles (preferred over bicycles because of substantial wind force); helicopters and light aircraft are used to round up steers and spot grazing herds.

## BAOTOU

The largest city in Inner Mongolia lies on the northernmost reaches of the Huang He (Yellow River), to the west of Hohhot. Previously set in an area of under-developed grasslands inhabited by the Mongols, the town underwent a radical change when the Communists came to power in 1949. In the next decade, an old 1923 railway line linking the town with Beijing was extended south-east to Yinchuan, and roads were constructed to facilitate access to the region's iron, coal and other mineral deposits. Today, Baotou is an industrial city of around 800,000 people.

The main tourist attraction is the large **Wudang Zhao Monastery** about two hours from the city by bus. The monastery is a Tibetan-style complex with flat-roofed buildings and is raved about by the travellers who have been there. CITS operates tours to the monastery, but there is also a local bus which will take you there.

## BAYAN OBO

About 150 to 200 km north of Baotou is Bayan Obo, an iron-ore centre. There's a railway line linking the two and though the train ride will probably be excrutiatingly slow, if you can get on board you'd get to see some of the scenery to the north – a rare opportunity to get off the track in Inner Mongolia. Bayan Obo's proximity to the Soviet border probably makes it a militarily sensitive area, so it's likely there'll be a clamp on taking photographs and even if you do get on the train they'll probably boot you off – don't say you weren't warned. It's worth noting though that one of the western tour companies (China Passage) organises bicycle tours which make the circular trip Hohhot-Bayun Obo-Baotou-Hohhot – so there may yet be hope for individual travel in the area.

## XILINHOT (ABAGNAR QI)

From all accounts, if you're interested in pursuing the topic of the disappearing Mongols, this sounds like the best bet. Xilinhot is 500 km north-east of Hohhot as the crow flies. Xilinhot is a town, the headquarters of the large Xilin Gol League, which is subdivided into 10 districts and over 100 communes. The League covers an area of 172,000 sq km, with a population of under a million – a quarter of whom are Mongolian. The Xilin Gol League was a centre of Mongolian nationalism in the 1930s but today the major occupation is the tending of sheep, cattle, goats, camels and horses – some 5 million of them. Industry is minimal, though petroleum deposits have been discovered. Ensconced in Xilinhot is the Beizimiao, a large Chinese-style lamasery, apparently dilapidated, dating from the Qing dynasty.

The only problem might be getting a permit for the place. Xilinhot was originally open to foreign tourists, but sometime in 1983 it was closed (although a few public security offices didn't get the message and one or two people got permits) – applications for permits will probably have to go through the public security office in Hohhot. If you do get a permit you'll probably be required to fly to Xilinhot from Hohhot; the fare is Y76. One Swiss couple who got out there in the middle of 1983 were allowed to take the bus back – and it seems they had a wow of a time grooving with the Mongolians on board. The frost-free period narrows at this latitude to about three months, with the best time to visit being June to August.

When the place was open, CITS had jeep excursions to communes 50 km and 130 km away, with overnight stops in yurts, tea-tasting, campfires. Should you strike a guaranteed Mongol you might get a cup of their cream tea. It's made of camel's milk and salt, and apparently tastes revolting – it's also most impolite to refuse a cup.

### Footnote

Over the Great Wall and below the Bamboo Curtain is the world's most ambitious reforestation and afforestation program – a shelter belt creeping toward its ultimate length of 6000 km. Known as 'The Green Wall', the belt is designed to protect precious farmland from the sands of the Gobi desert when the winter winds blow. It will eventually stretch from Xinjiang to Heilongjiang (China's last great timber preserve). This huge tree-planting program is only a small part of the PRC's schedule – there's a similar belt along the south-east coast to break the force of summer typhoons. It's an attempt to reverse the effects of centuries of careless tree cutting which, combined with slash-and-burn farming, has contributed to disastrous flooding and other ecological catastrophes. Tree planting is the duty of every able-bodied person in China; since the formation of communes and production brigades in 1958, forest cover has been raised from 9% to almost 13% (it should be pointed out here that in the early days of the PRC, forests were decimated *to* nine per cent). The goal by the year 2000 is for 20% cover, which would require tree planting on 70 million hectares. Planting in the northern frontier zones is done in 1 km wide strips; between 1978 and 1982, almost five million hectares were afforested with a survival rate of 55%, and a further 1.1 million hectares were added in 1983. Wasteland and barren hills are allocated to rural households for planting and farming (also done on a contract basis) and the government provides seeds, saplings and know-how.

# Ningxia

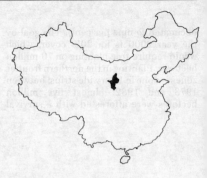

Ningxia was carved out as a separate administrative region in 1928 and remained a province until 1954. It was then absorbed into Gansu Province. In 1958 Ningxia re-emerged, this time as an 'Autonomous Region' with a large Hui population. The boundaries of the region have ebbed and flowed since then, once taking in a chunk of Inner Mongolia, now somewhat reduced. Almost four million people live in Ningxia, but only about a third are Hui, the rest are Han Chinese.

Part of the arid north-west of China, Ningxia is probably one of the poorest regions in China. It's a region of hard, cold winters and plummeting temperatures; blistering summers make irrigation an utter necessity. The network of irrigation channels that criss-cross the region have their beginnings as far back as the Han Dynasty, when the area was first settled by the Han Chinese in the 1st century BC.

The building of the Baotou-Lanzhou railway in 1958, cutting through Ningxia, helped relieve the isolation and also helped the development of some industry in this otherwise almost exclusively agricultural region.

The region opened up to tourism in 1983. The capital city of **Yinchuan** is open to individuals, along with a group of 108 Buddhist pagodas 78 km south of Yinchuan at Qingtang Gorge. The white-painted, vase-shaped brick pagodas have octagonal bases and were built in twelve rows; they were constructed during the Yuan Dynasty.

### Getting There

Yinchuan lies on the Lanzhou-Beijing railway which runs through Baotou, Hohhot and Datong. There are also flights from Baotou (Y50), Beijing (Y124), Lanzhou (Y43) and Xian (Y97) to Yinchuan.

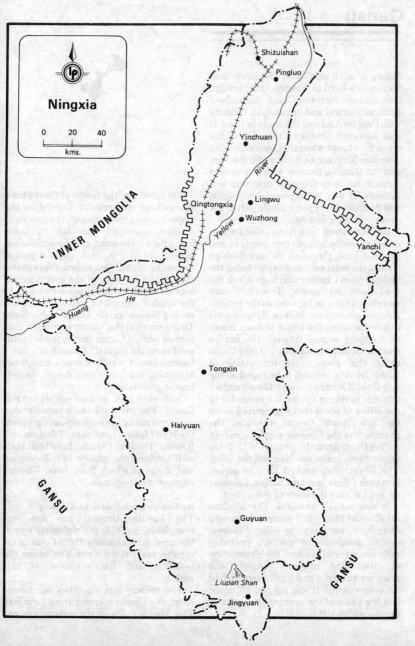

# Gansu

Gansu is a strange state. Desolate and barren, it's hard to imagine that through this narrow corridor China maintained political, cultural and commercial contacts with Central Asia and the lands beyond. It was, however, always on the edge of the empire – except when that empire spilled over into Xinjiang as it did under the Han and the Qing – a frontier with a semi-arid climate, liable to frequent droughts and famines. It was an impoverished region and its inhabitants played little part in the destiny of their country.

But the famed 'Silk Road', along which camel caravans would carry goods in and out of China, threaded its way through Gansu, the most common export being the highly prized Chinese silk, from which the road took its name. Travellers and merchants from as far away as the Roman Empire entered the Middle Kingdom via this route, using the string of oasis towns as stepping stones through the barren wastes. Buddhism was carried into China along this route, and the string of Buddhist cave temples to be found all the way from Xinjiang through Gansu and up through northern China is a reminder of the influx of ideas that was carried along the Silk Road. Gansu was also the boundary of the Chinese empire – except during those dramatic periods of Chinese imperialism under the Han and the Qing. The Great Wall snaked its way across northern China and into Gansu, finishing up not far past the town of Jiayuguan.

It was not all peaceful. The Moslem rebellion of 1862-1878 was put down with incredible savagery by the Chinese; untold numbers of people, probably millions, were killed and the destruction of cities and property brought the province to ruin – and finally established Chinese control. It was topped off in the last few years of the century by a massive famine which left its toll.

Traditionally, the towns of Gansu have always been the series of oases along the major caravan route, though the coming of modern transport has led to some industrial development and the exploitation of oil, iron ore and coal deposits. Agriculture is only possible in these oases, though the foothills of the mountainous regions which border Qinghai Province to the south do support a pastoral economy, raising horses, cattle, sheep and camels. To the north of the 'Gansu corridor' – that narrow part of Gansu that extends northwest from the capital of Lanzhou – lies a barren desert which extends into Inner Mongolia, much of it true desert, some it sparse grassland.

Just over 19½ million people inhabit Gansu. The province has a considerable variety of minority peoples; amongst them the Hui, Mongol herdsmen, Tibetans and Kazaks. The Han Chinese have built their own settlements, places like Jiayuguan and Jiuquan which have been Chinese outposts for centuries.

### By Rail through Gansu to Xinjiang

The Lanzhou-Urumqi rail line was completed in 1963. It's definitely one of the great achievements of the Communist regime, and has done much to relieve the isolation and backwardness of this region.

The railway line stretches north-west along the Gansu corridor from Lanzhou. The Marco Polos of the railway age can

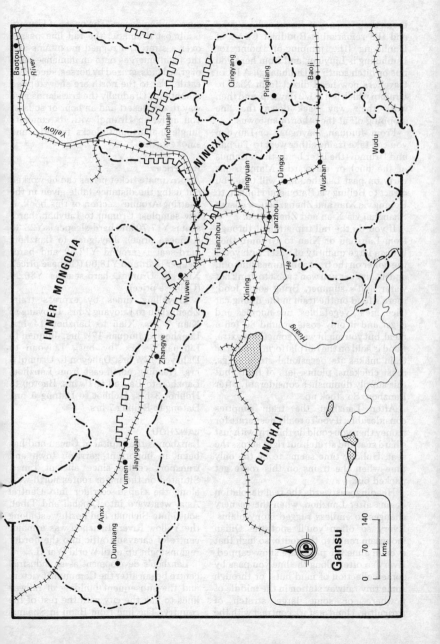

break their journey at Jiuquan, Jiayuguan and the remarkable Buddhist Caves of Dunhuang (the jumping-off point for Dunhuang is Liuyuan, and from here you bus or hitch south to Dunhuang). A lot of travellers now head direct from Xian to Urumqi which is a 2-1/2 day trip, and then work their way back down the line stopping off at the other open towns.

From Jiuquan, Jiayuguan or Liuyuan you can take trains either west to Turpan and Urumqi (the later being the terminus of the line) or eastwards. Many trains carry on past Lanzhou and will take you direct to Beijing via Batou and Hohhot, to Beijing via Xian and Zhengzhou, or east to Shanghai via Xian and Zhengzhou.

If you do the rail trip straight through from Lanzhou or Xian to Urumqi, then bring a large quantity of water with you – the boiler on the train sometimes runs out, and in any case you won't want to drink hot water if it's summer. Bring some food; there's food on the train in the dining car (rice, meat, vegetables, rice-noodles and eggs) and it only costs around 80 fen a meal, but you might want something extra. Food is sold on the rail platforms when the train makes its occasional stops (eggs, roast chickens, plums, jars of fruit), but this supply diminishes considerably after Lanzhou. So stock up.

After Lanzhou the train empties considerably; if you're really desperate for money then you could do this trip with just a hard seat and stretch out right across the seat. Holiday time seems to be the only time when the trains on this route get packed out.

Heading westwards the real desolation begins after Lanzhou, when the scenery changes to endless rugged stony plains. Every so often you'll spot the Qilian mountain range to the south; so high that even in June the peaks are snow-capped. Every so often along the line you pass by some collection of mud huts, or through some tiny railway station in the middle of nowhere, or some large stretch of agricultural land, a stark contrast with the surrounding desert. The onset of Urumqi is almost dramatic; the rail line passes over a stretch of rugged mountains and the train emerges onto an immense plain of grasslands, grazed by horses, sheep and cattle. Far to the north are snow-topped mountains. Gradually the grasslands give way to dry desert and an hour or so later you arrive in Urumqi with its concrete jungle of apartment blocks, factories and smokestacks.

### Rail Prices

Approximate ticket prices can be worked out using the distance table given in the 'Getting Around' section of this book. A few samples: Urumqi to Liuyuan, hard-seat is Y17.70 and hard-sleeper is Y28.30 (Chinese price). Jiayuguan to Lanzhou, hard-seat is around Y12.60 and hard-sleeper is around Y18.00 (Chinese price). Xian to Urumqi, hard-seat is Y36.90 (Chinese price).

Travelling times by express train: Zhengzhou to Luoyang 2 hrs, Luoyang to Xian 7 hrs, Xian to Lanzhou 14 hrs, Lanzhou to Jiuquan 17½ hrs, Jiuquan to Liuyuan 7 hrs (by bus), Liuyuan to Daheyon 13½ hrs, Daheyon to Urumqi 3 hrs. Heading north-east from Lanzhou, Lanzhou to Baotou is 17 hrs, Baotou to Hohhot 3 hrs, Hohhot to Datong 5 hrs, Datong to Beijing 7 hrs.

### LANZHOU

Lanzhou is the capital of Gansu and has been an important garrison town and transport centre since ancient times. Situated on the major routes north-west along the Gansu corridor into Central Asia, westward into Qinghai and Tibet, south into Sichuan and north-west along the Yellow River, Lanzhou was a major centre of caravan traffic into the border regions right up until World War II.

Lanzhou's development as an industrial centre began after the Communist victory and the subsequent building of railway lines to link the city with the rest of the country. The line from Baoji in Shaanxi

Top: A yurt in Inner Mongolia [MB]
Bottom: Mosque at Kashgar [AS]

Top: Jiayu fort at Jiayuguan, Gansu [AS]
Left: Mosque at Urumqi [AS]
Right: Grasslands of Inner Mongolia [MB]

was extended here in 1952, another from Baotou in 1958. Construction also began on the Lanzhou-Urumqi line, probably with the intention that it would one day join up with the Soviet Union. Another line was built linking Lanzhou with Xining. This transformed Lanzhou into a major industrial city, destined to become the principal industrial base of north-west China. 200,000 people lived in Lanzhou in 1949; by 1959 the number was 900,000 and today it stands at over two million.

## Information & Orientation
Most of Lanzhou is stretched out along the southern bank of the Yellow River. The eastern segment of town, between the railway station and the Xiguan traffic circle, is the centre of town, and in this area are most of the tourist facilities.

**CITS** (tel 49621) is in a building in a walled-in compound next to the Lanzhou Hotel –there's a gateway facing the street and a yellow CITS sign in English. Walk in past the bus garage on the right; the CITS offices are in Rms 201 and 202 of the modern building behind the garage. They're vaguely open from 8 am to 6.30 pm, probably with a couple of hours break in the middle of the day. Friendly people here but they don't speak much English.

**Public Security** is in a brown brick building next to the large red brick review platform on Dongfanghung Square. Friendly lot; once upon a time they gave permits to Lhasa, but alas no longer.

**CAAC** (tel 23432 or 23431) is at 46 Donggang Xilu, a five minute walk west of the Lanzhou Hotel. It's open 7.30 to 11.30 am and 3 to 6 pm.

**Bank** The Bank of China is at 70 Donggang Lu, just west of the Lanzhou Hotel.

**Post** There is a post office on the ground floor of the Friendship Hotel open 11.30 am to 3.00 pm and 6 to 9 pm.

**Friendship Store** is on the ground floor of the Friendship Hotel.

**Maps** Decent maps seem hard to come by; there is an excellent map of Lanzhou in Chinese showing the bus routes, but I've only seen it at the service counters of the Friendship Hotel. The commonly available map is a not very useful sketch map in one of the Chinese tourist leaflets on Lanzhou.

## Things to See
Lanzhou has few sights though there's an intrinsic interest about the place that makes it a worthwhile stop. If you do come here and if you get a chance *don't* miss the utterly brilliant Dance Ensemble of Gansu Province. Also not to be missed are the Bilingisi Buddhist Caves.

### Provincial Museum
The museum is directly across the street from the Friendship Hotel. The ground floor is totally devoted to exhibits on the life of Zhou Enlai, and has an interesting photo collection though if you've made it this far you've probably seen them all before.

More interesting are the exhibits on the third floor, which includes the entire skeleton of a mammoth exhumed in 1973, as well as fragments of skeletons, teeth and tusks from other extinct members of the pachyderm family.

There's an extensive display of decorated earthenware pottery showing the progression in design; the Gansu painted pottery dates from the Yangshuo and Majiayuo Culture of 4000-2000 BC. There are also exhibits from the Bilingisi Caves; glazed clay statues; model bronze chariots and mounted horsemen dug up from the Letai Han Tomb at Wuwei in Gansu–altogether 220 figures and chariots were unearthed including the 'Galloping Horse of Gansu'; Jin Dynasty fresco bricks which were found lining the walls of a tomb at Jiayuguan – each brick has a painted scene depicting hunting, cultivating, theatre performances, etc; plus the inevitable displays of bronze pots, urns and cooking vessels.

Photos are not permitted (the only English signs in the museum are 'Don't take picture') and you can buy a replica of the galloping horse for just Y1860 from the museum shop.

### Temple of the Town Gods

The temple is a ten minute walk east of Xiguan. It's been partially restored and is now used as a public park where old men sit around playing cards and chequers while sipping tea, often to the accompaniment of live music. There's another temple, also under restoration, just west of the bridge over to the White Pagoda Park.

### Baita Shan (White Pagoda Hill)

Baita Shan lies opposite the city on the north bank of the Yellow River. It's dotted with the usual Ming and Qing pavilions, though the white Buddhist shrine atop the mountains is considerably older. From the top of the hill you can get a panoramic view of the industrial haze that hangs heavy on this dusty town.

### Bilingisi Caves

The Bilingisi Buddhist Caves are located 35 km south-west of Yonging County in Gansu Province. The oldest caves date back to the Western Qin Dynasty of 385-431 AD, and since then have been repaired and added to on numerous occasions. The caves have been cut into a cliff face 60 metres high and stretch for about 200 metres. There are 183 caves which remain to this day and these contain 694 statues, 82 clay sculptures and a number of murals. Cave 169 is the oldest and contains one Buddha and two Bodhisattvas; inscriptions on the wall give the date of the statues as 420 AD. Most of the other caves were completed during the prosperous Tang period. The star of the caves is the 27 metre high seated statue of Maitreya, the coming Buddha.

Probably the only way you'll make it to the caves is on one of the tours which leaves from Lanzhou. If you buy your ticket from the CITS office the charge is Y45 for the tour, and you'll probably go down with one of the western or Overseas Chinese tour groups. They pick you up in a minibus from the Friendship Hotel at 7.30 am and bus you down to a dusty little industrial town where there's a dam and the Liuchiahsia Hydro-electric Power Station. On the way down you drive through immense stretches of steep, terraced hills which grow wheat and corn. The bus ride takes about two hours. On the way into the town you'll see one good reason for coming here if not for the caves – wild marijuana grows in abundance on the side of the road. The bus drives over the top of the dam to a stairway leading down to the boat. The boat takes you on a two-hour trip down the reservoir; a beautiful trip with blue-green water, red gravel embankments and jagged grey hills on either side.

You can also buy tickets from the Friendship Hotel in Lanzhou; they've offered travellers tickets for just Y23, and others for Y19.

Be warned that even though the ride to the caves is beautiful and the caves themselves are magnificent, you're likely to get no more than 45 minutes to one hour to look around them – if everything goes on time. Nor will they let you take photographs – and they do enforce that rule!

### Places to Stay

The *Friendship Hotel* (tel 30511) is an immense Russian-built structure with huge columns in the foyer supporting the roof. The hotel has two main blocks, one facing Xijin Xilu and one behind it – the rear block is used to stow away foreigners. Double rooms with attached bathroom are Y26, but if you're on your own you'll probably get it for Y13. They also have dormitory beds for Y6. To get there take bus No 1 for 12 stops from in front of the railway station – it's a long ride.

The *Lanzhou Hotel* is another cavernous construction, not as nice but rather better located than the Friendship Hotel. A bed in a triple is Y5 and there are private bathrooms with large bathtubs. The hotel is a 20 minute walk from the railway station or you could take bus No 1 two stops.

### Places to Eat

I guess there must be food in this city –I don't think two million people could be adequately fed each day by the *Friendship Hotel* restaurant. You can't help thinking that this is the only eating house in Lanzhou, a bit on the expensive side but OK. There is said to be another good restaurant, the Lanzhou Canting on Jiuquan Lu in the centre of town –if you can find it.

### Getting Around

Apart from hiring a taxi from the Friendship Hotel, there are buses and walking to choose from.

### Getting Away

**Train** Trains to Urumqi via the Gansu corridor; to Beijing via Baotou, Hohhot and Datong; to Golmud via Xining; to Shanghai via Xian and Zhengzhou; to Beijing via Xian and Zhengzhou

**Plane** Lanzhou is connected by air to Baotou (Y93), Beijing (Y198), Canton (Y284), Changsha (Y208), Dunhuang (Y161), Jiuquan (Y94), Nanjing (Y191), Qingyang (Y55), Shanghai (Y226), Taiyuan (Y129), Urumqi (Y226), Xian (Y63), Xining (Y24), Yinchuan (Y43), Zhengzhou (Y120).

### JIUQUAN

Jiuquan has been an administrative outpost of Chinese civilisation since the Han Dynasty. The name means 'Wine Spring' and the story goes that when the Western Han General Ho Qubing found he lacked sufficient wine for his army to celebrate a triumphant expedition, he poured what he had into a spring and the whole army drank from that.

### Things to See

In the middle of the city stands the large **Drum Tower** which was built in the middle of the fourth century. It was originally built as a watchman's tower on the eastern gate of the town, but expansion of the town pushed it into the centre and it was renamed the Drum Tower. During the Qing Dynasty the tower was renovated, and on each of the four sides of the tower were hung tablets inscribed with cute little phrases like 'Beckoning to the Hua Mountain in the east', 'Taking in a full view of the Qilian Mountains in the south', 'Westward, Yiwu can be reached' and 'The great desert stretches away in the north'. And a Chinese tourist leaflet says *From tower, one enjoys splendid views in all directions, along with a sense of elation that comes from being face to face with the infinite and sublime.*

Clusters of tombs dating back to the Wei Dynasty of the third century AD are dispersed along a narrow strip of land about 20 km from north to south and three km wide that runs between Jiuquan and the Jiayu Pass. At their southern tip are a number of tombs dating from the Eastern Jin Dynasty (317-420 AD), decorated with murals.

The other attractions of the locale are the **Wenshushan Buddhist Cave Temples** 15 km from the town. The earliest of these date back to the fifth century.

### Getting Away

Jiuquan lies on the Lanzhou-Urumqi railway line. There are also regular buses to Jiayuguan (a one hour drive) and there is a daily bus to Dunhuang. There are three flights per week from Jiuquan to Dunhuang and three flights per week to Lanzhou.

### JIAYUGUAN

Jiayuguan is an ancient Han Chinese outpost. The Great Wall once extended

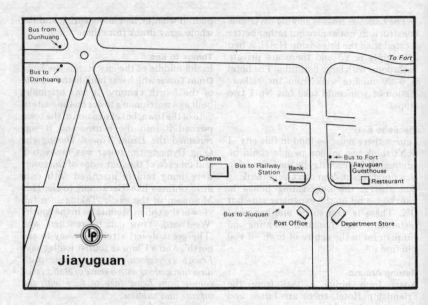

Bus from Dunhuang

Bus to Dunhuang

To Fort

Cinema

Bus to Railway Station

Bank

Bus to Fort
Jiayuguan Guesthouse

Restaurant

Bus to Jiuquan

Post Office

Department Store

Jiayuguan

beyond here, but in 1372 during the first few years of the Ming Dynasty a fortress was built here – from then on this was considered the terminus of the wall and the end of the empire.

The town lies on the Lanzhou-Urumqi rail line, and is mainly made up of bungalows and apartment blocks interspersed with factories and smokestacks. Not an unpleasant place, but very drab and dusty. The only attraction is the fort, and it's a worthy structure to stop off and have a look around.

### Information & Orientation
Someone has obviously given some thought to individual travellers because there are some signs in English up where you need them.

Jiayuguan is an easy place to find one's way around in since everything is easily accessible from the tourist-hotel. The railway station is to the north of the town and the local bus will take you straight to the hotel. The bank, department store and

post office are situated opposite the hotel and the public security office is a short distance away. The fort is a short distance from the town and the bus to the fort leaves from outside the hotel. The pick-up point for buses to Dunhuang is a 15 minute walk from the hotel. Directions for all these places are best ascertained from the map in this book.

**CITS** has a rep who floats around the Jiayuguan Binguan occasionally – or ask the staff at the reception desk.

**Public Security** is close to the hotel. Turn right at the front gate and then right again at the first crossroads. The public security compound is just around the corner and the office handling foreigners is just inside the gateway.

**Post** There is a post office diagonally opposite the hotel.

**Bank** The bank is opposite the hotel.

## Things to See

The **Jiayu Fort** is the attraction of Jiayuguan. The fort guards the Jiayu Pass which lies between the snow-capped Qilian Mountains and the Black Mountain of the Mazong Range. During the Ming Dynasty this was considered the terminus of the Great Wall, though the last few fragments can still be seen crumbling westwards.

The fort was dubbed by the Chinese as the 'Impregnable Defile Under the Sun' or the 'Impregnable Pass Under Heaven'. Although the Chinese often controlled territory far beyond Jiayuguan, this was the last major stronghold of the empire to the west.

The fort was first built in 1372, with additional towers and battlements added in subsequent years. The outer wall of the fort is about 733 metres in circumference and almost 10 metres high. At the eastern end of the fort is the **Guanghua Men (Gate of Enlightenment)** and in the west is the **Rouyuan Men (Gate of Concilliation)**. Over each gate stand towers which rise to a height of 17 metres, with upturned flying eaves. On the inside of each gate are horse lanes leading up to the top of the wall and at the four corners of the fort are blockhouses, bowmen's turrets and watch towers. Outside the Guanghua Men but inside the outer wall are three interesting buildings; the **Wenchang Pavilion** and the **Guandi Temple** which have been partly restored, and the unrestored open-air theatre stage.

There is a local bus which runs four times a day to the fort. You can pick it up from the stop outside the hotel (look for the orange sign with blue lettering in both Chinese and English). Buses depart from this stop at 9.30 am, noon, 2 pm and 4.30 pm. Extra buses run on public holidays. The fare is 15 fen and the ride takes about 15 minutes. Admission to the fort is 10 fen, and for some reason you have to sign your name in a book.

## Places to Stay

The *Jiayuguan Binguan* is a new hotel and is probably destined to be packed full of tour groups. Single rooms are Y6, doubles Y12 and a triple is Y18. They'll readily give you a bed in a triple for just Y6 if you're on your own. The staff are extremely friendly but speak little English. To get to the hotel from the railway station, take the local bus which leaves from outside the station; it stops across the road from the hotel and the fare is 15 fen. If you're coming in on the bus from Dunhuang it's within easy walking distance.

## Places to Eat

The only restaurant is around the corner from the hotel; turn left at the front gate,

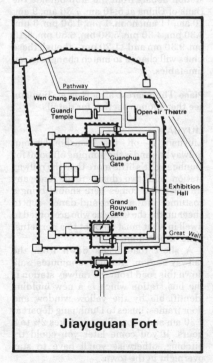

**Jiayuguan Fort**

then left again. It's an OK restaurant with OK food. The hotel will no doubt have a restaurant by the time this book is out.

### Getting Away
**Bus** Buses to Jiuquan leave from the stop just next to the post office diagonally across the road from the guest house. The fare is 60 fen. The first bus is at 6.30 am and the last at 7.45 pm, with buses departing at half to one hour intervals.

Buses to Dunhuang depart each morning at 7 am from the large intersection, a 15 minute walk from the guest house (refer to the map in this book for directions).

**Train** Jiayuguan lies on the Lanzhou-Urumqi railway line. Buses to the train station depart from the stop outside the Bank of China at 5.40 am, 7.30 am, 9 am, 10 am, 11 am, noon, 1 pm, 1.50 pm, 3 pm, 3.30 pm, 4.30 pm, 5.30 pm, 6.50 pm, 8.15 pm, 9.30 pm and 11.20 pm – though these times will change to match changes in rail timetables.

**Plane** The nearest airport is at Jiuquan; see the Jiuquan section for details.

## LIUYUAN
Liuyuan is on the Lanzhou-Urumqi railway line and is the jumping off point for Dunhuang. It's little more than the railway station and two dusty roads and any traveller who comes here should bring a costume and a song-and-dance act to cheer up the the Chinese who are forced to dwell in what must amount to a perpetual state of boredom.

A short road leads down from the railway station. About five minutes walk down this road from the railway station is the bus station which is a new building identifiable by the yellow window and door frames; buses to Dunhuang depart at 7.30 am and noon. The trip takes 2½ to 3 hours. If you come later you could try hitching, otherwise you'll have to stay overnight in the town.

There are two hotels to choose from, both on the main road. The first is a whitewashed building just a few minutes walk down from the train station on the right. The second hotel is further down on the same side of the road and looks marginally better – it's a grey brick building with two columns holding up a verandah over the front entrance and charges Y1 for a bed.

There is one OK place to eat, a small restaurant five minutes walk down from the second hotel. It's identifiable by a green fly-wire net hanging in the doorway. The people here are friendly.

## DUNHUANG
Dunhuang is a giant oasis stuck in the middle of the Gansu Desert, a three hour bus ride through the oblivion end of China south of the Lanzhou-Urumqi railway line. During the Han and Tang Dynasties this was a pivotal point of interchange between China and the outside world, a major staging post for both in-coming and outgoing trading caravans. Today it attracts visitors because it is the site of one of the greatest examples of Buddhist art in the world – the Magao Caves.

### Information & Orientation
The centre of Dunhuang is little more than two intersecting roads and all life-support systems are within easy walking distance of each other.

**CITS** The staff at the Dunhuang Hotel are CITS people. There's one guy at the front desk who is extremely helpful, friendly and gives accurate information, and speaks quite good English.

**Public Security** is walking distance from the hotel and hostel (see the map). It's open 7.30 am to noon and 3 to 6.30 pm but is closed on Sundays.

**CAAC** For air-tickets, book at CITS in the Dunhuang Hotel.

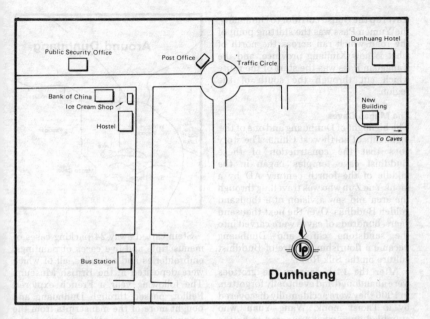

**Bank** You can change money at the Bank of China which is walking distance from the hotel and hostel (see the map). The bank is open 9.15 am to noon and 3 to 5.30 pm.

**Maps** There's a simple map of Dunhuang and the surrounding district in the foyer of the Dunhuang Hotel. Other than that there's nothing else around at the moment except for the sketch-map in this book.

### Things to See

The main attraction of Dunhuang are the Magao Caves and there is little to see in the oasis itself.

### The Southern Dunes

This ridge of vast sand dunes is to the south of the oasis. You can easily bicycle out to the edge of the ridge and then climb to the top. Alternatively, a bus is often organised by the hotel and hostel to take people, mainly Hong Kongers, out there in the evening. The cost is only Y1 for the round-trip. It's a *steep, hard* climb to the top of the dunes, but it affords a great view of the oasis in one direction and the infinite stretch of desert in the other. Behind the ridge is a much-touted lake which turns out to be a rather putrid little pool.

### Yangguan and Yumen Passes

62 km southwest of Dunhuang is the mountain pass of Yangguan. The Han Dynasty beacon towers which marked the route westwards for the camel caravans, and which warned the populace of invaders have almost disappeared under the drifting sand. Nearby are the ruins of the ancient Han town of Shouchang. To the north-west of Dunhuang is the Yumen Pass, also noted for its ancient ruins. To get to either of these passes you'd have to try hitching up with a tour group or hire a taxi from the hotel.

Caravans heading out of China would

travel up the Gansu corridor to Dunhuang; the Yumen Pass was the starting point of the road which ran across the north of what is now Xinjiang province, and the Yangguan Pass was the start of the route which cut through the south of the region.

## The Magao Caves

The highlight of Dunhuang and one of the highlights of north-west China. The story goes that the construction of these Buddhist cave temples began in the middle of the fourth century AD by a monk Yue Zun who was travelling through the area and saw a vision of a thousand golden Buddhas. Over the next thousand years, hundreds of caves were carved into the sandstone cliffs and Dunhuang became a flourishing centre of Buddhist culture on the Silk Road.

After the 14th century the grottoes were abandoned and eventually forgotten. In 1900 they were accidentally discovered by a Taoist monk, Wang Yuan ,who stumbled upon what appeared to be the former monastery library with its collection of scrolls, documents, embroideries and paintings that had been left behind by the Buddhist monks. Bricked up to prevent the contents falling into the hands of invaders, the dry desert air had preserved the paper and artworks.

Passing through the area in 1907, the British explorer Sir Aurel Stein heard a rumour of the hoard, tracked down the monk and was allowed to inspect the contents of the cave. It was an archaeological goldmine mainly of Buddhist texts in Chinese, Tibetan and many other Central Asian languages, some known and some long forgotten. There were paintings on silk and linen and what may be the oldest printed book in existence dating to 868 AD.

The sacking of the Dunhuang caves began in earnest. Stein convinced Wang to part with a large section of the library in return for a donation towards the restoration of some of the grottoes.

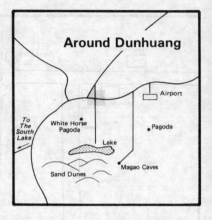

Stein carted away 24 packing cases of manuscripts and five cases of paintings, embroideries and art relics, all of which were deposited in the British Museum. The following year a French explorer, Pelliot, passed through Dunhuang and bought more of the manscripts from the monk. He was followed by others from the United States, Japan and Russia who all carted off their booty. News of the find filtered through to Beijing and the imperial court ordered the remainder of the collection to be transported to the capital. Many were pilfered whilst they sat in the Dunhuang government offices, and Stein reported in 1914 when he returned to the area that fine Buddhist manuscripts were brought to him for sale. He also said that Wang had regretted not taking up his original offer of parting with the collection *en bloc*.

For the Chinese it's another example of the plundering of the country by foreigners in the 19th and early 20th centuries; though one hates to think what would have happened to the collection if Stein had left it where it was – most likely it would have been looted and either destroyed or sold off piece-meal. Half the world seems to have ended up in the British Museum – the Greeks want their Parthenon back and the Chinese want the Dunhuang manuscripts back – though the manuscripts are probably better preserved where they are, and available to a far greater number of researchers than what they would be in the People's Republic.

The Magao Caves are located 25 km south-east of Dunhuang in a river valley between the Sanwei and Mingsha Mountains. The desert cliffs are completely exposed to the elements and the interiors of the caves have been severely damaged by wind and water erosion and many have collapsed. Cave 94 for example, is totally decimated and is now used to store junk. Today, 492 grottoes are still standing. The grottoes honeycomb a 1600 metre long cliff face which sits on a north-south axis. Altogther they contain over 2000 statues and over 45,000 separate murals. Cave 17 is where Wang discovered the hoard of manuscripts and artworks.

In 1961 the Dang River was diverted north of the grottoes to prevent further damage through flooding. Two years later the Tang and Song pavilions at the caves were rebuilt and the exterior walls of the caves were reinforced with concrete colonnades and blocks. Windows, walls, and doors were constructed to prevent further erosion from wind and drifting sand, and foundations were laid under many of the statues. Walkways were erected on the cliff face to allow access to all the caves.

Most of the Dunhuang art dates from the Northern and Western Wei, the Northern Zhou, the Sui and the Tang Dyansties, though examples from the Five Dynasties, Northern Song, Western Xia and the Yuan can also be found. The Northern Wei, the Western Wei and Northern Zhou, and the Tang caves are in the best state of preservation.

Many of the caves are rectangular or square-shaped with recessed, decorated ceilings. The focal point of each is the group of brightly-painted statues representing Buddha and the bodhisattvas or Buddha's disciples. Because the sandstone here was too soft for fine carving the smaller statues

are made of terracotta, coated with a sort of plaster surface and painted with mineral pigments. As with the caves constructed later at Datong and Luoyang, the main themes are the life of Buddha, religious stories and tales from Chinese mythology, and the walls of the caves are painted in intricate detail.

**The Northern Wei, Western Wei & Northern Zhou Dynasties (386 AD – 581 AD)** The Turkish-speaking Tobas who inhabited the region north of China invaded and conquered the country in the fourth century and founded the Northern Wei Dynasty around 386 AD. They deliberately adopted a policy of copying Chinese customs and lifestyle. But friction between groups who wanted to maintain the traditional Toba lifestyle and those who wanted to assimilate with the Chinese eventually split the Toba empire in two in the middle of the sixth century; the eastern part adopted the Chinese way of life and the rulers took the dynasty name of the Northern Qi. The western part tried to revert to Toba customs without success. The rulers took the dynasty name of Northern Zhou; by 567 they had defeated the Qi and taken control of all of northern China.

The fall of the Han Dynasty in 220 AD sent Confucianism into decline. With the turmoil produced by the Toba invasions Buddhism took on a particular appeal with its teachings of nirvana and personal salvation. The religion spread rapidly under the patronage of the new rulers, and made a new and decisive impact on Chinese art which can be seen in the Buddhist statues at Magao.

The art of this period is characterised by its attempt to depict people who had transcended the material world and entered onto some higher spiritual plane. The statues are characterised by broad faces and prominent cheekbones, thin lips and eyebrows and noses set high on the face – this indicating an Indian influence. The earlier Wei faces were originally painted vermilion, with chalk-white nose and eyes. But the vermilion oxidised and turned black, giving the figures even more unnatural an appearance.

Later Wei carvings depict figures in wide hats and elaborate dress, but in general the slender Wei figures are draped in clinging, light robes (like the bodhisattvas in the Northern Wei Caves 248 and 257), and the heads seem large in proportion to the bodies. Like the sculptures of the same period at Luoyang, the expressions on the faces of the Buddhas and the bodhisattvas are smiling and benevolently saccharine – Cave 259 of the Northern Wei period being a good example.

The Wei and Zhou paintings at Magao are some of the most interesting in the grottoes. The figures are simple, almost cartoon-like with round heads, elongated ears and puppet-like, segmented bodies which are boldly outlined. The female figures are all topless, with large breasts, which also suggests an Indian influence. The Northern Zhou Cave 299 shows musicians and dancers in this style and 290 shows flying celestial maidens. The paintings in the Northern Zhou Cave 428 are a good example of this style.

The wall painting in Northern Wei Cave 254 is done in this style and portrays the story of Buddha vanquishing Mara. It refers to the night that Buddha sat beneath a fig tree south of the Indian city of Patna, and entered into a deep meditation. Mara, the Evil One, the Devil, realising that Sakyamuni was on the verge of enlightenment, rushed to the spot. Mara tempted him with desire, parading three voluptuous goddesses before him, but Sakyamuni resisted. Then Mara assailed him with hurricanes, torrential rains and showers of flaming rocks, but the missiles turned to lotus petals. And finally Mara challenged his right to do what he was doing, but Buddha touched the earth with his fingertip and the roaring it summoned up drove away Mara and his demons. Sakyamuni had achieved enlightenment – but Mara was waiting with one last temptation; this time it was an appeal to reason, that speech-defying revelations could not be translated into words and no one would understand so profound a truth as the Buddha had attained. But Buddha said that there would be some who would understand, and Mara was finally banished forever.

### The Sui Dynasty (581 AD – 618 AD)

The throne of the Northern Zhou Dynasty was usurped by a general of Chinese or mixed Chinese-Toba origin. Prudently putting to death all the sons of the former emperor, he embarked on a series of wars which by 589 had reunited northern and southern China for the first time in 360 years. The Tobas simply disappeared from history, either mixing with other Turkish tribes from Central Asia or assimilating with the Chinese, marrying into Chinese families and adopting Chinese names.

The Sui was a short-lived dynasty and it did not leave any great masterpieces. It was more a transition period between the Wei and Tang periods. Again the best Sui art was of Buddhist origin. What separates the Sui style from the Wei is the rigidity of its sculpture. The figures of the Buddha and the bodhisattvas are rigid and immobile; their heads are curiously oversized and their torsos elongated. All of them are draped in Chinese robes with none of the Indian-inspired softness and grace of the Wei figures.

At Magao the Sui caves are located to the north of the Wei caves and in some instances the Sui have painted over the Wei. Ananda, the young disciple of Buddha, appears for the first time (as in Cave 419) and Kasyapa the older disciple of Buddha also appears (such as the grizzly-looking example in Cave 419). The lotus flower motif appears frequently. Stories from the life of Buddha provide the main themes of the wall paintings. Other Sui Caves include 204, 244, 302 and 427.

### The Tang Dynasty (618 AD – 907 AD)

The reign of the last Sui Emperor Yang Ti was characterised by imperial extravagance, cruelty and social injustice. Taking advantage of the inevitable peasant revolts which had arisen in eastern China, a noble family of Chinese-Turkish descent assassinated the emperor, took control of the capital, Changan, and assumed the throne taking the dynasty name of Tang.

During the Tang period China extended her domain by force of arms into Central Asia, pushing outward as far as Lake Balkhash in what is today Soviet Kazakhstan. Trade with the outside world expanded and foreign merchants and religions poured into the Tang capital of Changan. Tang art took on incomparable vigour, and the trend was towards realism and nobility of form. Buddhism had become prominent and Buddhist art reached its peak; the proud bearing of the Buddhist figures in the Magao caves reflect the feelings of the times, the prevailing image of the brave Tang warrior and the strength and steadfastness of the empire.

The Tang figures are notable for their awesomeness and overwhelming size and power; the best examples are the colossal Buddhas of caves 96 and 130 – the one in 96 is the taller, standing over 30 metres tall. The statues can be viewed from platforms constructed in the cave wall opposite their chests and faces. The roof and walls of Cave 130 are adorned with paintings.

The bodhisattvas, richly ornamented, were often modelled on local officials and lords. Warriors are well-muscled, aggressive and wear armour and helmets (Caves 46, 194 and 322). The supple bodies and flowing robes of the Tang figures suggest an element of sensuality influenced by Persian and Indian art. But unlike the figures of the Wei, Zhou and Sui periods, the Tang are realistic, lifelike with human expressions but with an all-pervading sense of nobility. One good example is the statue of Buddha's older disciple Kasyapa in Cave 45. But there are notable exceptions to this rule – such as the statues in Cave 16 with their heavy eyebrows, long slit eyes and enormous hands.

Cave 158 contains a huge statue of the reclining Sakyamuni Buddha at the time of his death. The face resembles a Tang Dynasty woman with a peaceful, serene composure. The figures painted on the walls surrounding the statue are his mourning disciples; they include Turks, Arabs and other barbarians, and their grief-stricken faces are unlike anything else in the caves.

Other Tang Dynasty Caves include 17, 45, 57, 103, 112, 156, 159, 196, 217, 220, 320, 321, 328 and 329. Cave 156 has an interesting wall mural showing a Tang army on the march.

**Later Dynasties** Since little space remained to carve out new caves, later dynasties resorted to either painting over or enlarging and restoring the art in earlier caves. Although the latter practice was particularly true of the Northern Song, there is one magnificent Song mural in Cave 361, a landscape in relief depicting the terrain, cities, towns, bridges, roads, temples and travellers of China's sacred Buddhist mountain, Wutai Shan.

During the Yuan Dynasty (1279 AD – 1368 AD) nine new caves were carved and others were restored. These caves were characterised by circular altars and, for the first time, frescoes; No 3 is an example of a Yuan Dynasty cave. Cave 346 is an example of a Five Dynasties cave. Cave 55 is another example of a Northern Song construction.

Except for the small niches (most of which are in very bad condition or are completely bare of both statues and paintings) all the caves have gates which are locked. Many of the locked caves are in such poor condition that they would simply not be worth opening to the general public. Some, like Cave 462 – the Mizong

Cave – contain Tantric art whose explicit sexual portrayals have been deemed too corrupting for the public to view. A few caves are presently in the process of being restored. Only 40 caves have been cleared for public view.

The guides show the groups of Chinese no more than a dozen caves. Admission to the caves is 10 fen, but it seems – according to a sign in Chinese near the entrance to the caves – that if you pay Y4 then you can see all 40 caves. The main problem is that the staff and guides are appallingly apathetic – they may have good reason to be, but if you come all the way across the desert and only see 12 caves then there's little reason to feel sympathetic. Your guide will only take you to the 12 caves which are normally shown to tourists, and requests to see any of the others (even the ones which are officially open) are simply met with a blunt 'NO'. The guides seem to be more informative with their Chinese groups but they won't tell westerners anything – even if you speak to them in Chinese! Westerners who show up in the afternoon are considered a dreadful imposition. Avoid going to the caves with a busload of Hong Kongers. They came to China to have fun and whilst they spend half an hour having their photos taken at the front entrance, you'll be sitting around twiddling your thumbs.

You're not allowed to take photos in the caves; you have to leave your camera and bags in the luggage hut near the entrance. Photos are sometimes permitted after payment of some appropriately vast sum of money. Banning flash photos is understandable, but you're not even allowed to take time-exposures. Instead there is a shop outside the cave selling slides, postcards and books . . . Bring your own torch as most of the caves are very dark and it's hard to see much of the detail without your own lighting – particularly in the niches in the sides of the main caves. Torches can be bought for a few yuan in China.

Getting to the caves is a bit of a hassle. There is a bus from Dunhuang's long-distance bus station which departs each morning at 8 am and the trip out takes about 45 minutes. The bus leaves the caves at 11.30 am, so in all you get about 2 hours to see what you can of the grottoes. There are no buses in the afternoon. Alternatively, you could hire a taxi at the Dunhuang Hotel to take you to the caves. It takes about 25 minutes to drive out there, and if you're away for a total of about four hours then the taxi will cost you about Y30 (at a rate of 50 fen per km plus a small waiting charge). You could ride a bicycle out there but be warned that half the ride is entirely through desert and would be absolute murder – don't say I didn't warn you!

### Places to Stay

The *Dunhuang Hotel* is the tourist joint, and it's a good place. It's Y10 for a bed in a four-bed room (Hmmmh!) –if you're a student in China it's only Y3.50 though they're very scrupulous about checking student cards. A double room is Y30, though if you're on your own they'll probably give you the room for Y15. To get to the hotel from the bus station, turn left out of the station and then right at the first T-intersection. The hotel is on the left, past the traffic circle.

There is a large hotel five minutes walk down from the bus station, on the way to the Dunhuang Hotel. It's a large red brick and yellow-concrete building with a wire fence and lamps on green-coloured poles. It *does* take foreigners. It's Y3 for dorm-bed and Y12 for a double room (they may give you the room for Y6 if you're on your own).

### Places to Eat

Food at the *Dunhuang Hotel* is good. Y3 for breakfast, Y6 lunch and Y6 dinner; they serve you little plates of various food. You have to tell them at each meal if you'll be eating at the next, and if you haven't they won't serve you –fair enough if you're the only person in the hotel, but even if they've got 20 Hong Kongers and a table of Japanese in the restaurant they still lack the spontaneity required to serve one stray back-packer – as if they carefully weigh the food out for every meal! It's the one sore point of this hotel.

The hotel also has *The Cafe* on the 3rd floor. Here you can sit around and watch TV and get drunk on Tsingtao or Lanzhou Piju or else sample such delights as 'Orong juice' 'Soole water' 'Luoky Cola' 'Ven Mouth Wine' and 'Five Smells Wine'.

There is an icecream and cold drinks shop on the corner of the T-intersection next to the large hostel.

### Getting Around
There are bicycles for hire from outside the hostel, and the guy only charges 30 fen per hour.

### Getting Away
**Bus & Train** Buses to Liuyuan depart from the long-distance bus station at 7 am and at 2.30 pm. The trip takes about 3½ hours and costs Y3.20. Liuyuan is on the Lanzhou-Urumqi railway line and is the

jumping-off point for Dunhuang. It's a miserable place and you should avoid going there if possible (see the Liuyuan section for a repeat of the miserable details).

To avoid the exotic Liuyuan diversion, there is a direct bus from from Dunhuang to Jiayuguan and then on to Jiuquan. It departs at 6.45 am. The fare to Jiayuguan is Y9.40 and the trip takes 9 hours. The fare to Jiaquan is Y9.90 and takes about another hour.

**Plane** Dunhuang is connected by air to Jiuquan (Y67) and to Lanzhou (Y161).

## MAIJISHAN
Maijishan lies in the far south-east of Gansu Province. The name means 'Corn Rick Mountain'; it has sheer cliff faces with soft, easily excavated rock. It was chosen sometime in the fifth century as the location for a series of Buddhist caves. The caves date back to the Northern Wei and Song Dynasties and contain clay figures and wall paintings. Stone sculptures have evidently been brought in from elsewhere, since the local rock is too soft for carving, as at Dunhuang.

# Xinjiang

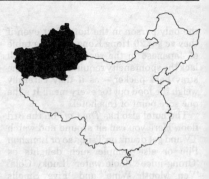

Xinjiang is one of China's 'Autonomous Regions', inhabited predominantly by the Turkish-speaking Moslem Uygur people whose autonomy from their Chinese overlords is in name only.

The history of this desolate north-western region has largely been one of continuing wars and conflicts between the native population, coupled with repeated Chinese invasions and subjugations.

The Chinese were interested in the region for two reasons. Firstly because a lucrative trade plied the 'Silk Roads' that cut through the oasis towns north and south of the Taklimakan Desert. Along this route camel caravans would carry goods from China to Central Asia – and which would eventually find their way to Europe. It was a trade which had been going on at least since Roman days when the silk, the principal Chinese export, was a prized possession amongst fashionable Roman ladies. Whoever controlled the oasis towns could also tax the flow of goods, and so the conquest of Xinjiang was indeed a profitable venture.

Secondly, subjugation of the region would also help to control the trouble-some nomadic border tribes, the 'barbarians', who made frequent raids into China to carry off prisoners and booty, thus acquiring goods and labour not available on the northern steppes.

The Chinese never really subdued the region and their hold over it waxed and waned with the power of the central government. The area was constantly subjected to waves of invasions by the Huns, Tibetans, and the Mongols under Genghis and later under his descendent Tamerlane.

The Han were the first Chinese rulers to conquer Xinjiang, between 73 and 97 AD, even crossing the Tian Mountains and marching a 70,000 man army as far as the Caspian Sea, although the Chinese only held onto an area somewhat further east of Lake Balkash. With the demise of the Han in the third century the Chinese once again lost control of the region until the Tang expeditions reconquered it and extended Chinese power as far as Lake Balkash.

Once again the region was lost to the Chinese with the fall of the Tang and it was not until the Qing Dynasty that it was recovered. That was achieved by the second Qing Emperor Kang-xi, who came to the throne at 16 years of age and reigned from 1661-1722. His long rule gave him enough time to conquer Mongolia and Tibet as well, extending Chinese power to the greatest extent it has ever known.

The 19th century was a bloody one for Xinjiang. If the newly arrived European barbarians were an affliction on the limbs of China then the internal barbarians were a disease of its vitals. Unrest was everywhere in China in the 19th century. There had been a raging rebellion between the Yellow and Yangtse Rivers between 1796-1805, followed by the massive Taiping Rebellion of 1851-1864. And there were two major Moslem rebellions; one in Yunnan from 1855-73 and another in the north-west from 1862-73 which spread across Shaanxi, Ningxia, Gansu and Xinjiang. Both were put down with extreme savagery by the Chinese. The north-western rebellion had grown out of decades of misrule by the Chinese,

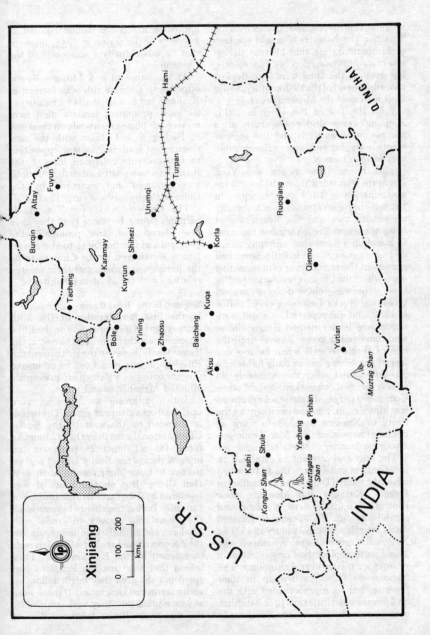

religious controversy and contact with the Taipings. The massacre of untold numbers of Moslems during this 11 year period celebrated the assertion of Chinese rule, but even as the Qing went into decline towards the end of the 19th century, so did their hold over the Moslem areas.

With the fall of the Qing in 1911, Xinjiang came under the rule of a succession of warlords and the governments in Beijing and later in Nanjing had very little influence.

The frst of these rulers was Yang Zhengxin who ruled from 1911 until his assassination in 1928 at a banquet in Ürümqi (the region's traditions of hospitality are all its own and the death-rate at banquets is appalling). Yang had managed to maintain a somewhat unhappy peace and his policy of isolationism had preserved the region from contaminating ideas which the Chinese revolution had let loose. He was followed by a second tyrannical overlord who was forced to flee in 1933, and was replaced by a still more oppressive leader named Sheng Shizai who remained in power almost until the end of World War II when he too was forced out. Sheng had initially followed a pro-Communist policy, then suddenly did a reverse and embarked on an anti-Communist purge. Amongst those executed was Mao Zemin, who had been sent by the Party to Xinjiang in 1938 to work as Sheng's financial adviser. Mao Zemin was a younger brother of Mao Zedong.

The only real attempt to establish an independent state was in the 1940s when a Kazakh named Osman led a rebellion of Uygurs, Kazakhs and Mongols, took control of south-western Xinjiang and established an independent Eastern Turkestan Republic in January 1945. The Nationalist government convinced the Moslems to abolish their new republic in return for a pledge of real autonomy. The Nationalists failed to live up to their promise, but soon preoccupied with the civil war they had little time to re-establish control over the region. They eventually appointed a Moslem named Burhan as governor of the region in 1948, unaware that he was actually a supporter of the Communists.

At the same time a Moslem league opposed to Chinese rule was formed in Xinjiang, but in August 1949 a number of its most prominent leaders died in a mysterious plane crash while on their way to Beijing to hold talks with the new Communist leaders. Moslem opposition to Chinese rule collapsed, though the Kazakh Osman continued to fight until he was captured and executed by the Chinese Communists in early 1951.

The Chinese hold over Xinjiang is certainly strong, but since 1949 they have been faced with two problems; the geographical location next to the Soviet Union, considered by the Chinese to be the paramount threat, and their volatile relations with the Moslem inhabitants.

## Xinjiang & the Great Game

In the first few decades of the 20th century, the Xinjiang region looked like becoming another unwilling player in the 'Great Game' between the British and the Russians. It was round two of an insane power struggle which had previously afflicted Afghanistan and Tibet.

British interests in Xinjiang were obvious from a glance at a map. The region is bounded on the west by the Soviet Union and on the north by Outer Mongolia (now, for all practical purposes, an integral part of the Soviet Union) and on the east by Inner Mongolia and north-west Han China. But on the south it was bordered by Tibet and British India. For centuries Indian merchants have crossed the Himalayan passes to trade with Kashgar, and so the British once again saw their economic and their strategic interests threatened by the Russian bear. They feared that now that the Russians had spied out the area they might follow up with a territorial annexation. If there were any such plans then they were stopped by the disastrous Russo-Japanese War of

1904, the revolution of 1917, the ensuing civil war, and the Nazi invasion.

In the end it was the Chinese who won out in the Great Game, and they had hardly been playing. Today the region bristles with Chinese troops and weapons. Some of them are there to keep down the ever-volatile Uygurs; others to hold back the real or imagined threat from the Soviet Union.

## The People

Xinjiang is inhabited by something like 15 or 16 of China's official total of 55 national minorities. The problem with the Chinese is that 50% of their country isn't even inhabited by them, but by minority people who mostly don't like them. What is more, these minority people inhabit the border regions; around Vietnam, India, Afghanistan, the USSR – all places of past or possible future conflict.

In 1955 the province of Xinjiang was renamed the 'Uygur Autonomous Region'. At that time more than 90% of the population were non-Chinese. But with the building of the Lanzhou-Ürümqi railroad and the development of industry in the region, there was a large influx of Chinese who now form a majority in the northern area whilst the Uygurs continue to predominate in the south.

In 1953 Xinjiang had a population of about 4.9 million of whom 3.6 million were Uygurs and only a very small number were Han Chinese. By 1970, the number of Hans was estimated to have grown to about four million. According to the 1982 census there are now 13 million people in Xinjiang of whom only about six million are Uygurs. It's a trend that will inevitably continue as the region develops, with the result that the Uygurs will be subjugated and pacified by sheer weight of numbers.

Relations between the Han and the minority people in the region tend to vary; the nomadic Kazakhs (better known as Cossaks on the other side of the Sino-Soviet border) were angered by the forced introduction of the communes; in 1962

60,000 are supposed to have crossed into the Soviet Union (it's a sizeable number – there are only 900,000 today spread across Xinjiang, Gansu and Qinghai). Relations with the Tajiks (numbering 26,000) are said to be better.

Unfortunately for the Chinese, relations with the majority-minority Uygurs can be best described as volatile. The Chinese have done a great deal to relieve the backwardness of the region, building roads, railways, hospitals and industrialising the towns, and their presence also prevents the Uygurs fighting amongst themselves, a problem whenever centralised rule has toppled. So it's difficult for the Chinese to understand the hostility with which they are greeted. Part of the hostility probably originates from centuries of Chinese misrule and from the savage way in which the 19th century rebellions were put down; part of it simply from the fact that the Uygurs just don't have *anything* in common with the Chinese. The Uygur religion is monotheic Islam, their written script is Arabic, their language is closely related to Turkish, their physical features are basically Caucasian and many could easily be mistaken for Greeks, southern Italians or other southern Europeans.

Part of the problem may also stem from the intentional or unintentional policy of the Chinese which could obliterate the Uygur culture. The Arabic script used by the Uygurs is no longer taught in schools, and although the children speak Uygur their inability to read the script will make huge parts of their culture inaccessible once the older people die. The Arabic script has been replaced by a romanised form, and granted that this will speed up the education process and increase literacy in the area, it will nevertheless make Arabic language books inaccessible to the younger generation of Uygurs. The Cultural Revolution inflicted itself here by closing down the mosques, slightly more than a sore point with a devoutly religious-thinking people like the Moslems.

With the death of Mao and the rise of a more liberal regime to power, the mosques have since been reopened.

The all-out rebellions of the past may be over – in fact, probably an impossibility with the influx of Chinese soldiers and settlers – but every year there is some sort of anti-Chinese riot or demonstration in one Xinjiang town or another. For the Uygurs the Chinese are very much a foreign occupation force.

## Minority Nationalities

The minority nationalities of Xinjiang are probably some of the most interesting in China. To the west of Ürümqi the Tian range divides and between the two mountain ranges is the Ili Valley. The population in the valley is a mixed bag of Kirghiz, Kazakhs, Chinese, and even includes a colony of Sibo, the descendants of the Manchu garrison which was stationed here after the conquests of the 18th century. Another peculiar army to hit Xinjiang were the refugee White Russian troops who fled after their defeat in the Russian Civil War. Some settled here and founded scattered colonies.

The most interesting minority has a population of one; in the 1930s there was a bizarre story that T.E Lawrence (of Arabia fame) was active in the British cause against the Russians in Xinjiang, and had gone wandering off with a band of local tribesmen to raise hell and high sandstorms. It was a rumour which continued even after Lawrence's fatal motorcycle accident in Britain in 1936 – the Xinjiang footnote being not the least fantastic part of the Lawrence legend.

## The Land

Xinjiang is divided into two major regions by the east-west Tian Mountain Range. To the north of the Tian range is the Junggar Basin, and to the south is the Tarim Basin.

The Tarim Basin is bordered to the north by the Tian range and to the south by the Kunlun range. It's a huge depression into which streams from the surrounding mountains lose themselves in the sands of the Taklimakan Desert which occupies the centre of the basin.

Other streams run from the Tian range into the Tarim River which flows eastward and empties into the vast saltmarsh and lake of Lop Nur. The boundaries of Lop Nur vary greatly from year to year as a result of climatic variation; it's an area of poor grassland and semi-desert and almost uninhabited. Since 1964 the Chinese have been testing their nuclear bombs here.

The Taklimakan Desert is a true desert. Cultivation is only possible in the oases of irrigated land which centre on the streams which flow into the basin from the surrounding mountains. These oases have had flourishing cultures of their own for 2000 years and were important stopover points on the 'Silk Road', the trading route which connected China to the land further west.

The oases of Xinjiang are largely populated by Uygur people and support a flourishing irrigated agricultural industry, based mainly on food grains and fruit. The grasslands of the foothills support an extensive pastoral industry rearing sheep and horses. The agriculture of places like the Turpan and Hami depressions depends entirely on irrigation with water drawn from underground streams. Only in the Ili Valley, west of Ürümqi, is rainfall sufficient to support a flourishing agricultural and pastoral industry.

The Junggar Basin is an area which has been the centre of extensive colonisation by the Chinese since the 1950s. Large state farms have been established on formerly uncultivated land. The major towns are Ürümqi, the capital of Xinjiang, Shihezi and Manas. Their importance grew with the completion of the Xinjiang railway from Lanzhou to Ürümqi in 1963, the rapid growth in the population and the exploitation of rich oil resources in the Junggar Basin.

The Junggar Basin extends north to the

high Atlay mountains on the Mongolian border. The Junggar is less arid than the Tarim Basin and most of it is grassland supporting a pastoral population. Most are either nomadic Kazakhs or Torgut Mongols, herding sheep, some horses, cattle and camels. The north and north-west of the Junggar Basin is bounded by the Atlay mountain range, of 3000 to 4000 metre high peaks. It's an area of substantial rainfall, and the mountains are either tree-covered or form rich pasture-land. The population is mainly nomadic Kazakh or Oirat Mongol herdsmen.

**Climate** Try to avoid going to Xinjiang either at the height of summer or the depths of winter. In summer, industrial Ürümqi is miserable and Turpan more than deserves the title of 'hottest place in China' – the maximums in Turpan get up to 47°C. In winter though this region is as formidably cold as anywhere else in northern China. In Ürümqi the average temperature in January is around –10°C, with minimums down to almost –30°C. Temperatures in Turpan are only slightly more favourable to human existence.

### DAHEYON

The jumping-off point for Turpan is a place on the railway line signposted 'Turpan Zhan'. In fact where you actually are is a place called Daheyon, and the Turpan oasis is an hour's drive south across the desert. Daheyon is *not* a place you'll want to hang around, so spare a thought for the Chinese who have to eke out a sane living here.

The bus station is a ten minute walk from the railway station. Walk up the road leading from the railway station and turn right at the first main intersection; the bus station is a few minutes walk up ahead on the left-hand side of the road. There are two buses a day to Turpan, one at 8 am and the other at 5 pm but these departure times depend on the relative position of the sun and the moon. There are lots of

trucks on these two roads and you may be able to hitch if you miss the bus; it's about an hour's drive to Turpan but the buses are said to take much longer! If you miss the bus and can't get there hitching you'll have to spend the night in this exotic outpost.

### TURPAN

East of Ürümqi the Tai Mountains split into a southern and a northern mountain range; between the two lies the Hami depression which falls to 200 metres below sea level and the Turpan to 160 metres. Both are practically rainless with searing hot summers.

Turpan county is inhabited by about 170,000 people, of whom about 120,000 are Uygurs and the rest mostly Chinese. The centre of the county is the large Turpan oasis. It's little more than a few main streets set in a vast tract of grain fields, and more importantly it's been spared the architectural horrors that have been inflicted on Ürümqi. Most of the streets are planted with trees and are lined with mud-brick walls enclosing mud houses. Open channels with flowing water run down the sides of the streets and from these the inhabitants draw water as well as using them to wash their clothes, dishes and kiddies.

Turpan is also the only place in Xinjiang officially open to foreigners which has any real Uygur history, unlike the Chinese settlements of Ürümqi and Shihezhi. Nearby Gaochang was once the capital of the Uygurs. It was an important staging post on the Silk Road and was a centre of Buddhism before being converted to Islam in the 8th century. During the Chinese occupation it served as a garrison town.

Turpan is a quiet place (one of the few in China) and the guest house is a good place to sit underneath the vine trellises, drink beer and contemplate the moon. The living is cheap, the food is good and the people are friendly, and there are a couple of interesting 'sights' scattered

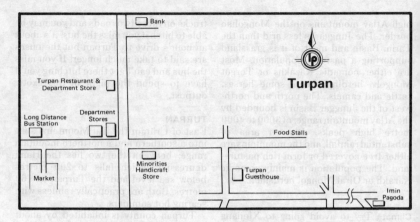

around to keep yourself occupied. Along with Hangzhou and Yangshuo it's one of the few places in the country where you can relax and withdraw a bit from China. And it's also the hottest; temperatures in summer have been known to reach 47°C!

### Information & Orientation
The 'centre' of the Turpan oasis is little more than two main roads and a couple of side streets where you'll find the shops, the market, the long-distance bus station, the tourist guest house and a couple of plodding donkey carts all within easy walking distance of each other. Most of the sights are scattered on the outskirts of the oasis or in the surrounding desert.

**CITS** is at the Turpan Guest House. The staff at the reception desk handle enquiries, some speak quite good English and are friendly and helpful.

**Public Security** has its foreign affairs office in the Turpan Guest House. The office is open when it's open and closed when it's closed (remember this is a laid-back town). In mid-1983 they'd cross out permits for Xining (which at the time was closed to individuals) and also Kashgar and any other towns that weren't officially open but which people had managed to

get permits for. But they'd readily give third extensions on visas and a few people even got two-month extensions – something none of the other public security offices were doing any more.

**CAAC** There are no flights to Turpan and the nearest airport is at Ürümqi.

**Bank** The only place to change money and travellers cheques is the Bank of China, a 20 minute walk from the Guest House (refer to the map in this book for directions).

**Post** There is a post office in the Turpan Guest House which is open 8 to 9.30 am, noon to 5 pm and 7 to 9.30 pm.

**Maps** There are no maps available of the oasis itself though there is supposed to be a large one hanging in a back room of the Guest House. The reception desk of the Guest House distributes a fairly good map (in Chinese) of the surrounding area, showing the little villages and the historical sites.

### Things to See
#### Imin Pagoda (Sugongta Mosque)
On the eastern outskirts of Turpan is this unusual mosque with its single minaret,

designed in a simple Afghani style and built in the late 1770s by a local ruler. The pagoda is circular, 44 metres high and tapering towards the top.

The mosque is a half hour walk from the Turpan Guest House. Turn left out of the hotel and left again at the first crossroads; this road leads straight down to the mosque. There is a hole in the wall at the side of the mosque so you can get into the main building. If you want to climb the pagoda you'll have to get the door to the stairway unlocked by the keeper who lives in the small whitewashed building at the side of the mosque.

### Gaochang

About 46 km east of Turpan are the ruins of Gaochang, the capital of the Uygurs when they moved into the Xinjiang region from Mongolia in the ninth century. It had originally been founded in the seventh century during the Tang Dynasty and became a major staging post on the Silk Road.

The walls of the city are clearly visible. They stood as much as 12 metres thick, formed a rough square 6 km in circumference, and were surrounded by a moat. The city was divided into an outer city, an inner city within the walls, and a palace and government compound. A large monastery in the south-west part of the city is in reasonable condition with some of its rooms, corridors and doorways still preserved.

### Atsana Graves

These are the graves where the dead of Gaochang are buried and they are to the north-west of the ancient city. Only three of the tombs are open to tourists and each of these is approached by a short flight of steps which leads down to the burial chamber about six metres below ground level.

One tomb has portraits of the people who are buried here painted on the walls, while another has paintings of birds. The third tomb contains three well-preserved

corpses like those in the museums at Ürümqi and Hangzhou. Some of the artefacts which have been excavated from the tombs date back as far as the Jin Dynasty of the third to fifth centuries AD. The finds included silks, brocades, embroideries and many funerary objects such as shoes, hats and sashes which were made of recycled paper. The last turned out to be quite a find for the archaeologists since the paper included deeds, records of slave purchases, orders for silk and other everyday transactions.

### Flaming Mountains

To the north of Gaochang lie the aptly-named Flaming Mountains, a 100 km long and 10 km wide and purplish-brown in colour – they look like they're on fire in the mid-day sun and hence the name.

### Bezelik 1000-Buddha Caves

Situated on the western side of the Flaming Mountains on a cliff face fronting a river valley are the remains of these Buddhist cave temples. All the caves are in dreadful condition, most having been devastated by Moslems or robbed by all and sundry. The large statues which stood at the rear of each cave have been destroyed or stolen and the faces of the Buddhas which ornament the walls have either been scrapped or completely gouged out. Particularly active in the export of murals was a German Albert von Le Coq, who removed whole frescoes from the stone walls and transported them back to the Berlin Museum – where Allied bombing wiped most of them out during World War II. Today the caves permit little more than a hint of what they were like in their heyday.

### Jiaohe

Jiaohe was established during the Han Dynasty as a garrison town used by the Chinese army to defend the border lands. The city was totally decimated by the Genghis Khan travelling roadshow but you'd be forgiven if you thought it had

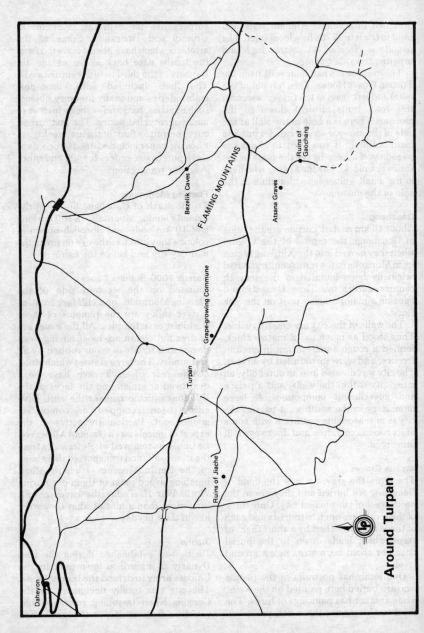

**Around Turpan**

Ruins of Gaochang

Atsana Graves

FLAMING MOUNTAINS

Bezelik Caves

Grape-growing Commune

Turpan

Ruins of Jiache

Daheyon

been struck by an A-bomb. The buildings are rather more obvious than the ruins of Gaochang though, and you can walk through the old streets and along the roads. A main road cuts through the city, and at the end is a large monastery with figures of Buddha still visible.

The ruins are 20 km east of Turpan and stand on an island bounded by two small rivers – thus the name Jiaohe, which means 'confluence of two rivers'. You can get out to the ruins on a donkey cart; it's about a 1½ hour ride from the hotel and the return trip will only cost you Y3 (or maybe Y4 if there are two of you). There's an artificial lake close to the ruins if you want to go swimming.

### Places to Stay

The *Turpan Binguan* is the only hotel you can stay at, and it's one of the most pleasant in China. There are a couple of older wings as well as a new wing which takes the soya sauce as one of the grossest buildings in the country – imitation red pillars, white plaster relief decorations, green walls with yellow trim and even domes on the roof. On the other hand the vine trellises are a good place to sit around at night contemplating the moon and saturating yourself with beer. When there's a tour group in town there's a performance of Uygur music, song and dancing in the courtyard under the grape trellises. It starts around 9.30 pm and is free to all. They're fun nights that usually end up with the front row of the audience being dragged out to dance with the performers, who must rate as some of the spunkiest girls in China.

Rates are Y5 for a dormitory bed, Y19 for a double room in the old wing, or Y30 for a double room (with shower and toilet) in the new wing. Double rooms will probably be readily given for half price if you're on your own. The common toilets and showers have doors and partitions, but the opening hours of the showers are utterly haphazard.

The hotel is a short walk from the long-distance bus station; turn left out of the station and walk down the main road, through the first cross-road and then turn right at the first T-intersection. The hotel is in a grey-washed compound down this road on the left.

### Places to Eat

The *Turpan Binguan* is the best place to eat – the food is excellent! Hotel meals are a flat Y3.50 each and more than worth the money. Breakfast is very good at a flat Y2. There is a small market down a lane approximately opposite the bus station where you can get shish kebab and flat bread and there are also some small food stalls here. The *Turpan Restaurant* on the same road which leads to the bank (see the map) might also be worth checking out.

### Getting Around

Public transport around Turpan is by donkey cart; there are no buses. If you walk then remember that Turpan is really spread out. You can believe those stories about this being the hottest place in China so take a water bottle with you! The middle of the day can be searing and the streets are almost bare of people.

There are three possible ways of getting to the sights which are scattered around Turpan. You can rent a taxi from the hotel at a rate of 50 fen per km. Or you may be able to go with a tour group, and you'll be charged about Y10 for this. Or you can get enough people together and hire a minivan from the hotel. These seat 12 people and a trip including the Gaochang ruins, Atsana Graves, Bezelik Caves, Flaming Mountains and the Iman Pagoda will cost each person about Y12. (If there's time left, you might also stop off at one of the grape-growing communes.) If you want to go on a minibus trip then look out for the Hong Kongers – they travel in little gangs and you should be able to tag along with them.

### Getting Away

Getting out of Turpan is a confused affair

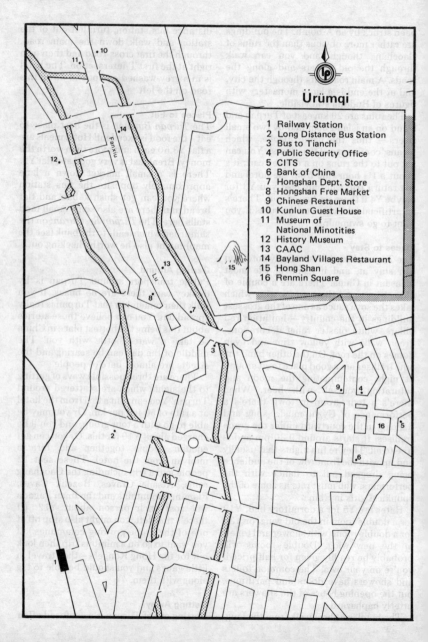

## Ürümqi

1 Railway Station
2 Long Distance Bus Station
3 Bus to Tianchi
4 Public Security Office
5 CITS
6 Bank of China
7 Hongshan Dept. Store
8 Hongshan Free Market
9 Chinese Restaurant
10 Kunlun Guest House
11 Museum of
   National Minotities
12 History Museum
13 CAAC
14 Bayland Villages Restaurant
15 Hong Shan
16 Renmin Square

but most people make it to the outside world by some means or another.

**Bus** The bus station is a nondescript grey-washed building with blue doors and window shutters on the main street. The ticket windows at the bus station never seem to be open. So just turn up early and buy your ticket on the day of departure from the guy who stands around outside selling them. Make sure you get to the station an hour or even more before departure, because absolutely *no one* seems to know when the buses depart! If you can find out you're a genius! There are buses from here to Ürümqi and to Daheyon.

Departure times for the buses to Ürümqi have been variously described as 7 am, 7.30 am, 8.30 am, 1 pm, and 6 pm – although there are only supposed to be two buses a day. My bus departed at 7.30 am, stopped for an hour at 10 am for a meal and arrived in Ürümqi at around 12.45 pm. It's great scenery along the way, passing by immense grey sand-dunes and there are snow-capped mountains visible in the distance as you approach Ürümqi. The fare to Ürümqi is Y4.90.

**Train** The nearest train line is the Ürümqi-Lanzhou line to the north of Turpan. The nearest railway station is at the small hole of Daheyon. Departure times for buses from Turpan to Daheyon have been given as 8 am, 8.30 am, 9 am, 5 pm, 5.30 pm, 6 pm although there are only supposed to be two buses a day. A departure time of around 7.30 am or 8 am as well as one at 6 pm are probably the best bet – and *apparently* it takes two hours for the bus to get to Daheyon! Try to avoid going to Daheyon (see that section for details).

**Plane** The nearest airport is Ürümqi (see that section for details).

## ÜRÜMQI

In the centre of Ürümqi is a desolate rocky outcrop called Hong Shan. Steps to the top lead to a small pavilion from which you can get a panoramic view of the great expanse of dusty roads, shimmering apartment blocks and smokestacks that have sprung out of the surrounding desolation. Ürümqi is an interesting place to visit but it's got to be one of the ugliest cities on the face of the earth!

The capital of Xinjiang, the city boomed after the Communists built the railway line from Lanzhou across the Xinjiang desert. 800,000 people live here now, 75% of them Han Chinese – though the place has always been a Chinese island in a sea of Moslems. The inspired concrete block architecture of Socialist Eastern China has been imported lock stock and barrel, and Ürümqi essentially looks little different from its northern Han China counterparts 1500 miles east, just uglier. There are few 'sights' as such, but there's an intrinsic interest to the place which makes it worth visiting.

Two and a half days up the rail line from Xian and in the same country, you couldn't hope to come across a people more different from the Chinese than the Uygurs. Ürümqi is the first place you'll see these swarthy-skinned Turkic descendants in any number; larger and heavier than the Han Chinese, their features resemble Caucasians and many of them could easily pass for southern Italians or for Greeks. The Uygur women wear skirts or dresses and brightly coloured scarves, in contrast to the slacks and baggy trousers of the Han Chinese, and they pierce their ears – a practice which repels the Han. The Uygur men must be the only men in China capable of growing beards. Arm's distance from the Uygurs are the Han Chinese immigrants as well as the PLA soldiers who are not only there to keep the Russians at bay and maintain Chinese control over Xinjiang but also to keep the tenuous peace between the Uygurs and the Han. It's hard not to feel you're in the provincial capital of a foreign occupation force.

## Information & Orientation

Ürümqi is a sort of blob-shaped city with an urban peninsula to the north. Most of the sights, tourist facilities and hotels are scattered across the city though they're all easily accessible by the local buses.

The railway station and long-distance bus station are in the south-eastern corner of the city, the main tourist hotel and a couple of museums are in the northern peninsula. There are two candidates for the title of 'city centre': one is the area around the large Hongshan Department Store where some of the major arteries intersect; the other is in the eastern part of the city which is the main shopping district and is also the location of useful things like the CITS office, Public Security and the Bank of China.

**CITS** (tel 5794) is opposite Renmin Square which lies in the eastern part of the city. The compound in which the office is located is across the road from the eastern side of the square. There is no sign, but the entrance to the compound is through two large green metal gates which lead to a car and bus park. The CITS office is in the yellow concrete building on your left as you enter the compound. The guy here speaks good English and is friendly and helpful. The office is open Monday to Saturday 9.30 am to 1 pm and 4 to 8 pm. It's closed on Sundays. A bus No 1 from the Kunlun Guest House will take you most of the way to the office.

**Public Security** is a ten-minute walk from the CITS office, in a large government building just to the north-west of Renmin Square (refer to the map in this book). To get there from the Kunlun Hotel take bus No 1 – it goes straight past the building.

**CAAC** is on Fanxiu Lu, the same road that the Kunlun Guest House is on, and it's open 10 am to 1.30 pm and 4 to 8 pm. Buses No 1 and No 2 from the guest house go straight past the office.

**Bank** The Bank of China is the only place to change money and travellers cheques. Take bus No 1 eight stops from the Kunlun Hotel and then retrace the tyre marks a hundred metres. The bank is a large grey colonnaded building.

**Post** There is a post office on the ground floor of the Kunlun Guest House. The main post office is a big Corinthian-colonnaded building directly across the the traffic circle from the Hongshan Department Store.

**Maps** There are good maps, in Chinese and showing the bus routes, available from the shop on the ground floor of the Kunlun Guest House.

## Things to See

As mentioned earlier, Ürümqi has few 'sights' as such and much of the interest of the city is intrinsic. Worth exploring, though, are two of the museums which house some interesting exhibits. A couple of hours drive from the city in the Tai Mountains is the stunning Lake of Heaven.

## Museum of National Minorities

Xinjiang covers 16% of China's total land surface. It is inhabited not only by the Han Chinese but also by 13 of China's official total of 55 minority peoples. The museum contains an interesting exhibition relating to some of the Xinjiang minority groups and it's well worth a look in. It's on Fanxiu Lu, a few minutes walk from the Kunlun Guest House, but on the opposite side of the road.

Notable amongst the exhibits are the Daur hats which are made of the heads of animals and have large fur rims – the Daur number about 94,000 and are spread across Xinjiang, Inner Mongolia and Heilongjiang. The Tajik exhibition features silver and coral beads supporting silver pendants – these people number about 26,500 and are found only in Xinjiang. The Kazakhs (better known on the other side of the border as Cossacks) number about 900,000 and their exhibition in the museum features a heavily furnished yurt. The Mongol exhibit includes particularly ornate silver bridles and saddles studded with semi-precious stones, stringed musical instruments and decorated boots.

## History Museum

This is probably one of the best museums in China – many of the captions are in English and the collection is quite large. Prime exhibits are the preserved bodies of two men and two women discovered in tombs in Xinjiang, similar to those you may have seen in the museum at Hangzhou. The collection of multi-coloured clay figurines unearthed from Turpan and dating back to the Tang Dynasty and the collection of silk fragments with various patterns from different dynasties are also interesting.

## The Southern Pastures

The southern pastures are a vast expanse of grazing land south of Ürümqi – it's probably the same area that the railway line passes through after crossing the Tian Mountains. The land is inhabited by Kazakh herdsmen who graze sheep, cattle and horses here during the summer months. Curious stories have been told of the gangs of Hong Kong Chinese who come down here by the minibus-load. Unused to vast open spaces or to the sight of animals almost in the wild, they leap from the bus and charge at the un-suspecting creatures who scatter in all directions. A distraught Kazakh herdsman rides up waving his arms in the air and shouting abuse, eventually having to be placated by the tour guide with apologies and cigarettes. I suppose such things happen . . .

There is said to be a local bus to the pasturelands – otherwise you'll probably have to hire a taxi from the Kunlun Guest House. The pastures are about 65 km from Ürümqi and the guest house charges 50 fen per km.

## Tianchi – the Lake of Heaven

The Lake of Heaven is a sight you'll never forget. Half-way up a mountain in the middle of a desert, it looks like a chunk of Switzerland or Canada that's been picked up and dumped in the oblivion end of China. It's a small deep-blue lake, surrounded by hills covered with fir trees and grazed by horses. Scattered around are the yurts of the Kazakh people who inhabit the mountains; in the distance are the snow-covered peaks of the Tian range and you can climb the hills right up to the snowline.

The Lake is situated 50 km east of Ürümqi on the 5445 metre high Bogda Feng, the Peak of God. The lake freezes over in Xinjiang's bitter winter and the roads up here are only open in the summer months.

There are daily buses from Ürümqi to Tianchi. You buy your ticket at a small booth on the northern side of the People's Park (Renmin Gongyuan) which is in the centre of Ürümqi. Buses depart from here at 7.50 am and the trip to Tianchi takes 3½ to 4 hours. They depart Tianchi for Ürümqi at 4 pm.

A one-way ticket costs Y2. A round-trip ticket costs Y5; this ticket is valid for any day but you only have a reserved seat if you come back on the same day. If you buy a return ticket and want to come back *another* day but still want a reserved seat, then it costs you Y7.50.

The bus will probably drop you off at the end of the lake – from there it's a 20 minute walk to the hotel which is on the banks of the lake. The bus back to Ürümqi leaves from a bus park just over a low ridge at the back of the hotel. The buses usually leave at 4 pm but they may go a little earlier. If you stay overnight then you'll have the place pretty much to yourself in the morning and after 4 pm since most people only come up here on day trips. Some people have hitched on trucks up to Tianchi.

The *Heavenly Lake Hotel* is situated right on the banks of the lake. It's a garish building utterly out of place with the blues and greens of the surroundings. There are rooms for six people at Y4 per bed, rooms for four people at Y8 per bed and double rooms for Y10 per bed. The manager here speaks some English and is very friendly. The hotel also has a little boat which takes people for a spin around the lake for Y1 each.

Just near where the bus from Ürümqi drops you off there is a camp site where you can stay in yurts for Y2 per person. The other possibility, of course, is to hike into the hills and go camping – it's a great opportunity, and a rare one in China. And the surrounding countryside is absolutely stunning!

The hotel seems to be the only place to eat. Lunch is Y5 – OK, but forgettable. The beer sells at Y1.10 a bottle, a tolerable brew but a bit tasteless.

### Shihezi

A couple of hours drive north-west of Ürümqi is the town of Shihezi (the name means Stony Creek); it's a Chinese outpost and almost all the inhabitants are Hans. The town is officially open to foreigners, though you need a permit, and you can get there by bus from Ürümqi (see the 'Getting Away' section).

### Places to Stay

The *Kunlun Guest House* is Ürümqi's main tourist joint. Cheapest accommodation is Y3 per bed in a four-bed room – the only problem is that apart from the small basin in the room there is nowhere to wash. Double rooms are Y30, with toilet and shower, and if you're on your own they'll readily give you the room for Y15. From the railway station take bus No 2 (the stop is right outside the station) and the bus will drop you off just a few minutes walk before the hotel.

If the Kunlun Guest House is full (and it sometimes is) there is another hotel around the corner which may put you up; ask the Kunlun staff to contact them first. To get there turn right out of the Kunlun

and right again at the first crossroads; the hotel is a brown brick, L-shaped building about a five minute walk down on the right-hand side of the road. It's Y2.50 for a bed in a three-bed room. It's a clean, modern place but very noisy.

The *Yanan Hotel* is a new tourist hotel in the south of the city, and double rooms go for around Y30; it's a long way from anything and you'd be better off staying at the Kunlun.

### Places to Eat

Although you won't starve, you're no more likely to find a marvellous banquet in Ürümqi than you are in any other Chinese city. For evening munchies, turn left out of the Kunlun Guest House and walk for about 15 minutes up the main street. You'll find lots of little stalls set up in the evening selling flat bread and shish kebab; 20 fen for the bread and 10 fen for each stick of shish kebab. Makes a great change from the rice and veggies.

For dumplings, try the *Bayland Villages Restaurant* (there's a sign in English) which is a little further up from the shish kebab stalls. According to the sign the restaurant serves a varied menu of 'Chinese & Western, Table D'Hote, Cheap Cold Dish, Convenient Snack'.

The restaurant on the ground floor of the *Kunlun Guest House* is best avoided except by the famished. For more flat bread and shish kebab try the *Hongshan Market* which is opposite the Hongshan Department Store. It's a bustling little covered market, with innumerable little food stalls and restaurants. There is a restaurant on the corner directly opposite the Public Security Office which serves reasonable Chinese food.

### Getting Around

From the east to the west, from the north to the south the wonders of Ürümqi are accessible by bus. Taxis are available for hire from the Kunlun Guest House.

### Getting Away

Escape from Ürümqi is by bus, train or plane – there are no boats.

**Bus** The long-distance bus station is in the western part of town. Buses depart for Shihezi at 8 am; the fare is Y4.00. Buses depart for Turpan at 9 am and the fare is Y4.90. Buses depart for Kashgar at 9 am and the fare is Y38.30 (Good luck!). Check out the colourful little mosque opposite the bus station while you're down there.

**Train** From Ürümqi there are trains running straight through to Beijing via Lanzhou, Yinchuan, Baotou, Hohhot and Datong; to Zhengzhou via Xian; to Beijing via Xian, Zhengzhou and Shijiazhuang; to Shanghai via Xian, Zhengzhou and Nanjing.

**Plane** Ürümqi is connected by air with Beijing (Y416), Lanzhou (Y226), Shanghai (Y452) and Xian (Y289). There are also flights from Ürümqi to the following places in Xinjiang; Fuyun, Altay, Karamay, Yining, Korla, Kuqa, Aksu, Kashgar, Hotan and Qiemo.

### KASHGAR

Kashgar, like Timbuktu, is one of those fabled cities that everyone seems to know about but no-one seems to get to. A thousand years ago it was a key centre on the Silk Road and Marco Polo passed through commenting that 'the inhabitants live by trade and industry. They have fine orchards and vineyards and flourishing estates. Cotton grows here in plenty, besides flax and hemp. The soil is fruitful and productive of all the means of life. The country is the starting-point from which many merchants set out to market their wares all over the world'.

In the early part of this century, Kashgar was a relatively major town on the edge of a vast nowhere and separated from the rest of China by an endless sandpit. Traders from India tramped to Kashgar via Gilgit and the Hunza Valley;

in 1890 the British sent a trade agent to Kashgar to represent their interests and in 1908 they established a consulate. Like Tibet in the 1890s the rumour machine soon spread the word that the Russians were on the verge of gobbling up Xinjiang.

To most people Kashgar, which is five or six weeks journey over 15,000 foot passes from the nearest railhead in India, must seem a place barbarously remote; but for us its outlandish name spelt civilisation. The raptures of arrival were unqualified. Discovery is a delightful process, but rediscovery is better; few people can ever have enjoyed a bath more than we did, who had not had one for five and a half months.

That is how Peter Fleming described his arrival in Kashgar back in 1935, after he and Kini Maillart had spent almost half a year on the backs of camels and donkeys getting there from Beijing.

Fleming described the city as being 'in effect run by the secret police, the Russian advisers, and the Soviet Consulate, and most of the high officials were only figureheads'. The rest of the foreign community consisted of the British Consul and his wife, their fifteen Hunza guards from the north of Pakistan, and a couple of Swedish missionaries.

Contact with the Soviet Union seemed to make sense given the geographical location of Kashgar. Ethnically, culturally, linquistically, and theologically the inhabitants of Kashgar had absolutely nothing in common with the Chinese and everything in common with the Moslem inhabitants on the other side of the border. Whereas it took a five month camel and donkey ride to get to Beijing and a five or six week hike to reach the nearest railhead in British India (although mail runners could do it in two), the Soviet railhead at Osh was more accessible. and from Kashgar strings of camels would stalk westward with their bales of wool and whatever, returning with cargoes of Russian cigarettes, matches and sugar.

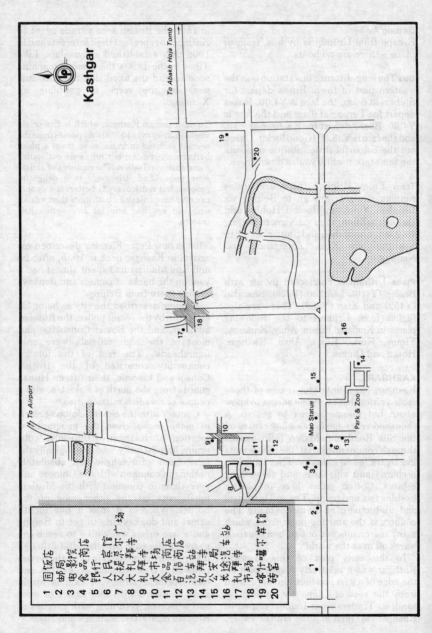

Kashgar

To Abakh Hoja Tomb

To Airport

To Abakh Hoja Tomb

Mao Statue

Park & Zoo

1 回饭店
2 邮局
3 电影院
4 食品商店
5 银行
6 人民饭店
7 提孜乃甫礼拜寺
8 大礼拜寺
9 大食品商店
10 礼拜寺
11 食品商店
12 百货商店
13 汽车站
14 礼拜寺
15 公安局
16 水途泛礼拜寺
17 市场
18 礼拜寺
19 喀什噶尔市场
20 砖窑

Rumours and also banquets seemed to be at their peak of eccentricity in Kashgar. Fleming describes his last night in Kashgar and a banquet given by the city officials 'half in their honour and half in ours . . . You never know what may not happen at a banquet in Kashgar and each of our official hosts had prudently brought his own bodyguard. Turkic and Chinese soldiers lounged everywhere; automatic rifles and executioner's swords were much in evidence, and the Mauser pistols of the waiters knocked ominously against the back of your chair as they leant over you with the dishes'. Speeches were made by just about everyone, feverishly translated into English, Russian, Chinese and Turkic and no one was assassinated.

The Kashgar of today has lost much the 'romantic' value that made eating there during the '30s a slightly nervous experience. When the Communists came to power the city walls were ripped down and a huge glistening white statue of Chairman Mao was erected on the main street. The statue stands today, hand outstretched to the sky above and the lands beyond, a constant reminder to the local populace of the alien regime that controls the city. About 120,000 people live here, and apart from the Uygur majority the number includes Tajiks, Kergezs and Uzbeks. The Han Chinese are relatively small in number, nothing like the horde that dominates Ürümqi, although PLA troops are always conspicuous. Nor does it take six months to reach

Kashgar; it's a three-day bus ride from Ürümqi or you can fly out in a couple of hours if you have more consideration for your bum. No longer so remote, nor so fabled, the city sounds like a disappointment—yet the peculiar quality of Kashgar is that every so often you chance to glance on some scene that suggests a different age and a world removed from China.

In some ways times seem to have changed little for the intrepid China traveller as Fleming relates. . .

One night we slept on the floor, drank tea in mugs, ate doughy bread, argued with officials, were stared at, dreaded the next day's heat; twenty-four hours later we were sitting in comforatable arm chairs with long drinks and illustrated ppers and a gramaphone playing, all cares and privations banished. It was a heavenly experience.

**Permits** As the situation stands in mid-1983 Kashgar is closed to westerners, though Hong Kongers are free to travel there and the occasional Overseas Chinese tour group is taken out. Sometime in mid-1983 Kashgar did a Lhasa and a couple of people got permits for the city; some of the Public Security Offices may have goofed up, been given incorrect information or the Chinese may even have deliberately given out permits just to see how much interest there was in the place. In any case it's hard to describe the childish sort of thrill you get coming away from a public security office clutching a little brown-paper permit to forbidden

| | | | |
|---|---|---|---|
| 1 | Tuen Parks Hotel | 11 | Foodstore |
| 2 | Post Office | 12 | Dept. Store |
| 3 | Cinema | 13 | Local Bus Station |
| 4 | Foodstore | 14 | Mosque |
| 5 | Bank | 15 | Public Security Office |
| 6 | Renmin Hotel | 16 | Long Distance Bus Station |
| 7 | Id Kah Square & Clock Tower | 17 | Mosque |
| 8 | Id Kah Mosque | 18 | Market |
| 9 | Mosque | 19 | Kashgar Guesthouse |
| 10 | Main Bazaar | 20 | Brick Kilns |

places, duly stamped with the sort of red seal that bank tellers use.

I got my permit in Luoyang and flew from Ürümqi to Kashgar; there was no trouble buying an air ticket and they checked my travel permit when I bought the ticket and again at the airport. I landed at Kashgar, took the bus to the centre and wandered around for three hours before encountering the police chief who hauled me off to Public Security. Friendly lot; they let me stay for three days, which was fair enough. From then on I was free to wander around where I wanted, though they told me not to leave Kashgar and not to go to the Pakistani/China border. And they let me take the bus back to Ürümqi.

Oddly enough, while I was in Kashgar there was an American tour group of about six people – they got here because they knew a foreign-expert friend in Beijing who knew someone in CITS. Another pair of American travellers who made it out on their own towards the end of 1983 were told by Public Security that they would have been allowed to carry on to Pakistan if they had visas for that country.

### Information & Orientation

The oasis only has two substantial thoroughfares, one running east-west and the other north-south. On the main intersection are three ugly yellow, colon-naded buildings dating back to 1956, rapidly transforming into archaeological ruins; on one corner is the Renmin Hotel, opposite is the **Bank of China** and diagonally opposite the hotel is a cinema.

North of the main intersection are a number of shops, a large department store adjacent to a bookstore and a large food store. The small streets to the right lead to the **bazaar**, and on the opposite side of the main road is the **Id Kah Square** and the large **Id Kah Mosque** from which a number of small market streets lead off in all directions. The main road leads to the airfield.

East of the main intersection is the huge **Mao statue**, and opposite is a large square and the **park and zoo**. Further down on the left is the **Public Security Office** in a whitewashed compound and on the right is the **long-distance bus station**. The road leads to the Kashgar Guest House. West of the main intersection is the **post office** and the **Tuen Parks Hotel**.

There are no maps of Kashgar available at the moment, though there's one (in Chinese) up in the waiting hall of the long-distance bus station which may help you orientate yourself.

### Things to See

Kashgar is a giant oasis. The focus of activity is the bazaar and the Id Kah mosque and square, and the 'suburbs' are the clusters of adobe houses congregated around the centre; beyond them lie the small villages scattered in the midst of huge tracts of wheatfields. The bus from the airfield takes you down the main road, where the uninspired architecture of socialist eastern China is making an impact in various stages of construction. It's hardly the bustling central Asian exotica you may have been expecting, but don't let these first impressions put you off.

Some of the best areas for walking are east of the main bazaar, and north-west of the Id Kah Mosque. To the south of the centre is a large cluster of mud brick houses covering a sort of plateau and these are worth a wander round. The streets are lined by continuous high walls, some of them white-washed, and the dusty streets are clogged with little children in hot pursuit of the strange foreigner! The adults don't tend to gather round foreigners like the Han Chinese, but the Uygur children do–and they come in plague proportions and if you've got a camera then spare plenty of film for photos of every kid on the block! A foreign face, rare as it is, is usually assumed to be an American – but quite often they'll ask you if you're a Pakistani, and three people

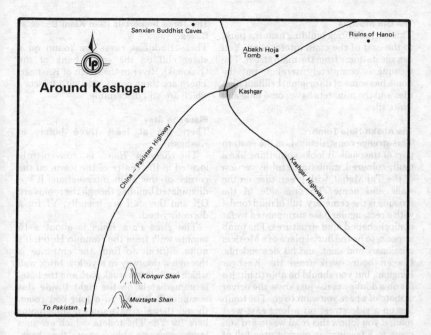

**Around Kashgar**

Sanxian Buddhist Caves

Ruins of Hanoi

Abakh Hoja Tomb

Kashgar

China – Pakistan Highway

Kashgar Highway

Kongur Shan

Muztagta Shan

To Pakistan

even asked if I was a 'Hindustani' (maybe it was the suntan?).

## The Bazaar

The bazaar is the focus of activity in Kashgar. The main market-street can be reached from the laneways opposite the Id Kah Square which run off the main north-south road. Kashgar is noted for its ornate knives which are sold in the bazaar and by hawkers in the streets. It's also a hat-making centre and the northern end of the street is devoted entirely to stalls selling embroidered caps and fur-lined headgear. Blacksmiths pound away on anvils here as if the Industrial Revolution was just a dream, colourfully painted wooden saddles can be bought, or you can pick your dinner from a choice line-up of goats' heads and hoofs. Old Asian men with long, thick beards, fur overcoats and high leather boots swelter in the sun. The Moslem Uygur women here dress in skirts and

stockings like the Uygur women in Ürümqi and Turpan, but there's a much greater prevalence of faces hidden behind long brown gauze veils. In the evening the Id Kah Square is a bustling marketplace and there are numerous market streets leading off from the square. Sunday is *the* time to be in Kashgar.

## The Id Kah Mosque

The Id Kah Mosque is a stark contrast to the Chinese-style architecture of the mosques in the east of the country, such as Canton and Xian. The Id Kah looks like it's been lifted out of Pakistan or Afghanistan and has the features which westerners usually associate with a mosque; the central dome and the flanking minarets. Prayer time is around 10 pm, though that may vary throughout the year. There are also smaller mosques scattered amongst the houses on the streets around the centre of Kashgar.

## The Old Mosque

This is a mud brick building near the park, to the east of the main intersection. You can see its dome from the main street. The mosque is completely derelict, but the dome has some of its original brilliant blue tiles and the minarets have some blue and white tiles.

## The Abakh Hoja Tomb

This strange construction is in the eastern part of the oasis. It looks something like a multi-coloured, miniature, stubby version of the Taj Mahal, with green tiles on the walls and dome. To one side of the mosque is the cemetery, full of mud tombs with a rectangular base surmounted by fat conical-shaped mud structures. The tomb appears to be the burial place of a Moslem missionary and saint, and his descendents. It's an hours walk from the Kashgar Binguan, but you should be able to hitch a lift on a donkey cart – just show the driver a photo of where you want to go. The tomb lies on a side street off a long east-west road; if you follow this road westward you come to a fascinating market area full of stalls and mud-brick houses and *nothing* to indicate you're in China!

## The Park and Zoo

The park is a pleasant place to sit down but the zoo is depressing. The kindest thing you could do for some of the animals here would be to put a bullet in their heads. In front of the entrance to the park is a large square and on the opposite side of the road is the massive glistening white statue of Mao Zedong.

## Hanoi

The ruins of this ancient city lie about 30 km east of Kashgar. The town reached its apex during the Tang and Song dynasties but appears to have been abandoned after the 11th century. To get out here you'll probably have to try and hire a jeep at the Kashgar Binguan – apparently it's a rough ride.

## The Three Immortals (San Xian) Buddhist Caves

These Buddhist caves are found on a sheer cliff on the south bank of the Qiakmakh River to the north of Kashgar. There are three caves, one with frescoes which are still discernible.

## Places to Stay

There are at least three hotels in Kashgar.

The *Renmin Hotel* is conveniently located in the centre of the town, on the corner of the main intersection. It's a dilapidated building though the rooms are OK and the staff are friendly; Y1 for a dormitory bed.

The *Tuen Park Hotel* is about a 15 minute walk from the Renmin Hotel. It's quite difficult to find; the entrance is through a doorway in a yellow brick wall which leads into a truck park and the hotel is immediately on the right inside this compound. It's Y2 in a four-bed room, though they also have some double rooms here for Y8. The toilets, which are in a large concrete block out the back, absolutely reek. There also seems to be nowhere to wash except for a few taps in the yard – a distinct disadvantage after you've been walking around this hot, dusty place all day.

The *Kashgar Binguan* is the best hotel in town and is up to the same good standard of any other basic Chinese tourist hotel further east. The problem with this place is that it's so far out from the middle of town – a good hour's walk to the main intersection and there's no bus. You can usually wave down a jeep or a truck or hitch a lift on a donkey cart. There are double rooms here in building No 1 for Y20 (with shower and toilet) but if you're alone they'll probably give one to you for Y10. A bed in a four-bed room in one of the other buildings is Y4 but it's very noisy. There's a little shop just inside the front gate which sells bottled fruit.

**Places to Eat**

You won't starve in Kashgar, but restaurant city it ain't!

The *Tuen Park Hotel* has a restaurant serving ordinary but OK Chinese food. The *Kashgar Binguan* serves Chinese meals for Y14 each(!) and the beer here is warm and Y2 a bottle.

Flat bread and shish kebab is sold at the little huddle of stalls on the main road, just west of the big square opposite the Mao statue. 20 fen for the bread and 10 fen for each kebab. There are a couple of excellent ice-cream stalls here too – about 20 fen for a glassful – very cold and very vanilla! There are more icecream stalls in the Id Kah Square and you should find eggs and roast chicken sold near the main intersection at night.

Jarred and canned fruit is available from the large food-store opposite the Id Kah Square on the main north-south road. There's a smaller store next to the cinema on the main intersection selling the same. You can buy eggs near the long-distance bus station; the ones painted red are hard-boiled.

There are some small restaurants right next to the Renmin Hotel which serve some tasty little morsels. Notable are the small rectangles of crisp pastry enveloping fried mince-meat. There are also some food stalls near the post office.

**Getting Around**

There are no city buses; to get around you have to walk or try waving down a jeep, truck or donkey cart. The most common transport in Kashgar is bicycle or donkey cart, and there's also the odd horse-drawn cart. There are jeeps at the Kashgar Binguan and you may be able to hire one and get out of town to see some of the more distant sights.

**Getting Away**

**Buses** There are buses from the long-distance bus station to Daheyon, Ürümqi, Aksu, Maralbixi, Hotan, Yingisar, Payziwat, Yopuria, Makit, Yakam and Kaoilik. The station is on a side-street off the main east-west road, and the ticket office and waiting hall is a large white building readily identifiable by its yellow doors and the Red Star over the main entrance.

There is a daily bus to Ürümqi via Aksu, Korla and Toksun. It's a 3½ day trip costing Y38.90. Tickets for the bus can only be bought one day before departure and the bus is scheduled to depart Kashgar at 8 am.

The bus to Turpan actually goes to Daheyon, stopping overnight at Aksu and Korla and going straight through Toksun on to Daheyon. The trip takes three days. Again, tickets for the bus can only be bought a day before departure. Daheyon is a small railway town on the Lanzhou-Ürümqi line and to get to nearby Turpan there are two buses a day – see the Daheyon section for details.

**Air** There are daily flights from Kashgar to Ürümqi and the fare is Y215. You fly out in a two-engined prop plane which stops briefly at Aksu to load and unload passengers. The flight takes about four to five hours including the stop at Aksu, and is worth doing at least once just to get some grasp of the immense desolation that is north-west China.

**KASHGAR to TURPAN – BY BUS**

**Day 1** The departure from Kashgar begins with a magnificent view of the Pamir Mountains spread out across the horizon. To the north of the road is the Tian Mountain range with its strange stratas of red, yellow and greenish-coloured rock and to the south is the endless southern desert. Every so often the bus pulls into some trucking stop where you can wash down some noodles and meat with a beer, watched by an ever-curious local gathering. At one of these miserable little stops somewhere out in the middle of utterly nowhere stood a large tattered stone column displaying a faded portrait of Chairman Mao – reminiscent of the pillars that Emperor Ashoka erected all over

India. It's a rough road, not recommended for those with bad backs.

The first big place you pass through is Aksu, and you may stop here or you may go straight through and overnight at another centre. Aksu is an enormous wind-swept oasis, a stark contrast to the surrounding desert.

My bus went through Aksu and overnighted further on. The hotel is at the bus station and is Y1.20 for a bed in an 8-bed dormitory. The bunk beds have thick quilts and you don't need a sleeping bag. Food at the hotel restaurant was surprisingly good, with none of that horrible musky odour permeating the air like you find in restaurants in eastern China. There's hot water for washing from two taps at the back of a shed near the hotel. Toilets were the usual partitionless squat-over holes in a block at the back of the hotel – the surrounding area has plenty of trees to hide behind if you prefer . . .

**Day 2** Departure was at 7.20 am. Mid-way between Aksu and Korla is Kuqa. From Kuqa runs the first highway to cross the previously impassable snow-capped Tianshan range. The asphalted highway is 532 km long and runs to Dushanzi, a new oil-drilling settlement on the north side of the range. Previously it took four days to transport oil from Dushanzi to Kuqa on the circuitous 1000 km route via Ürümqi and Korla, but the new highway cuts the travelling time down to a bit more than a day. The highway, on which construction started in 1974, crosses three rivers and tunnels through three mountains; the longest tunnel is just under 1900 metres. Most of the road is between 1000 and 3500 metres above sea level.

The bus arrives at Korla at about 8.30 pm. Korla is a flat industrial town and a railway line links the town with the Lanzhou-Ürümqi line. The hotel at the bus station was Y1 – though the beds were hard and the bedding fairly grubby. Toilets were clean and had the added luxury of concrete partitions.

**Day 3** The bus leaves Korla at 8 am and passes over a low range of hills after which the scenery is less desolate and interspersed with long stretches of pastureland. This changes dramatically as the bus begins its struggle into rocky hills which fast become increasingly desolate. We emerge on the other side into the Turpan Depression and the first major stop is the nondescript oasis of Toksan. If you're going to Ürümqi you *may* stop here overnight. Buses carrying on to Daheyon go straight through Toksan with only a brief stop, and arrive at Dahyeon around 6.00 pm –earlier or later depending on the enthusiasm of the driver and the decrepitude of the bus.

Be warned that bus schedules don't always run to time and you could take four days to do the trip, driving anything between eight and 14 hours a day depending on breakdowns or whatever. Most of the places you stop off at haven't seen a foreigner for years – at one stop two Americans were followed down the street by a crowd of 300. Suprisingly enough, although several police saw me at various places on the way back to Turpan, not one asked to look at my passport or travel permit – although they were obviously very curious.

As for hitching, traffic on the road between Kashgar and Ürümqi and Daheyon is light, but there are still enough trucks to make it worth considering if you really want to. There is a trucking stop down past the Kashgar long-distance bus station from which trucks head to Urumqi everyday – but I don't know how long this trip takes.

If you want to head out of Kashgar and towards the mountains, then you'll probably find that it's high security all the way in these sensitive border regions and you'll just be sent back – but you may be lucky and able to hitch up with one of the mountaineering troupes which occasionally come through here, but don't count on it.

# Tibet & Qinghai

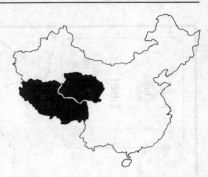

Westerners tend to imagine Tibet as some sort of Shangri-la – a strange projection of one of the world's most barren landscapes; isolated, desolate, bitterly cold in winter high plateau where the thin air can set the heart pounding and the lungs rasping. The Chinese can't understand why anyone would want to go to the oblivion end of their Middle Kingdom with its backward, barbarian people still weighed down with the remnants of their archaic feudal culture. But on the other hand the Chinese don't miss a chance to make a few bucks, and scratch their heads as they may they'll still let you into the place. That is, on a tour – a few lucky people have made it into the region on their own in the last few years but those days seem to be well and truly over. Parts of Qinghai have recently been opened up to individual travellers; the province lies on the north-east border of Tibet and is one of the great cartographical expressions of our time. For centuries this was part of the Tibetan world and today it's separated from the Tibetan homeland by colours on a Chinese-made map.

Most of Tibet is an immense plateau which lies at an altitude of between 4000 to 5000 metres. It's a desolate region broken by a series of east-west mountain ranges, and is completely barren except for some poor grasslands to the south-east. The plateau is bounded to the north by the Kunlun range which separates Tibet from Xinjiang Province and to the south the Himalayas and their peaks rising over 7000 metres.

The Qamdo region of Tibet in the east is a somewhat lower section of plateau, drained by the headwaters of the Salween, Mekong and Upper Yangtse Rivers. It's an area of considerably greater rainfall than the rest of Tibet and the climate is less extreme. Most of the Tibetan population lives in a number of valleys in the south of the country, where some agriculture is possible – the main crop being barley. On the uplands surrounding these valleys the inhabitants are mainly pastoralists, grazing sheep, yaks and horses.

Eastern Qinghai is a high grassland plateau rising between 2500 and 3000 metres above sea level, and slashed through by a series of mountain ranges whose peaks rise to 5000 metres – the source of the Yellow River. Most of the agricultural regions are concentrated in the east around the Xining area but the surrounding uplands and the regions west of Qinghai Lake have good pasturelands grazing sheep, horses and cattle.

North-west Qinghai is a great basin surrounded by mountains. It's littered with salt marshes and saline lakes, afflicted with harsh cold winters, and parts of it are barren desert, but it's also rich in mineral deposits, particularly oil.

Southern Qinghai is a high plateau 3500 metres above sea-level. It's separated from Tibet by a mountain range whose peaks rise to over 6500 metres and the Yangtse and the Mekong have their source here. Like Tibet the climate here is extreme, afflicted by long, bitterly cold winters. Most of the region is grassland and the population is composed almost entirely of semi-nomadic Tibetan herdsmen rearing goats, sheep and yaks.

The population of Tibet is almost 1,900,000 – the number comprises Tibetans as well as the pockets of Han

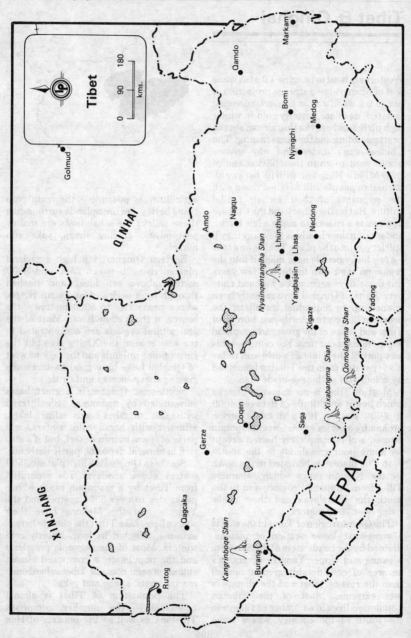

Chinese settlers who probably number around 120 or 130,000. There are, in fact, a total of almost 3,900,000 Tibetans spread out over Tibet, Sichuan, Qinghai, Gansu and Yunnan.

Qinghai has a total population of almost 3,500,000 – a number which may or may not include the unknown number of people imprisoned here in the province's labour camps. The region is a mixed bag of minorities including the Kazaks, Mongols, and Hui. The Tibetans are found throughout the province and the Han settlers are concentrated around the Xining area, the capital of the province.

### History

Recorded Tibetan history begins in the 7th century when the Tibetan armies were considered as great a scourge to their neighbours as the Huns were to Europe. Under King Srong-btsan Sgam-po the Tibetans occupied Nepal and collected tribute from parts of Yunnan Province. Shortly after his death the armies moved north and took control of the 'Silk Road' including the great city of Kashgar. Opposed by Chinese troops, who occupied all of Xinjiang under the Tang Dynasty, the Tibetans responded by sacking the imperial city of Changan. It was not until 842 that Tibetan expansion came to a sudden halt with the assassination of the King, and the region broke up into independent feuding principalities; never again would the Tibetan armies leave their high plateau.

As secular authority waned the power of the Buddhist clergy increased. Since the third century when Buddhism reached Tibet, it had to compete with *bon*, the traditional animistic religion of the region. Buddhism adopted many of the rituals of bon, like the flying of prayer flags and the turning of prayer wheels to form another variation on Buddhism known as 'Tantric Buddhism'. 'Lamaism' is the monastic side of the religion and revolves around the concerted meditation of the monks. The religion had spread through Tibet by the 7th century; after the 9th century the monasteries became increasingly politicised and in 1641 the Yellow Hat sect, a reformist movement advocating stringent monastic discipline, used the support of the Buddhist Mongols to crush the Red Hats, their rivals.

The Yellow Hats' leader adopted the title of Dalai Lama, or Ocean of Wisdom; religion and politics became inextricably entwined, presided over by the Dalai Lama – the God King. Each Dalai Lama was considered the reincarnation of the last; upon his death the monks searched the land for a new-born child who showed some sign of embodying his predecessor's spirit. The Yellow Hats won the Mongols to their cause by finding the fourth Dalai Lama in the family of the Mongol ruler. The Mongols however came to regard Tibet as their own domain and in 1705 ousted the Dalai Lama. Considered a threat to China, the Qing Emperor Kangxi sent an expedition to Tibet to expel the Mongols. The Chinese left behind representatives to direct Tibetan affairs and for the next two centuries the Chinese were to dominate the region.

With the fall of the Qing Dynasty in 1911 Tibet entered into a period of independence which was to last until 1950. In that year the PLA entered the region and occupied eastern Tibet. The Dalai Lama sent a delegation to Beijing which reached an agreement with the Chinese which allowed the PLA to occupy the rest of Tibet but left the existing political, social and religious organisation intact. The agreement was to last until 1959. In that year a rebellion broke out. Just why and how widespread depends on whether you believe the Chinese or the Tibetans – in any case the rebellion was suppressed by Chinese troops and the Dalai Lama and his retinue fled to India, and another 80,000 Tibetans scurried to India and Nepal. Tibet became an 'autonomous' region of China and over the next few years the political organisation of Tibet was altered drastically.

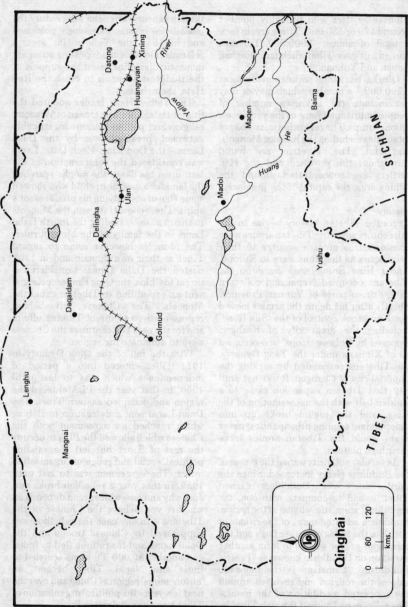

## Tibet & Qinghai Today

Tibetans and Chinese differ about the history of their countries; the Tibetans argue that they were long an independent country with their own language, religion, literature, and never really occupied by China. But to the Chinese the region is an 'inalienable' part of China. No effort is spared to reinforce that point, but the 'evidence' that the Chinese conjure up and expect you to believe is an insult to one's intelligence.

The Chinese contend that China and Tibet have known a peaceful and happy coexistence for the last 1300 years which linked them culturally and politically. Supporting this view are the marriages of Chinese feudal princesses to Tibetan warlord-kings and later in history the audiences the Son of Heaven granted to the Tibetan God-king. The Chinese point to the marriage of Princess Wen Chang, daughter of the Tang emperor Taizong, to Srong-btsan Sgam-po the King of Tibet in 641 AD. Then in 710 Princess Jin Cheng, the adopted daughter of the Tang Emperor Zhongong, was married to the Tibetan king. To 'prove' that Tibetans have always recognised their rule, the Chinese tell how the son of Heaven was visited by the Tibetan God-king, the Dalai Lama. Guides in the Potala point out a fresco which shows the visit of the 13th Dalai Lama to Beijing in 1908 to honour the corrupt Empress Dowager Cixi and the boy-emperor Puyi who was to be booted off the throne three years later. In the Hall of the fifth Dalai Lama they point out a fresco showing his visit to Beijing for an audience with the Qing emperor in 1652 – score a point to the Manchus?

The Tibetans were never really interested in making contact with foreigners, apart from those early armed annexations, and for centuries did their best to maintain their isolation on their high plateau. But Westerners have been captivated by Tibet's extraordinary isolation, its bizarre and fascinating culture. The Chinese see it as a dismal place of exile; their reconquest of Tibet in 1950 and the overthrow of the Dalai Lama in 1959 reinforced their view of themselves as a civilising force, liberators who overthrew a sadistic theocracy, ending a thousand years of feudalism.

Post-1959 Tibet saw the introduction of land reform – the great monastic estates were broken up and 1300 years of serfdom ended. But then came the ridiculous policies enforced during the Cultural Revolution; farmers were required to plant hopelessly alien lowland crops like wheat instead of the usual barley, in keeping with Chairman Mao's instruction to 'make grain the key link'. Strict limits were placed on the number of cattle that peasants could raise privately, equating prosperity with capitalism. Grain production slumped and the animal population declined. Then the Red Guards flooded in and wreaked their own havoc, but they did succeed in breaking the power of the monasteries. In 1959 there were at least 1600 monasterys operating in Tibet – by 1979 there were just ten. The Red Guards disbanded the monasteries and either executed or sent the monks to labour camps or to work in the fields.

Although they also built roads, schools and hospitals, the Chinese basically made a mess of Tibet – economically at least. Whether your average Tibetan peasant is any better off materially or any happier under the Chinese than under the former theocracy is a matter of opinion. Although the Chinese will never voluntarily relinquish control of Tibet – regardless of who or what faction holds power in Beijing – the present regime in Beijing has at least taken steps over the last few years to improve the living conditions in Tibet and the relations between the Tibetans and the Chinese. The Maoist Communist Party Chief in Tibet, General Ren Rong, was sacked in 1979. Most of the rural communes were disbanded and the land returned to private farmers; the farmers were allowed to grow or graze whatever they wanted and to sell their produce in free markets; taxes were reduced and state subsidies to the region increased. Some of the monasteries have been reopened on a limited basis and the Chinese continue to woo the Dalai Lama in the hope that he will return to Tibet. More likely he'll be given an office job in Beijing as a co-opted religious figurehead to try and legitimise Chinese control over Tibet.

Neighbouring Qinghai was part of the Tibetan region and except for the eastern area around the capital of Xining, the region was not incorporated into the Chinese empire until the early 18th century. Around 3,500,000 people live in the province, and that may or may not include an unknown number of prisoners who inhabit the highest concentration of labour camps in any province in China. Qinghai is a sort of Chinese Siberia where common criminals as well as political prisoners are incarcerated. These prisoners have included former Kuomintang army and police officers, 'rightists' arrested in the late 1950s after the Hundred Flowers had their blooms amputated, victims of the Cultural Revolution, former Red Guards arrested for their activities during the Cultural Revolution, supporters of the 'Gang of Four' and opponents of the present regime. Many of the Han Chinese settlers of the region are former prisoners; with a prison record behind them they have little or no future in eastern China and so choose to stay in Qinghai. Oddly, the exile of a Soviet dissident to Siberia is headline news in the USA or Europe, but when a Chinese dissident is exiled to Qinghai the story might be cut to a few paragraphs or not printed at all.

## Tourism in Tibet & Qinghai

If you had gone to China in 1981 or early 1982 then you could have gone to Tibet on your own – a few people did. At this time there were several public security offices (Qufu, Huang Shan, Hohhot, Baotou and Datong) who either didn't know that Tibet was officially closed to individual tourists,

didn't care or who just wanted to be accommodating – or the Chinese may have been issuing the permits deliberately to see how much interest there was in the region amongst travellers. Those who got permits generally either flew from Chengdu to Lhasa, took the bus or hitched. One lucky person even got a permit for Xining, Golmud and Lhasa and flew between each city.

That situation had changed by the second half of 1982 and by 1983 it seemed that no individual travellers had managed a permit for Lhasa. Tibet was simply out of the picture unless you were prepared to pay for a tour – and that looks like being the situation for a long time to come. Even if you could get a permit for Lhasa, it is unlikely that the CAAC office in Chengdu will sell you a ticket and if you do take the bus or hitch you'll probably be turned back – in early 1983 two guys tried hitching to Lhasa from Xinjiang Province, but were turned back half-way. Regardless, China is the sort of country where anything is possible and the only way the Chinese government will keep foreigners out of Tibet will be to ring the region with PLA guards at five metre intervals. *Someone* will always find a way of getting there.

It is virtually impossible to join a tour to Tibet once you are in China. If you want to go then you have to join one outside China. The following are the comments of a foreign expert who worked as teacher in Beijing, which should give you some idea of just how maddening the Chinese can be.

It was the Ministry of Education that got permission from the Lhasa/Tibetan Foreign Affairs Office for our 'foreign expert' group; it was not easy to come by and would not have been done at all if the initial request had not come from the French. (The French are all free to the Chinese, a gift of the French government, so Beijing does try occasionally to accommodate special requests). The request started in Wuhan, although three people were from Beijing, and one woman from Shanghai was given three days notice to join the group (she had had a request in for Tibet for three years), ... Our travel permits did not have Xigaze, but Lunze. We had been told that Xigaze was not possible because of PLA manoeuvres in the area. In Lhasa we were told that a mistake had been made and that we were going to Xigaze and that Lunze had never been open.

Our 'special' price was Y90 a day in Lhasa and Y100 in Xigaze (that's room, food and transport). In the eight days we also had a Y50 charge a piece for extra mileage. (It was indeed a special price – there was a tour group in Lhasa at the same time, paying US$200 a day, and their rooms and food were the same as those of the foreign experts).

The Chinese were up to their usual tricks. Upon arrival two days were taken away. We had been promised 10 full days in Tibet. To appease us, almost everything was left in the itinerary which meant we spent the whole day racing around. In addition to the usual monasteries we got to Ganden where immediately a Chinese official demanded papers from our guide. Theoretically no one can visit the monastery without authorisation; they are touchy about tourist reaction to the destruction still in evidence. The price one must pay to take pictures inside is a big rip-off, although one wouldn't mind so much if the money stayed with the monastery and didn't go to the Chinese. The standard price was Y20 per person. In the Jokhang we were allowed to take pictures of people free, the same in the Potala. At Sera it was a Y20 flat fee which allowed everyone to take pictures everywhere.

Our guides (with whom we were not even on speaking terms the last two days) said that in a couple of years Lhasa would be an open city, but I don't believe that for a minute. Even groups like ours (who've been working here to help China achieve the Four Modernisations!) can't get in; we're the first ones and two know at least a dozen experts from other cities who have been trying for a year or two. The news from Tibet as far as I could see is, no individual travellers. Our group was staying in the No 1 Guest House right in Lhasa and there was no one who was on their own. We were also in Xigaze and found no one else.

The Chinese have reason to be cautious; in a comparison between the Chinese and the Tibetans the Chinese don't fare well. A group like ours is even worse than tourists because after living here under their rules, it is very difficult to like this country at all.

It's worth considering whether going to Tibet at present is really worth it, both in terms of money and hassle. Part of the reason people want to go is simply because they're not allowed to go (except with a tour). If you want to see a bit of Tibet than you'll probably find it a lot easier just to go to Qinghai Province – the history, culture and people of the area is predominantly Tibetan and parts of the region are open to individual travellers. The labour camps may have been one of the reasons why the province was closed off to foreigners for so long – and it seems that it was not until about 1980 that any foreigners were taken there. Up until mid-1983 Qinghai was closed to individual travellers, though the occasional tour-group was taken to the capital of Xining and out to Qinghai Lake in the west. Today, Xining and Qinghai Lake are open to individual travellers. Some western agencies have mountaineering and trekking expeditions – if you can foot the bill.

Just why the Chinese don't want foreigners running around Tibet on their own is anyone's guess. It may be lack of hotels and food – the high cost of Tibetan tours is attributed to the cost of transporting supplies all the way from Chengdu, a two to three week trip by truck. Other people say it's because the Chinese don't want foreigners making close contact with the Tibetans. It may be because group tours make more money than individuals. The Chinese may also be worried about unaccompanied travellers coming down with severe altitude sickness – with all the accompanying hassle of having to hospitalise and move them back to eastern China. Most likely it's a combination of all these reasons. My prejudice is towards the money angle; Tibet was always the most coveted, most extraordinary, most unobtainable, most remote tourist destination in the world and the Chinese government and Western travel agencies will make more money by keeping it that way – no one will fork out a suitcase full of travellers cheques unless they feel privileged to do so.

Apart from Qinghai, if you want to see a slice of Tibet then consider the area of Ladakh in the far north of India – it was opened to travellers a few years ago and rapidly became one of the most popular tourist destinations in the country. It's a piece of Tibetan plateau under Indian control, complete with Tibetans and Tibetan monasteries – and you can go there anytime you want, weather permitting.

## LHASA

Lhasa has long been the capital of Tibet and remains the political centre, the most important city and the showpiece of the region. It lies a mere 3683 metres above sea level. Lhasa is actually two cities, one Chinese and one Tibetan. The Chinese city is the larger and is made up of the same inspired architecture that you see in eastern China; by contrast the Tibetan side is a ramshackle, scungy city of winding streets.

The chief attraction of Lhasa is the **Potala Palace**, once the centre of the Tibetan government and the winter residence of the Dalai Lama. This huge 17th-century edifice was built on the site of its – 7th-century forerunner. Also within the city limits is the golden-roofed **Jokhang Temple**, 1300 years old and one of Tibet's holiest of holy shrines. It was built in commemoration of the marriage of Tang princess Wen Chang to King Srong-btsan Sgam-po, and houses a pure gold Buddha which was brought to Tibet by the princess. About three km west of the Potala is the **Norbu Lingka** which used to be the summer residence of the Dalai Lama.

Outside the city are some interesting monasteries. The **Drepung Monastery**, which dates back to the early 15th century, is about five or six km outside Lhasa and is one of the 10 remaining monasteries in Tibet. In 1959 there were 10,000 monks living here, but the Chinese invasion and the Cultural Revolution put an end to that. Today there are maybe two

or three hundred monks in residence. The **Sera Monastery** is perhaps more interesting for what goes on behind rather than inside it. On a mountain top not far away is the site of the Tibetan 'sky burials' where the deceased are chopped up and then eaten by vultures. The funerals take place soon after dawn. The monastery is about six km north of Lhasa. The **Ganden Monastery** which is about 65 km east of Lhasa was razed during the Cultural Revolution but is apparently being rebuilt.

Lhasa is connected by road with Golmud and on to Dunhuang, and by road to Xining. It is also planned to build a railway line from Lhasa to Golmud to link up with the Golmud-Xining line. Lhasa is also connected by road with Chengdu in Sichuan Province, and back in the early days of individual travel to the region a number of foreigners got in this way. There is also a road connecting Lhasa with Nepal, via Xigatse, but the last time any foreigners made it through along that stretch was reportedly back in mid-1983. There has been some talk of the Chinese opening up tours to Lhasa from Kathmandu. Lhasa is also connected by air with Chengdu (Y322), Golmud (Y230) and Xian (Y390).

## XIGAZE

The second-largest urban centre in Tibet is Xigaze. This was formerly the seat of the Panchen Lama, second in the lamaist hierarchy to the Dalai Lama. The Panchen was taken to Beijing in 1965 and has lived there ever since, a supporter of Chinese policy in Tibet. The Tashilumpo Monastery in Xigaze used to be the residence of the Panchen and a number of monks still live here. The city controls the roads from Lhasa to western Tibet and into Nepal. There is a direct road from Xigaze to Lhasa, and another via Gyangze. The direct road is faster but the other route takes you over the 5000 metre high Kambla mountain pass and by the brilliant Lake Yamdrok Tso.

## GYANGZE

Gyangze is one of southern Tibet's chief centres. The road from Lhasa splits off here and one branch goes to Xigaze, while the other heads south into Sikkim via the town of Yadong.

## SAGYA

Sagya is 160 km west of Xigaze and about 22 km south of the main road. It's the site of a still-active monastery which was Tibet's most powerful 700 years ago.

## XINING

Xining is the only large city in Qinghai and is the capital of the province. It's a long-established Chinese city, and has been a military garrison and trading centre since the 16th century. It's always been an important transport centre with roads leading east to Lanzhou and south to Lhasa. Xining is now open to individual travellers, as is Huangzhong County where the Ta'er Monastery is sited.

There are a couple of sights in or near the city which probably rate as some of the highlights of China. The Dongguan (East City Gate) Mosque is located in eastern Xining. This mosque was built during the later part of the 14th century and is one of the largest mosques in China's north-west.

The Ta'er Lamasery is a large Tibetan monastery located in the town of Lusha'er about 25 km south-east of Xining – about an hour drive. It was once one of the six great monasteries of the Yellow Sect and was built in 1577. It's a pretty place and very popular with the local tourists – once they leave it's very pleasant. Great yoghurt and peaches available here and it may even be possible to stay overnight. The monastery is noted for its extraordinary sculptures in which human figures, animals and landscapes are carved out of yak butter! The art of butter sculpture probably dates back 1300 years in Tibet and was taken up by the Ta'er Lamasery in the last years of the 16th century.

Lake Qinghai, known as the 'Western Sea' in ancient times, is a large and beautiful saline lake lying 300 km west of Xining. There are bus tours from Xining, and the lake is also accessible by train – Ketu station is the jumping-off point and the lake is an hour's walk away. It appears that you're supposed to only go there on a bus tour from Xining, but give the train a go.

Xining is connected by rail to Lanzhou in Gansu Province. There are flights from Xining to Beijing (Y222), Lanzhou (Y24), Taiyuan (Y153), and Xian (Y87). There may be flights between Xining and Golmud.

## GOLMUD

Golmud is a town in the centre of Qinghai and is off-limits to foreigners. The road from Dunhuang in Gansu Province passes through here on its way to Lhasa; there is also a railway line connecting Golmud with Xining and it's planned to extend this line all the way from Golmud to Lhasa. There are flights between Golmud and Lhasa (Y230) and Xian (Y190) and there may be direct flights between Golmud and Xining.

# Index

---

### Tibet — a travel survival kit

When we published *China — a travel survival kit* Tibet was still off limits. Since then it has opened up and quickly became one of the most popular regions of China with travellers flocking there by a variety of routes — one of which requires 14 days of bus travel!

Michael Buckley, co-author of *China*, returned to China with Robert Strauss, a contributor to *China*, to research a new guidebook to Tibet. Between them they managed to cover Tibet from end to end and this comprehensive new guidebook covers all the routes into and out of Tibet including the Lhasa-Kathmandu route. With maps, charts, diagrams, illustrations, 16 pages of colour plates and a Tibetan language section this is the complete guidebook to the land of snows.

## Lonely Planet travel guides

*Africa on a Shoestring*
*Australia – a travel survival kit*
*Alaska – a travel survival kit*
*Bali & Lombok – a travel survival kit*
*Burma – a travel survival kit*
*Bushwalking in Papua New Guinea*
*Canada – a travel survival kit*
*China – a travel survival kit*
*Hong Kong, Macau & Canton*
*India – a travel survival kit*
*Japan – a travel survival kit*
*Kashmir, Ladakh & Zanskar*
*Kathmandu & the Kingdom of Nepal*
*Korea & Taiwan – a travel survival kit*
*Malaysia, Singapore & Brunei – a travel survival kit*
*Mexico – a travel survival kit*
*New Zealand – a travel survival kit*
*Pakistan – a travel survival kit*
*Papua New Guinea – a travel survival kit*
*The Philippines – a travel survival kit*
*South America on a Shoestring*
*South-East Asia on a Shoestring*
*Sri Lanka – a travel survival kit*
*Thailand – a travel survival kit*
*Tramping in New Zealand*
*Trekking in the Himalayas*
*Turkey – a travel survival kit*
*USA West*
*West Asia on a Shoestring*

## Lonely Planet phrasebooks

*Indonesia Prasebook*
*Nepal Phrasebook*
*Thailand Phrasebook*

Lonely Planet travel guides are available around the world. If you can't find them, ask your bookshop to order them from one of the distributors listed below. For countries not listed or if you would like a free copy of our latest booklist write to Lonely Planet in Australia.

**Australia**
  Lonely Planet Publications, PO Box 88, South Yarra, Victoria 3141.
**Canada**
  Milestone Publications, Box 2248, Sidney British Columbia, V8L 3S8.
**Denmark**
  Scanvik Books aps, Store Kongensgade 59 A, DK-1264 Copenhagen K.
**Hong Kong**
  The Book Society, GPO Box 7804.
**India & Nepal**
  UBS Distributors, 5 Ansari Rd, New Delhi.
**Israel**
  Geographical Tours Ltd, 8 Tverya St, Tel Aviv 63144.
**Japan**
  Intercontinental Marketing Corp, IPO Box 5056, Tokyo 100-31.
**Malaysia**
  MPH Distributors, 13 Jalan 13/6, Petaling Jaya, Selangor.
**Netherlands**
  Nilsson & Lamm bv, Postbus 195, Pampuslaan 212, 1380 AD Weesp.
**New Zealand**
  Roulston Greene Publishing Associates Ltd, Box 33850, Takapuna, Auckland 9.
**Papua New Guinea**
  Gordon & Gotch (PNG), PO Box 3395, Port Moresby.
**Singapore**
  MPH Distributors, 116-DJTC Factory Building, Lorong 3, Geylang Square, Singapore, 1438.
**Sweden**
  Esselte Kartcentrum AB, Vasagatan 16, S-111 20 Stockholm.
**Thailand**
  Chalermnit, 1-2 Erawan Arcade, Bangkok.
**UK**
  Roger Lascelles, 47 York Rd, Brentford, Middlesex, TW8 0QP.
**USA**
  Lonely Planet Publications, PO Box 2001A, Berkeley, CA 94702.
**West Germany**
  Buchvertrieb Gerda Schettler, Postfach 64, D3415 Hattorf a H.

# India
a travel survival kit

lonely planet